D1736660

ANTITRUST LAW IN PERSPECTIVE

CASES, CONCEPTS AND PROBLEMS IN COMPETITION POLICY

Third Edition

■ ■ ■

Andrew I. Gavil

Professor of Law
Howard University School of Law

William E. Kovacic

Global Competition Professor of Law and Policy
George Washington University Law School
Visiting Professor, King's College London
Non-Executive Director, United Kingdom Competition and Markets Authority

Jonathan B. Baker

Professor of Law
Washington College of Law
American University

Joshua D. Wright

University Professor & Executive Director, Global Antitrust Institute
Antonin Scalia Law School at George Mason University

AMERICAN CASEBOOK SERIES®

WEST
ACADEMIC
PUBLISHING

American Casebook Series is a trademark registered in the U.S. Patent and Trademark Office.

© West, Thomson business, 2002
© 2008 Thomson/West
© 2017 LEG, Inc. d/b/a West Academic
    444 Cedar Street, Suite 700
    St. Paul, MN 55101
    1-877-888-1330

Printed in the United States of America

ISBN: 978-0-314-26605-7

To my parents, Ruth and Irving, who gave me all they had to give, and to my wife, Judy, and my children, Justin, Noah and Zoe Ruth, who sustain me each day.

AIG

To my parents, Evan and Frances, and to my wife, Kathy.

WEK

To my sons, Danny and Alex, my wife, Susan, and my parents, Beverly and David.

JBB

To my children, James, Ella, and Olivia, my wife, Vinh, and my parents, Nelson and Sandra.

JDW

PREFACE TO THE THIRD EDITION

We are delighted to bring you the third edition of Antitrust Law in Perspective. Since the publication of the first edition in 2002 and the second in 2008, antitrust law, and competition policy more broadly, have continued to evolve, generating new and increasingly complex cases, new commentary, occasional controversy, and new challenges for antitrust professors and students. Some of our students are new to the subject matter, whereas others come to it with varying degrees of prior knowledge. Our goal for the third edition was not merely to update the cases and citations, but to bring some fresh thinking to how we conceptualize and convey the material to our students. We wanted to find better ways to engage them, stimulate their interest, hone their analytical skills, and hopefully facilitate their entry into the global competition policy community.

To that end, this edition provides more than just a comprehensive update of the second edition, adding a number of new principal cases, new or revised Notes and Sidebars, discussions of new or revised government guidelines and policy statements, and expanded treatment of some of the more thought-provoking antitrust issues of our day. We have also taken steps to more fully structure the book around the twin aims of modern antitrust law: collusion and exclusion. These revisions continue to develop a premise for the first edition: that today's antitrust law is moving away from reflexive categorization approaches to analyzing conduct, gravitating instead toward greater reliance on core concepts and frameworks informed by economics. In all of this, we have striven to strike a good balance between accessibility and sophistication of treatment.

We have reordered some of the chapters, combined some, and eliminated others. Chapter 1 still opens the book with an introduction to the essential economic concepts that guide modern antitrust analysis, but it also includes an expanded treatment of the role and impact of decision theory. Chapter 2, which again examines competitor agreements, has been significantly re-thought and restructured to more clearly present the rule of reason "continuum" in the way it is being implemented by the agencies and courts today. Chapter 3 streamlines the economics of collusion and features the two decisions in *In re Text Messaging Antitrust Litigation* that were authored by Judge Posner. These cases help orient students to better connect the legal analysis of "agreement" with the economics of collusion. Chapter 4 now introduces the economics of exclusion and the foundation of the modern law of monopolization, accelerating it from its later place in the previous editions. It now precedes Chapter 5 (mergers), allowing for a reintegration of the material on horizontal and vertical mergers into what we think is one of the most comprehensive and advanced merger chapters available, one well-suited both for introductory and advanced antitrust courses. Chapter 6 (anticompetitive distribution strategies) is an innovative integration of previous Chapters 4 and 7. By combining into a single chapter the material on "intrabrand" and "interbrand" restraints, which have traditionally been separated, the Chapter encourages consideration of the similarities and differences of various types of conduct based on economic effects, both anti- and procompetitive. Asking whether distribution strategies can facilitate collusion, for example, is more informative than asking whether it restricts "intra" or "inter" brand competition. We have also significantly revised and accelerated the treatment of innovation and technology-related issues in Chapter 7 (previous Chapter 10), and updated the material on jurisdiction and the state action doctrine in Chapter 8 (previous Chapter 9), which has been propelled forward by recent Supreme Court decisions. Current Chapter 8 has been dropped, although the portions of it that we thought were valuable have been integrated into other sections of the book. We have "test-driven" some of these changes in our own classes and hope you will agree that the book as a whole "teaches better" and provides a more up-to-date understanding of the concepts that drive modern antitrust analysis.

As with the previous editions, we are grateful to many of our adopters, who have freely given of their time and insights to improve this edition. We wish to express our deepest appreciation to Professor Steven C. Salop, who continues to be generous with his time, providing us with extensive and insightful comments that have improved the book in immeasurable ways. As in the past, we also thank Kathryn M. Fenton and Professor Spencer Weber Waller for updating their Sidebars. Valuable research assistance was provided by Marcus J. Bandy, Jarrell D. Blakemore, Hae-Sung Lee, and Vernon G. Ross at Howard, and Bernard Archbold, Demetrius Baefsky, Brady Cummins, Elyse Dorsey, Angela Diveley, Lindsey Edwards, Matt Lein, Elise Nelson, and Thomas Rucker at George Mason.

Finally, we more fully welcome our new co-author, former FTC Commissioner Joshua D. Wright. Josh began working with us with the 2011 Casebook Update, and had come to wonder whether we really intended to produce a third edition. Welcome Josh—we look forward to working with you on the fourth (starting now . . .)!

ANDREW I. GAVIL
WILLIAM E. KOVACIC
JONATHAN B. BAKER
JOSHUA D. WRIGHT

Washington, D.C.
October 2016

PREFACE TO THE SECOND EDITION

In the more than five years since the first edition was published, antitrust law has continued to evolve rapidly and in important ways. In the United States, the Supreme Court and lower courts have continued to look increasingly to economic analysis to refine and narrow the substantive rules of antitrust law. Internationally, competition law and policies have expanded to more than 100 nations which now participate to varying degrees in a still developing global competition policy system. These developments have together created new challenges for antitrust professors, but also exciting opportunities for greater perspective and deeper understanding for both experienced and new students to the subject.

We are very pleased, therefore, to bring you this thoroughly updated second edition. The book's basic structure and contents will be familiar to prior adopters and we hope inviting to new ones. As with the first edition, we have strived to make the second edition a compelling introduction to how antitrust is practiced today. To accommodate different styles of teaching and different degrees of emphasis on economics, we hope you will find it both user-friendly and sophisticated. In addition to updating throughout to reflect the latest court decisions, enforcement actions, and commentary (including Supreme Court antitrust decisions through the 2006–07 term), several chapters have been revamped more substantially. The treatment of antitrust economics in Chapter 1 has been expanded and now includes an appendix on cost concepts for those teachers inclined to delve more deeply into antitrust law's economic underpinnings. To reflect major areas of change, Chapter 4 (Distributional Relationships) has been significantly revised to take full account of the Supreme Court's 2007 decision in *Leegin*. Likewise, Chapter 6 (Dominant Firm Behavior) has been significantly updated to reflect the considerable developments that have taken place with respect to the treatment of single firm conduct. Finally, we have added several "Comparative Perspective Sidebars" to facilitate classroom discussion of competition law developments in the rest of the world, especially the European Union. Additional and significantly revised Notes and Sidebars also have been interspersed throughout the book.

We are grateful for the many suggestions we received from adopters of the first edition which have helped us to improve the second. In particular, we express our appreciation to Professors Peter C. Carstensen, Alvin K. Klevorick, James May, and Peter P. Swire. For updating their Sidebars, we also thank Kathryn M. Fenton and Professor Spencer Weber Waller. A very special note of thanks and our deep appreciation goes to Professor Steven

C. Salop, who provided us extensive comments, freely offered us the benefit of his extraordinary insights into antitrust economics and law, and even took up his pen on occasion to help us better frame some key issues.

We also thank the many students past and present who provided the research assistance and other support necessary to bring such a major undertaking to fruition. These include at Howard University, Nina R. Frant, Obinna C. Ihekweazu, Marques S. Johnson, and Michelle M. Yost, and at American University, Katherine Chesnut. We are especially grateful for the work at Howard of Kapil V. Pandit and Jack N.E. Pitts, Jr., who gave generously of their time, intellect, skill, and good spirits under often demanding deadlines to keep the book moving forward in the final months of preparation.

As with the first edition, a complete Teacher's Manual will be available to guide the use of the second and we encourage adopters to sign on to our Author's Forum in the West Education Network (TWEN), where we will post supplemental material and updates as needed. We look forward to hearing comments and reactions from established and new adopters, alike.

ANDREW I. GAVIL
WILLIAM E. KOVACIC
JONATHAN B. BAKER

Washington, D.C.
March 2008

PREFACE TO THE FIRST EDITION

In compiling and drafting this Casebook, our goal was to capture antitrust law as it is understood and practiced today. Hence, the book emphasizes the central role of concepts such as market power, efficiency, and entry across the full spectrum of competitively sensitive conduct. It does so in a flexible format that includes accessible narrative material, as well as charts, tables and figures that enable in-class teaching. We hope it will provide an engaging, contemporary, sophisticated and user-friendly vehicle for exploring the content and boundaries of modern "competition policy."

Reflecting our goals, the book has a number of distinctive features:

- **Immediate exposure to the core issues of antitrust law.** In a unique opening chapter, the book uses three case studies to introduce the core issues that shape competition policy. The case studies range from the hard core violations in the lysine and vitamin cartel cases, to the more complex Boeing-McDonnell Douglas merger. In addition, the chapter uses a hypothetical "Coffee Shop" problem to introduce the economics of "market power" and other fundamental economic concepts. The chapter also examines the Supreme Court's *Brunswick* decision to demonstrate at the outset how the analysis of "antitrust injury" has led modern courts increasingly to focus on broad economic concepts in defining anticompetitive effects. Through its case studies and case excerpts, the chapter quickly introduces the fundamentals of modern antitrust analysis, including the rich factual detail required to evaluate the reasonableness of most antitrust-sensitive conduct.

- **From categories to concepts.** Traditionally, antitrust rules and antitrust casebooks were organized by categories defined by the nature of the relationships among the parties (e.g., horizontal, vertical) and type of conduct at issue (e.g., concerted vs. unilateral). Although those categories continue to play a role in modern antitrust analysis, today's antitrust lawyers, enforcers and courts focus far more on the nature of the anticompetitive effects, and in private cases, the antitrust injuries, alleged. A major theme of the book, therefore, is that American antitrust law is evolving away from reliance on narrow doctrinal categories towards a more unitary analytical framework, driven by broad economic concepts such as market power, entry and efficiency. Reflecting that theme, the book separately groups conduct threatening collusive anticompetitive effects—including traditional horizontal agreements, vertical intrabrand agreements and horizontal mergers—and conduct threatening exclusionary effects—including dominant firm behavior, vertical interbrand restraints and vertical mergers.

- **Up-to-date and comprehensive treatment of horizontal merger analysis.** Because so much of the development of those concepts can be traced to modern merger practice, the casebook features one of the most comprehensive chapters on horizontal merger analysis to be found. It highlights the important lower court decisions that have supplanted older Supreme Court precedent in this important area, and is framed largely around the DOJ/FTC Horizontal Merger Guidelines.

- **New approaches to proving collusion.** In recognition of the renewed focus of courts, commentators and antitrust enforcers on domestic and international cartels, the book also includes one of the most comprehensive treatments available of the contemporary law and economics of proving collusion between rivals. Critical recent lower court decisions, such as *Blomkest* and *Toys-R-Us*, are excerpted and analyzed.

- **Contemporary approach to distribution practices.** Divided into two chapters, the book takes a sophisticated, yet practical and comprehensive approach to the antitrust issues that attend various distribution strategies.

- **Addresses role of antitrust in high-tech markets.** Our casebook recognizes the increasing importance of competitive effects involving innovation in antitrust analysis, and the contemporary ferment over the extent to which antitrust law can and should be harmonized with intellectual property law. The capstone chapter is devoted exclusively to antitrust in the new economy.

- **Fully integrates economic thinking.** Our casebook does not relegate modern economic analysis to occasional notes or to a discrete section on economics. Instead, we present the economics students need to know to practice antitrust today simply and clearly, and integrate economic thinking throughout the casebook. Differences between a Chicago school and post-Chicago perspective are noted where appropriate, as are other perspectives. On the other hand, we recognize that few students will have extensive backgrounds in economics, and that teachers, themselves, may have varying degrees of economic expertise. The economic content, therefore, is designed to be accessible, and adaptable to varying degrees of economic sophistication and varying styles of teaching.

- **Inclusive approach to the relevant cases.** Our casebook excerpts or discusses the traditional and familiar Supreme Court cases that have long been staples of the antitrust course. But the book also recognizes that much of the action in recent years has been in the lower courts. The casebook responds to that development by highlighting contemporary lower court decisions, especially with respect to mergers and the developing standards for proving market power and anticompetitive effects. Comprehensive treatment of the enduring aspects of the *Microsoft* litigation is also integrated throughout the book.

- **Beyond case law.** The sources of antitrust law encompass far more than just cases. The book relies upon a range of sources, not only to enhance its substantive content, but also to expose students to the full range of antitrust practice. Non-case materials include expert economic testimony, consent decrees, FTC Aids to Public Comment, business review letters, a complaint, and extensive treatment of government enforcement guidelines.

- **Sensitivity to antitrust's global context.** U.S. antitrust practitioners can no longer ignore developments in competition policy elsewhere in the world. Although comprehensive treatment of U.S. antitrust law remains the principal focus of the book, we provide an occasional counterpoint to the American approach by looking briefly at how other competition policy systems (primarily the E.U.) address similar issues. Moreover, beginning in the first chapter, we highlight the problems that the globalization of antitrust presents for firms that must manage compliance with multiple jurisdictions simultaneously.

- **Treatment of ethics.** Several Sidebars are specifically devoted to issues of ethics and professional responsibility in both the litigation and counseling context. These Sidebars allow interested teachers and students to explore how issues of professional responsibility can arise in and complicate antitrust practice. In addition to these substantive features of the book, teachers and students alike will notice some important, and, we hope, productive characteristics of the presentation.

- **"Sidebars" and "Notes".** We have banned the typical "notes" sections typified by numbered paragraphs following cases. All too often, our collective experience suggests that these notes reflect a counterproductive "hide the ball" approach to teaching, and can obscure important cases and concepts. In their place, we have prepared extensive narrative interstitial material in the form of "Sidebars" and "Notes." This material is accessible, informative, challenging and flexible. It serves many possible functions, including coverage of live controversies in the field, the historical development of antitrust concepts and thought, discussion of trends in the law, discussion of particular economic and legal issues in greater depth, and thoughts on future directions in our field.

- **Visual Learning.** In addition to the network of interstitial material, the book includes over 80 tables, charts and figures. Some simply summarize relevant factors, while others visually present more complex ideas, including relationships among parties to a case or transaction.

- **Attention to lawyering skills and problem solving.** Almost every chapter concludes with problems and exercises that develop lawyering skills as well as deepen the understanding of antitrust principles. The skills exercises also offer the opportunity to socialize students to the wide range of functions of antitrust lawyers and involve various litigation, counseling and regulatory settings.

As is common in any multi-authored book of this kind, no individual author necessarily agrees with every statement the book makes, even when we do not present multiple points of view. Moreover, we have at times chosen to emphasize perspectives we may not share for pedagogical reasons.

We believe that we have presented antitrust in an accessible yet sophisticated way that is consonant with modern antitrust practice. We hope you will agree, and look forward to hearing your comments and reactions.

ANDREW I. GAVIL
WILLIAM E. KOVACIC
JONATHAN B. BAKER

Washington, D.C.
October 2002

ACKNOWLEDGMENTS TO THE FIRST EDITION

On the day we received our contract offer from West Group, I called Bill Kovacic to report that there was "good news and bad news." The "good news"? We were on our way with our casebook concept. The "bad news"? He would be working with me on the casebook and updates for the rest of his life! I had no idea that the first phase of the rest of our working life together would take nearly six years! But here we finally are.

First and foremost, I want to thank my co-authors, Bill and Jon. All three of us share a true love for the subject, which I hope is revealed in the pages that follow. Those pages have been immeasurably enriched by the intellectual capital that Bill and Jon have brought to the book. Crossing paths with Bill Kovacic more than 15 years ago was one of the great fortunes of my life. He has been mentor, teacher, colleague, friend, and now co-author. I owe him a debt of gratitude that will be hard ever to repay. And Bill and I could not have been more delighted when Jon accepted our invitation to join the project after he left the FTC. The value he has added is incalculable in terms of the book's economic sophistication and clarity of presentation. It would not have been the same book without you, Jon. I have thoroughly enjoyed the many hours we three have spent dissecting and pondering antitrust's intricacies, and have learned so much from the both of you.

Bill, Jon and I also would like to collectively thank Kathryn M. Fenton, Steven C. Salop and Spencer Weber Waller, each of whom has made valuable contributions to the book that are noted in the text.

Of course, completing such a major project requires a great deal of support and research assistance. I am especially grateful to the Howard University School of Law for financial support over many years, and in particular to President H. Patrick Swygert and former Dean Alice Gresham Bullock for their consistent encouragement and support of my work. For the kind of unqualified and tireless encouragement one hopes to get from colleagues, I am also indebted to Professors Loretta C. Argrett, Rhea Ballard-Thrower, Cynthia Mabry, Laurence C. Nolan, Isiah Leggett, Okianer Christian Dark, Homer C. LaRue, Ziyad Motala, J. Clay Smith, Denise W. Spriggs, Andrew E. Taslitz and Frank H. Wu. A very special note of appreciation to the "other Andy"—to have found not only a colleague but a fellow Bronx traveler and best friend has been a source of persistent strength throughout our years together at Howard. Thanks, Taz!

Many students also have made significant contributions to the quality of the book. To my Howard students who, through the last several years, have cheerfully worked with earlier drafts of the manuscript, freely offering constructive comments, I thank you and hope the end product meets with your approval. To research assistants who have worked hard over the years, and frequently under tight deadlines, gratitude is also due. I want to especially thank Summeet Lall, Edrei Swanson, Darren P. Riley, Tyresse Horne, Sophiea C. Bailey, Esther R. Sailo, Nadine Jones-Francis, Natasha Yates and Charles W. Brumskine.

I have also been a very fortunate beneficiary of the wisdom and professionalism of some terrific antitrust lawyers in Chicago, Denver and Washington, D.C., who not only taught me a great deal, but encouraged my interest and enthusiasm for antitrust law. In particular, I want to express my gratitude to the late John T. ("Ted") Loughlin, and to Victor E. Grimm, John C. Christie, Jr., Michael Sennett, James E. Hartley, Larry R. Fullerton and Andrew J. Strenio, Jr..

To my "first fan," my sister Gale S. Wachs, boundless appreciation for a lifetime of confidence, encouragement and support. And finally, there is my family, to whom I dedicate it all. Without the unwavering support, love and encouragement of my wife, Judy Veis, and our children, Justin, Noah and Zoe Ruth, it could never have been done, and could hardly have been worth the effort.

ANDREW I. GAVIL

Washington, D.C.
October 2002

I want to express my gratitude to Andy and Jon. The vision for this book is first and foremost Andy's. In 1996 Andy and I traveled to Cairo to assist the Government of Egypt in developing a new competition law. Our Egyptian counterparts often pressed us to describe how academics, practitioners, and judges analyze antitrust issues in the United States and solicited our thoughts about the optimal design of competition policy institutions. Answering these questions required us to step back and reexamine competition policy in the United States and around the globe. On a day of tourism amid the pyramids at Giza, Andy said this introspection provided us an opportunity to develop a casebook that captured modern antitrust analysis. To Andy's wonderful concept Jon later added his unsurpassed appreciation of how economics has shaped contemporary antitrust doctrine and is likely to influence its future evolution. My gratitude for the chance to work with Andy and Jon is no less monumental than the antiquities that provided the setting for Andy's original proposal.

I also must note that Andy and Jon have borne the heaviest burdens in completing the casebook, especially after I came to the Federal Trade

Commission in June 2001. This was not because they had idle time to occupy. Rather, it demonstrates their unbounded generosity. Their kindness did not surprise me. On countless occasions since I met them in the mid-1980s Andy and Jon have carried me, whether teaching me economics and law, providing career advice, or simply supplying encouragement. Broad minds and great hearts.

I got lots of help from the university communities at George Mason and George Washington. No academic prospers without astute research assistants. My deepest thanks to Eric Berman, Neil Graham, Robin Moore, and Tom Mila for doing research and editing that made this a much better casebook. I am also grateful to my antitrust students at George Washington who used early versions of the manuscript and provided countless helpful suggestions.

Finally, I dedicate my efforts to my Father, who died soon before we began the project, to my Mother, and to my wife, Kathy.

WILLIAM E. KOVACIC

Washington, D.C.
October 2002

Thanks first to Andy and Bill for inviting me to join them in this project. "Free riding" works best with co-authors as hard-working and talented as both of you. Thanks also to Dean Claudio Grossman and the Washington College of Law for supporting my work on this casebook; to the students who tried out the manuscript in draft; to the Dean's Fellows who provided research assistance, Alexandra Cornhill, Arturo DeCastro, Sharmalee Rajakumaran and Traci Tyers; and to my many mentors and colleagues in antitrust.

JONATHAN B. BAKER

Washington, D.C.
October 2002

SUMMARY OF CONTENTS

TABLE OF CONTENTS

TABLE OF FIGURES

TABLE OF CASES

The principal cases are in bold type.

ANTITRUST LAW IN PERSPECTIVE

CASES, CONCEPTS AND PROBLEMS IN COMPETITION POLICY

Third Edition

CHAPTER 1

DEFINING COMPETITION POLICY
FOR A GLOBAL ECONOMY

■ ■ ■

INTRODUCTION

Antitrust law is an old subject with remarkable new life. In its contemporary form, antitrust law originated in North America amid forces of economic upheaval which, though distant in time, continue to reshape the world economy today. In the second half of the nineteenth century, parallel revolutions in communications (the telegraph) and transportation (the railroad) fused insular geographic regions into unified markets and spawned enterprises of unprecedented size to serve them. Using a new corporate instrument called the "trust," firms coordinated their business practices and established control of markets for basic commodities such as oil, sugar, and tobacco. The new leviathans menaced suppliers, crushed smaller rivals, and bent the political process to their will. In all things, they appeared to operate beyond the reach of social conventions and legal constraints that had governed commerce before.

The emergence of the trusts catalyzed intense demands for government intervention. Elected officials, editorial writers, and small businesses demanded action, and legislatures responded by enacting "antitrust" laws. Kansas began the movement in 1887 with the first of several state laws. But it quickly became apparent that the jurisdictional reach of the states was inadequate to police these national and international enterprises. National legislation soon followed in Canada in 1889 and then in the United States in 1890 with the Sherman Act. Supplemented at various times in later years, the Sherman Act remains the principal statutory foundation for the U.S. regime and a major focal point for study in this Casebook.

In fits and starts after 1890, antitrust law gradually became an important instrument of U.S. economic policy. Few other countries followed suit at first. Through most of the Sherman Act's first century, antitrust seemed destined to remain a largely American endeavor. By the late 1980s, roughly 30 jurisdictions had adopted antitrust laws in any form, and only a handful had built effective means for implementation.

All of that changed in a hurry. With the ascent of market-oriented economic policies after the fall of the Berlin Wall in 1989 and the collapse

1

of the Soviet Union in 1991, dozens of countries enacted competition laws. The total number of adopters now stands at approximately 130, with the number certain to climb to over 135 by 2020. In barely 25 years, roughly 100 jurisdictions have created antitrust systems. By historical standards, this represents an extraordinary transformation.

Behind the sheer numbers stand some impressive implementation programs. Many new regimes (for example, in emerging markets such as Brazil, China, India, Mexico, and South Africa) have credible, powerful enforcement mechanisms. China's Antimonopoly Law became effective in 2008, and the country's antitrust regime already has joined the EU and the United States on the short list of nations that multinational enterprises must consider in planning mergers and devising other business strategies.[1] Consequently, the study of antitrust law today has significance that was inconceivable only a few decades ago. For firms and their advisors, the global expansion of antitrust systems compels greater attention to antitrust concerns in carrying out mergers or other routine transactions and in crafting global strategies for the development, production, and sale of new products and services. More generally, the study of antitrust law provides a way to assess the role of public intervention in the economy, to understand forces that shape legal institutions, and to appreciate how nations with dissimilar legal and political systems can achieve needed levels of economic integration, cooperation, and legal consistency.[2]

To recognize the widespread global adoption of antitrust laws is not to assert the primacy or durability of competition as an organizing principle of economic policy. Two developments require attention in assessing the future significance of competition policy and its chief tool, antitrust law. First, the global financial crisis that began in 2008, and whose effects continue to grip many countries today, has inspired a vibrant debate about the value of market-oriented policies and of competition law as an ingredient of a market-based economic regime. The buoyant optimism about market reforms that prevailed in the 1990s has given way to more cautious reflection about the appropriate role of the government in the economy.

The second cautionary development is a modern variant of the economic revolution that inspired the adoption of the first antitrust laws in the 1880s and 1890s. The miraculous communications device of the 1800s was the telegraph; today the communications revolution takes the form of dramatic advances in information technology that can facilitate the rapid emergence of new products, services, and business models that can

---

[1] *See generally* Symposium, *Competition Law in China Today*, 3 J. ANTITRUST ENFORCEMENT 1 (Supp. 1 Oct. 2015).

[2] See generally William E. Kovacic & Marianela Lopez-Galdos, Lifecycles of Competition Systems: Explaining Variation in the Implementation of New Regimes, 79 J.L. & CONTEMP. PROBS. (Fall 2016).

displace existing ones and lead to the obsolescence of incumbent firms. The modern successors to the growth of railroads in the 1800s are the airplane and containerized shipping that lower the cost of moving goods around the world. Just as the communications and transportation breakthroughs of the 1800s transformed separate, local geographic areas into regional and national commercial markets in the United States, so too have their modern counterparts linked nations ever more closely into a global bazaar. It is increasingly common today for design and development work to be accomplished in one country, product components to be manufactured in multiple locations, and then the finished product to be assembled in yet another location from which it is ultimately distributed for sale throughout the globe.

Life in the global economic souk features many success stories, but also instances of acute discontent. In their role as consumers, citizens relish the competition that gives them an array of stunning new, better, and lower-cost products and services. In their role as workers or residents in individual communities, citizens can be ambivalent about competition, or outright antagonistic. As Joseph Schumpeter pungently observed nearly 75 years ago,[3] competition often achieves economic progress through creative destruction. It replaces existing firms and business models with new enterprises and new methods of production and service delivery. The process of replacement can obliterate existing companies and throw their workers and communities into turmoil. To this one must add the concern, expressed frequently in contemporary popular debate and scholarly discourse, that competition can yield results that disproportionately reward people of means, afflict the less fortunate with declining incomes, and simply ignore the dispossessed.[4]

In a fundamental way, antitrust law thus presents a paradox for consumers. Even as it promotes the competitive process that can bring new, less expensive, and more varied products and services to the market, it is no friend of the stability that citizens cherish as workers and residents of communities. This places antitrust agencies today, and antitrust policy more generally, in a politically and socially awkward role—to be the voice for pro-competitive policies that facilitate innovation-driven upheaval and to demonstrate, by logic and policy outcomes, that antitrust serves the best interests of all citizens, and not merely the favored few. In short, antitrust agencies must answer two basic questions from the larger public: How do we know that competition works, and works for us? To be sure, this is not the first era in which antitrust law has confronted these challenges, but

---

[3] JOSEPH A. SCHUMPETER, CAPITALISM, SOCIALISM, AND DEMOCRACY 84 (Harper & Bros. 3d ed., 1950) (1942).

[4] The possible roles of competition law and policy in addressing disparities in wealth are examined in Jonathan B. Baker & Steven C. Salop, *Antitrust, Competition Policy, and Inequality*, 104 GEO. L.J. ONLINE (2015) and Daniel A. Crane, *Antitrust and Wealth Inequality*, 101 CORNELL L. REV. 1171 (2015).

the urgency and intensity with which the issues are raised today requires that antitrust agencies not only be proficient technical analysts but also effective participants in public debates about the rationale for pro-competition policies.

As we have suggested here, antitrust has much to do with economics and economic policy. This makes antitrust a natural habitat for those keen on economics, but it ought not dismay those who come to the subject without formal training in the field. We believe that antitrust's core economic ideas are readily accessible to the specialist and the novice, alike. These principles will be, perhaps, most familiar to readers with long experience living in a market economy. Many economic ideas that provide the conceptual framework for antitrust law appear in daily life in the many nations that use markets to organize the production and sale of goods and services. We can understand many antitrust ideas intuitively from our daily exposure to and interaction with markets. At the same time, those who have lived and studied in economies guided heavily by central planning will often find the key ideas to be within reach, as they may reflect the incentives that influence common human behavior.

To introduce those ideas, we begin with two case studies. The first examines the prosecution in the 1990s of an international cartel that fixed the prices of the food additive lysine. The second is a hypothetical example involving retail sales of coffee. These case studies introduce many of the basic legal, institutional, and economic concepts that will preoccupy us throughout this Casebook, and illustrate its three principal themes. First, they suggest how antitrust law is evolving away from a formalistic analytical model that depends on separating conduct into discrete categories towards reliance on a set of core concepts that have been greatly influenced by economic theory. Although we present the traditional framework, it serves mainly as a step towards a more modern, concept-based vision of antitrust law and policy. The practical value of these economic concepts depends on their ability to support administrable standards that effectively distinguish "anticompetitive" from "procompetitive" business conduct.

Second, the international cartel case illustrates the dramatic trend toward the globalization of antitrust law and its concepts. The food additive cartel was a vast international enterprise, and the successful prosecution of its participants shows how anticompetitive conduct can implicate the antitrust laws of different jurisdictions. The globalization of antitrust law poses challenges of adapting antitrust law to varied settings, coordinating investigations and the prosecution of cases, and, to a degree consistent with the goals of antitrust enforcement, minimizing the burdens placed upon businesses subject to multiple competition law systems with sometimes dissimilar visions of the law and its purposes.

Third, the case studies illustrate the skills demanded of the modern antitrust lawyer. The successful private practitioner today must play several roles—analyze the likely treatment of business conduct under the laws of multiple jurisdictions, persuade antitrust agencies not to challenge a particular transaction, negotiate with potential litigants, and analyze the competitive effects of varied federal, state, and local regulations that may impede or facilitate competition. Attorneys and other public enforcement officials realize that successful policy outcomes often require cooperation with their counterparts in other countries. Paramount among the antitrust lawyer's associated skills is a basic knowledge of economics. The coffee shop case study emphasizes the centrality of economic principles in evaluating the competitive significance of business behavior.

At the outset, we raise a point of terminology. Our Casebook speaks of "antitrust law" or "antitrust policy" and "competition law" or "competition policy" somewhat interchangeably. A North American practitioner in this field likely calls herself an "antitrust lawyer"—a habit that reflects the vocabulary used in the United States since the late nineteenth century. In the rest of the world, specialists say that they practice "competition law," a phrase rooted in the experience of Europeans under the Treaty on the Functioning of the European Union and in the laws of the European Union's member states.

These terms sometimes are synonyms, but they can have different meanings. The term "antitrust law and policy" sometimes refers to the enforcement of prohibitions against certain conduct by private firms. By contrast, "competition law and policy" tends to embrace a larger range of intervention and policy tools. Examples include scrutiny of public restrictions on entry into a market or the design of an intellectual property system, by which a jurisdiction can influence the level of innovation and competition within its borders. The policy instruments beyond law enforcement include regulations, guidelines, competition advocacy, and speeches by enforcement agency personnel, all of which can influence the direction of competition policy. This Casebook focuses heavily on law enforcement, but it also draws attention to the broader array of public interventions that affect competition and emphasizes measures beyond law enforcement that antitrust agencies use to implement competition policy.

This Chapter has three Sections. Section A presents the facts and background information needed to begin considering the competition issues raised in the international lysine cartel prosecution. Section B presents four core issues that occupy our attention throughout the Casebook and introduces the basic economic concepts of modern antitrust law through our second case study, which involves the retail sale of coffee. Section C concludes, providing an introduction to the forms of economic proof and the role of decision theory that figure so prominently in modern antitrust analysis and which will be evident in all of the Chapters to come. An Appendix on Cost Concepts completes the Chapter.

A. "HARVEST KING"—THE LYSINE CARTEL

Most systems of competition law deal severely with agreements by rival firms to suppress production, raise prices, or retard innovation. This Section looks at one of the most notorious cartels in modern antitrust experience. The central player was Archer-Daniels-Midland Company (ADM), the world's largest producer of food additives, oils, and fibers derived from grains, soybeans, and other farm staples. From 1991 to 1995, ADM helped to orchestrate a global cartel to boost the price of lysine. With the help of a company insider, the Federal Bureau of Investigation (FBI) began an inquiry that ultimately spanned the globe in a case the FBI called "Harvest King." Few cases since 1890 have so influenced the way antitrust law is applied and practiced internationally. This is one of them.

UNITED STATES V. ANDREAS

United States Court of Appeals for the Seventh Circuit, 2000.
216 F.3d 645.

Before: KANNE, ROVNER, and EVANS, CIRCUIT JUDGES.

KANNE, CIRCUIT JUDGE.

For many years, Archer Daniels Midland Co.'s philosophy of customer relations could be summed up by a quote from former ADM President James Randall: "Our competitors are our friends. Our customers are the enemy." This motto animated the company's business dealings and ultimately led to blatant violations of U.S. antitrust law, a guilty plea and a staggering criminal fine against the company. It also led to the criminal charges against three top ADM executives that are the subject of this appeal. The facts involved in this case reflect an inexplicable lack of business ethics and an atmosphere of general lawlessness that infected the very heart of one of America's leading corporate citizens. Top executives at ADM and its Asian co-conspirators throughout the early 1990s spied on each other, fabricated aliases and front organizations to hide their activities, hired prostitutes to gather information from competitors, lied, cheated, embezzled, extorted and obstructed justice.

After a two-month trial, a jury convicted three ADM officials of conspiring to violate § 1 of the Sherman Antitrust Act, 15 U.S.C. § 1, which prohibits any conspiracy or combination to restrain trade. District Judge Blanche M. Manning sentenced defendants Michael D. Andreas and Terrance S. Wilson to twenty-four months in prison. They now appeal several issues related to their convictions and sentences, and the government counter-appeals one issue related to sentencing. We find no error related to the convictions, but agree with the government that the defendants should have received longer sentences for their leadership roles in the conspiracy.

I.   History

The defendants in this case, Andreas and Wilson, were executives at Archer Daniels Midland Co., the Decatur, Illinois-based agriculture processing company. Mark E. Whitacre, the third ADM executive named in the indictment, did not join this appeal. ADM, the self-professed "supermarket to the world," is a behemoth in its industry with global sales of $14 billion in 1999 and 23,000 employees. Its concerns include nearly every farm commodity, such as corn, soybeans and wheat, but also the processing of commodities into such products as fuel ethanol, high-fructose sweeteners, feed additives and various types of seed oils. ADM has a worldwide sales force and a global transportation network involving thousands of rail lines, barges and trucks. The company is publicly held and listed on the New York Stock Exchange.

The Andreas family has long controlled ADM. Dwayne Andreas is a director and the former CEO, G. Allen Andreas is the board chairman and president, and various other family members occupy other executive positions. Michael D. Andreas, commonly called "Mick," was vice chairman of the board of directors and executive vice president of sales and marketing. Wilson was president of the corn processing division and reported directly to Michael Andreas.

A.   The Lysine Industry

Lysine is an amino acid used to stimulate an animal's growth. It is produced by a fermentation process in which nutrients, primarily sugar, are fed to microorganisms, which multiply and metabolize. As a product of that process, the microorganisms excrete lysine, which is then harvested and sold to feed manufacturers who add it to animal feed. Feed manufacturers sell the feed to farmers who use it to raise chickens and pigs. The fermentation process tends to be very delicate, and utmost care must be used to keep the fermentation plant sterile.

Until 1991, the lysine market had been dominated by a cartel of three companies in Korea and Japan, with American and European subsidiaries. Ajinomoto Co., Inc. of Japan, was the industry leader, accounting for up to half of all world lysine sales. Ajinomoto had 50 percent interests in two subsidiaries, Eurolysine, based in Paris, and Heartland Lysine, based in Chicago. The other two producers of lysine were Miwon Co., Ltd. (later renamed Sewon Co., Ltd.) of South Korea, and Kyowa Hakko, Ltd. of Japan. Miwon ran a New Jersey-based subsidiary called Sewon America, and Kyowa owned the American subsidiary Biokyowa, Inc., which is based in Missouri.

Lysine is a highly fungible commodity and sold almost entirely on the basis of price. Pricing depended largely on two variables: the price of organic substitutes, such as soy or fish meal, and the price charged by other lysine producers. Together, the three parent companies produced all of the world's lysine until the 1990s, presenting an obvious opportunity for collusive behavior. Indeed the Asian cartel periodically agreed to fix prices, which at times reached as high as $3.00 per pound.

In 1989, ADM announced that it was building what would be the world's largest lysine plant. If goals were met, the Illinois facility could produce two or three times as much lysine as any other plant and could ultimately account for up to half of all the lysine produced globally. Even before the plant became operational, ADM embarked on an ambitious marketing campaign aimed at attracting large American meat companies, such as Tyson Foods, in part by capitalizing on anti-Asia sentiment prevalent at the time. Also around 1990, another South Korean company, Cheil Jedang Co., began producing lysine. Despite some early difficulties with the fermenting process, the ADM plant began producing lysine in 1991 and immediately became a market heavyweight, possibly even the industry leader. The two new producers created chaos in the market, igniting a price war that drove the price of lysine down, eventually to about 70-cents per pound. The Asian companies understandably were greatly concerned by developments in this once profitable field.

B. Start of the Conspiracy

Against this background, Kyowa Hakko arranged a meeting with Ajinomoto and ADM in June 1992. Mexico City was chosen as the site in part because the participants did not want to meet within the jurisdiction of American antitrust laws. Ajinomoto was represented by Kanji Mimoto and Hirokazu Ikeda from the Tokyo headquarters, and Alain Crouy from its Eurolysine subsidiary. Masaru Yamamoto represented Kyowa Hakko, and Wilson and Whitacre attended for ADM. Mimoto, Ikeda, Crouy and Yamamoto testified as government witnesses at trial. At this meeting, the three companies first discussed price agreements and allocating sales volumes among the market participants. Wilson, who was senior to Whitacre in the corporate hierarchy, led the discussion on behalf of ADM. The price agreements came easily, and all present agreed to raise the price in two stages by the end of 1992. According to internal Ajinomoto documents prepared after the meeting, the cartel's goal was to raise the price to $1.05 per pound in North America and Europe by October 1992 and up to $1.20 per pound by December, with other price hikes for other regions. The companies agreed to that price schedule and presumed that Ajinomoto and Kyowa would convince Sewon and Cheil to agree as well.

The sales volume allocation, in which the cartel (now including ADM) would decide how much each company would sell, was a matter of strong disagreement. In ADM's view, ADM should have one-third of the market, Ajinomoto and its subsidiaries should have one-third and Kyowa and the Koreans should have the remaining third. Ajinomoto—the historical industry leader—disagreed vehemently and thought ADM did not deserve an equal portion of the market and could not produce that much lysine in any case. Wilson also suggested each company pick an auditor to whom sales volumes could be reported so that the cartel could keep track of each other's business. The meeting ended without a sales volume allocation agreement, but two months later, at the recommendation of Whitacre, the cartel raised prices anyway, and prices rose from $.70 to $1.05 per pound.

Still, the cartel considered a price agreement without allocating sales volume to be an imperfect scheme because each company would have an incentive to cheat on the price to get more sales, so long as its competitors continued to sell at the agreed price. With cheating, the price ultimately would drop, and the agreement would falter. An effort had to be made to get the parties to agree to a volume agreement, and to that end, Whitacre invited Ajinomoto officials to visit ADM's Decatur lysine facility to prove that it could produce the volume ADM claimed. Mimoto, Ikeda and other Ajinomoto officials, including an engineer named Fujiwara, visited the plant in September 1992. At a meeting before the tour, Whitacre and Mimoto confirmed the price schedule to which the parties had agreed in Mexico City.

The cartel met again in October 1992, this time in Paris. All five major lysine producers attended, along with representatives of their subsidiaries. Wilson and Whitacre again represented ADM. To disguise the purpose of the meeting, the parties created a fake agenda, and later a fictitious lysine producers trade association, so they could meet and share information without raising the suspicions of customers or law enforcement agencies. According to the agenda, the group was to discuss such topics as animal rights and the environment. In reality, they discussed something much dearer to their hearts—the price of lysine. According to internal Ajinomoto documents, the "purpose of the meeting" was to "confirm present price level and reaction of the market, and 2, future price schedule."

Shortly after this meeting, under circumstances explained below, Whitacre began cooperating with the FBI in an undercover sting operation aimed at busting the price-fixing conspiracy. As a result, most of the meetings and telephone conversations involving Whitacre and other conspirators after October 1992 were audiotaped or videotaped.

Despite the cartel's efforts to raise prices, the price of lysine dropped in 1993. According to executives of the companies who testified at trial, without a sales volume agreement, each company had an incentive to underbid the agreed price, and consequently each company had to match the lower bids or lose sales to its underbidding competitors. This resulted in the price of lysine falling in the spring of 1993. The group, calling itself "G-5" or "the club," met in Vancouver, Canada, in June 1993 to deal with the disintegrating price agreement. Wilson and Whitacre again represented ADM. At this meeting, the Asian companies presented a sales volume allocation that limited each company to a certain tonnage of lysine per year. ADM, through Wilson, rejected the suggested tonnage assignment because it granted ADM less than one-third of the market. Ajinomoto still considered ADM's demands too high.

That summer's strong commodities market permitted frequent increases in the lysine price, to which each of the companies agreed, despite the absence of a volume allocation. The cartel's continued strong interest in a volume allocation to support the price agreement led to another meeting in Paris in October 1993. The failure to reach a volume schedule in Paris finally led to a call for a meeting between the top management at Ajinomoto and ADM: Kazutoshi Yamada and Mick Andreas.

In October 1993, Andreas and Whitacre met with Yamada and Ikeda in Irvine, California. With Whitacre's assistance, the meeting was secretly videotaped and audiotaped. Andreas threatened Yamada that ADM would flood the market unless a sales volume allocation agreement was reached that would allow ADM to sell more than it had the previous year. The four discussed the dangers of competing in a free market and hammered out a deal on volume allocations, with Andreas accepting less than a one-third share of the market in exchange for a large portion of the market's growth. Specific prices were not discussed, but Andreas acknowledged the price deal that had already been negotiated. Yamada agreed to present ADM's proposal to the other three Asian producers.

A central concern to Andreas was the difficulty he expected the Asian producers to encounter in maintaining their agreed price level. As Andreas explained at some length, the Asian companies had a more decentralized sales system that depended on agents making deals with customers. ADM featured a very centralized system in which agents played a small role in overall sales and had no discretion over price. In such an environment, maintaining control over price was easy; for the Japanese, Andreas feared it would be difficult and suggested that Ajinomoto move to a more ADM-like centralized pricing system. Andreas also expressed concern that customers could "cheat" the producers by bargaining down the price, apparently by claiming to have received lower bids from competing producers. Ikeda and Yamada agreed that customer cheating was a problem, and the four briefly discussed a quick-response system that would allow the producers to verify with each other the prices offered to particular customers.

After the Irvine meeting, the cartel met in Tokyo to work out the details of the Andreas-Yamada arrangement. All the companies except for

Cheil now agreed to both tonnage maximums and percentage market shares. The group excluded Cheil from this discussion because it considered Cheil's volume demand unreasonable. The cartel, expecting the lysine market to grow in 1994, thought it wise to agree on percentages of the market that each company could have since it was possible that all five producers could sell more than their allotted tonnage. With a total expected market of 245,000 tons for 1994, Ajinomoto was to sell 84,000 tons, ADM would sell 67,000 tons, Kyowa would sell 46,000 tons, Miwon would sell 34,000 tons and Cheil, if it eventually accepted the deal, would get 14,000 tons, according to the deal hammered out by Yamada and Andreas in Irvine.

As they had before the Andreas-Yamada meeting, Wilson and Whitacre attended these Tokyo meetings for ADM. In Tokyo, Wilson suggested, and the members agreed, that each producer report their monthly sales figures by telephone to Mimoto throughout the year, and if one producer exceeded its allocation, it would compensate the others by buying enough from the shorted members to even out the allocation. The producers also agreed on a new price of $1.20 for the United States market. The agreement to buy each other's unsold allocation cemented the deal by eliminating any incentive for a company to underbid the sales price. According to Mimoto: "Since there is an agreement on the quantity allocation, our sales quantity is guaranteed by other manufacturers of the lysine. So by matching the price, to us, lowering the price is very silly. We can just keep the price." With the agreement on prices and quantities in place, the lysine price remained at the agreed level for January and February 1994.

On March 10, 1994, the cartel met in Hawaii. At this meeting, attended by Wilson and Whitacre on behalf of ADM, the producers discussed the progress of the volume allocation agreement, reported their sales figures and agreed on prices. They also considered letting Cheil into the allocation agreement and agreed to grant the company a market share of 17,000 tons. Cheil accepted this arrangement at a meeting later that day, at which Wilson explained that the conspiracy would operate almost identically to the scheme used to fix prices in the citric-acid market. The cartel further agreed on prices for Europe, South America, Asia and the rest of the world, and discussed how the global allocations would work on a regional basis. According to the figures reported to Mimoto through May 1994, prices were maintained, and both ADM and Ajinomoto were on track to meet their sales volume limits.

In the summer of 1994, the producers met in Sapporo, Japan, for a routine cartel meeting. Whitacre represented ADM by himself. At this meeting, Sewon demanded a larger share of the market for 1995. This created a problem for the cartel, which necessitated another meeting between Andreas and Yamada. In October 1994, while on a separate business trip to the United States, Yamada met with Andreas in a private dining room at the Four Seasons Hotel in Chicago. Whitacre, Wilson and Mimoto also attended along with their bosses.

The cartel met in Atlanta in January 1995, using a major poultry exposition as camouflage for the producers being in the same place at the same time. The cartel, without the presence of Sewon, decided to cut Sewon out of the agreement for 1995 because of its unrealistic volume demand. Sewon then joined the meeting and agreed to abide by the set price, if not the volume. The group discussed the year-end sales figures for 1994, comparing them to each company's allocated volume, and discussed the new allotment for 1995. According to the 1994 numbers, each company finished fairly close to its allotted volume. The cartel met once more in Hong Kong before the FBI raided the offices of ADM in Decatur and Heartland Lysine in Chicago. These raids ended the cartel. Heartland Lysine immediately notified its home office in Japan of the search, and Ajinomoto began destroying evidence of the cartel housed in its Tokyo office. Mimoto overlooked documents stored at his home and later turned these over to the FBI. Included in these saved documents were copies of internal Ajinomoto reports of the Mexico and Paris meetings.

C. The Investigation

Mark E. Whitacre joined ADM in 1989 as president of its bioproducts division. That year, ADM announced that it would enter the lysine market dominated by Asian producers. Whitacre, who held a Ph.D. in biochemistry from Cornell University and degrees in agricultural science, answered directly to Mick Andreas. Just 32 years old when he joined the company, Whitacre's star clearly was rising fast at ADM, and some industry analysts thought he could be the next president of ADM.

In 1992, Whitacre began working with Wilson, and the two attended the first meetings of the lysine producers in Mexico City. Also in 1992, Whitacre began embezzling large sums of money from ADM and eventually stole at least $9 million from the company by submitting to ADM phony invoices for work done by outside companies, who would then funnel the money to Whitacre's personal offshore and Swiss bank accounts. To cover up the embezzlement, Whitacre hatched a scheme in the summer of 1992 to accuse Ajinomoto of planting a saboteur in ADM's Decatur plant. Whitacre would accuse the saboteur of contaminating the delicate bacterial environment needed for the production of lysine, a story made believable because of the many early difficulties the ADM lysine plant encountered.

In accordance with the plot, Whitacre told Mick Andreas that an engineer at Ajinomoto named Fujiwara had contacted him at his home and offered to sell ADM the name of the saboteur in exchange for $10 million. The story was a lie. However, Dwayne Andreas believed it and feared it could jeopardize relations between the United States and Japan. He called the CIA, but the CIA, considering the matter one of federal law enforcement rather than national security, directed the call to the FBI, which sent agents out to ADM to interview Whitacre and other officials about the extortion. Whitacre apparently had not expected this and realized quickly that his lie would be discovered by the FBI, particularly after Special Agent Brian Shepard asked Whitacre if he could tap Whitacre's home telephone to record the next extortion demand. Whitacre knew that when the extortionist failed to call, Shepard would know Whitacre had invented the story. Whitacre confessed the scheme to Shepard, but to save himself, he agreed to become an undercover informant to help the FBI investigate price fixing at ADM. He did not come totally clean with the FBI, however; he failed to mention the millions he embezzled and in fact continued to embezzle after he began working for the government. For the next two-and-a-half years, Whitacre acted as an undercover cooperating witness—legally a government agent—and secretly taped hundreds of hours of conversations and meetings with Wilson, Mick Andreas and the other conspirators. In addition, the FBI secretly videotaped meetings of the lysine producers.

* * *

———————

Mark Whitacre, the ADM executive featured in the Seventh Circuit's opinion, was a vexing informant for the Department of Justice (DOJ) as it investigated ADM's participation in the lysine cartel. The DOJ gradually learned that Whitacre aided the inquiry to deflect attention from his embezzlement of ADM funds. For all the trouble Whitacre's falsehoods caused the prosecutors, however, the information he provided was pure gold for building the government's case. *See generally* KURT EICHENWALD, THE INFORMANT (2000).

The most stunning evidence appeared in the videotapes Whitacre helped the DOJ to obtain by alerting them to the time and location of cartel meetings. Captured in grainy, black and white images were hours of discussions in which the lysine producers set price and output levels, argued over production quotas, and devised ways to audit compliance with their pact. In one memorable session in a hotel room in Atlanta, the competitors joked openly about the possibility that the FBI or the Federal Trade Commission (FTC) might detect their behavior.

Seldom had prosecutors obtained such damning evidence of an antitrust crime. Confronted with the evidence, ADM agreed to pay a criminal fine of $100 million—at that time, the largest criminal recovery in the history of the Sherman Act. The DOJ indicted ADM executives Michael Andreas, Terrence Wilson, and Mark Whitacre, the cooperating witness who violated his cooperation agreement through various deceits. A jury convicted all three men, and Andreas and Wilson contested their conviction on appeal. In the *Andreas* opinion excerpt we just read, the Seventh Circuit upheld their convictions and concluded that the trial judge erred by imposing excessively lenient (24 month) sentences. ADM later paid hundreds of millions of dollars in settlements to resolve private suits and claims pressed by foreign governments.

What motivated ADM and its co-conspirators to undertake the price-fixing scheme? How might it benefit them? What reasons might justify condemning this arrangement among competitors? Treating it as a crime? Would it harm consumers? How? If antitrust law seeks to prohibit such conduct, how can it do so? What should the scope of the offense be? The punishment? Should the conspirators be permitted any defenses? What if they set "reasonable" prices that stabilized their industry and helped keep employment high? What if the arrangement helped lower their production costs? What if their only defense was to increase their profits?

Consider the operation of the cartel. What was the mechanism used to fix prices, and what steps did the conspirators take to implement their agreement? Why did they keep coming back to discussions of "cheating," "quotas," and output allocations? How easy or hard is it to agree to fix prices? How often did the conspirators have to meet? Why did they meet *where* they met?

Sidebar 1–1:
"Vitamins, Inc."

In the course of investigating the lysine cartel, Whitacre told the FBI he had overheard conversations within ADM about arrangements to set production levels for another food additive, citric acid. Whitacre also knew that ADM executives met regularly with some of Europe's leading food additive producers, including Hoffmann-La Roche (Roche). Whitacre correctly perceived that ADM was working with Roche to rig citric acid production, but he did not imagine the full state of play in Europe. On a scale that dwarfed the lysine cartel, Roche, BASF, and Rhone-Poulenc had formed a covert consortium to control the production and pricing of vitamins. Observing ADM's success in boosting prices for food additives, the three European firms set out to replicate the model of industry-wide coordination for vitamins. They targeted the market for industrial quantities of Vitamins A, B, and C, which food companies bought and blended into products consumed by hundreds of millions of individuals every day.

The resulting scheme, which the participants called "Vitamins, Inc.," was a complex venture. Formed in the 1980s, the cartel met regularly in European resorts to identify global demand, set overall production levels, allocate sales quotas, and arrange for producers who exceeded their quotas to pay firms whose sales fell below the cartel's projections. Implementation of the cartel's strategic plan took place through committees organized by geography and product group. The committees met separately and reported to the cartel's board, which met in Switzerland each year to set a budget for the entire undertaking. The cartel enlisted a private consulting firm, Treuhand, to help administer the scheme and give advice on how to improve it.

As it closed in on the vitamins conspirators, the Justice Department soon realized the benefits of a new policy it had adopted earlier in the decade to disrupt the operation of cartels. Since the late 1970s, the DOJ had promised to reduce the punishment for companies and individuals who revealed their participation in antitrust crimes such as price-fixing. This first generation "leniency" program elicited weak cooperation from cartel insiders; leniency applicants had to reveal all that they knew in return for only partial dispensation from punishment. Their cooperation would only mitigate criminal sanctions, not avoid them completely.

To do better, the government sweetened the prize. In August 1993, under the direction of Anne Bingaman, the Assistant Attorney General for Antitrust, the DOJ announced that it would grant full immunity from criminal prosecution for the first company (other than the cartel ringmaster) to notify the government of a cartel in which it had participated. In August 1994 the DOJ expanded the new policy to include individuals engaged in criminal antitrust violations. The leniency polices are discussed at greater length in Sidebar 3–1, *infra*.

Late in 1997, the business press reported that the DOJ was investigating pricing patterns in the vitamins industry and was steadily gathering evidence. The reports caught the attention of Rhone-Poulenc, the smallest Vitamins, Inc. member. Fearing that the walls were closing in on the cartel, Rhone-Poulenc played the leniency card and told its story to the DOJ.

In return for full immunity from criminal prosecution for the company and its employees, Rhone-Poulenc revealed the details of the vitamins cartel and its operations. After sorting through a treasure trove of new information, the DOJ confronted Roche and BASF. The vitamins scheme greatly exceeded the lysine cartel in its financial scale and organizational intricacy. In 1999, Roche and BASF agreed to pay the Justice Department criminal fines of $500 million and $225 million, respectively, for colluding to set vitamin prices. At the time, the total payment of $725 million constituted the largest criminal fine ever recovered by the DOJ for any violation of a U.S. criminal statute. In addition, private parties overcharged by the vitamin cartel recovered an estimated $3–4 billion in damages. Government fines paid as a consequence of public enforcement actions in the U.S. and elsewhere totaled nearly $1.8 billion. A number of foreign citizens agreed to serve prison terms in the United States to resolve their participation in the illegal scheme. *See generally* JOHN M. CONNOR, GLOBAL PRICE FIXING (2d ed. 2007). In the rest of this Chapter, consider why the antitrust laws should treat the lysine and vitamins cartels so harshly.

In several parts of this Casebook, we will return to the issues of substantive doctrine and prosecutorial process that figured prominently in the lysine and vitamins cases. For now it is enough to underscore several features of these two episodes. First, the Sherman Act was among the earliest "white collar" criminal statutes, and today U.S. antitrust policy treats the behavior at issue—joint efforts by producers to restrict output as a means of raising prices—as so dangerous to the competitive process that it warrants prosecution as a felony. The modern U.S. antitrust system has relied on two interrelated strategies to detect and deter such cartels: a leniency program to promote detection by boosting the reward to cartel participants for reporting their own misconduct and severe sanctions for corporate and individual violators, including criminal sanctions (the maximum possible jail sentence for culpable individuals today is ten years). For data on the largest U.S. fine recoveries, see U.S. Dep't of Justice, Antitrust Division, *Sherman Act Violations Yielding a Corporate Fine of $10 Million or More, https://www.justice.gov/atr/sherman-act-violations-yielding-corporate-fine-10-million-or-more.*

Second, much of the illegal activity took place outside the United States in jurisdictions that previously had taken a less severe view of cartels. The DOJ's prosecution of the lysine and vitamins cartels catalyzed major changes in the treatment of such conduct abroad. The vitamins cartel had exploited the indifference of many European governments toward supplier collusion. The scheme's duration, the magnitude of harm, and the sheer volume of fines collected by the DOJ caused the European Union and other jurisdictions to reconsider and reshape policy. Many foreign authorities, including the EU, now assign the highest enforcement priority to the investigation and prosecution of cartels. The U.S. experience with leniency inspired widespread adoption. Nearly half of the world's 130 competition systems today have leniency programs, and most impose substantial fines for cartel activity. Roughly thirty jurisdictions treat the cartel offense as a crime, though successful application of the criminal enforcement powers has eluded all but a few countries. *See* CRIMINALISING CARTELS: CRITICAL STUDIES OF AN INTERNATIONAL REGULATORY MOVEMENT (Caron Beaton-Wells & Ariel Ezrachi eds., 2011).

Third, the lysine and vitamins case studies underscore the value of achieving a better understanding of how cartels operate and of the policy measures best suited to detect and deter them. Before the discovery of the lysine and vitamins cartels, a number of commentators had argued that cartels were unlikely to form, because they are difficult to establish and maintain. These cases demonstrated that cartels can persist over a number of years, even decades. *See* Margaret C. Levenstein & Valerie Y. Suslow, *Breaking Up is Hard to Do: Determinants of Cartel Duration*, 54 J. LAW & ECON. 455 (2011) (evaluating 81 cartels terminated by antitrust enforcement since 1890 and finding that they had an average duration of 8 years). The collusive schemes required the participants to establish intricate administrative machinery and to undertake elaborate measures to ensure the effective management of the cartel. *See generally* ROBERT MARSHALL & LESLIE MARX, THE ECONOMICS OF COLLUSION (2012). One can ask why business managers take the increasingly serious risks from participating in these arrangements, what public harms they cause, and what enhancements to detection tools and penalties would deter them from doing so. As the case studies indicate, solutions to the cartel problem are likely to benefit greatly from substantial cooperation among the enforcement authorities of different nations.

B. IDENTIFYING THE CORE QUESTIONS OF ANTITRUST LAW

Like few other contemporary antitrust matters, the international cartel cases led the antitrust bar and government officials to revisit basic issues surrounding the operation of antitrust systems and to confront the consequences of the globalization of competition. In this Section, we identify the core questions of antitrust law that were implicated in the cartel cases and that increasingly dominate the design and implementation of antitrust systems in the U.S. and abroad.

1. WHAT ARE THE PURPOSES OF COMPETITION LAW SYSTEMS?

A system of law has two basic elements: (1) *doctrine* embodied in statutes, administrative regulations, and judicial interpretations, and (2) *institutions* that implement legal commands. For most jurisdictions, the central antitrust institution is the public enforcement body. The system's effectiveness also depends on the contributions from other public and private institutions. These include courts that adjudicate cases; the provision (if any) for private rights of action; universities that teach antitrust economics and law and perform research about antitrust theory and practice; legal and economic societies that provide a forum for discussion about antitrust issues; and trade associations that provide channels for disseminating information about competition laws to businesses.

A central question about any antitrust system is "what are its goals?" Below, we explore the economic and non-economic goals an antitrust system might serve. For economic purposes, we consider what society expects to achieve through private markets. Antitrust law's economic purposes are important for contemporary policy making, especially in the United States. On the non-economic side, we explore some deeply embedded, historically persistent antitrust sub-themes, such as a fear of corporate bigness, a preference for commercial fairness, and a distrust of economic phenomena that could corrupt the political process. *See generally* Symposium, *The Goals of Antitrust*, 81 FORDHAM L. REV. 2151 (2013).

a. What Economic Purposes Can They Serve?

Nearly 40 years ago, Robert Bork underscored the importance of goals to the operation of an antitrust system. "Antitrust policy," Bork wrote, "cannot be made rational until we are able to give a firm answer to one question: What is the point of the law—what are its goals? Everything else follows from the answer we give." ROBERT H. BORK, THE ANTITRUST PARADOX 50 (1978).

Antitrust's chief economic aim is to prevent the acquisition, maintenance, or exercise of "market power," as microeconomics uses the term. A firm or firms exercise market power when they reduce output or otherwise restrict competition to raise price above the competitive level. Yet market power is not the reason for every price increase. The price of a good or service can rise by reason of an increase in the costs of producing and selling it, or due to inflation. Such price increases reflect the natural operation of markets, not the exercise of market power, and although they may concern policy-makers, they ordinarily are not the object of the antitrust laws. Below we present a hypothetical case that explains the economic basis of antitrust's concern with market power—the relationship between a reduction in output and higher prices—and describe the economic effects that result. As you read the Coffee Shop case, ask whether the higher prices the co-conspirators received in the lysine and vitamins cartels reflected the exercise of market power.

Market Power and Its Consequences:
The Case of the Coffee Shop

Stroll into an office complex and you are likely to find that one of the ground-floor tenants is a coffee shop. Customers stop by to choose from a selection of coffees and teas and at least to scan the display of freshly baked cookies, muffins, scones, and pastries. The shop owner likes her customers, but she also likes her income. As she sees patrons fill the shop every day, she wonders if she could get her customers to pay more if she reduced the total amount she produces each day. Below we explore the question of whether our shop owner has, or can exercise, "market power." Doing so allows us to introduce some basic ideas from microeconomics that are relevant to antitrust analysis.

i. *Demand*

If a reduction in output is to cause a price increase, the firm or firms cutting back on sales must face a downward-sloping demand function. A demand function is a schedule that describes the amount of a good or service buyers would be willing to purchase at varying prices in some time period. Figure 1–1 depicts the hypothetical demand for coffee in the morning at our coffee shop. At a price of $1 per cup, our coffee shop sells 100 cups in a typical morning. If the shop raised the price to $1.25 per cup without regard to what other coffee vendors nearby were doing, it would only sell 50 cups in a typical morning. If it lowered its price to 75 cents per cup, it would sell 150 cups. How can we know the likely effect of a price change on the shop's coffee sales? Perhaps the coffee shop experimented with raising or lowering price. We might also survey customers, study the experience of coffee shops in other office complexes, ask an industry expert (such as our coffee shop owner) to share her business judgment based on her experience, or ask an expert economist to study the available data and provide an opinion.

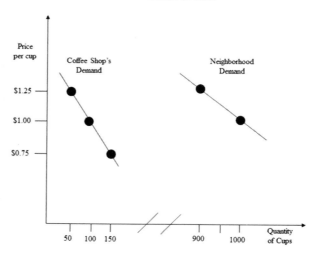

Figure 1–1:
Demand for Coffee

As the price rises, the quantity sold falls; this is what is meant by a "downward-sloping demand curve." Quantity falls because, as price rises, fewer buyers are willing to patronize the coffee shop. The demand function thus summarizes the economic force of *buyer substitution*. At the higher price, some buyers (half in the example) would continue to purchase coffee from the coffee shop before work. These are sometimes called "inframarginal" consumers. But the other half, sometimes called "marginal" consumers, would make other choices—that is, the "marginal consumers" are those that would change their behavior in some way in response to a small increase in price. Some may purchase coffee from some other vendor; some may make coffee in their office; some may drink coffee at home before work; some may switch to drinking tea or other beverages; and some may do without a morning beverage entirely. As Figure 1–1 also indicates, if the coffee shop lowers price below $1 per cup, its sales would likely rise as buyers purchase more coffee at that location. Some might shift their purchases from other vendors to the coffee shop, or from other beverages to coffee, while others might decide that at the lower price they can now afford to buy coffee at work or afford occasionally to have a second cup.

Buyers can be more or less sensitive to changes in price. The more sensitive they are—the greater the change in quantity generated by a small change in price—the less steep the slope of the demand curve. If the quantity demanded is extremely responsive to a small change in price, the demand curve will be a horizontal line. Conversely, the less the change in quantity generated by a small change in price, the steeper the slope of the demand curve. Buyer sensitivity to changes in price can be computed in terms of the *percentage* change in quantity generated by a small *percentage* change in price. This degree to which buyers respond to price changes is termed the "elasticity of demand." In Figure 1–1 the elasticity of demand is –2 at the initial sales level (approximated by the percentage change in the quantity demanded, –50%, divided by the percentage change in the price, 25%).[5]

Demand curves characterized by various elasticities are depicted in Figure 1–2. If a small percentage change in price leads to a very large percentage change in quantity demanded, demand is said to be highly "elastic." The demand for coffee from our coffee shop might be elastic in a business district where most workers would respond to a price increase by buying their coffee at other nearby coffee shops, or putting small coffee makers in their offices, or carrying a thermos of the beverage from home. If sellers would lose so many customers in response to a very small price increase as to make some or all of the demand curve a horizontal line, demand in the horizontal segment is said to be "perfectly elastic." For example, the demand for coffee sold in our coffee shop might be highly elastic if the same coffee were available at the same price from a coffee service that provided coffee machines for the offices of tenants in the office building. A demand curve might also vary in elasticity along its length. For example, the demand for coffee from our coffee shop might be perfectly elastic along some segment or segments along the demand curve, but not along a different segment, where price is higher or lower.

Conversely, if a small percentage change in price leads to only a small change in quantity demanded, demand is said to be highly "inelastic." Producers of a good or service facing inelastic demand can raise price without significantly reducing demand. For example, the demand for our coffee shop's variety of espresso might be relatively inelastic. This is because our owner has an unmatched skill at making a type of espresso viewed by coffee connoisseurs as so sublime that the product's price becomes less important to them. If the quantity demanded is so unresponsive to price as to make the demand curve a vertical line, demand is said to be "perfectly inelastic."

---

[5] The mathematically inclined will recognize that the elasticity of a demand curve is not the same thing as its slope, though the two concepts are related. Think of the demand curve as relating the quantity of the product demanded (Q) to the price charged (P). Then the slope of the demand curve can be written as $\Delta Q/\Delta P$ (where Δ represents the change), and the elasticity is written $(\Delta Q/Q)/(\Delta P/P)$, which is the percentage change in quantity divided by the percentage change in price, or, equivalently, as $(\Delta Q/\Delta P)(P/Q)$.

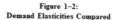

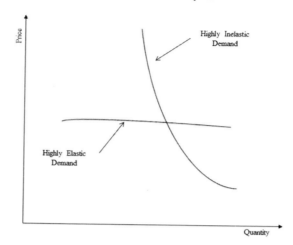

Notice that in each example above, the demand curve relates to both a product and a geographic region. In the case of the coffee shop, the extent of buyer substitution can depend upon the proximity of other coffee vendors, the acceptability to consumers of other beverages in the coffee shop, or some combination of both. In the aggregate, buyer willingness to substitute these and other alternatives to purchasing coffee in the coffee shop will determine the degree of the coffee shop's market power, if any, over coffee. Defining the range of reasonable geographic and product substitutes is the goal of "market definition," which can play an important role in the identification of market power.

Figure 1–1 also depicts a second demand function, the demand for morning coffee collectively faced by all the coffee shops and restaurants in the neighborhood. It shows that at a price of $1 per cup—charged by all vendors at once—1000 cups are sold in the typical morning. If the price rose to $1.25 per cup, 900 cups would instead be sold. Most buyers would continue to buy morning coffee (maybe while grumbling about the higher price), but some—100 in this example—would substitute other ways of getting coffee, switch to tea or other beverages, or forego a morning drink. Note that the demand curve facing an individual *firm* is often more elastic than the demand curve facing the *industry* as a whole, a circumstance illustrated in Figure 1–1. If the coffee shop alone raises price by a small percentage, it will lose a significant percentage of its customers to rival coffee vendors. But if all of the coffee shops in the neighborhood raise price together, they will be able to retain many of those customers.

ii. *Supply and Perfect Competition*

The demand curve describes how one important group of market participants, buyers, will respond to price changes. To understand what price is actually set in the market, we must also consider the behavior of the other important group of market participants, sellers.

Seller behavior generally depends both on each firm's costs and on the way the firms interact with each other. In a perfectly competitive market, the simplest case, each firm's supply decision depends only on its costs; it does not take into account the response of rivals in making its supply decisions. Such firms are sometimes termed "price-takers," because they decide how much output to supply based solely on comparing their costs to the market price.

In particular, a firm selling in a perfectly competitive market will produce an additional unit of output so long as the market price is at least as great as the cost of producing that incremental unit. The cost of producing an additional unit of output is termed the *marginal cost* of that unit. The key distinction is between costs that vary with the decision the firm is making (here, whether to produce additional output) and costs that do not. For example, if the coffee shop has already rented retail space, installed brewing equipment, hired its staff, and advertised its presence, the cost of producing and selling one more cup of coffee likely will be simply the cost of the extra beans, hot water, a paper cup, and the electricity required to brew one more cup. The marginal cost of producing one more cup would be those *variable costs* (costs that vary with the decision, here whether to produce an additional cup of coffee) associated with the incremental (additional) cup produced.

In many industries, the marginal cost of production increases with output (an upward sloping curve), as depicted for the firm in Figure 1–3. This might occur for the coffee shop, for example, if it costs more to buy coffee beans if they have to be purchased at the last minute, to serve a new customer. Marginal cost curves are often upward sloping, as drawn in the figure, but they do not have to be. In some industries, each additional unit can be produced at the same cost as the previous one, and in other industries, additional units can be produced for less.

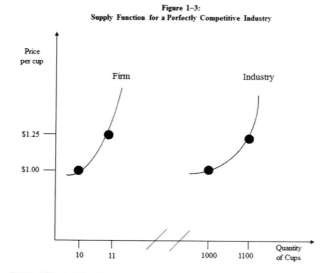

Figure 1–3:
Supply Function for a Perfectly Competitive Industry

Costs that do not vary with producing additional cups of coffee are termed *fixed costs*. If the firm was making a different decision, for example whether to expand the business by doubling the size of the retail space, adding more equipment and increasing the staff, some of the costs that are considered fixed with respect to selling an additional cup in a given morning would become variable, and, consequently, would matter in making that decision. Hence, from an economic perspective, the "cost" of a product like a cup of coffee depends on what decision the firm is making: whether to brew an additional cup this morning with the existing facility, staff and equipment, or whether to expand the operation in order to be able to produce and sell more cups every day in the future. (We will discuss these cost concepts in more detail, along with additional cost concepts, in the Appendix at the end of this Chapter.)

In a perfectly competitive market, each firm produces every unit of output for which the price exceeds or equals its marginal cost of production, because every such unit adds to the firm's profit. Under such circumstances, the amount that the industry as a whole will supply at any price depends only on the marginal cost functions of the individual firms. Figure 1–3 depicts the derivation of the industry supply function from the marginal cost functions of an industry composed of one hundred identical firms. For the representative firm, marginal cost rises with output. The tenth unit costs $1 to produce, while the eleventh unit costs $1.25. If the market price were $1, therefore, each firm would choose to produce ten units and the industry as a whole (all one hundred firms) would supply 1000 units. Similarly, at a market price of $1.25, the industry would supply 1100 units.

Under perfect competition, the market price is determined by the intersection of the industry supply function and the industry demand function, as depicted in Figure 1–4. If price were lower, buyers would want to purchase more than the sellers would supply, and the price would be bid up until supply equals demand. Similarly, if the price were higher, sellers would see a shortfall of willing buyers; price would be bid down until supply equals demand.

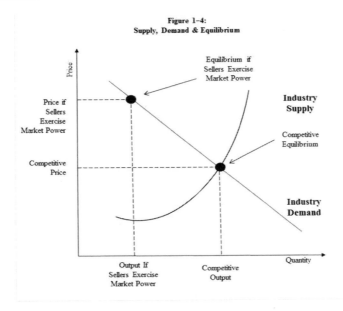

Figure 1–4:
Supply, Demand & Equilibrium

Price increases in a perfectly competitive model reflect higher seller costs. One reason the competitive price might rise is if the marginal costs of production increase for some or all firms. This might occur for the coffee shop, for example, if the price of coffee beans rises. Under such circumstances, firms will require a higher market price before they will produce the same amount of output as before. This is depicted graphically as a backward (or upward) shift in the industry supply function, and, as shown in Figure 1–5, it leads to a higher competitive price.

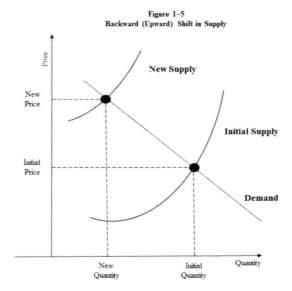

Figure 1–5
Backward (Upward) Shift in Supply

Another reason prices might rise in a competitive market is that buyers might increase their demand for coffee, desiring to purchase more than before at any price. This might occur, for example, if the number of office workers taking coffee breaks increased, or if a widely-reported study identified previously unknown health benefits to coffee drinking. This dynamic is depicted as an outward (or upward) shift in the demand curve. As shown in Figure 1–6, it leads to a higher price if the industry supply curve is rising. Here, the higher demand leads firms to expand output, and seller marginal costs rise as they do, leading to higher market prices.

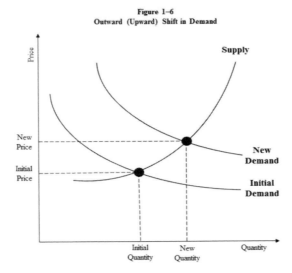

Figure 1–6
Outward (Upward) Shift in Demand

Both buyers and sellers benefit from participating in a competitive market. To see why, suppose, that the competitive price is $1 per cup, and at that price 1000 cups are sold by all firms participating in the market. Now consider the 500th unit produced and sold. Suppose that this unit is valued by its buyer at $2, and costs its producer only 60 cents to make. Pause on this point to marvel at the miracle of the market: it takes resources worth only 60 cents to the seller, and converts them into a product, here a cup of coffee, worth $2.00 to the buyer—for a gain to society of $1.40. If the competitive price is $1, then the buyer claims the majority of the total social gain: the buyer pays $1 for a product she values at $2, for a benefit of $1, and the seller receives $1 for producing something that costs it only 60 cents, for a benefit of 40 cents. This kind of calculation could be repeated for every unit produced and sold, as depicted in Figure 1–7. In the figure, the two shaded triangles collectively reflect the total social benefit of all the transactions in the market—the $1.40 benefit of the transaction involving the 500th unit, combined with the benefit to society of every other one of the 1000 units produced and sold. This area is termed the "aggregate surplus." It is divided into two parts: the "consumers' surplus" is the triangle above the market price, and the "producers' surplus" is the area below that triangle. The consumers' surplus and the producers' surplus reflect the portion of the aggregate surplus that accrues to buyers and sellers, respectively.

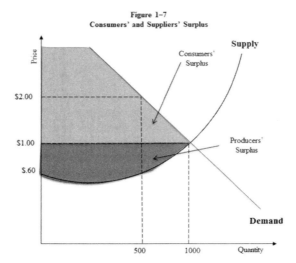

Figure 1–7
Consumers' and Suppliers' Surplus

iii. Market Power

The model of perfect competition was constructed by economists largely to illustrate the general properties of a decentralized allocation of goods and services guided by market prices. The model makes a number of simplifying assumptions to achieve that end, but was not intended to describe with precision all of the economic forces at work in real world markets. In this sense, all real world markets are "imperfect." For example, many firms in the modern economy face downward sloping demand for their products or services and are in consequence able to raise price by reducing output, potentially above a competitive level but not necessarily so.

When competition is not perfect, the firms participating in the market may be able to exercise what economists term "market power" by raising their price above the competitive level. In this case, the neighborhood coffee vendors could exercise market power if they reduced their sales and raised price—but only if they act together. If they collectively agreed to cut back sales by 10% (from 1000 to 900) and raise price by 25% (from $1 to $1.25), they would likely increase their profits, assuming that the higher price did not attract new competition. Whether they actually would find this strategy profitable, assuming for the moment that it were legal, depends not just on how many sales they would lose (the slope of the industry demand curve) but also on the profit margin (price less unit cost) on those lost sales.

For example, if it costs these vendors 60 cents to make a cup of coffee, each cup sold at $1.00 contributes 40 cents to profit. Their gross profit on sales of coffee at $1.00 per cup is $400 (1000 cups x 40 cents). By collectively raising their price from $1.00 to $1.25 they can increase their profits by $185 to a total of $585, even though they will be selling 100 fewer cups of coffee per day. Here's why. At $1.25 a cup, the coffee vendors will sell only 900 cups of coffee a day, but as a result of the 25 cent price increase their total revenues on the sale of those 900 cups will increase by $225 (25 cents x 900 cups). This gain of $225 would be partially offset by a loss of the 40 cents per cup they would have made selling an additional 100 cups at $1.00, for a revenue loss of $40 (40 cents x 100). Raising price from $1.00 to $1.25, therefore, would yield a net profit increase of $185 ($225–$40). The unit cost relevant to this analysis is an "incremental" or "marginal" cost that does not take into account fixed costs (up-front expenditures) unrelated to the number of cups sold, like rent and kitchen equipment.

The more attractive the substitution alternatives buyers have—that is, the more elastic industry demand—the more sales sellers would lose by raising price and the less profitable this strategy would become. For this reason, it is more likely that the group of coffee vendors would find it profitable to raise price collectively than that our coffee shop would choose to do so on its own. Acting alone, our coffee shop would gain 25 cents per cup on the 50 cups it continues to sell by raising price to $1.25 per cup (25 cents x 50 cups = $12.50), but would lose 40 cents per cup on the 50 cups it no longer sells each morning at $1.00 (40 cents x 50 cups = $20), for a net loss of $7.50. So the coffee shop acting alone cannot profitably exercise market power by reducing output to raise price. In contrast, the coffee shop may be able to exercise market power by colluding with other neighborhood sellers. This conclusion presumes that the coffee vendors could reach and implement an agreement to raise price, and that the higher price does not attract entry—for example, from restaurants adding a take-out coffee counter. As we learned with the lysine and vitamins cartels, and as we will see in later Chapters, there are a variety of ways in which firms, acting individually or collectively, can exercise market power, and there can be legal implications for that behavior.

It is worth noting that every firm, even a firm that exercises market power, has an incentive to change its output in response to shifts in marginal cost, leading to changes in price. If a firm's marginal cost increases, the firm will have an incentive not to sell as much as before, as the last units it previously sold would no longer be profitable to produce. The firm will cut back on output until the last unit sold becomes profitable again, as a result of a reduction in marginal cost (if marginal cost is less when the firm produces fewer units) or an increase in the market price (to the extent the reduction in firm output leads buyers to bid up the market price, along a downward sloping market demand curve) or both. If a firm's marginal cost of producing a product declines, similarly, the firm will have an incentive to produce and sell more, even if the addition to industry output leads to some decline in the market price. Indeed, even a monopolist, a firm without competition in its market, will find it profitable to lower price if its marginal cost declines (as might occur if input costs fall) and will raise price if its marginal cost increases.

iv. The Consequences of the Exercise of Market Power

Figure 1–8 depicts the economic consequences of the exercise of market power. (To facilitate computations, this figure assumes that the marginal costs of production are not increasing with the number of units produced, the assumption made previously, but instead remain the same for all units produced.) If the neighborhood coffee vendors collectively raise price from $1 to $1.25, the 900 daily buyers who continue to purchase coffee in the typical morning lose even though they stay in the market. They must pay 25 cents more per cup. This is a transfer of wealth from buyers to sellers. As a group, these buyers previously paid $900 for their morning coffee; now they pay $1125. The $225 extra that buyers pay to sellers is both a loss in consumers' surplus and a gain in producers' surplus. This transfer constitutes one effect of the exercise of market power.

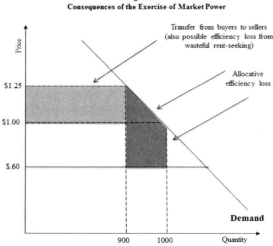

Figure 1–8:
Consequences of the Exercise of Market Power

In addition, when price exceeds the competitive price, society suffers an "allocative efficiency loss" or "deadweight loss." This loss is a reduction in aggregate surplus. It arises because some socially valuable purchases cannot be made. Some buyers—accounting for 100 daily coffee cups—were willing to pay at least $1 per cup, though less than $1.25 per cup, for a product that cost some seller only 60 cents to make. From a social point of view, the reduction in sales from 1000 cups to 900 thus means that society is not taking advantage of 100 opportunities to increase social welfare, by turning resources costing 60 cents per cup to a seller into a product worth at least $1 per cup to a buyer. These lost gains from trade cost society; it is as though society is throwing away at least 40 cents for each cup previously sold that is no longer sold. Put differently, resources such as coffee beans and labor that might have been used to make a product worth $1 will be put to some other use making something worth much less, or not put to any use at all, and buyers willing to pay $1 for a cup of coffee will use that dollar to acquire something else worth less to them.

Moreover, under some circumstances most of the wealth transfer could represent a loss to society. The profit to producers from exercising market power is $185, the $225 transfer less the lost profit of $40 on the units the firms must forgo selling in order to raise price (40 cents on each of 100 units). To sustain their ability to collectively raise price, the incumbent coffee vendors would be willing to spend up to $185 in order to keep out new coffee sellers, who might undercut the $1.25 price. They might, for example, lobby the zoning commission to prevent new coffee shops from opening. Such "rent-seeking" expenditures—if they are made—protect monopoly profits without helping the sellers produce cheaper or better coffee and represent an additional waste of social resources. Both the allocative efficiency loss and the possible efficiency loss from wasteful rent-seeking are depicted in Figure 1–8.[6]

Although the *exercise* of market power reduces social wealth and transfers resources from buyers to sellers, competition in the *pursuit* of market power can be beneficial. If a firm obtains market power, that situation presents an opportunity for rivals: if they can undersell the firm exercising market power slightly, they may be able to steal away most if its business, and earn much of the rewards sellers obtain from exercising market power. Of course, many firms may seek to follow this strategy, and the firm initially exercising market power may be led to protect its business by cutting price as well. Through competition among firms pursuing market power, the price could return to the competitive level, to the benefit of buyers and society as a whole. But this competitive dynamic, in which the pursuit of market power is beneficial, cannot occur unless existing rivals are able to expand output or new competitors are able to enter the market.

Similarly, the patent laws seek to enlist competition in the pursuit of a prize—the ability to exclude rivals, which may at times permit the patent holder to exercise market power—in order to spur innovation. Here again, the pursuit of market power could create a benefit to society. But, as we

---

[6] Richard Posner emphasized the possibility of an efficiency loss of monopoly from wasteful rent-seeking in Richard A. Posner, *The Social Costs of Monopoly and Regulation*, 83 J. POL. ECON. 807 (1975). Franklin Fisher clarified the conditions under which this might occur in Franklin M. Fisher, *The Social Costs of Monopoly and Regulation: Posner Reconsidered*, 93 J. POL. ECON. 410 (1985).

will examine in Chapter 7, this benefit is not unequivocal. The same patent laws which may generate a competitive race to innovate, may also discourage later innovation that builds upon the first new idea and may permit the owner of the intellectual property to exercise market power in pricing the product or process it patents.

v. *The Benefits of Competition*

The previous discussion and Figures 1–1 to 1–8 simplify the dimensions on which competition takes place to two: price and output. In actual markets, market power can be manifested not just by a reduction in output and increase in price, but also in other ways, such as a reduction in product quality (in effect selling less at the same price, which can be understood as effectively an increase in price), loss of product variety, or decrease in the resources devoted to pursuing innovation. For example, the neighborhood coffee vendors might agree to maintain the price of a small, medium, and large cup, but to shrink each cup size by one ounce. They might agree collectively to use lower quality coffee beans to cut costs, or not to add espresso drinks to the menu because they are difficult to make. These agreements would not provide customers with less expensive or better products; rather each would increase profits by reducing output and raising price, broadly defined, and thus reflect the exercise of market power.

In antitrust cases, the term market power is sometimes equated with a high market share. By "market share," the cases mean the percentage of aggregate sales, output or capacity accounted for by a firm or group of firms in a particular, "defined" market. That is not how economists use the term market power today and not how we will do so in this book. Market power in economics refers to the ability to profit by circumscribing some dimension of competition, as by raising price above the competitive level without losing so many sales that the price increase will be unprofitable. We will see later when and how a high market share might constitute indirect proof that a firm or group of firms has or can exercise market power. But a high share in an industry characterized by highly elastic demand, for example, might not. We also will follow the contemporary convention in economics of not distinguishing between market power and monopoly power, although the case law sometimes treats these terms differently. If there is a difference between market power and monopoly power, it is just a matter of degree.

The previous discussion has highlighted one efficiency benefit of competition relative to the exercise of market power: competition achieves allocative efficiency (avoids an allocative efficiency loss). Two other economic benefits of competition are worth highlighting, although they do not necessarily distinguish competitive industries from those exercising market power. First, competition ensures that goods are made by the firm which can produce them at lowest cost. Firms that can produce some units at high cost will be underbid, and find themselves unable to sell those units. Producers are driven, in consequence, to keep their costs low. This outcome is termed "production efficiency."[7] The possible loss from wasteful rent-seeking, discussed above, can be understood as a type of production inefficiency, by which the firms are spending more than necessary to make the units they sell. Second, competition ensures that the buyers who most value the goods get them. The buyers with the highest valuation will find it worthwhile to bid up the price until prospective buyers who value the goods less drop out of the bidding. This result is termed "consumption efficiency." (Note that consumption efficiency ignores differences in the distribution of wealth across buyers, which could affect how much those buyers are willing to bid for desired goods. Hence a competitive market, while ensuring consumption efficiency, may generate a distribution of goods across buyers that some may find undesirable, calling into question whether the "consumption efficiency" that results from consumption should invariably be seen as a benefit.)

The allocative efficiency loss depicted in Figure 1–8 was computed relative to a starting point in which price was $1.00 and 1000 cups of coffee were sold each morning. Buyers and sellers *collectively* would, however, be even better off if coffee sold at a lower price, at coffee's marginal cost of 60 cents per cup, because a number of buyers willing to pay at least marginal cost went unserved at the price of $1.00. Indeed, buyers and sellers *as a group* do better for this reason in the economist's model of perfect competition.

Under perfect competition, no firm has the power to raise price by reducing output. Each firm sells as much as it can profitably produce at the market price. Accordingly, the firm produces every unit of output for which the price exceeds or equals its marginal cost of production, and the amount that the industry as a whole will supply at any price depends only on the marginal cost functions of the individual firms. As we have already discussed, Figure 1–4 depicts the derivation of the industry supply function from the marginal cost functions of an industry composed of one hundred identical firms. For the representative firm, marginal cost rises with output. The tenth unit costs $1 to produce, while the eleventh unit costs $1.25. If the market price were $1, therefore, each firm would choose to produce ten units and the industry as a whole (all one hundred firms)

---

[7] Some authors also refer to "transactional" efficiencies (ways to minimize the cost of making transactions, as by lessening information costs or reducing the threat of opportunistic behavior or "hold ups") and "dynamic" efficiencies (ways to lower the costs of, and thus stimulating, the development of new and improved products and better production processes). In general, this Casebook does not distinguish these benefits from other aspects of production efficiency. However, transactional efficiencies will come up in Sidebar 5–14, *infra*, and dynamic efficiencies are the subject of Chapter 7.

would supply 1000 units. Similarly, at a market price of $1.25, the industry would supply 1100 units.

Under perfect competition, the market price is determined by the intersection of the industry supply function and the industry demand function, as depicted in Figure 1–4. If price were lower, buyers would want to purchase more than the sellers would supply, and the price would be bid up until supply equals demand. Similarly, if the price were higher, sellers would see a shortfall of willing buyers; price would be bid down until supply equals demand. At this competitive equilibrium, every seller would produce all units of output for which price is at least marginal cost, guaranteeing production efficiency; the buyers who value the product the most would obtain it, guaranteeing consumption efficiency; and every buyer willing to pay more than the production costs of a seller will obtain the product, guaranteeing allocative efficiency. As Figure 1–4 also shows, if the sellers can exercise market power, for example by collectively acting at least in part as though they were a monopolist, price will be higher and output lower than under perfect competition.

In some circumstances, markets that do not match the model of perfect competition may be considered workably competitive. For example, in an industry with high fixed costs relative to the size of the market and low marginal costs (a situation which might describe movie theaters, hotels, or computer software), marginal cost pricing may be too low to keep the firms profitably in business. In the competitive benchmark for these industries, against which the exercise of market power may be compared, prices to at least some customers will exceed marginal cost. This situation may still be workably competitive when free entry by new competitors caps those prices and prevents the firms from achieving monopoly profits. (Figure 1–8 can be interpreted as depicting this situation, if $1.00 is the competitive price and a price of $1.25 reflects the exercise of market power.) We will revisit the meaning of "competition" in this setting in Chapter 7, when we consider antitrust issues raised by high technology markets.

———————

The Coffee Shop case study highlights two economic consequences of the exercise of market power: a transfer of resources from buyers to sellers and an allocative efficiency loss. Standard welfare economics focuses on minimizing efficiency losses. An economy in which markets achieve allocative, production, and consumption efficiency can be thought of as maximizing aggregate wealth. [8] Thus, the allocative efficiency loss in Figure 1–8 is costly to society, and counts as an economic harm, because it

---

[8] Formal welfare economics is based on the concept of Pareto efficiency, which arises when there is no way to make any economic actor better off without making any other actor worse off. Pareto efficiency is not the same thing as wealth maximization, but the difference is not generally important for analyzing the welfare issues raised in this book.

reduces collective wealth. Welfare economics does not take a view on whether the consequences of wealth transfers from buyers to sellers create the kind of harms that ought to concern policy-makers and courts. Antitrust commentators dispute whether wealth transfers should count in antitrust policy-making. As will be discussed later in this Chapter, advocates of an "aggregate welfare standard" would not consider wealth transfers while advocates of a "consumer welfare standard" would.

b. What Non-Economic Purposes Can They Serve?

Thus far we have focused on the economic reasons to have antitrust laws, because today they dominate discussion of antitrust rules in the United States and figure prominently in discussions about antitrust law in other jurisdictions. The U.S. and other nations sometimes have used antitrust to promote non-economic goals, too, such as fairness, protection of small firms, social justice, equity, and political stability. These goals are "non-economic" in the sense that they are concerned with values other than the economic well-being of consumers or the economy as a whole. For example, eliminating smaller firms in favor of larger ones may benefit consumers if the larger firms can realize scale economies unavailable to smaller ones, i.e., if the larger firms can lower their per unit costs by expanding their output, and the consequence is lower prices. An antitrust policy motivated by the economic goal of "efficiency," therefore, might permit conduct that allows firms to grow to achieve economies of scale, even if that growth also eliminates some smaller, less efficient competitors.[9]

For non-economic reasons, one might prefer antitrust rules that preserve a market comprised of smaller firms. Such a preference might favor individual autonomy, greater entrepreneurship, local ownership, and "quality of life" gains associated with the service and variety offered by large numbers of smaller firms, a belief that smaller businesses increase aggregate employment, the fear that eliminating some smaller firms inevitably will lead to the elimination of others, or the fear that highly concentrated wealth can facilitate the corruption of the political process. An antitrust policy motivated by these non-economic values might treat harshly all conduct that diminishes the number of firms in a market, regardless of the conduct's immediate impact on consumers. In pursuing non-economic values, one might sacrifice to some extent the promise of lower consumer prices and other benefits associated with efficient markets.

---

[9] The elimination of small firms also could reduce economic efficiency, and these effects would need to be weighed against the productive efficiency gains from shifting output to the lower cost firms. This could happen, for example, if the smaller firms offer products that some consumers prefer to those of the larger firms, or the smaller firms have adopted new technologies that make them more efficient than incumbent firms, or give them the potential to lower their costs and compete more aggressively in the future. Even if the small firms have high costs, moreover, they may still constrain the prices that the larger firms charge if the latter have some ability to exercise market power; if so, their elimination could lead to higher prices.

Although less likely to prove influential today, in the past these kinds of non-economic goals consistently found expression in the antitrust decisions of the federal courts. In the first decade following adoption of the Sherman Act, the Supreme Court invoked those purposes in a much-quoted passage from its decision in *Trans-Missouri Freight*:

> [The result of a combination of capital controlling the price of a commodity] * * * is unfortunate for the country, by depriving it of the services of a large number of small but independent dealers, who were familiar with the business, and who spent their lives in it, and who supported themselves and their families from the small profits realized therein. * * * [I]t is not for the real prosperity of any country that such changes should occur which result in transferring an independent business man, the head of his establishment, small though it might be, into a mere servant or agent of a corporation for selling the commodities which he once manufactured or dealt in, having no voice in shaping the business policy of the company and bound to obey orders issued by others.

United States v. Trans-Missouri Freight Ass'n, 166 U.S. 290, 324 (1897). A similarly famous expression of this perspective appeared in *United States v. Aluminum Co. of America,* 148 F.2d 416, 428–29 (2d Cir. 1945), where Judge Learned Hand's opinion observed:

> We have been speaking only of the economic reasons which forbid monopoly; but * * * there are others, based upon the belief that great industrial consolidations are inherently undesirable, regardless of their economic results. * * * Throughout the history of [the federal antitrust laws] * * * it has been constantly assumed that one of their purposes was to perpetuate and preserve, for its own sake and in spite of possible cost, an organization of industry in small units which can effectively compete with each other.

There are many other examples in the older antitrust cases. But for the most part, modern U.S. antitrust jurisprudence has subordinated non-economic goals to the attainment of economic efficiency. Nevertheless, non-economic goals occasionally find expression in modern judicial decisions. In *United States v. Brown University*, 5 F.3d 658 (3d Cir. 1993), for example, the Department of Justice challenged the collective agreement of a group of elite universities to use a common formula to calculate the need-based aid to be provided to commonly admitted students and to prohibit merit-based aid. On appeal, the only non-settling school argued that the agreement enabled the schools to allocate more funds for needier applicants and thus promoted socio-economic diversity at member institutions. But it further argued that greater socio-economic diversity, in turn, "improved the quality of the education offered by the schools and therefore enhanced the consumer appeal of an Overlap education." *Id.* at

674. The court of appeals concluded that this justification, which appeared to align economic and non-economic goals, warranted further consideration:

> It is most desirable that schools achieve equality of educational access and opportunity in order that more people enjoy the benefits of a worthy higher education. There is no doubt, too, that enhancing the quality of our educational system redounds to the general good. To the extent that higher education endeavors to foster vitality of the mind, to promote free exchange between bodies of thought and truths, and better communication among a broad spectrum of individuals, as well as prepares individuals for the intellectual demands of responsible citizenship, it is a common good that should be extended to as wide a range of individuals from as broad a range of socio-economic backgrounds as possible. It is with this in mind that the Overlap Agreement should be submitted to the rule of reason scrutiny under the Sherman Act.

Id. at 678.

In Chapter 2 below, we will consider the range of justifications that the Supreme Court has deemed appropriate to be evaluated along with alleged anticompetitive effects. For now, ask whether the defendant and the Third Circuit made a persuasive case that the social and economic aims of the overlap policy were "pro-competitive" in some economic sense.

In Sidebar 1–2, which follows, we consider some of the traditional arguments for and against giving weight to non-economic goals and their current status under U.S. antitrust law. We also note various ways that non-economic goals continue to have influence outside of antitrust.

Sidebar 1–2:
Non-Economic Values and Competition Policy

Non-economic values can give rise to laws and regulations that serve a variety of purposes that can appear to conflict with the economic goals of competition policy. In this Sidebar, we consider some examples of such laws and regulations, as well as the arguments often made to oppose inclusion of non-economic goals in antitrust policy.

Trade Laws and Antitrust

Many nations use trade barriers to shield domestic industry from foreign rivals—even when the predictable result is higher domestic prices. Such a policy choice sometimes reflects the belief that foreign firms enjoy an unfair advantage over domestic firms, or that free trade will cause some domestic industry to falter, causing economic displacement, unemployment, and political unrest.

Although free trade might increase a nation's aggregate wealth, it also may affect the distribution of wealth: some citizens may benefit, but others, like established businesses and displaced workers, may suffer uncompensated losses. The perceived benefits of barring imports or impeding their entry by raising tariffs, therefore, might be seen as greater than the detriment of reduced domestic competition and higher domestic prices. But how much employment saved counterbalances what degree of higher prices to consumers? And what are the long term consequences for the competitiveness of domestic industries that rely on protection rather than competition?

These questions arise frequently in debates surrounding the negotiation of free trade agreements. Although such arrangements have never been free of controversy, there was a rough political consensus in the 1990s that such arrangements yielded net benefits to their signatories. The North American Free Trade Agreement (NAFTA), adopted after contentious political debate in the United States, was a major manifestation of that consensus. The contemporary mood has changed dramatically since that time. Today it is difficult to elect officials, in the United States and abroad, who speak in support of free trade agreements. At a minimum, the discontent with trade may mean that a necessary condition for the approval of new free trade agreements will be assurances of assistance, through various social policy instruments, for workers who lose their jobs by reason of trade liberalization.

Exemptions

Non-economic goals also receive expression in the form of exemptions from the antitrust laws. Exemptions can protect entire industries, particular firms, or specific transactions, and are often justified on the ground that competition will produce undesirable consequences or that other policies could best be served by lifting the legal mandate that firms compete vigorously. Under U.S. antitrust law, for example, statutory exemptions exist for the activities of labor unions undertaken in the context of collective bargaining and the business of insurance. On occasion, the courts also have recognized exemptions, such as with the non-statutory labor exemption and a long-standing exemption for major league baseball. *See infra* Figure 8–2 (listing major statutory and non-statutory exemptions).

Recognizing the role that the legislative process plays in establishing exemptions, the United States Supreme Court has on several occasions rejected defenses that amounted to "competition is destructive in our industry," characterizing them in one instance as a "frontal assault on the basic policy of the Sherman Act." *National Soc'y of Prof'l Eng'rs v. United States*, 435 U.S. 679, 695 (1978).

The mere availability of exemptions, or requirements that certain transactions receive government approval, either through legislative or administrative means, may induce firms to pursue a government-bestowed dispensation from the usual mandate of competition. In some systems, this also can foster a threat that bribery or other means will corrupt the mechanisms for antitrust enforcement.

Other Laws and Regulatory Schemes

Non-economic concerns associated with competition also are addressed through other laws, such as tax, employment, and corporation laws, or by creating specialized administrative agencies. Such agencies can be charged with public purposes that include or ignore competition concerns. In the United States such specialized agencies include the Federal Communications Commission, the Federal Energy Regulatory Commission, and the Federal Reserve Board. Congress has given these agencies concurrent authority with the DOJ and the FTC to review mergers or to police unfair and deceptive practices in specific sectors.

The Case Against Reliance on Non-Economic Goals as a Guide to Antitrust Policy

Defenders of an economic approach to antitrust assert that antitrust rules and exemptions guided by non-economic values are usually inconsistent with economic interests and impose significant aggregate costs on consumers. They also assert that such rules tend to be inflexible and prone to over-deterrence. If every reduction in the number of competitors is deemed undesirable, antitrust law would always condemn mergers of competitors, regardless of both the firm's ability to raise prices after the merger and the efficiency benefits that the merger might create. Similarly, conduct that results in the elimination of even a single competitor, such as a firm's decision to substitute one dealer for several, might constitute a violation. If enforcement agencies and courts are charged with weighing economic versus non-economic values, we may be demanding too much of them institutionally: how can an enforcement agency or a court effectively weigh the social harm of eliminating one competitor (as in the case of a merger) against the social benefits that may flow from the merger if it leads to efficiencies and lower prices for consumers? Or suppose that a jurisdiction's law has a public interest test that allows enforcement officials to approve an anticompetitive merger in return for the parties' agreement to take steps that advance other social policy goals, such as preserving jobs or providing advancement for historically disadvantaged classes of citizens? What calculus guides the agency in deciding what bundle of social policy commitments adequately offsets an increase in price attributable to the merger?[a] Some would argue that such decisions are better suited for the political and legislative process.

An additional argument against devising antitrust rules to pursue non-economic goals explicitly is that relying on economic rules of decision often may also serve non-economic goals, albeit indirectly or incompletely. A byproduct of blocking the merger of two substantial firms on economic grounds, for example, will be benefits for non-economic goals such as mitigating corporate concentration. Conduct barred on consumer welfare grounds often serves in part to protect other interests, such as equity, social justice, and controlling sheer corporate size. The converse is less likely to be true. Giving primacy to non-economic goals in framing rules of decision would more likely lead to conflict with economic goals.

Reliance on non-economic goals does not necessarily yield more, rather than less, antitrust enforcement. A decision to approve an otherwise anticompetitive merger, for example, because it may create a "national champion" better equipped to compete internationally, will result in non-enforcement of the competition law.

Conclusion

It is important to realize that contemporary U.S. antitrust analysis focuses almost solely on economic goals—preventing the acquisition, maintenance, or exercise of market power. Although courts sometimes have articulated non-economic

---

[a]   Such public interest provisions appear in a number of antitrust laws outside the U.S., especially in jurisdictions where an important aim of the law is to improve conditions for citizens who, by reason of official policy or social norms, previously were excluded from participating in the market or forced to subsist in its shadows. For example, the inclusion of a public interest test was indispensable to South Africa's adoption of a new competition law system in 1998. *See* David Lewis, THIEVES AT THE DINNER TABLE (2012). Commentators who have studied South Africa's experience in applying the public interest test in merger reviews have discerned possibilities for applying the standard in a way that is administrable and faithful to the legislative purpose behind the provision. *See* Harry First & Eleanor M. Fox, *Philadelphia National Bank, Globalization, and the Public Interest*, 80 ANTITRUST L.J. 307 (2015).

goals for U.S. antitrust law, their reliance on such goals as a source of useful guidance for deciding particular cases has waned since the early 1970s. Non-economic goals frequently conflict with economic aims, provide too little guidance for antitrust decision makers, and arguably are ill-suited to decision-making processes that rely on adjudication and the adversary system. It is equally important to appreciate that this was not always the case in the United States, may still not be the case in some isolated circumstances, and may not be the case universally in the world today.

2. WHAT CONDUCT, PUBLIC OR PRIVATE, CAN IMPAIR THE PROPER FUNCTIONING OF MARKETS?

As discussed above, we expect competitive markets to yield production, allocative, and consumption efficiency, and we associate efficiency with the maximization of consumer welfare. "Competitive" markets can take many forms, and competition often is a matter of degree. As a general matter, however, we associate competitive markets with certain structural features:

- Enough buyers and sellers to insure competitive pricing, features, quality, and innovation;

- Homogeneous (*i.e.*, undifferentiated) products or services;

- Easy entry, expansion, and exit by firms; and

- Relatively unhindered information and knowledge about market conditions on the part of sellers and buyers.

Markets are less likely to perform competitively if any of these features is lacking in whole or part, although markets also can be very competitive if all of these conditions are not "perfectly" present. More important, the significance to competition of each of these factors does not necessarily mean that antitrust law is concerned with them all. For example, deceptive advertising, a form of imperfect information, is usually addressed through consumer protection laws and the common law of fraud. Product differentiation is now widely accepted as a common feature of competitive markets, even though it can lead to some market power when consumers prove willing to spend more for a familiar or prestigious brand name. Efforts in the 1970s to challenge "brand proliferation" in the cereal industry, for example, were ultimately abandoned.

Antitrust law primarily focuses on two features associated with perfect competition: the number of buyers and sellers and conditions of entry. Private conduct intended to or having the actual effect of eroding competition by altering either of these requirements of competition frequently attracts antitrust scrutiny. Although public sector conduct, particularly extensive regulation as in public licensing of trades and professions, can also directly impair the functioning of markets, U.S. antitrust law largely does not reach it for reasons related to the legislative history of the Sherman Act and constitutional issues associated with federalism. But public sector conduct is often within the scope of the antitrust laws of other nations.

With this core set of concerns in mind, this Subsection develops a framework for identifying "anticompetitive conduct," and for evaluating such conduct in terms of its "anticompetitive effects."

a. What Do We Mean by "Anticompetitive" Conduct?

"Anticompetitive" cannot be defined without answering the question: "What goals do the antitrust laws intend to promote?" The predominance of economic analysis in the United States necessarily creates a link between "anticompetitive" and economic goals. Anticompetitive means conduct likely to lead to the creation, maintenance, or enhancement of market power, or that involves the actual exercise of market power. As the Coffee Shop hypothetical showed, "market power" in turn refers to the ability to raise price by reducing output, or to limit some other dimension of competition. It is typically associated with a departure from the conditions necessary for the optimal functioning of a market: a sufficient number of buyers or sellers, relatively easy conditions of entry and exit, or readily accessible information on market conditions.

Figure 1–9:

Comparison of Characteristics of
Competitive and Non-Competitive Markets

Characteristics of Competitive Markets	Associated Benefits
• Numerous sellers and buyers • Homogeneous products • Ease of entry and exit • Complete knowledge/information • Competitive levels of innovation, quality, variety	• Marginal cost pricing (production efficiency) • Societal resources are well allocated (allocative efficiency) • Consumer welfare is maximized (consumption efficiency)
Possible Variations from the Competitive Model	**Potential Anticompetitive Consequences**
• Fewer buyers and sellers • Impediments to entry • Limited access to information	• Higher prices • Lower product quality, less consumer choice, little product innovation • Consumer deception • Wealth transfers from consumers to producers

As Figure 1–9 indicates, competitive markets should produce a variety of economic benefits. As the Supreme Court has observed: "The assumption that competition is the best method of allocating resources in a free market recognizes that all elements of a bargain—quality, service, safety and durability—and not just the immediate cost, are favorably affected by the free opportunity to select among alternative offers." *National Soc'y of Prof'l Eng'rs* v. *United States*, 435 U.S. 679, 695 (1978). So "anticompetitive effects" in the form of higher prices, lower quality or less innovation can flow from conduct that alters any of the characteristic features of markets. What sorts of conduct have been recognized as producing these kinds of adverse effects?

i.   Introducing the Concept of "Antitrust Injury"

The centrality of this question in modern antitrust policy is highlighted in *Brunswick Corp. v. Pueblo Bowl-O-Mat, Inc.*, 429 U.S. 477, 97 S.Ct. 690 (1977). In *Brunswick*, the Supreme Court considered whether a competitor can use the anti-merger provisions of the antitrust laws to challenge the acquisition of its principal rival by an even larger rival for whom the acquisition was a means of entering the market. To answer the question, the Court had to ask two questions: (1) what makes an acquisition anticompetitive, and (2) who can an acquisition harm? By focusing on these questions, the Court sparked an era of more critical analysis of the core purposes of antitrust law that begins with an evaluation of their potential anticompetitive effects. Look for the answers to these two questions as you read *Brunswick*.

BRUNSWICK CORPORATION V. PUEBLO BOWL-O-MAT, INC.

Supreme Court of the United States, 1977.
429 U.S. 477, 97 S.Ct. 690, 50 L.Ed.2d 701.

MR. JUSTICE MARSHALL delivered the opinion of the Court.

This case raises important questions concerning the interrelationship of the antimerger and private damages action provisions of the Clayton Antitrust Act.

I

Petitioner is one of the two largest manufacturers of bowling equipment in the United States. Respondents are three of the 10 bowling centers owned by Treadway Companies, Inc. Since 1965, petitioner has acquired and operated a large number of bowling centers, including six in the markets in which respondents operate. * * *

* * *

Respondents initiated this action in June 1966, alleging, *inter alia*, that these acquisitions might substantially lessen competition or tend to create a monopoly in violation of § 7 of the Clayton Act, 15 U.S.C. § 18. Respondents sought damages, pursuant to § 4 of the Act, 15 U.S.C. § 15, for three times "the reasonably expectable profits to be made [by respondents] from the operation of their bowling centers." Respondents also sought a divestiture order, an injunction against future acquisitions, and such "other further and different relief" as might be appropriate under § 16 of the Act, 15 U.S.C. § 26.

* * *

II

The issue for decision is a narrow one. Petitioner does not presently contest the Court of Appeals' conclusion that a properly instructed jury could have found the acquisitions unlawful. Nor does petitioner challenge the Court of Appeals' determination that the evidence would support a finding that had petitioner not acquired these centers, they would have gone out of business and respondents' income would have increased. Petitioner questions only whether antitrust damages are available where the sole injury alleged is that competitors were continued in business, thereby denying respondents an anticipated increase in market shares.

To answer that question it is necessary to examine the antimerger and treble-damages provisions of the Clayton Act. Section 7 of the Act proscribes mergers whose effect "*may be* substantially to lessen competition, or *to tend* to create a monopoly." (Emphasis added.) It is, as we have observed many times, a prophylactic measure, intended "primarily to arrest apprehended consequences of intercorporate relationships before those relationships could work their evil. . . ."

Section 4, in contrast, is in essence a remedial provision. It provides treble damages to "[a]ny person who shall be injured in his business or property by reason of anything forbidden in the antitrust laws. . . ." Of course, treble damages also play an important role in penalizing wrongdoers and deterring wrongdoing, as we also have frequently observed. It nevertheless is true that the treble-damages provision, which makes awards available only to injured parties, and measures the awards by a multiple of the injury actually proved, is designed primarily as a remedy.[10]

* * *

Every merger of two existing entities into one, whether lawful or unlawful, has the potential for producing economic readjustments that adversely affect some persons. But Congress has not condemned mergers on that account; it has condemned them only when they may produce anticompetitive effects. Yet under the Court of Appeals' holding, once a merger is found to violate § 7, all dislocations caused by the merger are actionable, regardless of whether those dislocations have anything to do with the reason the merger was condemned. This holding would make § 4 recovery entirely fortuitous, and would authorize damages for losses which are of no concern to the antitrust laws.

Both of these consequences are well illustrated by the facts of this case. If the acquisitions here were unlawful, it is because they brought a "deep pocket" parent into a market of "pygmies." Yet respondents' injury—the loss of income that would have accrued had the acquired centers gone bankrupt—bears no relationship to the size of either the acquiring company or its competitors. Respondents would have suffered the identical "loss"—but no compensable injury—had the acquired centers instead obtained refinancing or been purchased by "shallow pocket" parents as the

---

[10] Treble-damages antitrust actions were first authorized by § 7 of the Sherman Act. The discussions of this section on the floor of the Senate indicate that it was conceived of primarily as a remedy for "[t]he people of the United States as individuals," especially consumers. Treble damages were provided in part for punitive purposes, but also to make the remedy meaningful by counterbalancing "the difficulty of maintaining a private suit against a combination such as is described" in the Act.

When Congress enacted the Clayton Act in 1914, it "extend[ed] the remedy under section 7 of the Sherman Act" to persons injured by virtue of any antitrust violation. * * *

Court of Appeals itself acknowledged. Thus, respondents' injury was not of "the type that the statute was intended to forestall."

But the antitrust laws are not merely indifferent to the injury claimed here. At base, respondents complain that by acquiring the failing centers petitioner preserved competition, thereby depriving respondents of the benefits of increased concentration. The damages respondents obtained are designed to provide them with the profits they would have realized had competition been reduced. The antitrust laws, however, were enacted for "the protection of *competition* not *competitors*," *Brown Shoe Co. v. United States*. It is inimical to the purposes of these laws to award damages for the type of injury claimed here.

* * *

We therefore hold that for plaintiffs to recover treble damages on account of § 7 violations, they must prove more than injury causally linked to an illegal presence in the market. Plaintiffs must prove *antitrust* injury, which is to say injury of the type the antitrust laws were intended to prevent and that flows from that which makes defendants' acts unlawful. The injury should reflect the anticompetitive effect either of the violation or of anticompetitive acts made possible by the violation. It should, in short, be "the type of loss that the claimed violations . . . would be likely to cause."

* * *

In the *Brunswick* Court's view, what is the essential "anticompetitive" characteristic of a merger? Brunswick acquired some of Pueblo's local rivals, which otherwise were scheduled to close. What, then, was the essence of Pueblo's complaint about the acquisition?

Pueblo asked for the "damages" it would suffer because of new competition from Brunswick, as compared to the market it would have faced if its local rivals had closed, ceding the market to Pueblo. As the Supreme Court explained, such injury stemmed from *increased*, not decreased competition. Pueblo was implicitly arguing that but for Brunswick's acquisition of its local rivals, the rivals would have exited, and Pueblo then would have enjoyed some degree of market power. Increased competition from its larger (perhaps more efficient) rival, Brunswick, eroded Pueblo's hoped-for increased profits. Seeking the difference between its pre-entry and post-entry profits was tantamount to asking the Court to protect Pueblo's hoped-for market power—hence the Court's response that to do so would be "inimical" to the purposes of the antitrust laws.

We will revisit *Brunswick* and the concept of "antitrust injury" later in the Casebook. For now, we emphasize that *Brunswick* proved to be a watershed case. Afterwards, it became increasingly important in antitrust cases to articulate a clear theory of anticompetitive harm in seeking relief for any challenged conduct. Note how *Brunswick* focused on the fundamental question: "what would make an acquisition or merger 'anticompetitive'?" For Brunswick's acquisitions to have been anticompetitive, they would have had to *decrease* competition.

Modern discourse between EU and U.S. government officials has featured many statements about the proper aims of competition law. The speeches of top agency leaders in both jurisdictions indicate broad agreement on the question of goals. Each jurisdiction accepts the general proposition that the central aim of competition law is "the objective of benefitting consumers." Consistent with a single-minded focus on "consumer welfare," EU and U.S. antitrust officials routinely disavow any purpose of applying competition laws to safeguard individual competitors as an end in itself. EU officials also are familiar with, by direct quotation or paraphrase, the Supreme Court's admonition in *Brunswick* that the proper aim of antitrust law is " 'the protection of *competition*, not competitors.' " *Brunswick Corp.,* 429 U.S. at 488 (*quoting Brown Shoe Co. v. United States*, 370 U.S. 294, 320 (1962) (emphasis in original)).

The habit of EU and U.S. officials to invoke consumer welfare and related expressions is a useful start to a larger and continuing discussion about the aims of competition law. As we will see, these phrases by themselves do not tell us much about the meaning that each jurisdiction attaches to them. Nor do the phrases deny each jurisdiction discretion to achieve varied policy ends through the process of interpretation and application.

ii. Distinguishing Collusive from Exclusionary Anticompetitive Effects

Anticompetitive conduct today is generally divided into two broad categories that are defined by the nature of the effects they can precipitate: *collusive* or *exclusionary*. The distinction flows not so much from the relationship between the parties as in the traditional cases, but from the *mechanism for producing anticompetitive effects*. "*Collusive*" effects, which are depicted below in Figure 1–10, directly impair markets and typically will involve coordinated action by competitors, which collectively possess market power and are attempting to emulate the behavior of a monopolist by restricting their own output and raising price.[10] Many of the boldest

---

[10] As described above in the Coffee Shop Hypothetical, economic theory predicts that a monopolist will seek to maximize its profits by reducing output and raising price. For policy reasons explored in Chapter 4, Section 2 of the Sherman Act does not outlaw "monopoly;" instead it bars "monopolization," the active pursuit of monopoly through improper exclusionary conduct. As a result, a firm that gains a monopoly through the superiority of its product may charge its profit maximizing price without interference under U.S. antitrust law—even though the economic effects (an allocative efficiency loss and a transfer of wealth from producers to consumers) are no different than those explained in the example of the coffee vendors colluding to raise price. In

examples of conduct having collusive effects involve price fixing, as in the lysine and vitamins cartel cases. When substantial competitors decide to agree on prices, or in some circumstances to merge rather than compete, the consequence is more likely to be less output and higher prices for consumers.[11] Such conduct does not depend for its anticompetitive impact on any subsequent or additional events; its effects are immediate and direct: output is reduced; prices are inflated. Such conduct directly impairs the market's mechanisms for determining output, price, product quality and characteristics, and innovation.

Figure 1–10:
Collusive Anticompetitive Effects

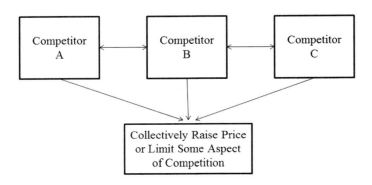

"*Exclusionary*" effects, which are depicted below in Figure 1–11, confer market power by restricting the output of a firm's or firms' rival, as by raising its costs (perhaps by cutting it off from key inputs to its production) or limiting its access to the market (perhaps by cutting off its access to a key channel of distribution). Exclusionary effects can result from the act of a single firm, or an agreement among a group of firms. In the latter instance, the relationship of the agreeing firms can vary, and can include horizontal as well as vertical coordination.

Whether perpetrated by a single firm or more than one firm, the effects of exclusionary conduct are always *indirect*: by excluding a rival, or impairing its ability to compete effectively, the predator hopes to obtain power over price or influence some other dimension of competition.

contrast, serious antitrust issues arise when firms try to achieve the same results by agreement or merger.

[11] As we will see in Chapter 5, we are not using "collusive" here the way "coordinated" is used in the Department of Justice/Federal Trade Commission Guidelines on Horizontal Mergers. "Coordinated" and "unilateral" anticompetitive effects, as those terms are used in the Guidelines, are both types of direct, "collusive" effects.

Exclusionary conduct will be condemned when, in impairing or excluding a rival, the conduct establishes conditions under which a firm or group of firms is able, or is very likely to be able, to exercise market power. Examples include unilateral efforts to exclude rivals through cost-raising strategies or predatory pricing, as well as coordinated efforts to restrict a rival's competitive options, such as exclusive dealing agreements, tying arrangements, and refusals to deal. In each instance, the common *direct* effect of the exclusionary conduct is its impact on one or more rivals. If that effect is significant enough, it may, by substantially diminishing the sources of competition, *indirectly* permit the excluding firm to harm competition by, for example, raising price or preventing the erosion of a supracompetitive price. As a consequence, exclusionary effects cases commence with an examination of the challenged conduct's tendency to exclude or impair rivals, and then move on to consider the consequences of that harm for competition more generally.

Figure 1–11:
Exclusionary Anticompetitive Effects

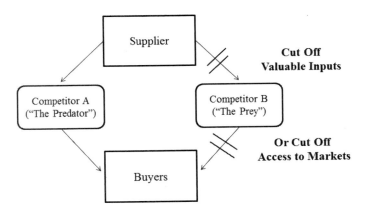

Firms, therefore, can directly or indirectly impede the operation of markets through conduct that produces *collusive* or *exclusionary effects*, or both. Appreciating these two categories of anticompetitive effects is central to comprehending the operation of modern antitrust laws, driven as it is by economic goals, and the burdens of proof associated with differing antitrust offenses. In a U.S. antitrust case today, the plaintiff (whether a government agency or a private party) must articulate a coherent theory of anticompetitive effects, and it bears the burden of linking particular conduct to those effects. In response, the defense will attempt to link that same conduct to neutral or procompetitive effects. In either event, the parties will have to address whether the conduct was collusive or exclusionary and whether it was intended to incapacitate the competitive process directly or indirectly. The nature of the evidence adduced in each instance may greatly vary, as will the relative burdens of pleading, production, and proof, but the end result, as is depicted below in Figure 1–12, is the same.

Figure 1–12:
Comparing Collusive and Exclusionary Anticompetitive Effects

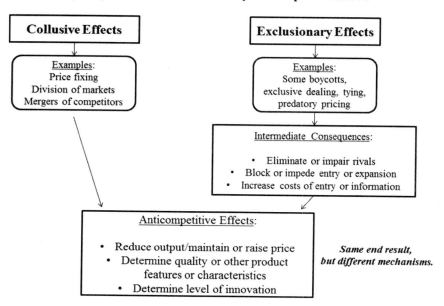

To apply the collusive-exclusionary distinction, let's first revisit the international cartel cases presented above. One anticompetitive hypothesis is that the two cartels would cause *collusive* anticompetitive effects. The participants in the lysine and vitamin cartels collectively had market power and acted in concert to curb the output of lysine and vitamins in order to raise prices. The impact of their conduct was *direct*: they restricted output and raised price.

At some point, however, the cartels might need to use concerted *exclusionary* strategies to ensure that the output restrictions boosted prices. Suppose an existing producer refused to go along with the cartel's plans or that there was a new entrant into the lysine or vitamins industry that refused to join the cartel. Such a "maverick" could destabilize the cartel. The existing cartel members might threaten to punish the maverick's customers or suppliers if the maverick undercut the cartel's prices in order to exclude it from the market entirely, or perhaps raise its costs just enough to neutralize its ability to undercut the cartel's preferred prices. In the lysine case, for example, ADM used its additional production capacity to discourage other cartel members from deviating from the agreed upon prices and output levels by threatening to raise its own output and lower market prices.

Anticompetitive strategies, therefore, may involve a mix of collusive and exclusionary effects, as is illustrated by the next case, which involved the efforts of a group of road paving firms to exclude a new rival that threatened to disrupt their bid-rigging cartel.

JTC PETROLEUM CO. v. PIASA MOTOR FUELS, INC.
United States Court of Appeals for the Seventh Circuit, 1999.
190 F.3d 775.

Before POSNER, CHIEF JUDGE, and EASTERBROOK and ROVNER, CIRCUIT JUDGES.

POSNER, CHIEF JUDGE.

The plaintiff seeks damages for violations of section 1 of the Sherman Act arising out of the road-repair business in southern Illinois. There are two groups of defendants: the road contractors themselves, called "applicators," and producers of the emulsified asphalt that the applicators apply to the surface of the roads. After the plaintiff, itself an applicator, settled with all three of the producers and three of the six applicator defendants, the district court granted summary judgment for the remaining applicator defendants, who are the appellees in this court.

* * *

The plaintiff presented evidence both that the applicator defendants had agreed not to compete with one another in bidding on local government contracts and that the producers had agreed not to compete among each other either, both agreements being (if proved) per se violations of section 1 of the Sherman Act. There is a long history of bid-rigging and related practices of collusion in the road construction and road maintenance business. These are local markets, with a limited number of competitors, selling a rather standardized service to local governments constrained to give their business to the lowest bidder, a constraint that makes it easy for colluding bidders to determine whether one of their number is cheating on the agreement to divide markets. The conditions are thus ripe for effective collusion, making it unsurprising that there is evidence that the applicator defendants in fact colluded with one another to allocate the applicator business in their region. * * *

As for the producers of the asphalt used by these applicators, the record contains evidence that the product is both heavy relative to value and prone to deteriorate when transported long distances, and that as a result the practical radius within which a plant can supply applicators is only about 70 miles. This has limited to three the number of producers that can supply applicators in the region served by the plaintiff and by the applicator defendants. The plants are specialized to the production of emulsified asphalt, meaning that they can't readily be switched to producing other products. This gives the producers an incentive to produce emulsified asphalt up to the capacity of their plants (because there is no profitable use of the plants other than producing this product), and, since it is a fungible product, about the only way of increasing output is by cutting price. But since the demand for emulsified asphalt is inelastic—that is, lower prices do not yield commensurate increases in volume—the effect of price competition would be to diminish profits. So the producers, like the applicators, have much to gain by eliminating competition among themselves. And since the product is standard and the number of competing producers few, an agreement not to compete should not be too difficult to enforce; that is, at the producer level as at the applicator level, cheating should be readily observable and hence quickly checked by a retaliatory price cut. Therefore a cartel agreement would not be quickly eroded by cheating, and so again the conditions for collusion are ripe and again the record contains evidence of such collusion.

* * *

* * * JTC has tried to show * * * that the applicators enlisted the producers in their conspiracy, assigning them the role of policing the applicators' cartel by refusing to sell to applicators who defied the cartel—such as JTC, which has bid for jobs that the cartel had assigned to other applicators. JTC, a maverick, was a threat to the cartel—but only if it could find a source of supply of emulsified asphalt. The claim is that the applicators got the producers to deny JTC this essential input into its business, and as a result injured it. The producer was the cat's paw; the applicators were the cat.

* * * [I]t might seem to make no sense from the producers' standpoint to shore up a cartel of their customers. Cartels * * * raise price above the competitive level and by doing so reduce the demand for their product. The less asphalt the members of the applicators' cartel sell (perhaps because the higher, cartel price induces municipalities to defer road maintenance), the less they will buy, and so the producers will be hurt. But if the producers have nowhere else to turn to sell their product, as may be the case here because of the specialized character of their plants and the limited radius within which they can ship their product from the plant, the applicator defendants may be able to coerce them into helping to police their cartel by threatening to buy less product from them or pay less for it * * *.

Alternatively, and more plausibly (at least on this record), the cartelists may have been paying the producers to perform the policing function, rather than coercing them, by threats, to do so. If by refusing to sell to mavericks the producers increase the profits of the applicators' cartel, they create a fund out of which the cartel can compensate them, in the form of a higher price for the purchase of the product, for their services to the cartel. The record contains evidence that one of the producers obtained from applicators in the cartel area prices that were 4 to 18 (or maybe even 28) percent higher than the prices it obtained from presumably noncolluding applicators in the adjacent region, though there is no suggestion that the producer's costs were any higher in that region. The evidence is contested by the defendants, but the resolution of the contest is for trial. There is also evidence (again contested, and again this is irrelevant to whether summary judgment was properly granted) that the reasons the producers gave for refusing to sell to JTC were pretextual, for example, that JTC was not a good credit risk, even though when JTC offered to pay cash the producers still refused to sell to it. This suggests that the real reason for the refusal was one that the producers didn't want to acknowledge—namely that they were being compensated by the cartel for refusing to sell to a customer whom otherwise they would have been happy to sell to. The combination of the price difference with the evidence of pretext supports an inference that the producers were being compensated by the applicators for shoring up the cartel by boycotting an applicator that was competing with the cartel. If so—if the producers were working for the cartel—they were part of the applicators' conspiracy, and for the injury that they inflicted on JTC as agents of the applicators' cartel by denying JTC a source of supply the members of the cartel, three of which are the remaining defendants, would be culpable under elementary principles of both conspiracy law and agency law.

There may be an innocent explanation for why producers would charge lower prices elsewhere or why they refused to sell to JTC. But the only issue for us, in reviewing the grant of summary judgment for these defendants, is whether a rational jury, having before it the evidence developed to date, could conclude * * * that the reason for the producers' refusal to deal with JTC was that they were in cahoots with the cartel to discourage competition in the applicator market. Given the evidence of cartelization at both the applicator and producer level, the suspicious producer price behavior (suggestive of the producers' having been "paid off" by the cartel to boycott JTC and other upstarts), and the pretextual character of the reasons the producers gave for the refusal to deal, a rational jury could conclude that JTC was indeed the victim of a producers' boycott organized by the applicator defendants.

* * *

Reversed.

Figure 1–13:
The Alleged JTC Conspiracy

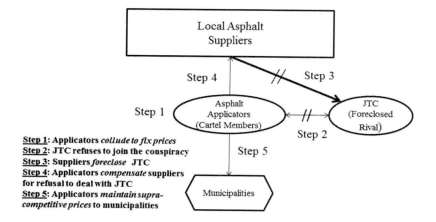

Step 1: Applicators *collude to fix prices*
Step 2: JTC refuses to join the conspiracy
Step 3: Suppliers *foreclose* JTC
Step 4: Applicators *compensate* suppliers for refusal to deal with JTC
Step 5: Applicators *maintain supra-competitive prices* to municipalities

Why is the conduct in *JTC* treated as categorically unlawful? The harsh treatment of the defendants' conduct in *JTC* appears to turn on the court of appeals' view that the applicators' conduct would have collusive effects, as with price fixing. Can the conduct also be viewed as exclusionary? How are the collusive and exclusionary effects, if any, inter-related?

Why does Judge Posner observe that industry conditions were ripe for collusion among the applicators (road contractors)? What role did the asphalt producers play in helping the applicators to collude, according to plaintiff JTC, leading Judge Posner to say that, under JTC's theory, "the producers were the cat's paw, and the applicators were the cat"? Why might the producers go along with the applicators' plan, given that a cartel, by raising prices, would reduce the demand for asphalt, leading the producers to sell less?

JTC helps us to understand the challenges that cartels must overcome to succeed. The first stage of a cartel involves formulating a consensus among its members. This is not always, or often, an easy task, as the participants must deal with the range of disagreements suggested in the lysine case study—for example, how to allocate shares of the cartel's output. Recall the bitter disagreements, recounted in the *Andreas* opinion above, among the lysine cartel participants about the establishment of sales quotas. Once the consensus is formed, the cartel not only must sustain the commitment of its own members, but it must deal with problems that arise from sources outside its membership, such as rivals and new entrants that refuse to join the cartel. It must also address pressure from suppliers, the threat of substitute products, and the possibility that powerful buyers may undermine the cartel by negotiating secretly with its members for better terms.

To deal with these second-stage problems, cartels often resort to techniques that, as we will see in Chapters 4 and 6, arise in the analysis of claims of illegal monopolization or attempted monopolization. The cartel might try to deny a rival access to needed inputs or customers. It might drop its prices to compete for the hold-out's customers. If the maverick resides off-shore and exports its products to the location of the cartel, the cartel members might file an anti-dumping action within their own borders. Or a cartel member simply might seek to acquire the maverick. *See* Randal D. Heeb et al., *Cartels as Two-Stage Mechanisms: Implications for Dominant Firm Conduct*, 10 CHICAGO J. INT'L L. 213 (2009); Margaret C. Levenstein & Valerie Y. Suslow, *What Determines Cartel Success?*, 44 J. ECON. LIT. 43, 75–79 (2006).

The Seventh Circuit's opinion and our discussion of *JTC Petroleum* highlight how colluding firms can employ exclusionary conduct to prevent erosion of their cartel by non-participating rivals. Suppose instead that there were only two road contractors: Piasa, a dominant firm, and JTC, which did not want to charge as high a price as Piasa would like. Suppose further that Piasa acted alone in soliciting the asphalt producers to refuse to deal with JTC, in order to raise road contracting prices. Would the economic consequences be any different than if Piasa were acting together with other members of the road contractors' cartel to exclude JTC? If not— if the economic harms from exclusionary conduct by a dominant firm would be similar to the economic harms from exclusionary conduct by several road contractors working together—should antitrust law treat the two situations differently? We return to the question of whether antitrust does and should scrutinize concerted action more closely than unilateral conduct at the start of Chapter 3.

The kinds of questions posed in this discussion of anticompetitive effects will occupy our attention throughout this Casebook.

b. Justifying Intervention: When Can Markets Be "Self-Correcting"?

Is all "anticompetitive conduct" worthy of condemnation? As with any area of government law enforcement, one must consider the costs and benefits of antitrust's legal rules. An antitrust system, therefore, might aspire for its rules to: (1) minimize the likelihood of both under-deterrence of anticompetitive conduct and over-deterrence of aggressive, but competitive conduct; (2) establish clear, easily ascertainable rules; (3) authorize administrative or judicial law enforcement only under circumstances likely to produce results that are superior to reliance on markets; and (4) create an enforcement scheme that is relatively easy and cost effective to administer. These aspirational goals for antitrust rules may not always be in alignment. A rule that fares well under one criterion may not fare well under another. In practice, antitrust rules, like other legal rules, may require difficult trade-offs. In the discussion below, we are not assuming the choice is between omniscient, perfectly executed government intervention, on the one hand, and rapid, complete market-generated correction on the other hand. We recognize that both methods have limitations, and the policy maker in practice must weigh the relative value of two imperfect techniques for correction.

First, antitrust rules should be adequate to deter anticompetitive conduct, but should not unduly inhibit procompetitive conduct. Excessively broad rules might condemn conduct that, while "aggressive," may reflect healthy, vigorous rivalry. Competition always will yield winners and losers. Competition generates great consumer benefits, but it also is disruptive. The better products, better services, and better prices provided by one seller tend to displace those of other sellers. The vanquished may attribute their failure to the competitive aggression of their rivals, but an antitrust law incapable of distinguishing socially productive "aggression" (e.g., the drive to achieve a dramatic qualitative improvement in a product) from truly anticompetitive conduct will condemn—and hence inhibit— desirable competitive instincts. Such "false positives" can be costly to consumers. Conduct that might lead to increased competition, lower prices, more services or other competitive benefits will be retarded due to antitrust enforcement—and consumers will be worse off. This was the accusation leveled forcefully by Robert H. Bork in a series of articles published in the 1960s and 1970s, culminating in his influential book, THE ANTITRUST PARADOX (1978). In Judge Bork's view the antitrust laws were paradoxically being interpreted in a way that hindered competition. "Certain of its doctrines," he wrote, "preserve competition, while others suppress it, resulting in a policy at war with itself." *Id.* at 7.

On the other hand, permissive rules or rules characterized by exceedingly demanding burdens of pleading, production, and proof, also can have substantial adverse consequences. "False negatives," concluding that anticompetitive conduct does not constitute an antitrust violation, also can injure consumers, especially if market imperfections impede correction by market forces, such as new entry. Permissive rules can lead to higher prices, lower quality, diminished service, and slower innovation. Discerning the appropriate line between over and under-deterrence, however, is difficult and is a source of much debate in antitrust circles.

Antitrust rules also should be reasonably certain and accessible for all market participants. Firms should be able to comply with the law without undue cost, delay, or uncertainty, and should be able to differentiate changes in market performance occasioned by competition from those that are the consequence of anticompetitive conduct. Vague, unduly complex, or non-transparent antitrust rules provide inferior guidance to firms and courts, may increase administrative and judicial intervention into private markets, and can increase compliance costs. Depending on their aversion to risk, some firms may forego procompetitive or otherwise desirable conduct for fear of antitrust liability; others may be emboldened by a lack of clarity to undertake anticompetitive conduct, either out of ignorance or in the hope of avoiding detection. Some may seek solace in the courts when they meet with failure in the marketplace; some may use the often high cost of judicial process itself as a tool to discourage victims of anticompetitive conduct from seeking redress.

Finally, the cost of enforcement should yield net benefits when compared to the cost of reliance on the market itself to provide a "cure" for the anticompetitive effects of conduct. As a general rule, some economists predict that the exercise of market power invites entry, which in turn erodes market power.

To the degree any particular market is viewed as producing extraordinary levels of profit, other firms will be attracted to and invest in that market. With entry, market power will quickly wither and competitive conditions will be restored. In this view, market power is an advertisement for entry, and will necessarily erode. Even better, if entry is easy, firms that might otherwise be capable of exercising market power could be deterred from doing so by this prospect, making correction through actual entry unnecessary.

The conclusion that market power will naturally erode depends upon several preconditions that may not always be present. *See generally* Jonathan B. Baker, *Taking the Error Out of "Error Cost" Analysis: What's Wrong with Antitrust's Right*, 80 ANTITRUST L.J. 1, 8–13 (2015). For example, entry may not be "easy;" resources for expansion may not be readily available; and strategic behavior by the firm with market power may discourage or otherwise hinder the efforts of new entrants. Strategic responses to entry can impede entry as it happens. In addition, the mere threat of future strategic responses, if credible, may influence the decision to enter. A firm contemplating entry will try to anticipate and predict the incumbent rival's response to its entry before reaching a decision on whether entry will be profitable. If the potential new entrant expects to face strategic behavior, perhaps because the incumbent firm has a past history of so meeting entrants, it may perceive its investment to be at risk and conclude that entry should not be attempted. Investors, too, may shy away from supporting the effort. This might especially be true when the entrant faces the prospect of incurring unrecoverable or "sunk" costs, which may be lost if exit becomes necessary as a consequence of strategic behavior. In these instances neither actual entry, nor the threat of entry, will suffice to deter the exercise of market power.

Moreover, even when markets function well, there will always be some "lag time" between the onset of market power and the emergence of new rivals. Strategic decisions about entry or expansion may take months, if not years. New or expanded plants and facilities may not be susceptible to rapid construction. Entry, if and when it comes, may not suffice to counteract the persistence of market power. These are difficult issues. As a matter of antitrust policy, we will need to decide whether a preference for market forces over government intervention justifies the risk associated with tolerating the exercise of market power for some period of time. If we choose the market as the best cure, how long are we willing to await correction through entry? And how can we know with some confidence that the entry, when it comes, will be adequate to mitigate the existing firm's market power?

If the alternative is litigation, however, it is important to assess its costs, as well, so they can be weighed against the price of leaving cures to the market. Litigation can be slow and costly. Although injunctive relief can quickly correct for a market problem that, if left to fester, could be difficult to undo, the full course of litigation from trial through appeals can be protracted. The *Matsushita* case (*see infra* Chapter 3), for example, alleged a conspiracy among Japanese consumer product manufacturers that began in 1953. The case was filed in 1974 and litigated vigorously and extensively until it was finally resolved on summary judgment in the U.S. Supreme Court in 1986. Even the government's 1998 case against Microsoft, remarkable for the pace at which it proceeded through discovery and trial, required enormous effort on the part of the parties and the court, and involved years of subsequent appeals and further proceedings. In both instances the cases demanded extensive evaluation of industry information and sometimes difficult judgments about the consequences of the alleged conduct.

Lag time also can permit the persistence of ultimately objectionable conduct, or it can delay and even deter conduct that after careful scrutiny may prove to be unobjectionable. Conversely, in the merger area, the mere announcement by the government of its intention to challenge a merger can prompt the parties to abandon the transaction, even if significant efficiencies may well be achievable.

Litigation also depends on the quality of advocates and judges, who may have little formal training in economic analysis. Although cross examination and the use of experts can compensate for the lack of judicial expertise, choosing between conflicting experts' testimony can be a daunting task. There is also the risk of "error" and the costs associated with it. Injunctive remedies such as barring specified conduct or ordering the divestiture or restructuring of a firm can lead to more, rather than less competitive markets, and require the courts to oversee industry behavior for years, as was the case with the 1982 settlement that decreed the breakup of the American Telephone & Telegraph Company. The federal court in *AT & T* oversaw many aspects of the telecommunications industry for more than a decade after the decree was entered. Choosing between antitrust law enforcement and the market, therefore, can be far from an easy task.

Many antitrust rules, even well settled ones, have fared poorly when carefully evaluated against these standards. When they have been so evaluated, the courts have either abandoned the rules, or amended them in various ways. Revisit the arguments outlined in this Section when you read cases such as *Continental T.V., Inc. v. GTE Sylvania Inc.*, 433 U.S. 36, 97 S.Ct. 2549 (1977) and *Leegin Creative Leather Prods., Inc. v. PSKS, Inc.*, 551 U.S. 877, 127 S.Ct. 2705 (2007) (*see infra* Chapter 6), and *Matsushita Elec. Indus. Co. v. Zenith Radio Corp.*, 475 U.S. 574 (1986) (*see infra* Chapter 3). We will revisit the significance of false positives, false negatives, and administrative costs associated with various alternative antitrust rules later in this Chapter in Sidebar 1–4, *Economics and the Development of Legal Rules.*

3. WHAT FORMS CAN ANTITRUST SYSTEMS TAKE?

An antitrust system's impact depends crucially on the means for its implementation. Adopting nominally powerful commands without effective means to enforce them will be ineffectual and could be harmful. Unenforceable or erratically applied laws create serious risks and costs for businesses and consumers. Hollow mandates foster public cynicism about the rule of law and raise doubts about the integrity of public administration. In this Subsection we introduce some key issues that a jurisdiction, such as a state or country, must address in designing a competition policy system. For additional and more in-depth discussions, see ANNETJE OTTOW, MARKET AND COMPETITION AUTHORITIES: GOOD AGENCY PRINCIPLES (2015); THE DESIGN OF COMPETITION LAW INSTITUTIONS: GLOBAL NORMS, LOCAL CHOICES (Eleanor M. Fox & Michael J. Trebilcock eds, 2013); DANIEL CRANE, THE INSTITUTIONAL STRUCTURE OF ANTITRUST ENFORCEMENT (2011); William E. Kovacic & David A Hyman, *Competition Agency Design: What's On the Menu?*, 8 EUR. COMPETITION J. 527 (2012).

A jurisdiction can use various institutional approaches to create and execute antitrust commands. The Sherman Act's chief innovation in 1890 was to replace a passive competition policy mechanism, in which common law courts merely refused to enforce anticompetitive private agreements, with a positive system of enforcement executed by public authorities and private entities. The new system also relied on the common law model, as reflected in the broadly drafted prohibitions of Sections 1 and 2 of the Sherman Act, and later in the provisions of the Clayton Act of 1914. As

William F. Baxter, the Assistant Attorney General for Antitrust from 1981 to 1984, observed, this was by design:

> These provisions contain the kernel of antitrust law. They are broadly phrased—almost constitutional in quality—embracing fundamental concepts with a simplicity virtually unknown in modern legislative enactments. In failing to provide more guidance, the framers of our antitrust laws did not abdicate their responsibility any more than did the Framers of the Constitution. The antitrust laws were written with awareness of the diversity of business conduct and with the knowledge that the detailed statutes which would prohibit socially undesirable conduct would lack the flexibility needed to encourage (and at times even permit) desirable conduct. To provide flexibility, Congress adopted what is in essence enabling legislation that has permitted a common-law refinement of antitrust law through an evolution guided by only the most general statutory directions.

William F. Baxter, *Separation of Powers, Prosecutorial Discretion, and the "Common Law" Nature of Antitrust Law*, 60 TEX. L. REV. 661, 662–63 (1982). Such a system makes some powerful institutional assumptions. It presumes the independence, competence, and integrity of both the judiciary and public enforcement agencies—elements frequently lacking to some degree in emerging markets that are seeking to establish competition policy systems. It also assigns to courts a degree of discretion incompatible with civil law regimes, which are accustomed to lengthy, detailed legislative enactments.

The need to understand the institutional foundations of antitrust policy has assumed ever greater significance for antitrust practice in today's increasingly market-dependent and global economy. Business conduct routinely implicates several national antitrust regimes and requires counselors to understand the varied institutional mechanisms through which different jurisdictions enforce competition policy commands.

Although antitrust's roots run deep historically, two distinct models have greatly influenced its contemporary form. The U.S. model relies chiefly upon a law enforcement model in which two national agencies (the Antitrust Division of the Department of Justice and the Federal Trade Commission), state attorneys general, and private plaintiffs bring cases in the federal courts. As we will see, the creation of the FTC in 1914 diversified this model by creating a mechanism for administrative adjudication of antitrust claims. As noted above, the U.S. model relies heavily upon a common law method of interpretation in the courts to define and develop doctrine.

In contrast, the European model, which dates from the creation of the European Union in 1957, is often called an administrative system of enforcement and is based on legal instruments that specify forbidden conduct more completely and vest greater authority for enforcement with an administrative body, the European Commission ("EC"). The EC implements the competition law provisions of the Treaty on the Functioning of the European Union ("TFEU") through its Directorate General-Competition ("DG Comp") by both conducting enforcement proceedings and adopting regulations that cover specific sectors of the economy or categories of conduct, such as mergers. Modernization reforms adopted in 2004 significantly expanded the enforcement role of the EU member states, and more recent reforms may lead to a greater role for private rights of action.

As we shall see, the U.S. and European models can differ in both substance and institutional design, and both have had substantial influence on the approximately 130 jurisdictions that today have competition law systems. By rough analogy to computer science, one can describe a competition system as having two basic ingredients: an operating system of institutions (e.g., enforcement agencies and courts) that provide the platform for policy implementation, and a body of applications that provide the analytical concepts and implementation techniques necessary to reach decisions in specific cases. William E. Kovacic, *The United States and Its Influence on Global Competition Policy*, 22 GEO. MASON L.REV. 1159, 1160–63 (2015). Variants of the EU model of administrative enforcement supply the operating system for most (over 80%) of the world's antitrust systems, many of which have civil law foundations, with which the EU institutional framework for competition law is most compatible.

Although the EU institutional model has a dominant share of the world's antitrust systems, the market for applications is highly competitive. Individual regimes can exercise substantial influence through the issuance of guidelines (e.g., for merger review) and experimentation with enforcement techniques (e.g., leniency programs). The design of new applications, rather than through the design of implementing institutions, is the means through which the United States exercises its greatest influence on what other competition agencies do.

a. The Structure of Legal Rules

One method for designing antitrust standards of conduct is to create general rules and rely chiefly on enforcement officials and courts to articulate the law's specific content. As we have already noted, the

Sherman Act assigns a pivotal role to the courts in adapting to changing views of what constitutes sound policy:

> * * * "[S]tare decisis is not an inexorable command." In the area of antitrust law, there is a competing interest, well-represented in this Court's decisions, in recognizing and adapting to changed circumstances and the lessons of accumulated experience. Thus, the general presumption that legislative changes should be left to Congress has less force with respect to the Sherman Act in light of the accepted view that Congress "expected the courts to give shape to the statute's broad mandate by drawing on common-law tradition." As we have explained, the term "restraint of trade," as used in § 1, also "invokes the common law itself, and not merely the static content that the common law assigned to the term in 1890." Accordingly, this Court has reconsidered its decisions construing the Sherman Act when the theoretical underpinnings of those decisions are called into serious question.

State Oil Co. v. Khan, 522 U.S. 3, 20–21 (1997). As Justice Sandra Day O'Connor suggested, drafting antitrust rules in general terms gives courts and enforcement agencies much discretion to shape policy and makes the law flexible and adaptable. Some legislatures might regard this degree of flexibility suspiciously if they think prosecutors will misuse their discretion or that courts will ignore the legislature's intent in interpreting the law.

An alternative is to draft more specific commands that leave courts and enforcement agencies with less discretion. Congress did that to a limited degree when it drafted the Clayton Act in 1914. Compared to the Sherman Act, the Clayton Act spells out anticompetitive conduct more fully. Another example of a more particularized approach to specifying prohibited conduct is Article 101 of the Treaty on the Functioning of the European Union ("TFEU"), the EU counterpart to Section 1 of the Sherman Act. Although Article 101 addresses some of the same acts that U.S. courts have condemned in applying Section 1, it does so more specifically. *See* Appendix A. Article 101's more complete codification of specific offenses is characteristic of civil law regimes and is also reflected in Article 102, TFEU, which addresses abuse of dominance.

b. Design of the Enforcement Mechanism

No less important than the choice of legal rules is the decision about who can enforce the law. As is depicted below in Figure 1–14, the U.S. antitrust system decentralizes the decision to prosecute to an unparalleled degree. By statute and by judicial interpretation, potential prosecutors in the U.S. include an executive department (the DOJ's Antitrust Division), an independent administrative agency (the FTC), the attorneys general of the 50 states and the District of Columbia, and aggrieved individuals, including consumers and competitors of the alleged violator.

Figure 1–14:
The Structure of the U.S. Antitrust Enforcement System

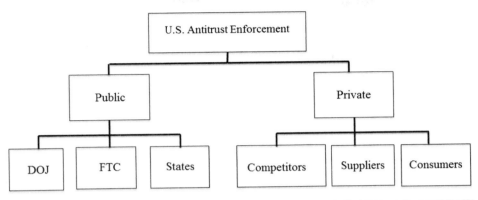

In cases involving regulated sectors such as telecommunications, other government bureaus, such as the Federal Communications Commission (FCC), exercise competition policy functions concurrently with the federal antitrust agencies. Mergers in the telecommunications industry, for example, can require the approval of the DOJ, the FCC, various state attorneys general, and state public service commissions. No other antitrust system distributes the power to enforce the law and shape competition policy so broadly. Why decentralize the power to prosecute so extensively? Sidebar 1–3 explores that and related questions.

Sidebar 1–3:
Ramifications of Decentralized Enforcement

Each authorized antitrust enforcer has distinctive institutional traits. Consider the choice of an executive department, like the DOJ, or an independent commission, like the FTC. Giving an *executive* department enforcement power increases presidential control over the law's implementation and makes policy more responsive to presidential election results. Executive branch participation also tends to be imperative in the roughly thirty countries (including the United States) which today treat some antitrust violations as crimes. By constitutional mandate or statute, the power to prosecute criminal charges tends to be vested in the executive branch.

Creating an independent agency, such as the FTC, gives the *legislature* more ability to shape competition policy and vests dispute resolution in an expert body. Compared to courts of general jurisdiction, administrative adjudication by an independent and specialized commission might expedite the decision of cases and build a more coherent, sensible body of competition doctrine. However, if some antitrust offenses are criminal and, as in the U.S., criminal enforcement can only be carried out by the executive branch, the creation of an independent administrative body will likely lead to a division of enforcement authority between two national agencies.

In addition to accommodating the institutional limits of administrative authority, diversifying prosecutorial power among two or more agents has several rationales. One basic reason to diversify is to increase the total resources devoted to antitrust enforcement. Vesting authority in a larger number of prosecutorial agents—political subdivisions such as state governments, private plaintiffs—can supplement expenditures by the national agency, yield more cases, and, by raising awareness of antitrust law, strengthen the jurisdiction's "competition culture." *See, e.g.*, Harry First & Spencer Weber Waller, *Antitrust's Democracy Deficit*, 81 FORDHAM L.REV. 2543 (2013). A second reason is to guard against default by a single prosecutorial agent. For example, a private right of action might ensure that the law is enforced if public officials, due to neglect, capture, inadequate resources, or a shift in the policy preferences of the public enforcement bodies, do not challenge behavior otherwise forbidden in the antitrust statute or by well-established judicial precedent. In another example, when the FTC deadlocked 2–2 due to one Commissioner's recusal in the earliest stages of its investigation of Microsoft in the 1990s, the case files were transferred to the Justice Department, which was able to continue the investigation. A third rationale involves the relative efficacy of private lawsuits. Compared to a government bureau, the victim of a price fixing cartel may be first to learn of a violation and may have stronger incentives to attack such conduct aggressively. The fourth rationale concerns the competitive benefits of diversification. Having two enforcement institutions (the DOJ and the FTC) "compete" can induce each agency to improve law enforcement by, for example, developing more effective ways to detect and attack harmful behavior or minimize compliance burdens by giving companies better guidance about contemplated business ventures.

In the 1980s, the Reagan Administration significantly retrenched several of the federal government's antitrust programs. Among other areas, the federal antitrust agencies relaxed controls on mergers and reduced scrutiny of restrictions that manufacturers impose upon their retailers. The Reagan White House also promoted the value of federalism. An unintended consequence of these policies was a dramatic increase in efforts by states to enforce the federal antitrust laws against behavior that the DOJ and the FTC refused to challenge. Some observers point to experience in the 1980s as demonstrating the value of diversifying the field of potential antitrust plaintiffs.

Decentralizing prosecutorial power also entails costs. Having two or more public enforcers entails some duplication in personnel and requires the agencies to spend some resource on liaison systems to avoid duplicative examination of the same potential misconduct. It also requires some mechanism for determining which matters will be handled by each enforcement authority.

Distributing authority across a number of prosecutorial agents also can reduce the clarity and predictability of competition law. If one agent's decision not to prosecute does not bind other agents, a firm must assume that the same conduct might still be investigated and/or challenged by other agents. This structure also curbs the ability of any single agent to narrow the scope of antitrust prohibitions by declining to invoke interpretations of the law that it deems to be overly expansive. Identifying and responding to the preferences of multiple prosecutorial agents may lead to greater uncertainty, which can increase compliance costs.

Diversification also raises the question of whether prosecutorial agents have adequate incentives to bring cases that serve consumer interests. One company might use the antitrust laws to sue a rival for conduct, such as aggressive, non-predatory pricing, that benefits consumers, but that decreases the plaintiff's sales. A state official might attack a competitively benign merger because the merging parties will close plants and eliminate jobs in her state. The rivalry that emerges between enforcement agencies, either within a single jurisdiction that has multiple agencies or between agencies in different jurisdictions, could lead to experiments with enforcement theories that raise an agency's visibility without improving antitrust policy. It might also lead to creative use of guidelines or novel cases that better serve consumer interests and advance the global dialogue about competition policy.

The U.S. competition policy system relies heavily on the courts to rationalize doctrine and constrain the discretion of prosecutorial agents. Although individual agents may proceed on different theories, judicial decisions establish binding principles that apply to all agents, at least with respect to federal antitrust laws.

Figure 1–15:
Institutional Enforcement Models

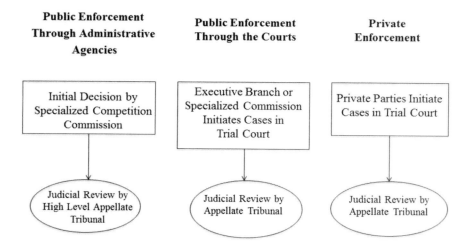

c. Remedies

A statute's impact often hinges on the nature of the remedies available for violations of the law and its remedial goals, which can include deterrence, compensation, remediation, and punishment.

The United States has a uniquely broad collection of remedies. The most powerful is the Sherman Act's treatment of violations as crimes, which prioritizes deterrence. The 1890 statute condemned infractions as misdemeanors and was amended in 1974 to make offenses felonies. Criminal enforcement has major institutional implications. As noted above, criminal sanctions ordinarily give a major prosecutorial role to the executive branch. A second implication involves defining forbidden conduct. Criminal punishment such as incarceration for individuals can greatly affect company behavior and have tremendous political ramifications. To retain political support and perceived legitimacy, in antitrust systems with criminal sanctions, criminal punishment ordinarily is reserved for well-defined categories of clearly pernicious conduct, such as price fixing by competitors.

The more common remedies are civil sanctions, which also serve the goal of deterrence, but can provide for compensation and remediation. These include civil monetary penalties, such as fines and damages, and equitable relief. Equitable relief, which can include mandatory and prohibitory injunctions, licensing of intellectual property, and asset divestitures, is the remedy most directly associated with remediation. Many countries, including the United States, permit independent commissions or other administrative bodies to impose civil sanctions, subject to judicial review. Another major element of U.S. civil enforcement is the availability of treble damages in private cases and the reimbursement by the defendant of the attorneys' fees and costs for prevailing private plaintiffs. 15 U.S.C. § 15. DOJ also can obtain treble damages where a federal procurement authority is the victim of a cartel. 15 U.S.C. § 15a. Damages serve to deter, but also provide a means for compensating victims of antitrust violations. Unlike the United States, many foreign countries expressly allow the government to recover civil monetary penalties for illegal behavior. In recent years, the DOJ and the FTC have recovered monetary penalties as restitution for antitrust violations (*see infra* Chapter 8).

Figure 1–16:
Possible Remedies for Antitrust Violations

Criminal	**Civil**
• Imprisonment	• Damages (single, double, treble or more)
• Fines (corporate and individual)	• Equitable (injunctive) relief
• Restitution	○ Conduct prohibitions
• Asset forfeitures	○ Divestiture or other structural relief
• Equitable (injunctive) relief	○ Disgorgement
• Director disqualification	• Attorneys' fees & costs of suit

d. The Role of the Courts

Competition laws usually give the courts a key role in developing antitrust principles. The role is most pronounced in the United States, which relies heavily on judicial interpretation to elaborate antitrust rules. Countries that rely on administrative adjudication before agencies such as the FTC typically permit the affected parties to seek judicial review of agency decisions. For example, decisions of the European Commission are reviewable by the General Court, with further appeals to the European Court of Justice.

The U.S. courts play a key role in shaping doctrine. With a highly decentralized system of prosecution, the courts are the chief means to clarify doctrine and reconcile any divergent views of enforcers and courts. Since the late 1970s, the preeminence of the U.S. courts in some areas of antitrust law has diminished as government enforcers have relied more heavily on non-litigation strategies—such as issuing guidelines and negotiating settlements—to shape policy. *See* Appendix B (collecting U.S. Guidelines and Policy Statements since 1980).

4. WHICH IDEAS INFLUENCE THE ANSWERS TO THE CORE QUESTIONS OF ANTITRUST POLICY?

In Section B1 we discussed economic and non-economic goals that competition laws might pursue. As was probably apparent, the choice among and between such goals frequently will be a function of one's ideas about the economic and political values that ought to inform the implementation of the law and economic regulation, generally. Antitrust, like many areas of public policy, has always been affected by contests of ideas. In this Section, we explore some of the principal schools of thought that have influenced modern antitrust doctrine and enforcement priorities.

In sketching the formative intellectual influences upon competition policy, we are walking into a bit of a minefield. To a large extent, modern U.S. antitrust history (indeed, earlier eras, as well) reflects a clash of opposing, timeless views about the respective roles of public intervention and private initiative in shaping the economy. To say that the answer lies in careful study of economics requires one to choose among competing economic views about the significance of business behavior and the capacity of public intervention to correct apparent failures of the market. Some areas of policy—for example, the development of increasingly powerful mechanisms to detect and punish cartels—feature broad-based, sustained agreement. Others—such as the treatment of conduct by dominant firms—bring commentators to the barricades.

Neither is there broad agreement about the content and meaning of "U.S. antitrust history." The popular discourse and scholarly literature on U.S. antitrust policy contains many "histories." They do not speak in one voice.[12] The narratives vary strikingly in their positive descriptions (what happened), clash in their interpretations of what causes adjustments in doctrine and enforcement (why it happened), and disagree (often strongly) in their normative assessments (did it help or hurt?). In many cases, the narrators played a part as public officials in shaping the policies at issue, and they have a point of view about whether their contributions improved the system.[13] What follows below is a necessarily simplified account of the complex mix of ideas that have influenced the U.S. antitrust system.

a. Changing Intellectual Foundations

Classical American political themes such as "tyranny," "autonomy," and "freedom" have long permeated antitrust discourse. In one colorful speech in support of the Sherman Act, the Act's namesake and supporter,

---

[12] These variations are apparent, for example, in Symposium: *Politics and Antitrust*, 79 ANTITRUST L.J. 557 (2014).

[13] All four co-authors of this Casebook have served in senior policy making positions in one or more of the federal institutions entrusted with antitrust enforcement. We are not always of one mind in our interpretation and assessment of various aspects of modern U.S. antitrust policy.

Senator John Sherman (R-OH) [14] charged that the early trusts were governed only by "[t]he law of selfishness, uncontrolled by competition," which "compels [them] to disregard the interest of the consumer." The trust, he argued, "dictates terms to transportation companies, it commands the price of labor without fear of strikes. . . ." He continued:

> If the concentrated powers of this combination are intrusted to a single man, it is a kingly prerogative, inconsistent with our form of government, and should be subject to strong resistance of the State and national authorities. If anything is wrong, this is wrong. If we will not endure a king as a political power, we should not endure a king over the production, transportation, and sale of any of the necessaries of life. If we would not submit to an emperor we should not submit to an autocrat of trade. * * *

21 CONG. REC. 2456–57 (1890) (statement of Sen. Sherman). This early association of antitrust with populist themes has remained an enduring feature of public debate over antitrust policy, and remains an important source of the continuing popular appeal of antitrust enforcement, especially against large firms. *See* Jonathan B. Baker, *Competition Policy as a Political Bargain*, 73 ANTITRUST L.J. 483 (2006).

On a number of occasions, the Supreme Court has echoed Sherman's vision in suggesting that the Sherman Act reflects social and political values and possesses a nearly constitutional stature in the American economy. In *Appalachian Coals, Inc. v. United States*, 288 U.S. 344, 359–60 (1933), the Court said the purpose of the Sherman Act was "to prevent undue restraints on interstate commerce, to maintain its appropriate freedom in the public interest, [and] to afford protection from subversive or coercive influences of monopolistic endeavor." It concluded that "[a]s a charter of freedom, the Act has a generality and adaptability comparable to that found to be desirable in constitutional provisions." A quarter-century later, in *Northern Pacific Railway Co. v. United States*, 356 U.S. 1, 4 (1958), the Court called the Sherman Act "a comprehensive charter of economic liberty" designed to promote economic progress "while at the same time providing an environment conducive to the preservation of our democratic, political and social institutions." Forward another 25 years, and the Court in *United States v. Topco Associates., Inc.*, 405 U.S. 596, 610 (1972) observed that "[a]ntitrust laws in general, and the Sherman Act in particular, are the Magna Carta of free enterprise." These measures, the Court declared, "are as important to the preservation of economic freedom and our free enterprise system as the Bill of Rights is to the protection of our fundamental personal freedoms." *Id.*

---

[14] Sherman came from a storied Ohio family and had a distinguished political career. He served as a senator, congressman, Secretary of the Treasury, and Secretary of State. *See* John Sherman—Biography, http://bioguide.congress.gov/scripts/biodisplay.pl?index=s000346. His brother, Maj. General William Tecumseh Sherman, was the famous Civil War general.

These and other expressions of purpose resonate with views about *political economy*. By the middle of the twentieth century, a distinct intellectual foundation for the U.S. antitrust system had emerged in the field of *economic theory*.[15] This is not to say that economics and antitrust were distinct fields prior to the 1950s—quite to the contrary, economics has always played a role in the development of antitrust law. But by the 1950s, more defined schools of economic thought began to exert increasing influence on antitrust enforcers and lawyers. By absorbing the economic teaching of their time and incorporating it into their work before the courts, these enforcers and lawyers played an important role in launching a pronounced and continuing trend towards greater reliance on economics, and economists, in developing antitrust law.

b. The Influence of Industrial Organization Economics

In the 1950s and 1960s, the rise of industrial organization economics greatly influenced antitrust. Industrial organization economists focused on three characteristics of markets, which they believed to be interrelated: structure, conduct, and performance. Sometimes labeled "structuralists," these economists heavily weighted the structure of markets—the number of buyers and sellers and conditions of entry—in predicting the likelihood of competitive problems. Based on skepticism about the ability of highly concentrated markets to perform competitively, many industrial organization economists presumed that concentrated markets usually would spawn anticompetitive conduct, leading to noncompetitive market performance. *See, e.g.,* CARL KAYSEN & DONALD F. TURNER, ANTITRUST POLICY: AN ECONOMIC AND LEGAL ANALYSIS (1959); REPORT OF THE ATTORNEY GENERAL'S NATIONAL COMMITTEE TO STUDY THE ANTITRUST LAWS (1955). They also doubted assertions of efficiency, which they saw as difficult to measure and prove, preferring the predictability of structural assumptions. *See* Derek C. Bok, *Section 7 of the Clayton Act and the Merging of Law and Economics*, 74 HARV. L. REV. 226 (1960).

The teachings of industrial organization economists permeated antitrust discourse and enforcement in the 1950s and 1960s, particularly for mergers. As we will see in Chapter 5, courts began to rely on "trends towards concentration" and "concentration ratios" as sufficient to make out a prima facie case for prohibiting mergers under Section 7 of the Clayton Act. Illustrative cases included *United States v. Philadelphia Nat'l Bank*, 374 U.S. 321 (1963); *United States v. Von's Grocery Co.*, 384 U.S. 270 (1966); and *United States v. Pabst Brewing Co.*, 384 U.S. 546 (1966).

The structuralist paradigm, and the decisions it spawned, attracted increasing criticism. Through reliance on concentration trends and aggregate concentration ratios, it encouraged condemnation of mergers of

---

[15] For an additional discussion, see William E. Kovacic & Carl Shapiro, *Antitrust Policy: A Century of Economic and Legal Thinking*, 14 J. ECON. PERSPS. 43 (2000).

firms with relatively small market shares (less than 10% in *Von's*; less than 6% in *Pabst*) and no likely ability to affect prices. Critics argued that these mergers were motivated by a desire to achieve economic efficiencies, rather than the "anticompetitive" scenario painted by the courts. Condemnation might well have meant higher prices for consumers. Moreover, by focusing on "trends" towards concentration, the courts ignored the possibility that some degree of increased concentration might enhance competition and lead to the realization of efficiencies that could lower prices. The stage was set for the rise of an alternative mode of analysis.

c.   The Chicago School of Antitrust

Structuralism represented one important fusion of economic concepts and legal principles. But economics itself is not static, and, as we have described, the antitrust laws were intentionally drafted in general terms to allow them to evolve over time. It is not surprising, therefore, that successive efforts to fuse economic concepts and legal principles would develop and that they would influence the evolution of antitrust law. In the early 1950s at the University of Chicago, a second formative "law and economics" emerged as a critical response to the principal tenets of the structuralist school of industrial organization economics. In what would become known as the "Chicago School of Antitrust," this new approach provided notably different policy proscriptions and spawned a lively debate about antitrust law's goals and analytical methods that continues today. *See generally* Richard A. Posner, *The Chicago School of Antitrust Analysis*, 127 U. PA. L. REV. 925 (1979).

The Chicago School emerged in the 1950s, but did not influence antitrust doctrine and enforcement policy significantly until the mid-to late 1970s. Its progenitors, Aaron Director, George Stigler, and Edward Levi of the University of Chicago, influenced a generation of advocates of a narrowly focused, economic approach to legal analysis, particularly antitrust analysis. Chicago School advocates, including Ward Bowman, Harold Demsetz, Benjamin Klein, John McGee, Lester Telser, and, later, Judges Robert Bork, Richard Posner, and Frank Easterbrook, as well as William F. Baxter, who headed the DOJ Antitrust Division in the first Reagan Administration, profoundly affected antitrust analysis.

In contrast to the structuralists, the Chicago School sought to apply the insights of price theory to antitrust law. "Price theory" is comprised of a set of theoretical assumptions about how competitive markets and firms behave. Firms will act to maximize profits; markets left unfettered by regulation will lead to productive and allocative efficiency. Together, profit maximizing firms and efficient markets will produce maximum "consumer welfare," which should serve as the principal goal of antitrust law. With these theoretical tools in hand, its advocates authored a series of influential articles and books challenging many accepted antitrust mores of the times.

The Chicago School viewed industrial structure as far less significant a predictor of anticompetitive conduct and performance. In its view, trends towards concentration might reflect a natural progression towards more efficient, and therefore more desirable, market structures, induced by the desire to achieve economies of scale. As a consequence, they tended to conclude that most markets were competitive, even those with few firms, and that true monopoly, when it did arise, would generally be self-correcting. As discussed in Section B2, above, it would soon invite entry and erode. Chicago School advocates also took the position that market entry and exit generally are easy, and that government regulation is the likeliest source of true barriers to entry. Finally, Chicago School advocates took particular aim at antitrust prohibitions of various arrangements directed at the distribution of products and services that in their view were far more likely to promote efficient distribution than result in a reduction in competition. The Chicago School thus questioned many of antitrust's traditional prohibitions and urged a more narrow focus on cartels and horizontal mergers of truly substantial competitors.

As suggested in the *Brunswick* decision, presented above, judicial antitrust perspectives had begun to change by the late 1970s. By the end of the decade, the shift in jurisprudence and the development of a new literature skeptical of intervention began to alter decision making within the federal antitrust agencies. *See, e.g.,* MARC ALLEN EISNER, ANTITRUST AND THE TRIUMPH OF ECONOMICS (1991). This reorientation accelerated in the early 1980s, when a broad-based and growing conservative political tide brought Ronald Reagan to the White House. Reagan named William Baxter to head DOJ's Antitrust Division and chose James C. Miller, III to be the first economist to chair the FTC. In his first term, Reagan also appointed Chicago-oriented academics such as Robert Bork, Frank Easterbrook, Douglas Ginsburg, Richard Posner, Antonin Scalia, and Stephen Williams to the federal bench. These moves gave the Chicago School powerful voices in antitrust enforcement and in the courts. While falling short of the total restructuring of antitrust doctrine it sought, the Chicago School reformulated antitrust rules in many areas, including most notably, mergers, vertical restrictions, and predatory pricing. The 1982 and 1984 federal Merger Guidelines, for example, reflected a major shift from the concentration concerns of the structuralist inspired 1968 Guidelines, to the market power and collusion focused Chicago School view.

Perhaps most important, the Chicago School altered the terms of antitrust debate. Many once controversial views gained wide acceptance. The Chicago School's call for antitrust to focus only on "consumer welfare" made many concepts that grounded Chicago School prescriptions—such as market power, entry, and efficiency—essential to antitrust analysis. *See, e.g.,* William M. Landes & Richard A. Posner, *Market Power in Antitrust Cases*, 94 HARV. L. REV. 937 (1981). Critics are compelled to anticipate their positions and respond. Courts continue to adopt their views and use their analytical approaches. This is not to say that the ascent of the Chicago School was uncontroversial. Quite to the contrary, it was accompanied first by intense criticism from defenders of the structuralist and populist approaches it challenged, and later by pointed economic criticisms based upon both theory and empirical evidence.

At the time Chicago emerged, critics charged that its models were exceedingly theoretical, ignored contrary evidence in particular cases, and imposed daunting burdens of proof on antitrust enforcers and private plaintiffs. As the Chicago School's influence waxed, the fortunes of antitrust plaintiffs unmistakably waned. Of course, Chicago School proponents responded that this outcome was as it should be—that many plaintiffs, including the government, were bringing economically unjustifiable cases. Critics also charged that the Chicago School's operative definition of "consumer welfare" was narrow, normative, and ignored concerns about the distribution of wealth. Criticism too came from those who questioned the efficacy of all antitrust law on the ground that, even as conceived by the Chicago School, it was still too interventionist and too easily subject to manipulation by interest groups. *See generally* FRED S. MCCHESNEY & WILLIAM F. SHUGART II, EDS., THE CAUSES AND CONSEQUENCES OF ANTITRUST: THE PUBLIC-CHOICE PERSPECTIVE (1995).

d. The Harvard School of Antitrust

By the mid-1980s, economists began to develop theoretical models and empirical evidence that, while accepting many of the Chicago School's basic microeconomic assumptions, questioned some of its central conclusions about the likelihood of anticompetitive conduct. But before moving on to discuss this important response to the Chicago School, it is necessary to consider another identifiable group of antitrust commentators, who evolved out of the structuralist school, but who, influenced by the Chicagoans, offered the basis for a more intervention-minded doctrinal approach and enforcement policy agenda than Chicago prescribed. These commentators, associated with the Harvard Law School, also had and continue to have substantial influence that is also likely to endure.

In the late 1950s, Professors Carl Kaysen and Donald Turner authored what was at the time the single most comprehensive and immediately authoritative treatise on antitrust law. Influenced in large part by the work of industrial organization economists, Kaysen & Turner's ANTITRUST POLICY (1959), sought to construct a coherent analytical framework for all areas of antitrust based upon the economic and legal teachings of the day. As a collaboration between an economist (Kaysen) and lawyer-economist (Turner) the work was unique, and represented an important step forward in the evolution of antitrust analysis. Although it reflected far more of an interventionist bent than did the contemporaneous work of the Chicago

School, it still departed from the arguably more populist antitrust of the pre and post-World War II period.

In the 1960s, Turner, as head of the Antitrust Division, successfully guided the drafting and adoption of the first Merger Guidelines in 1968, which reflected the industrial organization approach to merger analysis that developed from his work with Kaysen. As time went on, however, the views of Turner and his later co-author, Professor Phillip Areeda, began to evolve away from a rigid structuralist approach to include Chicago School perspectives, modified by their own insights. They authored a law review article on predatory pricing that gained immediate and broad judicial acceptance for the view that previous controls upon dominant firm price-cutting were unduly restrictive. Phillip Areeda & Donald F. Turner, *Predatory Pricing and Related Practices Under Section 2 of the Sherman Act*, 88 HARV.L. REV. 697 (1975). They produced the multi-volume treatise ANTITRUST LAW, which first appeared in 1978 and is today one of the most influential works on antitrust law ever written. ANTITRUST LAW demonstrated their willingness to incorporate myriad perspectives into their analysis, including those of the Chicago School. Their reasoned approach to integrating antitrust law and economics produced balanced, practical solutions to the antitrust challenges of the time, although over time they became increasingly non-interventionist based on their concerns about the administrability of various antitrust rules and the costs of likely errors by generalist judges and juries trying to implement them. Today, in the hands of their successor, Professor Herbert Hovenkamp, the treatise continues that tradition, and remains the most frequently cited source of antitrust analysis. *See generally Centennial Symposium in Honor of Professor Herbert Hovenkamp*, 100 IOWA L. REV. 1917 (2015).

From today's perspective, one can argue that the chief intellectual foundations of modern U.S. antitrust doctrine consists of two intertwined chains of ideas, one drawn from the Chicago School of Bork, Posner, and Easterbrook, and the other drawn from the Harvard School of Areeda, Turner, and Supreme Court Associate Justice Stephen G. Breyer. *See* William E. Kovacic, *The Intellectual DNA of Modern U.S. Competition Law for Dominant Firm Conduct: The Chicago/Harvard Double Helix*, 2007 COLUM. BUS. L. REV. 1. From this perspective, the combination of Chicago School and Harvard School views features shared prescriptions about the appropriate substantive theories for antitrust enforcement (the Chicago influence) and cautions about the administrability of legal rules and the capacity of the institutions entrusted with implementing them (the Harvard influence).For example, Areeda and Turner believed that private rights of action, with mandatory treble damages and jury trials, created a serious danger of over-deterrence in the U.S. antitrust system. Areeda played a formative role in devising the concept of antitrust injury that the Supreme Court endorsed in *Brunswick*. The Harvard perspective does not preclude enforcement, but it has supported the acceptance of presumptions that elevate the hurdles that private antitrust plaintiffs must clear to prevail in the courts.

e. Post-Chicago Antitrust Analysis, Game Theory, and Other Developments

Just as the Chicago School of antitrust evolved to challenge the dominant perspective of the industrial organization economics of the 1950s and 1960s, so too another school of law and economic thought emerged to challenge the antitrust views of Chicago commentators. One distinctive feature of this school, sometimes labeled "post-Chicago," is its greater concern with strategic conduct. This approach has gained significant influence among antitrust commentators, enforcers and courts in the U.S. and abroad since the mid-1980s.

Although the application to industrial organization economics of the modern economic theory of strategic behavior may be dated from the mid-1970s, particularly the work of economist A. Michael Spence, it has roots in the prior work of Joe S. Bain, Thomas Schelling, and others. Nineteenth century French economists Bertrand and Cournot developed models of industry conduct that recognized that oligopolists will take into account the responses of their rivals. Strategic considerations were important in Chicagoan George Stigler's analysis of collusion among oligopolists and Chicagoan Ronald Coase's path-breaking observation that a monopolist selling durable goods cannot price above competitive levels unless it can commit not to cut price in the future; otherwise buyers will expect prices to fall and delay purchases until then. Strategic considerations were also important to the Chicago view that price predation is unlikely because the predator cannot reasonably expect to recoup the lost profits from below-cost price through the later exercise of monopoly power. Nevertheless, strategic issues such as these played a lesser role in Chicago School economic analyses than they do in antitrust analysis today largely because the tools of game theory were not routinely used to facilitate their analysis before the final decades of the twentieth century.

"Game theory" is well suited to analyzing the conduct of oligopolists (firms facing a limited number of significant rivals), because it seeks to explain how economic actors interact when they recognize their interdependence. An atomistic competitor—a small wheat farmer in the Midwest, perhaps—knows that its output and price decisions will not affect the decisions of other sellers in the market. Consequently, as we learned in the Coffee Shop hypothetical, it maximizes profits by producing and selling its product so long as the market price exceeds its cost of bringing the last unit to market (that is, so long as price exceeds or equals marginal cost).

Business decisions are not so simple for firms large enough to recognize their interdependence. Coca-Cola and Pepsi-Cola each must think about the way the other will respond when considering key business decisions. As with an atomistic wheat farmer, a firm like Coke might consider reducing prices closer to costs as a method of increasing sales. But unlike the farmer, Coke might refrain from doing so for fear that its price reduction will set off a price war with Pepsi. Game theory provides mathematical tools for analyzing this sort of strategic consideration, and is widely employed in contemporary industrial organization economics.

Post-Chicago commentators generally propose qualifying rather than supplanting Chicago views. (But not always, as with the critique of the "single monopoly profit" argument discussed in Chapter 6 (see "*Note on the "Single Monopoly Profit" Theory* and Sidebar 6–5: *The Economics of Tying*). They tend to be more interventionist than Chicago School commentators, and question Chicago views that markets commonly self-correct, entry is commonly easy, firms cannot successfully coordinate, and government intervention can rarely succeed. Chicago-oriented scholars tended to focus their attention on explaining why the observed business practices could be efficient. But while the new models of strategic behavior tend to temper the pro-efficiency interpretations of business practices suggested by Chicago commentators, both schools rely on formal arguments from microeconomics and empirical research. In this respect, the new economic literature differs in spirit from the Chicago criticisms of the industrial organization economists of the structural school, whose prior dominance they challenged.

Post-Chicago economics has been reinforced by the development of new empirical tools for identifying the nature of strategic interactions among firms and measuring market power. This literature, sometimes called the "New Empirical Industrial Organization," originated in the work of Timothy Bresnahan and Robert Porter beginning in the early 1980s. In their antitrust applications, these new empirical tools have been particularly influential in shaping the analysis of mergers among sellers of differentiated products in branded consumer products industries because they can permit economists to determine whether the brands of the merging firms are particularly close substitutes.

Perhaps the greatest success of the post-Chicago school to date has been in persuading antitrust enforcement agencies in the U.S. and Europe, and to some extent the courts, to attach greater significance to claims of improper exclusion. *See* Steven C. Salop, *What Consensus? Why Ideology and Politics Still Matter in Antitrust*, 79 ANTITRUST L.J. 601 (2014); Jonathan B. Baker, *Exclusion as a Core Competition Concern*, 78 ANTITRUST L.J. 527 (2013). Chicagoans had accepted the theoretical possibility that exclusion could harm competition, but generally argued that the cure was worse than the disease: anticompetitive exclusion was probably rare, while antitrust rules attempting to prevent it would be prone to error in application by non-specialist judges and to misuse by rivals seeking to obtain inappropriate competitive advantage by chilling competition.

Post-Chicago influence is also apparent in the 1992 and 2010 revisions to the federal horizontal merger guidelines, especially in the conceptual paradigms set forth for the analysis of unilateral competitive effects of mergers and the likelihood of entry (*see infra* Chapter 5). The government's approach to unilateral competitive effects shaped a large number of consent settlements with merging firms during the 1990s, and some commentators consider it to have been vindicated in the government's successful effort to block the proposed merger of Staples and Office Depot. *Federal Trade Comm'n v. Staples, Inc.*, 970 F.Supp. 1066 (D.D.C.1997) (*see infra* Chapter 5).

Recall the *JTC Petroleum* decision, written by Judge Richard Posner, a leader of the Chicago School. In analyzing the conduct in that case, Judge Posner emphasized the possibility that the defendant applicators were colluding, and that the alleged conspiracy to exclude JTC was in part a way of preventing cheating on that cartel. In general, antitrust commentators associated with the Chicago School are more skeptical of exclusion cases than collusion cases, so it may be no accident that Judge Posner highlighted the possibility of collusion among applicators in his opinion. But suppose the defendant was a single, dominant firm rather than a group of firms, and that the defendant acted alone in soliciting the support of the producers for a refusal to deal with JTC. The exclusionary conduct in the case could still be understood as creating an "involuntary cartel"—allowing the defendant to maintain its market power by raising the cost of asphalt to a maverick firm that refused to go along with the defendant in keeping the price charged by applicators high. From a Chicago School perspective, the practical burden facing plaintiff in that case might be set higher, for fear of discouraging pro-competitive conduct. But under a Post-Chicago view, which is more comfortable with exclusion cases than the Chicagoans, the exclusionary conduct would likely be viewed as equally troublesome regardless of whether the exclusion was secured by a cartel or single firm.

f. Behavioral Economics

A more recent distinctive strand of economic thinking has examined antitrust policy by drawing on insights from behavioral economics. This body of scholarship draws upon the fields of psychology and information economics to reassess assumptions that underpin the rational actor model of human and organizational behavior. Behavioral economists have identified how psychological biases can move consumers to choose options that fail to serve their actual preferences or their best interests. For example, the complexity of information confronting consumers can lead them to rely upon rough rules of thumb (called "heuristics") that simplify decisionmaking but can guide consumers to make inferior choices. This literature also suggests that suppliers may be able to exploit these biases to earn supracompetitive returns, for example, by bundling together distinct products in ways that defeat consumer efforts to make price and quality comparisons. *See generally* RAN SPIEGLER, BOUNDED RATIONALITY AND INDUSTRIAL ORGANIZATION (2011) (surveying the implications of one important behavior economics idea for firm behavior). The literature also suggests how the biases of organizations (and not simply individuals) may discourage entry into markets where rational actor models would predict that entry will take place.

The practical relevance of behavioral economics insights for antitrust policy is contested. *Contrast* Avishalom Tor, *Understanding Behavioral Antitrust*, 92 TEXAS L. REV. 573 (2011) (identifying policy implications), *and* Amanda P. Reeves & Maurice E. Stucke, *Behavioral Antitrust*, 86 IND. L. J. 1531 (2011) (same) *with* Joshua D. Wright & Judd E. Stone II, *Misbehavioral Economics: The Case Against Behavioral Antitrust,* 33 CARDOZO L. REV. 1517 (2012) (questioning policy implications). An additional strand of scholarship examines how the insights of behavioral economics might explain the behavior of antitrust agencies and other regulatory bodies as they set priorities and make enforcement decisions. James C. Cooper & William E. Kovacic, *Behavioral Economics and Its Meaning for Antitrust Agency Decision Making*, 8 J. L. ECON. & POL'Y 779 (2012).

Antitrust will always be a product of the prevailing economic and political thinking of the times. This is no less true today than when Senator Sherman delivered his oratory on the floor of the Senate. The ubiquitous influence of political and economic thought throughout antitrust's history, combined with the longevity of some antitrust precedent, as well as the conflicting philosophies of contemporary federal judges and justices, guarantees that antitrust will continue to provide an arena for the clash of contemporary ideas on government and markets. The arena of that debate, however, is becoming increasingly global.

C. AN INTRODUCTION TO ECONOMIC PROOF

In modern antitrust law the core concepts of the field—including market power, anticompetitive effect, and procompetitive justifications—are understood to a great, even overwhelming extent as microeconomic concepts. As we observed in the Coffee Shop hypothetical, from an economic perspective, antitrust law aims to distinguish firm conduct that creates economic harms from benign or procompetitive conduct. In this Section of the Chapter, we more closely examine the theoretical and practical ramifications of integrating this perspective into antitrust law.

1. WHAT ARE THE EFFECTS OF BUSINESS CONDUCT ON ECONOMIC WELFARE?

The problem of economic proof arises because many of the practices subject to antitrust review can simultaneously create benefits and harms. An agreement among rivals, for example, can help the firms to lower costs or improve products, but it also can help them to exercise market power by acting collectively like a single firm. Mergers can create *both* market power and efficiencies. Dominant firms can engage in conduct that enhances the quality of the product they sell to customers, while simultaneously making it more difficult for their rivals to market competing products. Much of antitrust analysis involves the resolution of tradeoffs between procompetitive and anticompetitive effects of business decisions.

The possibility that firm conduct can both harm and benefit competition is depicted below, in Figure 1–17, a diagram introduced into antitrust commentary by economist Oliver Williamson. *See* Oliver E. Williamson, *Economies as an Antitrust Defense: The Welfare Tradeoffs*, 58 AM. ECON. REV. 18 (1968). The diagram depicts supply and demand within a market. (In Chapter 5 we will look at how "markets" are defined for antitrust purposes.) Using economic concepts we previously met in the coffee example, Figure 1–17 illustrates the effects on price, output, and economic welfare (efficiency) of firm conduct—whether unilateral or arising from agreement, whether collusive or exclusionary, whether merger or non-merger—that simultaneously raises price *and* generates cost savings.

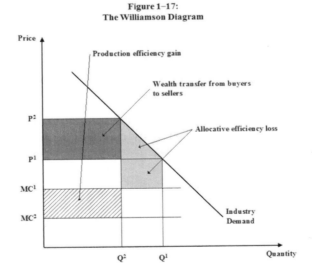

Figure 1–17:
The Williamson Diagram

Initially, the industry was selling Q1 units of output at a price P1. This price was in excess of the previous industry marginal cost (MC1), which can be thought of as the supply curve that would be observed if the market were characterized by perfect competition. (As with Figure 1–9, this figure assumes that the marginal costs of production are not increasing with the number of units produced, but instead remain the same for all units produced.) The conduct gives the firms in the market the ability to exercise market power by reducing output to Q2, leading price to rise along the industry demand curve to the post-conduct price P2. The conduct also generates cost savings, allowing the firms to reduce industry marginal cost to a lower level (MC2). (Although the conduct leads to an increase in price in the figure, that need not always be the case.)

As Figure 1–17 suggests, many of the business practices reviewed under antitrust law may simultaneously generate opposing incentives: (1) an incentive to raise price (or otherwise harm buyers) that may result from an increased ability to exercise market power; and (2) an incentive to lower price (or otherwise benefit buyers) that may derive from cost savings or other efficiencies. As a consequence, the market price may either rise or fall; the actual outcome will be based on the relative strength of these two incentives in particular cases.

Returning to Figure 1–17, the higher price creates a transfer from buyers to sellers (shaded rectangle in upper left), as buyers of Q2 units who formerly paid P1 now pay P2. (The figure and our discussion ignore the possibility that the transfer could be dissipated through wasteful rent-seeking, and thus that it also represents an efficiency loss.) The higher price also leads to an allocative efficiency loss (the shaded triangle and rectangle to the right of the transfer as indicated by the arrows), equal to the social gain no longer achieved after the exercise of market power. Before the business conduct under review, the market was able to convert resources that cost MC1 into products worth as indicated on the demand curve to buyers; the exercise of market power denies society this benefit for (Q1–Q2) units, generating an allocative efficiency loss.

But let us suppose that the business conduct also generates a production efficiency gain, depicted by the shaded rectangle in the lower left of the figure. The Q2 units that are still produced and sold after the merger are produced with less resources, as marginal cost falls to a lower level, which generates an efficiency gain. Fixed cost savings resulting from the conduct under review (e.g., a merger that reduces duplicative overhead expenditures like payroll) may also represent social resource savings but are not depicted.

As the Williamson diagram suggests, business conduct that raises price can simultaneously reduce social welfare (through the allocative efficiency loss) *and* increase it (as a result of the cost savings or other production efficiency gain). As drawn in Figure 1–17, the allocative efficiency loss exceeds the production efficiency gain arising from the cost savings, making the transaction objectionable on two grounds: (1) it will reduce aggregate social welfare; and (2) it will harm buyers by raising price. However, with different assumptions it is possible for the transaction simultaneously to increase aggregate social welfare (if the production efficiency gain exceeds the allocative efficiency loss) and harm buyers through higher prices (by generating a transfer from buyers to sellers).

In principle, this latter possibility may present a difficult policy tradeoff, even if competition law is understood as having an exclusively economic purpose. Some commentators argue that antitrust should be concerned with protecting the welfare of consumers (and other buyers). From this perspective, business conduct is harmful if it reduces consumers' surplus; this commonly is termed the "consumer welfare standard." This standard is defended primarily on grounds of distributional fairness to consumers.[16] Other commentators contend that antitrust should instead be concerned with protecting total surplus (consumers' and producers' surplus combined); this is commonly termed the "aggregate welfare standard" (or the "total welfare standard"). This standard is justified primarily as a means of increasing social wealth.[17] The antitrust enforcement agencies have consistently favored the consumer welfare standard, so a business practice that raises price can generally be expected to draw close scrutiny.

Conduct that harms consumer welfare often also harms aggregate welfare, and vice versa. The lysine cartel, for example, raised prices while generating no cost savings or other efficiency benefits, so harmed competition under both standards. However, some business practices would be beneficial under one standard but harmful under the other. For example, suppose certain business conduct is likely to generate a small price increase but also lead to large cost savings (or other efficiencies) that are not passed through to consumers, but instead accrue largely to the benefit of the firm and its shareholders. Should antitrust law prohibit or applaud that conduct? It would be deemed beneficial under the aggregate welfare standard but harmful under the consumer welfare standard.

---

[16] *See, e.g.*, Steven C. Salop, *Question: What is the Real and Proper Antitrust Welfare Standard? Answer: The True Consumer Welfare Standard*, 22 LOY. CONSUMER L. REV. 336 (2009); Robert H. Lande, *Chicago's False Foundation: Wealth Transfers (Not Just Efficiency) Should Guide Antitrust*, 58 ANTITRUST L.J. 631 (1989). A qualified consumer welfare standard has also been advocated on political economy grounds. Jonathan B. Baker, *Economics and Politics: Perspectives on the Goals and Future of Antitrust*, 81 FORDHAM L. REV. 2176–86 (2013) (explaining why the economic welfare standard debate is "unsatisfying" and connecting the economic goal with the need to preserve political support for efficiency-enhancing institutions).

[17] *See, e.g.*, ROBERT H. BORK, THE ANTITRUST PARADOX (1978); Ken Heyer, *Welfare Standards and Merger Analysis: Why Not the Best?*, 2 COMPETITION POL'Y INT'L, Autumn 2006, at 29; *cf.* LOUIS KAPLOW & STEVEN SHAVELL, FAIRNESS AND EFFICIENCY 29–38 (2002) (arguing that the policy analysis of legal rules outside those governing the tax and transfer system should generally focus on efficiency considerations rather than distributional ones). Bork uses the confusing terminology of "consumer welfare" to refer to what economists would term an aggregate welfare standard.

Changes in market price or output are often viewed as a guide to whether the conduct at issue harms economic welfare. These tests are particularly useful for applying the consumer welfare standard. In Figure 1–17, consumers' surplus falls (as a result of both the wealth transfer and the allocative efficiency loss), implying that competition is harmed, only if price increases. Similarly, consumers' surplus does not decline unless output decreases.

The analysis is somewhat more complicated for the aggregate welfare test. If price rises (thereby reducing consumer welfare), aggregate welfare could increase or decrease, and in particular may actually increase if cost savings are large. Those cost savings might arise from reductions in marginal cost, as are depicted in the figure, or from reductions in fixed cost, which are not. For similar reasons, even if output falls as a result of the business conduct under review, reducing consumer welfare, aggregate welfare could increase if the cost savings are large. The production efficiency gain from the cost savings would have to exceed the allocative efficiency loss arising from the output reduction. Moreover, aggregate welfare might fall even when consumer welfare rises. This could happen, for example, if a less efficient competitor enters the market. Its entry could lead prices to fall, but aggregate welfare may decrease if the shift of business from incumbents to the entrant leads to a sufficiently large increase in total industry production costs.

The two welfare standards may lead to different enforcement recommendations in a number of situations, including the following two. First, suppose a merger would likely allow the merged firm to raise price, creating a transfer of wealth to producers from consumers and an allocative efficiency loss. Suppose in addition that the merger permits the firms to obtain fixed cost savings, which would count as a production efficiency but would not confer a countervailing incentive to lower price, or variable cost savings that would also confer a production efficiency gain but would not be sufficient to lead the merged firm to lower price on net. If the production cost savings exceed the allocative efficiency loss, the merger would be beneficial under an aggregate welfare standard but harmful under a consumer welfare standard. Second, suppose that the exit of a less efficient rival would permit the remaining firms to increase prices, leading to a reduction in consumer welfare. But exit of the less efficient firm would lead many customers that would have purchased from it to buy instead from a more efficient (lower cost) producer. If the variable cost savings from shifting production to a lower cost firm are large enough, aggregate welfare would simultaneously rise. In this situation, exclusionary conduct by incumbent firms that leads to the exit of the inefficient rival would be beneficial under an aggregate welfare standard but harmful under a consumer welfare standard. In both situations, a consumer welfare advocate must justify enforcement when that decision would reduce total social wealth, and an aggregate welfare standard advocate must justify non-enforcement when that decision would lead to consumer harm.

These conclusions are subject to a number of qualifications. First, the analysis with respect to both welfare standards is more complicated if the conduct under review affects product quality. For example, if quality is reduced, the business practice could lead to a lower price in the marketplace, while harming competition. (To an economist, this is actually a situation in which the "quality-adjusted" price increases. But the quality-adjusted price may not be observed directly but would have to be established through economic analysis, perhaps involving expert economic testimony.) Or if quality is improved, output could in principle be lower, even though consumers benefit from the quality improvement and even though aggregate welfare rises. (Here, the economist would say that output increased in quality-adjusted units.)

Second, it is important to recognize that the "output" relevant for applying the output test is measured for the market as a whole, not just for the firm engaged in the practice under review. This point can be important particularly when the conduct at issue is exclusionary. If, for example, a dominant firm excludes one or more rivals, the result could be an increase in the market price resulting from a reduction in industry output—the exercise of market power. Yet the dominant firm could find that its own output has increased. Here, an output test based on the *dominant firm's* output would mislead, while an output test based on *market* output would not.

Third, some types of conduct may lessen economic welfare, however measured, in one market while increasing it in another. Commentators debate whether conduct likely to harm competition in one market may be saved by cost savings or other efficiencies benefitting buyers in other markets.

Finally, the comparisons between the aggregate welfare standard and the consumer welfare standard highlighted above focuses on short run considerations. Some advocates of the aggregate welfare standard argue that the short run benefits to producers recognized under the aggregate welfare standard, but excluded from consideration by the consumer welfare standard, will turn out to benefit consumers in the long run, making the aggregate welfare standard the better approach for protecting consumers in situations where business conduct that generates both market power and costs savings increases aggregate welfare but reduces consumer welfare. This could happen in two ways, but will not necessarily occur in either manner. First, cost-savings that are not passed through to consumers initially may lead in the long run to lower prices or other buyer benefits, if firms are led to confer those benefits on buyers through competition among sellers. But this outcome is based, controversially, on two assumptions unlikely to hold in general: that rivals rapidly and fully replicate the cost savings, and that competition works well in the market notwithstanding the ability of some firms to exercise market power in the short run. Second, the higher firm profits (both from the exercise of market power and from cost savings not passed through to buyers) could benefit buyers if they spur innovation. As will be discussed more fully in Chapter 7, this argument presumes, controversially, that the greater innovation incentives arising from the increased reward to a successful innovator outweighs the reduction in innovation incentives arising from the loss of competition. These possible long run dynamics are difficult to analyze in individual cases, so most commentators working within the economic approach to antitrust simply adopt either the consumer welfare standard or the aggregate welfare standard, and advocate application of that test across the board.

2. HOW CAN THE EFFECTS OF BUSINESS CONDUCT ON ECONOMIC WELFARE BE DEMONSTRATED?

Antitrust analysis would be a daunting task indeed if the determination of harm to competition required the computation of consumers' surplus or aggregate surplus in every case, and a determination of how either of those measures of economic welfare changed as a result of the business practice under review. This could be done in theory, but courts and enforcers have developed ways of simplifying the task in practice.

One common approach is to employ legal rules that employ reasonable inferences and presumptions based on limited factual showings, sometimes rebuttable and sometimes conclusive, to shift burdens of production. These kinds of rules appear in many forms in antitrust practice, including "per se" rules, "quick look" rules, and "presumptions" and will be discussed in greater depth at various points throughout the book.

When a detailed economic analysis cannot be avoided, a wider range of economic evidence may be brought to bear. Even then, economic evidence need not be quantitative, though it could be. As will be evident from reading the cases, the testimony of fact witnesses and documentary evidence from firm files can often be used to reach conclusions about market power, efficiencies, and the like. Economic evidence is often integrated into the decision-making process at agencies and courts through the testimony of economic experts. These experts may rely on qualitative and anecdotal evidence, as well as quantitative and systematic evidence.

Two intersecting trends have also complicated the development and presentation of proof in antitrust cases. First, as you will learn, the trend in antitrust case law for more than a generation has been to move away from bright line rules and standards that demand minimal levels of proof, towards more demanding standards of proof of competitive harm. That proof can consist of data, such as information about a firm's sales, profits, and performance, as well as communications and documents, such as letters, memoranda, and reports. Increasingly, such data and communications are likely to be digitized, what in civil procedure is referred to as Electronically Stored Information, or "ESI." The truck load of documents once associated with antitrust litigation is now likely to be replaced with digitized data and documents. In addition to letters and memoranda, parties are likely to be required to disclose emails, texts, and in some instances social media postings. Although the volume of information can be enormous, increased computing power and continually improving search tools have in many ways facilitated the task of identifying relevant material. It is as yet unclear, however, whether this expansion of available information will result in cost-effective, improved accuracy in decision-making.

Does antitrust law, with all its decision rules and with reliance on the adversarial process to test economic evidence, do a good job at evaluating the economic consequences of firm conduct? This is a lively subject of discussion in antitrust commentary and among economists.[18]

Before we conclude Chapter 1's introduction to the study of modern antitrust law, it is important to consider one other way in which economics and economic evidence influences antitrust-decision-making. Not only does it help us to evaluate market power, efficiencies, and the welfare effects of conduct, but it also provides a way of thinking about alternative legal standards that might be used when we integrate those concepts into a system of administrative or adversarial, litigation-based decision-making.

Sidebar 1–4:
Economics and the Development of Legal Rules[a]

Economics influences not only the substantive standards of antitrust laws, but also how courts and other policy-makers choose from among alternative legal standards. For example, what standard should be used to evaluate the legality under the Sherman Act of conduct such as the lysine and vitamins price fixing cartels we learned about earlier in this Chapter? One alternative would be to condemn such cartel activity "absolutely," under what is typically referred to as "per se" condemnation. As we will learn in the next Chapter, with per se analysis, actual anticompetitive effects are presumed and

---

[18] For a sample of the debate, compare Robert W. Crandall & Clifford Winston, *Does Antitrust Policy Improve Consumer Welfare? Assessing the Evidence*, 17 J. ECON. PERSPS. 3 (2003) with Jonathan B. Baker, *The Case for Antitrust Enforcement*, 17 J. ECON. PERSPS. 27 (2003).

[a] Portions of this Sidebar are adapted from Andrew I. Gavil, BURDEN OF PROOF IN U.S. ANTITRUST LAW, *in* I ABA Antitrust Section, ISSUES IN COMPETITION LAW AND POLICY 125 (2008) and Andrew I. Gavil, *Exclusionary Distribution Strategies by Dominant Firms: Striking a Better Balance*, 72 ANTITRUST L.J. 3, 65–68 (2004).

defenses are not permitted. To prove a violation under a per se approach, therefore, it is enough to establish that the defendants were rivals who fixed prices. That creates an "irrebuttable presumption" that the conduct was anticompetitive. *See* Sidebar 2–4, *Defining and Justifying the Contemporary Per Se Rule.*

Per se analysis is used, therefore, to condemn conduct that experience has suggested is very likely to be anticompetitive and very unlikely to be justifiable. What kind of conduct is likely to meet those criteria? If it does not, what alternative standards are possible? One alternative would be to require the plaintiff to present some proof of anticompetitive effects. Such proof would then shift a burden of production to the defendant, who would then be permitted to introduce evidence of legitimate justifications. Which approach should be used for cartels? Which approach would be best for exclusionary conduct, such as that presented in *JTC Petroleum* and mergers, which were the subject of *Brunswick*? For each kind of potentially anticompetitive conduct, often there is more than one possible standard for defining the line between the permissible and the impermissible. How can policy-makers and courts choose?

Drawing on economic reasoning and concepts, commentators have developed general models to assist in the choice of legal rules. These models have had particular appeal for antitrust, because as a general matter, it is an area of law that has been increasingly receptive to economic teachings. In selecting "optimal" legal rules, an economic analysis focuses on two factors: (1) the incidence and cost of error; and (2) the burden of processing, information, and administrative costs, sometimes referred to as "direct" costs. It postulates that legal commands, here rules for competitive conduct, should be designed to minimize the costs of incorrect decisions, either false convictions (referred to as "false positives") or false acquittals (referred to as "false negatives"), while also taking into account the costs of gathering, presenting, and processing the information needed to decide cases. *See generally* C. Frederick Beckner, III & Steven C. Salop, *Decision Theory and Antitrust Rules*, 67 ANTITRUST L.J. 41 (1999) ("Decision Theory"); Frank H. Easterbrook, *The Limits of Antitrust*, 63 TEX. L. REV. 1 (1984).[b]

---

[b]   This framework for economic analysis of legal rules has its roots in earlier writings on law and economics, especially the work of Judge Richard A. Posner. *See, e.g.*, Richard A. Posner, *The Behavior of Administrative Agencies*, 1 J. LEG. STUDIES 305 (1972); Richard A. Posner, *An Economic Approach to Legal Procedure and Judicial Administration*, 2 J. LEG. STUDIES 399 (1973)

What are the likely costs of "false positives?" If procompetitive or neutral conduct is condemned as anticompetitive, efficiencies may be lost to the economy and other firms considering similar conduct may be deterred from undertaking it. False negatives, on the other hand, may permit anticompetitive conduct to go un-checked, permitting some firms to exercise market power. And, as with false positives, false negatives may affect the conduct of firms that have not been charged with an antitrust violation. False negatives may encourage other firms to undertake similar conduct to the detriment of competition and require an increase in public and private resources being devoted to antitrust enforcement. Which kind of error is more costly, false positives or false negatives?

Typically, those arguing for more lenient antitrust rules (higher burdens of proof) argue that false positives are far more costly, because they result in immediate losses of efficiency. They also argue that even if market power is facilitated in some cases, it is likely to be temporary, because market power will be eroded by new competition absent government action to protect monopolists or cartels. In contrast, proponents of less lenient standards (lower burdens of proof, as with presumptions that can shift a burden of production to a defendant) argue that market power results in immediate harm to consumers and the exercise of market power is often long-lasting, even in private markets free from governmental interference. They tend to doubt that markets will correct for market power on their own. *See, e.g.*, Jonathan B. Baker, *Taking the Error Out of "Error Cost" Analysis: What's Wrong with Antitrust's Right*, 80 ANTITRUST L.J. 1 (2015).

Economic models for decision-making also must take into account the costs of administration associated with alternative legal rules, what have been labeled "direct costs." A "per se" approach, for example, might involve lower costs of administration than a more complete inquiry into effects and justifications, because less evidence must be discovered and presented than with a more expansive inquiry. It might be advantageous, therefore, from the point of view of direct costs. Yet if per se analysis sometimes or even often falsely condemns conduct that is beneficial for competition (or is unlikely to affect it significantly), then it might involve increased error costs. In more economic terms, it might be necessary to ask for any given

---

(hereafter "*Economic Approach to Procedure*"). *See also* William M. Landes, *An Economic Analysis of the Courts*, 14 J. LAW & ECON. 61 (1971).

legal standard whether the marginal contribution to accuracy of outcome (reduction of error) derived from additional process would be outweighed by the costs required to gather, present, and evaluate additional information.[c]

There may often be a trade-off between reduction of error and direct costs. It is frequently argued, for example, that the cure for error is additional information. Often this is argued by proponents of more demanding standards of proof. More and better economic evidence, however, can almost always be imagined and hence demanded, and it increases the direct costs of decision-making. For example, it might require more extensive discovery, longer trials, and more complex fact-finding and appeals. Will the reduction of false positives and false negatives through additional economic data necessarily reduce overall error costs? If not, imposition of the additional direct costs may be difficult to justify.

This kind of economic analysis of alternative legal rules and standards can be seductive in its seeming promise of mathematical precision. But it has limits. Can antitrust policy-makers assess the relevant costs—both error and direct costs—with sufficient precision to identify appropriate legal rules? How well can courts, in developing rules, assess tradeoffs in costs? For example, if courts seek to reduce error costs by demanding additional information from the litigants, how well can they compare the benefits from increased accuracy in their decisions with the costs imposed on the parties that must collect and present that evidence and the fact-finders that must evaluate it? Finally, if courts in developing legal rules focus only on economic costs, will litigants—especially losers in court—lose faith that the courts can produce fair and consistent results, what some commentators have labeled "procedural justice"? *See, e.g.*, John Thibault & Laurens Walker, *A Theory of Procedure*, 66 CAL. L. REV. 541 (1978); TOM R. TYLER, ED., PROCEDURAL JUSTICE (2005). Could the result be to undermine the political support for the existence of competition policy systems? *See* Jonathan B. Baker, *Competition Policy as a Political Bargain*, 73 ANTITRUST L.J. 483 (2006).

As you will see as this Casebook unfolds, this economic way of thinking about antitrust standards has been very influential. Beginning in the mid-to-late-1970s, the U.S. Supreme Court became persuaded that harsh antitrust prohibitions likely were

---

[c] At one extreme, false positives could be eliminated through repeal of all prohibitions. Likewise, all false negatives could be eliminated through sole reliance on per se prohibitions. The challenge in antitrust law as elsewhere in law is to aspire to "optimal" antitrust rules, taking into account the judicial process used to implement them.

leading to a high incidence of false positives and that those false positives were costly for the American economy. What followed was a generation of reconstruction of the content of many U.S. antitrust rules, a process that continues today. As you learn more about today's antitrust, consider why the Court altered direction, largely under the influence of economic criticism of older antitrust rules. Although there is general consensus that today's antitrust rules are superior to older rules that were more prone to produce false positives that were likely costly, consider also whether some of the newer standards have perhaps erred on the side of being prone to false negatives, in part because they are so demanding of economic proof.

You may recall reading the following case in your first year Civil Procedure course. In *Bell Atlantic Corp. v. Twombly*, the Supreme Court "retired" the "no set of facts" standard for pleading a claim for relief that had been in effect for fifty years. Although we will revisit the decision in Chapter 3 in connection with our discussion of conspiracy, read the excerpt provided here in light of Sidebar 1–4's discussion of decision theory. Are any of the components of decision theory evident in the Court's reasoning? If so, how did they influence the outcome of the case? If the Court is applying decision theory, is its application complete? What assumptions does it appear to make that bear on its application of decision theory? Does it cite any empirical evidence to support those assumptions?

BELL ATLANTIC CORP. V. TWOMBLY

Supreme Court of the United States, 2007.
550 U.S. 544, 127 S.Ct. 1955, 167 L.Ed.2d 929.

JUSTICE SOUTER delivered the opinion of the Court.

Liability under § 1 of the Sherman Act * * * requires a "contract, combination * * *, or conspiracy, in restraint of trade or commerce." The question in this putative class action is whether a § 1 complaint can survive a motion to dismiss when it alleges that major telecommunications providers engaged in certain parallel conduct unfavorable to competition, absent some factual context suggesting agreement, as distinct from identical, independent action. We hold that such a complaint should be dismissed.

* * *

II

A

Because § 1 of the Sherman Act "does not prohibit [all] unreasonable restraints of trade . . . but only restraints effected by a contract, combination, or conspiracy," "[t]he crucial question" is whether the challenged anticompetitive conduct "stem[s] from independent decision or from an agreement, tacit or express." While a showing of parallel "business behavior is admissible circumstantial evidence from which the fact finder may infer agreement," it falls short of "conclusively establish[ing] agreement or . . . itself constitut[ing] a Sherman Act offense." Even "conscious parallelism," a common reaction of "firms in a concentrated market [that] recogniz[e] their shared economic interests and their interdependence with respect to price and output decisions" is "not in itself unlawful." * * *

The inadequacy of showing parallel conduct or interdependence, without more, mirrors the ambiguity of the behavior: consistent with conspiracy, but just as much in line with a wide swath of rational and competitive business strategy unilaterally prompted by common perceptions of the market. *See, e.g.,* AEI-Brookings Joint Center for Regulatory Studies, Epstein, Motions to Dismiss Antitrust Cases: Separating Fact from Fantasy, Related Publication 06–08, pp. 3–4 (2006) (discussing problem of "false positives" in § 1 suits). Accordingly, we have previously hedged against false inferences from identical behavior at a number of points in the trial sequence. An antitrust conspiracy plaintiff with evidence showing nothing beyond parallel conduct is not entitled to a directed verdict; proof of a § 1 conspiracy must include evidence tending to exclude the possibility of independent action; and at the summary judgment stage a § 1 plaintiff's offer of conspiracy evidence must tend to rule out the possibility that the defendants were acting independently.

B

This case presents the antecedent question of what a plaintiff must plead in order to state a claim under § 1 of the Sherman Act. Federal Rule of Civil Procedure 8(a)(2) requires only "a short and plain statement of the claim showing that the pleader is entitled to relief," in order to "give the defendant fair notice of what the . . . claim is and the grounds upon which it rests." While a complaint attacked by a Rule 12(b)(6) motion to dismiss does not need detailed factual allegations, a plaintiff's obligation to provide the "grounds" of his "entitle[ment] to relief" requires more than labels and conclusions, and a formulaic recitation of the elements of a cause of action will not do. Factual allegations must be enough to raise a right to relief above the speculative level. * * *

In applying these general standards to a § 1 claim, we hold that stating such a claim requires a complaint with enough factual matter (taken as true) to suggest that an agreement was made. Asking for plausible grounds to infer an agreement does not impose a probability requirement at the pleading stage; it simply calls for enough fact to raise a reasonable expectation that discovery will reveal evidence of illegal agreement. And, of course, a well-pleaded complaint may proceed even if it strikes a savvy judge that actual proof of those facts is improbable, and "that a recovery is very remote and unlikely." * * *

* * *

We alluded to the practical significance of the Rule 8 entitlement requirement in *Dura Pharmaceuticals, Inc. v. Broudo,* 544 U.S. 336, 125 S.Ct. 1627, 161 L.Ed.2d 577 (2005), when we explained that something beyond the mere possibility of loss causation must be alleged, lest a plaintiff with " 'a largely groundless claim' " be allowed to " 'take up the time of a number of other people, with the right to do so representing an *in terrorem* increment of the settlement value.' " So, when the allegations in a complaint, however true, could not raise a claim of entitlement to relief, " 'this basic deficiency should . . . be exposed at the point of minimum expenditure of time and money by the parties and the court.' " * * * [*S]ee also . . .* Asahi Glass Co. v. Pentech Pharmaceuticals, Inc., 289 F.Supp.2d 986, 995 (N.D.Ill.2003) (Posner, J., sitting by designation) (*"[S]ome threshold of plausibility must be crossed at the outset before a patent antitrust case should be permitted to go into its inevitably costly and protracted discovery phase"*).

Thus, it is one thing to be cautious before dismissing an antitrust complaint in advance of discovery, but quite another to forget that proceeding to antitrust discovery can be expensive. As we indicated over 20 years ago in *Associated Gen. Contractors of Cal., Inc. v. Carpenters,* 459 U.S. 519, 528, n. 17, 103 S.Ct. 897, 74 L.Ed.2d 723 (1983), "a district court must retain the power to insist upon some specificity in pleading before allowing a potentially massive factual controversy to proceed." See also *Car Carriers, Inc. v. Ford Motor Co.,* 745 F.2d 1101, 1106 (C.A.7 1984) ("[T]he costs of modern federal antitrust litigation and the increasing caseload of the federal courts counsel against sending the parties into discovery when there is no reasonable likelihood that the plaintiffs can construct a claim from the events related in the complaint"); Note, Modeling the Effect of One-Way Fee Shifting on Discovery Abuse in Private Antitrust Litigation, 78 N.Y. & U. L.Rev. 1887, 1898–1899 (2003) (discussing the unusually high cost of discovery in antitrust cases); Manual for Complex Litigation, Fourth, § 30, p. 519 (2004) (describing extensive scope of discovery in antitrust cases); Memorandum from Paul V. Niemeyer, Chair, Advisory Committee on Civil Rules, to Hon. Anthony J. Scirica, Chair, Committee on Rules of Practice and Procedure (May 11, 1999), 192 F.R.D. 354, 357 (2000) (reporting that discovery accounts for as much as 90 percent of litigation costs when discovery is actively employed). That potential expense is obvious enough in the present case: plaintiffs represent a putative class of at least 90 percent of all subscribers to local telephone or high-speed Internet service in the continental United States, in an action against America's largest telecommunications firms (with many thousands of employees generating reams and gigabytes of business records) for unspecified (if any) instances of antitrust violations that allegedly occurred over a period of seven years.

It is no answer to say that a claim just shy of a plausible entitlement to relief can, if groundless, be weeded out early in the discovery process through "careful case management," * * * given the common lament that the success of judicial supervision in checking discovery abuse has been on the modest side. See, *e.g.*, Easterbrook, Discovery as Abuse, 69 B.U.L.Rev. 635, 638 (1989) ("Judges can do little about impositional discovery when parties control the legal claims to be presented and conduct the discovery themselves"). And it is self-evident that the problem of discovery abuse cannot be solved by "careful scrutiny of evidence at the summary judgment stage," much less "lucid instructions to juries." * * * [T]he threat of discovery expense will push cost-conscious defendants to settle even anemic cases before reaching those proceedings. Probably, then, it is only by taking care to require allegations that reach the level suggesting conspiracy that we can hope to avoid the potentially enormous expense of discovery in cases with no " 'reasonably founded hope that the [discovery] process will reveal relevant evidence' " to support a § 1 claim. * * *[6]

* * *

----

[6] The dissent takes heart in the reassurances of plaintiffs' counsel that discovery would be "phased" and "limited to the existence of the alleged conspiracy and class certification." * * * But determining whether some illegal agreement may have taken place between unspecified persons at different ILECs (each a multibillion dollar corporation with legions of management level employees) at some point over seven years is a sprawling, costly, and hugely time-consuming undertaking not easily susceptible to the kind of line drawing and case management that the dissent envisions. Perhaps the best answer to the dissent's optimism that antitrust discovery is open to effective judicial control is a more extensive quotation of the authority just cited, a judge with a background in antitrust law. Given the system that we have, the hope of effective judicial supervision is slim:

"The timing is all wrong. The plaintiff files a sketchy complaint (the Rules of Civil Procedure discourage fulsome documents), and discovery is launched. A judicial officer does not know the details of the case the parties will present and in theory *cannot* know the details. Discovery is used to find the details. The judicial officer always knows less than the parties, and the parties themselves may not know very well where they are going or what they expect to find. A magistrate supervising discovery does not—cannot—know the expected productivity of a given request, because the nature of the requester's claim and the contents of the files (or head) of the adverse party are unknown. Judicial officers cannot measure the costs and benefits to the requester and so cannot isolate impositional requests. Requesters have no reason to disclose their own estimates because they gain from imposing costs on rivals (and may lose from an improvement in accuracy). The portions of the Rules of Civil Procedure calling on judges to trim back excessive demands, therefore, have been, and are doomed to be, hollow. We cannot prevent what we cannot detect; we cannot detect what we cannot define; we cannot define 'abusive' discovery except in theory, because in practice we lack essential information." Easterbrook, Discovery as Abuse, 69 B.U.L.Rev. 635, 638–639 (1989) (footnote omitted).

D. CONCLUSION

This Chapter introduced the basic legal and economic concepts of modern antitrust law and sketched out the questions that antitrust policy is designed to ask; the remainder of the book seeks to answer those questions. A principal assumption of this book is that antitrust law has evolved from an approach that relied on sorting conduct into discrete categories to one focused on more common concepts, greatly influenced by economics. Today, those concepts (market power and market definition, entry, efficiency, and anticompetitive effect) cut across a wide variety of antitrust offenses. To answer the core questions of antitrust, therefore, our ultimate goal will be to identify, understand and obtain a working knowledge of these core concepts. We have only begun!

Appendix to Chapter 1

Cost Concepts

Antitrust analysis often relies on economic concepts of cost, nowhere more than in predatory pricing cases, which we will study in Chapter 4. A number of the ways that economists classify costs are set forth below.[19]

One way to explain cost concepts is to consider a hypothetical example. Consider a small stand selling ice cream on the boardwalk in a beach town during the summer. The owner of the business leases the location from the town over the 100-day summer season for $1000, or a rate of $10 per day. The rent covers utilities, including electricity and water. The stand is open every day of the week, but only in the afternoon, for four hours daily. It is staffed by a single worker, hired month by month. The owner pays the worker $1200 per month, which works out to be a rate of $10 per hour. The stand has very little equipment—a freezer and an ice cream scoop. The owner of the business purchased them for $500 at the start of the summer and they are likely to last five summers (500 operating days), and thus will cost the owner $1 per day.[20] Each cone of ice cream uses raw materials (two scoops of ice cream and the cone) that cost $1.

On a typical day, the stand sells 100 cones of ice cream. Given the above information, an accountant might record its costs on a per-day basis like this[21]:

---

[19] These cost concepts are discussed in more detail—usually with graphs—in most microeconomics or industrial organization economics texts. *See, e.g.,* DENNIS W. CARLTON & JEFFREY M. PERLOFF, MODERN INDUSTRIAL ORGANIZATION 29–47, 50–54 (4th ed. 2005).

[20] There are a number of methods of accounting for the cost associated with the decline in value of the equipment, as it grows more likely to break or becomes obsolete; this is the simplest.

[21] In computing total cost, an economist (but probably not an accountant) would also include a "normal" or "competitive" return on capital to the owner of the business. To keep the example simple, this component of economic cost is ignored.

Rent	$ 10
Wages	40
Cost of goods sold (raw materials)	100
<u>Equipment</u>	<u>1</u>
Total:	$151

Whether these figures appropriately represent the ice cream stand's costs depends on what question is being asked. They could even mislead, as the ice cream stand owner cannot save $10 (the rent on a per day basis) by choosing not to open the stand for a day, nor save $10 (the wage on a per-hour basis) by closing an hour early one day.

Total Cost and Average Cost

The accounting records indicate that the daily *total cost* (TC) of producing the 100 cones of ice cream sold on the typical day is $151. This implies that the daily *average cost* (AC) per cone is $1.51 ($151÷100).

Fixed Costs, Variable Costs, and Average Variable Cost

In economic terms, the total costs of a business can be divided into *fixed costs*, which the firm is committed to pay even if it produces nothing, and *variable costs*, which the firm would avoid by not producing. Here, if the stand was open but the day was cold and stormy, so the stand sold no ice cream at all, the owner would continue to pay rent, wages, and the costs of equipment, but it would not use up any raw materials. Accordingly, its daily total fixed costs are $51 ($10 + $40 + $1). On days when the weather is more typical, the stand sells 100 cones and also has daily total variable costs (TVC) of $100. Given that the stand sold 100 cones, the average variable cost (AVC) per cone is $1.00 ($100 ÷ 100). The distinction between average variable cost and average cost often arises when discussing price-cost comparisons in predatory pricing cases (*see infra* Chapter 4).

The classification between fixed costs and variable costs depends on what is contemplated in the assumption that the firm would not produce. The above example presumed that the stand was open, but sold no ice cream. If instead the business owner planned to shut down for one month of the summer, he or she could avoid paying wages too. With that decision in mind, wages would become a variable cost. Then the total variable cost (measured on a daily basis) would be $140 ($100 + $40) and the average variable cost would be $1.40 ($140 ÷ 10). If the business owner planned not to open for an entire season, he or she could avoid paying rent, making rent a variable cost as well.[22]

---

[22] Although labor is treated as a fixed cost in this simple example, it is more common in antitrust applications for it to be considered a variable cost.

Sunk Costs

Fixed costs can be classified further based on the extent to which they are *sunk costs*. Costs are sunk if they cannot be avoided by selling the asset or putting it to an alternative use. If the freezer could be sold for $500 used, then its costs are fixed but not sunk. If it has no resale value and cannot be shifted to use in some other business (like a coffee shop), then its costs are entirely sunk. If the business owner can recoup half its value in the event he or she exits the ice cream stand business, then its costs are half sunk. Similarly, if the stand were to shut down half-way through the season and the owner could not sublet the space to another business, then the rent would be a sunk cost. The distinction between fixed costs and sunk costs will arise when discussing entry in merger analysis (*see infra* Chapter 5).

Marginal Cost

The cost of producing an additional unit of output is termed the *marginal cost* of that unit. In the ice cream stand example, the 101st cone would cost the firm $1 (the cost of two scoops of ice cream and the cone), given the assumption that it is already making 100 units (and thus already has leased the stand for the summer and hired the worker for the month). In the example, marginal cost would also be $1 for every cone, whether the 20th unit or the 120th unit.

For some technologies, the magnitude of marginal cost instead would vary with the output level. For example, suppose the worker is more likely to spill ice cream and waste it when the stand is busy. Perhaps the worker never spills any ice cream when the stand sells 100 cones per day, but every tenth cone is wasted when the stand sells 150 or more cones per day, and the spillage rate is even greater (*e.g.*, 15%) when the stand sells 200 or more cones daily. Then marginal cost is an increasing function of output. It is $1 for the 100th unit sold, but $1.10 for the 150th unit ($1.00 plus 10% of $1.00), until 200 units are reached, at which point the marginal cost for the

200th unit (and subsequent units) rises to $1.15.[23] This marginal cost function is depicted in Figure 1–18:

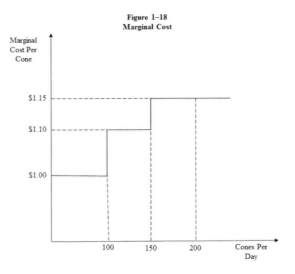

Figure 1–18
Marginal Cost

In the "textbook" model of perfect competition that beginning students of economics often learn, marginal cost is typically rising for individual firms, leading to an upward-sloping supply curve for the industry. This characterization of cost is plausible for an ice cream stand. In the oligopoly markets in which most antitrust enforcement arises, however, marginal cost can just as easily be constant or declining.

Even in the ice cream stand example, marginal cost could fall for larger levels of output, if, for example, the firm's ice cream supplier gives volume discounts. Perhaps the supplier would charge it $1.50 per cone for bulk ice cream if the stand bought only enough to sell up to 20 cones, but $1.00 per cone if the stand bought enough for 20 or more cones. Then marginal cost would be $1.50 for the 20th unit but would fall to $1.00 for the 21st (or more) cone. Marginal cost can even be declining in some range of firm output while increasing in other ranges.

In this example, putting aside the wastage and the volume discount, the ice cream stand's marginal cost ($1.00) of producing output is equal to its average variable cost and less than its average total cost ($1.50). Average variable cost will always be less than or equal to average total cost

---

[23] Capacity constraints can be represented by steeply increasing marginal costs. If the ice cream stand could not produce more than 250 cones per day without investing in additional production capacity (expanding its size, adding another worker, installing another freezer, etc.) then the marginal cost of the 251st unit would be much greater than the marginal cost of the 250th unit; its marginal cost would rise substantially when its output reached 250 cones per day, to include the costs of expansion. After expansion, though, marginal cost would fall.

(they can be identical only if there are no fixed costs). But marginal cost can be above, equal to, or below either measure of average cost. If the spillage rate increased as output rose, so that marginal cost increased with output, then there would be some number of cones sold such that marginal cost would equal average cost.[24]

Different Costs for Different Purposes

The economic concept of cost is always tied to a decision, in the above example a decision to produce one more unit of output. There are, as it is sometimes said, "different costs for different purposes."

When the ice cream stand's decision is whether to sell one more cone, it considers its marginal costs of $1 per cone. Selling one more unit would be profitable if the additional cone brought in more than $1 in revenue (that is, if the cone's price was more than $1).[25] For it to be profitable to open the stand for any period up to a month (the period after which the worker becomes a variable cost), the owner must expect to receive price in excess of $1.50 per cone (the average variable cost).

These measures no longer reflect cost well if the ice cream stand's decision is instead whether to extend its business hours by one more hour on holiday weekends. The cost of extending business hours would be just the cost of hiring a worker for an extra hour. If overtime is paid on an hourly basis (not contracted for monthly), and the ice cream stand owner pays the worker $20 per hour of overtime work, the cost for the typical holiday weekend day would be $20 per day. (This is the marginal cost of opening the stand for an extra hour.) If the stand expects to sell ten more ice cream cones during that extra hour, its average cost for those 10 extra cones is $3 ($1 per cone for the raw materials and $2 per cone for the worker). Accordingly, extending business hours would only be profitable if the price per cone exceeds $3.

The idea of focusing on different concepts of cost for different purposes often comes up when comparing a firm's decision to enter a business versus the decision to exit. In the ice cream stand example, if the issue is whether to open in the first place—purchase the freezer and scoops and lease the facility from the town—and the business expects to sell 100 cones per day (as it did in the example above), then its average cost would be $151 per day or $1.51 per cone. The firm would only enter the market if it anticipated being able to charge at least $1.51 per cone.

---

[24] In the "textbook" model of perfect competition, where marginal cost is increasing, the number of firms in the industry adjusts so that marginal cost equals average cost for the last firm to enter.

[25] This discussion assumes that the ice cream stand charges the same price to all buyers, thus ruling out the possibility that the ice cream stand faces a downward sloping demand curve or the possibility that it discriminates in price (*see infra* Chapter 6).

If the issue is instead whether to shut down the stand at the end of the first month of operation, and if the freezer cost is completely sunk and the owner could not sublease the stand, then the firm only would save the costs of the worker and the raw materials it no longer needs to purchase. Those saved costs are equal to $140 ($40 for the worker and $100 for the ice cream and the cone). Assuming that it would have sold 100 cones per day had it continued in business, the firm's relevant average cost would be $1.40 per cone ($140÷100), with respect to the shut down decision. That is, it would be profitable for the firm to stay in business so long as it anticipated that it could receive a price of at least $1.40 per cone for the remainder of the season. This figure is less than the $1.51 minimum price that was needed to make entry profitable before any costs were sunk. If the ice cream stand knew that it could not charge more than $1.50 per cone (perhaps because that is what rival ice cream vendors charge), the business owner would not have chosen to enter in the first place. But if the ice cream stand entered and then the other stands reduced price to $1.45, the owner would do better to cut its price and remain in business, rather than exit halfway through the season.

Scale Economies and Diseconomies

A firm experiences *economies of scale* if its average cost declines with output. This occurs when marginal cost is declining as output increases. It also occurs when marginal cost is constant and there are fixed costs. Returning to the original ice cream stand example, where fixed costs are $51 and marginal costs are $1 per cone, if the stand sold only one cone in a day, its total costs would be $52, and its average cost would be $52 as well ($52 ÷ 1). If the stand sold ten cones, its total cost would be $62 and its average cost would fall to $6.20 ($62 ÷ 10). At 100 cones sold in a day, average cost declines to $1.51, as previously noted.

If average cost is constant, the firm is said to experience *constant returns to scale*. If average cost is rising as output increases, the firm experiences *diseconomies of scale*. As with marginal cost, average cost can be declining in some ranges of firm output while increasing in other ranges.

In industries in which firms experience substantial scale diseconomies, firms will likely be small relative to the size of the market—it is simply too expensive for them to grow large. As a result, such industries commonly have many firms, and tend to behave competitively. By contrast, industries in which firms experience substantial scale economies may have few firms, each with a high market share. Small firms in such industries often cannot compete effectively without a differentiated (niche) product that is particularly valuable to some group of buyers, as they do not have the size needed to keep average costs low. Accordingly, in a market in which large firms obtain substantial cost savings as a result of their size, small firms often must offer a differentiated product to succeed.

Antitrust enforcement tends to be concentrated in oligopoly markets (those with a small number of large firms), where scale economies are often important. When rivals merge in such markets, they may seek to justify their transaction, which increases firm size, on the ground that it permits the firm to achieve greater economies of scale.[26]

Opportunity Cost

Suppose that a wealthy beach resident offers to rent the ice cream stand for a day for a private beach party. In order to decide whether to accept the offer (and at what price), the ice cream stand operator will need to consider and compare its options. If the stand is not rented for the party, it would likely serve 100 cones. The cost of giving up the daily business is the amount the stand owner would have received in revenue from selling those 100 cones less the variable costs of producing those costs. This difference is sometimes called the *contribution to profit*. If cones sell for $2.50, the contribution to profit from a regular day's operation would be $150 ($250 in revenues (100 x $2.50/cone) less $100 in costs of goods sold (100 x $1)). In order for the private party to be profitable, the wealthy resident would need to offer the stand owner more than $150 plus the cost of the ice cream needed to serve the private party guests. If the party guests would likely want only 50 cones, which cost $50 in raw materials (ice cream and cones), therefore, the wealthy resident would need to pay at least $200 ($150 + $50) to the ice cream stand owner.

As this example indicates, the cost of using the stand for a private party includes the foregone benefit from applying the resource in its best alternative use. That forgone benefit is termed an *opportunity cost*. Opportunity costs might be important in determining, to evaluate a predatory pricing claim, whether price is less than average cost or average variable cost. For example, if an airline adds a flight to a route, an economist would say that the cost of doing so includes the profits foregone by not using the aircraft on its most profitable alternative route.

---

[26] When firms sell multiple products, they sometimes can lower the cost of producing one by increasing their output of the other. If this situation arises, it is said to reflect *economies of scope*. The concept of average cost can be difficult to define when firms sell multiple products, raising problems for determining whether price is less than average cost or average variable cost, as some legal rules for evaluating predatory pricing allegations require.

CHAPTER 2

CONCERTED ACTION BY COMPETITORS

■ ■ ■

INTRODUCTION

Some of the cases discussed in Chapter 1 involved conduct by competitors that was clearly anticompetitive. It would be a mistake at the start of a course on competition policy to assume, however, that cooperative arrangements among competitors are predominantly anticompetitive. Partnerships, joint ventures, and strategic alliances among rivals are ubiquitous and rarely present serious competitive concerns. Quite to the contrary, they often provide a significant source of competitive vigor and innovation. As a matter of perspective, therefore, it is important to recognize that a course on antitrust law will necessarily tend to focus on those types of arrangements that have invited scrutiny because they present at least some arguable threat to competition. We carry out this sorting process aided by linguistic conventions: "cooperation" is used to describe desirable arrangements, whereas "collusion" is associated with the undesirable.

This Chapter examines agreements between competitors with a particular emphasis on agreements involving actual or threatened collusive effects. As we initially explored in Chapter 1, conduct can be anticompetitive because of either its "collusive" or direct effects on price, output, or innovation, or its "exclusionary" or indirect effects. We will turn to the examination of exclusionary agreements in Chapters 4 and 6. This Chapter will examine how over time courts have developed standards for effectively differentiating arrangements that present a threat of serious anticompetitive harm and those that may invigorate or perhaps have no significant effect on competition. Ideally, an effective standard will neither over-deter desirable collaborations nor under-deter undesirable collusion—but achieving the right balance can be challenging.

We begin by exploring the historical foundation of the principal standard developed by the courts to evaluate agreements under the Sherman Act: the "rule of reason." We will then move on to consideration of modern applications of the rule of reason, focusing on how courts have defined "anticompetitive effects" and established a procedural framework for allocating burdens between plaintiffs and defendants. Note as we proceed how the core concepts we examined in Chapter 1, especially "market power" and "efficiency," have become essential to the process.

A. HISTORICAL FOUNDATIONS: THE EMERGENCE OF THE RULE OF REASON

1. *STANDARD OIL* AND THE "RULE OF REASON"

The Sherman Act of 1890 was the first federal antitrust statute in the United States. Section 1 of the Act declares "[e]very contract, combination in the form of trust or otherwise, or conspiracy, in restraint of trade" to be unlawful, both civilly and criminally. *See infra* Appendix A. The language has long been interpreted to mean that there are two elements to an offense under Section 1: (1) concerted action—a "contract, combination . . . or conspiracy," and (2) an anticompetitive effect—a "restraint of trade." Section 2 of the Sherman Act, which we will examine in Chapter 4, also covers conspiracy, but in contrast to Section 1 its primary focus is on single firm conduct—usually the activities of actual or would-be monopolists. It, too, has been interpreted to require evaluation of the effects of allegedly anticompetitive conduct.

Chapter 3 focuses on the first requirement of Section 1, concerted action. This Chapter is concerned with the second requirement, "restraint of trade," and begins with the Supreme Court's earliest efforts to interpret it. In its first attempt to do so, the Court considered itself constrained by the seemingly plain meaning of the first word of the statute, "every." Although the defendants urged the Court to qualify "every" with a reasonableness standard, it declined to do so:

> When * * * the body of an act pronounces as illegal every contract or combination in restraint of trade or commerce among the several states, etc., the plain and ordinary meaning of such language is not limited to that kind of contract alone which is in unreasonable restraint of trade, but all contracts are included in such language, and no exception or limitation can be added without placing in the act that which has been omitted by congress.

United States v. Trans-Missouri Freight Ass'n, 166 U.S. 290, 328 (1897). Nevertheless, the Court acknowledged that the English and American common law, from which the phrase "restraint of trade" had been taken, allowed for exceptions. *Id.* at 329. In dissent, Justice Edward Douglass White unsuccessfully urged the Court to recognize the full import of that common law history by interpreting Section 1 as prohibiting only "unreasonable restraints of trade." *Id.* at 343–74 (WHITE, J., dissenting). *See also United States v. Joint-Traffic Ass'n*, 171 U.S. 505 (1898).

Trans-Missouri Freight's literal reading of the Sherman Act may have had the virtue of simplicity, but it also had the vice of over-inclusiveness. A prohibition of "every" agreement that restrained trade could encompass a full range of common, competitively insignificant or beneficial business arrangements, including most business partnerships and joint ventures, no matter how much they affect competition. Not surprisingly, therefore, little more than a decade after *Trans-Missouri Freight*, the Court reversed course in *Standard Oil Co. v. United States*, 221 U.S. 1 (1911), abandoning the literal reading of "every" relied upon in *Trans-Missouri Freight*.

Standard Oil was by far the most celebrated antitrust case yet to have been brought under the Sherman Act. Indeed, the term "anti-trust" had been coined with trusts such as Standard Oil in mind. The trust was a form of business organization that permitted rival firms to delegate to a single decision-maker, a "trustee," the authority to make decisions about industry-wide output and pricing. Without effectuating a formal merger, it permitted rivals to coordinate their production and pricing, in effect acting as a single firm, a monopoly. Its invention is often credited to Samuel C.T. Dodd, an attorney for Standard Oil, who first used the device to organize the Standard Oil Trust in 1882, see RON CHERNOW, TITAN: THE LIFE OF JOHN D. ROCKEFELLER, SR. 226–27 (1998), but it spread to other industries such as whiskey, railroads, and sugar.

Pitting the determined antitrust enforcers of the time against the financial interests of John D. Rockefeller and other prominent industrialists, the government's case against Standard Oil marked the end of antitrust law's adolescence in more ways than one. The record, reported the Court, "is inordinately voluminous, consisting of twenty-three volumes of printed matter, aggregating about 12,000 pages, containing a vast amount of confusing and conflicting testimony relating to innumerable, complex, and varied business transactions, extending over a period of nearly forty years." 221 U.S. at 30–31. By today's standards, the scope and complexity of the record seem greatly exaggerated, but the association of antitrust with complex litigation remains and can be traced to *Standard Oil*.

At the conclusion of the case, one of the most extensive trusts to emerge from the late nineteenth century became a casualty of the twentieth, disassembled into over thirty constituent parts. More importantly for current purposes, the Court did so after implying a reasonableness modification to the language of Section 1 of the Sherman Act. Now writing for the Court's majority and as its Chief Justice, White implemented the approach he had first outlined in his dissent in *Trans-Missouri Freight*: "the rule of reason." In so doing, the Court forever turned its back on the plain meaning approach, emphasizing instead the link between the Sherman Act and the English and American common law of restraint of trade:

> [Section 1 of the Sherman Act] necessarily called for the exercise of judgment which required that some standard should be resorted to for the purpose of determining whether the prohibition

contained in the statute had or had not in any given case been violated. Thus, not specifying, but indubitably contemplating and requiring a standard, it follows that it was intended that the standard of reason which had been applied at the common law and in this country in dealing with subjects of the character embraced by the statute was intended to be the measure used for the purpose of determining whether, in a given case, a particular act had or had not brought about the wrong against which the statute provided.

Standard Oil, 221 U.S. at 60.

Seven years later, the Court elaborated on the content of the rule of reason in our next case, *Bd. of Trade of Chicago v. United States*, 246 U.S. 231 (1918) ("*Chicago Board of Trade*"). In an opinion by Justice Louis Brandeis that remains influential today, the Court set out what has become the prevailing statement of that rule and the earliest example of its practical operation. As you read the case, try to answer the question: "what is the content of the rule of reason?" What factors does the Court identify as relevant to the rule of reason inquiry? How are those factors to be weighted? What defenses can be raised in rule of reason cases? How are burdens of production to be allocated among the plaintiffs and defendants under the rule of reason?

BOARD OF TRADE OF CITY OF CHICAGO V. UNITED STATES
Supreme Court of the United States, 1918.
246 U.S. 231, 38 S.Ct. 242, 62 L.Ed. 683.

MR. JUSTICE BRANDEIS delivered the opinion of the Court.

Chicago is the leading grain market in the world. Its Board of Trade is the commercial center through which most of the trading in grain is done.* * * Its 1600 members include brokers, commission merchants, dealers, millers, maltsters, manufacturers of corn products and proprietors of elevators. * * * The standard forms of trading are: (a) Spot sales; that is, sales of grain already in Chicago in railroad cars or elevators for immediate delivery by order on carrier or transfer of warehouse receipt. (b) Future sales; that is, agreements for delivery later in the current or in some future month. (c) Sales 'to arrive'; that is, agreements to deliver on arrival grain which is already in transit to Chicago or is to be shipped there within a time specified. On every business day sessions of the Board are held at which all bids and sales are publicly made. Spot sales and future sales are made at the regular sessions of the Board from 9:30 a. m. to 1:15 p. m., except on Saturdays, when the session closes at 12 m. Special sessions, termed the 'call,' are held immediately after the close of the regular session, at which sales 'to arrive' are made. These sessions are not limited as to duration, but last usually about half an hour. At all these sessions transactions are between members only; but they may trade either for themselves or on behalf of others. Members may also trade privately with one another at any place, either during the sessions or after, and they may trade with nonmembers at any time except on the premises occupied by the Board.

* * *

In 1906 the Board adopted what is known as the 'call' rule. By it members were prohibited from purchasing or offering to purchase, during the period between the close of the call and the opening of the session on the next business day, any wheat, corn, oats or rye 'to arrive' at a price other than the closing bid at the call. The call was over, with rare exceptions, by 2 o'clock. The change effected was this: Before the adoption of the rule, members fixed their bids throughout the day at such prices as they respectively saw fit; after the adoption of the rule, the bids had to be fixed at the day's closing bid on the call until the opening of the next session.

In 1913 the United States filed in the District Court for the Northern District of Illinois, this suit against the Board and its executive officers and directors, to enjoin the enforcement of the call rule, alleging it to be in violation of the Anti-Trust Law of July 2, 1890 [the Sherman Act]. The defendants admitted the adoption and enforcement of the call rule, and averred that its purpose was not to prevent competition or to control prices, but to promote the convenience of members by restricting their hours of business and to break up a monopoly in that branch of the grain trade acquired by four or five warehousemen in Chicago. On motion of the government the allegations concerning the purpose of establishing the regulation were stricken from the record. The case was then heard upon evidence; and a decree was entered which declared that defendants became parties to a combination or conspiracy to restrain interstate and foreign trade and commerce "by adopting, acting upon and enforcing" the "call" rule; and enjoined them from acting upon the same or from adopting or acting upon any similar rule.

* * * The government proved the existence of the rule and described its application and the change in business practice involved. It made no attempt to show that the rule was designed to or that it had the effect of limiting the amount of grain shipped to Chicago; or of retarding or accelerating shipment; or of raising or depressing prices; or of discriminating against any part of the public; or that it resulted in hardship to any one. The case was rested upon the bald proposition, that a rule or agreement by which men occupying positions of strength in any branch of trade, fixed prices at which they would buy or sell during an important part of the business day, is an illegal restraint of trade under the Anti-Trust Law. But the legality of an agreement or regulation cannot be determined by so simple a test, as whether it restrains competition. Every agreement concerning trade, every regulation of trade, restrains. To bind, to restrain, is of their very essence. The true test of legality is whether the restraint imposed is such as merely regulates and perhaps thereby promotes competition or whether it is such as may suppress or even destroy competition. To determine that question the court must ordinarily consider the facts peculiar to the business to which the restraint is applied; its condition before and after the restraint was imposed; the nature of the restraint and its effect, actual or probable. The history of the restraint, the evil believed to exist, the reason for adopting the particular remedy, the purpose or end sought to be attained, are all relevant facts. This is not because a good intention will save an otherwise objectionable regulation or the reverse; but because knowledge of intent may help the court to interpret facts and to predict consequences. The District Court erred, therefore, in striking from the answer allegations concerning the history and purpose of the call rule and in later excluding evidence on that subject. But the evidence admitted makes it clear that the rule was a reasonable regulation of business consistent with the provisions of the Anti-Trust Law.

First. The nature of the rule: The restriction was upon the period of price-making. It required members to desist from further price-making after the close of the call until 9:30 a.m. the next business day; but there was no restriction upon the sending out of bids after close of the call. Thus it required members who desired to buy grain "to arrive" to make up their minds before the close of the call how much they were willing to pay during the interval before the next session of the Board. The rule made it to their interest to attend the call; and if they did not fill their wants by purchases there, to make the final bid high enough to enable them to purchase from country dealers.

Second. The scope of the rule: It is restricted in operation to grain "to arrive." It applies only to a small part of the grain shipped from day to day to Chicago, and to an even smaller part of the day's sales; members were left free to purchase grain already in Chicago from any one at any price throughout the day. It applies only during a small part of the business day; members were left free to purchase during the sessions of the Board grain "to arrive," at any price, from members anywhere and from nonmembers anywhere except on the premises of the Board. It applied only to grain shipped to Chicago; members were left free to purchase at any price throughout the day from either members or non-members, grain "to arrive" at any other market. Country dealers and farmers had available in practically every part of the territory called tributary to Chicago some other market for grain "to arrive." * * *

Third. The effects of the rule: As it applies to only a small part of the grain shipped to Chicago and to that only during a part of the business day and does not apply at all to grain shipped to other markets, the rule had no appreciable effect on general market prices; nor did it materially affect the total volume of grain coming to Chicago. But within the narrow limits of its operation the rule helped to improve market conditions thus:

(a)　It created a public market for grain "to arrive." Before its adoption, bids were made privately. Men had to buy and sell without adequate knowledge of actual market conditions. This was disadvantageous to all concerned, but particularly so to country dealers and farmers.

(b)　It brought into the regular market hours of the Board sessions, more of the trading in grain "to arrive."

(c)　It brought buyers and sellers into more direct relations; because on the call they gathered together for a free and open interchange of bids and offers.

(d)　It distributed the business in grain "to arrive" among a far larger number of Chicago receivers and commission merchants than had been the case there before.

(e)　It increased the number of country dealers engaging in this branch of the business; supplied them more regularly with bids from Chicago; and also increased the number of bids received by them from competing markets.

(f)　It eliminated risks necessarily incident to a private market, and thus enabled country dealers to do business on a smaller margin. In that way the rule made it possible for them to pay more to farmers without raising the price to consumers.

(g)　It enabled country dealers to sell some grain to arrive which they would otherwise have been obliged either to ship to Chicago commission merchants or to sell for "future delivery."

(h)　It enabled those grain merchants of Chicago who sell to millers and exporters, to trade on a smaller margin and by paying more for grain or selling it for less, to make the Chicago market more attractive for both shippers and buyers of grain.

(i)　Incidentally it facilitated trading "to arrive" by enabling those engaged in these transactions to fulfill their contracts by tendering grain arriving at Chicago on any railroad, whereas formerly shipments had to be made over the particular railroad designated by the buyer.

* * * Every Board of Trade and nearly every trade organization imposes some restraint upon the conduct of business by its members. Those relating to the hours in which business may be done are common; and they make a special appeal where, as here, they tend to shorten the working day or, at least, limit the period of most exacting activity. The decree of the District Court is reversed with directions to dismiss the bill.

Reversed.

What is the test of "reasonableness" announced by the Court in *Chicago Board of Trade*? What factors are deemed relevant to the inquiry? Were the restrictions on trading imposed by the Board of Trade harmful to competition, pro-competitive, or competitively of little consequence? Did the Court consider factors other than competition in its analysis?

Consider the Court's observation that "On motion of the government the allegations concerning the purpose of establishing the regulation were stricken from the record." Why would the government urge the trial court to exclude evidence of purpose, and what rationale might justify its doing so? What were the consequences for the Board? Why did the Supreme Court refuse to follow the same approach?

Consider the following summary of the Court's holding:

Figure 2–1:

The *Chicago Board of Trade* Rule of Reason

Major Propositions:

(1) "The true test of legality is whether the restraint imposed is such as merely regulates and perhaps thereby promotes competition or whether it is such as may suppress or even destroy competition."

(2) Three Categories of Factors to Consider: Nature; Scope; Effect

Relevant Factors:

- **Facts peculiar to the business**
  - Conditions of business before and after restraint was imposed

- **Nature of restraint**
  - Its effect, actual or probable

- **History and purposes of the restraint**
  - Evil believed to exist
  - Reason for adopting particular remedy
  - Purpose or end sought to be attained
  - These are "all relevant factors"

Standard Oil and *Chicago Board of Trade* reflected aspects of a third formative decision, *United States v. Addyston Pipe & Steel Co.*, 85 F. 271 (6th Cir. 1898), *aff'd*, 175 U.S. 211 (1899). In an opinion by Judge William Howard Taft, the court divided restraints of trade into two categories. The first category included restraints that had no purpose other than restraining trade. These restraints were condemned absolutely at common law, and, the court reasoned, should be similarly condemned under the Sherman Act. In contrast to *Trans-Missouri Freight*, Taft's approach to "absolutely prohibited" agreements followed from the restraint's plainly anticompetitive effect rather than the language of the Sherman Act.

Taft's second category was constituted of restraints that were "ancillary" to an otherwise legitimate business transaction, such as the sale of a business. For example, the sale of a bakery might include a commitment by the seller that it will not re-enter the bakery business in competition with the buyer in the same town for a period of time after the sale. Such ancillary restraints, in this case a "covenant not to compete," facilitated the underlying, legitimate transaction and could be justified on the ground that they promoted trade if "reasonable." In this example, the sale would not sensibly go forward if the purchaser could not contractually protect against the possibility that the seller would promptly open a competing business proximate to that sold. Taft argued based on this and other common law examples that such ancillary restraints were and ought to be assessed for their reasonableness, because although restraining trade in some sense, they also tended to promote it, by facilitating the main transaction. They were deemed reasonable at common law, therefore, when both integral to and no greater than necessary to facilitate a legitimate transaction. The duration of the covenant not to compete, as well as its geographic scope, would have to be assessed and found to be "reasonable."

Taft's approach to the rule of reason differed from that later enunciated in *Standard Oil*. Under his approach, arrangements that only restrained trade, such as the price-fixing arrangement at issue in the case, were absolutely prohibited. "Reasonableness" only entered into the analysis of ancillary restraints:

> . . . [W]here the sole object of both parties in making the contract as expressed therein is merely to restrain competition, and enhance or maintain prices, it would seem that there was nothing to justify or excuse the restraint, that it would necessarily have a tendency to monopoly, and therefore would be void. In such a case there is no measure of what is necessary to the protection of either party, except the vague and varying opinion of judges as to how much, on principles of political economy, men ought to be allowed to restrain competition. There is in such contracts no main lawful

purpose, to subserve which partial restraint is permitted, and by which its reasonableness is measured, but the sole object is to restrain trade in order to avoid the competition which it has always been the policy of the common law to foster.

Addyston Pipe, 85 F. at 282–83. Taft further argued that courts were ill-equipped to evaluate broad arguments for reasonableness outside of the context of ancillary restraints and that to do so was to "set sail on a sea of doubt." *Id.* at 284. His views that some kinds of restraints should be absolutely prohibited and that ancillary restraints alone should be evaluated under a standard of reasonableness continue to influence application of the rule of reason in some circumstances and we will revisit them later in the Chapter in Sidebar 2–5.

As we have noted, *Addyston Pipe* preceded both *Standard Oil* (1911) and *Chicago Board of Trade* (1918), and those cases did not adopt Taft's approach in *Addyston Pipe*. Instead, they appeared to invite a wider inquiry into whether a particular restraint was reasonable or unreasonable That approach generated uncertainty about the content of the "rule of reason" and led to further development. In particular, three sets of questions remained in need of further consideration:

(1)   What factors matter to the rule of reason inquiry? Is the list provided in *Chicago Board of Trade* exhaustive or suggestive? Within its more general categories, such as "purpose," "nature," and "effect," are there more specific ones?

(2)   How are competing factors to be weighted? *Chicago Board of Trade* says nothing, for example, about how courts are to weigh conflicting evidence, such as evidence of competitive harm and competitive benefit, such as cost-reducing efficiencies. What if there is evidence that the "nature" of the agreement was anticompetitive, but that it also had some important and arguably procompetitive justifications? Is the agreement a reasonable or unreasonable restraint of trade?

(3)   How are burdens of production and proof to be allocated under the rule of reason? How much and what kind of evidence of "purpose, nature, and effect" will be sufficient to shift a burden of production to the defendant? How much and what kind of evidence can a defendant introduce to rebut?

The Court's failure to specify these particulars may have been due in part to its increased reliance in the years following *Chicago Board of Trade* on "per se" analysis, which continued to be applied expansively until the Supreme Court's watershed decision in *Continental T.V., Inc. v. GTE Sylvania Inc.*, 433 U.S. 36 (1977) (*see infra* Chapter 6). As this Chapter progresses, we will observe both trends.

Before moving on, however, it is also important to note the connection between the Sherman Act and the common law, which has influenced not just the content of the rule of reason, but the process that has allowed it to develop over time as our understanding of competition and economics changed. Reflected in both *Chicago Board of Trade* and *Addyston Pipe*, this inherent capacity to evolve is one of the Sherman Act's defining characteristics. As the Supreme Court later observed in a case we will read later in this Chapter:

> Congress * * * did not intend the text of the Sherman Act to delineate the full meaning of the statute or its application in concrete situations. The legislative history makes it perfectly clear that it expected the courts to give shape to the statute's broad mandate by drawing on common-law tradition. The Rule of Reason, with its origins in common-law precedents long antedating the Sherman Act, has served that purpose. It has been used to give the Act both flexibility and definition, and its central principle of antitrust analysis has remained constant.

Nat'l Soc'y of Prof'l Eng'rs v. United States, 435 U.S. 679, 688 (1978). *See also Bus. Elecs. Corp. v. Sharp Elecs. Corp.*, 485 U.S. 717, 732 (1988) ("The Sherman Act adopted the term 'restraint of trade' along with its dynamic potential. It invokes the common law itself, and not merely the static content that the common law had assigned to the term in 1890.").

In the next Section, we will see how this flexibility and adaptability allowed the Court to expand its reliance on "per se" analysis, which was an abbreviated application of the rule of reason. Later in the Chapter, however, we will observe as the Court retrenched on that reliance and returned to answer the questions left unanswered about the content and structure of a more complete rule of reason analysis.

2. ABBREVIATED APPLICATION OF THE RULE OF REASON: THE PER SE "RULE"

The Sherman Act's hostility to price fixing by competitors became more formalized after *Standard Oil* and *Chicago Board of Trade* and is embodied in a "per se rule"—an absolute prohibition—that began to take shape in 1927 and became well-settled by 1940. This per se rule was then extended to other kinds of conduct perceived as variants of price fixing, such as agreements to restrict output, agreements to divide markets, and collusive group boycotts. Each of these will be examined as we proceed through the Chapter.

In *United States v. Trenton Potteries Co.*, 273 U.S. 392 (1927), the Supreme Court reviewed the criminal convictions under the Sherman Act of producers of "sanitary pottery"—bathroom fixtures. There was no dispute that the producers had, through their trade association, fixed prices. Neither was there any dispute that they together accounted for 82% of the production of bathroom fixtures in the United States. While conceding these facts, the defendants argued in their defense that the prices they had set were "reasonable." Although the identical defense had been rejected in *Trans-Missouri Freight*, the defendants argued that *Standard Oil* and *Chicago Board of Trade* had reopened the door to broad based reasonableness defenses. But the Court rejected the approach, at least as it related to the treatment of price fixing under the Sherman Act:

> The aim and result of every price-fixing agreement, if effective, is the elimination of one form of competition. The power to fix prices, whether reasonably exercised or not, involves power to control the market and to fix arbitrary and unreasonable prices. The reasonable price fixed today may through economic and business changes become the unreasonable price of to-morrow. Once established, it may be maintained unchanged because of the absence of competition secured by the agreement for a price reasonable when fixed. *Agreements which create such potential power may well be held to be in themselves unreasonable or unlawful restraints, without the necessity of minute inquiry whether a particular price is reasonable or unreasonable* as fixed and without placing on the government in enforcing the Sherman Law the burden of ascertaining from day to day whether it has become unreasonable through the mere variation of economic conditions. Moreover, in the absence of express legislation requiring it, we should hesitate to adopt a construction making the difference between legal and illegal conduct in the field of business relations depend upon so uncertain a test as whether prices are reasonable—a determination which can be satisfactorily made only after a complete survey of our economic organization and a choice between rival philosophies.

Trenton Potteries, 273 U.S. at 397–98 (emphasis added).

Carefully consider the foregoing quotation from *Trenton Potteries*. In condemning the defendants' price fixing, does the Court assign any importance to factors other than the mere agreement to fix prices? For example, was it influenced by the defendants' share of the market or evidence of the actual effects of the agreement on prices? Consider the Court's statement that "[a]greements which *create such potential power* may well be held to be *in themselves* unreasonable or unlawful restraints." "In themselves" seems to be an endorsement of a per se prohibition of price fixing, but the reference to "power" and the Court's later assertion that "uniform price fixing *by those controlling in any substantial manner a trade or business* in interstate commerce is prohibited by the Sherman Law, despite the reasonableness of the particular prices agreed upon" suggest that the specific market context mattered. *Id.* at 398. If per se analysis applies only when the colluding firms possess market power and actually succeed in raising prices, how truly "per se" was the Court's approach? We will explore these questions in our next case, *Socony-Vacuum Oil*, and later in the Chapter in *Broadcast Music, Inc.*, after reflecting on the role of antitrust law during the Great Depression.

NOTE ON ANTITRUST LAW DEVELOPMENTS DURING THE GREAT DEPRESSION

Just two years after *Trenton Potteries* the Nation's economy began its plunge into the Great Depression. Industry after industry experienced "distressed" conditions, characterized by deteriorating demand, steep price cutting, and shrinking production. These conditions tested the Nation's commitment to competition policy and presented challenges for the application of antitrust laws.

Critics of competition called for government intervention to stabilize prices and halt the continuing de-stabilization of the economy. Congress responded in June 1933 with the National Industrial Recovery Act, 48 Stat. 195 ("NIRA"), which led to the creation of codes of "fair competition" negotiated by the firms in many industries and authorized the President to act in response to distressed conditions in particular industries. Our next case, *Socony-Vacuum Oil*, arose directly from efforts to organize the petroleum industry under the NIRA during the short period before the Act was declared unconstitutional by the Supreme Court in *A.L.A. Schecter Poultry Corp. v. United States*, 295 U.S. 495 (1935).

Even before the passage of the NIRA, however, some parties took matters into their own hands, often encouraged by state and local officials. In *Appalachian Coals, Inc. v. United States*, 288 U.S. 344 (1933), decided just six years after *Trenton Potteries* appeared to establish an absolute prohibition of price fixing by competitors, the Supreme Court rejected the government's attempt to enjoin the creation of an exclusive, joint selling agency by 137 Appalachian producers of bituminous coal. The producers, in response to what the district court termed "deplorable conditions resulting from overexpansion, destructive competition, wasteful trade practices, and the inroads of competing industries," 288 U.S. at 359, sought the Justice Department's approval of the creation of an exclusive, joint selling agent. The agent, which the producers had created, and through which they agreed to sell all of their production, would negotiate all sales on behalf of its shareholders, whose collective share of the market was reported to be somewhere between 12 and 74%, depending upon how broadly it was defined. *Id.* at 357. In structure, the sales agency looked much like the classic trusts—a new entity was created to handle all sales, and the defendant producers owned all of its capital stock in proportion to their production. *Id.* at 357–58.

As recounted by the Supreme Court, the producers insisted that "the primary purpose of the formation of the selling agency was to increase the sale, and thus the production, of Appalachian coal through better methods of distribution, intensive advertising and research, to achieve economies in marketing, and to eliminate abnormal, deceptive, and destructive trade practices." *Id.* at 359. The Court continued:

> Defendants contend that the evidence establishes that the selling agency will not have the power to dominate or fix the price of coal in any consuming market; that the price of coal will continue to be set in an open and competitive market; and that their plan by increasing the sale of bituminous coal from Appalachian territory will promote, rather than restrain, interstate commerce.

Id. The government argued in response, and the district court agreed, that although the selling agency would not lead to "monopoly control of any market nor the power to fix monopoly prices," it nevertheless "will * * * have a tendency to stabilize prices and to raise prices to a higher level than would prevail under conditions of free competition." *Id.* Indeed, that appeared to be its principal purpose.

Nevertheless, the Supreme Court turned to *Chicago Board of Trade*, not *Trenton Potteries*, and upheld the agency agreement as reasonable. Noting that "wherever their selling agency operates, it will find itself confronted by effective competition backed by virtually inexhaustive sources of supply, and will also be compelled to cope with the organized buying power of large consumers," the Court appeared to differ with the district court regarding its prediction that the agency would "stabilize" and raise prices on two grounds. First, it noted that there was no "monopolistic menace." The high figure of 74% used to describe the defendants' market share was a measure of their share of bituminous coal production in Appalachia—but most of their sales were made elsewhere, which meant that they lacked the ability to control "market prices." 288 U.S. at 373. The Court distinguished *Trenton Potteries*, pointing out that there the defendants had the power to set market prices, because they "controlled 82 per cent. of the business of manufacturing and distributing vitreous pottery in the United States." *Id.* at 375.

Undeniably, however, the Court was also greatly influenced by the conditions in the industry. Appearing to concede that some effect on prices might result from the agreement, the Court concluded that "the evidence fails to show * * * that any effect will be produced *which in the circumstances of this industry* will be detrimental to fair competition." *Id.* (emphasis added). The Court explained:

> The evidence leaves no doubt of the existence of the evils at which defendants' plan was aimed. The industry was in distress. It suffered from overexpansion and from a serious relative decline through the growing use of substitute fuels. It was afflicted by injurious practices within itself—practices which demanded correction. If evil conditions could not be entirely cured, they at least might be alleviated. The unfortunate state of the industry would not justify any attempt unduly to restrain competition or to monopolize, but the existing situation prompted defendants to make, and the statute did not

preclude them from making, an honest effort to remove abuses, to make competition fairer, and thus to promote the essential interests of commerce. The interests of producers and consumers are interlinked. When industry is greviously [sic] hurt, when producing concerns fail, when unemployment mounts and communities dependent upon profitable production are prostrated, the wells of commerce go dry. So far as actual purposes are concerned, the conclusion of the court below was amply supported that defendants were engaged in a fair and open endeavor to aid the industry in a measurable recovery from its plight.

Id. at 372.

Is the Court's application of the rule of reason consistent with either *Chicago Board of Trade* or *Trenton Potteries*? Is it subject to the kind of criticisms Judge Taft leveled in *Addyston Pipe*—was the Court now "setting sail on a sea of doubt"? How important was it to the Court's conclusion that the agency arrangement had yet to take effect? How did that fact affect the evidence it was able to consider? How important was the Court's perception that the producers lacked the ability to affect market prices? Wasn't affecting market prices an obvious goal of the arrangement? Do you find the Court's basis for distinguishing *Trenton Potteries* persuasive? Were there other grounds of distinction that could have been argued? Was the "per se" approach of *Trenton Potteries* effectively limited by the decision to cases in which additional evidence suggests some likelihood that "market" prices will be affected?

Trenton Potteries and *Appalachian Coals* together appeared to hold that price fixing by competitors was per se unlawful, but perhaps only when the defendants were in a position to affect market prices, *i.e.*, when they were in a position to exercise market power. Note that this synthesis of the two cases was reflected in the jury instructions used by the trial court in our next case, *Socony-Vacuum Oil*. But as we shall see, just seven years after *Appalachian Coals*, the Court appeared to reject any limitation on the per se prohibition of price fixing by competitors based on the actual effects of the agreement or the market share or market power of the firms involved.

UNITED STATES V. SOCONY-VACUUM OIL CO.

Supreme Court of the United States, 1940.
310 U.S. 150, 60 S.Ct. 811, 84 L.Ed. 1129.

[Like *Appalachian Coals*, *Socony-Vacuum Oil* arose out of the economic upheaval of the Great Depression, but it was a more direct consequence of federal government efforts to organize industries and stabilize prices pursuant to the NIRA. After the NIRA was struck down, the defendants, major oil companies, continued their organizing efforts through various means.

In a criminal indictment, the government charged that the defendants implemented two concerted gasoline buying programs that were designed to and had the effect of limiting the output and raising the price of gasoline in the Midwestern United States. Figure 2–2 depicts the organization of distribution in the industry. Gasoline production and sales involved four steps: (1) exploration and drilling; (2) refining; (3) distribution; and (4) retail sale. Only the major oil companies were fully integrated and performed all four functions. "Independents" were also engaged in refining, but sold their output to "jobbers," who acted as distributors. The major oil companies also sold to the jobbers, who supplied roughly 50% of the retail gasoline stations in the "Mid-Western area."

Independents sold to jobbers at "spot" market prices that constantly fluctuated; in contrast, the integrated firms sold to jobbers pursuant to long term contracts, but those contracts tied sale prices to spot market prices through a negotiated formula. As a consequence, deteriorating spot market prices due to increased supply from independents had a downward effect on all wholesale pricing.

The challenged agreements focused on the purchase of this surplus ("distress") gasoline from independent refiners, who accounted for virtually all of the gasoline sold in tank car quantities on the "spot market" in the Midwestern areas. Such sales amounted to less than 5% of all gasoline marketed there, but they produced a significant downward pressure on prices. The agreements orchestrated by the integrated major oil companies set up an informal system, termed "gentlemen's agreements," whereby each of the majors would select one or more independents with distress gasoline as a "dancing partner." It would then assume responsibility for purchasing its partner's distress supply. Because the majors had more substantial storage facilities than the independents, they could then hold the purchased surplus gasoline off of the market. Doing so had the effect of raising spot market prices, and ultimately stabilizing and raising prices market-wide. There was evidence that the defendants collectively shared a very substantial share of the market and that as a consequence of their actions prices actually increased. Eds.]

Figure 2–2:

The Structure of the Gasoline Industry in *Socony-Vacuum Oil*

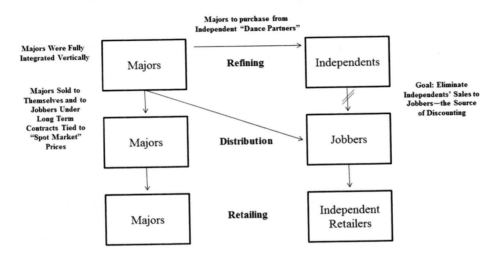

MR. JUSTICE DOUGLAS delivered the opinion of the Court.

* * *

III. The Alleged Conspiracy.

* * *

As a result of these buying programs it was hoped and intended that both the tank car and the retail markets would improve. The conclusion is irresistible that defendants' purpose was not merely to raise the spot market prices but, as the real and ultimate end, to raise the price of gasoline in their sales to jobbers and consumers in the Mid-Western area. Their agreement or plan embraced not only buying on the spot markets but also, at least by clear implication, an understanding to maintain such improvements in Mid-Western prices as would result from those purchases of distress gasoline. The latter obviously would be achieved by selling at the increased prices, not by price cutting. * * * In essence the raising and maintenance of the spot market prices were but the means adopted for raising and maintaining prices to jobbers and consumers.

* * *

V.   Application of the Sherman Act.

* * *

The [district] court charged the jury that it was a violation of the Sherman Act for a group of individuals or corporations to act together to raise the prices to be charged for the commodity which they manufactured where they controlled a substantial part of the interstate trade and commerce in that commodity. The court stated that where the members of a combination had the power to raise prices and acted together for that purpose, the combination was illegal; and that it was immaterial how reasonable or unreasonable those prices were or to what extent they had been affected by the combination. It further charged that if such illegal combination existed, it did not matter that there may also have been other factors which contributed to the raising of the prices.

* * *

The Circuit Court of Appeals held this charge to be reversible error, since it was based upon the theory that such a combination was illegal *per se*. In its view respondents' activities were not unlawful unless they constituted an unreasonable restraint of trade. Hence, since that issue had not been submitted to the jury and since evidence bearing on it had been excluded, that court reversed and remanded for a new trial so that the character of those activities and their effect on competition could be determined. In answer to the government's petition respondents here contend that the judgment of the Circuit Court of Appeals was correct, since there was evidence that they had affected prices only in the sense that the removal of the competitive evil of distress gasoline by the buying programs had permitted prices to rise to a normal competitive level; that their activities promoted rather than impaired fair competitive opportunities; and therefore that their activities had not unduly or unreasonably restrained trade.

* * *

In *United States v. Trenton Potteries Co.*, this Court sustained a conviction under the Sherman Act where the jury was charged that an agreement on the part of the members of a combination, controlling a substantial part of an industry, upon the prices which the members are to charge for their commodity is in itself an unreasonable restraint of trade without regard to the reasonableness of the prices or the good intentions of the combining units. * * * This Court reviewed the various price-fixing cases under the Sherman Act and said " * * * it has since often been decided and always assumed that uniform price-fixing by those controlling in any substantial manner a trade or business in interstate commerce is prohibited by the Sherman Law, despite the reasonableness of the particular prices agreed upon." This Court pointed out that the so-called "rule of reason" announced in *Standard Oil* and in *American Tobacco* had not affected this view of the illegality of price-fixing agreements.

* * *

Respondents seek to distinguish the *Trenton Potteries* case from the instant one. They assert that in that case the parties substituted an agreed-on price for one determined by competition; that the defendants there had the power and purpose to suppress the play of competition in the determination of the market price; and therefore that the controlling factor in that decision was the destruction of market competition, not whether prices were higher or lower, reasonable or unreasonable. * * *

But we do not deem those distinctions material.

In the first place, there was abundant evidence that the combination had the purpose to raise prices. And likewise, there was ample evidence that the buying programs at least contributed to the price rise and the stability of the spot markets, and to increases in the price of gasoline sold in the Mid-Western area during the indictment period. * * * Proof that there was a conspiracy, that its purpose was to raise prices, and that it caused or contributed to a price rise is proof of the actual consummation or execution of a conspiracy under § 1 of the Sherman Act.

Secondly, the fact that sales on the spot markets were still governed by some competition is of no consequence. For it is indisputable that that competition was restricted through the removal by respondents of a part of the supply which but for the buying programs would have been a factor in determining the going prices on those markets.

* * *

The elimination of so-called competitive evils is no legal justification for such buying programs. The elimination of such conditions was sought primarily for its effect on the price structures. Fairer competitive prices, it is claimed, resulted when distress gasoline was removed from the market. But such defense is typical of the protestations usually made in price-fixing cases. Ruinous competition, financial disaster, evils of price cutting and the like appear throughout our history as ostensible justifications for price-fixing. If the so-called competitive abuses were to be appraised here, the reasonableness of prices would necessarily become an issue in every price-fixing case. In that event the Sherman Act would soon be emasculated; its philosophy would be supplanted by one which is wholly alien to a system of free competition; it would not be the charter of freedom which its framers intended.

The reasonableness of prices has no constancy due to the dynamic quality of the business facts underlying price structures. Those who fixed reasonable prices today would perpetuate unreasonable prices tomorrow, since those prices would not be subject to continuous administrative supervision and readjustment in light of changed conditions. Those who controlled the prices would control or effectively dominate the market. And those who were in that strategic position would have it in their power to destroy or drastically impair the competitive system. But the thrust of the rule is deeper and reaches more than monopoly power. Any combination which tampers with price structures is engaged in an unlawful activity. Even though the members of the price-fixing group were in no position to control the market, to the extent that they raised, lowered, or stabilized prices they would be directly interfering with the free play of market forces. The Act places all such schemes beyond the pale and protects that vital part of our economy against any degree of interference. Congress has not left with us the determination of whether or not particular price-fixing schemes are wise or unwise, healthy or destructive. It has not permitted the age-old cry of ruinous competition and competitive evils to be a defense to price-fixing conspiracies. It has no more allowed genuine or fancied competitive abuses as a legal justification for such schemes than it has the good intentions of the members of the combination. If such a shift is to be made, it must be done by the Congress.

* * *

Nor is it important that the prices paid by the combination were not fixed in the sense that they were uniform and inflexible. Price-fixing as used in the *Trenton Potteries* case has no such limited meaning. * * * Hence, prices are fixed within the meaning of the *Trenton Potteries* case if the range within which purchases or sales will be made is agreed upon, if the prices paid or charged are to be at a certain level or on ascending or descending scales, if they are to be uniform, or if by various formulae they are related to the market prices. They are fixed because they are agreed upon. And the fact that, as here, they are fixed at the fair going market price is immaterial.

* * *

Under the Sherman Act a combination formed for the purpose and with the effect of raising, depressing, fixing, pegging, or stabilizing the price of a commodity in interstate or foreign commerce is illegal per se. Where the machinery for price-fixing is an agreement on the prices to be charged or paid for the commodity * * * the power to fix prices exists if the combination has control of a substantial part of the commerce in that commodity. Where the means for price-fixing are purchases or sales of the commodity in a market operation or, as here, purchases of a part of the supply of the commodity for the purpose of keeping it from having a depressive effect on the markets, such power may be found to exist though the combination does not control a substantial part of the commodity. In such a case that power may be established if as a result of market conditions, the resources available to the combinations, the timing and the strategic placement of orders and the like, effective means are at hand to accomplish the desired objective. But there may be effective influence over the market though the group in question does not control it. Price-fixing agreements may have utility to members of the group though the power possessed or exerted falls far short of domination and control. Monopoly power * * * is not the only power which the Act strikes down, as we have said. Proof that a combination was formed for the purpose of fixing prices and that it caused them to be fixed or contributed to that result is proof of the completion of a price-fixing conspiracy under § 1 of the Act.[59] The indictment in this case charged that this combination had that purpose and effect. And there was abundant evidence to support it. Hence the existence of power on the part of members of the combination to fix prices was but a conclusion from the finding that the buying programs caused or contributed to the rise and stability of prices.

* * *

Socony-Vacuum Oil settled the status of price fixing by competitors as unlawful under Section 1 of the Sherman Act, definitively placing it in the per se category. It did not matter that the mechanism was restriction of output, as opposed to fixing a price, because, as we learned in Chapter 1, lower industry output and higher industry prices go hand in hand. Moreover, in the text and in famous footnote 59, the Court strongly suggested that price fixing by competitors should be treated harshly regardless of the market power of the price fixers. The Court also declared that "[t]he elimination of so-called competitive evils is no legal justification for such buying programs." 310 U.S. at 220. Can the Court's statements on "competitive evils" and the irrelevance of market power be reconciled with *Appalachian Coals*? Did it effectively overrule it? *See Virginia Excelsior Mills, Inc. v. FTC*, 256 F.2d 538, 541 (4th Cir. 1958) (suggesting that

---

[59] Under this indictment proof that prices in the Mid-Western area were raised as a result of the activities of the combination was essential, since sales of gasoline by respondents at the increased prices in that area were necessary in order to establish jurisdiction. * * * But that does not mean that both a purpose and a power to fix prices are necessary for the establishment of a conspiracy under § 1 of the Sherman Act. * * * [I]t is well established that a person "may be guilty of conspiring, although incapable of committing the objective offense." In view of these considerations a conspiracy to fix prices violates § 1 of the Act though no overt act is shown, though it is not established that the conspirators had the means available for accomplishment of their objective, and though the conspiracy embraced but a part of the interstate or foreign commerce in the commodity. * * * Price-fixing agreements may or may not be aimed at complete elimination of price competition. The group making those agreements may or may not have power to control the market. But the fact that the group cannot control the market prices does not necessarily mean that the agreement as to prices has no utility to the members of the combination. The effectiveness of price-fixing agreements is dependent on many factors, such as competitive tactics, position in the industry, the formula underlying price policies. Whatever economic justification particular price-fixing agreements may be thought to have, the law does not permit an inquiry into their reasonableness. They are all banned because of their actual or potential threat to the central nervous system of the economy. * * * The existence or exertion of power to accomplish the desired objective * * * becomes important only in cases where the offense charged is the actual monopolizing of any part of trade or commerce in violation of § 2 of the Act. * * * An intent and a power to produce the result which the law condemns are then necessary.

Appalachian Coals was effectively overruled by *Socony-Vacuum Oil* and other subsequent pronouncements on price fixing).

Recall that just five years before *Socony-Vacuum Oil* the Court in *Schechter Poultry* had categorically rejected the National Industrial Recovery Act ("NIRA"), a cornerstone of the Roosevelt Administration's initial New Deal program. The NIRA sought to encourage the formation of industry "fair competition codes" in response to the Great Depression. Is the Court merely reemphasizing in *Socony-Vacuum Oil* that it will not endorse efforts, either public or private, to create exceptions to competition? Could historical context also explain *Appalachian Coals*, which pre-dated adoption of the NIRA? Are the two decisions "irreconcilable"? Do they reflect shifting views on the Court about government and private efforts to regulate the economy?

How does per se analysis operate as an application of the rule of reason? As we will examine in greater detail later in the Chapter, the Court appears to suggest that procedurally, per se analysis triggers a presumption that the challenged conduct is unreasonably anticompetitive. That is why the Court indicates in its famous footnote 59 that no further proof of competitive harm, such as market power, is required. The presumption, however, is not rebuttable, but irrebuttable: once the burden shifts to the defendant, no defenses are permitted.

What might be the economic rationale for such an irrebuttable presumption? The Court would later explain it this way:

> * * * [T]here are certain agreements or practices which because of their pernicious effect on competition and lack of any redeeming virtue are conclusively presumed to be unreasonable and therefore illegal without elaborate inquiry as to the precise harm they have caused or the business excuse for their use. This principle of per se unreasonableness not only makes the type of restraints which are proscribed by the Sherman Act more certain to the benefit of everyone concerned, but it also avoids the necessity for an incredibly complicated and prolonged economic investigation into the entire industry involved, as well as related industries, in an effort to determine at large whether a particular restraint has been unreasonable—an inquiry so often wholly fruitless when undertaken.

Northern Pac. Ry. Co. v. United States, 356 U.S. 1, 5 (1958). *See also FTC v. Superior Court Trial Lawyers Ass'n*, 493 U.S. 411, 433–34 (1990) ("In part, the justification for these *per se* rules is rooted in administrative convenience. They are also supported, however, by the observation that every speeder and every stunt pilot poses some threat to the community."). How might you use decision theory, as we discussed in Chapter 1, to support these arguments?

We will return to consider the operation and rationale for per se analysis in Sidebar 2–4. For now, as we proceed through the Chapter, consider how per se analysis under the rule of reason has evolved. How is it used and when? How much and what kind of evidence is present when it is invoked? Under what circumstances is it triggered by demonstrating the presence of a particular kind of pernicious agreement? Under what circumstances has the Court declined to invoke it, and why?

3. TRANSITIONING TO MODERN ECONOMIC ANALYSIS: FIRST PRINCIPLES

The breadth of the Court's decision in *Socony-Vacuum Oil* and its seemingly unequivocal condemnation of all forms of price-fixing posed some challenging questions for antitrust doctrine. It seemed to leave little room—and no rationale—for justifying common arrangements such as partnerships and joint ventures that "fix" prices as an incident to their integration. Thereafter, proof of a price fixing agreement alone arguably was sufficient to establish an offense under Section 1, and the only practical hope of avoiding condemnation was to have the challenged conduct classified as something other than "price fixing." This seemed to be in tension with *Chicago Board of Trade* and could be a difficult task, as "price-fixing" was being construed broadly by the courts. *See, e.g., Nat'l Macaroni Mfrs. Ass'n v. FTC*, 345 F.2d 421 (7th Cir. 1965) (agreement among rivals to reduce product quality—which could have the effect of lowering the price that the firms paid for a key production input or raising the effective (quality-adjusted) price of their output—was per se unlawful under *Socony*, even though the firms never discussed price).

At the same time, despite the Court's seemingly unequivocal language in both *Trenton Potteries* and *Socony-Vacuum Oil*, both decisions appeared to rely on extensive record evidence of market structure, market power, and competitive effects, at least raising a question about the potency of the Court's assertion in *Socony-Vacuum Oil* that proof of market power and actual anticompetitive effects was not required. With *Chicago Board of Trade* and *Appalachian Coals* also in the mix, there remained some lack of clarity as to the rule of reason's core concerns and its ability to make more nuanced judgments.

The Supreme Court's reliance on per se analysis reached a high point in *United States v. Topco Associates, Inc.*, 405 U.S. 596 (1972), a case that involved a practice called "market division," which we will discuss later in this Chapter. Reflecting the prevailing view of the Court majority at the time, the Court explained its reliance on per se analysis:

> Whether or not we would decide this case the same way under the rule of reason used by the District Court is irrelevant to the issue before us. The fact is that courts are of limited utility in

examining difficult economic problems.[10] Our inability to weigh, in any meaningful sense, destruction of competition in one sector of the economy against promotion of competition in another sector is one important reason we have formulated *per se* rules.

Id. at 609–10. Chief Justice Warren Burger dissented, foreshadowing the Court's later rejection of rigid application of per se analysis and its endorsement of the need to evaluate economic effects, especially efficiencies:

> With all respect, I believe that there are two basic fallacies in the Court's approach here. First, while I would not characterize our role under the Sherman Act as one of "rambl[ing] through the wilds," it is indeed one that requires our "examin[ation of] difficult economic problems." We can undoubtedly ease our task, but we should not abdicate that role by formulation of *per se* rules with no justification other than the enhancement of predictability and the reduction of judicial investigation. Second, from the general proposition that *per se* rules play a necessary role in antitrust law, it does not follow that the particular *per se* rule promulgated today is an appropriate one. Although it might well be desirable in a proper case for this Court to formulate a *per se* rule dealing with horizontal territorial limitations, it would not necessarily be appropriate for such a rule to amount to a blanket prohibition against all such limitations.

Id. at 622 (BURGER, C.J., dissenting).

Antitrust law entered its modern era in the late 1970s with several cases that sought to respond to the kind of issues that divided the Court in *Topco* and the mixed legacy of its early years, which had by that time been subjected to criticism by commentators. We next turn to two of the cases that focused on agreements between competitors. In *National Society of Professional Engineers*, the Court more firmly grounded the rule of reason, and federal antitrust law more generally, in concerns about competitive effects. And a year later, in *Broadcast Music, Inc.*, the Court sought to adjust for the potential excesses of *Socony-Vacuum Oil's* undiscriminating approach to agreements between competitors that affected price. Together, these two cases established the framework for modern analysis of all such agreements.

---

[10] * * * Without the *per se* rules, businessmen would be left with little to aid them in predicting in any particular case what courts will find to be legal and illegal under the Sherman Act. Should Congress ultimately determine that predictability is unimportant in this area of the law, it can, of course, make *per se* rules inapplicable in some or all cases, and leave courts free to ramble through the wilds of economic theory in order to maintain a flexible approach.

NATIONAL SOCIETY OF PROFESSIONAL ENGINEERS V. UNITED STATES

Supreme Court of the United States, 1978.
435 U.S. 679, 98 S.Ct. 1355, 55 L.Ed.2d 637.

MR. JUSTICE STEVENS delivered the opinion of the Court.

This is a civil antitrust case brought by the United States to nullify an association's canon of ethics prohibiting competitive bidding by its members. The question is whether the canon may be justified under the Sherman Act, because it was adopted by members of a learned profession for the purpose of minimizing the risk that competition would produce inferior engineering work endangering the public safety. The District Court rejected this justification without making any findings on the likelihood that competition would produce the dire consequences foreseen by the association. The Court of Appeals affirmed. * * * Because we are satisfied that the asserted defense rests on a fundamental misunderstanding of the Rule of Reason frequently applied in antitrust litigation, we affirm.

I

Engineering is an important and learned profession. There are over 750,000 graduate engineers in the United States, of whom about 325,000 are registered as professional engineers. * * * They perform services in connection with the study, design, and construction of all types of improvements to real property—bridges, office buildings, airports, and factories are examples. * * *

The National Society of Professional Engineers (Society) was organized in 1935 to deal with the nontechnical aspects of engineering practice, including the promotion of the professional, social, and economic interests of its members. Its present membership of 69,000 resides throughout the United States and in some foreign countries. * * *

The charges of a consulting engineer may be computed in different ways. He may charge the client a percentage of the cost of the project, may set his fee at his actual cost plus overhead plus a reasonable profit, may charge fixed rates per hour for different types of work, may perform an assignment for a specific sum, or he may combine one or more of these approaches. Suggested fee schedules for particular types of services in certain areas have been promulgated from time to time by various local societies. This case does not, however, involve any claim that the National Society has tried to fix specific fees, or even a specific method of calculating fees. It involves a charge that the members of the Society have unlawfully agreed to refuse to negotiate or even to discuss the question of fees until after a prospective client has selected the engineer for a particular project.

Evidence of this agreement is found in § 11(c) of the Society's Code of Ethics, adopted in July 1964.[3]

* * *

In 1972 the Government filed its complaint against the Society alleging that members had agreed to abide by canons of ethics prohibiting the submission of competitive bids for engineering services and that, in consequence, price competition among the members had been suppressed and customers had been deprived of the benefits of free and open competition. The complaint prayed for an injunction terminating the unlawful agreement.

In its answer the Society admitted the essential facts alleged by the Government and pleaded a series of affirmative defenses, only one of which remains in issue. In that defense, the Society averred that the standard set out in the Code of Ethics was reasonable because competition among professional engineers was contrary to the public interest. It was averred that it would be cheaper and easier for an engineer "to design and specify inefficient and unnecessarily expensive structures and methods of construction." * * * Accordingly, competitive pressure to offer engineering services at the lowest possible price would adversely affect the quality of engineering. Moreover, the practice of awarding engineering contracts to the lowest bidder, regardless of quality, would be dangerous to the public health, safety, and welfare. For these reasons, the Society claimed that its Code of Ethics was not an "unreasonable restraint of interstate trade or commerce."

* * *

II

* * *

A.   The Rule of Reason

One problem presented by the language of § 1 of the Sherman Act is that it cannot mean what it says. The statute says that "every" contract that restrains trade is unlawful. * * * But, as Mr. Justice Brandeis perceptively noted [in *Chicago Bd. of Trade*], restraint is the very essence of every contract; * * * read literally, § 1 would outlaw the entire body of private contract law. Yet it is that body of law that establishes the enforceability of commercial agreements and enables competitive markets—indeed, a competitive economy—to function effectively.

---

[3]   That section, which remained in effect at the time of trial, provided:

"Section 11—The Engineer will not compete unfairly with another engineer by attempting to obtain employment or advancement or professional engagements by competitive bidding. * * *

c.   He shall not solicit or submit engineering proposals on the basis of competitive bidding. * * *

Congress, however, did not intend the text of the Sherman Act to delineate the full meaning of the statute or its application in concrete situations. The legislative history makes it perfectly clear that it expected the courts to give shape to the statute's broad mandate by drawing on common-law tradition. The Rule of Reason, with its origins in common-law precedents long antedating the Sherman Act, has served that purpose. It has been used to give the Act both flexibility and definition, and its central principle of antitrust analysis has remained constant. Contrary to its name, the Rule does not open the field of antitrust inquiry to any argument in favor of a challenged restraint that may fall within the realm of reason. Instead, it focuses directly on the challenged restraint's impact on competitive conditions.

* * *

The Rule of Reason * * * has been regarded as a standard for testing the enforceability of covenants in restraint of trade which are ancillary to a legitimate transaction, such as an employment contract or the sale of a going business. Judge (later Mr. Chief Justice) Taft so interpreted the Rule in his classic rejection of the argument that competitors may lawfully agree to sell their goods at the same price as long as the agreed-upon price is reasonable. *United States v. Addyston Pipe & Steel Co.* That case, and subsequent decisions by this Court, unequivocally foreclose an interpretation of the Rule as permitting an inquiry into the reasonableness of the prices set by private agreement.

The early cases also foreclose the argument that because of the special characteristics of a particular industry, monopolistic arrangements will better promote trade and commerce than competition. That kind of argument is properly addressed to Congress and may justify an exemption from the statute for specific industries, but it is not permitted by the Rule of Reason. * * *

The test prescribed in *Standard Oil* is whether the challenged contracts or acts "were unreasonably restrictive of competitive conditions." Unreasonableness under that test could be based either (1) on the nature or character of the contracts, or (2) on surrounding circumstances giving rise to the inference or presumption that they were intended to restrain trade and enhance prices. * * * Under either branch of the test, the inquiry is confined to a consideration of impact on competitive conditions.

In this respect the Rule of Reason has remained faithful to its origins. From Mr. Justice Brandeis' opinion for the Court in *Chicago Board of Trade* [in 1918], to the Court opinion written by Mr. Justice Powell in *Continental T. V., Inc.* [in 1977], the Court has adhered to the position that the inquiry mandated by the Rule of Reason is whether the challenged agreement is one that promotes competition or one that suppresses competition. "The true test of legality is whether the restraint imposed is such as merely regulates and perhaps thereby promotes competition or whether it is such as may suppress or even destroy competition." [*Chicago Bd. of Trade*,] 246 U.S. at 238.

There are, thus, two complementary categories of antitrust analysis. In the first category are agreements whose nature and necessary effect are so plainly anticompetitive that no elaborate study of the industry is needed to establish their illegality—they are "illegal *per se*." In the second category are agreements whose competitive effect can only be evaluated by analyzing the facts peculiar to the business, the history of the restraint, and the reasons why it was imposed. In either event, the purpose of the analysis is to form a judgment about the competitive significance of the restraint; it is not to decide whether a policy favoring competition is in the public interest, or in the interest of the members of an industry. Subject to exceptions defined by statute, that policy decision has been made by the Congress.

B.   The Ban on Competitive Bidding

Price is the "central nervous system of the economy," and an agreement that "interfere[s] with the setting of price by free market forces" is illegal on its face. In this case we are presented with an agreement among competitors to refuse to discuss prices with potential customers until after negotiations have resulted in the initial selection of an engineer. While this is not price fixing as such, no elaborate industry analysis is required to demonstrate the anticompetitive character of such an agreement. It operates as an absolute ban on competitive bidding, applying with equal force to both complicated and simple projects and to both inexperienced and sophisticated customers. As the District Court found, the ban "impedes the ordinary give and take of the market place," and substantially deprives the customer of "the ability to utilize and compare prices in selecting engineering services." On its face, this agreement restrains trade within the meaning of § 1 of the Sherman Act.

The Society's affirmative defense confirms rather than refutes the anticompetitive purpose and effect of its agreement. The Society argues that the restraint is justified because bidding on engineering services is inherently imprecise, would lead to deceptively low bids, and would thereby tempt individual engineers to do inferior work with consequent risk to public safety and health.[19] The logic of this argument rests on the

---

[19] The Society also points out that competition, in the form of bargaining between the engineer and customer, is allowed under its canon of ethics once an engineer has been initially selected. It then contends that its prohibition of competitive bidding regulates only the *timing* of competition, thus making this case analogous to *Chicago Board of Trade*. * * * We find this reliance on *Chicago Board of Trade* misplaced for two reasons. First, petitioner's claim mistakenly treats negotiation between a single seller and a single buyer as the equivalent of competition between two or more potential sellers. Second, even if we were to accept the Society's equation of bargaining with price competition, our concern with *Chicago Board of Trade* is in its formulation of the proper

assumption that the agreement will tend to maintain the price level; if it had no such effect, it would not serve its intended purpose. The Society nonetheless invokes the Rule of Reason, arguing that its restraint on price competition ultimately inures to the public benefit by preventing the production of inferior work and by insuring ethical behavior. As the preceding discussion of the Rule of Reason reveals, this Court has never accepted such an argument.

It may be, as petitioner argues, that competition tends to force prices down and that an inexpensive item may be inferior to one that is more costly. There is some risk, therefore, that competition will cause some suppliers to market a defective product. Similarly, competitive bidding for engineering projects may be inherently imprecise and incapable of taking into account all the variables which will be involved in the actual performance of the project. Based on these considerations, a purchaser might conclude that his interest in quality—which may embrace the safety of the end product—outweighs the advantages of achieving cost savings by pitting one competitor against another. Or an individual vendor might independently refrain from price negotiation until he has satisfied himself that he fully understands the scope of his customers' needs. These decisions might be reasonable; indeed, petitioner has provided ample documentation for that thesis. But these are not reasons that satisfy the Rule; nor are such individual decisions subject to antitrust attack.

The Sherman Act does not require competitive bidding; it prohibits unreasonable restraints on competition. Petitioner's ban on competitive bidding prevents all customers from making price comparisons in the initial selection of an engineer, and imposes the Society's views of the costs and benefits of competition on the entire marketplace. It is this restraint that must be justified under the Rule of Reason, and petitioner's attempt to do so on the basis of the potential threat that competition poses to the public safety and the ethics of its profession is nothing less than a frontal assault on the basic policy of the Sherman Act.

The Sherman Act reflects a legislative judgment that ultimately competition will produce not only lower prices, but also better goods and services. "The heart of our national economic policy long has been faith in the value of competition." The assumption that competition is the best method of allocating resources in a free market recognizes that all elements of a bargain—quality, service, safety, and durability—and not just the immediate cost, are favorably affected by the free opportunity to select among alternative offers. Even assuming occasional exceptions to the

---

test to be used in judging the legality of an agreement; that formulation unquestionably stresses impact on competition. Whatever one's view of the application of the Rule of Reason in that case, the Court considered the exchange's regulation of price information as having a positive effect on competition. The District Court's findings preclude a similar conclusion concerning the effect of the Society's "regulation."

presumed consequences of competition, the statutory policy precludes inquiry into the question whether competition is good or bad.

* * *

* * * We adhere to the view * * * that, by their nature, professional services may differ significantly from other business services, and, accordingly, the nature of the competition in such services may vary. Ethical norms may serve to regulate and promote this competition, and thus fall within the Rule of Reason. But the Society's argument in this case is a far cry from such a position. We are faced with a contention that a total ban on competitive bidding is necessary because otherwise engineers will be tempted to submit deceptively low bids. Certainly, the problem of professional deception is a proper subject of an ethical canon. But, once again, the equation of competition with deception, like the similar equation with safety hazards, is simply too broad; we may assume that competition is not entirely conducive to ethical behavior, but that is not a reason, cognizable under the Sherman Act, for doing away with competition.

In sum, the Rule of Reason does not support a defense based on the assumption that competition itself is unreasonable. Such a view of the Rule would create the "sea of doubt" on which Judge Taft refused to embark in *Addyston*, and which this Court has firmly avoided ever since.

* * *

[Justice Brennan took no part in the consideration or decision of the case. The opinion of Mr. Justice Blackmun, with whom Mr. Justice Rehnquist joined, concurring in part and concurring in the judgment, is omitted, as is the opinion of Mr. Chief Justice Burger, concurring in part and dissenting in part. Eds.]

Suppose the NSPE had evidence that when engineers engaged in competitive bidding, the buildings and bridges they helped to build were more likely to have safety problems. For example, suppose—contrary to fact—that the NSPE only had members in half of the states, and it proffered an expert witness prepared to testify that in the 50% of states where the Society's Code of Ethics did not apply engineering services were lower in quality as well as lower in price. Should the NSPE have been permitted to introduce the expert's testimony? Why or why not?

Note that Justice Stevens' opinion restates several times that the focus of the inquiry under the rule of reason is impact of the challenged conduct on "competitive conditions." Why did the Court emphasize this repeatedly and what are its implications? What alternative focus might there be? Might the Court have been trying to focus the rule of reason on economic considerations and put to rest Judge Taft's concern that the rule of reason would permit any manner of "reasonableness" defense?

Consider, too, the Court's explanation of the relationship between per se analysis and the rule of reason. Per se analysis is discussed under the heading "Rule of Reason." And the Court describes "per se" and "rule of reason" not as two distinct "rules," but as "two complementary categories of antitrust analysis." The per se category covers "agreements whose nature and necessary effect are so plainly anticompetitive that no elaborate study of the industry is needed to establish their illegality;" in the second category are "agreements whose competitive effect can only be evaluated by analyzing the facts peculiar to the business, the history of the restraint, and the reasons why it was imposed," a reference to the *Chicago Board of Trade* factors. It notes that under both categories "the purpose of the analysis is to form a judgment about the competitive significance of the restraint." *NSPE* thus illustrates that there is no "per se *rule*" that stands apart from the rule of reason, but rather that per se *analysis* is but one way to apply the rule of reason. Figure 2–3 depicts this relationship. We will return to this point when we read the Court's opinions in *National Collegiate Athletic Association* and *California Dental Association* later in this Chapter.

Figure 2–3:

Visualizing the Dichotomous ("Bi-Polar") Rule of Reason

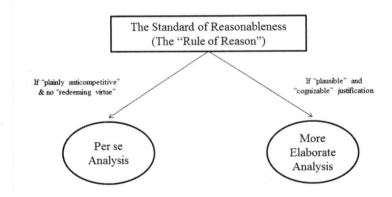

What approach did the Court take to conclude that the NSPE's ban on competitive bidding was an unreasonable restraint of trade? Did the court find it per se unlawful? Did it extend its analysis further to consider evidence of the ban's competitive effects and on NSPE's justifications? Or did it blend together features of the two "categories" of analysis, suggesting that they are less distinct than the Court's description might indicate? *Contrast Arizona v. Maricopa Cnty. Med. Soc'y*, 457 U.S. 332, 362 (1982) ("[I]n *National Society of Professional Engineers v. United States* . . . we held unlawful as a *per se* violation an engineering association's canon of ethics that prohibited competitive bidding by its members."), *with FTC v. Ind. Fed'n of Dentists*, 476 U.S. 447, 458 (1986) ("[W]e have been slow to condemn rules adopted by professional associations as unreasonable *per se*, see *National Society of Professional Engineers v. United States. . . .*"). What was the import of the Court's observation that NSPE's assertion that the ban was necessary to protect public safety was "nothing less than a frontal assault on the basic policy of the Sherman Act"?

In the Supreme Court term following *National Society of Professional Engineers*, the Court again visited the meaning and scope of the rule of reason. Recall that *Socony-Vacuum Oil* defined price-fixing very broadly, leaving little room for cooperating firms to argue that their conduct, once so characterized, was reasonable. In our next case, *Broadcast Music, Inc. v. Columbia Broadcasting System, Inc.*, 441 U.S. 1 (1979), the Court confronted the legacy of *Socony-Vacuum Oil*, concluding that not all practices that literally involve price-fixing are fairly characterized as "per se unlawful price-fixing."

As you read the decision, carefully consider the Court's reasons for doing so, and the prior cases that might support its departure from an arguably inflexible approach to price-fixing. What rationale prompts the Court to de-classify the blanket licensing arrangement challenged in *Broadcast Music,* Inc. as "price-fixing" and what are its broader implications for antitrust analysis? How does it reflect the Court's admonition in *National Society of Professional Engineer* that application of the Sherman Act should be guided by an assessment of competitive effect? More broadly, what does the decision teach us about how to apply the rule of reason once it has been determined that per se analysis should not apply to the conduct?

BROADCAST MUSIC, INC. v. COLUMBIA BROADCASTING SYSTEM, INC.

Supreme Court of the United States, 1979.
441 U.S. 1, 99 S.Ct. 1551, 60 L.Ed.2d 1.

MR. JUSTICE WHITE delivered the opinion of the Court.

This case involves an action under the antitrust and copyright laws brought by respondent Columbia Broadcasting System, Inc. (CBS), against petitioners, American Society of Composers, Authors and Publishers (ASCAP) and Broadcast Music, Inc. (BMI), and their members and affiliates. * * * The basic question presented is whether the issuance by ASCAP and BMI to CBS of blanket licenses to copyrighted musical compositions at fees negotiated by them is price fixing *per se* unlawful under the antitrust laws.

CBS operates one of three national commercial television networks,[1] supplying programs to approximately 200 affiliated stations and telecasting approximately 7,500 network programs per year. Many, but not all, of these programs make use of copyrighted music recorded on the soundtrack. CBS also owns television and radio stations in various cities.

* * *

I

Since 1897, the copyright laws have vested in the owner of a copyrighted musical composition the exclusive right to perform the work publicly for profit, * * * but the legal right is not self-enforcing. In 1914, Victor Herbert and a handful of other composers organized ASCAP because those who performed copyrighted music for profit were so numerous and widespread, and most performances so fleeting, that as a practical matter it was impossible for the many individual copyright owners to negotiate with and license the users and to detect unauthorized uses. * * * As ASCAP operates today, its 22,000 members grant it nonexclusive rights to license nondramatic performances of their works, and ASCAP issues licenses and distributes royalties to copyright owners in accordance with a schedule reflecting the nature and amount of the use of their music and other factors.

* * *

BMI, a nonprofit corporation owned by members of the broadcasting industry * * * was organized in 1939, [and] is affiliated with or represents some 10,000 publishing companies and 20,000 authors and composers, and operates in much the same manner as ASCAP. Almost every domestic copyrighted composition is in the repertory either of ASCAP, with a total of three million compositions, or of BMI, with one million.

Both organizations operate primarily through blanket licenses, which give the licensees the right to perform any and all of the compositions owned by the members or affiliates as often as the licensees desire for a stated term. Fees for blanket licenses are ordinarily a percentage of total revenues or a flat dollar amount, and do not directly depend on the amount or type of music used. Radio and television broadcasters are the largest users of music, and almost all of them hold blanket licenses from both ASCAP and BMI. Until this litigation, CBS held blanket licenses from both organizations for its television network on a continuous basis since the late

---

[1] [At the time of the action there were three principal national commercial television networks, the American Broadcasting Company ("ABC"), the Columbia Broadcasting System ("CBS"), and the National Broadcasting Company ("NBC"). Eds.]

1940's and had never attempted to secure any other form of license from either ASCAP * * * or any of its members.

* * *

The complaint filed by CBS charged * * * that ASCAP and BMI are unlawful monopolies and that the blanket license is illegal price fixing, an unlawful tying arrangement, a concerted refusal to deal, and a misuse of copyrights. The District Court, though denying summary judgment to certain defendants, ruled that the practice did not fall within the *per se* rule. * * * After an 8-week trial, limited to the issue of liability, the court dismissed the complaint, rejecting again the claim that the blanket license was price fixing and a *per se* violation of § 1 of the Sherman Act, and holding that since direct negotiation with individual copyright owners is available and feasible there is no undue restraint of trade. * * *

* * *

Though agreeing with the District Court's factfinding and not disturbing its legal conclusions on the other antitrust theories of liability * * * the Court of Appeals held that the blanket license issued to television networks was a form of price fixing illegal *per se* under the Sherman Act.

* * *

Because we disagree with the Court of Appeals' conclusions with respect to the *per se* illegality of the blanket license, we reverse its judgment and remand the cause for further appropriate proceedings.

II

In construing and applying the Sherman Act's ban against contracts, conspiracies, and combinations in restraint of trade, the Court has held that certain agreements or practices are so "plainly anticompetitive," and so often "lack ... any redeeming virtue," that they are conclusively presumed illegal without further examination under the rule of reason generally applied in Sherman Act cases. This *per se* rule is a valid and useful tool of antitrust policy and enforcement.[11] And agreements among competitors to fix prices on their individual goods or services are among those concerted activities that the Court has held to be within the *per se* category. But easy labels do not always supply ready answers.

---

[11] "This principle of per se unreasonableness not only makes the type of restraints which are proscribed by the Sherman Act more certain to the benefit of everyone concerned, but it also avoids the necessity for an incredibly complicated and prolonged economic investigation into the entire history of the industry involved, as well as related industries, in an effort to determine at large whether a particular restraint has been unreasonable—an inquiry so often wholly fruitless when undertaken." *Northern Pac. R. Co. v. United States.* * * *

A

To the Court of Appeals and CBS, the blanket license involves "price fixing" in the literal sense: the composers and publishing houses have joined together into an organization that sets its price for the blanket license it sells. But this is not a question simply of determining whether two or more potential competitors have literally "fixed" a "price." As generally used in the antitrust field, "price fixing" is a shorthand way of describing certain categories of business behavior to which the *per se* rule has been held applicable. The Court of Appeals' literal approach does not alone establish that this particular practice is one of those types or that it is "plainly anticompetitive" and very likely without "redeeming virtue." Literalness is overly simplistic and often overbroad. When two partners set the price of their goods or services they are literally "price fixing," but they are not *per se* in violation of the Sherman Act. *See United States v. Addyston Pipe & Steel Co.*, 85 F. 271, 280 (C.A.6 1898), *aff'd*, 175 U.S. 211, 20 S.Ct. 96, 44 L.Ed. 136 (1899). Thus, it is necessary to characterize the challenged conduct as falling within or without that category of behavior to which we apply the label "*per se* price fixing." That will often, but not always, be a simple matter.

Consequently, * * * "[i]t is only after considerable experience with certain business relationships that courts classify them as *per se* violations. . . ." We have never examined a practice like this one before. * * * And though there has been rather intensive antitrust scrutiny of ASCAP and its blanket licenses, that experience hardly counsels that we should outlaw the blanket license as a *per se* restraint of trade.

B

* * *

[Here the Court noted that the Department of Justice's Antitrust Division had previously challenged ASCAP's licensing practices under the Sherman Act. That litigation concluded with the entry of a consent decree in 1941 that was amended in 1950. Under the amended decree, which was still in effect at the time of this case, ASCAP's members were permitted to grant ASCAP only nonexclusive rights to license their works for public performance, retaining the "rights individually to license public performances, along with the rights to license the use of their compositions for other purposes." The decree also prohibited ASCAP from insisting that licensees accept the blanket license, and provided that "the fee for the per-program license * * * must offer the applicant a genuine economic choice between the per-program license and the more common blanket license." The Court further noted that "the blanket license continues to be the primary instrument through which ASCAP conducts its business under the decree" and that "[t]he courts have twice construed the decree not to require ASCAP to issue licenses for selected portions of its repertory." It observed that "the decree guarantees the legal availability of direct licensing of performance rights by ASCAP members" and noted that the lower courts had agreed "that there are no practical impediments preventing direct dealing by the television networks if they so desire. Historically, they have not done so. Since 1946, CBS and other television networks have taken blanket licenses from ASCAP and BMI. It was not until this suit arose that the CBS network demanded any other kind of license." Eds.]

* * * In these circumstances, we have a unique indicator that the challenged practice may have redeeming competitive virtues and that the search for those values is not almost sure to be in vain. Thus, although CBS is not bound by the Antitrust Division's actions, the decree is a fact of economic and legal life in this industry, and the Court of Appeals should not have ignored it completely in analyzing the practice. That fact alone might not remove a naked price-fixing scheme from the ambit of the *per se* rule, but * * * here we are uncertain whether the practice on its face has the effect, or could have been spurred by the purpose, of restraining competition among the individual composers.

* * *

III

* * *

As a preliminary matter, we are mindful that the Court of Appeals' holding would appear to be quite difficult to contain. If, as the court held, there is a *per se* antitrust violation whenever ASCAP issues a blanket license to a television network for a single fee, why would it not also be automatically illegal for ASCAP to negotiate and issue blanket licenses to individual radio or television stations or to other users who perform copyrighted music for profit? Likewise, if the present network licenses issued through ASCAP on behalf of its members are *per se* violations, why would it not be equally illegal for the members to authorize ASCAP to issue licenses establishing various categories of uses that a network might have for copyrighted music and setting a standard fee for each described use?

Although the Court of Appeals apparently thought the blanket license could be saved in some or even many applications, it seems to us that the *per se* rule does not accommodate itself to such flexibility and that the observations of the Court of Appeals with respect to remedy tend to impeach the *per se* basis for the holding of liability.[27]

---

[27] * * * The Court of Appeals would apparently not outlaw the blanket license across the board but would permit it in various circumstances where it is deemed necessary or sufficiently desirable. It did not even enjoin blanket licensing with the television networks, the relief it realized would normally follow a finding of *per se* illegality of the license in that context. Instead, as requested by CBS, it remanded to the District Court to require ASCAP to offer in addition to

CBS would prefer that ASCAP be authorized, indeed directed, to make all its compositions available at standard per-use rates within negotiated categories of use. But if this in itself or in conjunction with blanket licensing constitutes illegal price fixing by copyright owners, CBS urges that an injunction issue forbidding ASCAP to issue any blanket license or to negotiate any fee except on behalf of an individual member for the use of his own copyrighted work or works. Thus, we are called upon to determine that blanket licensing is unlawful across the board. We are quite sure, however, that the *per se* rule does not require any such holding.

B

In the first place, the line of commerce allegedly being restrained, the performing rights to copyrighted music, exists at all only because of the copyright laws. Those who would use copyrighted music in public performances must secure consent from the copyright owner. * * * Furthermore, nothing in the Copyright Act of 1976 indicates in the slightest that Congress intended to weaken the rights of copyright owners to control the public performance of musical compositions. Quite the contrary is true. Although the copyright laws confer no rights on copyright owners to fix prices among themselves or otherwise to violate the antitrust laws, we would not expect that any market arrangements reasonably necessary to effectuate the rights that are granted would be deemed a *per se* violation of the Sherman Act. * * *

C

More generally, in characterizing this conduct under the *per se* rule[33] our inquiry must focus on whether the effect and, here because it tends to show effect, the purpose of the practice are to threaten the proper operation of our predominantly free-market economy—that is, whether the practice facially appears to be one that would always or almost always tend to restrict competition and decrease output, and in what portion of the market, or instead one designed to "increase economic efficiency and render markets more, rather than less, competitive."

---

blanket licensing some competitive form of per-use licensing. But per-use licensing by ASCAP, as recognized in the consent decrees, might be even more susceptible to the *per se* rule than blanket licensing.

The rationale for this unusual relief in a *per se* case was that "[t]he blanket license is not simply a 'naked restraint' ineluctably doomed to extinction." To the contrary, the Court of Appeals found that the blanket license might well "serve a market need" for some. *Ibid.* This, it seems to us, is not the *per se* approach, which does not yield so readily to circumstances, but in effect is a rather bobtailed application of the rule of reason, bobtailed in the sense that it is unaccompanied by the necessary analysis demonstrating why the particular licensing system is an undue competitive restraint.

[33] The scrutiny occasionally required must not merely subsume the burdensome analysis required under the rule of reason, or else we should apply the rule of reason from the start. That is why the *per se* rule is not employed until after considerable experience with the type of challenged restraint.

The blanket license, as we see it, is not a "naked restrain[t] of trade with no purpose except stifling of competition," but rather accompanies the integration of sales, monitoring, and enforcement against unauthorized copyright use. As we have already indicated, ASCAP and the blanket license developed together out of the practical situation in the marketplace: thousands of users, thousands of copyright owners, and millions of compositions. Most users want unplanned, rapid, and indemnified access to any and all of the repertory of compositions, and the owners want a reliable method of collecting for the use of their copyrights. Individual sales transactions in this industry are quite expensive, as would be individual monitoring and enforcement, especially in light of the resources of single composers. Indeed, as both the Court of Appeals and CBS recognize, the costs are prohibitive for licenses with individual radio stations, nightclubs, and restaurants, and it was in that milieu that the blanket license arose.

A middleman with a blanket license was an obvious necessity if the thousands of individual negotiations, a virtual impossibility, were to be avoided. Also, individual fees for the use of individual compositions would presuppose an intricate schedule of fees and uses, as well as a difficult and expensive reporting problem for the user and policing task for the copyright owner. Historically, the market for public-performance rights organized itself largely around the single-fee blanket license, which gave unlimited access to the repertory and reliable protection against infringement. * * *

With the advent of radio and television networks, market conditions changed, and the necessity for and advantages of a blanket license for those users may be far less obvious than is the case when the potential users are individual television or radio stations, or the thousands of other individuals and organizations performing copyrighted compositions in public. But even for television network licenses, ASCAP reduces costs absolutely by creating a blanket license that is sold only a few, instead of thousands, of times, and that obviates the need for closely monitoring the networks to see that they do not use more than they pay for. ASCAP also provides the necessary resources for blanket sales and enforcement, resources unavailable to the vast majority of composers and publishing houses. Moreover, a bulk license of some type is a necessary consequence of the integration necessary to achieve these efficiencies, and a necessary consequence of an aggregate license is that its price must be established.

D

This substantial lowering of costs, which is of course potentially beneficial to both sellers and buyers, differentiates the blanket license from individual use licenses. The blanket license is composed of the individual compositions plus the aggregating service. Here, the whole is truly greater than the sum of its parts; it is, to some extent, a different product. The blanket license has certain unique characteristics: It allows the licensee immediate use of covered compositions, without the delay of prior individual negotiations and great flexibility in the choice of musical material. * * * Thus, to the extent the blanket license is a different product, ASCAP is not really a joint sales agency offering the individual goods of many sellers, but is a separate seller offering its blanket license, of which the individual compositions are raw material.[40] ASCAP, in short, made a market in which individual composers are inherently unable to compete fully effectively.

E

Finally, we have some doubt—enough to counsel against application of the *per se* rule—about the extent to which this practice threatens the "central nervous system of the economy," that is, competitive pricing as the free market's means of allocating resources. Not all arrangements among actual or potential competitors that have an impact on price are *per se* violations of the Sherman Act or even unreasonable restraints. Mergers among competitors eliminate competition, including price competition, but they are not *per se* illegal, and many of them withstand attack under any existing antitrust standard. Joint ventures and other cooperative arrangements are also not usually unlawful, at least not as price-fixing schemes, where the agreement on price is necessary to market the product at all.

Here, the blanket-license fee is not set by competition among individual copyright owners, and it is a fee for the use of any of the compositions covered by the license. But the blanket license cannot be wholly equated with a simple horizontal arrangement among competitors. ASCAP does set the price for its blanket license, but that license is quite different from anything any individual owner could issue. The individual composers and authors have neither agreed not to sell individually in any other market nor use the blanket license to mask price fixing in such other markets. Moreover, the substantial restraints placed on ASCAP and its members by the consent decree must not be ignored. The District Court found that there was no legal, practical, or conspiratorial impediment to CBS's obtaining individual licenses; CBS, in short, had a real choice.

With this background in mind, which plainly enough indicates that over the years, and in the face of available alternatives, the blanket license has provided an acceptable mechanism for at least a large part of the market for the performing rights to copyrighted musical compositions, we cannot agree that it should automatically be declared illegal in all of its

---

[40] Moreover, because of the nature of the product—a composition can be simultaneously "consumed" by many users—composers have numerous markets and numerous incentives to produce, so the blanket license is unlikely to cause decreased output, one of the normal undesirable effects of a cartel. And since popular songs get an increased share of ASCAP's revenue distributions, composers compete even within the blanket license in terms of productivity and consumer satisfaction.

many manifestations. Rather, when attacked, it should be subjected to a more discriminating examination under the rule of reason. It may not ultimately survive that attack, but that is not the issue before us today.

* * *

[The opinion of MR. JUSTICE STEVENS, concurring in part and dissenting in part, is omitted. Eds.]

———————

What factors accounted for the Court's conclusion in *Broadcast Music* that the blanket license should not be treated as per se unlawful price-fixing? Is its rationale persuasive? Would the case have fallen comfortably into the per se category if ASCAP and Broadcast Music had together agreed on the prices each would charge for comparable blanket licenses? If the individual composers had adopted a uniform licensing fee schedule for their individual compositions?

Note that the Court remands the case for further proceedings under the rule of reason. Given the extent of the record in the case, as well as the Court's conclusions regarding the nature, purpose and effect of the blanket license, what was left for the court of appeals to do? Could it have reached any conclusion other than that the blanket license was reasonable?

Justice Stevens concurred with the Court majority that the blanket license should not have been treated as per se unlawful. He dissented, in part, however, arguing that in lieu of a remand the Court should have affirmed the court of appeals, albeit on different grounds. He would have reached the analysis of the blanket license and found it to be unreasonable under a more complete rule of reason analysis. 441 U.S. at 25–38 (Stevens, J., concurring in part and dissenting in part). In Stevens' view, ASCAP and Broadcast Music possessed market power, the blanket license resulted in higher prices for many licensees, and joint pricing did not appear to be reasonably necessary to their efforts to monitor use of the copyrighted compositions within their respective repertories. *Id.* at 30–33. Moreover, Stevens rejected the Court's assumption that licenses on a per-composition or per-use basis were too costly to negotiate, arguing that there was no support in the district court's findings for that conclusion. *Id.* at 34. Therefore, in his view, "[s]ince the record describes a market that could be competitive and is not, and since that market is dominated by two firms engaged in a single, blanket method of dealing, it surely seems logical to conclude that trade has been restrained unreasonably." *Id.* Do you find Justice Stevens' points to be persuasive? For the resolution on remand, see *CBS, Inc. v. ASCAP*, 620 F.2d 930 (2d Cir. 1980).

In explaining the origins and purposes of the blanket license, the Supreme Court asserted that "[i]ndividual sales transactions in this industry are quite expensive, as would be individual monitoring and enforcement, especially in light of the resources of single composers." Yet for purposes of assessing the blanket license's impact on competition, the Court also observed that "[t]he District Court found that there was no legal, practical, or conspiratorial impediment to CBS's obtaining individual licenses; CBS, in short, had a real choice." Are these two propositions consistent? Mutually exclusive? How critical was resolution of this question to the rule of reason inquiry? *See CBS, Inc.*, 620 F.2d at 936–38 (discussing feasibility of individual licenses and concluding: " * * * the District Court has found that CBS can feasibly obtain individual licenses from competing copyright owners and that it incurs no risk in endeavoring to do so.").

NOTE ON THE RULE OF REASON AFTER NATIONAL SOCIETY OF PROFESSIONAL ENGINEERS AND BROADCAST MUSIC

The analytical framework described in *National Society of Professional Engineers* ("*NSPE*") had a significant impact on the allocation of the burdens of production and proof in antitrust cases. When per se analysis was applied, plaintiffs needed only to establish concerted action of a kind that fell within one of the recognized per se categories, which expanded from price fixing to include division of markets and certain group boycotts. The courts would then presume that such conduct had the requisite unreasonable anticompetitive effect and preclude the introduction of any justifications. Per se analysis thus created an irrebuttable presumption of unreasonableness.

Under more complete rule of reason analysis, *Chicago Board of Trade*'s approach called for a thorough-going, multi-factored analysis to prove that a given restraint was in fact unreasonable. When *Chicago Board of Trade* was combined with *NSPE*, it appeared that when the "full" (comprehensive) rule of reason was applied, the plaintiff would have to introduce evidence of likely or actual adverse competitive effects and the defendants would be permitted to introduce evidence to rebut the plaintiff's case. The scope of the defendant's rebuttal would not be restricted, provided it was directed at the issue of competitive effect. The Court made clear that "ruinous competition," like "reasonable prices," would not constitute a cognizable defense. Similarly, *NSPE* reaffirmed that defenses rooted in the premise that competition could lead to undesirable results were not cognizable. But beyond this limitation, the specific requirements of burden shifting remained to be addressed.

At least in theory, therefore, it was easier for a plaintiff to prevail using per se analysis than under a more complete rule of reason inquiry. In consequence, a court's determination as to whether the alleged conduct fell within or outside a category of per se conduct—a decision often termed "categorization" of the case—often was outcome determinative. The Court in *NSPE* twice emphasized, however, that under both approaches "the purpose of the analysis is to form a judgment about the competitive significance of the restraint." Even though the "rule of reason" and "per se rule" have at times been described as distinct "rules," as we have already observed, they are better understood as two paths to implementing the same underlying standard, the standard of "reasonableness."

Broadcast Music also provided additional content to the rule of reason. Whereas *NSPE* focused on the anticompetitive side of effects, *BMI* appeared to mandate consideration of pro-competitive efficiencies as well, both in characterizing the conduct to determine whether use of per se analysis was appropriate and, if not, in determining whether competition would be harmed under a more complete examination of the evidence. In so doing, the Court provided important guidance about what kinds of defenses would be cognizable in a rule of reason case. The Court concluded in *Broadcast Music* that the presence of plausible efficiencies—cost reducing and output expanding tendencies—could justify moving a case out from under the per se label.

NSPE and *Broadcast Music*, together with other Supreme Court decisions of the period, combined to reframe antitrust rules around core economic concepts of anticompetitive effect, market power, and efficiencies: (1) the core concern for antitrust was anticompetitive effect; (2) such effects are unlikely to arise absent significant market power; and (3) before condemning conduct, consideration must also be given to its potential to generate efficiencies, such as lower costs and increased output. This constituted a more focused and economically-grounded framework than had existed before and has guided the analysis of competitor agreements ever since.

B. EVOLUTION AND MODERN IMPLEMENTATION OF THE RULE OF REASON

Although the contemporary economic content of the rule of reason began to take shape with *NSPE* and *BMI*, some fundamental questions remained about how it could be administered within the context of the U.S. legal system. Recall, for example, that in our discussion of *Chicago Bd. of Trade*, we noted that the decision broadly identified a range of factors relevant to the rule of reason inquiry, but it did not specify how the courts were to weigh various factors or allocate burdens of pleading, production, and proof. Commentators thus questioned whether it provided a sufficiently clear and predictable basis for deciding cases under the Sherman Act. Given the rule of reason's focus on anticompetitive effect, courts began to ask a series of questions that helped to structure the rule of reason inquiry to address those concerns, especially in the context of litigation:

- What kind and amount of evidence of anticompetitive effect would be sufficient to shift the plaintiff's burden of production (for motions for summary judgment) or proof (for a case at trial) to the defendant?

- Under what circumstances might the courts rely on reasonable inferences and presumptions to do so, rather than proof of actual effects?

- Would those presumptions be rebuttable or irrebuttable?

- Once a burden shifts to a defendant, what kind and amount of evidence of procompetitive effects would be sufficient to shift the burden back to the plaintiff?

- What defenses would be cognizable?

- What defenses may not be cognizable (e.g., "reasonable" prices were set; competition will produce poor quality products or services)?

- How should courts respond when plaintiffs and defendants both provide evidence to support their positions?

In this Section of the Chapter, we will examine how courts have sought to answer these questions under the rule of reason.

1. PROVING ANTICOMPETITIVE EFFECTS BY IRREBUTTABLE PRESUMPTION: PER SE ANALYSIS

In the next three principal cases, we will examine the Supreme Court's use of per se analysis in the modern era. Although these cases have historically been categorized separately as price-fixing, division of markets, and group boycotts, as we shall see, the economic objection to the conduct in each case is the same and the anticompetitive effects comparatively obvious; so is the lack of any cognizable justification for the defendants' conduct. As you read each case, consider what factors led the Court to conclude that the conduct challenged warranted summary treatment using per se analysis. Note, too, that the first two, *Catalano* and *BRG of Georgia*, are *per curiam* decisions, but the third, *Superior Court Trial Lawyers Association* divided the Court. As you read the three cases together, consider what might explain the Court's greater difficulty in deciding that case.

a. Price Fixing

CATALANO, INC. v. TARGET SALES, INC.
Supreme Court of the United States, 1980.
446 U.S. 643, 100 S.Ct. 1925, 64 L.Ed.2d 580.

PER CURIAM.

* * *

* * * Petitioners allege that, beginning in early 1967, respondent [beer] wholesalers secretly agreed, in order to eliminate competition among themselves, that as of December 1967 they would sell to retailers only if payment were made in advance or upon delivery. Prior to the agreement, the wholesalers had extended credit without interest up to the 30-and 42-day limits permitted by state law. According to the petition, prior to the agreement wholesalers had competed with each other with respect to trade credit, and the credit terms for individual retailers had varied substantially. After entering into the agreement, respondents uniformly refused to extend any credit at all.

The Court of Appeals decided that the credit-fixing agreement should not be characterized as a form of price fixing. The court suggested that such an agreement might actually enhance competition in two ways: (1) "by removing a barrier perceived by some sellers to market entry," and (2) "by the increased visibility of price made possible by the agreement to eliminate credit." * * *

In dissent, Judge Blumenfeld expressed the opinion that an agreement to eliminate credit was a form of price fixing. * * * He reasoned that the extension of interest-free credit is an indirect price reduction and that the elimination of such credit is therefore a method of raising prices. * * **

Our cases fully support Judge Blumenfeld's analysis and foreclose both of the possible justifications on which the majority relied.[8] In *Broadcast Music, Inc. v. Columbia Broadcasting System, Inc.*, * * * we said:

> "In construing and applying the Sherman Act's ban against contracts, conspiracies, and combinations in restraint of trade, the Court has held that certain agreements or practices are so 'plainly anticompetitive,' *National Society of Professional Engineers * * *; Continental T. V., Inc. v. GTE Sylvania Inc.*, 433 U.S. 36, 50, 97 S.Ct. 2549, 2557 (1977), and so often 'lack . . . any redeeming virtue,' *Northern Pac. R. Co. v. United States*, 356 U.S. 1, 5, 78 S.Ct. 514, 518, 2 L.Ed.2d 545 (1958), that they are conclusively presumed illegal without further examination under the rule of reason generally applied in Sherman Act cases."[9]

A horizontal agreement to fix prices is the archetypal example of such a practice. It has long been settled that an agreement to fix prices is

---

[8]   Respondents nowhere suggest a procompetitive justification for a horizontal agreement to fix credit. Their argument is confined to disputing that settled case law establishes that such an agreement is unlawful on its face.

[9]   The quotation from *Northern Pacific R. Co.* * * * is drawn from the following passage: "[T]here are certain agreements or practices which because of their pernicious effect on competition and lack of any redeeming virtue are conclusively presumed to be unreasonable and therefore illegal without elaborate inquiry as to the precise harm they have caused or the business excuse for their use. This principle of *per se* unreasonableness not only makes the type of restraints which are proscribed by the Sherman Act more certain to the benefit of everyone concerned, but it also avoids the necessity for an incredibly complicated and prolonged economic investigation . . . -an inquiry so often wholly fruitless when undertaken. Among the practices which the courts have heretofore deemed to be unlawful in and of themselves [is] price fixing. . . ."

unlawful *per se.* It is no excuse that the prices fixed are themselves reasonable. *See, e. g., United States v. Trenton Potteries Co.,* * * * *United States v. Trans-Missouri Freight Assn.,* * * *.* In *United States v. Socony-Vacuum Oil Co.,* * * * we held that an agreement among competitors to engage in a program of buying surplus gasoline on the spot market in order to prevent prices from falling sharply was unlawful without any inquiry into the reasonableness of the program, even though there was no direct agreement on the actual prices to be maintained. In the course of the opinion, the Court made clear that

> "the machinery employed by a combination for price-fixing is immaterial."

> "Under the Sherman Act a combination formed for the purpose and with the effect of raising, depressing, fixing, pegging, or stabilizing the price of a commodity in interstate or foreign commerce is illegal *per se.*" * * *

Thus, we have held agreements to be unlawful *per se* that had substantially less direct impact on price than the agreement alleged in this case. For example, in *Sugar Institute v. United States,* 297 U.S. 553, 601–602, 56 S.Ct. 629, 643, 80 L.Ed. 859 (1936), the Court held unlawful an agreement to adhere to previously announced prices and terms of sale, even though advance price announcements are perfectly lawful and even though the particular prices and terms were not themselves fixed by private agreement. Similarly, an agreement among competing firms of professional engineers to refuse to discuss prices with potential customers until after negotiations have resulted in the initial selection of an engineer was held unlawful without requiring further inquiry. *National Society of Professional Engineers* * * *.* Indeed, a horizontal agreement among competitors to use a specific method of quoting prices may be unlawful. * * *

It is virtually self-evident that extending interest-free credit for a period of time is equivalent to giving a discount equal to the value of the use of the purchase price for that period of time. Thus, credit terms must be characterized as an inseparable part of the price. An agreement to terminate the practice of giving credit is thus tantamount to an agreement to eliminate discounts, and thus falls squarely within the traditional *per se* rule against price fixing. While it may be that the elimination of a practice of giving variable discounts will ultimately lead in a competitive market to corresponding decreases in the invoice price, that is surely not necessarily to be anticipated. It is more realistic to view an agreement to eliminate credit sales as extinguishing one form of competition among the sellers. In any event, when a particular concerted activity entails an obvious risk of anticompetitive impact with no apparent potentially redeeming value, the fact that a practice may turn out to be harmless in a particular set of circumstances will not prevent its being declared unlawful *per se.*

The majority of the panel of the Court of Appeals suggested, however, that a horizontal agreement to eliminate credit sales may remove a barrier to other sellers who may wish to enter the market. But in any case in which competitors are able to increase the price level or to curtail production by agreement, it could be argued that the agreement has the effect of making the market more attractive to potential new entrants. If that potential justifies horizontal agreements among competitors imposing one kind of voluntary restraint or another on their competitive freedom, it would seem to follow that the more successful an agreement is in raising the price level, the safer it is from antitrust attack. Nothing could be more inconsistent with our cases.

Nor can the informing function of the agreement, the increased price visibility, justify its restraint on the individual wholesaler's freedom to select his own prices and terms of sale. For, again, it is obvious that any industrywide agreement on prices will result in a more accurate understanding of the terms offered by all parties to the agreement. * * * * [T]here is a plain distinction between the lawful right to publish prices and terms of sale, on the one hand, and an agreement among competitors limiting action with respect to the published prices, on the other.

Thus, under the reasoning of our cases, an agreement among competing wholesalers to refuse to sell unless the retailer makes payment in cash either in advance or upon delivery is "plainly anticompetitive." Since it is merely one form of price fixing, and since price-fixing agreements have been adjudged to lack any "redeeming virtue," it is conclusively presumed illegal without further examination under the rule of reason.

* * *

Do you agree with the Court's reasoning in *Catalano?* Are credit terms a "component of price," such that an agreement among competitors to limit the extension of credit should be deemed the equivalent of price-fixing? Note how the Court used a combination of the foundation cases we have already studied, such as *Trenton Potteries* and *Socony-Vacuum Oil,* as well as *National Society of Professional Engineers* to support its application of per se analysis. Are there factors present in each of these cases that allow a confident prediction of when the Court will apply per se analysis? Did the Court in *Catalano* make any mention of the defendants' market share or market power? Could they have implemented their plan if they lacked market power?

What evidence supported shifting a burden to the defendants? Once it shifted, did the Court consider and reject the defenses offered on their merits? Conclude that they were not cognizable, such as the quality arguments made in *National Society of Professional Engineers*? If cognizable, why did the defenses fail to persuade the Court? Suppose defendants had rock-solid evidence that no retailer paid a higher total price after the wholesalers stopped offering credit (because the wholesalers invariably discounted the product price by precisely the right amount to compensate). Why not permit the wholesalers to offer that evidence to show that competition was not harmed? We will consider that question again in the next Sidebar.

Two years later, in *Arizona v. Maricopa County Medical Society*, 457 U.S. 332 (1982), the Court again reaffirmed application of the per se rule, but in a decision that, somewhat like *Topco*, is today viewed with skepticism in light of subsequent Court decisions. In the next Sidebar, we discuss the case with the added insights that can be gleaned from the private papers of two of the Supreme Court Justices who were critical to the outcome of the case, Thurgood Marshall and Lewis Powell.

Sidebar 2–1:
Maricopa as Seen Through the
Marshall and Powell Papers

The Decision

In *Maricopa*, the State of Arizona challenged maximum fee agreements among the competing physician members of foundations for medical care that had been organized "to promote fee-for-service medicine and to provide the community with a competitive alternative to existing health insurance plans." 457 U.S. at 332. Under the agreements, members agreed to abide by a schedule of maximum fees they could claim in full payment for health services provided by the policyholders of specified insurance plans. The parties disputed the effect of the fee schedules. Arizona claimed that the periodic upward revisions of the schedules tended to stabilize and increase the rates paid by insurance companies to the physicians, which in turn increased insurance premiums for insureds. The Society countered that the schedules helped to contain costs by imposing meaningful limits on physicians' fees-for-service and allowing the insurance companies to more efficiently and accurately predict their costs, which in turn lowered insurance rates. The membership comprised 70% of the physicians in Maricopa County.

In a 4–3 decision, the Court held that the schedules were per se unlawful price fixing. Justice John Paul Stevens authored the majority opinion. Justice Lewis Powell dissented, joined by Chief Justice Warren Burger, who, you will recall, also dissented in *Topco*, and Justice William Rehnquist. Justices Harry Blackmun and Sandra Day O'Connor took no part in the consideration of the case

Justice Stevens argued that the maximum fee schedules could not be distinguished from the kinds of agreements to set prices that the Court had previously prohibited in cases such as *Trenton Potteries* and *Socony-Vacuum Oil*, but that they *were* different from the blanket license analyzed in *Broadcast Music*. He thus rejected the defendants' argument that per se analysis should not apply:

> The respondents' principal argument is that the *per se* rule is inapplicable because their agreements are alleged to have procompetitive justifications. The argument indicates a misunderstanding of the *per se* concept. The anticompetitive potential inherent in all price-fixing agreements justifies their facial invalidation even if procompetitive justifications are offered for some. Those claims of enhanced competition are so unlikely to prove significant in any particular case that we adhere to the rule of law that is justified in its general application. Even when the respondents are given every benefit of the doubt, the limited record in this case is not inconsistent with the presumption that the respondents' agreements will not significantly enhance competition.

Id. at 351. Stevens further asserted that the Court's "adherence to the *per se* rule is grounded not only on economic prediction, judicial convenience, and business certainty, but also on a recognition of the respective roles of the Judiciary and the Congress in regulating the economy." *Id.* at 354.

Justice Powell viewed the foundation's principal arguments far more favorably, especially their proffered business justifications. In his view, the challenged agreements were novel, arose in an industry with which the Court had little experience, and did not foreclose any competition. In short, they appeared to be reasonable efforts at cost containment. He argued that in the medical services field, insurance companies stand in the shoes of consumers and have every incentive to reduce costs. He found it significant that the insurance companies that had contracted with the Maricopa Foundation had no objections to the fees it set and concluded that the plans benefitted consumers. *See Maricopa*, 457 U.S. at 357–67 (POWELL, J., dissenting).

Powell also was more receptive to the Foundation's arguments based on *Broadcast Music*:

> The Court * * * is content simply to brand this type of plan as "price fixing" and describe the agreement in *Broadcast Music*—which also literally involved the fixing of prices—as "fundamentally different."
>
> In fact, however, the two agreements are similar in important respects. Each involved competitors and resulted in cooperative pricing. Each arrangement also was prompted by the need for better service to the consumers. And each arrangement apparently makes possible a new product by reaping otherwise unattainable efficiencies. The Court's effort to distinguish *Broadcast Music* thus is unconvincing.

Id. at 364–65. Powell's dissent concluded with stern criticism of the majority:

> I believe the Court's action today loses sight of the basic purposes of the Sherman Act. As we have noted, the antitrust laws are a "consumer welfare prescription." In its rush to condemn a novel plan about which it knows very little, the Court suggests that this end is achieved only by invalidating activities that *may* have some potential for harm. But the little that the record does show about the effect of the plan suggests that it is a means of providing medical services that in fact benefits rather than injures persons who need them.
>
> In a complex economy, complex economic arrangements are commonplace. It is unwise for the Court, in a case as novel and important as this one, to make a final judgment in the absence of a complete record and where mandatory inferences create critical issues of fact.

Id. at 367.

The Court's Internal Deliberations

The papers of Justices Thurgood Marshall and Lewis Powell reveal how a case destined for relative obscurity instead exposed a significant rift in the Justices' evolving views of the continued vitality of per se analysis. The skirmish, triggered by an unexpectedly sweeping draft opinion by Justice Powell, thus provides insights into the Court's efforts in the 1970s and 1980s to delineate the role of per se analysis under the rule of reason.

The procedural history of *Maricopa* provides an important backdrop to the Supreme Court's deliberations. In 1979, at the request of the State of Arizona Attorney General, the U.S. District Court for the District of Arizona granted a temporary restraining order to enjoin the defendant physicians' network from implementing a maximum fee-setting arrangement. After a number of months, the district court dissolved the injunction and denied the plaintiff's motion for summary judgment on the question of liability. That motion, filed by the Arizona Attorney General, was premised on the argument that the fee caps constituted a per se illegal horizontal price-fixing agreement.

A divided panel of the U.S. Court of Appeals for the Ninth Circuit affirmed the trial court's ruling. 643 F.2d 553 (9th Cir. 1980). Relying on the Supreme Court's then recent decisions in *National Society of Professional Engineers* and *Broadcast Music*, the court of appeals majority emphasized the need for a full trial to gather and evaluate evidence of the actual purpose and effect of the relatively novel fee-setting agreement. In a concurring opinion, Judge (later Supreme Court Justice) Anthony Kennedy maintained that a fuller factual record was necessary to permit a proper assessment of the challenged restraint, though he cautioned that such an assessment would not necessarily exculpate the arrangement. The dissenting member of the Ninth Circuit panel argued that the restriction fell squarely within the per se ban of *Socony-Vacuum Oil* and, notwithstanding the distinctive circumstances of the market for health care services, warranted condemnation without further inquiry.

The Arizona Attorney General petitioned the Supreme Court for a writ of certiorari, and in 1981 the Court granted the petition. Following briefing and oral argument, the Court met to discuss the case. According to the Marshall and Powell papers, several justices initially expressed second thoughts about having granted certiorari in the first place. Powell's papers indicate that Chief Justice Burger and Justice Marshall were initially "firm votes for a DIG"—the informal acronym for announcing that certiorari has been "dismissed as improvidently granted." They were not alone, however, in expressing concern that the record below provided a sparse factual basis for deciding which legal standard should apply.

With Justices Harry Blackmun and Sandra Day O'Connor recused, only seven remained to decide the case. According to Powell's records, Justices Stevens and Brennan favored reversal, which would reassert the vitality of the per se rule, whereas Justice White "would remand without deciding whether there has been a per se violation or whether the rule of reason is applicable." Powell further indicated that "[b]oth Bill Rehnquist and I expressed views generally similar to those of Byron [White]." A fourth vote was needed to establish a Court majority.

Powell believed that the Chief Justice, who had expressed some interest in the idea of a DIG, could be persuaded in the alternative to remand the case, and on November 21, 1981 Powell wrote to him seeking his support for that approach:

> As we have only a seven member Court, there would be no Court opinion, unless you revert to your alternative vote which—as recorded in my notes—was to remand. You stated that summary judgment had been granted prematurely, and that the record before us is inadequate, a view that appears to be similar to that of Byron [White], Bill Rehnquist and mine.

Justices White and Rehnquist promptly responded in writing that Powell had accurately stated their positions. On November 27, the Chief Justice responded, indicating his support for the approach and asking Powell "to draft a dispositive Per Curiam on this case." A hand written note memorializes a conversation between the Chief Justice and Justice Powell in which they agreed that it would not be a "full opinion." Powell was directed to "keep it short."

But as Powell set about the task of drafting the short opinion that would seal the four-vote pact, he developed concerns about the wisdom of the approach. It would provide little guidance to the district court, which would still have to parse the three opinions generated by the court of appeals. The draft opinion grew to what Powell himself described as a "rather full memorandum" of fifteen single-spaced pages. Although it still left the ultimate disposition of the case to the district court, it reviewed the Court's recent Section 1 jurisprudence and underscored how *Sylvania* and *Broadcast Music* had questioned the analytical rigidity of per se analysis and demanded a more probing evaluation of business practices previously believed to be inimical to the competitive process.

The document appears to have startled several of Powell's colleagues. Justice John Paul Stevens called it a direct assault upon the per se prohibition of naked horizontal restraints. *Maricopa*, he said, was the place for the Court to decide whether the bright lines drawn in *Socony-Vacuum Oil* and nurtured by decades of judicial elaboration retained their vitality. Two days after Powell's draft was circulated, Stevens responded:

> The analysis in your memorandum is somewhat puzzling. If the maximum price fixing arrangement is illegal per se—as I believe it is—I do not understand how any of the three justifications can save it. If you are saying that an arrangement is not a "price fixing" agreement that deserves per se condemnation if the participants are motivated by any purpose except stifling competition, not much will remain of the per se doctrine. In any event, I intend to adhere to the position I took in Conference and will be writing in dissent as soon as I can.

What once seemed to be a case destined for an unremarkable dismissal of certiorari had become a pitched contest over the fundamentals of antitrust doctrine.

To Powell's seeming chagrin, both the Chief Justice and Justice White responded to Steven's promise of an alternate opinion by withholding their immediate support for Powell's draft. When completed, Stevens' "dissent" initially gained the support of Justices William Brennan and Thurgood Marshall. But on April 26, 1982, Justice Byron White (the author of *Broadcast Music*) wrote to Powell: "I have spent considerable time in this case and have decided, contrary to my conference vote, that the Court of Appeals should be reversed." With this fourth vote, Steven's "dissent" had become the majority opinion.

Not only did Stevens, Brennan, Marshall—and now White—oppose Powell's memorandum, but they believed the Court should decide the case on its merits and reverse the Ninth Circuit. Now joined only by the Chief Justice and Justice William Rehnquist, Justice Powell's presumptive majority decision became a dissent based largely upon the draft memorandum that had triggered the Court's internal debate. Four years later, in the context of preparing the majority opinion in *Matsushita* (*see infra* Chapter 3), Powell would write to Justice Rehnquist that "the Court's 4–3 decision in [*Maricopa*] could well be the most erroneous antitrust decision the Court has ever made."

What do the Powell and Marshall papers tell us about *Maricopa*'s significance? Is the decision best understood as an idiosyncratic consequence of efforts by some of the Court's members to control apparent overreaching by one of their colleagues? As you read further in this Chapter and Chapter 6, consider whether the behind the scenes history suggests that the case is an anomaly in a landscape in which *Sylvania* (1977) (*see infra* Chapter 6), *Broadcast Music* (1979), and *NCAA* (1984) (*see infra* Chapter 2) provide the more reliable guideposts to the direction of the Court's Section 1 jurisprudence. Or is *Maricopa* simply an indication that the Court always will strive to preserve a well-delineated zone of per se illegality, even if doing so requires making debatable judgments about certain types of practices? Had Justice Powell simply drafted a one page notice identifying categories of facts for the trial court to consider on remand, would this case (or a case like it) subsequently have made its way back to the Supreme Court—with the same result?

While the Powell and Marshall papers may not give us clear answers to these questions, they do reinforce one point that arguably can be distilled from a reading of the Court's modern Section 1 decisions. A doctrinal framework that seeks to preserve both the substantive and administrative benefits of bright line rules, yet still makes discriminating judgments about the competitive significance of business conduct, is certain to generate continuing debate about whether the bright lines are correctly placed.

We will re-visit the seeming tension between *Maricopa* and *Broadcast Music* later in this Chapter when we read the Supreme Court's decision in *NCAA*. Although at the time it was decided *Maricopa* put into question whether *Broadcast Music* was an anomaly or had significantly altered the law of *Socony-Vacuum Oil*, *NCAA* and later cases like *Dagher*, discussed in our next Note, strongly suggest that *Broadcast Music* was no outlier. Instead, it signaled the beginning of important changes of attitude at the Court about the standards for judging cooperative conduct and, more generally, the role of economic analysis. Today, it is clear that *Broadcast Music* narrowed the traditional per se rule to limit it to naked price-fixing: an agreement among rivals on price with no plausible efficiency justification. Indeed, it is unclear whether today's Supreme Court would still endorse the 4–3 decision in *Maricopa*, or would find Justice Powell's dissent the more persuasive approach.

Many of the cases we have already studied could be labelled "joint ventures," a term that is used to describe a wide range of business forms that involve shared ownership. Often, joint ventures are created through detailed agreements that describe the respective contributions of each of the joint venturers, as well as the benefits they will receive. It is also common for joint venture agreements to include restrictions that may affect competition, such as limitations on the ability of each venture participant to distribute the products of the venture and provisions that limit the use of any intellectual property that has been contributed to or that is generated by the venture. Joint ventures may also have to include provisions for how the price of any jointly produced or distributed product will be established.

The Chicago Board of Trade, the National Society of Professional Engineers, ASCAP and BMI might all be described as "joint ventures" of their members. Should the term also be used to describe cartel behavior, such as that involved in *Socony-Vacuum Oil* and *Catalano*? How can we distinguish joint ventures from cartels? What legal framework should we use to analyze the reasonableness of any specific provisions of a joint venture agreement that affect competition? The next Sidebar explores these questions.

Sidebar 2–2:
Joint Venture Analysis and the Supreme
Court's Decision in *Dagher* (2006)

A Taxonomy of Joint Ventures

The examples of joint ventures we have observed thus far in the Casebook do not exhaust the range of cooperative relationships that can be formed among firms. Although cooperative arrangements are ubiquitous and variable, they generally fall into one of three basic categories: (1) research and development joint ventures; (2) production joint ventures; and (3) distribution (marketing) joint ventures. Any given venture may fall exclusively into one of these categories, or combine features of more than one.

Research and Development ("R & D") Joint Ventures. R & D ventures pool the intellectual and financial resources of firms—often rivals—to pursue the development of new products, processes, or even basic scientific or technical knowledge. They may entail the sharing of an existing facility or funding the creation of a new one. Often, the cost of undertaking such research is daunting for a single firm, and a single firm may lack all of the know-how to pursue the research. Indeed, R & D ventures frequently involve the cross-licensing of intellectual property, such as patents or copyrights, and can lead to the creation of new intellectual property. Such ventures can accelerate the pace of innovation and lead to significant technological breakthroughs, topics that we will explore in greater depth in Chapter 7.

Production Joint Ventures. Production joint ventures involve an undertaking jointly to produce something, typically a new product. As with R & D ventures, production joint ventures may involve sharing production facilities or know-how, or, in combination with R & D, the joint development of new production methods. Production joint ventures may also facilitate the combination of complementary know-how or distribution capabilities. To further encourage R & D joint ventures, and some production ones, Congress has provided some limited exemptions from antitrust coverage in the National Cooperative Research and Production Act of 1993, 15 U.S.C. § 4301.

Distribution Joint Ventures. Distribution or marketing joint ventures combine the capabilities of firms to bring new or existing products or services to market. They may combine, improve upon or expand existing capabilities, or lead to the creation of new capabilities or methods.

All joint ventures share certain critical characteristics that illustrate their procompetitive potential. First, they involve an integration of assets, know-how or both to produce something that none of the venturers could produce on its own, at least not as cost-effectively. Second, they typically involve efficiencies—cost savings or product improvements that flow from combining efforts and sharing risks and costs. Finally, they typically require contractual restraints to ensure that the fruits of the venture are not exploited by one or more of the venturers.

For some of these same reasons, joint ventures can raise antitrust issues. Frequently, they arise between and among rivals. And because they almost always substitute some degree of cooperation for competition, the possibility exists that they will be used directly or indirectly to facilitate anticompetitive coordination of the sort we have examined in this Chapter. They can also provide opportunities to engage in exclusionary conduct. Characterizing the conduct under examination in each case as a "joint venture," therefore, does not help to answer the question whether it is anticompetitive. Indeed, the Supreme Court has reminded firms engaged in coordination that the "joint venture" label offers no immunity from antitrust scrutiny where competitive concerns are raised. *See, e.g., Timken*, 341 U.S. at 597–98.

Evaluating joint ventures thus requires an appreciation for the kinds of anticompetitive effects associated with different kinds of collaborations and the legal framework necessary to distinguish the legitimate from the illegitimate. As we have been learning, anticompetitive conduct can be usefully categorized as collusive or exclusionary. This is true as well for joint ventures.

Possible Anticompetitive Effects of Joint Ventures

In applying the collusive/exclusionary framework to joint ventures, it is useful to separately consider joint venture *formation* and *operation*. As is illustrated in Figure 2–2, the formation alone of a joint venture can lead to collusive or exclusionary effects. By combining the research, production, or marketing capabilities of competing firms that collectively possess market power, a joint venture can substitute joint for individual action—cooperation for competition. It can serve, therefore, as a vehicle for setting prices, reducing innovation, or restricting some other dimension of competition, just as the "trusts" once did. Competition among multiple joint ventures could be sufficient to protect buyers from non-competitive prices, however, even if each venture sets its own price and makes its own decisions about production and distribution.

Joint ventures also can involve a risk of harmful "spill over" effects. Ventures with entirely laudable goals can produce anticompetitive effects that surface as the rivals engage in direct conversation and cooperation. It may be difficult to confine such conversation to the legitimate aims of the venture. Specific practices and structural protections may be needed to insure that operation of the joint venture will not facilitate unrelated and unnecessary cooperation. For example, membership on the joint venture's board of directors could be limited and officers of the venture could be given autonomy to make pricing and output decisions. Important information concerning the venture, such as costs, pricing, product and R & D plans, might also be limited to specified persons, or circulated only in summary form to prevent sensitive data from being discussed jointly by the rival owners. There are many other examples of devices commonly used to keep joint ventures from wandering beyond their legitimate purposes.

Another critical issue will be *inclusiveness*—the broader the scope of the venture in terms of its membership, the greater the risk that it will attain market power. Can you think of any cases we have studied in this Chapter that would fit that description? If so, how would they be treated? As per se unlawful? Would it depend on the nature of their proposed actions? On the other restraints agreed to my members? For one approach to addressing these issues, see Federal Trade Commission & U.S. Department of Justice, Antitrust Guidelines for Collaborations Among Competitors (April 2000).

Another concern is *exclusion*. By including some firms, but excluding others, the formation of a joint venture can cause exclusionary effects. Under what circumstances might those effects give raise to significant competitive concerns? When would an excluded rival complain and why? Under what circumstances would such complaints signal significant concern about antitrust violations? We will revisit some of these issues in Chapters 4 and 6. For one example, see *United States v. VISA U.S.A., Inc.*, 344 F.3d 229 (2d Cir. 2003). NWS?

The *operation* of joint ventures also raises questions of both collusive and exclusionary effects. Here we have seen many examples—the call rule in *Chicago Board of Trade*, the blanket license in *Broadcast Music*, and the code of ethics in *National Society of Professional Engineers* were all examples of operational rules adopted by the organizations after they were formed.

Figure 2–4 summarizes some of the common competitive concerns associated with joint ventures. How would you use the chart to go about analyzing one? What cases from this Chapter would be most relevant? We will revisit the exclusion theories after we examine the law and economics of exclusion in greater depth in Chapters 4 and 6.

Figure 2–4:

Anticompetitive Theories Associated with Joint Ventures

Stage of Operations	Collusive Effects	Exclusionary Effects
Formation	<ul><li>Are the co-venturers rivals?</li><li>Will they be able to raise price or restrict some other aspect of competition?</li><li>Are there likely "spill-over" effects with respect to non-venture products?</li><li>Are there provisions that will prevent such actions?</li></ul>	<ul><li>Is the venture exclusive to its members?</li><li>How competitively significant will access to the venture be?</li><li>Will members enjoy advantages not reasonably obtainable by non-members?</li></ul>

Operation	• How do the venture documents contemplate operation of the venture? • Will the venturers share risks and rewards? • Will the venturers divide markets? • Are there provisions that will prevent or facilitate collusive effects?	• Do the venture documents contemplate exclusive dealing, licensing, or tying? • Are there features of the venture that in operation likely will impair or exclude non-members from access to input suppliers or dealers?

The Supreme Court's Decision in Dagher

As we have observed, many of the cases we have already studied, could be analyzed as joint ventures. The Supreme Court extended its decision in *Broadcast Music* in *Texaco Inc. v. Dagher*, 547 U.S. 1, 126 S.Ct. 1276 (2006), limiting use of per se analysis in the context of a joint venture. *Dagher* involved an agreement between Texaco and Shell to refine and sell gasoline jointly in the western United States. Pursuant to the agreement, the two previous rivals combined their refining and distribution networks into a new entity, Equilon, but maintained their distinct brand names at retail gasoline stations. Despite the fact that the FTC had earlier reviewed and declined to oppose the venture, a class of Texaco and Shell service station owners brought suit, alleging that the joint venturers' decision to permit Equilon to set joint prices for both brands constituted per se unlawful price fixing.

In an opinion authored by Justice Clarence Thomas, the Supreme Court reaffirmed the vitality of the per se ban on price-fixing, but concluded that it should not be applied to the joint price setting arrangement. Citing to *Maricopa* and *Broadcast Music*, the Court reasoned:

> * * * These cases do not present such * * * [a horizontal price-fixing] agreement * * * because Texaco and Shell Oil did not compete with one another

in the relevant market—namely, the sale of gasoline to service stations in the western United States—but instead participated in that market jointly through their investments in Equilon. In other words, the pricing policy challenged here * * * [is] not a pricing agreement between competing entities with respect to their competing products. Throughout Equilon's existence, Texaco and Shell Oil shared in the profits of Equilon's activities in their role as investors, not competitors. When 'persons who would otherwise be competitors pool their capital and share the risks of loss as well as the opportunities for profit . . . such joint ventures [are] regarded as a single firm competing with other sellers in the market.' *Arizona v. Maricopa County Medical Soc.,* 457 U.S. 332, 356 (1982). As such, though Equilon's pricing policy may be price fixing in a literal sense, it is not price fixing in the antitrust sense. *See Broadcast Music, Inc. v. Columbia Broadcasting System, Inc.,* 441 U.S. 1, 9 (1979) ("When two partners set the price of their goods or services they are literally 'price fixing,' but they are not *per se* in violation of the Sherman Act.").

547 U.S. at 5–6 (footnotes omitted). In the Court's view, as a matter of antitrust law it was not significant that the venturers each retained their distinct brand: "We see no reason to treat Equilon differently just because it chose to sell gasoline under two distinct brands at a single price. As a single entity, a joint venture, like any other firm, must have the discretion to determine the prices of the products that it sells, including the discretion to sell a product under two different brands at a single, unified price." *Id.* (footnote omitted). We will discuss the Court's treatment of "single entity" issues again in Chapter 3, when we consider the Court's decisions in *Copperweld Corp. v. Independence Tube Corp.,* 467 U.S. 752 (1984) and *American Needle, Inc. v. National Football League,* 560 U.S. 183 (2010), which examined the scope of Section 1's "concerted action" requirement.

Because the plaintiffs in *Dagher* elected to pursue their claims under the per se approach or not at all, the Court ordered that judgment be entered for the defendants. *See also In re Sulfuric Acid Antitrust Litigation,* 703 F.3d 1004 (7th Cir. 2013) (affirming dismissal of a case challenging certain joint venture conduct where the court concluded per se analysis was inappropriate and plaintiff elected not to pursue the case under a more complete rule of reason analysis).

Although there has been little criticism of *Dagher's* conclusion that per se analysis should not have been applied to the joint venture's pricing conduct, consider how the case could have been analyzed further under the rule of reason. The Court did not mention a number of facts in the record that were highlighted by the court of appeals. For example: (1) Equilon was not evenly owned by Shell and Texaco (Shell owned 56% whereas Texaco owned 44%); (2) the joint venture agreements permitted the two firms to dissolve Equilon at any time by mutual consent or, after an initial term of five years, unilaterally upon two years advance notice; (3) the specific decision to market both brands at the same price was not contained in the main joint venture agreements and there was some evidence that the two parties conceived of the joint pricing idea before the venture was formed; (4) there was some evidence that the joint pricing permitted Equilon to raise prices in at least two major metropolitan areas at a time when crude oil prices were low and stable; and (5) the alleged joint venture efficiencies of $800 million did not appear in any way related to the agreement on price. *See Dagher v. Saudi Refining, Inc.*, 369 F.3d 1108, 1111–13 (9th Cir. 2004). Do any of these facts alone or in combination suggest that the pricing provision could have been found anticompetitive under a more complete rule of reason analysis?

Conclusion

Use of the "joint venture" label in modern antitrust analysis, as we have noted, adds little to the analysis of specific restraints. As we shall see, that analysis focuses on the competitive effects of specific conduct, whether it is the creation of a cooperative arrangement or its operation. This can be understood as another example of how antitrust analysis has moved away from formalistic, categorical analysis, toward a more conceptual approach informed by economics. How might we use such a conceptual framework to explain the results in the various cases we have read thus far in the Chapter?

b. Market Division

Price fixing is not the only way competitors can emulate a monopolist—they can also do so by "dividing markets." When competitors divide markets they are agreeing to create monopolies of a sort for each other. They can do this geographically by agreeing not to compete in defined areas, by dividing up and assigning customers or customer categories, by agreeing not to solicit each other's customers, or by agreeing to divide product lines. The quid pro quo for Firm A staying away from the territory, customers or products of Firm B, is that Firm B will do the same. In this way, all of the colluding firms can obtain power over price and output—they can in effect insulate themselves from competition, thereby creating monopolies by agreement. Indeed, in one respect dividing markets can be more anticompetitive than price fixing. Price-fixing agreements may leave open the possibility of non-price competition, such as on quality, service, or innovation, but dividing markets will generally limit *all* competition, price and non-price.

As in the case of price fixing, however, such a scheme could not effectively convey power over price unless the parties to the arrangement collectively possess market power. In the absence of collective market power, any agreement to divide markets is unlikely to confer power over price since the participants in the agreement will still face competition from other firms not party to the understanding.

In *Timken Roller Bearing Co. v. United States*, 341 U.S. 593 (1951), the Supreme Court appeared to move division of markets by competitors into the per se category along with price fixing. There the government charged that the defendants, the world's principal manufacturers of "antifriction bearings," had over a period of some 40 years established "comprehensive agreements providing for a territorial division of the world markets." The agreements included allocating trade territories, fixing the price of products of one affiliate that were sold in the territory of another, cooperating to hinder new entry, and restricting imports and exports from the United States. Although the facts were somewhat complicated by the cross-ownership of the principal defendants, Timken Roller Bearing (U.S.), British Timken and French Timken, the Court viewed the group as a cartel, and the arrangements as merely an alternate method of price fixing.

The principle established in *Timken* later spread to factual contexts arguably distinct from the one the Court faced in *Timken*. In two important cases that predate *Broadcast Music*—*United States v. Sealy, Inc.*, 388 U.S. 350 (1967) and *United States v. Topco Associates, Inc.*, 405 U.S. 596 (1972), which we have already mentioned—the Supreme Court treated arrangements that were less clearly "horizontal" as nevertheless subject to the per se rule that was implicit in *Timken*. Although both cases challenged conduct that clearly met a literal definition of "dividing markets," it was less clear that the parties doing the dividing were truly "competitors" and that the arrangement could facilitate the exercise of market power. As a consequence of the invocation of the per se rule in both, however, the Court bypassed opportunities to explore efficiency based defenses that were raised by the parties.

In *Topco*, the Justice Department brought an action to enjoin some of the bylaws of a cooperative association of small to medium-size independent grocery chains. The association functioned largely as a purchasing agent for its members, procuring and distributing a wide range of products mostly sold under brand names owned by the association. The bylaws established various categories of territorial licenses that restricted Topco membership and the distribution of Topco-branded products by its members. The average market share of each member was 6%. *Id.* at 597–600.

The government challenged the bylaw provisions as a per se unlawful "division of markets," charging that they had the effect of eliminating competition between Topco members. Topco did not dispute the facts as alleged, but rather contended that "restricting competition in the sale of Topco-brand goods, the association actually increases competition by enabling its members to compete successfully with larger regional and national chains." *Id.* at 605. The district court applied the rule of reason and considered Topco's argument that, although its bylaws restricted competition between its members for the Topco brand (intrabrand competition), doing so strengthened them and facilitated competition between Topco's members and the larger retail chains (interbrand competition). The district court accepted these arguments, concluding that the bylaws were "procompetitive," but the Supreme Court reversed. In its view, the bylaws implemented a horizontal agreement to divide territories, which it described as one of the "classic examples of a *per se* violation of § 1." *Id.* at 608.

As we have already noted, it is unlikely that the Court would decide *Topco* similarly today. As Chief Justice Burger correctly pointed out in his dissenting opinion, in contrast to the Timken affiliates, the Topco members were not clearly competitors. In addition, the Topco brand was a product of cooperation that no individual member could have otherwise created and offered for sale, and the territorial restraints adopted by Topco were designed to permit its members to better compete against integrated national chains by offering a low cost private label brand, *i.e.*, to expand market output. The competition that existed among Topco members for the Topco brand, therefore, only existed by virtue of their agreement collectively to create the brand. The Supreme Court's later decisions in *Sylvania* (1977) (*see infra* Chapter 6) and *Broadcast Music* (1979), both demonstrated a far greater willingness to give weight to similar factors. Viewed in the light of these and other decisions subsequent to *Topco*, such as *Northwest Wholesale Stationers* (*see infra* Chapter 6) and *NCAA* (*see infra* Chapter 2), it is unlikely that the Court today would refuse as it did in *Topco* to consider Topco's defenses. Several appellate court decisions have made these arguments and treated *Topco* as having been effectively overruled, at least on similar facts. *See, e.g., Rothery Storage & Van Co. v.*

Atlas Van Lines, Inc., 792 F.2d 210, 229 (D.C.Cir. 1986) (Bork, J.); *Polk Bros., Inc. v. Forest City Enters., Inc.*, 776 F.2d 185, 188–89 (7th Cir. 1985) (Easterbrook, J.). *See also General Leaseways, Inc. v. National Truck Leasing Ass'n.*, 744 F.2d 588 (7th Cir. 1984) (Posner, J.) (implicitly following same approach). For a thoughtful defense of *Topco* arguing that it was carefully framed by the Justice Department and rightly decided on the facts, see Peter C. Carstensen & Harry First, *Rambling Through Economic Theory: Topco's Closer Look*, in ANTITRUST STORIES 171 (Eleanor M. Fox & Daniel A. Crane eds., 2007).

Regardless of the continued vitality of *Topco*, however, as we see in the next case, the simple legal principle announced in *Timken* and repeated in *Topco*—that division of markets by competitors is per se illegal—remains the law when the parties to the division are competitors and the conduct evidences no apparent competitive benefits.

PALMER V. BRG OF GEORGIA

Supreme Court of the United States, 1990.
498 U.S. 46, 111 S.Ct. 401, 112 L.Ed.2d 349.

PER CURIAM.

In preparation for the 1985 Georgia Bar Examination, petitioners contracted to take a bar review course offered by respondent BRG of Georgia, Inc. (BRG). In this litigation they contend that the price of BRG's course was enhanced by reason of an unlawful agreement between BRG and respondent Harcourt Brace Jovanovich Legal and Professional Publications (HBJ), the Nation's largest provider of bar review materials and lecture services. The central issue is whether the 1980 agreement between respondents violated § 1 of the Sherman Act. * * *

HBJ began offering a Georgia bar review course on a limited basis in 1976, and was in direct, and often intense, competition with BRG during the period from 1977 to 1979. BRG and HBJ were the two main providers of bar review courses in Georgia during this time period. In early 1980, they entered into an agreement that gave BRG an exclusive license to market HBJ's material in Georgia and to use its trade name "Bar/Bri." The parties agreed that HBJ would not compete with BRG in Georgia and that BRG would not compete with HBJ outside of Georgia.[2] Under the agreement, HBJ received $100 per student enrolled by BRG and 40% of all

---

[2] The 1980 agreement contained two provisions, one called a "Covenant Not to Compete" and the other called "Other Ventures." The former required HBJ not to "directly or indirectly own, manage, operate, join, invest, control, or participate in or be connected as an officer, employee, partner, director, independent contractor or otherwise with any business which is operating or participating in the preparation of candidates for the Georgia State Bar Examination." * * * The latter required BRG not to compete against HBJ in States in which HBJ currently operated outside the State of Georgia. * * *

revenues over $350. Immediately after the 1980 agreement, the price of BRG's course was increased from $150 to over $400.

On petitioners' motion for partial summary judgment as to the § 1 counts in the complaint and respondents' motion for summary judgment, the District Court held that the agreement was lawful. The United States Court of Appeals for the Eleventh Circuit, with one judge dissenting, agreed with the District Court that *per se* unlawful horizontal price fixing required an explicit agreement on prices to be charged or that one party have the right to be consulted about the other's prices. The Court of Appeals also agreed with the District Court that to prove a *per se* violation under a geographic market allocation theory, petitioners had to show that respondents had subdivided some relevant market in which they had previously competed. * * *

In *United States v. Socony-Vacuum Oil Co.*, we held that an agreement among competitors to engage in a program of buying surplus gasoline on the spot market in order to prevent prices from falling sharply was unlawful, even though there was no direct agreement on the actual prices to be maintained. We explained that "[u]nder the Sherman Act a combination formed for the purpose and with the effect of raising, depressing, fixing, pegging, or stabilizing the price of a commodity in interstate or foreign commerce is illegal *per se*."

The revenue-sharing formula in the 1980 agreement between BRG and HBJ, coupled with the price increase that took place immediately after the parties agreed to cease competing with each other in 1980, indicates that this agreement was "formed for the purpose and with the effect of raising" the price of the bar review course. It was, therefore, plainly incorrect for the District Court to enter summary judgment in respondents' favor. Moreover, it is equally clear that the District Court and the Court of Appeals erred when they assumed that an allocation of markets or submarkets by competitors is not unlawful unless the market in which the two previously competed is divided between them.

In *United States v. Topco Associates, Inc.* we held that agreements between competitors to allocate territories to minimize competition are illegal. * * * The defendants in *Topco* had never competed in the same market, but had simply agreed to allocate markets. Here, HBJ and BRG had previously competed in the Georgia market; under their allocation agreement, BRG received that market, while HBJ received the remainder of the United States. Each agreed not to compete in the other's territories. Such agreements are anticompetitive regardless of whether the parties split a market within which both do business or whether they merely reserve one market for one and another for the other. Thus, the 1980 agreement between HBJ and BRG was unlawful on its face.

The petition for a writ of certiorari is granted, the judgment of the Court of Appeals is reversed, and the case is remanded for further proceedings consistent with this opinion.

* * *

———

What justifies treating a division of markets by competitors as per se unlawful? How, economically, is it like price fixing? Under what circumstances might it have any justification worth evaluating? Should it be treated as per se unlawful even when there is a plausible efficiency-related justification for the conduct? Did HBJ or BRG appear to offer any?

Can *BRG* be distinguished from *Topco*? Do both cases present equally compelling cases for imposition of a per se rule? In answering that question, how significant is the evidence cited by the Court in *BRG* that the price of bar review courses increased almost threefold immediately after the agreement between the defendants was adopted? Does the increase in price suggest that BRG had market power? Is the Court in *BRG* implicitly suggesting that market power should be a prerequisite to application of the per se rule, or is an inquiry into market power unnecessary if the restraint is "naked," as suggested in *Socony-Vacuum Oil*? Is the division of markets in *BRG* fairly characterized as "naked," because the defendants had no plausible justification for their actions? Did the defendants in *Topco* offer a justification for their division of markets that would warrant different treatment?

c. Concerted Refusals to Deal ("Group Boycotts")

Like price-fixing and division of markets, the Supreme Court has applied per se analysis to a third kind of agreement among competitors, "group boycotts." Sometimes referred to as "concerted refusals to deal," group boycotts have a long and unsettled history that has included outright per se condemnation, qualified per se condemnation, and even more comprehensive treatment under the rule of reason. In keeping with this book's overall organizational approach, we have divided the treatment of boycotts based on the nature of their alleged anticompetitive effect: collusive or exclusionary. In this Section, we will discuss collusive group boycotts, but most of the prominent examples have involved exclusionary group boycotts. We will discuss more of the historical development of the Supreme Court's treatment of exclusionary boycotts, including *Northwest Wholesale Stationers, Inc. v. Pacific Stationery & Printing Co.*, 472 U.S. 284 (1985) and *Klor's v. Broadway-Hale Stores, Inc.*, 359 U.S. 207 (1959), in Chapter 4. Before reading our next case, *Superior Court Trial Lawyers Association,* however, we provide some additional background on the development of the law and on the lexicon that has been used to describe this kind of conduct.

All "concerted refusals to deal" are the product of "collusion," in the sense of "agreement." By "collusive group boycotts" we refer to concerted refusals to deal that result in collusive effects, *i.e.*, those that directly fix the output or the prices charged by the colluding firms. Principal examples of collusive group boycotts include an agreement among competitors to boycott a supplier in order to coerce acceptance of a lower price than the supplier would charge in a competitive market, or one to boycott a purchaser in order to coerce acceptance of a higher price than the purchaser would pay in a competitive market. In these instances, the target of the boycott is a customer or supplier of the colluding firms and the anticompetitive impact is a consequence of the boycotters' effort to affect output.

Characterization of the conduct as a boycott instead of mere price fixing may turn on little more than the presence of evidence of express, coercive demands—"meet our price or we will refuse to deal with you"— which can be understood as the means for enforcing an underlying agreement on price. Consider the Lysine cartel in Chapter 1, and *Catalano* in this Chapter, for example. In each case the parties to the price fixing agreement were in effect refusing to sell on terms other than those to which they had agreed. A collusive boycott's impact on output and price, therefore, as with all collusive anticompetitive effects, is *direct*.

The evidence relevant to a case of collusive group boycott will focus on the boycotters' demonstrated ability to secure their demanded price—their market power. This evidence might take the form of proof that the boycott actually led to higher prices (or lower prices in the case of a demand directed at a supplier), or circumstantial evidence, in the form of proof that the boycotters collectively command a significant share of a properly defined relevant market and that conditions of entry into that market are difficult. Justifications for the boycott may not prove convincing, and may not even be accepted into evidence.

Figure 2–5:

Typical Collusive Group Boycotts

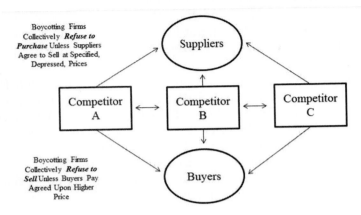

In Sidebar 2–3, immediately below, we consider some additional issues that have complicated the legal treatment of conduct characterized as a "boycott."

Sidebar 2–3:
Use of the "Group Boycott" Label

Many of the problems associated with application of per se analysis to concerted refusals to deal concern two factors. First, the terms "concerted refusal to deal" and "group boycott" can be used literally to describe a wide variety of benign and common business relationships. Every decision to purchase a good or service from one seller, for example, can be interpreted by another seller as an agreement between the buyer and seller not to deal with another seller.

Similarly, every decision to appoint a dealer as the representative of a particular manufacturer or to identify a sole source of supplies for a specific input, even when the selection follows a competitive bidding process, could too easily be labeled a "group boycott" of the firm or firms not selected. If per se analysis of refusals to deal covered all such relationships, it would prove to be quite expansive, disruptive, and costly. The Supreme Court thus limited reliance on per se analysis in *NYNEX Corp. v. Discon, Inc.*, 525 U.S. 128, 135 (1998):

> * * * [T]he specific legal question before us is whether an antitrust court considering an agreement by a buyer to purchase goods or services from one supplier rather than another should (after examining the

buyer's reasons or justifications) apply the *per se* rule if it finds no legitimate business reason for that purchasing decision. We conclude no boycott-related *per se* rule applies and that the plaintiff here must allege and prove harm, not just to a single competitor, but to the competitive process, *i.e.,* to competition itself.

See also U.S. Healthcare, Inc. v. Healthsource, Inc., 986 F.2d 589, 593–94 (1st Cir. 1993); *Rothery Storage & Van Co. v. Atlas Van Lines, Inc.,* 792 F.2d 210, 215–16 (D.C. Cir. 1986) (citing James A. Rahl, *Per Se Rules and Boycotts Under the Sherman Act: Some Reflections on the* Klor's *Case,* 45 VA. L. REV. 1165, 1172 (1959) ("All agreements to deal on specified terms mean refusal to deal on other terms;" hence any literal application of group boycott label would mean "that every restraint is illegal.")).

The courts also have recognized that the "group boycott" label can be abused if applied to totally non-commercial boycotts, such as those used in the pursuit of civil rights causes. For example, in *NAACP v. Claiborne Hardware Co.,* 458 U.S. 886 (1982), discussed immediately below in *Superior Court Trial Lawyers Association,* the Court overturned the Mississippi Supreme Court's imposition of civil, common law liability against a group of African-Americans engaged in a boycott of white merchants who segregated their customers by race. In the Court's view, the non-violent aspects of the boycott were constitutionally protected forms of association and speech. Damages for lost profits attributable to the boycott's success, therefore, could not provide a legitimate basis for antitrust liability.

Second, neither the term "group boycott," nor the Supreme Court's cases using it, explicitly distinguish as we have between concerted refusals to deal that have collusive anticompetitive effects and those that have exclusionary effects. But that distinction may help to explain why the courts have used different analytical approaches to assess different types of refusals to deal and why some might be more readily condemned than others. As a general matter, for example, courts appear to view collusive boycotts as better candidates for per se condemnation, especially when there is evidence of an underlying agreement to fix prices or divide markets, as we will see in our next case, *Superior Court Trial Lawyers Association.* In such instances it can be difficult to imagine a justification that would be worth considering. In contrast, the Court declined to use a per se approach in *F.T.C. v. Ind. Fed'n of Dentists*, 476 U.S. 447 (1986), a case that involved a variation of a collusive group boycott. There the FTC challenged a dental association's policy of refusing to supply x-rays to third-party insurers, who used the x-rays to verify treatment decisions and to determine consequent payments to the dentists for services rendered to their insureds. The purpose of the refusal seemed clear: frustrate efforts at cost containment by the third-party payers. Nevertheless, both the FTC and the Court declined to apply the per se rule:

> The policy of the Federation with respect to its members' dealings with third-party insurers resembles practices that have been labeled "group boycotts": the policy constitutes a concerted refusal to deal on particular terms with patients covered by group dental insurance. Although this Court has in the past stated that group boycotts are unlawful per se, we decline to resolve this case by forcing the Federation's policy into the "boycott" pigeonhole and invoking the per se rule. * * * [T]he category of restraints classed as group boycotts is not to be expanded indiscriminately, and the per se approach has generally been limited to cases in which firms with market power boycott suppliers or customers in order to discourage them from doing business with a competitor—a situation obviously not present here. Moreover, we have been slow to condemn rules adopted by professional associations as unreasonable per se, and, in general, to extend per se analysis to restraints imposed in the context of business relationships where the economic impact of certain practices is not immediately obvious. Thus, as did the FTC, we evaluate the restraint at issue in this case under the Rule of Reason rather than a rule of per se illegality.

Id. at 458–59. Note that the Court appears to suggest that use of the per se approach should be confined to certain *exclusionary* boycotts that are targeted at competitors. By the time the Court decided our next case, *Superior Court Trial Lawyers*, it recognized collusive group boycotts as a species of price-fixing and had more confidence that per se treatment would be appropriate.

The Supreme Court's fractured decision in *Hartford Fire Ins. Co. v. California*, 509 U.S. 764 (1993) presents the most comprehensive attempt to date by the Court to develop a taxonomy for refusals to deal. Justice Scalia traced the "boycott" label to its origins—an organized effort in 1880 by tenants on various estates in Ireland to reduce their rents and rid themselves of Captain Charles Boycott, the managing agent of the estates. Justice Scalia's opinion would confine the term "boycott" to its original context—coercive or "conditional" efforts to alter the conduct of another. Disagreement within the Court over use of "boycott," however, was largely influenced by the context of the narrow question before it—whether the defendants' conduct met the definition of a boycott as that term is used in Section 3(b) of the McCarren Ferguson Act. The Court's goal, therefore, was not specifically to synthesize and explain all of its prior decisions, something it may have occasion to do in the future.

In the Section that follows, we will explore the more contemporary treatment by the Court of collusive group boycotts, starting with perhaps the most easily identifiable, and controversial, recent case of a very visible, collusive group boycott. We will return to the topic in Chapter 6, where we examine boycotts having exclusionary effects.

As we have noted, many of the traditional Supreme Court cases associated with the application of per se analysis to group boycotts involved exclusionary, not collusive group boycotts. In our next case, however, the Court focused on a collusive group boycott. As you read the case, reflect on the issues we have just raised. Does the "group boycott" label add anything to the economic analysis of the conduct challenged in *SCTLA*? In economic terms, is it different from *Catalano* or *BRG of Georgia*? Separately, note too how the Court struggles with the fact that some boycotts may contain an expressive component that may be protected in part by the First Amendment.

FEDERAL TRADE COMMISSION V. SUPERIOR COURT TRIAL LAWYERS ASS'N

Supreme Court of the United States, 1990.
493 U.S. 411, 110 S.Ct. 768, 107 L.Ed.2d 851.

JUSTICE STEVENS delivered the opinion of the Court.

Pursuant to a well-publicized plan, a group of lawyers agreed not to represent indigent criminal defendants in the District of Columbia Superior Court until the District of Columbia government increased the lawyers' compensation. The questions presented are whether the lawyers' concerted conduct violated § 5 of the Federal Trade Commission Act and, if so, whether it was nevertheless protected by the First Amendment to the Constitution.

I

The burden of providing competent counsel to indigent defendants in the District of Columbia is substantial. During 1982, court-appointed counsel represented the defendant in approximately 25,000 cases. In the most serious felony cases, representation was generally provided by full-time employees of the District's Public Defender System (PDS). Less serious felony and misdemeanor cases constituted about 85 percent of the total caseload. In these cases, lawyers in private practice were appointed and compensated pursuant to the District of Columbia Criminal Justice Act (CJA).

Although over 1,200 lawyers have registered for CJA appointments, relatively few actually apply for such work on a regular basis. In 1982, most appointments went to approximately 100 lawyers who are described as "CJA regulars." These lawyers derive almost all of their income from representing indigents. * * *

In 1974, the District created a Joint Committee on Judicial Administration with authority to establish rates of compensation for CJA lawyers not exceeding the rates established by the federal Criminal Justice Act of 1964. After 1970, the federal Act provided for fees of $30 per hour for court time and $20 per hour for out-of-court time. * * * These rates accordingly capped the rates payable to the District's CJA lawyers, and could not be exceeded absent amendment to either the federal statute or the District Code.

Bar organizations began as early as 1975 to express concern about the low fees paid to CJA lawyers. Beginning in 1982, respondents, the Superior Court Trial Lawyers Association (SCTLA) and its officers, and other bar groups sought to persuade the District to increase CJA rates to at least $35 per hour. Despite what appeared to be uniform support for the bill, it did not pass. It is also true, however, that nothing in the record indicates that the low fees caused any actual shortage of CJA lawyers or denied effective representation to defendants.

* * *

At a SCTLA meeting [in the Summer of 1983], the CJA lawyers voted to form a "strike committee." The eight members of that committee promptly met and informally agreed "that the only viable way of getting an increase in fees was to stop signing up to take new CJA appointments, and that the boycott should aim for a $45 out-of-court and $55 in-court rate schedule."

On August 11, 1983, about 100 CJA lawyers met and resolved not to accept any new cases after September 6 if legislation providing for an increase in their fees had not passed by that date. Immediately following the meeting, they prepared (and most of them signed) a petition stating:

"We, the undersigned private criminal lawyers practicing in the Superior Court of the District of Columbia, agree that unless we are granted a substantial increase in our hourly rate we will cease accepting new appointments under the Criminal Justice Act."

On September 6, 1983, about 90 percent of the CJA regulars refused to accept any new assignments. Thereafter, SCTLA arranged a series of events to attract the attention of the news media and to obtain additional support. * * *

* * *

Within 10 days, the key figures in the District's criminal justice system "became convinced that the system was on the brink of collapse because of the refusal of CJA lawyers to take on new cases." On September 15, they hand-delivered a letter to the Mayor describing why the situation was expected to "reach a crisis point" by early the next week and urging the immediate enactment of a bill increasing all CJA rates to $35 per hour. The Mayor promptly met with members of the strike committee and offered to support an immediate temporary increase to the $35 level as well as a subsequent permanent increase to $45 an hour for out-of-court time and $55 for in-court time.

At noon on September 19, 1983, over 100 CJA lawyers attended an SCTLA meeting and voted to accept the $35 offer and end the boycott. The city council's Judiciary Committee convened at 2 o'clock that afternoon. The committee recommended legislation increasing CJA fees to $35, and the council unanimously passed the bill on September 20. On September 21, the CJA regulars began to accept new assignments and the crisis subsided.

II

The Federal Trade Commission (FTC) filed a complaint against SCTLA and four of its officers (respondents) alleging that they had "entered into an agreement among themselves and with other lawyers to restrain trade by refusing to compete for or accept new appointments under the CJA program beginning on September 6, 1983, unless and until the District of Columbia increased the fees offered under the CJA program." The complaint alleged that virtually all of the attorneys who regularly compete for or accept new appointments under the CJA program had joined the agreement. The FTC characterized respondents' conduct as "a conspiracy to fix prices and to conduct a boycott" and concluded that they were engaged in "unfair methods of competition in violation of Section 5 of the Federal Trade Commission Act."[2]

---

[2] [The FTC Act's prohibition of "unfair methods of competition" has been interpreted to include all Sherman Act offenses, but it is not limited to them and can extend further. Eds.]

After a 3-week hearing, the ALJ [Administrative Law Judge] found that the facts alleged in the complaint had been proved, and rejected each of the respondents' three legal defenses—that the boycott was adequately justified by the public interest in obtaining better legal representation for indigent defendants; that as a method of petitioning for legislative change it was exempt from the antitrust laws under our decision in *Eastern Railroad Presidents Conference v. Noerr Motor Freight, Inc.*, 365 U.S. 127 (1961) and that it was a form of political action protected by the First Amendment under our decision in *NAACP v. Claiborne Hardware Co.*, 458 U.S. 886 (1982). The ALJ nevertheless concluded that the complaint should be dismissed because the District officials, who presumably represented the victim of the boycott, recognized that its net effect was beneficial. * * *

The ALJ's pragmatic moderation found no favor with the FTC. Like the ALJ, the FTC rejected each of respondents' defenses. It held that their "coercive, concerted refusal to deal" had the "purpose and effect of raising prices" and was illegal *per se*. Unlike the ALJ, the FTC refused to conclude that the boycott was harmless, noting that the * * * boycott forced the city government to increase the CJA fees from a level that had been sufficient to obtain an adequate supply of CJA lawyers to a level satisfactory to the respondents. * * *

The Court of Appeals vacated the FTC order and remanded for a determination whether respondents possessed "significant market power." The court began its analysis by recognizing that absent any special First Amendment protection, the boycott "constituted a classic restraint of trade within the meaning of Section 1 of the Sherman Act." * * * The Court of Appeals was not persuaded by respondents' reliance on *Claiborne Hardware* or *Noerr*, or by their argument that the boycott was justified because it was designed to improve the quality of representation for indigent defendants. It concluded, however, that "the SCTLA boycott did contain an element of expression warranting First Amendment protection." It noted that boycotts have historically been used as a dramatic means of expression and that respondents intended to convey a political message to the public at large. It therefore concluded that under *United States* v. *O'Brien*, 391 U.S. 367 (1968), a restriction on this form of expression could not be justified unless it is no greater than is essential to an important governmental interest. This test, the court reasoned, could not be satisfied by the application of an otherwise appropriate *per se* rule, but instead required the enforcement agency to "prove rather than presume that the evil against which the Sherman Act is directed looms in the conduct it condemns." * * *

* * *

III

* * * We may assume that the preboycott rates were unreasonably low, and that the increase has produced better legal representation for indigent defendants. Moreover, given that neither indigent criminal defendants nor the lawyers who represent them command any special appeal with the electorate, we may also assume that without the boycott there would have been no increase in District CJA fees at least until the Congress amended the federal statute. These assumptions do not control the case, for it is not our task to pass upon the social utility or political wisdom of price-fixing agreements.

As the ALJ, the FTC, and the Court of Appeals all agreed, respondents' boycott "constituted a classic restraint of trade within the meaning of Section 1 of the Sherman Act." As such, it also violated the prohibition against unfair methods of competition in § 5 of the FTC Act. Prior to the boycott CJA lawyers were in competition with one another, each deciding independently whether and how often to offer to provide services to the District at CJA rates. The agreement among the CJA lawyers was designed to obtain higher prices for their services and was implemented by a concerted refusal to serve an important customer in the market for legal services and, indeed, the only customer in the market for the particular services that CJA regulars offered. "This constriction of supply is the essence of 'price-fixing,' whether it be accomplished by agreeing upon a price, which will decrease the quantity demanded, or by agreeing upon an output, which will increase the price offered." The horizontal arrangement among these competitors was unquestionably a "naked restraint" on price and output.

* * *

The social justifications proffered for respondents' restraint of trade thus do not make it any less unlawful. The statutory policy underlying the Sherman Act "precludes inquiry into the question whether competition is good or bad." Respondents' argument * * * ultimately asks us to find that their boycott is permissible because the price it seeks to set is reasonable. But it was settled shortly after the Sherman Act was passed that it * * * is no excuse that the prices fixed are themselves reasonable. * * *

Our decision in *Noerr* in no way detracts from this conclusion. In *Noerr*, we "considered whether the Sherman Act prohibited a publicity campaign waged by railroads" and "designed to foster the adoption of laws destructive of the trucking business, to create an atmosphere of distaste for truckers among the general public, and to impair the relationships existing between truckers and their customers." Interpreting the Sherman Act in the light of the First Amendment's Petition Clause, the Court noted that "at least insofar as the railroads' campaign was directed toward obtaining governmental action, its legality was not at all affected by any anticompetitive purpose it may have had."

It of course remains true that "no violation of the Act can be predicated upon mere attempts to influence the passage or enforcement of laws," even if the defendants' sole purpose is to impose a restraint upon the trade of their competitors. But in the *Noerr* case the alleged restraint of trade was the intended *consequence* of public action; in this case the boycott was the *means* by which respondents sought to obtain favorable legislation. The restraint of trade that was implemented while the boycott lasted would have had precisely the same anticompetitive consequences during that period even if no legislation had been enacted. In *Noerr*, the desired legislation would have created the restraint on the truckers' competition; in this case the emergency legislative response to the boycott put an end to the restraint.

* * *

IV

SCTLA argues that if its conduct would otherwise be prohibited by the Sherman Act and the Federal Trade Commission Act, it is nonetheless protected by the First Amendment rights recognized in *NAACP v. Claiborne Hardware Co.*, 458 U.S. 886 (1982). That case arose after black citizens boycotted white merchants in Claiborne County, Mississippi. The white merchants sued under state law to recover losses from the boycott. We found that the "right of the States to regulate economic activity could not justify a complete prohibition against a nonviolent, politically motivated boycott designed to force governmental and economic change and to effectuate rights guaranteed by the Constitution itself." * * *

* * *

The activity that the FTC order prohibits is a concerted refusal by CJA lawyers to accept any further assignments until they receive an increase in their compensation; the undenied objective of their boycott was an economic advantage for those who agreed to participate. * * * Those who joined the *Claiborne Hardware* boycott sought no special advantage for themselves. They were black citizens in Port Gibson, Mississippi, who had been the victims of political, social, and economic discrimination for many years. They sought only the equal respect and equal treatment to which they were constitutionally entitled. * * * As we observed, the campaign was not intended "to destroy legitimate competition." * * * Equality and freedom are preconditions of the free market, and not commodities to be haggled over within it.

The same cannot be said of attorney's fees. * * * [O]ur reasoning in *Claiborne Hardware* is not applicable to a boycott conducted by business competitors who "stand to profit financially from a lessening of competition in the boycotted market." * * *

* * *

V

* * *

The Court of Appeals, however, crafted a new exception to the *per se* rules, and it is this exception which provoked the FTC's petition to this Court. The Court of Appeals derived its exception from *United States v. O'Brien*, 391 U.S. 367 (1968). In that case O'Brien had burned his Selective Service registration certificate on the steps of the South Boston Courthouse. He did so before a sizable crowd and with the purpose of advocating his antiwar beliefs. We affirmed his conviction. We held that the governmental interest in regulating the "nonspeech element" of his conduct adequately justified the incidental restriction on First Amendment freedoms. * * *

However, the Court of Appeals held that, in light of *O'Brien*, the expressive component of respondents' boycott compelled courts to apply the antitrust laws "prudently and with sensitivity," . . . with a "special solicitude for the First Amendment rights" of respondents. The Court of Appeals concluded that the governmental interest in prohibiting boycotts is not sufficient to justify a restriction on the communicative element of the boycott unless the FTC can prove, and not merely presume, that the boycotters have market power. Because the Court of Appeals imposed this special requirement upon the government, it ruled that *per se* antitrust analysis was inapplicable to boycotts having an expressive component.

There are at least two critical flaws in the Court of Appeals' antitrust analysis: it exaggerates the significance of the expressive component in respondents' boycott and it denigrates the importance of the rule of law that respondents violated. Implicit in the conclusion of the Court of Appeals are unstated assumptions that most economic boycotts do not have an expressive component, and that the categorical prohibitions against price fixing and boycotts are merely rules of "administrative convenience" that do not serve any substantial governmental interest unless the price-fixing competitors actually possess market power.

It would not much matter to the outcome of this case if these flawed assumptions were sound. *O'Brien* would offer respondents no protection even if their boycott were uniquely expressive and even if the purpose of the *per se* rules were purely that of administrative efficiency. * * * The administrative efficiency interests in antitrust regulation are unusually compelling. The *per se* rules avoid "the necessity for an incredibly complicated and prolonged economic investigation into the entire history of the industry involved, as well as related industries, in an effort to determine at large whether a particular restraint has been unreasonable." If small parties "were allowed to prove lack of market power, all parties would have that right, thus introducing the enormous complexities of market definition into every price-fixing case." For these reasons, it is at least possible that the *Claiborne Hardware* doctrine, which itself rests in part upon *O'Brien*, exhausts *O'Brien's* application to the antitrust statutes.

In any event, however, we cannot accept the Court of Appeals' characterization of this boycott or the antitrust laws. Every concerted refusal to do business with a potential customer or supplier has an expressive component. At one level, the competitors must exchange their views about their objectives and the means of obtaining them. The most blatant, naked price-fixing agreement is a product of communication, but that is surely not a reason for viewing it with special solicitude. At another level, after the terms of the boycotters' demands have been agreed upon, they must be communicated to its target: "[W]e will not do business until you do what we ask." That expressive component of the boycott conducted by these respondents is surely not unique. On the contrary, it is the hallmark of every effective boycott.

At a third level, the boycotters may communicate with third parties to enlist public support for their objectives; to the extent that the boycott is newsworthy, it will facilitate the expression of the boycotters' ideas. But this level of expression is not an element of the boycott. * * *

In sum, there is thus nothing unique about the "expressive component" of respondents' boycott. A rule that requires courts to apply the antitrust laws "prudently and with sensitivity" whenever an economic boycott has an "expressive component" would create a gaping hole in the fabric of those laws. Respondents' boycott thus has no special characteristics meriting an exemption from the *per se* rules of antitrust law.

Equally important is the second error implicit in respondents' claim to immunity from the *per se* rules. In its opinion, the Court of Appeals assumed that the antitrust laws permit, but do not require, the condemnation of price fixing and boycotts without proof of market power. * * * The opinion further assumed that the *per se* rule prohibiting such activity "is only a rule of 'administrative convenience and efficiency,' not a statutory command." This statement contains two errors. The *per se* rules are, of course, the product of judicial interpretations of the Sherman Act, but the rules nevertheless have the same force and effect as any other statutory commands. Moreover, while the *per se* rule against price fixing and boycotts is indeed justified in part by "administrative convenience," the Court of Appeals erred in describing the prohibition as justified only by such concerns. The *per se* rules also reflect a longstanding judgment that the prohibited practices by their nature have "a substantial potential for impact on competition." * * *

* * *

The *per se* rules in antitrust law serve purposes analogous to *per se* restrictions upon, for example, stunt flying in congested areas or speeding. Laws prohibiting stunt flying or setting speed limits are justified by the State's interest in protecting human life and property. Perhaps most violations of such rules actually cause no harm. No doubt many experienced drivers and pilots can operate much more safely, even at prohibited speeds, than the average citizen.

If the especially skilled drivers and pilots were to paint messages on their cars, or attach streamers to their planes, their conduct would have an expressive component. High speeds and unusual maneuvers would help to draw attention to their messages. Yet the laws may nonetheless be enforced against these skilled persons without proof that their conduct was actually harmful or dangerous.

In part, the justification for these *per se* rules is rooted in administrative convenience. They are also supported, however, by the observation that every speeder and every stunt pilot poses some threat to the community. * * *

So it is with boycotts and price fixing.[16] Every such horizontal arrangement among competitors poses some threat to the free market. A small participant in the market is, obviously, less likely to cause persistent damage than a large participant. Other participants in the market may act quickly and effectively to take the small participant's place. For reasons including market inertia and information failures, however, a small conspirator may be able to impede competition over some period of time. Given an appropriate set of circumstances and some luck, the period can be long enough to inflict real injury upon particular consumers or competitors.

* * *

Of course, some boycotts and some price-fixing agreements are more pernicious than others; some are only partly successful, and some may only succeed when they are buttressed by other causative factors, such as political influence. But an assumption that, absent proof of market power, the boycott disclosed by this record was totally harmless—when

---

[16] "In sum, price-fixing cartels are condemned per se because the conduct is tempting to businessmen but very dangerous to society. The conceivable social benefits are few in principle, small in magnitude, speculative in occurrence, and always premised on the existence of price-fixing power which is likely to be exercised adversely to the public. Moreover, toleration implies a burden of continuous supervision for which the courts consider themselves ill-suited. And even if power is usually established while any defenses are not, litigation will be complicated, condemnation delayed, would be price-fixers encouraged to hope for escape, and criminal punishment less justified. Deterrence of a generally pernicious practice would be weakened. The key points are the first two. Without them, there is no justification for categorical condemnation." 7 P. Areeda, Antitrust Law ¶ 1509, pp. 412–413 (1986).

overwhelming testimony demonstrated that it almost produced a crisis in the administration of criminal justice in the District and when it achieved its economic goal—is flatly inconsistent with the clear course of our antitrust jurisprudence. Conspirators need not achieve the dimensions of a monopoly, or even a degree of market power any greater than that already disclosed by this record, to warrant condemnation under the antitrust laws.

* * *

[The opinion of JUSTICES BRENNAN and MARSHALL, concurring in part, and dissenting in part, is omitted, as is the opinion of MR. JUSTICE BLACKMUN, also concurring in part and dissenting in part. Eds.]

What makes *SCTLA* a case of "collusive" group boycott? Note that the challenged conduct could easily be viewed as a price fixing agreement among competitors—the members of the SCTLA collectively agreed upon a specific hourly rate for their services and demanded it from their customer, the District of Columbia. Yet the mechanism chosen to implement the price fixing scheme was a boycott of the buyer, the D.C. government. This point was emphasized near the end of the majority's opinion in response to an argument made by Justice Brennan in his dissent. Brennan argued that in fact not all boycotts had been deemed per se unlawful by the Court. Justice Stevens replied for the majority:

> In response to Justice Brennan's opinion, and particularly to its observation that some concerted arrangements that might be characterized as "group boycotts" may not merit per se condemnation * * * we emphasize that this case involves not only a boycott but also a horizontal price-fixing arrangement—a type of conspiracy that has been consistently analyzed as a per se violation for many decades. All of the "group boycott" cases cited in Justice Brennan's footnote involved nonprice restraints. There was likewise no price-fixing component in any of the boycotts listed [in] * * * Justice Brennan's opinion. Indeed, the text of the opinion virtually ignores the price-fixing component of respondents' concerted action.

493 U.S. at 436 n.19. Is the majority taking the position that collusive group boycotts should be treated as per se unlawful only when the boycott functions as a mechanism to enforce an underlying price fixing agreement?

Recall that in *Catalano* the Court struck down as price fixing a collective agreement by beer wholesalers who refused to continue offering short-term credit. Can the mechanism chosen by the wholesalers to enforce the agreement be characterized as a boycott? In a sense, didn't the wholesalers collectively refuse to deal with any beer retailer who would not pay in full either in advance or upon delivery? Should *Catalano* be categorized as a "boycott" or as a "price-fixing" case? Should it matter? Are the economic consequences of the conduct the same whether it bears one label or the other? Consider, too, the facts in *BRG Georgia*. Is every effective division of markets in effect an agreement that each party will refuse to deal with a purchaser that has been assigned to the other party?

Note that a significant portion of the Court's opinion in *SCTLA* has to do with the inter-relationship of the Sherman Act and the First Amendment. Why? Would the SCTLA have been immune from antitrust prosecution had its members simply lobbied the D.C. government for an increase in the statutory rate they were paid for their services as CJA lawyers, even if the lobbying was successful? What is the majority's response to the fact that SCTLA's conduct involved, but went beyond lobbying? We will examine the interaction of the Sherman Act and the First Amendment in the context of government petitioning activity in greater depth in Chapter 8, when we take up what has become known as the *Noerr-Pennington* doctrine.

The Majority's treatment of the First Amendment issue provoked a pointed dissent by Justices Brennan and Marshall. While concurring in the majority's conclusion that the SCTLA's actions were neither outside the scope of the Sherman Act, nor automatically immunized from antitrust regulation by the First Amendment, Justices Brennan and Marshall took issue with Part V of the majority's opinion—its discussion of *United States v. O'Brien*. In their view, the majority's endorsement of the FTC's use of the per se rule demonstrated insensitivity "to the venerable tradition of expressive boycotts as an important means of political communication." 493 U.S. at 782–83 (BRENNAN, J., dissenting).

Might the alignment of the justices in the decision have been affected by the injection of First Amendment issues? What fear regarding the First Amendment likely prompted Justices Brennan and Marshall to back away from the Court's application of per se analysis? Would that concern be relevant to all collusive group boycotts, or just to those involving "expressive" components? Might the majority have viewed the case as an opportunity to contain the scope of First Amendment protections? Considering both opinions—is it possible that the views of the majority and the dissent concerning the First Amendment explain more about their positions in the case than their views on antitrust enforcement? Is there a tension for both the majority and the dissent between their views on the scope of antitrust enforcement and their views of the scope of protected speech under the First Amendment?

We will return to this difficult area of antitrust law in Chapter 8, when we will again see that conduct that would appear to fall within the scope of the First Amendment can have significant anticompetitive consequences.

Finally, note that the SCTLA also argued that it should be treated as a labor union, immune from antitrust scrutiny under the exemptions set forth in the Norris LaGuardia Act, 29 U.S.C. § 101, et. seq. Why should labor unions be exempt from the coverage of the Sherman Act for their collective bargaining efforts, including the threat of strike? Why didn't SCTLA succeed in invoking the Act? We will return to the issue of statutory exemptions in Chapter 8.

Sidebar 2–4:
Defining and Justifying
Contemporary Per Se Analysis

Having examined some of the most influential cases that endorsed abbreviated analysis of patently anticompetitive agreements, it is useful to pause and ask "what is per se analysis?" As we have already suggested, that question can be addressed from both *legal* and *economic* perspectives.

What is per se analysis legally?

One way to look at per se analysis is as a rule of evidence, as opposed to one of substantive antitrust law. When anticompetitive effects are relatively obvious, they can give rise to a presumption that conduct will unreasonably restrain trade. If the probable effect of the conduct is likely to be especially pernicious, and it is unlikely that many instances of the conduct will be justifiable, the presumption might be irrebuttable. As we have already noted, the "per se rule" is thus not a distinct "rule" at all, but a particularized approach to applying the rule of reason.

Thought of in this way, per se analysis reduces the Section 1 inquiry to whether the defendants engaged in a "contract, combination or conspiracy" and whether that agreement falls into a recognized per se category, such as price-fixing or market division. Once such an agreement is proved, if per se analysis applies to the conduct at issue, anticompetitive effect is presumed and all defenses, *i.e.*, attempts to demonstrate "reasonableness," are precluded.

But what are the indicia of anticompetitive potential that justify invocation of the per se approach, and how much and what kind of evidence is needed to trigger the presumption?

A more searching analysis of the per se cases reveals that, although the courts surely viewed themselves as applying a rule of facial invalidity—at least with respect to agreements among competitors—the cases themselves frequently involved well-developed records. Note for example that in *Trenton Potteries* the Court observed that the alleged conspirators had a very substantial market share, an indication that they were capable of collectively raising prices. In *Socony-Vacuum Oil*, the Court had very extensive evidence of the alleged practice's impact on industry output and prices, even though in its famous footnote 59 the Court disavowed reliance on actual market effect as a prerequisite for invocation of per se analysis. Similarly in *Catalano*, *BRG of Georgia*, and *Superior Court Trial Lawyers Association* there was evidence—easily accessible and relatively apparent evidence—that the conduct had its intended effect. These are not the only prominent cases in which per se analysis has been successfully invoked in the presence of at least some evidence of harm to competition beyond just the nature of the agreement itself.

Professor Thomas Krattenmaker has sought to reinterpret some of these cases, arguing that there are no truly per se "offenses" under the antitrust laws; instead, he maintained, antitrust has identified certain *defenses*, such as "reasonable prices," that are per se inadmissible. *See* Thomas G. Krattenmaker, *Per Se Violations in Antitrust Law: Confusing Offenses With Defenses*, 77 GEO. L.J. 165 (1988). What is the practical consequence of characterizing per se analysis as one that precludes certain defenses as opposed to one that identifies certain offenses as indefensible? Another commentator has maintained that "in the modern context" per se analysis describes conduct that is "inherently suspect because it appears highly likely, absent an efficiency justification, to decrease the output of the collaborators or to increase their price." Timothy J. Muris, *The New Rule of Reason*, 57 ANTITRUST L.J. 859, 861 (1989). Which of these approaches best describes the Court's actions in the cases we have read? What are the consequences of the various approaches might be for allocating burdens of production and proof in the cases? Do both offer helpful perspectives?

What is per se analysis economically?

Per se analysis reflects a judgment about the likely threat that certain conduct poses to competition, as well as concerns for administrative convenience, judicial efficiency, and certainty for the business community. In the context of price fixing by competitors, for example, it reflects a judgment that the practice is so likely to prove to be unreasonably anticompetitive that it is not worth the cost, including time and judicial resources, to consider reasonableness defenses. The search for the exceptional case—the truly "reasonable" instance of price fixing—is so unlikely to prove fruitful, that it is not worth the cost of investigation and evaluation. In decision-theoretic terms, "false positives" are relatively unlikely and an alternate, more searching approach would be substantially more costly to administer yet unlikely to significantly reduce the already low incidence of false positives.

Also, as we noted at the outset of our discussion of per se analysis, it has been argued that it provides certainty and guidance to the business community and the courts. Bright line rules mean, for better or worse, that the law is relatively clear and compliance is seemingly easy. Accordingly, per se analysis makes the most economic sense when factors like the following are present:

- if permitted, the prohibited conduct will likely harm competition severely;
- if the conduct is reviewed for reasonableness rather than held illegal per se, defendants will frequently claim that their conduct is reasonable, it will be costly and time-consuming to evaluate those claims, and in the end, few such claims will prove to be valid; and
- little pro-competitive conduct will be deterred by establishing a rule that denies defendants the ability to prove that their conduct was reasonable.

So it is with price fixing by competitors and its variants. The consequences can be quite severe, as we saw in Chapter 1 when we considered the behavior of the lysine and vitamin cartels and the coffee suppliers, and as we have seen in the last three cases, *Catalano*, *BRG of Georgia*, and *SCTLA*. Successful price fixing conspiracies or agreements to divide markets can lead to very significant inefficiencies and transfers of wealth. On the other hand, truly "reasonable" instances of such conduct may be rare—but the cost of identifying them judicially could be substantial. In short, the social costs of condemning the rare instance of "reasonable" price fixing will likely be far outweighed by the benefits of a bright line prohibition. Those benefits include certainty—firms can readily discern the line between acceptable and unacceptable business behavior—and deterrence—instances of objectionable price fixing can be minimized. As one commentator has observed:

> From a law and economics perspective, per se rules may be preferred to a rule of reason when violations are expensive for a court to observe but are strongly correlated with observable behaviors that are cheaply observed, and when it would be expensive for a violator

> to break the law without engaging in the observable behavior. Under such circumstances, the judicial system would minimize enforcement costs by conditioning liability on the cheaply observable behavior, and the resulting enforcement errors, corporate compliance costs, and social costs of deterring socially beneficial actions, would not produce an efficiency loss.[a]
>
> Hence, when the defendants in *Trenton Potteries* argued to the Court that the rates they had agreed to were "reasonable," the Court refused to entertain their argument as a defense to price fixing. That reflected a presumption that the benefits of permitting such a defense are far outweighed by their costs, because they will be difficult to verify and are so unlikely to prove to be valid.

2. PROVING ANTICOMPETITIVE EFFECTS BY REBUTTABLE PRESUMPTION THROUGH EVIDENCE OF ACTUAL HARM

As we have explained, the custom of describing "per se" and "rule of reason" as two distinct "rules" has persisted for a very long time. On occasion it has distorted understanding of the relationship between per se analysis and the rule of reason; it also influences how cases are litigated. Application of the "per se rule" significantly enhanced the plaintiff's possibility of prevailing, whereas application of the "rule of reason," because that typically meant the derogatorily labelled "full blown" rule of reason (*i.e.* the comprehensive rule of reason), often led to victory for the defendants. Since the choice of "rule" could be outcome determinative, a great deal of effort went into categorizing conduct as being under one or the other as if they were two polar opposites.

Beginning with the Supreme Court's decision in *National Society of Professional Engineers*, the Court began to explore a more fluid approach to applying the rule of reason. Proceeding from the assumption that not all cases literally falling into the per se category warrant per se treatment—a conclusion that was apparent in *Broadcast Music*—the Court also appeared to recognize that not all cases excused from per se treatment deserved or required "full blown" rule of reason analysis under the *Chicago Board of Trade* approach. As a consequence, it began scouting out the ground

---

[a] Jonathan B. Baker, *Per Se Rules in the Antitrust Analysis of Horizontal Restraints*, 36 ANTITRUST BULL. 733, 740 n.29 (1991). *See also* F.M. SCHERER & DAVID ROSS, INDUSTRIAL MARKET STRUCTURE AND ECONOMIC PERFORMANCE 335–39 (3d ed. 1990) (discussing rationale for per se prohibition of price fixing); C. Frederick Beckner III & Steven C. Salop, *Decision Theory and Antitrust Rules*, 67 ANTITRUST L.J. 41 (1999) (proposing decision theoretic model to guide process of fact-gathering, decision-making, and rule choice in antitrust cases).

between abrupt per se condemnation and comprehensive rule of reason analysis—a development that has continued.

The Supreme Court and the lower courts also began to address the legacy of *Chicago Board of Trade's* rule of reason, searching for ways to better specify the facts most relevant to a rule of reason inquiry and the allocation of burdens between plaintiffs and defendants. This development also continues, especially as the cost of complex antitrust litigation has become an increasing concern of courts, commentators, and enforcers. As we shall see, this has resulted in efforts not only by the Supreme Court, but also by the lower courts and commentators, to develop a more structured approach that explicitly accounts for burden-shifting conventions. Such approaches can help to facilitate the use of procedural devices used to screen cases, especially motions to dismiss and motions for summary judgment.

In this Section and the two that follow, we will explore the development of these more fluid and more structured approaches to the rule of reason. As you read the next case and the note that follows, consider how each of the cases discussed easily could have been forced into one or the other of the traditional categories, per se or rule of reason—but to what end? Considered as a group, they suggest a unified framework for analyzing competitor conduct allegedly having collusive anticompetitive effects.

NATIONAL COLLEGIATE ATHLETIC ASS'N V. BOARD OF REGENTS OF THE UNIVERSITY OF OKLAHOMA

Supreme Court of the United States, 1984.
468 U.S. 85, 104 S.Ct. 2948, 82 L.Ed.2d 70.

JUSTICE STEVENS delivered the opinion of the Court.

The University of Oklahoma and the University of Georgia contend that the National Collegiate Athletic Association has unreasonably restrained trade in the televising of college football games. After an extended trial, the District Court found that the NCAA had violated § 1 of the Sherman Act and granted injunctive relief. The Court of Appeals agreed that the statute had been violated but modified the remedy in some respects. We granted certiorari, and now affirm.

I

The NCAA

Since its inception in 1905, the NCAA has played an important role in the regulation of amateur collegiate sports. It has adopted and promulgated playing rules, standards of amateurism, standards for academic eligibility, regulations concerning recruitment of athletes, and rules governing the size of athletic squads and coaching staffs. * * * With the exception of football, the NCAA has not undertaken any regulation of the televising of athletic events.

The NCAA has approximately 850 voting members. The regular members are classified into separate divisions to reflect differences in size and scope of their athletic programs. * * *

Some years ago, five major conferences together with major football-playing independent institutions organized the College Football Association (CFA). The original purpose of the CFA was to promote the interests of major football-playing schools within the NCAA structure. The Universities of Oklahoma and Georgia, respondents in this Court, are members of the CFA.

* * *

The Current Plan

The [television] plan adopted in 1981 for the 1982–1985 seasons is at issue in this case. This plan * * * recites that it is intended to reduce, insofar as possible, the adverse effects of live television upon football game attendance. * * * The plan recites that the television committee has awarded rights to negotiate and contract for the telecasting of college football games of members of the NCAA to two "carrying networks." * * *

In separate agreements with each of the carrying networks, ABC [the American Broadcasting Cos.] and the Columbia Broadcasting System (CBS), the NCAA granted each the right to telecast the 14 live "exposures" described in the plan, in accordance with the "ground rules" set forth therein. Each of the networks agreed to pay a specified "minimum aggregate compensation to the participating NCAA member institutions" during the 4-year period in an amount that totaled $131,750,000. In essence the agreement authorized each network to negotiate directly with member schools for the right to televise their games. The agreement itself does not describe the method of computing the compensation for each game, but the practice that has developed over the years and that the District Court found would be followed under the current agreement involved the setting of a recommended fee by a representative of the NCAA for different types of telecasts, with national telecasts being the most valuable, regional telecasts being less valuable, and Division II or Division III games commanding a still lower price. The aggregate of all these payments presumably equals the total minimum aggregate compensation set forth in the basic agreement. * * * [T]he amount that any team receives does not change with the size of the viewing audience, the number of markets in which the game is telecast, or the particular characteristic of the game or the participating teams. Instead, the "ground rules" provide that the carrying networks make alternate selections of those games they wish to televise, and thereby obtain the exclusive right to submit a bid at an essentially fixed price to the institutions involved.

The plan also contains "appearance requirements" and "appearance limitations" which pertain to each of the 2-year periods that the plan is in effect. The basic requirement imposed on each of the two networks is that it must schedule appearances for at least 82 different member institutions during each 2-year period. Under the appearance limitations no member institution is eligible to appear on television more than a total of six times and more than four times nationally, with the appearances to be divided equally between the two carrying networks. The number of exposures specified in the contracts also sets an absolute maximum on the number of games that can be broadcast.

Thus * * * the current plan * * * limits the total amount of televised intercollegiate football and the number of games that any one team may televise. No member is permitted to make any sale of television rights except in accordance with the basic plan.

Background of this Controversy

Beginning in 1979 CFA members began to advocate that colleges with major football programs should have a greater voice in the formulation of football television policy than they had in the NCAA. CFA therefore investigated the possibility of negotiating a television agreement of its own, developed an independent plan, and obtained a contract offer from the National Broadcasting Co. (NBC). This contract, which it signed in August 1981, would have allowed a more liberal number of appearances for each institution, and would have increased the overall revenues realized by CFA members.

In response the NCAA publicly announced that it would take disciplinary action against any CFA member that complied with the CFA-NBC contract. * * * On September 8, 1981, respondents commenced this action in the United States District Court for the Western District of Oklahoma and obtained a preliminary injunction preventing the NCAA from initiating disciplinary proceedings or otherwise interfering with CFA's efforts to perform its agreement with NBC. Notwithstanding the entry of the injunction, most CFA members were unwilling to commit themselves to the new contractual arrangement with NBC in the face of the threatened sanctions and therefore the agreement was never consummated.

* * *

[Here the Court described in detail the proceedings in the district court and the court of appeals. Although the district court had condemned the NCAA's plan, it did so after a lengthy trial, and it considered each of the NCAA's defenses. In contrast, the Court of Appeals held that the plan should have been treated as per se unlawful price fixing and that, in any event, the procompetitive justifications urged by the NCAA were not supported by the evidence. Eds.]

II

There can be no doubt that the challenged practices of the NCAA constitute a "restraint of trade" in the sense that they limit members' freedom to negotiate and enter into their own television contracts. In that sense, however, every contract is a restraint of trade, and as we have repeatedly recognized, the Sherman Act was intended to prohibit only unreasonable restraints of trade.

It is also undeniable that these practices share characteristics of restraints we have previously held unreasonable. * * * By participating in an association which prevents member institutions from competing against each other on the basis of price or kind of television rights that can be offered to broadcasters, the NCAA member institutions have created a horizontal restraint—an agreement among competitors on the way in which they will compete with one another. A restraint of this type has often been held to be unreasonable as a matter of law. Because it places a ceiling on the number of games member institutions may televise, the horizontal agreement places an artificial limit on the quantity of televised football that is available to broadcasters and consumers. By restraining the quantity of television rights available for sale, the challenged practices create a limitation on output; our cases have held that such limitations are unreasonable restraints of trade. Moreover, the District Court found that the minimum aggregate price in fact operates to preclude any price negotiation between broadcasters and institutions, thereby constituting horizontal price fixing, perhaps the paradigm of an unreasonable restraint of trade.

Horizontal price fixing and output limitation are ordinarily condemned as a matter of law under an "illegal per se" approach because the probability that these practices are anticompetitive is so high. * * * In such circumstances a restraint is presumed unreasonable without inquiry into the particular market context in which it is found. Nevertheless, we have decided that it would be inappropriate to apply a per se rule to this case. This decision is not based on a lack of judicial experience with this type of arrangement,[21] on the fact that the NCAA is organized as a nonprofit entity,[22] or on our respect for the NCAA's historic role in the

---

[21] While judicial inexperience with a particular arrangement counsels against extending the reach of *per se* rules, the likelihood that horizontal price and output restrictions are anticompetitive is generally sufficient to justify application of the *per se* rule without inquiry into the special characteristics of a particular industry. * * *

[22] There is no doubt that the sweeping language of § 1 applies to nonprofit entities. * * *

preservation and encouragement of intercollegiate amateur athletics.[23] Rather, what is critical is that this case involves an industry in which horizontal restraints on competition are essential if the product is to be available at all.

* * * What the NCAA and its member institutions market in this case is competition itself—contests between competing institutions. Of course, this would be completely ineffective if there were no rules on which the competitors agreed to create and define the competition to be marketed. * * * Moreover, the NCAA seeks to market a particular brand of football— college football. The identification of this "product" with an academic tradition differentiates college football from and makes it more popular than professional sports to which it might otherwise be comparable, such as, for example, minor league baseball. * * * Thus, the NCAA plays a vital role in enabling college football to preserve its character, and as a result enables a product to be marketed which might otherwise be unavailable. In performing this role, its actions widen consumer choice—not only the choices available to sports fans but also those available to athletes—and hence can be viewed as procompetitive.

Broadcast Music squarely holds that a joint selling arrangement may be so efficient that it will increase sellers' aggregate output and thus be procompetitive. Similarly, as we indicated in *Continental T.V., Inc. v. GTE Sylvania Inc.* [*see infra* Chapter 6], a restraint in a limited aspect of a market may actually enhance marketwide competition. Respondents concede that the great majority of the NCAA's regulations enhance competition among member institutions. Thus, despite the fact that this case involves restraints on the ability of member institutions to compete in terms of price and output, a fair evaluation of their competitive character requires consideration of the NCAA's justifications for the restraints.

Our analysis of this case under the Rule of Reason, of course, does not change the ultimate focus of our inquiry. Both *per se* rules and the Rule of Reason are employed "to form a judgment about the competitive significance of the restraint." *National Society of Professional Engineers.* * * *

Per se rules are invoked when surrounding circumstances make the likelihood of anticompetitive conduct so great as to render unjustified further examination of the challenged conduct. But whether the ultimate finding is the product of a presumption or actual market analysis, the essential inquiry remains the same—whether or not the challenged

---

[23] While as the guardian of an important American tradition, the NCAA's motives must be accorded a respectful presumption of validity, it is nevertheless well settled that good motives will not validate an otherwise anticompetitive practice.

restraint enhances competition.[26] Under the Sherman Act the criterion to be used in judging the validity of a restraint on trade is its impact on competition.

III

Because it restrains price and output, the NCAA's television plan has a significant potential for anticompetitive effects.[28] The findings of the District Court indicate that this potential has been realized. The District Court found that if member institutions were free to sell television rights, many more games would be shown on television, and that the NCAA's output restriction has the effect of raising the price the networks pay for television rights.[29] to all games, the NCAA creates a price structure that is unresponsive to viewer demand and unrelated to the prices that would prevail in a competitive market.[30] And, of course, since as a practical matter all member institutions need NCAA approval, members have no real choice but to adhere to the NCAA's television controls.[31]

The anticompetitive consequences of this arrangement are apparent. Individual competitors lose their freedom to compete. Price is higher and output lower than they would otherwise be, and both are unresponsive to consumer preference. This latter point is perhaps the most significant, since "Congress designed the Sherman Act as a 'consumer welfare prescription.'" A restraint that has the effect of reducing the importance of consumer preference in setting price and output is not consistent with this fundamental goal of antitrust law. Restrictions on price and output are the paradigmatic examples of restraints of trade that the Sherman Act was

---

[26] Indeed, there is often no bright line separating *per se* from Rule of Reason analysis. *Per se* rules may require considerable inquiry into market conditions before the evidence justifies a presumption of anticompetitive conduct. * * *

[28] In this connection, it is not without significance that Congress felt the need to grant professional sports an exemption from the antitrust laws for joint marketing of television rights. *See* 15 U.S.C. §§ 1291–1295. The legislative history of this exemption demonstrates Congress' recognition that agreements among league members to sell television rights in a cooperative fashion could run afoul of the Sherman Act. * * *

[29] "It is clear from the evidence that were it not for the NCAA controls, many more college football games would be televised. This is particularly true at the local level. * * * The evidence establishes the fact that the networks are actually paying the large fees because the NCAA agrees to limit production. If the NCAA would not agree to limit production, the networks would not pay so large a fee. Because NCAA limits production, the networks need not fear that their broadcasts will have to compete head-to-head with other college football telecasts, either on the networks or on various local stations. * * * "

[30] "Turning to the price paid for the product, it is clear that the NCAA controls utterly destroy free market competition. NCAA has commandeered the rights of its members and sold those rights for a sum certain. In so doing, it has fixed the minimum, maximum and actual price which will be paid to the schools appearing on ABC, CBS and TBS. * * * Because of the NCAA controls, the price which is paid for the right to televise any particular game is responsive neither to the relative quality of the teams playing the game nor to viewer preference." * * *

[31] Since, as the District Court found, NCAA approval is necessary for any institution that wishes to compete in intercollegiate sports, the NCAA has a potent tool at its disposal for restraining institutions which require its approval. * * *

intended to prohibit. At the same time, the television plan eliminates competitors from the market, since only those broadcasters able to bid on television rights covering the entire NCAA can compete. Thus, as the District Court found, many telecasts that would occur in a competitive market are foreclosed by the NCAA's plan.

Petitioner argues, however, that its television plan can have no significant anticompetitive effect since the record indicates that it has no market power—no ability to alter the interaction of supply and demand in the market.[38] We must reject this argument for two reasons, one legal, one factual.

As a matter of law, the absence of proof of market power does not justify a naked restriction on price or output. To the contrary, when there is an agreement not to compete in terms of price or output, "no elaborate industry analysis is required to demonstrate the anticompetitive character of such an agreement." *Professional Engineers*, 435 U.S., at 692.[39] * * * We have never required proof of market power in such a case. This naked restraint on price and output requires some competitive justification even in the absence of a detailed market analysis.[42]

As a factual matter, it is evident that petitioner does possess market power. The District Court employed the correct test for determining whether college football broadcasts constitute a separate market—whether there are other products that are reasonably substitutable for televised NCAA football games. Petitioner's argument that it cannot obtain supracompetitive prices from broadcasters since advertisers, and hence broadcasters, can switch from college football to other types of programming simply ignores the findings of the District Court. It found that intercollegiate football telecasts generate an audience uniquely

---

[38] Market power is the ability to raise prices above those that would be charged in a competitive market. * * *

[39] "The fact that a practice is not categorically unlawful in all or most of its manifestations certainly does not mean that it is universally lawful. * * * The essential point is that the rule of reason can sometimes be applied in the twinkling of an eye." P. Areeda, The "Rule of Reason" in Antitrust Analysis: General Issues 37–38 (Federal Judicial Center, June 1981). * * *

[42] The Solicitor General correctly observes:

"There was no need for the respondents to establish monopoly power in any precisely defined market for television programming in order to prove the restraint unreasonable. Both lower courts found not only that NCAA has power over the market for intercollegiate sports, but also that in the market for television programming—no matter how broadly or narrowly the market is defined—the NCAA television restrictions have reduced output, subverted viewer choice, and distorted pricing. Consequently, unless the controls have some countervailing procompetitive justification, they should be deemed unlawful regardless of whether petitioner has substantial market power over advertising dollars. While the 'reasonableness' of a particular alleged restraint often depends on the market power of the parties involved, because a judgment about market power is the means by which the effects of the conduct on the market place can be assessed, market power is only one test of 'reasonableness.' And where the anticompetitive effects of conduct can be ascertained through means short of extensive market analysis, and where no countervailing competitive virtues are evident, a lengthy analysis of market power is not necessary." Brief for United States as *Amicus Curiae* 19–20. * * *

attractive to advertisers and that competitors are unable to offer programming that can attract a similar audience. These findings amply support its conclusion that the NCAA possesses market power. Indeed, the District Court's subsidiary finding that advertisers will pay a premium price per viewer to reach audiences watching college football because of their demographic characteristics is vivid evidence of the uniqueness of this product. * * *[49] It inexorably follows that if college football broadcasts be defined as a separate market—and we are convinced they are—then the NCAA's complete control over those broadcasts provides a solid basis for the District Court's conclusion that the NCAA possesses market power with respect to those broadcasts. * * *

Thus, the NCAA television plan on its face constitutes a restraint upon the operation of a free market, and the findings of the District Court establish that it has operated to raise prices and reduce output. Under the Rule of Reason, these hallmarks of anticompetitive behavior place upon petitioner a heavy burden of establishing an affirmative defense which competitively justifies this apparent deviation from the operations of a free market. We turn now to the NCAA's proffered justifications.

IV

Relying on *Broadcast Music*, petitioner argues that its television plan constitutes a cooperative "joint venture" which assists in the marketing of broadcast rights and hence is procompetitive. While joint ventures have no immunity from the antitrust laws * * * a joint selling arrangement may "mak[e] possible a new product by reaping otherwise unattainable efficiencies." The essential contribution made by the NCAA's arrangement is to define the number of games that may be televised, to establish the price for each exposure, and to define the basic terms of each contract between the network and a home team. The NCAA does not, however, act as a selling agent for any school or for any conference of schools. * * * Thus, the effect of the network plan is not to eliminate individual sales of broadcasts, since these still occur, albeit subject to fixed prices and output limitations. Unlike *Broadcast Music's* blanket license covering broadcast rights to a large number of individual compositions, here the same rights are still sold on an individual basis, only in a noncompetitive market.

The District Court did not find that the NCAA's television plan produced any procompetitive efficiencies which enhanced the

---

[49] For the same reasons, it is also apparent that the unique appeal of NCAA football telecasts for viewers means that "from the standpoint of the consumer—whose interests the statute was especially intended to serve," there can be no doubt that college football constitutes a separate market for which there is no reasonable substitute. Thus we agree with the District Court that it makes no difference whether the market is defined from the standpoint of broadcasters, advertisers, or viewers. [The dissent took issue with the majority's conclusion on this point, arguing that the competitive effect of the NCAA's plan should have been judged in a broader "entertainment" market. He also urged the Court to consider the non-economic nature of the NCAA's program of self regulation. 468 U.S. at 131–33 (White, J., dissenting). Eds.]

competitiveness of college football television rights; to the contrary it concluded that NCAA football could be marketed just as effectively without the television plan. There is therefore no predicate in the findings for petitioner's efficiency justification. Indeed, petitioner's argument is refuted by the District Court's finding concerning price and output. If the NCAA's television plan produced procompetitive efficiencies, the plan would increase output and reduce the price of televised games. The District Court's contrary findings accordingly undermine petitioner's position. In light of these findings, it cannot be said that "the agreement on price is necessary to market the product at all." *Broadcast Music*, 441 U.S., at 23, 99 S.Ct., at 1564. In *Broadcast Music*, the availability of a package product that no individual could offer enhanced the total volume of music that was sold. Unlike this case, there was no limit of any kind placed on the volume that might be sold in the entire market and each individual remained free to sell his own music without restraint. Here production has been limited, not enhanced. No individual school is free to televise its own games without restraint. The NCAA's efficiency justification is not supported by the record.

Neither is the NCAA's television plan necessary to enable the NCAA to penetrate the market through an attractive package sale. Since broadcasting rights to college football constitute a unique product for which there is no ready substitute, there is no need for collective action in order to enable the product to compete against its nonexistent competitors.[55]* * *

V

Throughout the history of its regulation of intercollegiate football telecasts, the NCAA has indicated its concern with protecting live attendance. This concern, it should be noted, is not with protecting live attendance at games which *are* shown on television; that type of interest is not at issue in this case. Rather, the concern is that fan interest in a televised game may adversely affect ticket sales for games that will not appear on television.

* * * [T]he District Court found that there was no evidence to support that theory in today's market. Moreover, as the District Court found, the television plan has evolved in a manner inconsistent with its original design to protect gate attendance. Under the current plan, games are shown on television during all hours that college football games are played. The plan simply does not protect live attendance by ensuring that games will not be shown on television at the same time as live events.

---

[55] If the NCAA faced "interbrand" competition from available substitutes, then certain forms of collective action might be appropriate in order to enhance its ability to compete. Our conclusion concerning the availability of substitutes in Part III, *supra*, forecloses such a justification in this case, however.

There is, however, a more fundamental reason for rejecting this defense. The NCAA's argument that its television plan is necessary to protect live attendance is not based on a desire to maintain the integrity of college football as a distinct and attractive product, but rather on a fear that the product will not prove sufficiently attractive to draw live attendance when faced with competition from televised games. At bottom the NCAA's position is that ticket sales for most college games are unable to compete in a free market. The television plan protects ticket sales by limiting output—just as any monopolist increases revenues by reducing output. By seeking to insulate live ticket sales from the full spectrum of competition because of its assumption that the product itself is insufficiently attractive to consumers, petitioner forwards a justification that is inconsistent with the basic policy of the Sherman Act. * * *

VI

* * *

Our decision not to apply a *per se* rule to this case rests in large part on our recognition that a certain degree of cooperation is necessary if the type of competition that petitioner and its member institutions seek to market is to be preserved. * * * The specific restraints on football telecasts that are challenged in this case do not, however, fit into the same mold as do rules defining the conditions of the contest, the eligibility of participants, or the manner in which members of a joint enterprise shall share the responsibilities and the benefits of the total venture.

The NCAA does not claim that its television plan has equalized or is intended to equalize competition within any one league. The plan is nationwide in scope and there is no single league or tournament in which all college football teams compete. * * * The interest in maintaining a competitive balance that is asserted by the NCAA as a justification for regulating all television of intercollegiate football is not related to any neutral standard or to any readily identifiable group of competitors.

The television plan is not even arguably tailored to serve such an interest. It does not regulate the amount of money that any college may spend on its football program, nor the way in which the colleges may use the revenues that are generated by their football programs, whether derived from the sale of television rights, the sale of tickets, or the sale of concessions or program advertising. The plan simply imposes a restriction on one source of revenue that is more important to some colleges than to others. There is no evidence that this restriction produces any greater measure of equality throughout the NCAA than would a restriction on alumni donations, tuition rates, or any other revenue-producing activity. * * *

Perhaps the most important reason for rejecting the argument that the interest in competitive balance is served by the television plan is the District Court's unambiguous and well-supported finding that many more games would be televised in a free market than under the NCAA plan. The hypothesis that legitimates the maintenance of competitive balance as a procompetitive justification under the Rule of Reason is that equal competition will maximize consumer demand for the product. The finding that consumption will materially increase if the controls are removed is a compelling demonstration that they do not in fact serve any such legitimate purpose.

* * *

Affirmed.

[The dissenting opinion of Mr. Justice White, with whom Justice Rehnquist joined, is omitted. Eds.]

The Court in *NCAA* observes that the television plan, by restricting output and setting price, is indistinguishable from per se unlawful price fixing. Why then did it decline to apply per se analysis to the plan? In applying the rule of reason, how elaborate an inquiry did it undertake? In footnote 26 the Court says "there is often no bright line separating *per se* from Rule of Reason analysis." Is that proposition inconsistent with the Court's assertion in *National Society of Professional Engineers*, decided just six years before, that Section 1 cases fall into "two categories," per se or rule of reason? Read footnotes 39 and 42 and the related text carefully. What could Professor Areeda have meant when he suggested that the rule of reason could be "applied in the twinkling of an eye"? What did the Justice Department mean in its brief when it argued that "market power is only one test of 'reasonableness' "? What then distinguishes per se from rule of reason treatment?

What evidence did the Court cite in support of its conclusion that the plaintiffs had established the anticompetitive effects of the television plan? Note that once the Court concluded in Part III of its opinion that the plaintiffs had carried their burden of demonstrating anticompetitive effect, the burden shifted to the NCAA to respond with some procompetitive justification: "Under the Rule of Reason, these hallmarks of anticompetitive behavior place upon petitioner a heavy burden of establishing an affirmative defense which competitively justifies this apparent deviation from the operations of a free market." Parts IV and V thus turn to consideration of the NCAA's proffered defenses. Did the Court conclude that, as in *National Society of Professional Engineers*, the defenses were not cognizable? Or did the Court find that the NCAA failed to satisfy the burden that had shifted to it? These questions have recurred in the NCAA's later encounters with the Sherman Act, but with mixed results. *See, e.g., O'Bannon v. NCAA*, 802 F.3d 1049 (9th Cir. 2015) (applying rule of reason to affirm in part antitrust challenge to NCAA's athlete compensation rules); *Marucci Sports, L.L.C. v. NCAA*, 751 F.3d 368 (5th Cir. 2014) (dismissing complaint by baseball bat manufacturer challenging NCAA regulations for non-wood bats); *Agnew v. NCAA*, 683 F.3d 328 (7th Cir. 2012) (dismissing action by student athletes challenging regulations affecting student scholarships); *Law v. NCAA*, 134 F.3d 1010 (10th Cir. 1998) (applying rule of reason to conclude that NCAA's limit on compensation of college basketball coaches was an unlawful restraint of trade).

The Court observes in its discussion of the "Background to the Controversy" that the plaintiffs filed suit after they were threatened with disciplinary sanctions by the NCAA and that other schools, fearing similar action, did not join them under the alternative contract they had negotiated. Was the NCAA using the threat of disciplinary action to support its cartel by impeding the competitive efforts of its non-compliant members? Recall from our discussions of the lysine cartel and *JTC Petroleum* in Chapter 1 that collusion and exclusion can often occur together, because cartel members may need to control for competitive challenges or other changing market conditions. We will examine this issue in greater depth in Chapter 3.

How should the courts approach arrangements that include a multiplicity of restraints? What if no single restraint has a very significant impact on competition, but collectively they do? Should all be enjoined? Some? Restraints of trade can be found unreasonable either individually or collectively. How did the Court approach the restraints in *NCAA*? Did the Court here question the validity of the NCAA's formation? Any other aspects of its operation? Or was this a narrowly focused analysis solely of the competitive effects of the television contract?

In the Note that follows, we examine the ramifications and continued significance of *NCAA*. It was a watershed case that came to be associated with "quick look" or "abbreviated" application of the rule of reason. More broadly, it signaled the Court's movement towards a more fluid, "continuum" understanding of the rule of reason.

NOTE ON THE DEVELOPMENT OF THE "QUICK LOOK"

NCAA was later clarified in *FTC v. Ind. Fed'n of Dentists*, 476 U.S. 447 (1986) ("*IFD*"), which together with *NCAA* endorsed what has become known as the "quick look" or "truncated" rule of reason. With origins in Professor Philip Areeda's "twinkling of an eye" allusion cited by *NCAA* in its footnote 39, the quick look acknowledges that there are alternatives to the seemingly bipolar extremes of per se condemnation and "full-blown" rule of reason analysis. Just as efficiencies in cases like *Broadcast Music* demonstrated that rote application of the per se rule can be unwarranted, *NCAA* held that harm to competition can be so evident that a court will be justified in shifting the burden of production to the defendants to justify their conduct without undertaking any "elaborate industry analysis," an allusion to the full-blown rule of reason, which has become associated with additional evidence that would support an inference of anticompetitive effect, especially evidence of market power.

In *IFD*, the FTC challenged the Indiana Federation of Dentists' policy of refusing to supply x-rays to insurers, who used the x-rays to verify treatment decisions and to determine consequent payments to the dentists for services rendered to their insureds. Although the Federation argued that its actions were justified to ensure quality dental care, the FTC argued, and the Court found, that the refusal to supply x-rays frustrated efforts at cost containment by the insurance companies. The Federation also argued that it lacked market power, and that the FTC should have been required to define the relevant markets in which its members competed and demonstrate that it had market power in each of those markets as a basis for inferring probable anticompetitive effects.

As in *NCAA*, the Court rejected the Federation's demand that the FTC prove "market power" given the more direct record evidence of actual harm:

> Since the purpose of the inquiries into market definition and market power is to determine whether an arrangement has the potential for genuine adverse effects on competition, "proof of actual detrimental effects, such as reduction of output," can obviate the need for an inquiry into market power, which is but a "surrogate for detrimental effects." In this case, we conclude that the finding of actual, sustained adverse effects on competition in those areas where IFD dentists predominated, viewed in light of the reality that markets for dental services tend to be relatively localized, is legally sufficient to support a finding that the challenged restraint was unreasonable even in the absence of elaborate market analysis.

IFD, 476 U.S. at 460–61 (citations omitted).

Taken together, *NCAA* and *IFD* provided important additional guidance in applying the rule of reason. In both cases the Court re-emphasized its holding in *National Society of Professional Engineers* that the focus of all Section 1 inquiries is on proof of anticompetitive effects. But it recognized that such effects can be proven either with direct or circumstantial evidence. Circumstantial evidence—what was being demanded by the NCAA and the Federation—would consist of market definition, a calculation of market shares, and an inference from high market shares that the defendants had market power, *i.e.*, the capacity to harm competition. Direct evidence—what the plaintiffs proffered in both cases—was evidence of actual anticompetitive effects, of the exercise of market power, such as reduced output, higher prices, or diminished quality. Such direct evidence, because it is responsive to the ultimate question under Section 1, obviates the need for an inquiry into market power as evidenced circumstantially through inferences drawn from market shares and market power.

The Court's suggestion that "market power" is an alternative to proof of actual detrimental effects is sometimes a source of confusion. Another way to understand the Court's insight in the two cases is that market power is the source of the ability to inflict competitive harm, but in cases like *NCAA* and *IFD* where direct evidence of harm is available, the evidence demonstrates the actual exercise of that power, whereas in circumstantial evidence cases it is inferred. Hence, when direct evidence of actual effects is presented, there is no need for "elaborate industry analysis" in the form of market definition and market share calculations. Direct evidence is qualitatively superior to circumstantial evidence. Of course, a plaintiff could offer both, but the Court's principal point was that it should not have to do so. *See generally* Andrew I. Gavil, *Moving Beyond Caricature and Characterization: The Modern Rule of Reason in Practice*, 85 S. CAL. L. REV. 733 (2012).

The two cases also provided important guidance on two operational characteristics of the rule of reason: (1) the allocation of burdens; and (2) the scope of cognizable defenses.

First, like per se analysis, the "quick look" can be understood in evidentiary terms as a burden-shifting device. In both *NCAA* and *IFD*, the Court held that evidence of actual harm to competition provides the needed basis to shift a burden of production to the defendant. Because market power is highly probable if not inherent in the showing of actual harm to competition, plaintiffs who proffer such direct evidence need not also have to bear the burden of proving market power through circumstantial evidence—high market shares in a properly defined relevant market. In contrast to per se analysis, however, the quick look creates a rebuttable, not an irrebuttable, presumption of unreasonableness, typically because there is some potential and plausible efficiency justification for the conduct. This was evident in the Court's rationale for declining to apply per se analysis in both *Broadcast Music* and *NCAA*.

Second, the quick look narrowed the range of cognizable rebuttal evidence. Not only did the Court conclude that it was not necessary for the plaintiff to present circumstantial evidence in addition to direct evidence of harm, but it twice rejected a defendant's effort torebut a case based on evidence of actual harm by presenting circumstantial evidence of *lack* of market power, such as a diminutive market share.

Quick look analysis as applied in *NCAA* and *IFD* thus shares a common characteristic with per se analysis: once the plaintiff has met its burden, it is difficult for the defendant to rebut. Under per se analysis, that is because the presumption of harm is irrebuttable. With quick look analysis based on a showing of actual harm, it will be difficult for a defendant to argue based on circumstantial evidence that the court should infer lack of power in the face of evidence not only that it possesses it, but that it has exercised it. To rebut the showing of anticompetitive effects, a defendant must challenge the direct evidence of harm on its own terms. The Supreme Court reiterated the reasoning of *NCAA* and *IFD* in *Eastman Kodak Co. v. Image Technical Services, Inc.*, 504 U.S. 451, 469 & n.15 (1992), a case that involved claims of exclusionary conduct under both Sections 1 and 2. *See also Toys "R" Us, Inc. v. FTC*, 221 F.3d 928 (7th Cir. 2000). *But see Republic Tobacco Co. v. North Atlantic Trading Co.*, 381 F.3d 717 (7th Cir. 2004) (declining to apply direct evidence approach in non-horizontal case); Andrew I. Gavil, *A Comment on the Seventh Circuit's* Republic Tobacco *Decision: On the Utility of "Direct Evidence of Anticompetitive Effects,"* ANTITRUST, Spring 2005, at 59.

NCAA and *IFD* had three common features: (1) application of per se analysis was deemed inappropriate owing to the possibility of a plausible and cognizable justification for the challenged conduct; (2) a "quick" review of the evidence indicated that actual harm had occurred; and (3) the Court rejected efforts by the defendant to rebut the plaintiffs' evidence of actual harm by presenting circumstantial evidence of lack of market power. The two cases did not specify, however, what kind and how much evidence of actual effects would be sufficient to warrant a burden shift. Actual price effects, for example, could be relatively minor or substantial, and evidence of such effects may be relatively more persuasive or conjectural. Moreover, developing proof of actual detrimental effects to competition is not necessarily any "quicker" than presenting a fully developed circumstantial case based on market definition and market share analysis. It might be, but not necessarily. Finally, the approach could be faulted if it too readily permits a burden shift, even on the slightest bit of "actual effects" evidence. "Too quick" of a look could lead to more challenges based on relatively weak evidence in contexts where anticompetitive effects seem less likely.

These issues required further consideration and development, a process that continued in our next case, *California Dental Association ("CDA")*. Note how *NCAA* and *IFD* continued to evolve, and became recognized as establishing a more structured and focused approach to applying the rule of reason. What if anything does *CDA* add to that approach beyond recognizing it? Although the Court reaffirmed its commitment to the quick look concept, does it place any limitations on its use? If so, is the end result greater or lesser clarity in the use of the rule of reason?

CALIFORNIA DENTAL ASSOCIATION v. FEDERAL TRADE COMMISSION

Supreme Court of the United States, 1999.
526 U.S. 756, 119 S.Ct. 1604, 143 L.Ed.2d 935.

JUSTICE SOUTER delivered the opinion of the Court.

There are two issues in this case: whether the jurisdiction of the Federal Trade Commission extends to the California Dental Association (CDA), a nonprofit professional association, and whether a "quick look" sufficed to justify finding that certain advertising restrictions adopted by the CDA violated the antitrust laws. We hold that the Commission's jurisdiction under the Federal Trade Commission Act (FTC Act) extends to an association that, like the CDA, provides substantial economic benefit to its for-profit members, but that where, as here, any anticompetitive effects of given restraints are far from intuitively obvious, the rule of reason demands a more thorough enquiry into the consequences of those restraints than the Court of Appeals performed.

I

The CDA is a voluntary nonprofit association of local dental societies to which some 19,000 dentists belong, including about three-quarters of those practicing in the State. The CDA is exempt from federal income tax * * * although it has for-profit subsidiaries that give its members advantageous access to various sorts of insurance, including liability coverage, and to financing for their real estate, equipment, cars, and patients' bills. The CDA lobbies and litigates in its members' interests, and conducts marketing and public relations campaigns for their benefit.

The dentists who belong to the CDA through these associations agree to abide by a Code of Ethics (Code) including the following § 10:

> "Although any dentist may advertise, no dentist shall advertise or solicit patients in any form of communication in a manner that is false or misleading in any material respect. In order to properly serve the public, dentists should represent themselves in a manner that contributes to the esteem of the public. Dentists should not misrepresent their training and competence in any way that would be false or misleading in any material respect."

The CDA has issued a number of advisory opinions interpreting this section,[1] and through separate advertising guidelines intended to help

---

[1] The advisory opinions, which substantially mirror parts of the California Business and Professions Code, include the following propositions:

"A statement or claim is false or misleading in any material respect when it:

"a. contains a misrepresentation of fact;

"b. is likely to mislead or deceive because in context it makes only a partial disclosure of relevant facts;

"c. is intended or is likely to create false or unjustified expectations of favorable results and/or costs;

"d. relates to fees for specific types of services without fully and specifically disclosing all variables and other relevant factors;

"e. contains other representations or implications that in reasonable probability will cause an ordinarily prudent person to misunderstand or be deceived.

"Any communication or advertisement which refers to the cost of dental services shall be exact, without omissions, and shall make each service clearly identifiable, without the use of such phrases as 'as low as,' 'and up,' 'lowest prices,' or words or phrases of similar import.

"Any advertisement which refers to the cost of dental services and uses words of comparison or relativity-for example, 'low fees'-must be based on verifiable data substantiating the comparison or statement of relativity. The burden shall be on the dentist who advertises in such terms to establish the accuracy of the comparison or statement of relativity."

members comply with the Code and with state law the CDA has advised its dentists of disclosures they must make under state law when engaging in discount advertising.[2]

* * *

The Commission brought a complaint against the CDA, alleging that it applied its guidelines so as to restrict truthful, nondeceptive advertising, and so violated § 5 of the FTC Act. The complaint alleged that the CDA had unreasonably restricted two types of advertising: price advertising, particularly discounted fees, and advertising relating to the quality of dental services. An Administrative Law Judge (ALJ) * * * found that, although there had been no proof that the CDA exerted market power, no such proof was required to establish an antitrust violation under *In re Mass. Bd. of Registration in Optometry*, 110 F.T.C. 549 (1988), since the CDA had unreasonably prevented members and potential members from using truthful, nondeceptive advertising, all to the detriment of both dentists and consumers of dental services. He accordingly found a violation of § 5 of the FTC Act.

The Commission adopted the factual findings of the ALJ except for his conclusion that the CDA lacked market power, with which the Commission disagreed. The Commission treated the CDA's restrictions on discount advertising as illegal *per se*. In the alternative, the Commission held the price advertising (as well as the nonprice) restrictions to be violations of the Sherman and FTC Acts under an abbreviated rule-of-reason analysis. * * *

The Court of Appeals for the Ninth Circuit affirmed, sustaining the Commission's assertion of jurisdiction over the CDA and its ultimate conclusion on the merits. The court thought it error for the Commission to have applied *per se* analysis to the price advertising restrictions, finding analysis under the rule of reason required for all the restrictions. But the Court of Appeals went on to explain that the Commission had properly [applied an abbreviated version of the rule of reason]. * * *

The Court of Appeals thought truncated rule-of-reason analysis to be in order for several reasons. As for the restrictions on discount advertising, they "amounted in practice to a fairly 'naked' restraint on price competition

---

"Advertising claims as to the quality of services are not susceptible to measurement or verification; accordingly, such claims are likely to be false or misleading in any material respect." * * *

2   The disclosures include:

"1. The dollar amount of the nondiscounted fee for the service[.]

"2. Either the dollar amount of the discount fee or the percentage of the discount for the specific service[.]

"3. The length of time that the discount will be offered[.]

"4. Verifiable fees[.]

"5. [The identity of] [s]pecific groups who qualify for the discount or any other terms and conditions or restrictions for qualifying for the discount."

itself." The CDA's procompetitive justification, that the restrictions encouraged disclosure and prevented false and misleading advertising, carried little weight because "it is simply infeasible to disclose all of the information that is required," and "the record provides no evidence that the rule has in fact led to increased disclosure and transparency of dental pricing." As to non-price advertising restrictions, the court said that

> "[t]hese restrictions are in effect a form of output limitation, as they restrict the supply of information about individual dentists' services. The restrictions may also affect output more directly, as quality and comfort advertising may induce some customers to obtain nonemergency care when they might not otherwise do so. * * * Under these circumstances, we think that the restriction is a sufficiently naked restraint on output to justify quick look analysis."

* * *

II

[In Part II of its opinion, the Court affirmed the view of both the Commission and the Court of Appeals that the FTC Act provides the FTC with jurisdiction over not-for-profit associations like the CDA when they engage in activities that significantly enhance their members' "profits." Eds.]

III

The Court of Appeals treated as distinct questions the sufficiency of the analysis of anticompetitive effects and the substantiality of the evidence supporting the Commission's conclusions. Because we decide that the Court of Appeals erred when it held as a matter of law that quick-look analysis was appropriate (with the consequence that the Commission's abbreviated analysis and conclusion were sustainable), we do not reach the question of the substantiality of the evidence supporting the Commission's conclusion.[8]

In *National Collegiate Athletic Assn. v. Board of Regents of Univ. of Okla.*, we held that a "naked restraint on price and output requires some competitive justification even in the absence of a detailed market analysis." Elsewhere, we held that "no elaborate industry analysis is required to demonstrate the anticompetitive character of" horizontal agreements among competitors to refuse to discuss prices, *National Soc. of Professional Engineers v. United States*, or to withhold a particular desired service, *FTC v. Indiana Federation of Dentists*. In each of these cases, which have formed the basis for what has come to be called abbreviated or "quick-look"

---

[8] We leave to the Court of Appeals the question whether on remand it can effectively assess the Commission's decision for substantial evidence on the record, or whether it must remand to the Commission for a more extensive rule-of-reason analysis on the basis of an enhanced record.

analysis under the rule of reason, an observer with even a rudimentary understanding of economics could conclude that the arrangements in question would have an anticompetitive effect on customers and markets. * * * As in such cases, quick-look analysis carries the day when the great likelihood of anticompetitive effects can easily be ascertained.

The case before us, however, fails to present a situation in which the likelihood of anticompetitive effects is comparably obvious. Even on Justice Breyer's view that bars on truthful and verifiable price and quality advertising are *prima facie* anticompetitive, * * * and place the burden of procompetitive justification on those who agree to adopt them, the very issue at the threshold of this case is whether professional price and quality advertising is sufficiently verifiable in theory and in fact to fall within such a general rule. Ultimately our disagreement with Justice Breyer turns on our different responses to this issue. Whereas he accepts, as the Ninth Circuit seems to have done, that the restrictions here were like restrictions on advertisement of price and quality generally, it seems to us that the CDA's advertising restrictions might plausibly be thought to have a net procompetitive effect, or possibly no effect at all on competition. The restrictions on both discount and nondiscount advertising are, at least on their face, designed to avoid false or deceptive advertising[9] in a market characterized by striking disparities between the information available to the professional and the patient. * * *

The explanation proffered by the Court of Appeals for the likely anticompetitive effect of the CDA's restrictions on discount advertising began with the unexceptionable statements that "price advertising is fundamental to price competition," and that "[r]estrictions on the ability to advertise prices normally make it more difficult for consumers to find a lower price and for dentists to compete on the basis of price." The court then acknowledged that, according to the CDA, the restrictions nonetheless furthered the "legitimate, indeed procompetitive, goal of preventing false and misleading price advertising." The Court of Appeals might, at this juncture, have recognized that the restrictions at issue here are very far from a total ban on price or discount advertising, and might have considered the possibility that the particular restrictions on professional advertising could have different effects from those "normally" found in the commercial world, even to the point of promoting competition by reducing the occurrence of unverifiable and misleading across-the-board discount advertising. Instead, the Court of Appeals confined itself to the brief assertion that the "CDA's disclosure requirements appear to prohibit across-the-board discounts because it is simply infeasible to disclose all of the information that is required," followed by the observation that "the

---

[9]　That false or misleading advertising has an anticompetitive effect, as that term is customarily used, has been long established. * * *

record provides no evidence that the rule has in fact led to increased disclosure and transparency of dental pricing."

But these observations brush over the professional context and describe no anticompetitive effects. Assuming that the record in fact supports the conclusion that the CDA disclosure rules essentially bar advertisement of across-the-board discounts, it does not obviously follow that such a ban would have a net anticompetitive effect here. * * * [T]he CDA's rule appears to reflect the prediction that any costs to competition associated with the elimination of across-the-board advertising will be outweighed by gains to consumer information (and hence competition) created by discount advertising that is exact, accurate, and more easily verifiable (at least by regulators). As a matter of economics this view may or may not be correct, but it is not implausible, and neither a court nor the Commission may initially dismiss it as presumptively wrong.[12]

In theory, it is true, the Court of Appeals neither ruled out the plausibility of some procompetitive support for the CDA's requirements nor foreclosed the utility of an evidentiary discussion on the point. The court indirectly acknowledged the plausibility of procompetitive justifications for the CDA's position when it stated that "the record provides no evidence that the rule has in fact led to increased disclosure and transparency of dental pricing." But because petitioner alone would have had the incentive to introduce such evidence, the statement sounds as though the Court of Appeals may have thought it was justified without further analysis to shift a burden to the CDA to adduce hard evidence of the procompetitive nature of its policy; the court's aversion to empirical evidence at the moment of this implicit burden-shifting underscores the leniency of its enquiry into evidence of the restrictions' anticompetitive effects.

The Court of Appeals was comparably tolerant in accepting the sufficiency of abbreviated rule-of-reason analysis as to the nonprice advertising restrictions. The court began with the argument that "[t]hese restrictions are in effect a form of output limitation, as they restrict the supply of information about individual dentists' services." Although this sentence does indeed appear as cited, it is puzzling, given that the relevant output for antitrust purposes here is presumably not information or

---

[12] Justice Breyer suggests that our analysis is "of limited relevance," because "the basic question is whether this . . . theoretically redeeming virtue in fact offsets the restrictions' anticompetitive effects in this case." He thinks that the Commission and the Court of Appeals "adequately answered that question," but the absence of any empirical evidence on this point indicates that the question was not answered, merely avoided by implicit burden-shifting of the kind accepted by Justice Breyer. The point is that before a theoretical claim of anticompetitive effects can justify shifting to a defendant the burden to show empirical evidence of procompetitive effects, as quick-look analysis in effect requires, there must be some indication that the court making the decision has properly identified the theoretical basis for the anticompetitive effects and considered whether the effects actually are anticompetitive. Where, as here, the circumstances of the restriction are somewhat complex, assumption alone will not do.

advertising, but dental services themselves. The question is not whether the universe of possible advertisements has been limited (as assuredly it has), but whether the limitation on advertisements obviously tends to limit the total delivery of dental services. * * * If quality advertising actually induces some patients to obtain more care than they would in its absence, then restricting such advertising would reduce the demand for dental services, not the supply; and it is of course the producers' supply of a good in relation to demand that is normally relevant in determining whether a producer-imposed output limitation has the anticompetitive effect of artificially raising prices.[13]

Although the Court of Appeals acknowledged the CDA's view that "claims about quality are inherently unverifiable and therefore misleading," it responded that this concern "does not justify banning all quality claims without regard to whether they are, in fact, false or misleading." As a result, the court said, "the restriction is a sufficiently naked restraint on output to justify quick look analysis." The court assumed, in these words, that some dental quality claims may escape justifiable censure, because they are both verifiable and true. But its implicit assumption fails to explain why it gave no weight to the countervailing, and at least equally plausible, suggestion that restricting difficult-to-verify claims about quality or patient comfort would have a procompetitive effect by preventing misleading or false claims that distort the market. It is, indeed, entirely possible to understand the CDA's restrictions on unverifiable quality and comfort advertising as nothing more than a procompetitive ban on puffery.

The point is not that the CDA's restrictions necessarily have the procompetitive effect claimed by the CDA; it is possible that banning quality claims might have no effect at all on competitiveness. * * * And it is also of course possible that the restrictions might in the final analysis be anticompetitive. The point, rather, is that the plausibility of competing claims about the effects of the professional advertising restrictions rules out the indulgently abbreviated review to which the Commission's order was treated. The obvious anticompetitive effect that triggers abbreviated analysis has not been shown.

In light of our focus on the adequacy of the Court of Appeals's analysis, Justice Breyer's thorough-going, *de novo* antitrust analysis contains much to impress on its own merits but little to demonstrate the sufficiency of the

---

[13] Justice Breyer wonders if we "mea[n] this statement as an argument against the anticompetitive tendencies that flow from an agreement not to advertise service quality." But as the preceding sentence shows, we intend simply to question the logic of the Court of Appeals's suggestion that the restrictions are anticompetitive because they somehow "affect output," presumably with the intent to raise prices by limiting supply while demand remains constant. We do not mean to deny that an agreement not to advertise service quality might have anticompetitive effects. We merely mean that, absent further analysis of the kind Justice Breyer undertakes, it is not possible to conclude that the net effect of this particular restriction is anticompetitive.

Court of Appeals's review. The obligation to give a more deliberate look than a quick one does not arise at the door of this Court and should not be satisfied here in the first instance. Had the Court of Appeals engaged in a painstaking discussion in a league with Justice Breyer's (compare his 14 pages with the Ninth Circuit's 8), and had it confronted the comparability of these restrictions to bars on clearly verifiable advertising, its reasoning might have sufficed to justify its conclusion. Certainly Justice Breyer's treatment of the antitrust issues here is no "quick look." Lingering is more like it, and indeed Justice Breyer, not surprisingly, stops short of endorsing the Court of Appeals's discussion as adequate to the task.

Saying here that the Court of Appeals's conclusion at least required a more extended examination of the possible factual underpinnings than it received is not, of course, necessarily to call for the fullest market analysis. Although we have said that a challenge to a "naked restraint on price and output" need not be supported by "a detailed market analysis" in order to "requir[e] some competitive justification," *National Collegiate Athletic Assn.*, 468 U.S., at 110, 104 S.Ct. 2948, it does not follow that every case attacking a less obviously anticompetitive restraint (like this one) is a candidate for plenary market examination. The truth is that our categories of analysis of anticompetitive effect are less fixed than terms like *"per se,"* "quick look," and "rule of reason" tend to make them appear. We have recognized, for example, that "there is often no bright line separating *per se* from Rule of Reason analysis," since "considerable inquiry into market conditions" may be required before the application of any so-called *"per se"* condemnation is justified. *Id.* at 104, n.26, 104 S.Ct. 2948. "[W]hether the ultimate finding is the product of a presumption or actual market analysis, the essential inquiry remains the same—whether or not the challenged restraint enhances competition." *Id.*, at 104, 104 S.Ct. 2948. * * * As the circumstances here demonstrate, there is generally no categorical line to be drawn between restraints that give rise to an intuitively obvious inference of anticompetitive effect and those that call for more detailed treatment. What is required, rather, is an enquiry meet for the case, looking to the circumstances, details, and logic of a restraint. The object is to see whether the experience of the market has been so clear, or necessarily will be, that a confident conclusion about the principal tendency of a restriction will follow from a quick (or at least quicker) look, in place of a more sedulous one. And of course what we see may vary over time, if rule-of-reason analyses in case after case reach identical conclusions. For now, at least, a less quick look was required for the initial assessment of the tendency of these professional advertising restrictions. Because the Court of Appeals did not scrutinize the assumption of relative anticompetitive tendencies, we vacate the judgment and remand the case for a fuller consideration of the issue.

It is so ordered.

JUSTICE BREYER, with whom JUSTICE STEVENS, JUSTICE KENNEDY, and JUSTICE GINSBURG join, concurring in part and dissenting in part.

I agree with the Court that the Federal Trade Commission has jurisdiction over petitioner, and I join Parts I and II of its opinion. I also agree that in a "rule of reason" antitrust case "the quality of proof required should vary with the circumstances," that "[w]hat is required . . . is an enquiry meet for the case," and that the object is a "confident conclusion about the principal tendency of a restriction." But I do not agree that the Court has properly applied those unobjectionable principles here. In my view, a traditional application of the rule of reason to the facts as found by the Commission requires affirming the Commission—just as the Court of Appeals did below.

I

The Commission's conclusion is lawful if its "factual findings," insofar as they are supported by "substantial evidence," "make out a violation of Sherman Act § 1." To determine whether that is so, I would not simply ask whether the restraints at issue are anticompetitive overall. Rather, like the Court of Appeals (and the Commission), I would break that question down into four classical, subsidiary antitrust questions: (1) What is the specific restraint at issue? (2) What are its likely anticompetitive effects? (3) Are there offsetting procompetitive justifications? (4) Do the parties have sufficient market power to make a difference?

A

The most important question is the first: What are the specific restraints at issue? Those restraints do *not* include merely the agreement to which the California Dental Association's (Dental Association or Association) ethical rule literally refers, namely, a promise to refrain from advertising that is " 'false or misleading in any material respect.' " Instead, the Commission found a set of restraints arising out of the way the Dental Association implemented this innocent-sounding ethical rule in practice, through advisory opinions, guidelines, enforcement policies, and review of membership applications. As implemented, the ethical rule reached beyond its nominal target, to prevent truthful and nondeceptive advertising. In particular, the Commission determined that the rule, in practice:

(1) "precluded advertising that characterized a dentist's fees as being low, reasonable, or affordable,"

(2) "precluded advertising . . . of across the board discounts," and

(3) "prohibit[ed] all quality claims."

Whether the Dental Association's basic rule as *implemented* actually restrained the truthful and nondeceptive advertising of low prices, across-the-board discounts, and quality service are questions of fact. * * * [B]oth the ALJ and the Commission ultimately found against the Dental Association in respect to these facts. And the question for us—whether those agency findings are supported by substantial evidence—is not difficult.

* * *

B

Do each of the three restrictions mentioned have "the potential for genuine adverse effects on competition"? I should have thought that the anticompetitive tendencies of the three restrictions were obvious. An agreement not to advertise that a fee is reasonable, that service is inexpensive, or that a customer will receive a discount makes it more difficult for a dentist to inform customers that he charges a lower price. If the customer does not know about a lower price, he will find it more difficult to buy lower price service. That fact, in turn, makes it less likely that a dentist will obtain more customers by offering lower prices. And that likelihood means that dentists will prove less likely to offer lower prices. * * * The Commission thought this fact sufficient to hold (in the alternative) that the price advertising restrictions were unlawful *per se*. For present purposes, I need not decide whether the Commission was right in applying a *per se* rule. I need only assume a rule of reason applies, and note the serious anticompetitive tendencies of the price advertising restraints.

The restrictions on the advertising of service quality also have serious anticompetitive tendencies. This is not a case of "mere puffing." * * * [S]ome parents may still want to know that a particular dentist makes a point of "gentle care." Others may want to know about 1-year dental work guarantees. To restrict that kind of service quality advertisement is to restrict competition over the quality of service itself, for, unless consumers know, they may not purchase, and dentists may not compete to supply that which will make little difference to the demand for their services. That, at any rate, is the theory of the Sherman Act. And it is rather late in the day for anyone to deny the significant anticompetitive tendencies of an agreement that restricts competition in any legitimate respect, let alone one that inhibits customers from learning about the quality of a dentist's service.

Nor did the Commission rely solely on the unobjectionable proposition that a restriction on the ability of dentists to advertise on quality is likely to limit their incentive to compete on quality. Rather, the Commission pointed to record evidence affirmatively establishing that quality-based competition is important to dental consumers in California. Unsurprisingly, these consumers choose dental services based at least in part on "information about the type and quality of service." * * *

The FTC found that the price advertising restrictions amounted to a "naked attempt to eliminate price competition." It found that the service quality advertising restrictions "deprive consumers of information they value and of healthy competition for their patronage." It added that the "anticompetitive nature of these restrictions" was "plain." The Court of Appeals agreed. I do not believe it possible to deny the anticompetitive tendencies I have mentioned.

C

We must also ask whether, despite their anticompetitive tendencies, these restrictions might be justified by other procompetitive tendencies or redeeming virtues. This is a closer question—at least in theory. The Dental Association argues that the three relevant restrictions are inextricably tied to a legitimate Association effort to restrict false or misleading advertising. The Association, the argument goes, had to prevent dentists from engaging in the kind of truthful, nondeceptive advertising that it banned in order effectively to stop dentists from making unverifiable claims about price or service quality, which claims would mislead the consumer.

The problem with this or any similar argument is an empirical one. Notwithstanding its theoretical plausibility, the record does not bear out such a claim. The Commission, which is expert in the area of false and misleading advertising, was uncertain whether petitioner had even *made* the claim. It characterized petitioner's efficiencies argument as rooted in the (unproved) factual assertion that its ethical rule "challenges *only* advertising that is false or misleading." Regardless, the Court of Appeals wrote, in respect to the price restrictions, that "the record provides no evidence that the rule has in fact led to increased disclosure and transparency of dental pricing." With respect to quality advertising, the Commission stressed that the Association "offered no convincing argument, let alone evidence, that consumers of dental services have been, or are likely to be, harmed by the broad categories of advertising it restricts." * * *

With one exception, my own review of the record reveals no significant evidentiary support for the proposition that the Association's members must agree to ban truthful price and quality advertising in order to stop untruthful claims. The one exception is the obvious fact that one can stop untruthful advertising if one prohibits all advertising. But since the Association made virtually no effort to sift the false from the true, that fact does not make out a valid antitrust defense.

In the usual Sherman Act § 1 case, the defendant bears the burden of establishing a procompetitive justification. And the Court of Appeals was correct when it concluded that no such justification has been established here.

D

I shall assume that the Commission must prove one additional circumstance, namely, that the Association's restraints would likely have made a real difference in the marketplace. The Commission, disagreeing with the ALJ on this single point, found that the Association did possess enough market power to make a difference. In at least one region of California, the mid-Peninsula, its members accounted for more than 90% of the marketplace; on average they accounted for 75%. In addition, entry by new dentists into the market place is fairly difficult. Dental education is expensive * * * as is opening a new dentistry office. And Dental Association members believe membership in the Association is important, valuable, and recognized as such by the public.

These facts, in the Court of Appeals' view, were sufficient to show "enough market power to harm competition through [the Association's] standard setting in the area of advertising." And that conclusion is correct. Restrictions on advertising price discounts * * * may make a difference because potential patients may not respond readily to discount advertising by a handful (10%) of dentists who are not members of the Association. And that fact, in turn, means that the remaining 90% will prove less likely to engage in price competition. Facts such as these have previously led this Court to find market power—unless the defendant has overcome the showing with strong contrary evidence. I can find no reason for departing from that precedent here.

II

In the Court's view, the legal analysis conducted by the Court of Appeals was insufficient, and the Court remands the case for a more thorough application of the rule of reason. But in what way did the Court of Appeals fail? I find the Court's answers to this question unsatisfactory— when one divides the overall Sherman Act question into its traditional component parts and adheres to traditional judicial practice for allocating burdens of persuasion in an antitrust case.

Did the Court of Appeals misconceive the anticompetitive tendencies of the restrictions? * * *

* * * [T]he Court of Appeals * * * *rejected* the legal "treatment" customarily applied "to classic horizontal agreements to limit output or price competition"—*i.e.*, the FTC's (alternative) *per se* approach. It did so because the Association's "policies do not, on their face, ban truthful nondeceptive ads"; instead, they "have been enforced in a way that restricts truthful advertising." It added that "[t]he value of restricting false advertising . . . counsels some caution in attacking rules that purport to do so but merely sweep too broadly."

Did the Court of Appeals misunderstand the nature of an anticompetitive effect? * * *

* * * An agreement not to advertise, say, "gentle care" is anticompetitive because it imposes an artificial barrier against each dentist's independent decision to advertise gentle care. That barrier, in turn, tends to inhibit those dentists who want to supply gentle care from getting together with those customers who want to buy gentle care. There is adequate reason to believe that tendency present in this case.

Did the Court of Appeals inadequately consider possible procompetitive justifications? * * *

The Commission found that the defendant did not make the necessary showing that a redeeming virtue existed in practice. The Court of Appeals, asking whether the rules, as enforced, "augment[ed] competition and increase[d] market efficiency," found the Commission's conclusion supported by substantial evidence. * * *

The majority correctly points out that "petitioner alone would have had the incentive to introduce such evidence" of procompetitive justification. But despite this incentive, petitioner's brief in this Court offers nothing concrete to counter the Commission's conclusion that the record does not support the claim of justification. Petitioner's failure to produce such evidence itself "explain[s] why [the lower court] gave no weight to the . . . suggestion that restricting difficult-to-verify claims about quality or patient comfort would have a procompetitive effect by preventing misleading or false claims that distort the market."

* * * With respect to any of the three restraints found by the Commission, whether "net anticompetitive effects" follow is a matter of how the Commission, and, here, the Court of Appeals, have answered the questions I laid out at the beginning. Has the Commission shown that the restriction has anticompetitive tendencies? It has. Has the Association nonetheless shown offsetting virtues? It has not. Has the Commission shown market power sufficient for it to believe that the restrictions will likely make a real world difference? It has.

The upshot, in my view, is that the Court of Appeals, applying ordinary antitrust principles, reached an unexceptional conclusion. It is the same legal conclusion that this Court itself reached in *Indiana Federation*—a much closer case than this one. * * *

I would note that the form of analysis I have followed is not rigid; it admits of some variation according to the circumstances. The important point, however, is that its allocation of the burdens of persuasion reflects a gradual evolution within the courts over a period of many years. That evolution represents an effort carefully to blend the procompetitive objectives of the law of antitrust with administrative necessity. It represents a considerable advance, both from the days when the Commission had to present and/or refute every possible fact and theory, and from antitrust theories so abbreviated as to prevent proper analysis. The former prevented cases from ever reaching a conclusion, and the latter called forth the criticism that the "Government always wins." I hope that this case does not represent an abandonment of that basic, and important, form of analysis.

For these reasons, I respectfully dissent from Part III of the Court's opinion.

* * *

NCAA was decided by a vote of 7–2, with Justices White and Rehnquist dissenting. Justice White later authored the unanimous opinion of the Court in *IFD*. Note that the Court in *CDA* was again unanimous in endorsing use of quick look analysis and emphasizing that regardless of the mode of analysis, the rule of reason inquiry has a singular focus: competitive effects. But it divided 5–4 with respect to its application to the facts presented by the parties. What explains this division within the Court?

In answering that question, consider the implications of the quick look for the allocation of burdens between parties under the rule of reason. The majority and the dissent agreed that the plaintiff bore the initial burden of coming forward with evidence that the CDA's conduct was anticompetitive. They also agreed that once the quick look is triggered, the burden shifts to the defendant to come forward with evidence to support its defenses. But they disagreed about the parties' respective ability to meet their burdens under the specific facts of the case. In the view of the majority, the FTC had not presented sufficient evidence to warrant the quick look's burden shift: "the Court of Appeals may have thought it was justified without further analysis to shift a burden to the CDA to adduce hard evidence of the procompetitive nature of its policy; the court's adversion to empirical evidence at the moment of this implicit burden shifting underscores the leniency of its enquiry into evidence of the restrictions' anticompetitive effects." *See supra* Chapter 2, at 204. Why weren't the alleged anticompetitive effects of the CDA's restrictions obvious enough to warrant a burden shift that would have required CDA to support its assertions of procompetitive justifications? In contrast, Justice Breyer, joined by three other justices, concluded that the FTC had met its burden with respect to anticompetitive effect under the quick look, and hence that the burden shifted to the CDA, which was therefore required to support its argument that the restrictions either were procompetitive or that they had no impact on competition. *See supra* Chapter 2, at 209.

Note that once Justice Breyer concluded that the burden had shifted, he went on to consider whether the CDA had supported its assertion of procompetitive justifications, something the majority did not view as necessary given its view that the burden never shifted from the FTC to the CDA. Finding that evidence lacking, Justice Breyer would have affirmed the decisions of the court of appeals and the FTC. If the majority had agreed that the FTC had met its initial burden of production and the burden had shifted to the CDA, what evidence would the CDA have needed to produce in order to shift the burden of production back to the FTC? Given Justice Breyer's assessment of the record, would the majority have agreed that the CDA failed to support its defenses? If so, should the majority have been less demanding of the FTC's evidence of harm? From a decision-theoretic point of view, what are the consequences of allowing quick look analysis to be triggered too easily, as the majority feared? Too slowly, as the dissent feared?

CDA posed a question about the scope of quick look analysis: can it be triggered by a combination of economic reasoning and circumstantial evidence or is it only applicable in cases presenting evidence of actual competitive harm? As we have seen, when it comes to price-fixing and market division, courts have long been comfortable relying on facial analysis supported by economic reasoning to support an irrebuttable presumption that certain conduct will be anticompetitive. This was further discussed in Sidebar 2–4, which considered the contemporary justifications for per se analysis. Are "quick look" cases distinct?

The FTC had not relied on actual effects evidence, such as evidence of reduced output and higher prices, as in *NCAA*, but rather on its view that the anticompetitive effects of the CDA's restrictions on advertising were relatively obvious, so much so that a burden shift to the CDA that would require it to come forward with evidence of the procompetitive justifications for the restrictions was warranted. *See* Timothy J. Muris, California Dental Association v. Federal Trade Commission: *The Revenge of Footnote 17*, 8 SUP. CT. ECON. REV. 265 (2000) (arguing that the empirical literature concerning the consequences of restraining professional advertising should have been sufficient to support the conclusion that CDA's restraints on advertising were likely to lead to increased prices without any improvement in quality). In dissent, Justice Breyer agreed. He saw no reason to be cautious given the nature of CDA's restraints and the general evidence available regarding the competitive consequences of sweeping restrictions on advertising. In his view, the anticompetitive effects were likely enough to warrant a burden shift. *See also* HERBERT HOVENKAMP, THE ANTITRUST ENTERPRISE: PRINCIPLE AND EXECUTION 147 (2005):

> * * * As a matter of pure logic, the Court was certainly right when it said that competitor-created restraints on advertising could increase, decrease, or have no impact at all on the output of dental

services. As a matter of evidence and history, however, that position is myopic. * * * [A] fox going into a hen house at night might be intending to kill chickens, to take a harmless nap, or to gather eggs and clean cages. But the farmer, knowing the history of foxes in hen houses, need not wait until the fox's intentions are clear.

Id. at 147–48.

Since *CDA*, it has been common for defendants to argue that the decision limited reliance on the quick look to cases of actual harm. In support of that position, some commentators and later litigants point to the Court's observation that "quick look analysis carries the day when the great likelihood of anticompetitive effects can easily be ascertained" and its conclusion that "[t]he obvious anticompetitive effect that triggers abbreviated analysis has not been shown." (*See supra* Chapter 2, at 205). These statements, plus its reference to the court of appeals' "adversion to *empirical* evidence," could be cited to suggest that a quick look burden shift will only be appropriate when he plaintiff comes forward with evidence of actual adverse effects. But in footnote 12, the Court also stated: "before a *theoretical claim of anticompetitive effects can justify shifting to a defendant the burden to show empirical evidence of procompetitive effects*, as quick-look analysis in effect requires, there must be some indication that the court making the decision has properly identified the theoretical basis for the anticompetitive effects and considered whether the effects actually are anticompetitive." (*See supra* Chapter 2, at 204) (emphasis added). Here the Court seems to embrace the possibility that economic reasoning—perhaps when accompanied by certain circumstantial evidence (background facts suggesting a high probability of competitive harm)—can also support reliance on quick look analysis. This would seem to be consistent with Professor Areeda's idea that sometimes the rule of reason can be applied "in the twinkling of an eye," an idea that the Court had cited with approval in *NCAA*. Proving "actual effects" may not be "quick" and so a requirement of actual effects as a prerequisite for quick look burden shifting would seem to be at odds with one of the principal motivating purposes of quick look analysis: reducing the costs of administering the rule of reason.

Under this reading of *CDA*, the Court was not rejecting the possibility of quick look analysis based on some combination of facts and economic theory, but was more narrowly concluding that the record in the case, which included a plausible claim by the CDA that its advertising restrictions could be pro-competitive, did not lend itself to such abbreviated analysis. Footnote 12 may also suggest that the Court had some concern about even-handed treatment of the parties: perhaps some of the justices thought it would be wrong to allow the plaintiff to shift a burden to the defendant based on a "theoretical" basis, only to have the defendant face a burden of producing "empirical evidence." In both *NCAA* and *IFD*, the converse was the case: the defendants were unable to shift a burden back to the plaintiffs, who had produced evidence of actual harm, with a theoretical case of efficiencies based on circumstantial evidence of their lack of market power. Would it make economic sense, however, to require symmetry in the nature and quality of the evidence? As we shall see in our next Section, after *CDA*, the FTC brought several cases to test the limits of *CDA* and more firmly establish that evidence of actual harm was a sufficient, but not necessary, precondition for quick look burden shifting.

The Court concluded its opinion in *CDA* by trying to dispel the notion that applying the rule of reason is a function of choosing from among three distinct approaches: "The truth is that our categories of analysis of anticompetitive effect are less fixed than terms like *"per se,"* "quick look," and "rule of reason" tend to make them appear. . . . What is required . . . is an enquiry meet for the case, looking to the circumstances, details, and logic of a restraint." (*See supra* Chapter 2, at 206). Does this explanation provide any clarity to the rule of reason? What options were available to the court of appeals on remand to resolve the case in light of this standard? *See California Dental Ass'n v. FTC*, 224 F.3d 942 (9th Cir. 2000) (concluding that the FTC failed to demonstrate the anticompetitive effect of the CDA's advertising restrictions and was not entitled to remand to further develop the record). Recall that Justice Breyer sought to articulate a more structured approach to implementing the rule of reason by presenting four questions to guide the inquiry. (*See supra* Chapter 2, at 207.) Which approach, Justice Souter's or Justice Breyer's, seems like a superior way to approach rule of reason analysis? Writing for the Court in *FTC v. Actavis, Inc.*, 133 S.Ct. 2223 (2013), Justice Breyer, citing his opinion in *CDA*, declined to apply quick look analysis because the probability that the conduct at issue there would be anticompetitive depended largely on the characteristics of the industry and a range of specific factors, which he outlined. *Id.* at 2237.

Before we proceed to consider how the lower courts have responded to *NCAA*, *IFD*, and *CDA*, we consider some of the unique issues that have arisen in antitrust cases concerning professions and their trade groups.

NOTE ON ANTITRUST AND THE PROFESSIONS

How important is it to an understanding of *CDA* that it concerned self-regulation by a trade association of professionals? As we have already seen, the application of the antitrust laws to the professions has a long and contentious history. Cases like *National Society of Professional Engineers, Maricopa County Medical Society, Indiana Federation of Dentists,* and *CDA* all involved application of the antitrust laws to efforts by professions to regulate their own competitive activities.

In virtually all of these cases the defendants urged the Supreme Court to acknowledge that there were differences in the nature of competition among professionals that warranted departure from traditional antitrust rules in other industries. These arguments typically sought either relief from the per se rule, or special consideration under the rule of reason. Until *CDA*, these efforts largely failed. Indeed, there was a well-established line of cases harshly condemning obviously anticompetitive arrangements among professionals. *See, e.g., Goldfarb v. Virginia State Bar*, 421 U.S. 773 (1975) (minimum fee schedules adopted by Bar Association were per se unlawful). Indeed, a wide range of economic benefits and harms can come from various forms of professional industry self-regulation. The argument continues to surface in other industry contexts, such as sports leagues, higher education, and especially health care.

What characteristics of professions might distinguish them from other trades or industries? Professor Lao observes that "[d]emands for special antitrust rules pertaining to the professions are usually based on information asymmetries between professionals and their clients or patients." Marina Lao, Comment: *The Rule of Reason and Horizontal Restraints Involving Professionals*, 68 ANTITRUST L.J. 499, 512 (2000). What does she mean by "information asymmetries"? How might such asymmetries warrant treating industry self-regulating restraints, such as the advertising restraints in *CDA*, differently from similar restraints among other industries? Is there any question in your mind that an agreement between General Motors and Ford to refuse to advertise quality or price information to consumers would be presumptively unlawful? What arguments related to the professional context of the CDA's advertising regulations did the Court appear to accept in *CDA*? How might they explain the outcome of the case?

Some commentators have sought to limit the scope of *CDA* by confining it to its "professional" context. These commentators cite the Court's long-evident animosity towards professional advertising, and its tolerance of efforts to curb it. *See, e.g.,* Stephen Calkins, *California Dental Association: Not a Quick Look but not the Full Monty*, 67 ANTITRUST L.J. at 518 ("The Court majority's unhappiness with professional advertising is essential to an understanding of its opinion in CDA."). Do you agree? Is the opinion relevant only to agreements among professionals relating to advertising? Does it relate to all professional self-regulation, whether directed at advertising or otherwise? Or does it have general applicability to all horizontal cases? For a broader discussion of the FTC's efforts over time to police the professions, see John E. Kwoka, Jr., *The Federal Trade Commission and the Professions: A Quarter Century of Accomplishment and Some New Challenges*, 72 ANTITRUST L.J. 997 (2005) (including an analysis of *CDA*).

We will revisit the antitrust treatment of professionals again in Chapter 8, when we consider cases involving what has been labelled the "state action" doctrine. In those cases, the FTC has challenged the anticompetitive conduct of boards of professionals who are active market participants and who have been imbued by the state with a degree of authority to supervise their fellow professionals. That conduct can give rise to liability when it has not been adequately supervised by the state. *See, e.g., North Carolina State Bd. of Dental Examiners v. FTC*, 135 S.Ct. 1101 (2015).

---

3. PROVING ANTICOMPETITIVE EFFECTS BY REBUTTABLE PRESUMPTION USING ECONOMIC REASONING

As we have seen, the Court in *CDA* divided over the degree to which economic theory and circumstantial evidence drawn from other industries could support reliance on the quick look and result in a shift of burden. And as we noted, after *CDA*, some commentators and litigants argued that *CDA* confined use of the quick look to cases of actual anticompetitive effect.

As a response, the FTC brought the following case, which could be understood as an effort to revisit and test the limits of that restrictive reading of *CDA*. As you read the decision, consider not only how the FTC supported its use of abbreviated rule of reason analysis, but how the defendants and the court responded. Also note the court's presentation of the history and development of the rule of reason—much of which we have now covered in this Chapter—and its overall approach to structuring the inquiry and accounting for burden shifting. What was its response, in particular, to the defendants' assertion that the quick look can only be used in cases of actual anticompetitive effect?

POLYGRAM HOLDING, INC. V. FEDERAL TRADE COMMISSION

United States Court of Appeals for the District of Columbia Circuit, 2005.
416 F.3d 29.

Before: GINSBURG, CHIEF JUDGE, and EDWARDS and ROGERS, CIRCUIT JUDGES.

GINSBURG, CHIEF JUDGE.

PolyGram Holding, Inc. and several of its affiliates petition for review of an order of the Federal Trade Commission holding PolyGram violated § 5 of the Federal Trade Commission Act, 15 U.S.C. § 45. As detailed below, PolyGram entered into an agreement with Warner Communications, Inc. to distribute the recording of a concert to be given by "The Three Tenors" in 1998. The two companies later entered into a separate agreement to suspend, for ten weeks, advertising and discounting of two earlier Three Tenors concert albums, one distributed by PolyGram and the other by Warner. The Commission held the latter agreement unlawful and prohibited PolyGram from entering into any similar agreement in the future. We agree with the Commission that, although not a *per se* violation of antitrust law, the agreement was presumptively unlawful and PolyGram failed to rebut that presumption. We therefore deny PolyGram's petition for review.

I.   Background

* * * The Three Tenors—José Carreras, Placido Domingo, and Luciano Pavarotti—put on spectacular concerts coinciding with the World Cup soccer finals in 1990, 1994, and 1998. PolyGram distributed the recording of the 1990 concert, which became one of the best-selling classical albums of all time. Warner distributed the 1994 concert album, which also met with great success. Both albums remained on the top-ten classical list throughout 1994, 1995, and 1996.

In late 1997 PolyGram and Warner agreed jointly to distribute the recording of The Three Tenors' July 1998 concert. Warner, which had the worldwide rights, retained the United States rights but licensed to PolyGram the exclusive right to distribute the 1998 album outside the United States, and the companies agreed to share equally the worldwide profit or loss on the project. The agreement also obligated PolyGram and Warner to consult with one another on all "marketing and promotional activities" for the 1998 concert album, but each company was free ultimately to pursue its own marketing strategy and to continue exploiting its earlier Three Tenors concert album without limitation. * * *

Representatives of PolyGram and Warner first met in January 1998 to discuss "marketing and operational issues." One of PolyGram's representatives voiced concern about the effect of marketing the earlier Three Tenors albums upon the prospects for the 1998 concert album and suggested the two companies impose an "advertising moratorium" surrounding the 1998 release, which was scheduled for August 1. According to notes of their next meeting (in March) PolyGram and Warner representatives agreed that "a big push" on the earlier albums "shouldn't take place before November 15." After that meeting, each company instructed its affiliates to cease all promotion of the 1990 and 1994 Three Tenors albums for approximately six weeks, beginning in late July or early August.

Apparently Warner's overseas division did not get the message because in May it announced an aggressive marketing campaign, scheduled to run through December, to discount and to promote the 1994 album throughout Europe. When PolyGram learned of this, it threatened to "retaliate" by cutting the price of its 1990 album. Accusations then flew between the two companies about which had started the imminent price war. Meanwhile, in June the promoter of The Three Tenors concert informed PolyGram and Warner that the repertoire for the 1998 concert would substantially overlap those of the 1990 and 1994 concerts, which in the view of both PolyGram and Warner executives jeopardized the commercial viability of the forthcoming concert album.

By the time The Three Tenors performed in Paris on July 10, PolyGram and Warner had exchanged letters reaffirming their commitment to suspend advertising and discounting the 1990 and 1994 concert albums and agreeing the moratorium would run from August 1 through October 15. About a week later, however, PolyGram's Senior Marketing Director, who had passed on the details of the agreement to PolyGram's General Counsel, sent a memorandum around the company stating, "Contrary to any previous suggestion, there has been no agreement with [Warner] in relation to the pricing and marketing of the previous Three Tenors albums." Warner followed suit on August 10, sending a letter to PolyGram repudiating any pricing or advertising restrictions relative to its 1994 album. At the same time, however, PolyGram and Warner executives privately assured one another their respective companies intended to honor the agreement, and in fact the companies did substantially comply with the agreement through October 15, 1998.

* * *

II.   Analysis

* * *

The Commission's findings of fact are conclusive if supported by substantial evidence. *See* 15 U.S.C. § 45(c). The legal issues are "for the courts to resolve, although even in considering such issues the courts are to give some deference to the Commission's informed judgment that a particular commercial practice is to be condemned as 'unfair.'" *FTC v. Ind. Fed'n of Dentists,* 476 U.S. 447, 454 (1987) (*IFD*).

The Supreme Court's approach to evaluating a § 1 claim has gone through a transition over the last twenty-five years, from a dichotomous categorical approach to a more nuanced and case-specific inquiry. In 1978, just before the transition began, the Court summarized its doctrine as follows:

> There are . . . two complimentary categories of antitrust analysis. In the first category are agreements whose nature and necessary effect are so plainly anticompetitive that no elaborate study of the industry is needed to establish their illegality—they are "illegal per se." In the second category are agreements whose competitive effect can only be evaluated by analyzing the facts particular to the business, the history of the restraint, and the reasons why it was imposed.

Nat'l Soc'y of Prof'l Eng'rs v. FTC, 435 U.S. 679, 692 (1978).

Courts and commentators have recognized the trade-offs inherent in each category. *Per se* analysis, which requires courts to generalize about the utility of a challenged practice, reduces the cost of decision-making but correspondingly raises the total cost of error by making it more likely some practices will be held unlawful in circumstances where they are harmless or even procompetitive. The converse—increased litigation cost but reduced cost of error—obtains under the rule of reason, which requires an exhaustive inquiry into all the myriad factors "bearing on whether the conduct is on balance anticompetitive or procompetitive."

Since *Professional Engineers* the Supreme Court has steadily moved away from the dichotomous approach—under which every restraint of trade is either unlawful *per se,* and hence not susceptible to a procompetitive justification, or subject to full-blown rule-of-reason analysis—toward one in which the extent of the inquiry is tailored to the suspect conduct in each particular case. * * * [Here the court cited as examples *NCAA v. Board of Regents,* 468 U.S. 85 (1984) and *Indiana Federation of Dentists*, contrasting them with earlier cases that favored the per se approach, such as *United States v. Socony-Vacuum Oil Co.*, 310 U.S. 150 (1940) and *Klor's, Inc. v. Broadway-Hale Stores, Inc.,* 359 U.S. 207 (1959). Eds.]

At the same time, however, in *NCAA* and *IFD* the Court did not insist upon the elaborate market analysis ordinarily required under the rule of reason to prove the defendant had market power and the restraint it imposed had an anticompetitive effect. The Court instead adopted an intermediate inquiry, since dubbed the "quick look," to evaluate horizontal restraints of trade.

It would be somewhat misleading, however, to say the "quick look" is just a new category of analysis intermediate in complexity between "*per se* "condemnation and full-blown "rule of reason" treatment, for that would suggest the Court has moved from a dichotomy to a trichotomy, when in fact it has backed away from any reliance upon fixed categories and toward a continuum. The Court said as much in *California Dental Association v. FTC:*

> The truth is that our categories of analysis of anticompetitive effect are less fixed than terms like "*per se,*" "quick look," and "rule of reason" tend to make them appear. We have recognized, for example, that there is often no bright line separating *per se* from Rule of Reason analysis, since considerable inquiry into market conditions may be required before the application of any so-called "*per-se*" condemnation is justified.

526 U.S. 756, 779 (1999).

Rather than focusing upon the category to which a particular restraint should be assigned, therefore, the Court emphasized the basic point that under § 1 the essential inquiry is "whether . . . the challenged restraint enhances competition." In order to make that determination, a court must make "an enquiry meet for the case, looking to the circumstances, details, and logic of a restraint," which in some cases may not require a full-blown market analysis. The Court continued:

> The object is to see whether the experience of the market has been so clear, or necessarily will be, that a confident conclusion about the principle tendency of a restriction will follow from a quick (or at least quicker) look, in place of a more sedulous one. And of course what we see may vary over time, if rule-of-reason analyses in case after case reach identical conclusions.

In this case * * * the Commission analyzed PolyGram's conduct under the legal framework it had devised in [*In re Massachusetts Board of Optometry,* 110 F.T.C. 549 (1988)], which it maintains is consistent with the Supreme Court's teaching of more than a decade later in *California Dental* (1999). The *Mass. Board* analysis proceeds in several distinct steps: First, the Commission must determine whether it is obvious from the nature of the challenged conduct that it will likely harm consumers. If so, then the restraint is deemed "inherently suspect" and, unless the defendant comes forward with some plausible (and legally cognizable) competitive justification for the restraint, summarily condemned. "Such justifications," the Commission explained, "may consist of plausible reasons why practices that are competitively suspect as a general matter may not be expected to have adverse consequences in the context of the particular market in question, or they may consist of reasons why the practices are likely to have beneficial effects for consumers."

If the defendant does offer such an explanation, then the Commission "must address the justification" in one of two ways. First, the Commission may explain why it can confidently conclude, without adducing evidence, that the restraint very likely harmed consumers. Alternatively, the Commission may provide the tribunal with sufficient evidence to show that anticompetitive effects are in fact likely. If the Commission succeeds in either way, then the evidentiary burden shifts to the defendant to show the restraint in fact does not harm consumers or has "procompetitive virtues" that outweigh its burden upon consumers.

PolyGram argues the Commission's framework conflicts with Supreme Court precedent by condemning a restraint that is not *per se* illegal without the Commission having to prove the restraint actually harms competition. According to PolyGram, "proof of actual anticompetitive effect (or market power as its surrogate) is required in *any* Rule of Reason case."

* * * [W]e reject PolyGram's attempt to locate the appropriate analysis, and the concomitant burden of proof, by reference to the vestigial line separating *per se* analysis from the rule of reason. At bottom, the Sherman Act requires the court to ascertain whether the challenged restraint hinders competition; the Commission's framework, at least as the Commission applied it in this case, does just that.

We therefore accept the Commission's analytical framework. If, based upon economic learning and the experience of the market, it is obvious that a restraint of trade likely impairs competition, then the restraint is presumed unlawful and, in order to avoid liability, the defendant must either identify some reason the restraint is unlikely to harm consumers or identify some competitive benefit that plausibly offsets the apparent or anticipated harm. That much follows from the caselaw. * * *

Although the Commission uses the term "inherently suspect" to describe those restraints that judicial experience and economic learning have shown to be likely to harm consumers, we note that, under the Commission's own framework, the rebuttable presumption of illegality arises not necessarily from anything "inherent" in a business practice but from the close family resemblance between the suspect practice and another practice that already stands convicted in the court of consumer welfare. The Commission appears to acknowledge, as it must, that as economic learning and market experience evolve, so too will the class of restraints subject to summary adjudication.

That said, we have no difficulty with the Commission's conclusion that PolyGram's agreement with Warner in all likelihood had a deleterious effect upon consumers—unless, that is, PolyGram comes forward with some plausible explanation to the contrary. An agreement between joint venturers to restrain price cutting and advertising with respect to products not part of the joint venture looks suspiciously like a naked price fixing agreement between competitors, which would ordinarily be condemned as *per se* unlawful. The Supreme Court has recognized time and again that agreements restraining autonomy in pricing and advertising impede the "ordinary give and take of the market place."

PolyGram's fate in this case therefore rests upon the plausibility of the sole competitive justification it proffered for the moratorium agreement, namely, that the restrictions on discounting and advertising enhanced the long-term profitability of all three concert albums and promoted the "Three Tenors" brand. According to PolyGram, each company was concerned the other would "free ride" on the promotional activities of the joint venture by promoting its own earlier concert album; as a result fewer Three Tenors albums would be sold overall and the joint venture would be less likely to create future products, such as a "greatest hits" album or a boxed set. Thus, PolyGram likens the moratorium agreement here to the restraint at issue in *Polk Brothers, Inc. v. Forest City Enterprises,* 776 F.2d 185 (7th Cir. 1985), where two potential retail competitors collaborated to build a store offering some of each company's products but agreed not to sell competing products at the new store. Because the restraint arguably promoted productivity and output by controlling each participant's ability to free-ride on the other's promotional efforts, the court, rather than condemning the restraint summarily, went on to evaluate it under the rule of reason.

At first glance PolyGram's contention has some force; the moratorium appears likely to have mitigated the "spillover" effects that could be expected to follow an aggressive launch of the 1998 album. Absent the moratorium, that is, a consumer, after learning of the new album through the joint venture's advertising, might decide that he would be just as happy with an older concert album, especially if the older album were then available at a discount. The "free-riding" to be eliminated by the moratorium agreement, however, was nothing more than the competition of products that were not part of the joint undertaking. Why not an agreement by which PolyGram and Warner would eliminate advertising and price competition on all their records for a time while they focused exclusively upon promoting the new Three Tenors album? The "procompetitive" justification PolyGram offers is "nothing less than a frontal assault on the basic policy of the Sherman Act." *Nat'l Soc'y of Prof'l Engineers,* 435 U.S. at 695.

To take the Commission's example, if General Motors were vigorously to advertise the release of a new model SUV, other SUV manufacturers would no doubt reap some of the benefit of GM's efforts. But that would not mean General Motors and its competitors could lawfully agree to restrict prices and advertising on existing SUV models in return for General Motors giving its rivals a share of its profit on the new model. Nor would an agreement to restrain prices and advertising on existing SUVs be lawful if General Motors were to release the new model SUV as a joint venture with one of its competitors. A restraint cannot be justified solely on the ground that it increases the profitability of the enterprise that introduces the new product, regardless whether that enterprise is a joint venture or a solo undertaking. And it simply does not matter whether the new SUV would have been profitable absent the restraint; if the only way a new product can profitably be introduced is to restrain the legitimate competition of older products, then one must seriously wonder whether consumers are genuinely benefitted by the new product. As the Supreme Court said in *Catalano, Inc. v. Target Sales, Inc.,* 446 U.S. 643, 649 (1980),

> in any case in which competitors are able to increase the price level or to curtail production by agreement, it could be argued that the agreement has the effect of making the market more attractive to potential new entrants. If that potential justifies horizontal agreements among competitors imposing one kind of voluntary restraint or another on their competitive freedom, it would seem to follow that the more successful an agreement is in raising the price level, the safer it is from antitrust attack. Nothing could be more inconsistent with our cases.

In sum, because PolyGram has failed to identify any competitive justification for its agreement with Warner to refrain from advertising or discounting their competitive Three Tenors products, we hold it violated

§ 5 of the FTC Act. Hence, we need not go on to determine whether the Commission's findings of fact concerning actual competitive harm are supported by substantial evidence.

Finally, we hold the remedy ordered by the Commission was reasonable. The Commission found there was a significant risk that, if not prohibited from doing so, PolyGram would enter into similar arrangements in the future. That determination is supported by substantial evidence. The record shows the condition that gave rise to the moratorium agreement—namely, the company "fear[ed] that a new release by one of [its] recording artists may lose sales to the artist's older albums owned by a competitor"—is a recurrent one in the record industry; therefore, PolyGram would have the same incentive in the future to enter into other agreements to restrain advertising and price discounting. * * *

* * *

What was it about Polygram and Warner's conduct that made it "inherently suspect"? Why in the FTC and the court's view was it so likely to be anticompetitive? If that was true, why wasn't it deemed per se unlawful?

The FTC had applied a framework developed years earlier in *In re Massachusetts Bd. of Optometry,* 110 F.T.C. 549 (1988), which the court discusses. Does the court clearly endorse that approach? What does it mean when it states that it "accept[s] the Commission's analytical framework"? Are there other frameworks it might also "accept"? What components would they have to share with the *Mass. Board* framework in order also to be acceptable to the D.C. Circuit?

Recall that in *NCAA* and *IFD* the Supreme Court concluded that evidence of actual anticompetitive effects was sufficient to warrant a shift of burden to the defendant, who at that point had to present a justification—*i.e.*, meet a burden of production. That was the import of the "quick look": when actual anticompetitive effects are present, the plaintiff's initial burden of production is satisfied and the defendant must respond. As we discussed in the notes following *CDA*, it was possible to read *CDA* to suggest that the quick look could only be applied when there is evidence of actual anticompetitive effect.

Does *Polygram* recognize that quick look analysis is applicable in cases where there may not be evidence of actual effects, but there is a high likelihood of them? As the D.C. Circuit notes, Polygram and Warner objected to the "inherently suspect" approach, in part on the ground that it was inconsistent with the Supreme Court's "quick look" jurisprudence, which they claimed required proof of actual anticompetitive effects. The FTC maintained that there was in fact evidence of actual anticompetitive effect, but it took the position that it did not have to present that evidence given the high probability that the agreement was anticompetitive. The D.C. Circuit agreed.

How does the D.C. Circuit reconcile *Polygram* with *CDA*? Recall that near the conclusion of the majority opinion in *CDA*, the Court said "there is generally no categorical line to be drawn between restraints that give rise to an *intuitively obvious inference of anticompetitive effect* and those that call for more detailed treatment." In using the phrase "intuitively obvious inference," was the Court leaving open the possibility that some kinds of conduct—perhaps conduct such as the promotional moratorium at issue in *Polygram*—could be sufficient to warrant a shift of burden even in the absence of evidence of actual anticompetitive effects? Are "intuitively obvious" and "inherently suspect" two ways of describing the high probability that a restraint will have an unreasonably anticompetitive effect? Note that the D.C. Circuit expressed its support for shifting a burden of production to the defendant when its conduct appears anticompetitive "based upon economic learning and the experience of the market." Would *CDA* have been decided the same way if the Supreme Court had utilized the D.C. Circuit's approach?

What justification for the advertising moratorium did Polygram and Warner offer? Why did the FTC and the court agree that it was insufficient to shift a burden back to the FTC and force it to establish actual anticompetitive effects? The court declines to accept the parties' free-riding justification, although it acknowledges that absent the condemned practice, free riding of some sort could occur. On what basis does the court distinguish free riding that a joint venture may prohibit from free riding that it cannot lawfully prevent? Does a moratorium on promoting the earlier albums (as by cutting price) increase the incentive of each firm to market the new album in its territory, as defendants alleged? Or does it simply reduce the incentive of each to promote a competing product (the earlier albums), as the court found? For an argument that the court did not properly analyze free riding in this case, see Joshua D. Wright, *Singing Along: A Comment on Goldberg and Muris on the Three Tenors*, 1(3) REV. L. & ECON. 4 (2005). Would the court have come out differently in *Polygram* had it applied an ancillary restraints analysis? *See id.* (arguing that the moratorium agreement was ancillary to the joint venture and, in consequence, should not have been condemned on a quick look). A different way to understand ancillary restraint analysis is that it relies on a combination of facial analysis, economic reasoning, and prior experience to identify restraints for which the case for a cognizable justification should be presumed strong. When restraints are of this type, it would be difficult for plaintiff to overcome that presumption with evidence that competition has been harmed even if plaintiff is able to proffer sufficient evidence to satisfy an initial burden of production. Just as *Polygram* uses facial analysis, economic reasoning, and prior experience to identify conduct presumed harmful, this approach relies on similar factors to identify conduct that ought to be presumed efficient. Does the restraint in *Polygram* fall in this category? Does your answer depend on whether you think the court properly analyzed free-riding? We will revisit and discuss the contemporary role, if any, of ancillary restraint analysis in our next Sidebar, below.

Finally, note that the FTC's remedy was to enjoin the defendants from entering into similar agreements in the future. Was the remedy adequate to solve the competitive problem? Could someone who purchased the 1998 CD during the period of the ban on promotions of the 1990 and 1994 CDs bring suit against Polygram and Warner under the antitrust laws? What would be their theory of antitrust injury?

The Fifth Circuit joined the D.C. Circuit and also endorsed use of the FTC's "inherently suspect" framework in *North Texas Specialty Physicians v. FTC.*, 528 F.3d 346 (5th Cir. 2008).

Sidebar 2–5:
Revisiting *Addyston Pipe* and
Ancillary Restraint Analysis

Origins

As we discussed earlier in this Chapter in *United States v. Addyston Pipe & Steel Co.*, 85 F. 271, *aff'd*, 175 U.S. 211 (1899), Judge Taft looked to the common law to interpret Section 1 and proposed that "reasonable" restraints should be distinguished from "unreasonable" ones using "ancillary restraint" analysis. *See also* WILLIAM H. TAFT, THE ANTI-TRUST ACT AND THE SUPREME COURT (1914) (elaborating on his views in one of the first treatises on antitrust law). But his approach was not relied upon in either *Standard Oil* (1911) or *Chicago Bd. of Trade* (1918), the Supreme Court's formative decisions on the rule of reason. Although *Addyston Pipe* was affirmed by the Court, it therefore had little impact on application of the Sherman Act for decades.

As a purely legal construct—which was how it was offered by Taft—ancillary restraint analysis had two critical features. First, it distinguished pure or "naked" restraints from "ancillary" ones, and thus began with a characterization step. When nothing but restraint was apparent, as was the case in *Addyston Pipe*, a price-fixing case, little analysis was needed and a practice could be quickly condemned—an early manifestation of per se analysis. But where the restraint appeared to be derivative—"ancillary" to and "necessary" to support some broader and legitimate business purpose—

further inquiry into its reasonableness was warranted. 85 F. at 282.

Consistent with the legislative history of the Sherman Act, which revealed that Congress purposefully drew the phrase "restraint of trade" from the common law, Taft cited five common law examples to support his proposed approach. *Id.* at 281. These included apprenticeships, partnerships, and agreements for the sale of an ongoing business, all of which often included "covenants not to compete." In return for training an apprentice, for example, a tradesman might want contractual protection that the apprentice would not, once educated, take the knowledge and good will obtained and set up shop in competition with his trainer-mentor. A covenant not to compete would be condemned, therefore, only if it prohibited the apprentice from practicing his trade for an unreasonably long period of time or in an unreasonably broad geographic area— more than was necessary to protect the tradesman. As Taft explained: ". . .if the restraint exceeds the necessity presented by the main purpose of the contract, it is void for two reasons: First, because it oppresses the covenantor, without any corresponding benefit to the covenantee; and, second, because it tends to a monopoly." *Id.* Impact on competition was but one of the common law's concerns.

Taft, therefore, was thinking purely in terms of the common law and its operation, not necessarily about the economic implications of ancillary restraint analysis. But, to the extent the common law's approach to ancillary restraints sought to facilitate legitimate commerce, it clearly had economic consequences. "Reasonableness," it could be argued, was defined for Taft by the line separating agreements that tended to restrict output out of proportion to necessity from those that served to reasonably restrict it so as to expand it. By facilitating the formation of a partnership, the sale of a shop, or the securing of an apprentice, an ancillary restraint could facilitate the expansion of supply, even though it ostensibly also involved the restriction of some rivalry. Restraints on rivalry that served to promote economic expansion were "reasonable," for they restrained trade only as a means of creating commerce and only to the degree necessary to do so.

Revival

A more economic interpretation of *Addyston Pipe* proved appealing to some commentators, especially proponents of the Chicago School of antitrust, who sought support in historical antitrust for an approach to antitrust analysis that was more focused on economic efficiency. Responding to the Court's expansion of its reliance on per se analysis and relatively undemanding burdens of proof, these commentators saw in ancillary restraint analysis a legal framework that would support a more economically grounded approach to interpreting the rule of reason. As Robert Bork wrote in 1978, referring to Judge Taft's reference to the partnership example:

> This insight is, or should be, central to modern antitrust. It is useful, therefore, to put Taft's reasoning in modern terms and to generalize it. The integration of economic activities, which is indispensable to productive efficiency, always involves the implicit elimination of actual or potential competition. We allow it—indeed, should encourage it—because the integration creates wealth for the community. We should equally encourage those explicit and ancillary agreed-upon eliminations of rivalry that make the basic integration more efficient.

ROBERT H. BORK, THE ANTITRUST PARADOX 28 (1978). *See also* Thomas C. Arthur, *Farewell to the Sea of Doubt: Jettisoning the Constitutional Sherman Act*, 74 CAL. L. REV. 263 (1986). As Judge Easterbrook later elaborated in *Polk Bros., Inc. v. Forest City Enterprises, Inc.*, 776 F.2d 185, 189 (7th Cir. 1985):

> The evaluation of ancillary restraints under the Rule of Reason does not imply that ancillary agreements are not real horizontal restraints. They are. A covenant not to compete following employment does not operate any differently from a horizontal market division among competitors—not at the time the covenant has its bite, anyway. The difference comes at the time people enter beneficial arrangements. A legal rule that enforces covenants not to compete, even after an employee has launched his own firm, makes it easier for people to cooperate productively in the first place. Knowing that he is not cutting his own throat by doing so, the employer will train the employee, giving him skills, knowledge, and trade secrets that make the firm more productive. Once that employment ends, there is nothing left but restraint-but the aftermath is the wrong focus.
>
> A court must ask whether an agreement promoted enterprise and productivity at the time it was adopted.
> * * *

Proponents of ancillary restraint analysis in antitrust were also encouraged by the Supreme Court's decision in *Broadcast Music*, which appeared to at least implicitly allude to the kind of analysis endorsed by *Addyston Pipe*. *See Broadcast Music*, 440 U.S. at 20–21 (concluding that the blanket license was not a "naked restraint" but rather "accompanies the integration of sales, monitoring, and enforcement against unauthorized copyright use."). When federal judges associated with the Chicago School, including Judge Bork, were appointed to the bench, they wasted no time in reading *Broadcast Music* as an invitation to use *Addyston Pipe*'s ancillary restraint analysis to evaluate agreements among rivals for their tendency to promote output and productive efficiency. *See, e.g., Rothery Storage & Van Co. v. Atlas Van Lines, Inc.*, 792 F.2d 210 (D.C. Cir. 1986), *cert. denied*, 479 U.S. 1033 (1987) (Judge Bork); *Polk Bros., supra* (Judge Easterbrook). In both cases, the courts viewed *Broadcast Music* as a basis for jettisoning prior decisions such as *Topco*, in favor of a more structured, and economic framework for evaluating horizontal restraints derived from *Addyston Pipe*. By aggressively extending *Broadcast Music* from the price-fixing context to division of markets, moreover, these influential appellate judges promoted antitrust's movement away from narrowly tailored legal categories—like "price-fixing" and "division of markets"—towards more economically-grounded core concepts, such as "efficiency."

Contemporary Significance

The trend towards placing greater weight on economic analysis of a horizontal restraint's impact on efficiency, signaled by *Broadcast Music* and, with respect to vertical restraints, by *Sylvania* (1977), which we will read in Chapter 6, has proved durable and is now a widely accepted tenet of antitrust law. But the election to implement that economic analysis through *Addyston Pipe*'s ancillary restraint framework has largely been confined to joint ventures and neither the decision to use it nor its application has been uniform or consistent. *See, e.g., Major League Baseball Properties, Inc. v. Salvino, Inc.*, 542 F.3d 290 (2d Cir. 2008) (in reaching a unanimous conclusion upholding an alleged restraint adopted by Major League Baseball teams, the majority used a structured rule of reason approach, whereas then Judge Sonia Sotomayor concurred relying on ancillary restraint analysis).

More importantly, in a critical way, ancillary restraint analysis is now an historic artifact. Arguing that a restraint is

> "ancillary" and "necessary" to some legitimate purpose is conclusory, just another way of asserting that it promotes efficiency. Ancillary restraint analysis has been integrated, therefore, into the now prevalent structured approach to applying the rule of reason that focuses on competitive effects and procedurally is implemented through burden-shifting that allows for cognizable defenses, such as efficiency. This was already evident at the Supreme Court in both *Broadcast Music* and *NCAA*, neither of which explicitly relied on ancillary restraint analysis in applying the rule of reason, and in its most recent decisions, which continue to emphasize the primacy of structured rule of reason analysis. *See, e.g., FTC v. Actavis, Inc.,* 133 S.Ct. 2223, 2238 (2013). While some litigants and courts today may characterize restraints as "ancillary," therefore, that characterization is best understood as a rhetorical device for highlighting purported efficiencies. It is no longer necessary as a legal basis for injecting efficiency considerations and adds little to the rule of reason analysis of competitive effects.

4. PROVING ANTICOMPETITIVE EFFECTS BY REBUTTABLE PRESUMPTION USING CIRCUMSTANTIAL EVIDENCE

We began this Chapter by studying the foundations of the rule of reason and have now observed its development through more than a century of evolution. Since *Standard Oil* and *Chicago Board of Trade*, however, the cases have focused largely on application of per se and quick look analysis. Although *Broadcast Music* called for a more comprehensive rule of reason analysis, it did not elaborate on *Chicago Board of Trade*. The content of the rule of reason, therefore, has remained somewhat illusory, even though its focus on anticompetitive effects has come into focus. Some of the questions we posed early in the Chapter following the decision remain unanswered.

Our next case, *Realcomp II, Ltd. v. FTC*, 635 F.3d 815 (6th Cir. 2011), is a contemporary example of how courts apply the basic teaching of *Chicago Board of Trade*. Note how the court cites back to *Chicago Board's* emphasis on the nature, purpose, and effect of challenged conduct, but it does not stop there. Informed by later decisions, like *NSPE*, *NCAA*, *IFD*, and *CDA*, it synthesizes a structured rule of reason, including inferences and presumptions and burden shifting principles guided by the core economic concerns of modern competition analysis: market power, anticompetitive effect, and efficiencies. Look for parallels with the explanation of the state of the law that we just read in *Polygram*. Do you see consensus? Any points of difference?

As you will see in *Realcomp II*, the Commission again relied upon its "inherently suspect" formulation of the quick look, but as in *Polygram* it also presented additional evidence that in its view was sufficient to meet its burden under a more complete application of the rule of reason. What evidence did the FTC introduce? Why, in the court's view, did that evidence satisfy the rule of reason and demonstrate that the challenged conduct was an unreasonable restraint of trade? How did the court receive it and frame it under the rule of reason?

REALCOMP II, LTD. V. FTC
United States Court of Appeals for the Sixth Circuit, 2011.
635 F.3d 815.

Before: SILER, MOORE, and GRIFFIN, CIRCUIT JUDGES.

KAREN NELSON MOORE, CIRCUIT JUDGE.

Realcomp II, Ltd. ("Realcomp") is an association of local real-estate boards and associations located in southeastern Michigan, with a membership composed of local real-estate agents and brokers. Realcomp's primary service to its member brokers is its operation of the Realcomp Multiple Listing Service ("Realcomp MLS"), a database of property listings that can be viewed and searched by Realcomp members. Pursuant to its website policy, Realcomp prohibited information about exclusive agency and other nontraditional listings on Realcomp's MLS from being distributed to public real-estate advertising websites through its MLS feeds.

Reversing and vacating the Initial Decision of the Chief Administrative Law Judge ("ALJ"), the Federal Trade Commission ("Commission") ruled that Realcomp violated Section 5 of the Federal Trade Commission Act ("FTC Act"), by adopting anticompetitive policies—including the website policy—that limited the public distribution and display of limited-service property listings based on the nature of the listing contract. Realcomp petitions for review of the Commission's opinion and order with respect to only the website policy.

Under a full rule-of-reason analysis, we conclude that substantial evidence supports the Commission's findings that: 1) Realcomp's website policy gave rise to potential genuine adverse effects on competition due to Realcomp's substantial market power and the website policy's anticompetitive nature; 2) the website policy in fact caused actual anticompetitive effects; and 3) Realcomp's proffered procompetitive justifications were insufficient to overcome a prima facie case of adverse impact. These findings establish that Realcomp's website policy unreasonably restrained competition in the market for the provision of residential real-estate-brokerage services in southeastern Michigan and the Realcomp MLS area. Therefore, we deny Realcomp's petition for review.

I.   FACTS AND PROCEDURE

A.   Realcomp and the Real-Estate Market

Realcomp * * * is affiliated with the National Association of Realtors ("NAR"), and its bylaws require it to abide by NAR's rules. Realcomp's approximately 14,000 member brokers compete with one another to provide residential real-estate-brokerage service to home buyers and sellers. Any licensed real-estate broker who is a member of a Realcomp shareholder board, including brokers who offer discount services, may become a Realcomp member. Every Realcomp member, including those who offer alternative business models, pays the same quarterly membership fees.

Realcomp's primary service to its member brokers is its operation of the Realcomp MLS, the largest MLS in Michigan. An MLS is "a database of information about properties for sale (exclusive of FSBO [For Sale By Owner] properties) that can be viewed and searched by all other local brokers who practice in the area and participate in the MLS." By disseminating detailed listings, the Realcomp MLS facilitates the sharing of information among brokers representing buyers and brokers representing sellers. Real-estate listings on Realcomp's MLS, which include property details and offers of compensation, can be viewed by Realcomp members through Realcomp's online system, but not by the general public without the access of a member broker.

The Realcomp MLS also disseminates listing information to selected public websites that can be searched by members of the public. Thus, in addition to access to and advertisement on the MLS database itself, the Realcomp MLS offers its members internet advertising on the approved websites to which Realcomp provides information. Approved websites include MoveInMichigan.com, Realcomp IDX participant websites, and Realtor.com. To disseminate listings, Realcomp provides an IDX (Internet Data Exchange) feed each day which can be loaded onto websites of member brokers and which assembles selected MLS listing data from all brokers who have requested that their listings be distributed. Through Realcomp's IDX feed, brokers are able to display listing information from the Realcomp database on their individual websites so that consumers can search available properties on those websites.

The Commission contends that technological developments like the MLS data feed are enabling consumers to self-supply certain services and are exerting competitive pressure on the traditional model for brokerage services. Under the traditional model, home sales involving the use of real-estate brokers incorporate both a listing broker, who works with home sellers, and a cooperating broker, who works with home buyers. Although representing one party in a particular transaction, brokers do not often specialize as either a cooperating or listing broker and may represent either buyers or sellers. The agreement between a listing broker and home seller, called a listing agreement, specifies the duration of the contract, the types of services to be provided by the listing broker, the compensation to be paid to the listing broker, and the offer of compensation to be paid to any cooperating broker who secures the home purchaser. A listing broker is compensated either by a flat fee paid up-front at the time of the listing agreement or by commission based on the selling price of the home, or by some combination of the two. The home seller also compensates the cooperating broker, either directly or through payment to the listing broker.

There are two common types of listing agreements governing the bundle of services provided by and compensation paid to residential real-estate brokers: Exclusive Right to Sell ("ERTS") and Exclusive Agency ("EA") agreements. Under an ERTS listing agreement, the listing broker is appointed as the seller's exclusive agent for a specified period of time to sell the property on the owner's stated terms, and is provided the same compensation when the property is sold even if the owner or another broker, and not the ERTS listing agent, secures the property's sale. A cooperating broker, in contrast, typically is not paid directly by either the home seller or the home buyer, but instead is compensated indirectly by the home seller through the listing broker, who makes an offer of compensation carved from the listing broker's own compensation to any cooperating broker who finds the buyer that ultimately purchases the home. A common ERTS compensation structure includes a 6% commission to the listing broker and an offer of compensation of 3% by the listing broker to the cooperating broker. There are also flat-fee ERTS listings that provide higher fees to the listing agent than do flat-fee EA agreements.

Under an EA listing agreement, the listing broker acts as the exclusive agent of the home seller, but is paid less or no additional compensation if the property is sold without further assistance from the listing broker. Cooperating brokers are paid directly by the seller. EA contracts may offer a la carte, or unbundled, brokerage services, with a compensation structure characterized by an up-front fee to the listing broker rather than a commission, and a 3% offer of compensation from the seller directly to any cooperating broker.

In a commission-based ERTS transaction, if the home is sold to an unrepresented buyer, the listing broker retains the compensation that otherwise would have been paid to the cooperating broker, and the cost to the home seller remains the same. Under an EA agreement, in contrast, if the home is sold to an unrepresented buyer, the compensation to the listing broker remains the same, and the compensation that would have been paid to the cooperating broker is retained by the home seller. ERTS agreements typically govern a traditional package of full brokerage services, while EA agreements and flat-fee ERTS agreements are conducive to providing discounted, limited brokerage services. The traditional set of services provided by a listing broker to the home seller include showing and marketing the property, presenting and evaluating offers to the seller, and negotiating counteroffers. Full-service listing brokers in Realcomp's area typically charge commission rates around 6% and are compensated through commission-based ERTS contracts.

The discount, limited-service brokerage model exemplified by EA listings offers a lower-cost alternative to the traditional full-service model. A listing broker in a limited-service listing may provide any, but not all, of the services provided under a traditional brokerage model, according to the preferences of the home seller as consumer. As described by the ALJ, unbundled brokerage services "meet a consumer demand for lower cost brokerage services where consumers are willing to carry out some of the home selling tasks themselves that otherwise would be performed by real estate professionals." Home sellers may "purchase a subset of the full range brokerage services (such as listing in an MLS), while self-supplying other services" such as "show[ing] the property, hold[ing] open houses, negotiat[ing] with buyers, or clos[ing] the transaction . . . without broker assistance."

The expansion of the market share of limited-service brokers since 2003 has been attributed in part to the role of the internet in making it easier for brokers to market directly to home buyers and in enabling consumers to self-supply services. The development of the internet and MLS databases, the increase in the number of broker websites, and data feeds provided from the local MLS to public websites have enhanced the ability of brokers to share real-estate information and of members of the public to access it. As a result, the traditional brokerage model faces competitive pressure arising from the technological developments that enable consumers to self-supply certain services and from limited-service brokers who discount their fees in response to these developments.

B. Complaint Against Realcomp

On October 10, 2006, complaint counsel for the Commission issued an administrative complaint against Realcomp, alleging that Realcomp's * * * website policy and search-function policy injured consumers by explicitly limiting the publication and marketing of nontraditional listings, thereby eliminating certain forms of competition without cognizable and plausible efficiency justifications. The Commission argued that Realcomp had adopted restrictive policies in order to restrain the competition from limited-service brokers.

According to complaint counsel, pursuant to Realcomp's website policy, Realcomp prohibited information about EA listings and other nontraditional listings[2] on Realcomp's MLS from being distributed to public real-estate advertising websites through the MLS feeds. Adopted in 2001, the website policy was first enforced in 2004 when Realcomp incorporated the requirement that members designate a listing type for all listings. The policy violated an NAR rule forbidding member MLSs from excluding EA listings from their IDX feeds. But the Realcomp board voted against adopting the NAR IDX policy and retained its data-feed exclusions.

Pursuant to the search-function policy, adopted in 2003 and eliminated in 2007, EA and other nontraditional listings were excluded from the default search setting in the Realcomp MLS. As a result of the default settings on the MLS, a broker wanting to display EA listings in her search results had to select specifically to search all listings or the EA listings, or change permanently the search default by saving changes to her settings.

In addition to requiring members to disclose each listing's type, Realcomp implemented a minimum-service requirement which mandated that, in order for a listing to be labeled ERTS—and consequently included in data feeds to public websites and in the default search settings in the Realcomp MLS—brokers were required to provide full-service brokerage services in connection with the listing. The minimum-service requirement was adopted in 2004 and eliminated in 2007.

* * *

II. ANALYSIS

A. Standard of Review

When we review a decision of the Federal Trade Commission, the legal issues are "for the courts to resolve, although even in considering such issues the courts are to give some deference to the Commission's informed judgment that a particular commercial practice is to be condemned as 'unfair.'" The Commission's findings of fact are conclusive if supported by substantial evidence. When we review the Commission's findings, we may not "make [our] own appraisal of the testimony, picking and choosing for [ourselves] among uncertain and conflicting inferences." Rather, under the substantial-evidence standard, we uphold the Commission's findings "if . . . supported by 'such relevant evidence as a reasonable mind might accept as adequate to support a conclusion.'"

* * *

B. Restraint of Trade

Because "[t]he FTC Act's prohibition of unfair competition and deceptive acts or practices . . . overlaps the scope of § 1 of the Sherman Act

---

[2] The rules prohibit distribution to real-estate internet advertising sites of "Exclusive Agency, Limited Service and MLS Entry Only Listings."

... aimed at prohibiting restraint of trade," we rely upon Sherman Act jurisprudence in determining whether the challenged policies violated Section 5 of the FTC Act. To determine whether Realcomp's actions constitute a violation, we assess: (1) whether there was a contract, combination, or conspiracy—or, more simply, an agreement; and, if so, (2) whether the contract, combination, or conspiracy "unreasonably restrained trade in the relevant market." With respect to the first element, Realcomp is a combination of its members with respect to the challenged policies: Realcomp is owned by seven associations of competing real-estate brokers, is governed by members of those associations, and claims a membership of brokers competing in the market for real-estate-brokerage services. The website policy constitutes an agreement governing the Realcomp MLS among the Realcomp members. Realcomp is, therefore, a contract, combination, or conspiracy.

With respect to the second element, in evaluating whether Realcomp unreasonably restrained trade, the Supreme Court has explained that "a restraint may be adjudged unreasonable either because it fits within a class of restraints that has been held to be '*per se*' unreasonable, or because it violates what has come to be known as the 'Rule of Reason.'" Under per se analysis, "certain agreements or practices are so 'plainly anticompetitive,' . . . and so often 'lack . . . any redeeming virtue,' . . . that they are conclusively presumed illegal without further examination." "A court need not then inquire whether the restraint's authors actually possess the power to inflict public injury . . . , nor will the court accept argument that the restraint in the circumstances is justified by any procompetitive purpose or effect."

When restraints are not per se unlawful, and their net impact on competition not obvious, the conventional rule-of-reason approach requires courts to engage in a thorough analysis of the relevant market and the effects of the restraint in that market. A full rule-of-reason inquiry "may extend to a 'plenary market examination,'" which may include the analysis of "'the facts peculiar to the business, the history of the restraint, and the reasons why it was imposed,'" "as well as the availability of reasonable, less restrictive alternatives." If Realcomp's challenged policies are shown to have an anticompetitive effect, or if Realcomp is shown to have market power and to have adopted policies *likely* to have an anticompetitive effect, then the burden shifts to Realcomp to provide procompetitive justifications for the policies.

An abbreviated or quick-look analysis, however, does not require "elaborate industry analysis," and applies when "an observer with even a rudimentary understanding of economics could conclude that the arrangements in question would have an anticompetitive effect on customers and markets." Thus, when a restraint is not "conclusively presumed illegal," but "the likelihood of anticompetitive effects is . . .

obvious," the proponent of the restraint must provide "some competitive justification" for it, "even in the absence of a detailed market analysis" showing market power or market effects. Under a quick-look analysis, once a restraint is deemed facially anticompetitive, the burden shifts to its proponent for justification on procompetitive grounds.

Despite these different methods, "no categorical line" separates those "restraints that give rise to an intuitively obvious inference of anticompetitive effect and those that call for more detailed treatment." Rather, the Supreme Court has emphasized that "whether the ultimate finding is the product of a presumption or actual market analysis, the essential inquiry remains the same—whether or not the challenged restraint enhances competition." Accordingly, the Court has moved "away from . . . reliance upon fixed categories and toward a continuum," within which "the extent of the inquiry is tailored to the suspect conduct in each particular case." Therefore, we must make "an enquiry meet for the case, looking to the circumstances, details, and logic of a restraint." In all cases, "the criterion to be used in judging the validity of a restraint on trade is its impact on competition."

The FTC as a party and the Commission in its decision below both assert that the Realcomp website policy is "inherently suspect" and therefore subject to an abbreviated or quick-look review.[4] Because the Commission found that the website policy was inherently suspect, the Commission concluded that anticompetitive effects could be inferred without proof of Realcomp's market power or a demonstration of actual adverse impact. But, notwithstanding its initial quick-look analysis, the Commission alternatively invalidated the challenged restraints under a more searching inquiry, which included an assessment of Realcomp's market power and the actual, as well as likely, anticompetitive effects of its policies. Realcomp objects that the website policy should not be treated as inherently suspect, and that under any test, the website policy is not an unreasonable restraint of trade.

We uphold the Commission on the basis of the more extended rule-of-reason analysis without reaching the question of whether to apply quick-look analysis. * * *

C. Rule of Reason

Applying the rule of reason, we first look to see "whether [the] FTC has demonstrated 'actual detrimental effects' or 'the potential for genuine adverse effects on competition.'" Market power and the anticompetitive nature of the restraint are sufficient to show the potential for anticompetitive effects under a rule-of-reason analysis, and once this showing has been made, Realcomp must offer procompetitive justifications.

---

[4] The Commission applied the "inherently suspect" or "quick-look" analytical framework upheld by the D.C. Circuit in *Polygram Holding, Inc. v. FTC*, 416 F.3d 29 (D.C.Cir. 2005). * * *

Realcomp contends that, to the contrary, "the requirement for proof of market power can be obviated by evidence of actual anticompetitive effects, not the other way around," and so Realcomp urges that actual anticompetitive effects must be proven.

[The court rejected Realcomp's position that all rule of reason cases require proof of actual anticompetitive effects. Quoting the Supreme Court's decision in *Indiana Federation of Dentists*, it held that reliance on inferences drawn from market power and the nature of the conduct can serve as an alternative method of satisfying Section 1's requirement of an unreasonable restraint of trade: " 'the purpose of the inquiries into market definition and market power is to determine whether an arrangement has the *potential* for genuine adverse effects on competition,' and this is so precisely because actual anticompetitive effects may be difficult to demonstrate." Eds.]

Although the policy at issue in *Indiana Federation* was initially afforded abbreviated treatment, the Supreme Court also analyzed the restriction as if it were not sufficiently "naked" automatically to necessitate "some countervailing procompetitive virtue," and explained what must be shown to establish the illegality of less obviously anticompetitive restraints. Notably, *Indiana Federation* did *not* require proof of an anticompetitive effect—specifically, in that case, that the policy at issue resulted in the provision of more costly services than consumers otherwise would have chosen—because:

> [a] concerted and effective effort to withhold (or make more costly) information desired by consumers for the purpose of determining whether a particular purchase is cost justified is likely enough to disrupt the proper functioning of the price-setting mechanism of the market that it may be condemned even absent proof that it resulted in . . . the purchase of higher priced services[ ] than would occur in its absence.

Similarly, here, the website policy is alleged to be an "effort to withhold (or make more costly) information desired by consumers" that would result in "the purchase of higher priced [brokerage] services, than would occur in its absence." Thus, we next assess whether Realcomp's website policy resulted in " 'actual detrimental effects' or 'the *potential* for genuine adverse effects on competition.' " Under either inquiry, substantial evidence supports the Commission's findings.

1. Potential Adverse Effects

a. Market Power

The Commission adopted the ALJ's findings that Realcomp possessed substantial market power in the relevant markets, and Realcomp does not dispute those findings. The ALJ defined the relevant product market as real-estate-brokerage services and found that, for most home sellers and buyers, no reasonable substitutes for such services exist because of the significant advantages of using a real-estate broker to sell a home. Because of the local nature of real-estate markets, the ALJ found that counties in southeastern Michigan define the geographic scope of competition for real-estate-brokerage services. Because of the lack of substitutes for brokerage services, the ALJ found that a broker monopolist could profitably increase commissions significantly above competitive levels.

Defining the relevant input market as the supply of multiple listing services to real-estate brokers, the ALJ found that an MLS like Realcomp exhibits network effects, meaning that the value of the MLS increases as the number of other users of the service increases. The value of an MLS to home sellers (or their representatives) increases with the number of home buyers (or their representatives) using the site, and, similarly, the value to home buyers increases as more home sellers list their properties on the MLS. "Brokers without full access to an MLS would . . . be at a significant competitive disadvantage," "listing services with fewer users are not economically viable substitutes," and barriers to entry make it "improbable" for a rival MLS successfully to enter the market. Because the value of an MLS depends on the number of users, the ALJ observed that "market share is a good indicator of market power," and found that Realcomp possessed a large market share in each relevant county. In light of Realcomp MLS's market share, network effects, and barriers to entry, the ALJ concluded that Realcomp possessed substantial market power in the relevant markets.

Adopting these findings, the Commission agreed that "Realcomp possessed substantial market power in two relevant markets in Southeastern Michigan: the market for residential real estate brokerage services and the market for multiple listing services, which is a vital input into the brokerage services market." Given the extensive and undisputed market analysis undertaken by the ALJ and adopted by the Commission, substantial evidence supports the Commission's findings that Realcomp possessed substantial market power.

b.   Anticompetitive Nature

* * *

In establishing that Realcomp's policies "narrow consumer choice" and "hinder the competitive process," the Commission made the following relevant findings:

> (1) because of its database of listings, the Realcomp MLS is the most effective tool for the sale of residential real estate in Southeastern Michigan; (2) brokers offering limited service and brokers offering traditional, full-service brokers' services compete

with one another for new listings; (3) limited service brokers' services potentially cost less than the services of brokers offering only full-service listings (they not only unbundle the services offered but also unbundle the commission structure); (4) limited service brokers' listings consequently exert a 'price pressure' on full-service brokers' listings; (5) Realcomp's Website Policy, coupled with its Minimum Service Requirement, severely restricted consumers' access to limited service listings because, as a result of those policies, the listings were not available on the most popular websites.

These findings are supported by the evidence before the ALJ and the Commission that the website policy created barriers to the dissemination of discount listings to public websites—the entry point for many consumers in their online real-estate searches. This evidence showed that EA listings can be posted on some public websites, despite Realcomp's policies, but only by dual-listing with another MLS that does not impose similar restrictions. Moreover, such dual-listing raises costs for offering and advertising such discount services, and limited-service brokers testified that Realcomp's policies placed them at a competitive disadvantage. In addition, two of the top four public websites used by consumers in the relevant market can be accessed only through the Realcomp MLS; therefore, due to the website policy, EA listings cannot be placed on these websites. Consumers using these websites are not informed that the websites display only ERTS listings. Realcomp's website policy thus limited access to internet marketing and imposed additional costs on the marketing of discount listings.

Furthermore, the ALJ and Commission both found that limited-service listings exert price pressure on the full-service brokerage model; and brokers testified that discounted online and limited-service models have led to customers asking agents to reduce their commissions. Evidence that the website policy limited exposure of discount listings thus reveals "a concerted refusal to deal with [EA listings] on substantially equal terms" and establishes that the website policy is likely to protect its full-service brokers from competitive pricing pressure. Combining these findings with Realcomp's substantial market power, the Commission reasonably concluded that Realcomp's website policy is likely to be anticompetitive.

The ALJ observed that the Realcomp MLS alone reached about 80% of home buyers, and brokers could place EA listings on Realtor.com and reach approximately 90% of home buyers. The ALJ concluded that, consequently, the website policy prevented EA listings from reaching "only a relatively small additional percentage of home buyers"—the 10% who perused home listings on the inaccessible websites. To the contrary, however, by reducing by 10% the number of home buyers that are exposed to discount listings, the website policy may very well constitute an unreasonable restraint.

Restricting the online dissemination of home listings is especially pernicious because of the emerging competitive impact of the internet and of discounted brokerage services on the residential real-estate market. As the D.C. Circuit observed, "the exclusion of nascent threats is the type of conduct that is reasonably capable of contributing significantly to a defendant's continued monopoly power." *United States v. Microsoft Corp.,* 253 F.3d 34, 79 (D.C.Cir. 2001). The D.C. Circuit was analyzing a monopolization claim under Section 2 of the Sherman Act, rather than a horizontal restraint under Section 1. Substantial evidence shows, though, that "the exclusion of nascent threats" such as discount brokerage services and consumer access to online listings "is reasonably capable of contributing significantly" to anticompetitive effects.

* * *

* * * [S]imilar to excluding discount brokers from the MLS altogether, the website policy limits exposure of discount listings. "[L]istings [are] not . . . distributed as widely as possible" due to the website policy, "resulting in inefficient sales prices," which is the same kind of economic harm caused by MLS exclusions. In particular, the website policy—like exclusions found to be anticompetitive—"reduces the competition among brokers and could result in less competition for brokerage fees."

It is undisputed that the website policy restricted the public dissemination of Realcomp real-estate listings tending to offer consumers limited-brokerage services at reduced costs. The Commission concluded that "[the] finding of market power, coupled with [the] . . . determination that the tendency of the challenged policies was to suppress competition, provide 'indirect' evidence that those policies have or likely will have anticompetitive effects." Evaluating the website policy, the ALJ also notably found that "the nature of the restraint is such that it is likely to be anticompetitive." Given the significance of the Realcomp MLS to the advertising of real-estate listings, and given the role of the internet in providing consumers with the ability to self-provide certain real-estate services, substantial evidence supports the Commission's conclusion that Realcomp's website policy is likely to have an adverse impact on competition by restricting consumer access to discount listings.

2. Actual Adverse Effects

The Commission also examined direct evidence of competitive effects and concluded that Realcomp's policies adversely affected competition. We conclude that the Commission's findings of actual adverse effects are supported by "relevant evidence that a reasonable mind might accept as adequate to support [its] conclusion." Evidence described in Part II.C.1, *supra,* demonstrates that the website policy in fact limited access to internet marketing and imposed financial and administrative costs on brokers seeking to dual-list with other MLSs. Three quantitative analyses conducted by the Commission's economic expert, Dr. Darrell Williams, corroborated other record evidence showing substantial consumer harm— specifically, a reduction of the share of discount listings in the southeastern Michigan real-estate market.

A time-series analysis conducted by Dr. Williams established that the share of EA listings declined by 50% after the introduction of the Realcomp restrictions. The analysis compared the share of EA listings in the Realcomp MLS before and after the challenged policies went into effect and showed that, from May 2004 to October 2006, the monthly average share of EA listings fell from about 1.5% of total listings to about 0.75%. As the Commission noted, although the study showed a reduction in only 0.75 absolute percentage points, the share of EA listings had dropped by half, revealing that "non-traditional arrangements [were] losing their toehold in the market."[9]

While the time-series analysis documented the drop in EA listings, it could not rule out the influence of other economic factors that might have caused the decline. The conclusion that the drop was at least in part caused by Realcomp's restrictive policies was supported by other evidence. A benchmark study conducted by Dr. Williams compared the share of EA listings in the local MLSs of Metropolitan Statistical Areas (MSAs) without restrictions (labeled Control MSAs) to that of MSAs with restrictions (labeled Restriction MSAs). Control MSAs were selected based on a combination of economic and demographic factors that rendered the MSAs statistically similar to Detroit. The benchmark study revealed relatively low shares of EA listings in all the Restriction MSAs—averaging only 1.4% of MLS listings—despite differences among the MSAs with respect to other variables such as population size.

Dr. Williams also found that the weighted average share of EA listings in Control MSAs was higher than in Restriction MSAs—5.6% compared to 1.4%—and that Realcomp's MLS had a significantly smaller share of EA listings than each of the MLSs without similar restrictions. * * *

Attributing the decline in EA shares to a buyers' market, the ALJ credited testimony that "in a declining or distressed market, where both the value of a home and the seller's equity are declining, more home sellers would choose full service ERTS listings over EA listings because they want the professional marketing services of a full service broker." Indeed, the ALJ found that, between 2003 and 2005, EA listings grew from 2% to 15% of listings nationally, but between 2005 and 2006, fell from 15% to 8%. However, the ALJ also heard testimony that demand for the services of limited-service brokers increases in a softening housing market because

---

[9]   A decline in the share of EA listings would have real implications for consumers who would otherwise purchase those listings. Assuming an average home sale price of $200,000, and assuming that EA listings save home sellers half of the typical 6% commission, an EA listing would save an individual home seller, on average, $6,000.

the reduced cost appeals to home sellers without equity in their homes. Furthermore, as the Commission noted, prior to November 2006, NAR permitted members to adopt restrictive policies like Realcomp's, suggesting that such policies could have interfered with the prevalence of EA listings in MLSs nationwide. This evidence is sufficient to provide substantial evidence for the Commission's inferences.

Dr. Williams also conducted ten statistical-regression analyses to evaluate the effects of different factors, including Realcomp's policies, on the share of EA listings. Dr. Williams concluded that Realcomp's policies are associated with a reduction in the share of EA listings of between 5.47 and 6.15 percentage points, leading him to predict that the percentage of EA listings in Realcomp would be higher, and the percentage of ERTS listings would be lower, in the absence of Realcomp's policies. * * *

* * *

Dr. Williams's time-series, benchmark, and statistical-regression analyses thus provide substantial evidence in support of the Commission's findings of anticompetitive effects. And, even if the evidence of actual effects is inconclusive, the Commission also demonstrated the adverse potential of Realcomp's website policy by establishing Realcomp's market power and the anticompetitive tendencies of the website policy.

3.   Procompetitive Justifications

Realcomp might still prevail, despite evidence of actual or likely anticompetitive effects, by demonstrating "some countervailing procompetitive virtue—such as, for example, the creation of efficiencies in the operation of a market or the provision of goods and services." Giving "some deference" to the Commission's conclusion, we conclude that the Commission properly rejected Realcomp's proffered justifications as not "legitimate, plausible, substantial and reasonable."

The ALJ concluded that, without the website restrictions, home sellers with EA agreements "would free ride on the Realcomp members who invest and participate in the MLS through the payment of dues and who otherwise undertake to support the cooperative endeavor of the MLS." However, as the Commission found, the circumstances of this case do not establish free-riding. EA home sellers making use of the Realcomp MLS still must employ a listing broker who is a paying Realcomp member. Realcomp charges equal membership fees to all users. Therefore, Realcomp's services to EA home sellers are compensated through payments of the EA seller to her listing broker, who in turn pays Realcomp for the benefit of participation in the MLS.

Realcomp also erroneously argues that the EA home seller free-rides specifically on Realcomp cooperating agents because the EA home seller may act as her own cooperating broker. By not employing a cooperating broker, the argument goes, the EA home seller compensates Realcomp only through her payment to the listing broker, which does not cover all of Realcomp's costs. These costs are shared by cooperating brokers who pay dues to Realcomp in order to benefit from the business generated by the MLS. Thus, Realcomp asserts, cooperating brokers "subsidize the cost that property owners would otherwise incur to procure buyers who do not use cooperating brokers."

Cooperating brokers are compensated, however, for whatever services they do provide to the EA home seller, and the EA home seller receives no free services. If an EA home seller does choose to transact with a cooperating buyer, which the EA home seller does in 80% of EA listing transactions, compensation is provided for the cooperating broker by the terms of the EA listing contract, of which the cooperating broker is aware before the sale.

Moreover, the free-riding justification fails because a home seller may contract with an unrepresented buyer regardless of the type of listing contract, and under either EA or ERTS listing agreements, there is no compensation provided to cooperating brokers when the home seller chooses not to employ their services. ERTS listings include no requirement for the involvement of cooperating brokers, and, like EA listing agreements, flat-fee ERTS listings do not incorporate a cooperating broker's commission into the listing broker's compensation. Although there may be incentives for an EA home seller to transact with an unrepresented buyer in order to avoid additional payment to a cooperating broker, listing brokers in ERTS transactions also benefit from selecting an unrepresented buyer and retaining the commission that would otherwise be divided. Thus, Realcomp has not demonstrated a connection between the website policy and the prevention of free-riding.[16]

The website policy also purportedly eliminates a "bidding disadvantage" faced by a buyer represented by a cooperating broker when bidding against an unrepresented buyer in an EA transaction. But rather than enhance competition, such a policy insulates cooperating brokers' commissions from competitive pricing pressure. As the Commission found, the bidding-disadvantage justification "reinforces the conclusion that [the policies] have an anti-competitive effect" by deliberately protecting established commissions and preventing the reduction in the cost of selling a home. Even if there are financial incentives for a home seller to contract with an unrepresented buyer over a cooperating broker, Realcomp offers

---

[16] The Commission's analysis is persuasive on this point, noting that EA listings disadvantage not the cooperating brokers, but rather "the listing broker who signs an EA contract for less compensation than an ERTS contract would have provided, and the listing broker who insists upon an ERTS contract and loses a listing as a result. . . . In other words, these two categories of listing brokers are not losing money through free-riding; they are losing money through competition."

no meritorious procompetitive justification for protecting cooperating brokers from pressure to lower costs.[17] And, as with the free-riding justification, Realcomp fails to demonstrate how EA listings give rise to a greater "bidding disadvantage" than do ERTS listings given that a listing broker in an ERTS agreement presumably prefers to retain the cooperating broker's commission for herself by transacting with an unrepresented buyer.

III. CONCLUSION

* * * Therefore, we DENY Realcomp's petition for review.

How did the court in *Realcomp II* apply the "rule of reason"? How did it structure its inquiry? Allocate burdens between the parties? What methods of proof did the court identify as valid ways for a plaintiff to establish competitive harm? How did the court use inferences to establish likely competitive effect? Evidence of actual effects? How significant was it that the record included evidence of both likely and actual effects, and that both similarly suggested that Realcomp's policies were anticompetitive? How did complaint counsel and the FTC use economic expert evidence? Did the court engage in any "balancing" of pro-and anti-competitive effects?

How would you characterize the FTC's theory of competitive harm, collusive or exclusionary? Both? If so, are there similarities between *Realcomp II* and *JTC Petroleum*, which we read in Chapter 1? Did the MLS members, faced with a competitive challenge to their long-standing commission practices that created downward pricing pressure, seek to neutralize that challenge by excluding their new rivals? What did the court mean when it upheld the FTC's finding that Realcomp's conduct limited "consumer choice" and "hinder[ed] the competitive process"? Did it conclude that any reduction in the variety of brokerage services constituted competitive harm? Note that the court concluded that this conduct "is likely to protect [Realcomp's] full-service brokers from competitive pricing pressure." Did the court instead conclude that a reduction in product variety and consumer choice harms competition only when it is tantamount to raising prices or, as here, keeping prices from falling? Did the court conclude that conduct that limits consumer knowledge of lower cost brokerage options necessarily hinders the competitive process by lessening

---

[17] The ALJ also noted that the website policy reflects the greater value of ERTS over EA contracts to the MLS because cooperating brokers often must deal directly with EA home sellers rather than listing brokers when engaging in EA contracts, and, as a result, may be required to provide transactional services that would otherwise be performed by full-service listing brokers. We agree with the Commission, however, that Realcomp has failed to carry its burden of demonstrating how meeting the preferences of cooperating brokers ultimately benefits consumers, why the price for EA listings does not incorporate these costs, or how this policy in particular offers efficiency benefits. It is also worth noting that, despite Realcomp's assertions of the website policy's necessity, the NAR has ruled that MLSs may no longer exclude EA listings from their IDX feeds.

the competition between full service and limited service brokerage services, thereby protecting the full service brokers from competitive pressure that would have otherwise led them to reduce their prices?

How can a defendant rebut a showing of actual or probable anticompetitive harm? Will its burden differ depending on the kind of evidence presented by the plaintiff? What was deficient in the effort by Realcomp to establish its procompetitive justifications? One of Realcomp's principal defenses was that its policies eliminated "free-riding." We will examine the free-rider argument again and in greater depth in Chapter 6, but recall that a similar argument was raised by the defendants in *Polygram*. What was Realcomp's argument? Did the court conclude that the defense was not cognizable, or that it was not proven? Why was it significant, in the court's view that when services are paid for there cannot be a free rider problem? For a similar view of free-riding, see *In the Matter of Toys-"R"-Us, Inc.*, 126 F.T.C. 415, 601 (1998) (" '[w]hat gives this the name *free*-riding is the lack of charge. When payment is possible, free-riding is not a problem because the 'ride' is not free.' "), *quoting Chicago Prof'l Sports, Ltd. v. Nat'l Basketball Ass'n.*, 961 F.2d 667, 675 (7th Cir. 1992).

Sidebar 2–6:
The Contemporary Rule of Reason in Practice

In this Sidebar we provide a suggested roadmap for analysis under the modern rule of reason, one that integrates the principles and procedural devices that have been embraced by the courts. Although the rule of reason has been subjected to criticism over the years for being unpredictable and costly to administer, the Supreme Court has, in a variety of contexts, reiterated its support for application of the rule of reason under Section 1 of the Sherman Act. At the same time, however, it has encouraged the lower courts to develop more cost-effective, administrable, and structured approaches to its application that are tailored to the specific needs of the industry and practices at issue. *See, e.g., FTC v. Actavis, Inc.*, 133 S.Ct. 2223, 2237–38 (2013); *Leegin Creative Leather Prods., Inc. v. PSKS, Inc.*, 551 U.S. 877, 898–99 (2007). Increasingly, courts and the federal enforcement agencies have sought to do just that and have been moving toward a consistent, structured approach for determining whether agreements between competitors violate Section 1 of the Sherman Act. At the outset, consider these general principles, which are drawn from the material we have read in this Chapter:

- Section 1 prohibits only "unreasonable" restraints of trade;

- The purpose of the inquiry under this "rule of reason" is to reach a judgment about the probable or actual competitive effect of specific conduct;

- In the context of litigation, the rule of reason is a structured, step-by-step inquiry that integrates burden-shifting;[a]

- The plaintiff bears the initial burden of coming forward with evidence tending to demonstrate anticompetitive effect, but that burden can be satisfied in a variety of ways depending upon the nature and strength of the evidence of competitive harm;

- Once the plaintiff successfully demonstrates presumptive anticompetitive effect, the burden of providing a cognizable justification for the conduct shifts to the defendant;

- When the probability of harm is very high and the likelihood of justification very low, the presumption of harm will be irrebuttable;

- In all other cases, the presumption is rebuttable, and the defendant can rebut that presumption of harm either by successfully undermining the evidence that supports the presumption of harm (and consequent initial burden shift) or by introducing evidence tending to show that the conduct will have no effects or will be procompetitive;

- If both parties have met their respective burdens, the court will assess all of the evidence to reach a conclusion about the conduct's likely overall effects, taking into account that the burden of proof (persuasion) always remains with the plaintiff, so harm must be more likely than not.

At each stage of the process, rule of reason analysis is guided by two core economic concepts: anticompetitive effect and efficiency. Evidence of each, however, can vary, and typically includes some combination of lay and expert evidence, both data (such as financial and sales figures and economic models) and

---

[a]   It is important, however, not to overstate the degree to which parties and courts rigidly compartmentalize evidence to align with a burden shifting framework. Private parties and the government, in its exercise of prosecutorial discretion, will be informed by an evaluation of all of the evidence. Burdens of pleading, production, and proof, however, can influence how courts assess the evidence in the context of litigation through motions to dismiss, for summary judgment, and the rare antitrust trial. Moreover, once an antitrust case reaches trial—and that is a relatively rare occurrence—the plaintiff doesn't typically introduce the minimal evidence of harm necessary to satisfy an initial burden, wait for the defendant to put on its response, and then reply; the plaintiff usually puts in all of its best evidence in its case-in-chief, including rebuttal evidence. And it will later use cross-examination to rebut the defendant's evidence, as well.

communications (such as documents, reports, and emails). And as we have seen, an agreement might be analyzed as a whole or with attention to one or more particular provisions, depending on the plaintiff's theory of competitive harm. The fact that an agreement may be procompetitive when viewed as a whole will not save an anticompetitive provision or feature of the agreement. Conversely, the presence of some procompetitive provision will not save an agreement that is anticompetitive as a whole. The scope of the violation will also affect the probable remedies when a violation is found.

Reflecting back on the cases we have studied in this Chapter from *Chicago Board of Trade* to *Realcomp II*, we now consider how each party to a Section 1 claim can meet its respective burden under the rule of reason.

The Prima Facie Case: Anticompetitive Effects

As the Supreme Court instructed in *California Dental*, analysis of conduct under Section 1 of the Sherman Act should not be viewed as implementing three distinct "rules"—per se, quick look, and rule of reason. The rule of reason is the single "rule," but it can be applied through a continuum of options, what the Supreme Court in *CDA* labelled an "enquiry meet for the case." Moreover, as we have seen, a burden shift under the rule of reason can be triggered by different circumstances, and there may not be a bright line that separates each approach.

Although this leaves application of the rule of reason somewhat less predictable than it might otherwise be, it also provides needed flexibility, consistent with the Sherman Act's design, to evaluate different practices and different kinds of evidence. It should be remembered that at one time the Supreme Court relied heavily on bright line, per se analysis. But that reliance was criticized for being inflexible and over-inclusive, and for its tendency to exclude consideration of evidence of procompetitive effects that might change the outcome of some cases if credited. The "quick look," on the other hand, was seen as a corrective step to avoid imposing needless costs of administering comprehensive rule of reason analysis in cases of relatively obvious competitive harm and as a way to preserve some of the benefits of per se rules by providing guidance to firms and courts. The history of the rule of reason, therefore, is a history of continuing refinement and adaptation. Let's review, therefore, the guidance we can derive from the cases about: (1) what constitutes an "anticompetitive effect," and (2) what kind of evidence will be sufficient to warrant a presumption of competitive harm that is sufficient to shift a burden to the defending parties.

What do we mean by "anticompetitive effect"? The most frequently cited examples of anticompetitive effects are decreased output and increased price. Recall from Chapter 1 that this reflects fundamental economic principles about the relationship of supply, demand, and price. Almost all of the cases we read that resulted in a finding of violation involved such output and price effects—the strategy of buying up and storing "excess" oil in *Socony-Vaccuum Oil*, the television plan in *NCAA* that reduced the number of televised collegiate football games, and the division of markets in *BRG of Georgia*, are all examples. On the other hand, recall that when courts declined to find a violation, they often cited lack of evidence of output or price effects as the reason. *Chicago Board of Trade* and *Broadcast Music* are examples.

Output and price effects are not the only kinds of anticompetitive effects that concern antitrust law. Recall that in *National Society of Professional Engineers* the Court observed that competition benefits "quality, service, safety, and durability." Conduct that restricts one of these other dimensions of competition, therefore, can also give rise to antitrust concerns. In later Chapters we will also see that restrictions on innovation can be deemed anticompetitive. Each of these can manifest themselves as price effects, too, but may also be distinct.

Two of the cases we studied could be read also to reflect concerns about the adverse consequences of conduct that interferes with the market mechanisms that determine output and prices. In *National Society of Professional Engineers*, for example, the Court did not rely on evidence that the ban on competitive bidding had actually resulted in lower output and higher prices of engineering services. It readily inferred, however, that the level of output and prices would be adversely affected by the ban. Similarly, in *Realcomp II*, the court readily inferred that depriving consumers of information about a lower cost alternative service was so likely to discourage price competition that it warranted a burden shift. Handicapping the competitive process, therefore, can also constitute an anticompetitive effect when it is likely to lead to higher prices, lower output, or other adverse consequences.

How can a plaintiff establish anticompetitive effect? The cases suggest a range of answers. Establishing anticompetitive effect is a necessary prerequisite to shift a burden to the defendant. The effect can be probable (based on inferences) or actual (based on evidence of actual adverse effects). Here is a summary of the approaches that have worked to shift a burden to the defendant:

- An agreement that falls squarely within a traditional per se category
  - Facially obvious anticompetitive effect ("always or almost always" anticompetitive)
    - *E.g.*, Price fixing, division of markets, collusive boycotts by competitors
  - No plausible and cognizable efficiency justification
  - Actual harm may also be evident, although proof is not required
  - Case Examples: *Socony-Vaccum Oil*; *Catalano*; *BRG of Georgia*; *SCTLA*
- Due to a plausible efficiency, traditional per se analysis is inappropriate, but competitive harm is still relatively obvious
  - *Broadcast Music* and *NCAA* conveyed the message that per se analysis is inappropriate in the presence of a plausible efficiency
  - But the burden of production can still shift from plaintiff to defendant if there is a high probability of competitive harm based on the market context, judicial learning, and/or economic reasoning, or if there is evidence of actual harm
  - Case Examples: *National Society of Professional Engineers*, *NCAA*, *Indiana Federation of Dentists*, *Polygram*
- An agreement will likely permit a defendant firm or group of firms to exercise market power
  - Relatively less obvious basis for predicting anticompetitive effects than the previous approaches
  - Typical steps:
    - define a relevant market
    - calculate marker share
    - infer market power from "high" market share
    - infer incentive and ability to exercise market power (probability of competitive harm) from

              proof of market power and the nature of the conduct

- o Note that the typical steps incorporate a "double inference:" from market share to market power, and from market power to competitive harm, though in principle, market power could instead be demonstrated in other ways, leaving only the second inference *(see* Sidebar 4–5])

- o Comment: this approach to satisfying plaintiff's initial burden is typically the initial showing in a comprehensive rule of reason analysis

  - If plaintiff fails to meet this initial burden, there is no burden shift, so case ends in defendant's favor

  - If plaintiff adopts this route to satisfy its initial burden, defendants often seek dismissal or summary judgment on the ground that plaintiff is unable to prove a relevant market or a sufficiently high market share

  - Note that if defendants lack the ability to harm competition, there would be no basis to shift burden from plaintiff to defendants

    - If lack of market power is relatively obvious, proof by defendants (perhaps through showing low market shares) could serve as a quick look to exculpate

- o <u>Case Example:</u> *Realcomp II*

The plaintiff in a Section 1 case thus has a variety of means to meet and shift a burden to the defendant. Note how, consistent with the idea of a "continuum," the alternative approaches reflect a sliding scale that demands more evidence as the case for anticompetitive effects becomes less obvious. In decision-theoretic terms, one can understand this sliding scale as adjusting the plaintiff's burden to approximate the likelihood and type of error. In general, less evidence is required when the probability of harm is high; as the probability of harm becomes less obvious, the burden on the plaintiff increases. In this way, the sliding scale accounts for the increased possibility of a false positive. Increasing the burden on the plaintiff is not costless, however, so the sliding scale must strive to ensure that the increased costs imposed on the decision-making process yield proportionately improved decisions.

Note also that the concept of market power is integral to all of the approaches. Whether it is presumed or subject to proof, market power is typically the source of anticompetitive harm. As one court has explained, "[a]s a threshold matter, a plaintiff must show that the defendant has market power—that is, the ability to raise prices significantly without going out of business—without which the defendant could not cause anticompetitive effects on market pricing." *Agnew v. NCAA*, 683 F.3d 328, 335 (7th Cir. 2012). Proving market power through inference from a high market share, however, has not been without its critics, some of whom have argued that high market share alone is not enough to warrant such an inference. However, because a high market share suggests the absence of rivalry, it may justify the inference that a firm or firms can profitably charge prices above marginal cost, and hence a *presumption* that a firm possesses market power.[b] That presumption might still be subject to rebuttal, as we discuss below, but it is a reasonable inference. There have also been critics of any approach to proving anticompetitive effects that does not also include proving a relevant market, but as we have noted, that criticism was rejected by the Supreme Court in *NCAA* and *Indiana Federation of Dentists*, at least with respect to horizontal restraints.

Rebutting a Prima Facie Case: Cognizable Defenses

Once the plaintiff successfully shifts a burden to the defendant, the defendant faces a presumption that its conduct harmed competition. As we have seen, when per se analysis applies, that presumption is irrebuttable, meaning no defenses are allowed. In all other cases, the presumption is rebuttable and the defendant will then have the burden of responding. The defendant can do so in two ways: by seeking to undermine the plaintiff's case, as by, for example, challenging its market definition and estimation of the defendant's market power, and/or by introducing evidence tending to indicate that the practice will have no competitive effect at all or will be pro-competitive—what the courts have described as a "cognizable" defense.

What differentiates a "cognizable" from a non-cognizable defense? Recall that very early on the Supreme Court concluded

---

[b]   The ability to do so, however, will depend on the elasticity of demand. The greater the elasticity of demand (loosely, the flatter the demand curve), the less likely it is that a firm or firms with a high market share can restrict output and raise price without losing so many sales that it will prove to be an unprofitable strategy. *See, e.g.*, DENNIS W. CARLTON & JEFFREY M. PERLOFF, MODERN INDUSTRIAL ORGANIZATION 93 (4th ed. 2005) ("[T]he key element in an investigation of market power is the price elasticity of demand.").

that "reasonable prices" was not a cognizable defense to price fixing. Another example was the rejection in *National Society of Professional Engineers* of the engineers' argument that competition would result in lower quality engineering services, which the Court described as a "frontal assault" on the Sherman Act. The D.C. Circuit in *Polygram* also rejected as not cognizable an argument by Polygram that its agreement to suspend promotion of its previous albums would prevent free-riding by its rivals. These defenses were not cognizable because they did not tend to diminish the likelihood that those effects would occur; instead they sought to excuse them.

To better understand this distinction, we now consider the two mirror issues to those that face plaintiffs and were discussed above: (1) what constitutes a "procompetitive effect," and (2) what kind of evidence will be sufficient to shift a burden back to the plaintiff. When we study the treatment of horizontal mergers in Chapter 5 we will examine these questions again and in greater depth; here we offer just a few observations based on the cases we have studied.

What do we mean by "procompetitive" effect? The most obvious example of a procompetitive effect is cost reduction, which is a common example of what is referred to as increased "efficiency." Reducing costs can lead to a wide variety of competitive benefits, such as lower prices, improved quality, and enhanced service. It might also lead to innovation in products, services, or business methods, and reduced product development time. All of these might increase output, the inverse of the most obvious kind of anticompetitive effect.

Reducing a firm or firms' costs also can have some positive, indirect effects. It can reduce or eliminate any incentive to raise price and restrict output that might flow from increased market power, and it can diminish the incentive to coordinate with rival firms to raise prices. Shifting or combining production or distribution facilities to reduce marginal costs, for example, is a commonly recognized example of a cost reduction likely to be procompetitive. Another example is reduced transaction costs, as we observed in *Broadcast Music* and possibly *Chicago Board of Trade*. Recall that in *Broadcast Music* the Court found that the blanket license helped to reduce the cost of policing copyright infringement and contracting with licensees.

As we discussed in Sidebar 2–5, ancillary restraint analysis, which some courts still mention, can also be understood today as another way of describing procompetitive justifications. Robert Bork argued, for example, that ancillary restraint analysis was the common law's way of acknowledging that the "integration of economic activities, which is indispensable to productive efficiency" should be encouraged, not condemned. ROBERT H. BORK, THE ANTITRUST PARADOX 28 (1978). Here, Judge Bork relies on facial analysis, economic reasoning, and prior experience to identify restraints for which an efficiency justification is likely to be strong. As we have noted, by supporting some legitimate and procompetitive purpose, the restraint might promote output and be fairly viewed as efficiency-enhancing. It is doubtful, however, that continued reference to ancillary restraint analysis itself aids the inquiry.

How can a defendant establish procompetitive effect? As noted above, a defendant's first line of defense is often denial: it will challenge the plaintiff's prima facie case. Consider the strategic explanation: undermining the plaintiff's case will keep a burden from shifting and relieve the defendant of the burden of coming forward with evidence of a procompetitive justification. *California Dental* is an illustration of how a defendant can successfully challenge the plaintiff's case for a burden shift. Once the Court agreed with the Dental Association that the FTC had failed to meet its burden of demonstrating anticompetitive effect, the CDA was not required to support its claim that its restrictions on advertising improved competition.

As we provided above with respect to anticompetitive effect, here is a summary of how defendants can meet their burden, depending on the nature of the plaintiff's case:

- An agreement that falls squarely within a traditional per se category
    - Presumption is irrebuttable, so there can be no defense
    - Best strategy, when available, is to argue that categorization of the agreement as a good fit for per se analysis is inappropriate
    - <u>Case Examples</u>: *Chicago Board of Trade*; *Broadcast Music*; *NCAA*
- Due to plausible efficiency, per se analysis is inappropriate, but competitive harm is still relatively obvious
    - If the initial burden shift is based on evidence of actual harm

- It can be difficult to rebut these kinds of quick look cases unless the evidence of actual harm can be successfully challenged
- Cannot rebut with circumstantial evidence of the lack of market power (*NCAA*)
  - o If the initial burden shift is based on a combination of economic theory and background facts
    - Challenge the theory of harm, if possible (*California Dental*)
    - Introduce evidence of procompetitive effect (*Polygram*)
  - o Defendants' goal may be to impose the higher burden on plaintiff that is associated with a more comprehensive rule of reason analysis, or to prevail if the plaintiff is unwilling to proceed under a more complete rule of reason
- Agreement will likely permit firm or firms to exercise market power
  - o Challenge evidence of market power, if possible (as by challenging market definition or market share calculations, or arguing that conditions of entry are relatively easy)
  - o Introduce evidence of procompetitive effects (*Realcomp II*)

Note that the defendant's strategy will vary with the nature and strength of the plaintiff's case. In other words, the sliding scale approach affects both parties, and will influence the likelihood that the defendant will be able to shift a burden back to the plaintiff.

Although we have only alluded to it at this point, also note our mention of "conditions of entry." It is easy to understand its importance. The success of any effort to exercise market power may be undermined by the ability of rivals, current or new, to respond to a price increase by increasing the supply of goods or services to a market. Increased supply from new entrants, or from incumbents not involved in exercising market power who instead expand their output, can defeat any effort to increase price. Moreover, the incentive to raise price may be diminished if firms otherwise inclined to try are aware that entry responses will be swift and substantial. Conversely, the presence of "barriers to entry" can bolster the incentive to exercise market power, because they reduce the likelihood of supply responses from rivals. A plaintiff might address conditions of entry to support a circumstantial case of market power (by arguing conditions are difficult). A defendant might argue that anticompetitive effects are unlikely when conditions are easy. We will discuss the importance of conditions of entry at greater length when we examine exclusion in Chapter 4 and horizontal mergers in Chapter 5.

Resolving the Hardest Cases

Many courts, including the Supreme Court, have suggested that when both plaintiffs and defendants meet their respective burdens of production, the court will decide cases based on a "balancing" of harms and benefits. *See, e.g., Atl. Richfield Oil Co. v. USA Petroleum Co.*, 495 U.S. 328, 342 (1990) ("*Per se* and rule-of-reason analysis are but two methods of determining whether a restraint is "unreasonable," *i.e.,* whether its anticompetitive effects outweigh its procompetitive effects"). *See also Law v. NCAA*, 134 F.3d 1010, 1019 (10th Cir. 1998) ("Ultimately . . . the harms and benefits must be weighed against each other in order to judge whether the challenged behavior is, on balance, reasonable.") And in *CDA*, for example, the Court indicated that the goal of rule of reason analysis is to determine whether a restraint has a "net anticompetitive effect." *California Dental*, 526 U.S. at 774.[c]

Such "balancing" or the determination of a restraint's "net" effects' could be interpreted in a number of ways. If taken literally, it might suggest that harms and benefits must be quantified by both parties and compared to see which is larger. But requiring proof of quantifiable harm would appear inconsistent with the courts' endorsement of a wide variety of ways for plaintiffs to establish anticompetitive effect. There are no reported cases in the U.S. taking such an approach.

"Rule of reason balancing," therefore, in the sense of comparing of quantifiable harms, is something of an antitrust law myth. Although it is frequently described as the final step in the rule of reason analysis, most cases turn instead on the strength and weight of the evidence of adverse effects. One commentator has found that almost all Section 1 cases are resolved based on the strength of the evidence of anticompetitive effect. *See, e.g.,* Michael A. Carrier, *The Rule of Reason: An Empirical Update for the 21st Century*, 16 GEO. MASON. L. REV. 827 (2009) (noting trend in the cases towards

---

[c] For one effort to synthesize the cases (as of the time it was written) into a coherent framework, see Fed. Trade Com'n & U.S. Dep't of Justice, *Antitrust Guidelines for Collaborations Among Competitors* (Apr. 2000)("Collaboration Guidelines"), https://www.ftc.gov/system/files/documents/public_statements/300481/000407ftcdojguidelines.pdf.

using a structured, burden-shifting framework to resolve rule of reason cases which disposes of 97% of cases based on an evaluation of the evidence of anticompetitive effect); Michael A. Carrier, *The Rule of Reason: Bridging the Disconnect*, 1999 B.Y.U. L. REV. 1265 (concluding that "in an astonishing 96% of Rule of Reason cases, courts do not balance anything"). If a plaintiff can survive the initial motions challenging its evidence of anticompetitive effect, settlement is more likely than a trial on the merits.

In reaching a conclusion about whether a particular restraint is unreasonable, should it matter whether a firm's procompetitive goals can be accomplished through means that are less restrictive of competition? Some courts have taken this approach, integrating it into their statement of the framework for applying the rule of reason. *See, e.g., O'Bannon v. NCAA*, 802 F.3d 1049, 1070 (9th Cir. 2015) (once plaintiff meets its initial burden of demonstrating significant anticompetitive effects and defendant comes forward with evidence of procompetitive effects, "plaintiff must then show that any legitimate objectives can be achieved in a substantially less restrictive manner"); *U.S. v. Brown University*, 5 F.3d 658, 679 (3d Cir. 1993) (same). It can be understood as derivative of ancillary restraint analysis, which asked whether a restraint was ancillary, necessary, and no greater than necessary to achieve a legitimate purpose. *See* Collaboration Guidelines, § 3.36(b) (addressing less restrictive alternatives as part of the evaluation of reasonable necessity). But in modern application it is not limited to cases involving restraints that can be characterized as ancillary and can be understood as a variation on structured rule of reason analysis.

How should the presence of a less restrictive alternative be evaluated, if it is deemed relevant, and with what result? If one is available, does that support a finding that the restraint is unreasonable? Perhaps the availability of less restrictive means calls into question whether the agreement has a legitimate purpose in the first place and if there is a way to harm competition less without sacrificing efficiency benefits we would prefer that defendants do so. But what if there are no alternative means of achieving a procompetitive goal equally well, does that necessarily mean that the restraint is "reasonable," regardless of its adverse effects? Which party should bear the burden of introducing evidence of a less restrictive alternative, and at what stage of the rule of reason analysis? The case law and commentary are inconsistent and the approach is not uniformly followed. For a thorough evaluation of these issues and an argument that the analysis of less restrictive alternatives can provide needed substance to rule of reason balancing, see C. Scott Hemphill, *Less Restrictive Alternatives in Antitrust Law*, 116 COLUM. L. REV. 927 (2016).

Conclusion

How well does this structured, burden-shifting approach work? Does it adequately reduce the possibility of wrongly condemning beneficial conduct under the rule of reason, of false positives? Does it risk failing to condemn conduct that is harmful, false negatives? Is it likely to do a good job of moderating the costs of enforcing the Sherman Act?

Reflect back on everything you have read in this Chapter and the approach suggested in this Sidebar as you move on to the next, final Section of the Chapter, where we profile four challenging cases. Consider how you would apply what you have learned so far to decide those cases, and what approach you would take to evaluate whether the plaintiffs have provided enough evidence of harm to shift a burden to the defendants and, if they have, whether the defendants have successfully shifted that burden back.

C. MODERN CHALLENGES IN CHARACTERIZATION AND APPLICATION OF THE RULE OF REASON

As you can see from decisions like *Polygram* and *Realcomp II*, the rule of reason has significantly developed since the days of *Standard Oil* and *Chicago Board of Trade*. With greater focus on competitive effects, courts tend to apply a rigorous and structured approach that begins with an assessment of the plaintiff's evidence of anticompetitive effect. In doing so, litigants and courts seek to locate cases along the rule of reason "continuum," which influences whether and under what circumstances the plaintiff has succeeded in shifting a burden to the defendants to present evidence of procompetitive justifications for their conduct. Because the choice of approach can influence the outcome of cases, as we saw in *California Dental*, parties to antitrust cases still litigate vigorously over the issue.

In this Section of the Chapter we profile four cases that address this process. Although there is some overlap, the first two focus primarily on whether to apply per se analysis; the second two on whether quick look analysis was appropriate under the facts. In lieu of edited versions of the decisions, we present brief summaries of the facts followed by selected passages. As you review each profile, consider how each court addressed the parties' arguments for and against applying different approaches.

What factors persuaded the courts one way or the other? Are there common features of the cases that suggest courts are perhaps reaching consensus on how to use the rule of reason continuum? Are the cases consistent?

Per se or Not?

1. ***In re Sulfuric Acid Antitrust Litigation*, 703 F.3d 1004 (7th Cir. 2012),** involved a class action against two Canadian mining firms that produced sulfuric acid as a byproduct of other manufacturing processes. Those manufacturing processes, as well as certain Canadian government regulatory mandates, resulted in an excess of sulfuric acid production over the demand for it in Canada. Those processes also were less costly than the production methods common in the U.S. As a consequence, the Canadian defendants looked for opportunities to sell their excess to U.S. firms.

In lieu of trying to develop their own U.S. distribution network, the Canadian firms entered into agreements with U.S. sulfuric acid producers. Fearing that the Canadians would develop their own U.S. distribution network and sell at lower prices owing to their cost advantage, the U.S. firms agreed to curtail their own production and devote their distribution capacity to Canadian-produced sulfuric acid. In return, they each received exclusive U.S. territories in which to distribute the Canadian sulfuric acid.

The plaintiff class, U.S. sulfuric acid purchasers, challenged these "shutdown agreements" as a form of per se unlawful price fixing. The defendants, Canadian mining companies, responded that they had valid business justifications for the agreements: that the cost of establishing their own distribution network in the United States would have been substantial; that they needed some reassurances that the excess sulfuric acid they were producing could be sold at a profit in the U.S.; and that had they been forced to sell their excess sulfuric acid in the U.S. at a loss (perhaps to avoid expensive storage expenses in Canada), they could have been subject to anti-dumping claims. *Id.* at 1008–10.

Just prior to trial, the district court ruled that the case could not proceed based on per se analysis—the plaintiffs would need to try the case under a more complete rule of reason analysis. Both plaintiffs and the district court, therefore, appeared to be proceeding under the old bi-polar framework, assuming that there were but two analytic choices and that they were distinct: per se or rule of reason. The plaintiffs elected to appeal the ruling, apparently assuming that although the evidence they had was sufficient to satisfy per se analysis, under a rule of reason they would need to prove market power, something they would be unable to do despite almost nine years of litigation and discovery. They would go to trial under the per se approach or not at all.

In an opinion by Judge Richard Posner, the Court of Appeals agreed with the district court that per se analysis was a poor fit for the agreements:

> It is relevant that we have never seen or heard of an antitrust case quite like this, combining such elements as involuntary production and potential antidumping exposure. It is a bad idea to subject a novel way of doing business (or an old way in a new and previously unexamined context, which may be a better description of this case) to per se treatment under antitrust law.

The court was perplexed, however, by the plaintiffs' decision not to proceed under a more complete rule of reason analysis:

> The abiding puzzle of the plaintiffs' appeal is why the lawyers for the class, having spent almost nine years litigating the case in the district court, refused to go to trial. Though the trial would have been governed by the rule of reason, probably all that this would have meant in a case such as this is that the defendants would have had greater latitude for offering justifications for what the plaintiffs claim is a price-fixing conspiracy than if the standard governing the trial had been the per se rule, which treats price fixing by competitors as illegal regardless of consequences or possible justifications. *Texaco Inc. v. Dagher,* 547 U.S. 1, 5, 126 S.Ct. 1276, 164 L.Ed.2d 1 (2006). The plaintiffs do not concede that the conduct they challenge was reasonable and therefore lawful; but their refusal to go to trial under the rule of reason suggests that they expected a jury to find that it was.
>
> From remarks by their lawyer at the oral argument we infer that they think that in a trial governed by the rule of reason they would have had to prepare a radically different case in chief, proving not only that the defendants fixed prices (all they'd have to prove, besides damages, in a per se case), but also that the defendants had market power (that is, the power to raise price above the competitive level without losing so much business to other sellers that the price would quickly fall back to that level) and that their collusive activity was indeed anticompetitive. Doubtless in most cases the prima facie case under the rule of reason requires proof "that the defendant has sufficient market power to restrain competition substantially" * * *. But a plaintiff who proves that the defendants got together and agreed to raise the price (whether directly or by restricting output, which would have the same effect) that he pays them for their products—which is what the plaintiffs in this case would have had to prove under the per se rule to establish liability and obtain damages—has made a prima facie case that the defendants' behavior was

unreasonable. He need not prove market power; even though by definition without it a firm or group of firms can't harm competition, it is not a part of the prima facie case of illegal per se price fixing. E.g., *National Collegiate Athletic Association v. Board of Regents,* 468 U.S. 85, 109–10, 104 S.Ct. 2948, 82 L.Ed.2d 70 (1984). But even if a challenged practice doesn't quite rise to the level of per se illegality, it may be close enough to shift to the defendant the burden of showing that appearances are deceptive and really the behavior that the plaintiffs have challenged is not anticompetitive. Of course there would be more work for the plaintiffs if the defendants in this case were able to create a triable issue of justification, but, as we have just explained, probably less than they think.

703 F.3d at 1007–08.

Note that the court is applying the same kind of burden shifting framework we have seen in other cases and have just described. What is it suggesting about the plaintiff's burden in the case, even if per se analysis was inappropriate? What would it take to shift it to the defendants, requiring them to come forward with evidence to support their purported justifications? What does the court's analysis suggest about the "line" separating per se analysis from more complete rule of reason analysis? Why does it appear to believe that the plaintiffs (or at least their lawyers) gave up too easily on satisfying their burden?

Although not explicitly discussed, would the case have been a better fit for quick look analysis? Does the appellate court's reference to *NCAA* suggest that perhaps it would have been receptive to such an argument? Under a more complete application of the rule of reason, is the court also suggesting that certain reasonable assumptions can be made about probable anticompetitive effect that would allow a burden to shift to the defendant? Was there any suggestion that the plaintiffs would need to show actual effects to establish liability? To collect damages?

2. In *United States v. Apple Inc.,* **791 F.3d 290 (2d Cir. 2015)**[3], the Justice Department, joined by 33 states, alleged that Apple had entered into a per se unlawful agreement to raise, fix, and stabilize the price of electronic books (e-books) with a group of leading book publishers. The case focused on events surrounding the introduction by Apple of its tablet computer, the iPad, and its related entry into the market for e-book distribution through creation of the iBookstore.

There were two interrelated components of the agreements. First, Apple orchestrated an agreement among the publishers to change their method of distribution from a wholesale model, whereby they sold e-books

---

[3]   One of the Casebook authors, Jonathan B. Baker, worked on this case for the government plaintiffs.

to retailers who in turn determined book prices to consumers, to an agency model, under which the e-book publishers would set retail prices for their own books. The change was directed in large part at Amazon, which had pioneered the market for e-book distribution. All five publishers had been dissatisfied with what they perceived as the low prices of e-books sold by Amazon and the change to an agency model would deprive Amazon of continued retail pricing discretion. Apple also entered into "most-favored nation" or MFN agreements with the publishers, under which they guaranteed that the price of e-books sold through the iBookstore would be the lowest retail price available in the marketplace. This provided added incentive for all of the publishers to switch Amazon from the wholesale to an agency model. It also diminished the publishers' incentive to sell e-books at lower prices through Amazon than through any other retailer, especially Apple. Following the near simultaneous implementation of these changes by all five publishers, e-book prices increased substantially on Amazon.

All five publishers entered into consent decrees settling the claims, but Apple declined and instead took the case to trial. Apple "strenuously" objected to application of per se analysis on two grounds. First, it argued that it was a distributor, not a publisher, and hence its relationship to the publishers could not fairly be characterized as "horizontal," as in previous per se unlawful price fixing cases. Second, it was a new market entrant in the sale of e-books, not a dominant player, and thus, it contended, the agreements, by facilitating its entry, enhanced competition in a market dominated by Amazon.

The district court rejected these efforts to distinguish Apple's conduct, and ruled that the agreement was a per se violation of the Sherman Act or, in the alternative, that it unreasonably restrained trade under a more complete rule of reason analysis. In its view, the government had met its burden of demonstrating anticompetitive effects, which shifted the burden to Apple—and Apple failed to shift it back:

> In sum, the Plaintiffs have shown not just by a preponderance of the evidence, * * * but through compelling direct and circumstantial evidence that Apple participated in and facilitated a horizontal price-fixing conspiracy. As a result, they have proven a *per se* violation of the Sherman Act. * * * If it were necessary to analyze this evidence under the rule of reason, however, the Plaintiffs would also prevail.

> Apple has not shown that the execution of the Agreements had any pro-competitive effects. The form Agreements eliminated retail price competition, and there is no evidence that the Publisher Defendants have ever competed with each other on price. To the contrary, several of the Publishers' CEOs explained that they have not competed with each other on that basis. The

pro-competitive effects to which Apple has pointed, including its launch of the iBookstore, the technical novelties of the iPad, and the evolution of digital publishing more generally, are phenomena that are independent of the Agreements and therefore do not demonstrate any pro-competitive effects flowing from the Agreements. In any event, the Plaintiffs have shown that the Agreements did not promote competition, but destroyed it. The Agreements compelled the Publisher Defendants to move Amazon and other retailers to an agency model for the distribution of e-books, removed the ability of retailers to set the prices of their e-books and compete with each other on price, relieved Apple of the need to compete on price, and allowed the Publisher Defendants to raise the prices for their e-books, which they promptly did on both New Releases and NYT Bestsellers, as well as backlist titles.

U.S. v. Apple Inc., 952 F.Supp.2d 638, 694 (SDNY 2013).

The court of appeals affirmed liability by a 2–1 margin, with one judge concurring in part and concurring in the judgment and another dissenting.

On appeal, Apple argued again that it should not be subjected to per se analysis because its contracts were vertical, not horizontal, and that even if they were considered horizontal they "promoted 'enterprise and productivity,'" i.e., they helped facilitate its entry into the market for e-book retailing, which enhanced competition. It also contended that, even if horizontal, the agreements did not deserve per se condemnation as price fixing. *U.S. v. Apple Inc.*, 791 F.3d. 290, 321 (2d Cir. 2015).

Like the district court, the lead opinion, authored by Circuit Judge Debra Ann Livingston, rejected Apple's arguments and concluded that the agreements were unreasonable restraints of trade, whether analyzed as per se unlawful or under a more complete rule of reason that took into account Apple's proffered defenses. In Judge Livingston's view, with which the concurring judge agreed, "[t]he conspiracy among Apple and the Publisher Defendants comfortably qualifies as a horizontal price-fixing conspiracy." *Id.* at 327. As she explained, albeit with some evident hesitation, there was nevertheless some reason to consider Apple's defenses:

> * * * [N]either Apple nor the dissent has presented any particularly strong reason to think that the conspiracy we have identified should be spared *per se* condemnation. My concurring colleague would therefore affirm the district court's decision on that basis alone. I, too, believe that *per se* condemnation is appropriate in this case and view Apple's sloganeering references to "innovation" as a distraction from the straightforward nature of the conspiracy proven at trial. Nonetheless, I am mindful of Apple's argument that the nascent ebook industry has some new

and unusual features and that the *per se* rule is not fit for "business relationships where the economic impact of certain practices is not immediately obvious." [citing among other decisions *In re Sulfuric Acid*.] I therefore assume, for the sake of argument, that it is appropriate to apply the rule of reason and to analyze the competitive effects of Apple's horizontal agreement with the Publisher Defendants.

Id. at 329. Concluding that the agreements did not fit squarely within per se analysis, however, did not mean that a protracted application of the rule of reason was in order. She instead concluded that "the same evidence supporting our determination that *per se* condemnation is the correct way to dispose of this appeal also supports at most a "quick look" inquiry under the rule of reason" and maintained that "[c]ontrary to the dissent's suggestion, this approach does not somehow "taint" the rule-of-reason analysis." *Id.* at 330.

Judge Dennis Jacobs dissented and would have reversed the district court's finding of liability. He was receptive to Apple's principal argument that the agreements facilitated its entry and thus promoted competition, even though e-book prices increased. More fundamentally, he viewed Apple's conduct as no more than aggressive competition: "A further and pervasive error (by the district court and by my colleagues on this appeal) is the implicit assumption that competition should be genteel, lawyer-designed, and fair under sporting rules, and that antitrust law is offended by gloves-off competition." *Id.* at 342 (Jacobs, J., dissenting).

Judge Livingston responded forcefully:

Significantly, the dissent *agrees* that Apple intentionally organized a conspiracy among the Publisher Defendants to raise ebook prices. Nonetheless, it contends that Apple was entitled to do so because the conspiracy helped it become an ebook retailer. In arriving at this startling conclusion—based in large measure on an argument that Apple itself did not assert—the dissent makes two fundamental errors. The first is to insist that the vertical organizer of a horizontal price-fixing conspiracy may escape application of the *per se* rule. This conclusion is based on a misreading of Supreme Court precedent, which establishes precisely the opposite. The dissent fails to apprehend that the Sherman Act outlaws *agreements* that unreasonably restrain trade and therefore requires evaluating the nature of the restraint, rather than the identity of each party who joins in to impose it, in determining whether the *per se* rule is properly invoked. Finally (and most fundamentally) the dissent's conclusion rests on an erroneous premise: that one who organizes a horizontal price-fixing conspiracy—the "supreme evil of antitrust," * * *—among those competing at a different level of the market has somehow done less damage to competition than its co-conspirators.

The dissent's second error is to assume, in effect, that Apple was entitled to enter the ebook retail market on its own terms, even if these terms could be achieved only via its orchestration of and entry into a price-fixing agreement with the Publisher Defendants. The dissent tells a story of Apple organizing this price-fixing conspiracy to rescue ebook retailers from a monopolist with insurmountable retail power. But this tale is not spun from any factual findings of the district court. And the dissent's armchair analysis wrongly treats the number of ebook retailers at any moment in the emergence of a new and transformative technology for book distribution as the *sine qua non* of competition in the market for trade ebooks.

More fundamentally, the dissent's theory—that the presence of a strong competitor justifies a horizontal price-fixing conspiracy—endorses a concept of marketplace vigilantism that is wholly foreign to the antitrust laws. By organizing a price-fixing conspiracy, Apple found an easy path to opening its iBookstore, but it did so by ensuring that market-wide ebook prices would rise to a level that it, and the Publisher Defendants, had jointly agreed upon. Plainly, competition is not served by permitting a market entrant to *eliminate price competition* as a condition of entry, and it is cold comfort to consumers that they gained a new ebook retailer at the expense of passing control over all ebook prices to a cartel of book publishers—publishers who, with Apple's help, collectively agreed on a new pricing model precisely to *raise* the price of ebooks and thus protect their profit margins and their very existence in the marketplace in the face of the admittedly strong headwinds created by the new technology.

Id. at 297–98.

Circuit Judge Lohier concurred in the judgment, but saw no need to venture beyond per se analysis. He joined the majority opinion, therefore, except with respect to its application of the quick look rule of reason. In his view, per se analysis "clearly applies to the central agreement in this case (and the only agreement alleged to be unlawful): the publishers' horizontal agreement to fix ebook prices.* * * I would affirm on that basis alone." *Id* at 339–40 (Lohier, J., concurring in part and concurring in the judgment). As for Apple's proffered defenses, which found favor with the dissent, he added:

That said, I recognize that the publisher defendants, who used Apple both as powerful leverage against Amazon and to keep each other in collusive check, may appear to be more culpable than Apple. And there is also some surface appeal to Apple's argument that the ebook market, in light of Amazon's virtually uncontested dominance, needed more competition. But more corporate bullying is not an appropriate antidote to corporate bullying. It cannot have been lawful for Apple to respond to a competitor's dominant market power by helping rival corporations (the publishers) fix prices, as the District Court found happened here. However sympathetic Apple's plight and the publishers' predicament may have been, I am persuaded that permitting "marketplace vigilantism," Majority Op. at 9, would do far more harm to competition than good, would be disastrous as a policy matter, and is in any event not sanctioned by the Sherman Act.

Id. at 340.

Why were two of the three judges on the panel comfortable affirming liability based on per se analysis? Did they maintain that the agreements here were presumptively an unreasonable restraint of trade and that the presumption was irrebuttable, i.e. that the government had shifted a burden to Apple and that there was no defense available? Note that once the analysis switched from per se to quick look, the presumption of competitive harm became rebuttable. Judge Livingston, as we observed, thus considered Apple's defenses. Did she reject them because Apple failed to meet its burden, or did she conclude that they were not cognizable defenses? What approach was the dissent using?

What distinguishes the facts of *Apple* from those in *In re Sulfuric Acid*? Do you agree that *Apple* was a better candidate for per se analysis? Were both cases well suited for the quick look, which allowed some consideration of the defenses? Were the defenses proffered in *Sulfuric Acid* more likely cognizable than those argued by Apple?

Quick Look or Not?

3.   In *California v. Safeway, Inc.*, 651 F.3d 1118 (9th Cir. 2011), the majority of a divided *en banc* court declined to apply either per se or quick look analysis to the revenue sharing provision (RSP) of a mutual strike assistance agreement (MSAA) reached among a group of competing grocery chains in California. Anticipating negotiations with their common labor union over a new collective bargaining agreement, the grocers feared that the union would strike one, but not all of them as a tactic to coerce better terms in the next round of negotiations. As a counterstrategy, the MSAA included the RSP, which provided "that in the event of a strike/lockout, any grocer that earned revenues above its historical share relative to the other chains during the strike period would pay 15% of those excess revenues [an estimate of the grocers' incremental profit on each

additional dollar of revenue] as reimbursement to the other grocers to restore their pre-strike shares." *Id.* at 1123.

The State of California challenged the RSP as a violation of Section 1 of the Sherman Act, characterizing it as a "profit-pooling" or "market-allocation" agreement that should be condemned per se or under a quick look analysis. In its view, the RSP amounted to a competitive truce that would reduce the grocers' incentive to compete vigorously during any strike. If the union struck just one grocer, the others would know that any profits gained at the expense of that rival would have to be shared, which would diminish their incentive to actively seek to divert and capture that rival's customers. California moved for summary judgment on that basis, but its motion was denied. The district court ruled that it would have to satisfy a more complete rule of reason inquiry. For purposes of the appeal, California stipulated that it was not prepared to undertake a full rule of reason inquiry. If it could not secure per se or quick look analysis, it was prepared to abandon the case.[4]

In the majority's view, the RSP was distinguishable from arrangements that had previously been condemned per se, "[b]ecause the RSP was an agreement among some, but not all, of the competitors in the relevant market, and because by its terms the RSP had a limited and indefinite duration. . . ." *Id.* at 1136. The court continued:

> Quite apart from the lack of judicial experience with a restraint of this nature, we conclude that the application of a per se rule is not warranted in this case because the practice of temporary revenue sharing during the duration of a labor dispute among some competitors within a market does not "facially appear[ ] to be one that would always or almost always tend to restrict competition and decrease output." * * * In light of its particular features and context, the RSP is 'not a naked restraint of trade with no purpose except stifling of competition.' [quoting *Broadcast Music*].

Id. at 1136–37. Similarly, the court rejected California's argument that the RSP constituted per se unlawful market allocation. In contrast to classic examples of per se unlawful market division, "the RSP did not 'prevent any Defendant from actually making sales' to consumers. California does not assert that the RSP restricted customers from patronizing certain grocers. Moreover, the agreement did not prevent the grocers from selling any particular products, or limit the grocers to a particular set of customers or geographic regions." *Id.*

---

4   The grocers unsuccessfully argued in the district court and the court of appeals that their agreement was immune from antitrust scrutiny under what is known as the "non-statutory labor exemption," which supplements a statutory exemption for certain labor organization activities (*see* 15 U.S.C. § 17), and applies to certain agreements between labor and non-labor entities. For an explanation, see *Brown v. Pro Football, Inc.*, 518 U.S. 231 (1996). We discuss these exemptions in Chapter 8.

For the same reasons, the court also declined to treat the RSP under quick look analysis. In its view, the effects of the agreement on the grocers' "competitive behavior and incentives" was "uncertain," rendering any anticompetitive effects "not obvious." "To reach a confident conclusion on the anticompetitive effects of the RSP," the court reasoned, "further development of the record is required." *Id.* Quoting from *California Dental*, the court concluded that "[t]he features of the RSP * * * strongly suggest that the agreement 'might plausibly be thought to have a net procompetitive effect, or possibly no effect at all on competition.' " *Id.* at 1138. Although it acknowledged the economic theory behind California's challenge, the majority therefore declined to decide the case absent a complete analysis of effects and justifications:

> Can it be successfully argued, to the contrary, that because the RSP reduces the monetary risks of lost sales to participating grocers during a whipsaw strike, it is irretrievably anticompetitive in effect? We conclude that such an argument fails. If a competitor finds itself the target of a strike, which would cause it to lose sales to other competitors, then revenue sharing provides some cushion from the damaging monetary impact of the strike. But it is by no means "obvious" that the grocers that entered into the RSP would be motivated to reduce their competition on price. Although the immediate monetary risk of losing sales to competitors during a labor strike is reduced by revenue sharing, the remaining risks are still such that a rational competitor would be expected to continue to compete vigorously. While it is true that the arrangement provides a cushion that may arguably affect incentives to compete, that alone, absent evidence of actual anticompetitive impact on pricing, is not sufficient for us to resolve the RSP issue on a "per se" or "quick look" or any other abbreviated basis.

Id. at 1138–39. The majority concluded that "[b]ecause California has not met its burden to show that the RSP is obviously anticompetitive, we need not address the grocers' procompetitive justifications." *Id.* at 1138 n.17

Circuit Judge Reinhardt, joined by Judges Schroeder and Graber, dissented in part and concurred in part. Quoting from *California Dental*, he cautioned against treating the various modes of analysis under the rule of reason as "separate and unrelated" and professed to embrace a "mixed or blended approach" under which he had reached a "confident conclusion" that the RSP was a violation of Section 1. *Id.* at 1147. Applying that approach, he had no difficulty concluding that the RSP was very likely anticompetitive:

> * * * the fact that defendants' agreement provides for profits to be shared only during a labor dispute and a brief ensuing period does

not alter its inherently anticompetitive nature. Even during a strike period, a profit sharing agreement generates a "great likelihood of anticompetitive effects." For a vendor, the principal features of an employee strike are diminished consumer demand, as some customers choose not to cross the picket lines; a reduced workforce, because some workers at least are on strike; and a more urgent financial condition, as fixed costs remain at nonstrike levels, and revenues go down. While diminished demand, a reduced workforce, and a more urgent financial condition might affect defendants' competitive behavior during the strike, these potential effects would occur independent of the existence of a profit sharing agreement. None of these effects changes the basic impact of the agreement: defendants had little incentive to compete with one another while [the RSP] * * * was in effect because any profits earned on sales to another defendant's former customers would simply be redistributed back to the other defendants.

* * * Profit sharing necessarily serves to diminish the incentives to compete below whatever the level of competition would be in the absence of such an agreement; it is inherently, or as some courts have said, intuitively, anticompetitive and has the same, or a similar, effect on competition during a strike as it would have before the strike and after it ends.

Id. at 1156–57. Summarizing his conclusion and further echoing the standard enunciated in *California Dental*, he asserted:

It is evident from a rudimentary knowledge of economics, as well as from a reading of the case law, that neither the agreement's limited duration nor its failure to include the fragmented group of other firms operating in the market could do more than *reduce* the ordinary anticompetitive effects of such agreements. Certainly these factors would not *eliminate* such effects. An analysis of the details, logic, and circumstances of the particular profit sharing agreement, including its relationship to the anticipated strike, confirms that conclusion. The agreement's effect is necessarily anticompetitive and, like any other profit sharing agreement of limited duration among firms that control well over a majority, but less than 100% of the market, the anticompetitive effects might be reduced to some extent but they certainly would not be eliminated.

Id. at 1145.

Judge Reinhardt also rejected the grocers' demand for "empirical evidence" of actual harm: "neither per se nor quick look review ordinarily requires empirical evidence of anticompetitive effects, nor is it required for the combined or mixed per se/quick look approach that should be applied here." *Id.* at 1157. After noting that such evidence would likely be very difficult to obtain, *id.* at 1157–58, and again purporting to apply *California Dental*, he maintained: "Given the obviously anticompetitive nature of defendants' profit sharing agreement, no empirical data about the effects of the agreement are necessary for 'an enquiry meet for [this] case.' " *Id.* at 1160.

Because he found the case for anticompetitive effect to be persuasive, in his view the court should have shifted the burden to the grocers to test their principal "procompetitive" justification, which was supported by the testimony of an expert economist:

> At this point comes defendants' actual and least justifiable contention. The supermarkets assert that conduct that serves to reduce the cost of labor serves a procompetitive purpose, such as may excuse otherwise anticompetitive behavior. They contend that the procompetitive benefit of their agreement is that it increased their chances of winning the labor dispute and reducing the wages and benefits they would be required to pay to their employees, which in turn would increase their ability to lower prices and compete more effectively with other companies. * * * Defendants' proffered justification for their profit sharing arrangement is, in essence, a countervailing power defense that the restraint of trade is necessary in order to give them sufficient bargaining power to counteract the market power exercised by their striking workers and thereby to allow them to purchase their workers' labor at a lower price.

> As California points out, however, the chain of contingencies linking defendants' exercise of bargaining power to reduced prices for consumer purchases renders any such procompetitive benefits of their profit sharing agreement purely speculative. Rule of reason examination of defendants' countervailing power defense is accordingly unnecessary. 'Suffice it to say that the theoretical literature suggests that countervailing cartels seldom improve the welfare of consumers.'

Id. at 1160.

Whose position did you find more persuasive, California's or the grocers'? How relatively "obvious" was the RSP's anticompetitive effect? Would you have voted with the majority to require additional evidence before shifting a burden to the grocers? To what degree, if any, might the majority's view about California's ability to meet its burden of showing anticompetitive effect have been influenced by its reaction to the grocers' position that they were seeking a counter-strategy to better enable them to combat the union's demands? Is the decision more anti-union than anti-antitrust?

What additional evidence of anticompetitive effect would the majority have required before it would have permitted the burden to shift to the grocers? In refusing to rely on quick look analysis, the majority suggested an answer:

> To reach a confident conclusion on the anticompetitive effects of the RSP, further development of the record is required. One might want to permit expert testimony and examine facts about the degree to which the challenged revenue-sharing agreement may have suppressed incentives of the grocers to discount and otherwise compete for customers. One might want to have an understanding of the market impact of other competitors, not in the defendant group, whose pricing and terms of sale would have to be taken into account in a competitive market. It might be helpful to have an understanding whether other competitors were waiting in the wings to exploit any anticompetitive market by their entry, whether these potential new competitors were overseas, or in other regions of the United States, or were skilled in the developing concept of internet marketing of groceries or other novel techniques that might impose market pressures. Any of these inquiries might inform an evaluation whether, during the relevant period of its operation, the revenue-sharing provision had any anticompetitive effect. On a "quick look," none of this can be ascertained with reliability.

Id. at 1137–38. Is this a fair description of more comprehensive rule of reason analysis? How might implementation of this approach affect the parties and the courts? Was such an inquiry necessary under the facts of the case? Why did California appear to assume that it would not be able to meet such a burden?

Finally, were you persuaded by the grocers' purportedly procompetitive justification? Note that, as in *California Dental*, the majority did not consider the grocers' defenses, because California had failed to shift a burden to the defendants. As was true for Justice Breyer in *California Dental*, once Judge Reinhardt concluded that a burden shift was in order, he went on to consider the grocers' defense and he rejected it. Was his criticism of the proffered justification based on lack of evidence, or did he find the arguments presented by the grocers to be non-cognizable, like the engineers' "quality" defense in *National Society of Professional Engineers*? Was there any similarity between the "procompetitive" justifications offered by the grocers and Apple's defense that it acted to counter Amazon's market power? Under what circumstances, if any, do you think rivals or other firms in the market should be able to defend against a charge of violating the antitrust laws by asserting that they were seeking to neutralize the perceived market power of an adversary, thereby enhancing, not reducing, competition? For a critique of *Safeway*, see Andrew I. Gavil, *Moving Beyond Caricature and Characterization: The Modern Rule of Reason in Practice*, 85 S. CAL. L. REV. 733, 770–81 (2012).

4.   Our last case profile is *In re Southeastern Milk Antitrust Litigation*, **739 F.3d 262 (6th Cir. 2014)**, where the court agreed that per se analysis was inappropriate, but approved use of quick look analysis. It also had to address the defendant's effort to exclude the testimony of the plaintiff's expert witness, who the plaintiff intended to use to support its more complete rule of reason analysis.

The case arose following the merger of the two largest milk bottlers in the U.S., Dean Foods Company (Dean) and Suiza Food Corporation (Suiza), a merger that was approved by the Department of Justice subject to the divestiture of specified milk processing plants. According to the complaint, filed by two milk retailers, following the required divestments and the consummation of the merger, the merged firm (Dean/Suiza) conspired with the entity that had purchased the divested milk processing plants to divide markets and restrict output. The district court granted the defendant's motion for summary judgment, dismissing the plaintiffs' Section 1 claim, ruling that (1) per se analysis did not apply; (2) under a rule of reason analysis, the plaintiffs were required to prove a relevant geographic market, and that (3) the testimony of the economic expert witness on whom the plaintiffs intended to rely to establish a relevant market would be excluded. Absent the testimony of the economist, the plaintiffs were unable to meet their burden of production as to the anticompetitive effect of the agreements. The district court did not consider a quick look option.

The facts that gave rise to the antitrust complaint were complex. Prior to the merger, both Dean and Suiza purchased their raw milk from other entities—Dean largely from independent farmers and Suiza from a dairy farmer cooperative, Dairy Farmers of America (DFA). DFA also had a significant non-majority ownership interest in Suiza. As a condition of the merger of Dean and Suiza, Suiza bought out DFA's interest and transferred six of its bottling plants to DFA. DFA then transferred ownership of the six processing plants to a newly formed partnership that also acquired ownership of five of Dean's milk processing plants, for a total of eleven, making it the second largest milk bottler in the Southeast United States. Although DFA no longer had an ownership interest in Dean/Suiza, it came away with a 50% equity interest in the new entity and under the partnership agreement it had the power to veto major business decisions by the partnership. It also continued to supply raw milk to Dean/Suiza, so after all of the agreements were implemented, DFA was both a supplier to and a competitor of the merged firm. As described by the court:

Although DFA's [50%] ownership stake provides an obvious incentive to fully support * * * [the partnership's] fledgling enterprise, DFA's raw milk supply agreements with the merged company create fertile soil for the development of a conflict of interest. Supported by several disputed factual allegations, the essence of Plaintiffs' conspiracy claim is as follows:

> * * * [the partnership] knowingly accepted 'second best' plants, operated those plants at losses and eventually shuttered some of those plants in an unlawful agreement with its competitor Dean/Suiza because, in return, its parent company, DFA, received a commitment from Dean/Suiza to allow it to supply raw milk to each Dean/Suiza bottling plant, including the pre-merger Dean plants previously supplied by independent dairy farmers.

Id. at 269.

The court of appeals agreed with the district court that the case was a poor fit for per se analysis, but it reversed the grant of summary judgment for the defendants and remanded the case, ruling that the district court erred by not considering quick look analysis.

In the view of the court, per se analysis was inappropriate because of the complex structural features of the relationships and the potential for procompetitive justifications for some of the challenged conduct. Because of DFA's dual role as owner of a bottler and as supplier to Dean/Suiza, the agreements could not be easily categorized as "horizontal." There was also conflicting evidence in the record relating to the vigor with which the new partnership competed with Dean/Suiza and the possibility that the plant closures cited by the plaintiffs helped to reduce costs. *Id.* at 273–74. It also noted that the Department of Justice had apparently approved the overall arrangement.

Citing to *Polygram* and *Realcomp II*, however, the Sixth Circuit noted plaintiffs' argument that the district court's "simple logic equation overlooks the recent deterioration of clearly defined types of market analysis in favor of a more case-by-case approach." *Id.* at 274. The court acknowledged the quick look as a feature of this more recent trend and noted its implications for fixing the parties' relative burdens:

> In the same way that this analysis occupies territory between the *per se* and rule of reason tests, so the burdens and presumptions do as well. Once anticompetitive behavior is shown to a court's satisfaction, even without detailed market analysis, the burden shifts to the defendant who must justify the agreement at issue on procompetitive grounds by providing some "competitive justification" for the restraint at issue.

Id. at 275. The district court erred in failing to consider this option, and, therefore, in demanding proof of a relevant geographic market:

> * * * Under the quick-look standard, the Plaintiffs have met their burden of raising a genuine issue of material fact as to whether Dean Foods violated the antitrust laws even without establishing the relevant geographic market. In applying the summary judgment standard, the Court must review the facts and draw all reasonable inferences in favor of the non-moving party. * * * Accordingly, when construing the facts and record evidence in Plaintiffs' favor, the alleged unlawful conduct has obviously adverse, anticompetitive effects; and for purposes of summary judgment, the district court should have at least considered the fact that a more detailed market analysis may not have been required under these circumstances. *See Realcomp,* 635 F.3d at 825. While it is true that the vertical elements of the Defendants' agreement require a rule of reason analysis, the agreement between the horizontal competitors for the express purpose of limiting competition between them could be viewed as a "facially anticompetitive restraint," and the district court should consider this possibility on remand. *Realcomp,* 635 F.3d at 827. Even though Dean Foods' alleged conduct is not illegal *per se,* the evidence in the record and the allegations in Plaintiffs' complaint are sufficient to shift the burden to Dean Foods to present some procompetitive benefits of the alleged conduct. * * *

Id. Focusing specifically on the district court's insistence that the plaintiffs were required to prove a relevant market, the court went on to hold that "[u]nder a quick-look analysis, the Plaintiffs do not necessarily need to establish either product or geographic market evidence in order to defeat summary judgment." *Id.* at 275–76. Finally, because rule of reason analysis remained an option on remand, the court addressed the district court's decision to exclude the plaintiff's expert economist and also reversed that portion of its decision, because the district court's "reasoning in its decision to exclude [the expert's] * * * testimony rests on an incomplete review of the facts and the application of incorrect legal standards." *Id.* at 279.

Note that these four decisions were lengthy and in some ways complex. The brief profiles offered here, therefore, are not a substitute for a careful and complete reading of each of the four cases. All recount, as do *Polygram* and *Realcomp II,* the development of the law as we have studied it in this Chapter from *Chicago Board of Trade* to *California Dental,* illustrating how the rule of reason has evolved since it was first embraced in *Standard Oil* more than a century ago. All acknowledge the primacy of competitive effect, often citing *National Society of Professional Engineers* for that proposition. In recognition of *Broadcast Music*, all acknowledge that efficiencies must be considered in anything other than instances of per se liability. And all seek to implement *California Dental's* "continuum" approach, integrating inferences, presumptions, and burden shifting to structure the rule of reason analysis.

Nevertheless, is there any guidance you can glean about the current state of the rule of reason from these four case profiles? How are the courts allocating the respective burdens of the parties and implementing a burden-shifting framework under the guidelines established by the Supreme Court? What circumstances have led courts to rely on per se analysis? To shy away from it? When have the courts embraced or rejected the quick look, and what distinguishes the cases where they have been willing to use it? What is meant today by the "full blown" rule of reason? As a practical matter, what differentiates the evidence the parties have assembled and presented in each case?

Finally, consider how an understanding of the allocation of burdens would affect your preparation and presentation of an antitrust case under Section 1 of the Sherman Act. Do you think the plaintiffs in *In re Sulfuric Acid* and *Safeway* too easily concluded that they would not be able to meet a more demanding burden of production? In reaching that conclusion, were they perhaps relying on an outdated view of the rule of reason, one that was based on a more stark contrast between the per se "rule" and the "rule" of reason? Do you think they were influenced by the perceived costs and benefits of litigating their cases more fully?

D. CONCLUSION

Welcome to the study of antitrust law! Although it may not yet be apparent, you have already been exposed to some of the most enduring challenges of competition policy, and many of the core concepts that are used to resolve them. As we shall see in subsequent Chapters, the evolution of the rule of reason has influenced other areas of antitrust, both in terms of the substantive focus of the analysis and in the procedural framework used to evaluate a wide range of conduct that may affect competition. Before proceeding, however, take advantage of the Problems that follow to reinforce and further refine your appreciation for the material we have covered thus far.

E. PROBLEMS

Problem 2–1:
Mountain Medical

Mountain is the largest city in a rural Western state. Its 150,000 residents are served by two hospitals and 250 physicians, including general practitioners and a variety of sub-specialists, such as surgeons, cardiologists, gastroenterologists, and nephrologists. The nearest hospital outside of Mountain is located in a small town some 30 miles away. Roughly half of the doctors in Mountain are members of a single multi-specialty physician practice, which is owned by one of the two hospitals.

Most of the remaining, independent doctors formed an association, Mountain Medical (MM). The physicians in MM created a common practice name. They jointly marketed their availability to insurers and employers seeking to provide health insurance to their employees, but did not merge their practices, or share profits and financial risks. Were MM to contract with a health insurer or employer, each of its physician members would charge that doctor's individual fees, and those fees might differ. In contrast, the hospital-owned multi-specialty physician practice charged common fees based upon a schedule adopted by the hospital. MM forbade its members from negotiating individually with health insurers, like an HMO, and employers.

MM was approached by More Care, a Health Maintenance Organization ("HMO"), that had previously not served Mountain, and that wanted to sign up doctors in order to enter the Mountain market. MM and More Care engaged in extended, but ultimately fruitless negotiations. More Care never entered the Mountain market. MM also collected detailed fee information from member doctors, and used that information to suggest that some doctors seek higher fees from a health plan that wanted a group contract.

In light of the cases we have studied in Chapter 2, have the physicians who are members of MM reached any agreement that should be deemed illegal per se under Section 1 of the Sherman Act? If not, have they reached any agreement that otherwise would be deemed an unreasonable restraint of trade?

Problem 2–2:
Midwest Truck Leasing

Midwest Truck Leasing ("MTL") is a company engaged in the business of leasing trucks. It is also a member of the North American Truck Leasing Association ("NATLA"). The roughly 150 members of NATLA, including MTL, lease trucks to businesses on a "full service" basis. This means that the lessor rather than the lessee is responsible for maintaining the trucks and for repairing them if they break down. The leases are short term or long term, local or "over the road," which means that the lessee may drive the truck anywhere in the country. Over-the-road customers demand full service, nation-wide.

NATLA members, however, are local companies, none of which owns service facilities outside of its local area, nor could any afford to do so.

NATLA was created in order to set up and administer a reciprocal service arrangement that would enable each member to lease trucks on a full-service over-the-road basis and thus compete with the national truck-leasing companies, which have their own service depots all over the United States. NATLA requires each member to give the trucks of the other members prompt and efficient repair service, but it does not regulate the price of the service. NATLA also collects and disseminates information on prices, services, and other issues of interest to its members, and operates a joint fuel purchasing program on behalf of its members. By aggregating their fuel requirements, they can usually negotiate more favorable prices from fuel suppliers.

Each NATLA member operates under a franchise from NATLA that designates the particular location at which it may conduct business as a "National franchisee"—and it specifically forbids each member from doing business as a National franchisee at any other location. NATLA rules also forbid each member/franchisee to affiliate with any other full-service truck-leasing enterprise or association. Typically, authorized locations are placed more than 25 miles apart. NATLA members can open an outlet at an unauthorized location under a different name, but trucks rented under that name would not be entitled to reciprocal service; and even if the member were willing to forgo that advantage, it still could not open an outlet under license from another full-service truck-leasing enterprise without violating NATLA rules and risking expulsion. Because markets for full-service commercial truck leases are local—to facilitate regular maintenance on their vehicles lessees typically lease trucks from a firm having an outlet within a few miles (no more than 25) of the lessee's place of business—the overall effect of NATLA's rules is to severely limit over-the-road leasing competition between its members.

MTL decided to defy both the location and non-affiliation restrictions. Upon discovering those facts, NATLA gave MTL notice that it would be expelled from NATLA immediately.

In light of the cases we have studied in Chapter 2, has NATLA reached any agreement that should be deemed illegal per se under Section 1 of the Sherman Act? If not, has it reached any agreement that otherwise would be deemed an unreasonable restraint of trade?

CHAPTER 3

DISTINGUISHING CONCERTED FROM UNILATERAL ACTION

▪ ▪ ▪

INTRODUCTION

Many competition laws, including Section 1 of the Sherman Act and Article 101 of the Treaty on the Functioning of the European Union (TFEU), attach special significance to conduct involving "concerted action." Section 1 of the Sherman Act prohibits "[e]very contract, combination . . . or conspiracy" in restraint of trade, and imposes no liability on firms that act alone. Single firm conduct is addressed instead under Section 2, but only when it concerns monopolization or attempt to monopolize. Similarly, Article 101 only applies to "all agreements between undertakings, decisions by associations of undertakings and concerted practices," whereas Article 102 is directed at single-firm conduct, but only when it concerns a "dominant firm."

As we will see in Chapter 4, a monopolist operates outside the Sherman Act's reach when it merely cuts its own output and boosts prices above competitive levels, even though the economic effects can be the same as when rival firms form a price-fixing cartel. But if a cartel is detected, its participants risk the same fate that befell the ADM executives we observed in Chapter 1 in *Andreas*—imprisonment as felons and payment of substantial fines.

Recall also from Chapter 2 that concerted action alone does not offend Section 1 of the Sherman Act. To violate Section 1, a "contract, combination . . . or conspiracy" must unreasonably restrain trade. In the cases we studied in Chapter 2, the fact of agreement, of "concerted action," usually was conceded, leaving only the conduct's competitive effects to be evaluated. In *Socony Vacuum Oil* and *Broadcast Music*, for example, the defendants acknowledged they had acted in concert and focused their defense on proving the "reasonableness" of their joint conduct. Similarly, in *National Society of Professional Engineers* and *NCAA*, the defendants' concerted conduct was apparent and even took the form of formal contracts and bylaws.

By contrast, the *Andreas* defendants vigorously contested the existence of an agreement. In this and similar cases, plaintiffs, prosecutors, and courts alike have had to develop an analytical framework for defining what constitutes concerted action. In this Chapter we study why competition laws have viewed concerted action skeptically, and how courts and enforcement authorities have sought to distinguish collective conduct from independent action, especially when direct evidence of agreement is lacking in whole or part.

Implementing this distinction has given rise to two sets of issues in the law of conspiracy. The first stemmed from the development of harsh prohibitions against concerted trade restraints and concerns about the impact of such prohibitions on firm behavior. In early Sherman Act cases such as *Chicago Board of Trade*, *Trenton* Potteries, and *Socony Vacuum Oil* (*see supra* Chapter 2), courts rarely faced difficult "agreement" issues, as defendants felt no urgency to depict their conduct as being unilateral rather than concerted. Over time, courts interpreted Section 1 to condemn certain agreements categorically—as "per se" unlawful. Because such cases presumed unreasonableness, the fact of agreement became the focal point for litigating Section 1 offenses. Proving agreement meant establishing a violation. *See* Sidebar 2–4: *Defining and Justifying the Contemporary Per Se Analysis.*

Aggressive Sherman Act enforcement against some forms of concerted action drove many cartels underground. Cartel members exercised greater precautions to shield illicit collaboration from detection or they sought other ways to facilitate coordination without agreement—so called "tacit collusion." In turn, prosecutors and courts alike strove to: (1) develop ways to flush out direct evidence, such as testimony from a cartel insider or documents that show an agreement existed; and (2) develop analytical methods for establishing agreement without express or direct evidence.

To obtain direct evidence of collusion today, prosecutors rely on informants, as in *Andreas*, corporate leniency programs, and offers of immunity for cooperative witnesses. Yet direct evidence is frequently unavailable, so public and private plaintiffs also rely heavily on circumstantial evidence to establish the fact of agreement among rivals when they think collusion has been hidden.

The second set of issues resulted from increased reliance on circumstantial evidence and inference to establish conspiracy. When plaintiffs used circumstantial proof extensively, the courts faced an apparent economic anomaly: the Sherman Act did not reach unilateral conduct having the same economic effects as similar, but concerted conduct. Judges felt bound by Section 1 to reject challenges to rival conduct falling short of the law's definition of agreement, even when rival conduct appeared coordinated from an economic perspective. Economic models that demonstrated the common nature of the effects of tacit and express collusion triggered vigorous debate among commentators and courts, but ultimately proved inadequate to bring informal coordination within Section 1's ambit.

Section A begins by discussing the Supreme Court's *Copperweld* decision, which offers some traditional explanations for why U.S. antitrust law treats collective action more harshly than unilateral behavior. As we shall see, those explanations flow from two goals that sometimes conflict: (1) preserving the incentive of individual firms to compete aggressively—specifically by guarding their autonomy over pricing decisions; and (2) protecting against the effects of combined economic power—as when firms coordinate their competitive behavior.

Section B explores the modern economic framework for understanding how firms collude. Starting with some pioneering Chicago School commentary, antitrust policy gradually has embraced a more economically-grounded framework for analyzing the formation, maintenance, and detection of cartels. Although Chicago School commentary typically concluded that durable cartels were difficult to form and maintain, and were therefore rare, later commentary—and enforcement experiences such as the lysine and vitamins cases discussed in Chapter 1—have raised doubts about that skepticism. Nevertheless, economic analysis that builds on the Chicago School's earlier work continues to lead the vanguard in analyzing cartel problems today.

Section C examines how the prohibition of certain concerted acts induced firms to alter their methods for coordinating output decisions, and how antitrust conspiracy law tried to neutralize and provide legal means for exposing those efforts. Our discussion highlights the policy tension between concerns about permitting cooperative behavior to proceed unpunished and undeterred, and concerns about subjecting firms not cooperating to litigation costs and sanctions, and thereby chilling procompetitive conduct. We trace this tension in early cartel cases, comparing *Interstate Circuit* with *Theatre Enterprises*, in a famous debate during antitrust's structural era between two leading scholars, Donald Turner and Richard Posner, and in modern decisions shaping summary judgment and pleading standards, *Matsushita* and *Twombly*.

Section D examines how modern case law addresses this tension in applying legal rules governing the inference of conspiracy from circumstantial evidence that includes parallel conduct. More specifically, it traces the development and application of the "parallelism plus" doctrine that shapes judicial decisions in this area today. The latter discussion highlights the growing importance of economic "plus factors" related to the ability of firms to solve their "cartel problems."

Section E examines information exchanges and other means of facilitating price and output coordination, which often fall short of "agreement." This section also provides an overview of "incipient" conspiracy—the treatment of practices falling short of agreement, yet arguably designed to achieve the same economic effects.

A. ANTITRUST'S SPECIAL SCRUTINY OF COLLECTIVE ACTION

Antitrust rules seldom interfere with decisions to raise prices by firms acting alone. As we will see in Chapter 4, dominant firms usually are free to set prices as high as they wish to exploit the market power inherent in a superior product or process. Public utility price controls for natural monopolies and occasional European Commission attacks on exploitative pricing under Article 102 are rare exceptions to the rule that monopolists may restrict output unilaterally to raise prices.

The main cases in Chapter 2, and some of the cases in Chapters 4 and 6, show that the rules can change dramatically when firms act together. A monopolist legally can curb output to raise prices, but rival business executives risk criminal sanctions if they agree to pursue the same result in concert, regardless of whether their agreement raises prices in fact. A vertically integrated company incurs no liability when it sets the price its wholly-owned retail outlets may charge for products made in its own factories. But, as we will learn in Chapter 6, a manufacturer may commit a Section 1 offense if it agrees with an independent retailer to set a minimum price for the resale of its goods when the agreement unreasonably restrains competition.

In *Copperweld Corp. v. Independence Tube Corp.*, 467 U.S. 752 (1984), the Supreme Court addressed the rationale for this distinction in U.S. antitrust law. The case involved an alleged conspiracy among a parent corporation (Copperweld), its wholly-owned subsidiary (Regal), which manufactured structural steel tubing, and an unaffiliated supplier of steel tubing mills (Yoder) to impede the efforts of a new entrant, Independence Tube. It was undisputed that, at the behest of Copperweld, Yoder breached a contract with Independence to construct its mill, which resulted in a nine-month delay in its entry. When a jury concluded that there had been a conspiracy, but that Yoder had not been a party to it, all that was left to satisfy Section 1's agreement requirement was a conspiracy between Copperweld and Regal—a parent and its wholly owned subsidiary. *Id.* at 755–57. In analyzing whether acts by firms subject to common ownership might satisfy Section 1's collective action requirement, the Supreme Court had occasion to explain the different standards for judging unilateral and concerted action.

Copperweld held that a parent corporation and its wholly-owned subsidiary constitute but a single economic actor, and therefore lack the capacity to conspire for Sherman Act Section 1 purposes. The Court's analysis focused on the economic interests of the entities:

The distinction between unilateral and concerted conduct is necessary for a proper understanding of the terms "contract, combination . . . or conspiracy" in § 1. Nothing in the literal meaning of those terms excludes coordinated conduct among officers or employees of the same company. But it is perfectly plain that an internal "agreement" to implement a single, unitary firm's policies does not raise the antitrust dangers that § 1 was designed to police. The officers of a single firm are not separate economic actors pursuing separate economic interests, so agreements among them do not suddenly bring together economic power that was previously pursuing divergent goals. Coordination within a firm is as likely to result from an effort to compete as from an effort to stifle competition. In the marketplace, such coordination may be necessary if a business enterprise is to compete effectively. For these reasons, officers or employees of the same firm do not provide the plurality of actors imperative for a § 1 conspiracy.

Copperweld, 467 U.S. at 769.

In later decisions, the courts of appeals expanded *Copperweld*'s principles to hold that the acts of parents and their less than wholly-owned subsidiaries, sister corporations controlled by the same parent, and other forms of intra-enterprise conduct cannot be challenged under Sherman Act § 1. Through these decisions, the courts have substantially narrowed the intra-enterprise conspiracy doctrine, which had previously been accepted by the courts. But the Supreme Court has not extinguished the possibility that Section 1 could be used to challenge an intra-enterprise conspiracy. In 2010, it permitted a lawsuit to proceed challenging an agreement among the teams that were members of a professional sports league to license their trademarked names and logos to apparel manufacturers through a single entity. *American Needle, Inc. v. Nat'l Football League*, 560 U.S. 183 (2010). In that decision, the Court declared that prior decisions established a "functional" analysis of intra-enterprise conspiracy rather than a formalistic analysis determined by corporate form. *Id.* at 192. It held that an agreement among separate economic actors pursuing separate economic interests can be reviewed under Sherman Act § 1 if it deprives the marketplace of independent centers of decision-making—the source of diversity of entrepreneurial interests, and thus of actual or potential competition. *Id.* at 195–96. Hence the NFL was not a single entity with respect to marketing the teams' individually-owned intellectual property, though the Court suggested that it might be treated as a single entity with respect to other collective decisions made by the teams. *Id.* at 204. Would the Court's rationale permit a cardiologist denied hospital privileges at a "peer review" meeting of the cardiology staff to challenge that decision as an agreement between the hospital and its staff cardiologists? Would it matter whether the staff cardiologists were hospital employees, or whether they instead had staff privileges but ran their practices independently and made individual patient admission decisions?

In reaching its decision in *Copperweld*, the Supreme Court provided an extensive and influential analysis of the significance in antitrust law of the distinction between concerted and unilateral conduct. The Court observed that unilateral conduct is unlawful only when it threatens actual monopolization, in order to reduce the risk of chilling aggressive competitive conduct. By contrast, agreements among rivals that fall in traditional per se categories (horizontal price fixing and market division) are declared illegal without inquiry into the harm they caused. While other forms of concerted conduct, including mergers, joint ventures, and vertical agreements, are judged under the rule of reason, even in those cases, the Court noted, it is not necessary to prove that concerted activity threatens monopolization. It therefore concluded that there was a "gap" between Section 1 and Section 2: whereas concerted action that unreasonably restrains trade is subject to Section 1, unilateral conduct must rise to the level of monopolization to warrant condemnation under Section 2. A unilateral act that results in an unreasonably restraint of trade, as was the case in *Copperweld*, falls outside the reach of the Sherman Act. The Court thus assumed that an unreasonable restraint of trade could be distinguished from monopolization or attempt to monopolize. *Id.* at 774–76. It justified the distinction between concerted and independent action on policy grounds:

> The reason Congress treated concerted behavior more strictly than unilateral behavior is readily appreciated. Concerted activity inherently is fraught with anticompetitive risk. It deprives the marketplace of the independent centers of decisionmaking that competition assumes and demands. In any conspiracy, two or more entities that previously pursued their own interests separately are combining to act as one for their common benefit. This not only reduces the diverse directions in which economic power is aimed but suddenly increases the economic power moving in one particular direction. Of course, such mergings of resources may well lead to efficiencies that benefit consumers, but their anticompetitive potential is sufficient to warrant scrutiny even in the absence of incipient monopoly.

Copperweld, 467 U.S. at 768–69. *See also id.* at 775 ("Subjecting a single firm's every action to judicial scrutiny for reasonableness would threaten to discourage the competitive enthusiasm that the antitrust laws seek to promote.") *Copperweld*'s rationale is explored further in the following Note.

NOTE ON THE RATIONALE FOR
SCRUTINIZING CONCERTED ACTION

Fear of the anticompetitive effects of "collusion," especially by competing firms, has long preoccupied economists and competition laws. One of the earliest reported accounts of competition-type law enforcement, Lysias's "Against the Grain Dealers," concerned the prosecution of a grain buying cartel in ancient Greece, which sought to depress the prices paid to grain importers and raise the prices charged to Atticans for their grain. *See* Lambros E. Kotsiros, *An Antitrust Case in Ancient Greek Law*, 22 INT'L LAW. 451 (1988). And students of economics are well acquainted with Adam Smith's classic admonition that "People of the same trade seldom meet together, even for merriment and diversion, but the conversation ends in a conspiracy against the public, or in some contrivance to raise prices." ADAM SMITH, THE WEALTH OF NATIONS 144 (E. CANNON, ED. 1976) (1776). The broader dilemma, of course, is both conceptual and linguistic. We recognize that "cooperation" is essential to economic progress, but seek to distinguish the positive, "cooperation," from the nefarious, "conspiracy." Both involve "concerted action," but only one potentially warrants condemnation.

It is also well settled that Section 1 of the Sherman Act prohibits the act of conspiring, alone, and the offense is complete even though no party to the conspiracy ever undertakes "an overt act *in furtherance* of the conspiracy." The only essential "overt act" is the act of conspiring, itself. Moreover, venue can be proper in an antitrust conspiracy case in any district in which an overt act in furtherance of a conspiracy has occurred, even though no overt act is required to establish the offense. In a non-antitrust case, the Supreme Court reiterated these two long established propositions relevant to conspiracy under the Sherman Act and other federal conspiracy statutes that are modeled on the Sherman Act. *See Whitfield v. U.S.*, 543 U.S. 209 (2005). *See also United States v. Socony-Vacuum Oil Co.*, 310 U.S. 150, 224 n.59 (1940).

The Sherman Act sets forth a particular, compound formula in an attempt to distinguish cooperation from conspiracy, condemning any "contract, combination in the form of trust or otherwise, or conspiracy." *See* James A. Rahl, *Conspiracy and the Anti-Trust Laws*, 44 ILL. L. REV. 743 (1950). Why did the drafters choose such a seemingly redundant formulation? Some scholars have suggested that it was designed to capture the full range of arrangements, and progresses from the "tightest" to the loosest of "agreements." It can also be viewed as a continuum, leading from the most "formal" to the most "informal" of arrangements, or from the "express" to the tacit or illicit. *See, e.g.*, Robert H. Bork, *Legislative Intent and the Policy of the Sherman Act*, 9 J.L. & ECON. 7, 21–22 (1966). As we noted in the introduction to this Chapter, however, formal and express agreements rarely pose any serious questions of proof. Much of this Chapter, therefore, is instead concerned with the standards for proving "conspiracy," the illicit form of concerted conduct. In any event, the courts increasingly have come to view the Sherman Act's terms as coextensive, rarely attributing any significance to its precise words.

More broadly, what accounts for the suspicion of what *Copperweld* labeled "concerted action"? *Copperweld's* explanation for Section 1's treatment of concerted action is based upon the view that when separate economic actors combine, the threat to competition is often greater than when single firms act. Hence, the decision claims, we invoke a higher level of scrutiny for concerted action than unilateral conduct by requiring proof of more than an "unreasonable restraint of trade" before condemning the latter. Yet, as we will see below in Section C when we learn about "conscious parallelism" and the standards for pleading and summary judgment, a relatively lower proof requirement for concerted conduct is not necessarily a low proof requirement. Indeed, over time, the Supreme Court has raised procedural hurdles to plaintiffs asking courts to infer agreement from circumstantial evidence. Our discussion in Section C will address the way the Court balances its concern to prevent hidden conspiracies (avoid false negatives) and to limit the transaction costs of litigation with its concerns to avoid improperly condemning agreements between rivals that benefit competition (avoid false positives) and to ensure that rules are readily administrable.

Copperweld's rationale elevates the form of the conduct—whether it was the product of unilateral or concerted action—over its effect on price, output and other dimensions of conduct. Yet antitrust increasingly focuses on the effect of the conduct on competition rather than the legal categories into which the conduct falls. From this perspective, is *Copperweld's* distinction between concerted and unilateral action better understood as a proxy for a distinction between collusive and exclusionary conduct? The two distinctions are not identical: the conduct in *JTC Petroleum*, which we read in Chapter 1, and exclusionary group boycotts, which are examined in Chapter 4, both involve concerted action with an exclusionary purpose, and we will look at unilateral practices facilitating collusion later in this Chapter. But the conduct at issue in *Copperweld* itself, where the Court found the affiliated firms incapable of conspiring, was exclusionary while the concerted conduct with which the decision expresses the most concern, horizontal price fixing and market division, is collusive. Should *Copperweld* be read in light of the modern judicial trend toward focusing on conduct's competitive effects rather than its form to express greater concern about collusive effects over exclusionary effects?

Whether the *Copperweld* Court's fundamental concern is with the legal category of concerted action or the economic category of collusive conduct, it has the effect of assigning greater priority to some types of anticompetitive allegations (concerted or collusive) over others (unilateral or exclusionary). *See also Verizon Commc'ns Inc. v. Law Offices of Curtis V. Trinko, LLP*, 540 U.S. 398, 408 (2004) (identifying collusion as the "supreme evil" of antitrust). As you reflect upon the cases you read in this book, consider whether courts in fact do so, and whether they should. For an argument that antitrust should not and does not downplay exclusion relative to collusion, see Jonathan B. Baker, *Exclusion as a Core Competitive Concern*, 78 ANTITRUST L.J. 527 (2013). The remainder of this Chapter highlights the problems created by collusive effects and the standards for proving "concerted action" when collusive effects are alleged.

Sidebar 3–1:
Leniency Programs

As we noted at the outset of Chapter 1, the Sherman Act was one of the first "white collar" criminal statutes in the U.S. and it remains so today. Violations of Sections 1 and 2 can be prosecuted as felonies and convicted individuals can be subjected to jail time. Recent U.S. practice, however, has confined criminal enforcement to naked cartels under Section 1 of the Act, as we observed in the *ADM* case in Chapter 1. These criminal prosecutions fall exclusively within the purview of the Antitrust Division of the Justice Department ("DOJ"). For more information on the DOJ's criminal enforcement program, see https://www.justice.gov/atr/criminal-enforcement.

Somewhat in contrast to civil price fixing cases, which can rely on direct or circumstantial evidence of agreement, given the higher burden of proof in U.S. criminal cases (beyond a reasonable doubt), criminal price fixing cases tend to rely primarily on direct evidence to prove that the parties reached an agreement to fix price or divide territories. Such direct evidence can include "hot documents" that reveal the inner workings of the cartel or the testimony of informants. Although the direct evidence may be augmented by circumstantial evidence, courts in criminal cases are less likely to be asked to infer agreements exclusively from circumstantial evidence, the subject of later sections of this Chapter.

Since the early 1980s, the DOJ has resorted more frequently to investigation techniques such as wire-tapping and electronic surveillance and broadened cooperation with other law enforcement entities and government bureaus in the U.S. and abroad in order to increase its ability to detect and obtain direct evidence of collusion. It also has employed "leniency programs" that provide incentives for cartel participants to inform the government about episodes of collusion. In the U.S., these programs offer immunity from criminal prosecution to the first individual or organization to inform the government about the cartel's existence, as well as other benefits. Although the second party to inform might obtain a reduced punishment, the leniency program confers enormous advantages on the first to disclose a cartel. The Justice Department's leniency programs were expanded in 1993 and 1994, to cover both corporations and individuals. *See* U.S. DEP'T OF JUSTICE, ANTITRUST DIVISION, CORPORATE LENIENCY POLICY (Aug. 10, 1993), http://www.us

doj.gov/atr/public/guidelines/0091.htm; U.S. DEP'T OF JUSTICE, ANTITRUST DIVISION, INDIVIDUAL LENIENCY POLICY (Aug. 10, 1994), http://www.usdoj.gov/atr/public/guidelines/0092.htm.

To promote transparency with respect to the benefits and obligations associated with leniency applications, in 2008, the DOJ issued four model leniency letters to minimize applicant uncertainty during the leniency application process. The "Model Individual Conditional Leniency Letter" requires an individual leniency applicant to identify himself, the relevant Section 1 violation [e.g., price fixing, bid rigging, market allocation], and the affected product and geographic markets; the letter also defines the leniency eligibility requirements, the individual applicant's compliance obligations, and provides an assurance that the agreement is binding. *See U.S. DEP'T OF JUSTICE, ANTITRUST DIVISION, MODEL INDIVIDUAL CONDITIONAL LENIENCY LETTER* (Nov. 19, 2008), https://www. justice.gov/atr/model-individual-conditional-leniency-letter. The "Model Corporate Conditional Leniency Letter" contains the same conditions and requirements as the individual letter, but immunizes the firm as well as its corporate directors, officers, and employees against prosecution for the enumerated Section 1 violation. *See U.S. DEP'T OF JUSTICE, ANTITRUST DIVISION, MODEL CORPORATE CONDITIONAL LENIENCY LETTER* (Nov. 19, 2008), https://www.justice.gov/atr/model-corporate-conditional-leniency-letter.

The DOJ also created guidance for leniency applicants involved in more than one Section 1 violation. In the "Model Dual Investigations Leniency Letter," the DOJ retains the right to levy charges against a corporate applicant and its employees for any separate Section 1 violation not enumerated in the agreement. *See U.S. DEP'T OF JUSTICE, ANTITRUST DIVISION, MODEL DUAL INVESTIGATIONS LENIENCY LETTER* (Nov. 19, 2008), https://www.justice.gov/atr/model-dual-investigations-leniency-letter. In the former context, the "Model Dual Investigations Acknowledgement Letter For Employees" defines the scope of an employee's immunity. *See U.S. DEP'T OF JUSTICE, ANTITRUST DIVISION, MODEL DUAL INVESTIGATIONS ACKNOWLEDGEMENT LETTER FOR EMPLOYEES* (Nov. 19, 2008), https://www.justice.gov/atr/model-dual-investigations-acknow ledgement-letter-employees. In 2013, the DOJ also established a detailed "Model Annotated Corporate Plea Agreement" and "Model Annotated Individual Plea Agreement," which were revised in 2016. *See U.S. DEP'T OF JUSTICE, ANTITRUST DIVISION, MODEL ANNOTATED CORPORATE PLEA AGREEMENT* (Aug. 29, 2016), https://www.justice.gov/atr/file/889021

/download; U.S. DEP'T OF JUSTICE, ANTITRUST DIVISION, MODEL ANNOTATED INDIVIDUAL PLEA AGREEMENT (Aug. 29, 2016), https://www.justice.gov/atr/file/888481/download.

The government's experience with leniency has yielded some dramatic successes. In the *Vitamins, Inc.* prosecution detailed in Chapter 1, the Leniency Program motivated one of the cartel members (Rhone Poulenc) to disclose the operation of the cartel and greatly accelerated the Justice Department's negotiation of guilty pleas with the corporations and culpable individuals. The Leniency Program also played a key role in providing the Justice Department with evidence of a conspiracy between the world's two leading art auction houses, Christie's International and Sotheby's Holdings, to set commission rates. In return for an abatement of her own punishment, the former Sotheby's chief executive officer provided testimony against Sotheby's chairman of the board, who was convicted of price-fixing. *See United States v. Taubman*, 2002 WL 548733 (S.D.N.Y. 2002), *aff'd*, 297 F.3d 161 (2d Cir. 2002). More recent successes have included the *Auto Parts* and *Air Cargo* prosecutions, both of which have led to multiple prosecutions and fines.

The DOJ leniency program's success has inspired a number of other jurisdictions, including those that do not have criminal penalties for cartel formation, to adopt leniency programs. The European Commission's leniency policy—by its own account—has proven very effective in the fight against cartels. For further information about the EU's leniency program, see http://ec.europa.eu/competition/cartels/leniency/leniency.html. The UK's Competition and Markets Authority also has adopted a leniency policy along with extensive guidance. *See* https://www.gov.uk/government/publications/leniency-and-no-action-applications-in-cartel-cases. A 2014 study by the International Competition Network reported that over 40 jurisdictions have adopted leniency systems. *See* INTERNATIONAL COMPETITION NETWORK, ANTI-CARTEL ENFORCEMENT MANUAL, CHAPTER 2 DRAFTING AND IMPLEMENTING AN EFFECTIVE LENIENCY POLICY app. 2 (2014) (Leniency Policies), http://www.international competitionnetwork.org/uploads/library/doc1005.pdf. For a valuable collection of essays examining the role of leniency programs in modern cartel enforcement, see ANTI-CARTEL ENFORCEMENT IN A CONTEMPORARY AGE: LENIENCY RELIGION (Caron Beaton-Wells & Christopher Tran, eds., 2015).

To date, antitrust enforcement agencies have enlisted informants chiefly by offering leniency or immunity to offenders, or simply by relying on voluntary disclosures by non-culpable individuals (such as a sales manager who objects to a supervisor's instructions not to fulfill orders from a loyal customer) who are upset by what they perceive to be improper conduct. Beyond offering dispensations from criminal sanctions and encouraging pure volunteerism, the U.S. antitrust system provides no further incentives to gain the assistance of informers. Would offering additional rewards, such as the payment of bounties, elicit still greater detection of cartels? *See* William E. Kovacic, *Private Monitoring and Antitrust Enforcement: Paying Informants to Reveal Cartels*, 69 GEO. WASH. L. REV. 766 (2001).

Leniency, both corporate and individual, may be conditional, granted by the government in return for certain representations about the cartel participants' past conduct, or perhaps for promises of future cooperation. What happens, however, when in the government's view the conditions have not been satisfied? In *Stolt-Nielsen, S.A. v. United States*, 442 F.3d 177 (3d Cir. 2006), the court reversed a district court's order enjoining the Department of Justice from indicting a company and one of its officers, despite their having previously entered into leniency agreements. In the view of the government, they had breached the conditions of those agreements and were therefore subject to prosecution for their participation in criminal antitrust violations. In the Third Circuit's view, although a prior grant of immunity may be a defense to conviction, it was not a defense to indictment. Moreover, it was a violation of principles of separation of powers for the court to enjoin the indictment. *But see U.S. v. Stolt-Nielsen S.A.*, 524 F. Supp. 2d 586 (E.D. Pa. 2007) (concluding after an evidentiary hearing that Stolt-Nielsen and individual defendants did not breach their leniency agreements and dismissing the DOJ's indictment).

The Antitrust Criminal Penalty Enhancement and Reform Act of 2004 (ACPERA), Pub. L. No. 108–237, § 213(b), 118 Stat. 665, 666–67 (codified as amended at 15 U.S.C. § 1 note), increased Sherman Act criminal penalties to their current levels—$100 million for a convicted corporation, and $1 million for any other person or imprisonment for up to 10 years. It also sought to enhance the incentives for firms to submit amnesty applications under the DOJ's Corporate Leniency Program, by expanding the DOJ's discretion. Under Section 213 of Title II of the law, which is set out as notes to Section 1 of the Sherman Act, a leniency applicant can secure reduced damage exposure to civil damages in any related private litigation (de-trebling of damages and no joint and several liability with co-conspirators). These benefits, however, are only available to corporations that have entered into leniency agreements with the government and have met the standards for cooperating with the private plaintiffs. In 2010, ACPERA was extended through June 22, 2020 by Pub. L. No. 11–190, 124 Stat. 1275. As required by the legislation extending ACPERA, the GAO undertook a study of the impact of its provisions and issued a Report on its findings in July 2011. *See Criminal Cartel Enforcement: Stakeholder Views on Impact of 2004 Antitrust Reform Are Mixed, but Support Whistleblower Protection* (GAO–11–619 July 25, 2011), http://www.gao.gov/new.items/d11619.pdf.

The courts continue to explore and define ACPERA's boundaries and significance. *See, e.g., In re Capacitors Antitrust Litig.*, 106 F. Supp. 3d 1051 (N.D. Cal. 2015) (leniency application submitted under ACPERA not relevant to disposition of motion to dismiss given lack of transparency as to scope and contents of the application); *In re Polyurethane Foam Antitrust Litig.*, 2014 WL 6461355 (N.D. Ohio Nov. 17, 2014) (determination whether ACPERA's conditions had been satisfied by leniency applicant not ripe for determination at class certification stage of proceedings); *In re Aftermarket Auto. Lighting Prods. Antitrust Litig.*, 2013 WL 4536569 (C.D. Cal. Aug. 26, 2013) (concluding that defendants' cooperation was insufficient to warrant damage reduction benefits of ACPERA); *In re TFT-LCD Antitrust Litig.*, 618 F. Supp. 2d 1194, 1196 (N.D. Cal. 2009) (ACPERA does not compel an amnesty applicant to identify itself and cooperate with plaintiffs); *In re Sulfuric Acid Antitrust Litig.*, 231 F.R.D. 320 (N.D. Ill. 2005) (Cooperation Agreement did not compel compliance with all discovery requests).

B. THE MODERN ECONOMICS OF COLLUSION

Much antitrust law is concerned with the possibility that firms may choose not to compete aggressively, but may instead collude, acting collectively more as though they were a monopolist. Yet collusion may not be easy to accomplish, whether it involves an express exchange of assurances or tacit understandings.

Economists have explained that successful coordination in an oligopoly requires that the firms solve three "cartel problems:"

- reaching consensus on terms of coordination;

- deterring cheating on that consensus; and

- preventing new competition, whether in the form of expansion by fringe firms that are currently rivals but not part of the coordinated arrangement or in the form of new entry.

One way to think of these problems is that they emphasize a feature of collusive conduct evident in *JTC Petroleum* (*see supra* Chapter 1): colluding firms may need to exclude in order for their arrangement to succeed. The alleged conspiracy among applicators in that case required the colluding firms to eliminate competition among themselves and to prevent competition from a rival, JTC, who would not go along with the collusive arrangement. Under the theory of the case accepted by the appellate panel for the purpose of deciding whether to uphold a grant of summary judgment to the defendants, the colluding firms excluded JTC by arranging for the asphalt producers to refuse to sell it a key input. It does not take much of an imaginative leap for either coordinating firms considering whether to cheat or new entrants to look at the technique used to police JTC and recognize that the coordinating firms could readily apply the same method to them. As should be evident, collusive and exclusionary conduct are often and naturally combined by firms exercising market power, as happened in *JTC*. Indeed, a study of multiple cartels found that many "use[d] exclusionary behavior often featured in monopolization cases to ensure the effectiveness of [their] efforts to restrict output." Randal D. Heeb, William E. Kovacic, Robert C. Marshall & Leslie M. Marx, *Cartels as Two-Stage Mechanisms: Implications for the Analysis of Dominant-Firm Conduct,* 10 CHI. J. INT'L L. 213, 217 (2009). Moreover, firms may collude in order to exclude, as with the allegations in *Brooke Group* and *Visa,* which we will read in Chapter 4. Does the close relationship between collusion and exclusion call into question *Copperweld*'s view that concerted action calls for greater scrutiny than unilateral conduct?

These three economic problems incident to the formation and successful operation of a cartel must be solved regardless of whether the collusive conduct is express or tacit. For this reason, the legal differences between express and tacit collusion are generally unimportant economically, and economists today frequently employ the terms "coordination" or "collusion" to encompass both possibilities, without distinction. Indeed, throughout this Casebook and the case excerpts, the terms "collusion" (whether tacit or express), "cartel," and "coordination" are used interchangeably, although these concepts are technically distinct. For a discussion of the differences among them, see Jonathan B. Baker, *Two Sherman Act Section 1 Dilemmas: Parallel Pricing, the Oligopoly Problem, and Contemporary Economic Theory,* 38 ANTITRUST BULL. 143 (1993). A related economic concept of "parallel accommodating conduct" is discussed in connection with coordinated competitive effects of merger in Chapter 5. Firms may be able to coordinate to raise prices through parallel accommodating conduct without reaching consensus on terms of coordination and deterring cheating on those terms. To date, this possibility has not played a role in the antitrust analysis of coordinated conduct outside the merger context,[1] so it is not discussed further here.

In this Section, we explore the economic problems of collusion from multiple perspectives. We begin with two case studies that have different purposes. The first, a hypothetical example involving gasoline stations, identifies the economic obstacles that firms must surmount to collude and shows how firms can overcome them without an express agreement. The second, a hypothetical example involving delicatessens, relies on the principles developed in the previous case study to identify features of market structures that tend to facilitate or frustrate coordination. We then discuss why firms might coordinate their conduct imperfectly.

In brief summary, the case studies show how coordinating firms can solve their first problem, of reaching consensus, by identifying terms of coordination, such as the prices each firm will charge (or the rule the firms will apply to select prices), the reduction in output each firm will undertake, or the way the firms will allocate customers or territories. The case studies also show how coordinating firms can solve their second problem, of deterring deviation (cheating), by exploiting or creating a method of detecting firms that cheat on the consensus, and a means of punishing cheaters. Cheating is more likely to be deterred as its detection becomes more swift and certain and the punishment to cheaters becomes more severe. This assumes that the punishment threat is credible in the eyes of the potential cheater: not so costly to the punishing firms as to make the cheating firms reasonably question whether the punishing firms would be willing to carry it out. If the punishment threat is not credible, cheating will not be deterred. The third problem, preventing new competition, is mainly solved by making entry difficult. It is not necessary for the coordinating firms to take steps to do so, however, if entry barriers are already high. Moreover, coordination may succeed even if some new competition occurs, whether in the form of output expansion by fringe rivals or new entry, so long as the addition to industry output is not so great as to make coordination unprofitable.

1. THE PROBLEMS OF COLLUSION AND THEIR SOLUTIONS: TWO CASE STUDIES

We present two case studies to illuminate the problems inhibiting collusion and to suggest how colluding firms may act to overcome them.

---

[1] The concept of "conscious parallelism," discussed below in Section C, may be interpreted within the framework of the three "cartel problems" as a coordinated outcome that arises when firms reach consensus on terms of coordination through leader-follower conduct, in a market in which firms would have little incentive to cheat on a coordinated price. It could also be interpreted as the outcome of parallel accommodating conduct, which does not require reaching consensus or deterring cheating.

The insights developed through these case studies form the basis for identifying features of market structure that can facilitate or frustrate collusion.

CASE STUDY I: TACIT COORDINATION— A GASOLINE STATION HYPOTHETICAL

The *Andreas* opinion, which we read in Chapter 1, points to the difficulties that an express cartel, with all the advantages of direct communication, faces in overcoming its cartel problems. A hypothetical example involving gas stations highlights a point that goes the opposite way: even firms colluding tacitly, without reaching an express agreement, can overcome those problems and successfully reach a coordinated outcome.[2] The gas station hypothetical also explains how, as a matter of economics, firms can do so.

Suppose four gasoline stations are located at four corners of a busy intersection, with no other stations for miles. Assume that the zoning laws do not permit any other gas stations to enter nearby. The latter assumption puts aside the cartel problem of deterring new competition to focus on reaching consensus and deterring cheating.

Each gasoline station pays $1.00 per gallon for gas, and the typical industry markup between the wholesale price and retail pricing is 5 cents per gallon. Each of the four stations thus charges $1.05 per gallon when they are competing aggressively. Each posts that price on a large sign where it can be seen by motorists coming from all directions, as well as viewed by its three competitors.

One day, one station raises its posted price to $1.10 per gallon, although neither its costs nor those of its rivals have increased. The other three stations see the new price and match it. If the new price sticks, the four rivals will have found a price in excess of the competitive level; they will be exercising market power.

Will any of the gas stations find it in its interest to cheat on the new, higher price? Quite possibly not. Consider the alternatives each firm faces. On the one hand, it can stick with the $1.10 price, and earn an extra 5 cents per gallon on all the gasoline it sells, well into the future. This could be very profitable. On the other hand, it could cheat, perhaps by deciding to sell gasoline at $1.09 per gallon. Will price-cutting be more profitable to the firm than cooperating? In order to get more business by lowering price, the firm will need to post its lower price on its sign. Then drivers will see that it sells gasoline for less, and will fill up at its pumps, rather than those of its rivals. Its sales will go up.

---

[2] The antitrust implications of a similar example are considered in Dennis W. Carlton, Robert H. Gertner & Andrew M. Rosenfield, *Communication Among Competitors: Game Theory and Antitrust*, 5 GEO. MASON L. REV. 423 (1997).

But the profitability of price-cutting depends on how its rivals respond. They will see the lower price of $1.09 per gallon too, and can be expected to cut their own price to match before very many drivers learn about the discounting station and switch to the cheater. Because price-cutting will be rapidly detected and responded to by its rivals, the price-cutting firm will get very little additional business by lowering price. Against this small benefit, it will give up 1 cent per gallon on all its future gasoline sales. Based on this comparison, cheating appears less profitable than cooperation. Accordingly, each firm will most likely stick with the $1.10 price, and not undercut it. Thus, the cartel problem of deterring cheating may not be a problem for these firms: with rapid detection of cheating by rivals, and rapid response by rivals, the gains from cheating may be so limited as to make continued cooperation more attractive than cheating for all firms.

The incentive to cheat on a coordinated outcome is the economic force that generates competition. If the goal is to get the nations of the world to cooperate on arms control, cheating is a bad thing. But if the goal is to ensure low prices and high output, cheating is good. Some readers may recognize this incentive as arising in the "game theory" model of a prisoner's dilemma (*see infra* Sidebar 3–2). In order for firms to coordinate successfully, they must find a way to solve the prisoner's dilemma that competition creates.

The cartel problem of deterring cheating is not insoluble, even though the firms cannot write an enforceable contract to cut output and raise price. Cartel members can deter cheating in at least three ways. The first is through mechanisms to detect cheating and punish it if it occurs. The second is by developing mechanisms that reduce the incentive to cheat. The third is by developing internal norms that stigmatize cheating.

The first method is perhaps the most prominent in the economics literature: cheating can be made unprofitable if a firm's rivals find out quickly, and respond rapidly to impose costs on the cheating firm (commonly referred to in the economics literature as "punishment"). The more rapid the detection and punishment of cheating, and the more severe the likely punishment, the greater the likelihood that a firm will decide not to cheat in the first place. The ability of many cartels to deter cheating is demonstrated by evidence that cartels often last more than a decade. Margaret Levenstein & Valerie Y. Suslow, *Breaking Up Is Hard to Do: Determinants of Cartel Duration*, 54 J.L. & ECON. 455 (2011) (the median lifespan of a sample of cartels cut short by antitrust enforcement was seven years, twenty-eight percent lasted at least a decade, and ten percent lasted seventeen years or more). But many cartels are also short-lived, and in other markets, coordination has undoubtedly been prevented by the inability of market participants to solve their cartel problems, as well as by the deterrent effect of antitrust enforcement.

Repeated interaction among firms can make cheating less likely. If firms interact only a short, finite time and have no future interactions to worry about, cheating may well be more profitable for each than cooperation. But repeated interaction can make continued cooperation more profitable than cheating by increasing the likely punishment that the cheater's rivals can impose.[3] Simply by declining to cooperate in the future, they can deny the cheater the profits it would otherwise have obtained from a long period of coordination.

Even with repeated interaction among the firms, however, coordination will not always be more profitable than cheating. In particular, with less rapid and less severe punishment—a less steep price reduction or a punishment response that does not last forever—cheating might not be deterred and the cartel might not survive (or might never form in the first place). The greater the opportunity for secret cheating— cheating that would likely last a long time before detection by rivals—the more likely a cartel will be unstable and not form in the first place. For similar reasons, if cheating would occur on a large scale before its rivals would respond—if the cheater takes most of the market, for example, by making a long-term deal with a few large customers—the more likely cheating will be profitable, notwithstanding the repeated interaction among sellers.

Cartels may also deter cheating by crafting mechanisms that reduce the incentive to cheat. In particular, cartels may develop ways of sharing information and revenues that reduce the gains of cheating relative to the gains from continued cooperation, and thereby lessen the temptation of coordinating firms to cheat. For example, a recent study found that most cartels exchanged information on sales, production, and price; most limited the need to monitor each other by allocating territories or customers; and some required members that exceeded their sales quota to purchase product from members that fell short. Margaret Levenstein & Valerie Y. Suslow, *Breaking Up Is Hard to Do: Determinants of Cartel Duration*, 54 J.L. & ECON. 455 (2011). With devices that provide disincentive to cheating like these in place, only a minority of cartels took steps to discipline cheaters, as by cutting price in response to cheating or seeking to foreclose cheating rivals from access to key inputs or customers. *Id.* Third, cartels may deter cheating through internal norms that stigmatize it. That may have been what the lysine conspirators accomplished with the motto "Our competitors are our friends. Our customers are the enemy."

What about the remaining cartel problem of reaching consensus? After all, firms invariably have divergent interests as well as a common interest

---

[3] According to what economists refer to as the "folk theorem" for oligopoly interaction with repeated play, repeated interaction creates a more congenial environment for successful coordination than a one-time interaction when the firms expect to interact infinitely, or, more to the point, when they expect to interact for a finite time with an uncertain ending point.

in obtaining a higher price. While each wants price to rise, each also wants to increase its market share at the higher price. Moreover, the firms may differ in ways that increase the divergence in their interests. In the gas station example, one station may have a much larger number of self-service pumps than the rest and, uniquely, a convenience store. This station might prefer higher automobile traffic than its rivals, and thus prefer a lower cartel price (and higher industry sales) than they would.

Notwithstanding the possibility of divergent views, price leadership may suffice to solve the cartel problem of reaching consensus. The firms could settle on any of a number of cartel prices in excess of $1.05 per gallon. By selecting $1.10, the firm that raised price first establishes that price as one for its rivals to match. Each rival knows that if all the firms go along with $1.10, that price is likely to stick—they can go through the same analysis of incentives to cheat that we have undertaken. Nor do any of the firms take much financial risk in raising price before knowing whether the others will go along. The first firm to raise its prices will lose business while its rivals consider whether to raise price as well, but the rivals are likely to respond quickly. If some rivals do not match the price increase, the firm which first boosted prices knows that it can back down before much time has gone by. So once the first firm raises price to $1.10 per gallon, the other firms are likely to follow.

As this example suggests, reaching a consensus on the collective output reduction, the collusive price, and the allocation of production and profits among the firms may be facilitated by communication among the firms. That is why price-fixing conspirators often meet face-to-face. Communication is dangerous, however, because it makes it more likely that the firms will be found to have violated Sherman Act § 1. *See United States v. Kwik-Chek Food Stores, Inc.*, Crim. No. CR08–063–RAW (E.D. Okla. 2008) (criminal indictment charged that gas stations in Antlers, Oklahoma reached an explicit agreement through discussions of retail prices), https://www.justice.gov/atr/case-document/indictment–78. Absent such conversations, the firms may be able to reach a consensus by making some price or customer allocation "focal" (natural and obvious), in ways that do not necessarily violate the antitrust laws—such as the use of posted gasoline prices by the gas stations in this example. In other cases, customer or territorial allocations may plausibly be focal. Firms may see some customers as naturally theirs and other customers as belonging to their rivals. If so, they may reach a market allocation along the lines "I won't solicit your historical customers if you don't solicit mine" or "I won't do business on your side of town if you don't do business on mine."

If raising price is so easy, and cheating so unlikely, why would the firms ever stop? Why wouldn't price rise to $100 per gallon? Because the industry demand curve is not perfectly inelastic. At a high enough price for gasoline, enough people will cut back on their driving, or drive to neighboring cities to buy gas, as to make continued price increases unprofitable. Indeed, even a monopolist will stop raising its prices eventually.

The gas station example was crafted to make it plausible that the firms could solve their cartel problems. With different facts, that outcome could be made less likely. Suppose, for example, that the stations are in the same part of town but cannot see each other. That might make it more difficult for them to identify a consensus price and make it more difficult for the firms to monitor each other's price changes, thereby increasing the time that a cheating station would have to profit from any extra sales that a lower price brought in. If some stations are attached to restaurants, they could cheat in ways that could be difficult for rivals to monitor or respond to by offering free fill-ups to repeat restaurant customers. A station that services the corporate fleet of a large area employer may have an incentive to cheat by making that discount also available for employees using their personal vehicles. If zoning is not an issue, high prices may attract independent refiners to sponsor the entry of new stations offering discounted gasoline. The next case study, involving delicatessens, looks systematically at features of market structure that may facilitate or frustrate coordination.

CASE STUDY II: FACTORS FACILITATING OR FRUSTRATING COORDINATION—A DELICATESSEN HYPOTHETICAL

As with the previous case study, we focus here on the first two cartel problems, reaching consensus and deterring cheating; the most important aspect of the third problem, preventing new competition, is analyzed when entry conditions are discussed in later Chapters. Recall that we first visited some of these issues in Chapter 1 in connection with our reading of *Andreas*, and the hypothetical neighborhood coffee shop conspiracy. This hypothetical case study builds on the economic analysis developed in the previous two case studies to identify features of market structure that may facilitate or frustrate coordination.

To frame the discussion, consider the following hypothetical example. A number of office buildings are clustered in one downtown neighborhood in a large city. These buildings house, among other things, several large law firms, various business offices, and a law school. The neighborhood has a number of restaurants that are popular lunch time spots, as well as several delicatessens. Take-out food is available only from the delis. We assume that deli takeout is a relevant product market, and the neighborhood is a relevant geographic market. Were it otherwise, the delicatessens as a group would not find it profitable to raise prices; as was true in the coffee shop hypothetical in Chapter 1, a deli cartel would fail if buyers responded to higher prices by shifting their purchases elsewhere.

What economic factors would affect the ability of the delicatessens to collude, whether tacitly or expressly? A list of factors facilitating or frustrating collusion is a staple of textbooks in industrial organization economics, and we discuss some possibilities below. A similar list appears in the U.S. Horizontal Merger Guidelines (§ 7.2), which we will study in Chapter 5. For a recent book length treatment, see ROBERT C. MARSHALL & LESLIE M. MARX, THE ECONOMICS OF COLLUSION: CARTELS AND BIDDING RINGS (2012).

The factors sketched below are not comprehensive. Some of these factors make collusion more likely, others make collusion less likely, and still others could go either way. We caution that we are not presenting a checklist. The issue in determining whether collusion is likely is not how many factors are present and how many are not; it is whether they suggest, taken as a whole, that the firms can reasonably expect to reach a consensus and deter deviation (cheating). For this reason, it is important to understand why each factor might be relevant to evaluating whether the firms participating in a market could reasonably be expected to solve their cartel problems, and we will highlight the explanation in our discussion below.

Number of Firms

It is commonly thought that the greater the number of firms, the more difficult it will be for them to collude successfully. As the number of firms grows, reaching consensus and deterring deviation both may become more difficult. If there are only two or three delis in the neighborhood, their ability to work out a mutually acceptable arrangement (reach a consensus) will likely be easier than if there are a dozen delis, much as it is generally easier for a few friends to coordinate their calendars and arrange to meet for dinner at a restaurant than it is for a large group to do so. Moreover, the larger the number of firms seeking to coordinate their pricing or other actions, the more likely one will prefer cheating rather than cooperating. It may also be more likely that a cheater will be able to do so for a while, secretly—without its rivals noticing and responding. This possibility will increase each firm's temptation to cheat or compete rather than collude.

An empirical relationship between the number of firms and the likelihood that they will overcome their cartel problems and successfully coordinate is widely accepted, but it is hardly the only relevant factor. Tacit or express collusion has occurred even in markets with a large number of firms, and collusion may be unsuccessful even with as few as two firms in a market. Moreover, there is no fixed "critical" number of firms below which coordinated conduct becomes more likely or more effective. These caveats are discussed in more detail in Chapter 5 with respect to horizontal mergers, as this is the context in which the significance of the number of firms for the likelihood of collusion has undergone the most analysis and elaboration. (*See* Sidebar 5–2.)

Relatedly, the conditions of entry matter to whether collusion is likely to succeed. If new competitors can easily appear, and have entered in a way that would lead them to expand output, prices may fall back to the competitive level unless the new rivals are brought into the collusive arrangement. Accordingly, the relevant number of firms may include potential entrants as well as incumbents. Entry conditions and the role of new competition are discussed in more detail in Chapter 5.

Product Heterogeneity and Complex, Changing Products

It is plausible that the delicatessens have different menus, and that each firm's menu includes a large number of products. The delis may have different locations, some may be a longer walk for most of the workers and students looking for lunch, they may differ in perceived quality, and they may vary on features such as image, ambience, and helpfulness of staff. The resulting product heterogeneity may create problems for both reaching consensus and deterring cheating from it. The sheer complexity of negotiating a price for every menu item may be hard for the firms to overcome. In addition, product heterogeneity may create opportunities for cheating in ways that would be hard for rivals to detect quickly. For example, a deli could effectively cut price for a sandwich while leaving the list price on its menu unchanged by giving away drinks and cookies for free. These problems of reaching consensus and deterring cheating are likely exacerbated if products are changing. A deli that frequently refreshes its menu by altering its special sandwiches can come up with variants that are outside the price consensus and take business away from rivals. Thus, a successful delicatessen cartel may need to develop a mechanism to incorporate new products into its coordination arrangement. This may be difficult, especially if the agreement is only tacit.

While product heterogeneity is commonly thought to frustrate collusion, and similarity among firms and homogeneous products are often thought to facilitate coordination, these are at best general tendencies. Even similar firms selling identical products may have divergent interests, and they may not be able to reach a consensus or successfully deter cheating. Indeed, more similar firms may at times have a greater temptation to cheat than firms that are differentiated, because the former may have a greater ability to attract business from their rivals through price cuts.

Moreover, coordination can succeed notwithstanding the complexity and range of products offered by sellers. The firms may facilitate collusion by developing ways of *exchanging information* to help reach a consensus and deter cheating by avoiding secret transactions, making detection of cheating easier. (*See Note on the Economic Effects of "Most Favored Nation"*

Provisions, infra Chapter 6, which discusses most favored customer provisions, one practice firms could adopt to facilitate information exchange, and the discussion of information exchange as a facilitating practice later in this Chapter.) The delis could adopt the identical menus or post price lists online; steps like these might make it easier for the firms to compare prices. Alternatively, the firms could *follow simple, obvious rules* (also termed "focal" rules) to simplify negotiations, thereby simplifying their coordination task. For example, the delis could allocate the office buildings among themselves, perhaps by proximity to each deli's location, so that each deli would market the delivery of catered lunches exclusively to specified buildings. Or they could grandfather in the variation in prices and products on their current menus, and merely agree to raise all prices by 5% across the board, without altering product definitions. The resulting coordinated outcome may fall short of what a delicatessen monopolist would choose to do, but it may nevertheless involve prices substantially in excess of what would be expected from a competitive industry. (We discuss incomplete coordination later in this Section.)

Excess Capacity

A Firm's Own Excess Capacity. Some of the delicatessens may be very busy at lunch time, have lines out the door, and find themselves unable to serve many more customers within the confines of their retail space, even if they were to add workers. These delicatessens are operating at nearly full capacity. A firm unable to expand output beyond its current sales will lack both the incentive and ability to cheat.

In contrast, other delicatessens might readily be able to serve more customers; they may have a great deal of excess capacity. Cheating on a cartel may be more tempting for a firm with substantial excess capacity than for a firm with limited or no excess capacity. The gains from cheating typically come from diverting a great deal of business away from rivals; a firm that cannot serve many more customers than it handles already may not find price-cutting a tempting strategy. A firm's ability to take advantage of its excess capacity to expand sales will be limited, however, to the extent products are differentiated, sellers experience high costs of expanding output (*i.e.* excess capacity cannot be exploited inexpensively), or buyers experience costs of switching between sellers.

Moreover, any other feature of the industry that allows a firm to expand output rapidly and inexpensively operates much like a firm's own excess capacity in terms of its influence on the likelihood of successful coordination. Thus, under some circumstances, *vertical integration* or the sale of *complementary products* may encourage cartel cheating. For example, if one of the delicatessens was affiliated with a chain of coffee shops, it might have an ability to expand sales not shared by its unaffiliated rivals, and thus a unique ability to benefit from cheating on cartel prices, by preparing sandwiches in the morning and stocking a refrigerator at the coffee shops with food for sale during lunch.

Excess Capacity in the Hands of Multiple Firms. While a firm's own excess capacity may encourage it to cheat, excess capacity in the hands of rival firms may discourage it from cheating. At some point, those rivals will discover that the price-cutter has been cheating. When they do, their excess capacity gives them the ability to punish that price-cutting severely: they can cut price deeply themselves, without fear that they will find themselves unable to serve the higher demand that will predictably flow from a lower price. Because excess capacity in the hands of rivals represents a threat to punish cheating severely, the firm may be discouraged from cheating in the first place.[4] Recall from *Andreas*, in Chapter 1, that despite its excess capacity, ADM preferred coordination to cheating and used its excess capacity as a threat of punishment to discourage other lysine cartel members from cheating. Excess capacity will represent less of a punishment threat, however, if products are differentiated, sellers experience high costs of expanding output, or buyers experience costs of switching between sellers.

Firm and industry excess capacity may be an aspect of market structure. For example, it may be the product of declining demand or of firm decisions to expand plants in anticipation of demand growth that never arrived. But it can be an aspect of market conduct or performance, both because it results from prior capacity investment decisions and because the amount that the firms sell depends on the price they charge. If market demand does not increase for reasons independent of firm conduct, firms selling relatively homogenous products would likely experience greater excess capacity the more effectively they are able to coordinate, though the increase in excess capacity resulting from the exercise of market power could be small if market demand is highly inelastic.

Any feature of the industry that leads cheating firms to expect that a severe price war will result from the breakdown of a cartel operates much like excess capacity in the hands of rivals in terms of its influence on the likelihood of successful coordination. Thus, under some circumstances, *inelastic market demand* or *low marginal costs* relative to market prices may discourage cheating on a cartel.

Inelastic market demand (and low marginal costs relative to market prices, which may be an indicator of inelastic market demand) may also facilitate coordination for a second reason: it raises the firm's gains from participation in a coordinated arrangement, so makes it more worthwhile for the firm to work with its rivals to develop and implement ways of

---

[4] This discussion presumes that the rivals would find it profitable to follow through to punish the cheating firm severely were they to observe cheating. If a severe punishment is not a credible threat, the threat of a less severe punishment that is credible may still be sufficient to foster incomplete coordination, as discussed below in connection with incomplete coordination.

overcoming their cartel problems. But the gains to coordination suggested by inelastic market demand would be limited if non-coordinating rivals (or entrants) can and would expand rapidly in the event prices rose, which could be the case even if those non-coordinating firms' shares are low.

Public vs. Private Transactions

The delicatessens post the prices for the items on their take out menu and advertise those prices in flyers distributed to the nearby offices and law school. Transactions are public and open, in the sense that the delis could not change the prices they charge their walk-in customers without their rivals finding out. However, transactions are not completely open. The number of customers served remains private information, unavailable to rivals. Nevertheless, if one deli decides to cheat on a cartel by cutting price, its rivals will detect that cheating rapidly, perhaps within the day, and can respond by lowering their own prices rapidly, as soon as they can print new flyers and change prices on their posted in-store displays. Open transactions may thus facilitate collusion by discouraging cheating.

The delicatessens in the neighborhood sell to the walk-in crowd at lunch, and to this point we have emphasized that aspect of their business in our analysis. But now suppose that much of their business takes a second form, catering lunchtime meetings at law firms and other neighborhood businesses. The delis may give the law firms their take out menus, but they may also give the law firms discounts. A deli may tell an office manager: "If you let us cater all your meetings, we will give you a 10% discount off our regular prices." These discounts are private. (A savvy office manager may tell a second deli: "Your rival is offering us a 10% discount; you'll need to give us 15% off to get us to switch," but the rival need not believe the office manager, as her information may be inaccurate or strategically exaggerated.)

If the delis have historically offered businesses 10% off, and one of the delis decides to raise its discount to 15% in order to cheat, it may take a while for its rivals to catch on. They may notice they are losing some business and hear more law firm administrators than usual tell them that they must offer a larger discount to win their business, but they may not rapidly figure out that all the lost business is going to one particular price-cutting rival. Thus, when transactions are private, cheating is more likely to succeed for a while, firms are more likely to cheat on a cartel, and, recognizing this, cartels are less likely to form in the first place. For this reason, private or confidential transactions are a factor tending to frustrate collusion.

The relevant dimension on which privacy of transactions tends to frustrate collusion depends on the nature of the collusive agreement, however. If the delis had colluded by dividing markets (allocating customers) rather than by agreeing on price—for example, through an agreement that each deli was responsible for catering in specific office buildings, and would not deliver outside its assigned territory—then the degree of transparency of pricing for catering services would not affect incentives to cheat. All that would matter would be whether a deli could secretly deliver lunch to customers in office buildings assigned to its rivals.

Predictable vs. Unpredictable Demand

As the last example suggests, the delicatessens may learn about the possibility of rival cheating from what happens to their own business. If they are losing more customers than usual, they may suspect that cheating is the reason, and investigate further. That inference is facilitated by stable demand, or more generally by predictable demand. Thus, if deli demand always falls in the summer, when law school classes are out and many office workers take vacation, colluding delicatessens are unlikely to interpret a July falloff in sales as cheating by a rival unless they seem to be losing more sales than past experience would suggest.

But catering demand may instead be characterized by "background noise"—i.e., in the past, demand may often have fluctuated for no obvious reason and fallen to unusually low levels for a couple of months at a time. This "background noise" means that it may take several months before a cartel member discovers that something is amiss. Its law firm catering business may be down, but the deli may think nothing of it until much time has passed. This possibility means that a cheating firm can expect to get away with its price-cutting undetected for a longer period than if demand were more stable, encouraging cheating and discouraging cartel formation. This inhibition to coordination may be reduced, however, if the firms collude by allocating territories or customers, as that may make it easier for them to identify the source of lost business. It may also be reduced if the terms of coordination require cartel participants that have unusually high market shares to purchase products from other firms with unusually low shares, or if colluding firms otherwise create mechanisms that limit the financial benefit of price-cutting.

"Lumpy" Sales and Large Buyers

Suppose now that the bulk of each delicatessen's business is law firm and business lunch catering rather than walk-in lunch time sales. Suppose further that two large law firms together account for three-quarters of the catering business in the neighborhood, and that law firm catering is negotiated annually, resulting in a year-long contract. A successful delicatessen cartel will presumably need to fix the price of catering services, perhaps in the form of an agreement not to discount more than 10% off of the "list" price on the menu.

In this market, buyers are large and sales are "lumpy" in the sense that the business comes up for renewal only annually. Transactions are thus aggregated due to the nature of contracting practices and the demands of larger buyers. As a consequence, a cheating firm, by making only two deals, one with each large law firm, can attract a full year's worth of business accounting for three-quarters of the largest market segment. Even if its rivals detect what has happened, they cannot rapidly punish the cheating firm by cutting price and stealing the business back, as most of the market is tied up for a year. A firm considering cheating in such an industry will realize that it can take a large chunk of business easily, and do so free from the threat of rapid punishment, particularly if the two contracts come up for renewal at about the same time of year. This opportunity will encourage firms to cheat, and its threat will discourage cartel formation in the first instance. So industries in which rival firms vie for a few, large, and long-term contracts may be less prone to collusion. Relatedly, in high-technology markets in which firms compete through the successive introduction of technologically superior products, it may be difficult for coordinating firms to punish rivals that cheat, as by undercutting the quality-adjusted price when introducing new products.

Conversely, if the great majority of deli sales are individual sandwiches sold to walk-in customers, each deli will realize that it cannot obtain very much additional business through cheating before that act is detected by its rivals and they respond. When sales are small and frequent, cheating may thus be a less attractive strategy, facilitating coordination. For the same reason, cheating may be discouraged by *high customer switching costs*, which would make it difficult for firms to convince the customers of rivals to switch suppliers.

Prior Express Collusion

Although prior collusion is not, strictly speaking, an aspect of market structure, the Horizontal Merger Guidelines, which we will examine in Chapter 5, highlight its value as evidence that the market is vulnerable to coordination. That inference would be weakened if aspects of market structure have changed substantially in ways that would tend to frustrate coordination. The Horizontal Merger Guidelines also indicate that failed attempts to collude suggest that coordination was difficult, but not so difficult as to discourage attempts; if conditions have changed in ways that lessen the significance of the factors that undermined past efforts, the market could have become more vulnerable to coordination. In addition, the Horizontal Merger Guidelines indicate that prior express collusion involving the same product in other geographic markets suggests vulnerability to collusion if conditions in the geographic markets are similar, and that failed attempts to collude in those markets may also be instructive.

Figure 3–1 summarizes the factors we have just outlined. As previously noted, analysis of the ability of firms successfully to coordinate is not a matter of counting the factors in each column and reaching a conclusion based on which side predominates. Instead, all the factors must be considered as a whole.

Figure 3–1:
Some Factors Facilitating or Frustrating Coordination

Facilitating	Frustrating
Few firms	Many firms
Product homogeneity	Product heterogeneity
Simple products	Complex, changing products
Public (open & transparent) transactions	Private transactions
Excess capacity (multiple firms)	Excess capacity (individual firm)
Predictable demand	Unpredictable demand
Small transactions	"Lumpy" sales
Small buyers	Large buyers
Inelastic market demand	—
Low marginal costs relative to price	—
High customer switching costs	—
Prior express collusion	—
—	Vertical integration
—	Sale of complementary products

Sidebar 3–2:
Understanding Collusion as a Prisoner's Dilemma

One of the most basic and widely-studied models in game theory is that of the prisoner's dilemma. In addition to suggesting how the police can get suspects to confess—the setting in which the story is usually told—the model also explains why firms compete even though they would jointly profit from collusion. After describing the prisoner's dilemma in its original setting, we will sketch its application to competition. We previously relied on the underlying ideas in explaining how the hypothetical gasoline stations in Case Study I would solve their cartel problems.

Two hard cases, Biff and Rocky, are suspects in a bank robbery. The investigating police officers are virtually certain that the two committed the crime, as in fact they did. But the police know this in part through inadmissible evidence, and do not think they can secure a conviction without at least one confession.

Biff and Rocky are questioned separately. Each knows that if they both hang tough, and do not confess, they will be interrogated in jail for a while, then be allowed to go free. If both confess, they will both go to jail. And if one confesses while the other does not, the cooperating prisoner will be freed immediately (in exchange for helping to make a case against his partner), while the prosecutor will throw the book at the non-cooperating one. As a result, the non-cooperating prisoner will likely receive a much longer jail term than if both were to confess.

These outcomes ("payoffs" in game theoretic language) are sketched in the following chart.

	Rocky does not confess	Rocky confesses
Biff does not confess	Biff and Rocky are jailed for a short while, then go free	Rocky goes free immediately; long jail term for Biff
Biff confesses	Biff goes free immediately; long jail term for Rocky	Medium jail sentence for both Biff and Rocky

Recall that the prisoners are separated. Each must make a decision about whether to confess without communicating with his partner. What strategy would we expect Biff to pursue?

We could begin by analyzing the outcomes from the point of view of the partnership between Biff and Rocky. The best outcome for the two together is if neither confesses, as their aggregate jail time together is small. The worst outcome for the two together is if both confess, as they then both stay in jail for a medium term.

But now look at the outcomes from Biff's individual point of view. Biff may think this way: "Rocky will either confess or not confess. If Rocky is going to confess, the best thing for Biff to do is confess too; that way Biff will avoid a long jail sentence in favor of a medium jail sentence. If Rocky is instead going to hang tough, confession is still the best strategy for Biff to follow; that way Biff will go free immediately." In short, whichever strategy Rocky follows, the best strategy for Biff is to confess. Confession is thus a "dominant" strategy for Biff, in game theory language. Rocky will think the same way, and conclude that no matter what Biff does, the best strategy for Rocky is to confess. Accordingly, the most likely outcome is that both confess and both go to jail for a medium term, even though a better outcome (a short jail time during interrogation) was available to both. The two suspects are led by individual self-interest to confess.

The analogy to competition among firms can quickly be sketched. Biff Co. and Rocky, Inc. are the only two firms competing in a relevant market. The management team at each must decide whether to cooperate (collude) or compete. Collusion is attractive: if both firms decide to collude and charge a high price, they each earn substantial profits. If both instead compete, and expand output while charging a low price, they earn zero economic profits (no profits in excess of what is required to keep the assets in the market). A firm makes out best by cheating, charging a low price when its rival's price is high, but then its rival loses money. These outcomes are set forth in the table below.

	Rocky Inc. cooperates	Rocky Inc. competes
Biff Co. cooperates	Biff: $10 million profit Rocky: $10 million profit	Biff: $5 million loss Rocky: $20 million profit
Biff Co. competes	Biff: $20 million profit Rocky: $5 million loss	Biff: $0 profit Rocky: $0 profit

As before, joint profits are maximized when both cooperate—they then split $20 million—and joint profits are the least when both compete. Nevertheless, each has a powerful incentive to compete. Biff reasons: "Rocky can either cooperate or compete. If Rocky cooperates, I do best by competing; I make $20 million rather than $10 million. If Rocky instead competes, I do best by competing also; at least I break even rather than losing money. Either way, I want to compete." Rocky reasons the same way, and both are led to compete rather than cooperate. Both would do better if they could find a way to cooperate, but competition is nevertheless the marketplace outcome.

Note that this discussion assumes that Rocky Inc. and Biff
Co. have only one decision to make, whether to cooperate or
compete, just like Rocky and Biff. In the language of game
theory, the prisoner's dilemma problem set forth above is a
"one-shot" game. Repeated interaction (or "repeated play" in the
language of game theory) can alter the outcome, and make it
more likely that the firms will choose to cooperate in any period.
This point is discussed in Case Study I, above.

Cartels arise when competing firms overcome their
prisoner's dilemma. One way that antitrust enforcers attempt
to undermine collusion is by creating a new prisoner's dilemma
for participants, by offering firms leniency if they are the first
to disclose a naked cartel to enforcement agencies. *See supra*
Sidebar 3–1.

A final word: from the point of view of the firms in this
example, cooperation is the goal, not competition. Cooperation
leads to the greatest profits to split between the firms. But don't
forget that from the point of view of buyers and economic
efficiency, competition—not cooperation—is the goal. Antitrust
law enforcement can be understood as designed to discourage
tacit collusion by making it less profitable.

2. INCOMPLETE COORDINATION

As the above examples suggest, coordination may be partly successful,
but nevertheless fall short of replicating the price a monopolist would
charge and the output a monopolist would produce for a number of reasons,
including the following four.

First, coordinating firms may not be able to punish cheating rivals as
strongly as would be necessary to induce every cartel member to charge the
full monopoly price. In some industries, for example, the necessary
punishment may require that the punishing firms charge prices below their
marginal costs, yet this strategy may require that the cartel absorb
substantial losses, so it may not be credible. On the other hand, colluding
firms may well be willing to engage in punishment that merely returns
price to the competitive level—as would happen in any event were the
cartel to break down—and this response to cheating may be sufficient to
induce all the firms to charge a price substantially in excess of the
competitive level without cheating.

Second, coordinating firms may not be able to allocate the monopoly
profits they achieve in a manner satisfactory to all the participants,
because they may be unable to compensate each other directly. For
example, in Case Study I, the gas station hypothetical, if the competitive
price is $1.00 per gallon and most firms want a cartel price of $1.30, a firm

that instead prefers that the cartel stop raising price at $1.10 would be able to insist on that price. In theory, the other firms could still get price up to $1.30 by paying off the latter seller to accept a price in excess of $1.10; if $1.30 were much more profitable for them than $1.10, they may earn enough extra monopoly profits to make such a payment advantageous. In practice, however, such payments, termed "side payments" by economists, could be difficult to negotiate and impossible to enforce given the risk that a prosecutor and court would infer an unlawful (even criminal) agreement to fix price. Some successful cartels nevertheless rely on side payments, as by requiring colluding firms that exceed their sales quotas to purchase product from colluding firms that fall short.

Third, firms sometimes are uncertain about the strategies their rivals are pursuing, and have difficulty inferring cheating from marketplace observations (*i.e.*, against a "noisy" background in which prices frequently fall for other reasons like unexpected declines in demand, as discussed in Case Study II, the delicatessen hypothetical, under the heading "Predictable vs. Unpredictable Demand"). Here, the coordinating firms may find it necessary to undertake expensive strategies for deterring cheating. For example, they may reduce the gains to cheating by setting price below the level a monopolist would charge, or they may respond to the mere possibility of cheating by engaging in a price war for some time before returning to higher prices. Indeed, one of the surprising discoveries of the modern economic theory of coordinated behavior is that occasional price wars—on their face, the essence of competition—are not inconsistent with coordination and indeed may be part of the mechanism by which cheating is deterred during high price periods.

Fourth, the firms may have difficulty in identifying the price that a monopolist would set, especially when they must coordinate pricing and output over a large number of products or markets without communicating. As previously noted, however, under such circumstances, firms may employ simple rules like a common percentage or dollar price increase applied to a large class of products, rather than fine-tuning price changes product-by-product to maximize joint profits. Doing so may mean that the cartel sets the price for at least some products lower than what they would charge if able to coordinate completely.

These difficulties do not necessarily make coordination impossible. They may instead lead to occasional price reductions or price wars in response to shocks, or to pricing that is maintained above competitive levels but short of monopoly levels. Indeed, perfect coordination—in which the firms act collectively like a monopolist, then split the joint profits—is likely rare, and imperfect coordination—in which the firms earn some monopoly profits but fall short of replicating how a monopolist would behave—is likely the general rule when coordination is at all successful.

How do firms solve their cartel problems in practice? Recall our discussion of the lysine and vitamin cartels in Chapter 1. What steps did the firms involved in those cartels take to reach consensus, deter cheating, and prevent entry?

C. THE DEVELOPMENT OF TRADITIONAL CONSPIRACY LAW

In Section B we saw that the members of a cartel must accomplish three basic tasks to raise prices by restricting output. They must reach consensus on the terms of their collaboration, deter cheating on those terms, and forestall or co-opt new competition. The adoption of competition statutes does not change the importance to successful cartel coordination of executing these tasks, but antitrust laws can dramatically affect *how* firms go about accomplishing them.

Consider the legal environment confronting business managers in the United States before the passage of state antitrust laws in the 1880s and the Sherman Act in 1890. Many common law contract cases had decided that a rule of reason governed agreements by competitors to fix prices or allocate markets. At worst, a common law court might refuse to enforce the terms of a collusive undertaking. Damage awards to cartel victims or criminal sanctions for cartel members were out of the question. Business rivals met openly to coordinate their production and pricing decisions. Newspapers announced the time and place for firms in an industry to meet to discuss possibilities for creating cartels. *See* Louis Galambos, *Loose Combinations and Their Public Control Over Time, in* NATIONAL COMPETITION POLICY: HISTORIANS' PERSPECTIVES ON ANTITRUST AND BUSINESS RELATIONSHIPS IN THE UNITED STATES 143, 149–50 (FTC, Aug. 1981).

The culture of open cooperation often tolerated by the common law was slow to change even after the passage of the first antitrust statutes. In early Section 1 cases, the courts rarely confronted the question of whether challenged conduct resulted from concerted action or unilateral behavior. For example, the pipe manufacturers in *Addyston Pipe*, which we discussed in Chapter 2, did not dispute the Justice Department's contention that they coordinated their production and sales activities.

Why did the defendants in early Section 1 cases feel no urgency to show that they had acted independently? Three explanations come to mind. The first is uncertainty created by judicial efforts to define the rules for competitor collaboration from 1890 until the late 1930s. Not until 1940 in *Socony-Vacuum Oil* (*see supra* Chapter 2), did the Supreme Court make absolutely clear that some types of behavior would be prohibited categorically.

A second factor is a periodic U.S. ambivalence about the value of competition as an organizing principle for the economy. As we discussed in the *Note on Antitrust Law Developments During the Great Depression* in Chapter 2, in the first term of Franklin Roosevelt's presidency, various statutes and regulations sought to promote recovery from the Depression by relying on central planning and other forms of extensive cooperation between producers in the same industry. Government programs to displace or suppress competition probably led companies to question the intensity of the country's commitment to enforce the Sherman Act's controls on concerted behavior that restrains trade.

The third factor was the limited sanction for Sherman Act violations relative to what is available today. Consider the case of criminal penalties. In 1890, Congress made Sherman Act offenses punishable as misdemeanors and established a maximum criminal fine of $50,000. The Sherman Act's original menu of criminal sanctions remained largely unchanged until the early 1970s and private treble damage actions, although authorized by statute, were rare. Today Sherman Act violations are felonies and individual violators can be punished with prison terms of up to ten years and fines of up to $1 million. Corporate entities can be fined $100 million per offense or can pay significantly higher fines under the standards set forth in the Federal Sentencing Guidelines. *See* Sherman Act, § 1, *infra* Appendix A; UNITED STATES SENTENCING COMMISSION GUIDELINES MANUAL, § 2R1.1 (2015), http://www.ussc.gov/sites/default/files/pdf/guidelines-manual/2015/GLMFull.pdf. The two principal defendants in the vitamins price fixing cartel (Hoffmann-La Roche and BASF) paid a total of $725 million in fines to the Justice Department and saw several of their executives serve prison terms.

1. COLLUSION IN THE SHADOW OF ANTITRUST: COORDINATION STRATEGIES FOR THE FIRMS AND PROOF STRATEGIES FOR PLAINTIFFS

As the implementation of an antitrust regime creates greater dangers for certain agreements, firms desiring to coordinate output and pricing decisions with their rivals are likely to reconsider their strategies for collaboration. Recall how we used the example of a coffee shop owner in Chapter 1 to identify the basic economic purposes of antitrust law. Suppose that our coffee shop owner and four of her rivals wished to cooperate to collectively reduce output and increase prices. How might our coffee shop entrepreneurs accomplish their aims? The firms would have several options.

Form Immunized Overt Agreements with Competitors. Serious exposure for criminal and civil liability makes it hazardous for competitors to create readily observable cartel agreements. Today companies would pursue this course only if authorization by federal or state government bodies provided Sherman Act immunity. The ability of foreign, federal and state governments to immunize collective business conduct from antitrust prohibitions is discussed further in Chapter 8.

Form Overt Agreements Supported by Reasonable Business Justifications. Firms use overt agreements when they believe that their behavior conforms to antitrust standards and does not constitute a per se violation. Joint ventures, which we examined in Chapter 2, frequently are created by means of elaborate contractual documents, and their formation routinely is announced to the public. Similarly, trade and professional groups often adopt formal bylaws that may include provisions that affect competition, as we observed in cases like *National Society of Professional Engineers* and *NCAA*, also in Chapter 2. The fact of overt cooperation obviates the need for a court to devote attention to proof of concerted action.

Form Illegal Agreements Covertly with Competitors. Firms seeking to engage in forbidden concerted behavior could cooperate covertly and take precautions to avoid detection by law enforcement officials or private antitrust plaintiffs. The participants in the food additives and vitamins cartels we examined in Chapter 1 took this path. If they are careful, creative, and loyal, the cartel members can minimize the creation of direct evidence, in the form of documents or testimony by insiders, with which a plaintiff could establish the fact of collusion.

Even with precautions, cartel participants still must make difficult decisions about whether to make records of their understandings and about how to ensure that each conspirator remains faithful to the cause. The tasks of organizing and managing a cartel may be so complex that the members must maintain covert written records concerning the scheme's operation. Moreover, designing and implementing covert understandings can involve extensive communications and possible meetings among the cartel members.

Frequent communication and recourse to written records can create two nightmares for the cartel—that a prosecutor will obtain its written records, or that a disaffected cartel participant (or, perhaps, a participant's employee) will inform prosecutors and perhaps testify in court about its existence. These forms of documentary and testimonial proof, usually referred to as *direct evidence*, have sufficed in many instances to prove a conspiracy. The logic for public prosecutors to adopt amnesty, leniency, and other forms of immunity programs is to exploit the intuition of the "Prisoner's Dilemma" game, described in Sidebar 3–2 above, and induce cartel members to defect and provide direct evidence of conspiracy.

Skillful, well-disciplined cartels minimize the creation of incriminating written records and strive to hide their illicit activities from employees within their own firms. They also seek to defuse discontent among cartel members that could lead a disgruntled participant to divulge the cartel's existence. If a cartel adopts these safeguards, an antitrust plaintiff may be forced to rely entirely on *circumstantial* proof of concerted action.

When rivals have reached a covert agreement, a public prosecutor or a private plaintiff can take alternative paths to establish the existence of an illegal arrangement. The first relies on direct evidence. In *Andreas* in Chapter 1, an ADM insider (Mark Whitacre) voluntarily supplied the information that helped the Justice Department uncover the food additives cartel. Or, as Sidebar 3–1 on leniency has suggested, the public prosecutor can try to induce cartel participants to supply direct evidence of conspiracy by providing something of benefit to an informer.

Second, the plaintiff can rely on circumstantial evidence from which the finder of fact might infer concerted action. The rise of harsh penalties for cartel formation has driven would-be cartel participants to greater secrecy. This development has challenged antitrust policy to define the types of circumstantial proof that permit the finder of fact to infer that the defendants acted collectively.

Collectively Adopt "Facilitating Practices." Firms intent on coordinating their behavior might identify forms of coordinated activity that fall outside the zone of behavior that courts have denominated as per se offenses, yet which still "facilitate" coordination. Thus, firms might agree, perhaps in the guise of a trade association, to share current information about prices, production levels, costs, or inventories. They might do so in the hope that a court would (1) not deem an agreement to share such information to be a form of per se unlawful "price fixing;" (2) not permit an information-sharing agreement to serve as circumstantial evidence from which a fact finder could infer that the participants were engaging in a covert agreement to set prices themselves; and (3) not find the agreement unlawful as an unreasonable restraint on competition. The information exchange cases, which we study later in this Chapter, seek to address the third possibility.

Engage in "Conscious Parallelism." If there are sufficiently few suppliers in the industry, firms might try to coordinate their behavior and achieve higher than competitive prices simply by anticipating and responding to the moves of their rivals, as we discussed in Case Study I with respect to the four gasoline stations. In this scenario, the competitors do not form overt or covert agreements to restrict output, and they need not form overt or covert agreements to adopt facilitating practices. Instead, the oligopolists recognize and act upon their interdependence. They select strategies on the assumption that each industry member realizes that its counterparts will observe and be affected by each of its moves. They do so in the expectation that no firm will have incentives to compete more aggressively and the hope that courts will not treat the sequence of action and reaction as a form of "agreement."

For example, one firm, perhaps the largest, might act as a "price leader," while its rivals observe and quickly copy the leader's price increases. Under such circumstances, all firms may raise prices in parallel to a higher than competitive level. The result may be "parallel pricing," by which all firms raise and lower prices nearly simultaneously, and prices end up above the competitive price. Whether this conduct should be deemed an unlawful agreement on price has bedeviled antitrust for decades, as will be discussed further below.

Unilaterally Adopt Facilitating Practices. In a concentrated industry, a firm might try to enhance the quality of tacit coordination by unilaterally adopting a practice that signals to other industry members that the actor either is seeking to curb its discretion or is willing to punish rivals who compete too aggressively. The initial adopter of the practice may hope that its competitors will mimic its moves by embracing the practice as well. For example, a company might establish a widely known practice of promising to give its largest customers the benefit of any price cut given to any single customer. Because such a commitment may force a supplier to cut prices for a broad swath of its customer base if it reduces prices for any single buyer, using a "most favored nations" or "most favored customers" clause can be a way for a firm to tell its rivals that it will try to refrain from cutting prices. (*See Note on the Economic Effects of "Most Favored Nation" Provisions, infra* Chapter 6.) Because unilateral facilitating practices can be implemented without an agreement, they cannot be challenged under Section 1 of the Sherman Act. Legal strategies for scrutinizing such conduct are considered in Section E of this Chapter.

In the balance of this Chapter, we turn to how the legal system and case law have responded to the range of coordination strategies that firms have adopted in trying to avoid antitrust liability.

2.   CONSCIOUS PARALLELISM OR AGREEMENT?

In the second term of Franklin Roosevelt's presidency, the Justice Department undertook an ambitious expansion of antitrust enforcement, including a commitment to prosecute cartels aggressively. The new wave of cartel cases yielded several Supreme Court decisions that confronted the issue of identifying agreements where the plaintiff relied mainly on proof of circumstantial evidence to establish conspiracy. *Interstate Circuit, Inc. v. United States*, 306 U.S. 208 (1939), was one of the first.

Interstate Circuit involves inferring an agreement from circumstantial evidence that includes parallel price increases by rivals. In this respect it addresses an issue that courts have confronted repeatedly in the many decades since. The decision appears animated by a common concern of courts during antitrust's structuralist era, which began in the late 1930s and extended through the Chicago School revolution of the late 1970s: the fear that covert cartels and other anticompetitive conduct would go unpunished if the courts became overly cautious in identifying antitrust violations.

The agreement found in *Interstate Circuit* has an unusual structure, sometimes called a "hub and spoke" conspiracy, in which a single firm is said to have acted as a cartel manager, orchestrating an agreement among its suppliers (as in this case) or customers. The defendants conceded that they had formed vertical agreements linking film exhibitors and distributors. The legal issue was whether the distributors agreed with each other, horizontally, by making identical agreements in parallel.

INTERSTATE CIRCUIT, INC. V. UNITED STATES
Supreme Court of the United States, 1939.
306 U.S. 208, 59 S.Ct. 467, 83 L.Ed. 610.

MR. JUSTICE STONE delivered the opinion of the Court.

[This case grew out of a government lawsuit challenging the conduct of a number of firms involved in the motion picture industry in Texas during the 1930s. Two types of firms, distributors and exhibitors, were defendants. The distributors owned or controlled the copyrights for movies, and accounted for 75% of the "first-class feature films exhibited in the United States." Exhibitors, who owned local theaters, would show the films pursuant to license agreements with the distributors. Local theaters, in turn, could be divided into two groups: "first-run" theaters (that showed a film during its first exhibition in a given locality) and "second-run" theaters (that showed a film during a subsequent exhibition in that locality).

At the time of the events giving rise to this litigation, Interstate Circuit operated forty-three first-run and second-run theaters located in six Texas cities. It had a complete monopoly of first-run theaters in these cities, excepting one theater in Houston. Although Interstate operated twenty-two second-run theaters, its only second-run theater monopoly was in Galveston. In most cities, Interstate competed with other second-run theaters. Texas Consolidated operated sixty-six theaters, both first-run and second-run, all in cities different from those served by Interstate. In six leading cities, Texas Consolidated faced no competing first-run theaters. Interstate and Texas Consolidated dominated the exhibition business in the cities in which their theaters were located, together contributing more than 74% of all license fees paid by exhibitors in their territories to the leading distributors. Interstate and Texas Consolidated were affiliated with each other and both were affiliated with Paramount, one of the distributor defendants. Interstate and Consolidated were run by the same senior managers: Hoblitzelle (president of both) and O'Donnell (general manager of both). First-run theaters typically charged an admission price for adults of at least 40 cents, while second-run theaters typically charged 15 cents.

On July 11, 1934, O'Donnell sent to each of the eight branch managers of the distributor appellants a letter on Interstate's letterhead. Each letter named all eight distributor branch managers as addressees. In the letter, O'Donnell asked for compliance with two demands as a condition of Interstate's continued exhibition of the distributors' films in its 'A' or first-run theatres at a night admission of 40 cents or more. (Approximately half of the pictures released by the distributor defendants were Class "A" feature films.) One demand was that the distributors "agree that in selling their product to subsequent runs, that this 'A' product will never be exhibited at any time or in any theatre at a smaller admission price than 25 cents for adults in the evening." The other was that "on 'A' pictures which are exhibited at a night admission of 40 cents or more—they shall never be exhibited in conjunction with another feature picture under the so-called policy of double features." The letter added that with respect to the "Rio Grande Valley situation," with which Consolidated alone was concerned, "We must insist that all pictures exhibited in our 'A' theatres at a maximum night admission price of 35 cents must also be restricted to subsequent runs in the Valley at 25 cents."

Conferences followed between Hoblitzelle and O'Donnell, acting for Interstate and Consolidated, and the representatives of the various distributors. In these conferences each distributor was represented by its local branch manager and by one or more superior officials from outside the state of Texas. In the course of them each distributor agreed with Interstate to impose both the demanded restrictions upon their subsequent-run licensees in the six Texas cities served by Interstate, except Austin and Galveston, for the 1934–35 season. None of the distributors agreed to restrict subsequent runs in towns in the Rio Grande Valley served by Consolidated.

The issue presented was whether these facts established an agreement *among the distributors*. The evidence of agreement was entirely circumstantial. There was no direct testimony in the record that the distributors entered into any agreement with each other to impose the restrictions upon subsequent-run exhibitors. In order to establish agreement, the government was compelled to rely on inferences drawn from the course of conduct of the alleged conspirators. In addressing this question, the Court emphasized that each defendant was aware that Interstate was presenting the same demands to the others, and that Interstate's plan would not succeed unless all participated. Eds.]

* * *

The O'Donnell letter named on its face as addressees the eight local representatives of the distributors, and so from the beginning each of the distributors knew that the proposals were under consideration by the others. Each was aware that all were in active competition and that without substantially unanimous action with respect to the restrictions for any given territory there was risk of a substantial loss of the business and good will of the subsequent-run and independent exhibitors, but that with it there was the prospect of increased profits. There was, therefore, strong motive for concerted action, full advantage of which was taken by Interstate and Consolidated in presenting their demands to all in a single document.

There was risk, too, that without agreement diversity of action would follow. Compliance with the proposals involved a radical departure from the previous business practices of the industry and a drastic increase in admission prices of most of the subsequent-run theatres. Acceptance of the proposals was discouraged by at least three of the distributors' local managers. Independent exhibitors met and organized a futile protest which they presented to the representatives of Interstate and Consolidated. While as a result of independent negotiations either of the two restrictions without the other could have been put into effect by any one or more of the distributors and in any one or more of the Texas cities served by Interstate, the negotiations which ensued and which in fact did result in modifications of the proposals resulted in substantially unanimous action of the distributors, both as to the terms of the restrictions and in the selection of the four cities where they were to operate.

* * * [W]e are unable to find in the record any persuasive explanation, other than agreed concert of action, of the singular unanimity of action on the part of the distributors by which the proposals were carried into effect as written in four Texas cities but not in a fifth or in the Rio Grande Valley. Numerous variations in the form of the provisions in the distributors' license agreements and the fact that in later years two of them extended the restrictions into all six cities, do not weaken the significance or force of the nature of the response to the proposals made by all the distributor appellants. It taxes credulity to believe that the several distributors would, in the circumstances, have accepted and put into operation with substantial unanimity such far-reaching changes in their business methods without some understanding that all were to join, and we reject as beyond the range of probability that it was the result of mere chance.

* * *

This inference [that the distributors acted in concert and in common agreement] was supported and strengthened when the distributors, with like unanimity, failed to tender the testimony, at their command, of any officer or agent of a distributor who knew, or was in a position to know, whether in fact an agreement had been reached among them for concerted action. * * *

While the District Court's finding of an agreement of the distributors among themselves is supported by the evidence, we think that in the circumstances of this case such agreement for the imposition of the restrictions upon subsequent-run exhibitors was not a prerequisite to an unlawful conspiracy. It was enough that, knowing that concerted action was contemplated and invited, the distributors gave their adherence to the scheme and participated in it. Each distributor was advised that the others were asked to participate; each knew that cooperation was essential to successful operation of the plan. They knew that the plan, if carried out, would result in a restraint of commerce, which, we will presently point out, was unreasonable within the meaning of the Sherman Act, and knowing it, all participated in the plan. The evidence is persuasive that each distributor early became aware that the others had joined. With that knowledge they renewed the arrangement and carried it into effect for the two successive years.

It is elementary that an unlawful conspiracy may be and often is formed without simultaneous action or agreement on the part of the conspirators. * * * Acceptance by competitors, without previous agreement, of an invitation to participate in a plan, the necessary consequence of which, if carried out, is restraint of interstate commerce, is sufficient to establish an unlawful conspiracy under the Sherman Act. * * *

MR. JUSTICE FRANKFURTER took no part in the consideration or decision of this case.

[Dissenting opinion of JUSTICES ROBERTS, MCREYNOLDS, and BUTLER omitted. Eds.]

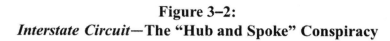

Figure 3–2:
Interstate Circuit—**The "Hub and Spoke" Conspiracy**

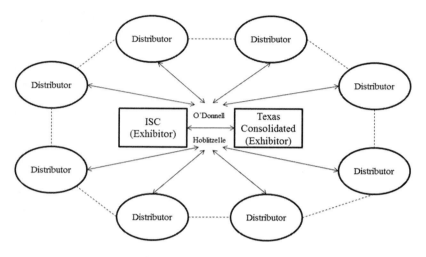

Today *Interstate Circuit* is commonly viewed as marking the outer limits of how far courts will go to infer an agreement from circumstantial evidence that includes parallel conduct. But the decision retains vitality, as shown by the Seventh Circuit's decision in *Toys "R" Us, Inc. v. FTC*, 221 F.3d 928 (7th Cir. 2000), which relied on *Interstate Circuit* to uphold an FTC decision involving a "hub and spoke" conspiracy. The FTC concluded that Toys "R" Us ("TRU") had used a series of vertical agreements with each of ten leading toy manufacturers to orchestrate a horizontal agreement among the manufacturers to boycott certain discounting retailers (warehouse club stores). In affirming the FTC, the circuit court wrote:

> [T]he TRU case if anything presents a more compelling case for inferring horizontal agreement than did *Interstate Circuit*, because not only was the manufacturers' decision to stop dealing with the warehouse clubs an abrupt shift from the past, and not only is it suspicious for a manufacturer to deprive itself of a profitable sales outlet, but the record here included the direct evidence of communications that was missing in *Interstate Circuit*.

Toys "R" Us, Inc., 221 F.3d at 935. More recently, in *United States v. Apple, Inc.*, 791 F.3d 290 (2d Cir. 2015), which we discussed in Chapter 2, the Second Circuit affirmed a district court's finding that Apple orchestrated a conspiracy among a group of major book publishers to raise the price of e-books in connection with Apple's launch of its iBookstore application and iPad tablet. Unlike *Interstate Circuit* and *Toys "R" Us*, the question at trial was not whether the firms along the "rim" of the alleged conspiracy (at the end of the "spokes") had agreed with each other; it was whether Apple, the firm said to be the "hub," had joined and facilitated an agreement along the rim among the book publishers.

Fifteen years after *Interstate Circuit*, the Supreme Court issued another decision on inferring agreement from circumstantial evidence involving parallel conduct that adopted a more cautious tone. In *Theatre Enters., Inc. v. Paramount Film Distrib. Corp.*, 346 U.S. 537 (1954), a private treble damage action, the Court considered the conduct of movie distributors who had refused to allow an exhibitor access to first-run films for showing in a suburban theater. The defendant distributors denied that they had acted in concert and offered economic justifications showing why each had chosen independently to follow the same course of action. Most importantly, at that time suburban theaters were served by limited public transportation facilities and had a much smaller drawing area than downtown theaters. Accordingly, "[t]he downtown theaters offer[ed] far greater opportunities for the widespread advertisement and exploitation of newly released features, which is thought necessary to maximize the overall return from subsequent runs as well as first-runs." *Id.* at 540. After trial, the jury returned a verdict for the defendants. On appeal, the suburban exhibitor urged that the trial judge should have directed a verdict in its favor. In sustaining the jury's verdict, the Supreme Court cautioned that "[c]ircumstantial evidence of consciously parallel behavior may have made heavy inroads into the traditional judicial attitude toward conspiracy; but 'conscious parallelism' has not read conspiracy out of the Sherman Act entirely." *Id.* at 541.

Interstate Circuit and *Theatre Enterprises* both accept that a court may apply the label of "concerted action" to interfirm coordination accomplished by means other than a direct exchange of assurances. They also both accept that courts may infer agreements from circumstantial proof suggesting that the challenged behavior more likely than not was the result of a jointly determined course of action. But they also establish that courts may not find concerted action where a plaintiff shows only that the defendants recognized their interdependence and simply mimicked their competitors' conduct. Additional evidence beyond parallel conduct, today termed "plus factors," would be required.

Theatre Enterprises signaled to the lower courts that they should be wary of deeming mere parallel conduct among oligopolists an "agreement" for purposes of the Sherman Act. Recall that *Theatre Enterprises* was written decades before *Broadcast Music* and *NCAA*, and thus during an era in which the per se prohibition against price-fixing was broadly read, as suggested by footnote 59 in *Socony-Vacuum Oil*. Could the Supreme Court's caution against inferring agreement simply from parallel conduct be interpreted as an adaptation to a substantive legal rule that made it very difficult for defendants to avoid liability once an agreement concerning price had been found? Or are other policy issues at stake? A famous and continuing academic debate on the topic, sketched in Sidebar 3–3, explored the policy concerns.

Sidebar 3–3:
The Turner/Posner Debate on Conscious Parallelism

The Supreme Court's agreement decisions from *Interstate Circuit* to *Theatre Enterprises* inspired a famous debate during the 1960s about the application of Section 1 to oligopoly behavior. The contestants were Donald F. Turner, a Harvard Law School professor who served as Assistant Attorney General for Antitrust in the mid-1960s, and Richard A. Posner, a professor at the University of Chicago Law School and subsequently a judge of the U.S. court of appeals. Endorsing the cautious approach of *Theatre Enterprises,* Turner argued that interdependent behavior should not be interpreted as an illegal conspiracy under Section 1. Donald F. Turner, *The Definition of Agreement Under the Sherman Act: Conscious Parallelism and Refusals to Deal*, 75 HARV. L. REV. 655 (1962). Turner explained that an oligopolist behaves exactly as a seller in a competitive industry, except that it also accounts for its rivals' reactions. From this he concluded that it would be unreasonable to interpret the Sherman Act to condemn rational and unavoidable unilateral behavior, even when the economic consequences mirrored those of conspiracy.

Even if oligopoly behavior were held illegal, Turner doubted that any remedy available under Section 1 would prove effective. Injunctive relief that directed defendants to ignore their rivals would be anomalous and counterproductive, for it would order them to make irrational price and output decisions. Commanding firms to price their goods at their marginal costs (*i.e.*, as if the market were competitive) would involve the courts in continuous regulation for which they are ill-equipped. These problems framing injunctive relief suggested a closely related problem with an aggressive approach to inferring an agreement from circumstantial evidence: if antitrust liability obtained for interdependent conduct, firms with only a handful of rivals, which necessarily recognize their interdependence, would appear to have no practical way to avoid liability.

Neither would dissolution or other structural solutions seem appropriate, since the essence of the Section 1 offense would be the interdependence theory, and this points to the seller's conduct (interdependent pricing) rather than market structure as ultimately being responsible for the result. In a later paper, though, Turner contended that the proper solution to the oligopoly problem would be to restructure oligopolists into smaller units, either by charging them with joint monopolization under Section 2 or by adopting special legislation. *See* Donald F. Turner, *The Scope of Antitrust and Other Economic Regulatory Policies*, 82 HARV. L. REV. 1207, 1217–31 (1969).

In contrast, Judge Posner suggested that these analytical difficulties might be overcome by an alternative theory. *See* Richard A. Posner, *Oligopoly and the Antitrust Laws: A Suggested Approach*, 21 STAN. L. REV. 1562 (1969). Posner argued that oligopoly markets involve concerted action in that they manifest a tacit output agreement among sellers. In a concentrated market, sellers must act voluntarily to translate their mutual dependence into oligopoly prices. This constitutes a meeting of the minds even though there is no overt communication among sellers. Each seller communicates its offer to the others by restricting output and thereby maintains its prices above the competitive level. If oligopoly pricing is to succeed, the seller's rivals must cooperate by curbing their output, as well. Posner argued that since "tacit collusion or noncompetitive pricing is not inherent in an oligopolistic market structure but, like conventional cartelizing, requires additional, voluntary behavior by the sellers," it violates Section 1. *Id.* at 1578. Nor did Posner find the problem of formulating an effective remedy under Section 1 insoluble. Posner believed that there were specific forms of behavior beyond the mere fact of interdependence that could be enjoined in a practical way. For an updated presentation of his critique of Turner, see RICHARD A. POSNER, ANTITRUST LAW 55–60 (2d ed. 2001).

The Turner/Posner debate arguably reflects a difference in judgment about the relative "error costs" of not finding agreement when firms are acting in ways that harm competition (false acquittals), versus finding agreement when firms are not harming competition or competition is harmed but there is no practical remedy (false convictions). From this perspective, Posner's view makes sense if firms that are able to solve their cartel problems (reaching consensus, deterring cheating and preventing new competition) to achieve higher than competitive prices through coordination almost invariably engage in explicit communication or other forms of conduct that can be enjoined. Turner's view makes sense if, in industries where firms can readily solve their cartel problems, high prices frequently result from leader-follower behavior that cannot practically be enjoined. For further discussion of the implications of the latter view, see Sidebar 3–5.

On the whole, Turner's position in the debate has prevailed in subsequent judicial treatments of the agreement issue in Section 1 litigation involving oligopolies. Courts consistently have held that conscious parallelism alone does not support an inference of agreement. *See, e.g., Bell Atl. Corp. v. Twombly*, 550 U.S. 544, 553–54 (2007). It bears repeating, though, that judges enjoy substantial discretion to define the elements of behavior that, when added to conscious parallelism, permit the fact finder to conclude that an agreement existed. After reciting the *Theatre Enterprises* admonition that conscious parallelism is not enough, some decisions have gone to great lengths to identify additional behavior from which an inference of agreement might be inferred.

Yet Posner's position continues to have adherents. Posner reignited the debate by reaffirming his views in *In re High Fructose Corn Syrup Antitrust Litigation*, 295 F.3d 651 (7th Cir. 2002) (Posner, J.). Professor Louis Kaplow has also taken Posner's side. Louis Kaplow, *An Economic Approach to Price Fixing*, 77 ANTITRUST L.J. 343 (2011); LOUIS KAPLOW, COMPETITION POLICY AND PRICE FIXING (2013). Kaplow observes that the right question is not "what is an agreement?", but rather what legal rule best promotes social welfare. He suggests that the social benefits from deterring oligopolistic price-elevation may be large, and contends that damage remedies for antitrust violations may deter undesirable conduct even when injunctions are difficult to craft. Kaplow recognizes that an approach that deems parallel price increases anticompetitive with relatively little additional evidence, and penalizes the firms involved with damages, may at times chill price increases when such conduct would be beneficial. For example, it may discourage a firm from raising its price when costs increase, particularly if the cost increase would be difficult to prove. But he argues that the social benefits of increased deterrence likely exceed the social costs of chilling beneficial conduct.

Kaplow's position has been criticized by Professor William Page, who ties the definition of agreement to objective evidence of communication. *See* William H. Page, *Objective and Subjective Theories of Concerted Action*, 79 ANTITRUST L.J. 215 (2013). *Cf.* Gregory J. Werden, *Economic Evidence on the*

Existence of Collusion: Reconciling Antitrust Law with Oligopoly Theory, 71 ANTITRUST L.J. 719, 780 (2004) (based on "policy and practical considerations" rather than modern economic theory, agreement should not be inferred absent evidence of communication among defendants) (predating Kaplow). Surprisingly, Judge Posner himself has questioned Kaplow's argument, both in scholarship and in writing an opinion for the Seventh Circuit we will read later in this Chapter. In reviewing Kaplow's book Posner said that in his earlier work, he "didn't sufficiently appreciate the force of Turner's doubts about the feasibility of an antitrust remedy for tacit collusion." Richard A. Posner, *Review of* KAPLOW, COMPETITION POLICY AND PRICE FIXING, 79 ANTITRUST L.J. 761 (2014). Posner expressed "sympathy with Kaplow's frustration at allowing tacit colluders to slip through the antitrust net," but "[no] confidence that punishing tacit colluders under antitrust law can produce net social benefits" because there is no good answer to the question of what courts should tell firms acting interdependently without communicating to do in order to avoid liability and exposure to damages. *Id.* at 767. Here, Posner suggests that Kaplow's approach is not administrable, and the costs of chilling procompetitive conduct are greater than Kaplow supposes. *Accord, In re Text Messaging Antitrust Litigation,* 782 F.3d 867, 873–74 (7th Cir. 2015) (Posner, J.).

As an example, return to the delicatessens described in Case Study II. If leader-follower conduct could be deemed an agreement, exposing the delis to treble damages, how would the firms be expected to act in response? Will delis avoid raising price or giving customers advance notice of future price increases for fear of being accused of soliciting collusion in the event rivals later raise prices too? Will they avoid even looking at rivals' prices, even if doing so would help them learn about changing market conditions in the same way that competitive firms would learn about market demand and costs through prices? If another deli raises price, will delis avoid raising prices as well to limit the threat of antitrust liability, and, in consequence, price below the competitive level? For how long will they be led to keep prices too low? If prices go up because costs have increased, would the delis be required to document those cost increases to avoid liability in the event costs increase for their rivals as well and all firms raise prices at the same time? Can they provide convincing documentation if the cost increases did not arise from higher wholesale prices of bread and lunch meat, but from an increase in the market demand for takeout and catering services that requires delis temporarily to use their wait staffs to make sandwiches, slowing their sit-down restaurant service and reducing the number of customers they can serve at tables? In short, if a court would have nothing to enjoin, can firms faced with the prospect of substantial damages practically alter their behavior to avoid liability without seriously chilling procompetitive conduct? Or is Kaplow right to suppose that any resulting social harms would be outweighed by the social benefits of increased deterrence of oligopolistic price-elevation?

Interstate Circuit and *Theatre Enterprises* reflect a tension in the interpretation of Sherman Act § 1. *Interstate Circuit* demands little evidence beyond parallel conduct before inferring conspiracy from circumstantial evidence, while *Theatre Enterprises* emphasizes the need for such evidence. The *Interstate Circuit* approach is particularly attractive if the primary policy concern is with deterring harmful conduct-cartels pushed underground by the Sherman Act's prohibition on conspiracy, or price elevation resulting from oligopolistic interdependence. The *Theatre Enterprises* caution is particularly attractive if the primary policy concern is with chilling procompetitive conduct—whether by discouraging aggressive competition among firms fearful of being found to have conspired, or by subjecting firms that have not harmed competition to possibly costly and time-consuming litigation or to settlements entered into in order to avoid litigation costs and the risks of continued litigation. This policy tension underlies the Posner-Turner debate, described in Sidebar 3–3.

The same policy tension arose in a different way in two Supreme Court decisions from the mid-1980s, *Monsanto* and *Matsushita*. In returning to the agreement question in these matters, the Supreme Court reflected both an awareness of developments in the economic literature concerning efforts by competitors to coordinate their activities and a heightened concern about the potential over-inclusiveness of certain antitrust rules that forbade agreements as illegal per se.

In *Monsanto Co. v. Spray-Rite Service Corp.*, 465 U.S. 752 (1984), which we will discuss in Chapter 6, the Court reaffirmed the proposition—since abandoned—that an agreement between a manufacturer and a distributor or retailer to set a minimum price for the resale of its products is illegal per se. More importantly, it focused on the standard of proof that plaintiffs must satisfy when they seek to establish the fact of such an agreement. In an influential passage, the Supreme Court observed:

The correct standard is that there must be evidence that tends to exclude the possibility of independent action by the [parties]. That is, there must be direct or circumstantial evidence that reasonably tends to prove that [the parties] had a conscious commitment to a common scheme designed to achieve an unlawful objective.

465 U.S. at 768.

In our next case, *Matsushita*, which was decided two years later, the Court extended *Monsanto*'s formulation of the agreement requirement to certain horizontal arrangements. The majority opinion was authored by Justice Lewis F. Powell, who also authored the Court's opinion in *Monsanto*.

MATSUSHITA ELECTRIC INDUSTRIAL CO. v. ZENITH RADIO CORP.

United States Supreme Court, 1986.
475 U.S. 574, 106 S.Ct. 1348, 89 L.Ed.2d 538.

JUSTICE POWELL delivered the opinion of the Court.

This case requires that we again consider the standard district courts must apply when deciding whether to grant summary judgment in an antitrust conspiracy case.

I

* * *

A.

Petitioners, defendants below, are 21 corporations that manufacture or sell "consumer electronic products" (CEPs)—for the most part, television sets. Petitioners include both Japanese manufacturers of CEPs and American firms, controlled by Japanese parents, that sell the Japanese-manufactured products. Respondents, plaintiffs below, are Zenith Radio Corporation (Zenith) and National Union Electric Corporation (NUE). Zenith is an American firm that manufactures and sells television sets. NUE is the corporate successor to Emerson Radio Company, an American firm that manufactured and sold television sets until 1970, when it withdrew from the market after sustaining substantial losses. Zenith and NUE began this lawsuit in 1974, claiming that petitioners had illegally conspired to drive American firms from the American CEP market. According to respondents, the gist of this conspiracy was a " 'scheme to raise, fix and maintain artificially *high* prices for television receivers sold by [petitioners] in Japan and, at the same time, to fix and maintain *low* prices for television receivers exported to and sold in the United States.' " These "low prices" were allegedly at levels that produced substantial losses for petitioners. The conspiracy allegedly began as early as 1953, and according to respondents was in full operation by sometime in the late 1960s. * * *

After several years of detailed discovery, petitioners filed motions for summary judgment on all claims against them. The District Court directed the parties to file, with preclusive effect, "Final Pretrial Statements" listing all the documentary evidence that would be offered if the case proceeded to trial. Respondents filed such a statement, and petitioners responded with a series of motions challenging the admissibility of respondents' evidence. In three detailed opinions, the District Court found the bulk of the evidence on which Zenith and NUE relied inadmissible.

The District Court then turned to petitioners' motions for summary judgment. In an opinion spanning 217 pages, the court found that the admissible evidence did not raise a genuine issue of material fact as to the existence of the alleged conspiracy. * * *

B.

The Court of Appeals for the Third Circuit reversed. * * *

We granted certiorari to determine (i) whether the Court of Appeals applied the proper standards in evaluating the District Court's decision to grant petitioners' motion for summary judgment, and (ii) whether petitioners could be held liable under the antitrust laws for a conspiracy in part compelled by a foreign sovereign. We reverse on the first issue, but do not reach the second.

II

We begin by emphasizing what respondents' claim is *not*. Respondents cannot recover antitrust damages based solely on an alleged cartelization of the Japanese market, because American antitrust laws do not regulate the competitive conditions of other nations' economies. Nor can respondents recover damages for any conspiracy by petitioners to charge higher than competitive prices in the American market. Such conduct would indeed violate the Sherman Act, *United States v. Trenton Potteries Co.*, 273 U.S. 392, 47 S.Ct. 377 (1927); *United States v. Socony-Vacuum Oil Co.*, 310 U.S. 150, 223, 60 S.Ct. 811, 844 (1940), but it could not injure respondents: as petitioners' competitors, respondents stand to gain from any conspiracy to raise the market price in CEPs. Finally, for the same reason, respondents cannot recover for a conspiracy to impose nonprice restraints that have the effect of either raising market price or limiting output. Such restrictions, though harmful to competition, actually *benefit* competitors by making supracompetitive pricing more attractive. * * *

Respondents nevertheless argue that these supposed conspiracies, if not themselves grounds for recovery of antitrust damages, are circumstantial evidence of another conspiracy that *is* cognizable: a conspiracy to monopolize the American market by means of pricing below the market level. The thrust of respondents' argument is that petitioners used their monopoly profits from the Japanese market to fund a concerted campaign to price predatorily and thereby drive respondents and other American manufacturers of CEPs out of business. Once successful, according to respondents, petitioners would cartelize the American CEP market, restricting output and raising prices above the level that fair competition would produce. The resulting monopoly profits, respondents contend, would more than compensate petitioners for the losses they incurred through years of pricing below market level.

The Court of Appeals found that respondents' allegation of a horizontal conspiracy to engage in predatory pricing, if proved, would be a *per se* violation of § 1 of the Sherman Act. Petitioners did not appeal from that conclusion. The issue in this case thus becomes whether respondents adduced sufficient evidence in support of their theory to survive summary judgment. We therefore examine the principles that govern the summary judgment determination.

III

To survive petitioners' motion for summary judgment, respondents must establish that there is a genuine issue of material fact as to whether petitioners entered into an illegal conspiracy that caused respondents to suffer a cognizable injury. Fed.Rule Civ.Proc. 56(e). * * * This showing has two components. First, respondents must show more than a conspiracy in violation of the antitrust laws; they must show an injury to them resulting from the illegal conduct. Respondents charge petitioners with a whole host of conspiracies in restraint of trade. Except for the alleged conspiracy to monopolize the American market through predatory pricing, these alleged conspiracies could not have caused respondents to suffer an "antitrust injury," * * * because they actually tended to benefit respondents. Therefore, unless, in context, evidence of these "other" conspiracies raises a genuine issue concerning the existence of a predatory pricing conspiracy, that evidence cannot defeat petitioners' summary judgment motion.

Second, the issue of fact must be "genuine." Fed.Rules Civ.Proc. 56(c), (e). * * * Where the record taken as a whole could not lead a rational trier of fact to find for the non-moving party, there is no "genuine issue for trial."

It follows from these settled principles that if the factual context renders respondents' claim implausible—if the claim is one that simply makes no economic sense—respondents must come forward with more persuasive evidence to support their claim than would otherwise be necessary. * * *

Respondents correctly note that "[o]n summary judgment the inferences to be drawn from the underlying facts . . . must be viewed in the light most favorable to the party opposing the motion." But antitrust law limits the range of permissible inferences from ambiguous evidence in a § 1 case. Thus, in *Monsanto Co. v. Spray-Rite Service Corp.*, 465 U.S. 752, 104 S.Ct. 1464 (1984), we held that conduct as consistent with permissible competition as with illegal conspiracy does not, standing alone, support an inference of antitrust conspiracy. To survive a motion for summary judgment or for a directed verdict, a plaintiff seeking damages for a violation of § 1 must present evidence "that tends to exclude the possibility" that the alleged conspirators acted independently. 465 U.S., at 764, 104 S.Ct., at 1471. Respondents in this case, in other words, must show that the inference of conspiracy is reasonable in light of the competing inferences of independent action or collusive action that could not have harmed respondents.

Petitioners argue that these principles apply fully to this case. According to petitioners, the alleged conspiracy is one that is economically irrational and practically infeasible. Consequently, petitioners contend, they had no motive to engage in the alleged predatory pricing conspiracy; indeed, they had a strong motive *not* to conspire in the manner respondents allege. Petitioners argue that, in light of the absence of any apparent motive and the ambiguous nature of the evidence of conspiracy, no trier of fact reasonably could find that the conspiracy with which petitioners are charged actually existed. This argument requires us to consider the nature of the alleged conspiracy and the practical obstacles to its implementation.

IV

A.

A predatory pricing conspiracy is by nature speculative. Any agreement to price below the competitive level requires the conspirators to forgo profits that free competition would offer them. The forgone profits may be considered an investment in the future. For the investment to be rational, the conspirators must have a reasonable expectation of recovering, in the form of later monopoly profits, more than the losses suffered. * * * [T]he success of such schemes is inherently uncertain: the short-run loss is definite, but the long-run gain depends on successfully neutralizing the competition. Moreover, it is not enough simply to achieve monopoly power, as monopoly pricing may breed quick entry by new competitors eager to share in the excess profits. The success of any predatory scheme depends on *maintaining* monopoly power for long enough both to recoup the predator's losses and to harvest some additional gain. Absent some assurance that the hoped-for monopoly will materialize, *and* that it can be sustained for a significant period of time, "[t]he predator must make a substantial investment with no assurance that it will pay off." For this reason, there is a consensus among commentators that predatory pricing schemes are rarely tried, and even more rarely successful.

These observations apply even to predatory pricing by a *single firm* seeking monopoly power. In this case, respondents allege that a large number of firms have conspired over a period of many years to charge below-market prices in order to stifle competition. Such a conspiracy is incalculably more difficult to execute than an analogous plan undertaken by a single predator. The conspirators must allocate the losses to be sustained during the conspiracy's operation, and must also allocate any gains to be realized from its success. Precisely because success is speculative and depends on a willingness to endure losses for an indefinite period, each conspirator has a strong incentive to cheat, letting its partners suffer the losses necessary to destroy the competition while sharing in any gains if the conspiracy succeeds. The necessary allocation is therefore difficult to accomplish. Yet if conspirators cheat to any substantial extent, the conspiracy must fail, because its success depends on depressing the market price for *all* buyers of CEPs. If there are too few goods at the artificially low price to satisfy demand, the would-be victims of the conspiracy can continue to sell at the "real" market price, and the conspirators suffer losses to little purpose.

Finally, if predatory pricing conspiracies are generally unlikely to occur, they are especially so where, as here, the prospects of attaining monopoly power seem slight. In order to recoup their losses, petitioners must obtain enough market power to set higher than competitive prices, and then must sustain those prices long enough to earn in excess profits what they earlier gave up in below-cost prices. Two decades after their conspiracy is alleged to have commenced, petitioners appear to be far from achieving this goal: the two largest shares of the retail market in television sets are held by RCA and respondent Zenith, not by any of petitioners. * * * Moreover, those shares, which together approximate 40% of sales, did not decline appreciably during the 1970's. Petitioners' collective share rose rapidly during this period, from one-fifth or less of the relevant markets to close to 50%. Neither the District Court nor the Court of Appeals found, however, that petitioners' share presently allows them to charge monopoly prices; to the contrary, respondents contend that the conspiracy is ongoing—that petitioners are still artificially *depressing* the market price in order to drive Zenith out of the market. The data in the record strongly suggest that that goal is yet far distant.

The alleged conspiracy's failure to achieve its ends in the two decades of its asserted operation is strong evidence that the conspiracy does not in fact exist. Since the losses in such a conspiracy accrue before the gains, they must be "repaid" with interest. And because the alleged losses have accrued over the course of two decades, the conspirators could well require a correspondingly long time to recoup. Maintaining supracompetitive prices in turn depends on the continued cooperation of the conspirators, on the inability of other would-be competitors to enter the market, and (not incidentally) on the conspirators' ability to escape antitrust liability for their *minimum* price-fixing cartel.[16] Each of these factors weighs more heavily as the time needed to recoup losses grows. If the losses have been substantial—as would likely be necessary in order to drive out the competition[17]—petitioners would most likely have to sustain their cartel for years simply to break even.

Nor does the possibility that petitioners have obtained supracompetitive profits in the Japanese market change this calculation. Whether or not petitioners have the *means* to sustain substantial losses in this country over a long period of time, they have no *motive* to sustain such losses absent some strong likelihood that the alleged conspiracy in this country will eventually pay off. The courts below found no evidence of any such success, and—as indicated above—the facts actually are to the contrary: RCA and Zenith, not any of the petitioners, continue to hold the largest share of the American retail market in color television sets. More important, there is nothing to suggest any relationship between petitioners' profits in Japan and the amount petitioners could expect to gain from a conspiracy to monopolize the American market. In the absence of any such evidence, the possible existence of supracompetitive profits in Japan simply cannot overcome the economic obstacles to the ultimate success of this alleged predatory conspiracy.[18]

B.

In *Monsanto,* we emphasized that courts should not permit factfinders to infer conspiracies when such inferences are implausible, because the effect of such practices is often to deter procompetitive conduct. Respondents, petitioners' competitors, seek to hold petitioners liable for damages caused by the alleged conspiracy to cut prices. Moreover, they seek to establish this conspiracy indirectly, through evidence of other combinations * * * whose natural tendency is to raise prices, and through evidence of rebates and other price-cutting activities that respondents argue tend to prove a combination to suppress prices.[19] But cutting prices

---

[16] The alleged predatory scheme makes sense only if petitioners can recoup their losses. In light of the large number of firms involved here, petitioners can achieve this only by engaging in some form of price fixing *after* they have succeeded in driving competitors from the market. Such price fixing would, of course, be an independent violation of § 1 of the Sherman Act. *United States v. Socony-Vacuum Oil Co.,* 310 U.S. 150, 60 S.Ct. 811 (1940).

[17] The predators' losses must actually *increase* as the conspiracy nears its objective: the greater the predators' market share, the more products the predators sell; but since every sale brings with it a loss, an increase in market share also means an increase in predatory losses.

[18] The same is true of any supposed excess production capacity that petitioners may have possessed. The existence of plant capacity that exceeds domestic demand does tend to establish the ability to sell products abroad. It does not, however, provide a motive for selling at prices lower than necessary to obtain sales; nor does it explain why petitioners would be willing to *lose* money in the United States market without some reasonable prospect of recouping their investment.

[19] Respondents also rely on an expert study suggesting that petitioners have sold their products in the American market at substantial losses. The relevant study is not based on actual cost data; rather, it consists of expert opinion based on a mathematical construction that in turn rests on assumptions about petitioners' costs. The District Court analyzed those assumptions in

in order to increase business often is the very essence of competition. Thus, mistaken inferences in cases such as this one are especially costly, because they chill the very conduct the antitrust laws are designed to protect. "[W]e must be concerned lest a rule or precedent that authorizes a search for a particular type of undesirable pricing behavior end up by discouraging legitimate price competition."

In most cases, this concern must be balanced against the desire that illegal conspiracies be identified and punished. That balance is, however, unusually one-sided in cases such as this one. As we earlier explained, predatory pricing schemes require conspirators to suffer losses in order eventually to realize their illegal gains; moreover, the gains depend on a host of uncertainties, making such schemes more likely to fail than to succeed. These economic realities tend to make predatory pricing conspiracies self-deterring: unlike most other conduct that violates the antitrust laws, failed predatory pricing schemes are costly to the conspirators. Finally, unlike predatory pricing by a single firm, *successful* predatory pricing conspiracies involving a large number of firms can be identified and punished once they succeed, since some form of minimum price-fixing agreement would be necessary in order to reap the benefits of predation. Thus, there is little reason to be concerned that by granting summary judgment in cases where the evidence of conspiracy is speculative or ambiguous, courts will encourage such conspiracies.

V

* * * [P]etitioners had no motive to enter into the alleged conspiracy. To the contrary, as presumably rational businesses, petitioners had every incentive *not* to engage in the conduct with which they are charged, for its likely effect would be to generate losses for petitioners with no corresponding gains. The Court of Appeals did not take account of the absence of a plausible motive to enter into the alleged predatory pricing conspiracy. It focused instead on whether there was "direct evidence of concert of action." The Court of Appeals erred in two respects: (i) the "direct evidence" on which the court relied had little, if any, relevance to the alleged predatory pricing conspiracy; and (ii) the court failed to consider the absence of a plausible motive to engage in predatory pricing.

The "direct evidence" on which the court relied was evidence of *other* combinations, not of a predatory pricing conspiracy. Evidence that petitioners conspired to raise prices in Japan provides little, if any, support for respondents' claims: a conspiracy to increase profits in one market does

---

some detail and found them both implausible and inconsistent with record evidence. Although the Court of Appeals reversed the District Court's finding that the expert report was inadmissible, the court did not disturb the District Court's analysis of the factors that substantially undermine the probative value of that evidence. We find the District Court's analysis persuasive. Accordingly, in our view the expert opinion evidence of below-cost pricing has little probative value in comparison with the economic factors * * * that suggest that such conduct is irrational.

not tend to show a conspiracy to sustain losses in another. Evidence that petitioners agreed to fix *minimum* prices * * * for the American market actually works in petitioners' favor, because it suggests that petitioners were seeking to place a floor under prices rather than to lower them. The same is true of evidence that petitioners agreed to limit the number of distributors of their products in the American * * *. That practice may have facilitated a horizontal territorial allocation, see *United States v. Topco Associates, Inc.,* 405 U.S. 596, 92 S.Ct. 1126, but its natural effect would be to raise market prices rather than reduce them. Evidence that tends to support any of these collateral conspiracies thus says little, if anything, about the existence of a conspiracy to charge below-market prices in the American market over a period of two decades.

That being the case, the absence of any plausible motive to engage in the conduct charged is highly relevant to whether a "genuine issue for trial" exists within the meaning of Rule 56(e). Lack of motive bears on the range of permissible conclusions that might be drawn from ambiguous evidence: if petitioners had no rational economic motive to conspire, and if their conduct is consistent with other, equally plausible explanations, the conduct does not give rise to an inference of conspiracy. Here, the conduct in question consists largely of (i) pricing at levels that succeeded in taking business away from respondents, and (ii) arrangements that may have limited petitioners' ability to compete with each other (and thus kept prices from going even lower). This conduct suggests either that petitioners behaved competitively, or that petitioners conspired to *raise* prices. Neither possibility is consistent with an agreement among 21 companies to price below-market levels. Moreover, the predatory pricing scheme that this conduct is said to prove is one that makes no practical sense: it calls for petitioners to destroy companies larger and better established than themselves, a goal that remains far distant more than two decades after the conspiracy's birth. Even had they succeeded in obtaining their monopoly, there is nothing in the record to suggest that they could recover the losses they would need to sustain along the way. In sum, in light of the absence of any rational motive to conspire, neither petitioners' pricing practices, nor their conduct in the Japanese market, nor their agreements respecting prices and distribution in the American market, suffice to create a "genuine issue for trial." Fed.Rule Civ.Proc. 56(e).[21]

On remand, the Court of Appeals is free to consider whether there is other evidence that is sufficiently unambiguous to permit a trier of fact to find that petitioners conspired to price predatorily for two decades despite the absence of any apparent motive to do so. The evidence must "ten[d] to

---

[21] We do not imply that, if petitioners had had a plausible reason to conspire, ambiguous conduct could suffice to create a triable issue of conspiracy. Our decision in *Monsanto Co. v. Spray-Rite Service Corp.,* 465 U.S. 752, 104 S.Ct. 1464 (1984), establishes that conduct that is as consistent with permissible competition as with illegal conspiracy does not, without more, support even an inference of conspiracy. *Id.,* at 763–764, 104 S.Ct., at 1470.

exclude the possibility" that petitioners underpriced respondents to compete for business rather than to implement an economically senseless conspiracy. *Monsanto,* 465 U.S. at 764, 104 S.Ct., at 1471. In the absence of such evidence, there is no "genuine issue for trial" under Rule 56(e), and petitioners are entitled to have summary judgment reinstated.

* * *

[Dissenting opinion of JUSTICES WHITE, BRENNAN, BLACKMUN, and STEVENS omitted. Eds.]

As in *Monsanto,* the Court's analysis of the agreement issue in *Matsushita* tried to reduce error costs associated with overly broad application of substantive liability standards. In *Matsushita* the alleged horizontal conspiracy consisted of a two-part concerted scheme by Japanese producers of consumer electronic equipment to price above costs in Japan: to use supracompetitive profits from the cartel in Japan to cross-subsidize collusive efforts to set prices at predatorily low levels in the United States, and later to raise prices above competitive levels in the United States once U.S. manufacturers had left the market. In such a setting, the Court emphasized that mistaken inferences of conspiracy could injure consumers by deterring firms from offering low prices.

At first glance, *Matsushita* might seem to have relatively limited application for Section 1 agreement jurisprudence. Few horizontal conspiracy cases allege that the defendants conspired to set prices below cost. The common horizontal restraint claim, as in the lysine and vitamins cartel prosecutions, argues that the defendants colluded to raise prices or restrict output-conduct that, unlike the asserted below cost pricing cartel in *Matsushita,* offers consumers fewer benefits and therefore, one might suppose, could be subject to more lenient standards of proof. The caution mandated by *Matsushita* might not be warranted where the challenged behavior poses greater dangers to the competitive process and enforcement false positives are less likely to harm society. But *Matsushita* has not been limited to its facts and instead has been read broadly in subsequent lower court decisions and by the Supreme Court, as is discussed in the Note following Sidebar 3–4. Sidebar 3–4 provides some additional insight into *Matsushita.*

Sidebar 3–4:
Matsushita-Perspectives from the Marshall Papers[a]

The papers of Justice Thurgood Marshall reveal that *Matsushita*, one of the most important pro-defendant Supreme Court decisions of the 1980s, very nearly was a plaintiff's victory.

After the Third Circuit reversed the district court's grant of summary judgment in 1983, the defendants filed a petition for a writ of certiorari with the Supreme Court. On April 1, 1985, the Court granted the writ, but soon had second thoughts. Several members of the Court found daunting the dispute's factual complexity and voluminous record—circumstances ultimately detailed in Justice Powell's majority opinion, excerpted above. By mid-June 1985, several justices seemed to conclude that the case was "factbound"—a decision so heavily dependent on idiosyncratic facts that it was poorly suited to serve as a vehicle for the Court to state principles of general application for future disputes. During a meeting on June 13, 1985, and in correspondence among the justices, the Court considered whether to "dismiss certiorari as improvidently granted" (or, in the Court's jargon, "DIG" the case). Fearing that a decision to DIG the case might create confusion about why the Court changed direction, the Court proceeded to hear argument and decide the matter.

Oral argument took place on November 12, 1985. The Marshall papers indicate that, soon after oral argument, five members of the court (Justices Blackmun, Brennan, Marshall, Stevens, and White) voted either to affirm the decision of the Third Circuit or to dismiss the original grant of certiorari as improvidently granted. Either outcome would have vindicated the plaintiffs by leaving in place the decision of the court of appeals. By the week's end, however, the alignment had changed. In a letter of November 15, 1985, Justice Marshall told Chief Justice Burger that "I have reexamined my position in this case and would like to change my vote from Affirm to Reverse." Informed of the switch in Justice Marshall's vote, Justice Powell proceeded to draft the majority opinion that would be joined by the Chief Justice and Justices Marshall, O'Connor, and Rehnquist.

Why did Justice Marshall change his vote and transform what had shaped up as a 5–4 plaintiff's victory into a 5–4 defendant's triumph? Perhaps it was simply the second thoughts of a Justice whose past decisions occasionally had revealed skepticism about the proper scope of antitrust private treble damage actions. Justice Marshall, after all, previously had authored the *Brunswick* decision (*see supra* Chapter 1) and constructed the modern antitrust injury test for private cases. Maybe it was the interaction with colleagues who believed the Third Circuit's decision was misguided. A further possibility, suggested in the Marshall papers, is that one of Justice Marshall's law clerks played a major role in persuading him to change his vote. Justice Marshall's papers contain a bench memorandum prepared by his clerk for oral argument that presents the argument that ultimately formed the core of Justice Powell's opinion. It is conceivable that the clerk continued to discuss the matter with Justice Marshall and finally persuaded him that the defendants had the better argument.

The Marshall papers on *Matsushita* raise interesting questions about what motivates a jurist's exercise of discretion in deciding cases. Is the dominant force a world view shaped by education and experience? Is it the quality of advocacy by the parties, especially their skill in writing briefs that assemble strong arguments and authorities for a favored proposition? For multi-member courts, is it the interaction with colleagues and the persuasiveness and personal appeal of individual tribunal members? Or is it the perspectives of the clerks whom the judge hires to assist in handling the tasks of chambers? The Marshall papers suggest that answering the larger question of why judges decide cases as they do can be complicated, and the solution may appear from directions that are hardly obvious to the observer who focuses solely on published decisions for clues.

Matsushita invited district court judges to conduct a preliminary assessment of the economic plausibility of a plaintiff's evidence of conspiracy at the summary judgment stage of litigation. If the plaintiff is incapable of producing evidence that "tends to exclude the possibility" of unilateral conduct, the Court indicates that summary judgment is warranted. This language could be read to encourage lower courts to dismiss cases with weak circumstantial evidence of agreement before trial. But the "tends to exclude" formulation does not change the evidentiary burden on plaintiffs to require near certainty: in a civil case, the inference of agreement still requires nothing more than a preponderance of the evidence. *See, e.g., In re Publication Paper Antitrust Litigation,* 690 F.3d 52, 62–63 (2d. Cir. 2012); *In re Brand Name Prescription Drugs Antitrust Litigation,* 186 F.3d 781, 787 (7th Cir. 1999) (Posner, C.J.).

---

[a] For a further elaboration of this Sidebar, see William E. Kovacic, *Antitrust in the O'Connor-Rehnquist Era: A View from Inside the Supreme Court*, ANTITRUST, Summer 2006, at 21, 22–24.

Courts have disagreed on whether *Matsushita's* "tends to exclude" standard should be applied equally in cases involving more typical cartel behavior that does not raise the kinds of economic plausibility concerns expressed in *Matsushita*, where the plaintiff alleged a decades-long predatory pricing scheme. Some courts have maintained that it should be applied to all allegations of conspiracy, without qualification. *See, e.g., Blomkest Fertilizer, Inc. v. Potash Corp. of Saskatchewan, Inc.*, 203 F.3d 1028, 1032 (8th Cir. 2000) ("We are among the majority of circuits to apply . . . *Matsushita,* broadly, and in both horizontal and vertical price fixing cases."). Others have offered a more measured interpretation, citing to the Court's observation that "if the factual context renders respondents' claim implausible—if the claim is one that simply makes no economic sense— respondents must come forward with more persuasive evidence to support their claim than would otherwise be necessary." 475 U.S. at 587. Under this alternate view, *Matsushita's* "more persuasive evidence" requirement applies only when the claim of conspiracy "makes no economic sense." This was an allusion in *Matsushita* to the demanding substantive standard for testing predatory pricing claims, especially predatory pricing conspiracy. It has been argued that this more demanding evidentiary approach should not be applied when the alleged agreement involves price fixing or market division among horizontal rivals. For example, in *In re Publication Paper*, the Second Circuit interpreted *Matsushita* as imposing a sliding scale linked to economic plausibility: "[W]here a plaintiff's theory of recovery is implausible, it takes 'strong direct or circumstantial evidence' to satisfy *Matsushita's* 'tends to exclude' standard. By contrast, broader inferences are permitted, and the 'tends to exclude' standard is more easily satisfied, when the conspiracy is economically sensible for the alleged conspirators to undertake and 'the challenged activities could not reasonably be perceived as procompetitive.'" 690 F.3d at 63. *See also Stanislaus Food Prods. v. USS-POSCO Indus.*, 803 F.3d 1084, 1089 (9th Cir. 2015) ("Implausible claims require a 'more persuasive' showing 'that tends to exclude the possibility' of independent action."); *In re Flat Glass Antitrust Litigation*, 385 F.3d 350, 357 (3d Cir. 2004) (*Matsushita* held that "the acceptable inferences which can be drawn from circumstantial evidence vary with the plausibility of the plaintiffs' theory and the dangers associated with such inferences").

Which approach, this sliding scale approach or the uniform approach, is more consistent with the evidentiary standards for proving a civil violation? Which approach strikes the better balance between avoiding false positives (not chilling beneficial conduct) and excessive transaction costs, and avoiding false negatives (failing to deter harmful conduct)?

Before *Matsushita*, the Court had long held that "summary procedures should be used sparingly in complex antitrust litigation where motive and intent play leading roles, the proof is largely in the hands of the alleged conspirators, and hostile witnesses thicken the plot." *Poller v. Columbia Broadcasting System, Inc*, 368 U.S. 464, 473 (1962). *Poller* thus viewed summary judgment as a disfavored procedure. *Matsushita* marked a clear departure from this attitude and in effect abrogated *Poller*.

As one of three landmark summary judgment cases decided by the Court during its 1985–86 term, *Matsushita* reflected the Court's general interest in re-invigorating use of summary judgment under Federal Rule of Civil Procedure 56, especially by defendants. *See also Celotex Corp. v. Catrett*, 477 U.S. 317 (1986); *Anderson v. Liberty Lobby, Inc.*, 477 U.S. 242 (1986). Collectively, these three cases evidenced serious concern on the part of the Court with increased caseloads, increased litigation costs, *in terrorem* settlements (settlements induced by a fear of costly discovery, treble damages, class actions, and jury trials), and inadequately aggressive case management by district court judges. In the antitrust area, *Matsushita* greatly expanded the use of summary judgment, which in turn focused a great deal of the effort that goes into antitrust litigation on preparation for and possible disposition of the case through summary judgment.

In our next principal case, *Bell Atlantic Corp. v. Twombly,* a decision we first discussed in Chapter 1 and that is read widely in civil procedure courses, the Supreme Court extended *Matsushita*'s plausibility screen backwards to the pleading stage of litigation. On the civil procedure issue, the Supreme Court held that, to survive a Federal Rule 12(b)(6) motion to dismiss for failure to state a claim, allegations of conspiracy must be "plausible" not merely possible. The decision was consistent with a trend in the courts to demand more substantial pleadings from plaintiffs in antitrust, as well as non-antitrust cases, but seemed to go further and led to an increased incidence of motions to dismiss. *See Ashcroft v. Iqbal*, 556 U.S. 662 (2009) (confirming that *Twombly* is not limited in application to antitrust cases).

As you read the decision, consider how the Court sought to balance the policy considerations that were addressed in *Interstate Circuit, Theatre Enterprises*, the Turner/Posner debate, *Monsanto*, and *Matsushita*. Those policies involve both the substantive standards of antitrust law (what evidence would be sufficient to prove an "agreement" for purposes of Section 1 of the Sherman Act) and pleading standards (what evidence would be sufficient to state a claim and permit plaintiff to proceed to discovery). Lower pleading standards might be favored because they allow plaintiffs to obtain the information they need to pursue claims they reasonably believe to be meritorious, thus encouraging lawsuits that would vindicate the antitrust laws, compensate victims, and deter anticompetitive conduct. In the specific case of conspiracy, such an approach also recognizes that the best evidence of conspiracy is likely to lie in the hands of the defendants. In contrast, the value of a higher pleading standard may lie in weeding out meritless suits that may never uncover circumstantial or direct evidence of agreement before they risk generating costly discovery and debilitating diversion of management time, and in reducing the threat that plaintiffs may file suit simply in order to extract settlements (to the extent those suits are not already discouraged by the summary judgment standards).

BELL ATLANTIC CORP. V. TWOMBLY
Supreme Court of the United States, 2007.
550 U.S. 544, 127 S.Ct. 1955, 167 L.Ed.2d 929.

JUSTICE SOUTER delivered the opinion of the Court.

* * * The question in this putative class action is whether a [Sherman Act] § 1 complaint can survive a motion to dismiss when it alleges that major telecommunications providers engaged in certain parallel conduct unfavorable to competition, absent some factual context suggesting agreement, as distinct from identical, independent action. We hold that such a complaint should be dismissed.

I

The upshot of the 1984 divestiture of the American Telephone & Telegraph Company's (AT & T) local telephone business was a system of regional service monopolies (variously called "Regional Bell Operating Companies," "Baby Bells," or "Incumbent Local Exchange Carriers" (ILECs)), and a separate, competitive market for long-distance service from which the ILECs were excluded. More than a decade later, Congress withdrew approval of the ILECs' monopolies by enacting the Telecommunications Act of 1996 (1996 Act), 110 Stat. 56, which "fundamentally restructure[d] local telephone markets" and "subject[ed] [ILECs] to a host of duties intended to facilitate market entry." In recompense, the 1996 Act set conditions for authorizing ILECs to enter the long-distance market.

"Central to the [new] scheme [was each ILEC's] obligation . . . to share its network with competitors," which came to be known as "competitive local exchange carriers" (CLECs). A CLEC could make use of an ILEC's network in any of three ways: by (1) "purchas[ing] local telephone services at wholesale rates for resale to end users," (2) "leas[ing] elements of the [ILEC's] network 'on an unbundled basis,' " or (3) "interconnect[ing] its own facilities with the [ILEC's] network." Owing to the "considerable expense and effort" required to make unbundled network elements available to rivals at wholesale prices, the ILECs vigorously litigated the scope of the sharing obligation imposed by the 1996 Act, with the result that the Federal Communications Commission (FCC) three times revised its regulations to narrow the range of network elements to be shared with the CLECs.

Respondents William Twombly and Lawrence Marcus (hereinafter plaintiffs) represent a putative class consisting of all "subscribers of local telephone and/or high speed internet services . . . from February 8, 1996 to present." In this action against petitioners, a group of ILECs,[1] plaintiffs seek treble damages and declaratory and injunctive relief for claimed violations of § 1 of the Sherman Act, which prohibits "[e]very contract, combination in the form of trust or otherwise, or conspiracy, in restraint of trade or commerce among the several States, or with foreign nations."

The complaint alleges that the ILECs conspired to restrain trade in two ways, each supposedly inflating charges for local telephone and high-speed Internet services. Plaintiffs say, first, that the ILECs "engaged in parallel conduct" in their respective service areas to inhibit the growth of upstart CLECs. Their actions allegedly included making unfair agreements with the CLECs for access to ILEC networks, providing inferior connections to the networks, overcharging, and billing in ways designed to sabotage the CLECs' relations with their own customers. According to the complaint, the ILECs' "compelling common motivatio[n]" to thwart the CLECs' competitive efforts naturally led them to form a conspiracy; "[h]ad any one [ILEC] not sought to prevent CLECs . . . from competing effectively . . . , the resulting greater competitive inroads into that [ILEC's] territory would have revealed the degree to which competitive entry by CLECs would have been successful in the other territories in the absence of such conduct."

Second, the complaint charges agreements by the ILECs to refrain from competing against one another. These are to be inferred from the ILECs' common failure "meaningfully [to] pursu[e]" "attractive business opportunit[ies]" in contiguous markets where they possessed "substantial competitive advantages," and from a statement of Richard Notebaert, chief executive officer (CEO) of the ILEC Qwest, that competing in the territory of another ILEC " 'might be a good way to turn a quick dollar but that doesn't make it right.' "

The complaint couches its ultimate allegations this way:

> "In the absence of any meaningful competition between the [ILECs] in one another's markets, and in light of the parallel course of conduct that each engaged in to prevent competition from CLECs within their respective local telephone and/or high speed internet services markets and the other facts and market

---

[1] The 1984 divestiture of AT & T's local telephone service created seven Regional Bell Operating Companies. Through a series of mergers and acquisitions, those seven companies were consolidated into the four ILECs named in this suit: BellSouth Corporation, Qwest Communications International, Inc., SBC Communications, Inc., and Verizon Communications, Inc. (successor-in-interest to Bell Atlantic Corporation). Together, these ILECs allegedly control 90 percent or more of the market for local telephone service in the 48 contiguous States.

circumstances alleged above, Plaintiffs allege upon information and belief that [the ILECs] have entered into a contract, combination or conspiracy to prevent competitive entry in their respective local telephone and/or high speed internet services markets and have agreed not to compete with one another and otherwise allocated customers and markets to one another."[2]

"Beginning at least as early as February 6, 1996, and continuing to the present, the exact dates being unknown to Plaintiffs, Defendants and their co-conspirators engaged in a contract, combination or conspiracy to prevent competitive entry in their respective local telephone and/or high speed internet services markets by, among other things, agreeing not to compete with one another and to stifle attempts by others to compete with them and otherwise allocating customers and markets to one another in violation of Section 1 of the Sherman Act."

The United States District Court for the Southern District of New York dismissed the complaint for failure to state a claim upon which relief can be granted. * * *

* * * The Court of Appeals for the Second Circuit reversed, holding that the District Court tested the complaint by the wrong standard. It held that "plus factors are not *required* to be pleaded to permit an antitrust claim based on parallel conduct to survive dismissal." * * *

We granted certiorari to address the proper standard for pleading an antitrust conspiracy through allegations of parallel conduct, and now reverse.

II

A

Because § 1 of the Sherman Act "does not prohibit [all] unreasonable restraints of trade . . . but only restraints effected by a contract, combination, or conspiracy," *Copperweld Corp. v. Independence Tube Corp.,* 467 U.S. 752, 775, 104 S.Ct. 2731, 81 L.Ed.2d 628 (1984), "[t]he crucial question" is whether the challenged anticompetitive conduct "stem[s] from independent decision or from an agreement, tacit or express," *Theatre Enterprises,* 346 U.S., at 540, 74 S.Ct. 257. While a showing of parallel "business behavior is admissible circumstantial evidence from which the

---

[2]   In setting forth the grounds for § 1 relief, the complaint repeats these allegations in substantially similar language:

"Beginning at least as early as February 6, 1996, and continuing to the present, the exact dates being unknown to Plaintiffs, Defendants and their co-conspirators engaged in a contract, combination or conspiracy to prevent competitive entry in their respective local telephone and/or high speed internet services markets by, among other things, agreeing not to compete with one another and to stifle attempts by others to compete with them and otherwise allocating customers and markets to one another in violation of Section 1 of the Sherman Act."

fact finder may infer agreement," it falls short of "conclusively establish[ing] agreement or . . . itself constitut[ing] a Sherman Act offense." *Id.*, at 540–541, 74 S.Ct. 257. Even "conscious parallelism," a common reaction of "firms in a concentrated market [that] recogniz[e] their shared economic interests and their interdependence with respect to price and output decisions" is "not in itself unlawful."

The inadequacy of showing parallel conduct or interdependence, without more, mirrors the ambiguity of the behavior: consistent with conspiracy, but just as much in line with a wide swath of rational and competitive business strategy unilaterally prompted by common perceptions of the market. Accordingly, we have previously hedged against false inferences from identical behavior at a number of points in the trial sequence. An antitrust conspiracy plaintiff with evidence showing nothing beyond parallel conduct is not entitled to a directed verdict, see *Theatre Enterprises, supra;* proof of a § 1 conspiracy must include evidence tending to exclude the possibility of independent action, see *Monsanto Co. v. Spray-Rite Service Corp.*, 465 U.S. 752, 104 S.Ct. 1464, 79 L.Ed.2d 775 (1984); and at the summary judgment stage a § 1 plaintiff's offer of conspiracy evidence must tend to rule out the possibility that the defendants were acting independently, see *Matsushita Elec. Industrial Co. v. Zenith Radio Corp.*, 475 U.S. 574, 106 S.Ct. 1348, 89 L.Ed.2d 538 (1986).

B

This case presents the antecedent question of what a plaintiff must plead in order to state a claim under § 1 of the Sherman Act. Federal Rule of Civil Procedure 8(a)(2) requires only "a short and plain statement of the claim showing that the pleader is entitled to relief," in order to "give the defendant fair notice of what the . . . claim is and the grounds upon which it rests," While a complaint attacked by a Rule 12(b)(6) motion to dismiss does not need detailed factual allegations, a plaintiff's obligation to provide the "grounds" of his "entitle[ment] to relief" requires more than labels and conclusions, and a formulaic recitation of the elements of a cause of action will not do. Factual allegations must be enough to raise a right to relief above the speculative level, on the assumption that all the allegations in the complaint are true (even if doubtful in fact).

In applying these general standards to a § 1 claim, we hold that stating such a claim requires a complaint with enough factual matter (taken as true) to suggest that an agreement was made. Asking for plausible grounds to infer an agreement does not impose a probability requirement at the pleading stage; it simply calls for enough fact to raise a reasonable expectation that discovery will reveal evidence of illegal agreement.[4] And,

---

[4] Commentators have offered several examples of parallel conduct allegations that would state a § 1 claim under this standard. See, *e.g.,* 6 Areeda & Hovenkamp ¶ 1425, at 167–185 (discussing "parallel behavior that would probably not result from chance, coincidence,

of course, a well-pleaded complaint may proceed even if it strikes a savvy judge that actual proof of those facts is improbable, and "that a recovery is very remote and unlikely." In identifying facts that are suggestive enough to render a § 1 conspiracy plausible, we have the benefit of the prior rulings and considered views of leading commentators, already quoted, that lawful parallel conduct fails to bespeak unlawful agreement. It makes sense to say, therefore, that an allegation of parallel conduct and a bare assertion of conspiracy will not suffice. Without more, parallel conduct does not suggest conspiracy, and a conclusory allegation of agreement at some unidentified point does not supply facts adequate to show illegality. Hence, when allegations of parallel conduct are set out in order to make a § 1 claim, they must be placed in a context that raises a suggestion of a preceding agreement, not merely parallel conduct that could just as well be independent action.

The need at the pleading stage for allegations plausibly suggesting (not merely consistent with) agreement reflects the threshold requirement of Rule 8(a)(2) that the "plain statement" possess enough heft to "sho[w] that the pleader is entitled to relief." A statement of parallel conduct, even conduct consciously undertaken, needs some setting suggesting the agreement necessary to make out a § 1 claim; without that further circumstance pointing toward a meeting of the minds, an account of a defendant's commercial efforts stays in neutral territory. An allegation of parallel conduct is thus much like a naked assertion of conspiracy in a § 1 complaint: it gets the complaint close to stating a claim, but without some further factual enhancement it stops short of the line between possibility and plausibility of "entitle[ment] to relief."

* * * [S]omething beyond the mere possibility of loss causation must be alleged, lest a plaintiff with " 'a largely groundless claim' " be allowed to " 'take up the time of a number of other people, with the right to do so representing an *in terrorem* increment of the settlement value.' " So, when the allegations in a complaint, however true, could not raise a claim of entitlement to relief, " 'this basic deficiency should . . . be exposed at the point of minimum expenditure of time and money by the parties and the court.' "

Thus, it is one thing to be cautious before dismissing an antitrust complaint in advance of discovery, but quite another to forget that proceeding to antitrust discovery can be expensive. * * * That potential

---

independent responses to common stimuli, or mere interdependence unaided by an advance understanding among the parties"); Blechman, Conscious Parallelism, Signalling and Facilitating Devices: The Problem of Tacit Collusion Under the Antitrust Laws, 24 N.Y.L. S. L.Rev. 881, 899 (1979) (describing "conduct [that] indicates the sort of restricted freedom of action and sense of obligation that one generally associates with agreement"). The parties in this case agree that "complex and historically unprecedented changes in pricing structure made at the very same time by multiple competitors, and made for no other discernible reason," would support a plausible inference of conspiracy.

expense is obvious enough in the present case: plaintiffs represent a putative class of at least 90 percent of all subscribers to local telephone or high-speed Internet service in the continental United States, in an action against America's largest telecommunications firms (with many thousands of employees generating reams and gigabytes of business records) for unspecified (if any) instances of antitrust violations that allegedly occurred over a period of seven years.

* * * Probably, then, it is only by taking care to require allegations that reach the level suggesting conspiracy that we can hope to avoid the potentially enormous expense of discovery in cases with no " 'reasonably founded hope that the [discovery] process will reveal relevant evidence' " to support a § 1 claim.

* * *

III

When we look for plausibility in this complaint, we agree with the District Court that plaintiffs' claim of conspiracy in restraint of trade comes up short. To begin with, the complaint leaves no doubt that plaintiffs rest their § 1 claim on descriptions of parallel conduct and not on any independent allegation of actual agreement among the ILECs. * * * The nub of the complaint, then, is the ILECs' parallel behavior, consisting of steps to keep the CLECs out and manifest disinterest in becoming CLECs themselves, and its sufficiency turns on the suggestions raised by this conduct when viewed in light of common economic experience.[11]

We think that nothing contained in the complaint invests either the action or inaction alleged with a plausible suggestion of conspiracy. As to the ILECs' supposed agreement to disobey the 1996 Act and thwart the CLECs' attempts to compete, we agree with the District Court that nothing in the complaint intimates that the resistance to the upstarts was anything more than the natural, unilateral reaction of each ILEC intent on keeping its regional dominance. The 1996 Act did more than just subject the ILECs to competition; it obliged them to subsidize their competitors with their own equipment at wholesale rates. The economic incentive to resist was powerful, but resisting competition is routine market conduct, and even if the ILECs flouted the 1996 Act in all the ways the plaintiffs allege, there is no reason to infer that the companies had agreed among themselves to do what was only natural anyway; so natural, in fact, that if alleging parallel decisions to resist competition were enough to imply an antitrust conspiracy, pleading a § 1 violation against almost any group of competing businesses would be a sure thing.

---

[11] The dissent's quotations from the complaint leave the impression that plaintiffs directly allege illegal agreement; in fact, they proceed exclusively via allegations of parallel conduct, as both the District Court and Court of Appeals recognized.

The complaint makes its closest pass at a predicate for conspiracy with the claim that collusion was necessary because success by even one CLEC in an ILEC's territory "would have revealed the degree to which competitive entry by CLECs would have been successful in the other territories." But, its logic aside, this general premise still fails to answer the point that there was just no need for joint encouragement to resist the 1996 Act; as the District Court said, "each ILEC has reason to want to avoid dealing with CLECs" and "each ILEC would attempt to keep CLECs out, regardless of the actions of the other ILECs."[12]

Plaintiffs' second conspiracy theory rests on the competitive reticence among the ILECs themselves in the wake of the 1996 Act, which was supposedly passed in the " 'hop[e] that the large incumbent local monopoly companies . . . might attack their neighbors' service areas, as they are the best situated to do so.' " Contrary to hope, the ILECs declined " 'to enter each other's service territories in any significant way,' " and the local telephone and high-speed Internet market remains highly compartmentalized geographically, with minimal competition. Based on this state of affairs, and perceiving the ILECs to be blessed with "especially attractive business opportunities" in surrounding markets dominated by other ILECs, the plaintiffs assert that the ILECs' parallel conduct was "strongly suggestive of conspiracy."

But it was not suggestive of conspiracy, not if history teaches anything. In a traditionally unregulated industry with low barriers to entry, sparse competition among large firms dominating separate geographical segments of the market could very well signify illegal agreement, but here we have an obvious alternative explanation. In the decade preceding the 1996 Act and well before that, monopoly was the norm in telecommunications, not the exception. The ILECs were born in that world, doubtless liked the world the way it was, and surely knew the adage about him who lives by the sword. Hence, a natural explanation for the noncompetition alleged is that the former Government-sanctioned monopolists were sitting tight, expecting their neighbors to do the same thing.

In fact, the complaint itself gives reasons to believe that the ILECs would see their best interests in keeping to their old turf. Although the complaint says generally that the ILECs passed up "especially attractive business opportunit[ies]" by declining to compete as CLECs against other

---

[12] From the allegation that the ILECs belong to various trade associations, the dissent playfully suggests that they conspired to restrain trade, an inference said to be "buttressed by the common sense of Adam Smith." If Adam Smith is peering down today, he may be surprised to learn that his tongue-in-cheek remark would be authority to force his famous pinmaker to devote financial and human capital to hire lawyers, prepare for depositions, and otherwise fend off allegations of conspiracy; all this just because he belonged to the same trade guild as one of his competitors when their pins carried the same price tag.

ILECs, it does not allege that competition as CLECs was potentially any more lucrative than other opportunities being pursued by the ILECs during the same period,[13] and the complaint is replete with indications that any CLEC faced nearly insurmountable barriers to profitability owing to the ILECs' flagrant resistance to the network sharing requirements of the 1996 Act. Not only that, but even without a monopolistic tradition and the peculiar difficulty of mandating shared networks, "[f]irms do not expand without limit and none of them enters every market that an outside observer might regard as profitable, or even a small portion of such markets." The upshot is that Congress may have expected some ILECs to become CLECs in the legacy territories of other ILECs, but the disappointment does not make conspiracy plausible. We agree with the District Court's assessment that antitrust conspiracy was not suggested by the facts adduced under either theory of the complaint, which thus fails to state a valid § 1 claim.

* * * Because the plaintiffs here have not nudged their claims across the line from conceivable to plausible, their complaint must be dismissed.

* * *

JUSTICE STEVENS, with whom JUSTICE GINSBURG joins except as to Part IV, dissenting.

In the first paragraph of its 23-page opinion the Court states that the question to be decided is whether allegations that "major telecommunications providers engaged in certain parallel conduct unfavorable to competition" suffice to state a violation of § 1 of the Sherman Act. The answer to that question has been settled for more than 50 years. If that were indeed the issue, a summary reversal citing *Theatre Enterprises, Inc. v. Paramount Film Distributing Corp.,* 346 U.S. 537, 74 S.Ct. 257, 98 L.Ed. 273 (1954), would adequately resolve this case. As *Theatre Enterprises* held, parallel conduct is circumstantial evidence admissible on the issue of conspiracy, but it is not itself illegal.

Thus, this is a case in which there is no dispute about the substantive law. If the defendants acted independently, their conduct was perfectly lawful. If, however, that conduct is the product of a horizontal agreement among potential competitors, it was unlawful. The plaintiffs have alleged such an agreement and, because the complaint was dismissed in advance

---

[13] The complaint quoted a reported statement of Qwest's CEO, Richard Notebaert, to suggest that the ILECs declined to compete against each other despite recognizing that it " 'might be a good way to turn a quick dollar.' " This was only part of what he reportedly said, however, and the District Court was entitled to take notice of the full contents of the published articles referenced in the complaint, from which the truncated quotations were drawn.

Notebaert was also quoted as saying that entering new markets as a CLEC would not be "a sustainable economic model" because the CLEC pricing model is "just . . . nuts." Another source cited in the complaint quotes Notebaert as saying he thought it "unwise" to "base a business plan" on the privileges accorded to CLECs under the 1996 Act because the regulatory environment was too unstable.

of answer, the allegation has not even been denied. Why, then, does the case not proceed? Does a judicial opinion that the charge is not "plausible" provide a legally acceptable reason for dismissing the complaint? I think not.

Respondents' amended complaint describes a variety of circumstantial evidence and makes the straightforward allegation that petitioners

"entered into a contract, combination or conspiracy to prevent competitive entry in their respective local telephone and/or high speed internet services markets and have agreed not to compete with one another and otherwise allocated customers and markets to one another."

The complaint explains that, contrary to Congress' expectation when it enacted the 1996 Telecommunications Act, and consistent with their own economic self-interests, petitioner Incumbent Local Exchange Carriers (ILECs) have assiduously avoided infringing upon each other's markets and have refused to permit nonincumbent competitors to access their networks. The complaint quotes Richard Notebaert, the former chief executive officer of one such ILEC, as saying that competing in a neighboring ILEC's territory " 'might be a good way to turn a quick dollar but that doesn't make it right.' " Moreover, respondents allege that petitioners "communicate amongst themselves" through numerous industry associations. In sum, respondents allege that petitioners entered into an agreement that has long been recognized as a classic *per se* violation of the Sherman Act.

Under rules of procedure that have been well settled since well before our decision in *Theatre Enterprises,* a judge ruling on a defendant's motion to dismiss a complaint "must accept as true all of the factual allegations contained in the complaint." But instead of requiring knowledgeable executives such as Notebaert to respond to these allegations by way of sworn depositions or other limited discovery—and indeed without so much as requiring petitioners to file an answer denying that they entered into any agreement—the majority permits immediate dismissal based on the assurances of company lawyers that nothing untoward was afoot. The Court embraces the argument of those lawyers that "there is no reason to infer that the companies had agreed among themselves to do what was only natural anyway"; that "there was just no need for joint encouragement to resist the 1996 Act"; and that the "natural explanation for the noncompetition alleged is that the former Government-sanctioned monopolists were sitting tight, expecting their neighbors to do the same thing".

The Court and petitioners' legal team are no doubt correct that the parallel conduct alleged is consistent with the absence of any contract, combination, or conspiracy. But that conduct is also entirely consistent with the *presence* of the illegal agreement alleged in the complaint. And the charge that petitioners "agreed not to compete with one another" is not just one of "a few stray statements"; it is an allegation describing unlawful conduct. As such, the Federal Rules of Civil Procedure, our longstanding precedent, and sound practice mandate that the District Court at least require some sort of response from petitioners before dismissing the case.

Two practical concerns presumably explain the Court's dramatic departure from settled procedural law. Private antitrust litigation can be enormously expensive, and there is a risk that jurors may mistakenly conclude that evidence of parallel conduct has proved that the parties acted pursuant to an agreement when they in fact merely made similar independent decisions. Those concerns merit careful case management, including strict control of discovery, careful scrutiny of evidence at the summary judgment stage, and lucid instructions to juries; they do not, however, justify the dismissal of an adequately pleaded complaint without even requiring the defendants to file answers denying a charge that they in fact engaged in collective decisionmaking. More importantly, they do not justify an interpretation of Federal Rule of Civil Procedure 12(b)(6) that seems to be driven by the majority's appraisal of the plausibility of the ultimate factual allegation rather than its legal sufficiency.

* * *

This case is a poor vehicle for the Court's new pleading rule, for we have observed that "in antitrust cases, where 'the proof is largely in the hands of the alleged conspirators,' . . . dismissals prior to giving the plaintiff ample opportunity for discovery should be granted very sparingly." Moreover, the fact that the Sherman Act authorizes the recovery of treble damages and attorney's fees for successful plaintiffs indicates that Congress intended to encourage, rather than discourage, private enforcement of the law. It is therefore more, not less, important in antitrust cases to resist the urge to engage in armchair economics at the pleading stage.

* * *

The Court does not suggest that an agreement to do what the plaintiffs allege would be permissible under the antitrust laws. Nor does the Court hold that these plaintiffs have failed to allege an injury entitling them to sue for damages under those laws. Rather, the theory on which the Court permits dismissal is that, so far as the Federal Rules are concerned, no agreement has been alleged at all. This is a mind-boggling conclusion.

As the Court explains, prior to the enactment of the Telecommunications Act of 1996 the law prohibited the defendants from competing with each other. The new statute was enacted to replace a monopolistic market with a competitive one. The Act did not merely require the regional monopolists to take affirmative steps to facilitate entry to new competitors; it also permitted the existing firms to compete with each other and to expand their operations into previously forbidden territory. Each of the defendants decided not to take the latter step. That was obviously an extremely important business decision, and I am willing to presume that each company acted entirely independently in reaching that decision. I am even willing to entertain the majority's belief that any agreement among the companies was unlikely. But the plaintiffs allege in three places in their complaint, that the ILECs did in fact agree both to prevent competitors from entering into their local markets and to forgo competition with each other. And as the Court recognizes, at the motion to dismiss stage, a judge assumes "that all the allegations in the complaint are true (even if doubtful in fact)."

The majority circumvents this obvious obstacle to dismissal by pretending that it does not exist. The Court admits that "in form a few stray statements in the complaint speak directly of agreement," but disregards those allegations by saying that "on fair reading these are merely legal conclusions resting on the prior allegations" of parallel conduct. The Court's dichotomy between factual allegations and "legal conclusions" is the stuff of a bygone era. That distinction was a defining feature of code pleading, but was conspicuously abolished when the Federal Rules were enacted in 1938.

Even if I were inclined to accept the Court's anachronistic dichotomy and ignore the complaint's actual allegations, I would dispute the Court's suggestion that any inference of agreement from petitioners' parallel conduct is "implausible." Many years ago a truly great economist perceptively observed that "[p]eople of the same trade seldom meet together, even for merriment and diversion, but the conversation ends in a conspiracy against the public, or in some contrivance to raise prices." A. Smith, An Inquiry Into the Nature and Causes of the Wealth of Nations, in 39 Great Books of the Western World 55 (R. Hutchins & M. Adler eds.1952). I am not so cynical as to accept that sentiment at face value, but I need not do so here. Respondents' complaint points not only to petitioners' numerous opportunities to meet with each other,[10] but also to Notebaert's curious statement that encroaching on a fellow incumbent's territory "might be a good way to turn a quick dollar but that doesn't make it right". What did he mean by that? One possible (indeed plausible) inference is that he meant that while it would be in his company's economic self-interest to compete with its brethren, he had agreed with his competitors not to do so.

---

[10] The Court describes my reference to the allegation that the defendants belong to various trade associations as "playfully" suggesting that the defendants conspired to restrain trade. Quite the contrary: An allegation that competitors meet on a regular basis, like the allegations of parallel conduct, is consistent with—though not sufficient to prove—the plaintiffs' entirely serious and unequivocal allegation that the defendants entered into an unlawful agreement. Indeed, if it were true that the plaintiffs "rest their § 1 claim on descriptions of parallel conduct and not on any independent allegation of actual agreement among the ILECs," there would have been no purpose in including a reference to the trade association meetings in the amended complaint.

According to the complaint, that is how the Illinois Coalition for Competitive Telecom construed Notebaert's statement, and that is how Members of Congress construed his company's behavior.

Perhaps Notebaert meant instead that competition would be sensible in the short term but not in the long run. That's what his lawyers tell us anyway. But I would think that no one would know better what Notebaert meant than Notebaert himself. Instead of permitting respondents to ask Notebaert, however, the Court looks to other quotes from that and other articles and decides that what he meant was that entering new markets as a competitive local exchange carrier would not be a " 'sustainable economic model.' " Never mind that—as anyone ever interviewed knows—a newspaper article is hardly a verbatim transcript; the writer selects quotes to package his story, not to record a subject's views for posterity. But more importantly the District Court was required at this stage of the proceedings to construe Notebaert's ambiguous statement in the plaintiffs' favor. The inference the statement supports—that simultaneous decisions by ILECs not even to attempt to poach customers from one another once the law authorized them to do so were the product of an agreement—sits comfortably within the realm of possibility. That is all the Rules require.

To be clear, if I had been the trial judge in this case, I would not have permitted the plaintiffs to engage in massive discovery based solely on the allegations in this complaint. On the other hand, I surely would not have dismissed the complaint without requiring the defendants to answer the charge that they "have agreed not to compete with one another and otherwise allocated customers and markets to one another." Even a sworn denial of that charge would not justify a summary dismissal without giving the plaintiffs the opportunity to take depositions from Notebaert and at least one responsible executive representing each of the other defendants.

Respondents in this case proposed a plan of " 'phased discovery' " limited to the existence of the alleged conspiracy and class certification. Two petitioners rejected the plan. Whether or not respondents' proposed plan was sensible, it was an appropriate subject for negotiation.[13]* * *

In short, the Federal Rules contemplate that pretrial matters will be settled through a flexible process of give and take, of proffers, stipulations, and stonewalls, not by having trial judges screen allegations for their plausibility *vel non* without requiring an answer from the defendant. * * *

* * *

---

[13] The potential for "sprawling, costly, and hugely time-consuming" discovery * * * is no reason to throw the baby out with the bathwater. The Court vastly underestimates a district court's case-management arsenal. * * *

IV

The transparent policy concern that drives the decision is the interest in protecting antitrust defendants—who in this case are some of the wealthiest corporations in our economy—from the burdens of pretrial discovery. * * * [I]n the final analysis it is only a lack of confidence in the ability of trial judges to control discovery, buttressed by appellate judges' independent appraisal of the plausibility of profoundly serious factual allegations, that could account for this stark break from precedent.

If the allegation of conspiracy happens to be true, today's decision obstructs the congressional policy favoring competition that undergirds both the Telecommunications Act of 1996 and the Sherman Act itself. More importantly, even if there is abundant evidence that the allegation is untrue, directing that the case be dismissed without even looking at any of that evidence marks a fundamental—and unjustified—change in the character of pretrial practice.

Accordingly, I respectfully dissent.

———————

Do the *Twombly* majority and dissent differ in the legal rule they think should apply, or in its application to the facts of the case? Do they differ in whether they are more concerned about the consequences of allowing anticompetitive conduct to take place free of challenge or the consequences of subjecting firms not harming competition to litigation costs and potential liability? Are the latter concerns greater today than they were at the time of *Interstate Circuit* because of the availability and costs of electronic discovery? The Supreme Court has also expressed concern about the costs and likelihood of errors in antitrust litigation in two other contexts: in specifying the standards for evaluating motions for summary judgment, as we saw in *Matsushita,* and in evaluating whether ongoing supervision of an industry by regulatory agencies should displace antitrust enforcement (*see infra* Chapter 8).

Note that the parallel conduct offered in support of inferring agreement in *Twombly* does not directly involve price: one claim is that the defendants acted in parallel ways to exclude entrants that might undermine a coordinated arrangement (recalling one aspect of *JTC Petroleum*), and the other claim involves parallel decisions not to expand the geographic regions in which they operate when doing so would mean competing directly with another defendant (a type of market division). Should the standards for inferring agreement from these types of conduct differ from the standards applied when inferring an agreement to fix prices when firms increase price in parallel?

The combination of *Twombly* and *Matsushita* may make the pursuit of an antitrust claim a costly and challenging undertaking for plaintiffs.

Indeed, *Twombly* is not confined to allegations of conspiracy any more than *Matsushita* was confined to claims of predatory pricing conspiracies. The pleading standard set forth in *Twombly* is being invoked by defendants and lower courts to demand more elaborate allegations of all elements of an antitrust claim, including antitrust injury, market definition, and competitive effects, and the Supreme Court has held that its principles are not limited in application to antitrust cases. *Ashcroft v. Iqbal*, 556 U.S. 662 (2009).

Do *Twombly* and *Matsushita* go too far in responding to the argument that antitrust cases can be very costly for defendants, difficult to comprehend by juries, and hence subject to abuse by plaintiffs seeking unwarranted settlements? Does it seem likely that plaintiffs, enticed by the promise of treble damages and attorney's fees, will lightly undertake the pursuit of a potentially years-long antitrust litigation in the hope of procuring a favorable settlement? Doesn't discovery have significant costs for plaintiffs as well as defendants? And is it likely that especially weak cases will pose a sufficiently credible threat to extract large settlements given the standards of substantive antitrust law that have become more favorable to defendants as they have evolved over the last thirty years? It is at least arguable that in the current atmosphere—as opposed to the atmosphere that prevailed until the late 1970s when per se analysis was far more commonly endorsed by the Court—truly innocent defendants are far less likely to be paying out large settlements to avoid the prospect of facing a jury.

The *Twombly* majority presumed that the alleged excesses of antitrust litigation are real. Are the citations it offers to support these views convincing? Is there any empirical evidence to support these assumptions about antitrust litigation, or any reason to assume that antitrust cases are any more complex and costly to process than other kinds of major federal litigation? Justice Stevens faults the majority for relying on "lawyers' arguments" made in briefs and papers in a case where no answer denying conspiracy had even been filed by the defendants and no evidence had been collected. Do you agree with his argument that even if these concerns are truly acute, Congress or the Federal Rules Advisory Committee are in a better position institutionally to gather objective evidence to assess and address those risks through revisions to the Rules than is the Court?

Courts are concerned at times with the interplay of doctrinal standards, standards of proof, and remedies. Judges uncomfortable with the potential over-inclusiveness of per se prohibitions may impose greater evidentiary demands on plaintiffs to prove collective action, because finding such action, by itself, can establish liability. Similarly, a judge who believes the antitrust remedial scheme is too severe—for example, in commanding that damages in private actions be trebled—also might increase the plaintiff's burden of pleading or proving agreement to diminish the likelihood that disfavored remedies might be applied. Historically, concern about the ability of the antitrust laws to reach all instances of tacit collusion was offered as a justification for a tough anti-merger policy, skeptical of all significant increases in market concentration; this approach was described as pursuing a "containment" policy that obstructs mergers threatening to create oligopolistic market structures. 6 PHILLIP E. AREEDA, ANTITRUST LAW ¶ 1432d (1986).

Consider the problem of inferring agreement from an economic or decision-theoretic perspective that focuses on relative "error costs" (*see supra* Sidebar 1–4). Do the policy considerations identified by the opinions in *Copperweld, Interstate Circuit, Matsushita, Twombly*, and the Turner/Posner debate point in a clear direction? If antitrust's substantive and procedural rules make it more difficult to infer an agreement from circumstantial evidence, that would risk "false negatives," not just in failing to find liability when firms have agreed to fix prices or divide markets in the cases litigated but also, and more importantly, in under-deterring such agreements by making them more difficult to prove. On the other hand, if antitrust rules make it easy to infer an agreement from circumstantial evidence, that would risk "false positives," not just in finding liability when rivals are engaging in procompetitive conduct but also, and more importantly, in chilling procompetitive conduct by firms seeking to comply with the rules and chilling beneficial joint ventures among rivals. Moreover, the degree of scrutiny antitrust gives alleged agreements among rivals affects the direct costs of litigation. If antitrust rules make it relatively easy for plaintiffs to survive a motion to dismiss or a motion for summary judgment, that could lead to excessive costs of discovery and litigation in non-meritorious cases, and lead some defendants to settle even though they have not harmed competition, especially if they fear application of those rules by juries. But if litigation cost considerations lead to antitrust rules that make it more difficult for plaintiffs, that could chill plaintiffs from bringing meritorious cases and undermine the social benefits of antitrust enforcement. As you read the remainder of this Chapter, consider whether antitrust law has set the line in the right place when balancing these competing concerns.

D. PROVING AGREEMENT THROUGH CIRCUMSTANTIAL EVIDENCE: "PARALLELISM PLUS"

In this Section we examine how modern judicial decisions have addressed longstanding questions about distinguishing concerted from unilateral conduct. We identify the approach modern courts apply when asked to infer an agreement to fix prices from circumstantial evidence.

1. ESTABLISHING PARALLELISM PLUS

Since *Interstate Circuit*, courts have struggled with whether parallel conduct that seems to flow from the recognition of interdependence should suffice, without more, to support an inference of agreement. Courts continue to hold, as the Supreme Court did in *Theatre Enterprises* in 1954, that mere conscious parallelism or oligopolistic interdependence does not permit an inference of conspiracy. Courts require plaintiffs to supplement proof of parallel conduct with additional facts ("plus factors") to justify an inference of agreement, and to make supplementary allegations of plus factors to justify that inference in the pleading context, as we saw in *Twombly*.

But what additional evidence do courts look for in order to make that inference? We introduce this question with *American Tobacco*, which the Supreme Court decided seven years after *Interstate Circuit*. In *American Tobacco*, the Court considered the concerted action issue in the context of reviewing conspiracy to monopolize charges brought under Section 2 of the Sherman Act against the country's leading producers of tobacco products. A jury had convicted defendants of violating Section 1 of the Sherman Act as well as Section 2, but the Supreme Court reviewed only the Section 2 convictions. Sherman Act § 2, which will be discussed more in Chapter 4, deals primarily with monopolization and attempt to monopolize, but also prohibits conspiracies to monopolize. The conspiracy to monopolize section is rarely invoked today, most likely because courts would be expected to apply the same standard for inferring an agreement as they rely upon when evaluating conduct challenged under Section 1, without requiring proof of specific intent to achieve a monopoly, an additional element of the Section 2 violation of attempted monopolization.

As in *Interstate Circuit*, the basis for the government's proof of conspiracy in *American Tobacco* was circumstantial evidence that included parallel price increases instituted by rival sellers. The Court did not infer agreement solely from evidence that each firm increased the list price of its leading brand identically on the same day. The additional factors it relied upon to sustain a finding of conspiracy when added to the fact of parallel conduct—what have come to be known as "plus factors"—are commonly thought of today as, at best, barely sufficient and at worst inadequate for inferring an agreement to fix prices. By modern standards, therefore, the inference that the defendants had conspired is adventurous on the facts in the record. As you read this decision, focus on identifying the "plus factors" that the Court relied upon.

AMERICAN TOBACCO CO. v. UNITED STATES

Supreme Court of the United States, 1946.
328 U.S. 781, 66 S.Ct. 1125, 90 L.Ed. 1575.

MR. JUSTICE BURTON delivered the opinion of the Court.

The petitioners are The American Tobacco Company, Liggett & Myers Tobacco Company, R. J. Reynolds Tobacco Company, American Suppliers, Inc., a subsidiary of American, and certain officials of the respective companies who were convicted by a jury, in the District Court of the United States for the Eastern District of Kentucky, of violating §§ 1 and 2 of the Sherman Anti-Trust Act * * * pursuant to an information filed July 24, 1940, and modified October 31, 1940.

* * * The conspiracy to monopolize and the monopolization charged here do not depend upon proof relating to the old tobacco trust [which was dissolved in 1911—Eds.] but upon a dominance and control by petitioners in recent years over purchases of the raw material and over the sale of the finished product in the form of cigarettes. The fact, however, that the purchases of leaf tobacco and the sales of so many products of the tobacco industry have remained largely within the same general group of business organizations for over a generation, inevitably has contributed to the ease with which control over competition within the industry and the mobilization of power to resist new competition can be exercised. A friendly relationship within such a long established industry is, in itself, not only natural but commendable and beneficial, as long as it does not breed illegal activities. Such a community of interest in any industry, however, provides a natural foundation for working policies and understandings favorable to the insiders and unfavorable to outsiders. The verdicts indicate that practices of an informal and flexible nature were adopted and that the results were so uniformly beneficial to the petitioners in protecting their common interests as against those of competitors that, entirely from circumstantial evidence, the jury found that a combination or conspiracy existed among the petitioners from 1937 to 1940, with power and intent to exclude competitors to such a substantial extent as to violate the Sherman Act as interpreted by the trial court.

* * * [A]lthough American, Liggett and Reynolds gradually dropped in their percentage of the national domestic cigarette production from 90.7% in 1931 to 73.3%, 71% and 68%, respectively, in 1937, 1938 and 1939, they have accounted at all times for more than 68%, and usually for more than 75%, of the national production. The balance of the cigarette production has come from six other companies. No one of those six ever has produced more than the 10.6% once reached by Brown & Williamson in 1939. * * *

* * *

With this background of a substantial monopoly, amounting to over two-thirds of the entire domestic field of cigarettes, and to over 80% of the field of comparable cigarettes, and with the opposition confined to several small competitors, the jury could have found from the actual operation of the petitioners that there existed a combination or conspiracy among them not only in restraint of trade, but to monopolize a part of the tobacco industry. * * *

* * *

II.

The verdicts show * * * that the jury found that the petitioners conspired to fix prices and to exclude undesired competition in the distribution and sale of their principal products. The petitioners sold and distributed their products to jobbers and to selected dealers who bought at list prices, less discounts. Almost all of the million or more dealers who handled the respective petitioners' products throughout the country consisted of such establishments as small storekeepers, gasoline station operators and lunch room proprietors who purchased the cigarettes from jobbers. The jobbers in turn derived their profits from the difference between the wholesale price paid by them and the price charged by them to local dealers. A great advantage therefore accrued to any dealer buying at the discounted or wholesale list prices. Selling to dealers at jobbers' prices was called 'direct selling' and the dealers as well as the jobbers getting those prices were referred to as being on the 'direct list.' The list prices charged and the discounts allowed by petitioners have been practically identical since 1923 and absolutely identical since 1928. Since the latter date, only seven changes have been made by the three companies and those have been identical in amount. The increases were first announced by Reynolds. American and Liggett thereupon increased their list prices in identical amounts.

The following record of price changes is circumstantial evidence of the existence of a conspiracy and of a power and intent to exclude competition coming from cheaper grade cigarettes. During the two years preceding June, 1931, the petitioners produced 90% of the total cigarette production in the United States. In that month tobacco farmers were receiving the lowest prices for their crops since 1905. The costs to the petitioners for tobacco leaf, therefore, were lower than usual during the past 25 years, and their manufacturing costs had been declining. It was one of the worst years of financial and economic depression in the history of the country. On June 23, 1931, Reynolds, without previous notification or warning to the trade or public, raised the list price of Camel cigarettes, constituting its leading cigarette brand, from $6.40 to $6.85 a thousand. The same day, American increased the list price for Lucky Strike cigarettes, its leading brand, and Liggett the price for Chesterfield cigarettes, its leading brand, to the identical price of $6.85 a thousand. No economic justification for this raise was demonstrated. The president of Reynolds stated that it was 'to express our own courage for the future and our own confidence in our industry.' The president of American gave as his reason for the increase, 'the opportunity of making some money.' He further claimed that because Reynolds had raised its list price, Reynolds would therefore have additional funds for advertising and American had raised its price in order to have a similar amount for advertising. The officials of Liggett claimed that they thought the increase was a mistake as there did not seem to be any reason for making a price advance but they contended that unless they also raised their list price for Chesterfields, the other companies would have greater resources to spend in advertising and thus would put Chesterfield cigarettes at a competitive disadvantage. This general price increase soon resulted in higher retail prices and in a loss in volume of sales. Yet in 1932, in the midst of the national depression with the sales of the petitioners' cigarettes falling off greatly in number, the petitioners still were making tremendous profits as a result of the price increase. Their net profits in that year amounted to more than $100,000,000. This was one of the three biggest years in their history.

* * *

III.

It was on the basis of such evidence that the Circuit Court of Appeals found that the verdicts of the jury were sustained by sufficient evidence on each count. * * *

It is not the form of the combination or the particular means used but the result to be achieved that the statute condemns. It is not of importance whether the means used to accomplish the unlawful objective are in themselves lawful or unlawful. Acts done to give effect to the conspiracy may be in themselves wholly innocent acts. Yet, if they are part of the sum of the acts which are relied upon to effectuate the conspiracy which the statute forbids, they come within its prohibition. No formal agreement is necessary to constitute an unlawful conspiracy. Often crimes are a matter of inference deduced from the acts of the person accused and done in pursuance of a criminal purpose. Where the conspiracy is proved, as here, from the evidence of the action taken in concert by the parties to it, it is all the more convincing proof of an intent to exercise the power of exclusion acquired through that conspiracy. The essential combination or conspiracy in violation of the Sherman Act may be found in a course of dealings or other circumstances as well as in any exchange of words. Where the circumstances are such as to warrant a jury in finding that the conspirators had a unity of purpose or a common design and understanding, or a meeting of minds in an unlawful arrangement, the conclusion that a conspiracy is established is justified. Neither proof of exertion of the power to exclude nor proof of actual exclusion of existing or potential competitors is essential to sustain a charge of monopolization under the Sherman Act.

* * *

In the present cases, the petitioners have been found to have conspired to establish a monopoly and also to have the power and intent to establish and maintain the monopoly. To hold that they do not come within the prohibition of the Sherman Act would destroy the force of that Act. Accordingly, the instructions of the trial court under § 2 of the Act are approved and the judgment of the Circuit Court of Appeals is affirmed.

JUSTICES REED and JACKSON took no part in the consideration or decision of these cases.

[Concurring opinion of MR. JUSTICE RUTLEDGE omitted. Eds.]

At the time of the events giving rise to the *American Tobacco* litigation, three firms accounted for the bulk of cigarette sales. The three manufacturers had "a friendly relationship" and the structure of the market had been stable for over a generation. The major tobacco firms implemented identical increases to cigarette list prices on the same day, June 23, 1931, with no economic justification. The firms increased their prices even though the costs of a key input were unusually low and manufacturing costs had been declining. As a result, the firms were highly profitable. List prices and discounts to dealers had been practically identical since 1923 and absolutely identical since 1928. The seven price changes since 1928 were identical in amount. Were any other facts important to the Court in upholding a jury verdict predicated on finding a conspiracy?

Does the Court believe that these facts rule out the possibility that the cigarette price increases came about through an oligopoly interaction short of agreement?[5] Or does it not care, on the view that such an interaction would constitute an unlawful conspiracy? (Note that this case was decided after *Interstate Circuit* but before *Theater Enterprises*, and before Turner and Posner debated the standards for proving conspiracy.)

----

[5] Firms would be expected to respond to a reduction in marginal cost by lowering their prices, all else being equal. The two most plausible economic explanations for higher prices in the face of declining costs here involve oligopoly conduct. Either (a) the cigarette producers acted less competitively than before (possibly through enhanced interfirm coordination), or (b) the cigarette oligopolists were always acting less than competitively (in a pre-existing oligopoly interaction possibly involving coordination) when market demand grew less elastic. With respect to the second explanation, the opinion reports that overall cigarette sales declined; this could be a response to higher prices, a response to lower consumer incomes during the Great Depression, or both. If the lost customers were more price-sensitive than those that remained, demand may have become less elastic. Either way, the conduct of the cigarette producers was likely inconsistent with perfect competition. The legal question is whether to deem that less-than-competitive outcome an agreement, subject to enforcement under Sherman Act § 1.

Should the facts recounted by the Court have been sufficient to infer an agreement? If so, on what basis? Does the opinion convince you that the major firms were acting pursuant to a covert express agreement when setting price? Does it convince you that the major firms were acting pursuant to a tacit understanding or meeting of the minds that was reasonable to deem an agreement? Does it convince you that the major firms had harmed competition by elevating price above competitive levels and that it was appropriate to reach that conduct regardless of whether the conduct would satisfy any particular definition of agreement?

If you do not believe these facts should have been sufficient, what additional evidence would you have required? More evidence of communication among the firms? A back-and-forth negotiation over terms of an agreement? A more complex change in prices—perhaps different price increases for different brands—that would be difficult to explain without communication?

Do policy considerations, such as those raised in the Turner-Posner debate, cut in favor or against finding an agreement? Should the Court have been more concerned with deterring anticompetitive conduct, or with chilling potentially beneficial conduct and preventing the unnecessary imposition of litigation costs? If, after this decision, a tobacco manufacturer raises prices, under what circumstances can a rival firm also raise prices (similarly in timing and amount) without risking violation of the antitrust laws? Should the Court have been more reluctant to find an agreement when the government sought a criminal sanction than it would if the government had brought the case civilly or if this had been a private treble damages action? Would your answer be different today, when criminal fines have grown much larger than they were at the time of the decision?

Historically, communication among firms, or the opportunity to communicate prior to an increase in industry prices, has been the most important plus factor relied upon by the courts to infer an agreement on price in a parallel pricing case. If firm representatives meet for dinner one day, and all raise price the next, courts may conclude that the firms reached an unlawful price-fixing deal over dessert. The significance of this plus factor is emphasized by a pre-*Matsushita* case, *United States v. Foley*. In *Foley* the court of appeals reviewed the criminal price-fixing conviction of ten leading suburban Washington D.C. realtors, which raised commission rates in the months following a dinner meeting among their principals at a country club.

UNITED STATES V. FOLEY

Unites States Court of Appeals for the Fourth Circuit, 1979.
598 F.2d 1323.

Before WINTER, CIRCUIT JUDGE, COWEN, SENIOR JUDGE and PHILLIPS, CIRCUIT JUDGE.

PHILLIPS, CIRCUIT JUDGE.

Six corporate and three individual defendants appeal their felony convictions for conspiracy to fix real estate commissions in Montgomery County, Maryland in violation of § 1 of the Sherman Act, 15 U.S.C. § 1. Finding no error, we affirm.

During the critical period in question all the defendants were realtors engaged as competitors in the business of "reselling" houses. When a person desired to sell his house in Montgomery County he listed it with a realtor, provided he did not decide to attempt to sell it directly. The listing provided that when the house was sold a fixed percentage of the sales price would be paid as a commission to the realtor. This commission was divided among the firms involved in the sale, a portion going to the firm that obtained the listing, another portion to the firm that produced the buyer. To facilitate the operation of this shared commission arrangement, each of the defendants belonged to the Montgomery County Board of Realtors, a trade association that operated a multiple listing service. In the case of almost all houses listed with a member realtor, the member sent a card to the listing service containing a picture of the house and certain pertinent information, including the commission. Thus all member realtors had available a fairly comprehensive list of houses on the market in the county.

During the summer of 1974, and for some time before, the prevailing commission rate in Montgomery County was six percent of the sales price. A few houses were listed at seven percent, but additional services were apparently provided for the higher rate. At this time the real estate brokerage business in the county was in difficult straits. While the number of houses listed with brokers for resale had continued to rise as it had for several previous years, the number of sales had fallen, mortgage funds were in short supply and increasing costs of stationery, telephone service, advertising and gasoline had reduced the profit margin.

On September 5, 1974, defendant John Foley, the president of defendant Jack Foley Realty, Inc., hosted a dinner party at the Congressional Country Club in Bethesda, Maryland. The guests were nine of the leading realtors in Montgomery County, including each of the three individual defendants and one representative of each of the corporate defendants in this appeal. Following the meal, Foley arose and, after making some other remarks, announced that his firm was raising its commission rate from six percent to seven percent. A discussion about the rate change ensued. Within the following months each of the corporate defendants substantially adopted a seven percent commission rate.

A United States grand jury for the district of Maryland indicted the nine defendants on April 1, 1977. Following a number of preliminary motions, the only one of which is of interest to this appeal being the denial of a motion to dismiss for lack of subject matter jurisdiction, a nine day jury trial was held in September 1977 before Judge Stanley Blair. All defendants were found guilty and this appeal ensued.

* * *

II. Conspiracy and Participation

Defendants * * * contend that there was insufficient evidence, although considered in the light most favorable to the government, to allow a jury to find the existence of a conspiracy and the participation of each defendant in it beyond a reasonable doubt. * * *

A. *The Evidence of Conspiracy*

Proof of a § 1 conspiracy need not be direct. "Acceptance by competitors of an invitation to participate in a plan, the necessary consequence of which, if carried out, is a restraint of commerce, is sufficient to establish an unlawful conspiracy under the Sherman Act, where each competitor knew that cooperation was essential to successful operation of the plan." While such evidence does not compel a finding of conspiracy, *Theatre Enterprises*, it does permit such a finding, *Interstate Circuit*. Within this principle, we find ample evidence to permit the finding of a conspiracy involving each of the defendants.

In the months preceding the September 5 dinner, several of the defendants were contemplating a change in commission rate, but were concededly afraid to undertake such a move for fear that they would be unable successfully to compete with firms still at six percent. Schick & Pepe had previously attempted to go to a seven percent rate and had failed because of competition. It was in this general climate of concern about competitive constraints that Foley called the meeting of September 5. At the dinner Foley rose, made some prefatory remarks and then stated that his firm was in dire financial condition. Saying that he did not care what the others did, he then announced that his firm was changing its commission rate from six percent to seven percent. Testimony as to what was said by various persons in the ensuing discussion is greatly in conflict, but there was evidence from which the jury could find that each of the individual defendants and a representative of each corporate defendant not represented by one of the individual defendants expressed an intention or gave the impression that his firm would adopt a similar change. The discussion also included reference to the earlier unsuccessful effort by Schick & Pepe to adopt a seven percent policy, from which the jury could conclude that defendants knew that their cooperation was essential. Evidence presented in the form of detailed charts with explanation by an economist qualified as expert witness showed that in the months following each defendant did in fact begin to take substantial numbers of seven percent listings. Moreover, the jury heard testimony of a number of instances in which members of the conspiracy sought after the September 5 dinner to hold their fellows to the "agreement." * * *

B. Connection of Each Defendant to the Conspiracy

(1) Jack Foley Realty, Inc. and John P. Foley, Jr.

Jack Foley hosted the September 5 dinner, inviting in addition to a few realtors who were close personal friends, those he regarded as the most active members of his profession. He had previously announced the commission change to his staff and on September 15 mailed a notice concerning it to all local realtors. By early October, Foley, Inc. had thirty percent of its listings at the higher rate; by December, the figure was in excess of seventy percent and remained in that neighborhood throughout 1975.

Allyn Rickman, vice president of Schick & Pepe and a guest at the September 5 dinner, testified that after Schick & Pepe took some six percent listings, Foley called him and told him that was a "mistake" because if they all did not hold the line none of them could get seven percent. Before the policy change, Foley's firm had accepted a house at a six percent listing. When the listing was renewed after the policy change, still at six percent, Foley, Inc. sent a card to the listing service which was in turn distributed to all the local realtors. A listing card was then received anonymously in the mail by Foley with a question mark on it. When the house was again relisted, the contract and the listing with the service were both at seven percent. John O'Keefe, a vice president at Foley, Inc., however, wrote a letter to the homeowner/seller informing him that Foley would reimburse him for the extra one percent. The letter contained the following explanation: "The reason I don't want (the listing) to go through showing 6% is our Firm was one of the leading Firms in changing from 6% to 7% and with Mr. Foley being the President of the Board of Realtors, I just don't want any unjust criticism of him or our Company for taking your listing at less than 7%."

(2) Colquitt-Carruthers, Inc. and John T. Carruthers, Jr.

John T. Carruthers of Colquitt-Carruthers, Inc. attended the dinner. The testimony conflicts on whether he said he was already at seven percent, or whether he was going to go to seven percent. His accountant testified that a policy change occurred between September 10 and September 24. Effective September 24, all listings other than at seven percent had to be accompanied by explanation; after November 1, they would not be accepted at less than seven percent. By October 1974,

Colquitt-Carruthers had sixty percent of its listings at the new rate and through the end of 1975 the figure was generally in excess of eighty percent.

There was testimony that Carruthers made several attempts to ensure the cooperation of other firms. William Ellis, vice president of Shannon & Luchs Co., a firm that delayed implementation of the seven percent policy, testified that Carruthers called him on three occasions. Around January 1, 1975, Carruthers called and asked about Ellis' "considerations." Ellis replied "You know I can't make the decision." Carruthers then offered to call the man who could make the decision. Later in January, Carruthers again called, this time explicitly asking about the change. Upon being told that Shannon & Luchs had adopted a seven percent policy, but had set no date for its implementation, Carruthers "threatened" Ellis with the loss of his job. In April when Shannon & Luchs' Gaithersburg, Maryland office took some six percent listings, Carruthers again called Ellis to complain.

Allyn Rickman, vice president of Schick & Pepe Realty, Inc., also testified that Carruthers called him to complain about some six percent listings that Schick & Pepe had accepted. He quoted Carruthers as saying "if we do not stay at seven percent, then it would be a slide back and . . . no one could get seven percent, because the competition would hurt us." There was also testimony that Carruthers complained to Robert Dorsey, a vice president at Bogley, Inc., about that firm having taken more six than seven percent listings.

* * *

(5)   Shannon & Luchs Co.

Shannon & Luchs did not officially adopt a seven percent policy until January 1975. At the dinner, its vice president, William Ellis, stated that they should not be discussing a rate increase and said that his firm was always the first to be investigated when something like this happened as it was the county's largest. He also stated that Shannon & Luchs would probably go to seven percent at a later date; Allyn Rickman remembered a possible mention of the first of the year. On September 9, Ellis told his managers not to turn down any seven percent listings they had an opportunity to get. In fact, the percentage of seven percent listings taken by Shannon & Luchs crept toward thirty percent by January 1975. Early in January, John T. Carruthers called Ellis and asked about his "considerations." Ellis told him that he, Ellis, did not make those decisions and Carruthers then offered to telephone the man who did; Ellis replied that he did not need help. On January 15, at Ellis' suggestion, Shannon & Luchs adopted a policy of taking seven percent listings unless some other rate were beneficial to the firm or otherwise appropriate. Although the new policy was not implemented until March 1, by that time forty percent of Shannon & Luchs' listings were at seven percent. By early April, the figure was about sixty-five percent and throughout 1975 it stood between eighty and ninety. In response to a comment from Carruthers in April, Ellis acknowledged that he had a "problem" in his Gaithersburg, Maryland office in implementing the policy. Shannon & Luchs did not adopt a seven percent policy for its offices in northern Virginia because of the threat of competition.

* * *

C.   Conclusion

We conclude that this evidence, here merely summarized and highlighted from a much more detailed body of proof adduced by the Government, was sufficient to permit the jury to find as it did against each of the defendants on the conspiracy issue. Defendants of course offered explanatory and exculpatory evidence, and on this appeal urge that the proper inferences to be drawn from all the evidence relieve their actions of criminal implications. Among these arguments is the interesting one that only by graceless refusals to accept Foley's invitation to dinner or by equally graceless withdrawals from it once its purpose was revealed could they have avoided the factual inferences required to implicate them in the conspiracy, and that to sustain their convictions will impose intolerable burdens on businessmen confronted with like dilemmas. This, with other arguments about the proper inferences to be drawn from the evidence, was undoubtedly presented to the jury by able counsel for the defendants. A properly composed jury of defendants' peers rejected this factual argument as well as others in reaching its verdict of guilty. That to sustain the jury finding on this issue may have the inhibitory effect on the conduct of others that is urged by defendants does not speak to the force of the evidence supporting the jury's finding in this case.

* * *

What plus factors did the court rely upon to infer an agreement from the parallel increase in real estate commission rates beyond the fact that the realtors had the opportunity to reach an agreement at a dinner meeting where, they admit, prices were discussed? Is it easy to come up with an innocent explanation for the later complaint calls, during which some realtors raised questions about price-cutting by others?

Suppose the only evidence of an agreement was statements at the dinner that simply restated the obvious, such as "We're all better off with high prices. If the rest of you match our commission rate, we'll all make money." Could a court reasonably infer that the subtext of those statements was the message "Please raise your rates to match?" If a court concluded that the firms had reached an unlawful agreement on price based solely on this evidence, what would the court enjoin if it sought to fashion an injunctive remedy? If the only remedy were damages, would the threat of damages deter firms in other markets from raising prices in similar situations, or would it merely deter them from making obvious statements at dinner while finding some other way to coordinate? And would the threat of a private action for damages chill legitimate and procompetitive cooperative behavior? For example, might senior executives avoid meeting to discuss improvements to the regional multiple listing service, for fear that enforcers or a class of customers might bring a price-fixing case if commissions rose shortly thereafter?

In the real estate industry, the seller and the buyer often have different agents, which must cooperate in a house sale and would then share the commission. What does this fact suggest about the likelihood that rivals would detect a realtor cutting the commission rate below an agreed-upon level? Would it have been possible for one of the realtors to cheat by signing up homeowners with a nominal 7% commission reported on the multiple listing service, then secretly rebating 1% back to the homeowner? Or would this practice likely be discovered before the cheating realtor increased its business significantly? If secret cheating was feasible, should that possibility have counted against the inference of an agreement in *Foley*? What does the need for cooperation between realtors suggest about the ability of colluding firms to punish a discounter?

The growth of the Internet has been changing the real estate industry. In 2008, the Justice Department settled a case it brought against the National Association of Realtors, an association of real estate brokers, alleging that association rules prevented the growth of brokers with Internet-based business models by restricting their access to the information about houses for sale available on multiple listing services. The Federal Trade Commission has also reached consent settlements with several local associations of real estate brokers involving similar practices. Recall, too, our consideration of the conduct of the realtors in *RealComp II*, which we studied in Chapter 2.

2. SYNTHESIZING THE PLUS FACTORS

Figure 3–3 summarizes the principal plus factors that courts use to illuminate the source of parallel conduct, including communication among the alleged conspirators, such as was described in *Foley*. Many of these factors are derived from the Supreme Court's opinions in *Interstate Circuit* and *American Tobacco*; others are highlighted in the appellate decisions we will read below.

Figure 3–3 organizes the plus factors that courts commonly rely upon into two broad groups. One group includes factors that tend to distinguish agreement from parallel conduct short of agreement directly. The other group includes factors that suggest that the industry is conducive to agreement.

The plus factors in the first group (*"Factors Tending to Distinguish Agreement from Conscious Parallelism Directly"*) aim to discriminate directly between consciously parallel conduct and conduct that would be deemed an agreement under the antitrust laws. (Recall the discussion of the Turner/Posner debate in Sidebar 3–3 and the discussion of what constitutes an agreement in Sidebar 3–5. Our framing implicitly adopts Turner's perspective; the Posner side of the debate might argue that the plus factors in the second set just as directly identify those instances of conscious parallelism that should be deemed an agreement.) The idea of the plus factors in this group—observed differences between the way firms behave and the way these firms would be expected to behave or similar firms did behave in competitive markets—is similar to the "single inference" method of inferring competitive effects discussed in Sidebar 4–5.

The plus factors in the first group are divided into three types. The first involves communication or the opportunity to communicate. Communication may take many forms, including meetings, phone calls, letters, text messages, and emails. It may take place directly between the firms, or through intermediaries such as trade associations. The mere fact of communication may support inferring an agreement without evidence of what was discussed, as may the opportunity to communicate without evidence that communication actually took place (though the latter may be less powerful as evidence that the firms covertly negotiated an express agreement). Communication involving competitively-sensitive information—perhaps including sales to specific customers, advance notice of price changes not disclosed to customers, or verification of the price the firm charged in specific past transactions—may lead to the inference that the firms communicated about other matters, such as the negotiation of prices or the allocation of territories, and thus may bear on the issue addressed by the first group of plus factors. Such communications may also suggest ways that the firms may have helped make the market conducive to coordination, and thus may bear on the issue addressed by the second group of plus factors.

The other two types of plus factors in the first group recognize that some types of conduct are difficult to understand as arising absent an agreement—because they are too complex to be explained by mere parallel behavior or hard to rationalize as having a legitimate business justification. It is impossible to provide a complete catalogue of these possibilities, but under some circumstances they might include, for example: a sudden and substantial change in industry conduct; complex and seemingly arbitrary revisions to the pattern of prices on price lists; firms purchasing products at wholesale from a competitor that they could have produced more cheaply internally; firms with excess low cost capacity declining to compete for the business of buyers that are customers of their rivals or declining to offer a secret discount to obtain a large increment of business; firms not adjusting prices when supply or demand conditions change substantially, as by declining to lower price high when costs and demand are falling; multiproduct producers raising prices substantially on products where their firm's demand is elastic but industry demand is less elastic; or rival firms standardizing or simplifying product grades, publishing price lists, or announcing price changes in advance in situations where these practices provide little or no customer benefit. Practices like these may look more suspicious—more difficult to understand as the product of independent action rather than an agreement—if they are introduced simultaneously and suddenly, or in the immediate wake of interfirm communication.

Defendants seeking to undermine an inference of conspiracy from the plus factors in the first group may argue that the factors have alternative and innocent explanations that are equally plausible. Rivals may communicate for a host of reasons unrelated to conspiracy, including advancing legitimate trade association activity, procompetitive collaborations, or charitable undertakings. Other practices mentioned above, such as issuing price lists or providing advance notice of price increases, may be valuable to customers. Conduct consistent with independent choice or conduct that accomplishes procompetitive or competitively neutral objectives may offer a less compelling basis for inferring an anticompetitive agreement even if the same conduct may also facilitate coordination.

The plus factors in the second group ("*Factors Suggesting the Industry is Conducive to Coordination*") are related to the economic question of whether the firms can successfully reach a coordinated outcome by reaching consensus on the terms of coordination, deterring deviation (cheating) from those terms, and preventing new competition.

Six types of factors are listed in this group. The first type includes industry features similar to those discussed previously in this Chapter as factors facilitating coordination. (*See* Case Study II and Figure 3–1.) The second type is concerned with a prior history of coordination.

Courts may also analyze whether defendants had a rational motive to engage in a conspiracy, as indicated by the third type of factors in the second grouping. When market demand is inelastic and entry is difficult, for example, the firms can increase industry revenues and profits by collectively reducing output and raising price. Under such circumstances, if the firms are not already colluding, they can profit by doing so. If instead they are already colluding, their coordination is almost surely imperfect and incomplete (as a monopolist facing inelastic demand would profit from raising price), so they could increase their anticompetitive profits by making coordination more effective. These "rational motive" factors may not be strongly probative taken alone—after all, firms in competitive markets would frequently find coordination profitable if only they could solve their cartel problems, but coordination is not inevitable in such settings. However, courts may find these factors more probative when considered in conjunction with the other plus factors in the second group (those suggesting more directly that the firms have found ways to solve the economic "cartel problems" of reaching consensus, deterring deviation, and preventing new competition).

The second group also includes a fourth type of economic factor that courts sometimes consider: aspects of market performance and conduct suggesting that firms have solved their cartel problems and are exercising market power. These might include, for example, evidence that prices are high relative to costs for products not strongly differentiated when firms have excess capacity, that prices rose when costs fell, or that market shares remained stable after substantial changes in the conditions of demand and supply. The fifth and sixth types of economic factors in the second group are reasons to think that if firms are exercising market power, they are doing so in a coordinated manner. These include the adoption of practices that might facilitate coordination, perhaps including pre-announcement of price increases, use of common price lists, or exchange of information about prices, costs, output, capacity or sales. They also include conduct that is hard to understand as being in a firm's self-interest unless also pursued by its rivals. These might include stability of prices despite substantial changes in market conditions.

Defendants using the plus factors in the second group to rebut the inference of conspiracy may argue (a) that collusion would be irrational (unprofitable because demand is elastic or entry is easy), (b) that collusion would be unsuccessful (because the firms cannot practically reach a consensus on terms of coordination, deter cheating, or prevent new competition), or (c) that collusion is inconsistent with industry conduct and performance (because the firms are behaving competitively). Coordination is not inevitable even if the industry structure appears conducive to it, and coordination is not unheard of in markets in which the market structure would appear not to be conducive to it (including markets with a large number of firms). Price increases may have explanations consistent with competition, as related to changes in cost and demand, without need to postulate coordination.

None of the plus factors, or types of plus factors, listed in Figure 3–3 should be looked at in isolation when considering whether the facts of a parallel conduct case support the inference of conspiracy. Moreover, some factors listed in each group and type may be more compelling than others. For example, evidence that prices rose when costs fell seems harder to rationalize as consistent with competitive behavior than evidence of stable market shares, although both could suggest that firms are exercising market power.

As a matter of economic logic, plus factors in the second group—which are largely concerned with market structure and performance—do not, alone, distinguish conscious parallelism from agreement. If prices are set above competitive levels in an industry that appears conducive to coordination, that outcome could be the product of interdependent conduct (such as leader-follower behavior) that today's courts, adopting the prevailing Turner view, would typically not deem an agreement. But these plus factors may support the inference of agreement when combined with plus factors in the first group.

Moreover, a defense argument based solely on plus factors in the second group—a claim that the inference of agreement is implausible because the market is not conducive to coordination—should not invariably prevail. Suppose, for example, that the market has features suggesting it is not conducive to coordination, such as many firms, non-transparent prices, volatile demand, and large buyers. Suppose further that the firms are thought to be exercising market power. Perhaps prices are nearly identical and rise together, firms do not discount prices, prices rose when costs fell, market shares are stable, and prices exceed the levels that prevailed at a time when firms were thought not to have been exercising market power. Should a court decline to infer an agreement on the ground that coordination was unlikely to succeed, notwithstanding the evidence that the firms were collectively exercising market power? Or should a court conclude that the firms could not have exercised market power without negotiating an agreement, perhaps through secret communications, and infer an agreement on price? The presence of plus factors in the first group (such as communication, complex conduct, and conduct lacking an efficiency justification) could make the latter inference the more compelling.

Figure 3–3:

Synthesizing the "Plus Factors" for Proving Conspiracy

Parallel Pricing +

Factors Tending to Distinguish Agreement from Conscious Parallelism Directly

- *Communication or opportunity to communicate*

  (*e.g.*, meetings, trade association conferences)

- *Conduct too complicated to be explained by mere parallel behavior*

  (*e.g.*, conduct that appears irrational absent agreement)

- *Conduct lacking an evident efficiency explanation*

  (*e.g.*, failure to price based on relative cost advantages)

Factors Suggesting the Industry is Conducive to Coordination (ability to solve "cartel problems" of reaching consensus, deterring cheating, and preventing new competition)

- *Industry features*

  (*e.g.*, few firms, homogeneous products, difficult entry conditions, large numbers of purchasers, small and frequent transactions, transparent prices)

- *Past history of industry coordination*

  (*e.g.*, historic evidence of successful interdependent or collusive action)

- *Rational motive to behave collectively*

  (*e.g.*, inelastic demand, difficult conditions of entry)

- *Factors suggesting firms are exercising market power*

  (*e.g.*, sustained and substantial profitability, persistently supra-competitive pricing, prices rise when costs fall, stability of market shares over time)

- *Facilitating factors*

  (*e.g.*, pre-announcement of price increases, other information exchange)

- *Actions contrary to self-interest unless pursued collectively*

  (*e.g.*, stability of prices notwithstanding substantial changes in supply or demand)

The most common plus factors are grouped in Figure 3–3, but they are not prioritized. Indeed, courts seldom rank plus factors by their probative value or specify the minimum critical mass of plus factors that will sustain an inference of concerted conduct. Moreover, some kinds of conduct could reasonably be categorized as bearing on the presence or absence of more than one plus factor. In addition, courts may differ on the relative weight they place on factors in the first group (those suggesting agreement as distinct from conscious parallelism) and the second group (those suggesting the industry is conducive to coordination). For example, when firms act in parallel and the industry appears conducive to coordination (based on analyzing plus factors in the second group), a court taking Posner's side of the Posner-Turner debate may demand less evidence from the first group of plus factors than a court taking Turner's side of the debate. These characteristics may suggest a great deal of ambiguity or judicial discretion in mapping from the facts of a parallel conduct case to a judgment about whether to infer an agreement pursuant to Sherman Act § 1.

3. INTEGRATING THE PLUS FACTORS INTO A NARRATIVE

The problem of integrating plus factors is discussed through the vehicle of the dueling opinions of a closely divided circuit court in *Blomkest Fertilizer, Inc. v. Potash Corp.*, 203 F.3d 1028 (8th Cir. 2000) (en banc) over whether the facts in that case support an inference of a tacit agreement to which Section 1 applies, or whether they merely reflect parallel pricing stemming from oligopolistic interdependence, which *Theatre Enterprises*, and later *Matsushita* and *Twombly*, regarded as insufficient to support an inference of agreement. The discussion highlights the way plus factors can be prioritized and weighed by integrating them into a narrative.

Blomkest involved allegations of a horizontal conspiracy to raise prices. The case concerned the production and sale of potash, a mineral used in fertilizer. A class of potash consumers alleged that eight potash producers, six Canadian and two American, had conspired to fix prices in violation of Sherman Act § 1 between April 1987 and July 1994. The case reached the circuit court on appeal from the district court's grant of summary judgment in favor of the defendant producers. By six votes to five, the Eight Circuit, sitting en banc, concluded that the facts, taken in the light most favorable to plaintiffs, would not support the inference of an agreement among the potash producers and affirmed the award of summary judgment to the defendants.

Prices rose in parallel early during the period of the alleged agreement. One Canadian firm, PCS, increased price suddenly and dramatically in early September 1987, and the remaining producers followed suit one week later. In January 1988, the Canadian producers reached an agreement with the U.S. Department of Commerce to suspend an investigation into complaints by U.S. potash producers that the Canadian firms had been "dumping" potash in the U.S. by selling it at prices well below market value in violation of international trade agreements. The Suspension Agreement set a price floor for Canadian potash sold in the U.S. Three days later, on January 11, PCS issued a new price list, setting prices below what it had charged in September 1987 but above the prior level. Most of the other producers followed PCS within eleven days.

PCS was originally owned by the government of the Canadian province of Saskatchewan. As a publicly owned firm, its goal was to maintain employment and local economic activity. From an economic point of view, it could be thought of as aiming to maximize output subject to not losing money, rather than maximizing profits, the usual goal of private firms. In 1986, a newly elected provincial government began steps to privatize the firm, appointing new management. Under new management PCS significantly reduced output and raised prices.

The circuit court majority declined to infer an agreement to raise price or maintain higher than competitive prices. There was no direct evidence of an agreement. A January 8 document describing new price lists to be issued on January 11 was not credited as probative because it was unclear who it was sent to or who saw it, and it was not uniformly followed by producers.

The majority also declined to infer an agreement after reviewing a range of possible plus factors. It did not find support for that inference in the evidence of communication among the firms. Price verification calls—evidence that high-level executives from one firm called their counterparts at other firms to verify prices in response to rumors that their rivals were discounting off of list prices—were dismissed along with evidence of meetings at trade shows because they were infrequent and sporadic. The price verification activity amounted to several dozen calls during a seven-year period during which the firms undertook tens of thousands of transactions. The majority also noted that these calls took place after the September 1987 price increase, that the firms were verifying prices on completed transactions (not calling before the price quotation to the customer), and that they would expect firms to verify prices given that this was an oligopolistic industry and transactions were often very large. The majority did not credit plaintiffs' argument that the producers signaled pricing intentions to each other through advance price announcements and the dissemination of price lists, terming this evidence too ambiguous to defeat summary judgment.

The majority found it impossible to reject an alternative explanation for the price increase not requiring an anticompetitive agreement. In its view, potash prices would naturally be expected to increase as the result of governmental action in the U.S. (the Suspension Agreement, which set a minimum sale price in the U.S.) and Saskatchewan (the steps taken toward privatizing PCS, which limited that firm's output). For the majority, the common price levels and rapid matching of price changes established no more than conscious parallelism. The uniform participation of Canadian producers in the suspension agreement was also not seen as puzzling: it was likely in the interest of all producers, even those with little exposure to possible penalties (low dumping margins), in order to avoid the cost of litigation and resolve uncertainty about the ultimate outcome of the dumping investigation.

The dissenting judges looked largely to the same plus factors, but saw the facts as instead supporting the conclusion that the defendants had reached an agreement on price. Their analysis of interfirm communications pointed first to evidence of solicitations to enter a price-fixing agreement, mostly by PCS. These included multiple complaints by PCS officials to their counterparts at rival firms about rival price cuts. In one instance, a PCS employee apologized to a senior executive at a rival firm for a low bid PCS had made by mistake, and said he hoped the low price would not spread in the marketplace. In another case, PCS cut prices for five days in December 1989 as part of what was termed a "market correction program." An executive from a rival firm testified that PCS communicated in advance that the purpose of the program was to "get [the] attention" of "cheating" competitors and thereby "stabilize" industry prices. In addition, the dissenters highlighted the price-verification calls dismissed by the majority. The calls began in 1987, they were often between high-level executives in a position to fix prices, and their number was more than trivial, according to the dissent.

The dissenters further explained that much of the conduct that concerned it had no legitimate justification, and was difficult to explain absent an agreement. Information about discounting, the subject of price verification calls, was shared with rivals not with customers, and the market correction program also appeared designed to discipline firms that had cheated on an agreement. Moreover, the dissent observed, the evidence showed that prices rose far more than what would have been expected from governmental intervention alone, and the Suspension Agreement did not dictate the actual price charged.

The dissenters highlighted aspects of market structure they saw as conducive to collusion. The potash industry was described as an oligopoly (eight firms). The dissenters also noted entry barriers, inelastic demand, and a standardized product. Another structural feature, industry excess capacity, cut the other way, spurring price competition during 1986 (the year before the alleged conspiracy began). In particular, individual attempts by four firms, including PCS, to initiate a price rise during 1986 had failed and the firms had engaged in a price war. The interfirm communications that the dissent saw as supporting the inference of agreement began during 1987.

Did the potash firms achieve a supracompetitive price through conduct that ought to be deemed an agreement to fix prices under Sherman Act § 1? As the six to five vote of the appellate panel emphasizes, *Blomkest* was a close case on the facts.

One way to approach this question is to think about the economic story the two sides told through their appeal to plus factors. Although the dissenters did not frame their argument this way, they appear to take the view that the producers were previously unable to collude successfully because they had difficulty solving one of their cartel problems: deterring cheating. The firms solved that problem in 1987, mainly through price verification calls. As a result, they were able to raise price above competitive levels (even above what was required by the Suspension Agreement). In this story, the firms primarily needed to prevent cheating in order to coordinate successfully. In *Foley,* which we previously read, and Problem 3–1 at the end of this Chapter, the coordinating firms also needed to solve a different cartel problem, reaching consensus.

The majority appears to tell two related economic stories. In the first story, the price increase was the natural result of governmental action in the U.S. and Saskatchewan that limited industry output. If so, it would not be necessary to posit an agreement in order to explain high prices. The dissent responded with evidence that prices rose substantially more than would have been expected from governmental intervention alone; the dispute on this point is in part over whether to give more weight to the timing of the governmental actions (as the majority does) or to the evidence as to their expected impact on the price level (as the dissent does).

The majority's second story would apply even if the 1987 price increase is thought to have exceeded the level that should have flowed from the governmental action. Under this story, the potash price increase was the natural result of independent decision-making under conditions of oligopolistic interdependence, so it is not necessary to posit an agreement to explain it. That is, the majority can be understood as making an argument of the form that Sidebar 3–5 suggests should insulate defendants from the inference of an agreement, namely: "Even if we are coordinating—which, of course, we do not admit—we did not need to agree in order to do so" or "We acknowledge that we each pay attention to our rival's prices when we make our own pricing decisions—we often follow the leader. But we make our decisions independently, and neither negotiate with our competitors nor exchange assurances with them about our prices." Consistent with this view, courts reviewing firm conduct in oligopolistic industries have historically declined to find conspiracy when parallel conduct is attributable simply to leader-follower behavior. This argument recalls Turner's position in the Turner/Posner debate (Sidebar 3–3), as it posits a gap between anticompetitive conduct among rivals and conduct that can or should be reached under Sherman Act § 1.

Even a Turnerite could question the second economic story we have attributed to the majority, however, by focusing on identifying the cartel problem that prevented the potash firms from coordinating successfully before 1987. The dissent can be understood as claiming that the key problem was deterring cheating, and that the firms solved it mainly through price verification calls introduced during that year. The majority's first economic story, associating the timing of the price increase with governmental action rather than the introduction of verification calls, would provide an alternative explanation for the timing, but not for the magnitude of the price increase (if the dissent's claim that it exceeded what the governmental action would have produced is credited), and neither of the majority's economic stories would explain why the firms were able to deter cheating in 1987 when they could not do so before. This discussion highlights the critical importance of the dissent's position on the evidence that price rose by more than what the change in PCS's management and Suspension Agreement would have produced.

The majority could have taken a different tack: accepting that the price verification calls permitted the firms to deter cheating, and arguing that at worst the facts would demonstrate an agreement among rivals to *verify* prices (not an agreement as to price). With such an agreement, the majority could have contended, oligopolistic interdependence would have led to substantial price increases without need to posit an agreement as to price (or an agreement not to discount, which would be a type of agreement as to price). Plaintiffs chose only to pursue the possibility of a price-fixing agreement in the potash litigation, and the possibility that firms agreed only to verify prices was not addressed by the court. We examine the law governing the possibility that an agreement to exchange information would be unreasonable because it facilitates coordination, and thus violate Sherman Act § 1, in the next Section of this Chapter.

Notice how our focus in the last few paragraphs on telling an economic story provides a framework for prioritizing the plus factors by integrating them into a narrative framed by the economics of cartel formation. The case for inferring agreement was tied to identifying the cartel problem the firms needed to solve in order to successfully coordinate, and the way they solved it. The key plus factors for the dissent supported that narrative—they were consistent with it and not with a benign alternative—and explained why the firms could not have solved their problem acting on their own. The case against inferring agreement was tied to alternative economic explanations for higher prices that did not require postulating an agreement: that they were the natural product of government action or that they were the natural result of oligopolistic interdependence. Similarly, in other cases, defendants might explain a price increase in terms of higher costs. With the plus factors integrated into an economic story, the question of which plus factors to credit is reinterpreted as a question of which narrative to credit, providing a way to synthesize and evaluate the plus factors rather than treating them as simply a category-by-category checklist. *Cf. In re High Fructose Corn Syrup Antitrust Litigation*, 295 F.3d 651, 655–56 (7th Cir. 2002) (Posner, J.) (even if no single item of evidence points unequivocally to conspiracy, the evidence as a whole can defeat a motion for summary judgment for defendant).

The majority's skepticism about inferring an agreement from circumstantial evidence in *Blomkest* is quite different from the court's attitude in *Foley*. This difference could be attributed to a difference in complexity of the economic narrative in the two cases. The economic story in *Foley* was simple. The key cartel problem inhibiting coordination among the realtors was likely reaching consensus, which the firms solved over a country club dinner. *Foley* tells the story of a covert agreement: the firms met secretly one day, and prices rose shortly thereafter. Communication was the most important plus factor for telling this story, and the court relied heavily on it. By contrast, the dissent's economic narrative in *Blomkest* was a more complex economic tale of cheating and cartel policing through occasional price verification calls. Was the inference of agreement in *Blomkest* more difficult, and ultimately rejected, because generalist judges have greater difficulty evaluating a complex economic case than evaluating a simple story of what happened at a dinner meeting?

Figure 3–4:

Contrasting the *Blomkest* Majority and Dissenting Narratives

Blomkest Majority (Summary Judgment for Defendants)	*Blomkest* Dissent (Would Deny Summary Judgment)
No direct evidence of agreement	Interfirm communications (solicitations; complaints about rival low pricing; references to cheating and price stabilization)
A circulated price list was of unknown origin and not followed by producers	No legitimate business justification for sharing of information about discounting, price verification calls, "market correction program"
Interfirm communications (price verification calls and trade show meetings)—infrequent and sporadic; limited to past transactions; too ambiguous	Prices increased more than would have been expected from government actions
Advance price announcements and dissemination of price lists— also too ambiguous to constitute signaling	Market structure (concentration, barriers to entry, inelastic demand, standardized product), but industry excess capacity spurred price competition
Independent business justifications (Suspension Agreement and Canadian government actions)	

4. MODERN TRENDS IN INFERRING AGREEMENT

Before *Matsushita*, courts rarely struggled with economic evidence when considering whether to infer an agreement to fix prices when prices rose in parallel. With *Matsushita*'s instruction to lower courts to weed out cases where the claims make "no economic sense," this has changed. This change is suggested by the extensive discussion of economic evidence by both the majority and dissent in *Blomkest*. Other recent appellate decisions on inferring agreement from circumstantial evidence also include extensive treatments of economic evidence. *Twombly* likely reinforced this trend. For a modern survey of plus factors, with a focus on economic evidence, see William E. Kovacic, Robert C. Marshall, Leslie M. Marx & Halbert L. White, Jr., *Plus Factors and Agreement in Antitrust Law*, 110 MICH. L. REV. 393 (2011).

The circuits differ in their willingness to infer conspiracy when evidence points both ways. In *In re High Fructose Corn Syrup Antitrust Litigation*, 295 F.3d 651 (7th Cir. 2002), the Seventh Circuit overturned a district court's award of summary judgment to defendants in an opinion written by Judge Richard Posner. According to the court, "all of [the] evidence is consistent with the hypothesis that [defendants] had a merely tacit agreement, which at least for purposes of this appeal the plaintiffs concede is not actionable under section 1 of the Sherman Act." *Id.* at 661. Yet the Seventh Circuit nevertheless found enough evidence for a reasonable jury to find an agreement to fix prices: "The evidence is not conclusive by any means—there are alternative interpretations of every bit of it—but it is highly suggestive of the existence of an explicit though of course covert agreement to fix prices." *Id.* at 663.

In *Williamson Oil Co. v. Philip Morris USA*, 346 F.3d 1287 (11th Cir. 2003), which we will read in Section E below, the appeals court affirmed a district court's entry of summary judgment in favor of defendants. The Eleventh Circuit held that the evidence, taken as a whole, did not distinguish between a conspiracy to fix prices and lawful "conscious parallelism." "Because [the plaintiffs] cannot demonstrate the existence of a plus factor," the Eleventh Circuit held, "they cannot establish an inference of conspiracy," as would be necessary to overturn the award of summary judgment to the defendants. *Id.* at 1323. Moreover, the defendants "would have rebutted any inference that they conspired to fix prices by demonstrating that the [plaintiff] class's conspiracy theory is utterly implausible." *Id. See also In re Flat Glass Antitrust Litigation*, 385 F.3d 350 (3d. Cir. 2004) (reversing district court award of summary judgment to plaintiffs, on the ground that the evidence was ambiguous as to whether the firms had agreed and, consequently, insufficient legally to support the inference of conspiracy).

Sidebar 3–5:
What Is an Agreement?

What is an agreement under the antitrust laws? In one view, an agreement is best understood as a process, involving negotiation and the exchange of assurances, not an outcome. This sidebar summarizes the argument for this perspective.[a]

It is tempting but ultimately unpersuasive to identify an agreement under the antitrust laws from circumstantial evidence in parallel pricing cases by applying common judicial definitions that sound in contract, like a "meeting of the minds" or "conscious commitment to a common scheme," which were used in some of the earlier Supreme Court cases. The reason: a court conscientiously applying these definitions would be led mistakenly to infer an agreement merely from the consciously parallel interaction among oligopolists. When one firm in an oligopoly raises its price, and each of the others follows that lead, the definitions are satisfied: the first price increase is an offer; those that follow are acceptances; as each observes the other's actions, they reach a common understanding.

Yet accepting this result by inferring an agreement whenever oligopolists price in parallel would be a mistake. As the Turner side argued in the debate discussed in Sidebar 3–3, it would permit a finding of unlawful conspiracy in situations where courts would often be unable to craft any effective injunctive remedy—there would be nothing practical that a court could order the parties to do to correct it. If agreement is evidenced by something beyond merely parallel price behavior, then a court can, in principle, enjoin that extra "something." But absent that extra "something," the only injunctive remedy is judicial price regulation—objectionable on a number of grounds. A damages remedy would still be available in principle, but if a court would have nothing to enjoin—if it cannot tell firms what conduct they must not undertake—firms seeking to comply with the Sherman Act would often find that they could avoid liability only by refraining from procompetitive conduct. To avoid that counterproductive outcome, to paraphrase the Supreme Court, conscious parallelism has not read "agreement" out of the Sherman Act.

The need to frame a satisfactory remedy generates other limits on the application of the antitrust laws. A firm or

---

[a] This sidebar is adapted from Jonathan B. Baker, *Identifying Horizontal Price Fixing in the Electronic Marketplace*, 65 ANTITRUST L. J. 41, 47–51 (1996). *See also* Jonathan B. Baker, *Two Sherman Act Section 1 Dilemmas: Parallel Pricing, the Oligopoly Problem, and Contemporary Economic Theory*, 38 ANTITRUST BULL. 143 (1993).

oligopoly that happens to charge prices above the competitive level does not for that reason alone violate Sherman Act Section 1. Moreover, mere leader-follower behavior is not illegal even if supracompetitive prices result. Return to the Gas Station Hypothetical (*see supra* Case Study I) with this issue in mind. Under contract law, a court could arguably find an implied-in-fact contract. Yet, at least in the Turner tradition, the gas stations would not be deemed to have reached an agreement under the antitrust laws.

An agreement under antitrust law is better defined by what the courts actually do in parallel pricing cases than by the words of the common legal definitions. Rather than deeming mere conscious parallelism an "agreement," courts look for certain additional features of firm behavior called "plus factors" to support an inference of agreement from circumstantial evidence. Plus factors are best thought of as evidence that the alleged conspirators have gone through a process of negotiation and exchange of assurances in addition to, or as the reason for, their parallel price behavior. They support a conclusion based on the totality of the circumstantial evidence that the parties have done more than merely watch each other's market behavior and respond to it independently, as leaders and followers, and, consequently, that the firms could have behaved differently.

This judicial methodology carries with it an important point: the legal idea of an agreement does not describe a result or equilibrium, but one particular process of reaching supracompetitive marketplace outcomes—what may be termed the "forbidden process" of negotiation and exchange of assurances. The forbidden process consists of behavior that can be enjoined. Thus, if the oligopoly reaches a high price equilibrium through the forbidden process that the law calls an agreement, Sherman Act Section 1 has been violated. If the same result were reached through leader-follower behavior, no agreement on price will be found.

Historically, the most important plus factors involved communications evidence suggesting that the firms were a hidden cartel, as in *Foley*. Secret and direct communications among the sellers just before prices rose suggest a cartel denied by its members and pushed underground by the Sherman Act. The list of plus factors has expanded as the critical task of determining whether firms pricing in parallel have engaged in the forbidden process has increasingly become an economic question. Recall that the Supreme Court in *Matsushita*, refused to permit an inference of conspiracy that did not make "economic sense."

In two situations, *Matsushita's* "economic sense" requirement should shield firms from claims of conspiracy. First, if the industry structure is not conducive to coordination—perhaps because entry is easy or because a firm could cut prices in secret and steal business from rivals—then a court should recognize that it would be irrational for a firm to risk prosecution by engaging in the forbidden process without any hope of gaining market power. Under such circumstances the inference of agreement from parallel pricing might not make economic sense. But, for example, a past history of coordination, or evidence that prices rose with no plausible economic justification would tend to suggest that coordination is feasible after all. The second group of plus factors listed in Figure 3–3 address whether coordination would be feasible.

Second, if the industry structure is conducive to coordination, a court should consider whether it was necessary for the firms to engage in the forbidden process to reach a coordinated, high-price equilibrium, or whether they could achieve (or have achieved) the same outcome through leader-follower behavior that does not carry the risk of liability. In the latter case, the firms can argue that "even if we are coordinating—which, of course, we do not admit—we did not need to agree in order to do so." In a parallel pricing case, the firms might also contend: "We acknowledge that we each pay attention to our rival's prices when we make our own pricing decisions—we often follow the leader. But we make our decisions independently, and neither negotiate with our competitors nor exchange assurances with them about our prices." If the facts support this argument, here, too, the inference of agreement would not make economic sense.

Under other circumstances, however, the inference of conspiracy could make economic sense. In particular, a court should be willing to infer an agreement in a parallel pricing case in an industry where entry and discounting are discouraged if the firms appear to have been doing more than merely following each other's market moves. Three types of indicators could help courts infer that firms have selected a coordinated equilibrium by engaging in the forbidden process of negotiation and exchange of assurances. First, firm behavior might be more complex than would be plausible if the outcomes had been reached absent the forbidden process, as through mere leader-follower behavior. A focal point or rule that developed from historic precedent or clear business imperatives would be expected to be obvious and straightforward—such as "we raise all our prices by a common percentage," or "we don't solicit each other's customers or in each other's territories." More complex relationships and rules might imply that the parties had engaged in active negotiation to reach an agreement. Second, the inference of agreement would be strengthened if the explanations offered by the parties about the putative legitimate business purposes are weak or even pretextual. Third, the inference of agreement would be strengthened if the rivals had an opportunity to communicate, and strengthened even more if their conduct includes overt communications spurring immediate responses, even if those communications and responses are not binding on the parties. These indicator types are reflected in the first group of plus factors listed in Figure 3–3, where they are described as helping distinguish agreement from conscious parallelism directly.

Recall the Turner/Posner debate discussed in Sidebar 3–3. Would you agree that the views expressed in this Sidebar generally coincide with those of Turner? If so, how would the Posner side have responded? For alternative modern views of "What is an Agreement" see the Kaplow, Page, and Werden references discussed in Sidebar 3–3.

We turn next to two appellate decisions in the same litigation which further illustrate the importance of economic evidence in cases where the evidence proffered to prove conspiracy is circumstantial. Note that the first decision related to a motion to dismiss ("*In re Text Messaging I*"), whereas the second arose later in the litigation on a motion for summary judgment ("*In re Text Messaging II*"). So the first applied *Twombly* and involved the burden of pleading; the second applied the principles of *Matsushita* and involved the burden of production. These decisions may prove to be especially influential to the evolution of post-*Twombly* antitrust conspiracy jurisprudence, because each was written by Judge Richard A. Posner and joined in by Judge Diane P. Wood, both of whom are regarded as antitrust experts.

IN RE TEXT MESSAGING ANTITRUST LITIGATION

United States Court of Appeals for the Seventh Circuit, 2010.
630 F.3d 622.

Before POSNER, WOOD, and TINDER, CIRCUIT JUDGES.

POSNER, CIRCUIT JUDGE.

A class action suit that has been consolidated for pretrial proceedings in the district court in Chicago charges the defendants with conspiring to fix prices of text messaging services in violation of federal antitrust law. The district court allowed the plaintiffs to file a second amended complaint despite the defendants' objection, based on *Bell Atlantic Corp. v. Twombly,* 550 U.S. 544, 127 S.Ct. 1955 (2007), that the second complaint like the first failed to state a claim. The defendants asked the district judge to certify, for interlocutory appeal under 28 U.S.C. § 1292(b), the question of the complaint's adequacy. The judge agreed. * * *

* * *

Our defendants contend that in this case * * * the complaint alleges merely that they are not competing. But we agree with the district judge that the complaint alleges a conspiracy with sufficient plausibility to satisfy the pleading standard of *Twombly.* * * *

The second amended complaint alleges a mixture of parallel behaviors, details of industry structure, and industry practices, that facilitate collusion. There is nothing incongruous about such a mixture. If parties agree to fix prices, one expects that as a result they will not compete in price-that's the purpose of price fixing. Parallel behavior of a sort anomalous in a competitive market is thus a symptom of price fixing, though standing alone it is not proof of it; and an industry structure that facilitates collusion constitutes supporting evidence of collusion. An accusation that the thousands of children who set up makeshift lemonade stands all over the country on hot summer days were fixing prices would be laughed out of court because the retail sale of lemonade from lemonade stands constitutes so dispersed and heterogeneous and uncommercial a market as to make a nationwide conspiracy of the sellers utterly implausible. But the complaint in this case alleges that the four defendants sell 90 percent of U.S. text messaging services, and it would not be difficult for such a small group to agree on prices and to be able to detect "cheating" (underselling the agreed price by a member of the group) without having to create elaborate mechanisms, such as an exclusive sales agency, that could not escape discovery by the antitrust authorities.

Of note is the allegation in the complaint that the defendants belonged to a trade association and exchanged price information directly at association meetings. This allegation identifies a practice, not illegal in itself, that facilitates price fixing that would be difficult for the authorities to detect. The complaint further alleges that the defendants, along with two other large sellers of text messaging services, constituted and met with each other in an elite "leadership council" within the association-and the leadership council's stated mission was to urge its members to substitute "co-opetition" for competition.

The complaint also alleges that in the face of steeply falling costs, the defendants increased their prices. This is anomalous behavior because falling costs increase a seller's profit margin at the existing price, motivating him, in the absence of agreement, to reduce his price slightly in order to take business from his competitors, and certainly not to increase his price. And there is more: there is an allegation that all at once the defendants changed their pricing structures, which were heterogeneous and complex, to a uniform pricing structure, and then simultaneously jacked up their prices by a third. The change in the industry's pricing structure was so rapid, the complaint suggests, that it could not have been accomplished without agreement on the details of the new structure, the timing of its adoption, and the specific uniform price increase that would ensue on its adoption.

A footnote in *Twombly* had described the type of evidence that enables parallel conduct to be interpreted as collusive: "Commentators have offered several examples of parallel conduct allegations that would state a [Sherman Act] § 1 claim under this standard . . . [namely,] 'parallel behavior that would probably not result from chance, coincidence, independent responses to common stimuli, or mere interdependence unaided by an advance understanding among the parties' . . . [;] 'conduct [that] indicates the sort of restricted freedom of action and sense of obligation that one generally associates with agreement.' The parties in this case agree that 'complex and historically unprecedented changes in pricing structure made at the very same time by multiple competitors, and made for no other discernible reason' would support a plausible inference of conspiracy." That is the kind of "parallel plus" behavior alleged in this case.

What is missing, as the defendants point out, is the smoking gun in a price-fixing case: direct evidence, which would usually take the form of an admission by an employee of one of the conspirators, that officials of the defendants had met and agreed explicitly on the terms of a conspiracy to raise price. The second amended complaint does allege that the defendants "agreed to uniformly charge an unprecedented common per-unit price of ten cents for text messaging services," but does not allege direct evidence of such an agreement; the allegation is an inference from circumstantial evidence. Direct evidence of conspiracy is not a sine qua non, however. Circumstantial evidence can establish an antitrust conspiracy. We need not decide whether the circumstantial evidence that we have summarized is sufficient to *compel* an inference of conspiracy; the case is just at the complaint stage and the test for whether to dismiss a case at that stage turns on the complaint's "plausibility."

The Court said in *Iqbal* that the "plausibility standard is not akin to a 'probability requirement,' but it asks for more than a sheer possibility that a defendant has acted unlawfully." This is a little unclear because plausibility, probability, and possibility overlap. Probability runs the gamut from a zero likelihood to a certainty. What is impossible has a zero likelihood of occurring and what is plausible has a moderately high likelihood of occurring. The fact that the allegations undergirding a claim could be true is no longer enough to save a complaint from being dismissed; the complaint must establish a nonnegligible probability that the claim is valid; but the probability need not be as great as such terms as "preponderance of the evidence" connote.

The plaintiffs have conducted no discovery. Discovery may reveal the smoking gun or bring to light additional circumstantial evidence that further tilts the balance in favor of liability. All that we conclude at this early stage in the litigation is that the district judge was right to rule that the second amended complaint provides a sufficiently plausible case of price fixing to warrant allowing the plaintiffs to proceed to discovery.

In re Text Messaging I illustrates the economically grounded approach to evaluating allegations of conspiracy common in the modern cases. Note how the court expressly looks for factors that make it more or less probable that the alleged conspirators could solve their cartel problems. Specifically, the decision relies on economic plus factors (here, prices rose while costs fell) to supplement communication (or opportunity to communicate, as with the trade association meetings and information exchanges). It also counts as a plus factor conduct that may be hard to understand unless the firms have engaged in negotiation (*i.e.* the simultaneous adoption of a uniform and simplified pricing structure, followed by a substantial price increase). Furthermore, *In re Text Messaging I* makes clear that direct evidence of agreement is unnecessary to support an allegation of conspiracy.

After remand and further discovery, however, the district court granted summary judgment for the defendants. The case was appealed and again Judge Posner wrote for the court. On a more complete record, he agreed with the district court that the case should not proceed owing to an absence of either direct evidence or circumstantial evidence sufficient to infer a conspiracy among the defendants. As you read the decision in *In re Text Messaging II*[6] note how once again the Seventh Circuit's analysis is

---

[6] One of the authors of this Casebook, Jonathan B. Baker, was an expert witness for one of the defendant firms.

informed by both the law of conspiracy, which differentiates conscious parallelism from agreement, and the economic analysis of collusion.

IN RE TEXT MESSAGING ANTITRUST LITIGATION

United States Court of Appeals for the Seventh Circuit, 2015.
782 F.3d 867.

Before WOOD, CHIEF JUDGE, and POSNER and TINDER, CIRCUIT JUDGES.

POSNER, CIRCUIT JUDGE.

This class action antitrust suit is before us for the second time. More than four years ago we granted the defendants' petition to take an interlocutory appeal * * * from the district judge's refusal to dismiss the complaint for failure to state a claim. But we upheld the judge's ruling. *In re Text Messaging Antitrust Litigation,* 630 F.3d 622 (7th Cir. 2010). Three years of discovery ensued, culminating in the district judge's grant of the defendants' motion for summary judgment, followed by entry of final judgment dismissing the suit, precipitating this appeal by the plaintiffs.

The suit is on behalf of customers of text messaging—the sending of brief electronic messages between two or more mobile phones or other devices, over telephone systems (usually wireless systems), mobile communications systems, or the Internet. (The most common method of text messaging today is to type the message into a cellphone, which transmits it instantaneously over a telephone or other communications network to a similar device.) Text messaging is thus an alternative both to email and to telephone calls. The principal defendants are four wireless network providers—AT & T, Verizon, Sprint, and T-Mobile—and a trade association, The Wireless Association, to which those companies belong. The suit claims that the defendants, in violation of section 1 of the Sherman Act * * * conspired with each other to increase one kind of price for text messaging service—price per use (PPU), each "use" being a message, separately priced. This was the original method of pricing text messaging; we'll see that it has largely given way to other methods, but it still has some customers and they are the plaintiffs and the members of the plaintiff class.

The defendants' unsuccessful motion to dismiss the complaint—the motion the denial of which we reviewed and upheld in the first appeal—invoked *Bell Atlantic Corp. v. Twombly,* 550 U.S. 544, 127 S.Ct. 1955, 167 L.Ed.2d 929 (2007), which requires a complaint to pass a test of "plausibility" in order to avoid dismissal. The reason for this requirement is to spare defendants the burden of a costly defense against charges likely to prove in the end to have no merit. We decided that the plaintiffs' second amended complaint passed the test. * * *

* * *

In short, we pointed to the small number of leading firms in the text messaging market, which would facilitate concealment of an agreement to fix prices; to the alleged exchanges of price information, orchestrated by the firms' trade association; to the seeming anomaly of a price increase in the face of falling costs; and to the allegation of a sudden simplification of pricing structures followed very quickly by uniform price increases.

With dismissal of the complaint refused and the suit thus alive in the district court, the focus of the lawsuit changed to pretrial discovery by the plaintiffs, which in turn focused on the alleged price exchange through the trade association and the sudden change in pricing structure followed by uniform price increases. Other factors mentioned in our first opinion—the small number of firms, and price increases in the face of falling costs—were conceded to be present but could not be thought dispositive. It is true that if a small number of competitors dominates a market, they will find it safer and easier to fix prices than if there are many competitors of more or less equal size. For the fewer the conspirators, the lower the cost of negotiation and the likelihood of defection; and provided that the fringe of competitive firms is unable to expand output sufficiently to drive the price back down to the competitive level, the leading firms can fix prices without worrying about competition from the fringe. But the other side of this coin is that the fewer the firms, the easier it is for them to engage in "follow the leader" pricing ("conscious parallelism," as lawyers call it, "tacit collusion" as economists prefer to call it)—which means coordinating their pricing without an actual agreement to do so. As for the apparent anomaly of competitors' raising prices in the face of falling costs, that is indeed evidence that they are not competing in the sense of trying to take sales from each other. However, this may be not because they've agreed not to compete but because all of them have determined independently that they may be better off with a higher price. That higher price, moreover—the consequence of parallel but independent decisions to raise prices—may generate even greater profits (compared to competitive pricing) if costs are falling, provided that consumers do not have attractive alternatives.

Important too is the condition of entry. If few firms can or want to enter the relevant market, a higher price generating higher profits will not be undone by the output of new entrants. Indeed, prospective entrants may be deterred from entering by realization that their entry might lead simply to a drastic fall in prices that would deny them the profits from having entered. And that drastic fall could well be the result of parallel but independent pricing decisions by the incumbent firms, rather than of agreement.

The challenge to the plaintiffs in discovery was thus to find evidence that the defendants had colluded expressly—that is, had explicitly agreed to raise prices—rather than tacitly ("follow the leader" or "consciously parallel" pricing). The focus of the plaintiffs' discovery was on the information exchange orchestrated by the trade association, the change in the defendants' pricing structures and the defendants' ensuing price hikes, and the possible existence of the smoking gun—and let's begin there, for the plaintiffs think they have found it, and they have made it the centerpiece—indeed, virtually the entirety—of their argument.

Their supposed smoking gun is a pair of emails from an executive of T-Mobile named Adrian Hurditch to another executive of the firm, Lisa Roddy. Hurditch was not a senior executive but he was involved in the pricing of T-Mobile's products, including its text messaging service. The first of the two emails to Roddy, sent in May 2008, said "Gotta tell you but my gut says raising messaging pricing again is nothing more than a price gouge on consumers. I would guess that consumer advocates groups are going to come after us at some point. It's not like we've had an increase in the cost to carry message to justify this or a drop in our subscription SOC rates? I know the other guys are doing it but that doesn't mean we have to follow." ("SOC" is an acronym for "system on a chip," a common component of cellphones.) The second email, sent in September 2008 in the wake of a congressional investigation of alleged price gouging by the defendants, said that "at the end of the day we know there is no higher cost associated with messaging. The move [the latest price increase by T-Mobile] was colusive [*sic*] and opportunistic." The misspelled "collusive" is the heart of the plaintiffs' case.

It is apparent from the emails that Hurditch disagreed with his firm's policy of raising the price of its text messaging service. (The price increase, however, was limited to the PPU segment of the service; we'll see that this is an important qualification.) But that is all that is apparent. In emphasizing the word "col[l]usive"—and in arguing in their opening brief that "Hurditch's statement that the price increases were collusive is thus dispositive. Hurditch's statement is a party admission and a co-conspirator statement"—the plaintiffs' counsel demonstrate a failure to understand the fundamental distinction between express and tacit collusion. Express collusion violates antitrust law; tacit collusion does not. There is nothing to suggest that Hurditch was referring to (or accusing his company of) express collusion. In fact the first email rather clearly refers to tacit collusion; for if Hurditch had thought that his company had agreed with its competitors to raise prices he wouldn't have said "I know the other guys are doing it but *that doesn't mean we have to follow*" (emphasis added). They would have to follow, or at least they would be under great pressure to follow, if they had agreed to follow.

As for the word "opportunistic" in the second email, this is a reference to the remark in the first email that T-Mobile and its competitors were seizing an opportunity to gouge consumers—and in a highly concentrated market, seizing such an opportunity need not imply express collusion.

Consider the last sentence in the second, the "colusive," email: "Clearly get why but it doesn't surprise me why public entities and consumer advocacy groups are starting to groan." This accords with another of Hurditch's emails, in which he predicted that the price increase would cause "bad PR [public relations]." Those concerns would be present whether the collusion among the carriers was tacit or express.

Nothing in any of Hurditch's emails suggests that he believed there was a conspiracy among the carriers. There isn't even evidence that he had ever communicated on any subject with any employee of any of the other defendants. The reference to "the other guys" was not to employees of any of them but to the defendants themselves—the companies, whose PPU prices were public knowledge.

The plaintiffs make much of the fact that Hurditch asked Roddy to delete several emails in the chain that culminated in the "colusive" email. But that is consistent with his not wanting to be detected by his superiors criticizing their management of the company. * * *

* * *

The problems with the plaintiff's case go beyond the inconclusiveness of the "colusive" email on which their briefs dwell at such length. The point that they have particular difficulty accepting is that the Sherman Act imposes no duty on firms to compete vigorously, or for that matter at all, in price. This troubles some antitrust experts, such as Harvard Law School Professor Louis Kaplow, whose book *Competition Policy and Price Fixing* (2013) argues that tacit collusion should be deemed a violation of the Sherman Act. That of course is not the law, and probably shouldn't be. A seller must decide on a price; and if tacit collusion is forbidden, how does a seller in a market in which conditions (such as few sellers, many buyers, and a homogeneous product, which may preclude nonprice competition) favor convergence by the sellers on a joint profit-maximizing price without their actually agreeing to charge that price, decide what price to charge? If the seller charges the profit-maximizing price (and its "competitors" do so as well), and tacit collusion is illegal, it is in trouble. But how is it to avoid getting into trouble? Would it have to adopt cost-plus pricing and prove that its price just covered its costs (where cost includes a "reasonable return" to invested capital)? Such a requirement would convert antitrust law into a scheme resembling public utility price regulation, now largely abolished.

And might not entry into concentrated markets be deterred because an entrant who, having successfully entered such a market, charged the prevailing market price would be a tacit colluder and could be prosecuted as such, if tacit collusion were deemed to violate the Sherman Act? What could be more perverse than an antitrust doctrine that discouraged new entry into highly concentrated markets? * * *

Further illustrating the danger of the law's treating tacit collusion as if it were express collusion, suppose that the firms in an oligopolistic market don't try to sell to each other's sleepers, "sleepers" being a term for a seller's customers who out of indolence or ignorance don't shop but instead are loyal to whichever seller they've been accustomed to buy from. Each firm may be reluctant to "awaken" any of the other firms' sleepers by offering them discounts, fearing retaliation. To avoid punishment under antitrust law for such forbearance (which would be a form of tacit collusion, aimed at keeping prices high), would firms be *required* to raid each other's sleepers? It is one thing to prohibit competitors from agreeing not to compete; it is another to order them to compete. How is a court to decide how vigorously they must compete in order to avoid being found to have tacitly colluded in violation of antitrust law? Such liability would, to repeat, give antitrust agencies a public-utility style regulatory role.

Or consider the case, of which the present one may be an exemplar, in which there are four competitors and one raises its price and the others follow suit. Maybe they do that because they think the first firm—the price leader—has insights into market demand that they lack. Maybe they're afraid that though their sales will increase if they don't follow the leader up the price ladder, the increase in their sales will induce the leader to reduce his price, resulting in increased sales by him at the expense of any firm that had refused to increase its price. Or the firms might fear that the price leader had raised his price in order to finance product improvements that would enable him to hold on to his existing customers—and win over customers of the other firms. If any of these reflections persuaded the other firms—without any communication with the leader—to raise their prices, there would be no conspiracy, but merely tacit collusion, which to repeat is not illegal * * *.

* * *

The collusion alleged by the plaintiffs spanned the period 2005 to 2008 (the year the suit was filed), and we must consider closely the evolution of the text messaging market in that period. Text messaging (a descendant of the old telex service) started in the 1990s and started slowly. In 2005, 81 billion text messages were sent in the United States, which sounds like a lot; in fact it was peanuts—for by 2008 the number had risen to a trillion and by 2011 to 2.3 trillion. One reason for the rapid increase was the advent and increasing popularity of volume-discounted text messaging plans. These plans entitled the buyer to send a large number of messages (often an unlimited number) at a fixed monthly price that made each message sent very cheap to the sender. We'll call these plans "bundles," and ignore the fact that often a text messaging bundle includes services in addition to text messaging, such as voice and video messaging. The pricing of text messaging bundles (for example charging a fixed monthly rate for unlimited messaging) largely replaced the original method of pricing text messages, which had been price per use (PPU), that is, price per individual message, not per month or per some fixed number of messages. Once text messaging bundles became popular, the PPU market shrunk to the relative handful of people who send text messages infrequently. The collusion alleged in this case is limited to that market.

In 2005 the price per use was very low—as low as 2 cents, though more commonly 5 cents. But between then and late 2008 all four defendant companies, in a series of steps (10 steps in all for the four companies), raised each of their PPUs to 20 cents. The increase attracted congressional concern and an investigation by the Justice Department's antitrust division, but neither legislative nor prosecutorial action resulted—only the series of class actions suits consolidated in 2009 in the suit before us.

The popularity of text messaging bundles took a big bite out of the PPU market. The consumers left in that market were as we said those who sent very few messages. The total cost to such users was very low. Each defendant company made, so far as appears, an independent judgment that PPU usage per customer was on average so low that the customer would not balk at, if he would even notice, an occasional increase of a few cents per message. * * *

Our earlier discussion of "sleepers" is relevant here. As heavy users of text messaging switched from PPU to bundles, the PPU market was left with the dwindling band of consumers whose use of text messaging was too limited to motivate them to switch to bundles or to complain about small increases in price per message. And they certainly weren't going to undergo the hassle of switching companies just because they would be paying a few dollars a year more for text messaging. This is no more than a plausible interpretation of the motive for and character of the price increases of which the plaintiffs complain, but the burden of establishing a prima facie case of explicit collusion was on the plaintiffs, and as the district judge found in his excellent opinion they failed to carry the burden.

Granted, the defendants overstate their case in some respects. They point out that each company conducted independent evaluations of the profitability of raising their PPUs, but one would expect such "independent" evaluations even if the firms were expressly colluding, as the "independent" evaluations would disguise what they were doing. The firms contend unnecessarily that the evaluations showed that the contemplated price increases would be profitable even if none of the other three carriers raised its PPU. That is overkill because it is not a violation of antitrust law for a firm to raise its price, counting on its competitors to do likewise (but without any communication with them on the subject) and fearing the consequences if they do not. In fact AT & T held back on raising its PPU for several months, fearing that Sprint's increase would have a bad effect on public opinion, and raised its own price only when the bad effect did not materialize.

The plaintiffs point out that the existence of express collusion can sometimes be inferred from circumstantial evidence, and they claim that they produced such evidence, along with Hurditch's emails, which they term direct evidence of such collusion—which, as we know, they are not. Circumstantial evidence of such collusion might be a decline in the market shares of the leading firms in a market, for their agreeing among themselves to charge a high fixed price might have caused fringe firms and new entrants to increase output and thus take sales from the leading firms. Circumstantial evidence might be inflexibility of the market leaders' market shares over time, suggesting a possible agreement among them not to alter prices, since such an alteration would tend to cause market shares to change. Or one might see a surge in nonprice competition, a form of competition outside the scope of the cartel agreement and therefore a possible substitute for price competition. Other evidence of express collusion might be a high elasticity of demand (meaning that a small change in price would cause a substantial change in quantity demanded), for this might indicate that the sellers had agreed not to cut prices even though it would be to the advantage of each individual seller to do so until the market price fell to a level at which the added quantity sold did not offset the price decrease.

The problem is that these phenomena are consistent with tacit as well as express collusion; their absence would tend to negate both, but their presence would not point unerringly to express collusion. And anyway these aren't the types of circumstantial evidence on which the plaintiffs rely. Rather they argue that had any one of the four carriers not raised its price, the others would have experienced costly consumer "churn" (the trade's term for losing customers to a competitor), and therefore all four dared raise their prices only because they had agreed to act in concert. For that would minimize churn—PPU customers would have no place to turn for a lower price. There is, however, a six-fold weakness to this suggested evidence of express collusion:

First, a rational profit-maximizing seller does not care about the number of customers it has but about its total revenues relative to its total costs. If the seller loses a third of its customers because it has doubled its price, it's ahead of the game because twice two-thirds is greater than one (4/3 > 3/3).

Second, in any case of tacit collusion the colluders risk churn, because no one would have committed to adhere to the collusive price. And yet tacit collusion appears to be common, each tacit colluder reckoning that in all likelihood the others will see the advantages of hanging together rather than hanging separately.

Third, the four defendants in this case did not move in lockstep. For months on end there were price differences in their services. * * * To eliminate all risk of churn the defendants would have had to agree to raise their prices simultaneously, and they did not.

Fourth, while there was some churn, this does not imply that each defendant had decided to raise its price so high as to drive away droves of customers had the other defendants not followed suit. T-Mobile, for example, appears not to have gained a significant number of customers from charging less for PPU service than Sprint. * * * Put differently, there is no evidence that PPU pricing is a major determinant of consumers' choice of carrier.

Fifth, the period during which the carriers were raising their prices was also the period in which text messaging caught on with the consuming public and surged in volume. Many PPU customers would have found that they were text messaging more, and the more one text messages the more attractive the alternative of a bundle plan. The defendants *wanted* their PPU customers to switch to bundles. * * *

And sixth, if the carriers were going to agree to fix prices, they wouldn't have fixed their PPU prices; why risk suit or prosecution for fixing such prices when the PPU market was generating such a slight—and shrinking—part of the carriers' overall revenues? The possible gains would be more than offset by the inevitable legal risks. * * *

The plaintiffs argue that many of the price increases were forced by senior management on the middle managers who would ordinarily be responsible for pricing decisions. The claim is that it would be the senior officials, few in number, at each company who would have negotiated the actual collusive agreement that the plaintiffs must prove. But what the record shows is merely (as in the Hurditch emails) that there was disagreement within each company about the optimal price to charge, obviously a speculative matter since no one could be certain how either competitors or consumers would react to any price change. There was plenty of evidence that proposals for price increases came from middle management. An economist would say (one of the defendants' economic experts did say) that as the price-sensitive users moved off PPU to bundles, leaving PPU to the sleepers, the overall demand for PPU became less elastic, meaning that a given percentage increase in the price of PPU service had a smaller negative effect on the demand for the service. That made raising the PPU a revenue winner.

It remains to consider the claim that the trade association of which the defendants were members, The Wireless Association (it has a confusing acronym—CTIA, reflecting the original name of the association, which was Cellular Telephone Industries Association), and a component of the association called the Wireless Internet Caucus of CTIA, were forums in which officers of the defendants met and conspired to raise PPU prices. Officers of some of the defendants attended meetings both of the association and of its caucus, but representatives of companies not alleged to be part of the conspiracy frequently were present at these meetings, and one of the plaintiffs' expert witnesses admitted that in the presence of non-conspirators "the probability of collusion would go away." Still, opportunities for senior leaders of the defendants to meet privately in these officers' retreats abounded. And an executive of one of the defendants (AT & T) told the president of the association that "we all try not to surprise each other" and "if any of us are about to do something major we all tend to give the group a heads up"—"plus we all learn valuable info from each other." This evidence would be more compelling if the immediate sequel to any of these meetings had been a simultaneous or near-simultaneous price increase by the defendants. Instead there were substantial lags. And as there is no evidence of what information was exchanged at these meetings, there is no basis for an inference that they were using the meetings to plot prices increases.

This and other circumstantial evidence that the plaintiffs cite are almost an afterthought. They have staked almost their all on Hurditch's emails. * * * The plaintiffs greatly exaggerate the significance of the emails, but apart from the emails the circumstantial evidence that they cite provides insufficient support for the charge of express collusion.

It is of course difficult to prove illegal collusion without witnesses to an agreement. And there are no such witnesses in this case. We can, moreover, without suspecting illegal collusion, expect competing firms to keep close track of each other's pricing and other market behavior and often to find it in their self-interest to imitate that behavior rather than try to undermine it—the latter being a risky strategy, prone to invite retaliation. The plaintiffs have presented circumstantial evidence consistent with an inference of collusion, but that evidence is equally consistent with independent parallel behavior.

We hope this opinion will help lawyers understand the risks of invoking "collusion" without being precise about what they mean. Tacit collusion, also known as conscious parallelism, does not violate section 1 of the Sherman Act. Collusion is illegal only when based on agreement. Agreement can be proved by circumstantial evidence, and the plaintiffs were permitted to conduct and did conduct full pretrial discovery of such evidence. Yet their search failed to find sufficient evidence of express collusion to make a prima facie case. The district court had therefore no alternative to granting summary judgment in favor of the defendants.

AFFIRMED.

In *In re Text Messaging II,* why did Judge Posner affirm the district court's decision that the evidence proffered by plaintiffs was insufficient to allow the case to be tried, after allowing discovery to proceed in *In re Text Messaging I*? What type of evidence was he looking for plaintiffs to find that did not turn up in discovery? In terms of the two groupings of plus factors set forth in Figure 3–3, does Judge Posner still think that the plaintiffs may be able to show that the market for PPU text messaging is conducive to coordination? Does he still think that the plaintiffs may be able to identify factors tending to distinguish agreement from conscious parallelism directly?

The decision in *In re Text Messaging II* emphasizes the distinction between an express agreement to fix prices (whether demonstrated by direct evidence or inferred from circumstantial evidence), which would violate the Sherman Act, and a tacit agreement, which would not. For example, the opinion states that that it was unnecessary for defendants to show that the price increases would have been profitable for each defendant even if none of the other firms followed suit "because it is not a violation of antitrust law for a firm to raise its price, counting on its competitors to do likewise (but without any communication with them on the subject) and fearing the consequences if they do not." Does Judge Posner emphasize this distinction because he thinks the evidence may be sufficient to show that the market is conducive to coordination, but that such a showing alone—lacking proof of plus factors in the first grouping (such as opportunity to communicate or conduct hard to understand unless the firms engaged in negotiation)—would be insufficient to infer agreement in a parallel pricing case? Is Judge Posner's concern with possible plus factors in both groups (not the second group alone) tied to his apparent conversion to Turner's side of the Turner/Posner debate? For a proposal to treat certain forms of behavior and industry conditions as strong circumstantial evidence of concerted action ("super" plus factors), see William E. Kovacic, Robert C. Marshall, Leslie M. Marx & Halbert White, *Plus Factors and Agreement in Antitrust Law,* 110 MICH. L. REV. 393 (2011).

When modern courts infer an agreement from circumstantial evidence, they may understand the agreement as a way to solve the economic problems impeding coordination (reaching consensus, deterring cheating, or preventing new competition). As previously discussed, the *Blomkest* dissent apparently took the view that the firms could successfully identify terms of coordination and prevent entry, but that an agreement (implemented through price verification calls) was needed to deter cheating. From this perspective, *In re Text Messaging I* appears to tell a story in which the firms could successfully deter cheating and prevent entry, but required an agreement to reach consensus on arguably complex terms of coordination involving the adoption of a uniform price structure.

By contrast, *In re Text Messaging II* appears to suppose, as the *Blomkest* majority may have believed on the facts of that case, that the firms could solve their cartel problems without reaching a covert express agreement. In particular, on a more complete record, Judge Posner seems to have taken the view that the firms could have reached consensus through parallel but independent decisions to raise prices, and that they should be insulated from liability as a result. Can the differing results in the two *Text Messaging* cases be explained by differences between the facts alleged in the complaint and the facts as they appeared after discovery (in both cases taken in a light most favorable to plaintiffs) with respect to the ability of the firms to reach terms of coordination?

The *Text Messaging* opinions do not explicitly discuss the legal standards for inferring agreement from circumstantial evidence. For example, they do not use the expression "plus factors" although a number of such factors are considered. Neither do they discuss burden of proof. Are they consistent with the way the Second Circuit interpreted *Matsushita* in *In re Publication Paper*, as requiring the plaintiff to offer stronger evidence of agreement, whether direct or circumstantial, the less plausible the plaintiff's economic theory? *See* 690 F.3d at 63. For example, can the differing results in the two *Text Messaging* cases be explained as resulting from differences in the plaintiff's burden of pleading as opposed to its burden of production? In other words, did Judge Posner make it more difficult for plaintiffs to prevail the second time around because he found plaintiffs' evidence of coordinated conduct less plausible than it appeared to him on the basis of the complaint alone?

E. INFORMATION EXCHANGE AND OTHER FACILITATING PRATICES

When courts interpret the antitrust laws to forbid horizontal agreements to set prices, firms seeking to coordinate their behavior may experiment with "second best" devices that fall short of reaching a consensus on output and prices but that help the firms approximate the result of an express price-fixing arrangement. To address these "facilitating practices," our discussion broadens this Chapter's legal lens beyond the problem of inferring agreements to fix prices from circumstantial evidence. The conduct at issue in this Section may be circumstantial evidence of an agreement to fix price (or some other agreement), but it also might be an unreasonable restraint of trade on its own. The first part of this Section addresses agreements to engage in practices that may harm competition by facilitating price coordination, as distinct from the agreements to fix prices discussed in previous Sections. The second part of this Section addresses the antitrust treatment of other practices, instituted unilaterally, that might facilitate coordination.

As we will see, conduct that might facilitate coordination can be unilateral or adopted by agreement. If adopted by agreement, the agreement can be horizontal or vertical. Moreover, facilitating practices can be challenged as an element of a broader agreement to fix prices or otherwise harm competition, or on a standalone basis. The range of legal categories potentially involved means that the practice could be evaluated for its reasonableness through abbreviated or more comprehensive analytical approaches, as we explored in Chapter 2.

We will also see that the conduct at issue in this Chapter can harm competition through a range of economic mechanisms. In some cases, for example, the practice may help firms achieve consensus on terms of coordination or detect (and thus deter) cheating by sharing information among rivals. In other cases, the practice may harm competition mainly by discouraging firms from competing aggressively with their rivals. In still others, it may facilitate coordination by excluding new competition, as by discouraging expansion by non-coordinating rivals. For that reason, some practices facilitating coordination may also be employed by dominant firms to create, protect, or enhance their monopoly power. (*See, e.g., Note on the Economic Effects of "Most Favored Nation" Provisions*, *infra* Chapter 6, which discusses most favored customer provisions.)

1. INFORMATION EXCHANGE

A number of Sherman Act decisions in the 1920s dealt with agreements, often reached in the context of a trade association, to share information on matters such as pricing, costs, inventories, and the terms of specific sales transactions. A combination of factors, notably the *Chicago Bd. of Trade* decision in 1918 (*see supra* Chapter 2) and encouragement from the Department of Commerce in the early 1920s for the development of information-sharing programs, led companies and entire industries to engage in various forms of cooperation that seemed to stop short of achieving an agreement on prices.

In a series of decisions beginning with two from that era, *American Column & Lumber Co. v. United States*, 257 U.S. 377 (1921) and *Maple Flooring Mfrs.' Ass'n v. United States*, 268 U.S. 563 (1925), the Supreme Court sought to define how Section 1 of the Sherman Act applied to these arrangements. As we shall see, because agreements to share information typically were express, these cases presented what appeared to be two distinct questions: (1) whether an express agreement to share information can provide a basis for inferring an illicit agreement to fix prices (potentially per se unlawful); and (2) whether an express agreement among rivals to exchange information could itself constitute an unreasonable restraint of trade under Section 1 of the Sherman Act (judged under the rule of reason). This seemingly clear differentiating line, however, became blurred in the cases and we will examine why that might be so.

American Column & Lumber involved a trade association comprised of 400 firms with hardwood lumber mills concentrated in the hardwood producing territory of the southwest United States. Although the members operated only 5% of the U.S. mills engaged in hardwood production, they produced one-third of the total national hardwood output. 257 U.S. at 391. Under the association's Open Competition Plan, to which 90% of its members subscribed, the firms were required to provide the association with extensive, detailed data about their businesses. For example, each firm was required to make daily reports to the association's secretary "of all sales actually made, with the name and address of the purchaser, the kind, grade and quality of lumber sold and all special agreements of every kind, very or written with respect thereto" and "a daily shipping report," "with exact copies of all the invoices, special agreements as to terms, grade, etc." *Id.* at 394–95. Firms were also required to submit monthly production and inventory reports, and current price lists. The reports were subject to audit by association representatives, and the association inspected the stocks of member firms from time to time to ensure consistency of grading across firms. "Plainly" according to the Supreme Court, "it would be very difficult to devise a more minute disclosure of everything connected with one's business than is here provided for by this Plan. * * * " *Id.* at 395–96.

The association assembled and digested this information, and provided reports to the members in a condensed and interpreted form. Members received weekly reports indicating the prices and sales in every individual transaction of all firms, and all shipments, and monthly reports indicating price lists, production and inventory holdings of all firms. Monthly meetings supplemented these extensive reports. In advance of the meetings, an association statistician compiled and distributed the results of a monthly survey of members indicating the expected future production of all firms. The association also suggested future prices and production levels to each firm every month. These reports went only to hardwood sellers. The information was not made available to buyers.

From the point of view of contemporary economic theory, these reports could be understood as helping the firms reach a consensus on price (as by suggesting prices) and deterring cheating on that consensus (by making secret price-cutting difficult). Moreover, the fact that the information went to sellers (and not to buyers) undermined many possible business justifications for the sharing of information. The Supreme Court majority saw the Open Competition Plan similarly, concluding that the members of the association had indeed "conspired" to fix prices:

> The Plan is, essentially, simply an expansion of the gentleman's agreement of former days, skillfully devised to evade the law. To call it open competition, because the meetings were nominally open to the public, or because some voluminous reports were transmitted to the Department of Justice, or because no specific

> agreement to restrict trade or fix prices is proved, cannot conceal the fact that the fundamental purpose of the Plan was to procure 'harmonious' individual action among a large number of naturally competing dealers with respect to the volume of production and prices, without having any specific agreement with respect to them * * *.

Id. at 410–11. *See also United States v. American Linseed Oil Co.,* 262 U.S. 371, 389–90 (1923).

In separate dissents, Justices Holmes and Brandeis asked an important question: How can competition be prevented without a binding agreement, *id.* at 412–13 (Holmes, J., dissenting), or without coercion, *id.* at 413–19 (Brandeis, J., dissenting)? Modern economic theory provides an answer. When firms know that their rivals will rapidly detect cheating and respond by also cutting price and expanding output, they may prefer not to compete aggressively, and thus collude tacitly. Justice Brandeis also suggested that the plan benefitted competition by placing small and isolated backwoods producers on a comparable informational footing with larger mills against whom they competed. *Id.* at 416 (Brandeis, J., dissenting).

Four years later, in *Maple Flooring*, the Supreme Court reviewed another information sharing agreement implemented by a trade association. In contrast to *American Column & Lumber*, the Court's analysis did not focus narrowly on the question of "agreement." In part because the government appeared to present its case in the alternative— either the information sharing facilitated an illicit agreement to fix uniform prices or it had undesirable effects itself—the Court did not carefully differentiate the two issues. In its view, the case failed for want of proof of uniform pricing, which undermined both of the government's theories. 268 U.S. at 567–68.

The defendants were 22 members of a trade association of lumber and flooring manufacturers, with mills mainly located in Michigan, Minnesota, and Wisconsin. Although a number of competing manufacturers were not members of the association, association members accounted for 70% of the total U.S. production of certain types of wood flooring in one of the subject years. *Id.* at 565–66.

The association's many activities "admittedly beneficial to the industry and to consumers," according to the Court, *id.* at 566, included cooperative advertising and the standardization and improvement of products. The government challenged other activities, however, including the computation and dissemination of aggregated information on price, inventory, and quantity sold, information on average cost of producing all dimensions and grades of flooring, and a booklet showing freight rates on flooring from Cadillac, Michigan to more than five thousand points of shipment in the United States. The flooring trade association held monthly meetings at which market conditions and input prices were discussed, but not past or future output prices. *Id.* at 566–67.

But unlike the trade association in *American Column & Lumber*, the Court noted that the flooring association did not identify the seller or customer when sharing information on past transactions, did not share current price quotations or information on future plans, and did not make recommendations as to future prices. *Id.* at 573–74. Moreover, the Court observed that the industry statistics gathered and disseminated by the trade association did not "differ in any essential respect from trade or business statistics which are freely gathered and publicly disseminated in numerous branches of industry producing a standardized product.* * * *" *Id.* at 574. The Court concluded, therefore, that the agreement to share prices did not violate the Sherman Act, but its analysis did not rest solely on the absence of a price-fixing agreement. It also discussed at length what it viewed as the competitively legitimate purposes of the information exchange and the absence of evidence that it affected costs or prices. *Id.* at 579–86.

As we shall discuss at greater length below, an economist's inquiry about information sharing today would focus on its impact on competition, not on a formal distinction regarding whether it provides circumstantial evidence of a price-fixing agreement or is unreasonable itself. (Compare Professor Kaplow's argument, in his contribution to the Turner/Posner debate (Sidebar 3–3), that antitrust should focus on whether firm conduct harmed competition not the definition of "agreement.") Figure 3–5 below compares the key traits of the information-sharing arrangements in *American Column & Lumber* and *Maple Flooring* from a modern economic perspective. Viewed in that way, the information exchange in *Maple Flooring* appears likely to have been substantially less effective in deterring cheating than the information shared in *American Column & Lumber*, notwithstanding that the association members accounted for a much larger share of the market in the flooring case (70% as compared with 33% in the lumber case). Detection of cheating would be more difficult after the information exchange, as the flooring firms would have to infer cheating by rivals from aggregated industry-wide information. In theory, however, the shared information about average costs and freight rates might help the firms reach a consensus by making one set of prices natural and obvious ("focal") in the event actual freight rates varied substantially from firm to firm. Although the government made a similar argument, *see* 268 U.S. at 572, the Supreme Court found instead that the firms had a legitimate business justification for sharing freight rate information:

> * * * [T]here were delays in securing quotations of freight rates from the local agents of carriers in towns in which the factories of defendants are located, which seriously interfered with prompt

quotations of delivered prices to customers; that the actual aggregate difference between local freight rates for most of defendants' mills and the rate appearing in defendants' freight rate book based on rates at Cadillac, Mich., were so small as to be only nominal, and that the freight rate book served a useful and legitimate purpose in enabling members to quote promptly a delivered price on their product by adding to their mill price a previously calculated freight rate which approximated closely to the actual rate from their own mill town.

Id. at 571.

The Court also defended the exchange of accurate information about business conditions among industry participants, sellers and buyers, as likely to facilitate the efficient adjustment of production levels to market conditions:

> * * * [T]he making available of such information tends to stabilize trade and industry, to produce fairer price levels and to avoid the waste which inevitably attends the unintelligent conduct of economic enterprise. 'Free competition' means a free and open market among both buyers and sellers for the sale and distribution of commodities. Competition does not become less free merely because the conduct of commercial operations becomes more intelligent through the free distribution of knowledge of all the essential factors entering into the commercial transaction.

Id. at 583.

Had the information exchange in this case been shown to be "the basis of agreement or concerted action to lessen production arbitrarily or to raise prices beyond the levels of production and price which would prevail if no such agreement or concerted action ensued," as in *American Column & Lumber*, it would have been enjoined. *Id.* at 587. But, as noted above, the Court held that the practices of the flooring trade association did not meet the requirements set out in *American Column & Lumber* and other decisions of the Court. *See also Sugar Inst., Inc. v. United States,* 297 U.S. 553, 598 (1936); *Cement Mfrs.' Protective Ass'n v. United States,* 268 U.S. 588, 602–03, 606 (1925).

Figure 3–5:

Information Sharing: *American Column & Lumber* and *Maple Flooring* Compared

American Column & Lumber (1921)	*Maple Flooring* (1925)
• Members' market share: 33%	• Members' market share: 70%

• Type of information disseminated by Association (monthly or weekly):
  • Current price lists
  • Output data
  • Inventory data
  • Data for each sale including quantity, price and buyer
	• Type of information disseminated by Association (at least monthly):
	  • Past sales (no current prices)
	  • Output data
	  • Inventory data
	  • No data on purchasers

• Form in which date was disseminated: Company by company.	• Form in which data was disseminated: Aggregated on Association-wide basis (specific sellers not identified).
• Distribution of data: to Association members only.	• Distribution of data: made available to public.
• Commentary on trends: Reports to members proposed future output and pricing levels.	• Commentary on trends: No effort to propose future output or pricing levels.
• Meetings: Members met monthly or weekly by area for "discussion of all subjects of interest."	• Meetings: Members met regularly, but no record evidence that meetings were occasions to fix prices.
• Effects Evidence: Information exchanges raised prices.	• Effects evidence: No evidence that information exchanges raised prices.
	• Freight book: Provided rates on shipment of flooring from Cadillac, MI to over 5000 destinations in United States. • No evidence in record that rate book was used to fix prices

American Column & Lumber and, to a significant extent, *Maple Flooring* both focused on whether the information exchanges at issue could provide a reasonable basis for inferring an illicit agreement to fix prices. Courts continue to face that question, *i.e.*, whether the exchange of certain types of information by rivals can fairly be viewed as circumstantial evidence—a "plus factor"—that tends to prove the existence of an agreement to fix prices. If proven, such an agreement to fix prices likely would be treated as per se unlawful.

In our next case, the plaintiff pointed to a number of alleged plus factors in an attempt to prove that the principal U.S. cigarette manufacturers conspired to fix prices. The excerpt focuses on the court's discussion of an information exchange plan that they collectively implemented. As you read the excerpt from the court's opinion, consider whether the court correctly analyzes the information exchange evidence from contemporary legal and economic perspectives. In particular, consider whether the court considers how information exchanges can help rivals to solve their cartel problems. Also note (1) the influence of the Supreme Court's *Matsushita* decision; and (2) the court's treatment of the testimony proffered by the plaintiff through its economic expert.

WILLIAMSON OIL CO., INC. V. PHILIP MORRIS USA

United States Court of Appeals for the Eleventh Circuit, 2003.
346 F.3d 1287.

MARCUS, CIRCUIT JUDGE.

This is an antitrust action brought pursuant to section 1 of the Sherman Act * * * by a class of several hundred cigarette wholesalers ("the class" or "the wholesalers") against Philip Morris, Inc. ("PM"), R.J. Reynolds Tobacco Co. ("RJR"), Brown & Williamson Tobacco Corp. ("B & W") and Lorillard Tobacco Co. ("Lorillard") (collectively "the manufacturers"). The class alleges that the manufacturers conspired between 1993 and 2000 to fix cigarette prices at unnaturally high levels, and that this collusion resulted in wholesale list price overcharges of nearly $12 billion. The district court ultimately entered summary judgment in favor of the manufacturers. It reasoned that the wholesalers had failed to demonstrate the existence of a "plus factor," as is necessary to create an inference of a price fixing conspiracy, and that even if the class had shown that a plus factor was present, the manufacturers were able to rebut fully the inference of collusion, as the economic realities of the 1990s cigarette market rendered the class's conspiracy theory untenable. Rather, the district court held that the manufacturers' pricing behavior evidenced nothing more than "conscious parallelism," a perfectly legal phenomenon commonly associated with oligopolistic industries.

On appeal, the wholesalers say that the district court misapplied the summary judgment standard, that they presented sufficient evidence to withstand the manufacturers' motions, and that the court erred by excluding portions of the testimony proffered by their primary expert witness. In the end, we conclude that none of the class's arguments are compelling and that the district court's treatment of the wealth of complicated issues in this case was nuanced, insightful and, ultimately, correct. Accordingly, we affirm the court's entry of final summary judgment in favor of PM, RJR, B & W and Lorillard.

I

The modern American tobacco industry is a classic oligopoly. Between 1993 and 1999, appellees-the nation's four largest cigarette manufacturers-along with Liggett Group, Inc. [which was not a party to the action] manufactured more than 97% of the cigarettes sold in the United States. Moreover, the composition of the industry has been remarkably stable over time, a condition that has resulted largely from the fact that during the twentieth century the major tobacco players engaged in minimal price competition. Because price fluctuations were relatively rare, smokers typically had no reason to change brands, brand loyalties were solidified and sizable market share shifts were uncommon.

During the early 1990s, however, a price gap widened between premium brands like Marlboro, Newport and Camel and discount and deep discount brands such as GPC, Basic and Doral. This price differential was the result of extremely competitive pricing of the non-premium brands, especially by B & W and RJR, which focused a large percentage of their competitive efforts on the discount and deep discount markets. This led some "premium smokers" to shift to one of the non-premium brands, and by 1993 these brands had captured over 40% of the United States market. At that time, there were 10 different wholesale list price points, *i.e.*, cigarette price tiers.

Although this trend toward the discount and deep discount brands benefitted RJR and B & W, it was extremely undesirable from the perspective of premium-intensive manufacturers like PM and Lorillard. As such, PM-which at the time was (and remains) the market leader, with a market share that ranged from 42% to 50% during the period of the alleged conspiracy—sought in April, 1992 to raise the price of its lowest tier products by $4 per thousand. This effort was unsuccessful, however, because RJR, B & W and Lorillard did not follow suit, and PM was forced to rescind its price increase. Although PM again attempted to increase its deep discount prices in March, 1993, this effort similarly was rebuffed by its competitors.

Though temporarily unsuccessful, PM continued looking for ways to reverse the trend toward discount cigarettes, and roughly one year after its failed $4 per thousand price increase it found one. On April 2, 1993, PM decided to take what appellants refer to as "the single boldest commercial move in U.S. cigarette market history": it announced that it was cutting the retail price of Marlboro cigarettes—which were by far the single best selling brand in America, enjoying a 21% market share—by 40 cents per pack and foregoing price increases on other premium brands "for the foreseeable future." April 2, 1993 subsequently became widely known throughout the industry as "Marlboro Friday." This highly competitive pricing decision was extremely significant for several reasons. First, it left no doubt that PM was willing to take drastic competitive measures (indeed, to sacrifice profits) in order to protect the market share of its flagship brand. Second and quite importantly, it slimmed the price gap between premium and discount cigarettes. Because this price differential was constricted, consumers suddenly had less of an economic incentive to purchase discount cigarettes, and as a result premium brands like Marlboro regained some of market share they had lost prior to Marlboro Friday.

Finally, it set off a price war among appellees, as RJR, B & W and Lorillard were immediately confronted with a need to respond in some way to PM's bold action. In order to remain competitive, these manufacturers matched PM's retail price reductions. Although these pricing actions cut into the market share held by discount brands generally, and thus led to a reduction in the overall share held by RJR and B & W, which, as stated, were more heavily invested in these brands, the decision to match PM's price reduction meant that no manufacturer suffered unduly large market share losses.

However, this vast decrease in cigarette prices was disastrous for PM, RJR, B & W and Lorillard alike in terms of profits, and appellees were forced to rethink their profitability strategies. Indeed, appellants recognize that this economic landscape became especially difficult in light of increasing regulation of the industry and the surge of health-related litigation. To exacerbate its competitors' predicament, on July 20, 1993, PM announced that its Marlboro Friday price reduction would be made permanent and expanded to all of its premium brands, *e.g.*, Parliament and Virginia Slims. Moreover, PM simultaneously lowered the wholesale price of its discount cigarettes and raised the wholesale price of its deep discount brands by 10 cents per pack, thereby consolidating the prices of these brand categories. This action reduced what had been 10 price points in the American cigarette market to four * * *. Again, PM's competitors promptly matched these newly announced prices. What's more, the very next day RJR announced that it would collapse the prices of its regular and 100 mm cigarettes, thereby reducing the price tiers to two: premium and discount. PM, B & W and Lorillard quickly followed suit.

Appellants contend that it is only at this point that PM, RJR, B & W and Lorillard began conspiring to fix and steadily increase prices to make up for the tremendous financial losses they suffered as a consequence of this price war. The class says that PM's actions on Marlboro Friday constructively informed its competitors that price discounting to gain market share would no longer be tolerated, and that only when such efforts were abandoned, and the premium/discount price gap narrowed, could prices again rise. By appellants' account, the manufacturers' conspiracy began in earnest when appellees began using trade press—*i.e.*, tobacco industry financial analysts * * * to "signal" each other regarding their willingness to comply with PM's implicit demands so as to facilitate price increases. For example, the class points to a statement made by * * * Martin Broughton, the CEO and Deputy Chairman of British American Tobacco ("BAT"), B & W's parent company, that "BAT may be one of those who started the price war in the U.S., but we have no wish to escalate it."[5] Appellants argue that this statement somehow was a signal sent by B & W to its competitors that B & W was willing to reduce or end price competition. The class alleges that RJR conveyed a similar message on November 2, 1993 by publicly announcing that it would no longer sacrifice profitability for market share.

Appellants say that PM signaled its acceptance of its competitors' overtures by putting its distributors on "permanent allocation"—that is, limiting the quantities of product the distributors could order—on November 5, 1993. Historically, this practice had been implemented as a temporary measure prior to a price increase, with the purpose being to prevent the wholesalers from engaging in "trade loading," *i.e.*, stocking up on cigarettes before the increase so as to deprive appellees of the benefit of their price adjustment. The class says that PM's placement of its wholesalers on permanent allocation actually was a signal that the price increase sought by RJR, B & W and Lorillard was coming.

Appellants suggest that RJR responded to PM's signal on November 8, 1993 with one last signal of its own. Specifically, the class argues that by announcing an increase of $2 per thousand cigarettes (4per pack) in both the premium and discount categories, and thus maintaining the constricted discount/premium price gap, RJR indicated that it was acceding to PM's conditions for increasing prices. By November 22, 1993, PM, B & W and Lorillard had matched RJR's increase. * * *

This initial RJR-led price increase was followed by eleven more parallel increases between May 4, 1995 and January 14, 2000. * * *

[Here the court described additional details of the plaintiffs' allegations and evidence and the defendants' arguments in response. Eds.]

* * *

Appellants also argue PM, RJR, B & W and Lorillard furthered their collusive enterprise by exchanging sales data through a common consultant, Management Science Associates ("MSA"), which allegedly

---

[5]   As the district court recognized * * * this statement is taken out of context. Broughton's full statement was that "BAT may be one of those who started the price war in the U.S., but we have no wish to escalate it. *But we shall be ready to respond tactically where necessary.*"

enabled appellees to ensure that all were adhering to their allocation programs and to detect and punish what plaintiffs' expert Franklin M. Fisher termed "defections from an industry understanding on price." The MSA system tracks shipments from the manufacturers to wholesalers and from the wholesalers to retailers and provides reports to each appellee regarding the shipments of its competitors. Appellants allege that although in 1994 PM began collecting sales data on RJR, B & W and Lorillard through MSA, and thereby incurred a great competitive advantage, in 1995 it inexplicably began sharing this system with its competitors. Moreover, the class posits, over time the MSA system has been modified to make the cigarette market more transparent, and all of these alterations have been implemented with the unanimous consent of PM, RJR, B & W and Lorillard.

* * *

II

* * *

1. *Appellants' Alleged Plus Factors*

After articulating the summary judgment standard in an antitrust case, the district court delineated eleven distinct factors that appellants had denominated "plus factors." These are: "(1) signaling of intentions; (2) permanent allocations programs; (3) monitoring of sales; (4) actions taken contrary to economic self-interest, including (a) little analysis of whether to follow price increases, (b) B & W and RJR pulling away from the discount cigarette market, (c) the May 1995 price increase lead by RJR and followed by Philip Morris, (d) Philip Morris' agreement to base the initial [Management Science Associates] . . . payments on market capitalization rather than market share, and (e) 'excessive' price increases after the MSA; (5) nature of the market; (6) strong motivation; (7) reduction in the number of price tiers; (8) opportunities to conspire; (9) pricing decisions made at high levels; (10) the smoking and health conspiracy; and (11) foreign conspiracies." * * * The district court ultimately concluded that none of them actually tended to exclude the possibility of independent behavior, and the class contests the correctness of the court's conclusions as to each factor. * * *

* * *

Appellants * * * raise two arguments related to the exchange by each appellee of wholesale-to-retail sales information through Management Science Associates. Around 1993–94, PM developed with MSA a system for tracking wholesale to retail shipments of its products, which it believed would afford it a great competitive advantage. Subsequently, in 1995, PM permitted MSA to share this service with its competitors. In exchange for their acceptance of the service, RJR, B & W and Lorillard agreed to share their own sales information.

Appellants first argue that PM's decision to share this service cannot be seen as being in its economic interest, and instead must be viewed as a means of facilitating the monitoring of the conspiracy by all of the conspirators. PM responds that by sharing the MSA service it shifted the financial burden of gathering sales and market share data for its competitors to RJR, B & W and Lorillard, and that as a result it actually realized an annual savings of millions of dollars. Viewed in the light most favorable to appellants, both explanations are plausible, and thus, at the most, this action by PM stands in equipoise; that is, it is equally consistent with collusion as with lawful competition, and accordingly * * * it cannot represent a plus factor. Second, appellants argue that the participation by all appellees in the MSA data sharing system was contrary to their respective interests.

Preliminarily (and quite significantly), we note that the evidence establishes that appellees exchanged only sales, *not pricing,* information through MSA. Simply put, it is far less indicative of a *price fixing* conspiracy to exchange information relating to sales as opposed to prices. Moreover, it plainly was economically beneficial for each individual appellee to keep tabs on the commercial activities of its competitors, so the receipt of information concerning their sales does not tend to exclude the possibility of independent action or to establish anticompetitive collusion. Indeed, as RJR argues, "[e]ven if one assumes that, all else being equal, RJR would prefer that data about its products not be available to its rivals . . ., that does not tell us that RJR acts irrationally if it concludes that the competitive benefit of obtaining its rivals' data outweighs whatever preference it has against sharing its own data."

Thus, although the sharing of information can be seen as suggesting conspiracy, as appellants allege, it also can be seen equally as a necessary means to the receipt of its competitors' information. If a particular manufacturer ceased providing its own information, its entitlement to that of its competitors would similarly end. To draw an analogy, each company's willingness to give its own information can be viewed as the ante in a poker game. To ante is irrational only if there is no legitimate reason why one would be playing the game; yet here, the game is oligopolistic competition, which everyone concedes is lawful, and the ante is perfectly consonant with the desire to play. For both of these reasons, the delivery of wholesale-to-retail sales information to MSA does not tend to exclude the possibility of independent action (or tend to establish a price fixing conspiracy), and thus cannot constitute a plus factor.

* * *

IV

Besides arguing that the district court erred by rejecting their arguments concerning plus factors, the class further contends that the court erroneously excluded the expert testimony of Professor Fisher on some of these points. Specifically, appellants say that the district court improperly excluded Fisher's conclusion that the manufacturers engaged in activities beyond mere conscious parallelism, which he expressed in the context of several of the particular actions on which appellants base their claims.[21]

[Here the court discussed the standards for the admissibility of expert economic testimony under Federal Rule of Evidence 702 and the Supreme Court's line of cases following *Daubert v. Merrell Dow Pharmaceuticals, Inc.,* 509 U.S. 579 (1993). Eds.]

> * * * Expert testimony may be admitted into evidence if: (1) the expert is qualified to testify competently regarding the matters he intends to address; (2) the methodology by which the expert reaches his conclusions is sufficiently reliable as determined by the sort of inquiry mandated in *Daubert*; and (3) the testimony assists the trier of fact, through the application of scientific, technical, or specialized expertise, to understand the evidence or to determine a fact in issue. * * *

In this case, the district court held that Fisher's opinions that collusive price fixing was afoot should be excluded because they were unhelpful and thus irrelevant, *i.e.*, they did not tend to make it any more probable that appellees were (or were not) engaged in a price fixing conspiracy. Additionally, the court held in at least one case that Fisher's testimony was unhelpful because he had misunderstood the evidence. More specifically, the district court excluded Fisher's ultimate opinion that there was an illegal price fixing conspiracy as irrelevant because Fisher did not differentiate between lawful, conscious parallelism and collusive price fixing. Accordingly, the court held, these conclusions were of absolutely no use to a factfinder.

* * *

Simply stated, we can perceive no abuse of discretion in the district court's decision to exclude some of Fisher's testimony. Fisher's conclusion was that plaintiffs participated in an illegal price fixing conspiracy, and he expressed this opinion in the context of several aspects of appellants' evidence, *e.g.*, by saying that the manufacturers' participation in the MSA information sharing system created an inference of collusion. However,

---

[21] Specifically, the district court excluded Fisher's testimony that appellees' alleged signaling was indicative of collusive price fixing; that their adoption of permanent allocation programs was indicative of price fixing; and that their exchange of information through MSA was part of a price fixing conspiracy.

Fisher defined "collusion" to include conscious parallelism. Put differently, he did not differentiate between legal and illegal pricing behavior, and instead simply grouped both of these phenomena under the umbrella of illegal, collusive price fixing. This testimony could not have aided a finder of fact to determine whether appellees' behavior was or was not legal, and the district court properly excluded it. * * *

* * *

V

Because appellants cannot demonstrate the existence of a plus factor, they cannot establish an inference of conspiracy, as they must to carry the burden imposed on them at the summary judgment stage of a collusive price fixing case. Moreover, appellees would have rebutted any inference that they conspired to fix prices by demonstrating that the class's conspiracy theory is utterly implausible. In addition, the court's exclusion of several portions of Fisher's testimony was in no sense an abuse of discretion, *i.e.*, did not constitute manifest error. Accordingly, we affirm in all respects the district court's final summary judgment in favor of the manufacturers.

———————

Do you agree with the Eleventh Circuit's analysis of the MSA information sharing system? Could the exchange help to facilitate an agreement on prices among the defendants? Also, do you agree with the court's observation that the information sharing here was equally consistent with unilateral and conspiratorial conduct, and hence insufficient to satisfy *Matsushita's* "tending to exclude the possibility" standard?

Cartel Problems, Courts, and Economists

The *Williamson* opinion did not discuss how sharing historical information about quantities shipped could facilitate collusion. Consider the following line of reasoning: Sales volume or market share data might serve as a useful surrogate for pricing data to identify cheating given that a firm that cheats on a collusive arrangement expands its output (and market share), resulting in a decline in the market price. In other words, if prices are not transparent—and wholesale prices may not be even if retail prices are—one way to tell if a firm is cheating on a price fixing agreement is to observe a significant increase in its share of sales. Even if retail prices are transparent, moreover, a firm might cheat secretly, *i.e.*, in ways that do not lead to a lower retail price, perhaps by giving retailers promotional incentives to display its brands more attractively or in better store locations. In either event, the firm's cheating may be observable in the form of increased sales volume, a higher market share, or increased shipments.

(Recall from the lysine cartel in Chapter 1 that the conspiring producers conferred to check sales volume and market shares at the end of each year).

Contrary to the court's conclusion, therefore, the exchange of historical sales information could facilitate cartel formation by helping the participants to solve their problem of deterring cheating through rapid detection and response. If that is true, might the exchange of such information also be circumstantial evidence of an underlying agreement on price? The testimony of the plaintiff's economist, Dr. Franklin Fisher, appeared to focus on some of these points. What was the court's response and why did the court exclude his testimony?

The court's treatment of Dr. Fisher's testimony highlights another challenge in addressing cases of alleged price-fixing in oligopolistic industries: because the Sherman Act only condemns "agreement," courts reviewing firm conduct in oligopolistic industries must differentiate between parallel conduct attributable simply to leader-follower behavior that has historically not been considered unlawful and "conspiracy." How can they do so, and what is the role of the economist in such a case?

Noting that "the definition of what qualifies as an 'agreement' is ultimately a question of law and driven by policy considerations," Professor Herbert Hovenkamp has suggested that, "nevertheless, an economist can contribute many observations relevant to the fact finder's determination." Herbert Hovenkamp, *Economic Experts in Antitrust Cases*, in 3 DAVID L. FAIGMAN ET AL., MODERN SCIENTIFIC EVIDENCE: THE LAW AND SCIENCE OF EXPERT TESTIMONY § 10.12 (2006). According to Hovenkamp, these observations include: (1) whether the market structure would make an agreement rational or worthwhile; (2) whether the market structure makes an agreement unnecessary; (3) whether a firm's actions are contrary to self-interest except on the supposition of an agreement; and (4) whether the degree of parallelism is sufficient that, when coupled with other factors, a fact inference of agreement is warranted. *Id.* Hovenkamp observes, however, "that much of what the economists have to say on the matter is theoretical and not subject to empirical falsification at all." *Id.* Do all four of his listed factors seem equally appropriate subjects of an economist's testimony? Does the fourth factor seem to invite the economist to offer an opinion on the ultimate legal question at issue, while the first three leave that issue to the fact-finder? *Cf.* Rebecca Haw Allensworth, *Law and the Art of Modeling: Are Models Facts?* 103 GEO. L. J. 825 (2015) (arguing that economic models should not be evaluated as facts).

The problem remains that all of these factors—legal and economic—might facilitate parallel pricing in an oligopolistic industry, but still not add up to the legal requirement of "agreement." Did the evidence and testimony in *Williamson* try to go further? Is Hovenkamp overlooking the role of facilitating practices? Might an economist be well-positioned to judge whether specific kinds of conduct—such as information sharing—are likely to facilitate cartel formation by solving cartel problems? Or was the court correct that Dr. Fisher's testimony still failed to differentiate between leader-follower behavior and "conspiracy"? As an economic matter, can an economist differentiate between the two situations? If not, what should an economist be permitted to say about the fact of "conspiracy"? We discuss the concept of "agreement" above in Sidebar 3–5.

The Impact of the Matsushita Standard

The *Williamson* court observed that sharing of past sales volume information was equally consistent with both unilateral and conspiratorial conduct. Invoking *Matsushita*, the court reasoned:

> If a particular manufacturer ceased providing its own information, its entitlement to that of its competitors would similarly end. To draw an analogy, each company's willingness to give its own information can be viewed as the ante in a poker game. To ante is irrational only if there is no legitimate reason why one would be playing the game; yet here, the game is oligopolistic competition, which everyone concedes is lawful, and the ante is perfectly consonant with the desire to play.

Williamson, 346 F.3d at 1313. Is the court conceding too much to oligopoly here? Is it accurate to describe a coordinated, cooperative effort to share information by rival oligopolists as "unilateral" conduct in any sense? Does that characterization ignore the cartel-facilitating theory presented by the plaintiffs?

Recall the Turner-Posner debate about the Sherman Act's ability to condemn "conscious parallelism." (*See supra* Sidebar 3–3.) One of Turner's points related to remedy. He argued that leader-follower behavior is difficult to remedy without disrupting normal strategic decision-making in an oligopolistic industry, arguing that there was in fact nothing to enjoin. Is that true in the case of coordinated facilitating practices, such as information exchanges? Couldn't the court in *Williamson* have enjoined the MSA information sharing system, potentially frustrating the defendants' ability to detect cheating? By dismissing the information sharing as normal oligopolistic behavior, does the court foreclose any rationale for condemning facilitating conduct? Is it reading *Matsushita* beyond its reasonable limits in doing so?

Although the court's analysis of information sharing can be critically examined, it is not clear that its ultimate conclusion was incorrect. Information sharing, alone, may not be sufficient to infer a conspiracy. In *Williamson*, it was only one factor addressed by the court, and as the court explains in other portions of its opinion omitted here, it did not agree with the plaintiffs that the tobacco industry defendants had gone beyond the kind of unilateral conduct one would expect from an oligopoly.

The Tobacco Industry and Antitrust.

As the court in *Williamson* describes, the American tobacco industry is recognized as an oligopoly that is prone to parallel behavior, especially with regard to pricing. That has long been the case, as you will recall from *American Tobacco.*

In the late 1990s, massive civil actions for damages were brought against tobacco firms by various states to recover the costs of health care to their citizens for tobacco-related illnesses. In connection with the first proposed settlement of the cases, which would have required Congressional action, the FTC prepared a report to Congress in September, 1997 on the conduct of the industry. Specifically, it discussed whether the industry structure was conducive to coordination and whether the proposed settlement would make coordination more likely or more effective. The report became moot when the states and the firms reached an alternative settlement that did not require Congressional intervention. The press release stated: "[the Report] identifies several features of the industry's past history and current structure that suggest why the industry is susceptible to coordinated price rises, including the tendency for price increases to consistently outpace cost increases, the small number of significant firms in the market, and the historical insulation of the cigarette industry from entry by new firms." *See Press Release, Substantial Profits for Tobacco Companies Could Result from Tobacco Settlement, Says FTC Staff,* https://www.ftc.gov/news-events/press-releases/1997/09/substantial-profits-tobacco-companies-could-result-tobacco

If the FTC was correct, did its findings tend to support the court or the plaintiffs in *Williamson?*

Note that the FTC Staff looked at some of the same factors identified by both Dr. Fisher and Professor Hovenkamp in concluding that the tobacco industry was "susceptible" to price-fixing. As a matter of proof, should such evidence ever be enough to prove that in fact an agreement was reached? We will revisit the challenges of evaluating competitively significant conduct in the tobacco industry in Chapter 4, in reading the Supreme Court's decision in *Brooke Group.*

NOTE ON CONTAINER CORP.: INFORMATION SHARING AS AN INDEPENDENT SHERMAN ACT VIOLATION

As was noted above at the beginning of this Section of the Chapter, agreements to share information often are express, leaving no question that the parties have reached an "agreement" for purposes of Section 1. The treatment of information sharing under the Sherman Act, therefore, has sometimes been viewed by courts and commentators as falling into two distinct categories: (1) cases in which the express information sharing agreement provides a basis for inferring an illicit agreement to fix prices; and (2) cases in which the agreement to share information is itself challenged as a standalone unreasonable restraint of trade. Although the two questions can be separated in theory, the line between them can be and historically has been blurred. In this Note, we further explore both the cases and some relevant economic commentary that illuminates the tension between these two seemingly distinct approaches, focusing on information sharing as a standalone violation.

Cases like *American Column & Lumber* and, more recently, *Williamson*, illustrate how information sharing agreements can be analyzed as circumstantial evidence of illicit agreements to fix prices. As one contemporary court has observed, however, "[t]here is a closely related but analytically distinct type of claim, also based on § 1 of the Sherman Act, where the violation lies in the information exchange itself—as opposed to merely using the information exchange as evidence upon which to infer a price-fixing agreement. This exchange of information is not illegal *per se,* but can be found unlawful under a rule of reason analysis." *Todd v. Exxon Corp.,* 275 F.3d 191, 198 (2d Cir. 2001). One way to understand the differing results in *American Column & Lumber* and *Maple Flooring* is to see them as addressing these two distinct issues: *American Column & Lumber* more clearly involved the inference of a price-fixing agreement, whereas *Maple Flooring's* greater focus on effects and justifications arguably suggests that it was evaluating information sharing as a standalone antitrust issue.

As *Todd* observes, it was not until the late 1960s, in *United States v. Container Corp.,* 393 U.S. 333 (1969), that the Supreme Court returned to the issues it first addressed in *American Column & Lumber* and *Maple Flooring,* and more clearly separated the two issues, when it held that an information exchange could itself constitute a violation of Section 1. The information exchange in *Container Corp.* was limited to price verification on demand. The defendants, who were rivals, would periodically request of each other verification of the prices they had most recently charged to a specific customer. The data was furnished by each defendant on the expectation that its rivals would comply with its requests for similar data, when made. 393 U.S. at 335. The Court barely paused to consider whether there was an agreement. It saw the case as "obviously quite different from the parallel business behavior condoned in *Theatre Enterprises, Inc. v. Paramount Film Distributing Corp.*" 393 U.S. at 335 n.2.

The concerted action identified by the Court in *Container* is best understood as an agreement to exchange price information. With an agreement established, the question was whether that agreement harmed competition. Writing for the Court, Justice Douglas analyzed the effect of the agreement this way:

> The result of this reciprocal exchange of prices was to stabilize prices though at a downward level. Knowledge of a competitor's price usually meant matching that price. The continuation of some price competition is not fatal to the Government's case. The limitation or reduction of price competition brings the case within the ban, for as

we held in United States v. Socony-Vacuum Oil Co., interference with the setting of price by free market forces is unlawful per se. Price information exchanged in some markets may have no effect on a truly competitive price. But the corrugated container industry is dominated by relatively few sellers. The product is fungible and the competition for sales is price. The demand is inelastic, as buyers place orders only for immediate, short-run needs. The exchange of price data tends toward price uniformity. For a lower price does not mean a larger share of the available business but a sharing of the existing business at a lower return. Stabilizing prices as well as raising them is within the ban of § 1 of the Sherman Act. As we said in United States v. Socony-Vacuum Oil Co., 'in terms of market operations stabilization is but one form of manipulation.' The inferences are irresistible that the exchange of price information has had an anticompetitive effect in the industry, chilling the vigor of price competition. The agreement in the present case, though somewhat casual, is analogous to those in American Column & Lumber Co. v. United States. * * *

393 U.S. at 336–38.

Justice Douglas appeared to find the Agreement's vice to be price stabilization without regard to whether the agreement harmed consumers through higher prices. A concurring opinion by Justice Fortas suggested a more modern analysis focused on how information exchange can facilitate coordination on prices by helping the firms deter cheating. Justice Fortas concluded that the agreement led to higher prices than would have otherwise occurred and that therefore application of a per se approach was unnecessary:

> * * * In summary, the record shows that the defendants sought and obtained from competitors who were part of the arrangement information about the competitors' prices to specific customers. '(I)n the majority of instances,' the District Court found, that once a defendant had this information he quoted substantially the same price as the competitor, although a higher or lower price would 'occasionally' be quoted. Thus the exchange of prices made it possible for individual defendants confidently to name a price equal to that which their competitors were asking. The obvious effect was to 'stabilize' prices by joint arrangement—at least to limit any price cuts to the minimum necessary to meet competition. In addition, there was evidence that, in some instances, during periods when various defendants ceased exchanging prices exceptionally sharp and vigorous price reductions resulted.

On this record, taking into account the specially sensitive function of the price term in the antitrust equation, I cannot see that we would be justified in reaching any conclusion other than that defendants' tacit agreement to exchange information about current prices to specific customers did in fact substantially limit the amount of price competition in the industry. That being so, there is no need to consider the possibility of a per se violation.

393 U.S. at 339–40 (FORTAS, J., concurring).

Justice Marshall's dissent argued that the government had not proved its case with evidence of anticompetitive effect, notwithstanding that the government "presented a convincing argument in theoretical terms." 393 U.S. at 345 (Marshall, J., dissenting). He emphasized that "The trial judge found that price decisions were individual decisions, and that defendants frequently did cut prices in order to obtain a particular order." In his view, "the absence of any price parallelism or price uniformity and the downward trend in the industry undercut the conclusion that price information was used to stabilize prices." 393 U.S. at 346 (Marshall, J., dissenting).

With *Container Corp.* and other antitrust decisions, it often is difficult to determine how specific judicial rulings actually affect business behavior. But in 1982 the Federal Trade Commission published a report on petroleum industry mergers that suggested how *Container Corp.* might have complicated efforts by direct rivals to coordinate pricing decisions. The FTC study quoted an undated document prepared by a petroleum industry company commenting on *Container Corp.*'s influence on the behavior of major integrated oil firms:

> It is difficult to over-estimate the significance of this [the *Container Corp.* decision] development. Previously, with price verification, the individual majors knew the price levels of the other majors and some stability and order was possible. Today, the only information available is the actual pump price at the station which is set by some relatively irresponsible dealers, and when instability sets in, a single major does not know if this is a move by the supplier or by a few dealers.

Federal Trade Commission, *Mergers in the Petroleum Industry* 291–92 (Sept. 1982). As this passage suggests, *Container Corp.* appears to have forced the petroleum firms to resort to more cumbersome methods—actually examining prices posted at individual retail outlets—to monitor pricing decisions of their competitors, potentially impeding coordination.

Justice Fortas's suggestion that per se analysis was not essential to the result in *Container Corp.* was later influential in persuading the Court that information exchanges in and of themselves should not be subject to per se condemnation. *See United States v. Citizens & Southern National Bank,* 422 U.S. 86, 113 (1975) ("the dissemination of price information is not itself a *per se* violation of the Sherman Act."). The Court explained its reasoning in *Citizens & Southern* several years later in *United States v. United States Gypsum Co.,* 438 U.S. 422 (1978):

> The exchange of price data and other information among competitors does not invariably have anticompetitive effects; indeed such practices can in certain circumstances increase economic efficiency and render markets more, rather than less, competitive. For this

> reason, we have held that such exchanges of information do not constitute a *per se* violation of the Sherman Act. A number of factors including most prominently the structure of the industry involved and the nature of the information exchanged are generally considered in divining the procompetitive or anticompetitive effects of this type of interseller communication.

Id. at 441 n.16. Citing to *American Column & Lumber, American Linseed,* and *Container,* the Court also observed, however, that "[e]xchanges of current price information, of course, have the greatest potential for generating anticompetitive effects and although not *per se* unlawful have consistently been held to violate the Sherman Act." *Id. See also Todd,* 275 F.3d at 199 (discussing the evolution of the cases in the Supreme Court).

In the wake of the information-sharing decisions discussed above, two generalizations can be made concerning the Sherman Act's application to agreements by competitors to share information about their operations. First, the case law may be interpreted as indicating that an agreement merely to share information—even information about current prices—is not illegal per se and would be judged by a reasonableness standard. From a contemporary perspective, this conclusion may be understood as consistent with the legal rule established in *Broadcast Music, Inc. (see supra* Chapter 2) and with the rule as articulated in *Gypsum.* 438 U.S. at 441 n. 16. It is also consistent with the way economists tend to view information sharing. From an economic point of view, Section 1's "agreement" requirement is less important than the effects and justifications for information sharing. *See, e.g.,* Dennis W. Carlton, et al., *Communication Among Competitors: Game Theory and Antitrust,* 5 GEO. MASON L. REV. 423, 424 (1997) ("There is, in general, no economic theory of the meaning of 'agreement' wherein one may determine easily when communication leads to anticompetitive results irrespective of the context of the events. Nor do we think this is the right problem to solve."). Moreover, some commentators have argued that information sharing by rivals can promote competition in a variety of settings. *Id. See also* David J. Teece, *Information Sharing, Innovation, and Antitrust,* 62 ANTITRUST L.J. 465, 466 (1994) (arguing that "information collection, dissemination, and exchange among 'competitors' . . . [in] dynamic environments where markets are experiencing rapid change, often induced by technological innovation," can promote innovation and hence competition); Richard A. Posner, *Information and Antitrust: Reflections on the* Gypsum *and* Engineers *Decisions,* 67 GEO. L.J. 1187, 1194 (1979) ("producers must be well informed about competitors' prices and plans if resources are to be allocated efficiently.").

Second, the reasonableness, and thus the validity, of an information sharing program depends heavily on several variables. Courts are more likely to approve information sharing arrangements if the participants:

- Collectively hold a relatively modest share of total sales in the relevant market;

- Share information concerning past, rather than current or future, transactions;

- Avoid exchanging information about prices or key cost elements that determine prices; and

- Share information that aggregates activities of all participants rather than transaction-specific and firm-specific data.

Todd, which involved the appeal of a district court's dismissal of plaintiff's claim that the defendant employers shared information concerning compensation arrangements for purpose of setting salaries at artificially low levels, illustrates this kind of synthesis of the previous cases. Relying in significant part on *Gypsum*, the court concluded that the complaint should not have been dismissed. In doing so, it evaluated the allegations of the plaintiff's complaint by looking at factors such as market definition, market power, evidence of actual effects, the susceptibility of the market to collusion, and the nature of the information exchanged. *Todd*, 275 F.3d at 199–214. On different facts, cases involving suppression of employee compensation have been challenged as price-fixing. *See, e.g., United States v. Adobe Systems, Inc.*, 2011 WL 10883994 (D.D.C. 2011) (final judgment prohibiting agreement among leading high-tech firms not to poach employees from rivals); *In re High-Tech Employee Antitrust Litig.*, 2015 WL 5159441 (N.D. Ca. 2015) (related private litigation granting approval of class action settlement).

2. UNILATERAL FACILITATING PRACTICES: INVITATIONS TO COLLUDE

In some industries, the main impediment to successful coordination among the firms may be reaching a consensus on terms of coordination. Under such circumstances, invitations to collude may be viewed as practices potentially facilitating coordination, even if the invitations are not accepted. By challenging such conduct, antitrust enforcers may discourage collusion by increasing the hazards of even inviting a competitor to engage in a collusive scheme. Although Section 1 of the Sherman Act reaches only actual agreements, the Justice Department in the mid-1980s sought to use Section 2's prohibition against attempted monopolization to attack an unaccepted invitation to collude where the offeror and the offeree together accounted for a substantial share of market activity.

UNITED STATES V. AMERICAN AIRLINES, INC.

United States Court of Appeals for the Fifth Circuit, 1984.
743 F.2d 1114.

W. EUGENE DAVIS, CIRCUIT JUDGE.

The question presented in this antitrust case is whether the government's complaint states a claim of attempted monopolization under section 2 of the Sherman Act against the defendants, American Airlines, and its president Robert L. Crandall, for Crandall's proposal to the president of Braniff Airlines that the two airlines control the market and set prices. * * *

I.

In February 1982, American Airlines (American) and Braniff Airlines (Braniff) each had a major passenger airline complex, or "hub" at the Dallas-Fort Worth International Airport (DFW).[1] These hubs enabled American and Braniff to gather passengers from many cities, concentrate them at DFW, and then arrange connections for them on American and Braniff flights to other cities. The hub systems gave American and Braniff a marked competitive advantage over other airlines that served or might wish to serve DFW. In addition, the limitations on arrivals imposed by the Federal Aviation Administration (FAA) after the 1981 air traffic controllers' strike impeded any significant expansion or new entry by airlines into service at DFW. These limitations helped enable American and Braniff to maintain their high market shares in relation to other competitors.

In February 1982, American and Braniff together enjoyed a market share of more than ninety percent of the passengers on non-stop flights between DFW and eight major cities, and more than sixty percent of the passengers on flights between DFW and seven other cities. The two airlines had more than ninety percent of the passengers on many flights connecting at DFW, when no non-stop service was available between the cities in question. Overall, American and Braniff accounted for seventy-six percent of monthly enplanements at DFW.

For some time before February 1982, American and Braniff were competing fiercely for passengers flying to, from and through DFW, by offering lower fares and better service. During a telephone conversation between Robert Crandall, American's president, and Howard Putnam, Braniff's president, the following exchange occurred:

---

[1] Many airlines structure their services around major airports in network complexes termed hubs. The term derives from the fact that the routes of an airline maintaining a hub operation resemble the hub and spokes of a wheel, with the major airport, for example, DFW, as the hub and the routes to other cities radiating like spokes.

Crandall: I think it's dumb as hell for Christ's sake, all right, to sit here and pound the * * * out of each other and neither one of us making a * * * dime.

Putnam: Well—

Crandall: I mean, you know, goddamn, what the * * * is the point of it?

Putnam: Nobody asked American to serve Harlingen. Nobody asked American to serve Kansas City, and there were low fares in there, you know, before. So—

Crandall: You better believe it, Howard. But, you, you, you know, the complex is here—ain't gonna change a goddamn thing, all right. We can, we can both live here and there ain't no room for Delta. But there's, ah, no reason that I can see, all right, to put both companies out of business.

Putnam: But if you're going to overlay every route of American's on top of over, on top of every route that Braniff has—I can't just sit here and allow you to bury us without giving our best effort.

Crandall: Oh sure, but Eastern and Delta do the same thing in Atlanta and have for years.

Putnam: Do you have a suggestion for me?

Crandall: Yes. I have a suggestion for you. Raise your goddamn fares twenty percent. I'll raise mine the next morning.

Putnam: Robert, we—

Crandall: You'll make more money and I will too.

Putnam: We can't talk about pricing.

Crandall: Oh bull * * *, Howard. We can talk about any goddamn thing we want to talk about.

Putnam did not raise Braniff's fares in response to Crandall's proposal; instead he presented the government with a tape recording of the conversation.

* * *

II.

The language of the Sherman Act, its legislative history, the general criminal law relating to attempt and the jurisprudence relating to attempt specifically under the Sherman Act, lead us to the same conclusion: the government need not allege or prove an agreement to monopolize in order to establish an attempted joint monopolization under section 2 of the Sherman Act.

* * *

* * * The offense of attempted monopolization * * * has two elements: (1) specific intent to accomplish the illegal result; and (2) a dangerous probability that the attempt to monopolize will be successful. When evaluating the element of dangerous probability of success, we do not rely on hindsight but examine the probability of success at the time the acts occur.

The government unequivocally alleged that Crandall proposed to enlist his chief competitor in a cartel so that American and Braniff, acting together, could control prices and exclude competition at DFW; as Crandall explained to Putnam, "we can both live here and there ain't no room for Delta." As a result of the monopolization, Braniff would "make more money and I will too."

Both Crandall and Putnam were the chief executive officers of their airlines; each arguably had the power to implement Crandall's plan. The airlines jointly had a high market share in a market with high barriers to entry. American and Braniff, at the moment of Putnam's acceptance, would have monopolized the market. Under the facts alleged, it follows that Crandall's proposal was an act that was the most proximate to the commission of the completed offense that Crandall was capable of committing. Considering the alleged market share of American and Braniff, the barriers to entry by other airlines, and the authority of Crandall and Putnam, the complaint sufficiently alleged that Crandall's proposal had a dangerous probability of success.

The requirement that an accused's conduct have a dangerous probability of success expresses a significant antitrust principle that the antitrust laws protect competition, not competitors, and its related principle that the Sherman Act does not reach practices only unfair, impolite, or unethical.

* * *

* * * We note * * * both that dangerous probability remains an element of attempted monopolization in this circuit and that in concluding that the government here stated a claim we do not retreat from its proof requirements. We see Crandall's alleged conduct as uniquely unequivocal and its potential, given the alleged market conditions, as being uniquely consequential. In sum, our decision that the government has stated a claim does not add attempt to violations of Section 1 of the Sherman Act or lower the incipiency gate of Section 2.

Finally, we note one final consequence of our reasoning. If a defendant had the requisite intent and capacity, and his plan if executed would have had the prohibited market result, it is no defense that the plan proved to be impossible to execute. As applied here, if Putnam from the beginning never intended to agree such fact would be of no aid to Crandall and American.

* * *

We * * * conclude that the better reasoned authorities support the view that a highly verbal crime such as attempted monopolization may be established by proof of a solicitation along with the requisite intent.

III.

Our decision that the government's complaint states a claim of attempted monopolization is consistent with the Act's language and purpose. The application of section 2 principles to defendants' conduct will deter the formation of monopolies at their outset when the unlawful schemes are proposed, and thus, will strengthen the Act.

Under appellees' construction of the Act, an individual is given a strong incentive to propose the formation of cartels. If the proposal is accepted, monopoly power is achieved; if the proposal is declined, no antitrust liability attaches. If section 2 liability attaches to conduct such as that alleged against Crandall, naked proposals for the formation of cartels are discouraged and competition is promoted.

Appellees argue that price fixing is an offense under section 1 of the Sherman Act and since the government charges that Crandall sought to have American and Braniff fix prices, the government's complaint in reality seeks to have us write an attempt provision into section 1. This argument is meritless. Appellees confuse the section 1 offense of price fixing with the power to control price following acquisition of monopoly power under section 2. Under the facts alleged in the complaint, Crandall wanted both to obtain joint monopoly power and to engage in price fixing. That he was not able to price fix and thus, has no liability under section 1, has no effect on whether his unsuccessful efforts to monopolize constitute attempted monopolization.

* * *

Conclusion

We hold that an agreement is not an absolute prerequisite for the offense of attempted joint monopolization and that the government's complaint sufficiently alleged facts that if proved would permit a finding of attempted monopolization by defendants. * * *

The court evaluated whether the "dangerous probability of success" element of the attempt to monopolize offense was satisfied by examining the aggregate market shares of American and Braniff rather than the market share of the defendant alone. Was this a creative and sensible approach to reaching egregious conduct? Or did the court stretch the offense of attempted monopolization too far to cover this case because there is no attempted collusion offense under the Sherman Act? We will examine the offense of attempt to monopolize more closely in Chapter 4.

How far does the *American Airlines* precedent extend? Suppose four airlines, not two, were significant competitors for airline travel out of Dallas, each accounting for about 25% of passengers and enplanements, and that the president of American Airlines made his price-fixing suggestion at a meeting at which the heads of all four carriers were present. Assuming that the other carriers did not go along with that suggestion, would the *American Airlines* precedent permit the government to bring an attempted monopolization case against American under such circumstances?

Since *American Airlines* was decided, the Justice Department has preferred to challenge attempted price-fixing or attempted bid rigging as violations of the wire fraud or mail fraud statutes rather than as attempts to monopolize. *See, e.g., United States v. Ames Sintering Co.*, 927 F.2d 232 (6th Cir. 1990).

It is also well-established that the Federal Trade Commission can reach invitations to collude under the unfair methods of competition prohibition of Section 5 of the Federal Trade Commission Act. *See In re Quality Trailer Products Corp.*, 115 F.T.C. 944, 945 (1992) (settling by consent agreement allegations that representatives from a major U.S. axle products manufacturer privately visited a competitor's headquarters and "told the competitor that its price for certain axle products was too low," and "that there was no need for the two companies to compete on price."). The Federal Trade Commission has most frequently used this authority to reach invitations to collude occurring in private communications between firms and in situations where an invitation, if accepted, would amount to a per se violation of Section 1 of the Sherman Act. Complaint, *In re Stone Container Corp.*, 125 F.T.C. 853, 854 (1998) ("The invitation, if accepted, was likely to result in higher prices, reduced output, and injury to consumers."); *In re Drug Testing Compliance Group LLC*, FTC File No. 151–0048, 2016 WL 406531, at *3–4 (Jan. 21, 2016) (prohibiting DTC from initiating any invitation to collude with competitors which, if successful, would constitute a per se violation of Section 1 of the Sherman Act); *In re Step N Grip, LLC*, FTC File No. 151–0181, 2015 WL 9412614, at *3–4 (Dec. 7, 2015) (barring competitors from engaging in practices that would, if successful, constitute a per se violation of Section 1 of the Sherman Act); *In re 680 Digital, Inc.*, FTC File No. 141–0036, 2014 WL 4380286, at *9 (Aug. 20, 2014) (preventing any communication about price or any agreement between Nationwide and its competitors that, if implemented, would constitute a per se Section 1 violation).

The FTC has also applied its unfair methods of competition authority to public statements potentially constituting invitations to collude. *See, e.g., In re Valassis Commc'ns, Inc.*, FTC File No. 051–0008, 2006 WL 1367833, at *1, 5 (Apr. 19, 2006) (resolving by consent order a Section 5 complaint alleging Valassis Communications encouraged its primary rival to collude by inviting the rival—during a public earnings conference call—to end a recent price war by mutually ceasing to solicit each other's customers and by restoring prices to pre-price war levels.); Complaint, *In re U-Haul Int'l, Inc.*, 150 F.T.C. 1, 1 (2010) ("U-Haul invited collusion employing both private communications and public statements. These actions endanger competition, and violate Section 5 of the FTC Act."). *See also Liu v. Amerco*, 677 F.3d 489 (1st Cir. 2015) (challenging invitation to collude under state unfair competition statute modelled after Section 5, but which unlike Section 5 allowed for consumer damage claims and class actions.). Sidebar 3–6, below, further discusses Section 5 of the FTC Act.

3. OTHER UNILATERAL FACILITATING PRACTICES

Another example of how firms can solve their cartel problems unilaterally, without agreement, comes from the experience of two large sellers of electrical equipment, General Electric and Westinghouse, during the 1960s. At the beginning of that decade, the two firms had been convicted of price-fixing (along with a third firm that later exited the market) in a famous scandal that sent executives to jail, and subjected the firms to expensive private lawsuits for treble damages. After the collapse of the price-fixing scheme, firm profitability fell. The companies wanted higher prices, but they did not want to risk another price-fixing conviction.

The two firms independently, but similarly, took several steps to restore profitability; we will focus on two. These steps can be understood as efforts to change the structure of the market to facilitate tacit collusion. First, the firms standardized their product definitions, and published price books setting forth list prices for the wide range of variants. These acts could simplify the coordination task by facilitating price leadership, much in the way simple, obvious rules did so in the hypothetical delicatessen example. The firms would no longer have to work out prices product-by-product in order to collude successfully; they could merely raise prices on all products across-the-board. Moreover, published price lists may make each firm's transactions more apparent to its rivals, creating more "open" pricing and thus discouraging cartel cheating.

Second, GE and Westinghouse promised customers that if any other electrical equipment customer got a lower price, the firm would retroactively give that lower price to the original customer, by refunding the difference. This practice is a type of "most favored nations" or "most favored customer" provision, and is discussed in more detail in Chapter 6 (*see Note on the Economic Effects of "Most Favored Nation" Provisions, infra*

Chapter 6). In brief, although such contractual agreements may appear favorable to individual buyers, their widespread use may be harmful to buyers as a group because they may facilitate coordination by discouraging cheating. Each firm that makes such a promise raises its own costs of cutting price. It effectively ties its own hands so that it won't have an incentive to cheat, making a price war less likely.

With these practices in place, prices and profits rose. Because the firms adopted these practices unilaterally, and neither was a monopolist, the Justice Department did not challenge them under the Sherman Act. But in the unique circumstances of this industry, the Justice Department was able to bring a case as a violation of the decree settling the earlier price-fixing convictions. *See* Proposed Modification of Existing Judgments, *United States v. General Electric Co.*, 42 Fed. Reg. 17,005 (1977); *see also* MICHAEL PORTER, CASES IN COMPETITIVE STRATEGY 102–18 (1983).

Unilateral facilitating practices among oligopolists cannot be challenged under Sherman Act § 1. Unlike the information exchange practices we considered earlier, they were not adopted through agreement. Neither can they be reached under Sherman Act § 2, so long as the industry lacks a dominant seller. At least this is the prevailing view today. During the 1970s, as part of a broad attack on market concentration discussed in Sidebar 4–3, the federal enforcement agencies explored the possibility of deconcentrating markets through "shared monopoly" cases. During the 1980s, the Federal Trade Commission saw the problem of unilateral facilitating practices among oligopolists as a gap in the Sherman Act that could potentially be filled through application of FTC Act § 5. Section 5 has long been recognized to reach conduct beyond Sherman and Clayton Act violations, including acts that violate the "spirit" of those antitrust statutes and even conduct that offends public values beyond the letter or spirit of the antitrust laws. *See, e.g., FTC. v. Indiana Federation of Dentists*, 476 U.S. 447, 454 (1986); *FTC v. Sperry & Hutchinson Co.*, 405 U.S. 233, 244 (1972); *FTC v. Brown Shoe Co.*, 384 U.S. 316, 320–21 (1966); *FTC v. Motion Picture Advertising Service Co.*, 344 U.S. 392, 394–95 (1953).

But in the *Du Pont (Ethyl)* case, decided in 1984, the Second Circuit held that FTC Act § 5 did not reach the challenged practices. *E.I. Du Pont De Nemours & Co. v. Federal Trade Commission (Ethyl)*, 729 F.2d 128 (2d Cir. 1984). The practices at issue in *Ethyl* included "most favored nations" clauses; the anticompetitive potential and procompetitive justifications for these provisions are considered in the *Note on the Economic Effects of "Most Favored Nation" Provisions* in Chapter 6. In its opinion, the appellate panel addressed both the scope of the FTC Act and the competitive effects of the practices that the FTC had held unlawful:

In our view, before business conduct in an oligopolistic industry may be labeled "unfair" within the meaning of § 5 a minimum standard demands that, absent a tacit agreement, at least some indicia of oppressiveness must exist such as (1) evidence of anticompetitive intent or purpose on the part of the producer charged, or (2) the absence of an independent legitimate business reason for its conduct. If, for instance, a seller's conduct, even absent identical behavior on the part of its competitors, is contrary to its independent self-interest, that circumstance would indicate that the business practice is "unfair" within the meaning of § 5. In short, in the absence of proof of a violation of the antitrust laws or evidence of collusive, coercive, predatory, or exclusionary conduct, business practices are not "unfair" in violation of § 5 unless those practices either have an anticompetitive purpose or cannot be supported by an independent legitimate reason. To suggest, as does the Commission in its opinion, that the defendant can escape violating § 5 only by showing that there are "countervailing procompetitive justifications" for the challenged business practices goes too far.

In the present case the FTC concedes that the petitioners did not engage in the challenged practices by agreement or collusively. Each acted independently and unilaterally. There is no evidence of coercive or predatory conduct. If the petitioners nevertheless were unable to come forward with some independent legitimate reason for their adoption of these practices, the Commission's argument that they must be barred as "unfair" when they have the effect of facilitating conscious price parallelism and interdependence might have some merit. But the evidence is overwhelming and undisputed, as the ALJ found, that each petitioner independently adopted its practices for legitimate business reasons which we have described.

Id. at 139–40. In a footnote, the court described its "some indica of oppressiveness" requirement as "comparable to the principle that there must be a 'plus factor' before conscious parallelism may be found to be conspiratorial in violation of the Sherman Act." *Id.* at 139 n. 10.

After the Second Circuit's *Ethyl* opinion, what room is left for the FTC to challenge unilateral facilitating practices under FTC Act § 5? To challenge facilitating practices under § 5, what showing must the FTC make before the defendant is required to present offsetting justifications? Could the FTC have brought *Ethyl* as an agreement case by adopting Judge Posner's views about inferring agreement from parallel conduct? (*See supra* Sidebar 3–3). Sidebar 3–6, which follows, further discusses the history and evolution of Section 5 of the FTC Act.

Sidebar 3–6:
Section 5 of the Federal Trade Commission Act[a]

Section 5 of the Federal Trade Commission Act forbids both unfair and deceptive acts and practices (sometimes referred to as "UDAP") and unfair methods of competition ("unfair methods" or "UMC"). 15 U.S.C. § 45(a)(1) (*See infra* Appendix A). The FTC's UDAP authority underpins its consumer protection function and is often relied upon to support claims of fraud and, more recently, issues related to information privacy. This Sidebar focuses on Section 5's UMC provision, which is associated with its antitrust enforcement authority.

This measure was integral to the FTC's establishment in 1914.[b] Congress intended Section 5 to be a tool for upgrading the U.S. antitrust system by permitting the FTC to reach behavior not necessarily proscribed by the Sherman Act or the Clayton Act. Section 5 would be applied by an expert administrative tribunal with power to impose prospective equitable relief (not monetary remedies or criminal sanctions); its decisions interpreting Section 5 would have no collateral effects in private litigation, and its work would be reviewed by appellate courts under a deferential standard.

In making this choice, Congress feared that the Sherman Act, at least as applied by the courts, would be too narrow to address the "trust" problem. Congress envisioned Section 5, in effect, as a means to adapt the antitrust system to new conditions, informed by the work of an administrative body which would apply the provision with a sophisticated understanding of business practices and their implications, gained both from its enforcement activities and its investigatory and study authority under Section 6 of the Act. 15 U.S.C. § 46 (*see infra* Appendix A). The FTC's administrative powers under Section 5 incorporated a significant trade-off. The Commission had broad authority to shape doctrine, but its remedial authority would be limited to equitable relief, such as injunctions.

In theory, Section 5 had the potential to help make the Commission, perhaps, the preeminent U.S. antitrust policy

---

[a] This sidebar is adapted in part from William E. Kovacic & Marc Winerman, *Competition Policy and the Application of Section 5 of the Federal Trade Commission Act*, 76 ANTITRUST L.J. 929 (2010).

[b] Marc Winerman, *The Origins of the FTC: Concentration, Cooperation, Control, and Competition*, 71 ANTITRUST L.J. 1, 58–92 (2003).

maker.[c] Through repeated exposure to competition policy problems, the FTC would use distinctive research and data collection powers to develop, apply, and assess doctrine. Expert commissioners would determine the appropriate standards of liability and over time firms would conform to those standards, and courts would eventually look to the Commission for guidance about how to frame and apply antitrust rules. By this design, the Department of Justice would gravitate toward focusing upon the prosecution of offenses deemed suitable for criminal punishment, along with some major monopolization cases. Other civil law enforcement would become the province of the FTC; Section 5's flexibility and the Commission's other institutional features would be a major reason for its specialized role.

Although the FTC does not have authority to enforce the Sherman Act, Section 5 has been consistently read to incorporate all Sherman Act offenses by reference. *See FTC v. Cement Institute*, 333 U.S. 683, 692 (1948). In addition, since 1914, the U.S. courts have interpreted Section 5 to permit the FTC to proscribe behavior beyond conduct prohibited by the other federal antitrust statutes.[d] Despite such rulings, the FTC's application of Section 5 has played a minor role in antitrust law. Since 1914, Sherman Act and Clayton Act litigation, rather than what are referred to as "stand-alone" Section 5 cases, has provided the main vehicle for setting doctrine. Relatively few Section 5 cases have had a notable impact in terms of antitrust doctrine or economic effects. Several factors explain why Section 5 has played so modest a role. Probably the most important is that the Sherman Act proved to be a far more flexible tool for setting antitrust rules than Congress expected in the early twentieth century. This is evident in the development of the rule of reason under Section 1 and doctrine governing single-firm conduct under Section 2. The potential breadth of the Sherman Act's prohibition on monopolization and attempted monopolization, for example, became apparent in *United States v. Aluminum Company of America (Alcoa)*[e] in 1945 and was reinforced by decisions such

---

[c] This was the expectation of some of the FTC Act's principal sponsors. Shortly before Congress passed the legislation in 1914, Senator Cummins predicted that the FTC "will be found to be the most efficient protection to the people of the United States that Congress has ever given the people by way of a regulation of commerce." 51 CONG. REC. 14,770 (1914).

[d] Neil W. Averitt, *The Meaning of "Unfair Methods of Competition" in Section 5 of the Federal Trade Commission Act,* 21 B.C. L. REV. 227, 239–40 (1980).

[e] 148 F.2d 416 (2d Cir. 1945).

as *American Tobacco Co. v. United States*[f] and *United States v. United Shoe Machinery Corp.*[g] These and other cases suggested that the Sherman Act could reach an especially wide range of business behavior.

These doctrinal trends raised questions about the utility of Section 5. There seemed little need for the elasticity of Section 5 when the Sherman Act was proving to be so elastic itself. In the period when courts were interpreting the Sherman and Clayton Acts expansively, it was not evident that Section 5 could make a useful contribution by reaching still further and adding to the mix. The Supreme Court had affirmed the FTC's authority to use Section 5 to prohibit behavior beyond the reach of the Sherman Act, but it was unclear if Section 5 would likely come into play except in relatively rare circumstances.

One possible application would be to fill gaps in coverage, such as to prohibit invitations to collude that neither constituted unlawful agreements within the reach of Section 1 of the Sherman Act nor violated the Sherman Act Section 2 ban on attempted monopolization. Such applications would serve to condemn behavior that posed the same competitive dangers as conduct proscribed by the other antitrust statutes, yet might evade effective control because it lacked some characteristic required by these measures. Among other hurdles, FTC cases seeking to serve this gap-filling function would have to overcome arguments that Congress purposefully created the gaps in question and did not intend that Section 5 be used to cure deliberate omissions in the coverage provided by the Sherman and Clayton Acts.

The general trend toward expansion in the interpretation of the Sherman Act that began in the 1940s ended in the late 1970s. This is particularly evident in the treatment of dominant firms. Judicial rulings in Section 2 cases over the past 40 years generally have narrowed the limits on single-firm behavior. Dominant firms today enjoy considerable freedom under U.S. law to select pricing, product development, and marketing tactics. Similarly, the Court has abandoned reliance on per se prohibitions in favor of a more flexible application of the rule of reason.

Several forces have propelled U.S. antitrust doctrine in permissive directions. One is commentary that offers procompetitive explanations for behavior once treated with suspicion. A second stimulus for retrenchment is the concern

---

[f]   328 U.S. 781 (1946).

[g]   110 F. Supp. 295 (D. Mass. 1953), *aff'd per curiam*, 347 U.S. 521 (1954).

that U.S. private rights of action and certain features of the U.S. litigation system generate overdeterrence, especially when used to challenge behavior that poses a complex mix of procompetitive and anticompetitive attributes. Modern Supreme Court decisions that have restricted the reach of the Sherman Act have emphasized this theme.[h]

Judicial skepticism in private Sherman Act cases has drawn attention back to Section 5. If Section 5 as a distinctive source of liability has limited utility in periods of Sherman Act doctrinal expansion, what happens when the reach of the Sherman Act shrinks, and shrinks dramatically, owing to judicial anxiety about overreaching in private litigation? Section 5 would seem to provide a possible institutional solution. Compared to the typical federal court, the FTC has superior tools to perform empirical and policy work that can inform the design of legal rules; it is a specialized tribunal whose decisions under Section 5 have far less collateral effect in private cases. In principle, administrative elaboration of doctrine by the FTC, subject to judicial review, should ameliorate many of the concerns that accompany the private litigation of antitrust cases before generalist courts.

Future FTC efforts to expand the use of Section 5 will confront a largely unhappy history. In the modern era, the FTC has relied upon Section 5 to achieve noteworthy settlements involving single-firm conduct[i] and invitations to collude,[j] but the FTC's record of appellate litigation involving applications of Section 5 that go beyond prevailing interpretations of the other antitrust laws is sobering. One needs to go back to the 1960s to find cases in which the FTC succeeded on appeal in an antitrust case premised entirely or largely upon a stand-alone Section 5 theory. These include challenges to full-line forcing in the sale of tires, batteries, and accessories,[k] a variant of exclusive dealing,[l] and a joint venture.[m] Before the 1960s, the list of FTC appellate successes is short, as well.

---

[h] *See, e.g.*, NYNEX Corp. v. Discon, Inc., 525 U.S. 128, 136–37 (1998) ("To apply the per se rule here . . . would transform cases involving business behavior that is improper for various reasons, say, cases involving nepotism or personal pique, into treble-damages antitrust cases.").

[i] *See, e.g.*, *In re* Negotiated Data Solutions LLC, C-4234, 2008 WL 4407246 (F.T.C. Sept. 22, 2008).

[j] *See, e.g.*, *In re* Valassis Communications, Inc., No. C-4160, 2006 WL 1367833 (F.T.C. Apr. 19, 2006).

[k] FTC v. Texaco, Inc., 393 U.S. 223 (1968); Atl. Refining Co. v. FTC, 381 U.S. 357 (1965).

[l] FTC v. Brown Shoe Co., 384 U.S. 316 (1966).

[m] Yamaha Motor Co. Ltd. v. FTC, 657 F.2d 971, 981 (8th Cir. 1981).

These results have not been for want of trying. In the 1970s the Commission premised several cases on distinctive Section 5 theories. Three of these matters—*Boise Cascade*,[n] *Official Airline Guides*,[o] and *Ethyl*[p] —resulted in court of appeals decisions adverse to the agency. The FTC also litigated and lost a case (*Abbott Laboratories*) in federal district court in the mid-1990s.[q] These federal court decisions in Section 5 cases reveal similar themes. Each court recognized that Section 5 allows the FTC to challenge behavior beyond the reach of the other antitrust laws, but each court also found that the agency had failed to sufficiently establish competitive harm of the sort being required in contemporary Sherman Act cases.

The more recent and the more distant cases reveal recurring judicial concerns about the outer bounds of Section 5. Courts have tended to endorse principles that strongly resemble standards familiar to them from Sherman Act and Clayton Act cases. The cost-benefit concepts devised in rule of reason cases supply the courts with natural default rules in the absence of something better. The apparent breadth of Section 5 also has spurred congressional efforts to restrain the FTC's use of its UMC authority. In the 1970s, for example, the FTC used Section 5 to challenge collective dominance in the breakfast cereal and petroleum sectors and sought extensive divestitures. These cases attracted hostile congressional scrutiny and criticism that the Commission was applying its mandate to assert unlimited control over the structure of American industry.[r]

In August 2015, the FTC sought to address concerns about the scope of its distinctive mandate by issuing a policy statement "to provide a framework for the Commission's exercise of its 'standalone' Section 5 authority to address acts or practices that are anticompetitive but may not fall within the scope of the Sherman or Clayton Act."[s] The statement observes that, in standalone Section 5 cases, the Commission (1) will be

---

[n] Boise Cascade Corp. v. FTC, 637 F.2d 573 (9th Cir. 1980).

[o] Official Airline Guides, Inc. v. FTC, 630 F.2d 920 (2d Cir. 1980).

[p] E.I. Du Pont De Nemours & Co. v. FTC, 729 F.2d 128 (2d Cir. 1984).

[q] FTC v. Abbott Labs., 853 F. Supp. 526 (D.D.C. 1994).

[r] William E. Kovacic, *The Federal Trade Commission and Congressional Oversight of Antitrust Enforcement*, 17 TULSA L.J. 587, 625–27, 666 (1982).

[s] FTC, *Statement of Enforcement Principles Regarding "Unfair Methods of Competition" Under Section 5 of the FTC Act* (Aug. 13, 2015), https//:www.ftc.gov/system/files/documents/public_statements/735201/150813section5enforcement.pdf. For one view on possible interpretation of the Statement by a former FTC Commissioner who voted for it, see Joshua D. Wright & Angela M. Diveley, *Unfair Methods of Competition After the 2015 Commission Statement*, ANTITRUST SOURCE (Oct. 2015), http://www.americanbar.org/content/dam/aba/publishing/antitrust_source/oct15_wright_10_19f.authcheckdam.pdf.

guided by the goal of promoting consumer welfare, (2) will evaluate challenged conduct under the rule of reason and will condemn only behavior that causes, or is likely to cause, harm to competition or the competitive process after accounting for cognizable efficiencies and business justifications, and (3) is less likely to use a standalone UMC theory if enforcement of the Sherman Act or Clayton Act is sufficient to address the competitive harm arising from a practice. By setting out these enforcement principles, the Commission has sought to provide firms, courts and legislators assurances about its enforcement intentions and, perhaps, has created a better foundation for future applications of its unique antitrust mandate.

F. CONCLUSION

In this Chapter, we have examined the law and economics of cartels, from both an historical and contemporary perspective. As we noted at the outset, the Sherman Act's distinction of unilateral and concerted action, combined with the impact of harsh treatment of price-fixing, has led to two sets of challenges. First, it became necessary to develop a framework for relying on circumstantial evidence of agreement to infer conspiracy. Second, even once such a framework developed, it remained essential to integrate that legal framework with modern economic concepts and principles. Doing so remains an ongoing challenge that continues to divide courts and commentators alike.

G. PROBLEMS AND EXERCISES

Problem 3–1:
Durab[7]

Many consumer electronics devices, such as radios and portable tape and compact disc players, are powered by small batteries, typically sold in different size categories, such as "D," "C," "A," "AA," and "AAA." The small battery industry is comprised of three main firms: Durab, Allthere, and Batteron. These firms account for approximately 90% of U.S. sales of small batteries. Durab and Allthere have 35% each and Batteron has 20%. These relative shares have been fairly stable for the past five years.

Recently a major camera company, Caman, entered the small battery market, but its sales have been limited due to its inability to gain sufficient retail distribution. A large Japanese battery company, Nisobat, has recently begun to import batteries from Japan. Nisobat's prospects for

---

[7]   This exercise is based on a problem created by Professor Steven C. Salop, and is used with his permission.

success are uncertain. The Nisobat brand name is well-regarded by consumers in general, and many of the firm's other products are sold through the same retailers that handle batteries, but the transportation costs of importing batteries are high.

Around 20% of all retail sales of batteries in the United States are made through Elec-City, a national chain of retail electronics stores. Most of the rest are made through large electronics and appliance superstores, department stores, and warehouse discounters. Some of these retailers, including Elec-City, also purchase private label batteries from the three major U.S. firms, and sell them side-by-side with the leading brands. Private label products carry the retailer's brand name (*e.g.*, "Elec-City"), not the manufacturer's brand name (*e.g.*, Durab). Private label batteries account for 5% of batteries sold nationwide. Retailers buy private label brands from battery manufacturers at a substantial discount below the standard wholesale list price for batteries carrying the manufacturer's brand name. (The wholesale price is the price a manufacturer charges for the product to the retailer. The retail price (usually higher) is the price the retailer charges to the consumer.)

Last December, the CEO of Durab gave a speech before securities analysts and the business press. The CEO's prepared remarks were followed by a question and answer session. A reporter for Consumer Electronics Daily, a leading trade publication, asked the Durab CEO about reports that wholesale battery prices would be rising soon. The CEO replied that costs had risen, and he thought prices should rise across-the-board, for all battery sizes. When asked how much he thought prices should rise, he replied "10–12%." This range was reported the next day in several news stories about the speech.

During January, the same reporter interviewed the CEO of Batteron and asked her about the Durab CEO's statement. She replied that she thought a 10% across-the-board price increase would be appropriate, except for size D batteries, which should go up 15%. That interview was reported in the January 24 edition of the Consumer Electronics Daily. On January 25, Durab announced that effective February 1, the wholesale price of batteries would rise by 10%, except that the price of size D batteries would increase by 12%. Two days later, on January 26, Batteron and Allthere announced similar wholesale price increases (10% for most batteries, 12% for size D), effective immediately. On February 1, Durab increased its wholesale price in accordance with its announcement. Nisobat and Caman did not announce price increases.

In response to complaints from various consumer groups, the Justice Department has undertaken a preliminary investigation of this episode. Initially, the question before the Division staff is whether a full-scale investigation of possible collusion in the small battery industry is warranted. What are the best arguments in favor and against doing so? What additional facts about the conduct or industry could the Justice Department pursue in discovery to make a better assessment?

Problem 3–2:
Ice Machines

Virtually all restaurants, bars, hotels, and other food and drink providers own commercial ice machines. More than one million commercial ice machines are in use in the U.S. Ice machines have a typical life expectancy of five years. Freeze, Chill, and Icy are the only manufacturers of ice machines selling in the U.S. Each accounts for approximately one-third of the ice machines sold annually, and their shares have not varied much from year to year.

Ice machines have a condenser unit (like an air conditioner) that chills water below the freezing point. The condenser is turned on and off by a lever in the ice bin that cuts off ice production when the bin is full. Ice machine technology had not changed for decades until mid-2010 when, coincidentally, three engineering labs at different universities each announced that they had developed and patented a new technology for ice machines.

One new technology allows the condenser to be water-cooled, making it possible to reduce ice machine size substantially relative to a traditional air-cooled machine that would produce ice at the same rate. Water-cooled machines would almost always be costlier to operate than air-cooled machines, however. This technology could allow an ice machine manufacturer to produce machines suitable for customers that have small food preparation spaces and high customer volumes, such as restaurants in food courts at shopping malls.

Another new technology introduces sophisticated electronic sensors and controls that vary the machine's internal temperature in order to create clear ice cubes. Electronic controls also allow the machine to adjust the rate at which ice is made to ensure that the ice in the bin is always fresh. This technology could allow a manufacturer to develop ice machines targeted to customers that particularly value clear and fresh ice, such as high-end restaurants and bars.

The third new technology blows highly filtered air into the bin, creating a pressure differential in the ice machine that keeps air potentially contaminated by outside microbes away from stored ice. This technology could permit an ice machine manufacturer to market "healthy" ice machines to customers particularly concerned to avoid airborne contamination, such as hospitals and schools.

During September and October 2010, the patent licensing office at each of the three universities contacted each U.S. ice machine manufacturer. They also contacted the two leading foreign ice machine manufacturers, Arctic and Globe. In dealing with the U.S. ice machine firms, each university had a similar experience: it noticed initial licensing interest from all three manufacturers, followed by a sudden loss of interest from two of the three in late November 2010. In early 2011 only one firm—a different firm in each case—chose to obtain a license from each university, and each negotiated to obtain exclusive U.S. rights for five years. Arctic and Globe have licensed all three patents for use in machines sold outside the U.S.

Every year, the three ice machine manufacturers purchase display booths at the annual meeting of the National Association of Restaurants (NAR), to show off their new models to prospective customers. The NAR meeting is always held during the second week of November. Each year at the NAR meeting, the CEOs of the three manufacturers have a private dinner.

At the most recent NAR meeting, in November 2012, each of the firms unveiled new models that augmented its traditional product line with one of the new technologies. Freeze added a line of small water-cooled ice machines. Chill introduced machines that produced clear and fresh ice using the variable temperature technology. Icy showed off its new healthy ice machines that used the positive pressure technology.

Restaurant News, the leading restaurant industry trade press publication, included an article on the new ice machines in its issue covering the NAR meeting. The article noted that restaurant representatives attending flocked to the display booths of all three firms, and suggested that machines using each new technology would appeal to a significant group of customers. The reporter questioned Chill's CEO about why it had licensed only one of the three new technologies. The CEO was quoted as saying that the firm wished it could develop machines using all three new technologies, but could only afford to develop one new type. In response to the same question, Icy's CEO stated that its marketing staff was very excited about selling healthy ice machines and its engineering staff had become expert in managing air flows.

The management culture at Freeze emphasizes undertaking detailed analysis before making decisions. In late 2010, the firm's senior marketing, engineering and finance executives evaluated its options. Their report concluded that there would be substantial markets for selling machines using all three technologies, that the development of new machines using each technology would present comparable engineering challenges, that the cost of a new machine would increase by about the same amount if each of the three technologies was incorporated, and that customers interested in new machines using each would be willing to pay a similar price premium over traditional machines. The report also made clear that Freeze would not be able to develop new models using more than one technology in time to introduce them in November 2012 without hiring additional engineers.

Did the three U.S. ice machine manufacturers reach an agreement to allocate customers for products made with the three the new ice machine technologies?

(Note that it is possible the manufacturers also or instead reached other agreements that could potentially be subject to antitrust scrutiny: to exclude Arctic and Globe, to engage in exclusive dealing with the effect of foreclosing Arctic and Globe, or to limit competition in licensing patents in order to avoid bidding up the licensing fee. These other possibilities implicate areas of antitrust law that will be considered in later Chapters; you may wish to return to this problem then.)

CHAPTER 4

EXCLUSIONARY CONDUCT

■ ■ ■

INTRODUCTION

In creating a national antitrust law in 1890, Congress sought to unravel supplier cartels and discourage producers from imposing unreasonable limits on the commercial freedom of their distributors and retailers. In Chapters 2 and 3 we learned how courts developed doctrines to address collective efforts by firms to restrain trade. An equally important congressional aim in establishing the U.S. antitrust system was to curb the power of individual, dominant corporate enterprises, particularly unreasonably exclusionary behavior.

The chief means for limiting such conduct in the United States is Section 2 of the Sherman Act, whose basic goal—barring efforts by single firms to unreasonably suppress competition—has been embraced by virtually every other competition law enforcement system in the world. The principal language and concepts of Section 2, like Section 1, derive from the common law, but their contemporary interpretation has evolved significantly in recent decades. Section 2's chief modern counterpart is Article 102 of the Treaty on the Functioning of the European Union (TFEU), which forbids the "abuse of a dominant market position." Article 102's abuse of dominance approach is the more common in competition law systems today.

Statutory Framework

Section 2 of the Sherman Act establishes three separate offenses: (1) monopolization, (2) attempt to monopolize, and (3) conspiracy to monopolize. As formulated by the Supreme Court in *United States v. Grinnell Corp.*, 384 U.S. 563, 570–71, 86 S.Ct. 1698, 1704 (1966):

> The offense of monopoly under § 2 of the Sherman Act has two elements: (1) the possession of monopoly power in the relevant market and (2) the willful acquisition or maintenance of that power as distinguished from growth or development as a consequence of a superior product, business acumen, or historic accident.

As we will see in the remainder of this Chapter, modern judicial decisions continue to employ this basic framework.

The controlling modern formulation of the offense of attempt to monopolize appears in *Spectrum Sports, Inc. v. McQuillan*, 506 U.S. 447, 456, 113 S.Ct. 884, 890 (1993), which we will read later in this Chapter, where the Supreme Court held:

> * * * [I]t is generally required that to demonstrate attempted monopolization a plaintiff must prove (1) that the defendant has engaged in predatory or anticompetitive conduct with (2) a specific intent to monopolize and (3) a dangerous probability of achieving monopoly power.

The rarely invoked conspiracy to monopolize offense traditionally required concerted action (like Section 1 of the Sherman Act) and specific intent to achieve a monopoly, but the plaintiff did not have to prove that the defendants have monopoly power. *See American Tobacco Co. v. United States*, 328 U.S. 781, 66 S.Ct. 1125 (1946). Modern courts have differed on the required elements, but have tended to be more demanding. Some have suggested that market power should be an element of the offense, arguing that it would be anomalous to require evidence of competitive harm for a Section 1 claim, but not for a Section 2 claim. *See, e.g., Dickson v. Microsoft Corp.*, 309 F.3d 193, 211 (4th Cir. 2002); Fraser v. Major League Soccer, LLC, 284 F.3d 47, 67–68 (1st Cir. 2002) (requiring proof of a relevant market and market power). Other courts have enumerated varying combinations of elements. *See, e.g., Howard Hess Dental Laboratories, Inc. v. Dentsply Int'l, Inc.*, 602 F.3d 237, 253 (3d Cir. 2010) (claim of conspiracy to monopolize requires proof of an agreement to monopolize, an overt act in furtherance of the conspiracy, specific intent to monopolize, and a causal connection between the conspiracy and the injury alleged); *Multistate Legal Studies, Inc. v. Harcourt Brace Jovanovich Legal and Professional Publications, Inc.*, 63 F.3d 1540, 1556 (10th Cir. 1995) (claim of conspiracy to monopolize requires proof of an agreement to monopolize, overt acts in furtherance, an "effect upon an appreciable amount of interstate commerce," and specific intent).

In contrast to the U.S. framework, Article 102 does not distinguish among monopolization, attempt to monopolize, and conspiracy to monopolize. It is directed at "abusive" conduct by "dominant" firms, which potentially sweeps more broadly than Section 2. For most offenses, however, Section 2 and Article 102 share a common formula: power (dominance) + conduct (abuse). But a dominant firm can also violate Article 102 through "exploitative" conduct, such as charging high prices, although exploitative conduct cases are increasingly rare. *See* Sidebar 4–11: *Comparative Perspectives: The Treatment of Anticompetitive Single Firm Conduct in the U.S. and E.U.*

In this Chapter we focus primarily on the offense of monopolization, but we will also consider attempted monopolization and abuse of dominance. As we shall see, to delineate each of these offenses, competition policy systems have had to address three basic issues. The first is to define *the status of "monopoly" or "dominance."* Section 2 and Article 102 are concerned with the exercise of substantial market power and ignore the conduct of commercially insignificant firms. In studying the market power requirement, we will return to a theme we introduced in examining the application of the rule of reason in Chapter 2: the use of market shares to infer market power, which depends crucially on how courts define the *relevant market* and evaluate the defendant's importance within that market.

The second basic issue is to define *improper behavior*. With the exception of exploitative conduct (the mere exercise of market power, as by raising price), antitrust laws rarely condemn monopoly itself. Making the mere possession of substantial market power illegal would ensnare firms that achieved preeminence through laudable means such as creating superior products and reducing costs. A competition system that punished such success inevitably would dampen the initiative to develop new products or processes that enhance competition and benefit consumers.

Implicit in the analysis of exclusionary conduct is an evaluation of its effects, both anticompetitive and procompetitive. In earlier cases, courts generally did not identify these considerations separately. Recent cases have tended to focus distinctly on each. The plaintiff offers a hypothesis of competitive harm and, if it is supported by evidence, the burden of production shifts to the defendant to offer evidence of a procompetitive reason for its acts. This trend in analysis highlights the third basic issue in our study of exclusionary behavior: *what constitutes a legitimate business justification for conduct asserted to be improper?* The inquiry associated with defining improper behavior and evaluating redeeming justifications is difficult in many cases. Much business behavior is competitively ambiguous, and courts have struggled to develop coherent principles for determining when the anticompetitive features of various practices are so pronounced as to render the behavior improper.

Three Perspectives on Exclusion

Antitrust's concern about possible harm to competition from exclusionary conduct has waxed and waned over time. These changes can most readily be appreciated by looking to the views of leading judges and commentators on allegations of exclusion by single, dominant firms.

Later in this Chapter, we will read Judge Learned Hand's influential 1945 *Alcoa* opinion. Judge Hand displayed deep concern about exclusionary conduct. Only if "exclusion" were interpreted very narrowly, he wrote, "as limited to maneuvers not honestly industrial, but actuated solely by a desire to prevent competition," could Alcoa's conduct in expanding capacity in advance of the growth of demand "be deemed not 'exclusionary.'" Hand refused to entertain such an interpretation, because to do so "would permit just such consolidations as [the Sherman Act] was designed to prevent." Judge Hand thus primarily feared *false acquittals* (sometimes referred to as "false negatives") and under-deterrence, the possibility that by failing to find violations in a monopolist's exclusionary conduct antitrust law could create a lethargic monopolist with little incentive to cut costs or innovate. Although his decision also included some often-quoted language warning of the consequences of *false convictions* (sometimes referred to as "false positives"), its predominant themes and holding illustrate the connection between a concern for false negatives and a relatively broad definition of "exclusionary" conduct.

In contrast to Judge Hand's vision is Robert H. Bork's in THE ANTITRUST PARADOX. First published in 1978, this volume set forth the Chicago School perspective on antitrust and expressed deep skepticism about exclusion as an antitrust theory, particularly as applied to dominant firm conduct. In the passage below, Bork assessed the possibility that a firm could exclude or foreclose its rivals by refusing to deal with certain suppliers or distributors:

> Where an *efficiency potential* appears in a case involving an individual refusal to deal, and there is *no clear evidence* that the purpose of the refusal was predatory, courts should generally find the refusal lawful, both because of tie-breaker considerations and because predation by an individual refusal to deal will be *very uncommon*.

ROBERT H. BORK, THE ANTITRUST PARADOX 346 (1978) (emphasis added). Note the "music" in this passage, and its implications for the relative evidentiary burdens of the parties to a monopolization case. To prove the benefits to competition, an efficiency "potential" is sufficient. To prove the harm, "clear evidence" would be required. The critical presumption: an anticompetitive outcome will be "very uncommon." Elsewhere in THE ANTITRUST PARADOX, Bork recognizes that firms can impede rivals in ways that harm competition:

> By disturbing optimal distribution patterns one rival can impose costs upon another, that is, force the other to accept higher costs. This may or may not be a serious cost increase, but if it is (and the matter can only be determined empirically), the imposition of costs *may conceivably* be a means of predation. The predator will suffer cost increases, too, and that sets *limits* to the types of cases in which this tactic will be used for predation. There is a further *complication*, moreover, in that the behavior involved will often be capable of creating efficiencies.

Id. at 156 (emphasis added). Note the skepticism resonating in Bork's phrase "may conceivably," and observe how Bork immediately turns from the anticompetitive theory to a limitation and a complication.

In discussing exclusion, therefore, Bork is describing a problem that he thinks is exceedingly rare. THE ANTITRUST PARADOX does identify one such case, the Supreme Court's decision in *Lorain Journal*, which we shall read later in this Chapter. Bork was also concerned in the book with the misuse of government processes as a method of exclusion. And two decades later he found another anticompetitive example in *United States v. Microsoft Corp.*, 253 F.3d 34 (D.C. Cir. 2001), where he personally represented one of Microsoft's excluded rivals (Netscape).

In sum, Bork's primary concern is the opposite of Judge Hand's. Bork is worried about *false convictions* (false positives) and over-deterrence, the possibility that enforcing antitrust rules against alleged episodes of exclusionary conduct will mistakenly punish and thereby chill aggressive competition. Bork fears that the primary consequence of opening the doors wide to exclusion allegations may be to keep prices high and discourage innovation, to deny consumers the benefits of efficiencies that may flow from a large firm's scale and scope, and to spur inefficient rivals to misuse the antitrust laws by bringing lawsuits after losing on the merits in the marketplace.

Under the influence of Bork and some of his Chicago School colleagues, as well as a number of other influential commentators, especially the late Phillip E. Areeda, who was associated with the "Harvard School," (*see supra* Chapter 1) courts today tend to approach exclusion cases with skepticism. Although we will read some cases in which plaintiffs prevailed, such as *Microsoft* and *Aspen Skiing*, most of the more recent monopolization decisions have been decided in favor of the defendants, reflecting more of Bork's concern about false positives than Hand's concern with false negatives. They also reflect a belief that markets will tend to self-correct when market power arises (because the promise of profit will attract new competition), whereas no such self-correction mechanism exists for inefficient or anticompetitive government action. They also reflect a concern, expressed by both Chicago and Harvard commentators, that courts are ill-equipped to make the kinds of complicated decisions required in many antitrust cases and will tend to err on the side of finding liability. For a discussion of the combined effect of Chicago and Harvard skepticism about challenges to dominant firm behavior, see William E. Kovacic, *The Intellectual DNA of Modern U.S. Competition Law for Dominant Firm Conduct: The Chicago/Harvard Double Helix*, 2007 COLUM. BUS. L. REV. 1 (2007).

The most influential contemporary antitrust commentary on exclusionary conduct takes a view between those of Hand and Bork. In 1986, Professors Thomas Krattenmaker and Steven Salop wrote that they:

> * * * do not believe that economic theory or antitrust policy suggests that virtually all exclusion claims are chimerical. Rather, * * * in carefully defined circumstances, certain firms can attain monopoly power by making arrangements with their suppliers that place their competitors at a cost disadvantage. * * * [C]laims of antitrust exclusion should be judged according to whether the challenged practice places rival competitors at a cost disadvantage sufficient to allow the defendant firm to exercise monopoly power by raising its price.

Thomas G. Krattenmaker and Steven C. Salop, *Anticompetitive Exclusion: Raising Rivals' Costs to Achieve Power over Price*, 96 YALE L.J. 209, 213–14 (1986); *see also* Steven C. Salop & David T. Scheffman, *Raising Rivals' Costs*, 73 AM. ECON. REV. 267 (1983) (introducing economic theory). Krattemaker and Salop recognize the efficiency potential of exclusionary conduct, and thus incorporate cost savings and other efficiencies in their analysis, although they call for such justifications to be proven rigorously rather than assumed or accepted upon a mere showing of plausibility. 96 YALE L.J. at 277–82. They also have more confidence in the capacity of courts to identify exclusionary conduct and are less confident that markets will "self-correct" when conduct raises competitors' costs and erects or fortifies barriers to entry. This intermediate perspective has been influential at the federal antitrust enforcement agencies and in the courts, as well as at the European Commission. Professor Jonathan Baker has added that exclusionary conduct should not be denigrated as a less important goal of the antitrust laws, but rather should be considered a "core" concern. *See* Jonathan B. Baker, *Exclusion as a Core Competition Concern*, 78 ANTITRUST L.J. 527 (2013).

But the intermediate perspective has not captured the field. The historic Chicago and Harvard Schools' skepticism about exclusion cases remains influential. As we will see later in this Chapter, the Supreme Court has expressed concern about the chilling effect of monopolization litigation on the legitimate business conduct of dominant firms and the danger that inefficient rivals will misuse the antitrust laws by bringing such cases. It has also extended the use of cost-based standards for defining predation. Moreover, there is a difference of perspectives as to whether empirical evidence supports the view that anticompetitive exclusion is much less common than other forms of anticompetitive conduct. *See, e.g.,* Jonathan B. Baker, *Taking the Error Out of "Error Cost" Analysis: What's Wrong with Antitrust's Right*, 80 ANTITRUST L.J. 1, 17–23 (2015); Joshua D. Wright, *Abandoning Antitrust's Chicago Obsession: The Case for Evidence-Based Antitrust*, 78 ANTITRUST L.J. 241 (2012); Francine

Lafontaine & Margaret Slade, *Exclusive Contracts and Vertical Restraints: Empirical Evidence and Public Policy*, in Handbook of Antitrust Economics 391 (Paoli Buccirossi ed., 2008); James C. Cooper et al., *Vertical Antitrust Policy as a Problem of Inference*, 23 J. Indus. Org. 639, 648 (2005). Differences of perspective have also developed between Democratic and Republican administrations, exhibited in speeches, amicus briefs, and enforcement actions, although the latter remain relatively infrequent regardless of administration. Figure 4–1 outlines some of the factors that can influence the advocacy of these various perspectives.

Figure 4–1:

Presumptions ("Priors") That Can Influence Perspectives

- *How often would exclusionary strategies be attempted absent enforcement constraints?*

  - Would attempts to exclude be rare?

  - Would attempts to exclude likely be unprofitable?

  - Do the potential victims have robust counterstrategies to deter or undo attempts to exclude at low cost?

  - Does exclusionary conduct tend to generate large efficiencies that will likely diminish or entirely eliminate any harm to competition and consumers from the exclusion?

- *How resilient are markets? How durable is likely market power achieved by exclusion?*

  - Are there market forces that will erode market power without the need for judicial intervention? Are markets "self-correcting"? Or, can market power be durable and thus difficult to dislodge without intervention?

  - Would the exclusionary conduct itself create impediments to market self-correction (e.g., barriers to entry; elimination of a maverick)?

  - If the firm gains or enhances its market power, would that lead to faster and better innovation? Or might it impede innovation by discouraging new entry or expansion?

- *How effective are courts and government at correctly identifying genuinely "exclusionary" acts?*

  - Can courts and agencies accurately differentiate between beneficial but aggressive competition and harmful exclusionary conduct?

- Will errors tend to deter more beneficial conduct or more harmful conduct?

- Are juries, courts and government enforcers biased against antitrust defendants?

Exclusionary Conduct and Dominant Firms

Debates about dominant firm conduct often focus on institutional, as well as doctrinal considerations. Views can differ about the capacity of the antitrust system: (1) to develop analytical tests that accurately identify anticompetitive behavior, and (2) to apply the tests sensibly in practice. As discussed in Chapter 1, the Chicago and Harvard Schools generally proscribe a narrower range of behavior than the Post-Chicago School, although conceptual differences between the groups about when exclusion is "improper" have diminished somewhat over time. Although there are differences of view between the Chicago and Harvard Schools, as a general matter they both have less confidence than the Post-Chicago School in the capacity of courts and enforcement agencies to accurately distinguish between anticompetitive and procompetitive behavior in practice. Fears about the magnitude of failures in implementation have led the Chicago School to prefer comparatively bright-line rules that err toward nonintervention. The Post-Chicago School is more sanguine about the prospects for accurate implementation and therefore entertains the use of more comprehensive reasonableness standards that create more possibilities for finding liability. The differing schools of thought also tend to disagree about the probable impact of relatively more or less interventionist liability standards on the respective competitive incentives of dominant firms and their rivals. Collectively, these differences of perspective tend to manifest themselves in differing views of the relative burdens of pleading, production, and proof of plaintiffs and defendants, reliance on inferences, and the assessment of probabilities.

As we shall learn, the debate has practical consequences for the selection of specific standards for judging exclusionary conduct, because those standards can be structured to hinder or facilitate claims of exclusion. For example, one's views about the likely market impact of specific conduct and the skill of courts and enforcement agencies in applying concepts in practice can be cast as presumptions. Observers who conclude that (a) successful efforts by a dominant firm to exclude equally or more efficient rivals are rare, and (b) attempts by courts and enforcement agencies to apply conceptually sound theories are excessively prone to misapplication, may adopt a strong presumption disfavoring intervention. That in turn may lead to demands for "rigorous" or "clear" proof of competitive harm and less reliance on inferences and presumptions when condemning conduct. Observers who conclude that (a) successful efforts to exclude by means other than efficiency are common enough to warrant serious attention, and (b) courts and enforcement agencies can make suitably accurate diagnoses and impose appropriate cures, are more likely to favor intervention when potentially harmful conduct is identified. These observers may be more willing to infer harm based on reasonable inferences from which the probability of harm is derived, and might demand more and better proof before crediting efficiencies. As you learn in this Chapter about the economics of exclusionary conduct, and the legal rules governing the conduct of such firms, you may find it instructive to consider whether legal doctrine is or should be based on either of these presumptions.

In Section A of this Chapter we explore the modern economic framework for understanding how firms may harm competition through exclusionary conduct. Section B turns the clock back to examine the origins and development of the traditional approach to analyzing exclusionary conduct, particularly *Grinnell's* power + exclusionary conduct formula and the pivotal role it assigns to market definition. Section C examines the leading modern court decisions on monopolization, which tend to follow one of two paradigms of exclusionary conduct: non-price exclusionary conduct and predatory pricing. Section D looks at other offenses under Section 2, specifically the controlling case law in attempt to monopolize cases. Section F concludes by discussing modern tools for analyzing, and appropriate methods of defining, anticompetitive exclusion, before turning to some Problems in Section G.

A. THE ECONOMICS OF EXCLUSION

Our discussion of *JTC Petroleum* in Chapter 1 and the economics of collusion in Chapter 3 illustrate the close relationship between collusion and exclusion. Collusion is threatened by the ability and willingness of rivals to deviate from (cheat on) the coordinated consensus. The economics of collusion revolves around whether and how rivals can be induced to cooperate rather than to compete, as by raising price and reducing their own output. This Section will show how a similar outcome to what might arise from successful collusion can be achieved if a dominant firm or a group of firms acts to exclude rivals that might otherwise not go along with collusive conduct. That is, the economics of exclusion can be understood simply as pointing out that collusive outcomes can be achieved indirectly, as by denying actual or would-be competitors access to low cost inputs or access to customers and reducing their output. Our window into the economics of exclusion is a leading Supreme Court decision concerning dominant firm conduct, *Lorain Journal*.

1. *LORAIN JOURNAL* CASE STUDY

During the late 1940s, the Justice Department challenged the efforts of the publisher of an Ohio newspaper, The Lorain Journal, to force its advertisers to refrain from placing advertisements with a local radio station with which the publisher competed to sell advertising services. The lawsuit relied upon an attempted monopolization theory to oppose the threatened refusal to deal. In 1951, the Supreme Court sustained the district court's finding that the threatened refusal to deal was improper and violated Section 2 of the Sherman Act. The economic question the case raises is whether the dominant firm harmed competition through actions that hindered the ability of its only rival to sell its services to an important class of customers.

LORAIN JOURNAL CO. v. UNITED STATES

United States Supreme Court, 1951.
342 U.S. 143, 72 S.Ct. 181, 96 L.Ed. 162.

MR. JUSTICE BURTON delivered the opinion of the Court.

* * *

This is a civil action, instituted by the United States in the District Court for the Northern District of Ohio, against The Lorain Journal Company, an Ohio corporation, publishing, daily except Sunday, in the City of Lorain, Ohio, a newspaper here called the Journal. * * *

The appellant corporation, here called the publisher, has published the Journal in the City of Lorain since before 1932. In that year it, with others, purchased the Times-Herald which was the only competing daily paper published in that city. Later, without success, it sought a license to establish and operate a radio broadcasting station in Lorain.

The court below describes the position of the Journal, since 1933, as 'a commanding and an overpowering one. It has a daily circulation in Lorain of over 13,000 copies and it reaches ninety-nine per cent of the families in the city.' * * * Lorain is an industrial city on Lake Erie with a population of about 52,000 occupying 11,325 dwelling units. The Sunday News, appearing only on Sundays, is the only other newspaper published there. * * *

* * *

From 1933 to 1948 the publisher enjoyed a substantial monopoly in Lorain of the mass dissemination of news and advertising, both of a local and national character. However, in 1948 the Elyria-Lorain Broadcasting Company, a corporation independent of the publisher, was licensed by the Federal Communications Commission to establish and operate in Elyria, Ohio, eight miles south of Lorain, a radio station whose call letters, WEOL, stand for Elyria, Oberlin and Lorain. Since then it has operated its principal studio in Elyria and a branch studio in Lorain. * * *

* * *

Substantially all of the station's income is derived from its broadcasts of advertisements of goods or services. * * *

The court below found that appellants knew that a substantial number of Journal advertisers wished to use the facilities of the radio station as well. For some of them it found that advertising in the Journal was essential for the promotion of their sales in Lorain County. It found that at all times since WEOL commenced broadcasting, appellants had executed a plan conceived to eliminate the threat of competition from the station. Under this plan the publisher refused to accept local advertisements in the Journal from any Lorain County advertiser who advertised or who appellants believed to be about to advertise over WEOL. The court found expressly that the purpose and intent of this procedure was to destroy the broadcasting company.

The court characterized all this as 'bold, relentless, and predatory commercial behavior.' * * * To carry out appellants' plan, the publisher monitored WEOL programs to determine the identity of the station's local Lorain advertisers. Those using the station's facilities had their contracts with the publisher terminated and were able to renew them only after ceasing to advertise through WEOL. The program was effective. Numerous Lorain County merchants testified that, as a result of the publisher's policy, they either ceased or abandoned their plans to advertise over WEOL.

"Having the plan and desire to injure the radio station, no more effective and more direct device to impede the operations and to restrain the commerce of WEOL could be found by the Journal than to cut off its bloodstream of existence—the advertising revenues which control its life or demise." " * * * [T]he very existence of WEOL is imperiled by this attack upon one of its principal sources of business and income."

* * *

The conduct complained of was an attempt to monopolize interstate commerce. It consisted of the publisher's practice of refusing to accept local Lorain advertising from parties using WEOL for local advertising. Because of the Journal's complete daily newspaper monopoly of local advertising in Lorain and its practically indispensable coverage of 99% of the Lorain families, this practice forced numerous advertisers to refrain from using WEOL for local advertising. That result not only reduced the number of customers available to WEOL in the field of local Lorain advertising and strengthened the Journal's monopoly in that field, but more significantly tended to destroy and eliminate WEOL altogether. Attainment of that sought-for elimination would automatically restore to the publisher of the Journal its substantial monopoly in Lorain of the mass dissemination of all news and advertising, interstate and national, as well as local. It would deprive not merely Lorain but Elyria and all surrounding communities of their only nearby radio station.

* * *

The publisher's attempt to regain its monopoly of interstate commerce by forcing advertisers to boycott a competing radio station violated Section 2. The findings and opinion of the trial court describe the conduct of the publisher upon which the Government relies. The surrounding circumstances are important. The most illuminating of these is the substantial monopoly which was enjoyed in Lorain by the publisher from 1933 to 1948, together with a 99% coverage of Lorain families. Those factors made the Journal an indispensable medium of advertising for many Lorain concerns. Accordingly, its publisher's refusals to print Lorain advertising for those using WEOL for like advertising often amounted to an effective prohibition of the use of WEOL for that purpose. Numerous Lorain advertisers wished to supplement their local newspaper advertising with local radio advertising but could not afford to discontinue their newspaper advertising in order to use the radio.

WEOL's greatest potential source of income was local Lorain advertising. Loss of that was a major threat to its existence. The court below found unequivocally that appellants' conduct amounted to an attempt by the publisher to destroy WEOL and, at the same time, to regain the publisher's pre-1948 substantial monopoly over the mass dissemination of all news and advertising.

To establish this violation of Section 2 as charged, it was not necessary to show that success rewarded appellants' attempt to monopolize. The injunctive relief under Section 4 sought to forestall that success. While appellants' attempt to monopolize did succeed insofar as it deprived WEOL of income, WEOL has not yet been eliminated. The injunction may save it. * * *

* * *

Assuming the interstate character of the commerce involved, it seems clear that if all the newspapers in a city, in order to monopolize the dissemination of news and advertising by eliminating a competing radio station, conspired to accept no advertisements from anyone who advertised over that station, they would violate Sections 1 and 2 of the Sherman Act. * * * It is consistent with that result to hold here that a single newspaper, already enjoying a substantial monopoly in its area, violates the 'attempt to monopolize' clause of Section 2 when it uses its monopoly to destroy threatened competition.[8]

---

[8] Appellants have sought to justify their conduct on the ground that it was part of the publisher's program for the protection of the Lorain market from outside competition. The

The publisher claims a right as a private business concern to select its customers and to refuse to accept advertisement from whomever it pleases. We do not dispute that general right. 'But the word 'right' is one of the most deceptive of pitfalls; it is so easy to slip from a qualified meaning in the premise to an unqualified one in the conclusion. Most rights are qualified.' The right claimed by the publisher is neither absolute nor exempt from regulation. Its exercise as a purposeful means of monopolizing interstate commerce is prohibited by the Sherman Act. The operator of the radio station, equally with the publisher of the newspaper, is entitled to the protection of that Act. '*In the absence of any purpose to create or maintain a monopoly*, the act does not restrict the long recognized right of trader or manufacturer engaged in an entirely private business, freely to exercise his own independent discretion as to parties with whom he will deal'. (Emphasis supplied.) United States v. Colgate & Co., 250 U.S. 300, 307, 39 S.Ct. 465, 468.

* * *

The Court concluded that the newspaper's conduct violated the antitrust laws because the defendant made it more difficult for the radio station, its only rival, to compete, threatening the radio station's existence, and because the newspaper was unable to provide a persuasive rationale for threatening to withhold cooperation from local advertisers if they placed advertisements with the radio station. Why would these facts imply that competition was harmed rather than simply that one competitor was injured?

Exclusionary tactics come in a wide range of varieties, many of which were separately categorized in traditional antitrust thinking.

- In *Lorain Journal*, the newspaper unilaterally refused to deal with certain other firms, namely those who also dealt with its rivals. Recall that Judge Bork was skeptical about whether *unilateral refusals to deal* should be viewed as anticompetitive, though he viewed *Lorain Journal* as having been properly decided.

---

publisher claimed to have refused advertising from Elyria or other out-of-town advertisers for the reason that such advertisers might compete with Lorain concerns. The publisher then classified WEOL as the publisher's own competitor from Elyria and asked its Lorain advertisers to refuse to employ WEOL as an advertising medium in competition with the Journal. We find no principle of law which required Lorain advertisers thus to boycott an Elyria advertising medium merely because the publisher of a Lorain advertising medium had chosen to boycott some Elyria advertisers who might compete for business in the Lorain market. Nor do we find any principle of law which permitted this publisher to dictate to prospective advertisers that they might advertise either by newspaper or by radio but that they might not use both facilities.

But the newspaper could have instead employed other tactics in its competitive battle for advertisers.

- The newspaper could have contracted with its advertisers for exclusivity, as by giving advertisers a lower price in exchange for their commitment not to advertise with any radio station located in the same part of the state. This is called *exclusive dealing*.

- The newspaper could have competed for advertisers by charging less for newspaper advertising or building a new radio station to compete with WEOL (note from the facts that they tried this, but were unable to secure the necessary broadcasting license). These strategies might have had the effect of drawing radio advertiser dollars away from WEOL, possibly harming WEOL and forcing it to exit the market. As we will see, there is a substantial debate as to when, if at all, price cutting or new product development should be viewed as harmful to competition.

- The newspaper could have cut price to a low level that the radio station was unable to match, forcing WEOL out of business. As we will see in the case law, this kind of tactic, which has been the subject of substantial attention in antitrust history and substantial debate as to its rationality, is called *predatory pricing* if the price is below the alleged monopolist's costs and other conditions are met.

- If the newspaper also owned a radio station, it could have offered an attractive package price to advertisers who advertised both in the newspaper and on its affiliated radio station, if their total advertising purchases exceeded a given threshold level. This offer might have shifted advertisers away from using WEOL and toward the affiliated radio station, possibly harming WEOL and forcing it to exit. This tactic involves both *bundling of services* and *loyalty discounts* (the discount for exceeding a threshold of purchases), and its treatment under antitrust principles has been the subject of recent controversy.

All of these tactics in some sense could exclude the competing radio station, WEOL. Some have greater exclusionary potential than others, and some would likely have stronger legitimate business justifications than others. But each can be understood through a single economic lens, the modern economic framework of "raising rivals' costs".

2. THE MODERN ECONOMICS OF EXCLUSION: TWO PARADIGMS

To understand how competition could be harmed by exclusionary conduct, we turn to the modern economic analysis of exclusion Today the terms "exclusion" and "foreclosure" are employed broadly to include practices beyond complete foreclosure that disadvantage rivals by raising their costs, reducing their revenues, or otherwise reducing their access to the market. As an economic matter, complete foreclosure is not necessary for exclusionary conduct to confer market power on the remaining firm or firms.

The modern economic literature on exclusionary practices can be organized around two paradigms: raising rivals' costs (using the terminology coined by Professors Krattenmaker and Salop), and predatory pricing. This Section of the Chapter discusses the raising rivals' costs framework. Later Sections turn to the predatory pricing paradigm, and consider cases that reveal a tension between the two.

Exclusionary practices can harm competition by leading rivals to participate in, or accede to, what might be termed an "involuntary" horizontal cartel. Suppose, for example, that firms A and B would like to collude with firm C, their only rival in a market protected from entry. Firms A and B cannot do so, because if A and B were to raise price, C would increase output and prevent the industry price from rising. If A could somehow raise C's marginal costs, or otherwise make it more difficult for C to sell more, then C would be led to do what it would not have done previously: reduce its output and go along with a higher price. Recall that this appeared to be the case in *JTC Petroleum*, which we read in Chapter 1.

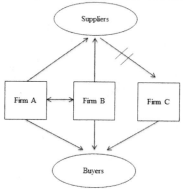

Figure 4–2:
Involuntary Cartel—Restricting Rival Access to Supply

1. Firms A and B are colluding;

2. Firm C either refuses to join Firms A & B, or
Firms A & B are not interested in inviting C to join;

3. Firms A & B secure agreement of their suppliers
to refuse to sell to Firm C, or at least to refuse to
sell to Firm C on equally desirable terms.

Firm A might be able to accomplish this end by foreclosing C from access to low cost sources of supply or distribution (input foreclosure), perhaps through exclusive contracts (or vertical merger) with input suppliers or distributors, or by making it more difficult for firm C to attract customers (customer foreclosure), perhaps by denying firm C access to complementary products (for example, as through tying). Exclusionary conduct can be thought of as raising firm C's "costs" even if it involves reducing that firm's access to customers or the market. These practices increase firm C's costs by making marketing more expensive. Hence our references to raising rivals' "costs" should be understood as including both input foreclosure and customer foreclosure. Predatory pricing, discussed later in the Chapter, can be thought of as a form of customer foreclosure: by lowering price, the predator makes it difficult for the excluded firm to obtain customers. But the economic literature and the courts generally treat it as a different way of excluding, so we do not refer to it here as a form of raising rivals' costs.

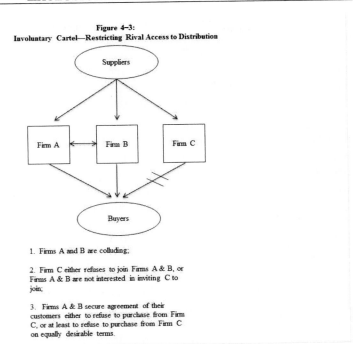

Figure 4–3:
Involuntary Cartel—Restricting Rival Access to Distribution

1. Firms A and B are colluding;

2. Firm C either refuses to join Firms A & B, or Firms A & B are not interested in inviting C to join;

3. Firms A & B secure agreement of their customers either to refuse to purchase from Firm C, or at least to refuse to purchase from Firm C on equally desirable terms.

Then, A and B could take advantage of the less aggressive competition from C to exercise market power.

Note that firm C need not be an incumbent producer. It could instead be a firm whose potential entry constrains anticompetitive behavior by firms currently in the market. By raising its costs, or reducing its access to the market, those firms can reduce output to raise price without fear of new competition. Note also that nothing in the example limits the firms to three. There may be multiple firms playing the roles of each actor (A, B, or C) in the hypothetical example. Some exclusionary practices, for example, may raise costs for a class of actual or potential rivals in the position of firm C.

For four reasons it is not a foregone conclusion that a raising rivals' costs strategy would work for firm A. First, firm C may have alternative ways to obtain supply or distribution at favorable costs. Suppose, for example, that firm A has paid a key input supplier only to sell to firm A, or, at a minimum, paid the supplier not to sell to firm C (without constraining the supplier's ability to sell to firm B). If firm C can obtain similar inputs at comparable cost and quality from another supplier, then firm A's conduct will not exclude firm C.

Second, if firm C can convince the supplier to terminate its exclusivity agreement with firm A, and sell to firm C after all, then firm C will again not be excluded. However, firm A may stack the deck against the latter method of evading firm A's strategy. If firm A's exclusionary contract with the supplier confers market power on firm A, and the market would otherwise be competitive, then firm A may be willing to pay more to the supplier to exclude firm C than the excluded firm would be willing to pay to avoid the foreclosure. Whereas firm C seeks to purchase just the input, firm A purchases both the input and profits from exercising market power. This would be so even if firm C is just as efficient a competitor as firm A.

Third, firm B may not go along with A in reducing output once C's ability to compete is impaired. Firm B instead may choose to "cheat" on what is effectively a cooperative agreement with firm A to raise price. This problem is not necessarily insurmountable. Firm A may be a monopolist—there may be no firm B, as in many of the dominant firm cases highlighted in this Chapter. Firm B may face capacity constraints or other barriers to expansion, or firms A and B may be able to deter deviation in much the way that some voluntary cartels are able to do so (*see supra* Chapter 3).

Finally, the strategy of excluding firm C may be unprofitable for firm A if it must bear the full costs of doing so (*e.g.*, the payments to suppliers needed to induce them not to deal with firm C), while firm A must share with firm B the benefits of any higher prices that may result. On the other hand, if firm A obtains a large fraction of the producer benefits from higher prices, perhaps because its market share is large, it may find it worthwhile to pay all of the costs, without requiring help from firm B.

Even if the raising rivals' costs strategy disadvantages firm C and reduces competition, it is not necessarily harmful economically on balance, as it may simultaneously confer efficiencies upon firm A. For example, a manufacturer may foreclose rivals from effective distribution by requiring its dealers not to handle the products of rival manufacturers, but the same practice may also lead the dealer to increase its promotional efforts, reduce dealer free-riding, and result in better dealer service to customers, all of which may lead to increased output by the manufacturer.

Notwithstanding these caveats, it should be clear that exclusionary arrangements with suppliers, distributors, or customers, or even for single-firm refusals to deal, sometimes may harm competition in much the same way that a voluntary cartel does. The main difference is that firm C does not go along with the industry output reduction voluntarily; it is coerced into doing so involuntarily. In this way, the modern analysis of exclusion suggests more of a concern with the anticompetitive dangers of exclusion than most Chicago School adherents might have supposed.

The modern view also suggests greater concern with chilling aggressive competition and denying consumers the benefits of efficiencies than Judge Hand perceived in *Alcoa*. As the involuntary cartel intuition emphasizes, the mere foreclosure of some rivals (or, more generally, raising rivals' costs) is not enough for exclusion to generate harm to competition. It is necessary also to show that the remaining rivals could and would take advantage by reducing output and raising price, and that the market price then would rise. It is also necessary to show that any resulting harm to competition would not be dissipated by any efficiencies resulting from the challenged conduct. For example, if cost saving resulting from the exclusionary conduct would lead the market price to fall on balance, notwithstanding the exclusionary potential for the conduct, competition would be enhanced.

Applying the Raising Rivals' Costs Framework

In applying the raising rivals' costs framework to analyze the cases, it is useful to break down the analysis into three steps. It is worth emphasizing that this is a framework for an economic analysis of the conduct. It could also be the framework for a legal analysis if a reasonableness assessment were employed, but other legal rules may call for various types of truncated analyses or burden-shifting.

Exclusion, or "Raising Rivals' Costs." The first step considers whether a firm in the role of firm C has been significantly impaired (excluded). How does the conduct alleged to harm competition in fact disadvantage some rival or rivals, by raising their costs or reducing their access to the market, causing those firms to become less aggressive competitors? This step of the inquiry commonly will focus on whether the impaired firm or firms have practical alternative means of obtaining supply or distribution at favorable costs.

Market Power, or "Power Over Price." Second, if the excluding firm or firms in the role of firm A are able to successfully disadvantage firms in the role of firm C, would the impact on firm C allow firm A to obtain or keep market power? One way to address this question is to begin by considering whether a hypothetical cartel composed of all sellers in the roles of firms A, B, and C would find it profitable to charge a price above the competitive level, whether such a hypothetical collusive arrangement is achieved voluntarily or involuntarily. In other words, are firms A, B, and C the only participants in a relevant market? If not, the exclusion of firm C may not confer market power on firm A. Even if the exclusion of sellers in the role of firm C would in principle confer market power on firm A, one must ask whether the exclusionary conduct would be profitable for firm A, taking into account the costs of the conduct, if any, and the monopoly profits firm A would reasonably expect to receive, and whether any sellers in the role of firm B would go along with the scheme as opposed to cheating on it.

Efficiency Justifications. The final step identifies any legitimate business justifications for the exclusionary conduct, and asks whether any resulting benefit to competition would give rise to contrary incentives that will likely dissipate the potential harm to competition demonstrated through the first two steps. If the exclusionary practice confers cost savings on firm A, for example, will firm A have an incentive to lower price that would offset any incentive to exercise market power by raising price?

Lorain Journal Revisited

With the raising rivals' costs framework in hand we return to the *Lorain Journal* decision, to see how it may be understood within the modern economic framework for analyzing exclusion. The Lorain Journal newspaper can be represented as a seller in the position of firm A. WEOL, the new radio station, is the excluded firm, in the role of firm C. There is no firm B. The exclusionary practice is the newspaper's unilateral refusal to accept advertisements from any Lorain County advertiser who advertises with WEOL.

Step 1: Raising Rivals' Costs. If advertisers are thought of as a radio station's customers—taking the view that the station uses its programming to create a listening audience, which it then sells to advertisers—then the conduct under review limits WEOL's access to key advertiser customers.[1] As a result, WEOL will find it more difficult to obtain advertising revenues (its revenues were reduced) and will become a less effective competitor. According to the Supreme Court, the Lorain Journal's conduct "tended to destroy and eliminate WEOL altogether." *Lorain Journal*, 342 U.S. at 150. There is no suggestion that WEOL had other ways to obtain advertising revenues.

Step 2: Market Power. The Supreme Court found that eliminating WEOL "would automatically restore to the publisher of the Journal its substantial monopoly in Lorain of the mass dissemination of all news and advertising, interstate and national, as well as local." *Id.* A market defined so that Lorain Journal and WEOL are the only rivals for local advertising is implicit in this conclusion. If one of the only two firms in a market protected from entry can exclude the other, it is immediately evident that the first will obtain monopoly power. The conduct at issue appears not to be very costly to the Lorain Journal. There is no suggestion, for example, that many advertisers chose to rely on WEOL exclusively. Thus, Lorain Journal's conduct did not reduce its advertising revenues.

Step 3: Efficiencies. The newspaper's justification for its conduct, dismissed by the court in a footnote, *id.* at n.8, appears to describe its desire to maintain its market power, not any effort to lower costs or otherwise obtain an efficiency. Commentators consistently treat this case as one in which the defendant presented no efficiency justification. *See, e.g.*, R. BORK, THE ANTITRUST PARADOX, at 345. Figure 4–4 summarizes this framework.

---

[1]   Note that, as was true in the case, we are assuming here that WEOL solely broadcasts over-the-air radio programming free of charge to its listeners. Eds.

Figure 4–4:

Applying the Raising Rival's Cost Framework

- *Harm to Competitors from Exclusion/Foreclosure*

  - Does the alleged conduct significantly disadvantage a rival's or rivals' ability to compete?

  - Totally exclude? Impair? Likely cause exit or marginalization?

  - By what mechanism? Raise costs? Reduce available customer base and revenues? Restrict ability to expand or invest; restrict breadth of distribution? Impede ability to achieve economies of scope or scale?

  - Do the rival(s) have practical alternative means of obtaining inputs or distribution at equally favorable costs and quality?

  - Excluded from most efficient channel of distribution or inputs?

  - Do the allegedly impaired rival(s) have the practical ability to engage in counter-strategies that would defeat any foreclosure effect and thereby deter the conduct?

- *Harm to Competition and Consumers from Exercise of Market Power ("Power over Price")*

  - Will the conduct facilitate the creation, enhancement, and/or maintenance of market power, including insulating it from erosion, by the firm(s) undertaking the challenged conduct?

  - Are there sufficient unimpaired rivals to maintain competition?

  - Will the impairment of the disadvantaged rival(s) facilitate collusion or tacit coordination?

  - Can consumers easily substitute alternative products/services without being harmed? Are there significant switching costs?

  - Is the exclusionary conduct likely profitable to the defendant(s)?

  - What is the cost of the conduct relative to its benefits?

- *Efficiency Justifications*

  - Does the firm have any cognizable efficiency benefits for its conduct?

- Does the conduct generate sufficient efficiencies such that the incentive to lower quality-adjusted prices will exceed the incentive to raise price from the exclusion so that consumers will not be harmed?

Accordingly, from a modern perspective, the *Lorain Journal* facts, as recounted by the Supreme Court, add up to a solid economic case of exclusionary conduct. The Lorain Journal created an involuntary cartel by excluding its only rival for advertising revenues, thereby protecting its monopoly power. The conduct had no efficiency justification, so it clearly harmed competition. As you read the other cases in this Chapter, consider whether the exclusionary practice at issue also harms competition according to the modern economic logic of raising rivals' costs, by creating an involuntary cartel.

Now consider the other, hypothetical tactics noted above that a newspaper might have employed to compete with rival radio station. These include exclusive contracts with advertisers, very low prices charged to advertisers, the construction of an affiliated radio station to compete with the rival, and bundling the price of advertising for advertisers that purchase space in the newspaper as well as time on its hypothetical affiliated radio station. Would each of these tactics be likely to foreclose WEOL from access to advertisers (raising that rival's costs)? Would each likely confer market power on the Lorain Journal newspaper? Would any appear to have a plausible efficiency justification?

As you consider the cases discussed in the remainder of this Chapter, it will be useful to apply this economic framework to consider whether the conduct they evaluate appears to harm competition. This economic framework could be understood as what a court would do were it to apply a structured reasonableness approach to evaluating dominant firm exclusionary conduct, implemented through burden-shifting as we observed in Chapter 2.

The courts increasingly incorporate presumptions or screens, much as the rule of reason was structured in analyzing horizontal agreements. In that context, per se rules, quick look rules and the like were defended as giving better guidance to courts and firms seeking to understand how to conduct their affairs within the law, and as reducing the transaction costs of resolving disputes. In the context of exclusionary conduct, some modern structured rules are designed particularly to give firms confidence that certain kinds of procompetitive conduct, particularly aggressive price-cutting, could not be challenged as anticompetitive. You will want to consider whether, in light of the economic framework for exclusion set forth here, the older rules may have too often discouraged procompetitive conduct, and whether the modern rules solve the problem. Do they strike the right balance between Bork's concerns about false positives with Hand's concern about false negatives?

B. HISTORICAL FOUNDATIONS: THE "POWER + CONDUCT" FRAMEWORK

1. THE ENDURING INFLUENCE OF JUDGE HAND'S DECISION IN *ALCOA*

Section 2 of the Sherman Act prohibits *"monopolization,"* not *"monopoly."* Courts have long-interpreted this to mean that monopoly alone, is not an offense. Rather Section 2 is concerned with *how* a firm obtains or protects a commanding position in the marketplace. As noted above in the Chapter Introduction, in *Grinnell* the Supreme Court therefore described the test for monopolization as being comprised of two distinct elements: (1) monopoly power; that was (2) willfully acquired or maintained. The conduct requirement can be understood as an effort to give effect to the language of Section 2. This two part approach has required courts to define what constitutes *monopoly* (or, in the modern language of antitrust economics and law, *substantial market power*) and to specify behavior that constitutes illegal monopolization (today such improper means are referred to as "predatory" or "exclusionary" conduct).

The two part test originated with one of the most controversial Section 2 prosecutions in U.S. antitrust history—the U.S. government's case against the Aluminum Corporation of America—"Alcoa." After its creation in 1888, Alcoa quickly became the nation's leading aluminum producer. The firm grew mainly by securing the rights to patents and patented processes that dramatically reduced the cost of producing aluminum. But Alcoa also used exclusionary techniques that caught the Justice Department's attention. It entered into what the court described as four successive "cartel" agreements whereby through restrictive covenants it divided markets with foreign manufacturers, limiting its own exports in return for their agreements to limit imports into the U.S. Moreover, making aluminum requires lots of electricity, and Alcoa's contracts with electric power companies forbade them to supply electricity to other aluminum manufacturers. In 1912, Alcoa and the Justice Department signed a consent decree invalidating the restrictive contract provisions and barring Alcoa from enforcing such arrangements with electricity suppliers.

From 1920 until the late 1930s, private and public efforts to enforce the Sherman Act's prohibition against monopolization fell into repose. The Supreme Court's decision in *United States v. U.S. Steel Corp.*, 251 U.S. 417 (1920), suggested that the Court had embraced a permissive view of dominant firm behavior and would intervene to correct only the most flagrant, persistent abuses of monopoly power.

From the onset of the Depression in 1929 until the mid-1930s, antitrust enforcement waned as the United States experimented with central planning and comprehensive regulation of prices and entry to spur economic recovery. The early New Deal of Franklin Roosevelt's presidency de-emphasized competition, including antitrust enforcement, in favor of planning measures such as the National Industrial Recovery Act to promote economic growth.

In the mid-1930s, Roosevelt heeded advisors who urged greater reliance on competition policy and renewed antitrust enforcement. Particularly under the leadership of Thurman Arnold as the Assistant Attorney General for Antitrust, the government initiated a number of major Section 2 cases. *Alcoa* was the first and most important.

By 1937, Alcoa had become the sole U.S. producer of virgin aluminum ingot. The Justice Department launched a new case, again alleging that the company had used exclusionary practices to perpetuate its monopoly position. Expanded demand for aluminum as a material for building airplanes, automobiles, home appliances, and ships had given Alcoa a position of great commercial prominence. The government alleged that Alcoa wrongly had discouraged entry and expansion by its competitors by adding substantially to its existing productive capacity in order to fulfill new demand. When Alcoa increased capacity, the government argued, its competitors feared they could not attract the minimum critical mass of customers necessary to support efficient operations. Alcoa's capacity additions also were said to reveal its willingness to boost output dramatically (and depress market prices) if its competitors tried to expand their sales by undercutting Alcoa's prices. Alcoa responded that only a perverse reading of Section 2 would bar a firm from adding facilities to supply new demand. The district court exonerated the company, finding that it neither held a monopoly nor behaved wrongfully.

The Supreme Court lacked a quorum to hear the direct appeal of the suit, as several Justices had played a role in the case before joining the Court and were hence recused. Congress passed a special law that made the U.S. Court of Appeals for the Second Circuit the court of last resort and authorized it to hear the case sitting "as the Supreme Court." The Second Circuit's opinion in the case, authored by Judge Learned Hand, thus carries the authority of a Supreme Court precedent. *See, e.g., American Tobacco Co. v. U.S.*, 328 U.S. 781, 811–12 (1946). As you shall see, the court first sought to determine whether Alcoa had monopoly power; it then turned to consider whether it acted improperly.

UNITED STATES V. ALUMINUM CO. OF AMERICA

Circuit Court of Appeals for the Second Circuit, 1945.
148 F.2d 416.

LEARNED HAND, CIRCUIT JUDGE.

* * *

I.

* * *

* * * [T]he most important question in the case is whether the monopoly in 'Alcoa's' production of 'virgin' ingot, secured by the two patents until 1909, and in part perpetuated between 1909 and 1912 by the unlawful practices, forbidden by the decree of 1912, continued for the ensuing twenty-eight years; and whether, if it did, it was unlawful under § 2 of the Sherman Act. It is undisputed that throughout this period 'Alcoa' continued to be the single producer of 'virgin' ingot in the United States; and the plaintiff argues that this without more was enough to make it an unlawful monopoly. It also takes an alternative position: that in any event during this period 'Alcoa' consistently pursued unlawful exclusionary practices, which made its dominant position certainly unlawful, even though it would not have been, had it been retained only by 'natural growth.' Finally, it asserts that many of these practices were of themselves unlawful, as contracts in restraint of trade under Sec. 1 of the [Sherman] Act. 'Alcoa's' position is that the fact that it alone continued to make 'virgin' ingot in this country did not, and does not, give it a monopoly of the market; that it was always subject to the competition of imported 'virgin' ingot, and of what is called 'secondary' ingot; and that even if it had not been, its monopoly would not have been retained by unlawful means, but would have been the result of a growth which the Act does not forbid, even when it results in a monopoly. We shall first consider the amount and character of this competition; next, how far it established a monopoly; and finally, if it did, whether that monopoly was unlawful under § 2 of the Act.

From 1902 onward until 1928 'Alcoa' was making ingot in Canada through a wholly owned subsidiary; so much of this as it imported into the United States it is proper to include with what it produced here. In the year 1912 the sum of these two items represented nearly ninety-one per cent of the total amount of 'virgin' ingot available for sale in this country. This percentage varied year by year up to and including 1938: in 1913 it was about seventy-two per cent; in 1921 about sixty-eight per cent; in 1922 about seventy-two; with these exceptions it was always over eighty per cent of the total and for the last five years 1934–1938 inclusive it averaged over ninety per cent. The effect of such a proportion of the production upon the market we reserve for the time being, for it will be necessary first to consider the nature and uses of 'secondary' ingot, the name by which the industry knows ingot made from aluminum scrap. This is of two sorts, though for our purposes it is not important to distinguish between them. One of these is the clippings and trimmings of 'sheet' aluminum, when patterns are cut out of it, as a suit is cut from a bolt of cloth. The chemical composition of these is obviously the same as that of the 'sheet' from which they come; and, although they are likely to accumulate dust or other dirt in the factory, this may be removed by well known processes. If a record of the original composition of the 'sheet' has been preserved, this scrap may be remelted into new ingot, and used again for the same purpose. It is true that some of the witnesses—Arthur V. Davis, the chairman of the board of 'Alcoa' among them—testified that at each remelting aluminum takes up some new oxygen which progressively deteriorates its quality for those uses in which purity is important; but other witnesses thought that it had become commercially feasible to remove this impurity, and the judge made no finding on the subject. Since the plaintiff has the burden of proof, we shall assume that there is no such deterioration. Nevertheless, there is an appreciable 'sales resistance' even to this kind of scrap, and for some uses (airplanes and cables among them), fabricators absolutely insist upon 'virgin': just why is not altogether clear. The other source of scrap is aluminum which has once been fabricated and the article, after being used, is discarded and sent to the junk heap, as for example, cooking utensils, like kettles and pans, and the pistons or crank cases of motorcars. These are made with a substantial alloy and to restore the metal to its original purity costs more than it is worth. However, if the alloy is known both in quality and amount, scrap, when remelted, can be used again for the same purpose as before. In spite of this, as in the case of clippings and trimmings, the industry will ordinarily not accept ingot so salvaged upon the same terms as 'virgin.' There are some seventeen companies which scavenge scrap of all sorts, clean it, remelt it, test it for its composition, make it into ingots and sell it regularly to the trade. There is in all these salvage operations some inevitable waste of actual material; not only does a certain amount of aluminum escape altogether, but in the salvaging process itself some is skimmed off as scum and thrown away. The judge found that the return of fabricated products to the market as 'secondary' varied from five to twenty-five years, depending upon the article; but he did not, and no doubt could not, find how many times the cycle could be repeated before the metal was finally used up.

There are various ways of computing 'Alcoa's' control of the aluminum market—as distinct from its production—depending upon what one regards as competing in that market. The judge figured its share—during the years 1929–1938, inclusive—as only about thirty-three percent; to do so he included 'secondary,' and excluded that part of 'Alcoa's own production which it fabricated and did not therefore sell as ingot. If, on the other hand, 'Alcoa's' total production, fabricated and sold, be included, and balanced against the sum of imported 'virgin' and 'secondary,' its share of the market was in the neighborhood of sixty-four per cent for that period. The percentage we have already mentioned—over ninety—results only if we both include all 'Alcoa's' production and exclude 'secondary'. That percentage is enough to constitute a monopoly; it is doubtful whether sixty or sixty-four percent would be enough; and certainly thirty-three per cent is not. Hence it is necessary to settle what he shall treat as competing in the ingot market. That part of its production which 'Alcoa' itself fabricates, does not of course ever reach the market as ingot; and we recognize that it is only when a restriction of production either inevitably affects prices, or is intended to do so, that it violates § 1 of the Act. However, even though we were to assume that a monopoly is unlawful under Sec. 2 only in case it controls prices, the ingot fabricated by 'Alcoa,' necessarily had a direct effect upon the ingot market. All ingot—with trifling exceptions—is used to fabricate intermediate or end, products; and therefore all intermediate, or end, products which 'Alcoa' fabricates and sell, pro tanto reduce the demand for ingot itself. The situation is the same, though reversed, as in Standard Oil Co. v. United States, 221 U.S. 1, 77, 31 S.Ct. 502, 523, where the court answered the defendant's argument that they had no control over the crude oil by saying that 'as substantial power over the crude product was the inevitable result of the absolute control which existed over the refined product, the monopolization of the one carried with it the power to control the other.' We cannot therefore agree that the computation of the percentage of 'Alcoa's' control over the ingot market should not include the whole of its ingot production.

As to 'secondary,' as we have said, for certain purposes the industry will not accept it at all; but for those for which it will, the difference in price is ordinarily not very great; the judge found that it was between one and two cents a pound, hardly enough margin on which to base a monopoly. Indeed, there are times when all differential disappears, and 'secondary' will actually sell at a higher price: *i.e.*, when there is a supply available which contains just the alloy that a fabricator needs for the article which he proposes to make. Taking the industry as a whole, we can say nothing more definite than that, although 'secondary' does not compete at all in some uses, (whether because of 'sales resistance' only, or because of actual metallurgical inferiority), for most purposes it competes upon a substantial equality with 'virgin.' On these facts the judge found that 'every pound of secondary or scrap aluminum which is sold in commerce displaces a pound of virgin aluminum which otherwise would, or might have been, sold.' We agree: so far as 'secondary' supplies the demand of such fabricators as will accept it, it increases the amount of 'virgin' which must seek sale elsewhere; and it therefore results that the supply of that part of the demand which will accept only 'virgin' becomes greater in proportion as 'secondary' drives away 'virgin' from the demand which will accept 'secondary.' (This is indeed the same argument which we used a moment ago to include in the supply that part of 'virgin' which 'Alcoa' fabricates; it is not apparent to us why the judge did not think it applicable to that item as well.) At any given moment therefore 'secondary' competes with 'virgin' in the ingot market; further, it can, and probably does, set a limit or 'ceiling' beyond which the price of 'virgin' cannot go, for the cost of its production will in the end depend only upon the expense of scavenging and reconditioning. It might seem for this reason that in estimating 'Alcoa's' control over the ingot market, we ought to include the supply of 'secondary,' as the judge did. Indeed, it may be thought a paradox to say that anyone has the monopoly of a market in which at all times he must meet a competition that limits his price. We shall show that it is not.

In the case of a monopoly of any commodity which does not disappear in use and which can be salvaged, the supply seeking sale at any moment will be made up of two components: (1) the part which the putative monopolist can immediately produce and sell; and (2) the part which has been, or can be, reclaimed out of what he has produced and sold in the past. * * * Thus, in the case at bar 'Alcoa' always knew that the future supply of ingot would be made up in part of what it produced at the time, and, if it was as far-sighted as it proclaims itself, that consideration must have had its share in determining how much to produce. How accurately it could forecast the effect of present production upon the future market is another matter. Experience, no doubt, would help; but it makes no difference that it had to guess; it is enough that it had an inducement to make the best guess it could, and that it would regulate that part of the future supply, so far as it should turn out to have guessed right. The competition of 'secondary' must therefore be disregarded, as soon as we consider the position of 'Alcoa' over a period of years; it was as much within 'Alcoa's' control as was the production of the 'virgin' from which it had been derived. * * * Finally, if 'Alcoa' is right, precisely the same reasoning ought to lead us to include that part of clippings and trimmings which a fabricator himself saves and remelts—'process scrap'—for that too pro tanto reduces the market for 'virgin.' It can make no difference whether the original buyer reclaims, or a professional scavenger. Yet 'Alcoa' itself does not assert that such 'process scrap' competes; indeed it was at pains to prove that this scrap was not included in its computation of 'secondary.'

We conclude therefore that 'Alcoa's' control over the ingot market must be reckoned at over ninety per cent; that being the proportion which its production bears to imported 'virgin' ingot. If the fraction which it did not supply were the produce of domestic manufacture there could be no doubt that this percentage gave it a monopoly—lawful or unlawful, as the case might be. The producer of so large a proportion of the supply has complete control within certain limits. It is true that, if by raising the price he reduces the amount which can be marketed—as always, or almost always, happens—he may invite the expansion of the small producers who will try to fill the place left open; nevertheless, not only is there an inevitable lag in this, but the large producer is in a strong position to check such competition; and, indeed, if he has retained his old plant and personnel, he can inevitably do so. There are indeed limits to his power; substitutes are available for almost all commodities, and to raise the price enough is to evoke them. Moreover, it is difficult and expensive to keep idle any part of a plant or of personnel; and any drastic contraction of the market will offer increasing temptation to the small producers to expand. But these limitations also exist when a single producer occupies the whole market: even then, his hold will depend upon his moderation in exerting his immediate power.

The case at bar is however different, because, for aught that appears there may well have been a practically unlimited supply of imports as the price of ingot rose. Assuming that there was no agreement between 'Alcoa' and foreign producers not to import, they sold what could bear the handicap of the tariff and the cost of transportation. For the period of eighteen years—1920–1937—they sold at times a little above 'Alcoa's' prices, at times a little under; but there was substantially no gross difference between what they received and what they would have received, had they sold uniformly at 'Alcoa's' prices. While the record is silent, we may therefore assume—the plaintiff having the burden—that, had 'Alcoa' raised its prices, more ingot would have been imported. Thus there is a distinction between domestic and foreign competition: the first is limited in quantity, and can increase only by an increase in plant and personnel; the second is of producers who, we must assume, produce much more than they import, and whom a rise in price will presumably induce immediately to divert to the American market what they have been selling elsewhere. It is entirely consistent with the evidence that it was the threat of greater foreign imports which kept 'Alcoa's' prices where they were, and prevented it from exploiting its advantage as sole domestic producer; indeed, it is hard to resist the conclusion that potential imports did put a 'ceiling' upon those prices. Nevertheless, within the limits afforded by the tariff and the cost of transportation, 'Alcoa' was free to raise its prices as it chose, since it was free from domestic competition, save as it drew other metals into the market as substitutes. * * *

* * * Having proved that 'Alcoa' had a monopoly of the domestic ingot market, the plaintiff had gone far enough; if it was an excuse, that 'Alcoa' had not abused its power, it lay upon 'Alcoa' to prove that it had not. But the whole issue is irrelevant anyway, for it is no excuse for 'monopolizing' a market that the monopoly has not been used to extract from the consumer more than a 'fair' profit. The [Sherman] Act has wider purposes. Indeed, even though we disregard all but economic considerations, it would by no means follow that such concentration of producing power is to be desired, when it has not been used extortionately. Many people believe that possession of unchallenged economic power deadens initiative, discourages

thrift and depresses energy; that immunity from competition is a narcotic, and rivalry is a stimulant, to industrial progress; that the spur of constant stress is necessary to counteract an inevitable disposition to let well enough alone. Such people believe that competitors, versed in the craft as no consumer can be, will be quick to detect opportunities for saving and new shifts in production, and be eager to profit by them. In any event the mere fact that a producer, having command of the domestic market, has not been able to make more than a 'fair' profit, is no evidence that a 'fair' profit could not have been made at lower prices. United States v. Corn Products Refining Co., 234 F. 964, 1014–15 (S.D.N.Y.1916). True, it might have been thought adequate to condemn only those monopolies which could not show that they had exercised the highest possible ingenuity, had adopted every possible economy, had anticipated every conceivable improvement, stimulated every possible demand. No doubt, that would be one way of dealing with the matter, although it would imply constant scrutiny and constant supervision, such as courts are unable to provide. Be that as it may, that was not the way that Congress chose; it did not condone 'good trusts' and condemn 'bad' ones; it forbad all. Moreover, in so doing it was not necessarily actuated by economic motives alone. It is possible, because of its indirect social or moral effect, to prefer a system of small producers, each dependent for his success upon his own skill and character, to one in which the great mass of those engaged must accept the direction of a few. These considerations, which we have suggested only as possible purposes of the Act, we think the decisions prove to have been in fact its purposes.

* * *

We have been speaking only of the economic reasons which forbid monopoly; but, as we have already implied, there are others, based upon the belief that great industrial consolidations are inherently undesirable, regardless of their economic results. In the debates in Congress Senator Sherman himself * * * showed that among the purposes of Congress in 1890 was a desire to put an end to great aggregations of capital because of the helplessness of the individual before them. * * * Throughout the history of [the antitrust] statutes it has been constantly assumed that one of their purposes was to perpetuate and preserve, for its own sake and in spite of possible cost, an organization of industry in small units which can effectively compete with each other. We hold that 'Alcoa's' monopoly of ingot was of the kind covered by § 2.

It does not follow because 'Alcoa' had such a monopoly, that it 'monopolized' the ingot market: it may not have achieved monopoly; monopoly may have been thrust upon it. If it had been a combination of existing smelters which united the whole industry and controlled the production of all aluminum ingot, it would certainly have 'monopolized' the market. * * * We may start therefore with the premise that to have combined ninety per cent of the producers of ingot would have been to 'monopolize' the ingot market; and, so far as concerns the public interest, it can make no difference whether an existing competition is put an end to, or whether prospective competition is prevented. The Clayton Act itself speaks in that alternative: 'to injure, destroy, or prevent competition.' § 13(a) 15 U.S.C.A. Nevertheless, it is unquestionably true that from the very outset the courts have at least kept in reserve the possibility that the origin of a monopoly may be critical in determining its legality; and for this they had warrant in some of the congressional debates which accompanied the passage of the Act. This notion has usually been expressed by saying that size does not determine guilt; that there must be some 'exclusion' of competitors; that the growth must be something else than 'natural' or 'normal'; that there must be a 'wrongful intent,' or some other specific intent; or that some 'unduly' coercive means must be used. At times there has been emphasis upon the use of the active verb, 'monopolize,' as the judge noted in the case at bar. What engendered these compunctions is reasonably plain; persons may unwittingly find themselves in possession of a monopoly, automatically so to say: that is, without having intended either to put an end to existing competition, or to prevent competition from arising when none had existed; they may become monopolists by force of accident. Since the Act makes 'monopolizing' a crime, as well as a civil wrong, it would be not only unfair, but presumably contrary to the intent of Congress, to include such instances. A market may, for example, be so limited that it is impossible to produce at all and meet the cost of production except by a plant large enough to supply the whole demand. Or there may be changes in taste or in cost which drive out all but one purveyor. A single producer may be the survivor out of a group of active competitors, merely by virtue of his superior skill, foresight and industry. In such cases a strong argument can be made that, although the result may expose the public to the evils of monopoly, the Act does not mean to condemn the resultant of those very forces which it is its prime object to foster: finis opus coronat ["the end crowns the work" Eds.]. The successful competitor, having been urged to compete, must not be turned upon when he wins. * * * 'Alcoa's' size was 'magnified' to make it a 'monopoly'; indeed, it has never been anything else; and its size, not only offered it an 'opportunity for abuse,' but it 'utilized' its size for 'abuse,' as can easily be shown.

It would completely misconstrue 'Alcoa's' position in 1940 to hold that it was the passive beneficiary of a monopoly, following upon an involuntary elimination of competitors by automatically operative economic forces. Already in 1909, when its last lawful monopoly ended, it sought to strengthen its position by unlawful practices, and these concededly continued until 1912. In that year it had two plants in New York, at which it produced less than 42 million pounds of ingot; in 1934 it had five plants (the original two, enlarged; one in Tennessee; one in North Carolina; one in Washington), and its production had risen to about 327 million pounds, an increase of almost eight-fold. Meanwhile not a pound of ingot had been produced by anyone else in the United States. This increase and this continued and undisturbed control did not fall undesigned into 'Alcoa's' lap; obviously it could not have done so. It could only have resulted, as it did result, from a persistent determination to maintain the control, with which it found itself vested in 1912. There were at least one or two abortive attempts to enter the industry, but 'Alcoa' effectively anticipated and forestalled all competition, and succeeded in holding the field alone. True, it stimulated demand and opened new uses for the metal, but not without making sure that it could supply what it had evoked. There is no dispute as to this; 'Alcoa' avows it as evidence of the skill, energy and initiative with which it has always conducted its business; as a reason why, having won its way by fair means, it should be commended, and not dismembered. We need charge it with no moral derelictions after 1912; we may assume that all it claims for itself is true. The only question is whether it falls within the exception established in favor of those who do not seek, but cannot avoid, the control of a market. It seems to us that that question scarcely survives its statement. It was not inevitable that it should always anticipate increases in the demand for ingot and be prepared to supply them. Nothing compelled it to keep doubling and redoubling its capacity before others entered the field. It insists that it never excluded competitors; but we can think of no more effective exclusion than progressively to embrace each new opportunity as it opened, and to face every newcomer with new capacity already geared into a great organization, having the advantage of experience, trade connections and the elite of personnel. Only in case we interpret 'exclusion' as limited to maneuvres not honestly industrial, but actuated solely by a desire to prevent competition, can such a course, indefatigably pursued, be deemed not 'exclusionary.' So to limit it would in our judgment emasculate the Act; would permit just such consolidations as it was designed to prevent.

* * *

In studying Alcoa's position in the aluminum industry, Judge Hand wrote against a backdrop of Supreme Court decisions that seemed to have set general boundaries for determining when market shares permitted an inference of substantial market power. In the Note that follows, we discuss those cases, as well as Judge Hand's analysis of market power in *Alcoa*.

NOTE ON THE ORIGINS OF ALCOA'S MARKET SHARE BENCHMARKS

Judge Hand's three market share benchmarks have proved to be extraordinarily influential and durable. But where did he get the idea that a 90% market share was certainly sufficient to establish a monopoly, but that

60–64% was doubtful and 33% was insufficient? The answer likely lies in his synthesis of several earlier Supreme Court cases involving prosecutions under Section 2.

Standard Oil and United States Steel

As we discussed at the outset of Chapter 2, the most important case in the early history of the U.S. antitrust laws is *Standard Oil Company of New Jersey v. United States*, 221 U.S. 1, 31 S.Ct. 502 (1911), which gave us the "rule of reason." In deliberations leading to passage of the Sherman Act of 1890, Standard Oil and its chief architect, John D. Rockefeller, provided a major target for congressional opprobrium. Following a series of highly critical accounts of Standard's behavior, first in a series of magazine articles and a book by journalist Ida M. Tarbell (*see* IDA M. TARBELL, THE HISTORY OF THE STANDARD OIL COMPANY (1904)), and later in official reports of the Federal Bureau of Corporations, President Theodore Roosevelt directed his attorney general to prepare a case against the petroleum giant.

In 1906, the Justice Department filed a civil action against Standard under Sections 1 and 2 of the Sherman Act. The government charged the company with monopolizing and attempting to monopolize the refining and marketing of petroleum products through various predatory means, including local price-cutting, bribery, obtaining rebates from railroads, and commercial espionage. After a fifteen-month trial, the U.S. district court in St. Louis issued a judgment for the government and ordered that the trust be dissolved.

Standard appealed the decision to the Supreme Court, attacking the trial court's conclusions that it had monopoly power and used improper business tactics. The company also assailed the district court's remedy, arguing that the forced dissolution of the firm into over 30 successor firms would yield economic chaos. On May 11, 1911, the Supreme Court upheld the trial court's finding of illegal monopolization and endorsed the dissolution decree. The Court's only concession to the defendant was to extend from 30 days to six months the period for executing the mandated divestitures.

In *Standard Oil*, both direct and circumstantial evidence led the Supreme Court to conclude that the defendant had substantial market power. Chief Justice Edward White's majority opinion spent little time defining a relevant market and analyzing the defendant's position in it. The parties agreed that the production of crude oil and the refining, transportation, and marketing of petroleum products constituted the relevant arenas of industrial activity. The Court accepted the government's allegation that Standard had achieved a 90 percent share of commerce in petroleum refining and had sustained its commanding position for well over a decade. The size and durability of the company's market share weighed decisively against its argument that it lacked a monopoly.

The Court did not require the government to show that Standard dominated all phases of the petroleum industry. Control over refining gave Standard power to govern the upstream (crude oil production) and downstream (marketing) segments. The Court's reliance on circumstantial evidence (Standard's share of activity) to determine the company's status proved influential. Later antitrust cases would treat a durable market share of 90 percent or more as creating a strong presumption of monopoly power.

The conclusion that Standard was a monopolist rested on more than market shares. In discussing Standard's dominance, the Court recited how the company *exercised* its power. The company preyed upon and then acquired competing refiners and secured its grip over refining by purchasing the transportation arteries (pipelines and rail tank cars) that linked refineries to crude oil production areas and to end users of products such as kerosene and gasoline. Here the Court suggested that proof of successful efforts to suppress and assimilate rivals—*direct evidence of the capacity to restrict competition*—could reinforce the inference of monopoly power derived from analyzing market shares. Thus Court planted the idea that evidence of a firm's actual success in subduing competitors could demonstrate its market power.

Standard Oil was one of many monopolization cases initiated by the Justice Department from 1905 through 1912. The targets of these cases, companies such as Standard, General Electric, DuPont, American Tobacco, International Harvester, and U.S. Steel, had exploited lax enforcement and favorable judicial interpretations to achieve market supremacy by purchasing competitors. In *United States v. E.C. Knight Co.*, 156 U.S. 1, 15 S.Ct. 249 (1895), the Supreme Court had rejected the Justice Department's challenge to a series of acquisitions that gave the defendant control of over 98 percent of the country's sugar refining capacity. It reached this result by concluding that "manufacturing" was not "commerce" under the Sherman Act and therefore left sugar refining outside the statute's reach. The decision helped trigger a massive wave of mergers that ended in 1904, when the Court upheld the government's effort in *Northern Securities Co. v. United States*, 193 U.S. 197, 24 S.Ct. 436 (1904) to undo the combination of the Great Northern and Northern Pacific railroads.

Among its efforts to reverse the effects of the turn-of-the-century merger wave, the Justice Department filed a monopolization case against U.S. Steel in 1911. The complaint in *United States v. United States Steel Corp.*, 251 U.S. 417, 40 S.Ct. 293 (1920), alleged that U.S. Steel had achieved monopoly power through anticompetitive mergers with competitors and requested the dissolution of the company. The trial court found that U.S. Steel had used a series of mergers to achieve market shares of 80 to 95 percent of U.S. production of numerous steel products, proceeded to raise prices dramatically, and realized extraordinary profits. The district court also reported that, from 1907 until 1911, U.S. Steel's president, E.H. Gary, organized regular dinners at which the company and its competitors met to cooperate in setting prices and production limits.

The district court nonetheless exonerated the defendant. Although U.S. Steel had attained market shares of 80 to 95 percent, the trial court emphasized that the company's share had fallen to 40.9 percent by the trial's end in 1917. The sharp decline in U.S. Steel's market share and the steady expansion by its rivals negated a finding of monopoly power. The court also downplayed the "Gary Dinners," noting that the gatherings had ceased before the government began its lawsuit. The Justice Department did not challenge, as a separate Section 1 offense, the participation by U.S. Steel and its rivals in the Gary Dinners. Nor did any competitors testify to decry oppression by the defendant. Instead, they appeared in droves to attest to U.S. Steel's adherence to decent methods of commerce.

By a 4–3 vote, the Supreme Court sustained the trial court's ruling and emphasized the absence of persuasive proof that U.S. Steel held substantial market power. Justice McKenna's majority opinion stated that the decline in U.S. Steel's market share, from 80–95 percent to about 41 percent, belied market preeminence. After all, how could a firm surrender half of its share of the market and still be considered "dominant"?

Beyond the circumstantial evidence (U.S. Steel's declining market share), the Court also pointed to the absence of direct proof of market power. U.S. Steel might have responded to entry and expansion by competitors with the sort of aggressive countermoves employed by Standard Oil. For example, U.S. Steel might have cut prices selectively in markets targeted by entrants or tried to deny competitors access to a vital input, such as iron ore. The Court said the government had introduced no evidence that U.S. Steel had abused its competitors or customers. Indeed, hundreds of U.S. Steel rivals had attested to the firm's propriety. U.S. Steel perhaps tried to persuade its rivals to collude, but the Court said these efforts seemed ineffective and had no impact on market conditions. The Court also dismissed the suggestion of the government's expert, an economist, that the uniformity of industry prices during the period in question probably resulted from actual or tacit collusion. The Court refused to rely on such "speculation" when U.S. Steel had produced so many testimonials from the company's rivals indicating that competition was robust.

The Court arguably misapprehended the significance of the Gary Dinners and the pricing patterns that followed them. The Gary Dinners may have helped develop understandings by which the producers organized their behavior. U.S. Steel may have announced its willingness to tolerate its rivals if they priced at or near the company's relatively high price. If so, it is hardly surprising, or inconsistent with the government's theory, that competitors would heap praise upon U.S. Steel. The defendant may have orchestrated a collusive pricing arrangement that let its rivals expand output gradually and obtain supra-competitive profits in the process. If U.S. Steel helped keep industry-wide prices above competitive levels, the rivals' gratitude was much deserved. For a thought-provoking analysis of the allegations of collusion and the record evidence in the case, see William H. Page, *The Gary Dinners and the Meaning of Concerted Action*, 62 S.M.U. L. REV. 597 (2009).

Judge Hand's 90 percent benchmark thus likely came from *Standard Oil*. For his view that 33 percent would be insufficient, he probably used *U.S. Steel* as the guidepost, for the Supreme Court had taken the decline in U.S. Steel's market share to roughly 41 percent as signifying a lack of monopoly power. Reflecting the paucity of case law addressing market shares of 40 to 90 percent, Hand further noted that "it is doubtful whether sixty or sixty-four percent would be enough." Figure 4–5 summarizes the results in cases that probably helped shape his thinking on this question.

Figure 4–5:

Pre-*Alcoa* Decisions and the Inference of Monopoly Power

Case	Defendant's Market Share	Monopoly Inferred?
Standard Oil (1911)	90%	Yes
American Tobacco (1911)	90%	Yes
International Harvester (1914)	85%	Yes
U.S. Steel (1920)	41%	No
Standard Oil of Indiana (1931)	26%	No
Appalachian Coals (1933)	12, 54, 64, or 74%; (de-pending on definition of relevant market)	No: (Decision suggests that proper market definition yielded share between 12% and 54% and no more than 64%.)

A Closer Look at Alcoa and Market Definition

The *Alcoa* court ultimately agreed with the government's claim that Alcoa's share of sales in a properly defined relevant market was 90 percent, well within the zone of concern that *Standard Oil* had identified in 1911. To reach 90 percent, the court made a number of difficult (and disputed) judgments about the relevant market's contours and Alcoa's share of activity in the market. The court had to decide whether to limit the product market to virgin ingot or combine virgin ingot and "secondary" (recycled) aluminum; to count aluminum that Alcoa produced but consumed itself to make aluminum products for later resale; and to treat foreign suppliers as being able to increase shipments to the United States if U.S. aluminum prices increased. Figure 4–6 indicates how sensitive the calculation of Alcoa's market share is to the assumptions the court made about the aluminum industry.

Figure 4–6:

Assumptions Underlying Calculation of Alcoa's Market Share

Relevant Market	Alcoa's Activity	Imports	Alcoa's Market Share
Virgin Ingot Only	External Output + Captive Production	10% only	90%
Virgin + Recycled	External Output + Captive Production	10% only	64%
Virgin + Recycled	External Output Only	10% only	33%
Any of Above	Any of Above	Unlimited	Uncertain, but smaller

One can quarrel with a number of the choices Judge Hand and his colleagues made in pegging Alcoa's market share at 90 percent. The record suggests that some purchasers of aluminum ingot (notably, aircraft manufacturers) regarded recycled aluminum as an unacceptable substitute for virgin ingot. Yet it also seems that many purchasers regarded virgin ingot and secondary aluminum as interchangeable. The court reasonably doubted the substitutability of secondary aluminum for all uses, but excluding all secondary aluminum from the market definition ignored the many customers for whom secondary was a suitable alternative. Alcoa presumably had some ability to adjust current output to account for competition in the secondary market, but it is unclear from the court's discussion why Judge Hand thought the company could wholly negate the constraining influence of recycling by cutting its new production. As is discussed in Sidebar 4–2, more contemporary economic research appears to justify Judge Hand's conclusion, albeit on different grounds that are more fully explained.

The decision to include all of Alcoa's "captive production"—aluminum that Alcoa produced and transferred to its wholly owned subsidiaries to fabricate aluminum parts and make finished products—also involves difficult judgments. The court reasoned that, if the price of aluminum ingot began to rise, Alcoa would divert its ingot away from its own fabricators and sell the ingot on the open market. Since Alcoa had an established network for selling virgin ingot, shifting output from internal consumption to external sales probably would have required a relatively modest effort. Not all companies might be able to make this switch fluidly. The ability to respond to price increases in the external market would depend on having an external sales network and substantial freedom to renege on commitments made to the firm's internal users of the product and, indirectly, to the customers who purchase the fabricated items that the firm produces.

The treatment of imports is a clearer issue in *Alcoa*. The court correctly noted that existing tariffs and quotas severely constrained the ability of foreign suppliers to respond to aluminum price increases in the United States. In recent times, the reduction of tariff and non-tariff barriers to trade through the World Trade Organization framework and other international agreements has boosted the ability of producers in many product markets to compete for sales worldwide. Today the geographic dimension of relevant markets that once were delimited by high trade barriers has become increasingly global.

Alcoa has exerted a profound, lasting impact on the analysis of monopoly power. The decision has anchored the analysis of market power in the process of defining relevant markets and calculating market shares as a surrogate for market power. *Alcoa* also emphasized—perhaps inordinately—the legal presumptions that flow from particular market share thresholds. Market definition became a high stakes, strategic battle that frequently determined litigation outcomes.

With so much depending on market definition, *Alcoa* also underscored the critical nature of certain industry data. Antitrust specialists need not agree or disagree with *Alcoa*'s market definition and market power analysis to recognize the importance of digging beneath the numbers where market shares are offered as proxies for market power. The exercises of defining a relevant market and attributing shares to individual market participants often rests upon a foundation of debatable assumptions. Where the basis for defining the relevant market or attributing market shares is uncertain, one should place less weight upon the resulting market shares as a basis for inferring the presence or absence of market power.

The next two Sidebars explore some of the many dimensions of *Alcoa*. Aided by an examination of the private papers of the panel that decided the case, Sidebar 4–1 reveals that the judges, especially Learned Hand, had serious reservations about the Sherman Act's approach to monopoly. Sidebar 4–2, which immediately follows, digs a bit deeper into some of the economic reasoning in the case from a contemporary perspective.

Sidebar 4–1:
Learned Hand, *Alcoa,* and the Reluctant
Application of the Sherman Act[a]

Alcoa is antitrust's closest equivalent to an epic poem. Though issued over 70 years ago, Judge Learned Hand's elegantly written opinion still permeates the vocabulary of antitrust law. Generations of antitrust students and practitioners have recited, and continue to invoke, its lyrical passages. Some quote the case to justify close scrutiny of dominant firms: "Many people believe that the possession of unchallenged economic power deadens initiative, discourages thrift and depresses energy; that immunity from competition is a narcotic, and rivalry is a stimulant, to economic progress; that the spur of constant stress is necessary to counteract an inevitable disposition to let well enough alone."[b] Others cite it to warn against punishing market preeminence gained by superior performance: "The successful competitor, having been urged to compete, must not be turned upon when he wins."[c]

Alcoa continues to figure prominently in debates about the ends and means of competition policy, and its symbolic significance extends beyond the specific holdings in the case. Commentators regard the case as one of the most powerful statements in antitrust jurisprudence for the robust efforts to constrain dominant firms. Discussions of the case often place Learned Hand at the center of attention and ascribe to Hand the views espoused in the Second Circuit's decision.[d]

Hand believed otherwise. He disliked the antitrust laws from his earliest days in public life. In a representative statement of his views, Hand wrote to a friend in 1914: "I do not agree by any means that the Sherman Act is of value or that the progressive party should take its position against monopoly. . . . I have always suspected that that there are monopolies possible which depend for their maintenance wholly upon economic efficiency and which it would be an economic blunder to destroy."[e] As a federal district judge, he discreetly carried these views into the political arena and took an active part in the 1912 presidential campaign of Theodore Roosevelt. Hand sympathized with the former president's caustic criticism of the antitrust laws,[f] which was a centerpiece of Roosevelt's campaign against Woodrow Wilson and William Howard Taft.

How did a Theodore Roosevelt Progressive, steeped in antipathy for the Sherman Act, come to write what has been taken as a soaring tribute to its value and an endorsement of its broad social mission? Why did Hand author an opinion that led his admirers and critics to identify him with an approach he disdained? Archival materials—especially Hand's published letters and the internal memoranda he exchanged with the other two judges on the *Alcoa* panel, Augustus Hand and Thomas Swan—help provide the answer.

In their internal deliberations, Hand and his colleagues repeatedly belittled the case as a tedious burden rather than an opportunity to shape the course of antitrust law. Hand wrote to Felix Frankfurter, then a member of the Supreme Court, that the case was "a dirty job."[g] Soon before the oral argument in 1944, Hand told a friend that the appeal involved 1500 pages of briefs and a trial record of 47,000 pages, "which I hope to not have to look at all."[h] His cousin and fellow panel member, Augustus Hand, called the case horrible and monstrous.[i]

---

[a]   This Sidebar is adapted from Marc Winerman & William E. Kovacic, *Learned Hand,* Alcoa, *and the Reluctant Application of the Sherman Act,* 79 ANTITRUST L.J. 295 (2013).

[b]   United States v. Aluminum Co. of Am., 148 F.2d 416, 427 (2d Cir. 1945).

[c]   *Id.* at 430.

[d]   Recall that due to recusals, the Supreme Court lacked a quorum to hear the appeal and Congress passed legislation authorizing the Second Circuit to sit "as" the Supreme Court for purposes of resolving the case. It therefore has the precedential value of a Supreme Court decision, which has amplified its influence.

[e]   Letter from Learned Hand to Amos R.E. Pinchot (May 29, 1914), in REASON AND IMAGINATION: THE SELECTED CORRESPONDENCE OF LEARNED HAND: 1897–1961, at 48 (Constance Jordan ed., 2013) (hereinafter *SELECTED CORRESPONDENCE*). Hand wrote this letter as Congress was considering bills that would become the Clayton Act and the Federal Trade Commission Act.

[f]   In accepting the nomination of the Progressive Party for the presidency in 1912, Roosevelt denounced an antitrust policy that "has occasionally done good, has usually accomplished nothing, but generally left the worst conditions wholly unchanged, and has been responsible for a considerable amount of downright and positive evil." Theodore Roosevelt, Address at the National Convention of the Progressive Party: A Confession of Faith (Aug. 6, 1912), in 17 THE WORKS OF THEODORE ROOSEVELT 254, 279 (Hermann Hagedorn ed., Nat'l ed., 1926). As Winerman and Kovacic observe, he advocated the creation of a government agency with broad authority:

> Though he [Roosevelt] would make antitrust "genuinely . . . effective against every big concern tending to monopoly or guilty of antisocial practices," a commission should supplement antitrust, exercising "complete power to regulate and control all the great industrial concerns engaged in interstate business." Its mandate would be broad. It would address competitive issues such as artificially high prices and low output and it would protect consumers, but it would also protect shareholders and labor. The proposal was central to TR's campaign, though it was controversial even within his new party.

79 ANTITRUST L.J. at 312 (footnotes omitted).

[g]   Letter from Learned Hand to Felix Frankfurter (Mar. 24, 1945), in SELECTED CORRESPONDENCE, at 255.

[h]   Letter from Learned Hand to Louis Henkin (Sept. 21, 1944), in SELECTED CORRESPONDENCE, at 247, 248.

[i]   Augustus Hand lamented that the records in the case "have become such a mess as to overwhelm everyone who does not have a century to live with the monstrous brood: 'Ingens horrendum cui lumen ademptum.'" Pre-Conference Memorandum from Augustus N. Hand to Learned Hand and Thomas W. Swan at 4, *United States v. Aluminum Co. of Am.,* 148 F.2d 416 (2d Cir. 1945) (No. 144) (Feb. 3, 1945) (on file in the Learned Hand Papers, Harvard Law School Library, Box 207, Folder 17). Augustus Hand adapted the text from the description in Virgil's Aeneid of the blinded cyclops Polyphemus.

Concluding that wartime developments meant that "no decree of dissolution and no injunction could properly be directed now," Thomas Swan told his colleagues that the appeal was "shadow boxing by the Department of Justice in order to 'save face' with the public. It is disgusting and maddening to spend weeks of futile labor on such a case."[j]

As Swan's comment suggests, the panel members believed the government's case was misguided. They deplored the use of antitrust law to address what they regarded as complex industrial phenomena. In one memo to his colleagues, Learned Hand described the unpalatable task before them:

> Alcoa has had undisputed control of the ingot market from the start; it has kept it deliberately and indeed in the face of some efforts to break in. If we hold that it is not a monopoly, deliberately planned and maintained, everyone who does not get entangled in the legal niceties and in the incredible nonsense that has emanated from the Supreme Court, will, quite rightly I think, write us down as asses. Wherever the line of size should be drawn, it must include a company such as this, if the [Sherman] Act is to be enforced. I despise this whole method of dealing with a very real and very serious problem in industrial life; but that is the way we have chosen, and we ought not to wince, because of the vagueness of the outlines, when we are faced with so clear an instance.[k]

In a separate memorandum, Learned Hand noted "There are two possible ways of dealing with [monopolies]: to regulate, or to forbid, them. Since we have no way of regulating them, we forbid them. I don't think much of that way, but I didn't set it up; and now the ordinary run of our fellow-citizens—some, even of the 'rugged individualists'—regard the Sherman Act as the palladium of their liberties."[l]

Left to give effect to their own policy preferences, the panel might well have affirmed the district court's dismissal of the suit. In writing the decision, however, consistent with their oath of office as Article III judges the three suppressed their own beliefs and instead strove to fulfill their duty to apply the Sherman Act as they perceived Congress to have intended. The opinion reflected their sense of obedience to the Sherman Act's aims,[m] not the panel's doubtful view of the statute.[n] Hand may have "despised" the Sherman Act as a solution to the monopoly problem, but he and his colleagues recognized that it was the solution "we have chosen."

Sidebar 4–2:
Durable Goods Monopoly—Three Economic Issues

Alcoa has prompted economists to study several issues raised directly or indirectly by the case. This Sidebar briefly surveys the literature on three of these issues.

Competition From Used or Recycled Products

Judge Learned Hand considered whether competition from sellers of secondary aluminum constrains the pricing of virgin aluminum in the context of market definition. The secondary product is ingot made from aluminum scrap. This is an instance of the more general question of whether recycled or used products should be counted as substitutes for new production.

Judge Hand addressed this question in the context of market definition. He recognized that secondary product competes with virgin in ingot market, probably setting a ceiling on the price of virgin aluminum. But Hand also observed that Alcoa knows that some of its virgin production will later return to the market, recycled from scrap. That consideration must affect Alcoa's decision as to present production. "The competition of 'secondary' must therefore be disregarded, as soon as we consider the position of 'Alcoa' over a period of years; it was as much within 'Alcoa's' control as was the production of 'virgin' from which it had been derived." Accordingly, Judge Hand excluded secondary aluminum from the relevant product market. Had he done otherwise, Alcoa's market share would have been calculated as 64% rather than 90%.

---

[j]   Pre-Conference Memorandum from Judge Thomas W. Swan to Judges Learned Hand and Augustus N. Hand at 5, *Alcoa*, 148 F.2d 416 (2d Cir. 1945) (No. 144) (Jan. 29, 1945) (on file in Learned Hand Papers, Harvard Law School Library, Box 207, Folder 17).

[k]   Pre-Conference Memorandum from Judge Learned Hand to Judges Augustus N. Hand and Thomas W. Swan at 13–14, *Alcoa*, 148 F.2d 316 (2d Cir. 1945) (No. 144) (undated) (on file in the Learned Hand Papers, Harvard Law School Library, Box 207, Folder 17.

[l]   Pre-Conference Memorandum from Judge Learned Hand to Judges Augustus N. Hand and Thomas W. Swan Second Memo on the Question of Monopoly at 8, *Alcoa*, 148 F.2d 416 (2d Cir. 1945) (on file in the Learned Hand Papers, Harvard Law School Library, Box 207, Folder 17).

[m]   In one passage of the decision, the court observes: "It is possible, because of its indirect social or moral effect, to prefer a system of small producers, each dependent for his success upon his own skill and character, to one in which the great mass of those engaged must accept the direction of a few. These considerations, which we have suggested only as possible purposes of the Act, we think the decisions prove to have been in fact its purposes." *Alcoa*, 148 F.2d at 427.

[n]   The style of the *Alcoa* opinion indirectly hints at the panel's own beliefs. The decision's most famous statements of the contributions of an egalitarian vision of antitrust policy are cast in the passive voice or in the third person. Thus, the court in key passages speaks of what "many people believe" or what "some think" or say that a matter "is believed." The panel stopped short of saying that *they* believed these propositions.

In part, the question of whether competition from used or recycled products constrains the potential exercise of market power by producers of new products turns on two familiar considerations. One comes up in market definition: do buyers consider the two products close substitutes? (Perhaps not. Metal produced from scrap could have additional impurities, making them unsuitable for some buyers. Relatedly, many new car buyers probably do not consider used cars close substitutes at current prices, though others likely do.) Another may arise in analyzing the significance of market shares. Can sellers of used or recycled products expand their output cheaply, or are they effectively constrained as to how much they put on the market?

The economics literature spawned by Judge Hand's analysis of the competitive role of secondary aluminum focuses upon an additional consideration that arises in durable goods markets, where the products at issue are not just any substitutes, but are derived from new production in the past. The new issue is whether the secondary product has been recovered from discarded scrap, or whether it was sold as used every time it previously changed hands. The recovery of discarded products is merely an alternative production process using different inputs, over which the producer of new products has no control. But if buyers of new products place value on them when they are used, by selling used goods to other buyers (some of whom may recondition them for sale in competition with new products), then a new product monopolist will recognize (as Hand observed) that it can restrict the supply of used goods in the future by reducing output in the present. Under such circumstances, the presence of a substantial market in used products can constrain the price of new products, but a new product monopolist may be able offset this procompetitive force to a significant degree by reducing new production in anticipation of its future return to the marketplace. *See generally*, Darius W. Gaskins, Alcoa *Revisited: The Welfare Implications of a Secondhand Market*, 7 J. ECON. THEORY 254 (1974); Peter L. Swan, Alcoa*: The Influence of Recycling on Monopoly Power*, 88 J. POL. ECON. 76 (1980), Robert E. Martin, *Monopoly Power and the Recycling of Raw Materials*, 30 J. INDUS. ECON. 405 (1982). *Cf.* Dennis W. Carlton & Robert Gertner, *Market Power and Mergers in Durable-Good Industries*, 32 J. L. & ECON. S203 (1989) (Pt. 2, October) (analyzing additional complications arising when the new product industry has an oligopoly market structure); Carl

Shapiro, *Comment on Carlton and Gertner*, 32 J. L. & ECON. S227 (1989) (Pt. 2, October).

These threads were integrated in an empirical study of Alcoa itself by economist Valerie Suslow, using modern empirical methods unavailable at the time the *Alcoa* case was litigated. Suslow finds that Alcoa possessed substantial market power: it recognized that it faced a downward sloping demand curve, and could therefore elevate price by reducing output. In consequence, she finds, Alcoa's markup of price over its marginal cost was equal to about 60% of price during the 1930s. (She does not specifically identify the competitive price, however.) This market power was not significantly undermined by competition with secondary aluminum recovered from scrap, but not primarily because Alcoa restricted virgin aluminum production in order to limit the future supply of the secondary product (Judge Hand's argument). The recycled product did not come onto the market for five to twenty-five years after the virgin aluminum was sold; in a growing market, therefore, secondary aluminum production would always be small relative to virgin aluminum and have little influence on virgin aluminum prices. Rather, competition from secondary aluminum was not a big threat to Alcoa for a more pedestrian reason: mainly because secondary aluminum was only an imperfect substitute to buyers of virgin aluminum. Valerie Y. Suslow, *Estimating Monopoly Behavior With Competitive Recycling: An Application to* Alcoa, 17 RAND J. ECON. 389 (1986).

Can the Monopolist Commit to High Future Prices?

Nobel Prize-winning economist Ronald Coase highlighted the significance of another important issue unique to durable goods markets: time. The buyer of a durable good like a computer or an automobile makes use of her purchase over a period of time. Often, the buyer has the option of purchasing immediately, or waiting a while (while continuing to use her existing car or computer) in the hope that the delay will allow her to purchase the product at a lower price in the future.

A monopolist seller, in turn, must decide how much to produce (and charge) both initially and in the future. It might want to keep output low, and charge a price well in excess of the competitive level. If it charges a high price initially, however, it will end up selling only to those buyers who value the product the most. The seller will then be tempted by another profit opportunity: by cutting price, it can sell even more to customers who didn't purchase initially (when the price was so high) but are nevertheless willing to pay more than seller's cost. In other words, the durable goods monopolist has an incentive to price discriminate over time. Initially, the monopolist would charge a monopoly price, but over time it would maximize profits by gradually lowering price, selling more and more until price falls to the competitive level.

Ronald Coase argued that this strategy would not be successful. Buyers—even those willing to pay a great deal— would recognize that the seller has a powerful incentive to lower price in the future, and would find it worth their while to delay purchases awaiting the price cuts. If so, the monopoly seller would be unable ever to charge a price greater than the competitive level. The durable goods monopolist, in effect, competes with its future self, and, notwithstanding its monopoly, cannot exercise market power! Ronald Coase, *Durability and Monopoly*, 15 J. L. & ECON. 143 (1972). This proposition—that a durable goods monopolist will be unable to exercise market power because rational buyers will balk at paying monopoly prices—is widely known as the "Coase conjecture" (and is a proposition distinct from the same economist's "Coase theorem" at the core of modern law and economics).

An extensive economics literature has identified factors that may preserve some ability for the durable goods monopolist to exercise market power, notwithstanding its Coase conjecture incentive not to raise price. If the durable goods monopolist can commit not to cut price in the future, buyers will not delay their purchases in anticipation of a price reduction, so the monopolist will be able to successfully charge a high price today. Sellers can make such commitments, for example, by limiting capacity (an artist making only so many prints before destroying the plates), or by contracting to pay a penalty if it cuts price in the future (*see Note on the Economic Effects of "Most Favored Nation" Provisions* in Chapter 6). Adjustment costs that keep sellers from adjusting price quickly might also lessen buyer incentives to wait for prices to fall. In addition, sellers can avoid competing with themselves by leasing rather than selling the durable product, making it impossible for buyers to obtain any advantage from delaying their purchase. Or they can reduce the problem by limiting durability through "planned obsolescence" (as through frequent product upgrades).

Excess Capacity as a Barrier to Entry

Judge Hand argued that Alcoa's policy of expanding capacity in anticipation of demand deterred entry by prospective rivals, and thus insulated Alcoa from competition. This is an example of a class of theories that economists have come to term "*strategic entry deterrence.*"

The central idea behind strategic entry deterrence is simple: if an incumbent firm can convince its potential rivals that their entry will lead to a competitive marketplace with a low post-entry price, then potential competitors will refrain from entry no matter how high the pre-entry price charged by the incumbent. To set up this threat, an incumbent must make irreversible investments in instruments of entry deterrence. These might include excess low cost capacity (Judge Hand's suggestion in *Alcoa*), brand proliferation, high advertising, or contract provisions with its customers whereby the incumbent agrees to match good-faith offers by its rivals. These investments are often costly to the monopolist, but the payoff is greater if they guarantee that the monopolist can protect a high price by deterring new competition.

Theories like these are well-established as possibilities in the economics literature. *See generally* Steven C. Salop, *Strategic Entry Deterrence,* 69 AM. ECON. REV. 335 (Papers & Proceedings 1979); Richard J. Gilbert, *Mobility Barriers and the Value of Incumbency, in* 1 HANDBOOK OF INDUSTRIAL ORGANIZATION 475 (Richard Schmalensee & Robert Willig, eds. 1989); Robert H. Smiley, *Empirical Evidence on Strategic Entry Deterrence,* 6 INT'L J. INDUS. ORG. 167 (1988) (survey of firms suggested that practices such as these are prevalent); Marvin B. Lieberman, *Excess Capacity as a Barrier to Entry: An Empirical Appraisal,* 35 J. INDUS. ECON. 607 (1987) (empirical study of thirty-eight chemical product industries called into question the specific method of entry deterrence that concerned Judge Hand in *Alcoa*, finding that incumbent firms in that industry rarely built excess capacity preemptively in an effort to deter entry). As we noted at the outset of this Chapter, however, whether exclusionary conduct is fairly viewed as prevalent or uncommon continues to be the focus of debate by antitrust commentators.

Judge Hand's opinion in *Alcoa* inspired extensive and continuing discussions among courts and commentators about the reach of Section 2. One focus of debate is Hand's evaluation of antitrust's goals. Hand provided a memorable statement of the reason for curbing monopolies ("Many people believe that possession of unchallenged economic power deadens initiative, discourages thrift and depresses energy. . . .") and supplied an elegant synthesis of the non-economic aims that motivated Congress to adopt the Sherman Act. Yet Hand also recognized the hazards of a rule of law that condemned commercial preeminence without regard to the means of its attainment ("The successful competitor, having been urged to compete, must not be turned upon when he wins."). Judge Hand resolved this dilemma—how to deter monopoly without diminishing incentives to compete—by embracing a vision of antitrust that favored strict limits on dominant firm conduct to promote economic decentralization and to achieve a more egalitarian political and social environment.

Judge Hand condemned Alcoa's strategy of anticipating and responding to new demand for aluminum by expanding its own production capacity on the ground that it preempted entry and expansion by competing aluminum producers. Such conduct, Judge Hand concluded, satisfied the behavioral element of the monopolization offense. Because Judge Hand dismissed other allegations of wrongful acts, 148 F.2d at 432–39, this behavior alone supplied the ingredient of bad conduct. Many commentators have assailed Hand's analysis. Should Alcoa have deferred increases in capacity and simply let rivals build new plants and serve all new demand? Was it rational for Alcoa, or any firm, to ignore increases in demand and remain content with its existing productive capabilities? And couldn't failure to expand output have resulted in even higher prices? How, in any event, were business managers to know when the addition of new capacity had gone too far? For an examination of the case aided by Hand's personal papers, see Marc Winerman & William E. Kovacic, *Learned Hand, Alcoa, and the Reluctant Application of the Sherman Act*, 79 ANTITRUST L.J. 295 (2013).

The historical context of the case amplifies its significance. Aluminum was used to build all kinds of military hardware, especially aircraft, and became an essential input into the United States' ability to wage war in World War II. Would it have served the interests of the United States in the 1930s if Alcoa, especially after Adolph Hitler's rise to power in Germany in 1933, had built no new plants until 1938, when the Justice Department filed its antitrust case?

In *American Tobacco Co. v. United States*, 328 U.S. 781, 66 S.Ct. 1125 (1946), the first Section 2 case to reach the Supreme Court after *Alcoa*, the Court endorsed Judge Hand's opinion and adopted *Alcoa*'s expansive view of when dominant firm conduct is improper. Two years after *American Tobacco*, in *United States v. Griffith*, 334 U.S. 100, 107, 68 S.Ct. 941, 945 (1948), the Court in dicta seemed to approve some of *Alcoa*'s fullest implications when it said monopoly power, however acquired, "may itself constitute an evil and stand condemned under § 2 even though it remains unexercised." The *Griffith* Court, however, also condemned the practice of the defendant theater owners of buying film distribution rights for all their movie theaters as a block. Since some of Griffith's theaters had monopoly power and others did not, block purchasing abused the defendant's dominant position by allowing it to gain an advantage in competitive markets. (As we shall see, this latter theory has since been rejected by the Supreme Court. *See infra Note on the Status of Essential Facilities and Leveraging After Trinko.*)

As blessed by *American Tobacco* and *Griffith*, *Alcoa* revitalized government efforts to enforce the Sherman Act's ban upon monopolization. In a number of cases, the government's theory of liability sought to define, in the tradition of *Alcoa*, broad limits on dominant firm behavior. Litigation involving United Shoe Machinery provides a major illustration. In *United States v. United Shoe Mach. Corp.*, 110 F. Supp. 295 (D. Mass. 1953), *aff'd per curiam*, 347 U.S. 521, 74 S.Ct. 699 (1954), the government challenged the country's largest producer of machines used to produce footwear. United Shoe's share of shoe machinery output was 75 to 85 percent, and the trial court found that the company had monopoly power. In a famous opinion by Judge Charles Wyzanski, the district court went on to condemn United Shoe's policy of leasing (and refusing to sell) its machines and its imposing lease terms that forced its customers to obtain maintenance and service on leased machines from United Shoe only. The court found that the lease-only and service practices improperly impeded entry by rival shoe machinery producers and discouraged competition from independent service organizations. 110 F. Supp. at 345–46.

At trial, United Shoe strived to show that its success was attributable to superior research and to its skill in meeting customer needs, not to any oppressive behavior. As the following passage indicates, Judge Wyzanski declined to find that the absence of obviously "predatory" conduct could exculpate United Shoe:

> It is only fair to add that the more than 14,000 page record, and the more than 5,000 exhibits, representing the diligent seven year search made by Government counsel aided by this Court's orders giving them full access to United's files during the last 40 years, show that United's power does not rest on predatory practices. Probably few monopolies could produce a record so free from any taint of that kind of wrong-doing. The violation with which United is now charged depends not on moral considerations, but on solely economic considerations. United is denied the right to exercise effective control of the market by business policies that are not the inevitable consequences of its capacities or its natural advantages. That those policies are not immoral is irrelevant.

> Defendant seems to suggest that even if its control of the market is not attributable exclusively to its superior performance, its research, and its economies of scale, nonetheless, United's market control should not be held unlawful, because only through the existence of some monopoly power can the thin shoe

machinery market support fundamental research of the first order, and achieve maximum economies of production and distribution.

　　To this defense the shortest answer is that the law does not allow an enterprise that maintains control of a market through practices not economically inevitable, to justify that control because of its supposed social advantage. It is for Congress, not for private interests, to determine whether a monopoly, not compelled by circumstances, is advantageous. And it is for Congress to decide on what conditions, and subject to what regulations, such a monopoly shall conduct its business.

110 F. Supp. at 345. Notwithstanding United Shoe's benign explanations, Judge Wyzanski concluded that the government had established an antitrust violation.

　　Like Judge Hand's analysis of Alcoa's capacity expansion efforts, Judge Wyzanski's evaluation of United Shoe's leasing and service policies—and his suggestion that a dominant firm risks Section 2 liability when it "maintains control of a market through practices not economically inevitable"—have inspired extensive debate. Some observers have argued that the challenged leasing terms may have helped assure the quality of the shoe machinery and enabled United Shoe to provide better services and information to its customers. The service agreements may have supplied an important source of feedback by which United spotted possibilities for improving its existing machines and used its research and development program to implement. Evidence recited by Judge Wyzanski indicated that many customers found United Shoe's leasing and service practices agreeable—an indication, perhaps, that the company's asserted justification was genuine. *Compare* Scott E. Masten & Edward A. Snyder, United States v. United Shoe Machinery Corporation: *On the Merits*, 36 J.L. & ECON. 33 (1993) (emphasizing efficiency grounds for leasing terms) *with* Joseph F. Brodley & Ching-to Albert Ma, *Contract Penalties, Monopolizing Strategies, and Antitrust Policy*, 45 STAN. L. REV. 1161 (1993) (rejecting efficiency interpretation of *United Shoe's* terms). For a contemporary account and analysis of the case by the economist who served as Judge Wyzanski's "law clerk," see CARL KAYSEN, UNITED STATES V. UNITED SHOE MACHINERY CORPORATION: AN ECONOMIC ANALYSIS OF AN ANTITRUST CASE (1956).

Sidebar 4–3:
The Section 2 Conduct Standard After
Alcoa—**Flirting with No Fault**

The issuance of the *Alcoa* decision in 1945 and its validation by the Supreme Court in *American Tobacco* in 1946 galvanized commentators and enforcement officials to consider a renewed campaign to use Section 2 to challenge dominant enterprises. *See* William E. Kovacic, *Failed Expectations: The Troubled Past and Uncertain Future of the Sherman Act as a Tool for Deconcentration*, 74 IOWA L. REV. 1105, 1118–19, 1133–36 (1989).

From academia came two influential papers in 1947 that made the case for a Section 2 renaissance. Declaring that *Alcoa* and *American Tobacco* "mark the new birth of Section 2," Eugene Rostow of the Yale Law School faculty proposed a new campaign of monopolization cases to deconcentrate American industry and "eliminate the wastes, the non-use of capacity, and the restrictionism of monopolistic industrial organization." Eugene Rostow, *The New Sherman Act: A Positive Instrument of Progress*, 14 U. CHI. L. REV. 567, 577, 568 (1947). Edward Levi, the Dean of the University of Chicago Law School, said that *Alcoa* and *American Tobacco* raised prospects for "a new interpretation of the Sherman Act" that "can give the act strength *against monopolies as such*, and also against control by three, four, or five corporations acting together." Edward Levi, *The Antitrust Laws and Monopoly*, 14 U. CHI. L. REV. 153, 183 (1947) (emphasis added). As Rostow and Levi envisioned it, employing Section 2 *against monopolies as such* meant reducing—perhaps eliminating—attention to the means by which monopolies took shape and instead embracing a "no-fault" interpretation of the statute—directly attacking substantial, persistent monopoly power.

From 1947 until the mid-1950s, the Department of Justice pursued an impressive array of cases against dominant firms. The government declined the invitation of Levi and Rostow to press no-fault theories of liability, but federal prosecutors took full advantage of the attenuated conduct requirement that emerged from *Alcoa* and *American Tobacco*. Key subjects of Justice Department monopolization actions included the distribution and exhibition of motion pictures, cellophane, shoe machinery, Pullman sleeping cars, telephone equipment, film processing, and bananas. Despite occasional setbacks such as the loss on liability in *du Pont (Cellophane)*, the government usually prevailed on liability issues. Nonetheless, a widespread perception that the remedial results in these matters had been ineffectual led to renewed calls by blue ribbon commissions and individual commentators for more aggressive measures to attack monopoly power directly and to break dominant firms into smaller successor companies.

Modern consideration of proposals to deconcentrate oligopolies originated in Carl Kaysen's and Donald Turner's ANTITRUST POLICY: AN ECONOMIC AND LEGAL ANALYSIS, which appeared in 1959. Viewed as the leading synthesis of antitrust law and economics of its time, the Kaysen-Turner volume declared that "[t]he principal defect of present antitrust law is its inability to cope with market power created by jointly acting oligopolists." *Id.* at 110. The two scholars called for new legislation to restructure concentrated industries and provided the foundation for similar recommendations by a host of legislative committees, blue ribbon task forces, and individual commentators in the 1960s and 1970s. In general terms, the deconcentration proposals would have broken up oligopolistic industries unless existing concentration resulted solely from lawful patents or unless dissolution would cause the loss of substantial scale economies. The deconcentration enthusiasts also urged that the government bring more Section 2 cases with structural relief as the preferred remedy.

These deconcentration proposals yielded no legislation, but they had a powerful (and unintended) impact on the future direction of antitrust. From 1969 to 1982 the Federal Trade Commission and the Justice Department undertook a new wave of dominant firm exclusionary conduct cases. Such matters did not employ no-fault concepts, but, in the tradition of *Alcoa*, they rested upon relatively broad views of what constitutes improper exclusionary conduct. In this period the federal antitrust authorities brought abuse of dominance cases against major firms in the computer, telecommunications, petroleum, food, photocopier, chemical, and tire industries. With rare exceptions, such as the Justice Department's restructuring of AT&T and an FTC consent decree that diminished the market power of Xerox in the copier industry, the government failed to establish liability in these matters.

The deconcentration proposals of the late 1950s and the 1960s had another important effect. They stimulated research and discussion concerning the structuralist assumptions that had guided antitrust policy since *Alcoa*. As the evidence (much of it assembled by Chicago School figures such as Yale Brozen, Harold Demsetz, and Richard Posner) began to mount that broad-based assaults on concentration were neither analytically justified nor costless, serious opposition arose within academia, government agencies, and the business community. A catalyzing event took place in 1974 in what came to be known as the Airlie House Conference. *See* INDUSTRIAL CONCENTRATION: THE NEW LEARNING (Harvey J. Goldschmid et al., eds., 1974) (collecting papers and proceedings at Airlie House Conference). At the Airlie House meeting, critics of structuralism synthesized a developing literature that challenged the economic basis for deconcentration. The results of the conference and related research were widely seen as refuting major elements of structuralist oligopoly theory and discrediting efforts to deconcentrate industries. By drawing critical scrutiny to structuralism, the deconcentration proposals indirectly helped inject Chicago School views into the mainstream of antitrust analysis and thus helped foster a broader conservative redirection of antitrust.

Until the mid-1970s, *Alcoa*'s expansive concept of improper exclusion influenced antitrust policy and jurisprudence concerning dominant firms. By the end of the 1970s, however, the ascent of Chicago School and other academic perspectives in the antitrust literature and in the courts provided different answers to the Section 2 policy questions framed in Judge Hand's opinion. Decisions in this era reflect increased concern with efficiency, with preserving incentives for dominant firms to compete aggressively, and supplying clear rules by which companies can plan operations to minimize antitrust risk. Two landmarks in this development stand out. The first is *Berkey Photo, Inc. v. Eastman Kodak Co.*, 603 F.2d 263 (2d Cir. 1979). In largely rejecting a private challenge to Kodak's conduct in the amateur film and camera markets, the court of appeals harshly criticized *Alcoa* and called Judge Hand's analysis of the monopolization conduct element a standardless "wishing well" that lent itself to ready manipulation. 603 F.2d at 273.

The second landmark appeared in 1980, as the Federal Trade Commission contributed to the new, efficiency-oriented jurisprudence in resolving its challenge to Du Pont's conduct in the chemical industry. The Commission alleged that Du Pont violated Section 5 of the FTC Act by attempting to monopolize the market for titanium dioxide, a chemical pigment used in making white paint. When the FTC issued its administrative complaint in 1978, Du Pont accounted for 42 percent of titanium dioxide sales. The complaint alleged that the company had acted illegally by announcing new expansions of capacity to capture all anticipated increases in demand—the same kind of conduct condemned as monopolization in *Alcoa*. In prosecuting the case, the FTC staff introduced internal Du Pont documents indicating that the company believed its announcements of new capacity would discourage entry and expansion by its rivals and enable Du Pont to charge supra-competitive prices. An administrative trial absolved the company of liability, and the Commission voted 5–0 to dismiss its complaint.

We now turn to some additional and important foundation developments that have influenced the courts' approach to the question of power. We will return to the related issue of conduct when we look at more contemporary developments in the law of monopolization in Section C, *infra*.

2. ECONOMIC ANALYSIS OF MARKET DEFINITION: THE *CELLOPHANE* DECISION (AND FALLACY)

A competition policy system could take many approaches to defining "monopoly." Modern economics treats *market power* as the ability to charge prices above a competitive level without suffering an immediate and unprofitably substantial loss of sales. By this measure, however, many firms have some market power. An antitrust system that scrutinized all instances of market power would require an immense investment in enforcement resources and would likely deter some procompetitive activities. As a concession to administrative necessity and in order to target the most serious market imperfections, antitrust systems ordinarily equate monopoly or dominance with *substantial and durable* market power.

Even with broad agreement on this principle, one must devise practical methods for deciding whether a firm possesses substantial market power. In evidentiary terms, we can think of the two principal methods of proof in two categories: *direct* evidence and *circumstantial* evidence. The main direct techniques for identifying substantial market power are to (a) measure the elasticity of demand for the products of the firm believed to possess a monopoly or (b) show that the alleged monopolist actually has used business methods other than superior performance to exclude its rivals from the market.

Problems in using direct evidence to identify monopoly power have elevated the importance of circumstantial proof. For nearly a century, courts have used the defendant's share of sales—its "market share"—as the chief circumstantial measurement tool. *Alcoa* illustrated that to use market shares to measure market power, one first must define a *relevant market*. As we learn in Chapter 5, which addresses mergers, the relevant market has *product* and *geographic* dimensions. Courts typically determine the product dimension by identifying the array of products that customers regard as acceptable substitutes for the defendant's product. The relevant market's geographic bounds are set by studying the location of suppliers from which a customer might purchase products deemed to be acceptable substitutes for the alleged monopolist's products. After drawing the relevant market's boundaries, the court calculates the defendant's market share by comparing its activity in the relevant product (measured by sales, units, or capacity) to the activity of all firms in the relevant market.

The value of market shares as proxies for measuring market power depends on the soundness of the market definition. Has the court correctly decided which products customers regard as acceptable substitutes for the defendant's products? Has it properly identified, and assigned proper market shares to all suppliers who serve the relevant market? Does a modest market share conclusively establish the lack of substantial market power? Does the presence of a high share invariably prove that defendant is a monopolist? The reliability of the answers given to these questions deeply influences the importance one should credit to market shares, as we have already observed in *Alcoa*.

As is discussed in Sidebar 4–3, the Justice Department's success in achieving a finding of liability in *Alcoa* inspired a new wave of efforts following World War II to enforce Section 2 of the Sherman Act. One of the most important of these initiatives was the *Cellophane* case, which we turn to now. In a complaint filed in 1947, the government charged du Pont with monopolization, attempted monopolization, and conspiracy to monopolize in a market consisting of cellophane. The trial court ruled for du Pont on all issues, and the government appealed to the Supreme Court.

The pivotal issue before the Court was whether du Pont had monopoly power. The company argued that buyers of cellophane routinely turned to other flexible packaging materials when du Pont attempted to raise the price of cellophane. Because cellophane appeared to face competition from numerous close substitutes, du Pont contended that the relevant market consisted of a wide range of flexible wrapping materials, in which cellophane was but one product. In such a market, du Pont's market share would fall well below the threshold of concern articulated in cases such as *Standard Oil* (1911) and *Alcoa* (1945). *See supra Note on the Origins of Alcoa's Market Share Benchmarks.*

Both the trial court and the Supreme Court found du Pont's view persuasive. The case provided the Supreme Court with its own opportunity to further explain the methodology courts should use to define markets and calculate market shares. Although the Court's analysis of the evidence concerning the flexible packaging materials sector has attracted extensive criticism, its doctrinal formula for defining the relevant market remains the basic test that courts and enforcement agencies use today in a variety of antitrust cases. As you review the case excerpt below, consider the methodology the Court uses to define du Pont's market share, and look for possible flaws in its analysis. Consider also how and why the analysis of market power and market definition are so integral to monopolization analysis and, as we shall see in the next Chapter, to merger analysis.

UNITED STATES V. E. I. DU PONT DE NEMOURS & CO.
United States Supreme Court, 1956.
351 U.S. 377, 76 S.Ct. 994, 100 L.Ed. 1264.

MR. JUSTICE REED delivered the opinion of the Court.

* * *

* * * The appeal, as specifically stated by the Government, 'attacks only the ruling that du Pont has not monopolized trade in cellophane.' At issue for determination is only this alleged violation by du Pont of § 2 of the Sherman Act.

During the period that is relevant to this action, du Pont produced almost 75% of the cellophane sold in the United States, and cellophane constituted less than 20% of all 'flexible packaging material' sales. * * *

The Government contends that, by so dominating cellophane production, du Pont monopolized a 'part of the trade or commerce' in violation of § 2. Respondent agrees that cellophane is a product which constitutes 'a 'part' of commerce within the meaning of Section 2.' But it contends that the prohibition of § 2 against monopolization is not violated because it does not have the power to control the price of cellophane or to exclude competitors from the market in which cellophane is sold. The court below found that the 'relevant market for determining the extent of du Pont's market control is the market for flexible packaging materials,' and that competition from those other materials prevented du Pont from possessing monopoly powers in its sales of cellophane.

The Government asserts that cellophane and other wrapping materials are neither substantially fungible nor like priced. For these reasons, it argues that the market for other wrappings is distinct from the market for cellophane and that the competition afforded cellophane by other wrappings is not strong enough to be considered in determining whether du Pont has monopoly powers. Market delimitation is necessary under du Pont's theory to determine whether an alleged monopolist violates Section 2. The ultimate consideration in such a determination is whether the defendants control the price and competition in the market for such part of trade or commerce as they are charged with monopolizing. Every manufacturer is the sole producer of the particular commodity it makes but its control in the above sense of the relevant market depends upon the availability of alternative commodities for buyers: i.e., whether there is a cross-elasticity of demand between cellophane and the other wrappings. This interchangeability is largely gauged by the purchase of competing products for similar uses considering the price, characteristics and adaptability of the competing commodities. The court below found that the flexible wrappings afforded such alternatives. This Court must determine whether the trial court erred in its estimate of the competition afforded cellophane by other materials.

The burden of proof, of course, was upon the Government to establish monopoly. This the trial court held the Government failed to do, upon findings of fact and law stated at length by that court. For the United States to succeed in this Court now, it must show that erroneous legal tests were applied to essential findings of fact or that the findings themselves were 'clearly erroneous' * * *.

I.   *Factual Background.*—For consideration of the issue as to monopolization, a general summary of the development of cellophane is useful.

In the early 1900's, Jacques Brandenberger, a Swiss chemist, attempted to make tablecloths impervious to dirt by spraying them with liquid viscose (a cellulose solution available in quantity from wood pulp) and by coagulating this coating. His idea failed, but he noted that the coating peeled off in a transparent film. This first 'cellophane' was thick, hard, and not perfectly transparent, but Brandenberger apparently foresaw commercial possibilities in his discovery. By 1908 he developed the first machine for the manufacture of transparent sheets of regenerated cellulose. The 1908 product was not satisfactory, but by 1912 Brandenberger was making a saleable thin flexible film used in gas masks. He obtained patents to cover the machinery and the essential ideas of his process.

* * *

In 1917 Brandenberger assigned his patents to La Cellophane Societe Anonyme and joined that organization. Thereafter developments in the production of cellophane somewhat paralleled those taking place in artificial textiles. Chemical science furnished the knowledge for perfecting the new products. The success of the artificial products has been enormous. Du Pont was an American leader in the field of synthetics and learned of cellophane's successes through an associate, Comptoir des Textiles Artificiel.

In 1923 du Pont organized with La Cellophane an American company for the manufacture of plain cellophane. The undisputed findings are that:

> 'On December 26, 1923, an agreement was executed between duPont Cellophane Company and La Cellophane by which La Cellophane licensed duPont Cellophane Company exclusively under its United States cellophane patents, and granted duPont Cellophane Company the exclusive right to make and sell in North and Central America under La Cellophane's secret processes for

cellophane manufacture. DuPont Cellophane Company granted to La Cellophane exclusive rights for the rest of the world under any cellophane patents or processes duPont Cellophane Company might develop.'

* * *

Sylvania, an American affiliate of a Belgian producer of cellophane * * *, began the manufacture of cellophane in the United States in 1930. * * * Since 1934 Sylvania has produced about 25% of United States cellophane.

An important factor in the growth of cellophane production and sales was the perfection of moistureproof cellophane, a superior product of du Pont research and patented by that company through a 1927 application. Plain cellophane has little resistance to the passage of moisture vapor. Moistureproof cellophane has a composition added which keeps moisture in and out of the packed commodity. This patented type of cellophane has had a demand with much more rapid growth than the plain.

In 1931 Sylvania began the manufacture of moistureproof cellophane under its own patents. After negotiations over patent rights, du Pont in 1933 licensed Sylvania to manufacture and sell moistureproof cellophane produced under the du Pont patents at a royalty of 2% of sales. These licenses with the plain cellophane licenses, from the Belgian company, made Sylvania a full cellophane competitor, limited on moistureproof sales by the terms of the licenses to 20% of the combined sales of the two companies of that type by the payment of a prohibitive royalty on the excess. There was never an excess production. The limiting clause was dropped on January 1, 1945, and Sylvania was acquired in 1946 by the American Viscose Corporation with assets of over two hundred million dollars.

Between 1928 and 1950, du Pont's sales of plain cellophane increased from $3,131,608 to $9,330,776. Moistureproof sales increased from $603,222 to $89,850,416, although prices were continuously reduced. It could not be said that this immense increase in use was solely or even largely attributable to the superior quality of cellophane or to the technique or business acumen of du Pont, though doubtless those factors were important. The growth was a part of the expansion of the commodity-packaging habits of business, a by-product of general efficient competitive merchandising to meet modern demands. The profits, which were large, apparently arose from this trend in marketing, the development of the industrial use of chemical research and production of synthetics, rather than from elimination of other producers from the relevant market. * * *

* * *

III. *The Sherman Act, § 2.* * * * If cellophane is the 'market' that du Pont is found to dominate, it may be assumed it does have monopoly power over that 'market.' Monopoly power is the power to control prices or exclude competition. It seems apparent that du Pont's power to set the price of cellophane has been limited only by the competition afforded by other flexible packaging materials. Moreover, it may be practically impossible for anyone to commence manufacturing cellophane without full access to du Pont's technique. However, du Pont has no power to prevent competition from other wrapping materials. The trial court consequently had to determine whether competition from the other wrappings prevented du Pont from possessing monopoly power in violation of Section 2. Price and competition are so intimately entwined that any discussion of theory must treat them as one. It is inconceivable that price could be controlled without power over competition or vice versa. This approach to the determination of monopoly power is strengthened by this Court's conclusion in prior cases that, when an alleged monopolist has power over price and competition, an intention to monopolize in a proper case may be assumed.

If a large number of buyers and sellers deal freely in a standardized product, such as salt or wheat, we have complete or pure competition. Patents, on the other hand, furnish the most familiar type of classic monopoly. As the producers of a standardized product bring about significant differentiations of quality, designed, or packaging in the product that permit differences of use, competition becomes to a greater or less degree incomplete and the producer's power over price and competition greater over his article and its use, according to the differentiation he is able to create and maintain. A retail seller may have in one sense a monopoly on certain trade because of location, as an isolated country store or filling station, or because no one else makes a product of just the quality or attractiveness of his product, as for example in cigarettes. Thus one can theorize that we have monopolistic competition in every nonstandardized commodity with each manufacturer having power over the price and production of his own product. However, this power that, let us say, automobile or soft-drink manufactures have over their trademarked products is not the power that makes an illegal monopoly. Illegal power must be appraised in terms of the competitive market for the product.

Determination of the competitive market for commodities depends on how different from one another are the offered commodities in character or use, how far buyers will go to substitute one commodity for another. For example, one can think of building materials as in commodity competition but one could hardly say that brick competed with steel or wood or cement or stone in the meaning of Sherman Act litigation; the products are too different. This is the interindustry competition emphasized by some economists. On the other hand, there are certain differences in the formulae for soft drinks but one can hardly say that each one is an illegal monopoly. Whatever the market may be, we hold that control of price or competition establishes the existence of monopoly power under Section 2. Section 2 requires the application of a reasonable approach in determining the existence of monopoly power just as surely as did Section 1. This of course does not mean that there can be a reasonable monopoly. Our next step is to determine whether du Pont has monopoly power over cellophane: that is, power over its price in relation to or competition with other commodities. The charge was monopolization of cellophane. The defense, that cellophane was merely a part of the relevant market for flexible packaging materials.

IV. *The Relevant Market.*—When a product is controlled by one interest, without substitutes available in the market, there is monopoly power. Because most products have possible substitutes, we cannot, as we said in *Times-Picayune Pub. Co. v. United States,* * * * give 'that infinite range' to the definition of substitutes. Nor is it a proper interpretation of the Sherman Act to require that products be fungible to be considered in the relevant market.

The Government argues:

'we do not here urge that in no circumstances may competition of substitutes negative possession of monopolistic power over trade in a product. The decisions make it clear at the least that the courts will not consider substitutes other than those which are substantially fungible with the monopolized product and sell at substantially the same price.'

But where there are market alternatives that buyers may readily use for their purposes, illegal monopoly does not exist merely because the product said to be monopolized differs from others. If it were not so, only physically identical products would be a part of the market. To accept the Government's argument, we would have to conclude that the manufactures of plain as well as moistureproof cellophane were monopolists, and so with films such as Pliofilm, foil, glassine, polyethylene, and Saran, for each of these wrapping materials is distinguishable. These were all exhibits in the case. New wrappings appear, generally similar to cellophane, is each a monopoly? What is called for is an appraisal of the 'cross-elasticity' of demand in the trade. The varying circumstances of each case determine the result. In considering what is the relevant market for determining the control of price and competition, no more definite rule can be declared than that commodities reasonably interchangeable by consumers for the same purposes make up that 'part of the trade or commerce', monopolization of which may be illegal. As respects flexible packaging materials, the market geographically is nationwide.

* * * In determining the market under the Sherman Act, it is the use or uses to which the commodity is put that control. The selling price

between commodities with similar uses and different characteristics may vary, so that the cheaper product can drive out the more expensive. Or, the superior quality of higher priced articles may make dominant the more desirable. Cellophane costs more than many competing products and less than a few. But whatever the price, there are various flexible wrapping materials that are bought by manufacturers for packaging their goods in their own plants or are sold to converters who shape and print them for use in the packaging of the commodities to be wrapped.

Cellophane differs from other flexible packaging materials. From some it differs more than from others. The basic materials from which the wrappings are made * * * are aluminum, cellulose acetate, chlorides, wood pulp, rubber hydrochloride, and ethylene gas. It will adequately illustrate the similarity in characteristics of the various products by noting here * * * glassine. Its use is almost as extensive as cellophane, and many of its characteristics equally or more satisfactory to users.

It may be admitted that cellophane combines the desirable elements of transparency, strength and cheapness more definitely than any of the others. * * *

But, despite cellophane's advantages it has to meet competition from other materials in every one of its uses. * * * Food products are the chief outlet, with cigarettes next. The Government makes no challenge to [the trial court's finding] that cellophane furnishes less than 7% of wrappings for bakery products, 25% for candy, 32% for snacks, 35% for meats and poultry, 27% for crackers and biscuits, 47% for fresh produce, and 34% for frozen foods. Seventy-five to eighty percent of cigarettes are wrapped in cellophane. Thus, cellophane shares the packaging market with others. The over-all result is that cellophane accounts for 17.9% of flexible wrapping materials, measured by the wrapping surface.

Moreover a very considerable degree of functional interchangeability exists between these products * * *. It will be noted * * * that except as to permeability to gases, cellophane has no qualities that are not possessed by a number of other materials. Meat will do as an example of interchangeability. Although du Pont's sales to the meat industry have reached 19,000,000 pounds annually, nearly 35%, this volume is attributed 'to the rise of self-service retailing of fresh meat.' In fact, since the popularity of self-service meats, du Pont has lost 'a considerable proportion' of this packaging business to Pliofilm. Pliofilm is more expensive than cellophane, but its superior physical characteristics apparently offset cellophane's price advantage. While retailers shift continually between the two, the trial court found that Pliofilm is increasing its share of the business. One further example is worth noting. Before World War II, du Pont cellophane wrapped between 5 and 10% of baked and smoked meats. The peak year was 1933. Thereafter du Pont was unable to meet the competition of Sylvania and of greaseproof paper. Its sales declined and the 1933 volume was not reached again until 1947. It will be noted that greaseproof paper, glassine, waxed paper, foil and Pliofilm are used as well as cellophane. * * *

An element for consideration as to cross-elasticity of demand between products is the responsiveness of the sales of one product to price changes of the other. If a slight decrease in the price of cellophane causes a considerable number of customers of other flexible wrappings to switch to cellophane, it would be an indication that a high cross-elasticity of demand exists between them; that the products compete in the same market. The court below held that the '(g)reat sensitivity of customers in the flexible packaging markets to price or quality changes' prevented du Pont from possessing monopoly control over price. The record sustains these findings.

We conclude that cellophane's interchangeability with the other materials mentioned suffices to make it a part of this flexible packaging material market.

The Government stresses the fact that the variation in price between cellophane and other materials demonstrates they are noncompetitive. As these products are all flexible wrapping materials, it seems reasonable to consider, as was done at the trial, their comparative cost to the consumer in terms of square area. * * *. Cellophane costs two or three times as much, surface measure, as its chief competitors for the flexible wrapping market, glassine and greaseproof papers. Other forms of cellulose wrappings and those from other chemical or mineral substances, with the exception of aluminum foil, are more expensive. The uses of these materials * * * are largely to wrap small packages for retail distribution. The wrapping is a relatively small proportion of the entire cost of the article. Different producers need different qualities in wrappings and their need may vary from time to time as their products undergo change. But the necessity for flexible wrappings is the central and unchanging demand. We cannot say that these differences in cost gave du Pont monopoly power over prices in view of the findings of fact on that subject.

It is the variable characteristics of the different flexible wrappings and the energy and ability with which the manufacturers push their wares that determine choice. A glance at 'Modern Packaging,' a trade journal, will give, by its various advertisements, examples of the competition among manufacturers for the flexible packaging market. The trial judge visited the 1952 Annual Packaging Show at Atlantic City, with the consent of counsel. He observed exhibits offered by 'machinery manufacturers, converters and manufacturers of flexible packaging materials.' He stated that these personal observations confirmed his estimate of the competition between cellophane and other packaging materials. * * *

The facts above considered dispose also of any contention that competitors have been excluded by du Pont from the packaging material market. That market has many producers and there is no proof du Pont ever has possessed power to exclude any of them from the rapidly expanding flexible packaging market. The Government apparently concedes as much, for it states that 'lack of power to inhibit entry into this so-called market (i.e., flexible packaging materials), comprising widely disparate products, is no indicium of absence of power to exclude competition in the manufacture and sale of cellophane.' The record shows the multiplicity of competitors and the financial strength of some with individual assets running to the hundreds of millions. Indeed, the trial court found that du Pont could not exclude competitors even from the manufacture of cellophane, an immaterial matter if the market is flexible packaging material. Nor can we say that du Pont's profits, while liberal (according to the Government 15.9% net after taxes on the 1937–1947 average), demonstrate the existence of a monopoly without proof of lack of comparable profits during those years in other prosperous industries. Cellophane was a leader over 17%, in the flexible packaging materials market. There is no showing that du Pont's rate of return was greater or less than that of other producers of flexible packaging materials.

The 'market' which one must study to determine when a producer has monopoly power will vary with the part of commerce under consideration. The tests are constant. That market is composed of products that have reasonable interchangeability for the purposes for which they are produced—price, use and qualities considered. While the application of the tests remains uncertain, it seems to us that du Pont should not be found to monopolize cellophane when that product has the competition and interchangeability with other wrappings that this record shows.

On the findings of the District Court, its judgment is affirmed.

[JUSTICE FRANKFURTER's concurring opinion is omitted. Eds.]

[The dissenting opinion of MR. CHIEF JUSTICE WARREN, with whom MR. JUSTICE BLACK and MR. JUSTICE DOUGLAS joined, is omitted. Eds.]

NOTE ON THE CONTRIBUTION OF DU PONT TO OUR UNDERSTANDING OF MARKET DEFINITION

The outcomes in both *Alcoa* and *du Pont* (*Cellophane*) hinged on the definition of the relevant market, because the courts were using market share to infer monopoly power. In *Alcoa*, the court reached its conclusion that Alcoa's market share was 90%, and hence sufficient, only by including Alcoa's virgin ingot and internal fabrication, but excluding all secondary and recycled aluminum. In *duPont*, if the market was limited to cellophane, du Pont held a market share of nearly 75 percent, and the Supreme Court would have deemed it to have monopoly power. In a market defined as all flexible packaging materials, du Pont's market share was less than 20 percent—far below the threshold earlier cases had associated with dominance. The Supreme Court majority chose the second of these definitions and absolved the company of Section 2 liability.

When market power is inferred from market shares, courts must define markets. Market definition is often a critical step in antitrust litigation, therefore, and frequently the substantive issue on which the outcome of cases turns. Once markets are defined, courts can identify the firms participating in those markets, and determine each firm's share of sales revenues, units sold or produced, capacity, or other measure of competitive significance.

Market definition involves specifying both a product and a geographic region. On both dimensions an antitrust market collects goods and locations that are not literally identical. If the product market were defined as soft drinks, for example, it would collect carbonated beverages in a range of flavors (cola, lemon-lime, etc.); if the geographic market were defined as the United States, it would collect locations as distant as Alaska, California, Florida, and Maine. The primary basis for market definition in antitrust law, established by *du Pont* (*Cellophane*)), is *buyer substitution*: an antitrust market is a collection of products that buyers view as reasonably interchangeable (at current or likely future prices) and locations they view as reasonably interchangeable for purchasing products.

This brief sketch ignores a wide range of issues and qualifications we will meet when we study market definition in greater detail in Chapter 5 in connection with mergers. We will learn there, for example, about the types of evidence courts rely upon to define markets. We will also meet "price discrimination" markets, which are defined by targeted customers as well as by products and locations. Chapter 5 also discusses the use and misuse of "submarkets" (markets narrowly defined within broad markets), an approach to market definition based on identifying a "cluster of services," the "hypothetical monopolist" test for market definition employed by the U.S. government's Horizontal Merger Guidelines, and the use of "critical loss analysis" for defining markets. That Chapter also notes that in non-merger cases some courts define markets based upon seller alternatives (supply substitution) as well as based upon buyer substitution (as in *Cellophane*). Readers interested in the cross-price elasticity of demand, which the *Cellophane* case referred to as an element it considered when defining markets, should consult the *Note on Cross-Price Elasticity of Demand* in Chapter 5, *infra*.

Notwithstanding the doctrinal importance of the market definition approach adopted in *Cellophane,* which established that a market is a collection of products reasonably interchangeable by buyers, the Supreme Court's application of that test to the facts in *Cellophane* has been criticized.

Today, commentators refer to this criticism as the *"Cellophane* fallacy" or *"Cellophane* trap." The issue is discussed in Sidebar 4–4.

> ## Sidebar 4–4:
> ## The *Cellophane* Fallacy
>
> The Court majority's conclusion in *Cellophane* that other flexible packaging materials such as glassine and pliofilm significantly constrained du Pont in setting cellophane prices aroused considerable criticism. The Court majority reasoned that, because du Pont's efforts to raise cellophane prices induced users to switch to other products, the company lacked substantial market power. The flaw in this analysis is that the switching to other products may have taken place after du Pont already had set cellophane prices at monopoly levels and was trying to boost them still further. Because buyers grow more likely to switch away from a product as its price increases, evaluating their switching behavior at the price a monopolist charges can lead to the mistaken inference that the dominant firm does not have market power when the firm is actually exercising it.
>
> A hypothetical (and unrealistic) example will help clarify the point. If prices for trans-Atlantic airline tickets were to rise, some customers who would fly today would instead cross the ocean by steamship—with more travelers substituting ship travel for air travel the higher the airlines charge for flying. Steamships would become a better substitute for airlines the higher the price of airline tickets. To keep the example simple, assume further that there are no other plausible demand substitutes for airlines.
>
> Suppose a court is deciding an antitrust case challenging an agreement among airlines that has yet to take effect, or a proposed merger between two major airlines. In those hypothetical cases, the allegation likely involves the *prospective* exercise of market power—whether the conduct would likely lead to the exercise of market power (or, at least, greater market power than before) and higher prices in the future. In evaluating such allegations, it would be important to know whether buyer substitution to steamships today would or would not constrain the airlines from raising price. That question would be evaluated when the market is defined.
>
> Market definition in a prospective case would NOT raise the concern termed the *Cellophane* fallacy. If the possibility of buyer substitution to steamships would prevent the airlines

from raising price even if they were to attempt to exercise market power, the court should define an *all* trans-Atlantic travel product market, one broader than trans-Atlantic air travel that encompasses steamship travel as well. The consequence would be to reduce the market share of the firms engaged in the conduct under review (agreement or merger); if the shares are low enough they may suggest that it is implausible that the conduct would allow firms to exercise market power. But if buyer substitution to steamships would be insufficient to deter the airlines from raising price, the court should define a trans-Atlantic *airline* travel product market. If defendants have a high share in that market, that evidence may suggest that the firms could exercise market power.

Now suppose instead that the antitrust allegation involves the *retrospective* exercise of market power. That is, suppose the plaintiff claims, as in *Cellophane,* that the defendant is currently exercising market power. In the hypothetical example, a retrospective market power allegation might arise in a monopolization case, in which a dominant airline is said to have raised price for trans-Atlantic flights above competitive levels, or in a non-monopolization case, in which several airlines are said to have acted collectively in the past to adopt a practice that allowed them to raise price. Because plaintiff is alleging pre-existing market power, the *Cellophane* fallacy could arise.

In a prospective harm case, the extent to which trans-Atlantic travelers view steamship service as a substitute for airline service at current prices helps determine whether the anticompetitive theory is more likely than an alternative competitive theory. Not so in a retrospective harm case. Focusing for simplicity on the monopolization setting, plaintiff's theory is that past conduct allowed the defendant to raise price above competitive levels (if the allegation is that defendant obtained market power), or else that defendant's present conduct prevented an outbreak of competition from rivals or potential entrants that would lead to lower, and more competitive prices (if the allegation is that defendant maintained market power). If either of these anticompetitive theories is correct, the price of air travel today would be well above the competitive level; the price has presumably risen to the point at which customer substitution to steamships would make a further price increase unprofitable. At that price, many buyers would view steamships as substitutes for airlines.

The problem facing the court in this retrospective harm case is that the plaintiff's supposition that steamship travel would not be a good substitute for airline travel at a competitive price for airline service may be incorrect. Perhaps the current price *is* the competitive price, as the defendant would likely claim, and the conduct under review neither permitted defendant to raise price above the competitive level nor prevented new competition from eroding current prices. Moreover, the defendant may contend, it is the possibility of buyer substitution to steamship travel that has prevented airline prices from rising above the competitive level all along. If the defendant is correct, we would expect to find that many buyers view steamships as substitutes for airlines—just as we had previously found when assuming that the plaintiff is correct. Hence, buyer substitution to steamships today (at current prices) would not discriminate between plaintiff's and defendant's theory of the case; we would expect to see such substitution regardless of whether the defendant is currently exercising market power or not.

Under such circumstances, the extent of buyer substitution to steamships at current prices (or more precisely, to anticipate the discussion of market definition under the Merger Guidelines in Chapter 5, the extent of buyer substitution in the event of a price increase from the current level) would not show whether steamships constrain the alleged exercise of market power by airlines. If a court broadens the product market beyond airlines to steamships based on observing buyer substitution in this retrospective case, it may conclude that the defendant has a low market share, and, in consequence, no market power, when it is possible that the defendant is actually exercising market power. The mistaken inference would arise if defendant had previously raised the price of airline tickets to a monopoly level, at which steamship travel became a substitute for air travel for many consumers. Critics of the Supreme Court's *Cellophane* decision say that the Court made just this mistake: it used a market definition method that would necessarily lead it to define a broad product market, and reject plaintiffs' claims, regardless of whether plaintiff or defendant was correct.

What can a court do to avoid this criticism when defining markets in a retrospective case? In addition to evaluating buyer substitution at current prices, as it would do in a prospective case, the court could seek to evaluate the extent to which buyer substitution from airlines to steamships would decline as the price of airline travel decreases. As airline travel becomes less expensive relative to steamship travel, one would expect fewer buyers to view the two as substitutes. If the extent to which air travelers view steamship service as a substitute falls off rapidly as the price of air travel declines, that would suggest that buyer substitution would not have prevented the anticompetitive price increase alleged by plaintiffs and lead a court to exclude steamships from the product market. Although the defendant may have a high share in a product market limited to air travel, it may still be able to resist the inference of market power, for example by proffering direct evidence that would overcome the implication of the market share evidence or by showing that entry was easy.

Conversely, if the extent to which air travelers view steamship service as a substitute does not fall off much as the price of air travel declines, that would suggest that buyer substitution to steamship travel could prevent an anticompetitive price increase in trans-Atlantic air travel, and thus lead a court to include steamship service along with airline service in a product market defined as all trans-Atlantic travel. Although the defendant airline will likely have a lower share in this product market than in a market limited to air travel, its share may still be high enough to prove market power, and even if it is not, the plaintiff may be able to prove market power or anticompetitive effects through direct evidence that overcomes the implication of a low market share.

In the *Cellophane* case, the Supreme Court majority found that various types of flexible packaging materials are substitutes for cellophane, relied on that finding to define a broad flexible packaging materials product market, found that defendant du Pont had a small share (less than 20%) in that market, and concluded that du Pont lacked monopoly power and was not liable for monopolization. Is the substitution evidence relied upon by the Court equally consistent with the possibility that du Pont was a monopolist of cellophane (with a share of nearly 75%), and, by exercising market power, that it raised the price of cellophane above the competitive level to a point at which other wrapping materials became substitutes for many buyers?

For further discussion of these issues, and other approaches to addressing the *Cellophane* fallacy, see Lawrence J. White, *Market Power and Market Definition in Monopolization Cases,* in II ABA SECTION OF ANTITRUST LAW, ISSUES IN COMPETITION LAW AND POLICY 913 (2008); Jonathan B. Baker, *Market Definition: An Analytical Overview*, 74 ANTITRUST L.J. 129, 162–66 (2007). On the broader lesson of this controversy, involving the importance of relating market definition to the allegation of harm to competition, see Steven C. Salop, *The First Principles Approach to Antitrust,* Kodak, *and Antitrust at the Millennium*, 68 ANTITRUST L.J. 187 (2000).

C. THE CONTEMPORARY LAW AND ECONOMICS OF MONOPOLIZATION

As we indicated earlier, Section 2 of the Sherman Act does not prohibit the status of monopoly. Monopolization doctrine requires the plaintiff to show that the defendant used improper exclusionary acts to gain or sustain substantial market power. How should the law define what behavior is improper? Developing and selling a superior product—for example, introducing jet aircraft that make propeller-driven airliners obsolete—can drive inferior products and their makers from the market. Such behavior takes sales away from rivals and can "exclude" them, yet the means of exclusion (creating new and superior products) yields great benefits to society. An undiscriminating ban on all conduct that excludes could encompass virtually any business tactic that increased a firm's sales, no matter how much the practice in question increased consumer well-being by reducing prices or improving product quality. Perhaps the chief analytical challenge in establishing standards of conduct for dominant firms, therefore, is to determine whether specific acts (or certain classes of conduct) that may result in significant exclusion also have competitively redeeming features that might warrant shielding them from liability. Hence conduct that merely excludes must be differentiated from what the law condemns as "exclusionary" conduct.

The traditional framework developed in *Alcoa* and other cases such as *Grinnell* suggested that the issue of conduct should be judged in isolation as part of a two stage inquiry. The "power *plus*-conduct" formulation, *i.e.*, considering first whether the defendant has monopoly power, and only then whether it has "willfully acquired or maintained" that power, encouraged this analytical division. Conduct in turn has often been judged based on evidence of its effects on competition. One way to understand the raising rival's cost framework, for example, is to recognize that it examines *conduct* to see if it raises rival's costs; it examines *effects* of that conduct to see if it may confer power over price.

Yet power, conduct, and effects are almost always interrelated: power represents the potential to cause anticompetitive effects through conduct; observed anticompetitive effects evidence the exercise of power through conduct. The traditional power-plus-conduct formula did not readily lend itself to this kind of simultaneous evaluation of power, conduct, and effects. Sometimes the same evidence tends to establish both power and effects.

In contrast to the traditional two-step approach, Professor Steven Salop has argued for an integrated, "first principles" approach to analyzing alleged antitrust offenses:

> * * * The first principles approach centers on an examination of the competitive effects of the conduct at issue. This is appropriate because competitive effect is the true core of antitrust. Although market power and market definition have a role in antitrust analysis, their proper roles are as parts of and in reference to the primary evaluation of the alleged anticompetitive conduct and its likely market effects. They are not valued for their own sake, but rather for the roles they play in an evaluation of market effects.
>
> Market power and market definition, therefore, should not be analyzed in a vacuum or in a threshold test divorced from the conduct and allegations about its effects. Instead, market power should be measured as the power profitably to raise or maintain price above the competitive benchmark price, which is the price that would prevail in the absence of the alleged anticompetitive restraint. The competitive benchmark may be the current price, the perfectly competitive price, or some other in-between price, depending on the particular allegations of anticompetitive effect being asserted. This integrated approach to antitrust analysis is the first principles approach.

Steven C. Salop, *The First Principles Approach to Antitrust,* Kodak*, and Antitrust at the Millennium*, 68 ANTITRUST L.J. 187, 188–89 (2000).

This "first principles" approach is consistent with the Supreme Court's observation in *National Society of Professional Engineers* (*see supra* Chapter 2) that the relevant inquiry under Section 1 of the Sherman Act "focuses directly on the challenged restraint's impact on competitive conditions." 435 U.S. at 688. It is also consonant with the observation in *Indiana Federation of Dentists* that "[s]ince the purpose of the inquiries into market definition and market power is to determine whether an arrangement has the potential for genuine adverse effects on competition, 'proof of actual detrimental effects, such as a reduction of output,' can obviate the need for an inquiry into market power, which is but a 'surrogate for detrimental effects.' " *FTC v. Indiana Fed'n of Dentists*, 476 U.S. 447, 460–61 (1986) (*see supra* Chapter 2). The Court's observations in these two cases highlight two fundamental insights of the First Principles approach: (1) the central goal of antitrust analysis is to evaluate likely or actual anticompetitive effects; and (2) evaluation of power, conduct, and effects are necessarily interrelated. Assessment of the competitive effects of conduct involves evaluation of the constraints on the firm's exercise of market power. Conduct cannot be assessed without knowing whether the firm can exercise market power. Similarly, market definition and market power cannot be assessed without reference to the conduct and the competitive effects alleged (as we saw with respect to the *Cellophane* fallacy).

In this Section of the Chapter, therefore, we have excerpted a variety of the leading cases on monopolization without regard to the traditional, dichotomous framework. As you read the cases, note how the inquiries into power, conduct, and effects—even when formally divided—are necessarily interrelated.

1. NON-PRICE EXCLUSIONARY CONDUCT

Lorain Journal involved efforts by an incumbent firm to encumber a competitor's efforts to establish access to customers whose trade was essential to its survival. Other cases have posed the problem of a refusal to deal in the context of the incumbent's efforts to cease or adjust an existing pattern of cooperation with a competitor.

In our next case, Aspen Skiing, the owner of three of the four mountain slopes in Aspen, Colorado, decided to withdraw from a joint marketing arrangement with Aspen Highlands Skiing, the owner of the fourth slope. The two firms together had for some time offered an all-Aspen ticket that entitled skiers to ski any of the Aspen slopes for a single price. When Aspen Skiing ended the relationship, Aspen Highlands attacked the refusal to continue dealing as illegal monopolization. In one of its most important modern analyses of dominant firm conduct, the Supreme Court unanimously upheld the trial court's finding of liability.

Aspen Skiing's significance, however, is not limited to the narrow context of addressing refusals to deal. As you read the case, note how the Court moves beyond the traditional *Alcoa-Grinnell* formulation of "willful acquisition or maintenance" to more specifically define "exclusionary" conduct. Note too how the Court utilizes a structured framework for evaluating the effects—both pro- and anti-competitive—of allegedly exclusionary conduct. Finally, consider the economic theory behind the Court's conclusion that Aspen Skiing's conduct was properly labeled as "exclusionary."

ASPEN SKIING CO. V. ASPEN HIGHLANDS SKIING CORP.

United States Supreme Court, 1985.
472 U.S. 585, 105 S.Ct. 2847, 86 L.Ed.2d 467.

JUSTICE STEVENS delivered the opinion of the Court.

In a private treble-damages action, the jury found that petitioner Aspen Skiing Company (Ski Co.) had monopolized the market for downhill skiing services in Aspen, Colorado. The question presented is whether that finding is erroneous as a matter of law because it rests on an assumption that a firm with monopoly power has a duty to cooperate with its smaller rivals in a marketing arrangement in order to avoid violating § 2 of the Sherman Act.

* * *

Aspen is a destination ski resort with a reputation for "super powder," "a wide range of runs," and an "active night life," including "some of the best restaurants in North America." Between 1945 and 1960, private investors independently developed three major facilities for downhill skiing: Aspen Mountain (Ajax), Aspen Highlands (Highlands), and Buttermilk. A fourth mountain, Snowmass, opened in 1967.

The development of any major additional facilities is hindered by practical considerations and regulatory obstacles. The identification of appropriate topographical conditions for a new site and substantial financing are both essential. Most of the terrain in the vicinity of Aspen that is suitable for downhill skiing cannot be used for that purpose without the approval of the United States Forest Service. That approval is contingent, in part, on environmental concerns. Moreover, the county government must also approve the project, and in recent years it has followed a policy of limiting growth.

Between 1958 and 1964, three independent companies operated Ajax, Highlands, and Buttermilk. In the early years, each company offered its own day or half-day tickets for use of its mountain. In 1962, however, the three competitors also introduced an interchangeable ticket.[7] The 6-day, all-Aspen ticket provided convenience to the vast majority of skiers who visited the resort for weekly periods, but preferred to remain flexible about what mountain they might ski each day during the visit. It also emphasized the unusual variety in ski mountains available in Aspen.

As initially designed, the all-Aspen ticket program consisted of booklets containing six coupons, each redeemable for a daily lift ticket at Ajax, Highlands, or Buttermilk. * * * The revenues from the sale of the 3-area coupon books were distributed in accordance with the number of coupons collected at each mountain.

In 1964, Buttermilk was purchased by Ski Co., but the interchangeable ticket program continued. In most seasons after it acquired Buttermilk, Ski Co. offered 2-area, 6-or 7-day tickets featuring Ajax and Buttermilk in competition with the 3-area, 6-coupon booklet. Although it sold briskly, the all-Aspen ticket did not sell as well as Ski Co.'s

---

[7]   Friedl Pfeiffer, one of the developers of Buttermilk, initiated the idea of an all-Aspen ticket at a luncheon with the owner of Highlands and the President of Ski Co. Pfeiffer, a native of Austria, informed his competitors that " '[i]n St. Anton, we have a mountain that has three different lift companies—lifts owned by three different lift companies. . . . We sell a ticket that is interchangeable.' It was good on any of those lifts; and he said, 'I think we should do the same thing here.' " * * *

multiarea ticket until Ski Co. opened Snowmass in 1967. Thereafter, the all-Aspen coupon booklet began to outsell Ski Co.'s ticket featuring only its mountains.

In the 1971–1972 season, the coupon booklets were discontinued and an "around the neck" all-Aspen ticket was developed. This refinement on the interchangeable ticket was advantageous to the skier, who no longer found it necessary to visit the ticket window every morning before gaining access to the slopes. Lift operators at Highlands monitored usage of the ticket in the 1971–1972 season by recording the ticket numbers of persons going onto the slopes of that mountain. Highlands officials periodically met with Ski Co. officials to review the figures recorded at Highlands, and to distribute revenues based on that count.

* * *

* * * Highlands' share of the revenues from the ticket was 17.5% in 1973–1974, 18.5% in 1974–1975, 16.8% in 1975–1976, and 13.2% in 1976–1977.[8] During these four seasons, Ski Co. did not offer its own 3-area, multi-day ticket in competition with the all-Aspen ticket.[9] By 1977, multiarea tickets accounted for nearly 35% of the total market. Holders of multiarea passes also accounted for additional daily ticket sales to persons skiing with them.

Between 1962 and 1977, Ski Co. and Highlands had independently offered various mixes of 1-day, 3-day, and 6-day passes at their own mountains. In every season except one, however, they had also offered some form of all-Aspen, 6-day ticket, and divided the revenues from those sales on the basis of usage. Nevertheless, for the 1977–1978 season, Ski Co. offered to continue the all-Aspen ticket only if Highlands would accept a 13.2% fixed share of the ticket's revenues.

Although that had been Highlands' share of the ticket revenues in 1976–1977, Highlands contended that that season was an inaccurate measure of its market performance since it had been marked by unfavorable weather and an unusually low number of visiting skiers. Moreover, Highlands wanted to continue to divide revenues on the basis of actual usage, as that method of distribution allowed it to compete for the daily loyalties of the skiers who had purchased the tickets. Fearing that the alternative might be no interchangeable ticket at all, and hoping to persuade Ski Co. to reinstate the usage division of revenues, Highlands

---

[8]   Highlands' share of the total market during those seasons, as measured in skier visits was 15.8% in 1973–1974, 17.1% in 1974–1975, 17.4% in 1975–1976, and 20.5% in 1976–1977.

[9]   In 1975, the Colorado Attorney General filed a complaint against Ski Co. and Highlands alleging, in part, that the negotiations over the 4-area ticket had provided them with a forum for price fixing in violation of § 1 of the Sherman Act and that they had attempted to monopolize the market for downhill skiing services in Aspen in violation of § 2. In 1977, the case was settled by a consent decree that permitted the parties to continue to offer the 4-area ticket provided that they set their own ticket prices unilaterally before negotiating its terms.

eventually accepted a fixed percentage of 15% for the 1977–1978 season. * * *

In the 1970's the management of Ski Co. increasingly expressed their dislike for the all-Aspen ticket. They complained that a coupon method of monitoring usage was administratively cumbersome. They doubted the accuracy of the survey and decried the "appearance, deportment, [and] attitude" of the college students who were conducting it. In addition, Ski Co.'s president had expressed the view that the 4-area ticket was siphoning off revenues that could be recaptured by Ski Co. if the ticket was discontinued. In fact, Ski Co. had reinstated its 3-area, 6-day ticket during the 1977–1978 season, but that ticket had been outsold by the 4-area, 6-day ticket nearly two to one.

In March 1978, the Ski Co. management recommended to the board of directors that the 4-area ticket be discontinued for the 1978–1979 season. The board decided to offer Highlands a 4-area ticket provided that Highlands would agree to receive a 12.5% fixed percentage of the revenue— considerably below Highlands' historical average based on usage. Later in the 1978–1979 season, a member of Ski Co.'s board of directors candidly informed a Highlands official that he had advocated making Highlands "an offer that [it] could not accept."

Finding the proposal unacceptable, Highlands suggested a distribution of the revenues based on usage to be monitored by coupons, electronic counting, or random sample surveys. If Ski Co. was concerned about who was to conduct the survey, Highlands proposed to hire disinterested ticket counters at its own expense—"somebody like Price Waterhouse"—to count or survey usage of the 4-area ticket at Highlands. Ski Co. refused to consider any counterproposals, and Highlands finally rejected the offer of the fixed percentage.

As far as Ski Co. was concerned, the all-Aspen ticket was dead. In its place Ski Co. offered the 3-area, 6-day ticket featuring only its mountains. In an effort to promote this ticket, Ski Co. embarked on a national advertising campaign that strongly implied to people who were unfamiliar with Aspen that Ajax, Buttermilk, and Snowmass were the only ski mountains in the area. For example, Ski Co. had a sign changed in the Aspen Airways waiting room at Stapleton Airport in Denver. The old sign had a picture of the four mountains in Aspen touting "Four Big Mountains" whereas the new sign retained the picture but referred only to three.

Ski Co. took additional actions that made it extremely difficult for Highlands to market its own multiarea package to replace the joint offering. Ski Co. discontinued the 3-day, 3-area pass for the 1978–1979 season, and also refused to sell Highlands any lift tickets, either at the tour operator's discount or at retail. Highlands finally developed an alternative product, the "Adventure Pack," which consisted of a 3-day pass at

Highlands and three vouchers, each equal to the price of a daily lift ticket at a Ski Co. mountain. The vouchers were guaranteed by funds on deposit in an Aspen bank, and were redeemed by Aspen merchants at full value. Ski Co., however, refused to accept them.

Later, Highlands redesigned the Adventure Pack to contain American Express Traveler's Checks or money orders instead of vouchers. Ski Co. eventually accepted these negotiable instruments in exchange for daily lift tickets. Despite some strengths of the product, the Adventure Pack met considerable resistance from tour operators and consumers who had grown accustomed to the convenience and flexibility provided by the all-Aspen ticket.

Without a convenient all-Aspen ticket, Highlands basically "becomes a day ski area in a destination resort." Highlands' share of the market for downhill skiing services in Aspen declined steadily after the 4-area ticket based on usage was abolished in 1977: from 20.5% in 1976–1977, to 15.7% in 1977–1978, to 13.1% in 1978–1979, to 12.5% in 1979–1980, to 11% in 1980–1981. Highlands' revenues from associated skiing services like the ski school, ski rentals, amateur racing events, and restaurant facilities declined sharply as well.

II

In 1979, Highlands filed a complaint in the United States District Court for the District of Colorado naming Ski Co. as a defendant. Among various claims, the complaint alleged that Ski Co. had monopolized the market for downhill skiing services at Aspen in violation of § 2 of the Sherman Act, and prayed for treble damages. The case was tried to a jury which rendered a verdict finding Ski Co. guilty of the § 2 violation and calculating Highlands' actual damages at $2.5 million.

In her instructions to the jury, the District Judge explained that the offense of monopolization under § 2 of the Sherman Act has two elements: (1) the possession of monopoly power in a relevant market, and (2) the willful acquisition, maintenance, or use of that power by anticompetitive or exclusionary means or for anticompetitive or exclusionary purposes. Although the first element was vigorously disputed at the trial and in the Court of Appeals, in this Court Ski Co. does not challenge the jury's special verdict finding that it possessed monopoly power.[20] Nor does Ski Co. criticize the trial court's instructions to the jury concerning the second element of the § 2 offense.

On this element, the jury was instructed that it had to consider whether "Aspen Skiing Corporation willfully acquired, maintained, or used

---

[20] The jury found that the relevant product market was "[d]ownhill skiing at destination ski resorts," that the "Aspen area" was a relevant geographic submarket, and that during the years 1977–1981, Ski Co. possessed monopoly power, defined as the power to control prices in the relevant market or to exclude competitors.

that power by anti-competitive or exclusionary means or for anti-competitive or exclusionary purposes." The instructions elaborated:

"In considering whether the means or purposes were anti-competitive or exclusionary, you must draw a distinction here between practices which tend to exclude or restrict competition on the one hand and the success of a business which reflects only a superior product, a well-run business, or luck, on the other. The line between legitimately gained monopoly, its proper use and maintenance, and improper conduct has been described in various ways. It has been said that obtaining or maintaining monopoly power cannot represent monopolization if the power was gained and maintained by conduct that was honestly industrial. Or it is said that monopoly power which is thrust upon a firm due to its superior business ability and efficiency does not constitute monopolization.

"For example, a firm that has lawfully acquired a monopoly position is not barred from taking advantage of scale economies by constructing a large and efficient factory. These benefits are a consequence of size and not an exercise of monopoly power. Nor is a corporation which possesses monopoly power under a duty to cooperate with its business rivals. Also a company which possesses monopoly power and which refuses to enter into a joint operating agreement with a competitor or otherwise refuses to deal with a competitor in some manner does not violate Section 2 if valid business reasons exist for that refusal.

"In other words, if there were legitimate business reasons for the refusal, then the defendant, even if he is found to possess monopoly power in a relevant market, has not violated the law. We are concerned with conduct which unnecessarily excludes or handicaps competitors. This is conduct which does not benefit consumers by making a better product or service available—or in other ways—and instead has the effect of impairing competition.

"To sum up, you must determine whether Aspen Skiing Corporation gained, maintained, or used monopoly power in a relevant market by arrangements and policies which rather than being a consequence of a superior product, superior business sense, or historic element, were designed primarily to further any domination of the relevant market or sub-market."

The jury answered a specific interrogatory finding the second element of the offense as defined in these instructions.

Ski Co. filed a motion for judgment notwithstanding the verdict, contending that the evidence was insufficient to support a § 2 violation as a matter of law. In support of that motion, Ski Co. incorporated the arguments that it had advanced in support of its motion for a directed verdict, at which time it had primarily contested the sufficiency of the evidence on the issue of monopoly power. Counsel had, however, in the course of the argument at that time, stated: "Now, we also think, Judge, that there clearly cannot be a requirement of cooperation between competitors."[22] The District Court denied Ski Co.'s motion and entered a judgment awarding Highlands treble damages of $7,500,000, costs and attorney's fees.[23]

The Court of Appeals affirmed in all respects. 738 F.2d 1509 (C.A.10 1984). The court advanced two reasons for rejecting Ski Co.'s argument that " 'there was insufficient evidence to present a jury issue of monopolization because, as a matter of law, the conduct at issue was pro-competitive conduct that a monopolist could lawfully engage in.' " First, relying on *United States v. Terminal Railroad Assn. of St. Louis*, 224 U.S. 383, 32 S.Ct. 507 (1912), the Court of Appeals held that the multiday, multiarea ticket could be characterized as an "essential facility" that Ski Co. had a duty to market jointly with Highlands. 738 F.2d, at 1520–1521. Second, it held that there was sufficient evidence to support a finding that Ski Co.'s intent in refusing to market the 4-area ticket, "considered together with its other conduct," was to create or maintain a monopoly. Id., at 1522.

In its review of the evidence on the question of intent, the Court of Appeals considered the record "as a whole" and concluded that it was not necessary for Highlands to prove that each allegedly anticompetitive act was itself sufficient to demonstrate an abuse of monopoly power. Id., at 1522, n.18.[25] The court noted that by "refusing to cooperate" with Highlands, Ski Co. "became the only business in Aspen that could offer a multi-day multi-mountain skiing experience"; that the refusal to offer a 4-

---

[22] Counsel also appears to have argued that Ski Co. was under a legal obligation to refuse to participate in any joint marketing arrangement with Highlands: "Aspen Skiing Corporation is required to compete. It is required to make independent decisions. It is required to price its own product. It is required to make its own determination of the ticket that it chooses to offer and the tickets that it chooses not to offer."

In this Court, Ski Co. does not question the validity of the joint marketing arrangement under § 1 of the Sherman Act. Thus, we have no occasion to consider the circumstances that might permit such combinations in the skiing industry. See generally National Collegiate Athletic Assn. v. Board of Regents of Univ. of Okla., 468 U.S. 85, 113–115, 104 S.Ct. 2948, 2966–2968 (1984); Broadcast Music, Inc. v. Columbia Broadcasting System, Inc., 441 U.S. 1, 18–23, 99 S.Ct. 1551, 1561–1564 (1979); Continental T.V., Inc. v. GTE Sylvania, Inc., 433 U.S. 36, 51–57, 97 S.Ct. 2549, 2558–2561 (1977).

[23] The District Court also entered an injunction requiring the parties to offer jointly a 4-area, 6-out-of-7-day coupon booklet substantially identical to the "Ski the Summit" booklet accepted by Ski Co. at its Breckenridge resort in Summit County, Colorado. The injunction was initially for a 3-year period, but was later extended through the 1984–1985 season by stipulation of the parties. Highlands represents that "it will not seek an extension of the injunction." No question is raised concerning the character of the injunctive relief ordered by the District Court.

[25] See Continental Ore Co. v. Union Carbide & Carbon Corp., 370 U.S. 690, 699, 82 S.Ct. 1404, 1410 (1962); Associated Press v. United States, 326 U.S. 1, 14, 65 S.Ct. 1416, 1421 (1945).

mountain ticket resulted in "skiers' frustration over its unavailability"; that there was apparently no valid business reason for refusing to accept the coupons in Highlands' Adventure Pack; and that after Highlands had modified its Adventure Pack to meet Ski Co.'s objections, Ski Co. had increased its single ticket price to $22 "thereby making it unprofitable . . . to market [the] Adventure Pack." Id., at 1521–1522. In reviewing Ski Co.'s argument that it was entitled to a directed verdict, the Court of Appeals assumed that the jury had resolved all contested questions of fact in Highlands' favor.

III

In this Court, Ski Co. contends that even a firm with monopoly power has no duty to engage in joint marketing with a competitor, that a violation of § 2 cannot be established without evidence of substantial exclusionary conduct, and that none of its activities can be characterized as exclusionary. It also contends that the Court of Appeals incorrectly relied on the "essential facilities" doctrine and that an "anticompetitive intent" does not transform nonexclusionary conduct into monopolization. In response, Highlands submits that, given the evidence in the record, it is not necessary to rely on the "essential facilities" doctrine in order to affirm the judgment.

"The central message of the Sherman Act is that a business entity must find new customers and higher profits through internal expansion— that is, by competing successfully rather than by arranging treaties with its competitors." *United States v. Citizens & Southern National Bank*, 422 U.S. 86, 116, 95 S.Ct. 2099, 2116 (1975). Ski Co., therefore, is surely correct in submitting that even a firm with monopoly power has no general duty to engage in a joint marketing program with a competitor. Ski Co. is quite wrong, however, in suggesting that the judgment in this case rests on any such proposition of law. For the trial court unambiguously instructed the jury that a firm possessing monopoly power has no duty to cooperate with its business rivals.

The absence of an unqualified duty to cooperate does not mean that every time a firm declines to participate in a particular cooperative venture, that decision may not have evidentiary significance, or that it may not give rise to liability in certain circumstances. The absence of a duty to transact business with another firm is, in some respects, merely the counterpart of the independent businessman's cherished right to select his customers and his associates. The high value that we have placed on the right to refuse to deal with other firms does not mean that the right is unqualified.[27]

---

[27] Under § 1 of the Sherman Act, a business "generally has a right to deal, or refuse to deal, with whomever it likes, as long as it does so independently." Monsanto Co. v. Spray-Rite Service

In *Lorain Journal Co. v. United States*, 342 U.S. 143, 72 S.Ct. 181 (1951), we squarely held that this right was not unqualified. Between 1933 and 1948 the publisher of the Lorain Journal, a newspaper, was the only local business disseminating news and advertising in that Ohio town. In 1948, a small radio station was established in a nearby community. In an effort to destroy its small competitor, and thereby regain its "pre-1948 substantial monopoly over the mass dissemination of all news and advertising," the Journal refused to sell advertising to persons that patronized the radio station. Id., at 153, 72 S.Ct., at 186.

In holding that this conduct violated § 2 of the Sherman Act, the Court dispatched the same argument raised by the monopolist here:

> "The publisher claims a right as a private business concern to select its customers and to refuse to accept advertisements from whomever it pleases. We do not dispute that general right. 'But the word "right" is one of the most deceptive of pitfalls; it is so easy to slip from a qualified meaning in the premise to an unqualified one in the conclusion. Most rights are qualified.' . . . The right claimed by the publisher is neither absolute nor exempt from regulation. Its exercise as a purposeful means of monopolizing interstate commerce is prohibited by the Sherman Act. The operator of the radio station, equally with the publisher of the newspaper, is entitled to the protection of that Act. 'In the absence of any purpose to create or maintain a monopoly, the act does not restrict the long recognized right of trader or manufacturer engaged in an entirely private business, freely to exercise his own independent discretion as to parties with whom he will deal.' (Emphasis supplied.) *United States v. Colgate & Co.*, 250 U.S. 300, 307. * * * "

The Court approved the entry of an injunction ordering the Journal to print the advertisements of the customers of its small competitor.

In Lorain Journal, the violation of § 2 was an "attempt to monopolize," rather than monopolization, but the question of intent is relevant to both offenses. In the former case it is necessary to prove a "specific intent" to accomplish the forbidden objective—as Judge Hand explained, "an intent which goes beyond the mere intent to do the act." *United States v. Aluminum Co. of America*, 148 F.2d 416, 432 (C.A.2 1945). In the latter case evidence of intent is merely relevant to the question whether the challenged conduct is fairly characterized as "exclusionary" or "anticompetitive"—to use the words in the trial court's instructions—or "predatory," to use a word that scholars seem to favor. Whichever label is used, there is agreement on the proposition that "no monopolist

Corp., 465 U.S. 752, 761, 104 S.Ct. 1464, 1469 (1984); United States v. Colgate & Co., 250 U.S. 300, 307, 39 S.Ct. 465, 468 (1919).

monopolizes unconscious of what he is doing." As Judge Bork stated more recently: "Improper exclusion (exclusion not the result of superior efficiency) is always deliberately intended."[29]

The qualification on the right of a monopolist to deal with whom he pleases is not so narrow that it encompasses no more than the circumstances of Lorain Journal. In the actual case that we must decide, the monopolist did not merely reject a novel offer to participate in a cooperative venture that had been proposed by a competitor. Rather, the monopolist elected to make an important change in a pattern of distribution that had originated in a competitive market and had persisted for several years. The all-Aspen, 6-day ticket with revenues allocated on the basis of usage was first developed when three independent companies operated three different ski mountains in the Aspen area. It continued to provide a desirable option for skiers when the market was enlarged to include four mountains, and when the character of the market was changed by Ski Co.'s acquisition of monopoly power. Moreover, since the record discloses that interchangeable tickets are used in other multimountain areas which apparently are competitive,[30] it seems appropriate to infer that such tickets satisfy consumer demand in free competitive markets.

Ski Co.'s decision to terminate the all-Aspen ticket was thus a decision by a monopolist to make an important change in the character of the market.[31] Such a decision is not necessarily anticompetitive, and Ski Co. contends that neither its decision, nor the conduct in which it engaged to implement that decision, can fairly be characterized as exclusionary in this case. It recognizes, however, that as the case is presented to us, we must interpret the entire record in the light most favorable to Highlands and give to it the benefit of all inferences which the evidence fairly supports,

---

[29] R. Bork, The Antitrust Paradox 160 (1978) (hereinafter Bork).

[30] Ski Co. itself participates in interchangeable ticket programs in at least two other markets. For example, since 1970, Ski Co. has operated the Breckenridge resort in Summit County, Colorado. Breckenridge participates in the "Ski the Summit" 4-area interchangeable coupon booklet which allows the skier to ski at any of the four mountains in the region: Breckenridge, Copper Mountain, Keystone, and Arapahoe Basin. In the 1979–1980 season Keystone and Arapahoe Basin—which are jointly operated—had about 40% of the Summit County market, and the other two ski mountains each had a market share of about 30%. During the relevant period of time, Ski Co. also operated Blackcomb Mountain, northeast of Vancouver, British Columbia, which has an interchangeable ticket arrangement with nearby Whistler Mountain, an independently operated facility. Interchangeable lift tickets apparently are also available in some European skiing areas.

[31] "In any business, patterns of distribution develop over time; these may reasonably be thought to be more efficient than alternative patterns of distribution that do not develop. The patterns that do develop and persist we may call the optimal patterns. By disturbing optimal distribution patterns one rival can impose costs upon another, that is, force the other to accept higher costs." Bork 156.

In § 1 cases where this Court has applied the per se approach to invalidity to concerted refusals to deal, "the boycott often cut off access to a supply, facility or market necessary to enable the boycotted firm to compete, . . . and frequently the boycotting firms possessed a dominant position in the relevant market." Northwest Wholesale Stationers, Inc. v. Pacific Stationery & Printing Co., 472 U.S. 284, 294, 105 S.Ct. 2613, 2619.

even though contrary inferences might reasonably be drawn. *Continental Ore Co. v. Union Carbide & Carbon Corp.*, 370 U.S. 690, 696, 82 S.Ct. 1404, 1409 (1962).

Moreover, we must assume that the jury followed the court's instructions. The jury must, therefore, have drawn a distinction "between practices which tend to exclude or restrict competition on the one hand, and the success of a business which reflects only a superior product, a well-run business, or luck, on the other." Supra, at 2854. Since the jury was unambiguously instructed that Ski Co.'s refusal to deal with Highlands "does not violate Section 2 if valid business reasons exist for that refusal," we must assume that the jury concluded that there were no valid business reasons for the refusal. The question then is whether that conclusion finds support in the record.

IV

The question whether Ski Co.'s conduct may properly be characterized as exclusionary cannot be answered by simply considering its effect on Highlands. In addition, it is relevant to consider its impact on consumers and whether it has impaired competition in an unnecessarily restrictive way.[32] If a firm has been "attempting to exclude rivals on some basis other than efficiency,"[33] it is fair to characterize its behavior as predatory. It is, accordingly, appropriate to examine the effect of the challenged pattern of conduct on consumers, on Ski Co.'s smaller rival, and on Ski Co. itself.

Superior Quality of the All-Aspen Ticket

The average Aspen visitor "is a well-educated, relatively affluent, experienced skier who has skied a number of times in the past. . . ." Over 80% of the skiers visiting the resort each year have been there before—40% of these repeat visitors have skied Aspen at least five times. Over the years, they developed a strong demand for the 6-day, all-Aspen ticket in its various refinements. Most experienced skiers quite logically prefer to purchase their tickets at once for the whole period that they will spend at the resort; they can then spend more time on the slopes and enjoying apres-ski amenities and less time standing in ticket lines. The 4-area attribute of the ticket allowed the skier to purchase his 6-day ticket in advance while reserving the right to decide in his own time and for his own reasons which mountain he would ski on each day. It provided convenience and flexibility, and expanded the vistas and the number of challenging runs available to him during the week's vacation.[34]

---

[32] "Thus, 'exclusionary' comprehends at the most behavior that not only (1) tends to impair the opportunities of rivals, but also (2) either does not further competition on the merits or does so in an unnecessarily restrictive way." 3 P. Areeda & D. Turner, Antitrust Law 78 (1978).

[33] Bork 138.

[34] Highlands' expert marketing witness testified that visitors to the Aspen resort "are looking for a variety of skiing experiences, partly because they are going to be there for a week and they

While the 3-area, 6-day ticket offered by Ski Co. possessed some of these attributes, the evidence supports a conclusion that consumers were adversely affected by the elimination of the 4-area ticket. In the first place, the actual record of competition between a 3-area ticket and the all-Aspen ticket in the years after 1967 indicated that skiers demonstrably preferred four mountains to three. Highlands' expert marketing witness testified that many of the skiers who come to Aspen want to ski the four mountains, and the abolition of the 4-area pass made it more difficult to satisfy that ambition. A consumer survey undertaken in the 1979–1980 season indicated that 53.7% of the respondents wanted to ski Highlands, but would not; 39.9% said that they would not be skiing at the mountain of their choice because their ticket would not permit it.

Expert testimony and anecdotal evidence supported these statistical measures of consumer preference. A major wholesale tour operator asserted that he would not even consider marketing a 3-area ticket if a 4-area ticket were available.[35] During the 1977–1978 and 1978–1979 seasons, people with Ski Co.'s 3-area ticket came to Highlands "on a very regular basis" and attempted to board the lifts or join the ski school.[36] Highlands officials were left to explain to angry skiers that they could only ski at Highlands or join its ski school by paying for a 1-day lift ticket. Even for the affluent, this was an irritating situation because it left the skier the option of either wasting 1 day of the 6-day, 3-area pass or obtaining a refund which could take all morning and entailed the forfeit of the 6-day discount. An active officer in the Atlanta Ski Club testified that the elimination of the 4-area pass "infuriated" him.

Highlands' Ability to Compete

The adverse impact of Ski Co.'s pattern of conduct on Highlands is not disputed in this Court. Expert testimony described the extent of its pecuniary injury. The evidence concerning its attempt to develop a

---

are going to get bored if they ski in one area for very long; and also they come with people of varying skills. They need some variety of slopes so that if they want to go out and ski the difficult areas, their spouses or their buddies who are just starting out skiing can go on the bunny hill or the not-so-difficult slopes." The owner of a condominium management company added: "The guest is coming for a first-class destination ski experience, and part of that, I think, is the expectation of perhaps having available to him the ability to ski all of what is there; *i.e.*, four mountains vs. three mountains. It helps enhance the quality of the vacation experience."

[35] "Our philosophy is that . . . to offer [Aspen] as a premier ski resort, our clients should be offered all of the terrain. Therefore, we would never consciously consider offering a three-mountain ticket if there were a four-mountain ticket available."

[36] For example, the marketing director of Highlands' ski school reported that one frustrated consumer was a dentist from "the Des Moines area [who] came out with two of his children, and he had been told by our base lift operator that he could not board. He became somewhat irate and she had referred him to my office, which is right there on the ski slopes. He came into my office and started out, 'Well, I want to go skiing here, and I don't understand why I can't.' When we got the situation slowed down and explained that there were two different tickets, well, what came out is irritation occurred because he had intended when he came to Aspen to be able to ski all areas. . . ."

substitute product either by buying Ski Co.'s daily tickets in bulk, or by marketing its own Adventure Pack, demonstrates that it tried to protect itself from the loss of its share of the patrons of the all-Aspen ticket. The development of a new distribution system for providing the experience that skiers had learned to expect in Aspen proved to be prohibitively expensive. As a result, Highlands' share of the relevant market steadily declined after the 4-area ticket was terminated. The size of the damages award also confirms the substantial character of the effect of Ski Co.'s conduct upon Highlands.[38]

Ski Co.'s Business Justification

Perhaps most significant, however, is the evidence relating to Ski Co. itself, for Ski Co. did not persuade the jury that its conduct was justified by any normal business purpose. Ski Co. was apparently willing to forgo daily ticket sales both to skiers who sought to exchange the coupons contained in Highlands' Adventure Pack, and to those who would have purchased Ski Co. daily lift tickets from Highlands if Highlands had been permitted to purchase them in bulk. The jury may well have concluded that Ski Co. elected to forgo these short-run benefits because it was more interested in reducing competition in the Aspen market over the long run by harming its smaller competitor.

That conclusion is strongly supported by Ski Co.'s failure to offer any efficiency justification whatever for its pattern of conduct.[39] In defending the decision to terminate the jointly offered ticket, Ski Co. claimed that usage could not be properly monitored. The evidence, however, established that Ski Co. itself monitored the use of the 3-area passes based on a count taken by lift operators, and distributed the revenues among its mountains on that basis. Ski Co. contended that coupons were administratively cumbersome, and that the survey takers had been disruptive and their work inaccurate. Coupons, however, were no more burdensome than the credit cards accepted at Ski Co. ticket windows. Moreover, in other markets Ski Co. itself participated in interchangeable lift tickets using coupons. As for the survey, its own manager testified that the problems were much overemphasized by Ski Co. officials, and were mostly resolved as they

---

[38] In considering the competitive effect of Ski Co.'s refusal to deal or cooperate with Highlands, it is not irrelevant to note that similar conduct carried out by the concerted action of three independent rivals with a similar share of the market would constitute a per se violation of § 1 of the Sherman Act. See Northwest Wholesale Stationers, Inc. v. Pacific Stationery & Printing Co., 105 S.Ct. 2613, 2619–2620. Cf. Lorain Journal Co. v. United States, 342 U.S. 143, 154, 72 S.Ct. 181, 187 (1951).

[39] "The law can usefully attack this form of predation only when there is evidence of specific intent to drive others from the market by means other than superior efficiency and when the predator has overwhelming market size, perhaps 80 or 90 percent. Proof of specific intent to engage in predation may be in the form of statements made by the officers or agents of the company, evidence that the conduct was used threateningly and did not continue when a rival capitulated, or evidence that the conduct was not related to any apparent efficiency. These matters are not so difficult of proof as to render the test overly hard to meet." Bork 157.

arose. Ski Co.'s explanation for the rejection of Highlands' offer to hire—at its own expense—a reputable national accounting firm to audit usage of the 4-area tickets at Highlands' mountain, was that there was no way to "control" the audit.

In the end, Ski Co. was pressed to justify its pattern of conduct on a desire to disassociate itself from what it considered the inferior skiing services offered at Highlands. The all-Aspen ticket based on usage, however, allowed consumers to make their own choice on these matters of quality. Ski Co.'s purported concern for the relative quality of Highlands' product was supported in the record by little more than vague insinuations, and was sharply contested by numerous witnesses. Moreover, Ski Co. admitted that it was willing to associate with what it considered to be inferior products in other markets.

Although Ski Co.'s pattern of conduct may not have been as " 'bold, relentless, and predatory' " as the publisher's actions in *Lorain Journal*, the record in this case comfortably supports an inference that the monopolist made a deliberate effort to discourage its customers from doing business with its smaller rival. The sale of its 3-area, 6-day ticket, particularly when it was discounted below the daily ticket price, deterred the ticket holders from skiing at Highlands. The refusal to accept the Adventure Pack coupons in exchange for daily tickets was apparently motivated entirely by a decision to avoid providing any benefit to Highlands even though accepting the coupons would have entailed no cost to Ski Co. itself, would have provided it with immediate benefits, and would have satisfied its potential customers. Thus the evidence supports an inference that Ski Co. was not motivated by efficiency concerns and that it was willing to sacrifice short-run benefits and consumer goodwill in exchange for a perceived long-run impact on its smaller rival.

Because we are satisfied that the evidence in the record,[44] construed most favorably in support of Highlands' position, is adequate to support the verdict under the instructions given by the trial court, the judgment of the Court of Appeals is

Affirmed.

JUSTICE WHITE took no part in the decision of this case.

Aspen Skiing's holding that a monopolist can violate Section 2 by changing its distribution pattern—and that as a remedy a monopolist can

---

[44] Given our conclusion that the evidence amply supports the verdict under the instructions as given by the trial court, we find it unnecessary to consider the possible relevance of the "essential facilities" doctrine, or the somewhat hypothetical question whether nonexclusionary conduct could ever constitute an abuse of monopoly power if motivated by an anticompetitive purpose. If, as we have assumed, no monopolist monopolizes unconscious of what he is doing, that case is unlikely to arise.

be required to cooperate with its competitors in a joint marketing arrangement—has stimulated extensive debate among commentators and courts. Some have suggested that such a standard raises the risks associated with undertaking legitimate collaboration with a direct rival (e.g., a research and development joint venture), as a lawsuit could accompany the decision later to terminate or otherwise alter such an arrangement. By raising the potential costs of abandoning such relationships, *Aspen* might make it less likely that collaborative arrangements will be formed in the first place.

Some lower courts sought to confine *Aspen Skiing* by depicting its outcome as the product of unusual facts and a frail defense by the monopolist. Aspen Skiing does not seem to have contested the plaintiff's suggestion that the relevant market consisted of downhill skiing in the Aspen area of Colorado—a market definition that excluded other ski resorts and gave Aspen a market share from which substantial market power easily would be inferred. In *Olympia Equip. Leasing Co. v. Western Union Tel. Co.*, 797 F.2d 370, 379 (7th Cir. 1986), the Seventh Circuit observed that "[i]f [*Aspen*] stands for any principle that goes beyond its unusual facts, it is that a monopolist may be guilty of monopolization if it refuses to cooperate with a competitor in circumstances where some cooperation is indispensable to effective competition."

In *Verizon Commc'ns Inc. v. Law Offices of Curtis V. Trinko, LLP*, 540 U.S. 398 (2004), the Supreme Court appeared to significantly limit the scope of *Aspen Skiing*, and with it the degree to which the antitrust laws will support a duty to deal, especially with rivals. We will read the case later in this Chapter when we consider refusals to deal in greater depth. In relation to its holding that rivals may have a duty to deal only under limited circumstances, the Court identified *Aspen Skiing* as being "at or near the outer boundary of § 2 liability." But it did not discuss *Aspen Skiing's* definition of exclusionary conduct or its approach to structuring a Section 2 monopolization inquiry and thus appeared implicitly to reject a call by the defendant and amici to adopt a more restrictive general definition of "exclusionary."

Note that the framework embraced in *Aspen Skiing* called for a consideration of the monopolist's "business justifications," such as efficiencies, which can be related to *Alcoa's* observation that liability should not attach to competitive successes occasioned by skill, foresight, business acumen, or luck. In evaluating asserted efficiency rationales, courts will consider whether the record shows that theoretically plausible justifications in fact motivated the defendant's refusal to deal. This approach to the analysis of efficiencies was also evident in *Eastman Kodak Co. v. Image Tech. Servs., Inc.*, 504 U.S. 451 (1992), which we discuss in the next Note.

Kodak focused on Kodak's policy of selling replacement parts for Kodak photocopiers and micrographic equipment only to customers who used Kodak service or repaired their own machines. Image Technical, an independent service organization (ISO), alleged that Kodak adopted the policy, which was a change from its past conduct, to eliminate ISOs from the continued servicing of Kodak equipment. Kodak sought summary judgment, arguing that it could not sensibly charge existing, "locked-in" users of Kodak machines supracompetitive prices for parts or service, because it lacked market power in the market for sales of original equipment (the record on appeal so stipulated). If it did, it would quickly acquire a reputation for gouging its customers in the aftermarket for parts and services and lose sales to rival new equipment manufacturers.

The Supreme Court began the analysis of the Section 2 claims by observing that Image Technical had "presented evidence that Kodak took exclusionary action to maintain its parts monopoly and used its control over parts to strengthen its monopoly share of the Kodak service market. Liability turns, then, on whether 'valid business reasons' can explain Kodak's actions." 504 U.S. at 483, *citing Aspen Skiing Co.*, 472 U.S. at 605; and *Alcoa*, 148 F.2d at 432. *Kodak* repeated *Aspen Skiing*'s admonition that a monopolist may refuse to deal with rivals "only if there are legitimate competitive reasons for the refusal." *Id.* at 483 n.32. In rejecting Kodak's argument, the Supreme Court said "Kodak's theory does not explain the actual market behavior revealed in the record," pointing to evidence that Kodak in fact had raised service prices for its customers without losing equipment sales. 504 U.S. at 473.

Justice Scalia dissented from the Court majority's ruling, but he endorsed the view that the conduct of a monopolist is to be judged by a more demanding standard than that applied to a firm lacking market power: "Where a defendant maintains substantial monopoly power, his activities are examined through a special lens: Behavior that might otherwise not be of concern to the antitrust laws—or that might be viewed as procompetitive—can take on exclusionary connotations when practiced by a monopolist." 504 U.S. at 488 (SCALIA, J., dissenting).

In the Note that follows, we examine the economics of market power in the kind of "aftermarkets" at issue in *Kodak*. As we shall see, as in *Aspen Skiing*, the Supreme Court attached considerable importance to Kodak's refusal to continue to sell parts to ISOs—a departure from its previous policy. Had Kodak never sold parts and service separate from its original equipment (for example, by bundling parts and service together with the copier in structuring the product's warranty), it would have faced no Sherman Act liability. Like the *Aspen Skiing* decision, the Court's opinion suggests that dominant firms should devote greater care in deciding whether to work with or supply competitors. The decision also illustrates the importance of being able to articulate a cognizable business justification for the termination of a relationship once formed and showing that it is consistent with the evidence.

NOTE ON KODAK AND THE ECONOMICS OF MARKET POWER IN AFTERMARKETS

Kodak sold copiers in an original equipment market (OEM) in competition with Canon, Xerox, and other rivals. Kodak also sold aftermarket parts and service to its "installed base" of customers, firms that had previously purchased a Kodak copier. Originally, Kodak competed with a number of independent service organizations (ISOs) in providing aftermarket parts and service to its equipment. The ISO plaintiffs alleged that Kodak thereafter sought to exclude them from competing in the aftermarket for parts and service, which allowed Kodak to raise prices above competitive levels. In its defense, Kodak argued, among other things, that because the original equipment market for copiers was competitive, it could not have been profitable for it to exercise market power in the aftermarket. This note examines the economic conditions under which it could have been profitable for Kodak to increase aftermarket prices above the competitive level—*i.e.*, to exercise market power—notwithstanding a competitive original equipment market.[2]

Assume, as the Court majority supposed, that the typical buyer of Kodak copiers is locked-in to that brand. That is, the buyer cannot substitute parts from other brands of copiers or service technicians trained on other copiers, and it cannot sell its Kodak copiers in the used market.[3] Assume further, as the Court also presumed, that the OEM market is competitive and that Kodak obtains a monopoly in the aftermarket.

Finally, suppose for the moment, as Kodak claimed, that most buyers of new equipment are well-informed about the likely cost of aftermarket parts and service at the time they make their original equipment purchase. These customers have a good understanding of the probability that a copier will need service over its lifetime and the likely cost of that service. When choosing between a Kodak copier and a rival brand, these informed customers compare "lifecycle costs," which include both the cost of acquisition and the costs of aftermarket parts and service. This assumption connects Kodak's OEM sales and its aftermarket prices. If Kodak raises aftermarket prices, it will lose new original equipment sales to informed buyers that recognize that their lifecycle costs have risen above the competitive level.

The profitability to Kodak of raising aftermarket prices above the competitive level depends on tallying up all the gains and losses from doing so. Higher aftermarket prices would allow Kodak to earn more on parts and

---

[2] Aftermarkets are common in durable products like copiers or automobiles. But they also arise in other settings. Suppose that a university decides to require its students to live in dormitories, and that it simultaneously raises the price of room and board. Could the higher price of housing have an anticompetitive motive?

[3] The analysis would be the same if there were a market for used Kodak copiers, so long as used products sold at a large discount, making it expensive for the buyer to switch copier brands once it adopted Kodak products.

service sold to its "installed base" of customers who had previously purchased a Kodak copier; these customers are locked-in and, assuming high switching costs, would not switch to other copiers. But higher aftermarket prices would lower aftermarket sales, as some copier owners would choose not to repair an old copier. And, more importantly, a higher aftermarket price would discourage some new purchasers from choosing the Kodak brand, driving them to products sold by Kodak's rivals. The profitability to Kodak of raising aftermarket prices, therefore, turns on whether the increase in profits earned in supplying parts and service to its installed base exceeds the reduction in profits arising from losses of sales both in the parts and service aftermarket and in the original equipment market.

The dominant effect of higher aftermarket prices could be to increase profits for Kodak if the original equipment market is very important to Kodak relative to the aftermarket. In a declining original equipment market, for example, Kodak might not lose very much even if higher aftermarket prices led most OEM customers to prefer other brands. Then Kodak might have a strong incentive to engage in "installed-base opportunism" by raising aftermarket prices above competitive levels. By contrast, if copier sales are rapidly growing, the market for new equipment would likely be more important to Kodak than aftermarket sales to its installed base, making it less likely that installed base opportunism would be profitable. Accordingly, if Kodak's new copier sales growth had begun to slow, that development might have made it profitable for the company to change its business strategy and raise the price of copier parts and service.

Kodak might also find it profitable to raise aftermarket prices even if original equipment sales are important to it, if the link between higher aftermarket prices and lower original equipment sales is weak. That might happen if, contrary to what Kodak urged the court to assume, many customers are not well-informed. If a substantial fraction of copier buyers are not well-informed, Kodak would not be penalized significantly in the OEM market if it charges a monopoly price for aftermarket services.[4]

It is possible that most copier buyers would be informed, and, in consequence, would make copier decisions by comparing lifecycle costs across brands. In particular, large firms that purchase many copiers likely have the ability and incentive to work out lifecycle cost projections and use those estimates when making OEM purchase decisions.[5] The *Kodak* majority was

---

[4]   Another way to attenuate the link between OEM sales and aftermarket prices is to suppose that Kodak can identify which OEM customers are well-informed, and that it can discriminate in price in the copier market against those who are not. Then Kodak would profit by raising the price in the aftermarket, and simultaneously lowering prices in the OEM market by a compensating amount, but only to the well-informed customers, diminishing the incentive for well-informed customers to switch to rival copiers. This scheme would allow Kodak to take advantage of the uninformed customers in its installed base without raising lifecycle prices to the well-informed customers.

[5]   It may be particularly easy for buyers to understand lifecycle costs in markets for other types of durable equipment (but apparently not for copiers), where manufacturers offer buyers long term service contracts at the time of the original equipment purchase. The price of those

skeptical of this argument, however, in part because it saw little evidence that Kodak lost OEM sales when it raised the price of service to its installed base. This observation suggested to the Court that a substantial fraction of copier buyers were not well-informed about lifecycle costs, perhaps because the buyers found it too expensive to gather the necessary information. If the typical copier buyer was becoming less informed than in the past—for example, if copiers were increasingly being purchased by small businesses unlikely to engage in lifecycle costing—Kodak could have found it profitable to alter its business strategy by raising aftermarket prices.

For two economic perspectives on Kodak's argument that competition in original equipment markets prevents anticompetitive harm in aftermarkets, see Severin Borenstein, Jeffrey K. MacKie-Mason & Janet S. Netz, *Antitrust Policy in Aftermarkets*, 63 ANTITRUST L. J. 455 (1995) and Carl Shapiro, *Aftermarkets and Consumer Welfare: Making Sense of* Kodak, 63 ANTITRUST L. J. 483 (1995). For an economic argument that Kodak's refusal to deal with the independent service organizations was not installed-base opportunism facilitated by imperfect information, but instead an effort to discriminate in price by charging more to customers that use their copiers the most intensively (and thus would need parts and service more frequently), see Benjamin Klein, *Market Power in Antitrust: Economic Analysis after* Kodak, 3 SUP. CT. ECON. REV. 43 (1993). *See also* David A.J. Goldfine & Kenneth M. Vorrasi, *The Fall of the Kodak Aftermarket Doctrine: Dying a Slow Death in the Lower Courts*, 72 ANTITRUST L.J. 209 (2004) (surveying post-*Kodak* lower court cases asserting similar theories and concluding that few cases survived summary judgment). The economics of price discrimination are sketched in Sidebar 5–4. For a discussion of the potential relevance of *Kodak* to patent hold-up cases, see *infra* Chapter 7.

We will return to the consideration of the treatment of refusals to deal as exclusionary conduct in Section C3b, *infra*. As noted above, *Aspen Skiing* was also significant for its definition of "exclusionary conduct" and its framework for analyzing power, conduct, and effects. We now return to a focus on those elements of the monopolization offense.

Our next case arose out of the governments' prosecution in the late 1990s of Microsoft Corporation for monopolizing the market for Intel-compatible PC operating systems. The case, which was initiated in May 1998, and settled by the federal government and some of the states that had joined in the prosecution in November 2002, was one of the most closely watched and debated monopolization cases in history. As you read the excerpt that follows, note how the court of appeals structured its analysis, but also how its inquiries

-----

contracts would inform buyers about the expected lifecycle cost of aftermarket parts and service. It is possible that what economists call a "moral hazard" problem—the concern that firms with service contracts will not take care of their machines, raising the costs of repair—makes it unprofitable for copier manufacturers to offer such contracts.

into power, conduct, and effects are intertwined. Note also how the court addresses efficiency justifications.

UNITED STATES V. MICROSOFT CORP.

United States Court of Appeals for the District of Columbia Circuit, 2001.
253 F.3d 34.

Before: EDWARDS, CHIEF JUDGE, WILLIAMS, GINSBURG, SENTELLE, RANDOLPH, ROGERS and TATEL, CIRCUIT JUDGES.

Opinion for the Court filed PER CURIAM.

* * *

II.   Monopolization

* * *

A.   Monopoly Power

While merely possessing monopoly power is not itself an antitrust violation, it is a necessary element of a monopolization charge. The Supreme Court defines monopoly power as "the power to control prices or exclude competition." *United States v. E.I. du Pont de Nemours & Co.*, 351 U.S. 377, 391, 76 S.Ct. 994, 100 L.Ed. 1264 (1956). More precisely, a firm is a monopolist if it can profitably raise prices substantially above the competitive level. Where evidence indicates that a firm has in fact profitably done so, the existence of monopoly power is clear. *See Rebel Oil Co. v. Atl. Richfield Co.*, 51 F.3d 1421, 1434 (9th Cir. 1995); *see also FTC v. Indiana Fed'n of Dentists*, 476 U.S. 447, 460–61, 106 S.Ct. 2009, 90 L.Ed.2d 445 (1986) (using direct proof to show market power in Sherman Act § 1 unreasonable restraint of trade action). Because such direct proof is only rarely available, courts more typically examine market structure in search of circumstantial evidence of monopoly power. Under this structural approach, monopoly power may be inferred from a firm's possession of a dominant share of a relevant market that is protected by entry barriers. "Entry barriers" are factors (such as certain regulatory requirements) that prevent new rivals from timely responding to an increase in price above the competitive level.

The District Court considered these structural factors and concluded that Microsoft possesses monopoly power in a relevant market. Defining the market as Intel-compatible PC operating systems, the District Court found that Microsoft has a greater than 95% share. It also found the company's market position protected by a substantial entry barrier.

Microsoft argues that the District Court incorrectly defined the relevant market. It also claims that there is no barrier to entry in that market. Alternatively, Microsoft argues that because the software industry is uniquely dynamic, direct proof, rather than circumstantial evidence, more appropriately indicates whether it possesses monopoly power. Rejecting each argument, we uphold the District Court's finding of monopoly power in its entirety.

1. Market Structure

a. Market definition

"Because the ability of consumers to turn to other suppliers restrains a firm from raising prices above the competitive level," *Rothery Storage & Van Co. v. Atlas Van Lines, Inc.*, 792 F.2d 210, 218 (D.C.Cir. 1986), the relevant market must include all products "reasonably interchangeable by consumers for the same purposes." In this case, the District Court defined the market as "the licensing of all Intel-compatible PC operating systems worldwide," finding that there are "currently no products—and . . . there are not likely to be any in the near future—that a significant percentage of computer users worldwide could substitute for [these operating systems] without incurring substantial costs." Calling this market definition "far too narrow," Microsoft argues that the District Court improperly excluded three types of products: non-Intel compatible operating systems (primarily Apple's Macintosh operating system, Mac OS), operating systems for non-PC devices (such as hand-held computers and portal websites), and "middleware" products, which are not operating systems at all.

We begin with Mac OS. Microsoft's argument that Mac OS should have been included in the relevant market suffers from a flaw that infects many of the company's monopoly power claims: the company fails to challenge the District Court's factual findings, or to argue that these findings do not support the court's conclusions. The District Court found that consumers would not switch from Windows to Mac OS in response to a substantial price increase because of the costs of acquiring the new hardware needed to run Mac OS (an Apple computer and peripherals) and compatible software applications, as well as because of the effort involved in learning the new system and transferring files to its format. The court also found the Apple system less appealing to consumers because it costs considerably more and supports fewer applications. Microsoft responds only by saying: "the district court's market definition is so narrow that it excludes Apple's Mac OS, which has competed with Windows for years, simply because the Mac OS runs on a different microprocessor." This general, conclusory statement falls far short of what is required to challenge findings as clearly erroneous. Microsoft neither points to evidence contradicting the District Court's findings nor alleges that supporting record evidence is insufficient. And since Microsoft does not argue that even if we accept these findings, they do not support the District Court's conclusion, we have no basis for upsetting the court's decision to exclude Mac OS from the relevant market.

Microsoft's challenge to the District Court's exclusion of non-PC based competitors, such as information appliances (handheld devices, etc.) and portal websites that host serverbased software applications, suffers from the same defect: the company fails to challenge the District Court's key factual findings. In particular, the District Court found that because information appliances fall far short of performing all of the functions of a PC, most consumers will buy them only as a supplement to their PCs. The District Court also found that portal websites do not presently host enough applications to induce consumers to switch, nor are they likely to do so in the near future. Again, because Microsoft does not argue that the District Court's findings do not support its conclusion that information appliances and portal websites are outside the relevant market, we adhere to that conclusion.

This brings us to Microsoft's main challenge to the District Court's market definition: the exclusion of middleware. * * *

Operating systems perform many functions, including allocating computer memory and controlling peripherals such as printers and keyboards. Operating systems also function as platforms for software applications. They do this by "exposing"—*i.e.*, making available to software developers—routines or protocols that perform certain widely-used functions. These are known as Application Programming Interfaces, or "APIs." * * * Software developers wishing to include [any] function in an application need not duplicate it in their own code. Instead, they can "call"—*i.e.*, use—the Windows API. Windows contains thousands of APIs, controlling everything from data storage to font display.

Every operating system has different APIs. Accordingly, a developer who writes an application for one operating system and wishes to sell the application to users of another must modify, or "port," the application to the second operating system. This process is both time-consuming and expensive.

"Middleware" refers to software products that expose their own APIs. Because of this, a middleware product written for Windows could take over some or all of Windows's valuable platform functions—that is, developers might begin to rely upon APIs exposed by the middleware for basic routines rather than relying upon the API set included in Windows. If middleware were written for multiple operating systems, its impact could be even greater. The more developers could rely upon APIs exposed by such middleware, the less expensive porting to different operating systems would be. Ultimately, if developers could write applications relying exclusively on APIs exposed by middleware, their applications would run on any operating system on which the middleware was also present. Netscape Navigator and Java—both at issue in this case—are middleware products written for multiple operating systems.

Microsoft argues that, because middleware could usurp the operating system's platform function and might eventually take over other operating system functions (for instance, by controlling peripherals), the District Court erred in excluding Navigator and Java from the relevant market. The District Court found, however, that neither Navigator, Java, nor any other middleware product could now, or would soon, expose enough APIs to serve as a platform for popular applications, much less take over all operating system functions. Again, Microsoft fails to challenge these findings, instead simply asserting middleware's "potential" as a competitor. The test of reasonable interchangeability, however, required the District Court to consider only substitutes that constrain pricing in the reasonably foreseeable future, and only products that can enter the market in a relatively short time can perform this function. Whatever middleware's ultimate potential, the District Court found that consumers could not now abandon their operating systems and switch to middleware in response to a sustained price for Windows above the competitive level. Nor is middleware likely to overtake the operating system as the primary platform for software development any time in the near future.

Alternatively, Microsoft argues that the District Court should not have excluded middleware from the relevant market because the primary focus of the plaintiffs' § 2 charge is on Microsoft's attempts to suppress middleware's threat to its operating system monopoly. According to Microsoft, it is "contradict[ory]," to define the relevant market to exclude the "very competitive threats that gave rise" to the action. The purported contradiction lies between plaintiffs' § 2 theory, under which Microsoft preserved its monopoly against middleware technologies that threatened to become viable substitutes for Windows, and its theory of the relevant market, under which middleware is not presently a viable substitute for Windows. Because middleware's threat is only nascent, however, no contradiction exists. Nothing in § 2 of the Sherman Act limits its prohibition to actions taken against threats that are already well-developed enough to serve as present substitutes. Because market definition is meant to identify products "reasonably interchangeable by consumers," and because middleware is not now interchangeable with Windows, the District Court had good reason for excluding middleware from the relevant market.

b. Market power

Having thus properly defined the relevant market, the District Court found that Windows accounts for a greater than 95% share. The court also found that even if Mac OS were included, Microsoft's share would exceed 80%. Microsoft challenges neither finding, nor does it argue that such a market share is not predominant.

Instead, Microsoft claims that even a predominant market share does not by itself indicate monopoly power. Although the "existence of [monopoly] power ordinarily may be inferred from the predominant share of the market," *Grinnell*, 384 U.S. at 571, we agree with Microsoft that because of the possibility of competition from new entrants, looking to current market share alone can be "misleading." In this case, however, the District Court was not misled. Considering the possibility of new rivals, the court focused not only on Microsoft's present market share, but also on the structural barrier that protects the company's future position. That barrier—the "applications barrier to entry"—stems from two characteristics of the software market: (1) most consumers prefer operating systems for which a large number of applications have already been written; and (2) most developers prefer to write for operating systems that already have a substantial consumer base. This "chicken-and-egg" situation ensures that applications will continue to be written for the already dominant Windows, which in turn ensures that consumers will continue to prefer it over other operating systems.

Challenging the existence of the applications barrier to entry, Microsoft observes that software developers do write applications for other operating systems, pointing out that at its peak IBM's OS/2 supported approximately 2,500 applications. This misses the point. That some developers write applications for other operating systems is not at all inconsistent with the finding that the applications barrier to entry discourages many from writing for these less popular platforms. Indeed, the District Court found that IBM's difficulty in attracting a larger number of software developers to write for its platform seriously impeded OS/2's success.

Microsoft does not dispute that Windows supports many more applications than any other operating system. It argues instead that "[i]t defies common sense" to suggest that an operating system must support as many applications as Windows does (more than 70,000, according to the District Court) to be competitive. Consumers, Microsoft points out, can only use a very small percentage of these applications. As the District Court explained, however, the applications barrier to entry gives consumers reason to prefer the dominant operating system even if they have no need to use all applications written for it:

> The consumer wants an operating system that runs not only types of applications that he knows he will want to use, but also those types in which he might develop an interest later. Also, the consumer knows that if he chooses an operating system with enough demand to support multiple applications in each product category, he will be less likely to find himself straitened later by having to use an application whose features disappoint him. Finally, the average user knows that, generally speaking, applications improve through successive versions. He thus wants an operating system for which successive generations of his favorite applications will be released—promptly at that. The fact

that a vastly larger number of applications are written for Windows than for other PC operating systems attracts consumers to Windows, because it reassures them that their interests will be met as long as they use Microsoft's product.

Findings of Fact ¶ 37. Thus, despite the limited success of its rivals, Microsoft benefits from the applications barrier to entry.

* * *

Microsoft next argues that the applications barrier to entry is not an entry barrier at all, but a reflection of Windows' popularity. It is certainly true that Windows may have gained its initial dominance in the operating system market competitively—through superior foresight or quality. But this case is not about Microsoft's initial acquisition of monopoly power. It is about Microsoft's efforts to maintain this position through means other than competition on the merits. Because the applications barrier to entry protects a dominant operating system irrespective of quality, it gives Microsoft power to stave off even superior new rivals. The barrier is thus a characteristic of the operating system market, not of Microsoft's popularity, or, as asserted by a Microsoft witness, the company's efficiency. *See* Direct Testimony of Richard Schmalensee ¶ 115.

Finally, Microsoft argues that the District Court should not have considered the applications barrier to entry because it reflects not a cost borne disproportionately by new entrants, but one borne by all participants in the operating system market. According to Microsoft, it had to make major investments to convince software developers to write for its new operating system, and it continues to "evangelize" the Windows platform today. Whether costs borne by all market participants should be considered entry barriers is the subject of much debate. We need not resolve this issue, however, for even under the more narrow definition it is clear that there are barriers. When Microsoft entered the operating system market with MS-DOS and the first version of Windows, it did not confront a dominant rival operating system with as massive an installed base and as vast an existing array of applications as the Windows operating systems have since enjoyed. Moreover, when Microsoft introduced Windows 95 and 98, it was able to bypass the applications barrier to entry that protected the incumbent Windows by including APIs from the earlier version in the new operating systems. This made porting existing Windows applications to the new version of Windows much less costly than porting them to the operating systems of other entrants who could not freely include APIs from the incumbent Windows with their own.

2. Direct Proof

Having sustained the District Court's conclusion that circumstantial evidence proves that Microsoft possesses monopoly power, we turn to

Microsoft's alternative argument that it does not behave like a monopolist. Claiming that software competition is uniquely "dynamic," the company suggests a new rule: that monopoly power in the software industry should be proven directly, that is, by examining a company's actual behavior to determine if it reveals the existence of monopoly power. According to Microsoft, not only does no such proof of its power exist, but record evidence demonstrates the absence of monopoly power. The company claims that it invests heavily in research and development, and charges a low price for Windows (a small percentage of the price of an Intel compatible PC system and less than the price of its rivals).

Microsoft's argument fails because, even assuming that the software market is uniquely dynamic in the long term, the District Court correctly applied the structural approach to determine if the company faces competition in the short term. Structural market power analyses are meant to determine whether potential substitutes constrain a firm's ability to raise prices above the competitive level; only threats that are likely to materialize in the relatively near future perform this function to any significant degree. The District Court expressly considered and rejected Microsoft's claims that innovations such as handheld devices and portal websites would soon expand the relevant market beyond Intel-compatible PC operating systems. Because the company does not challenge these findings, we have no reason to believe that prompt substitutes are available. The structural approach, as applied by the District Court, is thus capable of fulfilling its purpose even in a changing market. Microsoft cites no case, nor are we aware of one, requiring direct evidence to show monopoly power in any market. We decline to adopt such a rule now.

Even if we were to require direct proof, moreover, Microsoft's behavior may well be sufficient to show the existence of monopoly power. Certainly, none of the conduct Microsoft points to—its investment in R & D and the relatively low price of Windows—is inconsistent with the possession of such power. The R & D expenditures Microsoft points to are not simply for Windows, but for its entire company, which most likely does not possess a monopoly for all of its products. Moreover, because innovation can increase an already dominant market share and further delay the emergence of competition, even monopolists have reason to invest in R & D. Microsoft's pricing behavior is similarly equivocal. The company claims only that it never charged the short-term profit-maximizing price for Windows. Faced with conflicting expert testimony, the District Court found that it could not accurately determine what this price would be. In any event, the court found, a price lower than the short-term profit-maximizing price is not inconsistent with possession or improper use of monopoly power. Microsoft never claims that it did not charge the long-term monopoly price. Microsoft does argue that the price of Windows is a fraction of the price of an Intel-compatible PC system and lower than that of rival operating systems, but these facts are not inconsistent with the District Court's finding that Microsoft has monopoly power. *See Findings of Fact* ¶ 36 ("Intel-compatible PC operating systems other than Windows [would not] attract[ ] significant demand . . . even if Microsoft held its prices substantially above the competitive level.").

More telling, the District Court found that some aspects of Microsoft's behavior are difficult to explain unless Windows is a monopoly product. For instance, according to the District Court, the company set the price of Windows without considering rivals' prices, something a firm without a monopoly would have been unable to do. The District Court also found that Microsoft's pattern of exclusionary conduct could only be rational "if the firm knew that it possessed monopoly power." It is to that conduct that we now turn.

B. Anticompetitive Conduct

* * *

* * * [A]fter concluding that Microsoft had monopoly power, the District Court held that Microsoft had violated § 2 by engaging in a variety of exclusionary acts to maintain its monopoly by preventing the effective distribution and use of products that might threaten that monopoly. Specifically, the District Court held Microsoft liable for: (1) the way in which it integrated IE ["Internet Explorer" Internet browser, Eds.] into Windows; (2) its various dealings with Original Equipment Manufacturers ("OEMs"), Internet Access Providers ("IAPs"), Internet Content Providers ("ICPs"), Independent Software Vendors ("ISVs"), and Apple Computer; (3) its efforts to contain and to subvert Java technologies; and (4) its course of conduct as a whole. Upon appeal, Microsoft argues that it did not engage in any exclusionary conduct.

Whether any particular act of a monopolist is exclusionary, rather than merely a form of vigorous competition, can be difficult to discern: the means of illicit exclusion, like the means of legitimate competition, are myriad. The challenge for an antitrust court lies in stating a general rule for distinguishing between exclusionary acts, which reduce social welfare, and competitive acts, which increase it.

From a century of case law on monopolization under § 2, however, several principles do emerge. First, to be condemned as exclusionary, a monopolist's act must have an "anticompetitive effect." That is, it must harm the competitive *process* and thereby harm consumers. In contrast, harm to one or more *competitors* will not suffice. * * *

Second, the plaintiff, on whom the burden of proof of course rests, must demonstrate that the monopolist's conduct indeed has the requisite anticompetitive effect. In a case brought by a private plaintiff, the plaintiff must show that its injury is "of 'the type that the statute was intended to forestall,' " *Brunswick Corp. v. Pueblo Bowl-O-Mat, Inc.*, 429 U.S. 477, 487–88, 97 S.Ct. 690, 50 L.Ed.2d 701 (1977); no less in a case brought by the Government, it must demonstrate that the monopolist's conduct harmed competition, not just a competitor.

Third, if a plaintiff successfully establishes a *prima facie* case under § 2 by demonstrating anticompetitive effect, then the monopolist may proffer a "procompetitive justification" for its conduct. If the monopolist asserts a procompetitive justification—a nonpretextual claim that its conduct is indeed a form of competition on the merits because it involves, for example, greater efficiency or enhanced consumer appeal—then the burden shifts back to the plaintiff to rebut that claim.

Fourth, if the monopolist's procompetitive justification stands unrebutted, then the plaintiff must demonstrate that the anticompetitive harm of the conduct outweighs the procompetitive benefit. In cases arising under § 1 of the Sherman Act, the courts routinely apply a similar balancing approach under the rubric of the "rule of reason." * * *

Finally, in considering whether the monopolist's conduct on balance harms competition and is therefore condemned as exclusionary for purposes of § 2, our focus is upon the effect of that conduct, not upon the intent behind it. Evidence of the intent behind the conduct of a monopolist is relevant only to the extent it helps us understand the likely effect of the monopolist's conduct.

With these principles in mind, we now consider Microsoft's objections to the District Court's holding that Microsoft violated § 2 of the Sherman Act in a variety of ways.

1. *Licenses Issued to Original Equipment Manufacturers*

The District Court condemned a number of provisions in Microsoft's agreements licensing Windows to OEMs, because it found that Microsoft's imposition of those provisions (like many of Microsoft's other actions at issue in this case) serves to reduce usage share of Netscape's browser and, hence, protect Microsoft's operating system monopoly. The reason market share in the browser market affects market power in the operating system market is complex, and warrants some explanation.

Browser usage share is important because * * * a browser (or any middleware product, for that matter) must have a critical mass of users in order to attract software developers to write applications relying upon the APIs ["Application Programming Interfaces," Eds.] it exposes, and away from the APIs exposed by Windows. Applications written to a particular browser's APIs, however, would run on any computer with that browser, regardless of the underlying operating system. If a consumer could have access to the applications he desired—regardless of the operating system he uses—simply by installing a particular browser on his computer, then he would no longer feel compelled to select Windows in order to have access to those applications; he could select an operating system other than Windows based solely upon its quality and price. In other words, the market for operating systems would be competitive.

Therefore, Microsoft's efforts to gain market share in one market (browsers) served to meet the threat to Microsoft's monopoly in another market (operating systems) by keeping rival browsers from gaining the critical mass of users necessary to attract developer attention away from Windows as the platform for software development. * * *

In evaluating the restrictions in Microsoft's agreements licensing Windows to OEMs, we first consider whether plaintiffs have made out a *prima facie* case by demonstrating that the restrictions have an anticompetitive effect. In the next subsection, we conclude that plaintiffs have met this burden as to all the restrictions. We then consider Microsoft's proffered justifications for the restrictions and, for the most part, hold those justifications insufficient.

a.   Anticompetitive effect of the license restrictions

The restrictions Microsoft places upon Original Equipment Manufacturers are of particular importance in determining browser usage share because having an OEM pre-install a browser on a computer is one of the two most cost-effective methods by far of distributing browsing software. The District Court found that the restrictions Microsoft imposed in licensing Windows to OEMs prevented many OEMs from distributing browsers other than IE. In particular, the District Court condemned the license provisions prohibiting the OEMs from: (1) removing any desktop icons, folders, or "Start" menu entries; (2) altering the initial boot sequence; and (3) otherwise altering the appearance of the Windows desktop.

The District Court concluded that the first license restriction—the prohibition upon the removal of desktop icons, folders, and Start menu entries—thwarts the distribution of a rival browser by preventing OEMs from removing visible means of user access to IE. The OEMs cannot practically install a second browser in addition to IE, the court found, in part because "[p]re-installing more than one product in a given category . . . can significantly increase an OEM's support costs, for the redundancy can lead to confusion among novice users." * * *

Microsoft denies the "consumer confusion" story; it observes that some OEMs do install multiple browsers and that executives from two OEMs that do so denied any knowledge of consumers being confused by multiple icons.

Other testimony, however, supports the District Court's finding that fear of such confusion deters many OEMs from pre-installing multiple browsers. Most telling, in presentations to OEMs, Microsoft itself represented that having only one icon in a particular category would be "less confusing for endusers." Accordingly, we reject Microsoft's argument that we should vacate the District Court's Finding of Fact 159 as it relates to consumer confusion.

As noted above, the OEM channel is one of the two primary channels for distribution of browsers. By preventing OEMs from removing visible means of user access to IE, the license restriction prevents many OEMs from pre-installing a rival browser and, therefore, protects Microsoft's monopoly from the competition that middleware might otherwise present. Therefore, we conclude that the license restriction at issue is anticompetitive. * * *

The second license provision at issue prohibits OEMs from modifying the initial boot sequence—the process that occurs the first time a consumer turns on the computer. Prior to the imposition of that restriction, "among the programs that many OEMs inserted into the boot sequence were Internet sign-up procedures that encouraged users to choose from a list of IAPs assembled by the OEM." *Findings of Fact* ¶ 210. Microsoft's prohibition on any alteration of the boot sequence thus prevents OEMs from using that process to promote the services of IAPs, many of which— at least at the time Microsoft imposed the restriction—used Navigator rather than IE in their internet access software. Microsoft does not deny that the prohibition on modifying the boot sequence has the effect of decreasing competition against IE by preventing OEMs from promoting rivals' browsers. Because this prohibition has a substantial effect in protecting Microsoft's market power, and does so through a means other than competition on the merits, it is anticompetitive. * * *

Finally, Microsoft imposes several additional provisions that, like the prohibition on removal of icons, prevent OEMs from making various alterations to the desktop: Microsoft prohibits OEMs from causing any user interface other than the Windows desktop to launch automatically, from adding icons or folders different in size or shape from those supplied by Microsoft, and from using the "Active Desktop" feature to promote third-party brands. These restrictions impose significant costs upon the OEMs; prior to Microsoft's prohibiting the practice, many OEMs would change the appearance of the desktop in ways they found beneficial.

The dissatisfaction of the OEM customers does not, of course, mean the restrictions are anticompetitive. The anticompetitive effect of the license restrictions is, as Microsoft itself recognizes, that OEMs are not able to promote rival browsers, which keeps developers focused upon the APIs in Windows. This kind of promotion is not a zero-sum game; but for the restrictions in their licenses to use Windows, OEMs could promote multiple IAPs and browsers. By preventing the OEMs from doing so, this type of license restriction, like the first two restrictions, is anticompetitive:

Microsoft reduced rival browsers' usage share not by improving its own product but, rather, by preventing OEMs from taking actions that could increase rivals' share of usage.

b.   Microsoft's justifications for the license restrictions

Microsoft argues that the license restrictions are legally justified because, in imposing them, Microsoft is simply "exercising its rights as the holder of valid copyrights." Microsoft also argues that the licenses "do not unduly restrict the opportunities of Netscape to distribute Navigator in any event."

Microsoft's primary copyright argument borders upon the frivolous. The company claims an absolute and unfettered right to use its intellectual property as it wishes * * *. That is no more correct than the proposition that use of one's personal property, such as a baseball bat, cannot give rise to tort liability. As the Federal Circuit succinctly stated: "Intellectual property rights do not confer a privilege to violate the antitrust laws." *In re Indep. Serv. Orgs. Antitrust Litig.*, 203 F.3d 1322, 1325 (Fed. Cir. 2000).

Although Microsoft never overtly retreats from its bold and incorrect position on the law, it also makes two arguments to the effect that it is not exercising its copyright in an unreasonable manner, despite the anticompetitive consequences of the license restrictions discussed above. In the first variation upon its unqualified copyright defense, Microsoft cites two cases indicating that a copyright holder may limit a licensee's ability to engage in significant and deleterious alterations of a copyrighted work. The relevance of those two cases for the present one is limited, however, both because those cases involved substantial alterations of a copyrighted work, and because in neither case was there any claim that the copyright holder was, in asserting its rights, violating the antitrust laws.

The only license restriction Microsoft seriously defends as necessary to prevent a "substantial alteration" of its copyrighted work is the prohibition on OEMs automatically launching a substitute user interface upon completion of the boot process. We agree that a shell that automatically prevents the Windows desktop from ever being seen by the user is a drastic alteration of Microsoft's copyrighted work, and outweighs the marginal anticompetitive effect of prohibiting the OEMs from substituting a different interface automatically upon completion of the initial boot process. We therefore hold that this particular restriction is not an exclusionary practice that violates § 2 of the Sherman Act.

In a second variation upon its copyright defense, Microsoft argues that the license restrictions merely prevent OEMs from taking actions that would reduce substantially the value of Microsoft's copyrighted work: that is, Microsoft claims each license restriction in question is necessary to prevent OEMs from so altering Windows as to undermine "the principal value of Windows as a stable and consistent platform that supports a broad range of applications and that is familiar to users." Microsoft, however, never substantiates this claim, and, because an OEM's altering the appearance of the desktop or promoting programs in the boot sequence does not affect the code already in the product, the practice does not self-evidently affect either the "stability" or the "consistency" of the platform. * * * Therefore, we conclude Microsoft has not shown that the OEMs' liberality reduces the value of Windows except in the sense that their promotion of rival browsers undermines Microsoft's monopoly—and that is not a permissible justification for the license restrictions.

Apart from copyright, Microsoft raises one other defense of the OEM license agreements: It argues that, despite the restrictions in the OEM license, Netscape is not completely blocked from distributing its product. That claim is insufficient to shield Microsoft from liability for those restrictions because, although Microsoft did not bar its rivals from all means of distribution, it did bar them from the cost-efficient ones.

* * *

2. Integration of IE and Windows

* * *

Technologically binding IE to Windows, the District Court found, both prevented OEMs from pre-installing other browsers and deterred consumers from using them. In particular, having the IE software code as an irremovable part of Windows meant that pre-installing a second browser would "increase an OEM's product testing costs," because an OEM must test and train its support staff to answer calls related to every software product preinstalled on the machine; moreover, pre-installing a browser in addition to IE would to many OEMs be "a questionable use of the scarce and valuable space on a PC's hard drive."

* * * [The District Court] findings of fact in support of that conclusion center upon three specific actions Microsoft took to weld IE to Windows: excluding IE from the "Add/Remove Programs" utility; designing Windows so as in certain circumstances to override the user's choice of a default browser other than IE; and commingling code related to browsing and other code in the same files, so that any attempt to delete the files containing IE would, at the same time, cripple the operating system.

a. Anticompetitive effect of integration

As a general rule, courts are properly very skeptical about claims that competition has been harmed by a dominant firm's product design changes. In a competitive market, firms routinely innovate in the hope of appealing to consumers, sometimes in the process making their products incompatible with those of rivals; the imposition of liability when a monopolist does the same thing will inevitably deter a certain amount of innovation. This is all the more true in a market, such as this one, in which the product itself is rapidly changing. Judicial deference to product innovation, however, does not mean that a monopolist's product design decisions are per se lawful.

The District Court first condemned as anticompetitive Microsoft's decision to exclude IE from the "Add/Remove Programs" utility in Windows 98. Microsoft had included IE in the Add/Remove Programs utility in Windows 95, but when it modified Windows 95 to produce Windows 98, it took IE out of the Add/Remove Programs utility. This change reduces the usage share of rival browsers not by making Microsoft's own browser more attractive to consumers but, rather, by discouraging OEMs from distributing rival products. Because Microsoft's conduct, through something other than competition on the merits, has the effect of significantly reducing usage of rivals' products and hence protecting its own operating system monopoly, it is anticompetitive * * *.

Second, the District Court found that Microsoft designed Windows 98 "so that using Navigator on Windows 98 would have unpleasant consequences for users" by, in some circumstances, overriding the user's choice of a browser other than IE as his or her default browser. Plaintiffs argue that this override harms the competitive process by deterring consumers from using a browser other than IE even though they might prefer to do so, thereby reducing rival browsers' usage share and, hence, the ability of rival browsers to draw developer attention away from the APIs exposed by Windows. Microsoft does not deny, of course, that overriding the user's preference prevents some people from using other browsers. Because the override reduces rivals' usage share and protects Microsoft's monopoly, it too is anticompetitive.

Finally, the District Court condemned Microsoft's decision to bind IE to Windows 98 "by placing code specific to Web browsing in the same files as code that provided operating system functions." Putting code supplying browsing functionality into a file with code supplying operating system functionality "ensure[s] that the deletion of any file containing browsing-specific routines would also delete vital operating system routines and thus cripple Windows. . . ." * * * [P]reventing an OEM from removing IE deters it from installing a second browser because doing so increases the OEM's product testing and support costs; by contrast, had OEMs been able to remove IE, they might have chosen to pre-install Navigator alone.

Microsoft denies, as a factual matter, that it commingled browsing and non-browsing code, and it maintains the District Court's findings to the contrary are clearly erroneous. * * *

* * *

In view of the contradictory testimony in the record, some of which supports the District Court's finding that Microsoft commingled browsing and non-browsing code, we cannot conclude that the finding was clearly erroneous. Accordingly, we reject Microsoft's argument that we should vacate Finding of Fact 159 as it relates to the commingling of code, and we conclude that such commingling has an anticompetitive effect * * *.

b.   Microsoft's justifications for integration

Microsoft proffers no justification for two of the three challenged actions that it took in integrating IE into Windows—excluding IE from the Add/Remove Programs utility and commingling browser and operating system code. Although Microsoft does make some general claims regarding the benefits of integrating the browser and the operating system, it neither specifies nor substantiates those claims. Nor does it argue that either excluding IE from the Add/Remove Programs utility or commingling code achieves any integrative benefit. Plaintiffs plainly made out a *prima facie* case of harm to competition in the operating system market by demonstrating that Microsoft's actions increased its browser usage share and thus protected its operating system monopoly from a middleware threat and, for its part, Microsoft failed to meet its burden of showing that its conduct serves a purpose other than protecting its operating system monopoly. Accordingly, we hold that Microsoft's exclusion of IE from the Add/Remove Programs utility and its commingling of browser and operating system code constitute exclusionary conduct, in violation of § 2.

As for the other challenged act that Microsoft took in integrating IE into Windows—causing Windows to override the user's choice of a default browser in certain circumstances—Microsoft argues that it has "valid technical reasons." Specifically, Microsoft claims that it was necessary to design Windows to override the user's preferences when he or she invokes one of "a few" out "of the nearly 30 means of accessing the Internet." * * * The plaintiff bears the burden not only of rebutting a proffered justification but also of demonstrating that the anticompetitive effect of the challenged action outweighs it. In the District Court, plaintiffs appear to have done neither, let alone both; in any event, upon appeal, plaintiffs offer no rebuttal whatsoever. Accordingly, Microsoft may not be held liable for this aspect of its product design.

[The court's extensive discussion of the remaining categories of conduct found to be anticompetitive by the district court—agreements with Internet Service Providers, dealings with Internet Access Providers, Internet Content Providers, Independent Software Vendors and Apple Computer, and conduct affecting Sun Microsystems's Java and Intel—were also largely upheld. Eds.]

* * *

C. Causation

As a final parry, Microsoft urges this court to reverse on the monopoly maintenance claim, because plaintiffs never established a causal link between Microsoft's anticompetitive conduct, in particular its foreclosure of Netscape's and Java's distribution channels, and the maintenance of Microsoft's operating system monopoly. This is the flip side of Microsoft's earlier argument that the District Court should have included middleware in the relevant market. According to Microsoft, the District Court cannot simultaneously find that middleware is not a reasonable substitute and that Microsoft's exclusionary conduct contributed to the maintenance of monopoly power in the operating system market. Microsoft claims that the first finding depended on the court's view that middleware does not pose a serious threat to Windows, while the second finding required the court to find that Navigator and Java would have developed into serious enough cross-platform threats to erode the applications barrier to entry. We disagree.

Microsoft points to no case, and we can find none, standing for the proposition that, as to § 2 liability in an equitable enforcement action, plaintiffs must present direct proof that a defendant's continued monopoly power is precisely attributable to its anticompetitive conduct. * * *

* * * To require that § 2 liability turn on a plaintiff's ability or inability to reconstruct the hypothetical marketplace absent a defendant's anticompetitive conduct would only encourage monopolists to take more and earlier anticompetitive action.

We may infer causation where exclusionary conduct is aimed at producers of nascent competitive technologies as well as when it is aimed at producers of established substitutes. Admittedly, in the former case there is added uncertainty, inasmuch as nascent threats are merely *potential* substitutes. But the underlying proof problem is the same— neither plaintiffs nor the court can confidently reconstruct a product's hypothetical technological development in a world absent the defendant's exclusionary conduct. To some degree, "the defendant is made to suffer the uncertain consequences of its own undesirable conduct." 3 AREEDA & HOVENKAMP, ANTITRUST LAW ¶ 651c, at 78.

Given this rather edentulous test for causation, the question in this case is not whether Java or Navigator would actually have developed into viable platform substitutes, but (1) whether as a general matter the exclusion of nascent threats is the type of conduct that is reasonably capable of contributing significantly to a defendant's continued monopoly power and (2) whether Java and Navigator reasonably constituted nascent threats at the time Microsoft engaged in the anticompetitive conduct at issue. As to the first, suffice it to say that it would be inimical to the purpose of the Sherman Act to allow monopolists free reign to squash nascent, albeit unproven, competitors at will—particularly in industries marked by rapid technological advance and frequent paradigm shifts. As to the second, the District Court made ample findings that both Navigator and Java showed potential as middleware platform threats.

Microsoft's concerns over causation have more purchase in connection with the appropriate remedy issue, *i.e.*, whether the court should impose a structural remedy or merely enjoin the offensive conduct at issue. As we point out later in this opinion, divestiture is a remedy that is imposed only with great caution, in part because its long-term efficacy is rarely certain. Absent some measure of confidence that there has been an actual loss to competition that needs to be restored, wisdom counsels against adopting radical structural relief. * * *

* * *

Note how much of the evidence relied upon by the court in resolving the monopoly power issue in *Microsoft*, and how much of the argument it weighed, originated with the testimony of the economic experts. Which of the government's approaches to establishing monopoly power proved persuasive to the court and why? What particular evidence did the court find persuasive? What legal standard did it use? How did the court integrate economic concepts, legal theory and the evidence to reach its conclusions? And finally, how did the court respond to Microsoft's expert's positions on monopoly power? Why were they rejected? Consider Figure 4–7, which follows, and summarizes the government's positions, Microsoft's, and the court of appeals'.

In the final portion of the case excerpt, the D.C. Circuit was unequivocal in its conclusion that the antitrust laws should be able to reach conduct that threatens to forestall or completely impede emerging competitive threats. But how developed and concrete must those threats be? Would the court's conclusion have been altered had Navigator and Java never actually made it to market? In other words, how "nascent" and how "imminent" must the competitive threat be before the plaintiff can satisfy the Sherman Act's threshold requirements of substantiality?

More broadly, what are the permissible boundaries of a dominant firm's responses to new competition? Can the standards of proof for a violation of Section 2 inhibit a dominant firm's incentives to aggressively respond to new sources of competition? Must it sit back and avoid aggressive responses for fear that it will cross the line of legality? If so, will the cost in terms of diminished competitive vigor outweigh the value of too strict a standard? On the other hand, what are the risks of adopting a liability standard that is too permissive, i.e. that demands some higher burden of proof before condemning a dominant firm's responses to a rival that threatens its dominance? Could such a standard inhibit the incentives of firms (and their investors) who would challenge well-established dominant firms, especially those who have signaled their intention to respond aggressively? Given what we have read about Microsoft's conduct, would you agree with Microsoft's position that its hands were being tied unfairly by the court, impeding Microsoft's own ability to innovate without promoting innovation by its rivals? Did it successfully articulate and support innovation-related defenses for the specific conduct challenged by the government? Or were Netscape and Java the innovators and Microsoft the firm whose conduct, if permitted, would have perpetuated its monopoly and discouraged competition, especially from innovative new products and services? For a more complete account of the case and further examination of these questions, see ANDREW I. GAVIL & HARRY FIRST, THE MICROSOFT ANTITRUST CASES: COMPETITION POLICY FOR THE TWENTY-FIRST CENTURY (2014). *See also* William H. Page & John E. Lopatka, THE *MICROSOFT* CASE: ANTITRUST, HIGH TECHNOLOGY, AND CONSUMER WELFARE (2007).

What limits, if any, does the court put on its own analysis of causation? Of what significance is the court's suggestion that somewhat attenuated claims of causation may not defeat liability in a case seeking injunctive relief, but could influence the choice of remedy? How would it affect a private action brought seeking treble damages? We will return to that statement and examine its impact on the remedial portion of the decision later in this Chapter.

Figure 4–7:

Proving Microsoft's Market Power

Governments	Microsoft	Court of Appeals

• Persistent high share of defined relevant market (double inference)
• Barriers to entry
  • Sunk costs
  • Scale economies
  • Switching costs
  • Network effects
  • Applications
• Conduct constituting the exercise of market power (single inference) *and* actual anticompetitive effects
  • Exclusionary
  • Collusive
    • Prices
    • Profit margins
    • Equity Value
	• No market power in any relevant market ("behavioral" approach)
	  • Leap-frog competition
	  • Innovation
	  • Intense competition
	• No significant barriers to entry
	  • Sunk costs
	  • Switching costs
	  • Network effects
	  • Applications
	• Not possible to define a relevant market and calculate market shares
	  • Middleware
	  • Servers
	  • Other Oss
	• Profits and margins normal for software
	• Conduct evidencing vibrant competition
	  • Investment in R&D
	  • Low price for Windows
		• Persistent high share in properly defined relevant market
		• Barriers to entry
		  • Applications
		• Conduct constituting the exercise of market power (single inference) *and* actual anticompetitive effects

Recall that under the traditional framework, a finding of monopoly power alone does not constitute a violation of Section 2 of the Sherman Act.

In addition, the plaintiff, in this instance the federal government and nineteen states, also had to establish that the monopoly power found was either willfully acquired or willfully maintained. "Willfulness," as we have learned, means achieved or maintained by some predatory or exclusionary means. Although some of the many private cases filed against Microsoft in the wake of the governments' cases questioned the means whereby it achieved its monopoly position, note that the governments' cases focused on its "maintenance" of that power.

Note that to satisfy the "monopoly power" element of a Section 2 claim for monopolization, the D.C. Circuit relied on both circumstantial evidence (a defined relevant market in which it calculated market shares) and direct evidence (evidence of the actual exercise of market power). But evidence of the actual exercise of market power is not always available. In Section 1 and Section 2 Sherman Act cases, anticompetitive effects often are either presumed—as in the per se offenses of Section 1—or inferred from evidence of market power, typically high market shares, and other supporting evidence, such as barriers to entry. In many other antitrust offenses, a challenge is authorized before the full effects of conduct are felt, *e.g.*, attempt to monopolize, and all of the incipiency offenses under the Clayton Act. Merger challenges, for example, are almost always inferential/circumstantial cases because they are most often brought prospectively.

The field of mergers, which we will examine in Chapter 5, has laid the foundation for two general methods for inferring anticompetitive effects from evidence of market power. In the first, direct evidence of market power is used to infer anticompetitive effects. Thus, where price/cost ratios, direct measures of demand elasticities, or econometric analysis of prices supports the assertion that a firm or firms possess market power, the inference of anticompetitive effects can be made, provided it is linked to conduct that cannot be justified as legitimate. We describe this approach as the "*single inference*" method: from direct evidence of market power, anticompetitive effects are inferred. The evidence of market power is direct, but the conclusion as to anticompetitive effects is the product of inference: "market power," as opposed to evidence of actual price increases or the exclusion of rivals, justifies the presumption that illegitimate conduct will have anticompetitive consequences. It shifts a burden of production to the defending party. This single inference method is explored more fully in Sidebar 4–5.

In the second methodology, neither evidence of actual anticompetitive effects nor direct evidence of market power is available. In such circumstances, market power can be inferred from market share calculations, which in turn are derived after a relevant market is defined. In a sense, this method involves a "*double inference*:" from evidence of high market shares, market power is inferred, and from evidence of market power, anticompetitive harm is inferred. As we observed earlier in this Chapter in *Alcoa* and *Cellophane*, this approach has long been a staple of monopolization analysis. Note how the court in *Microsoft* relied on both single and double inference methods in its analysis of monopoly power. Linked with evidence of exclusionary conduct, monopoly power permits the inference of "monopolization," which can be interpreted as a kind of anticompetitive effect. In merger analysis, the double inference approach is the basis for the *Philadelphia Nat'l Bank* presumption, which we will study in Chapter 5. Similarly, in our study of Sherman Act Section 1 in Chapter 2, we saw how the approach is used in comprehensive rule of reason analysis, as it was in *RealComp II*.

In both instances, there can be disagreement in specific cases about the reliability and probative value of inferences from certain types of direct or circumstantial evidence, particularly with respect to inferences of market power from persistently high profits or high market shares. It is worth emphasizing that the inference of anticompetitive effect from direct evidence of market power is merely an *inference*. In principle, evidence of entry conditions and efficiencies can be used to rebut that inference.

Sidebar 4–5:
The "Single Inference" Method for
Inferring Anticompetitive Effects

The single inference method of inferring anticompetitive effect relies on direct evidence of market power and infers anticompetitive effect from that evidence. Although the evidence of market power is direct, the evidence as to anticompetitive effect is circumstantial—it requires an inference drawn from the direct proof of market power. At least three types of direct evidence of market power have been discussed in the case law and the economic literature:

- price and conduct comparisons across markets and over time;
- direct measures of the structure of demand; and
- accounting estimates of margins and profits.

Price and Conduct Comparisons Across Markets and Over Time

Often the most persuasive evidence of market power comes from direct comparisons of prices between the markets in question and comparable markets thought to perform competitively. These might be based upon different regions of the country, or a "before and after" comparison with the same market at an earlier time, for example. When a competitive benchmark is available, this type of comparison constitutes a "natural experiment" that can identify the presence or absence of market power.

The examples discussed in detail below illustrate the power of direct evidence on pricing for demonstrating market power. Two factors are critical in making such comparisons persuasive. The first is whether the benchmark market is likely to perform competitively, or at least more competitively than the market under review, if the anticompetitive theory is correct, so that the comparison between them provides a natural experiment. In a before-and-after comparison, for example, the benchmark would be the period before the conduct under review has occurred, and the comparison would ask whether price is higher in the period after the conduct took place. In a comparison across markets, the benchmark market might be relatively unconcentrated, and the comparison would ask whether prices are higher in more concentrated markets. The second factor is whether differences in price between the benchmark market and the market under review could have explanations other than market power, most importantly differences in cost. More generally, the observed differences in price must be greater than can be accounted for by differences in cost or other factors. Another innocent explanation that might apply in some cases is that the observed differences in price merely reflect price discrimination in competitive markets.

1. *Bid Rigging Illustration: Addyston Pipe*

One example of direct evidence of market power, from which anticompetitive effect can be inferred, comes from *Addyston Pipe.* Our discussion of this decision in Chapter 2 focused on its influence on the evolution of the rule of reason. The underlying facts can be quickly sketched. The defendants were six manufacturers of cast iron pipe, who commonly participated in procurement auctions run by local gas and water utilities. Instead of competing against each other when customers put out pipe orders for bid, the firms reached an agreement to divide up a number of markets in the southern and central part of the country, city-by-city, for two years. The Court observed: "[t]he record is full of instances * * * in which, after the successful bidder had been fixed by the 'auction pool,' or had been fixed by the arrangement as to 'reserve' cities, the other defendants put in bids at the public letting as high as the selected bidder requested, in order to give the appearance of active competition between the defendants." *Addyston Pipe*, 85 F. at 275. Territory more than 500 miles from the firms' foundries was called "free" territory, as opposed to "pay" territory, where the reserved cities were located. In free territory, the firms were allowed to bid any price.

The evidence concerning price variation across cities provided a direct basis for inferring that the firms exercised market power. Prices were higher in the reserved cities than the free cities, even though costs appeared to be lower in reserved cities, demonstrating directly that the firms had exercised market power. 85 F. at 277. This outcome was particularly hard to rationalize as derived innocently from differences in the cost of serving the various locations, because shipping costs were substantial, typically on the order of 10% to 25% of price.[a] This was far from the only evidence from which anticompetitive effect was inferred in *Addyston Pipe*—indeed, the agreement in that case would today likely be held illegal per se, as an agreement among rivals concerning price that lacked any business justification, without regard to the presence or absence of evidence of injury to competition. The case nevertheless provides a useful example of the "single inference" method.

The kind of comparison used to infer market power in *Addyston Pipe* has been used to distinguish bid rigging, a form of price-fixing, from competitive bidding in formal auctions. This approach compares the behavior of the firms under investigation to the behavior of a class of firms that are assumed *not* to be involved in bid rigging. The methodology requires that the firms bid in multiple auctions, as for different road building contracts, school milk procurements, forest timber sales, oil drilling tracts, etc. The analyst looks at the way the competitive firms alter their bids in response to variation in the characteristics across auctions, and infers that the firms under investigation are conspiring rather than bidding competitively—that they are making phantom bids that feign competition, as with the firms in *Addyston Pipe*—if they do not alter their bids across auctions in similar ways. *See, e.g.,* Patrick Bajari & Garrett Summers, *Detecting Collusion in Procurement Auctions: Select Survey of Recent Research,* 70 ANTITRUST L. J. 143 (2002); J. Douglas Zona & Robert H. Porter, *Detection of Bid Rigging in Procurement Auctions,* 101 J. POL. ECON. 518 (1993); J. Douglas Zona & Robert H. Porter, *Ohio*

---

[a] According to the appellate court, the defendants also claimed that "the prices at a city like St. Louis, in which the specifications were detailed and precise, were higher because pipe had to be made especially for the job, and they could not use stock on hand." 85 F. at 278. In theory, this possibility could have provided a cost-related explanation for high prices in the reserved cities, and thus undermined the direct evidence of market power. But it was apparently not a major focus of the litigation.

Milk Markets: An Analysis of Bidding, 30 RAND J. ECON. 263 (1999).

2. *Merger Illustration: Staples*

A modern example comes from the *Staples* merger case, which we will study in Chapter 5. According to George Cary, the then Senior Deputy Director of the FTC's Bureau of Competition and the FTC's lead counsel when the preliminary injunction hearing was held, the FTC had a "one-fact case." The key fact was what the trial court called the "compelling" pricing evidence. *Staples*, 970 F. Supp. at 1076. That evidence showed that Staples charged significantly higher prices—at least 5 percent and as much as 13 percent higher—in geographic markets (cities) where it had no office supply superstore competition than in markets where it competed with the two other superstore chains, notwithstanding the presence of a wide range of non-superstore retailers of office supplies in single superstore markets. *Id.* at 1075–76. The direct evidence on pricing was not limited to comparisons of prices across markets. The court also relied on before and after comparisons, finding that Staples changed price zones to lower prices when faced with the entry of another superstore, but not for other retailers. *Id.* at 1077–78.

The direct evidence on pricing was a key basis for defining a product market limited to "consumable office supplies sold through office superstores" and predicting that the proposed merger of Staples and one of its superstore rivals would likely be anticompetitive. Within this market, the proposed merger would have been a merger to monopoly in many metropolitan area geographic markets, and it increased concentration substantially in many other markets where a third superstore chain would remain as a competitor. In this way, direct evidence on *market power*—the likely market power of superstores acting collectively—provided circumstantial evidence of *anticompetitive effect*, making *Staples* a single inference case. Alternatively, if the decision is understood as using the pricing evidence to define the product market, to infer market power from high concentration (often merger to monopoly) in the various geographic markets, and to infer anticompetitive effects from market power, it is a double inference case.

But the district court also recognized that the pricing evidence provided *direct evidence of anticompetitive effect*. The FTC showed that prices were higher when Staples was the only superstore chain in the market, relative to prices when Staples competed with Office Depot, its merger partner, and no other superstore chain. The FTC also showed that prices were higher when Staples competed head to head with Office Max, the third major superstore chain. The lowest prices were consistently evident only when Staples, Office Depot, and Office Max were all competing. *See generally* Jonathan B. Baker, *Econometric Analysis in* FTC v. Staples, 18 J. PUB. POL. & MARKETING 11 (1999) ("*Econometric Analysis*"). According to the court:

> * * * [D]irect evidence shows that by eliminating Staples' most significant, and in many markets only, rival, this merger would allow Staples to increase prices or otherwise maintain prices at an anticompetitive level. The merger would eliminate head-to-head competition between the two lowest cost and lowest priced firms in the superstore market.

Staples, 970 F.Supp. at 1082–83 (footnote omitted). To the extent the court relied on direct evidence of anticompetitive effect, it was not engaging in either a single inference or a double inference method of inferring anticompetitive effects from market power. Thus, in *Staples,* the pricing evidence lent support *both* to proof of likely anticompetitive effects, and single or double inference proof of market power from which anticompetitive effects could be inferred. These alternative methods of proving anticompetitive effect, therefore, were aligned, which made the evidence especially compelling.[b]

The merging firms' response to the pricing evidence in *Staples* is instructive as to the significance and probative value of direct evidence of market power. They contended that superstores were constrained by competition from a wide range of non-superstore retailers of office supplies. They argued that if the product market were defined properly, to encompass the sale of consumable office supplies by all sellers, not just office superstores, the resulting low market shares for the merging firms—a combined share of only 5.5% nationwide—would properly reflect the low potential for anticompetitive effect from the proposed acquisition. In short, the parties argued that the *double inference* method of inferring anticompetitive effect should be preferred to the *single inference* method proposed by the F.T.C. and adopted by the court. They asked the court to

---

[b] It is worth noting that a court may find it valuable or necessary to define a market even when it does not employ the double inference method of proving harm to competition. Market definition allows for the identification of market participants, which a court may need to know in order to determine, for example, whether demand elasticities are properly estimated (without omitting the influence of a key rival) or to identify the maverick whose incentives may be relevant to analysis of coordinated competitive effects.

prefer circumstantial evidence of anticompetitive effect based on market shares and a disputed market definition to circumstantial evidence of anticompetitive effect based on direct evidence of market power from pricing comparisons across markets and over time.[c]

3. *Price Discrimination*

Economic price discrimination—charging different prices for the same product to different customers—also can provide direct evidence of market power based on pricing. *See* GEORGE STIGLER, THE ORGANIZATION OF INDUSTRY 14 (1968) (describing "the absence of systematic price discrimination" as evidence of competition). *But cf.* Symposium: *Competitive Price Discrimination*, 70 ANTITRUST L.J. 593 (2003) (debating whether price discrimination should be deemed to reflect market power when entry is easy and anticompetitive effects are absent). When firms discriminate in price, they charge a higher price to those customers willing to pay more, or to a group of buyers with relatively inelastic demand. (The economics of price discrimination are discussed in more detail in Sidebar 5–4, *infra*.) Evidence of price discrimination can arise through a comparison of the price charged different customers or in different markets for similar products. Or it can come from before and after comparisons of pricing in the same market, when market demand is thought to vary in elasticity over time.

To be probative of market power, such comparisons must involve similar products, or otherwise control for product differences likely to affect the price. This issue would arise in determining the extent of a price increase resulting from price discrimination by airlines, for example. If business passengers pay more for a ticket on the same aircraft than leisure passengers, who buy their tickets weeks in advance, the two groups of travelers are buying a somewhat different product. The business traveler is purchasing more than a seat on the aircraft; she is also acquiring the ability to decide whether or not to fly at the last minute.

Before terming the price difference economic price discrimination, and treating it as direct evidence of market power, one must first ask whether the higher last-minute price reflects price discrimination against a group of buyers with inelastic demand, or whether it instead reflects the added cost

---

[c] The merging firms further contended that the F.T.C. had drawn the wrong inference from the pricing data because it failed to control for differences in cost across cities. *See generally* Baker, *Econometric Analysis, supra.*

to the airline of holding the seat open until the last minute, where it might not be filled. Of course, both factors might prove to be important. *Cf. Blue Cross & Blue Shield United of Wisconsin v. Marshfield Clinic*, 65 F.3d 1406, 1412 (7th Cir. 1995) (questioning inference of market power from high prices on the ground that the higher priced product was higher quality). Price comparisons over time similarly require accounting for cost differences over time when used to identify market power. *See generally* Jonathan B. Baker & Timothy F. Bresnahan, *Empirical Methods of Identifying and Measuring Market Power*, 61 ANTITRUST L.J. 3 (1992).

4. *Conduct*

As we observed in Chapter 2 in connection with our examination of the modern rule of reason, courts increasingly have found evidence of actual anticompetitive effects sufficient to shift the burden of production from a plaintiff to a defendant in a range of antitrust cases. In each such instance, however, the effect followed from certain *conduct*. Evidence of conduct that produces an actual output reduction, including a reduction in non-price dimensions of competition such as product variety and innovation, would constitute proof of market power, and so allow the inference of anticompetitive effect. After all, a firm or group of firms that raise price by reducing industry output are almost by definition *exercising market power. See NCAA v. Bd. of Regents of Univ. of Oklahoma*, 468 U.S. 85, 104–05 n.29 (1984) ("The evidence establishes the fact that the networks are * * * paying * * * large fees because the NCAA agrees to limit production.").

Direct Measures of the Structure of Demand (Buyer Substitution)

As we first learned in Chapter 1, the power to raise price by reducing output is closely related to the responsiveness of buyers to higher prices—that is to the *elasticity of buyer demand*. Moreover, observations on the historical response of buyers to price changes can permit economic experts to learn about demand elasticities, as will be discussed in Chapter 5, in connection with market definition under the Horizontal Merger Guidelines.

Similar issues arise in proving a dominant firm's market power under Sherman Act § 2. In an influential article on market power, Landes and Posner pointed out that if direct evidence of elasticities is available, it can be used "to measure the firm's market power directly," in which case "no market share criterion of market power is either necessary or appropriate." William M. Landes & Richard A. Posner, *Market*

Power in Antitrust Cases, 94 HARV. L. REV. 937, 953 (1981) (showing how the elasticity of demand facing a dominant firm can be inferred from knowledge of the market elasticity of demand, firm market share, and the elasticity of supply of the competitive fringe).

One common use of direct evidence of prospective market power involves the analysis of mergers among sellers of differentiated products. Here, as will be discussed in Chapter 5, prospective market power may be inferred from evidence that the products of the merging firms are close substitutes for buyers.

Accounting Estimates of Margins and Profits

At one time, accounting estimates of firm profit rates were thought to provide strong direct evidence of market power, and thus circumstantial evidence of anticompetitive effect. During the 1970s, according to Professor Elzinga, antitrust came close to adopting accounting rates of return as "a primary device for unmasking monopoly." Kenneth G. Elzinga, *Unmasking Monopoly, in* ECONOMICS AND ANTITRUST POLICY 18 (Robert J. Larner & James W. Meehan, Jr. eds., 1989).

This initiative foundered for several reasons. First, high profit rates, even if measured successfully, do not necessarily derive from the exercise of market power. They may be related to success in lowering costs or other efficiencies, such as superior product design or superior distribution, and may be consistent with competitive returns in an industry in which firms must make substantial, but risky investments. As the literature on finance explains, high average returns on investment may be required to induce investors to accept high risks. Elzinga makes the point with an example:

> If ten wildcatters drill for oil and nine strike out instead of striking oil, the rate of return earned by the one successful driller provides no information for diagnosing the presence of monopoly rents for that firm. The risk-adjusted rate of return on invested funds for the entire set of wildcatters could be modest (or normal) even if the rate of return on invested funds for the fortunate driller was substantial.

Id. at 20. Conversely, if a monopolist is not forced by competition to keep costs low, but takes its reward for monopoly in the form of what economist J.R. Hicks termed "a quiet life," its inefficient methods of production may lead it to earn low, not high, profits.

Second, accounting measures of profitability may deviate substantially from the relevant economic concepts. The way accountants spread costs over time and adjust asset values for depreciation means, according to two influential commentators, that "there is no way in which one can look at accounting rates of return and infer anything about relative economic profitability or, a fortiori, about the presence or absence of monopoly profits." Franklin M. Fisher & John J. McGowan, *On the Misuse of Accounting Rates of Return to Infer Monopoly Profits*, 73 AM. ECON. REV. 82, 90 (1983).

These problems loom so large that antitrust today does not rely heavily on profitability measures in making inferences about market power. Judge Posner summarized the current consensus view this way:

> * * * [I]t is always treacherous to try to infer monopoly power from a high rate of return. * * * [N]ot only do measured rates of return reflect accounting conventions more than they do real profits (or losses), as an economist would understand these terms, but there is not even a good economic theory that associates monopoly power with a high rate of return. Firms compete to become and to remain monopolists, and the process of competition erodes their profits. Conversely, competitive firms may be highly profitable merely by virtue of having low costs as a result of superior efficiency, yet not sufficiently lower costs than all other competitors to enable the firm to take over its market and become a monopolist.

Blue Cross & Blue Shield United of Wisconsin v. Marshfield Clinic, 65 F.3d 1406, 1412 (1995) (citations omitted).

Finally, the relationship between price and marginal cost, termed price-cost margins, has also been proposed as a form of direct evidence of market power. Economists often report price-cost margins in terms of the Lerner Index, defined as the difference between price and marginal cost, expressed as a ratio of price. If price equals marginal cost, the Lerner Index equals zero. As marginal cost becomes a very small fraction of price, the Lerner Index approaches one. In one case cited by Professor Elzinga, for example, an economist testified that "a Lerner Index so close to its theoretical maximum of 1.0 makes the inference of market power indisputable." Kenneth G. Elzinga, *Unmasking Monopoly, supra* at 18.

One problem with relying on the Lerner Index as evidence of market power involves difficulties measuring marginal cost.

Average variable cost is a common proxy, but, for reasons set forth in our next Sidebar, a discussion of price-cost comparisons employed to detect predatory pricing, the proxy may not capture marginal cost well. On the other hand, the Horizontal Merger Guidelines regard accounting evidence of price-cost margins as sufficiently reliable to use in computing measures of upward pricing pressure in evaluation mergers between sellers of differentiated products. *See infra* Sidebar 5–8.

Putting aside problems with measuring marginal cost, interpreting high price-cost margins as evidence of market power raises issues similar to those involved in inferring market power from price comparisons across markets and over time, and those involved in inferring market power from high profits. For example, to interpret the Lerner Index as a gauge of market power, it is necessary to assume that the competitive price would be equal to marginal cost. But, as discussed above in connection with price discrimination, that may not be a good assumption for industries with high fixed cost and low marginal costs—the very industries in which the Lerner Index would be very high. Competitive benchmarks derived from before-and-after comparisons and cross-market "natural experiments" may be more convincing.

Notwithstanding these difficulties, price-cost margins continue to be relied on in some aspects of antitrust analysis. They are used to calibrate demand elasticities, for market definition and for simulating the price rise under the unilateral theory of competitive effect for mergers among sellers of differentiated products. *See generally* Gregory J. Werden, *Demand Elasticities in Antitrust Analysis*, 66 ANTITRUST L. J. 363 (1998); Gregory J. Werden & Luke M. Froeb, *Unilateral Competitive Effects of Horizontal Mergers, in* HANDBOOK OF ANTITRUST ECONOMICS (Paolo Buccirossi, ed. 2008).

Conclusion

Methods of inferring anticompetitive effect from direct evidence of market power often appear more complex than the indirect double inference approach of inferring anticompetitive effect from market shares, which provide indirect evidence of market power. Direct evidence of market power also may not be available, may be very costly to develop, and when it is available it may not be strongly probative. But the single inference approach to assessing anticompetitive effect is important in antitrust practice, on its own or in conjunction with market share evidence (as in *Microsoft*), because it offers the possibility

> of greater precision in identifying and measuring market power.

As we have learned, monopoly power alone is not an offense under Section 2, there must also be anticompetitive conduct, although as Sidebar 4–5 explains, sometimes the evidence of power and conduct can overlap. How did the court structure its inquiry into Microsoft's conduct? How did it allocate burdens of production and proof? Consider the following Figure, which summarizes the court's approach.

Figure 4-8
Microsoft's Structured Analysis

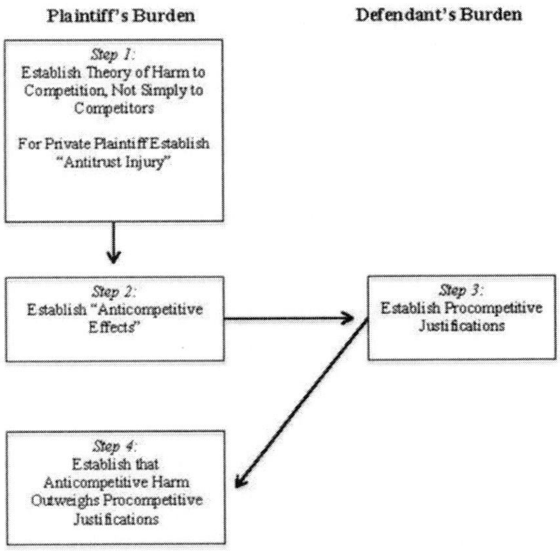

Plaintiff's Burden   Defendant's Burden

Step 1:
Establish Theory of Harm to Competition, Not Simply to Competitors

For Private Plaintiff Establish "Antitrust Injury"

Step 2:
Establish "Anticompetitive Effects"

Step 3:
Establish Procompetitive Justifications

Step 4:
Establish that Anticompetitive Harm Outweighs Procompetitive Justifications

Would the same structure apply whether the case was one under Section 1 or Section 2 of the Sherman Act? How does the court's approach compare to the one we considered at the end of Chapter 2 in connection with the rule of reason? To the implicit framework used by the Supreme Court in *Aspen Skiing*? What did the court of appeals mean when it stated: "In cases arising under § 1 of the Sherman Act, the courts routinely apply a similar balancing approach under the rubric of the 'rule of reason' "?

How distinct were the two traditional elements of power and conduct in the monopolization cases we have read thus far? To illustrate the point, consider the excerpts from *Aspen Skiing* and especially *Microsoft*. How distinct was the court's analysis of power and conduct in each case? What role did evidence of actual effects play in assessing both power and conduct? In *Microsoft*, did the court rely upon distinct evidence of each, or did the relevant evidence overlap? If the latter, what could explain such an "overlap"? Are there common concepts at work that cut across and possibly unify the two traditional legal factors under Section 2? What does it suggest about the continued distinctiveness of the elements of a Section 1 and Section 2 Sherman Act violation when evidence of actual anticompetitive effects is presented?

Does the court offer any specific definition of "exclusionary," as did the Court in *Aspen Skiing*? What does it mean when it says that "to be condemned as exclusionary, a monopolist's act must have an "anticompetitive effect"? Note that it goes on to say: "That is, it must harm the competitive *process* and thereby harm consumers. In contrast, harm to one or more *competitors* will not suffice." Is this different than the approach to definition taken in *Aspen Skiing*? If so, does it improve upon that approach? In what sense?

Consider finally whether there is a downside to "structured" analysis. Does it really reflect an "improvement" over previous, more open-ended approaches? If so, how so? Will it tend to be too rigid? Does it generally favor plaintiffs or defendants, which might perpetuate fears of over and under-deterrence and consequent costs of error, *i.e.*, incorrect judgments? Does it significantly clarify the relevant factors and the relative burdens of production and proof? Will it reliably include all of the useful evidence, or possibly exclude information that could affect the outcome of particular cases? Does it provide clear guidance to business firms, and if it does not, what costs are associated with complying with antitrust rules that do not?

In the wake of *Aspen Skiing* and *Kodak*, some commentators debated whether the two cases could be read as allowing an inference of harm to competition to arise from the absence of a legitimate business justification for the monopolist's conduct, even in the absence of affirmative evidence of anticompetitive effects. *Compare* Jonathan B. Baker, *Promoting Innovation Competition Through the* Aspen/Kodak *Rule*, 7 GEO. MASON. L. REV. 495 (1999) (arguing that the cases establish a truncated rule) *with* Timothy J. Muris, *The FTC and the Law of Monopolization*, 67 ANTITRUST L. J. 693 (2000) (arguing that they do not). Does *Microsoft* support either of these two views?

By the time the government actions against Microsoft were initiated in May, 1998 in the United States, the European Commission had begun its own investigation of Microsoft's anticompetitive conduct in Europe, which eventually led to more than one case against Microsoft. In the Note that follows, we explore the similarities and differences in the conduct challenged and the remedies ordered in the U.S. and E.U. cases against Microsoft.

NOTE ON MICROSOFT PROSECUTIONS IN THE EUROPEAN UNION

In December of 1998, after the U.S. antitrust case against Microsoft was under-way, Sun Microsystems filed a complaint with the Directorate General for Competition ("DG-Comp") of the European Commission ("EC") in Brussels alleging that Microsoft was refusing to supply it with interoperability information necessary to permit its work group server operating system software to interoperate with Microsoft's dominant PC operating system. [6] Under EC procedures, receipt of the complaint triggered an initial investigation by the EC. The following February, the Commission expanded the scope of that investigation to include allegations that Microsoft had tied its new media player, Windows Media Player, to Windows, much in the way that the U.S. case was considering allegations that it had tied its Internet browser, Internet Explorer ("IE"), to Windows. (The D.C. Circuit's resolution of the governments' tying allegations is reproduced in Chapter 6, *infra*.)

As a consequence of its investigation, which continued for several years, the EC ultimately presented Microsoft with three "Statements of Objections," [7] the rough equivalent in the U.S. of an administrative complaint. Collectively, the three statements alleged that Microsoft had abused its dominant position in the European Union ("E.U.") by failing to supply interoperability information to Sun and others and by tying its Windows Media Player to Windows, which impaired competition for media players. Under EC procedures, Microsoft then had a period of time to respond.

Ultimately rejecting those responses as inadequate, on March 24, 2004 the Commission issued its decision, concluding that Microsoft had in fact violated Article 82 (now Article 102 of the Treaty on the Functioning of the European Union ("TFEU")). As a remedy, the EC ordered Microsoft: (1) to produce an un-bundled version of Windows that did not include Windows Media Player in order to permit OEMs and consumers to substitute their own choice of media player, such as those from RealNetworks and Apple; (2) to disclose information sufficient to permit rival producers of work group server operating systems to produce software that would more easily interoperate with Windows client software; and (3) requiring it to pay a record fine of 497 million. *See* Commission Decision of 24.03.2004, relating to a proceeding under Article 82 of the E.U. Treaty (Case Comp/C-3/37.792 Microsoft), http://ec. europa.eu/competition/antitrust/cases/dec_docs/37792/37792_4177_1.pdf.

The case was appealed to the European Court of First Instance ("CFI"— now renamed the "General Court") and, in a comprehensive decision that was widely perceived as a very significant victory for the EC, the CFI affirmed the EC's decision in all substantive respects on September 17, 2007. *See* Case T-

---

[6] Portions of this chronology of events are adapted from a more comprehensive detailing of the development of the EC's initial investigation and prosecution of Microsoft on its website. *See* http://ec.europa.eu/competition/sectors/ICT/microsoft/investigation.html.

[7] These statements were issued on August 1, 2000, August 30, 2001, and August 6, 2003.

201/04, *Microsoft v. Commission*, Judgment of the Court of First Instance (Grand Chamber) of 17 September 2007, O.J. 2007 C269/45.

The EC's case against Microsoft involved some of the same facts and theories that had been raised in the U.S. Both cases proceeded from the critical assumption that Microsoft had obtained and was seeking to abuse its monopoly power in the market for Intel-compatible PC operating systems. Both the U.S. enforcement authorities and courts, as well as the EC and the CFI, readily concluded that Microsoft had durable monopoly power and that it was insulated from competition by significant barriers to entry. Both also readily concluded that Microsoft had undertaken conduct to fortify its monopoly from still developing competitive threats (although they were more fully formed in Europe) and that it lacked any legitimate justifications for its actions.

But there were also differences, some that were important. Whereas the U.S.'s case challenged a wide range of Microsoft's conduct as both tying and monopolization, the EC's case was relatively more narrowly drawn. Also, whereas the U.S. case focused on Microsoft's tying of its IE Internet browser to Windows, the EC's case focused on the tying of Windows Media Player to Windows.[8] Uniquely, the EC's case challenged Microsoft's refusal to provide information necessary to facilitate interoperability between Windows and work group servers running non-Microsoft operating systems.

More fundamentally, the core of the U.S. case (as it emerged from the court of appeals) proceeded from the theory that Microsoft's conduct, even when directed outside of the market for Intel-compatible PC operating systems ("PC OS"), had the effect of maintaining Microsoft's PC OS monopoly and hence constituted unlawful "monopoly maintenance" under Section 2. The court of appeals reversed the district court's judgment that Microsoft had attempted to monopolize a distinct Internet browser "market" because it failed to prove two requirements for a successful claim of attempt to monopolize: (1) the existence of a distinct relevant market for Internet browsers; and (2) that the "market" is protected from competition by substantial entry barriers. *Microsoft Corp.*, 253 F.3d at 80–84. In contrast, the EC's case, based on the "abuse of dominance" provisions in Article 82, was focused more on Microsoft's use of its monopoly power in PC OS to gain a competitive advantage in the markets for work group server operating systems and media players. In the U.S., such claims must satisfy the seemingly more stringent requirements of the offense of attempted monopolization.

Perhaps the most substantial point of difference between the two cases concerned remedy. As we shall learn later in this Chapter, the district court's order that Microsoft be broken up into two companies was vacated by the D.C. Circuit and, following remand, the U.S. case settled and a consent decree was entered. In contrast to the EC's case, Microsoft was not required to unbundle

---

[8]   As we shall see in Chapter 6, the D.C. Circuit reversed the district court's finding of liability based on Microsoft's tying of IE to Windows, because in the court's view the district court had improperly applied a per se standard. Because the case was settled after remand, the tying claims were never re-tried.

its Internet browser from Windows. Other, less invasive steps were agreed to that in theory could facilitate greater competition for browsers. Also, no major fines were imposed on Microsoft in the U.S., because U.S. enforcement agencies lack the same authority that the EC has to impose them.

The European Commission initiated a new antitrust challenge to Microsoft in early 2009. Like the 1998 U.S. case, the new case focused on Microsoft's bundling of its Internet Explorer browser (IE) with its Windows operating system. The Commission's Statement of Objections (SO) characterized that bundling as tying and expressed its preliminary view that the practice constituted an abuse of dominant position in violation of Article 82 (now 102). The case was settled when Microsoft agreed to provide Windows users with a browser "Choice Screen" that would provide consumers with a more readily accessible means of changing their choice of default browser from IE to other competitive products. A similar remedy had been ordered by the Korea Fair Trade Commission in its tying case against Microsoft.

We will more fully explore the law and economics of tying in Chapter 6, including further consideration of the *Microsoft* cases in the U.S. and the E.U. We will also examine the issues posed by refusals to share information, such as Microsoft's interoperability information, later in this Chapter.

Finally, recall that the court in Microsoft observed that although "anticompetitive intent" was not an element of the offense, evidence of intent could be used to inform the inquiry into effects. Our next Sidebar further explores the role of intent evidence in antitrust offenses.

Sidebar 4–6:
The Role of Intent in Antitrust Analysis

It might seem logical to assume that "intent" also would be a factor, if not a required element, of many antitrust offenses. After all, if the point of antitrust analysis frequently is to distinguish between "hard competition" and "predation," subjective intent would appear to be relevant to the inquiry. Defendants could be expected to offer exculpatory evidence of their "good," *i.e.*, competitive, intentions, whereas prosecutors and plaintiffs alike would try to focus attention on evidence suggesting a desire to injure consumers or vanquish rivals.

But evidence of intent can at once be both revealing and unreliable. Documents and testimony referring colorfully to a defendant's seeming intent to "drive out the competition" or "crush" its rivals, may be commonplace in the files of many a firm. Consider for example, the following deposition colloquy, reported in *Blair Foods, Inc. v. Ranchers Cotton Oil*, 610 F.2d

665 (9th Cir. 1980), a case alleging attempt to monopolize under Section 2, as well as conspiracy claims under Section 1:

> Q. There was no doubt in your mind that Blair [the plaintiff] was a part of the business scene?
>
> A. He (sic) was making himself a part of it at that time.
>
> Q. Did you have any objection to that?
>
> A. I would like to see all of my competitors bow out of business.
>
> Q. You would?
>
> A. Yes.
>
> Q. You would like the entire Northern California area for yourself?
>
> A. The whole world, yes. Wouldn't that be nice?
>
> Q. Have you always felt that way?
>
> [The Questioning Attorney]: Let the record show the witness is laughing at this. Counsel is taking it up as a serious matter.
>
> The Witness: You ask a silly question, you get a silly answer.

Id. at 667 n.1.

Critics of reliance on these sorts of statements point out that they could be as consistent with hard competition as with predation, and by themselves reveal little about the nature of the conduct undertaken and its consequences, especially in cases of alleged exclusionary conduct. *See, e.g.,* Frank H. Easterbrook, *On Identifying Exclusionary Conduct*, 61 NOTRE DAME L. REV. 972 (1986). The same statements could be found in the files of a firm that realized the goal of vanquishing its rival through efficiencies and innovation and one that did so through true predation. Antitrust standards that too readily rely on this sort of evidence, therefore, easily could dampen legitimately aggressive competitive spirits for fear of antitrust exposure.

On the other hand, to completely discount evidence of intent might be to ignore relevant and probative evidence with respect to the effects of conduct and possible justifications for it. In fact, evidence of intent may be most useful when it explains and illuminates the utility and efficacy of specific conduct. In such circumstances, internal documents describing the goals of particular conduct may well facilitate the investigation of its impact. This might be especially true where collusive effects are at issue. Evidence discussing intended effects on prices, for example, may not exhibit the inherent ambiguity of aggressive talk of injuring rivals. Some kind of "balance" therefore may be needed between the two extreme positions. *See generally* Marina Lao, *Reclaiming a Role for Intent Evidence in Monopolization Analysis*, 54 AM. U. L. REV. 151 (2004).

"Intent," therefore, has played varying roles in antitrust. But those roles vary with the civil or criminal nature of the alleged violation, and with the particular offense alleged under Section 1 or 2 of the Sherman Act.

Intent and Criminal Antitrust

Owing in large part to its origins as a "white collar" criminal statute, the Sherman Act has been read to incorporate the traditional requirement of the criminal law of "intent" or "mens rea." Hence the Supreme Court, relying on that tradition, has held that

> * * * [A]n effect on prices, without more, will not support a criminal conviction under the Sherman Act. * * * Rather, we hold that a defendant's state of mind or intent is an element of a criminal antitrust offense which must be established by evidence and inferences drawn therefrom and cannot be taken from the trier of fact through reliance on a legal presumption of wrongful intent from proof of an effect on prices.

United States v. U.S. Gypsum Co., 438 U.S. 422, 435 (1978). The Court concluded that it was "unwilling to construe the Sherman Act as mandating a regime of strict-liability criminal offenses." *Id.* at 436. Having concluded that intent was an element of a criminal Section 1 Sherman Act violation, the Court endorsed use of the traditional criminal law's "bifurcated" concept— intent could be established *either* by (1) purpose to bring about an anticompetitive result *or* (2) knowledge of the probable consequences of the conduct—*both* were not required. *Id.* at 444–45 & n.21. The Court reasoned:

> The business behavior which is likely to give rise to criminal antitrust charges is conscious behavior normally undertaken only after a full consideration of the desired results and a weighing of the costs, benefits, and risks. A requirement of proof not only of this knowledge of likely effects, but also of a conscious desire to bring them to fruition or to violate the law would seem, particularly in such a context, both unnecessarily cumulative and unduly burdensome. *Where carefully planned and calculated conduct is being scrutinized in the context of a criminal*

prosecution, the perpetrator's knowledge of the anticipated consequences is a sufficient predicate for a finding of criminal intent.

Id. at 445–46 (emphasis added).

Gypsum involved an alleged agreement to fix prices, which was largely evidenced by an exchange of price information by gypsum board producers. In defense of their actions, the producers asserted that the price information exchanges were undertaken for purposes of complying with the Robinson-Patman Act and were therefore exempt from Sherman Act scrutiny. Although this defense was ultimately rejected, its incorporation in the case meant it was not presented as a true "per se" price fixing indictment—a defense was considered and rejected.

Today, criminal prosecutions under Section 1 of the Sherman Act are almost exclusively reserved for per se offenses, such as price fixing, bid-rigging and division of markets. *See* ANTITRUST DIVISION MANUAL § IIIC5 ("Standards for Determining Whether to Proceed by Civil or Criminal Investigation"); Donald I. Baker, *To Indict or Not To Indict: Prosecutorial Discretion in Sherman Act Enforcement*, 63 CORNELL L. REV. 405 (1978). But does *Gypsum's* formulation of an intent requirement make sense for a per se offense? Would it make more sense for a rule of reason offense? How likely is it that the government would criminally prosecute a rule of reason offense? Can you see any problems that would arise in doing so? *See, e.g., United States v. Brown*, 936 F.2d 1042, 1045–46 (9th Cir. 1991) (*Gypsum* intent requirement inapplicable to per se case).

Intent in Civil Antitrust Cases

As we have noted, Section 2 of the Sherman Act prohibits three distinct offenses: monopolization, attempt to monopolize and conspiracy to monopolize. Here again we see the influence of the traditional criminal law approach to addressing matters of intent.

"Monopolization," constituting the *completed* offense, has consistently been interpreted as a "general intent" offense, *i.e.,* "no intent is relevant except that which is relevant to any liability, criminal or civil: *i.e.,* an intent to bring about the forbidden act." *United States v. Aluminum Co. of Am.*, 148 F.2d 416, 432 (2d Cir. 1945). Noting that "the question of intent is relevant" to both the offense of attempt to monopolize and monopolization, the Supreme Court elaborated on *Alcoa* in *Aspen Skiing*:

> In the former case [attempt to monopolize] it is necessary to prove a "specific intent" to accomplish the forbidden objective—as Judge Hand explained, "an intent which goes beyond the mere intent to do the act." United States v. Aluminum Co. Of America, 148 F.2d 416, 432 (C.A.2 1945). In the latter case [monopolization] evidence of intent is merely relevant to the question whether the challenged conduct is fairly characterized as "exclusionary" or "anticompetitive" * * * or "predatory" * * *. Whichever label is used, there is agreement on the proposition that "no monopolist monopolizes unconscious of what he is doing."

Aspen Skiing, 472 U.S. at 602 (quoting *Alcoa*). To the extent general intent is a formal requirement, therefore, it is readily inferred from the fact that the defendant has engaged in a predatory or exclusionary act constituting monopolization.

As *Aspen Skiing* also points out, however, in contrast, the offense of attempt to monopolize requires a showing of "specific intent." As we learned in Chapter 6, Justice Holmes is largely responsible for reading "specific intent" into the offense of attempted monopolization. *See Spectrum Sports, Inc. v. McQuillan*, 506 U.S. 447, 454–55 (1993) (discussing *Swift & Co. v. United States*, 196 U.S. 375, 396 (1905)). *Swift* was influenced by the common law origins of the Sherman Act and its status as a criminal statute. Given Justice Holmes' status as a scholar of the common law, it is not surprising that these facts would add up to a specific intent requirement—attempt crimes at common law were generally associated with "specific intent." Courts typically demand evidence of specific intent as well in cases alleging conspiracy to monopolize.

Sorting out the role of intent in civil Section 1 cases, however, has proved to be more of a challenge. You may recall from Chapter 2, that the Supreme Court's *Chicago Bd. of Trade* decision set forth the earliest and most significant definition of the rule of reason. The oft quoted language from *Chicago Bd. of Trade*, which invited evaluation of the history, purpose and effect of restraints of trade as part of the rule of reason inquiry, incorporated a role for purpose and intent:

> The history of the restraint, the evil believed to exist, the reason for adopting the particular remedy, *the purpose or end sought to be attained*, are all relevant

> facts. This is not because a good intention will save an
> otherwise objectionable regulation or the reverse, but
> because knowledge of intent may help the court to
> interpret facts and to predict consequences.

246 U.S. at 238 (emphasis added).

Over time, this portion of *Chicago Bd. of Trade* has
spawned several rules of thumb regarding intent in Sherman 1
cases: (1) good intentions are not a defense to a Sherman Act
violation—*i.e.*, when an agreement is established and there is
evidence that the agreement unreasonably restrained trade,
good intentions should be given no weight; (2) conversely, bad
intentions alone cannot make a violation out of conduct that
does *not* unreasonably restrain trade; but (3) evidence of intent
remains relevant to the extent it makes an inference of
anticompetitive effects more or less probable. The Ninth Circuit
summarized them in the remand in *California Dental Ass'n*, a
Supreme Court decision we studied in Chapter 2. Note how the
Ninth Circuit appears to incorporate all of the rules of thumb
outlined above:

> Our prior opinion held that the CDA constituted
> an agreement among its members. We did not dwell on
> the issue of intent, however, observing that "whatever
> its motivation, the point of the advertising policy was
> clearly to limit the types of advertising in which
> dentists could engage." We then observed that good
> "motives will not validate an otherwise
> anticompetitive practice," citing *NCAA v. Board of
> Regents*, 468 U.S. 85, 101 n. 23, 104 S.Ct. 2948, 82
> L.Ed.2d 70 (1984). This truncated discussion of intent
> reflects the well-established pattern of the Supreme
> Court to examine intent only in those close cases
> where the plaintiff falls short of proving that the
> defendant's actions were anticompetitive. Even then,
> "an admitted intention to limit competition will not
> make illegal conduct that we know to be pro-
> competitive or otherwise immune from antitrust
> control." 7 Phillip E. Areeda, Antitrust Law § 1506
> (1986). And, while "smoking gun" evidence of an intent
> to restrain competition remains relevant to the court's
> task of discerning the competitive consequences of a
> defendant's actions, "ambiguous indications of intent
> do not help us 'predict [the] consequences [of a
> defendant's acts]' " and are therefore of no value to a
> court analyzing a restraint under the rule of reason,

where the court's ultimate role is to determine the net effects of those acts. *Id.* Under such circumstances, we apply the rule of reason without engaging in the relatively fruitless inquiry into a defendant's intent.

* * *

We do see substantial evidence that the CDA intended to restrict certain types of advertising, but in light of the CDA's plausibly procompetitive justifications for the restrictions, such intent has no bearing on the question of whether those restrictions are in fact likely to prove anticompetitive or procompetitive. And the record reveals no unambiguous evidence that the CDA intended to restrain trade, so further analysis of CDA's intent becomes superfluous. Under such circumstances, intent "drops out" of our rule-of-reason inquiry, just as it did in our prior opinion, and the case hinges on the actual economic consequences of the CDA's restrictions.

California Dental Ass'n. v. FTC, 224 F.3d 942, 947–48 (9th Cir. 2000).

Based on the Ninth Circuit's approach, when would evidence of intent be relevant under the rule of reason? What kinds of intent evidence might be relevant? How can intent make a finding of anticompetitive effect more or less likely? Should exculpatory be as relevant as inculpatory evidence of intent? If so, is there a way to avoid creating an incentive for firms to routinely paper their files with manufactured "good intent" evidence? Should the answers to these questions vary depending upon whether the case is based on collusive or exclusionary effects? On whether the case is brought under Section 1, as were *Chicago Bd. of Trade* and *California Dental*, or as a monopolization case under Section 2?

Consider the following statement from the monopolization analysis in *United States v. Microsoft Corp.*:

> * * * [I]n considering whether the monopolist's conduct on balance harms competition and is therefore condemned as exclusionary for purposes of § 2, our focus is on the effect of that conduct, not upon the intent behind it. Evidence of the intent behind the conduct of a monopolist is relevant only to the extent it helps us understand the likely effect of the monopolist's conduct. [*citing* both *Chicago Bd. of Trade*

> (a Section 1 rule of reason case) and *Aspen Skiing Co.*
> (a Section 2 monopolization case)]
>
> 253 F.3d. at 59. Is the D.C. Circuit's approach consistent with the Ninth Circuit's in *California Dental?* Should it be? The *Microsoft* litigation renewed debate about the role of intent in monopolization cases. *Contrast* Steven C. Salop & R. Craig Romaine, *Preserving Monopoly: Economic Analysis, Legal Standards, and Microsoft*, 7 GEO. MASON L. REV. 617, 652 (1999) (no need for separate intent requirement in monopolization cases where firm engages in exclusionary conduct with insufficient offsetting efficiencies) *with* Ronald A. Cass & Keith Hylton, *Antitrust Intent*, 74 S. CAL. L. REV. 657 (2001) (advocating limited use of objective specific intent requirement in monopolization cases, even where evidence of anticompetitive effect is present). *See also McWane, Inc. v. FTC*, 783 F.3d 814, 840 (11th Cir. 2015) (citing *Microsoft* and *Chicago Board of Trade* for the proposition that "[a]nticompetitive intent alone, no matter how virulent, is insufficient to give rise to an antitrust violation. But, as this Court has said, "[e]vidence of intent is highly probative 'not because a good intention will save an otherwise objectionable regulation or the reverse; but because knowledge of intent may help the court to interpret facts and to predict consequences.' ").
>
> *California Dental* and *Microsoft*, however, appear to reflect the general rule—whether for purposes of monopolization under Section 2, or restraint of trade under Section 1, evidence of intent may aid the judgment of effects, but intent without effects will not suffice. Why would that be so? How might very specific evidence of intent tied to particular conduct illuminate its actual or likely effects? Are there no possible instances of unambiguous, anticompetitive intent evidence that might aid antitrust analysis in such cases? What would be lost if very strong evidence of anticompetitive intentions was deemed sufficient to support a finding of violation, even in the absence of evidence that the defendant was able to realize its goals? Would legitimate conduct be deterred?

2. PREDATORY PRICING

As we noted at the outset of this Chapter, the standards for judging non-price, as opposed to price-related exclusionary conduct, have followed two paradigms, although both can be understood in terms of their impact on rival access to suppliers and customers. Sometimes, they are differentiated by label: "exclusionary" being applied to non-price conduct and "predatory" being applied to price-specific conduct. Here we explore the development of the law and economics of "predatory pricing."

Traditionally, antitrust doctrine provided only murky guidance to dominant firms on pricing practices such as how much they could increase output and how low they could set their prices in response to entry or expansion by a competitor. Antitrust law provides two mechanisms for challenging such "predatory pricing:" Section 2 of the Sherman Act and Section 2(a) of the Clayton Act, as amended by the 1936 Robinson-Patman Act, which forbids certain forms of price discrimination. In the 1950s and 1960s, cases interpreting these provisions often accepted the idea that a dominant firm could use its "deep pockets" to finance below-cost sales to drive competitors from the market. A number of decisions displayed solicitude for the smaller, vanquished target of the dominant firm's pricing strategy.

Utah Pie Co. v. Continental Baking Co., 386 U.S. 685, 87 S.Ct. 1326 (1967) reflects this traditional view. In *Utah Pie* the Supreme Court used Section 2(a) of the Robinson-Patman Act to condemn the pricing conduct of Continental Baking, a national supplier of baked goods, in entering the Salt Lake City market for frozen dessert pies. The plaintiff, Utah Pie, was a local firm that held two-thirds of the Salt Lake City frozen pie market before Continental appeared on the scene. Continental priced its pies in Salt Lake City much lower than the company charged in nearby California and in other parts of the country. Utah Pie's share fell to under 50 percent of the market, and it sued Continental for predatory pricing.

The Supreme Court ruled that Utah Pie had produced enough evidence to sustain a jury verdict of unlawful price discrimination. The Court noted that, in support of its claim of probable competitive injury, Utah Pie had shown that Continental: (1) charged prices "less than its direct cost plus an allocation for overhead," 386 U.S. at 698, which (2) created a "drastically declining price structure;" and (3) that it did so with anticompetitive intent, which was evident from its "persistent sales below cost and radical price cuts themselves discriminatory." *Id.* at 702 & n.14. The Court's reasoning suggested that a firm might incur liability for setting its prices below its average total costs. Critics called *Utah Pie* a formula for shielding local firms (including those with high market shares) from competitive challenges by external suppliers.

Partly in response to *Utah Pie*, the 1970s and 1980s featured extensive academic literature about the appropriate antitrust standard for predatory pricing, and four schools of thought emerged:

- The *cost-based school* proposed that courts focus on the relationship between the dominant firm's costs and prices. The most influential cost-based approach, offered by Phillip Areeda and Donald Turner, recommended that courts adopt presumptions that pricing below a firm's *average variable costs* is illegal and that pricing at or above average variable cost is lawful. *See* Phillip A. Areeda & Donald F. Turner, *Predatory Pricing and Related Practices Under Section 2 of the Sherman Act*, 88 HARV. L. REV. 697 (1975).

- The *recoupment school* suggested that courts first ask whether the market's structural features, such as entry barriers, would permit the dominant incumbent to charge supra-competitive prices after it subdues its rivals. Only if such conditions exist would a court analyze the relationship between the dominant firm's prices and costs. *See, e.g.,* Paul L. Joskow & Alvin K. Klevorick, *A Framework for Analyzing Predatory Pricing*, 89 YALE L.J. 213 (1979).

- The *per se lawful school* urged courts to find no Section 2 liability based on predatory pricing. *See, e.g.,* ROBERT H. BORK, THE ANTITRUST PARADOX 154 (1978). Per se lawful advocates emphasized the rarity of the phenomenon due to the ability of entrants to neutralize the incumbent's predatory pricing tactics and warned that aggressive policing of price cuts would harm consumers by discouraging dominant firms from lowering prices. They also cautioned that courts too often will condemn benign behavior by mistake (false positives), and were willing to sacrifice the occasional meritorious accusation of predatory pricing for the sake of avoiding policies that would chill desirable price-cutting.

- The *game theoretic school* proposed that courts use a full, fact-specific analysis of the incumbent's response to entry (including evidence of its intent) and market conditions. Game theorists argued that predatory pricing could be a rational strategy and warned that under some circumstances incumbents can exclude equally efficient rivals by setting prices at or above average variable cost. *See, e.g.,* JEAN TIROLE, THE THEORY OF INDUSTRIAL ORGANIZATION 361–88 (1988).

From the mid-1970s through the early 1990s, courts generally accepted the idea that price-cost tests should anchor predatory pricing analysis. Most tribunals treated pricing at or above average variable cost as creating a rebuttable presumption of legality. Many cases endorsed the recoupment school's view that plaintiffs be required to prove that the defendant was likely to recoup its investment in below-cost pricing—for example, by showing that entry into the market was difficult and new challengers would not arise to face the incumbent. No court embraced the per se lawful approach, but the perspective of the per se lawful proponents was very influential and persuaded courts to impose tougher evidentiary burdens on predatory pricing plaintiffs. *See, e.g., Matsushita Elec. Indus. Co. v. Zenith Radio Corp.*, 475 U.S. 574, 106 S.Ct. 1348 (1986) (*see supra* Chapter 3).

The Supreme Court reformulated its predatory pricing test significantly in 1993. As in *Utah Pie*, the context again was a Robinson-Patman Act price discrimination dispute—this time a complaint pressed by Liggett & Myers (later acquired by Brooke Group) against Brown & Williamson (B & W). Liggett had tried to halt the decline of its cigarette business by offering cheap generic cigarettes in competition with popular brands. Liggett alleged that B & W unlawfully used below-cost sales in the form of rebates to cigarette wholesalers to punish Liggett and force it to raise the price it charged for generics. Liggett's sales of generic cigarettes had eroded B & W's branded sales. B & W had a market share of only 12 percent, but Liggett argued that every dollar B & W spent on below-cost pricing was rewarded with more than a dollar gained by stopping the loss of branded cigarette sales. A jury awarded Liggett nearly $149 million in damages. The trial court then set aside the verdict, the Fourth Circuit affirmed, and the Supreme Court agreed that no reasonable jury could have concluded that B & W's conduct was illegal.

BROOKE GROUP LTD. V. BROWN & WILLIAMSON TOBACCO CORP.

United States Supreme Court, 1993.
509 U.S. 209, 113 S.Ct. 2578, 125 L.Ed.2d 168.

MR. JUSTICE KENNEDY delivered the opinion of the Court.

* * *

I.

In 1980, Liggett pioneered the development of the economy segment of the national cigarette market by introducing a line of "black and white" generic cigarettes. The economy segment of the market, sometimes called the generic segment, is characterized by its bargain prices and comprises a variety of different products: black and whites, which are true generics sold in plain white packages with simple black lettering describing their contents; private label generics, which carry the trade dress of a specific purchaser, usually a retail chain; branded generics, which carry a brand name but which, like black and whites and private label generics, are sold at a deep discount and with little or no advertising; and "Value-25s," packages of 25 cigarettes that are sold to the consumer some 12.5% below the cost of a normal 20-cigarette pack. By 1984, when Brown & Williamson entered the generic segment and set in motion the series of events giving rise to this suit, Liggett's black and whites represented 97% of the generic segment, which in turn accounted for a little more than 4% of domestic cigarette sales. Prior to Liggett's introduction of black and whites in 1980, sales of generic cigarettes amounted to less than 1% of the domestic cigarette market.

* * * Cigarette manufacturing has long been one of America's most concentrated industries, and for decades, production has been dominated by six firms: R.J. Reynolds, Philip Morris, American Brands, Lorillard, and the two litigants involved here, Liggett and Brown & Williamson. R.J. Reynolds and Philip Morris, the two industry leaders, enjoyed respective market shares of about 28% and 40% at the time of trial. Brown & Williamson ran a distant third, its market share never exceeding 12% at any time relevant to this dispute. Liggett's share of the market was even less, from a low of just over 2% in 1980 to a high of just over 5% in 1984.

The cigarette industry also has long been one of America's most profitable, in part because for many years there was no significant price competition among the rival firms. List prices for cigarettes increased in lock-step, twice a year, for a number of years, irrespective of the rate of inflation, changes in the costs of production, or shifts in consumer demand. Substantial evidence suggests that in recent decades, the industry reaped the benefits of prices above a competitive level, though not through unlawful conduct of the type that once characterized the industry.

By 1980, however, broad market trends were working against the industry. Overall demand for cigarettes in the United States was declining, and no immediate prospect of recovery existed. As industry volume shrank, all firms developed substantial excess capacity. This decline in demand, coupled with the effects of nonprice competition, had a severe negative impact on Liggett. Once a major force in the industry, with market shares in excess of 20%, Liggett's market share had declined by 1980 to a little over 2%. With this meager share of the market, Liggett was on the verge of going out of business.

* * *

II.

Liggett contends that Brown & Williamson's discriminatory volume rebates to wholesalers threatened substantial competitive injury by furthering a predatory pricing scheme designed to purge competition from the economy segment of the cigarette market. This type of injury, which harms direct competitors of the discriminating seller, is known as primary-line injury. We last addressed primary-line injury over 25 years ago, in *Utah Pie Co. v. Continental Baking* Co., 386 U.S. 685, 87 S.Ct. 1326 (1967). * * *

Utah Pie has often been interpreted to permit liability for primary-line price discrimination on a mere showing that the defendant intended to harm competition or produced a declining price structure. The case has been criticized on the grounds that such low standards of competitive injury are at odds with the antitrust laws' traditional concern for consumer welfare and price competition. We do not regard the *Utah Pie* case itself as having the full significance attributed to it by its detractors. *Utah Pie* was an early judicial inquiry in this area and did not purport to set forth explicit, general standards for establishing a violation of the Robinson-Patman Act. As the law has been explored since *Utah Pie*, it has become evident that primary-line competitive injury under the Robinson-Patman Act is of the same general character as the injury inflicted by predatory pricing schemes actionable under § 2 of the Sherman Act. * * * There are, to be sure, differences between the two statutes. For example, we interpret § 2 of the Sherman Act to condemn predatory pricing when it poses "a dangerous probability of actual monopolization," whereas the Robinson-Patman Act requires only that there be "a reasonable possibility" of substantial injury to competition before its protections are triggered. But whatever additional flexibility the Robinson-Patman Act standard may imply, the essence of the claim under either statute is the same: A business rival has priced its products in an unfair manner with an object to eliminate or retard competition and thereby gain and exercise control over prices in the relevant market.

Accordingly, whether the claim alleges predatory pricing under § 2 of the Sherman Act or primary-line price discrimination under the Robinson-Patman Act, two prerequisites to recovery remain the same. First, a plaintiff seeking to establish competitive injury resulting from a rival's low prices must prove that the prices complained of are below an appropriate measure of its rival's costs.[1] *See, e.g., Cargill, Inc. v. Monfort of Colorado, Inc.*, 479 U.S. 104, 117, 107 S.Ct. 484, 493 (1986); *Matsushita Elec. Industrial Co. v. Zenith Radio Corp.*, 475 U.S. 574, 585, n. 8, 106 S.Ct. 1348, 1355 (1986) * * *. Although *Cargill* and *Matsushita* reserved as a formal matter the question " 'whether recovery should ever be available . . . when the pricing in question is above some measure of incremental cost,' " the reasoning in both opinions suggests that only below-cost prices should suffice, and we have rejected elsewhere the notion that above-cost prices that are below general market levels or the costs of a firm's competitors inflict injury to competition cognizable under the antitrust laws. "Low prices benefit consumers regardless of how those prices are set, and so long as they are above predatory levels, they do not threaten competition. . . . We have adhered to this principle regardless of the type of antitrust claim involved." As a general rule, the exclusionary effect of prices above a

---

[1] Because the parties in this case agree that the relevant measure of cost is average variable cost, however, we again decline to resolve the conflict among the lower courts over the appropriate measure of cost. *See Cargill, Inc. v. Monfort of Colorado, Inc.*, 479 U.S. 104, 117–118, n. 12, 107 S.Ct. 484, 493, n. 12 (1986); *Matsushita Elec. Industrial Co. v. Zenith Radio Corp.*, 475 U.S. 574, 585, n. 8, 106 S.Ct. 1348, 1355, n. 8 (1986).

relevant measure of cost either reflects the lower cost structure of the alleged predator, and so represents competition on the merits, or is beyond the practical ability of a judicial tribunal to control without courting intolerable risks of chilling legitimate price-cutting. * * * "To hold that the antitrust laws protect competitors from the loss of profits due to such price competition would, in effect, render illegal any decision by a firm to cut prices in order to increase market share. The antitrust laws require no such perverse result."

Even in an oligopolistic market, when a firm drops its prices to a competitive level to demonstrate to a maverick the unprofitability of straying from the group, it would be illogical to condemn the price cut: The antitrust laws then would be an obstacle to the chain of events most conducive to a breakdown of oligopoly pricing and the onset of competition. Even if the ultimate effect of the cut is to induce or reestablish supracompetitive pricing, discouraging a price cut and forcing firms to maintain supracompetitive prices, thus depriving consumers of the benefits of lower prices in the interim, does not constitute sound antitrust policy.

The second prerequisite to holding a competitor liable under the antitrust laws for charging low prices is a demonstration that the competitor had a reasonable prospect, or, under § 2 of the Sherman Act, a dangerous probability, of recouping its investment in below-cost prices. *See Matsushita*, 475 U.S., at 589, 106 S.Ct., at 1357; *Cargill*, 479 U.S., at 119, n. 15, 107 S.Ct., at 494, n. 15. "For the investment to be rational, the [predator] must have a reasonable expectation of recovering, in the form of later monopoly profits, more than the losses suffered." *Matsushita*, 475 U.S., at 588–589, 106 S.Ct., at 1356–1357. Recoupment is the ultimate object of an unlawful predatory pricing scheme; it is the means by which a predator profits from predation. Without it, predatory pricing produces lower aggregate prices in the market, and consumer welfare is enhanced. Although unsuccessful predatory pricing may encourage some inefficient substitution toward the product being sold at less than its cost, unsuccessful predation is in general a boon to consumers.

That below-cost pricing may impose painful losses on its target is of no moment to the antitrust laws if competition is not injured: It is axiomatic that the antitrust laws were passed for "the protection of competition, not competitors." *Brown Shoe Co. v. United States*, 370 U.S. 294, 320, 82 S.Ct. 1502, 1521 (1962). * * * Even an act of pure malice by one business competitor against another does not, without more, state a claim under the federal antitrust laws; those laws do not create a federal law of unfair competition or "purport to afford remedies for all torts committed by or against persons engaged in interstate commerce."

For recoupment to occur, below-cost pricing must be capable, as a threshold matter, of producing the intended effects on the firm's rivals, whether driving them from the market, or, as was alleged to be the goal here, causing them to raise their prices to supracompetitive levels within a disciplined oligopoly. This requires an understanding of the extent and duration of the alleged predation, the relative financial strength of the predator and its intended victim, and their respective incentives and will. * * * The inquiry is whether, given the aggregate losses caused by the below-cost pricing, the intended target would likely succumb.

If circumstances indicate that below-cost pricing could likely produce its intended effect on the target, there is still the further question whether it would likely injure competition in the relevant market. The plaintiff must demonstrate that there is a likelihood that the predatory scheme alleged would cause a rise in prices above a competitive level that would be sufficient to compensate for the amounts expended on the predation, including the time value of the money invested in it. As we have observed on a prior occasion, "[i]n order to recoup their losses, [predators] must obtain enough market power to set higher than competitive prices, and then must sustain those prices long enough to earn in excess profits what they earlier gave up in below-cost prices." *Matsushita*, 475 U.S., at 590–591, 106 S.Ct., at 1358.

Evidence of below-cost pricing is not alone sufficient to permit an inference of probable recoupment and injury to competition. Determining whether recoupment of predatory losses is likely requires an estimate of the cost of the alleged predation and a close analysis of both the scheme alleged by the plaintiff and the structure and conditions of the relevant market. If market circumstances or deficiencies in proof would bar a reasonable jury from finding that the scheme alleged would likely result in sustained supracompetitive pricing, the plaintiff's case has failed. In certain situations—for example, where the market is highly diffuse and competitive, or where new entry is easy, or the defendant lacks adequate excess capacity to absorb the market shares of his rivals and cannot quickly create or purchase new capacity—summary disposition of the case is appropriate.

These prerequisites to recovery are not easy to establish, but they are not artificial obstacles to recovery; rather, they are essential components of real market injury. As we have said in the Sherman Act context, "predatory pricing schemes are rarely tried, and even more rarely successful," *Matsushita*, 475 U.S., at 589, 106 S.Ct., at 1357, and the costs of an erroneous finding of liability are high. "[T]he mechanism by which a firm engages in predatory pricing—lowering prices—is the same mechanism by which a firm stimulates competition; because 'cutting prices in order to increase business often is the very essence of competition . . . [;] mistaken inferences . . . are especially costly, because they chill the very conduct the antitrust laws are designed to protect.'" *Cargill*, 479 U.S., at 122, n. 17, 107 S.Ct., at 495, n. 17 (quoting Matsushita, 475 U.S., at 594, 106 S.Ct., at 1360). It would be ironic indeed if the standards for predatory pricing liability were so low that antitrust suits themselves became a tool for keeping prices high.

Liggett does not allege that Brown & Williamson sought to drive it from the market but that Brown & Williamson sought to preserve supracompetitive profits on branded cigarettes by pressuring Liggett to raise its generic cigarette prices through a process of tacit collusion with the other cigarette companies. Tacit collusion, sometimes called oligopolistic price coordination or conscious parallelism, describes the process, not in itself unlawful, by which firms in a concentrated market might in effect share monopoly power, setting their prices at a profit-maximizing, supracompetitive level by recognizing their shared economic interests and their interdependence with respect to price and output decisions.

In *Matsushita*, we remarked upon the general implausibility of predatory pricing. *Matsushita* observed that such schemes are even more improbable when they require coordinated action among several firms. *Matsushita* involved an allegation of an express conspiracy to engage in predatory pricing. The Court noted that in addition to the usual difficulties that face a single firm attempting to recoup predatory losses, other problems render a conspiracy "incalculably more difficult to execute." In order to succeed, the conspirators must agree on how to allocate present losses and future gains among the firms involved, and each firm must resist powerful incentives to cheat on whatever agreement is reached.

However unlikely predatory pricing by multiple firms may be when they conspire, it is even less likely when, as here, there is no express coordination. Firms that seek to recoup predatory losses through the conscious parallelism of oligopoly must rely on uncertain and ambiguous signals to achieve concerted action. The signals are subject to misinterpretation and are a blunt and imprecise means of ensuring smooth cooperation, especially in the context of changing or unprecedented market circumstances. This anticompetitive minuet is most difficult to compose and to perform, even for a disciplined oligopoly.

From one standpoint, recoupment through oligopolistic price coordination could be thought more feasible than recoupment through monopoly: In the oligopoly setting, the victim itself has an economic incentive to acquiesce in the scheme. If forced to choose between cutting prices and sustaining losses, maintaining prices and losing market share, or raising prices and enjoying a share of supracompetitive profits, a firm may yield to the last alternative. Yet on the whole, tacit cooperation among oligopolists must be considered the least likely means of recouping predatory losses. In addition to the difficulty of achieving effective tacit coordination and the high likelihood that any attempt to discipline will produce an outbreak of competition, the predator's present losses in a case like this fall on it alone, while the later supracompetitive profits must be shared with every other oligopolist in proportion to its market share, including the intended victim. In this case, for example, Brown & Williamson, with its 11–12% share of the cigarette market, would have had to generate around $9 in supracompetitive profits for each $1 invested in predation; the remaining $8 would belong to its competitors, who had taken no risk.

* * *

To the extent that the Court of Appeals may have held that the interdependent pricing of an oligopoly may never provide a means for achieving recoupment and so may not form the basis of a primary-line injury claim, we disagree. A predatory pricing scheme designed to preserve or create a stable oligopoly, if successful, can injure consumers in the same way, and to the same extent, as one designed to bring about a monopoly. However unlikely that possibility may be as a general matter, when the realities of the market and the record facts indicate that it has occurred and was likely to have succeeded, theory will not stand in the way of liability. *See Eastman Kodak Co. v. Image Technical Services, Inc.*, 504 U.S. 451, 466, 467, 112 S.Ct. 2072 (1992).

* * *

III.

* * *

Liggett's theory of competitive injury through oligopolistic price coordination depends upon a complex chain of cause and effect: Brown & Williamson would enter the generic segment with list prices matching Liggett's but with massive, discriminatory volume rebates directed at Liggett's biggest wholesalers; as a result, the net price of Brown & Williamson's generics would be below its costs; Liggett would suffer losses trying to defend its market share and wholesale customer base by matching Brown & Williamson's rebates; to avoid further losses, Liggett would raise its list prices on generics or acquiesce in price leadership by Brown & Williamson; higher list prices to consumers would shrink the percentage gap in retail price between generic and branded cigarettes; and this narrowing of the gap would make generics less appealing to the consumer, thus slowing the growth of the economy segment and reducing cannibalization of branded sales and their associated supracompetitive profits.

Although Brown & Williamson's entry into the generic segment could be regarded as procompetitive in intent as well as effect, the record contains sufficient evidence from which a reasonable jury could conclude that Brown & Williamson envisioned or intended this anticompetitive course of events. * * * There is also sufficient evidence in the record from which a reasonable jury could conclude that for a period of approximately 18 months, Brown & Williamson's prices on its generic cigarettes were below its costs and that this below-cost pricing imposed losses on Liggett that Liggett was unwilling to sustain, given its corporate parent's effort to locate a buyer for the company. Liggett has failed to demonstrate competitive injury as a matter of law, however, because its proof is flawed in a critical respect: The evidence is inadequate to show that in pursuing this scheme, Brown & Williamson had a reasonable prospect of recovering its losses from below-cost pricing through slowing the growth of generics. * * *

No inference of recoupment is sustainable on this record, because no evidence suggests that Brown & Williamson—whatever its intent in introducing black and whites may have been—was likely to obtain the power to raise the prices for generic cigarettes above a competitive level. Recoupment through supracompetitive pricing in the economy segment of the cigarette market is an indispensable aspect of Liggett's own proffered theory, because a slowing of growth in the economy segment, even if it results from an increase in generic prices, is not itself anticompetitive. Only if those higher prices are a product of nonmarket forces has competition suffered. If prices rise in response to an excess of demand over supply, or segment growth slows as patterns of consumer preference become stable, the market is functioning in a competitive manner. Consumers are not injured from the perspective of the antitrust laws by the price increases; they are in fact causing them. Thus, the linchpin of the predatory scheme alleged by Liggett is Brown & Williamson's ability, with the other oligopolists, to raise prices above a competitive level in the generic segment of the market. Because relying on tacit coordination among oligopolists as a means of recouping losses from predatory pricing is "highly speculative," competent evidence is necessary to allow a reasonable inference that it poses an authentic threat to competition. The evidence in this case is insufficient to demonstrate the danger of Brown & Williamson's alleged scheme.

Based on Liggett's theory of the case and the record it created, there are two means by which one might infer that Brown & Williamson had a reasonable prospect of producing sustained supracompetitive pricing in the generic segment adequate to recoup its predatory losses: first, if generic output or price information indicates that oligopolistic price coordination in fact produced supracompetitive prices in the generic segment; or second, if evidence about the market and Brown & Williamson's conduct indicate that the alleged scheme was likely to have brought about tacit coordination and oligopoly pricing in the generic segment, even if it did not actually do so.

In this case, the price and output data do not support a reasonable inference that Brown & Williamson and the other cigarette companies elevated prices above a competitive level for generic cigarettes. Supracompetitive pricing entails a restriction in output. In the present setting, in which output expanded at a rapid rate following Brown & Williamson's alleged predation, output in the generic segment can only have been restricted in the sense that it expanded at a slower rate than it would have absent Brown & Williamson's intervention. Such a counterfactual proposition is difficult to prove in the best of circumstances; here, the record evidence does not permit a reasonable inference that output would have been greater without Brown & Williamson's entry into the generic segment.

Following Brown & Williamson's entry, the rate at which generic cigarettes were capturing market share did not slow; indeed, the average rate of growth doubled. During the four years from 1980 to 1984 in which Liggett was alone in the generic segment, the segment gained market share at an average rate of 1% of the overall market per year, from 0.4% in 1980 to slightly more than 4% of the cigarette market in 1984. In the next five years, following the alleged predation, the generic segment expanded from 4% to more than 15% of the domestic cigarette market, or greater than 2% per year.

While this evidence tends to show that Brown & Williamson's participation in the economy segment did not restrict output, it is not dispositive. One could speculate, for example, that the rate of segment growth would have tripled, instead of doubled, without Brown & Williamson's alleged predation. But there is no concrete evidence of this. Indeed, the only industry projection in the record estimating what the segment's growth would have been without Brown & Williamson's entry supports the opposite inference. In 1984, Brown & Williamson forecast in an important planning document that the economy segment would account for 10% of the total cigarette market by 1988 if it did not enter the segment. In fact, in 1988, after what Liggett alleges was a sustained and dangerous anticompetitive campaign by Brown & Williamson, the generic segment accounted for over 12% of the total market. Thus the segment's output expanded more robustly than Brown & Williamson had estimated it would had Brown & Williamson never entered.

Brown & Williamson did note in 1985, a year after introducing its black and whites, that its presence within the generic segment "appears to have resulted in . . . a slowing in the segment's growth rate." * * * But this statement was made in early 1985, when Liggett itself contends the below-cost pricing was still in effect and before any anticompetitive contraction in output is alleged to have occurred. Whatever it may mean, this statement has little value in evaluating the competitive implications of Brown & Williamson's later conduct, which was alleged to provide the basis for recouping predatory losses.

In arguing that Brown & Williamson was able to exert market power and raise generic prices above a competitive level in the generic category through tacit price coordination with the other cigarette manufacturers, Liggett places its principal reliance on direct evidence of price behavior. This evidence demonstrates that the list prices on all cigarettes, generic and branded alike, rose to a significant degree during the late 1980's. From 1986 to 1989, list prices on both generic and branded cigarettes increased twice a year by similar amounts. Liggett's economic expert testified that these price increases outpaced increases in costs, taxes, and promotional expenditures. The list prices of generics, moreover, rose at a faster rate than the prices of branded cigarettes, thus narrowing the list price differential between branded and generic products. Liggett argues that this would permit a reasonable jury to find that Brown & Williamson succeeded in bringing about oligopolistic price coordination and supracompetitive prices in the generic category sufficient to slow its growth, thereby preserving supracompetitive branded profits and recouping its predatory losses.

A reasonable jury, however, could not have drawn the inferences Liggett proposes. All of Liggett's data are based upon the list prices of various categories of cigarettes. Yet the jury had before it undisputed evidence that during the period in question, list prices were not the actual prices paid by consumers. As the market became unsettled in the mid-1980's, the cigarette companies invested substantial sums in promotional schemes, including coupons, stickers, and giveaways, that reduced the actual cost of cigarettes to consumers below list prices. This promotional activity accelerated as the decade progressed. Many wholesalers also passed portions of their volume rebates on to the consumer, which had the effect of further undermining the significance of the retail list prices. Especially in an oligopoly setting, in which price competition is most likely to take place through less observable and less regulable means than list prices, it would be unreasonable to draw conclusions about the existence of tacit coordination or supracompetitive pricing from data that reflect only list prices.

Even on its own terms, the list price data relied upon by Liggett to demonstrate a narrowing of the price differential between generic and full-priced branded cigarettes could not support the conclusion that supracompetitive pricing had been introduced into the generic segment. Liggett's gap data ignore the effect of "subgeneric" cigarettes, which were priced at discounts of 50% or more from the list prices of normal branded cigarettes. Liggett itself, while supposedly under the sway of oligopoly power, pioneered this development in 1988 with the introduction of its "Pyramid" brand. * * * By the time of trial, five of the six major manufacturers offered a cigarette in this category at a discount from the full list price of at least 50%. Thus, the price difference between the highest priced branded cigarette and the lowest price cigarettes in the economy segment, instead of narrowing over the course of the period of alleged predation as Liggett would argue, grew to a substantial extent. * * *

It may be that a reasonable jury could conclude that the cumulative discounts attributable to subgenerics and the various consumer promotions did not cancel out the full effect of the increases in list prices, and that actual prices to the consumer did indeed rise, but rising prices do not themselves permit an inference of a collusive market dynamic. Even in a concentrated market, the occurrence of a price increase does not in itself permit a rational inference of conscious parallelism or supracompetitive pricing. Where, as here, output is expanding at the same time prices are increasing, rising prices are equally consistent with growing product demand. Under these conditions, a jury may not infer competitive injury from price and output data absent some evidence that tends to prove that output was restricted or prices were above a competitive level.

Quite apart from the absence of any evidence of that sort, an inference of supracompetitive pricing would be particularly anomalous in this case, as the very party alleged to have been coerced into pricing through oligopolistic coordination denied that such coordination existed: Liggett's own officers and directors consistently denied that they or other firms in the industry priced their cigarettes through tacit collusion or reaped supracompetitive profits. Liggett seeks to explain away this testimony by arguing that its officers and directors are businesspeople who do not ascribe the same meaning to words like "competitive" and "collusion" that an economist would. This explanation is entitled to little, if any, weight. * * *

Not only does the evidence fail to show actual supracompetitive pricing in the generic segment, it also does not demonstrate its likelihood. At the time Brown & Williamson entered the generic segment, the cigarette industry as a whole faced declining demand and possessed substantial excess capacity. These circumstances tend to break down patterns of oligopoly pricing and produce price competition. The only means by which Brown & Williamson is alleged to have established oligopoly pricing in the face of these unusual competitive pressures is through tacit price coordination with the other cigarette firms.

Yet the situation facing the cigarette companies in the 1980's would have made such tacit coordination unmanageable. Tacit coordination is facilitated by a stable market environment, fungible products, and a small number of variables upon which the firms seeking to coordinate their pricing may focus. Uncertainty is an oligopoly's greatest enemy. By 1984, however, the cigarette market was in an obvious state of flux. The introduction of generic cigarettes in 1980 represented the first serious price competition in the cigarette market since the 1930's. This development was bound to unsettle previous expectations and patterns of market conduct and to reduce the cigarette firms' ability to predict each other's behavior.

The larger number of product types and pricing variables also decreased the probability of effective parallel pricing. When Brown & Williamson entered the economy segment in 1984, the segment included Value-25s, black and whites, and branded generics. With respect to each product, the net price in the market was determined not only by list prices, but also by a wide variety of discounts and promotions to consumers and by rebates to wholesalers. In order to coordinate in an effective manner and eliminate price competition, the cigarette companies would have been required, without communicating, to establish parallel practices with respect to each of these variables, many of which, like consumer stickers or coupons, were difficult to monitor. Liggett has not even alleged parallel behavior with respect to these other variables, and the inherent limitations of tacit collusion suggest that such multivariable coordination is improbable.

In addition, R.J. Reynolds had incentives that, in some respects, ran counter to those of the other cigarette companies. It is implausible that without a shared interest in retarding the growth of the economy segment, Brown & Williamson and its fellow oligopolists could have engaged in parallel pricing and raised generic prices above a competitive level. * * *

Even if all the cigarette companies were willing to participate in a scheme to restrain the growth of the generic segment, they would not have been able to coordinate their actions and raise prices above a competitive level unless they understood that Brown & Williamson's entry into the segment was not a genuine effort to compete with Liggett. If even one other firm misinterpreted Brown & Williamson's entry as an effort to expand share, a chain reaction of competitive responses would almost certainly have resulted, and oligopoly discipline would have broken down, perhaps irretrievably. * * *

Liggett argues that the means by which Brown & Williamson signaled its anticompetitive intent to its rivals was through its pricing structure. According to Liggett, maintaining existing list prices while offering substantial rebates to wholesalers was a signal to the other cigarette firms that Brown & Williamson did not intend to attract additional smokers to the generic segment by its entry. But a reasonable jury could not conclude that this pricing structure eliminated or rendered insignificant the risk that the other firms might misunderstand Brown & Williamson's entry as a competitive move. The likelihood that Brown & Williamson's rivals would have regarded its pricing structure as an important signal is low, given that Liggett itself, the purported target of the predation, was already using similar rebates, as was R.J. Reynolds * * *. And despite extensive discovery of the corporate records of R.J. Reynolds and Philip Morris, no documents appeared that indicated any awareness of Brown & Williamson's supposed signal by its principal rivals. Without effective signaling, it is difficult to see how the alleged predation could have had a reasonable chance of success through oligopoly pricing.

Finally, although some of Brown & Williamson's corporate planning documents speak of a desire to slow the growth of the segment, no objective evidence of its conduct permits a reasonable inference that it had any real prospect of doing so through anticompetitive means. It is undisputed that when Brown & Williamson introduced its generic cigarettes, it offered them to a thousand wholesalers who had never before purchased generic cigarettes. The inevitable effect of this marketing effort was to expand the segment, as the new wholesalers recruited retail outlets to carry generic cigarettes. Even with respect to wholesalers already carrying generics, Brown & Williamson's unprecedented volume rebates had a similar expansionary effect. Unlike many branded cigarettes, generics came with no sales guarantee to the wholesaler; any unsold stock represented pure loss to the wholesaler. By providing substantial incentives for wholesalers to place large orders, Brown & Williamson created strong pressure for them to sell more generic cigarettes. In addition, * * * many wholesalers passed portions of the rebates about which Liggett complains on to consumers, thus dropping the retail price of generics and further stimulating demand. Brown & Williamson provided a further, direct stimulus, through some $10 million it spent during the period of alleged predation placing discount stickers on its generic cartons to reduce prices to the ultimate consumer. In light of these uncontested facts about Brown & Williamson's conduct, it is not reasonable to conclude that Brown & Williamson threatened in a serious way to restrict output, raise prices above a competitive level, and artificially slow the growth of the economy segment of the national cigarette market.

* * *

IV.

We understand that the chain of reasoning by which we have concluded that Brown & Williamson is entitled to judgment as a matter of law is demanding. But a reasonable jury is presumed to know and understand the law, the facts of the case, and the realities of the market. We hold that the evidence cannot support a finding that Brown & Williamson's alleged scheme was likely to result in oligopolistic price coordination and sustained supracompetitive pricing in the generic segment of the national cigarette market. Without this, Brown &

Williamson had no reasonable prospect of recouping its predatory losses and could not inflict the injury to competition the antitrust laws prohibit. The judgment of the Court of Appeals is *affirmed*.

[The dissenting opinion of JUSTICES STEVENS, WHITE, and BLACKMUN is omitted. Eds.]

Under *Brooke Group*, a plaintiff alleging predatory pricing under Section 2 of the Sherman Act or Section 2(a) of the Robinson-Patman Act must satisfy a two-part test. It must show that the defendant set its prices below an "appropriate measure" of its costs and enjoyed a "dangerous probability" of recouping its investment in below-cost sales once the episode of predation had ended. Although Liggett established that Brown & Williamson had priced below its average variable cost, the Court concluded that it was entitled to judgment as a matter of law on the question of recoupment.

Together, *Matsushita* and *Brooke Group* have proven to be formidable hurdles to the successful prosecution of predatory pricing cases. Since *Matsushita* was decided in 1986, no plaintiff, including the Department of Justice, has succeeded in satisfying the two prong "below cost + recoupment" standard. What might explain the paucity of successful challenges to predatory pricing during that time? One explanation is that, as critics of predatory pricing urged, the practice is rarely successful and hence rarely tried. Another explanation could be that *Brooke Group* established a standard that, even if economically sound in theory, is too demanding as an evidentiary matter. As is discussed in Sidebar 4–7, which follows, some commentators have argued that it might also mean that the theory is not entirely sound as a matter of economics, or is simply not complete.

First note that the Court in *Brooke Group* did not specify a measure of cost that should be used in predatory pricing costs, although most lower courts have assumed it should be average variable cost. Determining whether a dominant firm's prices are "below cost," however, has proven to be a challenging task. *See, e.g., United States v. AMR Corp.*, 335 F.3d 1109 (10th Cir. 2003) (affirming summary judgment for American Airlines and rejecting all four tests of cost proffered by the Department of Justice). For an arguably more receptive view of predatory pricing claims, see *Spirit Airlines, Inc. v. Northwest Airlines, Inc.*, 431 F.3d 917, 945 (6th Cir. 2005) (reversing district court's award of summary judgment to the defendant airline and remanding for trial, concluding that the jury, not the court, should referee what one expert witness termed an "intellectual disagreement" over the appropriate measure of average variable costs).

Second, as was true in *Brooke Group*, it has proven difficult for plaintiffs to prove probability of recoupment. *See, e.g., Energy Conversion Devices Liquidation Trust v. Tina Solar Ltd.*, 2016 WL 4394564 (6th Cir. 2016). Moreover, the *Brooke Group* Court's emphasis on recoupment continues to raise questions for the analysis of predatory pricing in the typical monopolization case, where the plaintiff must prove that the defendant has substantial market power. It is unclear, for example, whether *Brooke Group* meant to suggest that the recoupment test imposes an element of proof above and beyond the plaintiff's showing that the defendant has monopoly power. A well-reasoned finding that a defendant has monopoly power ought to rest partly on the conclusion that entry barriers are high and that rivals cannot readily enter the market and compete away the defendant's monopoly profits. In consequence, a finding of durable monopoly power could suggest that recoupment is likely and would obviate the need for a separate recoupment inquiry. *See, e.g., Multistate Legal Studies, Inc. v. Harcourt Brace Jovanovich Legal and Professional Publications, Inc.*, 63 F.3d 1540 (10th Cir. 1995) (plaintiff created a triable issue of fact concerning recoupment by offering sufficient evidence that entry into the market was difficult). Perhaps the Court anticipated circumstances where a firm that already has monopoly power invests in predation to maintain such power, rather than to gain it in the first place. In such a case, one might ask whether the anticipated returns from predation (preserving the flow of monopoly profits) was likely to exceed the investment in predation. If not, then the low price might not be considered exclusionary.

Separately, the Court expressed its skepticism of the plaintiff's theory of oligopoly recoupment, remarking that "[t]his anticompetitive minuet is most difficult to compose and to perform, even for a disciplined oligopoly." 509 U.S. at 228. In his dissent, Justice John Paul Stevens responded:

> Also as a matter of economics, the Court insists that a predatory pricing program in an oligopoly is unlikely to succeed absent actual conspiracy. Though it has rejected a somewhat stronger version of this proposition as a rule of decision, * * * the Court comes back to the same economic theory, relying on the supposition that an "anticompetitive minuet is most difficult to compose and to perform, even for a disciplined oligopoly" * * *. I would suppose, however, that the professional performers who had danced the minuet for 40 to 50 years would be better able to predict whether their favorite partners would follow them in the future than would an outsider, who might not know the difference between Haydn and Mozart. In any event, the jury was surely entitled to infer that at the time of the price war itself, B & W reasonably believed that it could signal its intentions to its fellow oligopolists * * * assuring their continued cooperation.

Id. at 257–58 (STEVENS, J., dissenting) (footnote omitted). Which position do you find more persuasive?

An additional and related issue concerns intent evidence. Suppose that the plaintiff uncovers documents from the defendant's files suggesting the defendant's belief that it is succeeding in recouping its investment in predatory pricing. Imagine that the plaintiff obtains an annual strategic plan prepared for the defendant's Board of Directors in which the defendant's top officials describe how a below-cost pricing scheme actually yielded net benefits in the form of higher profits or other gains to the company. *Brooke Group* does not say whether the fact finder should accept such a document at face value as proving the dangerous probability—indeed, the certainty—of recoupment. Liggett believed that it had provided exactly such evidence of B & W's awareness of the success of its strategy, yet the Supreme Court majority discounted such evidence as being inconsistent with observable behavior in the market.

Finally, as is probably apparent from *Brooke Group* and these notes, predatory pricing as a theory of monopolization has engendered a great deal of legal and economic controversy. In *Brooke Group* and *Matsushita* and *Cargill, Inc. v. Monfort of Colorado, Inc.*, 479 U.S. 104, 107 S.Ct. 484 (1986), which preceded it, the Supreme Court appeared to embrace the notion that to be predatory a price must be "below cost." But can an above cost price ever be predatory? These four issues are explored at greater length in Sidebar 4–7, which follows a Note on the Supreme Court's extension of *Brooke Group's* analytical framework in *Weyerhaeuser*.

NOTE ON *WEYERHAEUSER* AND *PREDATORY OVERBUYING*

In *Weyerhaeuser Co. v. Ross-Simmons Hardwood Lumber Co.*, 549 U.S. 312, 127 S.Ct. 1069 (2007), the Supreme Court applied *Brooke Group* to decide a case alleging predatory bidding. The case involved two firms with hardwood lumber mills that processed red alder logs in the Pacific Northwest. Weyerhaeuser bought 65% of the logs in the region. Ross-Simmons, a rival to Weyerhaeuser, lost money and exited the market as the price of its key input, alder sawlogs, rose, and the price for its output, finished hardwood lumber, fell.

Ross-Simmons filed an antitrust complaint charging Weyerhaeuser with monopolization. In particular, Ross-Simons alleged that Weyerhaeuser had engaged in predatory bidding in order to exercise monopsony power. Its theory was that Weyerhaeuser bid up the price of logs to exceed the competitive level, presumably by overbuying, in order to force Ross-Simmons to exit. Ross-Simmons claimed that Weyerhaeuser would eventually recoup the short term losses from paying a higher than competitive price for logs by restricting its purchases of logs, forcing log prices below the competitive level. A jury returned a verdict in favor of Ross-Simmons, and the Ninth Circuit affirmed. The Supreme Court vacated that judgment on the ground that the lower courts should have applied *Brooke Group* to evaluate the claim. In particular, the

Court held that to prevail on a predatory bidding claim, the plaintiff must prove an analogue to the price-cost test employed for predatory pricing—namely that "the alleged predatory bidding led to below-cost pricing of the predator's outputs"—and plaintiff must prove that recoupment is likely. *Id. at* 1078.

The application of the below-cost pricing test to Ross-Simmons' allegations in this case is subtle. The problem is that predatory bidding could raise the price of logs in a localized region without leading to an increase in the price of finished wood. The price of finished wood would not rise because Weyerhaeuser sells the latter product in a national market in competition with firms that purchase logs elsewhere, where the price of logs did not change. Even if the price of finished wood does not change, and no other firms are charging prices below cost for finished wood, Weyerhaeuser could nevertheless be charging below *its* marginal cost of producing finished wood during the predatory bidding stage, satisfying the below-cost pricing test. Weyerhaeuser's marginal cost would rise because it bid up the price it pays for logs. Note that this test may not work if Weyerhaeuser exercises market power in the finished wood market, raising its price for finished wood above the competitive level. Under such circumstances, it is possible for Weyerhaeuser to engage in predatory bidding, and increase the price it pays for logs, without raising its marginal cost above the price it receives for finished wood.

The Court applied *Brooke Group* to predatory bidding because it saw the practice as analogous to predatory pricing, the conduct at issue in *Brooke Group*. As in *Brooke Group*, the Court was concerned with the possibility that if it adopted a test that was easier for plaintiffs to satisfy, it would chill procompetitive conduct, such as the acquisition of logs by an efficient sawmill seeking to expand. Although it recognized that the short-run benefit of predatory buying goes to log suppliers, and not necessarily to consumers, *id.* at 1077 n.4, it did not view that observation as sufficient reason to limit *Brooke Group* to predatory pricing. It is noteworthy, moreover, that the Court extended *Brooke Group* without considering the recent academic commentary noted by some appeals courts that highlights settings in which price predation could be a rational business strategy. For a further discussion of the issues posed by buyer market power, including anticompetitive overbuying, see Symposium, *Buyer Power and Antitrust*, 72 ANTITRUST L.J. 505 (2005).

Sidebar 4–7:
The Economic Debate About Predatory
Pricing: A Short History[a]

Predatory pricing is a common feature of popular accounts of monopolization, and was widely considered a serious problem during the early decades of the twentieth century. The "academic model of the classic predator," widely accepted before the 1960s, "was a firm of such unequal size and financial strength that a drastic cut of price in some small part of its territory, sustained with monopoly profits earned elsewhere, could eliminate a smaller competitor, leaving the predator to raise its prices and recoup its losses in that market." Terry Calvani & James M. Lynch, *Predatory Pricing Under the Robinson-Patman and Sherman Acts: An Introduction*, 51 ANTITRUST L.J. 375, 376 (1982). In business folklore, the "paradigm case" was *Standard Oil* (*see* discussion *supra* Chapter 2). Predatory pricing also is a concern under the abuse of dominance principles of other antitrust jurisdictions, and has even been the object of enforcement guidelines. *See, e.g.,* European Comm'n, Guidance on the Commission's Enforcement Priorities in Applying Article 82 [102] of the EC Treaty to Abusive Exclusionary Conduct by Dominant Undertakings, 2009 O.J. (C 45) ¶¶ 23–27 (Feb. 24, 2009), http://eur-lex.europa.eu/legal-content/EN/TXT/PDF/?uri=CELEX: 52009XC0224% 2801% 29&from=EN.

In this Sidebar, we expand upon the brief introduction to the various approaches to predatory pricing outlined at the beginning of this section of the Chapter, just before *Brooke Group*. To do so, we explore some of the considerable body of literature directed at evaluating the profitability, and hence the likelihood, of predatory pricing as an exclusionary strategy.

The Chicago School Challenge

The traditional view of predatory pricing was challenged by Chicago School commentators. John McGee exhaustively reviewed the trial record in *Standard Oil*, and found no evidence of price predation. John S. McGee, *Predatory Price Cutting: The* Standard Oil *(N.J.) Case* 1 J. L. & ECON. 137 (1958). More generally, Chicago-oriented commentators argued that below-cost pricing was irrational because the predator could not reasonably expect to recoup its initial losses from doing so.[b] *See, e.g.,* ROBERT H. BORK, THE ANTITRUST PARADOX 144–55 (1978). *But cf.* RICHARD A. POSNER, ANTITRUST LAW 208–10 (2d ed. 2001) (recognizing that predatory pricing in one market could be profitable if it deters entry or competition in other markets).

Recoupment is implausible, in the Chicago view, because it is so uncertain. The profits expected to follow the exit of the prey must substantially exceed the certain losses that come from below-cost pricing, given both the time value of money and the risk that the future profits will not be achieved. The predator's low price may not induce its rival or rivals to exit, acquiesce to a takeover, or compete less aggressively. Moreover, even if the victims exit, the predatory pricing scheme will not have been worthwhile unless the later monopoly price is high enough for long enough to generate profits that would more than offset the initial losses. Yet before recoupment is complete, the predator's product may become obsolete or otherwise undesirable to buyers, or the subsequent monopoly price may induce new entry. For example, if the prey is forced to exit from the market, the purchaser of its assets may be a plausible candidate for new entry. Or a large customer, fearing that successful predation may lead to an increase in the price of a product it buys, could sign a long-term contract with a new entrant or the prey, at a price above the predatory price, in order to preserve future competition. In other words, there may be events beyond the control of the predator, including counter-strategies by the prey, that will ultimately undermine the scheme, which makes it all the more risky to undertake. *See, e.g.,* Frank H. Easterbrook, *Predatory Strategies and Counterstrategies*, 48 U. CHI. L. REV. 263 (1981).

The Areeda-Turner Test

If the Chicago School is correct that predatory pricing as implausible and therefore unlikely to be pursued as an exclusionary strategy, aggressive antitrust enforcement against low prices, for fear that they are predatory, may do more harm than good. Under such circumstances, antitrust enforcement may be more likely to chill robust competition than to prevent harmful monopolization. Mainstream antitrust commentators responded to this criticism by developing cost-based tests for distinguishing between predatory pricing, which

---

[a] Some of the material in this Sidebar was adapted from Jonathan B. Baker, *Predatory Pricing After* Brooke Group: *An Economic Approach*, 62 ANTITRUST L.J. 585 (1994).

[b] As noted in the introductory material to this Chapter, Chicago School commentators have, however, been somewhat less hostile to the possibility of non-price predation (discussing the views of Robert H. Bork). Indeed, *Standard Oil* is today understood as exemplifying this anticompetitive possibility by Chicago-oriented commentators. Elizabeth Granitz & Benjamin Klein, *Monopolization by "Raising Rivals' Costs": The* Standard Oil *Case*, 39 J. L. & ECON. 1 (1996). As the title of Granitz and Klein's article suggests, the idea of non-price predation has been generalized in the "raising rivals' costs" framework for analyzing exclusionary conduct.

could harm competition, and robust competition, which should be permitted. The most influential test was proposed by Professors Areeda and Turner from the Harvard School in 1975. *See* Phillip Areeda & Donald F. Turner, *Predatory Pricing and Related Practices Under Section 2 of the Sherman Act*, 88 HARV. L. REV. 697 (1975). *See also* James D. Hurwitz & William E. Kovacic, *Judicial Analysis of Predation: The Emerging Trends*, 35 VAND. L. REV. 63 (1982) (describing the range of tests proposed for identifying predatory pricing); Joseph F. Brodley, et al., *Predatory Pricing: Strategic Theory and Legal Policy*, 88 GEO. L. J. 2239, 2250–62 (2000) (describing evolution of legal standards) ("*Strategic Theory*").

Areeda and Turner reasoned that a profit-maximizing firm not attempting to drive out its rivals is unlikely to set price below its own marginal cost—the incremental cost of making and selling the last unit of output—as doing so would require the seller to sacrifice short run profits. But they did not propose prohibiting prices set below a firm's marginal cost, as marginal cost is too difficult to infer from accounting records. Areeda and Turner saw average variable cost as a reasonable surrogate for marginal cost, and one that is practical to determine using historical accounting records. Accordingly, Areeda and Turner proposed that allegations of price predation be tested by comparing the monopolist's price with its average variable cost. Prices below that level would be presumed unlawful. As implemented by the courts, however, the presumption went the other way: prices above the monopolist's average variable cost would be presumed lawful.

Even this test was too harsh on price-cutters for many Chicago School commentators. In their view, which takes predatory pricing to be irrational and, therefore, implausible, episodes in which price appears to be less than marginal cost or average variable cost almost always reflect errors in the measurement of cost or competition, not price predation.[c] For example, it is frequently difficult to determine cost while the alleged predator is making substantial investments in acquiring physical capital, research and development, or developing a brand reputation (as through advertising). If accountants record such investments as expenses in the period they are made, revenues may fall short of accounting expenses during that period, so average revenue (price) will be less than some measure of cost. Such expenditures are not an appropriate

---

[c]   Here, as elsewhere in the analysis of predation, Richard Posner is an exception, accepting the practical possibility of price predation, at least as a method of maintaining (as opposed to obtaining) a monopoly. RICHARD A. POSNER, ANTITRUST LAW 207–23 (2d ed. 2001).

basis for an antitrust violation, they argued, even if accounting practice suggests that price is less than cost during the investment period, unless the investments themselves harm competition. Similarly, a competitive firm's investments might include investments in market share, undertaken through temporary or permanent price reductions. Again, in their view this practice would not necessarily be an appropriate basis for an antitrust violation. Some hypothetical examples suggested by business settings found in the case law illustrate this point:

- Competing spark plug manufacturers might sell their product to automobile manufacturers for incorporation into new vehicles at a price below marginal or average variable cost, in order to attract buyers of replacement spark plugs. Such a strategy might be effective if many replacement buyers will stick with the original brand even when charged a price above marginal cost.

- Competing photocopier manufacturers might price copiers below cost in order to attract buyers who can later be charged above-cost prices for dedicated replacement parts, and service.

- Competing firms producing both cameras and film might set camera prices below cost in order to sell more film at high price-cost margins.

- Competing sellers of some types of computer software might price their product below cost when high switching costs impede migration of the installed base to rival software, in order to increase the number of customers to whom they can later sell high-margin product upgrades.

- Competing computer manufacturers might price a new product below its initial variable cost in order to generate the scale economies and cost reductions from learning-by-doing that would justify the low price.

In all these cases, the reduction of price below cost may reflect a procompetitive investment in future competition, not price predation. Moreover, they illustrate how reliance on short term losses could lead to false positives, because the overall strategy is profitable without exclusion.

Although the Areeda-Turner standard for testing predatory pricing won influence in the courts, Chicago commentators thus were concerned that it swept in too much procompetitive conduct, and would in consequence chill procompetitive price-cutting. In response to this criticism, and following another suggestion of Areeda and Turner,[d] the Supreme Court has required that a plaintiff alleging predatory pricing by a monopolist prove more than that the price was below an appropriate measure of cost (although it has never endorsed any particular measure). In a series of decisions including *Matsushita* (*see supra* Chapter 3) and *Brooke Group*, the Court made clear that a predatory pricing plaintiff must also demonstrate that the predator had a reasonable prospect of recouping the costs of predation through the later exercise of market power. Kenneth G. Elzinga & David E. Mills, *Trumping the Areeda-Turner Test: The Recoupment Standard in* Brooke Group, 62 ANTITRUST L.J. 559 (1994).

If Chicago School commentators are correct in their view that price predation is almost invariably irrational because recoupment is almost always implausible, then this additional element of the predatory pricing offense provides a nearly insurmountable hurdle for plaintiffs to overcome, and properly so. Indeed, after *Brooke Group*, it is easier to make the case that the legal standard for proof of monopolization through price predation has chilled predatory pricing complaints than to make the case that the law chills aggressive price-cutting. For an examination and critique of the application of the recoupment prong of the test, see Christopher R. Leslie, *Predatory Pricing and Recoupment*, 113 COLUM. L. REV. 1695 (2013).

Critical Responses to the Brooke Group Framework

Beginning in the late 1970s and early 1980s, economists developed new theories that challenged the Chicago School view that price predation was irrational as a business strategy. These theories took on directly the claim that recoupment is almost never plausible. *See generally* Paul Milgrom & John Roberts, *New Theories of Predatory Pricing*, *in* INDUSTRIAL STRUCTURE IN THE NEW INDUSTRIAL ECONOMICS 112–37 (Giacomo Bonanno & Dario Brandolini, eds. 1990); Janusz Ordover & Garth Saloner, *Predation, Monopolization, and Antitrust*, *in* 1 HANDBOOK OF INDUSTRIAL ORGANIZATION 537–96 (Richard Schmalensee & Robert Willig, eds. 1989); Brodley, et al., *Strategic Theory, supra.*

---

    d   *See* Herbert J. Hovenkamp, *Predatory Pricing Under the Areeda-Turner Test* (U. Iowa Legal Studies Research Paper No. 15–06, 2015), https://ssrn.com/abstract=2422120 (tracing the below cost pricing and recoupment tests to Areeda and Turner, describing their subsequent history, and identifying implementation problems).

One contemporary recoupment theory,[e] in which predation occurs in one market while recoupment occurs rapidly and profitably in many others, is suggested by the following hypothetical example. Suppose a chain store faces local non-chain rivals in each of a large number of towns. The chain cuts price drastically in a few towns. When the chain's rivals in those towns either exit or begin to compete less aggressively with the chain, the price war ends, and high prices are restored. In addition, the chain store's rivals in all the other towns, in which the chain did not cut prices, also respond by avoiding aggressive competition with the chain. As a result, prices also increase in the towns in which predation did not occur.

In the example, the firm developed a reputation as a predator by reducing price in a small number of markets ("reputation effect" predation). In effect, it engaged in selective, targeted predation. The rivals in the markets in which predation occurred may have ended up crippled or destroyed. But rivals competing against the predator in markets in which predation did not occur were not injured directly. They never experienced a price war—but they were intimidated by the threat of a price war into engaging in less aggressive behavior than they would otherwise have found most profitable.

In other modern theories, the predator succeeds (1) by convincing investors or lenders no longer to support the prey ("deep pocket" or "financial market" predation); (2) by convincing a prospective entrant that the predator's costs are too low to make entry profitable (predation through "cost-signaling"); or (3) by convincing a prospective entrant that it's product will not be attractive to buyers ("test market" predation). *See generally* Brodley, et al., *Strategic Theory, supra*; DOUGLAS G. BAIRD, ROBERT H. GERTNER & RANDAL C. PICKER, GAME THEORY AND THE LAW 180–86 (1994).

The less skeptical view of predatory pricing suggested by these modern theories has been supported by empirical economic studies that identified examples of successful predatory pricing during periods when antitrust enforcement against the practice was lax. *See, e.g.*, Malcolm R. Burns, *Predatory Pricing and the Acquisition Cost of Competitors*, 94 J. POL. ECON. 266 (1986); David Genesove & Wallace P. Mullin, *Predation and Its Rate of Return: The Sugar Industry, 1887–1914*, 37 RAND J. ECON. 47 (2006); Kenneth G. Elzinga & David E. Mills, *Predatory Pricing in the Airline Industry:* Spirit

---

[e] Although this theory was new in terms of formal economic modeling, it had been anticipated by Richard Posner. RICHARD A. POSNER, ANTITRUST LAW 186 (1976).

Airlines v. Northwest Airlines *(2005)*, *in* THE ANTITRUST REVOLUTION: ECONOMICS, COMPETITION, AND POLICY 219 (John E. Kwoka, Jr. & Lawrence J. White eds., 5th ed. 2009); Josh Lerner, *Pricing and Financial Resources: An Analysis of the Disk Drive Industry, 1980–88*, 77 REV. ECON. & STAT. 585 (1995); Fiona Scott Morton, *Entry and Predation: British Shipping Cartels 1879–1929*, 6 J. ECON. & MGMT. STRATEGY 679 (1997); David F. Weiman & Richard C. Levin, *Preying for Monopoly? The Case of Southern Bell Telephone Company, 1894–1912*, 102 J. POL. ECON. 103 (1994). For a critique questioning the policy relevance of these studies, see Bruce H. Kobayashi, *The Law and Economics of Predatory Pricing, in* ANTITRUST LAW AND ECONOMICS 116 (Keith N. Hylton ed., 2d ed. 2010).

Concerns that the modern theories of price predation can pose substantial problems of evidence and proof were addressed by law professor Joseph Brodley and his economist co-authors, Patrick Bolton and Michael H. Riordan. Their article seeks to develop administrable methods of discriminating between predatory and competitive pricing, informed by post-Chicago developments in economics and by examples taken from the economic literature and the case law. Brodley, et al., *Strategic Theory, supra. See also* Joseph F. Brodley, et al., *Predatory Pricing: Response to Critique and Further Elaboration*, 89 GEO. L.J. 2495 (2001).

For example, in the modern economic theories, the successful predator's price cuts need not necessarily go below any particular measure of cost for it to discourage the prey from aggressive competition.[f] Brodley, Bolton and Riordan would nevertheless effectively require a plaintiff to demonstrate that the predator has lowered price below a measure of the predator's incremental costs. Brodley, et al., *Strategic Theory*, 88 GEO. L. J. at 2271–74. They also suggest ways of demonstrating that a monopolist or coordinating oligopoly has

---

[f] *Cf.* Aaron S. Edlin, *Stopping Above-Cost Predatory Pricing*, 111 YALE L.J. 941 (2002) (a (natural) monopolist with a cost advantage over its potential rivals can deter entry notwithstanding its high pre-entry price; predatory incumbent responses arise in response to mistakes by entrants, who may not realize that the incumbent's costs are so low or that market demand is low). For a reply, see Einer Elhauge, *Why Above-Cost Price Cuts to Drive Out Entrants are not Predatory—and the Implications for Defining Costs and Market Power*, 112 YALE L. J. 681 (2003). In part, the debate between Edlin and Elhauge turns on whether antitrust should primarily be concerned with consumer welfare or aggregate economic welfare (*see Note on Efficiencies and Consumer Welfare, supra* Chapter 5). If antitrust law condemns above-cost price reductions that exclude entrants, Elhauge emphasizes, it risks encouraging entry by high-cost producers, and thus a loss of production efficiency. In contrast, Edlin emphasizes that even high-cost entry can lower consumer prices, especially when the incumbent is exercising market power.

engaged in each of four predatory strategies, and that recoupment is likely.

These modern economic theories of predatory pricing have thus far had little influence in the courts. Brodley, et al., *Strategic Theory*, 88 GEO. L.J. at 2258–60. *But see Spirit Airlines, Inc. v. Northwest Airlines, Inc.*, 431 F.3d 917 (6th Cir. 2005). *Cf. Advo, Inc. v. Philadelphia Newspapers, Inc.*, 51 F.3d 1191, 1196 n.4 (3d Cir. 1995) (modern reputational effect theory "makes economic sense," but was not supported on the facts). Moreover, Chicago-oriented commentators question whether the new theories can be practically applied, and whether the competitive problems they identify are sufficiently common as to make increased antitrust enforcement worthwhile in light of the risk of chilling aggressive price competition. Brodley, et al., *Strategic Theory*, *supra*. *See also* Adriaan ten Kate & Gunnar Niels, *On the Rationality of Predatory Pricing: The Debate Between Chicago and Post-Chicago*, 47 ANTITRUST BULL. 1 (2002) (questioning practical applicability of modern predatory pricing theories); RICHARD A. POSNER, ANTITRUST LAW 221 (2d ed. 2001) (the conditions required for one modern theory to apply are "too exacting to make it an answer to the claim that predatory pricing can be a rational strategy for a monopolist").

As we have seen in this Chapter, the modern law of monopolization has developed along two lines. Today's law of predatory pricing is shaped largely by the Supreme Court's decisions in *Matsushita*, which we read in Chapter 3, *and Brooke Group*. In these two cases, the Supreme Court developed a two part test for predatory pricing. To be actionable under the antitrust laws, such pricing must be (1) below some appropriate measure of cost, and (2) it must be probable that the alleged predator will be able to recoup its losses through the later exercise of market power. This paradigm assumes that successful predatory pricing is a two-step process. In stage one, the "short run," the predator lowers its price below cost, sacrificing all profit and incurring losses, in order to exclude or discipline its rivals. In stage two, the "long run," the predator, having vanquished or humbled its rivals, will be in a position to exercise market power and hence "recoup" its short run losses.

Non-price exclusionary conduct, on the other hand, has been defined by *Aspen*, *Microsoft*, and to some degree the Supreme Court's decision in *Verizon*, which we will read later in this Chapter. Recall that the standard for judging non-price exclusionary conduct took shape in *Aspen*, where the Court reasoned:

The question whether Ski Co.'s conduct may properly be characterized as exclusionary cannot be answered by simply considering its effect on Highlands. In addition, it is relevant to consider its impact on consumers and whether it has impaired competition in an unnecessarily restrictive way.[9] If a firm has been "attempting to exclude rivals on some basis other than efficiency,"[10] it is fair to characterize its behavior as predatory. It is, accordingly, appropriate to examine the effect of the challenged pattern of conduct on consumers, on Ski Co.'s smaller rival, and on Ski Co. itself.

From the first quoted sentence, it seems clear that in the Court's view of "exclusion" is not the same as "exclusionary." Competition on the merits and exclusionary conduct alike will produce winners and losers. So to judge whether conduct that excludes is exclusionary, the majority directs us to consider the impact of the conduct on consumers, the targeted rival, and on the alleged predator. This distinction was reflected in *Microsoft*, where the court appeared to associate "exclusion" with impact on a competitor, and "exclusionary" with impact on competition, the competitive process, and consumers.

Inherent in this approach is a framework that involves shifting burdens of production: the plaintiff demonstrates exclusion or impairment of rivals and consequent actual or likely impact on consumers (injury to competition). The defendant must then come forward with "business justifications." As the D.C. Circuit noted in *Microsoft*, the approach is suggestive of the rule of reason under Section 1 of the Sherman Act, at least when the defendant can meet its burden of production by presenting evidence of a cognizable, procompetitive justification. But in practice, resolving such cases turns more on the relative strength of the evidence of effects and justifications rather than some dollar-for-dollar comparison or balancing of consumer and producer surplus.

The standards for judging price predation and non-price exclusionary conduct, therefore, are arguably distinct today and in tension, even though both share a common purpose: to identify situations in which exclusion is likely to facilitate the exercise of market power. The price predation standard, which focuses on measures of cost and theories of recoupment, has proven to be very difficult to satisfy. In contrast, the standard for proving non-price exclusionary conduct has led to some significant plaintiff's victories, although not many. The choice of standard, therefore, can make a difference in the outcome of specific cases and thus has led to significant litigation and commentary when the alleged conduct shares characteristics of both price and non-price behavior. Such conduct has been described as "Conditional Pricing Practices" and typically involves a

---

[9] "Thus 'exclusionary' comprehends at the most behavior that not only (1) tends to impair the opportunities of rivals, but also (2) either does not further competition on the merits or does so in an unnecessarily restrictive way." 3 P. Areeda & D. Turner, Antitrust Law 78 (1978).

[10] Bork [The Antitrust Paradox] 138.

combination of some price inducement (or penalty) which can be secured only upon a "condition." For example, "loyalty discounts" involve a supplier's offer of a lower price in return for a purchaser's agreement to buy a specified percentage of its needs from the supplier. "Bundled rebates" can involve sellers of a range of products and might involve a similar offer of price concession in return for the purchase of some specified "bundle" of products. These arrangements can take many forms.

Often, plaintiffs challenging such practices urge the courts to focus on the "condition" and apply the same kind of framework we have studied in *Aspen Skiing* and *Microsoft*, and will see further developed in Chapter 6 in connection with exclusive dealing. Defendants argue that because the conduct involves a "discount," it should be examined under the predatory pricing standards of *Brooke Group*. Both sides understand that the choice of approach can be outcome determinative. As we have learned, the standards of *Brooke Group* have proven very difficult to satisfy. Although the rule of reason approach is not a guarantee of victory for plaintiffs, the chances of prevailing appear to be decidedly better than under a price-cost test. But commentators also have disagreed about which approach is the most appropriate as a matter of economics for purposes of identifying anticompetitive uses of these practices. Critics of the use of a price-cost test for CPPs argue that it will be prone to false negatives, because the price is not necessarily the mechanism of exclusion. They argue that a rule of reason approach utilizing a raising rival's cost framework is more likely to produce accurate results. We shall examine Conditional Pricing Practices like these in Chapter 6. For present purposes, it is important to understand that the "two paradigms" can intersect and that when they do conflict can arise. For some of the key case examples, see *LePage's Inc. v. 3M Company*, 324 F.3d 141 (3d Cir. 2003) (declining to apply price-cost test to a bundled rebate and finding a violation); *Cascade Health Solutions v. PeaceHealth*, 479 F.3d 726 (9th Cir. 2007) (applying a price-cost test to bundling, but declining also to require proof of probable recoupment and concluding that the practice was lawful); *ZF Meritor, LLC v. Eaton Corp.*, 696 F.3d 254 (3d Cir. 2012) (declining to apply price-cost test and finding long-term loyalty discounts unlawful) (*see infra* Chapter 6); *Eisai, Inc. v. Sanofi Aventis U.S., LLC*, 821 F.3d 394 (3d Cir. 2016) (declining to apply price-cost test to challenged marketing strategy, but concluding that plaintiff failed to satisfy its burden of showing anticompetitive effect under a rule of reason approach).

Sidebar 4–8:
Should There Be a Unitary Standard
for Judging Exclusionary Conduct?

The very general standards of *Alcoa* ("skill, foresight, luck or business acumen") and *Grinnell* ("willful acquisition or maintenance") can be of limited use in differentiating aggressive, but legitimate competitive strategies from those deserving condemnation under Section 2. Other tests and standards developed to help divine that line with greater economic sophistication and reliability with respect to particular types of conduct, especially in *Aspen Skiing* for non-price conduct ("non-efficiency based competition" that "unnecessarily excludes") and in *Brooke Group* for predatory pricing (below cost pricing plus a dangerous probability of recoupment).

Perhaps multiple standards targeting specific classes of conduct are preferable to a unitary standard because they are flexible, which allows for some fine-tuning for categories of conduct that are more or less likely to be pernicious. Was *Brooke Group* correct in concluding that price predation warrants a unique and elevated standard of proof, because the likely incidence and consequences of false positives is especially great when price reducing strategies are challenged? On the other hand, the case law involving Conditional Pricing Practices (noted *supra* and discussed more fully in Chapter 6, *infra*) suggest that the use of multiple standards under Section 2 will place a premium on "characterization" and hence lead to increased and arguably pointless litigation. Would it be better to have a unitary standard for judging all instances of exclusionary conduct?

Enforcers and commentators have debated the propriety of using a unitary standard for all claims of exclusionary conduct. Such a standard could supersede the traditional formulations from *Alcoa* and *Grinnell* and resolve the current tension between *Aspen Skiing* and *Brooke Group*.

Three proposed unitary tests have been inspired by *Brooke Group*. The first, the "profit sacrifice" test, has two elements: it asks whether the challenged conduct "is profitable to the defendant in light of its incremental costs and incremental benefits," and, if so, "whether the conduct enabled the defendant to gain additional market power or a dangerous probability thereof." *See, e.g.,* A. Douglas Melamed, *Exclusive Dealing Agreements and Other Exclusionary Conduct—Are There Unifying Principles?*, 73 ANTITRUST L.J. 375, 389–403

(2006) ("*Unifying Principles*"). The underlying idea is similar to that underlying the below-cost pricing standard used to evaluate predatory pricing claims: conduct that is costly to a firm in the short run may be difficult to justify as "efficient." Critics argue that the profit sacrifice test focuses on the wrong question (the predator's profits rather than the conduct's exclusionary effects), that it is too hard to measure profits (which must be assessed relative to the profits available from some specific, alternative business strategy), that it would fail to condemn exclusionary conduct that is inexpensive for the predator (*see infra Note on Cheap Exclusion*, and that a plaintiff cannot be expected to offer proof on issues likely to turn on evidence solely within the hands of the defendant. For a comprehensive presentation of these objections, see Steven C. Salop, *Exclusionary Conduct, Effect on Consumers, and the Flawed Profit-Sacrifice Standard*, 73 ANTITRUST L.J. 311 (2006) ("*Flawed Profit-Sacrifice Standard*"). *See also* Andrew I. Gavil, *Exclusionary Distribution Strategies by Dominant Firms: Striking a Better Balance*, 72 ANTITRUST L.J. 3 (2004) ("*Exclusionary Distribution Strategies*"). For a further defense and response to objections, see Melamed, *Unifying Principles*, 73 ANTITRUST L.J. at 393–403.

The profit sacrifice test is related to a second test inspired by *Brooke Group*: the "no economic sense" test ("NES"). The NES test asks: would the monopolist have undertaken the conduct but for its anticompetitive effects? Put another way, it asks whether there was any legitimate business reason for the conduct. For a defense of the NES test, see Gregory J. Werden, *Identifying Exclusionary Conduct Under Section 2: The "No Economic Sense" Test*, 73 ANTITRUST L.J. 413 (2006) ("*No Economic Sense*"). *See also id.* at 422–25 (distinguishing NES from profit sacrifice and arguing that profit sacrifice "is neither necessary nor sufficient for conduct to be exclusionary"). The NES test has not been expressly embraced by any court and has been subjected to some of the same criticisms as the profit sacrifice test. *See* Salop, *Flawed Profit-Sacrifice Standard*, *supra* 318–28; Gavil, *Exclusionary Distribution Strategies*, *supra*, at 52–55. The NES test also seems to provide a monopolist with a complete defense to conduct that excludes, so long as it can point to some efficiency gains. It is seemingly indifferent to the amount of those gains (provided they are sufficient to justify the conduct in some sense) and the degree to which the challenged conduct also may have resulted in significant anticompetitive effects. Even if the overwhelmingly predominant effect of the conduct is to facilitate the exercise of market power, the conduct could be immunized from challenge.

The third test inspired by *Brooke Group*, the "equally efficient rival" test, is associated with the work of Judge Richard A. Posner. It condemns a monopolist's conduct if it could exclude "an equally or more efficient competitor," unless "the practice is, on balance, efficient." RICHARD A. POSNER, ANTITRUST LAW 18–21 (2d ed. 2001). This approach rules out Section 2 challenges by rivals that are unsuccessful because they are inefficient, by presuming that they wrongly blame the dominant firm's practices for their own competitive failure. Although no court has embraced Posner's standard as proposed, some have included considerations about rival efficiency in their tests. *See, e.g., Cascade Health Solutions v. PeaceHealth*, 515 F.3d 883, 905–09 (9th Cir. 2008) (discussing role of equally efficient competitor standard in connection with the analysis of bundled rebates). Critics have questioned this proposal on the ground that it implicitly presumes that the exclusion of a *less* efficient rival will be harmless, even though a less efficient rival can limit the extent to which the monopolist exercises market power and that the rival may be on a path toward achieving scale economies or otherwise becoming as efficient as the monopolist. *Cf.* Einer Elhauge, *Defining Better Monopolization Standards*, 56 STAN. L. REV. 253 (2003) (arguing for standard that distinguishes between conduct that improves monopolist's own efficiency, which would be permitted, and conduct that impairs rivals' efficiency and results in market-wide anticompetitive effects, which would be prohibited). They also point out that it initially redirects the inquiry away from a focus on the competitive effects of the challenged practice to the efficiency of the plaintiff, and that it can be difficult to determine whether a hypothetical competitor is "equally efficient." *See* Salop, *Flawed Profit-Sacrifice Standard, supra* at 328–29 (critique of equally efficient rival standard); Gavil, *Exclusionary Distribution Strategies, supra*, at 58–61 (same).

Three other unitary tests that have been proposed were inspired by *Aspen Skiing* and *Microsoft*. First, building on *Aspen Skiing* and other cases, *Microsoft* sets forth a reasonableness standard to define exclusionary conduct that uses burden-shifting to reduce the error costs as well as the direct transaction costs of litigation. It initially looks to plaintiff's burden of production to demonstrate anticompetitive harm to screen out claims that might lead to false positives. If that burden is met, it considers the defendant's procompetitive justifications, if any, defined as "a form of competition on the merits because it involves . . . greater efficiency or enhanced consumer appeal." If that burden is met and is not rebutted, "the plaintiff must demonstrate that the anticompetitive harm of the conduct outweighs the procompetitive benefit." The court described this overall framework as "similar" to the "balancing approach" associated with the rule of reason in Section 1 Sherman Act cases. *Microsoft*, 253 F.3d at 58–59. It ultimately recognizes, therefore, that false positives and false negatives are both concerns.

Second, the "disproportionality" test, which has been attributed to Professor Herbert Hovenkamp, modifies the reasonableness standard by limiting the definition of exclusionary conduct to actions that produce disproportionate harms.[a] This test recognizes the need to evaluate both the competitive harms and competitive benefits of exclusionary conduct, but relative to the reasonableness approach, it imposes a higher burden on plaintiffs and thus places a "thumb on the scale" in favor of defendants. The "disproportionality" qualification to reasonableness analysis can be understood as a concession to the concerns about false positives recognized in *Brooke Group* and in the *Brooke Group*-derived tests discussed above.[b]

Third, the "consumer welfare effect" standard proposed by Professor Steven C. Salop asks whether the exclusionary conduct harms consumers, as distinct from reducing aggregate efficiency. *See supra Note on Efficiencies and Consumer Welfare.* Analogizing to the rule of reason under Section 1 of the Sherman Act, as did the D.C. Circuit in *Microsoft*, Salop explains that "consumer welfare analysis is more geared towards comparing the magnitudes of various effects to predict the likely overall impact on *consumers.*" Salop, *Flawed Profit-Sacrifice Standard*, *supra* at 331–32 (emphasis original). Doing so, Salop argues, would focus the test "on the effect of the conduct on the market, that is, consumers and the competitive process." *Id.* Advocates of the NES and profit sacrifice tests

---

[a] 3 PHILLIP AREEDA & HERBERT HOVENKAMP, ANTITRUST LAW ¶ 651a, at 98 (4th ed. 2015). Professor Hovenkamp's definition of "monopolistic conduct" includes acts "reasonably capable of creating, enlarging or prolonging monopoly power by impairing the opportunities of rivals" if they: "do not benefit consumers at all," "are unnecessary for the particular consumer benefits claimed for them," or "produce harms disproportionate to any resulting benefits." *Id.*

[b] A disproportionality standard was endorsed by the Justice Department in a report issued during the administration of President George W. Bush, but withdrawn early in the Obama administration. U.S. DEP'T OF JUSTICE, COMPETITION AND MONOPOLY: SINGLE-FIRM CONDUCT UNDER SECTION 2 OF THE SHERMAN ACT 45–47 (2008) (advocating disproportionality test where a conduct-specific test would not apply) www.justice.gov/atr/public/reports/236681.pdf, *withdrawn*, Press Release, U.S. Dep't of Justice, Justice Department Withdraws Report on Antitrust Monopoly Law (May 11, 2009), www.justice.gov/atr/public/press_releases/2009/245710.pdf.

criticize this approach, the disproportionality test, and the reasonableness standard, on the ground that they provide less guidance to dominant firms, are less likely to produce consistent results, and are costly to implement because they are so fact-intensive. For a sampling of the criticisms, see Melamed, *Unifying Principles, supra* at 379–83; Werden, *No Economic Sense, supra* at 428–32. For a response to these criticisms, see Salop, *Flawed Profit-Sacrifice Standard, supra* at 330–33.

The question of whether a unitary standard should cover all types of exclusionary conduct has produced a lively debate. Which if any of the cases we have read in this Chapter turned on the choice of standard? Would they have been decided differently if one of the above standards had been adopted? Would the plaintiffs have prevailed in *Lorain Journal*, *Aspen Skiing*, or *Microsoft* if one of the *Brooke Group*-inspired tests had applied? Would defendants have still won *Brooke Group* if one of the *Aspen Skiing/Microsoft*-inspired tests had applied?

How do these various tests reflect the three "perspectives" we discussed at the outset of the Chapter? Which of the tests reflects a greater concern with false positives? False negatives? Which reflects greater confidence in the ability of markets to self-correct and skepticism about the capacity of courts? Which reflects greater concern that market power may prove durable? Do the tests differ substantially in the litigation costs they impose? Would it be better not to employ a unitary standard and instead rely on conduct-specific standards, as antitrust already does for predatory pricing? Does selective use of conduct-specific standards allow for a degree of tailoring to account for variations in the likely incidence and consequences of error?

3. CONCERTED AND UNILATERAL REFUSALS TO DEAL

Chapter 2's discussion of refusals to deal or "boycotts" focused on those having collusive effects and culminated with our examination of the Supreme Court's 1990 decision in *Superior Court Trial Lawyers* ("*SCTLA*"). *SCTLA* was controversial owing in large part to the political and constitutional context of the lawyers' actions. Nevertheless, it aptly illustrates how a boycott can be used by competing firms as a method of implementing an agreement to fix prices. The "boycott" label in those circumstances serves simply as a description of the means utilized to implement an agreement on price: "we will not sell to you unless you agree to pay the price we have collectively agreed upon." Arguably, the label adds nothing to the analysis of competitive effect. Viewed as such, a collusive group boycott is indistinguishable from any price fixing agreement and, therefore, warrants per se treatment, especially when there is evidence that it achieved its desired result, *i.e.*, higher prices.

Here we turn our attention to group boycotts having exclusionary effects. The modern exclusionary boycott is more complex to evaluate than the collusive boycott for two reasons: (1) its effects may be less obvious, and (2) its potentially legitimate justifications can be more varied. We will also need to consider how it fits within the contemporary framework for assessing exclusion.

Figure 4–9 depicts some common examples of concerted, exclusionary refusals to deal. As you read about the foundation and modern cases, consider how they match up with the examples presented here.

Figure 4–9:
Exclusionary Group Boycotts—Three Scenarios

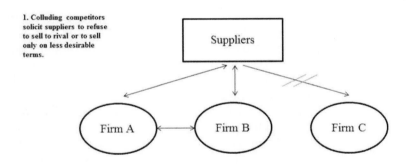

1. Colluding competitors solicit suppliers to refuse to sell to rival or to sell only on less desirable terms.

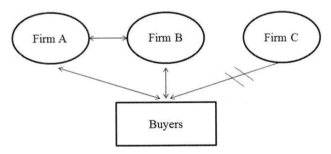

2. Colluding competitors solicit buyers to refuse to purchase from rival or to purchase only on less desirable terms.

3. Colluding competitors themselves refuse to deal or associate with rival, or to deal with it only on less desirable terms.

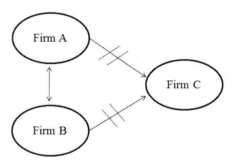

a.   Foundation Cases: From *Eastern States* to *Klor's*

Exclusionary group boycotts have a long history under U.S. antitrust laws. In *Eastern States Retail Lumber Dealers' Ass'n v. United States*, 234 U.S. 600 (1914), the Supreme Court affirmed a decree enjoining a group of retail lumber dealers from collectively refusing to purchase supplies from wholesalers engaged in the practice of "dual distributing," *i.e.*, selling lumber at both wholesale and retail. The boycott, which was organized under the auspices of the retailers' trade association, was designed to coerce dual distributors into exiting the retail end of the business, where their vertical integration into wholesaling promised them a decided cost advantage. The boycott took the form of a "blacklist," which identified dual distributors. The list was circulated to association members and customers, who in turn agreed not to purchase supplies from the listed firms. With reference to *Standard Oil's* "rule of reason," the Court condemned the boycott:

> A retail dealer has the unquestioned right to stop dealing with a wholesaler for reasons sufficient to himself, and may do so because he thinks such dealer is acting unfairly in trying to undermine his trade. * * *

> [But] [w]hen the retailer goes beyond his personal right, and, conspiring and combining with others of like purpose, seeks to obstruct the free course of * * * commerce and to unduly suppress competition by placing obnoxious wholesaler dealers under the coercive influence of a condemnatory report circulated among others, or possible customers of the offenders, he exceeds his lawful rights. * * *

Id. at 614.

Was the boycott in *Eastern States* collusive or exclusionary? Emphasizing the probability that the retail dealers were parties to a price fixing cartel, Judge Posner appears to have suggested that the essential anticompetitive character of the refusal to deal in *Eastern States* was its tendency to produce collusive effects. *See, e.g., JTC Petroleum Co. v. Piasa Motor Fuels, Inc.*, 190 F.3d.775, 778 (7th Cir. 1999) (*see supra* Chapter 1). But Justice Scalia has characterized the conduct as exclusionary. It was targeted at and intended to disadvantage wholesalers that were also retail rivals of association members. In contrast to *JTC*, there was no allegation of any ongoing cartel among the boycotting association members. As such, its "success," *i.e.*, its anticompetitive effect, depended upon the ability of the colluding firms either to coerce their rivals into abandoning dual distribution or to exclude them effectively. *See Hartford Fire Ins. Co. v. California*, 509 U.S. 764, 803 (1993) (viewing *Eastern States* as a conditional boycott). Which interpretation of *Eastern States* is more compelling? Does it matter from the point of view of antitrust analysis? Might it affect the analysis of *antitrust injury* for purposes of a private civil action initiated by an excluded firm?

The Supreme Court similarly condemned a boycott in *Fashion Originators' Guild of America v. FTC*, 312 U.S. 457 (1941) ("FOGA"), making clear that group boycotts would be condemned regardless of their direct relationship to price fixing. In doing so, it ruled inadmissible the Guild's defenses—that the agreement at issue had not "fixed or regulated prices, parcelled out or limited production, or brought about a deterioration in quality." *Id.* at 466. This brought the Court much closer in *FOGA* than in *Eastern States* to condemning boycotts as per se violations of the Sherman Act.

FOGA involved a boycott organized by designers and manufacturers of women's garments, primarily "high fashion" dresses, that was organized through their trade association, the Fashion Originators' Guild of America. The members objected to the sale by some of their retailing customers, such as department stores, of "pirated" designs, which were sold by lower cost manufacturers, who allegedly copied the designs of Guild members and sold them for less, having avoided the design costs. The members of FOGA agreed that they would boycott retailers that also sold such "pirated designs." More than 12,000 retailers signed agreements to "cooperate" with the boycott, and the record disclosed that more than half did so because they felt "constrained by threats that Guild members would not sell to retailers who failed to yield to their demands." According to the Court, "In 1936, [the 176 members of the Guild] sold in the United States more than 38% of all women's garments wholesaling at $6.75 and up, and more than 60% of those at $10.75 and above." *Id.* at 462.

But the Guild's conduct went beyond the boycott. The Court observed that it also (1) prohibited its members from participating in retail advertising; (2) regulated the discount they may allow; (3) prohibited their selling at retail; (4) cooperated with local guilds in regulating days upon which special sales were held; (5) prohibited its members from selling women's garments to persons who conduct businesses in residences, residential quarters, hotels or apartment houses; and (6) denied the benefits of membership to retailers who participated with dress manufacturers in promoting fashion shows unless the merchandise used was actually purchased and delivered. *Id.* at 463. According to the Court, collectively, the boycott and these other acts had actual anticompetitive effects:

> * * * [A]mong the many respects in which the Guild's plan runs contrary to the policy of the Sherman Act are these: it narrows the outlets to which garment and textile manufacturers can sell and the sources from which retailers can buy; subjects all retailers and manufacturers who decline to comply with the Guild's program to an organized boycott; takes away the freedom of action of members by requiring each to reveal to the Guild the intimate details of their individual affairs; and has both as its necessary tendency and as its purpose and effect the direct suppression of competition from the sale of unregistered textiles and copied designs. * * *

Id. at 465. The Court specifically rejected the defendants' plea that no violation could be found absent a finding that the Guild "fixed or regulated prices, parcelled out or limited production, or brought about a deterioration in quality," declaring that "action falling into these three categories does not exhaust the types of conduct banned by the Sherman and Clayton Acts." *Id.* at 466. It also rejected FOGA's defense that its actions were "reasonable," justified by its desire to protect against design pirates, affirming the Commission's decision to exclude most of the defendants' justification-related evidence. *Id.* at 467–68. For another example of the Court's treatment of concerted group boycotts, see *Associated Press v. United States*, 326 U.S. 1, 12 (1945) (by-laws of cooperative news gathering agency that precluded members from sharing gathered news with non-members unreasonably restrained trade "on their face," citing *FOGA* and *Socony-Vacuum Oil*).

Per se treatment of group boycotts did not become fully cemented in antitrust law, however, until the Court's 1959 decision in *Klor's v. Broadway-Hale Stores, Inc.*, 359 U.S. 207 (1959). Klor's operated a retail radio, television, and appliance store. It claimed that its rival Broadway-Hale, which operated a chain of department stores (one of which was next door to Klor's), conspired with ten leading national manufacturers and some of their distributors to refuse to deal with Klor's, or to deal with it only on less favorable terms than Broadway-Hale. Klor's maintained that this boycott violated Sections 1 and 2 of the Sherman Act. *Id.* at 208–09.

As the Court detailed, the defendants did not contest the main of Klor's' allegations. Yet they sought summary judgment on the ground that "there were hundreds of other household appliance retailers, some within a few blocks of Klor's who sold many competing brands of appliances, including those the defendants refused to sell to Klor's," in essence arguing that even if the allegations were true, the boycott could have no effect on competition. *Id.* at 209–10. The District Court agreed and dismissed the complaint, characterizing it as a " 'purely private quarrel' between Klor's and Broadway-Hale, which did not amount to a 'public wrong proscribed by the [Sherman] Act.' " *Id.* at 209–10. The Supreme Court reversed, firmly locating "group boycotts" in the "per se" category of cases:

> Group boycotts, or concerted refusals by traders to deal with other traders, have long been held to be in the forbidden category. They have not been saved by allegations that they were reasonable in the specific circumstances, nor by a failure to show that they "fixed or regulated prices, parcelled out or limited production, or brought about a deterioration in quality." Even when they operated to lower prices or temporarily to stimulate competition they were banned. * * *

> Plainly the allegations of this complaint disclose such a boycott. This is not a case of a single trader refusing to deal with another nor even of a manufacturer and a dealer agreeing to an exclusive distributorship. Alleged in this complaint is a wide combination consisting of manufacturers, distributors and a retailer. This combination takes from Klor's its freedom to buy appliances in an open competitive market and drives it out of business as a dealer in the defendants' products. It deprives the manufacturers and distributors of their freedom to sell to Klor's at the same prices and conditions made available to Broadway-Hale and in some instances forbids them from selling to it on any terms whatsoever. * * * It clearly has, by its "nature" and "character," a "monopolistic tendency." As such it is not to be tolerated merely because the victim is just one merchant whose business is so small that his destruction makes little difference to the economy. Monopoly can as surely thrive by the elimination of such small businessmen, one at a time, as it can by driving them out in large groups. In recognition of this fact the Sherman Act has consistently been read to forbid all contracts and combinations "which 'tend to create a monopoly,' " whether "the tendency is a creeping one" or "one that proceeds at full gallop."

Id. at 212–14 (footnotes omitted).

Did *Klor's* involve a collusive or an exclusionary group boycott? Can you tell from the evidence relied upon by the Court? Was the case really *horizontal*, focused on the competitive relationship between Klor's and Broadway-Hale, or was it *vertical*, more likely focused on the relationships between the major appliance manufacturers and Klor's? Recall that in *FOGA*, the boycotting manufacturers constituted a very substantial share of the market for women's dresses, making their threat of boycott a credible weapon against individual retailers. Is the same true in *Klor's*? Is it likely that Broadway-Hale was in a position to coerce such well known appliance manufacturers as General Electric and RCA not to sell to Klor's? If not, what might explain their decision to discontinue sales to Klor's? *See also Radiant Burners, Inc. v. Peoples Gas Light & Coke Co.*, 364 U.S. 656, 81 S.Ct. 365 (1961) (applying *Klor's* to the refusal by a standards setting group to test and consider for approval the plaintiff's gas burner where the standards group's membership included a number of the plaintiff's rival manufacturers).

One explanation long entertained by commentators is that Klor's was a discounter who was free riding on the promotional efforts of Broadway-Hale. As we will learn in Chapter 6, free riders can undermine a manufacturer's ability to attract aggressive and service-oriented retailers. Assume, for example, that Broadway-Hale engaged in a great deal of promotional activities, had well-trained sales people, and maintained attractive showrooms. Obviously, that level of service is costly, but may increase sales overall for the retailer as well as the manufacturers. If Klor's simply placed a sign in its window that said "Buy It Here for Less," and undertook none of the efforts that Broadway-Hale did, it might have been able to divert enough customers from Broadway-Hale to make its efforts uneconomical. Customers would learn all they needed to know about the product from Broadway-Hale, then buy from Klor's. If as a consequence Broadway-Hale gave up on its efforts, sales overall might actually decrease, hurting the manufacturers' efforts to increase output. Viewing the arrangement as "horizontal," and invoking the per se rule might not allow for such a justification. For a more convincing example of a dealer cartel soliciting its supplier to refuse to deal with discounters, see *United States v. General Motors Corp.*, 384 U.S. 127 (1966) (unlawful for associations of automobile dealers to agree with manufacturer to refuse to deal with discounting dealers).

There is no suggestion in *Klor's*, however, that this scenario in fact was the case. We are left, therefore, with something of a puzzle: why did the manufacturers go along with Broadway-Hale's request to boycott Klor's? The defendants offered no apparent justification, relying instead on the argument that Klor's' elimination could not affect competition given the many other retailers in the area. One commentator has suggested, therefore, that the outcome might be justified because the boycott did not yield any identifiable efficiencies and took from consumers a retailer that they apparently liked. *See* Robert H. Bork, THE ANTITRUST PARADOX 332

(1978). On the other hand, as we will learn in Chapter 6, today the law generally provides manufacturers with greater autonomy in structuring their dealer relations, and specifically allows them to refuse to sell to free riding retailers. Hence in *NYNEX Corp. v. Discon, Inc.*, 525 U.S. 128 (1998), it seemed clear that from the Supreme Court's perspective, the continued vitality of *Klor's* depends upon its status as a "horizontal," collusive effects case, which seems to require some stretching of its facts.

b. Contemporary Treatment of Exclusionary Concerted Refusals to Deal: *Northwest Wholesale Stationers* (1985) and *Visa* (2003)

Eastern States, *FOGA*, and *Klor's* established that group boycotts, also known as "concerted refusals to deal," were per se unlawful. But collectively, those decisions did not provide a coherent framework for differentiating collusive boycotts, which perhaps are more obviously deserving of harsh treatment, from boycotts that exclude, but which in some fashion could be subject to legitimate justifications. Recall the material we read at the outset of this Chapter on the economics of exclusion. How might exclusionary group boycotts fit into that framework? Are they objectionable because they can raise rival's costs and confer power over price on the boycotting firms? Are there examples of "naked" exclusionary boycotts that are objectionable because they lack any legitimate business justification?

The Supreme Court faced some of these issues in *Northwest Wholesale Stationers, Inc. v. Pacific Stationery & Printing Co.*, 472 U.S. 284, 105 S.Ct. 2613 (1985), where the Court sought to maintain the applicability of a per se approach to exclusionary "boycotts," but imposed some important conditions on its use.

Many of the basic facts in the case were uncontested. Northwest Wholesale Stationers was a purchasing cooperative of roughly 100 office supply retailers in the Pacific Northwest. It acted as the primary wholesaler for the retailers and, although non-member retailers could purchase their supplies from Northwest at the same price as members, members received a distribution of profits at the end of each year that effectively lowered their wholesale costs significantly. Northwest also provided warehousing facilities that permitted the cooperative to realize economies of scale in purchasing and warehousing that otherwise would not have been available to them. Pacific was a long-standing member of Northwest and was a "dual distributor," i.e., it was both a retailer and a wholesaler to other retailers, including non-members. The controversy arose when Northwest amended its bylaws to prohibit members from engaging in both retail and wholesale operations. Although a grandfather clause preserved Pacific's membership rights despite the change, when it later violated another of Northwest's bylaws by failing to notify it of a change in ownership, its membership was terminated without notice, an explanation, or any opportunity to contest the decision. Pacific challenged its expulsion in this fashion as a per se unlawful concerted refusal to deal. *Id.* at 286–87.

Recall from Chapter 2 that by the time this case came before the Court (1985), the Court had begun to modulate its use of per se analysis in cases like *Broadcast Music* (*see supra* Chapter 2) and to move the rule of reason beyond the simple per se vs. rule of reason model, as we saw in *NCAA* (*see supra* Chapter 2). It framed the issues before it, therefore, as including "whether a *per se* violation of § 1 of the Sherman Act occurs when a cooperative buying agency comprising various retailers expels a member without providing any procedural means for challenging the expulsion," but also "broader questions as to when *per se* antitrust analysis is appropriately applied to joint activity that is susceptible of being characterized as a concerted refusal to deal." *Id.* at 285–86.

The Court acknowledged that it had "long held that certain concerted refusals to deal or group boycotts are so likely to restrict competition without any offsetting efficiency gains that they should be condemned as *per se* violations of § 1 of the Sherman Act.[11] Quoting from *Broadcast Music*, however, it observed that "[w]holesale purchasing cooperatives such as Northwest are not a form of concerted activity characteristically likely to result in predominantly anticompetitive effects. Rather, such cooperative arrangements would seem to be 'designed to increase economic efficiency and render markets more, rather than less, competitive.'" *Id.* at 289–90. Noting, however, that Pacific was not challenging the legality of the cooperative as a whole, but more narrowly the act of expulsion, it further observed that it is "the action of expulsion that must be evaluated to determine whether *per se* treatment is appropriate. The act of expulsion from a wholesale cooperative does not necessarily imply anticompetitive animus and thereby raise a probability of anticompetitive effect." *Id.* at 295–96. It therefore sought to define something of a middle ground. Synthesizing a test drawn from observations about the specific facts in its previous decisions, it identified preconditions to the use of per se analysis for cases involving conduct that is susceptible to the "refusal to deal" label:

> Cases to which this Court has applied the *per se* approach have generally involved joint efforts by a firm or firms to disadvantage competitors by "either directly denying or persuading or coercing suppliers or customers to deny relationships the competitors need in the competitive struggle." In these cases, the boycott often cut off access to a supply, facility, or market necessary to enable the

---

[11] In support of this proposition, the Court cited *Klor's, General Motors, Fashion Originator's Guild,* and *Eastern States,* as well as *Radiant Burners, Inc. v. Peoples Gas Light & Coke Co.,* 364 U.S. 656, 81 S.Ct. 365 (1961) and *Associated Press v. United States,* 326 U.S. 1, 65 S.Ct. 1416 (1945).

boycotted firm to compete, and frequently the boycotting firms possessed a dominant position in the relevant market. In addition, the practices were generally not justified by plausible arguments that they were intended to enhance overall efficiency and make markets more competitive. Under such circumstances the likelihood of anticompetitive effects is clear and the possibility of countervailing procompetitive effects is remote.

Although a concerted refusal to deal need not necessarily possess all of these traits to merit *per se* treatment, not every cooperative activity involving a restraint or exclusion will share with the *per se* forbidden boycotts the likelihood of predominantly anticompetitive consequences. * * *

472 U.S. at 294. Based on the facts already in the record, it sided with the district court, agreeing that per se analysis was inappropriate for the expulsion, concluding:

A plaintiff seeking application of the *per se* rule must present a threshold case that the challenged activity falls into a category likely to have predominantly anticompetitive effects. The mere allegation of a concerted refusal to deal does not suffice because not all concerted refusals to deal are predominantly anticompetitive. When the plaintiff challenges expulsion from a joint buying cooperative, some showing must be made that the cooperative possesses market power or unique access to a business element necessary for effective competition.

Id. at 298. Because the case was decided on cross-motions for summary judgment and what the Court described as a "sparse" record, it was remanded for further consideration under these stated standards.

Note how the framework set forth in *Northwest Wholesale Stationers* appears to create a "quasi" or "qualified" per se rule for exclusionary group boycotts: the per se rule can only be invoked under specified conditions that make it more likely that the conduct will be anticompetitive. The Court's approach can be understood as an acknowledgement of a point we discussed in Sidebar 2–3, that the label "group boycott" can be applied to many different kinds of conduct, not all of which warrant per se treatment. It also connects *Northwest Wholesale Stationers* to *Broadcast Music*, where the Court cautioned that "easy labels do not always supply ready answers." *Broadcast Music*, 441 U.S. at 8 (noting that not all "literal" price fixing warrants treatment as per se unlawful price fixing) (*see supra* Chapter 2). The framework is summarized in Figure 4–10:

Figure 4–10:

Framework for Analyzing Exclusionary Group Boycotts Under *Northwest Wholesale Stationers*

"Cases to which this Court has applied the *per se* approach have generally involved joint efforts by a firm or firms to disadvantage competitors by . . ."

Three Steps/Requirements:

- Cutting off access to a supply, facility, or market necessary to enable the boycotted firm to compete (*Exclusionary Conduct*)

- Frequently the boycotting firms possessed a dominant position in the relevant market (*Market Power*)

- No plausible arguments that the boycott enhanced overall efficiency (*No Procompetitive Justification*)

How might a concerted refusal to deal "disadvantage competitors"? Does the Court require that all three elements be satisfied to condemn an exclusionary group boycott under this approach or does the decision leave open the possibility that a violation could be found if some, but not all, of these factors are present? Can this approach be fairly labeled as a "per se" application of the rule of reason? Does it more closely resemble a structured and abbreviated form of the rule of reason? If the latter, how does it relate to the Supreme Court's "quick look" approach, which we explored in Chapter 2? How does the suggested framework differ from a more complete application of the rule of reason? Could you prove a violation under a more complete rule of reason analysis if one of these preconditions was missing? How does it compare to the approach of the D.C. Circuit in *Microsoft*?

What is the economic rationale behind the three conduct examples provided by the Court? Would imposing the same conditions on boycotts having collusive effects make sense? How do the conditions distinguish the analysis of boycotts having exclusionary effects from boycotts having collusive ones? Does including a requirement of market power effectively move it out of the per se category? Would a finding of market power enable a "quick look" approach, as the Court had taken in *NCAA*? Finally, consider how the Court tries to situate its discussion of boycotts relative to the foundation cases we discussed above.

Consider as well the economic rationale for differentiating the treatment of group boycotts having exclusionary effects from those having collusive effects, like *Superior Court Trial Lawyers*. What justifies treating them differently? Why might group boycotts having collusive effects be more deserving of per se condemnation than those having exclusionary effects? Are there possible justifications more likely to be associated with the latter? Are the factors identified by the Court in *Northwest Wholesale Stationers* tailored to identifying exclusionary boycotts likely to produce unacceptable levels of anticompetitive effects? How might you analyze them in relation to minimizing the incidence of false positives?

Finally, review Figure 4–9. Which of the three scenarios portrayed best reflects *Northwest Wholesale Stationers*? Would the framework set forth in *Northwest Wholesale Stationers* work equally well for all three scenarios? Should it? For a later application of *Northwest Wholesale Stationers*, see *Toys "R" Us, Inc. v. FTC*, 221 F.3d 928, 936 (7th Cir. 2000) (concluding that its conditions had been met and that a violation had been established). *See also Craftsman Limousine, Inc. v. Ford Motor Co.*, 363 F.3d 761 (8th Cir. 2004) (finding a violation for an alleged concerted refusal to deal under the rule of reason, but declining to apply a per se approach).

In thinking about the role of exclusionary boycotts, recall from Chapter 1 that exclusion and collusion can be very much interdependent, as they were in *JTC Petroleum* and in some of the cases we studied in Chapter 2. How might exclusionary group boycotts be used to solve the "cheating" problem that can threaten to undermine many conspiracies, which we studied in Chapter 3? The colluders might be willing to share some of the excess profits obtained through price fixing with one or more suppliers willing to refuse to deal with a maverick rival that refuses to join in the price fixing scheme. In this scenario, illustrated in Figure 4–9(1), the boycott can be an effective tool for policing or enforcing an underlying agreement to fix prices or divide territories among the boycotting firms. If effective, the maverick will be forced to choose between joining the cartel and remaining free of the cartel while being forced to compete less aggressively. If it continues to compete, it will reduce output and raise price, because it must endure the higher costs associated with identifying alternative suppliers, if they are available at all. It will act as though it has joined the cartel, but its participation in the cartel's collective industry output reduction is "involuntary." The end result in terms of competitive effects is the same. Consider the example in Chapter 1 of *JTC Petroleum*. Recall that the road pavers paid the asphalt producers not to deal with their rival, JTC—an example of an exclusionary boycott being used to dissuade or exclude a competitor so the boycotting rivals could maintain their cartel.

An exclusionary (cartel-policing) boycott is still distinguishable from a collusive one, however, because its target is a rival of the colluders, not a customer or supplier, and the crucial evidence will still turn on the tendency of the boycott to exclude the rival, and the likelihood that the exclusion will lead to higher prices. *See Hartford Fire Ins. Co. v. California*, 509 U.S. 764, 800–11 (1993) (Scalia, J.) (distinguishing between collective refusals to deal on specified terms—what we describe as refusals to deal having collusive effects—and "conditional boycotts," which have as their goal the coercion of another competing firm in order to alter its conduct—what we describe as a concerted refusal to deal having exclusionary effects, or an "involuntary cartel").

In our next case, the Second Circuit faced allegations that the two largest credit card networks, Visa and MasterCard, prohibited their member banks from dealing with rival issuers of credit cards. Note how in analyzing the facts of the case, the court articulates a framework for evaluating exclusionary restraints undertaken in connection with the operation of an otherwise legitimate joint venture. How does that framework compare to the approach outlined by the Court in *Northwest Wholesaler Stationers*? Is it similar to the framework adopted by the D.C. Circuit in *Polygram*, (*see supra* Chapter 2) or in *Microsoft*? If so, does it suggest that it may be possible to articulate a common framework for evaluating both collusive and exclusionary conduct, at least in the context of joint ventures? How would such a framework account for the differing economic issues that arise in collusive vs. exclusionary effects cases?

UNITED STATES V. VISA U.S.A., INC.
United States Court of Appeals for the Second Circuit, 2003.
344 F.3d 229.

Before: OAKES, LEVAL, and CABRANES, CIRCUIT JUDGES.

LEVAL, CIRCUIT JUDGE.

* * * The U.S. Department of Justice ("DOJ") brought this civil enforcement action challenging the organizational structure of two of the nation's four major payment card systems. The complaint charged that MasterCard and Visa U.S.A., which are organized as joint ventures owned by their member banking institutions, conspired to restrain trade in two ways: (1) By enacting rules permitting a member-owner of one to function as a director of the other (an arrangement the government described as "dual governance") (Count I); and (2) by enacting and enforcing "exclusionary rules," which prohibit their member banks from issuing American Express ("Amex") or Discover cards (Count II).

After a 34-day trial, the court, in a commendably comprehensive and careful opinion, ruled in the defendants' favor as to dual governance (Count I). As to Count II, however, the court held that Visa U.S.A. and MasterCard violated * * * [Section 1 of the Sherman] Act by enforcing their respective versions of the exclusionary rule, barring their member banks from issuing Amex or Discover cards. * * *

* * *

For the reasons set forth below, we affirm the judgment.

Background

I.   Description of the General Purpose Payment Card Industry

A.   *The Structure of the Visa and MasterCard Networks*

Visa U.S.A. and MasterCard are two of the United States's four major network systems in the payment card industry, the other two being Amex and Discover.[2] Visa U.S.A. and MasterCard are organized as open joint ventures, owned by the numerous banking institutions that are members of the networks. * * * MasterCard is owned by its approximately 20,000 member banks; Visa U.S.A. is owned by its approximately 14,000 member banks. Because MasterCard allows its member banks to issue Visa cards, and Visa U.S.A. likewise allows its members to issue MasterCard cards, many of Visa U.S.A.'s 14,000 members are also members of the MasterCard network. * * *

The member banks of the MasterCard and Visa U.S.A. card networks may function either as "issuers" or "acquirers" or both. A member bank serving as an "issuer" issues cards to cardholders; it serves as the liaison between the network and the individual cardholder. A member bank serving as an "acquirer" acquires the card-paid transactions of a merchant; a particular acquiring bank acts as liaison between the network and those merchants accepting the network's payment cards with whom it has contracted.

When a consumer uses a Visa card or a MasterCard card to pay for goods or services, the accepting merchant relays the transaction information to the acquiring bank with whom it has contracted. The acquirer processes and packages that information and transmits it to the network (Visa U.S.A. or MasterCard). The network then relays the transaction information to the cardholder's issuing bank, which approves the transaction if the cardholder has a sufficient credit line. Approval is sent by the issuer to the acquirer, which relays it to the merchant.

Payment requests are sent by the merchant to the acquirer, which forwards the requests to the issuer. The issuer then pays the acquiring bank the amount requested, less what is called an "interchange fee"—typically 1.4%. The acquirer retains an additional fee—approximately .6%. Thus, the issuing bank and the acquirer withhold an aggregate of approximately 2% of the amount of the transaction from the merchant. This is known as the "merchant discount." For a $100 sale, the merchant typically will receive $98, the issuing bank retaining $1.40, while the acquiring bank retains 60 cents.

---

[2]   The four major systems each issue credit and charge cards. A *charge card* requires that the balance be paid in full at the end of every billing cycle. A *credit card* allows customers to pay only a portion of the monthly balance, charging interest on the unpaid balance.

Both MasterCard and Visa are *open* joint ventures, meaning that there is no limit to the number of banks that may become members, either as issuers or as acquirers. Any member may serve as both an issuer and as an acquirer. Members agree to abide by their association's by-laws and other regulations.

A member of either the Visa U.S.A. or MasterCard network may also be a member of the other network. Thus a bank that is a member of Visa U.S.A.'s network and issues Visa cards may also be a member of the MasterCard network and issue MasterCard cards. On the other hand, both MasterCard and Visa U.S.A. have promulgated rules that prohibit their members from issuing American Express or Discover cards. Those rules— Visa's by-law 2.10(e) and MasterCard's Competitive Programs Policy ("CPP")[3]—are the focus of this action, and were held by the district court to violate the Sherman Act.

B. The Structure of the American Express and Discover Networks

American Express and Discover, the other two major card systems in the United States, are quite differently organized. They are not joint venture membership associations. Rather, each is a vertically integrated entity, acting for profit, which combines issuing, acquiring, and network functions. (The parties and the District Court occasionally refer to this structure as a "closed loop.") Amex and Discover deal directly with consumers (by issuing cards), and with merchants (by acquiring and processing transactions). When a consumer makes a purchase with an American Express card, for example, the merchant contacts Amex directly, and if the customer has sufficient credit available, Amex approves the sale. Amex then pays the merchant directly, retaining a percentage—usually 2.73%. (Discover is organized similarly to Amex. Its merchant discount is usually 1.5%.)

Since at least 1995, American Express has sought to change its structure by soliciting banks to issue American Express cards. This effort has been successful outside of the continental United States and abroad, where banks such as Puerto Rico's Banco Popular have begun issuing Amex-branded cards. In the continental United States, in contrast, Amex has been unsuccessful in its attempt to solicit outside issuers. Because of Visa U.S.A.'s and MasterCard's exclusionary rules, any bank that undertook to issue Amex-branded cards would be forced to give up issuing

---

[3] Visa U.S.A.'s by-law 2.10(e), passed in 1991, states,

The membership of any Member shall automatically terminate in the event it, or its parent, subsidiary or affiliate, issues, directly or indirectly, Discover Cards, or American Express Cards, or any other card deemed competitive by the Board of Directors. E-2897; SPA 97.

MasterCard's CPP, passed in 1996, provides that

With the exception of participation in Visa, which is essentially owned by the same member entities, and several pre-existing programs to the extent individual members participate . . . members of MasterCard may not participate either as issuers or acquirers in competitive general purpose card programs. E-2265; SPA 101.

both Visa and MasterCard cards—a move no U.S. bank has been willing to make.

* * *

II. Competition in the General Purpose Payment Card Industry

Competition in the payment card industry takes place at the "network" level, as well as at the "issuing" and "acquiring" levels. At the network level, the four brands compete with one another to establish brand loyalty in favor of the Visa, MasterCard, Amex, or Discover card. At the issuing level, approximately twenty thousand banks that issue Visa and MasterCard cards to customers compete with one another and with Amex and Discover. Unlike the network services market, which has only four major participants, approximately 20,000 entities compete for customers in the issuing market, and no single participant is dominant. American Express is the largest single card issuer in the United States, as measured by transaction volume. By the same measure, Discover is the fifth largest issuer. The other large issuers are member banks in the Visa and MasterCard networks.

III. The Challenged Regulations

* * *

Discussion

* * *

For the government to prevail in a rule of reason case under Section 1, the district court concluded, and the parties do not argue otherwise, that the following must be shown: As an initial matter, the government must demonstrate that the defendant conspirators have "market power" in a particular market for goods or services.[4] Next, the government must demonstrate that within the relevant market, the defendants' actions have had substantial adverse effects on competition, such as increases in price, or decreases in output or quality. Once that initial burden is met, the burden of production shifts to the defendants, who must provide a procompetitive justification for the challenged restraint. If the defendants do so, the government must prove either that the challenged restraint is not reasonably necessary to achieve the defendants' procompetitive justifications, or that those objectives may be achieved in a manner less restrictive of free competition.

---

[4] Some authorities suggest that the market power requirement is unnecessary. *See, e.g., FTC v. Indiana Fed'n of Dentists,* 476 U.S. 447, 460, 106 S.Ct. 2009, 90 L.Ed.2d 445 (1986); * * * *NCAA v. Bd. of Regents,* 468 U.S. 85, 110 n. 42, 104 S.Ct. 2948, 82 L.Ed.2d 70 (similar). * * * Whether market power is a necessary element is of no moment here; the district court found that the defendants had market power in the relevant markets, and as indicated below, we see no reason to question that finding.

* * *

I.   Relevant Markets and Market Power

The district court determined, and we agree, that this case involves two interrelated, but separate, product markets: (1) what the court called the general purpose card market, consisting of the market for charge cards and credit cards, and (2) the network services market for general purpose cards.

A distinct product market comprises products that are considered by consumers to be "reasonabl[y] interchangeab[le]" with what the defendant sells. *Eastman Kodak Co. v. Image Tech. Servs., Inc.,* 504 U.S. 451, 482, 112 S.Ct. 2072, 119 L.Ed.2d 265 (1992); *United States v. E.I. du Pont de Nemours & Co.,* 351 U.S. 377, 404, 76 S.Ct. 994, 100 L.Ed. 1264 (1956). After hearing substantial expert testimony, the district court found as a matter of fact that other forms of payment—such as cash, checks, debit cards, and proprietary cards (*e.g.,* the Sears or Macy's cards)—are not considered by most consumers to be reasonable substitutes for general purpose credit or charge cards. As the government's expert witness explained, based on empirical analysis of consumer preferences, if prices for general purpose payment cards were to rise significantly, cardholders would likely pay the increased fees, rather than abandon their cards in favor of other forms of payment. Thus, general purpose payment cards constitute a distinct market, separate from the market for such other payment alternatives. We find no reason to doubt the court's conclusion.

Further, we agree with the district court that the four payment card networks compete with one another in a market for "network services." General purpose card networks * * * "provide the infrastructure and mechanisms through which general purpose card transactions are conducted, including the authorization, settlement, and clearance of transactions." Whereas in the market for general purpose *cards,* the issuers are the sellers, and cardholders are the buyers, in the market for general purpose card *network services,* the four networks themselves are the sellers, and the issuers of cards and merchants are the buyers. Issuing banks purchase network services from MasterCard and/or Visa U.S.A., and those two brands compete with Amex and Discover for the banks' business. Networks also compete for merchants, because the price merchants pay for acceptance of payment cards (the merchant discount) is affected by the size of the interchange fee, which is set by the network.

The district court found, on the basis of expert testimony, that there are no products reasonably interchangeable, in the eyes of issuers or merchants, with the network services provided by the four major brands. This was a reasonable finding: (1) Network-level costs are so high that banks and merchants cannot provide these services for themselves, and (2) issuance and acceptance of credit and charge cards is so profitable (and network service fees so negligible in comparison) that even a large increase in network fees would not provide a rational financial incentive to abandon the business of issuing or accepting payment cards.

We agree with the district court's finding that Visa U.S.A. and MasterCard, jointly and separately, have power within the market for network services. Market power has been defined by the Supreme Court to mean the "power to control prices or exclude competition." *du Pont,* 351 U.S. at 391, 76 S.Ct. 994. *NCAA,* at 109 n. 38, 104 S.Ct. 2948. Such power may be proven through evidence of specific conduct undertaken by the defendant that indicates he has the power to affect price or exclude competition. Alternatively, market power may be presumed if the defendant controls a large enough share of the relevant market. [The district court judge] * * * based her finding of market power first on the fact that merchants testified that they could not refuse to accept payment by Visa or MasterCard, even if faced with significant price increases, because of customer preference. Indeed, despite recent increases in both networks' interchange fees, no merchant had discontinued acceptance of their cards. In addition, the court inferred market power from the defendants' large shares of a highly concentrated market: In 1999, Visa U.S.A. members accounted for approximately 47% of the dollar volume of credit and charge card transactions, while MasterCard members accounted for approximately 26%. (American Express accounted for 20%; Discover, for 6%.)

The evidence relied on by the district court was sufficient to sustain a finding of market power. In addition, Amex, despite repeated recent attempts, has been unable to persuade any issuing banks in the continental United States to utilize its network services because the exclusivity rule would require such issuing banks to give up membership in the Visa and MasterCard consortiums, and banks are unwilling to do so. In short, Visa U.S.A. and MasterCard have demonstrated their power in the network services market by effectively precluding their largest competitor from successfully soliciting any bank as a customer for its network services and brand.

II. Harms to Competition

* * * The district court found that Visa U.S.A. and MasterCard's exclusionary rules harm competition by "reducing overall card output and available card features," as well as by decreasing network services output and stunting price competition. We cannot say that these conclusions were erroneous.

The most persuasive evidence of harm to competition is the total exclusion of American Express and Discover from a segment of the market for network services. As noted, there are only four major payment card network providers in the United States. While competition among (and within) these networks is robust at the issuing level (where 20,000 separate issuers compete to provide products to consumers), at the network level (where four major networks seek to sell their technical, infrastructure, and financial services to issuer banks) competition has been seriously damaged by the defendants' exclusionary rules. * * * The district court cited evidence that three major U.S. issuer banks—Banco Popular, Advanta, and Bank One—would have contracted with American Express to issue Amex cards in the United States but for the exclusionary rules. In addition, Banco Popular has contracted with Amex to issue its cards in Puerto Rico, where no exclusionary rules apply.

As a result, then, of the challenged policies, only two rival networks are effectively able to compete for the business of issuer banks. Testimony at trial revealed that Visa U.S.A. and MasterCard "pay millions of dollars in incentive payments in the form of discounts from the price for network services to selected issuing banks to compete for their business and [that] the banks play Visa and MasterCard against [each] other to obtain lower net prices and higher value for card network services." With only two viable competitors, however, such price and product competition is necessarily limited. Trial testimony strongly indicated that price competition and innovation in services would be enhanced if four competitors, rather than only two, were able to compete in this manner for issuing banks. Indeed, the district court found, based on testimony from Visa U.S.A. and MasterCard executives, that both defendants would "respond to . . . greater network competition by offering new and better products and services." * * *

In foreign countries, where Visa International rather than Visa U.S.A. operates the Visa network, and no exclusionary rule applies, Amex has succeeded in convincing banks that issue Visa cards also to issue Amex cards. This has caused Visa International to "proactively strengthen" its product offerings to member banks abroad. In addition, an internal Visa International memorandum cautions that Visa U.S.A. would have to compete more vigorously for market share if Amex were permitted to partner with its member banks: "To date, AmEx has been precluded from partnering with U.S. banks, although that situation could change. Since bank partners could significantly increase [Amex's] acceptance and cards, Visa needs to monitor the situation and counter with competitive products that meet banks['] needs."

The district court also found that product innovation and output has been stunted by the challenged policies. By excluding Amex and Discover from the market for outside card issuers, Visa U.S.A. and MasterCard effectively deny consumers access to products that could be offered only by a network in partnership with individual banks. Such products include cards that are able to link "to transaction accounts, to asset management accounts, to sale of mortgages or other financial products that [banks] offer [ ]."

We find no error in the district court's finding that competition has been harmed by the defendants' exclusionary rules.

III. The Defendants' Arguments

* * *

A. *Harms to Competition*

First, the defendants argue that the district court erred by mistaking harm to a *competitor* for harm to *competition*. They cite the familiar formula that the "antitrust laws protect competition, not competitors." Visa U.S.A. contends, for example, that "[t]he decision and remedy in this case will not benefit consumer welfare. Instead, virtually the sole beneficiary will be AmEx which hopes to gain not by offering lower prices or better products but largely by undermining its major brand competitors."

Defendants contend the exclusionary rules are akin to "exclusive distributorship" arrangements, which we have held are "presumptively legal." We find this argument unpersuasive.

Defendants are certainly correct that the proper inquiry is whether there has been an "*actual* adverse effect on competition as a whole in the relevant market." We have held that competition is not adversely affected if, despite an exclusive dealership arrangement, "competitors can reach the ultimate consumer of the product by employing existing or potential alternative channels of distribution."

The defendants argue that the harms identified by the district court as stemming from their exclusionary rules—that the types of cards that consumers can get from their banks are limited and [that] banks are prevented from combining their particular issuing skills with the AmEx brand—are not harms to Amex's ability to compete as a network (or Discover's), but rather harms to its distributive capacity, in much the same way Pepsi-Cola's distributive capacity might be limited by an exclusive arrangement between Coca-Cola and its truckers. For an exclusive dealership arrangement to cause a harm to competition (and overcome the presumption of legality), it must prevent competitors from getting their products to consumers at all. There is no question, the defendants argue, that Amex and Discover can get their products to consumers, as evidenced by the fact that they are respectively the largest and fifth largest issuers of payment cards in the United States.

The analogy to an exclusive arrangement between Coca-Cola and its truckers is not persuasive. The basic flaw in the analogy is that it depicts Visa U.S.A. (or MasterCard) as a single entity (like Coca-Cola) demanding a restrictive provision in its contract with a supplier of services to it. Visa

U.S.A. and MasterCard, however, are not single entities; they are consortiums of competitors. * * * These competitors have agreed to abide by a restrictive exclusivity provision to the effect that in order to share the benefits of their association by having the right to issue Visa or MasterCard cards, they must agree not to compete by issuing cards of Amex or Discover. The restrictive provision is a horizontal restraint adopted by 20,000 competitors.

* * * Each has agreed not to compete with the others in a manner which the consortium considers harmful to its combined interests. Far from being "presumptively legal," such arrangements are exemplars of the type of anticompetitive behavior prohibited by the Sherman Act.

In the market for *network services,* where the four networks are sellers and issuing banks and merchants are buyers, the exclusionary rules enforced by Visa U.S.A. and MasterCard have absolutely prevented Amex and Discover from selling their products at all.

Without doubt the exclusionary rules in question harm competitors. The fact that they harm competitors does not, however, mean that they do not also harm competition. We find no fault with the district court's finding that the exclusion of Amex and Discover from the ability to market their cards and programs to banks has harmed competition in the market for network services, and that Visa U.S.A. and MasterCard would be impelled to design and market their products more competitively if the banks to which they sell their services were free to purchase network services from Amex and Discover. Nor do we fault the district court's determination that certain types of products combining unique features of cards offered by Amex and Discover with the advantages of linkage to cardholders' bank accounts would likely become available. The district court was justified in finding harm to competition.

B.   *Procompetitive Justifications*

* * * The defendants assert that the principal benefit of the exclusionary rules is to promote "cohesion" within the MasterCard and Visa U.S.A. networks, so that those networks may compete effectively in the marketplace. Thus, the defendants argue, the exclusionary rules are ancillary to legitimate, procompetitive business strategies. * * *

The district court found no evidence to suggest that allowing member banks to issue cards of rival networks would endanger cohesion in a manner adverse to the competitive process. MasterCard members have long been permitted to issue Visa cards, and vice versa, without such consequences. Moreover, as the district court noted, there is no evidence that the defendants' network cohesion has been harmed overseas, where, in the absence of exclusionary rules, Amex has contracted with Visa and MasterCard member banks to issue Amex-branded payment cards.

In sum, the defendants have failed to show that the anticompetitive effects of their exclusionary rules are outweighed by procompetitive benefits.

* * *

———————

The analysis of exclusionary conduct in *Visa* raises a number of interesting questions. First, note that the court does not use the word "boycott" at all to describe the challenged conduct, nor does it refer to any of the classic boycott cases, such as *Eastern States*, *FOGA*, or *Klor's*. Neither does it mention *Northwest Wholesale Stationers*. But could the exclusionary rule adopted by Visa and MasterCard literally have been described as a "boycott" of firms like American Express and Discover? If so, why did the court steer clear of all suggestion that it was viewing the conduct as a boycott, subject to any of these cases?

One answer may lie in the analytical framework the court sets out in Section III of its opinion. How similar or different is it from the framework advocated in *Northwest Wholesale Stationers*? Does the court's framework draw attention to similarities in the analysis of conduct having collusive and exclusionary effects? Note the role of market power in both *Northwest Wholesale Stationers* and *Visa*, as well as evidence of both anticompetitive effects and business justifications, all of which have been increasingly important to the cases we have seen in Chapter 2 and here in Chapter 4. Is it fair to say that the framework can be the same for collusive and exclusionary effects cases, although the economic analysis of competitive effects and justifications differs? Would applying the label "boycott" and invoking the older cases have added anything to this analysis?

In Section II of the Discussion, what "harms to competition" does the court associate with the exclusionary rule? As we did with the court's finding of market power, consider here what evidence the court cites in support of that conclusion. Is the evidence cited related to exclusionary effects? Collusive effects? Both? Why does the court deem it significant that competition was different outside of the United States, where the exclusionary rule did not apply? If the exclusionary rule made economic sense to Visa U.S.A. and MasterCard in the United States, why do you suppose Visa Int'l and MasterCard did not implement the exclusionary rule outside of the United States? Finally, what arguments did the defendants offer to justify the exclusionary rule? Why did the court reject them?

The competitive analysis of conduct in the credit card industry is complicated by the fact that it involves what has been described as a "two-sided" market. Sidebar 4–9 discusses the economic issues associated with such markets.

Sidebar 4–9:
The Economics of Two-Sided
Platforms with Network Effects

Payment systems are an example of what economists term "two-sided" platforms with network effects.[a] They are an intermediary (or product "platform") in which there are two types of end users, each of whom finds the platform more desirable if the platform does well in attracting the other type of end user. "Network effects" arise when the value of a product to a buyer depends on the number of other users. Communications systems are an example: a telephone is more valuable the more numbers you can call. Software can also exhibit network effects: its value may be higher the more other users there are, with whom compatible files can be exchanged. When network effects are strong, there is often a tendency for one product to dominate the market. Network effects are discussed more fully in Chapter 7.

Payment systems like the Visa, Master Card, American Express, and Discover networks are two-sided platforms with network effects. Payment systems simultaneously attempt to attract cardholders to use their card, and merchants to accept it. In addition, merchants are more likely to accept a payment system's card the greater its number of cardholders, and cardholders are more likely to obtain a card the greater the number of merchants that accept it.

Newspapers and magazines are also two-sided platforms with network effects. These publications earn revenue by selling advertising space to advertisers and subscriptions to consumers who read the publications. The advertisers value the publication because it provides access to consumers, and the consumers may value the ads directly (because they value advertising information) or indirectly (because they value the content that the ads make possible). Other examples might include shopping malls, which attract retailers and shoppers, securities exchanges, which attract buyers and sellers, and computer operating systems, which attract both computer users and developers of applications software.

In many industries served by two-sided platforms, such as payment systems, the end users often employ multiple platforms, notwithstanding the way network effects often lead one product or service to dominate. Many consumers have cards

---

[a] In this context, the term "market" is used in a general way, not necessarily in the way the term is used in antitrust analysis. Accordingly, some authors writing about antitrust issues prefer the term "two-sided platforms."

from more than one network in their wallets, and most merchants accept more than one type of card. But card brands are differentiated to some extent, and not all merchants accept all cards.

Two-sided platforms have multiple ways of charging for their services. A payment system may charge cardholders an annual fee and charge merchants a specified percentage of each transaction (the "merchant discount").[b] Some newspapers and magazines are free and earn all their revenue from advertising, whereas others charge fees to both advertisers and subscribers. Some have a great deal of advertising and a low subscription price, while others earn most of their revenue from subscriptions. A shopping mall may charge retailers a rent based on their sales volume and may make implicit payments to shoppers by offering them free parking and other services.

Several forces affect the platform's pricing decisions. A platform will want to keep the price to one group of end users (*e.g.*, the cardholders, as opposed to the merchants) relatively low, or even to subsidize those users, if that group of end users is more highly responsive to price or if attracting more of that group of end users would make a relatively larger difference in attracting the other group of end users (*e.g.*, the merchants). The result may be that the price to one group of end users is high relative to the marginal cost of serving those end users, while the price to the other group of end users is low relative to the marginal cost of serving them (or even below that marginal cost).

This pricing pattern—a high price cost margin on some services, perhaps even accompanied by below-cost pricing on others—would not necessarily reflect the exercise of market power if there is adequate competition among platforms. Magazines may provide an example. In that situation, the platform as a whole, taking into account the revenues it receives from both groups of users, would not earn supracompetitive profits. However, if competition is more limited, so the platforms are able to exercise market power, then the prices for one or both services would be greater than those that would obtain under competition. One would expect the price to rise more on the side of the market where end user demand is less responsive to price, and where demand by those end users is more highly sensitive to the loss of the other group of end users.

---

[b]   As was explained in *Visa*, the merchant discount is the sum of the "interchange fee" charged by Master Card or Visa plus a small fee paid to the bank that processes transactions for the merchant.

To apply this framework to payment systems pricing, suppose that cardholders are more price-sensitive than merchants, and that merchants care more about whether the payment systems platform attracts cardholders than the reverse. Then fees to cardholders would be low (or even negative, for example if the platform pays cardholders to sign up through rewards programs) and merchant discounts high. This would be true whether there is competition among payment systems or whether there is a payment systems monopoly. A payment systems monopolist also would be most likely to look more to higher merchant discounts in order to exercise market power, and look relatively less to increasing cardholder fees.

How does the idea of two-sided platforms with network effects help in understanding the payment card industry and the *Visa* litigation? First, should a court be cautious about inferring market power solely from a high merchant discount? Trends in interchange fees and merchant discounts are interpreted from a two-sided platform perspective by economists who worked for Visa in Benjamin Klein, et al., *Competition in Two-Sided Markets: The Antitrust Economics of Payment Card Interchange Fees*, 73 ANTITRUST L.J. 571 (2006).

Second, in the *Visa* case, the court defines a market for "network services," where the four networks are sellers and issuing banks and merchants are buyers. Is doing so consistent with the market definition approach of the Merger Guidelines? Is it appropriate to consider demand substitution from one group of buyers (merchants) in defining markets while ignoring the other group of buyers (cardholders)? Is there a sensible way to consider both while defining markets, or would it be better only to consider one side at a time while defining the market, and then account for the interaction between the two sides of the platform in evaluating anticompetitive effects and efficiencies? In a later decision involving a Justice Department challenge to American Express's "anti-steering" restraints, which prohibited merchants from diverting consumers proffering American Express cards to less costly (from the merchant's perspective) means of payment, the Second Circuit held that the district court had erred in limiting the relevant market to network services, the market defined in *Visa*, and in concluding that the restraints were unreasonably anticompetitive. Although the district court claimed to have taken the two-sided nature of the platform into account in its analysis of market definition, it had declined to define the market to "encompass the entire multi-sided platform." In the Second Circuit's view, that was reversible error, "because the price charged to merchants necessarily affects cardholder demand, which in turn has a feedback effect on merchant demand (and thus influences the price charged to merchants)." *United States v. American Express Co.*, ___ F.3d. ___, 2016 WL 5349734 at *14 (2d. Cir. 2016). Similarly, in the court's view, this error undermined the district court's conclusion that the anti-steering provisions were unreasonably anticompetitive. *Id.* at *15–16. For a discussion of how the Justice Department analyzes market definition in payment systems cases that predates *American Express*, see Renata B. Hesse & Joshua H. Soven, *Defining Relevant Product Markets in Electronic Payment Network Antitrust Cases*, 73 ANTITRUST L.J. 709 (2006).

Third, the appeals court in *Visa* affirmed the district court's conclusion that the Visa and Master Card networks (including member banks) collectively exercised market power, raising what they charge merchants or cardholders (or both) above the competitive level, by impairing the ability of American Express or Discover to compete. How do the concepts of two-sided platforms and network effects illuminate the analysis of that competitive effects question?

For further discussion of the economic issues raised by two-sided platforms, see Jean-Charles Rochet & Jean Tirole, *Two-Sided Markets: A Progress Report*, 37 RAND J. ECON. 645 (2006); Mark Armstrong, *Competition in Two-Sided Markets*, 37 RAND J. ECON. 667 (2006); Marc Rysman, *The Economics of Two-Sided Markets*, 23 J. ECON. PERSPS. 125 (2009). For a discussion of various antitrust issues that two-sided platforms may raise, see Marc Rysman & Julian Wright, *The Economics of Payment Cards,* 13 REV. NETWORK ECONS. 303 (2014); David Evans & Richard Schmalensee, *The Industrial Organization of Markets with Two-Sided Platforms*, 3 COMPETITION POL'Y INT'L 151 (2007); Janusz Ordover, *Comments on Evans & Schmalensee's "The Industrial Organization of Markets with Two-Sided Platforms,"* 3 COMPETITION POL'Y INT'L 181 (2007).

c. Unilateral Refusals to Deal: *Trinko* (2004)

Since the earliest days of monopolization cases under Section 2 of the Sherman Act, the courts have been required to judge the legality of refusals by dominant firms to deal with their rivals, customers, or suppliers. For the most part, courts have declined to require monopolists to cooperate with another business entity. This general policy took shape in *United*

States v. Colgate & Co., 250 U.S. 300, 39 S.Ct. 465 (1919), where the Supreme Court provided a much-quoted statement about the extent of a firm's freedom to choose its commercial partners:

> In the absence of any purpose to create or maintain a monopoly, the [Sherman] act does not restrict the long recognized right of trader or manufacturer engaged in an entirely private business, freely to exercise his independent discretion as to parties with whom he will deal.

Id. at 307. The question of whether a firm has lost the immunity of *Colgate* by seeking to "create or maintain a monopoly" has inspired many antitrust disputes.

Claims of "refusal to deal" have arisen in three different fact patterns, although there are variations. The first includes cases in which a dominant firm threatens to cease cooperation with a customer or supplier that is considering forming a relationship with the dominant firm's competitors. *Lorain Journal*, which we considered at the beginning of this Chapter, is an example. The second consists of challenges to a dominant firm's attempt to withdraw from an existing contractual relationship or to impose new terms on an existing relationship. *Aspen Skiing* and *Kodak* are examples of this pattern. The third concerns the refusal of a dominant firm to provide access to a facility—sometimes called an "essential facility"—that a rival requires in order to compete with the dominant firm. One well-known instance of this pattern was *MCI Commc'ns Corp. v. American Tel. & Tel. Co.*, 708 F.2d 1081 (7th Cir. 1983).

In each of these cases, the plaintiff typically is seeking injunctive relief from the court, ordering the dominant firm to deal. Courts, commentators and parties, therefore, often pose the issue in such cases as whether a court should impose a "duty to deal" on dominant firms. Such duty to deal issues can arise, however, regardless of whether the allegedly exclusionary conduct is a refusal to deal. Imposed dealing also has been ordered as a remedy for other kinds of exclusionary conduct. Recall, for example, that although a refusal to deal was not one of the kinds of conduct challenged in the U.S. case against Microsoft, it was the basis for a portion of the European Commission's case. Yet both the Commission and the U.S. Justice Department deemed forced dealing—sharing of communications protocols by Microsoft to facilitate interoperability between Microsoft's Windows and other software—as an appropriate remedy. *See supra Note on the Microsoft Prosecution in the European Union.*

In our next case, the Supreme Court appeared to significantly limit the scope of *Aspen Skiing*, and with it the degree to which the U.S. antitrust laws will support a finding of liability for a dominant firm's refusal to deal with one of its rivals. As you read the case, however, consider its potentially broader implications for Section 2. What assumptions does the Court make, for example, about the competitive incentives of monopolists and their rivals? Are those assumptions similar or different that the assumptions Judge Hand made in *Alcoa*? Recall the three "perspectives" that we explored at the beginning of this Chapter. Does Trinko reflect a change of perspective at the Supreme Court when compared to *Alcoa*? More specifically, does the Court appear to be more concerned with false positives than false negatives? What attitude does it reflect about the value of private antitrust enforcement? How might concerns about private antitrust enforcement have influenced its approach to liability standards? On the other hand, are there ways in which the decision invites a narrow interpretation? For example, how significant to the Court's rationale is the regulatory context in which the case arose? Would the Court be more receptive to an antitrust-imposed "duty to assist rivals" in other contexts? As a remedy for other kinds of exclusionary conduct?

VERIZON COMMUNICATIONS INC. V. LAW OFFICES OF CURTIS V. TRINKO, LLP

United States Supreme Court, 2004.
540 U.S. 398, 124 S.Ct. 872, 157 L.Ed.2d 823.

JUSTICE SCALIA delivered the opinion of the Court.

The Telecommunications Act of 1996 imposes certain duties upon incumbent local telephone companies in order to facilitate market entry by competitors, and establishes a complex regime for monitoring and enforcement. In this case we consider whether a complaint alleging breach of the incumbent's duty under the 1996 Act to share its network with competitors states a claim under § 2 of the Sherman Act.

I

Petitioner Verizon Communications Inc. is the incumbent local exchange carrier (LEC) serving New York State. Before the 1996 Act, Verizon, like other incumbent LECs, enjoyed an exclusive franchise within its local service area. The 1996 Act sought to "uproo[t]" the incumbent LECs' monopoly and to introduce competition in its place. Central to the scheme of the Act is the incumbent LEC's obligation to share its network with competitors, including provision of access to individual elements of the network on an "unbundled" basis. New entrants, so-called competitive LECs, resell these unbundled network elements (UNEs), recombined with each other or with elements belonging to the LECs.

Verizon, like other incumbent LECs, has taken two significant steps within the Act's framework in the direction of increased competition. First, Verizon has signed interconnection agreements with rivals such as AT & T, as it is obliged to do [under the Act]. * * *

Second, Verizon has taken advantage of the opportunity provided by the 1996 Act for incumbent LECs to enter the long-distance market (from which they had long been excluded). That required Verizon to satisfy, among other things, a 14-item checklist of statutory requirements, which includes compliance with the Act's network-sharing duties. * * *

Part of Verizon's UNE obligation is the provision of access to operations support systems (OSS), a set of systems used by incumbent LECs to provide services to customers and ensure quality. Verizon's interconnection agreement and long-distance authorization each specified the mechanics by which its OSS obligation would be met. As relevant here, a competitive LEC sends orders for service through an electronic interface with Verizon's ordering system, and as Verizon completes certain steps in filling the order, it sends confirmation back through the same interface. Without OSS access a rival cannot fill its customers' orders.

In late 1999, competitive LECs complained to regulators that many orders were going unfilled, in violation of Verizon's obligation to provide access to OSS functions. The PSC [New York's Public Service Commission] and FCC [Federal Communications Commission] opened parallel investigations, which led to a series of orders by the PSC and a consent decree with the FCC. Under the FCC consent decree, Verizon undertook to make a "voluntary contribution" to the U.S. Treasury in the amount of $3 million; under the PSC orders, Verizon incurred liability to the competitive LECs in the amount of $10 million. Under the consent decree and orders, Verizon was subjected to new performance measurements and new reporting requirements to the FCC and PSC, with additional penalties for continued noncompliance. In June 2000, the FCC terminated the consent decree. The next month the PSC relieved Verizon of the heightened reporting requirement.

Respondent Law Offices of Curtis V. Trinko, LLP, a New York City law firm, was a local telephone service customer of AT&T. The day after Verizon entered its consent decree with the FCC, respondent filed a complaint in the District Court for the Southern District of New York, on behalf of itself and a class of similarly situated customers. The complaint, as later amended, alleged that Verizon had filled rivals' orders on a discriminatory basis as part of an anticompetitive scheme to discourage customers from becoming or remaining customers of competitive LECs, thus impeding the competitive LECs' ability to enter and compete in the market for local telephone service. * * * The complaint sought damages and injunctive relief for violation of § 2 of the Sherman Act pursuant to the remedy provisions of §§ 4 and 16 of the Clayton Act. * * *

The District Court dismissed the complaint in its entirety. As to the antitrust portion, it concluded that respondent's allegations of deficient assistance to rivals failed to satisfy the requirements of § 2. The Court of

Appeals for the Second Circuit reinstated the complaint in part, including the antitrust claim. We granted certiorari, limited to the question whether the Court of Appeals erred in reversing the District Court's dismissal of respondent's antitrust claims.

II

To decide this case, we must first determine what effect (if any) the 1996 Act has upon the application of traditional antitrust principles. The Act imposes a large number of duties upon incumbent LECs—above and beyond those basic responsibilities it imposes upon all carriers. * * *

That Congress created these duties, however, does not automatically lead to the conclusion that they can be enforced by means of an antitrust claim. Indeed, a detailed regulatory scheme such as that created by the 1996 Act ordinarily raises the question whether the regulated entities are not shielded from antitrust scrutiny altogether by the doctrine of implied immunity. * * *

Congress, however, precluded that interpretation. Section 601(b)(1) of the 1996 Act is an antitrust-specific saving clause providing that "nothing in this Act or the amendments made by this Act shall be construed to modify, impair, or supersede the applicability of any of the antitrust laws." This bars a finding of implied immunity. As the FCC has put the point, the saving clause preserves those "claims that satisfy established antitrust standards."

But just as the 1996 Act preserves claims that satisfy existing antitrust standards, it does not create new claims that go beyond existing antitrust standards; that would be equally inconsistent with the saving clause's mandate that nothing in the Act "modify, impair, or supersede the applicability" of the antitrust laws. We turn, then, to whether the activity of which respondent complains violates pre-existing antitrust standards.

III

The complaint alleges that Verizon denied interconnection services to rivals in order to limit entry. If that allegation states an antitrust claim at all, it does so under § 2 of the Sherman Act, which declares that a firm shall not "monopolize" or "attempt to monopolize." It is settled law that this offense requires, in addition to the possession of monopoly power in the relevant market, "the willful acquisition or maintenance of that power as distinguished from growth or development as a consequence of a superior product, business acumen, or historic accident." *United States v. Grinnell Corp.*, 384 U.S. 563, 570–71, 86 S.Ct. 1698, 16 L.Ed.2d 778 (1966). The mere possession of monopoly power, and the concomitant charging of monopoly prices, is not only not unlawful; it is an important element of the free-market system. The opportunity to charge monopoly prices—at least for a short period—is what attracts "business acumen" in the first place; it induces risk taking that produces innovation and economic growth. To safeguard the incentive to innovate, the possession of monopoly power will not be found unlawful unless it is accompanied by an element of anticompetitive *conduct*.

Firms may acquire monopoly power by establishing an infrastructure that renders them uniquely suited to serve their customers. Compelling such firms to share the source of their advantage is in some tension with the underlying purpose of antitrust law, since it may lessen the incentive for the monopolist, the rival, or both to invest in those economically beneficial facilities. Enforced sharing also requires antitrust courts to act as central planners, identifying the proper price, quantity, and other terms of dealing—a role for which they are ill-suited. Moreover, compelling negotiation between competitors may facilitate the supreme evil of antitrust: collusion. Thus, as a general matter, the Sherman Act "does not restrict the long recognized right of [a] trader or manufacturer engaged in an entirely private business, freely to exercise his own independent discretion as to parties with whom he will deal." *United States v. Colgate & Co.*, 250 U.S. 300, 307, 39 S.Ct. 465, 63 L.Ed. 992 (1919).

However, "[t]he high value that we have placed on the right to refuse to deal with other firms does not mean that the right is unqualified." *Aspen Skiing Co. v. Aspen Highlands Skiing Corp.*, 472 U.S. 585, 601, 105 S.Ct. 2847, 86 L.Ed.2d 467 (1985). Under certain circumstances, a refusal to cooperate with rivals can constitute anticompetitive conduct and violate § 2. We have been very cautious in recognizing such exceptions, because of the uncertain virtue of forced sharing and the difficulty of identifying and remedying anticompetitive conduct by a single firm. The question before us today is whether the allegations of respondent's complaint fit within existing exceptions or provide a basis, under traditional antitrust principles, for recognizing a new one.

The leading case for § 2 liability based on refusal to cooperate with a rival, and the case upon which respondent understandably places greatest reliance, is *Aspen Skiing*. * * * We upheld a jury verdict for the plaintiff, reasoning that "[t]he jury may well have concluded that [the defendant] elected to forgo these short-run benefits because it was more interested in reducing competition . . . over the long run by harming its smaller competitor."

Aspen Skiing is at or near the outer boundary of § 2 liability. The Court there found significance in the defendant's decision to cease participation in a cooperative venture. The unilateral termination of a voluntary (*and thus presumably profitable*) course of dealing suggested a willingness to forsake short-term profits to achieve an anticompetitive end. Similarly, the defendant's unwillingness to renew the ticket *even if compensated at retail price* revealed a distinctly anticompetitive bent.

The refusal to deal alleged in the present case does not fit within the limited exception recognized in *Aspen Skiing*. The complaint does not allege that Verizon voluntarily engaged in a course of dealing with its rivals, or would ever have done so absent statutory compulsion. Here, therefore, the defendant's prior conduct sheds no light upon the motivation of its refusal to deal—upon whether its regulatory lapses were prompted not by competitive zeal but by anticompetitive malice. The contrast between the cases is heightened by the difference in pricing behavior. In *Aspen Skiing*, the defendant turned down a proposal to sell at its own retail price, suggesting a calculation that its future monopoly retail price would be higher. Verizon's reluctance to interconnect at the cost-based rate of compensation available tells us nothing about dreams of monopoly.

The specific nature of what the 1996 Act compels makes this case different from *Aspen Skiing* in a more fundamental way. In *Aspen Skiing*, what the defendant refused to provide to its competitor was a product that it already sold at retail—to oversimplify slightly, lift tickets representing a bundle of services to skiers. Similarly, in *Otter Tail Power Co. v. United States*, 410 U.S. 366, 93 S.Ct. 1022, 35 L.Ed.2d 359 (1973), another case relied upon by respondent, the defendant was already in the business of providing a service to certain customers (power transmission over its network), and refused to provide the same service to certain other customers. In the present case, by contrast, the services allegedly withheld are not otherwise marketed or available to the public. The sharing obligation imposed by the 1996 Act created "something brand new"—"the wholesale market for leasing network elements." The unbundled elements offered pursuant to [the Act] exist only deep within the bowels of Verizon; they are brought out on compulsion of the 1996 Act and offered not to consumers but to rivals, and at considerable expense and effort. New systems must be designed and implemented simply to make that access possible—indeed, it is the failure of one of those systems that prompted the present complaint.[3]

We conclude that Verizon's alleged insufficient assistance in the provision of service to rivals is not a recognized antitrust claim under this Court's existing refusal-to-deal precedents. This conclusion would be unchanged even if we considered to be established law the "essential facilities" doctrine crafted by some lower courts, under which the Court of Appeals concluded respondent's allegations might state a claim. We have never recognized such a doctrine, and we find no need either to recognize it or to repudiate it here. It suffices for present purposes to note that the

---

[3] Respondent also relies upon *United States v. Terminal Railroad Assn. of St. Louis*, 224 U.S. 383, 32 S.Ct. 507, 56 L.Ed. 810 (1912), and *Associated Press v. United States*, 326 U.S. 1, 65 S.Ct. 1416, 89 L.Ed. 2013 (1945). These cases involved concerted action, which presents greater anticompetitive concerns and is amenable to a remedy that does not require judicial estimation of free-market forces: simply requiring that the outsider be granted nondiscriminatory admission to the club.

indispensable requirement for invoking the doctrine is the unavailability of access to the "essential facilities"; where access exists, the doctrine serves no purpose. * * * Respondent believes that the existence of sharing duties under the 1996 Act supports its case. We think the opposite: The 1996 Act's extensive provision for access makes it unnecessary to impose a judicial doctrine of forced access. To the extent respondent's "essential facilities" argument is distinct from its general § 2 argument, we reject it.

IV

Finally, we do not believe that traditional antitrust principles justify adding the present case to the few existing exceptions from the proposition that there is no duty to aid competitors. Antitrust analysis must always be attuned to the particular structure and circumstances of the industry at issue. Part of that attention to economic context is an awareness of the significance of regulation. * * * "[A]ntitrust analysis must sensitively recognize and reflect the distinctive economic and legal setting of the regulated industry to which it applies." *Concord v. Boston Edison Co.*, 915 F.2d 17, 22 (C.A. 1 1990) (Breyer, C.J.)(internal quotation marks omitted).

One factor of particular importance is the existence of a regulatory structure designed to deter and remedy anticompetitive harm. Where such a structure exists, the additional benefit to competition provided by antitrust enforcement will tend to be small, and it will be less plausible that the antitrust laws contemplate such additional scrutiny. Where, by contrast, "[t]here is nothing built into the regulatory scheme which performs the antitrust function," *Silver v. New York Stock Exchange*, 373 U.S. 341, 358, 83 S.Ct. 1246, 10 L.Ed.2d 389 (1963), the benefits of antitrust are worth its sometimes considerable disadvantages. Just as regulatory context may in other cases serve as a basis for implied immunity, it may also be a consideration in deciding whether to recognize an expansion of the contours of § 2.

The regulatory framework that exists in this case demonstrates how, in certain circumstances, "regulation significantly diminishes the likelihood of major antitrust harm." *Concord v. Boston Edison Co., supra*, at 25. Consider, for example, the statutory restrictions upon Verizon's entry into the potentially lucrative market for long-distance service. To be allowed to enter the long-distance market in the first place, an incumbent LEC must be on good behavior in its local market. Authorization by the FCC requires state-by-state satisfaction of [the Act's] competitive checklist, which as we have noted includes the nondiscriminatory provision of access to UNEs. * * *

* * *

The regulatory response to the OSS failure complained of in respondent's suit provides a vivid example of how the regulatory regime operates. When several competitive LECs complained about deficiencies in Verizon's servicing of orders, the FCC and PSC responded. The FCC soon concluded that Verizon was in breach of its sharing duties, imposed a substantial fine, and set up sophisticated measurements to gauge remediation, with weekly reporting requirements and specific penalties for failure. * * *

Against the slight benefits of antitrust intervention here, we must weigh a realistic assessment of its costs. Under the best of circumstances, applying the requirements of § 2 "can be difficult" because "the means of illicit exclusion, like the means of legitimate competition, are myriad." Mistaken inferences and the resulting false condemnations "are especially costly, because they chill the very conduct the antitrust laws are designed to protect." *Matsushita Elec. Industrial Co. v. Zenith Radio Corp.*, 475 U.S. 574, 594, 106 S.Ct. 1348, 89 L.Ed.2d. 358 (1986). The cost of false positives counsels against an undue expansion of § 2 liability. One false-positive risk is that an incumbent LEC's failure to provide a service with sufficient alacrity might have nothing to do with exclusion. Allegations of violations of [1996 Act] duties are difficult for antitrust courts to evaluate, not only because they are highly technical, but also because they are likely to be extremely numerous, given the incessant, complex, and constantly changing interaction of competitive and incumbent LECs implementing the sharing and interconnection obligations. *Amici* States have filed a brief asserting that competitive LECs are threatened with "death by a thousand cuts,"—the identification of which would surely be a daunting task for a generalist antitrust court. Judicial oversight under the Sherman Act would seem destined to distort investment and lead to a new layer of interminable litigation, atop the variety of litigation routes already available to and actively pursued by competitive LECs.

Even if the problem of false positives did not exist, conduct consisting of anticompetitive violations of [the 1996 Act] may be, as we have concluded with respect to above-cost predatory pricing schemes, "beyond the practical ability of a judicial tribunal to control." *Brooke Group Ltd. v. Brown & Williamson Tobacco Corp.*, 509 U.S. 209, 223, 113 S.Ct. 2578, 125 L.Ed.2d 168 (1993). Effective remediation of violations of regulatory sharing requirements will ordinarily require continuing supervision of a highly detailed decree. We think that Professor Areeda got it exactly right: "No court should impose a duty to deal that it cannot explain or adequately and reasonably supervise. The problem should be deemed irremedia[ble] by antitrust law when compulsory access requires the court to assume the day-to-day controls characteristic of a regulatory agency." * * * An antitrust court is unlikely to be an effective day-to-day enforcer of these detailed sharing obligations.[4]

The 1996 Act is in an important respect much more ambitious than the antitrust laws. It attempts *"to eliminate the monopolies enjoyed by the inheritors of AT & T's local franchises."* Section 2 of the Sherman Act, by contrast, seeks merely to prevent *unlawful monopolization.* It would be a serious mistake to conflate the two goals. The Sherman Act is indeed the "Magna Carta of free enterprise," but it does not give judges *carte blanche* to insist that a monopolist alter its way of doing business whenever some other approach might yield greater competition. We conclude that respondent's complaint fails to state a claim under the Sherman Act.[5]

* * *

[The concurring opinion of JUSTICE STEVENS, with whom JUSTICE SOUTER and JUSTICE THOMAS joined is omitted. Eds.]

Trinko attracted a great deal of attention even before it was decided, and the Supreme Court's decision triggered a great deal of discussion in the antitrust community. On the one hand, it addresses a very narrow legal question in a very unique setting: courts should be reluctant to utilize the antitrust laws to scrutinize purely unilateral refusals to assist rivals by firms in industries subject to extensive, competition-focused regulation that includes specific mechanisms to require dealings with rivals by incumbent monopolists. Some lower courts have adopted this narrow view of the case. *See, e.g., Covad Commc'ns Co. v. Bell Atl. Corp.*, 398 F.3d 666 (D.C. Cir. 2005) (*Trinko* does not affect a claim by a rival that the dominant firm refused to deal with the rival's customers); *Nobody v. Clear Channel Commc'ns, Inc.*, 311 F. Supp. 2d 1048, 1112–14 (D. Colo. 2004) (reading *Trinko* narrowly). *But see MetroNet Services Corp. v. Qwest Corp.*, 383 F.3d 1124 (9th Cir. 2004).

However, the language and rationale of *Trinko* are far more sweeping. For example, the Court constructed its ultimately dismissive view of Trinko's complaint by articulating some key assumptions about antitrust law and the limits of antitrust enforcement: (1) "forced" sharing tramples on the dominant firm's "right" to be free to choose its trading partners, and erodes its incentive to innovate; (2) the presence of an elaborate regulatory

---

[4] The Court of Appeals also thought that respondent's complaint might state a claim under a "monopoly leveraging" theory * * *. We disagree. To the extent the Court of Appeals dispensed with a requirement that there be a "dangerous probability of success" in monopolizing a second market, it erred, *Spectrum Sports, Inc. v. McQuillan*, 506 U.S. 447, 459, 113 S. Ct. 884, 122 L.Ed.2d 247 (1993). In any event, leveraging presupposes anticompetitive conduct, which in this case could only be the refusal-to-deal claim we have rejected.

[5] Our disposition makes it unnecessary to consider petitioner's alternative contention that respondent lacks antitrust standing.

scheme directed at competition obviates the need for private antitrust enforcement; and (3) antitrust rules must be crafted to minimize the threat of false positives, the danger of which is amplified by the institutional limitations of courts. It also analogized refusals to deal to predatory pricing and, citing to *Brooke Group*, maintained that judging such claims would likely be "beyond the practical ability" of courts. These are hardly self-evident assertions, and each is subject to debate. Moreover, the case was appealed based on Verizon's motion to dismiss for failure to state a claim under Federal Rule of Civil Procedure 12(b)(6), so there is no record upon which the Court's detailed discussion rests. For a critique of the case that elaborates on these points, see Andrew I. Gavil, *Exclusionary Distribution Strategies by Dominant Firms: Striking a Better Balance*, 72 ANTITRUST L.J. 3 (2004).

On the other hand, was the Court justified in its reluctance to use antitrust law to impose upon dominant firms a duty to deal with their rivals? What reasons does it cite for that reluctance? Are those reasons persuasive? In all cases? Did you find the Court's distinction of *Aspen Skiing* persuasive? What did the Court mean when it suggested that *Aspen* lies "at or near the outer boundary of § 2 liability"? Do *Aspen Skiing* and *Kodak* provide a viable, alternative framework for evaluating refusals to deal?

Finally, what are the decision's implications for other areas of federal government regulation that involve conduct that might also fall within the scope of the antitrust laws? *Trinko*'s skepticism about the value of antitrust enforcement, especially through private, civil treble damage actions, and its expressed preference for government regulation, quickly resurfaced when the Supreme Court endorsed implied antitrust immunity in a case that presented some parallel questions of whether private rights of action under the antitrust laws should be permitted against conduct already the subject of regulation by the Securities and Exchange Commission. *See Credit Suisse Sec. (USA) LLC v. Billing*, 551 U.S. 264, 127 S.Ct. 2383 (2007). For a discussion of the negative impact of *Trinko* and *Credit Suisse* on the ability of plaintiffs to enforce the antitrust laws in regulated industries, and an argument that their rationale should not apply to public enforcement agencies, see Howard A. Shelanski, *The Case for Rebalancing Antitrust and Regulation*, 109 MICH. L. REV. 683 (2011).

Unilateral refusals to deal that take the form of a refusal to license intellectual property also have a long and sometimes complicated history that includes changing attitudes about the relationship of antitrust to intellectual property law. We will examine those issues in Chapter 7.

NOTE ON "PRICE SQUEEZES": THE INTERSECTION
OF BROOKE GROUP AND TRINKO

In *Pac. Bell Tel. Co. v. Linkline Commc'ns., Inc.*, 555 U.S. 438 (2009), the Supreme Court rejected Section 2 claims brought by a class of Internet service providers (ISPs) who sold Internet-based digital subscriber line (DSL) access to retail customers. The ISPs alleged that the incumbent telephone companies, who also sold DSL services in competition with them and who owned the infrastructure and facilities needed to provide DSL service, monopolized and attempted to monopolize the regional DSL market by engaging in a "price squeeze," i.e., charging such a high wholesale access price to the ISPs that they could not effectively compete with the telephone companies at retail.

The Supreme Court extended its decisions in *Brooke Group* and *Trinko*, holding that absent a duty to deal at all, and absent satisfaction of the two elements of the *Brooke Group* standard (proof that the telephone companies set their retail DSL prices below cost and that they had a reasonable probability of recouping their losses), "price squeeze" claims were not cognizable under Section 2. The Court reasoned that absent a duty to deal and evidence of predatory pricing, a dominant firm has no duty to maintain its rivals' profit margins by offering access to its infrastructure, let alone at prices low enough to facilitate competition with itself at the retail level. Indeed, the Court held, an upstream monopolist can charge a monopoly price to its rivals.

Alcoa also had involved a claim of "price squeeze" and, although the court did not base its finding of liability on that ground, it appeared to accept the theory as a potential basis for Section 2 liability. In *LinkLine*, however, the Court cast doubt on the continued precedential value of *Alcoa* and drew instead on both *Brooke Group* and *Trinko* to support its conclusion, arguing in large part that any other rule would not be administrable by courts.[12] To find liability based on a price squeeze theory, courts would have to look at both wholesale and retail prices and reach a conclusion about what constitutes reasonable profit margins, which would draw the court into difficult, regulatory judgments about reasonable prices and price margins. For a response to the Court's reasoning on this point, and an argument that a price squeeze standard for an unregulated, vertically integrated monopolist involves no more complicated issues than the long recognized below-cost test endorsed by *Brooke Group*, see Steven C. Salop, *Refusals to Deal and Price Squeezes by*

---

[12] Referring specifically to Alcoa's observations regarding price squeeze claims, the Court stated: "Given developments in economic theory and antitrust jurisprudence since *Alcoa*, we find our recent decisions in *Trinko* and *Brooke Group* more pertinent to the question before us." 555 U.S. at 452 n.3 For a further discussion of this footnote and of the continued vitality of *Alcoa* as a general matter, see Marc Winerman & William E. Kovacic, *Learned Hand,* Alcoa, *and the Reluctant Application of the Sherman Act*, 79 ANTITRUST L.J. 295, 301–02 (2013). The authors argue that:

> Since the late 1970s, the power of *Alcoa* as precedent for the interpretation of Section 2 has waned as the courts of appeals and the Supreme Court have adopted increasingly permissive interpretations of Section 2 of the Sherman Act. In doing so, the modern jurisprudence has walked away from the pluralist view of goals that *Alcoa* embraced and has focused almost single-mindedly on the attainment of superior efficiency.

an Unregulated, Vertically Integrated Monopolist, 76 ANTITRUST L.J. 709 (2010).

Salop proposes as an administrable price benchmark the wholesale price of access (more generally, the input price) that would permit an equally efficient competitor that competes only in the retail market (more generally, the downstream market) to break even. This benchmark is based on the monopolist's price and cost. For the case of differentiated products, the price benchmark could be adjusted downward based on evidence of the degree of substitution between the monopolist's and competitor's product, or based on the monopolist's market share in the downstream market. According to Salop, this benchmark would facilitate entry and competition by more cost-efficient and differentiated product competitors that would benefit consumers, while maintaining innovation incentives for both the monopolist and the new competitors.

Trinko also affected two other traditional theories of antitrust liability: the "essential facilities" doctrine, which had been thought to constitute one basis for judicially mandated dealing, and "monopoly leveraging," which involves the alleged use of monopoly power to obtain a competitive advantage in an adjacent or complementary product market. The Sidebar that follows examines the status of these two possibilities for liability under Section 2 after *Trinko*.

Sidebar 4–10:
The Status of Essential Facilities
and Leveraging After *Trinko*

Essential Facilities

In the final paragraph of Part III of its opinion, *Trinko* holds that the "essential facilities" doctrine, sometimes also referred to as the "bottleneck" doctrine, would not alter its conclusion that the antitrust laws did not impose a duty to deal with rivals on Verizon, given that the Telecommunications Act already did so. The Court also asserted that the doctrine was a creature of lower courts, and that the Supreme Court "never recognized such a doctrine." It concluded that there was "no need either to recognize it or to repudiate it here," however, and concluded: "[i]t suffices for present purposes to note that the indispensable requirement for invoking the doctrine is the unavailability of access to the 'essential facilities'; where access exists, the doctrine serves no purpose." 540 U.S. at 410–11.

Prior to *Trinko,* it was widely believed that the Court had in fact long endorsed the essential facilities doctrine, albeit in very limited circumstances. *See* Robert Pitofsky, et al., *The*

Essential Facilities Doctrine Under U.S. Antitrust Law, 70 ANTITRUST L.J. 443 (2002) ("The essential facilities doctrine has a long and respected history as part of U.S. antitrust law."). The doctrine was associated with a line of Supreme Court decisions beginning with *United States v. Terminal Railroad Assn.*, 224 U.S. 383, 32 S.Ct. 507, 56 L.Ed. 810 (1912), and continuing through later decisions such as *Associated Press v. United States*, 326 U.S. 1, 65 S.Ct. 1416, 89 L.Ed. 2013 (1945), *United States v. Griffith*, 334 U.S. 100, 68 S.Ct. 941 (1948), and *Otter Tail Power Co. v. United States*, 410 U.S. 366, 93 S.Ct. 1022, 35 L.Ed.2d 359 (1973). It was generally viewed as a narrow exception to the general principle repeated in both *Aspen Skiing* and *Trinko*, that the antitrust laws in general do not impose upon a monopolist any duty to deal with its rivals. Essential facilities claims thus have been rare and are evenly more rarely successful. *See, e.g., Blue Cross & Blue Shield United of Wisconsin v. Marshfield Clinic*, 65 F.3d 1406 (7th Cir. 1995); *Alaska Airlines, Inc. v. United Airlines, Inc.*, 948 F.2d 536 (9th Cir. 1991).

As noted at the outset of our discussion of refusals to deal, the essential facilities doctrine was never really distinct from the general law of refusals to deal. It functioned more like a specialized application of the law concerning such refusals, triggered by a monopolist's control over some physical plant, access to which was necessary if there was to be any meaningful competition at all. Under one widely-cited articulation, the essential facility doctrine required the plaintiff to prove (1) control of an essential facility by a monopolist, (2) the inability of a competitor reasonably to duplicate the essential facility, (3) the denial of use of the facility to a competitor, and (4) the feasibility of providing access to the facility. *MCI Commc'ns Corp. v. American Tel. & Tel. Co.*, 708 F.2d 1081, 1132–33 (7th Cir. 1983). The influence of this formulation on the law of concerted refusals to deal is evident in *Northwest Wholesale Stationers, supra,* noted that per se unlawful concerted refusals to deal typically involve efforts to disadvantage competitors by " 'either directly denying or persuading or coercing suppliers or customers to deny relationships the competitors need in the competitive struggle' " 472 U.S. at 294, and later concluded that a critical factor in applying per se analysis would be "exclusive access to an element essential to effective competition." *Id.* at 296.

Trinko's skepticism about the essential facilities doctrine reflects the influence of an important critique of the doctrine by the late Professor Phillip Areeda, which was cited by the Court in *Trinko*. *See* Phillip Areeda, *Essential Facilities: An Epithet in Need of Limiting Principles*, 58 ANTITRUST L.J. 841 (1989) ("*Essential Facilities*"). Areeda suggested, for example, that the Supreme Court had never actually used the phrase "essential facility" and had not expressly endorsed its use. He also reasoned that many of the Supreme Court cases often cited to support the doctrine involved concerted action, not unilateral action, and thus raised more substantial competitive concerns not present in unilateral cases.

Perhaps most importantly, Areeda argued that court-imposed duties to deal undermine incentives to innovate. For the monopolist, fear that it will be ordered to share the fruits of its work with its rivals may inhibit it from undertaking research and development in the first place; the incentives of the rival might also be undermined if instead of relying on its own skill, it seeks to free ride on the monopolist's efforts with the help of court intervention. Areeda also articulated one last powerful point: imposing a duty to deal may be especially difficult to administer and may require continuing supervision by the courts. *See Trinko*, 540 U.S. at 415 ("An antitrust court is unlikely to be an effective day-to-day enforcer of these detailed sharing obligations.") This is especially true in cases where the monopolist has never offered access to the specific "facility" to anyone, in which case the court would have to determine and then periodically evaluate prices and terms of sale. *Trinko* referred to almost all of these points either expressly or implicitly in its brief discussion of the essential facilities doctrine. *Id.* at 410 n.3 & 410–11. For an additional critique and suggestions for limiting principles, see Abbott B. Lipsky, Jr. & J. Gregory Sidak, *Essential Facilities*, 51 STAN. L. REV. 1187 (1999).

Trinko surely narrowed the circumstances under which courts may impose a duty on a monopolist to deal. Moreover, some commentators have read its discussion of the essential facilities doctrine to signal the doctrine's formal demise, or at least to signal its inapplicability in the context of a regulated industry that involves provisions for access. Even Professor Areeda, however, acknowledged that the doctrine could play a useful role in antitrust, provided it is narrowly tailored. *See* Areeda, *Essential Facilities*, *supra* at 852. In fact, Areeda appeared to approve of the result in *MCI*. *Id.* at 845 n.21 ("*MCI* * * *, which rests on the essential facilities notion, is probably correct.") In addition, some commentators recently have tried to address the challenge of providing a methodology for determining the prices and conditions under which a vertically integrated monopolist could be required to deal with an unintegrated rival in its output market. *See* Steven C. Salop, *Refusals to Deal and Price Squeezes by an Unregulated, Vertically Integrated Monopolist*, 76 ANTITRUST L.J. 709 (2010). It remains to be seen, therefore, whether under appropriate and limited circumstances, the Court would approve the imposition of a duty to deal on a monopolist whose control of a facility effectively barred all competition.

Monopoly Leveraging

Prior to *Trinko*, there was some case law supporting the idea that a monopolist can violate Section 2 when it "leverages" its monopoly power in one market to gain a competitive advantage in a second, adjacent or complementary market, where it competes but does not achieve a monopoly position. Such claims were raised in *Berkey Photo, Inc. v. Eastman Kodak Co.*, 603 F.2d 263 (2d Cir. 1979) as well as in *Microsoft*.

In the final portion of its opinion, *Trinko* also rejected the plaintiff's claim that Verizon could be found liable under Section 2 based on a theory of "monopoly leveraging." Referencing its standards for claims of attempt to monopolize, the Court held: "[t]o the extent the Court of Appeals dispensed with a requirement that there be a 'dangerous probability of success' in monopolizing a second market, it erred, *Spectrum Sports, Inc. v. McQuillan*, 506 U.S. 447, 459, 113 S.Ct. 884, 122 L.Ed.2d 247 (1993). In any event, leveraging presupposes anticompetitive conduct, which in this case could only be the refusal-to-deal claim we have rejected." *Trinko*, 540 U.S. at 415 n.4. *See also Doe 1 v. Abbott Labs*, 571 F.3d 930 (9th Cir. 2009) (applying *Trinko* and *LinkLine* to dismiss allegations of unlawful monopoly leveraging in two distinct markets, because in the first the plaintiff failed to allege an unlawful refusal to deal within the parameters of *Trinko* and in the second it failed to allege below cost pricing and a probability of recoupment as required by *Brooke Group* and *LinkLine*).

Although as noted above there is some possibility that the essential facilities doctrine survived *Trinko* under the right circumstances, this holding appears to be unequivocal: there is no distinct offense of "monopoly leveraging" apart from attempt to monopolize. We will revisit the offense of attempt to monopolize later in this Chapter when we read *Spectrum Sports*.

NOTE ON "CHEAP EXCLUSION"

Exclusionary conduct cases may be the most contested area in antitrust. Disputes extend, for example, over the standards for identifying exclusionary or predatory conduct ("bad acts") in monopolization cases; whether unilateral refusals to deal should ever be the basis for antitrust liability, particularly when the dominant firm's conduct involves goods protected by intellectual property; whether new product introductions should ever be the basis for antitrust liability; and over the standards for identifying exclusionary group boycotts—all issues discussed in this Chapter. Those favoring antitrust intervention in these areas often emphasize that anticompetitive exclusion can be as harmful as anticompetitive collusion. Those skeptical of such intervention point out that much conduct that appears exclusionary in fact promotes competition, that it can be difficult to tell whether the anticompetitive harm outweighs the procompetitive benefit, and that antitrust intervention in this area risks chilling legitimate and beneficial firm conduct.

In 2005, several members of the senior antitrust enforcement staff at the Federal Trade Commission attempted to describe the enforcement priorities supported by the case law to develop a consensus norm around the idea of "cheap exclusion." *See generally* Susan A. Creighton, et al., *Cheap Exclusion*, 72 ANTITRUST L.J. 975 (2005). Under this view, anticompetitive exclusion is most likely to occur, and most clearly anticompetitive, if it is "cheap" in two senses: inexpensive for the excluding firms to undertake, and undertaken without a legitimate business justification.

Examples of cheap exclusion may include abuse of governmental processes, such as obtaining a patent by fraud, abuse of voluntary standard setting agreements to exclude rivals, or product redesign to create incompatibility for rivals with no benefit for buyers. The idea of cheap exclusion sharply distinguishes predatory pricing, which is both expensive for the predator (as it must initially make sales below cost) and beneficial to buyers (who purchase at a low price). Exclusive dealing. examined in Chapter 6, lies in-between. Under some circumstances it could be both an inexpensive strategy to implement and confer little benefit on buyers, and in consequence represent a good target for antitrust intervention.

How well does the idea of "cheap exclusion" rationalize the exclusionary conduct cases? Does it tend to describe those that are the most convincing examples of anticompetitive conduct, and not those that are less convincing? Was any of the conduct in *Microsoft* an example of cheap exclusion?

The authors also argued that a focus on cheap exclusion was warranted from the point of view of allocating scarce government enforcement resources:

> * * * In the efficient allocation of always-scarce enforcement resources, exclusionary conduct that is likely to be common (relative to other forms of exclusion), and lacks any legitimate competitive benefit, makes an attractive target. Put differently, when fishing, the

best place to fish is where the fish are plentiful, and the things you catch are likely to be fish.

Id. at 978. In this passage, can the "cheap" in "cheap exclusion" also be read as referring to the cost of prosecuting such cases? Based on what you have seen so far of antitrust, and particularly of Section 2, does the theory of cheap exclusion represent a realistic assessment of the relative costs of bringing antitrust suits? Is it true that cases in which firms undertake conduct that excludes inexpensively (as opposed to the more costly kinds of conduct, such as predatory pricing) and for which they offer no legitimate business justification, will be easy to bring? Recall that under the framework set out in *Microsoft*, a defendant does not have to meet a burden of production with regard to its legitimate business justifications until the government has first offered evidence that the defendant is a monopolist and that its conduct resulted in a significant anticompetitive effect. If the plaintiff, private or public, must still prove monopoly power and anticompetitive effect, will cheap exclusion cases necessarily be relatively more simple to bring?

Perhaps then, these government enforcers were trying to lay the intellectual foundation for a simpler brand of antitrust, where obviously anticompetitive conduct is more easy to reach and condemn. We have seen examples of this effort in cases such as *Polygram* (*see supra* Chapter 2). If so, perhaps inherent in the idea of cheap exclusion is a confession that the cost of bringing more complex cases involving more ambiguous conduct has become increasingly prohibitive, even for the government, and that the antitrust laws are in need of a correction of sorts that makes it easier to skewer the bad fish.

Sidebar 4–11:
Comparative Perspectives:
The Treatment of Anticompetitive Single
Firm Conduct in the U.S. and E.U.

As we have discussed at various points in this Chapter, Article 102 of the Treaty on the Functioning of the European Union (TFEU), which prohibits "abuse of a dominant position," is a counterpart to Section 2 of the Sherman Act, which bans monopolization, attempt to monopolize, and conspiracy to monopolize. Although Article 102 and Section 2 share some common core concepts, they have some important differences. Article 102 generally sweeps more broadly than Section 2, and its broader reach highlights an important element of divergence among the world's competition law systems. This Sidebar examines the U.S. and E.U; approaches toward single firm conduct as a way to understand the challenges to global convergence on common standards of competition law.[a]

Monopoly vs. Dominance

As we already have seen, Section 2's prohibition of monopolization applies to firms with "monopoly power." As explored later in this Chapter, the offense of attempted monopolization requires a showing that the defendant has a "dangerous probability" of achieving monopoly power. Roughly speaking, U.S. cases have associated market shares of at least 70 percent and above with monopoly power. In the past twenty years, litigated decisions finding liability (notably, the Department of Justice prosecution of Microsoft) have tended to feature defendants with market shares at or near 90 percent. Cases involving attempted monopolization generally have not found the requisite dangerous probability of success unless the defendant has a market share of at least 50 percent. Direct measures of market power have played an increasing role in Section 2 cases and other areas of U.S. antitrust analysis, but market shares still are influential in informing judicial judgments about whether the firm in question is a monopolist. Whatever the approach taken, Section 2 as it has been interpreted imposes a formidable market power threshold.

"Dominance" under Article 102 reaches further than Section 2's concept of monopoly power. In a formative early judgment, the European Court of Justice recognized that "very large shares are in themselves, and save in exceptional circumstances, evidence of the existence of a dominant position." *Hoffmann-La Roche v. Commission*, Case 85/76 1979 [ECR] 461, at ¶ 41. Later judgments have established a presumption that dominance exists at market shares of 50 percent or above, absent exceptional circumstances showing the absence of significant market power. *See Akzo v. Commission*, Case C-62/86 [1991] ECR I-3359, ¶ 60. Older and newer decisions have found dominance where the defendant had a market share of between 40 and 50 percent. *See United Brands v. Commission*, Case 27/76 [1978] ECR 207; *AstraZeneca AB v. Commission*, [2010] ECR-II 2805, upheld on appeal, Case C-457-10 P EU:C:2012:770.

---

[a]   The authors are grateful to Professors Ariel Ezrachi, Alison Jones, and Richard Whish for many informative discussions about EU law and policy governing single firm conduct. Their texts on European competition law are among the most illuminating in the field. *See* ARIEL EZRACHI, EU COMPETITION LAW: AN ANALYTICAL GUIDE TO THE LEADING CASES (3d ed. 2012); ALISON JONES & BRENDA SUFRIN, EU COMPETITION LAW: TEXT, CASES AND MATERIALS (6th ed. 2016); RICHARD WHISH & DAVID BAILEY, COMPETITION LAW (8th ed. 2015).

The E.U. jurisprudence creating a presumption of dominance at shares of 40 or 50 percent has elicited critical commentary that suggests the thresholds are too stringent. *See, e.g.*, JOHN O'DONOHUE & JORGE PADILLA, THE LAW AND ECONOMICS OF ARTICLE 102 TFEU (2d ed. 2013). Such criticism seems to have resonated to some degree with the drafters of the *European Commission's Guidance on Article 102 Enforcement Priorities*, which appeared in February 2009. The document did not set out guidelines for the application of Article 102; it only described how the Commission intended to use its discretion in deciding whether to pursue Article 102 cases. The Guidance document did not mention the *Akzo* market share presumption and indicated, more generally, that an inference of market power depended on the height of market shares and their durability. Two leading commentators have noted that this approach is "perhaps suggesting that [the Commission] is not keen on a presumption that attaches such weight to a market share figure." RICHARD WHISH & DAVID BAILEY, COMPETITION LAW 193 (8th ed. 2015).

Despite the difference between the establishment of dominance in an Article 102 abuse case and a Section 2 monopolization case, it is possible to see some convergence between the E.U. and U.S. systems when the Sherman Act's attempt offense is taken into account. In the U.S., the existence of the attempt offense arguably informs firms with at least 50 percent of the market that the Sherman Act allows scrutiny of the practices the firm may use to boost a 50 percent market share to high levels. Article 102 has no such incipiency offense (no equivalence of "attempt"), but the interpretation of dominance under the article has demonstrated that shares of 50 percent (and as low as 40 percent) are significant.

Monopolization vs. Abuse

Similarities and differences also arise in the scope of the conduct that can fall within the reach of each jurisdiction's approach. Both jurisdictions do not treat the existence of dominance as an offense; the E.U. and the U.S. systems require an ingredient of improper behavior. Both jurisdictions also agree, in principle, that competition law should not condemn firms which subdue their rivals by reason of superior performance. *Compare Alcoa with Post Danmark A/S Konkurrenceradet*, Case C-209/10, EU:C:2012:172, ¶ 22.

Both systems treat various forms of improper exclusion as satisfying this improper conduct requirement. Article 102 goes further than the Sherman Act by condemning "exploitative abuses," such as the charging of excessive prices. The European Commission rarely brings claims of excessive pricing, but various E.U. member states have been more willing to prosecute such cases, especially where the dominant firm (e.g., a public utility) owes its position to longstanding forms of government intervention. Although occasional accusations of "price gouging" arise in the U.S., judicial interpretations of Section 2 have rejected the possibility that high prices can alone constitute an infringement.

Both the E.U. and the U.S. have moved away from categorical rules that determine liability and have embraced an analytical framework that requires analysis of competitive effects. The two jurisdictions vary, however, in defining the types of proof or market conditions that will support an inference that the defendant's conduct has caused, or is likely to cause, adverse competitive effects. For example, the judgment in Case T-286/09 *Intel Corp. v. Commission* EU:T2014:547 (General Court), appeal pending before the Court of Justice, Case C-413/14 P *Intel Corp. v. Commission*, suggested that a strong inference of adverse effects might be premised upon proof that the dominant firm used certain pricing rebate schemes, without requiring additional proof of actual effects.

In general, E.U. jurisprudence and policy have created a wider zone of liability for dominant firms under Article 102 than the decisions of U.S. courts in Sherman Act Section 2 cases. Compared to cases such as *Brooke Group*, the E.U. jurisprudence treats predatory pricing as a more plausible theory of exclusion and has refused to adopt the Brooke Group requirement that the plaintiff show that the defendant is likely to recoup its investment in predation once its rival has been vanquished or chastened. *See France Telecom SA v. Commission*, Case T-340/03 [2007] ECR II-107. EU jurisprudence also has treated rebate schemes with greater skepticism than U.S. courts, *see Manufacture Francaise des Pneumatiques Michelin v. Commission* [2003] ECR II-4071 ("*Michelin II*"). In *British Airways PLC v. Commission*, Case C-95/04 P [2007] ECR I-2331, the Court of Justice found that British Airways had abused a dominant position by employing rebate practices which largely resembled conduct that supported a monopolization claim that a U.S. court of appeals had rejected in the same period. *Virgin Atlantic Airways Ltd. v. British Airways plc*, 257 F.3d 256 (2d Cir. 2001). E.U. law also has been more receptive than U.S. doctrine to challenges to single firm refusals to deal and margin squeezes. Compare

> *Trinko* and *linkLine* to the European judgments in the Microsoft litigation (refusals to deal deemed to be abuse) and *Deutsche Telecom v. Commission*, Case C-280/08 P [2010] ECR I-9555 (finding liability based on margin squeeze).
>
> In all of these matters, the E.U. approach weighs concerns about false positives less heavily than U.S. courts. E.U. judgments also reveal less anxiety about the administrative burdens associated with certain forms of intervention (e.g., setting access terms to an essential facility) and less concern about the competence of courts to make difficult judgments about the competitive consequences of dominant firm behavior. From a review of E.U. cases, "it is clear that a dominant firm (or one that fears it might be characterized as dominant must behave on the market with great caution." WHISH & BAILEY, COMPETITION LAW, *supra*, at 187. Companies operating in the United States need not be as cautious.

NOTE ON BUSINESS TORTS AND THE ANTITRUST LAWS

Some critics of the use of the antitrust laws to police exclusionary conduct have suggested that antitrust is unnecessary given that much exclusionary conduct can be challenged by the victim as a business tort. For example, if one firm destroys its rival's in-store product displays, that conduct could be tort. If it also satisfies the elements of an antitrust offense, and in particular if it leads to harm to competition, the same conduct could also form the basis for an antitrust complaint. Under this view, the main effect of introducing antitrust liability is to elevate damages in such cases from single to treble, leading private plaintiffs to bring too many frivolous lawsuits. More generally, the Supreme Court has referred derisively to "private state tort suits masquerading as antitrust actions" in the hope of securing treble damages. *Copperweld Corp. v. Independence Tube Corp.*, 467 U.S. 752, 777 (1984). One way to understand the potent slogan repeated so often by the Court, that the antitrust laws "protect competition not competitors" is as an expression of this difference. Tort laws protect competitors; the antitrust laws protect competition.

Consider the following response from four F.T.C. officials:

[W]hile claims of tortious conduct are frequently heard, the elements of actual monopolization under Section 2 (where the conduct is usually unilateral) are considerably more difficult to establish. The antitrust plaintiff must prove that the alleged predator has acquired monopoly power and that the effect of the conduct is anticompetitive exclusion, not simply the imposition of costs on a competitor. That a competitor has been harmed can justify a tort suit by that competitor, if the other relevant elements of the tort are established, but to show an antitrust violation one must prove harm to competition. But the point remains that when all the elements of monopolization, including injury to competition, are present, tortious conduct—rarely, if ever, an efficiency-enhancing form of "competition on the merits"—can be a cheap form of exclusion.

Susan A. Creighton, et al., *Cheap Exclusion*, 72 ANTITRUST L.J. 975, 990 (2005) (footnotes omitted). Would consumers be better off if the conduct viewed as a basis for a Section 2 violation in *Alcoa, Lorain Journal, Aspen Skiing, Brooke Group*, or *Microsoft* (most plaintiff victories) could not be reached under the antitrust laws, but could only be challenged under tort law? Can it be persuasively argued that public enforcement of antitrust, even with respect to tortious behavior, can add value, in part because where the conduct is not only tortious (harm to competitor) but also anticompetitive (harm to competition), a single competitor may not necessarily suffer the same harm consumers suffer and therefore its incentives to pursue the matter may be inadequate to protect the public interest?

4. PATTERN OR PRACTICE: PREPARING A "MONOPOLY BROTH"

Part of the urgency to develop a new framework for analyzing monopolization claims stems from cases in which the dominant firm is said to have used a variety of improper tactics to exclude rivals. The case prosecuted by the Justice Department and the state governments against Microsoft illustrates the point. The government plaintiffs alleged that Microsoft had used a multi-faceted strategy to suppress competition from other actual or potential producers of software. As no single business tactic would forestall competition, the company was said to have used a variety of means—including exclusive dealing, tying, and threats to punish firms engaged in new product development—to extinguish "middleware" threats to the Windows operating system. The government plaintiffs argued that the courts should not examine each element of Microsoft's conduct in insolation, but instead should consider the "pattern or practice" of alleged misconduct.

The legal foundation for the "pattern or practice" concept (sometimes called the "monopoly broth" theory by commentators and courts) first appeared in *Continental Ore Co. v. Union Carbide & Carbon Corp.*, 370 U.S. 690, 82 S.Ct. 1404 (1962). In *Continental Ore*, the Supreme Court confronted allegations that the defendants had violated Sections 1 and 2 of the Sherman Act through a broad collection of improper acts. The Supreme Court wrote that "plaintiffs should be given the full benefit of their proof without tightly compartmentalizing the various factual components and wiping the slate clean after scrutiny of each. * * * [T]he duty of the jury was to look at the whole picture and not merely at the individual figures in it." 370 U.S. at 699.

Continental Ore creates an important possibility for plaintiffs alleging unlawful exclusion. Assume that the plaintiff alleges that the defendant engaged in wrongful acts A, B, and C. Suppose further that none of the acts, examined individually, provides the requisite element of improper conduct to support a finding of monopolization liability. *Continental Ore* appears to teach that the court should examine the entire pattern of the defendant's behavior and can assemble the subcritical elements of behavior—A and B and C—into a critical mass of improper conduct that might be called ABC.

Applying the pattern or practice theory poses the challenging task of defining what quantum of individual acts suffices to create the critical mass of illegality. Suppose, again, that the plaintiff accuses the defendant of improper acts A, B, and C. The plaintiff argues that even if A, B, and C do not individually support a finding of illegality, the combination of ABC does. If the defendant shows there is no basis for allegation A, does the combination of B and C supply the necessary pattern of illegality? A court might find it difficult to provide operational criteria that give business managers a clear sense of when a collection of aggressive tactics will be considered an illegal pattern or practice. The result could be a very general form of guidance that an aggregation of tactics could constitute, at some undefined point, an improper course of conduct.

The *Microsoft* case might have provided an occasion for the D.C. Circuit to examine the pattern or practice concept—the district court expressly relied upon Continental Ore to conclude that Microsoft was separately liable under Section 2 for its "general course of conduct." But the court of appeals declined to address the issue, "because the District Court did not point to any series of acts, each of which harms competition only slightly but the cumulative effect of which is significant enough to form an independent basis for liability." *United States v. Microsoft Corp.*, 253 F.3d 34, 78 (D.C. Cir. 2001). This conclusion, however, did not significantly alter the outcome of the case, which largely rested upon findings that a number of the defendant's practices individually supported a finding of monopolization liability.

D. THE OFFENSE OF ATTEMPT TO MONOPOLIZE

Up until this point in the Chapter we have focused on the offense of "monopolization." Section 2 of the Sherman Act also proscribes attempts to monopolize and conspiracies to monopolize. Like monopolization, the attempt offense can be prosecuted as a felony, but few cases have explored this avenue of enforcement. Justice Holmes provided an early formative statement on attempts to monopolize in *Swift & Co. v. United States*, 196

U.S. 375, 25 S.Ct. 276 (1905). Drawing closely on the criminal law analogue, he concluded that attempted monopolization consisted of conduct that closely approaches but does not quite attain completed monopolization, plus a wrongful intent to monopolize. Thus conduct amounts to an attempt to monopolize if there is a "specific intent" to monopolize and a "dangerous probability" that, if unchecked, such conduct will ripen into monopolization. Beyond these formulas lurk difficult questions: what kinds of evidence will be relevant to an inquiry into "specific intent"? How much market power must a defendant have before there is a "dangerous probability" that its conduct threatens to achieve monopoly? What kind of conduct will support an accusation of "attempt to monopolize" if it is normal in the competitive process for firms to strive to secure a competitive advantage over their rivals?

For most of the twentieth century, the Supreme Court shed little light on these issues, and lower court decisions reflected considerable disarray. As the offense of monopolization expanded—especially in *Alcoa*—the role of attempt to monopolize became uncertain. As with monopolization, efforts to develop a legal test for attempt displayed tension between prohibiting undesirable business conduct that is likely to result in monopoly and avoiding the suppression of desirable rivalry. Since many business practices support both inferences, actions to punish attempts require close scrutiny of the market context and any justifications for the defendant's conduct. In 1993, the Supreme Court provided an important clarification of the attempt offense in *Spectrum Sports, Inc. v. McQuillan*, our next case.

SPECTRUM SPORTS, INC. V. MCQUILLAN

Supreme Court of the United States, 1993.
506 U.S. 447, 113 S.Ct. 884, 122 L.Ed.2d 247.

JUSTICE WHITE delivered the opinion of the Court.

Section 2 of the Sherman Act makes it an offense for any person to "monopolize, or attempt to monopolize, or combine or conspire with any other person or persons, to monopolize any part of the trade or commerce among the several States. . . ." The jury in this case returned a verdict finding that petitioners had monopolized, attempted to monopolize, and/or conspired to monopolize. The District Court entered a judgment ruling that petitioners had violated § 2, and the Court of Appeals affirmed on the ground that petitioners had attempted to monopolize. The issue we have before us is whether the District Court and the Court of Appeals correctly defined the elements of that offense.

I

Sorbothane is a patented elastic polymer whose shock-absorbing characteristics make it useful in a variety of medical, athletic, and equestrian products. BTR, Inc. (BTR), owns the patent rights to sorbothane, and its wholly owned subsidiaries manufacture the product in the United States and Britain. Hamilton-Kent Manufacturing Company (Hamilton-Kent) and Sorbothane, Inc. (S.I.), were at all relevant times owned by BTR. S.I. was formed in 1982 to take over Hamilton-Kent's sorbothane business. Respondents Shirley and Larry McQuillan, doing business as Sorboturf Enterprises, were regional distributors of sorbothane products from 1981 to 1983. Petitioner Spectrum Sports, Inc. (Spectrum), was also a distributor of sorbothane products. Petitioner Kenneth B. Leighton, Jr., is a co-owner of Spectrum. Kenneth Leighton, Jr., is the son of Kenneth Leighton, Sr., the president of Hamilton-Kent and S.I. at all relevant times.

In 1980, respondents Shirley and Larry McQuillan signed a letter of intent with Hamilton-Kent, which then owned all manufacturing and distribution rights to sorbothane. The letter of intent granted the McQuillans exclusive rights to purchase sorbothane for use in equestrian products. Respondents were designing a horseshoe pad using sorbothane.

In 1981, Hamilton-Kent decided to establish five regional distributorships for sorbothane. Respondents were selected to be distributors of all sorbothane products, including medical products and shoe inserts, in the Southwest. Spectrum was selected as distributor for another region.

In January 1982, Hamilton-Kent shifted responsibility for selling medical products from five regional distributors to a single national distributor. In April 1982, Hamilton-Kent told respondents that it wanted them to relinquish their athletic shoe distributorship as a condition for retaining the right to develop and distribute equestrian products. As of May 1982, BTR had moved the sorbothane business from Hamilton-Kent to S.I. In May, the marketing manager of S.I. again made clear that respondents had to sell their athletic distributorship to keep their equestrian distribution rights. At a meeting scheduled to discuss the sale of respondents' athletic distributorship to petitioner Leighton, Jr., Leighton, Jr., informed Shirley McQuillan that if she did not come to agreement with him she would be " 'looking for work.' " Respondents refused to sell and continued to distribute athletic shoe inserts.

In the fall of 1982, Leighton, Sr., informed respondents that another concern had been appointed as the national equestrian distributor, and that they were "no longer involved in equestrian products." In January 1983, S.I. began marketing through a national distributor a sorbothane horseshoe pad allegedly indistinguishable from the one designed by respondents. In August 1983, S.I. informed respondents that it would no longer accept their orders. Spectrum thereupon became national distributor of sorbothane athletic shoe inserts. Respondents sought to obtain sorbothane from the BTR's British subsidiary, but were informed by that subsidiary that it would not sell sorbothane in the United States. Respondents' business failed.

Respondents sued petitioners seeking damages for alleged violations of §§ 1 and 2 of the Sherman Act * * *.

The case was tried to a jury * * *. All of the defendants were found to have violated § 2 by, in the words of the verdict sheet, "monopolizing, attempting to monopolize, and/or conspiring to monopolize." * * * The jury awarded $1,743,000 in compensatory damages on each of the violations found to have occurred. This amount was trebled under § 4 of the Clayton Act. The District Court also awarded nearly $1 million in attorney's fees and denied motions for judgment notwithstanding the verdict and for a new trial.

The Court of Appeals for the Ninth Circuit affirmed the judgment in an unpublished opinion. The court expressly ruled that the trial court had properly instructed the jury on the Sherman Act claims and found that the evidence supported the liability verdicts as well as the damages awards on these claims. * * * On the § 2 issue that petitioners present here, the Court of Appeals, noting that the jury had found that petitioners had violated § 2 without specifying whether they had monopolized, attempted to monopolize, or conspired to monopolize, held that the verdict would stand if the evidence supported any one of the three possible violations of § 2. The court went on to conclude that a case of attempted monopolization had been established.[4] The court rejected petitioners' argument that attempted monopolization had not been established because respondents had failed to prove that petitioners had a specific intent to monopolize a relevant market. The court also held that in order to show that respondents' attempt to monopolize was likely to succeed it was not necessary to present evidence of the relevant market or of the defendants' market power. In so doing, the Ninth Circuit relied on *Lessig v. Tidewater Oil Co.*, 327 F.2d 459 (CA9), cert. denied, 377 U.S. 993, 84 S.Ct. 1920 (1964), and its progeny. The Court of Appeals noted that these cases, in dealing with attempt to monopolize claims, had ruled that "if evidence of unfair or predatory conduct is presented, it may satisfy both the specific intent and dangerous probability elements of the offense, without any proof of relevant market or the

---

[4]　The District Court's jury instructions were transcribed as follows:

"In order to win on the claim of attempted monopoly, the Plaintiff must prove each of the following elements by a preponderance of the evidence: first, that the Defendants had a specific intent to achieve monopoly power in the relevant market; second, that the Defendants engaged in exclusionary or restrictive conduct in furtherance of its specific intent; third, that there was a dangerous probability that Defendants could sooner or later achieve [their] goal of monopoly power in the relevant market; fourth, that the Defendants' conduct occurred in or affected interstate commerce; and, fifth, that the Plaintiff was injured in the business or property by the Defendants' exclusionary or restrictive conduct.

"If the Plaintiff has shown that the Defendant engaged in predatory conduct, you may infer from that evidence the specific intent and the dangerous probability element of the offense without any proof of the relevant market or the Defendants' marketing *[sic]* power." * * *

defendant's marketpower *[sic]*." If, however, there is insufficient evidence of unfair or predatory conduct, there must be a showing of "relevant market or the defendant's marketpower *[sic]*." The court went on to find:

> "There is sufficient evidence from which the jury could conclude that the S.I. Group and Spectrum Group engaged in unfair or predatory conduct and thus inferred that they had the specific intent and the dangerous probability of success and, therefore, McQuillan did not have to prove relevant market or the defendant's marketing power."

The decision below, and the *Lessig* line of decisions on which it relies, conflicts with holdings of courts in other Circuits. Every other Court of Appeals has indicated that proving an attempt to monopolize requires proof of a dangerous probability of monopolization of a relevant market. We granted certiorari * * * to resolve this conflict among the Circuits. We reverse.

II

While § 1 of the Sherman Act forbids contracts or conspiracies in restraint of trade or commerce, § 2 addresses the actions of single firms that monopolize or attempt to monopolize, as well as conspiracies and combinations to monopolize. Section 2 does not define the elements of the offense of attempted monopolization. Nor is there much guidance to be had in the scant legislative history of that provision, which was added late in the legislative process. *See* 1 E. Kintner, Legislative History of the Federal Antitrust Laws and Related Statutes 23–25 (1978); 3 P. Areeda & D. Turner, Antitrust Law ¶ 617, pp. 39–41 (1978). * * *

This Court first addressed the meaning of attempt to monopolize under § 2 in *Swift & Co. v. United States,* 196 U.S. 375, 25 S.Ct. 276 (1905). The Court's opinion, written by Justice Holmes, contained the following passage:

> "Where acts are not sufficient in themselves to produce a result which the law seeks to prevent—for instance, the monopoly—but require further acts in addition to the mere forces of nature to bring that result to pass, an intent to bring it to pass is necessary in order to produce a dangerous probability that it will happen. * * * But when that intent and the consequent dangerous probability exist, this statute, like many others and like the common law in some cases, directs itself against that dangerous probability as well as against the completed result." *Id.,* at 396, 25 S.Ct., at 279.

The Court went on to explain, however, that not every act done with intent to produce an unlawful result constitutes an attempt. "It is a question of proximity and degree." *Id.,* at 402, 25 S.Ct., at 281. *Swift* thus indicated that intent is necessary, but alone is not sufficient, to establish the dangerous probability of success that is the object of § 2's prohibition of attempts.

The Court's decisions since *Swift* have reflected the view that the plaintiff charging attempted monopolization must prove a dangerous probability of actual monopolization, which has generally required a definition of the relevant market and examination of market power. * * *

* * * [T]his Court reaffirmed in *Copperweld Corp. v. Independence Tube Corp.,* 467 U.S. 752, 104 S.Ct. 2731 (1984), that "Congress authorized Sherman Act scrutiny of single firms only when they pose a danger of monopolization. Judging unilateral conduct in this manner reduces the risk that the antitrust laws will dampen the competitive zeal of a single aggressive entrepreneur." *Id.,* at 768, 104 S.Ct., at 2740. Thus, the conduct of a single firm, governed by § 2, "is unlawful only when it threatens actual monopolization." *Id.,* at 767, 104 S.Ct., at 2739.

The Courts of Appeals other than the Ninth Circuit have followed this approach. Consistent with our cases, it is generally required that to demonstrate attempted monopolization a plaintiff must prove (1) that the defendant has engaged in predatory or anticompetitive conduct with (2) a specific intent to monopolize and (3) a dangerous probability of achieving monopoly power. See 3 Areeda & Turner, *supra,* ¶ 820, at 312. In order to determine whether there is a dangerous probability of monopolization, courts have found it necessary to consider the relevant market and the defendant's ability to lessen or destroy competition in that market.

Notwithstanding the array of authority contrary to *Lessig,* the Court of Appeals in this case reaffirmed its prior holdings; indeed, it did not mention either this Court's decisions discussed above or the many decisions of other Courts of Appeals reaching contrary results. Respondents urge us to affirm the decision below. We are not at all inclined, however, to embrace *Lessig's* interpretation of § 2, for there is little, if any, support for it in the statute or the case law, and the notion that proof of unfair or predatory conduct alone is sufficient to make out the offense of attempted monopolization is contrary to the purpose and policy of the Sherman Act.

* * *

* * * The purpose of the [Sherman] Act is not to protect businesses from the working of the market; it is to protect the public from the failure of the market. The law directs itself not against conduct which is competitive, even severely so, but against conduct which unfairly tends to destroy competition itself. It does so not out of solicitude for private concerns but out of concern for the public interest. *See, e.g., Brunswick Corp. v. Pueblo Bowl-O-Mat, Inc.,* 429 U.S. 477, 488, 97 S.Ct. 690, 697 (1977); *Cargill, Inc. v. Monfort of Colorado, Inc.,* 479 U.S. 104, 116–117,

107 S.Ct. 484, 492–493 (1986); *Brown Shoe Co. v. United States,* 370 U.S. 294, 320, 82 S.Ct. 1502, 1521 (1962). Thus, this Court and other courts have been careful to avoid constructions of § 2 which might chill competition, rather than foster it. It is sometimes difficult to distinguish robust competition from conduct with long-term anticompetitive effects; moreover, single-firm activity is unlike concerted activity covered by § 1, which "inherently is fraught with anticompetitive risk." *Copperweld,* 467 U.S., at 767–769, 104 S.Ct., at 2739–2740. For these reasons, § 2 makes the conduct of a single firm unlawful only when it actually monopolizes or dangerously threatens to do so. *Id.,* at 767, 104 S.Ct., at 2739. The concern that § 2 might be applied so as to further anticompetitive ends is plainly not met by inquiring only whether the defendant has engaged in "unfair" or "predatory" tactics. Such conduct may be sufficient to prove the necessary intent to monopolize, which is something more than an intent to compete vigorously, but demonstrating the dangerous probability of monopolization in an attempt case also requires inquiry into the relevant product and geographic market and the defendant's economic power in that market.

III

We hold that petitioners may not be liable for attempted monopolization under § 2 of the Sherman Act absent proof of a dangerous probability that they would monopolize a particular market and specific intent to monopolize. In this case, the trial instructions allowed the jury to infer specific intent and dangerous probability of success from the defendants' predatory conduct, without any proof of the relevant market or of a realistic probability that the defendants could achieve monopoly power in that market. In this respect, the instructions misconstrued § 2, as did the Court of Appeals in affirming the judgment of the District Court. Since the affirmance of the § 2 judgment against petitioners rested solely on the legally erroneous conclusion that petitioners had attempted to monopolize in violation of § 2 and since the jury's verdict did not negate the possibility that the § 2 verdict rested on the attempt to monopolize ground alone, the judgment of the Court of Appeals is reversed, * * * and the case is remanded for further proceedings consistent with this opinion.

———

Summarizing the elements of the attempt offense, the Court in *Spectrum Sports* said the plaintiff must prove that (1) the defendant has engaged in predatory or anticompetitive conduct with (2) a specific intent to monopolize and (3) a dangerous probability of achieving monopoly power. Repudiating the view of the Ninth Circuit's earlier *Lessig* decision that a dangerous probability of success could be inferred from proof of predatory conduct alone, the Court held that satisfying the dangerous probability element required an assessment of the defendant's market power.

A finding that the defendant possessed a dangerous probability of success can occur at market share thresholds well below those needed to establish actual monopolization. Although results in individual cases vary, courts generally have presumed that market shares below 50 percent do not show the requisite dangerous probability of attaining a monopoly. As with monopolization cases, courts in attempt disputes adjust the inferences to be drawn from market shares depending on the height of entry barriers.

E. REMEDIES

To this point we have primarily discussed the liability standards under Section 2. What remedies are available once a violation has been found? What purposes do they serve? These issues are addressed in greater depth in Chapter 8; here we briefly consider the issues unique to monopolization cases.

Remedies can serve three main purposes: they can deter the same or similar conduct, compensate victims of an antitrust violation, as with private actions for damages, or "remediate"—seek to repair the damage done by the anticompetitive conduct. With the exception of damages, antitrust remedies are typically achieved through equitable relief— injunctions. As a general matter, injunctive remedies fall into two categories: behavioral and structural. Behavioral or "conduct" remedies require a change of behavior, typically an injunction will either prohibit specified conduct or mandate specific acts (as with a duty to deal). Structural remedies, as the label suggests, typically involve a transfer of property that serves to restructure a violator's business. Perhaps the most common example is a "divestiture"—the sale of some part of a business, but mandatory licensing of intellectual property can also be understood as a structural remedy, as it leads to a change of ownership rights.

As we explore in the next Note and the case discussions that follow, it has been difficult to evaluate the success of remedies in monopolization cases. As you read the material, consider how we should define "success" when remedies are fashioned. How should we evaluate it?

NOTE ON THE SUCCESS OF CONDUCT REMEDIES IN MONOPOLIZATION CASES[13]

Though frequently imposed, conduct remedies do not enjoy a favorable reputation in the antitrust literature, particularly in the case of dominant firm behavior. One often-voiced criticism, particularly in older commentary, is that

---

[13] This Note is adapted from William E. Kovacic, *Failed Expectations: The Troubled Past and Uncertain Future of the Sherman Act as a Tool of Deconcentration*, 74 IOWA L. REV. 1105 (1989).

conduct remedies do little to unravel existing accumulations of market power and provide feeble alternatives to structural solutions, such as divestiture, that directly dismantle positions of dominance. This critique reflects the strong influence of the structuralist school of antitrust, which posits market structure as the key determinant of competitive vigor and tends to equate concentrated markets with a lack of competition. In the view of structuralists, conduct remedies that have not reduced the defendant's market share dramatically—below 50 percent, to use a rough rule of thumb—have failed their essential purpose.

Experience with the *United States v. United Shoe Mach. Corp.*, 110 F. Supp. 295 (D. Mass. 1953), *aff'd per curiam*, 347 U.S. 521, 74 S.Ct. 699 (1954) litigation sometimes is offered to illustrate this point. In a monopolization case concluded in the early 1950s, the DOJ prevailed on the issue of liability, but failed to persuade the court to order divestiture. Emphasizing that the defendant owned a single facility, the court forbad the continuation of United's lease-only policy and required United to unbundle service from the supply of its machines. United's market share fell to the low 60s until 1968, when the Supreme Court granted the government's request for divestiture. The failure to grant divestiture in the original 1950s proceeding is offered as an example of the weakness of conduct remedies and the relative superiority of divestiture.

Criticism of the remedial history of the *United Shoe Machinery* litigation may rest on questionable assumptions derived from structuralist economic models that enjoyed widespread acceptance in the 1950s and 1960s. One point for reconsideration is whether a fall from roughly 85 percent to 60 percent constitutes a remedial failure. The Supreme Court's 1968 opinion treats United's market share as the sole index of remedial effectiveness. Such an approach ignores other data—such as industry patterns of entry, profitability, and innovation—that might provide a more reliable measure of the remedy's impact.

A second basic concern with conduct remedies is that they can entail extensive judicial supervision and continuing intervention to interpret remedial commands and see that they are obeyed. This possibility is perhaps most evident where the court seeks to force an incumbent dominant firm to grant access to a valuable commercial asset. For example, in *Otter Tail Power Co. v. United States*, 410 U.S. 366 (1973), the Supreme Court ordered an integrated electric utility to "wheel" bulk power over its long distance transmission lines to municipally-owned distribution systems. If a court decides to mandate access to a key asset, it must be prepared to specify the price and quality terms on which the defendant must provide access. In setting appropriate access charges, courts may find themselves enmeshed in ratemaking exercises for which they are institutionally ill-suited. Similarly, the consent decree between the Justice Department and AT & T, which was entered in 1982 and resulted in the dismantling of the "Bell System," required continuing oversight by the federal district court until the enactment of the Telecommunications Act of 1996.

Perhaps the most dramatic form of judicial intervention in civil cases is the entry of an order that requires the defendant to be restructured into two or more entities or to divest substantial assets to another purchaser. Divestiture orders offer the possibility of swiftly dissipating the defendant's market power by introducing new competitors into the market. In some instances, the divestiture remedy may involve a single instance of judicial intervention and avoid the need to exercise continuing oversight responsibilities associated with some controls on conduct.

Divestiture orders are most common, and the least controversial, in merger challenges, and it is easy to see why. As we shall see in Chapter 5, mergers that present substantial competitive concerns are often permitted to go forward on the condition that the merging firms divest specified assets, such as entire product lines, plants, or subsidiaries. Similarly, when a court concludes that a merger will be anticompetitive, it enjoins the merger, *i.e.*, it prohibits the combining of the firms or assets at issue. When it reaches such a conclusion after a merger or acquisition has already been consummated, it will typically seek to undo the effort through divestiture. Although it can sometimes be difficult to "unscramble the eggs," *i.e.*, disentangle assets that have already been commingled, the mere fact that the assets once existed separately provides the court with at least some guidance as to how to achieve the divestiture with minimal damage to the efficient operation of the firms.

Similarly, divestiture has been a common and generally accepted remedy for Section 2 monopolization cases where the monopolist became dominant at least in part through acquisitions, even though the acquisitions themselves were not independent violations. Again, it is easy to see why. When a monopolist acquired its dominant position at least in part through the acquisition of rivals, a remedy for abusing that position might include dismantling its monopoly. As in the case of illegal mergers, the fact that its constituent parts once existed independently provides the court with valuable guidance in approaching the divestiture process.

Nevertheless, divestiture remains a drastic and rarely employed remedy outside of these narrow circumstances. It is almost unheard of in Section 1 cases, and remains controversial in Section 2 cases—especially when the dominant firm achieved its dominance through internal growth as opposed to acquisitions. Courts in civil cases, especially abuse of dominance matters, have tended to regard divestiture as a riskier form of intervention than conduct controls. The perceptions of risk are most acute where a restructuring might result in the loss of valuable efficiencies. Courts also might fear that a divestiture will reduce employment and impose significant losses on investors. Divestitures that do not succeed might also be difficult to reverse, especially if the divested assets exit the market, as with bankruptcy, whereas conduct orders can be amended over time. Because courts tend to see divestiture as entailing greater risks, plaintiffs are well-advised to devote additional effort to demonstrating that a divestiture plan will produce substantial net competitive benefits without substantial adverse effects.

Divestiture measures also can be difficult to administer. In the simplest type of divestiture, a court can order existing organizational units within the firm to be spun off as separate entities. Such a move ordinarily will require some difficult judgments about how to allocate personnel and assets that serve the company as a whole, but there generally will be no need to sever existing design or production teams, and perhaps no need to separate physical facilities. In the harder case, the firm's operations are carried out in fully integrated teams. If a restructuring program is to be carried out, the court will have to decide how personnel who serve in the unitary teams will be allocated to the new enterprise, and how equipment and physical facilities will be divided. And although courts may have jurisdiction to require defendants to implement specific measures, they are unlikely to have any ability to control the choices of key personnel, who might elect to seek alternative employment rather than support the restructuring.

Divestitures must also meet financial market tests for practicality and value. Whereas divestiture of assets may be appealing as an economic matter, the assets must have value in the market sufficient to attract buyers at reasonable prices. For example, it may be difficult to sell off assets deemed to be over-priced or lacking in value. Older physical facilities may be economically inefficient, out of date and unattractive to purchasers. Finding purchasers for assets ordered to be divested, therefore, may not always be a simple matter, and courts often turn to Special Masters to oversee divestiture orders over some specified period of time.

If the plaintiff proposes a structural solution, how should the court determine whether structural relief is appropriate? In 2001 the court of appeals decision in *United States v. Microsoft Corp.* devoted extensive attention to the duties of the trial judge in such instances. As we saw earlier in this Chapter, the D.C. Circuit affirmed much of the trial court's ruling that Microsoft had violated Section 2 of the Sherman Act by using improper means to preserve monopoly power in the software sector. In addition to extensive conduct remedies, the district court had endorsed the government's proposal that Microsoft—a unitary firm that had achieved its dominance through internal growth—be broken into two. As you will see, the court of appeals reversed and remanded the district court's remedial order.

UNITED STATES V. MICROSOFT CORP.

United States Court of Appeals for the District of Columbia, 2001.
253 F.3d 34.

PER CURIAM.

* * *

V.   Trial Proceedings and Remedy

* * * We conclude * * * that the District Court's remedies decree must be vacated for three independent reasons: (1) the court failed to hold a remedies-specific evidentiary hearing when there were disputed facts; (2) the court failed to provide adequate reasons for its decreed remedies; and (3) this Court has revised the scope of Microsoft's liability and it is impossible to determine to what extent that should affect the remedies provisions.

A.   Factual Background

On April 3, 2000, the District Court concluded the liability phase of the proceedings by the filing of its Conclusions of Law holding that Microsoft had violated §§ 1 and 2 of the Sherman Act. The court and the parties then began discussions of the procedures to be followed in the imposition of remedies. Initially, the District Court signaled that it would enter relief only after conducting a new round of proceedings. In its Conclusions of Law, the court stated that it would issue a remedies order "following proceedings to be established by further Order of the Court." And, when during a post-trial conference, Microsoft's counsel asked whether the court "contemplate[d] further proceedings," the judge replied, "Yes. Yes. I assume that there would be further proceedings." The District Court further speculated that those proceedings might "replicate the procedure at trial with testimony in written form subject to crossexamination."

On April 28, 2000, plaintiffs submitted their proposed final judgment, accompanied by six new supporting affidavits and several exhibits. In addition to a series of temporary conduct restrictions, plaintiffs proposed that Microsoft be split into two independent corporations, with one continuing Microsoft's operating systems business and the other undertaking the balance of Microsoft's operations. Microsoft filed a "summary response" on May 10, contending both that the proposed decree was too severe and that it would be impossible to resolve certain remedies-specific factual disputes "on a highly expedited basis." Another May 10 submission argued that if the District Court considered imposing plaintiffs' proposed remedy, "then substantial discovery, adequate time for preparation and a full trial on relief will be required." * * *

After the District Court revealed during a May 24 hearing that it was prepared to enter a decree without conducting "any further process," Microsoft renewed its argument that the underlying factual disputes between the parties necessitated a remedies-specific evidentiary hearing. In two separate offers of proof, Microsoft offered to produce a number of pieces of evidence. * * *

[Here the court summarized Microsoft's offers of proof concerning the likely adverse effects of the plaintiffs' proposed remedies. Microsoft had offered testimony by several economic experts, an investment bank, and Microsoft executives, including the company's chairman, Bill Gates. Eds.]

Over Microsoft's objections, the District Court proceeded to consider the merits of the remedy and on June 7, 2000 entered its final judgment. The court explained that it would not conduct "extended proceedings on the form a remedy should take," because it doubted that an evidentiary hearing would "give any significantly greater assurance that it will be able to identify what might be generally regarded as an optimum remedy." The bulk of Microsoft's proffered facts were simply conjectures about future events, and "[i]n its experience the Court has found testimonial predictions of future events generally less reliable even than testimony as to historical fact, and cross-examination to be of little use in enhancing or detracting from their accuracy." Nor was the court swayed by Microsoft's "profession of surprise" at the possibility of structural relief. "From the inception of this case Microsoft knew, from well-established Supreme Court precedents dating from the beginning of the last century, that a mandated divestiture was a possibility, if not a probability, in the event of an adverse result at trial."

The substance of the District Court's remedies order is nearly identical to plaintiffs' proposal. The decree's centerpiece is the requirement that Microsoft submit a proposed plan of divestiture, with the company to be split into an "Operating Systems Business," or "OpsCo," and an "Applications Business," or "AppsCo." OpsCo would receive all of Microsoft's operating systems, such as Windows 98 and Windows 2000, while AppsCo would receive the remainder of Microsoft's businesses, including IE [Internet Explorer Internet browser] and Office [Microsoft Office]. The District Court identified four reasons for its "reluctant[ ]" conclusion that "a structural remedy has become imperative." First, Microsoft "does not yet concede that any of its business practices violated the Sherman Act." Second, the company consequently "continues to do business as it has in the past." Third, Microsoft "has proved untrustworthy in the past." And fourth, the Government, whose officials "are by reason of office obliged and expected to consider—and to act in—the public interest," won the case, "and for that reason alone have some entitlement to a remedy of their choice."

* * *

[The court of appeals concluded that the trial court's efforts to accelerate the conduct of the case on the merits by limiting the number of witnesses for each side did not constitute error. Eds.]

C. Failure to Hold an Evidentiary Hearing

* * * It is a cardinal principle of our system of justice that factual disputes must be heard in open court and resolved through trial-like evidentiary proceedings. Any other course would be contrary "to the spirit which imbues our judicial tribunals prohibiting decision without hearing." A party has the right to judicial resolution of disputed facts not just as to the liability phase, but also as to appropriate relief. Normally, an evidentiary hearing is required before an injunction may be granted." Other than a temporary restraining order, no injunctive relief may be entered without a hearing. *See generally* Fed. R. Civ. P. 65. A hearing on the merits—*i.e.*, a trial on liability—does not substitute for a relief-specific evidentiary hearing unless the matter of relief was part of the trial on liability, or unless there are no disputed factual issues regarding the matter of relief.

This rule is no less applicable in antitrust cases. The Supreme Court "has recognized that a 'full exploration of facts is usually necessary in order (for the District Court) properly to draw (an antitrust) decree' so as 'to prevent future violations and eradicate existing evils.' " *United States v. Ward Baking Co.*, 376 U.S. 327, 330–31, 84 S.Ct. 763 (1964). Hence a remedies decree must be vacated whenever there is "a bona fide disagreement concerning substantive items of relief which could be resolved only by trial." *Id.* at 334, 84 S.Ct. 763 * * *

Despite plaintiffs' protestations, there can be no serious doubt that the parties disputed a number of facts during the remedies phase. In two separate offers of proof, Microsoft identified 23 witnesses who, had they been permitted to testify, would have challenged a wide range of plaintiffs' factual representations, including the feasibility of dividing Microsoft, the likely impact on consumers, and the effect of divestiture on shareholders. To take but two examples, where plaintiffs' economists testified that splitting Microsoft in two would be socially beneficial, the company offered to prove that the proposed remedy would "cause substantial social harm by raising software prices, lowering rates of innovation and disrupting the evolution of Windows as a software development platform." And where plaintiffs' investment banking experts proposed that divestiture might actually increase shareholder value, Microsoft proffered evidence that structural relief "would inevitably result in a significant loss of shareholder value," a loss that could reach "tens—possibly hundreds—of billions of dollars."

Indeed, the District Court itself appears to have conceded the existence of acute factual disagreements between Microsoft and plaintiffs. The court acknowledged that the parties were "sharply divided" and held "divergent opinions" on the likely results of its remedies decree. The reason the court declined to conduct an evidentiary hearing was not because of the absence of disputed facts, but because it believed that those disputes could be resolved only through "actual experience," not further proceedings. But a prediction about future events is not, as a prediction, any less a factual issue. Indeed, the Supreme Court has acknowledged that drafting an antitrust decree by necessity "involves predictions and assumptions concerning future economic and business events." *Ford Motor Co. v. United States*, 405 U.S. 562, 578, 92 S.Ct. 1142 (1972). Trial courts are not excused from their obligation to resolve such matters through evidentiary hearings simply because they consider the bedrock procedures of our justice system to be "of little use."

* * *

Plaintiffs further argue—and the District Court held—that no evidentiary hearing was necessary given that Microsoft long had been on notice that structural relief was a distinct possibility. It is difficult to see why this matters. Whether Microsoft had advance notice that dissolution was in the works is immaterial to whether the District Court violated the company's procedural rights by ordering it without an evidentiary hearing. To be sure, "claimed surprise at the district court's decision to consider permanent injunctive relief does not, alone, merit reversal." But in this case, Microsoft's professed surprise does not stand "alone." There is something more: the company's basic procedural right to have disputed facts resolved through an evidentiary hearing.

* * *

D. Failure to Provide an Adequate Explanation

We vacate the District Court's remedies decree for the additional reason that the court has failed to provide an adequate explanation for the relief it ordered. The Supreme Court has explained that a remedies decree in an antitrust case must seek to "unfetter a market from anticompetitive conduct," *Ford Motor Co.*, 405 U.S. at 577, 92 S.Ct. 1142, to "terminate the illegal monopoly, deny to the defendant the fruits of its statutory violation, and ensure that there remain no practices likely to result in monopolization in the future," *United States v. United Shoe Mach. Corp.*, 391 U.S. 244, 250, 88 S.Ct. 1496 (1968); *see also United States v. Grinnell Corp.*, 384 U.S. 563, 577, 86 S.Ct. 1698 (1966).

The District Court has not explained how its remedies decree would accomplish those objectives. Indeed, the court devoted a mere four paragraphs of its order to explaining its reasons for the remedy. They are: (1) Microsoft "does not yet concede that any of its business practices violated the Sherman Act"; (2) Microsoft "continues to do business as it has in the past"; (3) Microsoft "has proved untrustworthy in the past"; and (4) the Government, whose officials "are by reason of office obliged and expected to consider—and to act in—the public interest," won the case, "and for that reason alone have some entitlement to a remedy of their choice." Nowhere did the District Court discuss the objectives the Supreme Court deems relevant.

* * *

F.　On Remand

As a general matter, a district court is afforded broad discretion to enter that relief it calculates will best remedy the conduct it has found to be unlawful. This is no less true in antitrust cases. *See, e.g.*, Ford Motor Co., 405 U.S. at 573, 92 S.Ct. 1142 ("The District Court is clothed with 'large discretion' to fit the decree to the special needs of the individual case."); *Md. & Va. Milk Producers Ass'n, Inc. v. United States*, 362 U.S. 458, 473, 80 S.Ct. 847 (1960) ("The formulation of decrees is largely left to the discretion of the trial court. . . ."). And divestiture is a common form of relief in successful antitrust prosecutions: it is indeed "the most important of antitrust remedies." See, e.g., *United States v. E.I. du Pont de Nemours & Co.*, 366 U.S. 316, 331, 81 S.Ct. 1243 (1961).

On remand, the District Court must reconsider whether the use of the structural remedy of divestiture is appropriate with respect to Microsoft, which argues that it is a unitary company. By and large, cases upon which plaintiffs rely in arguing for the split of Microsoft have involved the dissolution of entities formed by mergers and acquisitions. On the contrary, the Supreme Court has clarified that divestiture "has traditionally been the remedy for Sherman Act violations whose heart is intercorporate *combination and control*," du Pont, 366 U.S. at 329, 81 S.Ct. 1243 (emphasis added), and that "[c]omplete divestiture is particularly appropriate where asset or stock *acquisitions* violate the antitrust laws," *Ford Motor Co.*, 405 U.S. at 573, 92 S.Ct. 1142 (emphasis added).

One apparent reason why courts have not ordered the dissolution of unitary companies is logistical difficulty. As the court explained in *United States v. ALCOA*, 91 F. Supp. 333, 416 (S.D.N.Y.1950), a "corporation, designed to operate effectively as a single entity, cannot readily be dismembered of parts of its various operations without a marked loss of efficiency." A corporation that has expanded by acquiring its competitors often has preexisting internal lines of division along which it may more easily be split than a corporation that has expanded from natural growth. Although time and corporate modifications and developments may eventually fade those lines, at least the identifiable entities preexisted to create a template for such division as the court might later decree. With reference to those corporations that are not acquired by merger and acquisition, Judge Wyzanski accurately opined in *United Shoe*:

United conducts all machine manufacture at one plant in Beverly, with one set of jigs and tools, one foundry, one laboratory for machinery problems, one managerial staff, and one labor force. It takes no Solomon to see that this organism cannot be cut into three equal and viable parts.

United States v. United Shoe Machinery Corp., 110 F. Supp. 295, 348 (D.Mass.1953).

Depending upon the evidence, the District Court may find in a remedies proceeding that it would be no easier to split Microsoft in two than United Shoe in three. Microsoft's Offer of Proof in response to the court's denial of an evidentiary hearing included proffered testimony from its President and CEO Steve Ballmer that the company "is, and always has been, a unified company without free-standing business units. Microsoft is not the result of mergers or acquisitions." Microsoft further offered evidence that it is "not organized along product lines," but rather is housed in a single corporate headquarters and that it has

> only one sales and marketing organization which is responsible for selling all of the company's products, one basic research organization, one product support organization, one operations department, one information technology department, one facilities department, one purchasing department, one human resources department, one finance department, one legal department and one public relations department.

If indeed Microsoft is a unitary company, division might very well require Microsoft to reproduce each of these departments in each new entity rather than simply allocate the differing departments among them.

In devising an appropriate remedy, the District Court also should consider whether plaintiffs have established a sufficient causal connection between Microsoft's anticompetitive conduct and its dominant position in the OS market. "Mere existence of an exclusionary act does not itself justify full feasible relief against the monopolist to create maximum competition." Rather, structural relief, which is "designed to eliminate the monopoly altogether . . . require[s] a clearer indication of a *significant causal connection* between the conduct and creation or maintenance of the market power." Absent such causation, the antitrust defendant's unlawful behavior should be remedied by "an injunction against continuation of that conduct."

* * * [W]e have found a causal connection between Microsoft's exclusionary conduct and its continuing position in the operating systems market only through inference. Indeed, the District Court expressly did not adopt the position that Microsoft would have lost its position in the OS market but for its anticompetitive behavior. *Findings of Fact* § 411 ("There is insufficient evidence to find that, absent Microsoft's actions, Navigator and Java already would have ignited genuine competition in the market for Intel-compatible PC operating systems."). If the court on remand is unconvinced of the causal connection between Microsoft's exclusionary conduct and the company's position in the OS market, it may well conclude that divestiture is not an appropriate remedy.

While we do not undertake to dictate to the District Court the precise form that relief should take on remand, we note again that it should be tailored to fit the wrong creating the occasion for the remedy.

* * *

How should a court decide the scope of equitable remedies once an antitrust violation has been found? What should the scope of those remedies be? In *Microsoft*, the district court had ordered a combination of "behavioral" or "conduct" remedies, as well as "structural" remedies. What might lead a court to select one or the other, or, as the *Microsoft* district court did, both? Why did the court of appeals conclude that an evidentiary hearing is required before an order of divestiture can be entered? Would the same reasoning require a hearing before *any* equitable remedy is entered?

Recall from our earlier readings on *Microsoft* in this Chapter that before reaching its decision to remand the question of remedy, the D.C. Circuit affirmed in part, reversed in part, and remanded in part the district court's conclusion that Microsoft had violated Sections 1 and 2 of the Sherman Act. On remand the Antitrust Division, under leadership that had changed due to the presidential election of 2000, quickly announced that it would neither pursue any of the remanded claims of liability, nor seek a break up of Microsoft. Thereafter, it and nine of the remaining eighteen litigating states reached a settlement with Microsoft that involved a variety of conduct remedies and no structural relief. But nine other states rejected the settlement as inadequate and asked the district court to proceed with the remand, urging broader conduct remedies.

Faced with an unprecedented situation, the district court divided the proceedings into two "tracks." Track 1 focused on the required procedures for federal court approval of a government negotiated consent decree under the Tunney Act, 15 U.S.C. § 16(e). Track 2 proceeded to trial on the remanded question of remedy, in which the nine non-settling states sought to augment the agreement reached with Microsoft by the Department of Justice and joined in by the nine settling states. The district court ultimately approved the settlement of the case in the Tunney Act proceeding, and ordered little in the way of additional relief in the remedy trial pursued in the end solely by the State of Massachusetts. The D.C. Circuit affirmed in almost all respects. On the merits it found no abuse of discretion by the district court, instead praising its handling of the complex two track proceedings. *See Massachusetts v. Microsoft Corp.*, 373 F.3d 1199 (D.C. Cir. 2004). For further discussion of the Tunney Act, see *infra* Sidebar 8–7.

What challenges confronted the district court in working on two "tracks"? How might it be possible to enter a remedial decree pursuant to a settlement, yet to also order additional remedial steps in a second and independent judicial proceeding?

Although the initial consent decree was to last five years, it was extended by the court and did not expire until May 2011. How should its "success" be judged? Should compliance with the decree itself constitute success? Should the success of decrees intended to remediate, i.e. to restore competition, instead be measured by their effects on competition? For a critical analysis and assessment of the decree in the *Microsoft* case, as well as the other remedies faced by Microsoft in a plethora of private civil cases and the cases brought by the European Commission, see ANDREW I. GAVIL & HARRY FIRST, THE MICROSOFT ANTITRUST CASES: COMPETITION POLICY FOR THE TWENTY-FIRST CENTURY 235–79 (2014).

F. CONCLUSION

Jurisprudence concerning dominant firm behavior reflects a fundamental dilemma in economics and law about the design of policies governing large business enterprises. Judge Learned Hand displayed that ambivalence memorably in *Alcoa*. Hand warned that "unchallenged economic power deadens initiative, discourages thrift and depresses energy," yet he also cautioned that the "[s]uccessful competitor, having been urged to compete, must not be turned upon when he wins." How is a competition policy system to discourage overreaching by dominant enterprises without promoting passivity as a way of commercial life?

Efforts to resolve the dilemma have proceeded on two basic fronts. The first is to refine tools used to identify conditions of genuine dominance. Aided in large measure by analytical advances in the U.S. merger guidelines that we will study in Chapter 5, antitrust agencies and courts have improved their capacity to measure market power accurately and directly. There still remain, however, difficult measurement problems in industries undergoing rapid technological change or other forms of dynamism.

The second frontier of activity involves the definition of unreasonable exclusion. *Alcoa* defined improper conduct expansively and reflected an implicit assumption that aggressive intervention to police dominant firms was appropriate because firms rarely gained or sustained dominance through superior performance. By the late 1970s and early 1980s, courts and enforcement agencies in varying degrees had begun to heed the cautions of critics about (1) possible justifications for acts previously deemed to constitute improper means of exclusion; (2) the role of superior performance in yielding dominance; and (3) the capacity of judges and antitrust officials to correctly diagnose competitive maladies and impose useful cures. Through the 1980s and 1990s, debate surfaced in which some commentators, operating within an efficiency framework, have suggested new possibilities for intervention and sought to develop analytical tools that courts and enforcement bodies can administer successfully.

The modern ferment in analysis reflects dissatisfaction with formalistic, traditional methodologies that, by placing specific methods of exclusion in discrete categories, sometimes diverted attention from questions that should supply the foundation for evaluating all allegations of dominant firm misconduct.

G. PROBLEMS AND EXERCISES

Problem 4–1:
Amerinet

Amerinet is the largest Internet service provider ("ISP") in the United States. Amerinet is the leading provider of "Jiffy Messaging" ("JM") services, which permit individuals to send and receive electronic messages in real time with other members of their "crony lists." Amerinet is pursuing a series of business initiatives (part of the company's "Amerinet Anywhere" strategy) that would permit wireless access to Amerinet's services through a portable, handheld device that has voice and JM capabilities. Amerinet calls the new handheld device and related services by the name of "AmeriPhone." To carry out its plans, Amerinet intends to use the following approaches.

(a) Amerinet intends to contract with the most popular mobile telephone manufacturers to supply the hardware for the AmeriPhone. The manufacturers will be required to agree that they will not produce or sell a similar device to any competitor of Amerinet.

(b) Amerinet will sell its AmeriPhone and related services through independent distributors. Amerinet will require all of its distributors to agree that the AmeriPhone service can be sold only to customers of Amerinet's basic Internet access service. Amerinet plans to configure its wireless Internet service so that it only works with the branded Amerinet handset.

(c) To encourage retail sales of the AmeriPhone service, Amerinet wants to initiate a nationwide marketing campaign for the service. The campaign would feature a highly promoted, uniform, low monthly price. Amerinet wants this price to be available to customers at all of its retail outlets, including its independent distributors.

You are an Assistant General Counsel at Amerinet. You have been asked to advise Amerinet about the possible antitrust consequences of proceeding with these business strategies. Draft a memorandum of no more than five (5) pages evaluating the legality of the proposed strategies based on the cases we have studied. Identify for Amerinet any additional information you might need to know about the market to evaluate its proposals.

Problem 4–2:
Mountain Air

Mountain Air and Icarus Air have 85% and 5%, respectively, of a properly defined relevant market consisting of passenger airline traffic through Denver, Colorado. Icarus is a small, low-cost airline, and it recently emerged from a bankruptcy reorganization after one of its planes crashed with a large loss of life.

Last winter Icarus offered discounted fares to induce vacationers to fly Icarus to Denver. Mountain swiftly matched these fares. Icarus believes Mountain's discounted fares fail to recover Mountain's short-run average variable costs. Icarus had identified witnesses who will testify that a Mountain official told a large travel agency: "We'll give seats away to melt Icarus's revenues, and then raise fares later once Icarus has fallen to earth." If Icarus quits Denver, the City of Denver (which owns Denver's airport) will insist that Icarus's gates and other airport assets be sold to an airline other than Mountain.

Before its bankruptcy, Icarus formed a code-sharing arrangement with Mountain by which the two firms jointly served routes west of Denver that Mountain did not serve but Icarus did. After Icarus emerged from bankruptcy, Mountain ended the agreement and began serving the routes by itself. Mountain has gotten complaints from customers who say Icarus provided better service. Mountain has told the public that it fears harm to its reputation by working with an airline that had a recent crash. Mountain's internal marketing studies (a) predict lucrative profits from taking over Icarus's routes, (b) conclude that customers view Icarus as being at least as safe as Mountain, and (c) say Icarus "needs code-sharing with Mountain to sustain operations in Denver."

In the past, when Mountain has perceived that a low-cost entrant such as Icarus might offer service on routes served by Mountain, Mountain has publicly announced that it has future plans to greatly increase its own service on the routes that the entrant is thinking of serving. Mountain's internal marketing studies indicate that Mountain believes such announcements discourage entrants from initiating service. Mountain sometimes adds the capacity and service that its advance announcements promise, but sometimes it withdraws its promise if it appears that the entrant is not going to enter the market after all.

You are a private attorney and have been retained by Mountain to evaluate its possible antitrust vulnerability for these practices in the United States. Mountain also would like your views about whether the same strategies it has used in the United States would be acceptable in the European Union. Prepare a brief memorandum of no more than five (5) pages advising Mountain on each of the questions it has posed.

CHAPTER 5

MERGERS AND ACQUISITIONS

■ ■ ■

INTRODUCTION

When a firm buys some or all of the stock or assets of another, the transaction is termed an "acquisition." If all of a firm is acquired, the two companies are said to have "merged." Mergers and acquisitions among rivals can reduce competition because they alter the structure of markets by changing the number, identity, size, and other characteristics of firms. Most of the more than 100 competition enforcement authorities in the world have adopted some form of merger control mechanism as part of their antitrust laws. As a consequence, acquisitions involving multinational corporations with significant worldwide operations commonly are subject to review by more than one jurisdiction, and sometimes are subject to review by dozens of jurisdictions.

Mergers and acquisitions frequently are categorized as "horizontal," "vertical," or "conglomerate." Like horizontal agreements, horizontal mergers and acquisitions involve sellers of substitutes, *i.e.*, competitors. Like vertical agreements, vertical mergers and acquisitions involve firms and their suppliers, customers, or other sellers of complements. Conglomerate mergers involve firms that sell neither substitutes nor complements. Typically, a conglomerate is engaged in many unrelated lines of business. This Chapter focuses on horizontal mergers and emphasizes "collusive" rather than "exclusionary" competitive concerns. Section D considers vertical mergers, which more commonly may raise exclusionary concerns, and the Chapter discusses conglomerate mergers in Sidebar 5–12.

As will be evident in both the organization and content of this Chapter, the development of merger law in the U.S. illustrates the antitrust field's shift in perspective from narrow doctrinal categories to broad, overarching concepts like market power, entry, and efficiency. Indeed, under the influence of government Merger Guidelines, the shift toward a more concept-oriented approach to antitrust analysis arguably took place first and most extensively in the merger area, especially since the early 1980s. The influence of the Merger Guidelines has been enhanced by the fact that the Supreme Court has not decided a substantive merger case since the mid-1970s. Although we will review some early cases, much of the Chapter focuses on how merger law and merger lawyers operate today—by applying economic concepts to make often complex judgments about the likely performance of markets affected by mergers.

A. A PRIMER ON MERGER ANALYSIS IN THE U.S.

1. INTRODUCTION TO THE STATUTORY FRAMEWORK

Most mergers are reviewed under Section 7 of the Clayton Act, 15 U.S.C. § 18 (*see infra* Appendix A). The original version, enacted in 1914, was restricted to stock acquisitions. Congress closed the resulting loophole in 1950, amending the section so that it also covered asset acquisitions. The 1950 amendments also removed earlier language that had arguably limited the text to anticompetitive horizontal mergers, thus making clear that the statute applied equally to horizontal, vertical, and conglomerate mergers. *See generally Brown Shoe Co. v. United States*, 370 U.S. 294 (1962) (excerpted later in this Chapter).

Mergers also can be challenged under other federal statutes. They may violate the Sherman Act, as Section 1 agreements in restraint of trade or under Section 2 as monopolization or attempts or conspiracies to monopolize. They may also be viewed as unfair methods of competition in violation of Section 5 of the FTC Act. Interlocking directorates—the presence of common directors on the boards of rival firms—can also be an antitrust violation under Section 8 of the Clayton Act, 15 U.S.C. § 19. The distinguishing characteristic of the anti-merger prohibitions of the Clayton Act is its objection to mergers that "*may* * * * substantially * * * lessen competition" (emphasis added). As we shall see when we read *Brown Shoe* later in this Chapter, in the wake of the 1950 Amendments, this language was seized upon by the Supreme Court as providing the authority to go beyond the Sherman Act by "arresting mergers at a time when the trend to a lessening of competition in a line of commerce was still in its *incipiency*" (emphasis added). The "may" language also provides a basis for challenging mergers before they lead to actual anticompetitive effects, *i.e.*, before they are consummated.

The Clayton Act, like the Sherman Act (but not the FTC Act), may be enforced by states and private parties, as well as by the federal antitrust enforcement agencies. Private plaintiffs challenging mergers, as when making other claims under federal antitrust laws, must demonstrate that they are harmed as a result of the practice they challenge as anticompetitive. We first encountered this "antitrust injury" requirement in Chapter 1, when we read *Brunswick*, itself a private merger challenge. In practice, most merger enforcement is conducted by the federal antitrust agencies, sometimes joined by state enforcers.

Some mergers in certain industries, mainly those currently or previously subject to extensive federal regulation, also may be reviewed on competition grounds by federal agencies other than the Justice Department and Federal Trade Commission, although typically with their input. In some cases, the transaction may be reviewed concurrently by an antitrust agency and by an industry regulator. Examples include railroads (Surface Transportation Board), communications (Federal Communications Commission), energy producers (Federal Energy Regulatory Commission), and banking (Federal Reserve Board). Mergers involving national security interests are subject to antitrust review and to an additional regulatory regime under the Exon-Florio Amendment to the Defense Production Act of 1950 ("Exon-Florio"), 50 U.S.C. App. § 2170.

Largely owing to the passage of the Hart-Scott-Rodino ("HSR") Antitrust Improvements Act in 1976, which created a system of pre-merger notification, mergers today commonly are challenged prior to consummation or "closing," before any possible adverse competitive effects can occur. *See* Sidebar 5–3. Before 1976, it was more common for acquisitions to be challenged only after consummation. But retrospective merger review often made the remedy a difficult problem because it required a court to unscramble integrated business assets and activities. Moreover, challenges after consummation created uncertainty for the merged entity and its employees for a substantial period of time. On the other hand, retrospective review avoided consummation delays for mergers subject to extensive investigation and, in theory, permitted courts to judge mergers based upon their actual effects. In practice, however, courts often discounted favorable post-transaction evidence on the ground that the firm's managers were aware that government investigation and judicial review were pending.

Prospective merger review requires enforcers and courts to make a prediction about the likely competitive effects of the deal. How might they do so? One traditional solution has been the "structural presumption," which predicts anticompetitive effects based on significant increases in market concentration. This presumption, the subject of the first cases we study in the next section, can be understood as a legal device for making predictions about the competitive effects of horizontal mergers in an environment of uncertainty. As you read the cases and learn of the law's evolution, consider the advisability of structuring horizontal merger review this way, and the different choices that have been made by courts in different eras. Also consider whether the various factors highlighted in those decisions—including high post-merger market concentration, a sizeable increase in concentration, and a trend toward concentration—are likely to serve as reliable indicators of future adverse competitive effects.

Although most merger challenges today occur before consummation, the legal authority for post-consummation challenges was unaffected by the enactment of the HSR pre-merger notification system. Today, the federal enforcement agencies occasionally undertake post-consummation challenges, either with respect to transactions that were not reportable under the pre-merger notification regime (perhaps because they were too small), or to mergers and acquisitions that may not have appeared to present competitive problems at the time they were reported but raise concerns later. *See* John D. Harkrider & Rachel D. Adcox, *Closing at Your Peril: Post-Consummation Merger Challenges*, 12 THE THRESHOLD 52 (Summer 2012), http://www.axinn.com/media-articles–155.html (between 2002 and 2012, the agencies challenged thirty mergers post-consummation). Merging firms are more likely to litigate post-consummation challenges, because delays in resolving the agency challenge are typically less costly to them after they have combined their assets than when they must wait to do so. *See, e.g., United States v. Bazaarvoice, Inc.*, 2014 WL 203966 (N. D. Cal. Jan. 8, 2014); *St. Alphonsus Med. Ctr. v. St. Luke's Health Sys.*, 778 F.3d 775 (9th Cir. 2015).

2. MOTIVES FOR MERGER AMONG RIVALS

Before we begin our study of the cases, we examine why firms might seek to merge or to acquire each other's assets. Firms commonly seek to make acquisitions for a number of reasons that do not raise antitrust concerns, including:

- to reduce costs or improve products in ways unavailable to the merger partners individually;

- to improve the profitability of the acquired assets by replacing ineffective management;

- to obtain tax advantages in some situations; and

- to satisfy the "hubris" of some managers, who obtain personal satisfaction from creating and controlling large corporate empires.

The vast majority of mergers and acquisitions are motivated by reasons such as these and are commonly considered benign from an antitrust standpoint. Indeed, in a typical year, the federal antitrust enforcement agencies identify no antitrust problem in nearly all of the mergers and acquisitions that they review. Although this Chapter looks at the antitrust law issues that arise from mergers and acquisitions, such transactions may also raise other legal issues, including tax, securities, and corporate law questions. Accordingly, legal counseling for merging firms commonly draws upon the expertise of attorneys practicing in all these fields.

Some mergers among rivals do raise antitrust concerns and may be motivated in whole or part by the desire to obtain market power. A horizontal acquisition may permit the merger partners to obtain market power in three ways (not mutually exclusive):

- *Coordinated Competitive Effects.* By reducing the number of competitors, a merger may make it easier for rivals in a market to collude tacitly or achieve higher prices through consciously parallel conduct after the merger. Such mergers would raise the same kind of concern about "collusive" conduct that might also arise, for example, in agreements among rivals to fix prices or divide markets.

- *Unilateral Competitive Effects.* If the merging firms are the only two participants in the relevant market, their "merger to monopoly" could result in "unilateral competitive effects" because once merged, the merged firm could raise price without needing to coordinate with any other firms. Even when the merging firms are not the only market participants, a merger may allow two firms that sell products that are close substitutes to coordinate their business strategies, lessening the competitive constraint the sellers pose for each other and leading to higher prices even if other sellers in the market do not change their strategies. These "unilateral" competitive effects may also be understood as reflecting a "collusive" competitive concern (as opposed to an exclusionary competitive concern).[1] If other sellers participating in the market respond to the higher prices arising from unilateral competitive effects by competing less aggressively, the merger could be understood as generating both unilateral and coordinated competitive effects.

- *Exclusionary Anticompetitive Effects.* A merger may allow firms to obtain market power by impairing rivals' access to key inputs or distribution channels.

Mergers that generate antitrust scrutiny may simultaneously permit the exercise of market power and allow the merging firms to lower costs or otherwise achieve efficiencies. This observation raises a frequent challenge in the antitrust analysis of mergers, and, indeed, in antitrust generally: how to evaluate conduct that appears likely to generate both

---

[1]   Although this terminology should by now be familiar to students who have read our earlier Chapters, it may be confusing to other readers steeped in the Merger Guidelines who look at this Chapter first. In brief, this Casebook distinguishes between "collusive" and "exclusionary" competitive concerns. Anticompetitive conduct is termed "collusive" if it harms competition directly, and termed "exclusionary" if it does so indirectly, as a result of the elimination or impairment of rivals. We do not use the term "collusive" synonymously with "coordinated" competitive effects. Rather, we describe two of the major categories of competitive effects discussed in the Merger Guidelines, "coordinated" and "unilateral," as different types of "collusive" competitive effects.

anticompetitive harm and procompetitive efficiencies. One policy tradeoff that may result in the merger context is depicted in Figure 5–1. This type of figure originated with economist Oliver Williamson and is sometimes referred to as the "Williamson diagram."[2]

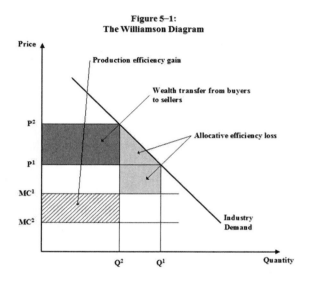

Figure 5–1:
The Williamson Diagram

Figure 5–1 illustrates the effects on price, output, and economic welfare (efficiency) of a merger that simultaneously raises price *and* generates cost savings, using economic concepts we previously met in the coffee example in Chapter 1. Initially, the industry was selling Q^1 units of output at a price P^1. This price was in excess of pre-merger industry marginal cost (MC^1). The merger gives the firms participating in the market the ability to exercise market power by reducing output to Q^2, leading price to rise along the industry demand curve to the post-merger price P^2. Although the merger leads to an increase in price in the figure, it need not always do so.

As Figure 5–1 suggests, a merger may create opposing incentives for the merging firms: (1) an incentive to raise price, which may result from an increased ability to exercise market power; and (2) an incentive to lower

---

[2] Economics students will recognize that Figure 5–1 incorporates a number of assumptions that are made to simplify the graph and that do not qualify the general observations made in the text. For example, the possibility of product differentiation is ignored; marginal cost is assumed not to vary with output; the industry is assumed to price in excess of marginal cost pre-merger; complications that arise when firms sell multiple products or are investing in the development of next generation products are ignored; and the figure implicitly assumes that demand and costs would not have changed absent the merger. Note as well that the only costs depicted in the figure are variable (marginal) costs; fixed costs are not shown. (In this aspect, the figure differs from Williamson's original presentation, which worked with average costs.) The figure also does not show how the monopolist's price and output are determined (*i.e.* its marginal revenue is not depicted).

price, which may derive from efficiencies (here depicted as marginal cost savings). As a consequence, the post-merger price may either rise or fall; the actual outcome will be based on the relative strength of these two incentives in particular cases. If the post-merger price is likely to fall, the merger may be deemed procompetitive, making the antitrust enforcer's job easy. A merger likely to raise price, in contrast, can be expected to draw enforcer scrutiny, and may raise some of the policy issues sketched below.

Returning to Figure 5–1, the higher price creates a transfer from buyers to sellers (shaded rectangle in upper left), as buyers of Q^2 units who formerly paid P^1 are forced to pay P^2.[3] It also leads to an allocative efficiency loss (the shaded triangle and rectangle to the right of the transfer as indicated by the arrows), equal to the social gain achieved pre-merger but no longer achieved after the exercise of market power. Before the merger, the market was able to convert resources that cost MC^1 into products worth as indicated on the demand curve to buyers; the exercise of market power denies society this benefit for (Q1–Q2) units, generating an allocative efficiency loss.

But the merger also will generate a production efficiency gain. This gain arises from the cost savings depicted by the shaded rectangle in the lower left of the figure. In particular, the Q^2 units that are still produced and sold after the merger are produced with fewer resources because marginal cost falls to a lower level. This generates an efficiency gain. Fixed cost savings resulting from the merger (*e.g.*, from the reduction in duplicative overhead expenditures like payroll) may also represent social resource savings but these savings are not depicted in Figure 5–1.

Because marginal cost declines, it is possible that the merger could cause the price to fall. For example, if the merger did not confer additional market power on the remaining industry participants, and the lower costs instead led producers to expand output, then output would rise and price would fall. This possible outcome—in which Q^2 exceeds Q^1 and P^2 is below P1—is not depicted in the figure. It would represent a merger that is unambiguously procompetitive.

A merger that raises price can simultaneously reduce social welfare (through the allocative efficiency loss) *and* increase it (through the production efficiency gain). As drawn in Figure 5–1, the allocative efficiency loss exceeds the production efficiency gain, making the transaction objectionable on two grounds: (1) it will reduce aggregate social welfare; and (2) it will harm buyers by raising price. However, with different assumptions it is possible for the transaction to simultaneously increase aggregate social welfare (if the production efficiency gain exceeds

---

[3]   The figure and our discussion ignores the possibility, suggested in Chapter 1, that the transfer could be dissipated through wasteful rent-seeking, and thus also represents an efficiency loss.

the allocative efficiency loss), and harm buyers through higher prices (by generating a transfer from buyers to sellers).

In principle, the latter possibility may present a difficult policy tradeoff. Commentators and courts debate whether a merger, likely to generate a small price increase, may be saved by large cost savings (or other efficiencies) when those savings are not passed through to consumers but instead accrue to the benefit of shareholders. They also debate whether a merger, likely to raise price in one market, may be saved by cost savings or other efficiencies benefitting consumers in other markets. We will return to these issues when efficiencies are considered later in this Chapter.

3. HISTORICAL PERSPECTIVES ON MERGER ENFORCEMENT

While mergers and acquisitions are routine in a dynamic economy, mergers sometimes come in waves. The U.S. is commonly thought to have experienced unusual clusters of mergers around 1900, during the late 1920s, during the late 1960s, during the 1980s, and during the late 1990s through 2000. Although these were all periods of economic expansion and strong stock market performance, merger waves seem largely unpredictable as they did not arise at other times when the economy grew and the stock market boomed.

The characteristics of merging firms have varied from one era to the next. Many of the "trusts" that give "antitrust" law its name—including the Standard Oil and American Tobacco trusts that were the subject of high profile monopolization cases in the early twentieth century—were formed through mergers among rivals. During the 1990s, certain sectors of the economy—defense, energy, financial services, health care, pharmaceuticals, and telecommunications—accounted for a substantial proportion of the mergers that occurred, particularly the largest transactions. These sectors were buffeted by outside forces such as deregulation, technological change, and the end of the Cold War—leading firms to alter their business strategies and, as a consequence, to reconfigure their assets.

In most recent years, between 1,000 and 2,000 mergers and acquisitions were reported to the federal enforcement agencies annually pursuant to the premerger notification requirements of the Hart-Scott-Rodino Antitrust Improvements Act, discussed in Sidebar 5–3. The number can vary substantially from year to year.

B. HORIZONTAL MERGERS: THE EMERGENCE AND EROSION OF THE STRUCTURAL PARADIGM

1. GUIDE TO THE CASES

Before the 1970s, the "oligopoly problem" loomed large in the thinking of courts and commentators concerned with the review of horizontal mergers under the antitrust laws. Coordination and supracompetitive pricing were commonly thought to be nearly inevitable when an industry had only a small number of firms, but frequently unreachable under Sherman Act § 1 because it could be accomplished through price leadership or other methods that might not constitute an "agreement." Economists schooled in the "structure-conduct-performance" paradigm emphasized the way market structure—primarily concentration of sellers, but also entry conditions, product differentiation, vertical integration, and other factors— affected firm conduct (the pricing, advertising, investment, product variety, research and development, and other behavior of firms) and market performance (firm profits, economic welfare, and other measures).

In this intellectual environment, antitrust law accepted a strong presumption of economic harm from high market concentration and identified competitive concerns at concentration levels that were low by today's standards. These views, combined with non-economic concerns to protect small business and avoid the adverse political consequences thought to arise from the aggregation of economic power, led Congress and the courts to look to merger law as a vehicle for preventing increased market concentration in its incipiency. These concerns are highlighted by the Supreme Court in *Brown Shoe's* discussion of the legislative history of the 1950 amendments to the Clayton Act. The Court's decision in *United States v. Philadelphia Nat'l Bank*, 374 U.S. 321 (1963), which we will read after *Brown Shoe*, codified them doctrinally by setting forth a legal presumption of anticompetitive effects from a horizontal merger that would increase market concentration.

The legislative concern to prevent the growth of harmful concentration in its incipiency changed the focus of the antitrust review of mergers away from an *ex post* review of their actual effects to an *ex ante* review of their likely future effects. Antitrust law's focus on future effects was heightened by the pre-merger notification requirements enacted in 1976 and is discussed below in Sidebar 5–3.

The modern era in merger analysis can be dated from the Justice Department's 1982 Merger Guidelines, which accepted the structural presumption from *Philadelphia Nat'l Bank* and other controlling Supreme Court precedent but also endorsed the idea from *United States v. General Dynamics Corp.*, 415 U.S. 486 (1974), that the presumption can be rebutted by also considering factors that might facilitate or frustrate the anticompetitive effects of mergers such as entry and efficiencies. These are factors that must be assessed in making a predictive determination about likely competitive effects. The new approach went beyond the existing cases, however, and also reflected new thinking about oligopoly among economists, influenced importantly by the Nobel Prize-winning Chicago economist George Stigler. Stigler and others no longer saw coordination as inevitable in an oligopoly, but instead sought to analyze whether the firms in the market could overcome the difficulties of reaching a consensus and deterring deviation (cheating) from it, as was discussed in Chapter 3.

Although the Merger Guidelines were conceived as a guide to the exercise of prosecutorial discretion, the conceptual framework they adopt has greatly influenced merger analysis in the courts. The courts of appeals thus took the lead in working through the implications of the new Chicago School economic perspective for horizontal merger law, under the framework set forth in the Merger Guidelines. In *United States v. Waste Management, Inc.*, 743 F.2d 976 (2d Cir. 1984), excerpted later in this Chapter, the Second Circuit allowed ease of entry to rebut the structural presumption of harm to competition derived from concentration statistics. In *FTC v. University Health*, 938 F.2d 1206 (11th Cir. 1991), the Eleventh Circuit suggested that efficiencies could do so as well.

The final two horizontal merger cases excerpted in this section are from the U.S. Court of Appeals for the D.C. Circuit. Both *United States v. Baker Hughes, Inc.*, 908 F.2d 981 (D.C. Cir. 1990) and *FTC v. H.J. Heinz Co.*, 246 F.3d 708 (D.C. Cir. 2001), reaffirmed that the structural presumption set forth in *Philadelphia Nat'l Bank* remains controlling precedent. While *Baker Hughes* emphasizes how that presumption can be rebutted, *Heinz* highlights its importance when market concentration is very high. As you read these decisions, ask yourself whether they are consistent, or whether they suggest different answers to one of the central doctrinal questions in horizontal merger analysis today: how far has the structural presumption eroded in the years since *Philadelphia Nat'l Bank*?

2. THE EMERGENCE OF THE STRUCTURAL PRESUMPTION

BROWN SHOE CO. V. UNITED STATES

Supreme Court of the United States, 1962.
370 U.S. 294, 82 S.Ct. 1502, 8 L.Ed.2d 510.

[This case involved the proposed merger of two firms in the shoe business: Brown Shoe Company, Inc. proposed to acquire the G.R. Kinney Company, Inc. Both companies were vertically integrated, participating in both shoe manufacturing and shoe retailing.

Brown was the fourth largest shoe manufacturer in the country, accounting for about 4% of total domestic production and 6% of wholesale shoes sold nationally. It was also the Nation's third largest shoe retailer, controlling 1,230 retail shoe outlets. Of these, 470 were company owned and operated, and the rest were mainly independently-owned stores operating under the Brown franchise program. Most retail shoe stores were independent of any manufacturer: the 1,230 retail shoe outlets controlled by Brown accounted for only 20% of the firm's approximately 6,000 retail customers.

Kinney was primarily in the retail business, though it also was the twelfth largest domestic shoe manufacturer with about a 0.5% share. Kinney was the country's eighth largest retailer with over 350 retail outlets, accounting for 1.2% of shoes sold (and 2% of children's shoes sold). Kinney-manufactured products accounted for about one fifth of the company's retail sales. Brown was the largest outside supplier of the shoes sold in Kinney's retail outlets, supplying nearly 8% of those products.

After the merger, the four leading shoe manufacturers in the U.S. would account for about 23% of domestic production, and the 24 leading manufacturers would produce about 35% of the Nation's shoes. The district court found a "definite trend" among shoe manufacturers to acquire retail outlets, and for vertically integrated firms to supply an ever-increasing percentage of the retail outlets' needs, thereby foreclosing other manufacturers from effectively competing for the retail accounts. In consequence, the available outlets for independent shoe producers were "drying up" and the number of firms manufacturing shoes was falling, from 1,077 in 1947 to 970 by 1954. Brown had a history of acquiring independent retail outlets, purchasing seven over the previous five years, and then changing their product mix to favor Brown shoes.

The district court enjoined the merger, and the Supreme Court affirmed. In analyzing the vertical aspects of the merger, the Court concluded that the "trend toward vertical integration in the shoe industry, when combined with Brown's avowed policy of forcing its own shoes upon its retail subsidiaries, may foreclose competition from a substantial share of the markets for men's, women's, and children's shoes, without producing any countervailing competitive, economic, or social advantages." Accordingly, it held that the shoe industry "is being subjected to * * * a cumulative series of vertical mergers which, if left unchecked, will be likely 'substantially to lessen competition.'" The excerpts below describe the Court's analysis of the legislative history of the Clayton Act, and its analysis of the horizontal aspects of the merger. Eds.]

MR. CHIEF JUSTICE WARREN delivered the opinion of the court.

* * *

III.

LEGISLATIVE HISTORY.

This case is one of the first to come before us in which the Government's complaint is based upon allegations that the appellant has violated § 7 of the Clayton Act, as that section was amended in 1950. * * *

The dominant theme pervading congressional consideration of the 1950 amendments was a fear of what was considered to be a rising tide of economic concentration in the American economy. Apprehension in this regard was bolstered by the publication in 1948 of the Federal Trade Commission's study on corporate mergers. Statistics from this and other current studies were cited as evidence of the danger to the American economy in unchecked corporate expansions through mergers. Other considerations cited in support of the bill were the desirability of retaining 'local control' over industry and the protection of small businesses. Throughout the recorded discussion may be found examples of Congress' fear not only of accelerated concentration of economic power on economic grounds, but also of the threat to other values a trend toward concentration was thought to pose. * * *

* * * [I]t is apparent that a keystone in the erection of a barrier to what Congress saw was the rising tide of economic concentration, was its provision of authority for arresting mergers at a time when the trend to a lessening of competition in a line of commerce was still in its incipiency. Congress saw the process of concentration in American business as a dynamic force; it sought to assure the Federal Trade Commission and the courts the power to brake this force at its outset and before it gathered momentum. * * *

* * * [A]t the same time that it sought to create an effective tool for preventing all mergers having demonstrable anti-competitive effects, Congress recognized the stimulation to competition that might flow from particular mergers. When concern as to the Act's breadth was expressed, supporters of the amendments indicated that it would not impede, for example, a merger between two small companies to enable the combination to compete more effectively with larger corporations dominating the relevant market, nor a merger between a corporation which is financially healthy and a failing one which no longer can be a vital competitive factor in the market. The deletion of the word 'community' in the original Act's description of the relevant geographic market is another illustration of Congress' desire to indicate that its concern was with the adverse effects of a given merger on competition only in an economically significant 'section' of the country. Taken as a whole, the legislative history illuminates congressional concern with the protection of competition, not competitors, and its desire to restrain mergers only to the extent that such combinations may tend to lessen competition. * * *

* * * Congress used the words 'may be substantially to lessen competition' (emphasis supplied), to indicate that its concern was with probabilities, not certainties. Statutes existed for dealing with clear-cut menaces to competition; no statute was sought for dealing with ephemeral possibilities. Mergers with a probable anticompetitive effect were to be proscribed by this Act. * * *

* * *

V.

THE HORIZONTAL ASPECTS OF THE MERGER.

* * *

* * * In an industry as fragmented as shoe retailing, the control of substantial shares of the trade in a city may have important effects on competition. If a merger achieving 5% control were now approved, we might be required to approve future merger efforts by Brown's competitors seeking similar market shares. The oligopoly Congress sought to avoid would then be furthered and it would be difficult to dissolve the combinations previously approved. Furthermore, in this fragmented industry, even if the combination controls but a small share of a particular market, the fact that this share is held by a large national chain can adversely affect competition. Testimony in the record from numerous independent retailers, based on their actual experience in the market, demonstrates that a strong, national chain of stores can insulate selected outlets from the vagaries of competition in particular locations and that the large chains can set and alter styles in footwear to an extent that renders the independents unable to maintain competitive inventories. A third significant aspect of this merger is that it creates a large national chain which is integrated with a manufacturing operation. The retail outlets of integrated companies, by eliminating wholesalers and by increasing the volume of purchases from the manufacturing division of the enterprise, can market their own brands at prices below those of competing independent retailers. Of course, some of the results of large integrated or chain operations are beneficial to consumers. Their expansion is not rendered unlawful by the mere fact that small independent stores may be adversely affected. It is competition, not competitors, which the Act protects. But we cannot fail to recognize Congress' desire to promote competition through the protection of viable, small, locally owned business. Congress appreciated that occasional higher costs and prices might result from the maintenance of fragmented industries and markets. It resolved these competing considerations in favor of decentralization. We must give effect to that decision.

Other factors to be considered in evaluating the probable effects of a merger in the relevant market lend additional support to the District

Court's conclusion that this merger may substantially lessen competition. One such factor is the history of tendency toward concentration in the industry. As we have previously pointed out, the shoe industry has, in recent years, been a prime example of such a trend. Most combinations have been between manufacturers and retailers, as each of the larger producers has sought to capture an increasing number of assured outlets for its wares. Although these mergers have been primarily vertical in their aim and effect, to the extent that they have brought ever greater numbers of retail outlets within fewer and fewer hands, they have had an additional important impact on the horizontal plane. By the merger in this case, the largest single group of retail stores still independent of one of the large manufacturers was absorbed into an already substantial aggregation of more or less controlled retail outlets. As a result of this merger, Brown moved into second place nationally in terms of retail stores directly owned. Including the stores on its franchise plan, the merger placed under Brown's control almost 1,600 shoe outlets, or about 7.2% of the Nation's retail 'shoe stores' as defined by the Census Bureau, and 2.3% of the Nation's total retail shoe outlets. We cannot avoid the mandate of Congress that tendencies toward concentration in industry are to be curbed in their incipiency, particularly when those tendencies are being accelerated through giant steps striding across a hundred cities at a time. In the light of the trends in this industry we agree with the Government and the court below that this is an appropriate place at which to call a halt.

* * *

Brown Shoe arguably sets forth inconsistent themes. On one hand, the Court notes congressional recognition of "the stimulation to competition that might flow from particular mergers," such as a merger of two small firms that would allow those sellers "to compete more effectively with larger corporations dominating the relevant market." When pursuing this theme, the Court emphasizes congressional concern with "the protection of competition, not competitors." On the other hand, the Supreme Court's focus on preventing a trend toward concentration in an industry could be understood as a mandate to protect competitors, particularly small businesses, against the possibility that they would be swallowed up in what has been termed the "market for corporate control," even at the price of an efficiency loss to the economy. The Court explains that "Congress appreciated that occasional higher costs and prices might result from the maintenance of fragmented industries and markets." In the past, some commentators have read the passages pursuing the latter theme as suggesting that mergers could harm competition by *lowering* costs. As we shall see, however, modern courts and commentators no longer view an "efficiency offense" as a viable basis for a claim under the antitrust laws.

Philadelphia Nat'l Bank, which was handed down one year after *Brown Shoe*, highlights the second theme in creating the structural presumption that has since framed horizontal merger analysis in the courts. *Philadelphia Nat'l Bank*'s approach to merger analysis was also consistent with influential commentary by Derek Bok published two years before *Brown Shoe*. Derek C. Bok, *Section 7 of the Clayton Act and the Merging of Law and Economics*, 74 HARV. L. REV. 226 (1960). Bok had emphasized the conflict between the desire to make an accurate economic analysis of probable competitive effect and the need to adopt simple and predictable rules to facilitate workable judicial administration. To resolve that conflict, he proposed a simple standard for merger review based upon market concentration.

UNITED STATES V. PHILADELPHIA NATIONAL BANK

Supreme Court of the United States, 1963.
374 U.S. 321, 83 S.Ct. 1715, 10 L.Ed.2d 915.

[The Philadelphia National Bank, the second largest commercial bank in the four-county Philadelphia metropolitan area, proposed to merge with the Girard Trust Corn Exchange Bank, the third largest commercial bank in the region. The United States challenged the transaction. After a district court decision in favor of the merging banks, the government appealed to the Supreme Court.

The Supreme Court analyzed this merger within a product market consisting of "the cluster of products (various kinds of credit) and services (such as checking accounts and trust administration) denoted by the term 'commercial banking'." The Court explained that the services in the cluster were insulated from effective competition, some because they were "so distinctive," others because of "cost advantages," and the rest because they enjoy a "settled consumer preference." The Court defined a geographic market consisting of the four-county Philadelphia metropolitan area, notwithstanding its observation that some banking services were "more local in nature than others." Eds.]

MR. JUSTICE BRENNAN delivered the opinion of the Court.

I.   THE FACTS AND PROCEEDINGS BELOW.

* * *

* * * Were the proposed merger to be consummated, the resulting bank would be the largest in the four-county area, with (approximately) 36% of the area banks' total assets, 36% of deposits, and 34% of net loans. It and the second largest (First Pennsylvania Bank and Trust Company, now the largest) would have between them 59% of the total assets, 58% of deposits, and 58% of the net loans, while after the merger the four largest banks in the area would have 78% of total assets, 77% of deposits, and 78% of net loans.

The present size of both PNB and Girard is in part the result of mergers. Indeed, the trend toward concentration is noticeable in the Philadelphia area generally, in which the number of commercial banks has declined from 108 in 1947 to the present 42. Since 1950, PNB has acquired nine formerly independent banks and Girard six * * *. During this period, the seven largest banks in the area increased their combined share of the area's total commercial bank resources from about 61% to about 90%.

* * *

The Government's case in the District Court relied chiefly on statistical evidence bearing upon market structure and on testimony by economists and bankers to the effect that, notwithstanding the intensive governmental regulation of banking, there was a substantial area for the free play of competitive forces; that concentration of commercial banking, which the proposed merger would increase, was inimical to that free play; that the principal anticompetitive effect of the merger would be felt in the area in which the banks had their offices, thus making the four-county metropolitan area the relevant geographical market; and that commercial banking was the relevant product market. The defendants, in addition to offering contrary evidence on these points, attempted to show business justifications for the merger. They conceded that both banks were economically strong and had sound management, but offered the testimony of bankers to show that the resulting bank, with its greater prestige and increased lending limit,[9] would be better able to compete with large out-of-state (particularly New York) banks, would attract new business to Philadelphia, and in general would promote the economic development of the metropolitan area.[10]

* * *

III. The Lawfulness of the Proposed Merger Under Section 7.

The statutory test is whether the effect of the merger 'may be substantially to lessen competition' 'in any line of commerce in any section of the country.' We analyzed the test in detail in *Brown Shoe Co. v. United*

---

[9] See 12 U.S.C. § 84 * * *. The resulting bank would have a lending limit of $15,000,000, of which $1,000,000 would not be attributable to the merger but to unrelated accounting factors.

[10] There was evidence that Philadelphia, although it ranks fourth or fifth among the Nation's urban areas in terms of general commercial activity, ranks only ninth in terms of the size of its largest bank, and that some large business firms which have their head offices in Philadelphia must seek elsewhere to satisfy their banking needs because of the inadequate lending limits of Philadelphia's banks; First Pennsylvania and PNB, currently the two largest banks in Philadelphia, each have a lending limit of $8,000,000. Girard's is $6,000,000. Appellees offered testimony that the merger would enable certain economies of scale, specifically, that it would enable the formation of a more elaborate foreign department than either bank is presently able to maintain. But this attempted justification, which was not mentioned by the District Court in its opinion and has not been developed with any fullness before this Court, we consider abandoned.

States, 370 U.S. 294, 82 S.Ct. 1502, 8 L.Ed.2d 510, and that analysis need not be repeated or extended here, for the instant case presents only a straightforward problem of application to particular facts.

* * *

Having determined the relevant market, we come to the ultimate question under § 7: whether the effect of the merger 'may be substantially to lessen competition' in the relevant market. Clearly, this is not the kind of question which is susceptible of a ready and precise answer in most cases. It requires not merely an appraisal of the immediate impact of the merger upon competition, but a prediction of its impact upon competitive conditions in the future; this is what is meant when it is said that the amended § 7 was intended to arrest anticompetitive tendencies in their 'incipiency.' Such a prediction is sound only if it is based upon a firm understanding of the structure of the relevant market; yet the relevant economic data are both complex and elusive. See generally Bok, Section 7 of the Clayton Act and the Merging of Law and Economics, 74 Harv.L.Rev. 226 (1960). And unless businessmen can assess the legal consequences of a merger with some confidence, sound business planning is retarded. So also, we must be alert to the danger of subverting congressional intent by permitting a too-broad economic investigation. And so in any case in which it is possible, without doing violence to the congressional objective embodied in § 7, to simplify the test of illegality, the courts ought to do so in the interest of sound and practical judicial administration. This is such a case.

We noted in *Brown Shoe Co.* that '[t]he dominant theme pervading congressional consideration of the 1950 amendments [to § 7] was a fear of what was considered to be a rising tide of economic concentration in the American economy.' This intense congressional concern with the trend toward concentration warrants dispensing, in certain cases, with elaborate proof of market structure, market behavior, or probable anticompetitive effects. Specifically, we think that a merger which produces a firm controlling an undue percentage share of the relevant market, and results in a significant increase in the concentration of firms in that market is so inherently likely to lessen competition substantially that it must be enjoined in the absence of evidence clearly showing that the merger is not likely to have such anticompetitive effects.

Such a test lightens the burden of proving illegality only with respect to mergers whose size makes them inherently suspect in light of Congress' design in § 7 to prevent undue concentration. Furthermore, the test is fully consonant with economic theory. That '[c]ompetition is likely to be greatest when there are many sellers, none of which has any significant market share,' is common ground among most economists, and was undoubtedly a premise of congressional reasoning about the antimerger statute.

The merger of appellees will result in a single bank's controlling at least 30% of the commercial banking business in the four-county Philadelphia metropolitan area. Without attempting to specify the smallest market share which would still be considered to threaten undue concentration, we are clear that 30% presents that threat. Further, whereas presently the two largest banks in the area (First Pennsylvania and PNB) control between them approximately 44% of the area's commercial banking business, the two largest after the merger (PNB-Girard and First Pennsylvania) will control 59%. Plainly, we think, this increase of more than 33% in concentration must be regarded as significant.[42]

* * *

There is nothing in the record of this case to rebut the inherently anticompetitive tendency manifested by these percentages. There was, to be sure, testimony by bank officers to the effect that competition among banks in Philadelphia was vigorous and would continue to be vigorous after the merger. We think, however, that the District Court's reliance on such evidence was misplaced. This lay evidence on so complex an economic-legal problem as the substantiality of the effect of this merger upon competition was entitled to little weight, in view of the witnesses' failure to give concrete reasons for their conclusions.[43]

Of equally little value, we think, are the assurances offered by appellees' witnesses that customers dissatisfied with the services of the resulting bank may readily turn to the 40 other banks in the Philadelphia area. In every case short of outright monopoly, the disgruntled customer has alternatives; even in tightly oligopolistic markets, there may be small firms operating. A fundamental purpose of amending § 7 was to arrest the trend toward concentration, the tendency to monopoly, before the consumer's alternatives disappeared through merger, and that purpose would be ill-served if the law stayed its hand until 10, or 20, or 30 more Philadelphia banks were absorbed. This is not a fanciful eventuality, in view of the strong trend toward mergers evident in the area; and we might

---

[42] It is no answer that, among the three presently largest firms (First Pennsylvania, PNB, and Girard), there will be no increase in concentration. If this argument were valid, then once a market had become unduly concentrated, further concentration would be legally privileged. On the contrary, if concentration is already great, the importance of preventing even slight increases in concentration and so preserving the possibility of eventual deconcentration is correspondingly great.

[43] The fact that some of the bank officers who testified represented small banks in competition with appellees does not substantially enhance the probative value of their testimony. * * * In an oligopolistic market, small companies may be perfectly content to follow the high prices set by the dominant firms, yet the market may be profoundly anticompetitive.

note also that entry of new competitors into the banking field is far from easy.[44]

* * *

We turn now to three affirmative justifications which appellees offer for the proposed merger. The first is that only through mergers can banks follow their customers to the suburbs and retain their business. This justification does not seem particularly related to the instant merger, but in any event it has no merit. There is an alternative to the merger route: the opening of new branches in the areas to which the customers have moved—so-called de novo branching. Appellees do not contend that they are unable to expand thus, by opening new offices rather than acquiring existing ones, and surely one premise of an antimerger statute such as § 7 is that corporate growth by internal expansion is socially preferable to growth by acquisition.

Second, it is suggested that the increased lending limit of the resulting bank will enable it to compete with the large out-of-state banks, particularly the New York banks, for very large loans. We reject this application of the concept of 'countervailing power.' If anticompetitive effects in one market could be justified by procompetitive consequences in another, the logical upshot would be that every firm in an industry could, without violating § 7, embark on a series of mergers that would make it in the end as large as the industry leader. For if all the commercial banks in the Philadelphia area merged into one, it would be smaller than the largest bank in New York City. This is not a case, plainly, where two small firms in a market propose to merge in order to be able to compete more successfully with the leading firms in that market. Nor is it a case in which lack of adequate banking facilities is causing hardships to individuals or businesses in the community. The present two largest banks in Philadelphia have lending limits of $8,000,000 each. The only business located in the Philadelphia area which find such limits inadequate are large enough readily to obtain bank credit in other cities.

This brings us to appellees' final contention, that Philadelphia needs a bank larger than it now has in order to bring business to the area and stimulate its economic development. We are clear, however, that a merger the effect of which 'may be substantially to lessen competition' is not saved because, on some ultimate reckoning of social or economic debits and credits, it may be deemed beneficial. A value choice of such magnitude is beyond the ordinary limits of judicial competence, and in any event has been made for us already, by Congress when it enacted the amended § 7. Congress determined to preserve our traditionally competitive economy. It

---

[44] Entry is, of course, wholly a matter of governmental grace. In the 10-year period ending in 1961, only one new bank opened in the Philadelphia four-county area. That was in 1951. At the end of 10 years, the new bank controlled only one-third of 1% of the area's deposits.

therefore proscribed anticompetitive mergers, the benign and the malignant alike, fully aware, we must assume, that some price might have to be paid.

* * *

NOTE ON VON'S GROCERY AND PABST BREWING

Two Supreme Court cases decided in 1966, three years after *Philadelphia Nat'l Bank*, represent the high water mark of judicial efforts to halt the rising tide of industrial concentration. In both *United States v. Von's Grocery Co.*, 384 U.S. 270, 86 S.Ct. 1478, 16 L.Ed.2d 555 (1966) and *United States v. Pabst Brewing Co.*, 384 U.S. 546, 86 S.Ct. 1665, 16 L.Ed.2d 765 (1966), the Court prohibited mergers among firms which, by present-day standards, had small market shares in largely unconcentrated markets.

Von's involved the acquisition of one grocery store chain serving Los Angeles, Shopping Bag Food Stores, by another, Von's Grocery Company. In 1958, the year before the merger, the largest chain in the metropolitan area had 8% of retail sales, Von's was third largest with 4.7%, and Shopping Bag was sixth with 4.2%. In 1960, the merging firms together accounted for only 7.5% of the total. But chain stores were growing rapidly and the number of single grocery stores in Los Angeles decreased from 5,365 in 1950 to 3,590 in 1963. In an opinion written by Justice Black, the Court majority observed:

> * * * While the grocery business was being concentrated into the hands of fewer and fewer owners, the small companies were continually being absorbed by the larger firms through mergers. * * * Moreover, * * * acquisitions and mergers in the Los Angeles retail grocery market have continued at a rapid rate since the merger. These facts alone are enough to cause us to conclude contrary to the District Court that the Von's-Shopping Bag merger did violate § 7. Accordingly, we reverse.

> The facts of this case present exactly the threatening trend toward concentration which Congress wanted to halt.

384 U.S. at 273–74, 277. Justice Stewart responded in dissent:

> I believe that even the most superficial analysis of the record makes plain the fallacy of the Court's syllogism that competition is necessarily reduced when the bare number of competitors has declined. In any meaningful sense, the structure of the Los Angeles grocery market remains unthreatened by concentration. Local competition is vigorous to a fault, not only among chain stores themselves but also between chain stores and single-store operators. * * * And, most important of all, the record simply cries out that the numerical decline in the number of single-store owners is the result of transcending social and technological changes that positively

preclude the inference that competition has suffered because of the attrition of competitors.

Section 7 was never intended by Congress for use by the Court as a charter to roll back the supermarket revolution. Yet the Court's opinion is hardly more than a requiem for the so-called 'Mom and Pop' grocery stores—the bakery and butcher shops, the vegetable and fish markets—that are now economically and technologically obsolete in many parts of the country.

In a single sentence and an omnibus footnote at the close of its opinion, the Court pronounces its work consistent with the line of our decisions under § 7 since the passage of the 1950 amendment. The sole consistency that I can find is that in litigation under § 7, the Government always wins.

384 U.S. at 287–88, 301 (Stewart, J. dissenting).

The *Pabst* case, decided during the same Court term, involved the merger of what was in 1958 the Nation's tenth largest brewer, Pabst, and its eighteenth largest brewer, Blatz. The Supreme Court reversed a district court judgment in favor of the merging firms, in an opinion also written by Justice Black:

> * * * [The] facts show a very marked thirty-year decline in the number of brewers and a sharp rise in recent years in the percentage share of the market controlled by the leading brewers. If not stopped, this decline in the number of separate competitors and this rise in the share of the market controlled by the larger beer manufacturers are bound to lead to greater and greater concentration of the beer industry into fewer and fewer hands. The merger of Pabst and Blatz brought together two very large brewers competing against each other in 40 States. In 1957 these two companies had combined sales which accounted for 23.95% of the beer sales in Wisconsin, 11.32% of the sales in the three-state area of Wisconsin, Illinois, and Michigan, and 4.49% of the sales throughout the country. In accord with our prior cases, we hold that the evidence as to the probable effect of the merger on competition in Wisconsin, in the three-state area, and in the entire country was sufficient to show a violation of § 7 in each and all of these three areas.

384 U.S. at 551–52.

Rapid consolidation was a key feature of the industries in which the structural presumption was developed: banking (*Philadelphia Nat'l Bank*), supermarkets (*Von's Grocery*), and beer (*Pabst*). But was that consolidation driven by a desire to create a monopoly, and tending to result in higher prices, as the Court predicted?

A trend toward consolidation could instead arise from firm efforts to reduce costs by obtaining greater economies of scale and scope (*see supra* Appendix to Chapter 1). Some firms may be able to achieve such cost savings more quickly through acquisition than through internal expansion. (Section C.4 of this Chapter discusses whether to credit this possibility as a defense.) Still another explanation for industry trends toward concentration has been suggested by economist John Sutton. Technological developments that lower the costs of transportation and communication lead some markets to grow in size. For example, as automobile ownership became widespread, food consumers were no longer limited to the corner grocery. Sometimes larger markets facilitate the entry of new sellers; under such circumstances, concentration may fall. But in other cases, firms in expanding markets may find it profitable to make substantial investments in advertising or research and development, for example by developing regional or national brand names or new and better products, in order to attract a larger share of the growing market demand. In such industries, Sutton finds, markets become more concentrated as they grow in size. Increasing industry output suggests that prices will decline (see the discussion of demand in Chapter 1), even though the number of firms is shrinking. Sutton finds this pattern in a wide range of industries, highlighting many examples from the food and drink sector. JOHN SUTTON, SUNK COSTS AND MARKET STRUCTURE: PRICE COMPETITION, ADVERTISING AND THE EVOLUTION OF CONCENTRATION (1991).

---

3.   THE EROSION OF THE STRUCTURAL PRESUMPTION

Our next principal case, *United States v. General Dynamics Corp.*, 415 U.S. 486 (1974), foreshadowed a change in direction for merger analysis toward taking factors beyond market concentration into account. After years of litigation under Clayton Act § 7 in which, as Justice Stewart wrote in dissent in *Von's Grocery*, "the Government always wins," the Supreme Court decided a merger case in favor of allowing the acquisition, with Justice Stewart writing the majority opinion. By a 5–4 vote, the Supreme Court in *General Dynamics* made clear that the presumption of anticompetitive effects derived from concentration is rebuttable.

UNITED STATES V. GENERAL DYNAMICS CORPORATION
Supreme Court of the United States, 1974.
415 U.S. 486, 94 S.Ct. 1186, 39 L.Ed.2d 530.

MR. JUSTICE STEWART delivered the opinion of the Court.

[In 1959, Materials Service Corp., which was later itself purchased by General Dynamics, acquired the United Electric Coal Co. Both firms produced and sold coal in the state of Illinois, and in the Eastern Interior Coal Province Sales Area, a coal distribution area recognized by the industry comprising Illinois, Indiana, and parts of six neighboring states. The government challenged the acquisition based on evidence showing that in both markets, the coal industry was concentrated among a small number of leading producers and that the trend had been toward increasing concentration. For example, the top four firms accounted for 43% of the Eastern Interior Coal Province market in 1957, and nearly 63% in 1967. Over the same ten year period, the share accounted for by the top four firms in Illinois rose from 55% to 75%. The Supreme Court noted that the statistics on the degree of concentration in the two coal markets, and the percentage increase in concentration, were roughly comparable to those found in *Von's Grocery*. Eds.]

II

* * *

In prior decisions involving horizontal mergers between competitors, this Court has found prima facie violations of § 7 of the Clayton Act from aggregate statistics of the sort relied on by the United States in this case. * * *

The effect of adopting this approach to a determination of a 'substantial' lessening of competition is to allow the Government to rest its case on a showing of even small increases of market share or market concentration in those industries or markets where concentration is already great or has been recently increasing, since 'if concentration is already great, the importance of preventing even slight increases in concentration and so preserving the possibility of eventual deconcentration is correspondingly great.' *United States v. Aluminum Co. of Am.*, 377 U.S. 271 (1964) (citing *United States v. Philadelphia Nat'l Bank*, 374 U.S. at 365 n.42).

While the statistical showing proffered by the Government in this case, the accuracy of which was not discredited by the District Court or contested by the appellees, would under this approach have sufficed to support a finding of 'undue concentration' in the absence of other considerations, the question before us is whether the District Court was justified in finding that other pertinent factors affecting the coal industry and the business of the appellees mandated a conclusion that no substantial lessening of competition occurred or was threatened by the acquisition of United Electric. We are satisfied that the court's ultimate finding was not in error.

In *Brown Shoe v. United States*, we cautioned that statistics concerning market share and concentration, while of great significance, were not conclusive indicators of anticompetitive effects * * *.

Much of the District Court's opinion was devoted to a description of the changes that have affected the coal industry since World War II. On the basis of more than three weeks of testimony and a voluminous record, the court discerned a number of clear and significant developments in the industry. First, it found that coal had become increasingly less able to compete with other sources of energy in many segments of the energy market. * * *

Second, the court found that to a growing extent since 1954, the electric utility industry has become the mainstay of coal consumption. * * *

Third, and most significantly, the court found that to an increasing degree, nearly all coal sold to utilities is transferred under long-term requirements contracts, under which coal producers promise to meet utilities' coal consumption requirements for a fixed period of time, and at predetermined prices. * * *

* * * In markets involving groceries or beer, as in *Von's Grocery*, and *Pabst*, statistics involving annual sales naturally indicate the power of each company to compete in the future. Evidence of the amount of annual sales is relevant as a prediction of future competitive strength, since in most markets distribution systems and brand recognition are such significant factors that one may reasonably suppose that a company which has attracted a given number of sales will retain that competitive strength.

In the coal market, as analyzed by the District Court, however, statistical evidence of coal production was of considerably less significance. The bulk of the coal produced is delivered under long-term requirements contracts, and such sales thus do not represent the exercise of competitive power but rather the obligation to fulfill previously negotiated contracts at a previously fixed price. The focus of competition in a given time frame is not on the disposition of coal already produced but on the procurement of new long-term supply contracts. In this situation, a company's past ability to produce is of limited significance, since it is in a position to offer for sale neither its past production nor the bulk of the coal it is presently capable of producing, which is typically already committed under a long-term supply contract. A more significant indicator of a company's power effectively to compete with other companies lies in the state of a company's uncommitted reserves of recoverable coal. A company with relatively large supplies of coal which are not already under contract to a consumer will have a more important influence upon competition in the contemporaneous negotiation of supply contracts than a firm with small reserves, even though the latter may presently produce a greater tonnage of coal. In a market where the availability and price of coal are set by long-term contracts rather than immediate or short-term purchases and sales, reserves rather than past production are the best measure of a company's ability to compete.

The testimony and exhibits in the District Court revealed that United Electric's coal reserve prospects were 'unpromising.' United's relative position of strength in reserves was considerably weaker than its past and current ability to produce. While United ranked fifth among Illinois coal producers in terms of annual production, it was 10th in reserve holdings, and controlled less than 1% of the reserves held by coal producers in Illinois, Indiana, and western Kentucky. Many of the reserves held by United had already been depleted at the time of trial, forcing the closing of some of United's midwest mines. Even more significantly, the District Court found that of the 52,033,304 tons of currently mineable reserves in Illinois, Indiana, and Kentucky controlled by United, only four million tons had not already been committed under long-term contracts. United was found to be facing the future with relatively depleted resources at its disposal, and with the vast majority of those resources already committed under contracts allowing no further adjustment in price. In addition, the District Court found that 'United Electric has neither the possibility of acquiring more (reserves) nor the ability to develop deep coal reserves,' and thus was not in a position to increase its reserves to replace those already depleted or committed.

Viewed in terms of present and future reserve prospects—and thus in terms of probable future ability to compete—rather than in terms of past production, the District Court held that United Electric was a far less significant factor in the coal market than the Government contended or the production statistics seemed to indicate. While the company had been and remained a 'highly profitable' and efficient producer of relatively large amounts of coal, its current and future power to compete for subsequent long-term contracts was severely limited by its scarce uncommitted resources. Irrespective of the company's size when viewed as a producer, its weakness as a competitor was properly analyzed by the District Court and fully substantiated that court's conclusion that its acquisition by Material Service would not 'substantially . . . lessen competition. . . . * * *

General Dynamics was decided in 1974, before Supreme Court decisions like *GTE Sylvania* (1977) (*see infra* Chapter 6) and *Broadcast Music* (1979) (*see supra* Chapter 2) that appeared to embrace the Chicago School perspective on the importance of efficiency considerations and before the 1982 Merger Guidelines. In part for this reason, it appears more like a modern merger decision in retrospect than it likely did at the time. Although the case made clear that the structural presumption was rebuttable, the successful rebuttal was arguably on narrow grounds: that concentration was measured incorrectly, using the wrong units in an unusual case in which market shares based upon production capacity (here, coal reserves) differed markedly from market shares computed in terms of past sales. These are, as Judge Posner has observed, "highly unusual facts." *Hospital Corp. of Am. v. Federal Trade Comm'n*, 807 F.2d 1381, 1385 (7th Cir. 1986) (Posner, J.). Accordingly, Posner continued, this decision could be understood as "carv[ing] only a limited exception[ ] to the broad holdings of some of the merger decisions of the 1960s." *Id.* As you read the appeals court decisions that follow, notice how they instead read *General Dynamics* more broadly, to permit a wide-ranging analysis of whether market shares accurately reflect the merging firms' ability to compete and provide a sufficient basis to predict anticompetitive effects.

NOTE ON THE STRUCTURAL PRESUMPTION AND THE 1982 MERGER GUIDELINES

The Justice Department's first merger guidelines were promulgated in 1968, before *General Dynamics*. Assistant Attorney General Donald Turner, who issued the 1968 Guidelines, chose to set enforcement standards at concentration levels less stringent than those *Pabst* and *Von's Grocery* might have permitted, though at levels that were still exceedingly strict by modern standards. In 1982, the U.S. Department of Justice, under the leadership of Assistant Attorney General William F. Baxter, issued merger guidelines that replaced Turner's guidelines. In doing so, and in many other ways, Baxter led the way in revising antitrust enforcement in light of Chicago School views, which the Supreme Court had just begun to incorporate into the case law. Because the Court had not issued a major merger decision since *General Dynamics* (and, since the 1982 Guidelines, still has not done so), Baxter had to devise a way to harmonize the old precedents, rooted in antitrust's structural era, with the approach of the Chicago School. The 1982 Guidelines accomplished this task by declaring that concentration was highly influential but not outcome-determinative in evaluating acquisitions among rivals. In taking this view, Baxter was undoubtedly aware that economists had questioned the inevitability of tacit collusion in concentrated markets, as we learned in Chapter 3, and that the empirical groundings of the structural presumption had also been challenged (*see* Sidebar 5–2).

In the decades since the 1982 Merger Guidelines were issued, they have been revised multiple times. (The current government Horizontal Merger Guidelines can be accessed at http://www.justice.gov/atr/public/guidelines/hmg–2010.html and are discussed in more detail in Section C of this Chapter.) But the problem they address—harmonizing the older structural era decisions with contemporary and still evolving economic thinking—remains central to horizontal merger analysis today. Although the Supreme Court has not revisited the question, several appeals courts have done so. The D.C. Circuit opinion that we shall read next, *United States v. Baker Hughes*, may be the most authoritative, as it was written by one future Supreme Court justice and joined by another (and the two are from opposite wings of many Court splits). Footnote 12 and the accompanying text expressly frame the *Baker Hughes* decision as harmonizing *General Dynamics* and *Philadelphia Nat'l Bank* with the newer economic thinking endorsed by the Supreme Court in other antitrust decisions. (We will discuss the *Baker Hughes* court's analysis of entry later in this Chapter.)

Sidebar 5–1:
The Sound of Silence: The Supreme Court
and Merger Policy Since 1975

Imagine that a lawyer born and trained outside of the United States was asked to write a paper summarizing the current state of federal merger law in the United States. How should the foreign observer describe U.S. merger doctrine and policy today? The answer would depend on where she looks.

The standard research methodology for tackling a question like this would follow the traditional hierarchy of authority in the U.S. legal system. The researcher would focus first upon statutes enacted by Congress and decisions of the Supreme Court interpreting those statutes. Like most of the U.S. antitrust laws, Section 7 of the Clayton Act is "open textured." Section 7's key operative terms—"may be substantially to lessen competition"—are not self-defining. This characteristic gives the judiciary considerable discretion to give specific substantive meaning to the statute and to determine the outcome of specific cases through interpretation of Section 7's relatively open-ended language. As seen thus far in Chapter 5, the trail of Supreme Court decisions interpreting the amended Section 7 begins with *Brown Shoe* in 1962 and effectively ends with *General Dynamics* in 1974 (formally ending one year later with *Citizens & Southern*).[a] It has been decades since the Court commented upon the anti-merger provision's substantive liability standard.

A research project confined to analyzing the Supreme Court's Section 7 horizontal merger jurisprudence from 1962 through 1975 would reveal a strict set of limits on combinations involving rival firms. To such a reader, the Court's rulings might be distilled into three core principles:

- The plaintiff in a Section 7 case can create a presumption of illegality by demonstrating a trend toward concentration, a significant increase in concentration, and that post-acquisition market shares have exceeded a specific level. *See Philadelphia National Bank*. The relevant threshold of concern may be as low as 4.49%. *See Pabst*.

---

[a]   Although the Supreme Court issued substantive antitrust merger decisions in three bank cases shortly after *General Dynamics*, in *United States v. Marine Bancorporation*, 418 U.S. 602 (1974), *United States v. Connecticut Nat'l Bank*, 418 U.S. 656 (1974), and *United States v. Citizens & Southern Nat'l Bank*, 422 U.S. 86 (1975), *General Dynamics* is generally treated as the last major Supreme Court interpretation of Clayton Act § 7.

- The presumption of illegality created by market share data is virtually conclusive. In unusual circumstances, however, the defendant can rebut the presumption of illegality by showing that the plaintiff has calculated market shares based upon a measure of commercial activity that fails to give an accurate picture of the merging parties' capability to compete for future sales. *See General Dynamics.*

- Courts should subordinate efficiency considerations in favor of attaining a more decentralized commercial environment. *See Brown Shoe.*

In offering this restatement, a counselor would have to caution that the more recent Supreme Court decisions, such as *General Dynamics* (1974) and *Marine Bancorporation* (1974), had shown a tendency to favor defendants after a long, previously unbroken string of government victories that started with *Brown Shoe* (1962).

A second exercise would ignore the Supreme Court's jurisprudence and instead focus solely on the merger decisions of the lower courts and on government merger policy, especially as articulated in the federal merger guidelines. As you will see in decisions such as *Baker Hughes*, *infra*, the lower courts have not adhered closely to the letter or spirit of the Supreme Court's merger jurisprudence. Lower court decisions since 1975 hardly have blessed all horizontal mergers, but they (a) have raised the market share thresholds for presuming illegality, and (b) have shown that the nominal opportunity, suggested in *Philadelphia Nat'l Bank*, for defendants to rebut the presumption can be exercised successfully. In addition, discussions of the political and social values of preferring economic decentralization at the possible cost of economic efficiency have vanished from the district court and court of appeals decisions.

In taking these steps, our researcher might observe, the courts often have relied on the framework presented in the federal merger guidelines issued in 1982 and modified in 1984, 1992, 1997, and 2010. The federal guidelines use the structural presumption of *Philadelphia Nat'l Bank*, but with several vital qualifications. The federal guidelines emphasize that the examination of market shares is far from the only inquiry. The guidelines underscore the need to assess other variables that shed light on whether the merging parties, acting alone or in coordination with rivals, could raise prices. The federal guidelines also set the threshold of concern well above the 4.49% that the Supreme Court found sufficient in *Pabst*.

In applying their guidelines since 1982, the DOJ and the FTC have tended to sue only when a merger reduces the number of significant companies in the market to fewer than four. The cases we study later in this Chapter—matters such as *Staples* and *Heinz* (both three-to-two mergers)—suggest where the federal agencies, in effect, have drawn the line when they go to court. This is a great distance from *Brown Shoe* where, as we saw earlier in this Chapter, the Justice Department challenged a merger that would have yielded a combined market share of 5%.

Should our hypothetical researcher conclude that merger decisions of the lower federal courts and the enforcement policies of the federal antitrust agencies constitute civil disobedience that ignores the commands of Supreme Court Section 7 decisions? Two considerations suggest not. The first is that Congress has not amended Section 7 to forestall the drift away from the tenets of the Court's merger cases. Congressional committees responsible for antitrust issues pay close attention to merger policy. Congress could have embedded the precepts of 1960s Supreme Court merger analysis in the Clayton Act if it disapproved of the move by lower courts and enforcement bodies since 1975 to accept more permissive approaches. That Congress has not acted to arrest this development may suggest its general acceptance of modern trends in interpreting and applying Section 7.

A second reason comes from reading Supreme Court antitrust decisions in non-merger matters since 1975. As a whole, these decisions provide grounds for inferring that the Court approves of the evolution of lower court merger jurisprudence and agency enforcement practice. *Broadcast Music*, *Matsushita*, and other Court decisions since 1975 have consistently expressed the view that antitrust analysis should consider efficiencies along with market power, making it difficult to imagine today's Court endorsing the views it expressed in *Brown Shoe*, *Von's Grocery*, and *Pabst*. When U.S. antitrust lawyers tell their clients to attempt mergers at thresholds well above levels condemned in *Von's Grocery* and *Pabst*, the Court's non-merger cases support the common prediction that "the Court would decide those cases differently today."

The prediction is almost certainly correct. After all, two members of the unanimous *Baker Hughes* court of appeals panel—Ruth Bader Ginsburg and Clarence Thomas—now sit on the Supreme Court. No member of today's Court participated in any of the tribunal's previous merger decisions, and all have seemingly acquiesced, with varied degrees of enthusiasm, in the efficiency-oriented perspective that governs the Court's non-merger decisions. Still, the Court has never directly repudiated the teaching of its merger decisions. A researcher familiar with the hierarchy of authority in the U.S. legal system could be forgiven for being perplexed that the foundations of modern U.S. merger policy rest upon the assumption, without the benefit of the Court's own direct guidance, that the Court no longer means what it once said.

UNITED STATES V. BAKER HUGHES, INC.

United States Court of Appeals for the District of Columbia Circuit, 1990.
908 F.2d 981.

Before RUTH B. GINSBURG, SENTELLE, and THOMAS, CIRCUIT JUDGES.

CLARENCE THOMAS, CIRCUIT JUDGE.

Appellee Oy Tampella AB, a Finnish corporation, through its subsidiary Tamrock AG, manufactures and sells hardrock hydraulic underground drilling rigs (HHUDRs) in the United States and throughout the world. Appellee Baker Hughes Inc., a corporation based in Houston, Texas, owned a French subsidiary, Eimco Secoma, S.A. (Secoma), that was similarly involved in the HHUDR industry. In 1989, Tamrock proposed to acquire Secoma.

The United States challenged the proposed acquisition, charging that it would substantially lessen competition in the United States HHUDR market in violation of section 7 of the Clayton Act, 15 U.S.C. § 18. * * *

The basic outline of a section 7 horizontal acquisition case is familiar. By showing that a transaction will lead to undue concentration in the market for a particular product in a particular geographic area,[2] the government establishes a presumption that the transaction will substantially lessen competition. The burden of producing evidence to rebut this presumption then shifts to the defendant. If the defendant successfully rebuts the presumption, the burden of producing additional evidence of anticompetitive effect shifts to the government, and merges with the ultimate burden of persuasion, which remains with the government at all times.

---

[2] The parties in this case do not seriously contest the district court's definition of the relevant markets. The court defined the geographic market as the entire United States, and the relevant product as three types of HHUDRs: face drills ("jumbos"), long-hole drills, and roof-bolting drills, as well as associated spare parts, components, and accessories, and used drills. * * *

By presenting statistics showing that combining the market shares of Tamrock and Secoma would significantly increase concentration in the already highly concentrated United States HHUDR market, the government established a prima facie case of anticompetitive effect.[3] The district court, however, found sufficient evidence that the merger would not substantially lessen competition to conclude that the defendants had rebutted this prima facie case. The government did not produce any additional evidence showing a probability of substantially lessened competition, and thus failed to carry its ultimate burden of persuasion.

In this appeal, * * * [t]he government's key contention is that the district court * * * failed to apply a sufficiently stringent standard. The government argues that, as a matter of law, section 7 defendants can rebut a prima facie case *only by a clear showing that entry into the market by competitors would be quick and effective.* Because the district court failed to apply this standard, the government submits, the court erred in concluding that the proposed acquisition would not substantially lessen future competition in the United States HHUDR market.

We find no merit in the legal standard propounded by the government. It is devoid of support in the statute, in the case law, and in the government's own Merger Guidelines. Moreover, it is flawed on its merits in three fundamental respects. First, it assumes that ease of entry by competitors is the only consideration relevant to a section 7 defendant's rebuttal. Second, it requires that a defendant who seeks to show ease of entry bear the onerous burden of proving that entry will be "quick and effective." Finally, by stating that the defendant can rebut a prima facie case only by a clear showing, the standard in effect shifts the government's ultimate burden of persuasion to the defendant. Although the district court in this case did not expressly set forth a legal standard when it evaluated the defendants' rebuttal, we have carefully reviewed the court's thorough analysis of competitive conditions in the United States HHUDR market, and we are satisfied that the court effectively applied a standard faithful to section 7. Concluding that the court applied this legal standard to factual findings that are not clearly erroneous, we affirm the court's denial of a permanent injunction and its dismissal of the government's section 7 claim.

I.

It is a foundation of section 7 doctrine, disputed by no authority cited by the government, that evidence on a variety of factors can rebut a prima facie case. These factors include, but are not limited to, the absence of significant entry barriers in the relevant market. In this appeal, however,

---

[3] From 1986 through 1988, Tamrock had an average 40.8% share of the United States HHUDR market, while Secoma's share averaged 17.5%. In 1988 alone, the two firms enjoyed a combined share of 76% of the market. * * * The acquisition thus has brought about a dramatic increase in the Herfindahl-Hirschman Index (HHI)—a yardstick of concentration—for this market. * * * This acquisition has increased the HHI in this market from 2878 to 4303.

the government inexplicably imbues the entry factor with talismanic significance. If, to successfully rebut a prima facie case, a defendant *must* show that entry by competitors will be quick and effective, then other factors bearing on future competitiveness are all but irrelevant. The district court in this case considered at least two factors in addition to entry: the misleading nature of the statistics underlying the government's prima facie case and the sophistication of HHUDR consumers. These non-entry factors provide compelling support for the court's holding that Tamrock's acquisition of Secoma was not likely to lessen competition substantially. We have concluded that the court's consideration of these factors was crucial, and that the government's fixation on ease of entry is misplaced.

Section 7 involves *probabilities*, not certainties or possibilities.[5] The Supreme Court has adopted a totality-of-the-circumstances approach to the statute, weighing a variety of factors to determine the effects of particular transactions on competition. That the government can establish a prima facie case through evidence on only one factor, market concentration, does not negate the breadth of this analysis. Evidence of market concentration simply provides a convenient starting point for a broader inquiry into future competitiveness; the Supreme Court has never indicated that a defendant seeking to rebut a prima facie case is restricted to producing evidence of ease of entry. Indeed, in numerous cases, defendants have relied entirely on non-entry factors in successfully rebutting a prima facie case.

* * *

Indeed, that a variety of factors other than ease of entry can rebut a prima facie case has become hornbook law. * * *

It is not surprising, then, that the Department of Justice's own Merger Guidelines contain a detailed discussion of non-entry factors that can overcome a presumption of illegality established by market share statistics. According to the Guidelines, these factors include changing market conditions (§ 3.21), the financial condition of firms in the relevant market (§ 3.22), special factors affecting foreign firms (§ 3.23), the nature of the product and the terms of sale (§ 3.41), information about specific transactions and buyer market characteristics (§ 3.42), the conduct of firms in the market (§ 3.44), market performance (§ 3.45), and efficiencies (§ 3.5).[4]

---

[5] See *Brown Shoe Co. v. United States* ("Congress used the words '*may* be substantially to lessen competition' (emphasis supplied), to indicate that its concern was with probabilities, not certainties. Statutes existed for dealing with clear-cut menaces to competition; no statute was sought for dealing with ephemeral possibilities. Mergers with a *probable* anticompetitive effect were to be proscribed by this Act.") (footnote omitted) (emphasis added).

[4] [The court's references here are to the 1984 version of the Merger Guidelines. Eds.]

Given this acknowledged multiplicity of relevant factors, we are at a loss to understand on what basis the government has decided that "[t]o rebut the government's prima facie case, the defendants were *required* to show that *entry* would be both quick and effective in preventing supracompetitive prices." Brief for Appellants at 11–12 (emphasis added).
* * *

The district court's analysis of this case is fully consonant with precedent and logic. The court reviewed the evidence proffered by the defendants as part of its overall assessment of future competitiveness in the United States HHUDR market. As noted above, the court gave particular weight to two non-entry factors: the flawed underpinnings of the government's prima facie case and the sophistication of HHUDR consumers. The court's consideration of these factors was not only appropriate, but imperative, because in this case these factors significantly affected the probability that the acquisition would have anticompetitive effects.

With respect to the first factor, the statistical basis of the prima facie case, the court accepted the defendants' argument that the government's statistics were misleading. Because the United States HHUDR market is minuscule, market share statistics are "volatile and shifting," and easily skewed. In 1986, for instance, only 22 HHUDRs were sold in the United States. In 1987, the number rose to 43, and in 1988 it fell to 38. Every HHUDR sold during this period, thus, increased the seller's market share by two to five percent. A contract to provide multiple HHUDRs could catapult a firm from last to first place. * * * High concentration has long been the norm in this market. For example, only four firms sold HHUDRs in the United States between 1986 and 1989. Nor is concentration surprising where, as here, a product is esoteric and its market small. Indeed, the trial judge found that "[c]oncentration has existed for some time [in the United States HHUDR market] but there is no proof of overpricing, excessive profit or any decline in quality, service or diminishing innovation."

The second non-entry factor that the district court considered was the sophistication of HHUDR consumers. HHUDRs currently cost hundreds of thousands of dollars, and orders can exceed $1 million. These products are hardly trinkets sold to small consumers who may possess imperfect information and limited bargaining power. HHUDR buyers closely examine available options and typically insist on receiving multiple, confidential bids for each order. This sophistication, the court found, was likely to promote competition even in a highly concentrated market.

* * * These findings provide considerable support for the district court's conclusion that the defendants successfully rebutted the government's prima facie case. Because the defendants also provided compelling evidence on ease of entry into this market, we need not decide whether these findings, without more, are sufficient to rebut the government's prima facie case. The foregoing analysis of non-entry factors is intended merely to underscore that, contrary to the government's assumption, these factors are relevant, and can even be dispositive, in a section 7 rebuttal analysis.

II.

The existence and significance of barriers to entry are frequently * * * crucial considerations in a rebuttal analysis. In the absence of significant barriers, a company probably cannot maintain supracompetitive pricing for any length of time. The district court in this case reviewed the prospects for future entry into the United States HHUDR market and concluded that, overall, entry was likely, particularly if Tamrock's acquisition of Secoma were to lead to supracompetitive pricing. The government attacks this conclusion, asserting that, as a matter of law, the court should have required the defendants to show clearly that entry would be "quick and effective." We reject this novel and unduly onerous standard. The district court's factual findings amply support its determination that future entry into the United States HHUDR market is likely. This determination, in turn, supports the court's conclusion that the defendants successfully rebutted the government's prima facie case.

As authority for its "quick and effective" entry test, the government relies primarily on *United States v. Waste Management, Inc.*, 743 F.2d 976, 981–84 (2d Cir. 1984). This reliance is misplaced. Neither *Waste Management* nor any other case purports to establish a categorical "quick and effective" entry requirement. The Second Circuit in *Waste Management* simply noted that the defendant had successfully rebutted the government's prima facie case by showing that entry into the Dallas/Fort Worth trash collection market was "easy." That a defendant *may* successfully rebut a prima facie case by showing quick and effective entry does not mean that successful rebuttal *requires* such a showing. We are at a loss to understand how the government derived from *Waste Management* (where, lest the irony be missed, the government lost) the proposition that "a defendant arguing supposed ease of entry can rebut the government's prima facie case *only* by clearly showing that entry will be both quick and effective at preventing supracompetitive pricing."

That the "quick and effective" standard lacks support in precedent is not surprising, for it would require of defendants a degree of clairvoyance alien to section 7, which, as noted above, deals with probabilities, not certainties. Although the government disclaims any attempt to impose upon defendants the burden of proving that entry actually will occur, we believe that an inflexible "quick and effective" entry requirement would tend to impose precisely such a burden. A defendant cannot realistically be expected to prove that new competitors will "quickly" or "effectively" enter unless it produces evidence regarding specific competitors and their plans. Such evidence is rarely available; potential competitors have a strong interest in downplaying the likelihood that they will enter a given market. When the government sarcastically "wonders how slow and ineffective entry rebuts a prima facie case," it misses a crucial point. If the totality of a defendant's evidence suggests that entry will be slow and ineffective, then the district court is unlikely to find the prima facie case rebutted. This is a far cry, however, from insisting that the defendant must invariably show that new competitors will enter quickly and effectively.

Furthermore, the supposed "quick and effective" entry requirement overlooks the point that a firm that *never* enters a given market can nevertheless exert competitive pressure on that market. If barriers to entry are insignificant, the *threat* of entry can stimulate competition in a concentrated market, regardless of whether entry ever occurs. If a firm that *never* enters a market can keep that market competitive, a defendant seeking to rebut a prima facie case certainly need not show that any firm *will* enter the relevant market.

* * *

Having rejected the "quick and effective" entry standard itself, we turn briefly to the government's more general argument that the district court's findings regarding ease of entry failed to support its conclusion that the defendants had rebutted the prima facie case. The district court in this case discussed a number of considerations that led it to conclude that entry barriers to the United States HHUDR market were not high enough to impede future entry should Tamrock's acquisition of Secoma lead to supracompetitive pricing. First, the court noted that at least two companies, Cannon and Ingersoll-Rand, had entered the United States HHUDR market in 1989, and were poised for future expansion. Second, the court stressed that a number of firms competing in Canada and other countries had not penetrated the United States market, but could be expected to do so if Tamrock's acquisition of Secoma led to higher prices.[9] Because the market is small, "[i]t is inexpensive to develop a separate sales and service network in the United States." Third, these firms would exert competitive pressure on the United States HHUDR market even if they never actually entered the market. Finally, the court noted that there had been tremendous turnover in the United States HHUDR market in the 1980s. Secoma, for example, did not sell a single HHUDR in the United States in 1983 or 1984, but then lowered its price and improved its service,

---

[9] Some of these firms have already tried, but failed, to penetrate the United States HHUDR market. As the district court correctly noted, however, failed entry in the past does not necessarily imply failed entry in the future: if prices reach supracompetitive levels, a company that has failed to enter in the past could become competitive.

becoming market leader by 1989. Secoma's growth suggests that competitors not only can, but probably will, enter or expand if this acquisition leads to higher prices. The district court, to be sure, also found some facts suggesting difficulty of entry,[10] but these findings do not negate its ultimate finding to the contrary.

In sum, we see no error—legal or factual—in the district court's determination that entry into the United States HHUDR market would likely avert anticompetitive effects from Tamrock's acquisition of Secoma. The court's determination on entry, considered along with the findings discussed in section I of this opinion, suffices to rebut the government's prima facie case.

III.

Finally, we consider the strength of the showing that a section 7 defendant must make to rebut a prima facie case. The district court simply reviewed the evidence that the defendants presented and concluded that the acquisition was not likely to substantially lessen competition. The government argues that the court erred by failing to require the defendants to make a "clear" showing. The relevant precedents, however, suggest that this formulation overstates the defendants' burden. We conclude that a "clear" showing is unnecessary, and we are satisfied that the district court required the defendants to produce sufficient evidence.

The government's "clear showing" language is by no means unsupported in the case law. In the mid-1960s, the Supreme Court construed section 7 to prohibit virtually any horizontal merger or acquisition. At the time, the Court envisioned an ideal market as one composed of many small competitors, each enjoying only a small market share; the more closely a given market approximated this ideal, the more competitive it was presumed to be.

This perspective animated a series of decisions in which the Court stated that a section 7 defendant's market share measures its market power, that statistics alone establish a prima facie case, and that a defendant carries a heavy burden in seeking to rebut the presumption established by such a prima facie case. The Court most clearly articulated this approach in *Philadelphia Bank* * * *.

In *United States v. Von's Grocery Co.*, the Court further emphasized the weight of a defendant's burden. * * *

---

[10] The court, for instance, noted that HHUDRs are custom-made, and thus are not readily interchangeable or replaceable. Buyers, therefore, tend to return to sellers from whom they have purchased in the past. The court also found that HHUDR customers typically place great importance on assurances of product quality and reliable future service—considerations that may handicap new entrants. It also noted the significant economies of scale involved in manufacturing HHUDRs.

Although the Supreme Court has not overruled these section 7 precedents, it has cut them back sharply. In *General Dynamics*, the Court affirmed a district court determination that, by presenting evidence that undermined the government's statistics, section 7 defendants had successfully rebutted a prima facie case. In so holding, the Court did not expressly reaffirm or disavow *Philadelphia Bank*'s statement that a company must "clearly" show that a transaction is not likely to have substantial anticompetitive effects. The Court simply held that the district court was justified, based on all the evidence, in finding that "no substantial lessening of competition occurred or was threatened by the acquisition."

General Dynamics began a line of decisions differing markedly in emphasis from the Court's antitrust cases of the 1960s. Instead of accepting a firm's market share as virtually conclusive proof of its market power, the Court carefully analyzed defendants' rebuttal evidence.[12] These cases discarded *Philadelphia Bank*'s insistence that a defendant "clearly" disprove anticompetitive effect, and instead described the rebuttal burden simply in terms of a "showing." Without overruling *Philadelphia Bank*, then, the Supreme Court has at the very least lightened the evidentiary burden on a section 7 defendant.

In the aftermath of *General Dynamics* and its progeny, a defendant seeking to rebut a presumption of anticompetitive effect must show that the prima facie case inaccurately predicts the relevant transaction's probable effect on future competition. The more compelling the prima facie case, the more evidence the defendant must present to rebut it successfully. A defendant can make the required showing by affirmatively showing why a given transaction is unlikely to substantially lessen competition, or by discrediting the data underlying the initial presumption in the government's favor.

By focusing on the future, section 7 gives a court the uncertain task of assessing probabilities. In this setting, allocation of the burdens of proof assumes particular importance. By shifting the burden of producing evidence, present law allows both sides to make competing predictions about a transaction's effects. If the burden of production imposed on a defendant is unduly onerous, the distinction between that burden and the

---

[12] Judge Posner has elucidated this point:

The most important developments that cast doubt on the continued vitality of such cases as *Brown Shoe* and *Von's* are found in other cases, where the Supreme Court, echoed by the lower courts, has said repeatedly that the economic concept of competition, rather than any desire to preserve rivals as such, is the lodestar that shall guide the contemporary application of the antitrust laws, not excluding the Clayton Act. . . . Applied to cases brought under Section 7, this principle requires the district court . . . to make a judgment whether the challenged acquisition is likely to hurt consumers, as by making it easier for the firms in the market to collude, expressly or tacitly, and thereby force price above or farther above the competitive level.

Hospital Corp. of Am. v. FTC, 807 F.2d 1381, 1386 (7th Cir. 1986), cert. denied, 481 U.S. 1038 (1987).

ultimate burden of persuasion—always an elusive distinction in practice—disintegrates completely. A defendant required to produce evidence "clearly" disproving future anticompetitive effects must essentially persuade the trier of fact on the ultimate issue in the case—whether a transaction is likely to lessen competition substantially. Absent express instructions to the contrary, we are loath to depart from settled principles and impose such a heavy burden.

Imposing a heavy burden of production on a defendant would be particularly anomalous where, as here, it is easy to establish a prima facie case. The government, after all, can carry its initial burden of production simply by presenting market concentration statistics. To allow the government virtually to rest its case at that point, leaving the defendant to prove the core of the dispute, would grossly inflate the role of statistics in actions brought under section 7. The Herfindahl-Hirschman Index cannot guarantee litigation victories.[13] Requiring a "clear showing" in this setting would move far toward forcing a defendant to rebut a probability with a certainty.

* * *

The appellees in this case presented the district court with considerable evidence regarding the United States HHUDR market. The court credited the evidence concerning the sophistication of HHUDR consumers and the insignificance of entry barriers, as well as the argument that the statistics underlying the government's prima facie case were misleading. This evidence amply justified the court's conclusion that the prima facie case inaccurately depicted the probable anticompetitive effect of Tamrock's acquisition of Secoma. Because the government did not produce sufficient evidence to overcome this successful rebuttal, the district court concluded that "it is not likely that the acquisition will substantially lessen competition in the United States either immediately or long-term." 731 F. Supp. at 12. The government has given us no reason to reverse that conclusion.

For the foregoing reasons, the judgment of the district court is

Affirmed.

---

[13] We refer the government to its own Merger Guidelines, which recognize that "[i]n a variety of situations, market share and market concentration data may either understate or overstate the likely future competitive significance of a firm or firms in the market." Although the Guidelines disclaim "slavish[ ] adhere[nce]" to such data, we fear that the Department of Justice has ignored its own admonition. The government does not maximize scarce resources when it allows statistics alone to trigger its ponderous enforcement machinery.

NOTE ON BUYER POWER

The appeals court in *Baker Hughes* cited "the sophistication of HHUDR consumers" as a non-entry factor tending to rebut the government's *prima facie* case and observed that the government's Merger Guidelines in force at the time recognize "information about specific transactions and buyer market characteristics" as among the "non-entry factors that can overcome a presumption of illegality established by market share statistics." The government's current Merger Guidelines similarly recognize that powerful buyers "are often able to negotiate favorable terms with their suppliers," both because it may be less costly for sellers to serve large buyers and because large buyers may have the bargaining leverage to induce "price discrimination in their favor." *Horizontal Merger Guidelines* § 8 (2010). How could powerful, large, or sophisticated buyers make anticompetitive effects from merger unlikely? There are at least two possible scenarios.

First, recall from Chapter 3 that when buyers are large and sales are "lumpy," coordination may be frustrated. A firm considering cheating in such an industry may realize that it can easily take a large chunk of business and do so free from the threat of rapid punishment. This opportunity may encourage firms to cheat, and its threat may discourage cartel formation in the first instance. Second, a large buyer may be able to take advantage of its scale of purchases to integrate vertically into the upstream industry, creating new upstream rivalry that undermines the post-merger exercise of market power. Similarly, a large buyer may be able to help a small upstream seller become a substantial, low cost rival to the merged firm. Here the role of the large buyer is to facilitate entry or expansion upstream, creating additional rivalry for the merged firm. The first of these scenarios could arise when the competitive concern is with post-merger coordination; in the second scenario, the response of large buyers could potentially address a wider range of competitive concerns. When the court in *Baker Hughes* discusses the role of sophisticated buyers, does it have either of these possibilities in mind?

The antitrust agencies have expressed caution about crediting the argument that the presence of powerful buyers would rebut a concern about the competitive consequences of an acquisition. Even if large buyers were able to negotiate favorable terms before their suppliers merged, the merger may lessen that ability by making it impossible for buyers of any size to play off the merger partners against each other. *See Horizontal Merger Guidelines* § 8 (2010) ("Normally, a merger that eliminates a supplier whose presence contributed significantly to a buyer's negotiating leverage will harm that buyer."). The agencies also raise the possibility that the large buyer would exploit its ability to negotiate favorable terms with suppliers simply to protect itself, but not also to prevent harm to other buyers. *Id.* ("[E]ven if some powerful buyers could protect themselves, the Agencies also consider whether market power can be exercised against other buyers."). Did the court in *Baker Hughes* adequately address these caveats?

Eleven years after *Baker Hughes*, the D.C. Circuit revisited the structure of horizontal merger analysis in *Heinz*.[5] In reading this decision, consider the extent to which the court's approach to merger analysis is consistent with that of *Baker Hughes*.

FEDERAL TRADE COMMISSION V. H.J. HEINZ CO.

United States Court of Appeals for the District of Columbia Circuit, 2001.
246 F.3d 708.

Before: HENDERSON, RANDOLPH and GARLAND, CIRCUIT JUDGES.

KAREN LeCRAFT HENDERSON, CIRCUIT JUDGE.

On February 28, 2000 H.J. Heinz Company (Heinz) and Milnot Holding Corporation (Beech-Nut) entered into a merger agreement. The Federal Trade Commission (Commission or FTC) sought a preliminary injunction pursuant to section 13(b) of the Federal Trade Commission Act (FTCA), to enjoin the consummation of the merger. The injunction was sought in aid of an FTC administrative proceeding which was subsequently instituted by complaint to challenge the merger as violative of, *inter alia*, section 7 of the Clayton Act. The district court denied the preliminary injunction and the FTC appealed to this court. For the reasons set forth below, we reverse the district court and remand for entry of a preliminary injunction against Heinz and Beech-Nut.

I. BACKGROUND

* * * The baby food market is dominated by three firms, Gerber Products Company (Gerber), Heinz and Beech-Nut. Gerber, the industry leader, enjoys a 65 per cent market share while Heinz and Beech-Nut come in second and third, with a 17.4 per cent and a 15.4 per cent share respectively. The district court found that Gerber enjoys unparalleled brand recognition with a brand loyalty greater than any other product sold in the United States. Gerber's products are found in over 90 per cent of all American supermarkets.

By contrast, Heinz is sold in approximately 40 per cent of all supermarkets. Its sales are nationwide but concentrated in northern New England, the Southeast and Deep South and the Midwest. * * * Heinz lacks Gerber's brand recognition; it markets itself as a "value brand" with a shelf price several cents below Gerber's.

Beech-Nut has a market share (15.4%) comparable to that of Heinz (17.4%) * * * Beech-Nut maintains price parity with Gerber, selling at about one penny less. It markets its product as a premium brand. Consumers generally view its product as comparable in quality to Gerber's.

---

[5] Two of the authors of this Casebook, Jonathan B. Baker and William E. Kovacic, were involved in the *Heinz* litigation, both on the side of the merging firms.

Beech-Nut is carried in approximately 45 per cent of all grocery stores. Although its sales are nationwide, they are concentrated in New York, New Jersey, California and Florida.[3]

* * *

II. ANALYSIS

* * *

'Whenever the Commission has reason to believe that a corporation is violating, or is about to violate, Section 7 of the Clayton Act, the FTC may seek a preliminary injunction to prevent a merger pending the Commission's administrative adjudication of the merger's legality.' Section 13(b) provides for the grant of a preliminary injunction where such action would be in the public interest—as determined by a weighing of the equities and a consideration of the Commission's likelihood of success on the merits. * * *

To determine likelihood of success on the merits we measure the probability that, after an administrative hearing on the merits, the Commission will succeed in proving that the effect of the Heinz/Beech-Nut merger "may be substantially to lessen competition, or to tend to create a monopoly" in violation of section 7 of the Clayton Act. This court and others have suggested that the standard for likelihood of success on the merits is met if the FTC "has raised questions going to the merits so serious, substantial, difficult and doubtful as to make them fair ground for thorough investigation, study, deliberation and determination by the FTC in the first instance and ultimately by the Court of Appeals." * * *

In *United States v. Baker Hughes Inc.*, we explained the analytical approach by which the government establishes a section 7 violation. First the government must show that the merger would produce "a firm controlling an undue percentage share of the relevant market, and [would] result[ ] in a significant increase in the concentration of firms in that market." *Philadelphia Nat'l Bank.* Such a showing establishes a "presumption" that the merger will substantially lessen competition. To rebut the presumption, the defendants must produce evidence that "show[s] that the market-share statistics [give] an inaccurate account of the [merger's] probable effects on competition" in the relevant market. *United States v. Citizens & S. Nat'l Bank*, 422 U.S. 86, 120, 95 S.Ct. 2099, 45 L.Ed.2d 41 (1975).[7] "If the defendant successfully rebuts the

---

[3] Although Heinz and Beech-Nut introduced evidence showing that in areas that account for 80% of Beech-Nut sales, Heinz has a market share of about 2% and in areas that account for about 72% of Heinz sales, Beech-Nut's share is about 4%, the FTC introduced evidence that Heinz and Beech-Nut are locked in an intense battle at the wholesale level to gain (and maintain) position as the second brand on retail shelves.

[7] To rebut the defendants may rely on "[n]onstatistical evidence which casts doubt on the persuasive quality of the statistics to predict future anticompetitive consequences" such as "ease

presumption [of illegality], the burden of producing additional evidence of anticompetitive effect shifts to the government, and merges with the ultimate burden of persuasion, which remains with the government at all times." Although *Baker Hughes* was decided at the merits stage as opposed to the preliminary injunctive relief stage, we can nonetheless use its analytical approach in evaluating the Commission's showing of likelihood of success. Accordingly, we look at the FTC's prima facie case and the defendants' rebuttal evidence.

Merger law "rests upon the theory that, where rivals are few, firms will be able to coordinate their behavior, either by overt collusion or implicit understanding, in order to restrict output and achieve profits above competitive levels." * * * Increases in concentration above certain levels are thought to "raise[ ] a likelihood of 'interdependent anticompetitive conduct.' " * * *

[The court then examined market concentration, employing the Herfindahl-Hirschman Index (HHI), a measure set forth in the Horizontal Merger Guidelines. It found that the baby food industry was "highly concentrated" pre-merger and that the merger would increase that concentration in excess of a threshold set forth in the Guidelines.—Eds.][10] * * * This creates, by a wide margin, a presumption that the merger will lessen competition in the domestic jarred baby food market.[11] * * * Here, the FTC's market concentration statistics[12] are bolstered by the indisputable fact that the merger will eliminate competition between the two merging parties at the wholesale level, where they are currently the only competitors for what the district court described as the "second position on the supermarket shelves." * * *

Finally, the anticompetitive effect of the merger is further enhanced by high barriers to market entry. * * *

As far as we can determine, no court has ever approved a merger to duopoly under similar circumstances.

In response to the FTC's prima facie showing, the appellees make three rebuttal arguments, which the district court accepted in reaching its conclusion that the merger was not likely to lessen competition

---

of entry into the market, the trend of the market either toward or away from concentration, and the continuation of active price competition." * * * In addition, the defendants may demonstrate unique economic circumstances that undermine the predictive value of the government's statistics. *See United States v. General Dynamics Corp.* * * *.

[10] To determine the HHI score the district court first had to define the relevant market. The court defined the product market as jarred baby food and the geographic market as the United States. The parties do not challenge the court's definition.

[11] The FTC argues that this finding alone—that it is certain to establish a prima facie case—entitles it to preliminary injunctive relief * * *. We disagree * * *.

[12] The Supreme Court has cautioned that statistics reflecting market share and concentration, while of great significance, are not conclusive indicators of anticompetitive effects. *See General Dynamics* * * *.

substantially. For the reasons discussed below, these arguments fail and thus were not a proper basis for denying the FTC injunctive relief. * * *

[The three rebuttal arguments cited by the court involved claims that (1) "there is little competitive loss from the merger" because "Heinz and Beech-Nut do not really compete against each other at the retail level;" (2) "the anticompetitive effects of the merger will be offset by efficiencies resulting from the union of the two companies, efficiencies which they assert will be used to compete more effectively against Gerber;" and (3) "the merger is required to enable Heinz to innovate, and thus to improve its competitive position against Gerber." With respect to the second of these arguments, the appeals court noted that the district court had identified "substantial cost savings" from consolidating baby food product in Heinz' underutilized production plant and had accepted that Heinz would obtain quality improvements from recipe consolidation.—Eds.]

In a footnote the district court dismissed the likelihood of collusion derived from the FTC's market concentration data. "[S]tructural market barriers to collusion" in the retail market for jarred baby food, the court said, rebut the normal presumption that increases in concentration will increase the likelihood of tacit collusion. The court's sole citation, however, was to testimony by the appellees' expert, Jonathan B. Baker, a former Director of the Bureau of Economics at the FTC, who testified that in order to coordinate successfully, firms must solve "cartel problems" such as reaching a consensus on price and market share and deterring each other from deviating from that consensus by either lowering price or increasing production. He opined that after the merger the merged entity would want to expand its market share at Gerber's expense, thereby decreasing the likelihood of consensus on price and market share. In his report, Baker elaborated on his theory, explaining that the efficiencies created by the merger will give the merged firm the ability and incentive to take on Gerber in price and product improvements. He also predicted that policing and monitoring of any agreement would be more difficult than it is now, due in part to a time lag in the ability of one firm to detect price cuts by another. But the district court made no finding that any of these "cartel problems" are so much greater in the baby food industry than in other industries that they rebut the normal presumption. * * *

The combination of a concentrated market and barriers to entry is a recipe for price coordination. * * * The creation of a durable duopoly affords both the opportunity and incentive for both firms to coordinate to increase prices. * * * Because the district court failed to specify any 'structural market barriers to collusion' that are unique to the baby food industry, its conclusion that the ordinary presumption of collusion in a merger to duopoly was rebutted is clearly erroneous. * * *

* * *

* * * The FTC demonstrated that the merger to duopoly will increase the concentration in an already highly concentrated market; that entry barriers in the market make it unlikely that any anticompetitive effects will be avoided; that pre-merger competition is vigorous at the wholesale level nationwide and present at the retail level in some metropolitan areas; and that post-merger competition may be lessened substantially. These substantial questions have not been sufficiently answered by the appellees. As we said in *Baker Hughes*, "[t]he more compelling the prima facie case, the more evidence the defendant must present to rebut it successfully." In concluding that the FTC failed to make the requisite showing, the district court erred in a number of respects. Regarding the contention of lack of pre-merger competition, it made a clearly erroneous factual finding and misunderstood the law with respect to the import of competition at the wholesale level. Regarding the proffered efficiencies defense, the court failed to make the kind of factual findings required to render that defense sufficiently concrete to rebut the government's prima facie showing. Finally, as to the contention that the merger is necessary for innovation, the court clearly erred in relying on evidence that does not support its conclusion. Because the district court incorrectly assessed the merits of the appellees' rebuttal arguments, it improperly discounted the FTC's showing of likelihood of success.

* * *

The *Heinz* panel expressly rejected the FTC's contention that high concentration in a market with entry barriers alone entitles the government to a preliminary injunction and accepted that a successful rebuttal requires evidence showing that market share statistics provide "an inaccurate account of the [merger's] probable effects on competition." In both respects, the decision was consistent with *Baker Hughes*. But can these two cases be fully reconciled?

In *Baker Hughes*, the court stated, "Evidence of market concentration simply provides a convenient starting point for a broader inquiry into future competitiveness." Consistent with that observation, the *Heinz* court approached its inquiry into the likely competitive effects of the baby food industry merger by beginning with concentration. But in doing so, the *Heinz* panel gave the concentration evidence substantial weight. The court treated the proposed transaction as reducing the number of firms from three to two ("a merger to duopoly"), and viewed the resulting high concentration as creating a strong presumption that the merger would harm competition. It observed: "[t]he combination of a concentrated market and barriers to entry is a recipe for price coordination. * * * The creation of a durable duopoly affords both the opportunity and incentive for both firms to coordinate to increase prices."

Moreover, the *Heinz* panel arguably incorporated its view of the likely consequences of a merger to duopoly into the legal standard it applied to test the defendants' rebuttal evidence. To successfully rebut the government's *prima facie* case with evidence that the industry participants were unlikely to successfully solve their "cartel problems," and thus that post-merger tacit collusion would be unlikely, the defense in *Heinz* was required to make a specific showing not explicitly mentioned in *Baker Hughes*: that "these 'cartel problems' are so much greater in the baby food industry than in other industries that they rebut the normal presumption" that collusion is likely in a merger to duopoly. Is this test consistent with the observation in *Baker Hughes* that "[t]he more compelling the [government's] prima facie case [based on market shares], the more evidence the defendant must present to rebut it successfully," or does it set forth a different standard?

In giving concentration such great weight, did the court in *Heinz* merely conduct a "totality-of-the-circumstances" analysis, as called for by *Baker Hughes*? Or did the *Heinz* court strengthen the structural presumption, relative to how the presumption was treated in *Baker Hughes*, even to the point of making it unrebuttable in practice when a merger reduces the number of firms to as few as two? Would *Baker Hughes*, in which post-merger market concentration was also high, have come out the same way had the court in that case adopted the approach suggested in *Heinz*, and explicitly inquired as to whether entry conditions were less congenial to the exercise of market power in the hardrock hydraulic underground drilling rig industry than in other industries? For a discussion of the economic evidence in *Heinz*, see Jonathan B. Baker, *Efficiencies and High Concentration: Heinz Proposes to Acquire Beech-Nut*, *in* THE ANTITRUST REVOLUTION 157 (John E. Kwoka, Jr. & Lawrence J. White eds., 5th ed. 2008).

The burden shifting framework developed in *Baker Hughes* and *Heinz* is arguably artificial because it suggests a stilted approach in which each side introduces limited evidence intended solely to meet its burden of production. "In practice * * * the government usually introduces all of its evidence at one time, and the defendant responds in kind." *Chicago Bridge & Iron Co. v. FTC*, 534 F.3d 410, 424 (5th Cir. 2008). What are the implications of this practice for sorting out the parties' relative burdens of production and proof? According to *Chicago Bridge & Iron*, to accommodate the "practical difficulties in separating the burden to persuade and the burdens to produce" in such cases, courts use a more flexible approach, which "allows the Commission to preserve the prima facie presumption if the respondent * * * fails to satisfy the burden of production in light of contrary evidence in the prima facie case." 534 F.3d at 425. Is the court in *Chicago Bridge & Iron* confusing the burden of production with a totality of the circumstances approach to evaluating the government's ability ultimately to satisfy its burden of persuasion?

Relying on *Baker Hughes*, the *Heinz* court held that " '[t]he more compelling the prima facie case, the more evidence the defendant must present to rebut it successfully.' " *Heinz*, 246 F.3d at 725. With reference to this "sliding scale" language, *Chicago Bridge & Iron* adds that to the extent the government anticipates the merging firms' likely rebuttal evidence and responds to it in its case-in-chief, "the prima facie case is very compelling and significantly strengthened." 534 F.3d. at 426. Is this a reasonable interpretation of *Heinz*? Does *Heinz* stand for the proposition that the defendant must proffer more evidence to satisfy its initial burden on rebuttal the stronger the government's prima facie case? Or is the sliding scale language a statement about how the court should evaluate the evidence after respondent has satisfied its burden of production? *See FTC v. Arch Coal, Inc.*, 329 F. Supp.2d 109, 129 (D.D.C. 2004) ("although the FTC has satisfied its prima facie case burden, the FTC's prima facie case is not strong. Certainly less of a showing is required from defendants to rebut a less-than-compelling prima facie case.")

The burden-shifting framework established in *Baker Hughes* and reaffirmed in *Heinz* is routinely relied upon by district courts, even outside the D.C. Circuit. *See, e.g., United States v. Bazaarvoice, Inc.*, 2014 WL 203966 (N.D. Cal. 2014); *FTC v. OSF Healthcare System*, 852 F. Supp. 2d 1069 (N.D. Ill. 2012); *FTC v. Foster*, 2007 WL 1793441 (D.N.M. 2007). In litigating merger challenges since *Baker Hughes* and *Heinz,* moreover, the Justice Department and Federal Trade Commission have routinely relied upon the structural presumption. Is the government correct to see a continuing litigation advantage in demonstrating high market concentration after *Baker Hughes* and *Heinz*? To what extent has that advantage dissipated with the erosion of the structural presumption since the 1960s? The enforcement agencies also routinely explain why evidence other than market concentration supports what can be inferred from market shares. After *Baker Hughes* and *Heinz*, is it likely that the government could prevail by simply resting on the structural presumption, without proving more than high and increasing concentration in a properly-defined market?

The erosion of the structural presumption reflects in part changing economic views about the strength of the connection between market concentration and market power since the time of *Philadelphia National Bank* that are surveyed in Sidebar 5–2. As you learn more about the way the current merger guidelines analyze coordinated and unilateral competitive effects, consider whether presumptions based on market concentration should be supplemented or replaced by presumptions based on other characteristics of horizontal mergers and the markets in which they take place. Also consider the extent to which the most recent government merger guidelines move in that direction. For commentary advocating doing so, see generally Jonathan B. Baker & Carl Shapiro, *Reinvigorating Horizontal Merger Enforcement, in* WHERE THE CHICAGO SCHOOL OVERSHOT THE MARK: EFFECT OF CONSERVATIVE ECONOMIC ANALYSIS ON U.S. ANTITRUST 235, 258–66 (Robert Pitofsky, ed., 2008); Steven C. Salop, *The Evolution and Vitality of Merger Presumptions: A Decision-Theoretic Approach*, 80 ANTITRUST L. J. 301 (2015). *See also* Douglas H. Ginsburg & Joshua D. Wright, *Philadelphia National Bank: Bad Economics, Bad Law, Good Riddance*, 80 ANTITRUST L. J. 201 (2015) (encouraging the enforcement agencies to explore potential bases for presumptions other than concentration).

Sidebar 5–2:
Inferring Market Power from Market Concentration:
The Economics of the Structural Presumption[a]

Economists have long attempted to identify empirically the relationship between market concentration and market power. Those efforts arguably provide some justification for the structural presumption, but the relationship between concentration and market power is no longer thought to be as strong as was believed at the time of *Philadelphia National Bank.*

The original efforts at identifying the relationship, mainly published during the 1960s, sought to relate market concentration to firm profits. But these studies were subject to devastating criticism. The most important problem was emphasized by economist Harold Demsetz: if firms with high market shares have high price-cost margins (and thus high profits), is it because the large firms are able to exercise market power or because the large firms have obtained efficiencies that allow them to lower both costs and prices relative to their rivals? Harold Demsetz, *Two Systems of Belief About Monopoly, in* INDUSTRIAL CONCENTRATION: THE NEW LEARNING 164 (H.J. Goldschmid, H.M. Mann & J.F. Weston eds., 1974). Accordingly, a review of the studies finds: "The relation, if any, between seller concentration and profitability is weak statistically, and the estimated concentration effect is usually small. The estimated relation is unstable over time and space and vanishes in many multivariate studies." Richard Schmalensee, *Inter-Industry Studies of Structure and Performance, in* 2 HANDBOOK OF INDUSTRIAL ORGANIZATION 976 (R. Schmalensee & R. Willig eds., 1989) (Stylized Fact 4.5).

---

[a]   This Sidebar was adapted from Jonathan B. Baker, *Mavericks, Mergers, and Exclusion: Proving Coordinated Competitive Effects Under the Antitrust Laws*, 77 N.Y.U. L. REV. 135 (2002).

In response, empirical economists led by Leonard Weiss sought to address these problems by relating market concentration to price. This approach had some success, particularly in analyses of different markets within the same industry. Critics of these studies emphasize two problems: it may be difficult to measure market concentration and to account adequately for the reverse effect of price on concentration. Still, the studies appear to find a relationship between market concentration and industry price. Thus, a modern survey concluded that "[i]n cross-section comparisons involving markets in the same industry, seller concentration is positively related to the level of price." Schmalensee, *Inter-Industry Studies*, *supra*, at 988 (Stylized Fact 5.1).

More recent studies, using empirical methodologies and data unavailable to Weiss, make clear that increases in concentration, particularly substantial ones, may generate large increases in prices. For example, the results reported in Timothy F. Bresnahan & Valerie Y. Suslow, *Oligopoly Pricing with Capacity Constraints*, 15/16 ANNALES D'ECONOMIE ET DE STATISTIQUE 267 (1989), suggest that a merger in the North American aluminum industry during the 1960s and 1970s would have led to a price increase of 2.7% during cyclical downturns, when the firms were operating at excess capacity, for every 100-point increase in the Herfindahl-Hirschman Index (HHI) of market concentration. Similarly, the FTC's econometric evidence showed that the proposed merger between Staples and Office Depot—which would have reduced the number of firms from three to two in some markets and two to one in others—would have raised price on average by about 8%. Jonathan B. Baker, *Econometric Analysis in* FTC v. Staples, 18 J. PUB. POL'Y & MARKETING 11 (1999). These studies make careful efforts to account for differences in the competitive roles played by various firms and distinguish between high costs and market power as the explanation for high prices.

But the empirical economic evidence does not support the structuralist view that high market concentration makes tacit collusion inevitable. While market concentration appears related to price, and improved prospects for tacit collusion offer one possible explanation, concentration is far from the only factor relevant to the assessment of whether the disappearance of a firm, through merger or exclusion, will facilitate coordination. The economic studies make it clear that other industry-specific and market-specific factors beyond concentration (such as the elasticity of market demand, the ability of firms to solve cartel problems, and the ease of entry

> and rival repositioning) are also important in determining price and the competitive effects of mergers. Moreover, the empirical research does not reliably identify any particular concentration level common across industries at which price increases kick in or raise particular competitive concerns. That is, there is no well-established "critical" concentration ratio.

C. HORIZONTAL MERGER ANALYSIS UNDER THE DOJ/FTC MERGER GUIDELINES

The Merger Guidelines promulgated by the federal antitrust enforcement agencies are designed to describe how the Justice Department and Federal Trade Commission will exercise their prosecutorial discretion in evaluating mergers, not to articulate the applicable legal standard that should or would be applied by a court. They bind the agencies but not the courts. The Guidelines are nevertheless influential with judges, as we will see in the case excerpts below, because they set forth a systematic approach to the analysis of mergers that has been informed by the case law and contemporary economic thinking and because the Supreme Court has not decided a merger case on the merits since the mid-1970s.

The first Justice Department Merger Guidelines were issued in 1968. They have been revised several times since in response to experience and broad policy challenges. The 1982 Merger Guidelines were developed out of a need to harmonize the then-ascendant Chicago School economic learning with the pre-existing case law, which was rooted in prior, structural era thinking. The 1984 Merger Guidelines sought to resolve a national political debate over the Justice Department's handling of politically-sensitive mergers among large steel producers faced with foreign competition. The revision clarified geographic market definition analysis for firms competing with foreign rivals and expressed more sympathy toward an efficiency justification for acquisitions.

The 1992 Horizontal Merger Guidelines, issued for the first time jointly by the Justice Department and the FTC, followed a series of Antitrust Division losses in the courts (including *Baker Hughes*). After study, the Justice Department concluded that those losses were a consequence of overemphasis by the government on market structure in litigation rather than on articulating a compelling competitive effects story, and of the government's lack of success in explaining the distinction between market participants that happen to have no sales but likely would if prices rose even slightly and entry of new firms induced by the merger. These deficiencies were addressed by the revisions. The 1992 Guidelines also educated the bar, economic consultants, judges, and agency staff alike on new methods of analysis that the enforcement agencies had begun to employ internally, most notably involving the analysis of unilateral competitive effects, that were stimulated by then-contemporary developments in microeconomics. Agency interest in clarifying the role of efficiencies in merger analysis, the subject of the 1997 revisions, followed FTC hearings on Competition Policy in the New High-Tech, Global Marketplace and the resulting recognition that courts were becoming increasingly receptive to the possibility of an efficiency defense. In 2006, the agencies supplemented the Horizontal Merger Guidelines with a new document, the *Commentary on the Horizontal Merger Guidelines*, which provided a more detailed explication of how the agencies apply the guidelines, mainly through detailed case illustrations.

The Horizontal Merger Guidelines were revised again in 2010. These revisions have several themes. One is to emphasize further the analysis of competitive effects over market structure (particularly market concentration). This is evident from the start: after an overview, the Guidelines lead with a new section that sets forth sources and types of evidence of adverse competitive effects and treats market shares and concentration as just one of a number of ways to identify those effects, though also noting that high and increasing concentration in a market can create a rebuttable presumption that a merger of firms in that market will enhance market power.

A second theme is to recognize multiple methods by which mergers can harm competition—identifying not just unilateral and coordinated effects, but subcategories of each, and adding exclusionary effects of horizontal mergers to the mix. A third theme is to incorporate clarifying examples and discussions of relevant evidence; here the 2010 Guidelines follow the approach of the 2006 commentary. A fourth theme is more subtle. The 1992 Guidelines had a rigid, flow-chart aesthetic: they mapped a sequential path for making merger decisions that was conceptually precise, though in some respects difficult to apply in practice. The 2010 Guidelines are more holistic, flexible, and user-friendly, and they back off from conceptual precision in areas where the prior approach had misled or confused practitioners (as with the analysis of entry). For an explanation of the approach taken in the 2010 Guidelines by one of the drafters, see Carl Shapiro, *The 2010 Horizontal Merger Guidelines: From Hedgehog to Fox in Forty Years*, 77 ANTITRUST L.J. 701 (2010).

The 2010 Guidelines are limited to the analysis of horizontal mergers. Earlier Justice Department guidelines also addressed vertical mergers; the sections of the 1984 guidelines dealing with that subject remain in force at that agency, but have rarely been invoked. However, as discussed below in Section D, challenges to vertical mergers are less common than regulatory opposition to horizontal mergers.

The influence of the federal Merger Guidelines has prompted the development of similar guidelines by many foreign regulators,[6] and led the federal agencies to develop guidelines for other areas of antitrust practice. The reasons for the success of the 1982 Merger Guidelines are explored in William Blumenthal, *Clear Agency Guidelines: Lessons from 1982*, 68 Antitrust L.J. 5 (2000).

Agency practice in merger analysis is also important because few federal merger challenges are litigated, and even fewer merger cases brought by state governments or by private parties have yielded judicial decisions. With so little merger litigation, merger law is shaped primarily by federal agencies through the government's promulgation of guidelines and negotiation of consent decrees in individual cases.

The federal agencies no longer base enforcement decisions on factors such as trends toward industry concentration or the loss of small businesses, which were prominent in older Supreme Court decisions like *Brown Shoe*. The Merger Guidelines instead focus on market power as the source of concern about mergers under the antitrust laws: the possibility that a merger will "create, enhance, or entrench market power or . . . facilitate its exercise." *Horizontal Merger Guidelines* § 1 (2010). The resulting adverse effects are not limited to higher prices, but also may include "non-price terms and conditions that adversely affect customers, including reduced product quality, reduced product variety, reduced service, or diminished innovation." *Id.* In adopting this approach, the Guidelines are consistent with the modern case law, which interprets Clayton Act § 7's concern with acquisitions that "substantially . . . lessen competition" as tethering the statute to the economic concept of market power.

The Horizontal Merger Guidelines "are intended to assist the business community and antitrust practitioners by increasing the transparency of the analytical process underlying the Agencies' enforcement decisions." *Id.* Although "[t]hey may also assist the courts in developing an appropriate framework for interpreting and applying the antitrust laws in the

---

6   The European Commission adopted its first Merger Regulation in 1989 and a significantly amended one in 2004. *See* Council Regulation (EC) No 139/2004 of 20 January 2004 on the control of concentrations between undertakings. O.J. L. 24, 29.01.2004. Because the competition prohibitions of the Treaty of Rome did not include a separate merger provision like Section 7 of the Clayton Act in the U.S., the EC Merger Regulation is anchored to Article 102's prohibition of the abuse of dominant position. Shortly after the adoption of the revised EC Merger Regulation, the Commission also adopted Horizontal Merger Guidelines. *See* Guidelines on the assessment of horizontal mergers under the Council Regulation on the control of concentrations between undertakings, O.J. L.C 31, 05.02.2004. The European Commission also adopted guidelines for non-horizontal mergers in 2007 and guidelines on the definition of the relevant market which apply generally, including to merger analysis. A separate implementing regulation was adopted in 2004 and later amended in 2008 and 2013. The Merger Regulation and the Implementing Regulation are available at http://ec.europa.eu/competition/mergers/legislation/regulations.html. The various guidance documents can be found here: http://ec.europa.eu/competition/mergers/legislation/notices_on_substance.html.

horizontal merger context," *id.*, they do not explicitly address the burdens of production and proof that the government expects courts to apply in litigation. They do reflect the framework applied by the courts, however, when they state, "Mergers that cause a significant increase in concentration and result in highly concentrated markets are presumed to be likely to enhance market power, but this presumption can be rebutted by persuasive evidence showing that the merger is unlikely to enhance market power." *Horizontal Merger Guidelines* § 2.1.3 (2010).

Sidebar 5–3:
Pre-Merger Notification and the Merger Enforcement Process in the U.S.

The Hart-Scott-Rodino Antitrust Improvements Act, enacted in 1976 and amended most recently in 2000, requires that merging firms provide the FTC and Justice Department with information about planned transactions that exceed a certain size threshold. 15 U.S.C. § 18a. Merging firms falling within those thresholds also must delay consummation to permit prior agency review. In recent years, between 1,000 and 2,000 transactions have been reported annually.

The statute responded to two problems that limited the effectiveness of antitrust enforcement. First, most mergers and acquisitions do not generate headlines, even in the industry trade press, and therefore do not come to the attention of the FTC or Justice Department prior to consummation. Second, before 1976, mergers were often consummated before an enforcement agency investigation was complete, and before any possible court case. As a result, even if the agency successfully challenged a merger, the assets of the merging firms would often have been integrated, increasing the likelihood that a divestiture remedy would be impractical. As is often said in explanation, it is difficult to "unscramble scrambled eggs."

The statute generally requires that firms report all stock or asset acquisitions, including those involved in the formation of a joint venture, above certain thresholds based on the size of the transaction and the size of the parties. The thresholds are indexed for inflation. As of 2016, acquisitions of voting securities or assets valued above $312.6 million must be reported, and smaller transactions that exceed $78.2 million in value must also be reported if the annual sales or assets of the parties exceed certain thresholds. Acquisitions of goods and real estate in the ordinary course of business, stock purchases solely for the purpose of investment, and mere intra-corporate transfers are exempted. Filing parties must pay a fee that varies between $45,000 and $280,000, depending on the value of the transaction. Failure to file may result in penalties. Extensive regulations dictate the form, timing, and procedure of HSR filings. 16 C.F.R. § 801 *et seq.*

Once a merger is reported to government antitrust enforcers, the transaction may not be closed and joint operations may not begin for several weeks (*see* Figure 5–2). During that period, the Justice Department and FTC determine which agency will review the transaction, and that agency undertakes an initial review of the acquisition and decides whether a more extensive inquiry is called for. When the agencies negotiate "clearance," historical expertise plays a major role. The resulting industry allocations can seem arbitrary: the FTC tends to investigate soft drink and spirits mergers, whereas the Justice Department tends to review beer mergers; and in recent years, the FTC tends to investigate hospital mergers, whereas the Justice Department tends to review mergers between health insurers. In some industries, such as technology and defense, both agencies have extensive expertise, and either agency may review the transaction.

Figure 5–2:

Stages of Merger Review at the Federal Antitrust Agencies

1. *Filing*: Transaction filed with the FTC and DOJ.

2. *Clearance*: DOJ and FTC decide which agency (if any) will investigate. If neither agency wishes to investigate, and early termination has been requested by the parties, it will generally be granted.

3. *Initial waiting period*: the investigating agency decides whether to issue a "second request." The merging firms cannot close (consummate) their transaction for 30 days following the date of their filing (15 days for a cash tender offer or an acquisition in bankruptcy), unless early termination of the waiting period is granted. The waiting period is extended if there is a second request.

4. *Second request*: the investigating agency may request additional information. The second request is typically extensive, although it may be reduced by mutual agreement, and parties may take weeks or sometimes months to comply with it.

5. *Second waiting period*: the investigating agency decides whether to challenge the deal. The parties may not close their

transaction until they have substantially complied with the second request and a second waiting period of thirty (30) days (ten (10) days for a cash tender offer or an acquisition in bankruptcy) is complete. If the agency brings a court challenge, it will typically seek a temporary restraining order (or negotiate one with the parties) to prevent consummation of the transaction while the preliminary injunction hearing is pending.[7]

The vast majority of reported transactions are not investigated beyond the initial waiting period. Indeed, most filing parties request and are granted "early termination," or agency notification that its investigation has closed before the initial waiting period has ended. The agencies can, however, extend their review beyond the initial waiting period by issuing a request for additional information—commonly referred to as a "second request"—to both parties to the acquisition. The second request typically includes extensive interrogatories and document requests, though its scope is often modified in negotiations with the parties in order to satisfy the agencies' information needs with less burden to the merging firms. Party responses to the second request are confidential, although some information may be made public if presented as evidence in a judicial proceeding and not then covered by a court-issued protective order. Once the parties have complied substantially with the second request, the parties may consummate their transaction after a second waiting period is complete, unless doing so is enjoined by a court. This prevents the agencies from scuttling the transaction by delaying their review.

After reviewing the merging firms' response to a second request, the agencies may identify competitive concerns. When they do, agency concerns are generally resolved through negotiation, not litigation. Sometimes the parties will withdraw their filing, restructure their transaction to avoid agency concerns, and refile. More often, the agency and parties will negotiate a limited divestiture of some of the merged firm's assets to resolve the agency's competitive concerns. That divestiture agreement is usually formalized in a consent decree, accepted by a district court (for DOJ challenges) or the Federal Trade Commission after public comment. Although the agencies prepare complaints and typically provide an analysis to aid public comment, the factual record is not as developed as it would be in a litigated case. Merging firms often have an incentive to settle in order to avoid delay in consummating the merger, particularly when agency concerns relate to a small part of a large transaction.

---

[7] Each year the agencies issue an Annual Report to Congress on the pre-merger notification system. It includes extensive statistical data on the number and kinds of filings they have received, the number of cases receiving second requests, and the number of challenges brought. *See* https://www.ftc.gov/policy/reports/policy-reports/annual-competition-reports.

In cases where the enforcement agency has competitive concerns but a settlement cannot be reached, the agencies typically file a complaint to enjoin the merger preliminarily in federal district court (generally along with a request for a temporary restraining order to preserve the firms as separate entities). Often the merging firms will choose to abandon the transaction, in part to avoid the delay and expense associated with litigation. The two federal enforcement agencies at most litigate only a handful of merger challenges in a typical year. In the event the matter proceeds beyond a preliminary injunction to a trial on the merits, that trial would be before an FTC administrative law judge in an FTC case and before the federal court in a Justice Department case (where it usually is consolidated with the preliminary injunction hearing). Consent settlements are much more common than litigated challenges; for this reason, some commentators view merger control in the U.S. as more a regulatory activity than a judicial one.

State attorneys general and private parties may also challenge mergers in court, though such actions are also rare. But the states in particular are active in merger review, often investigating a transaction simultaneously with the federal investigation (and often coordinating their efforts with the relevant federal agency). The states can also participate as an amicus or party in the event of a federal challenge. States also may challenge transactions on their own if the federal agencies choose not to do so, *e.g.*, *New York v. Kraft Gen. Foods, Inc.*, 926 F. Supp. 321 (S.D.N.Y. 1995), or even after a federal agency has resolved its concerns by consent order. *California v. American Stores Co.*, 495 U.S. 271 (1990). Private parties may also challenge mergers regardless of the outcome of the federal enforcement agency review. In rare cases, a mergers may be challenged jointly by a federal agency, a state, and a private party. *See Saint Alphonsus Med. Ctr-Nampa, Inc. v. St. Luke's Health System, Ltd.*, 778 F.3d 775 (9th Cir. 2015) (successful challenge to hospital merger by FTC, State of Idaho, and rival hospital).

In planning a transaction or cooperating to complete the HSR premerger review process, the parties to a proposed consolidation must exercise care not to coordinate their affairs in a manner that assumes the deal is an accomplished fact. Until the transaction is closed, the parties retain the legal status of independent entities and therefore are bound by restrictions that Section 1 of the Sherman Act imposes upon relations between competitors. For example, efforts by the merging parties to set prices jointly or allocate common customers before the transaction is consummated is considered to be "gun-jumping" and, if discovered, is likely to be challenged by the federal antitrust agencies as illegal horizontal collusion, a violation of the mandatory HSR waiting periods, or both. Antitrust doctrine permits the purchaser to gather information from the seller to perform "due diligence" tasks necessary to verify the seller's financial condition, but well-counseled companies generally enlist corporate outsiders (such as law firms and accounting firms) to perform these tasks and take precautions to ensure that company insiders who receive due diligence information are precluded from transmitting such data to other company insiders.

———————

After an overview (§ 1), the Merger Guidelines set up the discussion of competitive effects with four sections providing important background information. One describes the types and sources of evidence the agencies rely on (§ 2), another explains the possible significance of price discrimination for merger analysis (§ 3), the next sets forth the agencies' methodology for defining markets (§ 4), and the following section explains how the agencies identify market participants, calculate their market shares, and measure concentration in the market as a whole (§ 5). The heart of the Guidelines is found in the next two sections, on unilateral competitive effects (§ 6) and coordinated competitive effects (§ 7). The next four sections discuss how the agencies evaluate several issues that would be considered possible sources of rebuttal arguments if a merger challenge was litigated: powerful buyers (§ 8), entry (§ 9), efficiencies (§ 10), and failure and exiting assets (§ 11). The final two sections discuss extensions of the Guidelines methodology to evaluate mergers of buyers (§ 12) and partial acquisitions (§ 13). The Guidelines make clear that the sections are ordered this way for expositional convenience, and their order is not intended to force the analysis into a rigid list of steps. This is nowhere more clear than in the discussion of market definition, where the Guidelines state that merger analysis "need not start with market definition," note that some of the analytical tools they rely on do not require market definition, and observe that "[e]vidence of competitive effects can inform market definition, just as market definition can be informative regarding competitive effects." *Horizontal Merger Guidelines* § 4 (2010).

Our presentation of modern merger analysis follows the order of the Guidelines with certain omissions. It begins in Section C.1 with market definition, the identification of market participants, and the measurement of firm shares and market concentration. Section C.2 turns to competitive effects, both coordinated and unilateral. Section C.3 deals with supply substitution and entry. Section C.4 covers efficiencies, and Section C.5 covers failing firms and exiting assets. The Guidelines sections not explicitly listed in this structure are nevertheless relevant to our discussion; students will find the entire Guidelines document worth reading, not just the Guidelines sections with titles most closely related to the Chapter section titles. With respect to those other Guidelines sections: we integrate a discussion of sources and types of evidence into our presentation, discuss the possibility of price discrimination most extensively in connection with market definition (*see infra Note on Issues in Market Definition: Submarkets, Price Discrimination Markets, Cluster Markets, and Critical Loss Analysis*), sketch issues related to powerful buyers (*see supra Note on Buyer Power*; *infra Note on Mergers that Enhance Buyer Market Power*), address mergers among buyers in the introduction to our discussion of competitive effects, and do not treat partial acquisitions except insofar as they are covered by our prior discussion of joint ventures in Chapter 2.

1. MARKET DEFINITION, MARKET PARTICIPANTS, AND MARKET CONCENTRATION (HORIZONTAL MERGER GUIDELINES §§ 4–5)

Since the creation of the pre-merger notification program, the competitive consequences of mergers have generally been evaluated prospectively, i.e. prior to consummation. As we saw in *Brown Shoe*, *Philadelphia Nat'l Bank*, *Baker Hughes*, and *Heinz*, to make these predictions about a merger's likely competitive effects, the courts and Merger Guidelines have relied upon inferences drawn from evidence of market power, such as market shares and market concentration. In the absence of actual effects evidence, which is unavailable when a merger is challenged before consummation, the court must use evidence such as this to make a prediction of the likely competitive effects of the transaction.

We will study market definition in detail below, but before we do so it is important to reiterate that this approach—defining markets and determining market shares—is not the only way to demonstrate market power, and that measurement of market power is not the only way to prove anticompetitive effect in antitrust analysis. The Horizontal Merger Guidelines make this point in several ways. They say that that in a merger enforcement action, the agencies "normally" identify one or more relevant markets in which the merger may substantially lessen competition, leaving open the possibility that market definition could be unnecessary under unusual circumstances. *Horizontal Merger Guidelines* § 4 (2010). The Guidelines state explicitly that "[t]he measurement of market shares and market concentration is not an end in itself, but is useful to the extent it illuminates the merger's likely competitive effects." *Id.* Accordingly, merger analysis "need not start with market definition" and [s]ome of the analytical tools used by the Agencies to assess competitive effects do not rely on market definition." *Id.* Notwithstanding this language, the common practice of the enforcement agencies is to define markets when challenging mergers, regardless of whether those challenges are litigated or settled by consent. Moreover, even if tools that do not require market definition are employed to analyze competitive effects, an "evaluation of competitive alternatives available to customers is always necessary at some point in the analysis." *Id.*

In order to determine market concentration, it is necessary to define the *relevant market* and identify the *firms participating in the market*, as well as their individual *market shares*. A "relevant market" (one defined for the purpose of the antitrust analysis of market power) always has two components: a "relevant *product* market" and a "relevant *geographic* market." It thus specifies both the products and the regions to which a buyer could turn for substitutes. Doing so is consistent with the language of Clayton Act § 7, which specifies that an unlawful acquisition be found likely to harm competition "in any line of commerce * * * in any section of the country." After studying competitive effects analysis later in this Chapter, it will be instructive to return to this language and consider whether it would require a court to identify the scope of a market with precision in an unusual case—one that the Merger Guidelines consider possible but has not yet been litigated—in which harm to competition is demonstrated entirely through means other than inference from high and increasing market concentration. *Cf. Horizontal Merger Guidelines* § 4 (2010) ("Relevant markets need not have precise metes and bounds."). When price discrimination is possible, moreover, a relevant market is described not just by its products and geographic area; it is also described by a class of targeted buyers, as will be discussed below.

The probative value of market shares as a proxy for measuring market power depends importantly on various assumptions about the soundness of the market definition exercise. Has the court correctly decided which products customers regard as acceptable substitutes for the defendant's products? Has it properly identified, and assigned proper market shares to, all sellers that serve the relevant market? Does a modest market share conclusively establish the lack of substantial market power, and does the presence of a high share invariably prove that the defendant has market power? If so, how high a share suggests how strong an inference? As a general rule, antitrust plaintiffs in merger litigation tend to advocate more narrow markets than antitrust defendants, because market concentration tends to be greater in more narrow markets. But occasionally the roles will be reversed: an antitrust defendant may advocate a narrow market that includes the products of one merging firm but not the other, in order to suggest the absence of a significant horizontal rivalry between the firms.

Market definition has been the subject of a great deal of attention in the academic literature. For a detailed survey of market definition issues predating the 2010 Guidelines, see Jonathan B. Baker, *Market Definition: An Analytical Overview*, 74 ANTITRUST L.J. 129 (2007). More recently, Professor Louis Kaplow has argued that market definition is conceptually incoherent and should be abandoned entirely. Louis Kaplow, *Why (Ever) Define Markets?*, 124 HARV. L. REV. 437 (2010). For responses and replies, see Gregory J. Werden, *Why (Ever) Define Markets? An Answer to Professor Kaplow*, 78 ANTITRUST L.J. 729 (2013); Louis Kaplow, *Market Definition:*

Impossible and Counterproductive, 79 ANTITRUST L.J. 361 (2013); Gregory J. Werden, *The Relevant Market: Possible and Productive* (April 11, 2014), http://ssrn.com/abstract=2423933.

The Supreme Court established the legal standard for defining markets in *United States v. E. I. du Pont de Nemours & Co.*, 351 U.S. 377 (1956) (*Cellophane*), a monopolization case discussed in Chapter 4. The Justice Department brought the case as a challenge to du Pont's position as the leading supplier of cellophane.

The pivotal issue before the Court was whether du Pont possessed monopoly power. The government argued that the relevant market was limited to cellophane, and hence that du Pont had a market share in excess of 70%, conferring market power. The company defended itself by arguing that buyers of cellophane routinely turned to other flexible packaging materials when du Pont attempted to raise the price of cellophane, and that therefore the market was more properly defined to include a wider range of flexible wrapping products in which cellophane accounted for less than 20% of sales, well below the threshold of concern articulated in previous monopolization cases. *See Note on the Origins of Alcoa's Market Share Benchmarks, supra* Chapter 4. Both the trial court and the Supreme Court found du Pont's view persuasive. Although the Court's analysis of the evidence concerning the flexible packaging materials sector has attracted extensive criticism for reasons already discuss in Chapter 4, its doctrinal formula for defining the relevant market remains the basic test that courts and enforcement agencies use today in merger and non-merger cases:

> [W]here there are market alternatives that buyers may readily use for their purposes, illegal monopoly does not exist merely because the product said to be monopolized differs from others. If it were not so, only physically identical products would be a part of the market. To accept the Government's argument, we would have to conclude that the manufactures of plain as well as moistureproof cellophane were monopolists, and so with films such as Pliofilm, foil, glassine, polyethylene, and Saran, for each of these wrapping materials is distinguishable. * * * *In considering what is the relevant market for determining the control of price and competition, no more definite rule can be declared than that commodities reasonably interchangeable by consumers for the same purposes make up that 'part of the trade or commerce', monopolization of which may be illegal.* * * *.

351 U.S. at 394–95 (emphasis added). The Court further explained: "The 'market' which one must study to determine when a producer has monopoly power * * * is composed of products that have reasonable interchangeability for the purposes for which they are produced—price, use and qualities considered." *Id.* at 404.

The doctrinal test adopted in *Cellophane* focuses upon *buyer substitution* possibilities. As it suggests, market definition seeks to identify the products (and geographic locations) that encompass the practical alternatives available to buyers, considering the price, use, and qualities of those choices. The Court highlighted the economic concept of buyer substitution by equating its "reasonably interchangeable" in demand formulation for market definition doctrine with "cross-elasticity of demand between products," an economic concept (discussed further below) which, the Court explains, relates to "the responsiveness of the sales of one product to price changes of the other." 351 U.S. at 380, 400. *Accord Brown Shoe Co. v. United States*, 370 U.S. 294, 325 (1962).

The Court reiterated its emphasis on buyer substitution possibilities as the linchpin of market definition in 1964, when it issued a merger decision placing insulated copper conductor and insulated aluminum conductor in separate markets because of insufficient demand substitution over a vigorous dissent that highlighted extensive supply substitution (production flexibility) between the two. *United States v. Aluminum Co. of Am.*, 377 U.S. 271 (1964) (*Rome Cable*). This demand-side orientation—delineating the product market according to the customer's view of which products (or geographic locations) are acceptable substitutes for each other—continues to provide the basic framework for delineating relevant markets today.[8]

Some contemporary courts follow the lead of the *Rome Cable* dissent and expand markets to account for supply substitution as well as demand substitution. *See, e.g., Menasha Corp. v. News America Marketing In-Store, Inc.*, 354 F.3d 661 (7th Cir. 2004) (Easterbrook, J.). Deviation from an exclusive demand-side focus is rarely employed when markets are defined for the purpose of analyzing mergers, however. (*Menasha* was decided under the Sherman Act, as were the two monopolization cases referenced in the first paragraph of Sidebar 5–10, below, where markets were also broadened to account for the possibility of supply substitution.) For a defense of the demand-side orientation of market definition, see Jonathan B. Baker, *Market Definition: An Analytical Overview*, 74 ANTITRUST L.J. 129, 132–38 (2007).

NOTE ON CROSS-PRICE ELASTICITY OF DEMAND

In *Cellophane*, the Supreme Court looked to the cross-price elasticity of demand when defining a market. It explained the concept this way:

> An element for consideration as to cross-elasticity of demand between products is the responsiveness of the sales of one product to price

---

[8]   In defining antitrust markets in both merger and monopolization settings, courts have historically treated as relevant authority cases decided under Sherman Act § 2 (*Cellophane*) and those decided under Clayton Act § 7 (*Rome Cable, Brown Shoe*). Doing so is consistent with the concept-oriented perspective of modern antitrust, and we follow that practice here.

changes of the other. If a slight decrease in the price of cellophane causes a considerable number of customers of other flexible wrappings to switch to cellophane, it would be an indication that a high cross-elasticity of demand exists between them; that the products compete in the same market.

351 U.S. at 400.

The elasticity of demand discussed in Chapter 1 is what economists term the *own*-price elasticity of demand. It asks how responsive a product's buyers are, in the aggregate, to changes in the product's own price. If price rises, do buyers tend to stick with the product (making demand relatively inelastic) or do they tend to reduce their purchases (making demand relatively elastic)? As the coffee discussion in Chapter 1 suggested, if the demand for a product is highly elastic (extremely responsive to changes in its own price), even a monopolist of that product would find it unprofitable to exercise market power. This economic insight underlies the market definition formula of the Merger Guidelines, which we will meet shortly.

The *cross*-price elasticity of demand asks a different question: how responsive are a product's buyers to changes in the price of a *different* product. If the quantity of brown paper wrapping sold, for example, increases when the price of cellophane rises, the two products are *substitutes* in demand. [9] Quantitatively, the cross-price elasticity of demand between products A and B can be expressed as the percentage change in quantity for product A, divided by the percentage change in price for product B. Cross-elasticities need not be symmetric: it is possible, for example, that the quantity of cellophane sold increases a great deal when the price of brown paper wrapping rises (high cross-elasticity), but, simultaneously, that the quantity of brown paper wrapping sold does not rise very much in response to an increase in the price of cellophane (low cross-elasticity). If a product outside a proposed relevant market has a high cross-elasticity with the products included in the market, then the excluded product provides a relatively close substitute to buyers of the included products, and the excluded product is a candidate for inclusion by expanding the market. Demand cross-elasticities are also relevant to the analysis of unilateral effects among sellers of differentiated products, as will be discussed below in Section C.2.b of this Chapter.

a.　Market Definition Under the Merger Guidelines

Under the Horizontal Merger Guidelines, market definition takes into account only the economic force of demand (or buyer) substitution: the possibility that buyers would defeat an attempt by sellers to exercise

---

[9]　Products could instead be *complements* in demand. If peanut butter and jelly are usually used together to make sandwiches, one might expect that peanut butter sales would fall when the price of jelly rises (as would jelly sales). In short: if the price of one good rises, that will lead to an increase in quantity sold for substitute products and a decrease in quantity sold for demand complements (as well as a decrease in quantity sold of the good itself).

market power by purchasing alternative products in place of those for which price has risen. Other economic forces relevant to merger analysis are accounted for in other analyses set forth in the Guidelines. In particular, supply substitution (also called production flexibility) is examined in the identification of market participants and in the analysis of entry, and the nature of rivalry among the firms in the market is addressed in competitive effects analysis.

Through this approach to market definition, market concentration statistics are connected to the economic concept of market power, for which concentration is a surrogate. Thus, for example, it would probably make no sense to define a geographic market for restaurants limited to one block in a large city, and stop a merger of the only two restaurants in that block on the ground that their combination would create a firm with a 100% market share. Many diners probably would be willing to substitute restaurants in the next block, or go out to eat in a different part of town, in the event lunch and dinner prices were to rise on the block where the merging restaurants were located. As a consequence, it would be unlikely that the post-merger price increase would be profitable, which calls into question whether it was appropriate to define the city block as a relevant geographic market. Conversely, it may also be inappropriate to analyze the merger of two primary care hospitals in Chicago's northern suburbs only within a geographic market that encompasses a broadly-defined "Chicagoland" metropolitan area extending from Indiana to Wisconsin. Doing so could mean that the market participants may include relatively distant substitutes with little competitive significance for the merging firms, leading to misleadingly low market shares that would understate the possible competitive threat from the transaction.

The Guidelines' focus on demand substitution as the basis of market definition is consistent with the Supreme Court's doctrinal formulation in *Cellophane* that product markets are collections of goods with "reasonable interchangeability" in demand. But the Guidelines go beyond the case law by suggesting a metric—a conceptual answer to the question of "how much buyer substitution would be sufficient to preclude a proposed market definition." In particular, the Merger Guidelines use what is referred to as the "*hypothetical monopolist test*," which defines a market as a collection of products or services, and a geographic region, that would form a valuable monopoly. Were a hypothetical monopolist of the products and region in the market to raise price, that act would likely be profitable, as most buyers would pay more rather than respond by substituting alternatives outside the market. *Horizontal Merger Guidelines* §§ 4.1, 4.2 (2010).

The approach to market definition employed by the Merger Guidelines can also be understood as an algorithm. It begins by specifying as a candidate market each product sold by either merging firm and the location at which it is sold. A candidate market is recognized as a relevant antitrust market if a hypothetical monopolist pursuing maximum profits would increase the price of some or all of the products, at some or all of the locations, by a *"small but significant and nontransitory"* amount (referred to as a "SSNIP") relative to the prices that would likely prevail but-for the merger under review (usually pre-merger prices). If the hypothetical monopolist would not find a SSNIP profitable, the candidate market is expanded, normally by adding the next-best substitute. Then the new candidate market is tested to determine whether it constitutes a relevant antitrust market, and so on until a market is identified. More simply, if it would not be profitable to monopolize the candidate market, the market is expanded by adding products or regions until it would be profitable to do so. Because the hypothetical monopolist test is applied to a group of products within a geographic region, product and geographic market definition are often interrelated in practice even when they are discussed as separate inquiries. When a merger involves firms selling multiple products or services, this process would be undertaken for each candidate market to determine the degree, if any, of competitive overlap between the merging firms.

The Guidelines caution that "[r]elevant antitrust markets defined according to the hypothetical monopolist test are not always intuitive and may not align with how industry members use the term 'market'." *Id.* at § 4. For example, the test "may identify a group of products as a relevant market even if customers would substitute significantly to products outside that group in response to a price increase. *Id.* § 4.1.1.

The market definition process set forth in the Horizontal Merger Guidelines does not necessarily lead to a unique market. A merger may be evaluated within any relevant market that satisfies the hypothetical monopolist test "guided by the overarching principle that the purpose of defining the market and measuring market shares is to illuminate the evaluation of competitive effects." *Horizontal Merger Guidelines* § 4.1.1 (2010). To avoid overstating the competitive significance of distant substitutes, the Guidelines say, the agencies usually rely on market shares and concentration measures within the smallest market satisfying the hypothetical monopolist test. *Id.* In practice, though, the government does not necessarily define the most narrow, defensible market. For example, in its 2013 complaint challenging the US Airways/American Airlines merger, the Justice Department did not seek to define a product market more narrow than "scheduled air passenger service" (when it is possible that it could have separated, for example, business and leisure travel or first class and economy service). And in its 2011 complaint challenging the proposed AT&T/T-Mobile merger, the Justice Department did not seek to define a product market more narrow than "mobile wireless telecommunications services" (when it is possible that it could have separated, for example, prepaid and postpaid wireless service). Indeed, if a transaction would harm competition within a larger market, the presence of a smaller relevant market that could have been defined should not stand in the way of identifying an anticompetitive effect in the larger market. Moreover, the existence of a large market in which the merging firms have low market shares and the transaction appears not to harm competition does not preclude the possibility that the transaction would be found to harm competition within a smaller market defined by the hypothetical monopolist test that is nested within it. See the discussion of "submarkets" below.

In most contexts, the SSNIP is a price increase of 5% lasting for the foreseeable future. This 5% figure is a benchmark for a conceptual experiment defining markets, not a tolerance level. A merger within a relevant market may be considered anticompetitive if it appears likely to lead to any increase in price, no matter how small.[10] Thus, potential substitutes that would not become available in time to prevent a hypothetical monopolist from raising price profitably in the short run would be excluded from the market. *See United States v. Microsoft Corp.*, 253 F.3d 34, 53–54 (D.C. Cir. 2001) (stating that market definition requires that a court "consider only substitutes that constrain pricing in the reasonably foreseeable future, and only products that can enter the market in a relatively short time can perform this function").

The market definition approach of the Horizontal Merger Guidelines generally begins with the prevailing prices of the products of the merging firms and possible substitutes for those products. But if prices are likely to change without the merger, for example because of innovation, entry, or the likely breakdown of pre-merger coordination, anticipated future prices absent the merger may instead be employed as the benchmark when applying the hypothetical monopolist test. *Horizontal Merger Guidelines* § 4.1.2 (2010).[11]

---

[10] In practice, however, the enforcement agencies and courts would not be expected to challenge mergers when the adverse effect is thought to be small. It is hard to be confident that competition would be harmed when the competitive effect could be small given difficulties measuring effects with precision and the possibility that small adverse effects could be outweighed by procompetitive benefits. Moreover, as a matter of public policy, it is generally not worth using social resources to pursue violations with small economic impact. A government case intended to establish an important precedent, and thereby deter a great deal of harmful conduct by other firms, might be an exception.

[11] This approach generally grandfathers in any existing market power in the industry, and focuses the competitive effects analysis on the question of whether the merger will likely make the exercise of market power worse. It does not emphasize the possibility that the merger would prevent the erosion of market power and a decline in price, though that possibility could be accounted for by basing the benchmark on anticipated future prices that are lower than prevailing prices. This type of adjustment is rarely employed in practice, however, because of the difficulty in identifying the likely time path of prices absent the merger. For this reason, the Guidelines do not explicitly address the possibility of committing the *Cellophane* fallacy (*see supra* Sidebar 4–3), although that possibility would justify their approach of using anticipated future prices as the benchmark.

NOTE ON MARKET DEFINITION IN PRACTICE

Although some have criticized the Guidelines' approach to market definition as difficult to implement in practice, the federal enforcement agencies have become adept at developing evidence related to answering the Guidelines' central "hypothetical monopolist" question. An example of how a disputed market definition might be resolved will suggest some types of evidence that might be brought to bear. Other examples predating the 2010 Guidelines appear in the 2006 Commentary on the Horizontal Merger Guidelines, issued jointly by the Justice Department and the Federal Trade Commission.

When the Federal Trade Commission sought a preliminary injunction against Coca-Cola's proposed acquisition of the Dr Pepper soft drink brand in the mid-1980s, the FTC staff proposed an "all carbonated soft drink" product market, in which the merging firms would have a combined market share of 42%, while Coke proposed a broader product market consisting of "all beverages," in which the merger partners would have a much lower combined market share, and the transaction would not appear likely to raise a competitive problem.[12]

To decide between alternatives such as these, the Merger Guidelines focus on whether a hypothetical collusive price increase among sellers of a product would be profitable, or whether it would be made unprofitable by buyers responding to the high price by switching their purchases to other products or consuming less. The relevant evidence may be grouped into five categories, which encompass most of the types of evidence mentioned by the Guidelines. *Horizontal Merger Guidelines* §§ 4.1.3, 4.2.1 (2010) (providing examples of types of evidence on which the enforcement agencies often rely when evaluating buyers' likely responses to higher prices).

First, direct evidence of demand substitution might be obtained by *asking buyers about their likely responses* if price were to increase. This information could be obtained through informal customer interviews or by surveying a sample of buyers. Buyers might be asked questions like these: "Would a 5% or 10% increase in the price of the merging firms lead you to switch to another product? For what fraction of your purchases? Would an increase in the price of a broader collection of products (such as all cola-flavored soft drinks, or all carbonated soft drinks) lead you to substitute other products?"

Second, evidence about *the response of buyers to past price changes* may bear on the extent of likely buyer substitution in response to a hypothetical future price increase. Such evidence could be anecdotal (*e.g.*, a marketing executive's assessment of the consequences of a past price change) or systematic (*e.g.*, from an econometric (statistical) analysis of pricing data

---

[12] Although the district court that reviewed the FTC's preliminary injunction request did not report concentration estimates for the market alleged by Coke, it did observe that carbonated soft drinks accounted for less than one fourth (approximately 22.3%) of per capita beverage consumption in the U.S. at the time of the litigation. *FTC v. Coca-Cola Co.*, 641 F. Supp. 1128, 1133 (D.D.C. 1986), *vacated and remanded mem.*, 829 F.2d 191 (D.C. Cir. 1987).

collected from sellers of the product). It may include studies of the elasticity of demand (*see supra* Chapter 1) or a comparison of the price in monopolized markets with the price in otherwise similar markets thought to perform competitively (see the discussion of *Staples* later in this Chapter).

The third class of relevant evidence may be available if buyer substitution patterns are known to depend on the characteristics of products or geographic locations. Under such circumstances, the extent of demand substitution might be *inferred from information about the distribution of those characteristics*. For example, if a large group of soft drink buyers were known to consider carbonation a very important product attribute, then sparkling water might be a more plausible substitute, and thus a more plausible candidate for inclusion in the market, than fruit juices. In other industries, information about the nature and distribution of buyer switching costs (for product market definition) or product shipment costs (for geographic market definition) might permit similar inferences.

Fourth, *the conduct of sellers*, who have an economic interest in understanding buyer substitution patterns, may provide indirect evidence on the likely extent of buyer substitution. Such evidence may appear in marketing documents of the merging firms or testimony of their marketing executives that shows whether the firms track and respond to the prices of beverages other than soft drinks. The focus is on identifying which rivals the firms routinely monitor and respond to as a guide to seller views about likely buyer substitution responses to price increases. This may differ from the scope of the "market" identified by the sellers in their documents, as the relevant market for antitrust purposes need not be the same as what firms and their executives call the market for different purposes. Moreover, the price-cost margins chosen by sellers reflect in part seller views about the extent of buyer substitution. In particular, high margins imply that sellers do not believe buyers are sensitive to changes in price. The role of margins in market definition is examined in more detail in connection with the discussion of "Critical Loss Analysis" (*see infra Note on Issues in Market Definition: Submarkets, Price Discrimination Markets, Cluster Markets, and Critical Loss Analysis*). On the other hand, if the costs of producing a set of products rises and prices remain unchanged, that observation suggests that sellers view the demand for that collection of products as highly sensitive to price changes.

Finally, indirect evidence as to likely buyer substitution patterns in the event prices were to rise may also be found in the *testimony of industry experts*, in this case perhaps experienced soft drink merchandisers at grocery stores or other beverage firms.

Evidence of similarities or differences in product prices is sometimes discussed by courts, but it is generally not indicative of likely buyer substitution responses. After all, in many settings, buyers may choose between high-price/high-quality products and low-price/low-quality products. For example, some buyers of high-priced custom suits might respond to a price increase for that product by switching to less expensive suits sold off-the-rack (or vice versa, responding to higher department store prices by switching to a custom tailor). If many (but not necessarily most) buyers would view these products as substitutes, it would not be appropriate to use a high price (or a low price) as a basis for market definition. However, if evidence not involving product price points demonstrates that most or all buyers of high-priced/high-quality pens, for example, would not switch to low-priced/low-quality pens in the event the price of high-quality pens were to rise, high-quality pens might constitute a product market—and the bounds of that market might conveniently be described in terms of fountain pens priced above a certain level. *See United States v. Gillette Co.*, 828 F. Supp. 78, 81–83 (D.D.C. 1993) (defining market for premium writing instruments as those priced between $50 and $400).

Typically, no one type of evidence is dispositive, and a wide range of information not listed here may also bear on the market definition question. Moreover, the probative value of direct and indirect evidence and the probative value of quantitative and qualitative evidence may vary from case to case; the classification scheme presented here is an aid to understanding, not a ranking indicating the types of evidence that are to be preferred.

When the 1986 Coke/Dr Pepper merger case was tried, the district court agreed with the FTC on a carbonated soft drink product market, and enjoined the merger. In support of its product market definition, the court noted that the major soft drink producers "make pricing and marketing decisions based primarily on comparisons with rival carbonated soft drink products, with little if any concern about possible competition from other beverages such as milk, coffee, beer or fruit juice." *FTC v. Coca-Cola Co.*, 641 F. Supp. 1128, 1133 (D.D.C. 1986), *vacated and remanded mem.*, 829 F.2d 191 (D.C. Cir. 1987).

The soft drink merger example focuses on product market definition. The same kinds of evidence are equally relevant to geographic market definition. Is the Washington, D.C. metropolitan area a relevant geographic market for analyzing a merger among soft drink producers? Under the Merger Guidelines' approach to answering this question, a court would be led to ask whether a hypothetical soft drink monopoly in Washington would be made unprofitable by consumers traveling to Baltimore or other out-of-town locations to buy soft drinks. The possibility that Baltimore firms would respond by opening stores to sell soft drinks in Washington is a supply substitution response that is relevant to analyzing the competitive effects of the merger, but would not be accounted for in the market definition step of the analysis under the Guidelines' approach. Evidence of demand substitution away from Washington in response to a price rise could come from many sources, including the following: buyer responses to past price increases in Washington (when the price in Baltimore did not change); a survey of likely buyer responses to a price hike in Washington; information about the distribution of buyer and product characteristics (*e.g.*, the fraction of Washington area residents that live very close to Baltimore area retailers or commute to Baltimore frequently); evidence concerning the locations sellers monitor and respond to (*e.g.*, whether

Washington area sellers pay attention to what Baltimore sellers charge for soft drinks); and views of industry experts.

How much demand substitution would be too much to make a price increase unprofitable? Evidence about the extent of demand substitution in response to a price increase (the elasticity of demand) is often calibrated in relationship to accounting measures of price-cost margins. *See generally* Gregory J. Werden, *Demand Elasticities in Antitrust Analysis*, 66 ANTITRUST L.J. 363 (1998). One approach to structuring that calibration, "critical loss analysis," is discussed below (*see infra Note on Issues in Market Definition: Submarkets, Price Discrimination Markets, Cluster Markets, and Critical Loss Analysis*).

The *H & R Block* decision, a merger case decided after the 2010 Guidelines were issued, illustrates the application of Merger Guidelines principles. Which of the five categories of evidence set forth above are most represented? To what extent does the court evaluate the probative value of the sources of evidence considered? What does the court say about the following types of evidence it considered when defining markets, and how does each bear on the extent of buyer substitution: the views of Tax Act's investment bankers, merging firm documents indicating which rivals' prices and other business decisions the firms monitor, differences in convenience in manual and digital do it yourself tax preparation, the survey of buyers proffered by the merging firms, and buyer switching data?

The excerpt from *H & R Block* includes the court's discussion of market definition and coordinated competitive effects. The section of the opinion entitled "Coordinated Effects" is not directly relevant to market definition, but will be discussed later in this Chapter in connection with coordinated competitive effects and may be read then.

UNITED STATES V. H & R BLOCK, INC.

United States District Court for the District of Columbia, 2011.
833 F. Supp. 2d 36.

BERYL A. HOWELL, DISTRICT JUDGE.

* * * In this case, the United States, through the Antitrust Division of the Department of Justice, seeks to enjoin a proposed merger between two companies that offer tax software products—H & R Block ["HRB"] and TaxACT—on the grounds that the merger violates the antitrust laws and will lead to an anticompetitive duopoly in which the only substantial providers of digital tax software in the marketplace would be H & R Block and Intuit, the maker of the popular "TurboTax" software program. After carefully considering all of the evidence, including documents and factual and expert testimony, the applicable law, and the arguments before the

Court, the Court will enjoin the proposed merger for the reasons explained in detail below.

* * *

* * * Broadly speaking, there are three methods for preparing a tax return. The "pen and paper" or "manual" method includes preparation by hand and with free, electronically fillable forms available on the IRS website. A second method, known as "assisted" preparation, involves hiring a tax professional—typically either a certified public accountant ("CPA") or a specialist at a retail tax store. HRB operates the largest retail tax store chain in the United States. The companies Jackson-Hewitt and Liberty Tax Service also operate well-known retail tax stores. Finally, many taxpayers now prepare their returns using digital do-it-yourself tax preparation products ("DDIY"), such as the popular software product "TurboTax." DDIY preparation is becoming increasingly popular and an estimated 35 to 40 million taxpayers used DDIY in 2010.

The three most popular DDIY providers are HRB, TaxACT, and Intuit, the maker of TurboTax. According to IRS data, these three firms accounted for approximately 90 percent of the DDIY-prepared federal returns filed in tax season 2010.[3] The next largest firm is TaxHawk, also known as FreeTaxUSA, with 3.2 percent market share, followed by TaxSlayer, with 2.7 percent. The remainder of the market is divided among numerous smaller firms. Intuit accounted for 62.2 percent of DDIY returns, HRB for 15.6 percent, and TaxACT for 12.8 percent. DDIY products are offered to consumers through three channels: (1) online through an internet browser; (2) personal computer software downloaded from a website; and (3) personal computer software installed from a disk, which is either sent directly to the consumer or purchased by the consumer from a third-party retailer. In industry parlance, DDIY products provided through an internet browser are called "online" products, while software applications downloaded onto the user's computer via the web or installed from a disk are referred to as "software" products.

The proposed acquisition challenged in this case would combine HRB and TaxACT, the second and third most popular providers of DDIY products, respectively. According to the government, this combination would result in an effective duopoly between HRB and Intuit in the DDIY market, in which the next nearest competitor will have an approximately 3 percent market share, and most other competitors will have less than a 1 percent share. The government also alleges that unilateral anticompetitive effects would result from the elimination of head-to-head competition between the merging parties.

---

[3]　* * * "[T]ax season 2010" refers to returns filed primarily in early 2010, corresponding to income earned in "tax year 2009."

Thus, the DOJ alleges that because the proposed acquisition would reduce competition in the DDIY industry by eliminating head-to-head competition between the merging parties and by making anticompetitive coordination between the two major remaining market participants substantially more likely, the proposed acquisition violates Section 7 of the Clayton Act, 15 U.S.C. § 18. Accordingly, the government seeks a permanent injunction blocking HRB from acquiring TaxACT.

* * *

* * * Over the years, TaxACT has emphasized high-quality free product offerings as part of its business strategy. * * * [F]rom the beginning, TaxACT's business strategy relied on promoting "free" or "freemium" products, in which a basic part of the service is offered for free and add-ons and extra features are sold for a price. * * *

Currently, TaxACT's free product offering allows customers to prepare, print, and e-file a federal tax return completely for free. TaxACT's "Deluxe" edition, which costs $9.95, contains additional features, such as the ability to import data from a return filed the prior year through TaxACT. Customers who use TaxACT to prepare a state tax return in addition to a federal return pay either $14.95 for the state return in combination with the free federal product or $17.95 for the state return in combination with the "Deluxe" federal product. * * *

* * *

III. DISCUSSION

A. The Relevant Product Market

"Merger analysis begins with defining the relevant product market." "Defining the relevant market is critical in an antitrust case because the legality of the proposed merger [ ] in question almost always depends upon the market power of the parties involved." Indeed, the relevant market definition is often "the key to the ultimate resolution of this type of case because of the relative implications of market power."[7]

The government argues that the relevant market in this case consists of all DDIY products, but does not include assisted tax preparation or pen-and-paper. Under this view of the market, the acquisition in this case would result in a DDIY market that is dominated by two large players—H & R Block and Intuit—that together control approximately 90 percent of

---

[7] "A relevant market has two components: (1) the relevant product market and (2) the relevant geographic market. . . . The 'relevant geographic market' identifies the geographic area in which the defendants compete in marketing their products or services." The parties have stipulated that the relevant geographic market in this case is worldwide. DDIY products are provided online and can be used by any individual worldwide—either within the United States or abroad—who needs to prepare and file a U.S. tax return. The products at issue in this case are not used for preparation of foreign tax returns. The Court accepts the parties' stipulation as to the relevant geographic market.

the market share, with the remaining 10 percent of the market divided amongst a plethora of smaller companies. In contrast, the defendants argue for a broader market that includes all tax preparation methods ("all methods"), comprised of DDIY, assisted, and pen-and-paper. Under this view of the market, the market concentration effects of this acquisition would be much smaller and would not lead to a situation in which two firms control 90 percent of the market. This broader view of the market rests primarily on the premise that providers of all methods of tax preparation compete with each other for the patronage of the same pool of customers—U.S. taxpayers. After carefully considering the evidence and arguments presented by all parties, the Court has concluded that the relevant market in this case is, as the DOJ contends, the market for digital do-it-yourself tax preparation products.

A "relevant product market" is a term of art in antitrust analysis. The Supreme Court has set forth the general rule for defining a relevant product market: "The outer boundaries of a product market are determined by the reasonable interchangeability of use [by consumers] or the cross-elasticity of demand between the product itself and substitutes for it." *Brown Shoe*, 370 U.S. at 325, 82 S.Ct. 1502; *see also United States v. E.I. du Pont de Nemours & Co.*, 351 U.S. 377, 395, 76 S.Ct. 994, 100 L.Ed. 1264 (1956). In other words, courts look at "whether two products can be used for the same purpose, and, if so, whether and to what extent purchasers are willing to substitute one for the other."

A broad, overall market may contain smaller markets which themselves "constitute product markets for antitrust purposes."[8] * * * Traditionally, courts have held that the boundaries of a relevant product market within a broader market "may be determined by examining such practical indicia as industry or public recognition of the [relevant market] as a separate economic entity, the product's peculiar characteristics and uses, unique production facilities, distinct customers, distinct prices, sensitivity to price changes, and specialized vendors." These "practical indicia" of market boundaries may be viewed as evidentiary proxies for proof of substitutability and cross-elasticities of supply and demand.

An analytical method often used by courts to define a relevant market is to ask hypothetically whether it would be profitable to have a monopoly over a given set of substitutable products. If so, those products may constitute a relevant market. This approach—sometimes called the "hypothetical monopolist test"—is endorsed by the Horizontal Merger Guidelines issued by the DOJ and Federal Trade Commission.[10] In the

---

[8]   Courts have sometimes referred to such markets-within-markets as "submarkets." Other courts and commentators have criticized this "submarket" terminology as unduly confusing, however.

[10]   The Merger Guidelines are not binding upon this Court, but courts in antitrust cases often look to them as persuasive authority.

merger context, this inquiry boils down to whether "a hypothetical profit-maximizing firm, not subject to price regulation, that was the only present and future seller of those products . . . likely would impose at least a small but significant and non-transitory increase in price ("SSNIP") on at least one product in the market, including at least one product sold by one of the merging firms." The "small but significant and non-transitory increase in price," or SSNIP, is typically assumed to be five percent or more.

Thus, the question here is whether it would be hypothetically useful to have a monopoly over all DDIY tax preparation products because the monopolist could then profitably raise prices for those products by five percent or more; or whether, to the contrary, there would be no reason to monopolize all DDIY tax preparation products because substitution and price competition with other methods of tax preparation would restrain any potential DDIY monopolist from profitably raising prices. In other words, would enough DDIY users switch to the assisted or pen-and-paper methods of tax preparation in response to a five-to-ten percent increase in DDIY prices to make such a price increase unprofitable?

In evaluating the relevant product market here, the Court considers business documents from the defendants and others, the testimony of the fact witnesses, and the analyses of the parties' expert economists. This evidence demonstrates that DDIY is the relevant product market in this case.

1. The Defendants' Documents Show That DDIY Is The Relevant Product Market.

When determining the relevant product market, courts often pay close attention to the defendants' ordinary course of business documents. The government argues that the defendants' ordinary course of business documents in this case "conclusively demonstrate that competition with other [DDIY] firms drive Defendants' pricing decisions, quality improvements, and corporate strategy" for their own DDIY products—thus supporting the government's view of the relevant market. The defendants contend that the government has relied on "select, 'out-of-context' snippets from documents," and that the documents as a whole support the defendants' view that the relevant product market is all methods of tax preparation. The Court finds that the documentary evidence in this case supports the conclusion that DDIY is the relevant product market.

Internal TaxACT documents establish that TaxACT has viewed DDIY offerings by HRB and TurboTax as its primary competitors, that it has tracked their marketing, product offerings, and pricing, and that it has determined its own pricing and business strategy in relation to those companies' DDIY products. Confidential memoranda prepared by TaxACT's investment bankers for potential private equity buyers of TaxACT identify HRB and TurboTax as TaxACT's primary competitors in a DDIY market. These documents also recognize that TaxACT's strategy for competing with Intuit and HRB is to offer a lower price for what it deems a superior product.

While, as defendants point out, parts of these TaxACT documents also discuss the broader tax preparation industry, these documents make clear that TaxACT's own view—and that conveyed by its investment bankers to potential buyers—is that the company primarily competes in a DDIY market against Intuit and HRB and that it develops its pricing and business strategy with that market and those competitors in mind. These documents are strong evidence that DDIY is the relevant product market.

Internal HRB documents also evidence HRB's perception of a discrete DDIY market or market segment. HRB and its outside consultants have tracked its digital competitors' activities, prices, and product offerings. Documents from HRB's DDIY business have also referred to HRB, TaxACT, and TurboTax as the "Big Three" competitors in the DDIY market. Finally, the documents show that, in connection with a proposed acquisition of TaxACT, HRB identified the proposed transaction as a way to grow its digital "market share" and has measured TaxACT's market share in a DDIY market. All of these documents also provide evidence that DDIY is a relevant product market.

The defendants acknowledge that "the merging parties certainly have documents that discuss each other and digital competitors generally, and even reference a digital market and the 'Big Three,'" but contend this evidence is insufficient to prove a market. Rather, the defendants argue that the documents show that the relevant market is all methods of tax preparation, especially in light of documented competition between DDIY providers and assisted providers for the same overall pool of U.S. taxpayers who are potential customers. As discussed below, the Court disagrees and finds that the relevant product market is DDIY products.

2. The Relevant Product Market Does Not Include Assisted Tax Preparation Or Manual Preparation.

It is beyond debate—and conceded by the plaintiff—that all methods of tax preparation are, to some degree, in competition. All tax preparation methods provide taxpayers with a means to perform the task of completing a tax return, but each method is starkly different. Thus, while providers of all tax preparation methods may compete at some level, this "does not necessarily require that [they] be included in the relevant product market for antitrust purposes." DDIY tax preparation products differ from manual tax preparation and assisted tax preparation products in a number of meaningful ways. As compared to manual and assisted methods, DDIY products involve different technology, price, convenience level, time investment, mental effort and type of interaction by the consumer. Taken together, these different attributes make the consumer experience of using

DDIY products quite distinct from other methods of tax preparation. The question for this court is whether DDIY and other methods of tax preparation are "reasonably interchangeable" so that it would not be profitable to have a monopoly over only DDIY products.

a. Assisted Tax Preparation Is Not in the Relevant Product Market.

Apart from the analysis of their economic expert, the defendants' main argument for inclusion of assisted tax preparation in the relevant market is that DDIY and assisted companies compete for customers.[11] As evidence for this point, the defendants emphasize that Intuit's marketing efforts have targeted HRB's assisted customers. While the evidence does show that companies in the DDIY and assisted markets all generally compete with each other for the same overall pool of potential customers—U.S. taxpayers—that fact does not necessarily mean that DDIY and assisted must be viewed as part of the same relevant product market. DDIY provides customers with tax preparation services through an entirely different method, technology, and user experience than assisted preparation. As Judge Tatel explained in *Whole Foods:*

> [W]hen the automobile was first invented, competing auto manufacturers obviously took customers primarily from companies selling horses and buggies, not from other auto manufacturers, but that hardly shows that cars and horse-drawn carriages should be treated as the same product market. * * *

The key question for the Court is whether DDIY and assisted products are sufficiently close substitutes to constrain any anticompetitive DDIY pricing after the proposed merger. Evidence of the absence of close price competition between DDIY and assisted products makes clear that the answer to that question is no—and that DDIY is the relevant product market here. Significantly, despite some DDIY efforts to capture tax store customers, none of the major DDIY competitors sets their prices based on consideration of assisted prices. Indeed, there are quite significant price disparities between the average prices of DDIY and assisted products. The average price of TurboTax, the most popular DDIY brand is approximately $55. The average price of HRB's DDIY products is approximately $25. Overall, the DDIY industry average price is $44.13. In contrast, the typical price of an assisted tax return is significantly higher, in the range of $150–200. A 10 percent or even 20 percent price increase in the average price of DDIY would only move the average price up to $48.54 or $52.96, respectively—still substantially below the average price of assisted tax products. The overall lack of evidence of price competition between DDIY

---

[11] The defendants' primary argument for inclusion of both assisted and pen-and-paper in the relevant market is based upon their economic expert's analysis of data derived from two consumer surveys commissioned by the defendants. The Court will analyze the arguments of the defendants' expert economist separately below.

and assisted products supports the conclusion that DDIY is a separate relevant product market for evaluating this transaction, despite the fact that DDIY assisted firms target their marketing efforts at the same pool of customers.

The defendants point to some evidence that HRB sets prices for certain assisted products to compete with DDIY. For example, defendants note that in 2009, HRB "reduced prices on its assisted tax preparation services to $39 for federal 1040EZ preparation and $29 for state tax preparation to compete with and {redacted}" to DDIY. These are limited product offerings for which prices appear well below even the 25th percentile price for HRB's assisted products. Relatedly, the defendants' claim that prices for assisted and DDIY products "significantly overlap" is not strongly supported and relies on a comparison of the most limited, low-end assisted products with DDIY products generally. In sum, while defendants' have identified isolated instances in which assisted product offerings are priced lower than the average prices for typical assisted products, they do not and cannot demonstrate that this is generally the case.

Testimony from HRB executives further supports treating DDIY as a relevant product market in evaluating this transaction. HRB's DDIY and assisted businesses are run as separate business units. * * *

Finally, defendants argue that their broad relevant market is appropriate because there is "industry movement toward 'hybrid' products that combine some elements of both digital and assisted tax preparation." Based on the evidence presented at the hearing, however, it would be premature for the Court to identify any trend toward hybrid products. In fact, neither Intuit nor TaxACT presently offers a hybrid product and the defendants openly concede that HRB's current hybrid product has had "somewhat limited success," which defendants attribute to "technical issues" and a "lack of consistent marketing." {T}he Court finds it unlikely that there will be a sufficiently large scale shift into these products in the immediate future to compel the conclusion that DDIY and assisted products make up the same relevant product market.

b.   Manual Tax Preparation Is Not
in the Relevant Product Market.

The defendants also argue that manual tax preparation, or pen-and-paper, should be included in the relevant product market. At the outset, the Court notes that pen-and-paper is not a "product" at all; it is the task of filling out a tax return by oneself without any interactive assistance. Even so, the defendants argue pen-and-paper should be included in the relevant product market because it acts as a "significant competitive constraint" on DDIY. The defendants' argument relies primarily on two factors. First, the defendants' cite the results of a 2011 email survey of TaxACT customers. For reasons detailed in the following section, the Court declines to rely on this email survey. Second, the defendants point to documents and testimony indicating that TaxACT has considered possible diversion to pen-and-paper in setting its prices.

The Court finds that pen-and-paper is not part of the relevant market because it does not believe a sufficient number of consumers would switch to pen-and-paper in response to a small, but significant increase in DDIY prices. The possibility of preparing one's own tax return necessarily constrains the prices of other methods of preparation at some level. For example, if the price of DDIY and assisted products were raised to $1 million per tax return, surely all but the most well-heeled taxpayers would switch to pen-and-paper. Yet, at the more practical price increase levels that trigger antitrust concern—the typical five to ten percent price increase of the SSNIP test—pen-and-paper preparation is unlikely to provide a meaningful restraint for DDIY products, which currently sell for an average price of $44.13.

The government well illustrated the overly broad nature of defendants' proposed relevant market by posing to the defendants' expert the hypothetical question of whether "sitting at home and drinking chicken soup [would be] part of the market for [manufactured] cold remedies?" The defendants' expert responded that the real "question is if the price of cold medicines went up sufficiently, would people turn to chicken soup?" As an initial matter, in contrast to the defendants' expert, the Court doubts that it would ever be legally appropriate to define a relevant product market that included manufactured cold remedies and ordinary chicken soup. This conclusion flows from the deep functional differences between those products. Setting that issue aside, however, a price has increased "sufficiently" to trigger antitrust concern at the level of a five to ten percent small, but significant non-transitory increase in price. Just as chicken soup is unlikely to constrain the price of manufactured cold remedies sufficiently, the Court concludes that a SSNIP in DDIY would not be constrained by people turning to pen-and-paper. First, the share of returns prepared via pen-and-paper has dwindled over the past decade, as the DDIY market has grown. Second, while pen-and-paper filers have been a net source of new customers for DDIY companies, both HRB and {redacted} executives have testified that they do not believe their DDIY products compete closely with pen-and-paper methods. * * *

* * *

While some diversion from DDIY to manual filing may occur in response to a SSNIP, the Court finds that it would likely be limited and marginal. The functional experience of using a DDIY product is meaningfully different from the self-service task of filling out tax forms independently. Manual completion of a tax return requires different tools, effort, resources, and time investment by a consumer than use of either DDIY or assisted methods. * * *

* * *

The defendants' proposed relevant market of all methods of tax return preparation is so broadly defined that, as the plaintiff's expert testified, there are no conceivable alternatives besides going to jail, fleeing to Canada, or not earning any taxable income. As the plaintiff's expert put it, "if you're talking about the market for all tax preparation, you're talking about a market where, in economist terms, demand is completely [in]elastic. There are no alternatives." In such circumstances, the usual tools of antitrust analysis—such as the hypothetical monopolist test— cease being useful because it is self-evident that a monopolist of all forms of tax preparation, including self-preparation, could impose a small, but significant price increase. Indeed, a monopolist in that situation could essentially name any price since taxpayers would have no alternative but to pay it. As the plaintiff's expert testified, defining a market that broadly negates the entire purpose of defining a relevant market in an antitrust case. * * *

3.   The Economic Expert Testimony Tends to Confirm That DDIY Is the Relevant Product Market.

Both the plaintiff and the defendants presented testimony from expert economists to support their view of the relevant product market. In addition to their testimony at the hearing, these expert witnesses also provided a detailed expert report and an affidavit summarizing their analysis and conclusions.

The Court finds that the analysis performed by the plaintiff's expert tends to confirm that DDIY is a relevant product market, although the available data in this case limited the predictive power of the plaintiff's expert's economic models. The Court also finds that it cannot draw any conclusions from defendants' expert's analysis because of severe shortcomings in the underlying consumer survey data upon which the defendants' expert relied.

* * *

* * * Switching refers to the number of consumers who switch between different products for any reason. In any given year, many taxpayers switch from the tax preparation method they used in the prior year to a new method. Since the IRS processes all U.S. tax returns each year and tracks data about the methods of tax preparation that taxpayers used, there is ample, reliable data that market analysts can use to see how many taxpayers switched between methods each year. The IRS data, however, provides little direct insight about *why* any given taxpayer switched methods of preparation. The switch could have been for reasons of price,

convenience, changes in the consumer's personal situation, an increase or decrease in tax complexity, a loss of confidence in the prior method of preparation, or any other reason.

As opposed to switching, diversion refers to a consumer's response to a measured increase in the price of a product.[13] In other words, diversion measures to what extent consumers of a given product will switch (or be "diverted") to other products in response to a price increase in the given product. The IRS switching data does not directly measure diversion because switching can occur for any number of reasons, many of which may not involve price.

Unfortunately, no direct, reliable data on diversion exists in this case. The plaintiff's expert argues, however, that the IRS switching data can provide at least some estimate of diversion. While this approach is not without its limitations, as discussed further below, the Court finds that the switching data is at least somewhat indicative of likely diversion ratios. Moreover, the IRS data is highly reliable because (1) the sample size is enormous, since it encompasses over 100 million taxpayers, and (2) the data reflects actual historical tax return filing patterns as opposed to predicted behavior.

The defendant's expert, who criticizes reliance on this switching data, suggests instead that a better analysis can be based upon simulated diversion data derived from consumer surveys commissioned by the defendants. As described more fully below, however, the shortcomings of these survey-derived diversion data are so substantial that the Court cannot rely on them.

* * *

b. Coordinated Effects

[Within the worldwide DDIY market, the court found that the three leading firms had premerger market shares of 62.2% for Intuit, 15.6% for HR, and 12.5% for TaxACT. The merger would give the combined firm a share of 28.4%, and would raise the HHI by approximately 400 to 4691. Given these concentration levels, the court found that the government "has established a *prima facie* case of anticompetitive effects." Eds.]

---

[13] [The argument between the experts was in part over the best source of data for quantifying "diversion:" the extent to which consumers would substitute to other forms of tax preparation in the event that price of DDIY products were to rise. The plaintiffs' expert relied on switching data from the IRS to measure diversion. He incorporated his diversion rate estimates into his testimony on market definition in part by applying a "Critical Loss Analysis" framework, which is discussed *infra* in the *Note on Controversies in Market Definition: Submarkets, Price Discrimination Markets, Cluster Markets, and Critical Loss Analysis.* The expert also incorporated those estimates into his testimony on unilateral competitive effects (not included in the Casebook excerpt). Diversion ratios are related to demand cross-elasticities, and are discussed *infra* in the *Note on the Economics of Unilateral Effects in Differentiated-Product Markets: The Merger of Crunchies and Fruities.* Eds.]

Merger law "rests upon the theory that, where rivals are few, firms will be able to coordinate their behavior, either by overt collusion or implicit understanding in order to restrict output and achieve profits above competitive levels." The government argues that the "elimination of TaxACT, one of the 'Big 3' Digital DIY firms" will facilitate tacit coordination between Intuit and HRB. "Whether a merger will make coordinated interaction more likely depends on whether market conditions, on the whole, are conducive to reaching terms of coordination and detecting and punishing deviations from those terms." Since the government has established its *prima facie* case, the burden is on the defendants to produce evidence of "structural market barriers to collusion" specific to this industry that would defeat the "ordinary presumption of collusion" that attaches to a merger in a highly concentrated market. *See Heinz,* 246 F.3d at 725.

The defendants argue the primary reason that coordinated effects will be unlikely is that Intuit will have no incentive to compete any less vigorously post-merger. The defendants assert that the competition between Intuit and HRB's retail stores would be "fundamentally nullified if Intuit decided to reduce the competitiveness of TurboTax." Further, defendants contend that Intuit has no incentive to reduce the competitiveness of its free product because it views its free product as a critical driver of new customers. Therefore, the defendants conclude that if HRB does not compete as aggressively as possible with its post-merger products, it will lose customers to Intuit.

The most compelling evidence the defendants marshal in support of these arguments consists of documents and testimony indicating that Intuit engaged in a series of "war games" designed to anticipate and defuse new competitive threats that might emerge from HRB post-merger. The documents and testimony do indicate that Intuit and HRB will continue to compete for taxpayers' patronage after the merger—indeed, in the DDIY market, they would be the only major competitors. This conclusion, however, is not necessarily inconsistent with some coordination. As the Merger Guidelines explain, coordinated interaction involves a range of conduct, including unspoken understandings about *how* firms will compete or refrain from competing. *See* Merger Guidelines § 7.

In this case, the government contends that coordination would likely take the form of mutual recognition that neither firm has an interest in an overall "race to free" in which high-quality tax preparation software is provided for free or very low prices. Indeed, the government points to an outline created as part of the Intuit "war games" regarding post-merger competition with HRB that also indicates an Intuit employee's perception that part of HRB's post-merger strategy would be to "not escalate free war:

Make free the starting point not the end point for customers."[30] Since, as defendants point out, DDIY companies have found "free" offers to be a useful marketing tool, it is unlikely that free offers would be eliminated. Rather, the government argues, it is more likely that HRB and Intuit may find it "in their mutual interest to reduce the quality of their free offerings . . . offer a lower quality free product and maintain higher prices for paid products. . . ."

The government points to a highly persuasive historical act of cooperation between HRB and Intuit that supports this theory. *Cf.* Merger Guidelines § 7.2 ("[M]arket conditions are conducive to coordinated interaction if firms representing a substantial share in the relevant market appear to have previously engaged in express collusion."). After TaxACT launched its free-for-all offer in the FFA, Intuit proposed that the firms in the market limit their free FFA offers, a move which TaxACT opposed and which Mr. Dunn believed was an illegal restraint on trade. HRB, Intuit, and others then joined together and successfully lobbied the IRS for limitations on the scope of the free offers through the FFA—limitations that remain in place today. This action illustrates how the pricing incentives of HRB and Intuit differ from those of TaxACT and it also shows that HRB and Intuit, although otherwise competitors, are capable of acting in concert to protect their common interests.

The defendants also argue that coordinated effects are unlikely because the DDIY market consists of differentiated products and has low price transparency. To the contrary, the record clearly demonstrates that the players in the DDIY industry are well aware of the prices and features offered by competitors. Since DDIY products are marketed to a large swath of the American population and available via the Internet, DDIY firms can easily monitor their competitors' offerings and pricing. The fact that competitors may offer various discounts and coupons to some customers via email hardly renders industry pricing "not transparent," as defendants submit. Moreover, while collusion may, in some instances, be more likely in markets for homogenous products than differentiated products, product differentiation in this market would not necessarily make collusion more difficult. *See Heinz,* 246 F.3d at 716–17, 724–25 (finding likelihood of coordinated effects in product market differentiated by brand) * * *.

---

[30] The government also cites an informal analysis written by Adam Newkirk, an analyst for HRB's DDIY business. Mr. Newkirk's analysis hypothesized that one possible reason for HRB to acquire TaxACT was that HRB and Intuit would jointly control a large DDIY market share post-merger and would "both obviously have great incentive to keep this channel profitable," while other potential purchasers of TaxACT "could decide to cut prices even further. . . ." The Court finds that the government overemphasized the importance and relevance of Mr. Newkirk's analysis. The hearing testimony showed that Mr. Newkirk is a data analyst who had no decision-making role or authority in relation to the merger and that his discussion about the rationales for the merger was informal speculation. Even so, this reasoning—independently reached by Intuit—is essentially a précis of the government's coordinated effects concern.

Other indicia of likely coordination are also present in the DDIY market. Transactions in the market are small, numerous, and spread among a mass of individual consumers, each of whom has low bargaining power; prices can be changed easily; and there are barriers to switching due to the "stickiness" of the DDIY products.

Finally, the Court notes that the "merger would result in the elimination of a particularly aggressive competitor in a highly concentrated market, a factor which is certainly an important consideration when analyzing possible anti-competitive effects." The evidence presented at the hearing from all parties demonstrated TaxACT's impressive history of innovation and competition in the DDIY market. Mr. Dunn's trial testimony revealed him to be a dedicated and talented entrepreneur and businessman, with deep knowledge and passion for providing high-quality, low-cost tax solutions. TaxACT's history of expanding the scope of its high-quality, free product offerings has pushed the industry toward lower pricing, even when the two major players were not yet ready to follow—most notably in TaxACT's introduction of free-for-all into the market.

The government presses the argument that TaxACT's role as an aggressive competitor is particularly important by urging this Court to find that TaxACT is a "maverick." In the context of antitrust law, a maverick has been defined as a particularly aggressive competitor that "plays a disruptive role in the market to the benefit of customers." Merger Guidelines § 2.1.5. The most recent revision of the Merger Guidelines endorses this concept and gives a few examples of firms that may be industry mavericks, such as where "one of the merging firms may have the incentive to take the lead in price cutting or . . . a firm that has often resisted otherwise prevailing industry norms to cooperate on price setting or other terms of competition." *Id.*

The parties have spilled substantial ink debating TaxACT's maverick status. The arguments over whether TaxACT is or is not a "maverick"—or whether perhaps it once was a maverick but has not been a maverick recently—have not been particularly helpful to the Court's analysis. The government even put forward as supposed evidence a TaxACT promotional press release in which the company described itself as a "maverick." This type of evidence amounts to little more than a game of semantic gotcha. Here, the record is clear that while TaxACT has been an aggressive and innovative competitor in the market, as defendants admit, TaxACT is not unique in this role. Other competitors, including HRB and Intuit, have also been aggressive and innovative in forcing companies in the DDIY market to respond to new product offerings to the benefit of consumers.

The government has not set out a clear standard, based on functional or economic considerations, to distinguish a maverick from any other aggressive competitor. At times, the government has emphasized

TaxACT's low pricing as evidence of its maverick status, while, at other times, the government seems to suggest that almost any competitive activity on TaxACT's part is a "disruptive" indicator of a maverick. For example, the government claims that "[m]ost recently, TaxACT continued to disrupt the Digital DIY market by entering the boxed retail software segment of the market, which had belonged solely to HRB and [Intuit]." Credible evidence at the hearing, however, showed {otherwise}. Moreover, the Court credits Mr. Dunn's explanation that TaxACT has little interest in selling boxed retail software because he believes this market segment is {redacted} not particularly significant.

What the Court finds particularly germane for the "maverick" or "particularly aggressive competitor" analysis in this case is this question: Does TaxACT consistently play a role within the competitive structure of this market that constrains prices? The Court finds that TaxACT's competition does play a special role in this market that constrains prices. Not only did TaxACT buck prevailing pricing norms by introducing the free-for-all offer, which others later matched, it has remained the only competitor with significant market share to embrace a business strategy that relies primarily on offering high-quality, full-featured products for free with associated products at low prices.

Moreover, as the plaintiff's expert, Dr. Warren-Boulton, explained, the pricing incentives of the merged firm will differ from those of TaxACT pre-merger because the merged firm's opportunity cost for offering free or very low-priced products will increase as compared to TaxACT now. In other words, the merged firm will have a greater incentive to migrate customers into its higher-priced offerings—for example, by limiting the breadth of features available in the free or low-priced offerings or only offering innovative new features in the higher-priced products.

While the defendants oppose the government's maverick theory, they do not deny that TaxACT has been an aggressive competitor. Indeed, they submit that "that's why H & R Block wants to buy them." HRB contends that the acquisition of TaxACT will result in efficiencies and management improvements that "will lead to better, more effective, and/or cheaper H & R Block digital products post-merger" that are better able to compete with Intuit. This argument is quite similar to the argument of the defendants in *Heinz,* which some commentators have described as arguing that the merger would create a maverick. While the district court in *Heinz* accepted this argument that the merger would enhance rather than stifle competition, the D.C. Circuit reversed, finding that the "district court's analysis [fell] short of the findings necessary for a successful efficiencies defense" in that case. As explained more fully in Section III.B.2.d below, the defendants' efficiency arguments fail here for some of the same reasons the D.C. Circuit identified in *Heinz.*

Finally, the defendants suggest that coordinated effects are unlikely because of the ease of expansion for other competitors in the market. As detailed above in the Court's discussion of barriers to entry and expansion, the Court does not find that ease of expansion would counteract likely anticompetitive effects.

Accordingly, the defendants have not rebutted the presumption that anticompetitive coordinated effects would result from the merger. To the contrary, the preponderance of the evidence suggests the acquisition is reasonably likely to cause such effects. *See [Heinz]* at 711–12 (finding, in market characterized by high barriers to entry and high HHI figures, that "no court has ever approved a merger to duopoly under similar circumstances.").

NOTE ON ISSUES IN MARKET DEFINITION: SUBMARKETS, PRICE DISCRIMINATION MARKETS, CLUSTER MARKETS, AND CRITICAL LOSS ANALYSIS

This note discusses four controversies involving market definition: submarkets, price discrimination markets, cluster markets, and critical loss analysis.

Submarkets

Some modern decisions refer to an early list of evidence potentially relevant to market definition that the Supreme Court provided in *Brown Shoe* in connection with the Court's endorsement of the possibility of "submarkets" within a broader market:

> The outer boundaries of a product market are determined by the reasonable interchangeability of use or the cross-elasticity of demand between the product itself and substitutes for it. However, within this broad market, well-defined submarkets may exist which, in themselves, constitute product markets for antitrust purposes. The boundaries of such a submarket may be determined by examining such practical indicia as industry or public recognition of the submarket as a separate economic entity, the product's peculiar characteristics and uses, unique production facilities, distinct customers, distinct prices, sensitivity to price changes, and specialized vendors. Because § 7 of the Clayton Act prohibits any merger which may substantially lessen competition "in *any* line of commerce" (emphasis supplied), it is necessary to examine the effects of a merger in each such economically significant submarket to determine if there is a reasonable probability that the merger will substantially lessen competition. If such a probability is found to exist, the merger is proscribed.

Brown Shoe, 370 U.S. at 325 (footnotes and citation omitted). Several of the seven *Brown Shoe* "practical indicia" appear related to the identification of buyer substitution patterns. Others appear related to the possibility of supply (seller) substitution, accounted for in the contemporary Horizontal Merger Guidelines in the identification of market participants or the analysis of entry. Still others relate to the possibility of "price discrimination" markets (discussed later in this Note) or unilateral adverse competitive effects of mergers (discussed later in this Chapter).

In addition to its value in pointing lower courts toward potentially relevant evidence of buyer substitution patterns, this paragraph from *Brown Shoe* was influential in its endorsement of "submarkets." Submarkets continue to be defined by lower courts, as we will see later in this Chapter when we read *FTC v. Staples*, where the court defined a product market with reference to a particular distribution channel ("the sale of consumable office supplies through office supply superstores").

Defenders observe that defining submarkets is appropriate when the resulting markets are consistent with Merger Guidelines principles. If the hypothetical monopolist test is satisfied for a more narrow group of products and locations, those products and locations are also appropriately considered a "market." But this practice has been criticized. Critics emphasize that when the *Brown Shoe* practical indicia are applied blindly, without reference to the economic goal of identifying buyer substitution possibilities, they may allow courts to define inappropriately narrow submarkets within the outer bounds of markets properly defined with reference to substitution possibilities. For a survey of the uses and abuses of antitrust submarkets, see Jonathan B. Baker, *Stepping Out in an Old Brown Shoe: In Qualified Praise of Submarkets*, 68 ANTITRUST L. J. 203 (2000).

Price Discrimination Markets

The Merger Guidelines employ the term "price discrimination market" to describe the situation in which a hypothetical monopolist (of a group of products and geographic locations) would likely charge different prices to different groups of buyers and in consequence would raise prices to a class of targeted customers. *Horizontal Merger Guidelines* §§ 3, 4.1.4, 4.2 (2010). For example, if a passenger airline monopolist would find it profitable to raise fares to business passengers (buying unrestricted tickets) on city-pair routes by a small but significant amount, then business fares (unrestricted tickets) on those routes would constitute a relevant market. This market could be described as a price discrimination market: the product market would be passenger air travel; the geographic market would be the city-pairs, and business travelers would constitute the set of targeted customers. This approach to market definition recognizes that a hypothetical monopolist may find it profitable to raise prices to targeted customers even if a price increase for all customers would not be profitable because too many other customers would substitute away. If prices are negotiated individually with customers, markets defined according to Merger Guidelines principles may be as narrow as individual customers. *Id.* § 4.1.4.

In order for price discrimination to be successful in the airline example, the airline must be able to sort buyers by how much they are willing to pay: they must be able to distinguish reliably between those buyers willing to pay a high price (here business travelers) and those that are not. The introduction of tickets with fare restrictions might be a way of sorting out leisure travelers from business passengers, for example. If doing so is impossible, the ability of leisure travelers to substitute connecting flights or driving for non-stop travel on a city-pair route might make it unprofitable for the airline to raise fares on that route. In addition, the buyers charged a low price must be unable to resell the product cheaply to the buyers charged a high price. (Limited reselling may not be sufficient defeat the profitability of price discrimination, but substantial reselling would.) In the airline industry, the necessary prohibition on buyer arbitrage is enforced by the requirement that passengers present identification at the airport consistent with the name on their ticket. *Cf. Spirit Airlines, Inc. v. Northwest Airlines, Inc.* 431 F.3d 917 (6th Cir. 2005) (finding that a reasonable trier of fact could have defined a leisure airline passenger market). For further discussion of the economics of price discrimination, see Sidebar 5–4, *infra.*

Targeted buyers are often distinguished by their uses or locations. For example, one court limited a product market to latex condoms sold through retail outlets in the United States, excluding condom sales to the U.S. Agency for International Development (USAID) for distribution free of charge in third-world countries. *Ansell Inc. v. Schmid Laboratories, Inc.*, 757 F. Supp. 467 (D.N.J. 1991), *aff'd*, 941 F.2d 1200 (3d Cir. 1991). Another court upheld a market defined as the sale of new components for automotive electrical units to production-line rebuilders, excluding sales to repair shops. *Avnet, Inc. v. FTC*, 511 F.2d 70, 78–79 (7th Cir. 1975), *cert. denied*, 423 U.S. 833 (1975). In merger litigation, a court defined a market described as "broadline foodservice distribution to national customers." *FTC v. Sysco Corp.* 113 F. Supp. 3d. 1 (D.D.C. 2015).

Cluster Markets

In several bank merger cases in the 1960s and 1970s, beginning with *Philadelphia Nat'l Bank*, the Supreme Court employed a different approach to market definition, collecting into one product market the commercial banking "cluster of services." The Court determined that commercial banking activity— including loans and other types of credit, deposit accounts, checking services, and trust administration—constituted a unique cluster of products and services, distinct from those offered by savings and loans, finance companies, credit unions, and other financial institutions. According to the Court in *Philadelphia Nat'l Bank*, banking services were clustered because distinctiveness, cost advantages, and "a settled consumer preference" insulated each commercial banking product from competition.

Lower courts have applied the cluster concept to define markets in a handful of other industry settings, including traditional grocery supermarkets, department stores, and "acute inpatient care" hospital services. The hospital example is instructive: courts have defined cluster markets in order to analyze hospital mergers even though the individual services that comprise the cluster are commonly recognized as relevant product markets in non-merger antitrust cases involving medical services provided by hospitals, as with anesthesiology services in *Jefferson Parish* (*see infra* Chapter 6). The cluster market concept deviates from the demand substitution approach of the main line of Supreme Court market definition precedents and the Merger Guidelines because it includes in the same market products or services that are not substitutes from the standpoint of buyers. Cluster markets are most likely to mislead when firms selling a partial line of products and services, but not all the services in the cluster, provide a significant competitive constraint on firms selling some or all of the full line of products. Defining a broad hospital market cluster could, for example, lead a court to understate the competitive significance of outpatient clinics in restraining some forms of coordinated conduct; this particular danger would be avoided by limiting the cluster to acute inpatient care, but the latter cluster may still exclude inpatient facilities specializing in, for example, cancer care, and thus potentially understate their competitive significance.

All products are, in a sense, combinations of products that are not substitutes. In an appropriate case, automobiles could constitute a product market for antitrust analysis (perhaps, for example, if General Motors were accused of monopolization or if General Motors and Ford proposed to merge), even though a car combines a chassis, tires, engine, radio, etc. In fact, automobiles could be an appropriate product market for analyzing some allegations even though tires are relevant markets for analyzing other allegations (an agreement between Michelin and Goodyear to exchange information, perhaps). An automobile product market would be appropriate, notwithstanding that it aggregates products that are not substitutes, because the buyers alleged to have been harmed by the conduct under review purchase the aggregated product. Cluster markets are not defined by what buyers purchase, however. They are defined by the group of products that multi-product sellers offer.

Some commentators view cluster markets as merely a matter of analytical convenience: why bother to define separate markets for a large number of individual services when market shares and entry conditions are similar for each (or when data limitations will effectively require that the same proxy, such as number of hospital beds, be employed to estimate the market share for each individual service)? Other commentators suggest greater continuity with the judicial focus on demand substitution and argue that clusters are properly defined when a seller can offer buyers substantial transactions costs savings from "one-stop shopping." From either perspective, a proposed cluster market would be called into question when competition from sellers of a partial line of products or services can constrain the pricing of the full line of sellers offering the cluster.

Critical Loss Analysis

The hypothetical monopolist test in the Merger Guidelines is sometimes implemented with an approach called Critical Loss Analysis (CLA). CLA bases market definition on a simple numerical comparison between what is termed the "Critical Loss" and the "Predicted Loss."[14] The goal is to evaluate the profitability of a small but significant and non-transitory increase in price (SSNIP) within the candidate market. As will be explained, the 2010 Merger Guidelines reject a simple version of CLA that had been employed in the past, but accept a modified version of CLA as a possible method of organizing information about market definition and structuring the implementation of the hypothetical monopolist approach.

A numerical example involving product market definition illustrates the computation for a simple case. Suppose that all the products sold in a candidate market have the same pre-merger price of $20. Suppose further that all the firms in the candidate market have a marginal cost of $12 that does not vary with the level of output. Then for each unit sold, the hypothetical monopolist would earn an incremental dollar profit margin (i.e., contribution to profit per unit) of $8, which is computed by subtracting marginal cost from price. With these numbers, the percentage margin would be 40%, where the margin is expressed as a percentage of price.[15] Assume further that before the merger, the collective quantity sold by participants in the candidate market is 100 units and the firms collectively are earning an aggregate dollar profit contribution of $800 (i.e., 100 units times an $8 profit-margin per unit).

Suppose that the hypothetical monopolist increases price by a SSNIP equal to 5%, from $20 to $21. At the new price, the profit margin would rise to $9. The SSNIP would be profitable if the actual loss in sales attributable to the price increase was sufficiently small to make the dollar contribution more than $800. This would require retained sales of at least 88.9 units (88.9 units at $9 just exceeds $800), or a loss of no more than 11.1 units. With an initial output of 100, the "critical loss" is 11.1%.[16] These calculations are summarized in Figure 5–3:

---

[14] The latter concept has also been termed the "Actual Loss."

[15] This measure is also termed the Lerner Index. The use of the Lerner Index as indicator of market power is discussed in Sidebar 4–5: The Single Inference Method of Inferring Anticompetitive Effects.

[16] The same numbers imply that the "critical elasticity" of demand for the products in the candidate market is −2.2. Recall from the Coffee Shop example in Chapter 1 that the own-price elasticity of demand can be approximated by the ratio of the percent change in quantity sold to the percent change in price. Accordingly, the SSNIP would be profitable so long as the demand for the candidate product is not more elastic than the critical elasticity (not greater than −2.2 in absolute value). As this example suggests, CLA can alternatively be implemented by comparing a "critical elasticity" with the observed elasticity of demand. This alternative approach summarizes the evidence on buyer substitution in an estimated elasticity of demand rather than in an estimate of the "Predicted Loss."

Figure 5–3:

Calculation of Critical Loss for Market Definition

Price, cost, industry output, and industry profit contribution premerger:

Price	$20
Marginal cost	$12
Incremental dollar profit margin ($20–$12)	$8
Percentage profit margin ($8/$20)	40%
Quantity sold (industry)	100
Aggregate dollar profit contribution (100 x $8)	$800

Critical loss calculation for candidate market:

Price (after SSNIP of $1 (5%))	$21
Marginal cost	$12
Incremental dollar profit margin	$9
Quantity sold (industry) to preserve prior	88.9
dollar profit contribution	
(*i.e.* 88.9 x $9 = 100 x $8 = $800)	
Critical loss (in units) (100–88.9)	11.1
Critical loss (percentage of initial output of 100)	11.1%

The critical loss is then compared to the "predicted loss." The "predicted loss" is an estimate of the fraction of sales that the hypothetical monopolist likely would lose in the event of the SSNIP. That fraction depends on the predicted magnitude of buyer substitution out of the candidate market from the price increase, that is, on the own-price elasticity of demand for the products in the candidate market. If the "predicted loss" arising from the SSNIP is smaller than the "critical loss," then the set of products in the candidate market comprise a relevant market. But if the predicted loss is instead more than 11%, then the SSNIP would not be profitable and the market definition would be rejected.[17]

---

[17] In *U.S. v. Bazaarvoice, Inc.*, 2014 WL 203966 (N.D. Cal. Jan. 8, 2014), the court described the CLA test in an alternative but equivalent way: as a comparison between a critical loss threshold and a "recapture rate." According to the court, "In order for a SSNIP imposed by a hypothetical monopolist to be profitable, the recapture rate ("the percentage of sales lost by one product in the candidate market, when its price alone rises, that is recaptured by other products in the candidate market") must be high enough that the incremental profits from the increased

The Merger Guidelines recognize that the margin itself provides useful information about the likely magnitude of the predicted loss. A profit-maximizing firm not engaged in coordinated conduct normally raises price more above marginal cost on those products for which consumers are less price sensitive (i.e., demand is less elastic). Hence a high price-cost margin implies that buyers are not sensitive to price and, in consequence, the predicted loss likely is small. To account for this relationship, the Merger Guidelines "require that estimates of the predicted loss be consistent with [all evidence of consumer substitution], including the pre-merger margins of products in the candidate market used to calculate the critical loss." *Horizontal Merger Guidelines* § 4.1.3 (2010).

This requirement addresses an important difficulty. In the simple approach to Critical Loss Analysis sketched above, a high price-cost margin implies that the critical loss is small.[18] Under such circumstances, it would not take a large predicted loss to defeat the candidate market, so high price-cost margins would seemingly tend to lead to broad market definitions. The Merger Guidelines recognize that this implication is often incorrect: higher margins may imply a low critical loss, but they may also imply a low predicted loss.[19]

The use of CLA sometimes raises other complications. First, CLA requires measurement of marginal cost. Yet it may not be obvious which costs should be considered variable and which should be considered fixed for this purpose.[20] In addition, if marginal costs vary with the level of output (*e.g.*, if there are scale economies or rising costs), or if opportunity costs (*e.g.*, lost profits from diverting output from one market to another) are an important component of

---

price plus the incremental profits from the recaptured sales that goes to other products in the candidate market exceeds the profits lost to products outside the candidate market." *Id.* at 30 (quoting *Horizontal Merger Guidelines* § 4.1.3 (2010)). The proposed market definition was supported by evidence that the recapture rate exceeded the threshold (minimum rate) needed to show a relevant market. In *H & R Block*, the court applied the same framework, but employed the term "aggregate diversion ratio" instead of "recapture rate."

[18] Conversely, a low price-cost margin implies that the critical loss is larger. For example, if marginal cost in the example above were $19 instead of $12, the profit margin would be only $1 per unit, which is lower than the original $8 figure. In this case, a $1 SSNIP would double the margin to $2, and the aggregate contribution to profit would rise as long as retained sales exceeded 50 units. The critical loss would be 50%, which is higher than the previously calculated 11% critical loss.

[19] Although "high pre-merger margins normally indicate that each firm's product individually faces demand that is not highly sensitive to price," Horizontal Merger Guidelines § 4.1.3 (2010), the relationship between the price-cost margin and the demand elasticity will not always be easy to evaluate. If firms are coordinating pre-merger, for example, that may allow them to achieve high margins even when each firm's demand is highly elastic. Moreover, the demand elasticity cannot be inferred in a simple way from price-cost margins when firms sell products that are substitutes or complements for the product in the candidate market as well as that product. Nor can the demand elasticity be inferred from margins in a simple way if firms set current prices low in order to sell more in the short run, as they may do in order to reduce future costs when scale economies or learning are important or to increase future demand when buyers develop brand loyalty.

[20] For example, capital costs are often considered fixed, but they may be considered variable for a growing firm that faces capacity constraints. The distinction between fixed and variable costs, and the link between the economic concept of cost and a decision by the firm, are discussed further in the Appendix to Chapter 1 on Cost Concepts.

marginal cost, then marginal costs can be more difficult to estimate, even with detailed accounting data. Problems with using accounting data on average variable cost to infer marginal cost were discussed in connection with predatory pricing in Chapter 4, *supra*.

Second, CLA assumes that the hypothetical monopolist raises price uniformly for all the products within the candidate market. But, a profit-maximizing hypothetical monopolist might choose to raise the prices of some products by more than others. Under such circumstances, CLA might reject a candidate market even though post-merger price discrimination would be profitable.[21]

While these complications often can be addressed within the CLA framework, critics suggest that these problems would be more easily recognized and minimized if the CLA framework is not employed. Those critics also suggest that in practice, CLA may tend to elevate in importance quantitative measures of demand elasticity over qualitative evidence concerning buyer substitution, which may be more probative in some mergers. For more extensive discussions of these issues, and citations to the relevant economic literature, compare David Scheffman & Joseph Simons, *The State of Critical Loss Analysis: Let's Make Sure We Understand the Whole Story*, ANTITRUST SOURCE, November 2003, http://www.abanet.org/antitrust/at-source/03/11/scheffman.pdf (supporting critical loss analysis) with Joseph Farrell & Carl Shapiro, *Improving Critical Loss Analysis*, ANTITRUST SOURCE, February 2008, http://faculty.haas.berkeley.edu/shapiro/critical2008.pdf (criticizing the misuse of critical loss analysis).

Sidebar 5–4:
The Economics of Price Discrimination

As suggested by the recognition of price discrimination markets in the Horizontal Merger Guidelines, price discrimination in the economic sense is ubiquitous in the economy. It is particularly prevalent in industries where producers face high fixed costs and low marginal costs, so long as the seller has a way of sorting customers based on their willingness to pay for the product. For example, the marginal cost to a movie theater of filling any seat in its auditorium is probably very small if some seats would otherwise go empty, as the major costs—facility construction, film rental, on-site staff, food for resale—do not appear to vary with the number of seats filled. With marginal cost near zero, the business would probably not be profitable were the theater to set price equal to marginal cost; the industry would likely not survive unless the theaters charged some price in excess of marginal cost.

---

[21] To address this problem, CLA could be used to evaluate a SSNIP applied to some but not all of the products in the candidate market.

But the theaters can do even better if they can sort their patrons into a price-insensitive group (relatively inelastic demand, *e.g.*, those who come to the movie theater on weekend evenings) and a price-sensitive group (relatively elastic demand, *e.g.*, those willing to come at other times), and charge a higher price to the first group. Moreover, such price discrimination is not necessarily inconsistent with competition, where competition in this context is understood as free entry. The high price charged to the price-insensitive group would then be limited by the threat of new competition, and the firm as a whole would not earn more than competitive profits. *See In re Brand Name Prescription Drugs Antitrust Litig.*, 288 F.3d 1028 (7th Cir. 2002) (Posner, J.) (explaining that sellers of prescription drugs may charge different prices to different customers or different customer groups without exercising monopoly power).

Price discrimination and related practices like producing products in multiple versions—all ways of selling a product at different prices to different consumers according to how much they are willing to pay for it—are often a natural way to recover the high fixed costs of information and information technology. *See generally* CARL SHAPIRO & HAL R. VARIAN, INFORMATION RULES: A STRATEGIC GUIDE TO THE NETWORK ECONOMY 19–81 (1999) (chapters on pricing information and versioning information). As with price discrimination generally, the licensing of intellectual property at a price above its marginal cost (often zero) is not necessarily inconsistent with competition, and thus does not necessarily reflect the exercise of market power (*see infra* Chapter 7).

Price discrimination can be harmful or beneficial to buyers. *See, e.g., Jefferson Parish Hosp. Dist. No. 2 v. Hyde*, 466 U.S. 2, 36 n.4 (1984) (O'Connor, J., concurring). It is harmful if it permits the seller to raise price to a group of buyers; it is beneficial if it encourages the seller to serve a previously unserved group of buyers. To see why either possibility could occur, consider the following hypothetical example involving price discrimination by a monopolist.

Eastern is the only airline flying between Washington, D.C. and Boston. It is thus a monopolist. There are two kinds of passengers, business and leisure. All business passengers are identical, and would be willing to pay $200 for a one-way ticket. All leisure passengers are identical, and would be willing to pay $100 for a one-way ticket. All costs are fixed (none vary with the number of passengers): the plane costs $1000 per flight to operate regardless of the number of passengers who fly. (The numbers in the example are wildly unrealistic; they have been chosen to make the math simple!)

First, it is possible that price discrimination would benefit buyers by making a product available to a group of buyers who otherwise would be unserved. To see why, assume that the typical flight carries 10 business passengers and 5 leisure passengers. The carrier compares the following two alternatives—no price discrimination and price discrimination—and selects the alternative that leads to the highest profit.

If price discrimination were prohibited, the airline could charge only one price. What price would it select? The best price must either be $100 (in which case Eastern will serve both business and leisure passengers) or $200 (in which case it will serve only business passengers). Eastern evaluates these alternatives by comparing the resulting profit. If the price is $100, 15 passengers will fly (both groups). Eastern will receive revenues of $1500 and earn a profit of $500. If the price is instead $200, 10 fly (only business passengers). Eastern will receive revenues of $2000 and earn a profit of $1000. Comparing these alternatives, Eastern would pick a price of $200 if it is limited to one price (*i.e.*, prevented from discriminating in price). Leisure travelers would not fly; only business travelers would be served.

With price discrimination, Eastern can do better, and so may some customers. Suppose that the airline offers two types of tickets: restricted tickets (*e.g.*, with advance purchase requirements and limited refundability) and unrestricted tickets. Business travelers will only purchase unrestricted tickets (assuming the price is no more than $200). Leisure travelers will purchase either restricted or unrestricted, and choose the type with the lowest price (assuming the price is no more than $100).

Eastern's best strategy now is to sell unrestricted tickets for $200 and restricted tickets for $100. The 10 business travelers will buy $200 (unrestricted) tickets, generating $2000 in revenue. The 5 leisure travelers will buy $100 (restricted) tickets, generating $500 more revenue. Eastern's total revenue now is $2500, and it earns a profit of $1500. In this example, permitting price discrimination may induce Eastern to serve the leisure customers, who previously would have gone unserved, without charging more to its business customers.

But price discrimination need not necessarily benefit Eastern's buyers. It may instead allow the seller to charge more to a group of buyers lacking attractive alternatives (and thus facing inelastic demand). To see why, assume (contrary to what was previously supposed) that the typical flight carries 5 business passengers and 10 leisure passengers.

If the airline can charge only one price, what price would be best under these assumptions? As before, the best price must either be $100 (in which case Eastern will serve both business and leisure passengers) or $200 (in which case it will serve only business passengers). If the price is $100, 15 passengers will fly (both groups). Eastern will receive revenues of $1500 and earn a profit of $500. If the price is instead $200, 5 fly (only business passengers). Eastern will receive revenues of $1000 and earn a profit of $0. Comparing these alternatives, Eastern would pick a price of $100 if it is limited to one price (prevented from discriminating in price). Both leisure travelers and business travelers would be served.

To understand the consequences of price discrimination in the second example, suppose that the airline offers two types of tickets, restricted and unrestricted. Eastern's best strategy is again to sell unrestricted tickets for $200 and restricted tickets for $100. The 5 business travelers will buy $200 (unrestricted) tickets, generating $1000 in revenue. The 10 leisure travelers will buy $100 (restricted) tickets, generating $1000 more revenue. Eastern's total revenue now is $2000, and it earns a profit of $1000. In this second example, price discrimination induces Eastern to sort out the business travelers and charge them a higher price, while still serving the leisure travelers. In the example, price discrimination harms the business passengers (who pay more) without benefitting the leisure travelers (who are still served at the prior price), so passengers collectively are made worse off.

In this simple example, price discrimination has distributional consequences—it transfers wealth from business travelers to the airline—but does not create an allocative efficiency loss because all fifteen passengers fly regardless of Eastern's pricing policy. This special feature of the example need not hold in general, in which case price discrimination would also reduce economic efficiency. Suppose, for example, that when the airline set a price of $100 for all seats, some of the five leisure passengers were spouses or other companions, who decided to join a business traveler at the last minute. When Eastern decides to discriminate in price, these leisure passengers would no longer buy tickets—they are too late to purchase restricted tickets and unwilling to pay the high price for unrestricted seats. Price discrimination would remain profitable for Eastern, but now some passengers who would previously have purchased tickets are no longer served (output is reduced), generating an efficiency loss.

In more complex examples, price discrimination may benefit some consumers while harming others, and may generate either an efficiency gain or efficiency loss overall. For example, if Eastern's marginal cost declines as its output rises, price discrimination would confer a production efficiency if it leads Eastern to serve more passengers. Moreover, as illustrated in both examples above, price discrimination increases Eastern's profits. If the firm would be unable to cover its avoidable fixed costs absent the higher profits it would earn by discriminating in price, it would need to do so in order to stay in business.

The sports and entertainment industries are increasingly shifting from setting a single price to discriminating in price, for example by charging higher prices for the most popular concerts or games. Is this change in business practice likely pro-competitive or anticompetitive?

b. Identifying Market Participants

After defining product and geographic markets, it is necessary to determine what firms sell in those markets before market concentration can be calculated. The Merger Guidelines count as firms participating in the market all firms that currently earn revenues from the market, as well as firms that do not yet earn revenues but are committed to entering the market in the near future. *Horizontal Merger Guidelines* § 5.1 (2010). This definition also recognizes as market participants vertically integrated firms, which may transfer the relevant product internally to a downstream division rather than selling it to an outside buyer, "to the extent that their inclusion accurately reflects their competitive significance."

Firms not currently earning revenues from the relevant product in the relevant geographic area may be counted as participating in the market if they would very likely enter the market quickly in the event of a SSNIP "with direct competitive impact," and enter without the prospect of incurring significant sunk costs. These firms are termed *"rapid entrants."* (Such firms were termed "uncommitted entrants" in the 1992 Horizontal Merger Guidelines.)

Sunk expenditures are investments that would not be recoverable in the event the firm were later to exit the market. Investments in office equipment might not be sunk, at least to the extent the firm could recover some or all of those expenditures were it to sell the equipment in the used market. But investments in signage, letterhead and business cards specific to the firm at some specific location, or tools and dyes specific to the firm's production process, would be sunk to the extent they cannot be used by other firms, or by this firm in other plants selling to other markets. The significance of sunk expenditures is discussed more fully later in this Chapter in connection with the analysis of entry. A firm that can enter quickly and without substantial sunk expenditures—a "rapid entrant"—is likely to enter the market in response to a short term profit opportunity. It can be thought of, therefore, as a "hit and run" entrant—available nimbly to come into the market with little delay in response to even a small increase in price, and ready to leave the market quickly in the event that supply increases so much that price returns to its lower, pre-merger level.

As previously noted in this Chapter, some courts deviate from the Merger Guidelines' approach to market definition by expanding markets to reflect seller substitution (production flexibility). In the Merger Guidelines, this important economic force is not addressed in market definition but is divided and treated in two places: the identification of market participants (through the inclusion of "rapid entrants" as participants), a subject of this section, and the analysis of entry, which will be discussed in a later section of this Chapter.

c.　Measuring Market Concentration

With a market defined and market participants identified—including both incumbent sellers and uncommitted entrants—the stage is set to measure market concentration. Market shares are usually measured in terms of annual historical sales revenues, but may instead be based upon projected rather than historical data, data covering longer periods, physical units rather than dollars, sales to recent customers rather than all customers, or shipments, production, capacity, or reserves instead of sales, if these alternatives would better reflect the future competitive significance of the firms. *Horizontal Merger Guidelines* § 5.2 (2010). The choice of units does not usually make much difference to the picture of concentration that emerges, although the choice between sales and reserves did matter in *General Dynamics*.

Market participants that are not currently producing may be assigned shares if a measure of their competitive significance comparable to what is employed for current producers is available. When market shares are based on firms' readily available capacities, as might make sense for rapid entrants (or for all firms in homogeneous product markets), capacity is excluded to the extent it is committed or so profitably employed outside the relevant market or so costly that it would not likely be used to respond to an increase in price in the relevant market. But a measure of divertible capacity would likely overstate the competitive significance of a rapid entrant if its products are differentiated from those of other firms or its marginal cost of production and distribution would increase as it expands sales within the relevant market.

The Merger Guidelines suggest three tools for measuring market concentration: a simple count of the number of significant rivals in the market, the combined market share of the merging firms, and the Herfindahl-Hirschman Index (HHI). *Horizontal Merger Guidelines* § 5.3 (2010). Among the three approaches, the Guidelines emphasize the HHI. A comparison of the HHI measured pre-merger and post-merger provides a method for evaluating the impact of the transaction on the structure of the relevant market.

The HHI takes into account both the number and relative size of the firms in the market. It is computed by squaring the market share of each firm, and summing the resulting numbers. Thus, in a three firm market, in which firms have market shares a, b, and c, the HHI equals $a^2 + b^2 + c^2$. The HHI ranges from 0 to 10,000. An atomistic industry, with no firm having as much as 1% of the market, would have an HHI near zero. A monopolist, with 100% of the market, would have an HHI of 10,000 ($100^2 = 10,000$).

In the first example presented in Figure 5–4, markets 1 and 2 have a different number of firms and a different structure—one with three similarly-sized firms and two smaller sellers, the other with one firm twice the size of the next largest sellers—but their market concentration is summarized by the same HHI number. In contrast, markets 3 and 4 have the same number of firms, but very different HHIs. In reviewing these examples, ask yourself whether antitrust law should treat markets 1 and 2 as similarly structured, and markets 3 and 4 as differently structured, for the purpose of reviewing the likely competitive consequences of a horizontal merger.[22]

One difference between the HHI and the leading prior approach to measuring concentration, "concentration ratios" that sum the market shares for a specified number of the largest firms, is that the HHI takes into account the size of all of the firms. The Supreme Court relied on the two-firm concentration ratio in *Philadelphia National Bank* and cited the two-firm, four-firm, and ten-firm concentration ratios in *General Dynamics*. For example, the four-firm concentration ratio (abbreviated C4 or CR4) is the sum of the market shares of the four firms with the greatest

---

[22] If all firms in an industry were identically sized, the HHI would equal 10,000 divided by the number of firms. For example, a market with five identical firms, each holding 20%, would be characterized by an HHI of 2000 ($20^2 + 20^2 + 20^2 + 20^2 + 20^2 = 2000 = 10,000/5$). This mathematical property suggests that each HHI can be interpreted as a *numbers equivalent*: 10,000 divided by the HHI equals the number of identically-sized firms that would produce the same degree of market concentration measured by the HHI. For example, an HHI of 2550 has a numbers equivalent of 3.9 ($10,000/2550 = 3.9$), suggesting that the various market structures producing that HHI are roughly equivalent to an industry with slightly less than four equally-sized firms.

market shares. Note that markets 3 and 4 in Figure 5–4 would be represented by the identical C4 (of 95%), but would have very different HHIs. Which index seems to you to capture best the extent of similarity or differences between these market structures?

Figure 5–4:

Understanding the HHI

Market 1

Firm	Market Share	Market Share Squared
A	30%	900
B	30%	900
C	25%	625
D	10%	100
E	5%	25
Total	**100%**	**HHI=2550**

Market 2

Firm	Market Share	Market Share Squared
A	40%	1600
B	20%	400
C	20%	400
D	10%	100
E	5%	25
F	5%	25
Total	**100%**	**HHI=2550**

Market 3

Firm	Market Share	Market Share Squared
A	80%	6400
B	5%	25
C	5%	25
D	5%	25
E	5%	25
Total	**100%**	**HHI=6500**

Market 4

Firm	Market Share	Market Share Squared
A	25%	625
B	25%	625
C	25%	625
D	20%	400
E	5%	25
Total	**100%**	**HHI=2300**

Calculating the Effect of a Merger on the HHI:
Two Examples from Market 1

Example 1: Firm C acquires Firm D

Firm	Pre-Merger Market Share	Pre-Merger Market Share Squared	Post-Merger Market Share	Post-Merger Market Share Squared
A	30%	900	30%	900
B	30%	900	30%	900
C	25%	625	35%	1225
D	10%	100	—	—
E	5%	25	5%	25
Total	**100%**	**HHI=2550**	**100%**	**HHI=3050**

Notes:

Change in HHI from merger (also called "delta HHI" or "Δ HHI"): 3050–2550 = 500

Alternate calculation method for change in HHI (double the product of the merging firms' market shares): 2(25)(10) = 500.

Example 2: Firms A and B Merge

Firm	Pre-Merger Market Share	Pre-Merger Market Share Squared	Post-Merger Market Share	Post-Merger Market Share Squared
A	30%	900	60%	3600
B	30%	900	–	–
C	25%	625	25%	625
D	10%	100	10%	100
E	5%	25	5%	25
Total	100%	HHI=2550	100%	HHI=4350

Notes:

Change in HHI from merger (also called "delta HHI" or "Δ HHI"): 4350–2550 = 1800

Alternate calculation method for change in HHI (double the product of the merging firms' market shares): 2(30)(30) = 1800.

———————

The Merger Guidelines specify safe harbors for mergers in relatively unconcentrated markets or for mergers in more concentrated markets that do not increase concentration very much. *Horizontal Merger Guidelines* § 5.3 (2010). In particular, mergers are unlikely to be challenged if the post-merger HHI is below 1500 (unconcentrated markets) or, regardless of post-merger concentration level, if the HHI rises by less than 100 points as a consequence of the merger. The Guidelines distinguish between moderately concentrated markets (post-merger HHI between 1500 and 2500) and highly concentrated markets (post-merger HHI above 2500). The Guidelines state that mergers resulting in highly concentrated markets that increase the HHI by more than 200 points "will be presumed to be likely to enhance market power," though that presumption "may be rebutted by persuasive evidence showing that the merger is unlikely to enhance market power." The reference to a rebuttable presumption appears to reflect a desire to invoke the structural presumption from *Philadelphia National Bank* in litigation, notwithstanding other aspects of the Guidelines that downplay reliance on market shares as a firm predictor of competitive effects.

These concentration levels are not closely tied to empirical economic studies relating market concentration to price, though they are not inconsistent with such studies. (*See* Sidebar 5–2). Rather, they were chosen to reflect recent agency practice. For mergers that do not fall within safe harbors based on low market concentration, the Merger Guidelines call for further competitive analysis, with market shares taken into account to the extent they bear on the likely competitive effects of the transaction.

Courts analyzing mergers today commonly rely on market concentration in the first instance as the method by which the government establishes its prima facie case, consistent with the legal framework set forth in *Baker Hughes* and *Heinz*. For example, a 2009 district court opinion preliminarily enjoining a proposed acquisition challenged by the FTC began its analysis with concentration:

> As defense counsel admitted at the inception of this case, the HHIs in these markets are "very, very, high." Because of the high market concentrations and HHIs in the [two] pre- and post-merger * * * markets, the FTC has established a strong *prima facie* case that a merger between [defendants] would violate Section 7 of the Clayton Act. But that is just the beginning of the inquiry.

FTC v. CCC Holdings Inc., 605 F. Supp. 2d 26, 46 (D.D.C. 2009). Courts also commonly consider concentration in evaluating coordinated competitive effects, as with this example from the same district court opinion:

> In a highly concentrated market, with stable market shares, low growth rates and significant barriers to entry, there are few incentives to engage in healthy competition. * * * Nevertheless, Defendants have made a strong argument that despite these characteristics, the market dynamics create a number of incentives to compete, and indeed, have maintained a competitive marketplace to this day. Although Defendants present several arguments why coordination is not likely to occur despite their merger, the FTC has responded with substantial evidence of significant barriers to entry as well as credible evidence that coordination is possible, and even likely, in these markets.

Id. at 66–67.

But courts tend to emphasize evidence other than concentration when analyzing unilateral competitive effects, entry, and efficiencies, and concentration played no explicit role in the court's analysis of these issues in *CCC Holdings*.

Concentration is an important determinant of merger enforcement at the Federal Trade Commission, according to statistics released by the FTC. Federal Trade Commission, *Horizontal Merger Investigation Data, Fiscal Years 1996–2011* (Jan. 2013), http://www.ftc.gov/reports/horizontal-merger-investigation-data-fiscal-years–1996–2011. The Justice Department likely behaves similarly to the FTC, but DOJ has not released comparable data. The data concern horizontal merger investigations in which a "second request" was issued (*see supra* Sidebar 5–3). The study looked at the frequency with which such investigations resulted in enforcement actions—a term that includes consent settlements, litigation, or abandonment of the transaction once the agency expressed its concern that the transaction would have adverse competitive effects.

The importance of concentration is evident whether concentration is measured by the HHI or the number of firms. The study also shows that when concentration was neither very high nor very low, the frequency of enforcement increased when the agency uncovered "hot documents"—such as an internal memorandum of the merging firm that states, "this merger will permit us to raise prices." Such documents are commonly thought to improve the agency's litigation prospects in the event of a court challenge. The frequency of enforcement also increased when the agency received strong customer complaints. (The use and significance of customer views is discussed below in Sidebar 5–7.) An analysis of FTC second requests similarly shows the importance of market concentration, entry barriers, hot documents, and customer complaints in focusing that agency's investigative effort. Darren S. Tucker, *A Survey of Evidence Leading to Second Requests at the FTC*, 78 ANTITRUST L.J. 591, 599 (2013).

2. COMPETITIVE EFFECTS

The previous section, on defining markets, identifying market participants, assigning market shares, and determining the post-merger HHI and the increase in HHI from merger describes the methodology employed by the Merger Guidelines to identify how a horizontal merger alters market structure. The Guidelines go on to suggest a number of ways that the change in market structure resulting from merger among rivals might reduce competition; these are termed "competitive effects" theories. The competitive effects theories considered in the Merger Guidelines are grouped into two classes: "coordinated" and "unilateral." We follow that division in this Casebook, and discuss coordinated competitive effects in the first subsection below. (We take up the two classes of theories in the opposite order from which they are presented in the Guidelines.) It is possible for a merger to raise both unilateral and coordinated effects issues simultaneously, for example unilateral effects in a narrow market and coordinated effects in a broader one, so both possibilities may have to be analyzed. Figure 5–5 illustrates these two theories of competitive harm.

Figure 5–5:
Two Horizontal Merger Scenarios

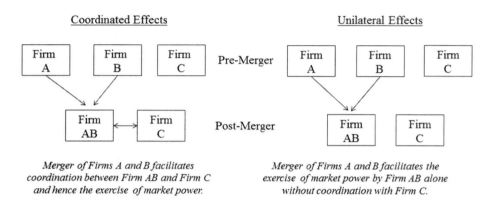

Coordinated Effects   Unilateral Effects

Merger of Firms A and B facilitates   *Merger of Firms A and B facilitates the*
coordination between Firm AB and Firm C   *exercise of market power by Firm AB alone*
and hence the exercise of market power.   *without coordination with Firm C.*

The Guidelines focus on collusive mergers; they do not provide a framework for analyzing ways in which a merger among rivals might lead to the exercise of market power through the exclusion of other rivals, although they point out the possibility and make clear that it should be considered in an appropriate case. We note here without further analysis that it is possible for horizontal mergers to harm competition by making it easier for the merged firm to exclude rivals. For example, a horizontal merger might create a dominant firm and confer on it the bargaining leverage it needs to obtain exclusive contracts from key input suppliers. This could harm competition by making it more difficult for fringe rivals to expand output inexpensively and compete aggressively. We discuss harmful exclusionary effects of mergers below in connection with vertical mergers and discuss conglomerate mergers in Sidebar 5–11.

This Chapter follows the Merger Guidelines by emphasizing the possibility that sellers with enhanced market power through merger would exercise that power by raising price. But, as the Guidelines note, "[e]nhanced market power can also be manifested in non-price terms and conditions that adversely affect customers, including reduced product quality, reduced product variety, reduced service, or diminished innovation." *Horizontal Merger Guidelines* § 1. As one former senior government official (who helped draft the 2010 Guidelines when he returned to the government) has emphasized:

> * * * [E]ven if antitrust analysis *appears* to focus on price effects, this can and should be understood as *synecdoche*: the part standing for the whole. That is, there are reasons to expect competitive effects in different dimensions (innovation, quality, price), and their net effect, usually to go together. The shifts in incentives that are fundamental in antitrust economics apply

quite broadly, so that a price analysis can often proxy for a fuller competitive analysis.

Joseph Farrell, *Thoughts on Antitrust and Innovation* (January 25, 2001), http://www.usdoj.gov/atr/public/speeches/7402.htm. Examples of government enforcement actions against mergers thought to reduce competition in the development of new products are presented in Chapter 7.

NOTE ON MERGERS THAT ENHANCE BUYER MARKET POWER (MONOPSONY POWER)

Firms may also exercise market power as buyers, by depressing the price they pay for an input. Economists term this possibility the exercise of "monopsony" power (as opposed to the "monopoly" power firms exercise when raising the price they sell to their customers). Firms exercise monopsony power by reducing their purchases of an input, driving down the price paid to suppliers. The reduction in quantity below the competitive level makes the harm to the suppliers exceed the gain to the buyers, creating an efficiency loss in the market.

If a merger permits firms in an industry to exercise monopsony power, the lower input prices the merging firms pay do not necessarily benefit the consumers who buy the merging firms' products, for two reasons. First, firms may have buying power in dealing with their suppliers, but may sell in competitive markets also served by rivals that did not achieve lower costs; if so, their exercise of monopsony power may not affect the price they charge downstream. Professor Marius Schwartz, formerly a senior economics official in the Antitrust Division, has made this point using the example of a merger of two textile producers that are major employers in a small town. The merged firm may be able to drive down local wages, but the price of textiles to consumers may remain unchanged if it is determined in a world market by the decisions of numerous other textile producers.

Second, lower input prices resulting from the exercise of monopsony power typically mean that the input quantity utilized falls, inducing the merged firm to *reduce* the output of the good it sells to consumers and *raise* its price. In contrast, lower production costs that arise from efficiencies are likely to benefit consumers of the merging firms' products, to the extent the reduction in production costs induces the merged firm to *expand* output of the good it sells to consumers and *lower* its price.

Even without harm to consumers, Professor Schwartz contends, antitrust enforcement is warranted because of the harm to suppliers and loss in overall welfare (efficiency loss). He sees little economic basis for opposing the exercise of market power against individuals in their capacity as buyers of products but not as sellers of their resources. Marius Schwartz, *Buyer Power Concerns and the Aetna-Prudential Merger* (Oct. 20, 1999), http://www.usdoj.gov/atr/public/speeches/3924.htm.

The 2010 Merger Guidelines take a similar view, recognizing the possibility that a merger could harm competition by enhancing market power among buyers. *Horizontal Merger Guidelines* § 12 (2010). The Guidelines say this concern is analyzed through "essentially the same framework" as is employed to analyzing the possibility that a transaction could enhance market power among sellers. *Id.*

---

a.   Coordinated Competitive Effects

The Merger Guidelines recognize that a merger "may diminish competition by enabling or encouraging post-merger coordinated interaction among firms in the relevant market that harms consumers." *Horizontal Merger Guidelines* § 7 (2010). The term "coordinated" competitive effects is defined as "conduct among multiple firms that is profitable for each of them only as a result of the accommodating reactions of the others." *Id.* This definition encompasses three types of firm behavior.

First, it incorporates the possibility that the firms in a market might collectively act to harm competition through conduct that would violate Sherman Act § 1: tacit or express collusion (*e.g.*, price-fixing or market division) among rivals that recognize their interdependence.

Second, coordinated competitive effects also include higher prices that would result from "conscious parallelism" and price leadership which, as we saw in Chapter 3, can have the same economic consequences as price-fixing without involving conduct that would satisfy the "agreement" requirement of Sherman Act § 1. The Horizontal Merger Guidelines describe this type of coordinated interaction as "a similar common understanding [among rivals] that is not explicitly negotiated but would be enforced by the detection and punishment of deviations that would undermine the coordinated interaction." *Id.* Here, the Guidelines are describing firms that achieve higher than competitive pricing by solving their "cartel problems" of reaching consensus and deterring cheating, as was discussed in Chapter 3.

Third, "coordinated effects" in the Merger Guidelines also includes the possibility of "parallel accommodating conduct not pursuant to a prior understanding." *Id.* This third possibility, introduced in the 2010 Guidelines, captures mergers that would lead firms to compete less aggressively for reasons unconnected with either an express agreement or with the threat of punishment for cheating from a market outcome adopted by consensus. *Cf.* Eric Maskin & Jean Tirole, *A Theory of Dynamic Oligopoly III: Cournot Competition*, 31 EUR. ECON. REV. 947 (1987) (dampened competition in the Markov perfect equilibrium of a duopoly model with adjustment costs). For a possible case illustration of this third possibility, see Complaint, *United States v. Int'l Paper Co.*, No. 1:12–cv–00227 (D.D.C. Feb. 10, 2012), http://www.justice.gov/atr/cases/f280100/280127.pdf; Competitive Impact Statement, *United States v. Int'l Paper Co.*, No. 1:12–cv–00227 (D.D.C. Feb. 10, 2012), http://www.justice.gov/atr/cases/f280100/280135.pdf.

Sidebar 5–5 considers what can be learned from criminal cartel prosecutions for the analysis of the coordinated competitive effects of horizontal mergers.

Sidebar 5–5:
Criminal Cartel Prosecutions and
Coordinated Competitive Effects

The Department of Justice prosecutes cartels criminally and reviews mergers for their potential to facilitate coordination. Not surprisingly, therefore, government enforcers have evaluated their experiences detecting and prosecuting criminal cartels to determine whether those experiences can aid them in predicting the likelihood of future coordination as a consequence of mergers of competitors. Careful analysis of the factors that allowed cartel participants to solve their "cartel problems" might help to identify markets and mergers more susceptible to future coordination.

In the following excerpted speech, then Deputy Assistant Attorney General William J. Kolasky offered some "Lessons Learned from Criminal Cartel Prosecutions" to inform the prediction of future coordinated effects in horizontal mergers.[a] One lesson drawn from the mere incidence of cartels is that coordination is perhaps more easily achieved than had previously been thought. If so, that "lesson" might suggest that a higher level of scrutiny would be in order for mergers in industries that possess some of the same coordination-facilitating characteristics as those found in the cartel cases.

As you read the speech, consider whether factual or legal differences between cartel prosecutions and mergers might diminish to some degree the value of the lessons drawn. For example, as we saw in Chapters 1 and 3, the kinds of cartels that qualify for criminal prosecution are often express. Tacit coordination, alone, might not rise to the level of agreement that would justify even a civil prosecution. Yet, as we shall shortly see, evidence that a post-merger market will be

---

[a]   William J. Kolasky, *Coordinated Effects in Merger Review: From Dead Frenchmen to Beautiful Minds and Mavericks* (April 24, 2002), http://www.usdoj.gov/atr/public/speeches/11050.htm.

significantly more susceptible to tacit collusion might warrant a prediction of probable future coordinated effects, satisfying the standards of Section 7 of the Clayton Act. Should this difference in legal standards limit the relevance of the cartel experience for mergers? Would you agree with Kolasky's assertion that "whether cartels are express or tacit, they have to reach a consensus and deter cheating, so what we learn from them can inform merger analysis, where the concern is as much about tacit collusion as express"? Might efforts to refocus merger analysis on the kinds of evidence found in the cartel cases perhaps unintentionally tend to elevate, rather than simply inform, the standards for predicting coordinated effects? What impact might it have on the continued vitality of the *Philadelphia Nat'l Bank* presumption?

"For those who may be tempted to argue that coordination is too difficult to occur in the real world, I should not have to do more than to point to the large number of multinational cartels we've successfully prosecuted in [the] last seven years to show why such arguments will fall on deaf ears. Beyond that, I think there are at least ten important lessons to be drawn from those cases that should help inform our review of future mergers. While our criminal cartel cases involve express cartels, whether cartels are express or tacit, they have to reach a consensus and deter cheating, so what we learn from them can inform merger analysis, where the concern is as much about tacit collusion as express.

First, cartels can involve a fairly large number of firms. The number of participants in several of the cartels we prosecuted were surprisingly high. Five or six members were not uncommon and occasionally we have uncovered cartels with 10 or more members. This appears to be due in part at least to fringe players in the market feeling they will profit more by going along with the cartel than by trying to take share away from the larger firms by undercutting their prices.

Second, industry concentration matters. As expected, the industries in which we have detected cartels are usually highly concentrated with the largest firms acting as ringleaders and the fringe players following along. In one case, there was evidence that the industry had attempted unsuccessfully to coordinate prices for several years before the cartel finally got off the ground after the industry consolidated down to approximately six players.

Third, cartels often use multiple tools to enforce compliance. Just as Stigler observed, cartels can take many forms, with the choice of form being determined in part at least by balancing the comparative cost of reaching and enforcing the collusive agreement against the risk of detection. Past empirical studies of price-fixing cases found that multiple instruments of coordination are frequently employed. Our multinational cartel cases over the last seven years found that this pattern continues. The vitamin cartel of the 1990s (whose prosecution led to the largest Sherman Act fines in history), for example, included price-fixing, bid-rigging, customer and territorial allocations, and coordinated total sales.

Fourth, the ability of large sophisticated buyers to defeat cartel activity may be overrated. In merger analysis, some assume that large purchasers in the market will provide sufficient discipline to prevent cartels. Our experience shows to the contrary that many successful cartels sell to large, sophisticated buyers. In the lysine cartel, the buyers included Tysons Foods and Con Agra; in citric acid, the buyers included Coca-Cola and Procter & Gamble; and in graphite electrodes, the victims included every major steel producer in the world. What is particularly ironic is that the perpetrators and victims of the citric acid cartel included some of the very same firms that the district court found were unlikely to engage in or be vulnerable to cartel activity in refusing to enjoin an acquisition by ADM of one of its leading rivals in the high fructose corn syrup market back in 1991.[b]

Fifth, excess capacity in the hands of leading firms can be an effective tool for punishing cheating and thereby enforcing collusive agreements. In lysine, ADM, which had substantial excess capacity, repeatedly threatened to flood the market with lysine if the other producers refused to agree to a volume allocation agreement proposed by ADM. In another case where competitors bought from one another, the cartel member with the extra capacity threatened to not sell to a competitor who was undercutting the cartel.

Sixth, cartels are more durable than sometimes thought. After the ADM plea, the Wall Street Journal stated "If colluders push prices too high, defectors and new entrants will set things right." Our experience has shown that this is not the case. Several of the cartels we prosecuted had been in existence for over ten years, including one (sorbates) that lasted 17 years, from 1979 to 1996.

Seventh, large, publicly traded companies are not immune from the temptation to engage in cartel activity. Our cases have

---

[b]   U.S. v. Archer-Daniels-Midland Co., 781 F.Supp. 1400 (S.D. Iowa, 1991).

turned up hard-core cartel activity by top management at some of the world's largest corporations and most respected corporations including Christies/Sotheby's, ADM, Hoffmann-La Roche, BASF, ABB, and a host of others. We have repeatedly found that even the largest companies have become sloppy about their antitrust compliance programs and that they are not doing all they should to educate managers about the risks at which they put themselves and their companies by engaging in cartel activity.

Eighth, trade associations and industry publications that report detailed market information are important in facilitating cartel activity. Cartel members will often use trade associations as a cover for their cartel meetings. In both lysine and citric acid, the conspirators created a working group within a legitimate trade association. This group's sole purpose was to provide false, but facially legitimate, explanations as to why they were meeting. Similarly, in some of our chemical investigations, a widely read weekly newspaper was used as the way of announcing price increases to other cartel members, which they were to follow. Other investigations have turned up a one-time agreement to incorporate a public index into a formula; so, as a newspaper announces a commodity price index change, the conspirators do not need to communicate again.

Ninth, cartel participants tend to be recidivists. The most notorious example is Hoffmann-La Roche, which continued its participation in the vitamin conspiracy even as it was entering into a plea agreement for its participation in the citric acid cartel.

Tenth, and finally, while product homogeneity and high entry barriers may facilitate cartel behavior, they are not essential to it. While the products in our cartel cases tend to be fungible, there are sometimes exceptions. One case we prosecuted involved bid rigging on school bus bodies. School bus bodies have many options, but the conspirators were able to work out a formula that incorporated the options and trade-in value to determine a price at or below which the designated winning bidder was supposed to bid. Similarly, while most of our cartel cases involve industries in which entry tends to be difficult, there are notable exceptions, such as in the Division's many bid-rigging cases in the road building industry. The road building industry, at least at the time of the conspiracies, was not difficult to enter, yet the Division turned up numerous cartels."

With respect to coordinated competitive effects, the Guidelines state that the enforcement agencies are likely to challenge a merger if (1) market concentration is high and increasing, (2) the market shows signs of vulnerability to coordinated conduct, and (3) the merger may enhance that vulnerability. *Horizontal Merger Guidelines* § 7.1 (2010). Although the Guidelines do not explain why the level and change in market concentration matters, our previous discussion of coordination in Chapter 3 provides one reason: the fewer the firms, the easier it may be for the remaining sellers to work out any differences over the terms of coordination, or to identify rapidly a firm that attempts to cheat on such a consensus and thus make punishment for cheating more likely. From this perspective, the probability that a merger will diminish competition is the greatest when post-merger concentration is high and concentration has increased markedly.

In analyzing the second factor, the agencies presume conditions are conducive to coordination if firms have previously engaged in express collusion (unless competitive conditions have since changed significantly) or if firms have colluded in another market with very similar characteristics. Conditions would also be conducive if, after the merger, the firms can overcome their "cartel problems" of reaching a consensus on the terms of coordination such as price and market shares, and discouraging cheating on those terms (as through rapid detection and punishment of deviation). Because the Guidelines also concerned with the market's vulnerability to parallel accommodating conduct, they do not organize the market conditions they list explicitly in terms of "cartel problems," but many track the factors considered previously in Chapter 3. *See id.* § 7.1.

The Guidelines observe that an acquisition eliminating a "maverick firm" in a market vulnerable to coordinated conduct is likely to harm competition (*see infra* Sidebar 5–6). *Id.* § 7.2. This would provide a way to demonstrate that the merger would enhance the market's vulnerability to coordination.

Court decisions evaluating coordinated competitive effects typically analyze market concentration and its change from merger, and evaluate factors determining the likelihood that market participants can solve their "cartel problems." These were the focus of Judge Posner's opinion in our next case. The enforcement agencies and courts have not grappled with the litigation challenges associated with proving that the merger will enhance the prospects for parallel accommodating conduct to the extent that concept goes beyond express and tacit collusion.

HOSPITAL CORPORATION OF AMERICA
V. FEDERAL TRADE COMMISSION

United States Court of Appeals for the Seventh Circuit, 1986.
807 F.2d 1381.

Before POSNER and FLAUM, CIRCUIT JUDGES, and CAMPBELL, SENIOR DISTRICT JUDGE.

POSNER, CIRCUIT JUDGE.

Hospital Corporation of America, the largest proprietary hospital chain in the United States, asks us to set aside the decision by the Federal Trade Commission that it violated section 7 of the Clayton Act * * * by the acquisition in 1981 and 1982 of two corporations, Hospital Affiliates International, Inc. and Health Care Corporation. * * *

* * *

If all the hospitals brought under common ownership or control by the two challenged acquisitions are treated as a single entity, the acquisitions raised Hospital Corporation's market share in the Chattanooga area from 14 percent to 26 percent. This made it the second largest provider of hospital services in a highly concentrated market where the four largest firms together had a 91 percent market share compared to 79 percent before the acquisitions. * * * Nor would expressing the market shares in terms of the Herfindahl index alter the impression of a highly concentrated market.

* * *

* * * Hospital Corporation has argued the case to us as if we were the FTC, which assuredly we are not. Our only function is to determine whether the Commission's analysis of the probable effects of these acquisitions on hospital competition in Chattanooga is so implausible, so feebly supported by the record, that it flunks even the deferential test of substantial evidence.

* * *

When an economic approach is taken in a section 7 case, the ultimate issue is whether the challenged acquisition is likely to facilitate collusion. In this perspective the acquisition of a competitor has no economic significance in itself; the worry is that it may enable the acquiring firm to cooperate (or cooperate better) with other leading competitors on reducing or limiting output, thereby pushing up the market price. * * * There is plenty of evidence to support the Commission's prediction of adverse competitive effect in this case; whether we might have come up with a different prediction on our own is irrelevant.

The acquisitions reduced the number of competing hospitals in the Chattanooga market from 11 to 7. True, this calculation assumes that the hospitals that came under the management although not ownership of Hospital Corporation should be considered allies rather than competitors of Hospital Corporation; but the Commission was entitled to so conclude. The manager (Hospital Corporation) sets the prices charged by the managed hospitals, just as it sets its own prices. Although the pricing and other decisions that it makes in its management role are subject to the ultimate control of the board of directors of the managed hospital, there is substantial evidence that the board usually defers to the manager's decisions. If it were not inclined to defer, it would not have a management contract; it would do its own managing, through officers hired by it. A hospital managed by Hospital Corporation is therefore unlikely to engage in vigorous or perhaps in any price competition with Hospital Corporation—or so at least the Commission was entitled to conclude.

The reduction in the number of competitors is significant in assessing the competitive vitality of the Chattanooga hospital market. The fewer competitors there are in a market, the easier it is for them to coordinate their pricing without committing detectable violations of section 1 of the Sherman Act, which forbids price fixing. This would not be very important if the four competitors eliminated by the acquisitions in this case had been insignificant, but they were not; they accounted in the aggregate for 12 percent of the sales of the market. As a result of the acquisitions the four largest firms came to control virtually the whole market, and the problem of coordination was therefore reduced to one of coordination among these four.

Moreover, both the ability of the remaining firms to expand their output should the big four reduce their own output in order to raise the market price (and, by expanding, to offset the leading firms' restriction of their own output), and the ability of outsiders to come in and build completely new hospitals, are reduced by Tennessee's certificate-of-need law. Any addition to hospital capacity must be approved by a state agency. The parties disagree over whether this law, as actually enforced, inhibits the expansion of hospital capacity. * * * Should the leading hospitals in Chattanooga collude, a natural consequence would be the creation of excess hospital capacity, for the higher prices resulting from collusion would drive some patients to shorten their hospital stays and others to postpone or reject elective surgery. If a noncolluding hospital wanted to expand its capacity so that it could serve patients driven off by the high prices charged by the colluding hospitals, the colluders would have not only a strong incentive to oppose the grant of a certificate of need but also substantial evidence with which to oppose it—the excess capacity (in the market considered as a whole) created by their own collusive efforts. At least the certificate of need law would enable them to delay any competitive sally by a noncolluding competitor. Or so the Commission could conclude (a refrain we shall now stop repeating). We add that at the very least a certificate of need law forces hospitals to give public notice, well in advance, of any plans to add capacity. The requirement of notice makes it harder for the member of a hospital cartel to "cheat" on the cartel by adding capacity in advance of other members; its attempt to cheat will be known in advance, and countermeasures taken.

All this would be of little moment if, in the event that hospital prices in Chattanooga rose above the competitive level, persons desiring hospital services in Chattanooga would switch to hospitals in other cities, or to nonhospital providers of medical care. But this would mean that the Chattanooga hospital market, which is to say the set of hospital-services providers to which consumers in Chattanooga can feasibly turn, * * * includes hospitals in other cities plus nonhospital providers both in Chattanooga and elsewhere; and we do not understand Hospital Corporation to be challenging the Commission's market definition, which is limited to hospital providers in Chattanooga. Anyway, these competitive alternatives are not important enough to deprive the market shares statistics of competitive significance. Going to another city is out of the question in medical emergencies; and even when an operation or some other hospital service can be deferred, the patient's doctor will not (at least not for reasons of price) send the patient to another city, where the doctor is unlikely to have hospital privileges. Finally, although hospitals increasingly are providing services on an out-patient basis, thus competing with nonhospital providers of the same services (tests, minor surgical procedures, etc.), most hospital services cannot be provided by nonhospital providers; as to these, hospitals have no competition from other providers of medical care.

In showing that the challenged acquisitions gave four firms control over an entire market so that they would have little reason to fear a competitive reaction if they raised prices above the competitive level, the Commission went far to justify its prediction of probable anticompetitive effects. Maybe it need have gone no further. *See United States v. Philadelphia Nat'l Bank*, supra, 374 U.S. at 362–63, 83 S.Ct. at 1740–41. * * * But it did. First it pointed out that the demand for hospital services by patients and their doctors is highly inelastic under competitive conditions. This is not only because people place a high value on their safety and comfort and because many of their treatment decisions are made for them by their doctor, who doesn't pay their hospital bills; it is also because most hospital bills are paid largely by insurance companies or the federal government rather than by the patient. The less elastic the demand for a good or service is, the greater are the profits that providers can make by raising price through collusion. A low elasticity of demand means that raising price will cause a relatively slight fall in demand, with the result that total revenues will rise sharply. * * *

Second, there is a tradition, well documented in the Commission's opinion, of cooperation between competing hospitals in Chattanooga. Of course, not all forms of cooperation between competitors are bad. *See, e.g., Broadcast Music, Inc. v. Columbia Broadcasting System, Inc.*, 441 U.S. 1, 99 S.Ct. 1551, 60 L.Ed.2d 1 (1979). But a market in which competitors are unusually disposed to cooperate is a market prone to collusion. The history of successful cooperation establishes a precondition to effective collusion—mutual trust and forbearance, without which an informal collusive arrangement is unlikely to overcome the temptation to steal a march on a fellow colluder by undercutting him slightly. That temptation is great. A seller who makes a profit of $10 on each sale at the cartel price, and then cuts price by $1 and thereby (let us suppose) doubles his output, will increase his total profits by 180 percent.

The management contracts between Hospital Affiliates (itself an owner as well as manager of hospitals) and two other hospitals in Chattanooga—contracts that when taken over by Hospital Corporation gave it virtual control over the pricing and other decisions of two of its competitors, at least for a time—illustrate the unusual degree of cooperation in this industry; imagine Ford's signing a management contract with General Motors whereby General Motors installed one of its officers (who would remain an officer of GM) as Ford's manager. Hospitals routinely exchange intimate information on prices and costs in connection with making joint applications to insurers for higher reimbursement schedules. Such cooperation may be salutary but it facilitates collusion and therefore entitles the Commission to worry even more about large horizontal acquisitions in this industry than in industries where competitors deal with each other at arm's length.

Third, hospitals are under great pressure from the federal government and the insurance companies to cut costs. One way of resisting this pressure is by presenting a united front in negotiations with the third-party payors—which indeed, as we have just said, hospitals in Chattanooga have done. * * *

All these considerations, taken together, supported—we do not say they compelled—the Commission's conclusion that the challenged acquisitions are likely to foster collusive practices, harmful to consumers, in the Chattanooga hospital market. Section 7 does not require proof that a merger or other acquisition has caused higher prices in the affected market. All that is necessary is that the merger create an appreciable danger of such consequences in the future. A predictive judgment, necessarily probabilistic and judgmental rather than demonstrable * * * is called for. Considering the concentration of the market, the absence of competitive alternatives, the regulatory barrier to entry (the certificate of need law), the low elasticity of demand, the exceptionally severe cost pressures under which American hospitals labor today, the history of collusion in the industry, and the sharp reduction in the number of substantial competitors in this market brought about by the acquisition of four hospitals in a city with only eleven (one already owned by Hospital Corporation), we cannot say that the Commission's prediction is not supported by substantial evidence.

But of course we cannot just consider the evidence that supports the Commission's prediction. We must consider all the evidence in the record. We must therefore consider the significance of the facts, pressed on us by Hospital Corporation, that hospital services are complex and heterogeneous, that the sellers in this market are themselves heterogeneous because of differences in the services provided by the different hospitals and differences in the corporate character of the hospitals (some are publicly owned, some are proprietary, and some are private but nonprofit), that the hospital industry is undergoing rapid technological and economic change, that the payors for most hospital services (Blue Cross and other insurance companies, and the federal government) are large and knowledgeable, and that the FTC's investigation which led to this proceeding was touched off by a complaint from a competitor of Hospital Corporation. Most of these facts do detract from a conclusion that collusion in this market is a serious danger, but it was for the Commission—it is not for us—to determine their weight.

The first fact is the least impressive. It is true that hospitals provide a variety of different services many of which are "customized" for the individual patient, but the degree to which this is true seems no greater than in other markets. Although collusion is more difficult the more heterogeneous the output of the colluding firms, there is no established threshold of complexity beyond which it is infeasible and Hospital Corporation made no serious effort to show that hospital services are more complex than products and services in other markets, such as steel, building materials, and transportation, where collusion has been frequent.

The heterogeneity of the sellers has two aspects: the hospitals in Chattanooga offer different mixtures of services; and they have different types of ownership—private for-profit ("proprietary"), private not-for-profit, public. The significance of these features is unclear. Concerning the first, if one assumes that collusion is practiced on a service-by-service basis, the fact that hospitals provide different mixtures of service seems irrelevant to the feasibility of collusion. True, since different types of service may not be substitutable—open-heart surgery is not a substitute for setting a broken leg—specialized hospitals might not compete with one another. But that is not Hospital Corporation's argument. Its argument is that the different mixture of services in the different hospitals would make it difficult for their owners to fix prices of competing services, and this we don't understand.

Different ownership structures might reduce the likelihood of collusion but this possibility is conjectural and the Commission was not required to give it conclusive weight. The adoption of the nonprofit form does not change human nature, * * * as the courts have recognized in rejecting an implicit antitrust exemption for nonprofit enterprises. * * *

* * *

The economic and technological ferment in the hospital industry may make collusion more difficult, but also more urgent, since risk-averse managers may be strongly inclined to stabilize, if necessary through collusion, whatever features of an uncertain environment they are able to bring under their control. Regarding the weighing of such imponderables as this, much must be left to the judgment of the Commission.

The concentration of the buying side of a market does inhibit collusion. The bigger a buyer is, the more easily and lucratively a member of the cartel can cheat on his fellows; for with a single transaction, he may be able to increase his sales and hence profits dramatically. But with all the members thus vying for the large orders of big buyers, the cartel will erode. * * * Hospital Corporation argues that the effective buyers of most hospital services are large and knowledgeable institutions rather than the patients who are the nominal buyers. But the role of the third-party payor is not quite that of a large buyer. * * * [A]s a practical matter Blue Cross could not tell its subscribers in Chattanooga that it will not reimburse them for any hospital services there because prices are too high. As a practical matter it could not, if the four major hospital owners in the city, controlling more than 90 percent of the city's hospital capacity, raised their prices, tell its subscribers that they must use the remaining hospitals—whose aggregate capacity would be completely inadequate and, for reasons discussed earlier, could not readily, or at least rapidly, be expanded—if they want to be reimbursed. * * *

Hospital Corporation's most telling point is that the impetus for the Commission's complaint came from a competitor—a large nonprofit hospital in Chattanooga. A rational competitor would not complain just because it thought that Hospital Corporation's acquisitions would facilitate collusion. Whether the competitor chose to join a cartel or stay out of it, it would be better off if the cartel were formed than if it were not formed. For the cartel would enable this seller to raise its price, whether or not to the cartel level. By staying out of the cartel and by pricing just below the cartel price, the competitor might, as we noted earlier, do even better than by joining the cartel.

The hospital that complained to the Commission must have thought that the acquisitions would lead to lower rather than higher prices—which would benefit consumers, and hence, under contemporary principles of antitrust law, would support the view that the acquisitions were lawful.

But this is just one firm's opinion. It was not binding on the Commission, which having weighed all the relevant facts concluded that the acquisitions had made collusion in this market significantly more likely than before. Since, moreover, the complainant was a nonprofit hospital, in attributing the complaint to fear of lower prices Hospital Corporation is contradicting its argument that the non-profit sector of the hospital industry does not obey the laws of economic self-interest.

* * *

The Commission's order is affirmed and enforced.

―――――――

As you reflect on Judge Posner's analysis of coordinated competitive effects in *Hospital Corp. of America*, recall the discussion of tacit collusion in Chapter 3. If the firms in an oligopoly are able to achieve high prices without reaching an agreement, for example by reaching a consensus through price leadership, they may exercise market power without violating Sherman Act § 1. "Conscious parallelism" leading to higher than competitive prices is not a violation of the antitrust laws. But an acquisition that appears likely to facilitate tacit collusion violates Clayton Act § 7, even if the coordinated behavior that results would not itself be subject to attack under the Sherman Act. From this perspective, Section 7 is prophylactic, intended to limit the spread of coordinated pricing. This is sometimes called the "containment" justification for merger enforcement.

Coordinated competitive effects analysis in merger review is closely related to the problem of identifying price-fixing studied in Chapter 3, because the underlying economic problem is the same. Successful collusion, whether tacit or express, generally requires that the firms solve their "cartel problems" of reaching a consensus, deterring cheating, and preventing entry; these economic problems were discussed in that Chapter. Accordingly, it is no surprise that Judge Posner, in his opinion in *Hospital Corp. of America*, pays a great deal of attention to the range of factors that might bear on whether industry participants could reasonably be expected to collude tacitly. How does Posner's list of factors match up with the factors discussed in Chapter 3? With those discussed by Kolasky in Sidebar 5–5?

Note also Judge Posner's observation that "Hospital Corporation made no serious effort to show that hospital services are more complex than products and services in other markets . . . where collusion has been frequent." 807 F.2d at 1390. Recall that the D.C. Circuit, in *Heinz*, found similarly that "the district court made no finding that any of [the asserted] 'cartel problems' are so much greater in the baby food industry than in other industries that they rebut the normal presumption [that increases in concentration will increase the likelihood of tacit collusion]." How in practice could the merging firms make these required comparative showings?

The framework set forth in the Merger Guidelines for evaluating coordinated effects has three elements. The Guidelines first ask whether concentration is high and increasing. Second, the Guidelines ask whether the post-merger market is vulnerable to coordination, as would be the case if the firms can likely reach a consensus on terms of coordination and deter cheating on those terms. This issue was emphasized by Judge Posner. Under what circumstances, if any, should vulnerability of the market to coordination form the basis of a presumption of coordinated effects from merger? Should a history of collusion create such a presumption? Should the presence of large and sophisticated buyers prevent the assertion of such a presumption? Third, the Guidelines ask whether the merger makes a difference, as by increasing the likelihood that firms in the market can successfully raise price through coordination or by making ongoing coordination more effective.

The third issue—the incremental impact of the merger on coordinated conduct—can be addressed in various ways. A substantial increase in market concentration is generally thought to increase the probability that firms can reach consensus and deter cheating. In addition, the merger may alter certain factors facilitating or frustrating coordination to improve the prospects of coordination. For example, if a merger leads to greater symmetry among the firms in the market, as by reducing differences among sellers in the attributes of their products or seller costs, the odds of successful coordination may increase. Andrew R. Dick, *Coordinated Interaction: Pre-Merger Constraints and Post-Merger Effects*, 12 GEO. MASON L. REV. 65 (2003).

In some cases, moreover, a merger may make coordination more likely or more effective by leading a "maverick" firm in the relevant market to compete less aggressively. The Merger Guidelines point out that when coordinated interaction in the pre-merger market is prevented or limited by a "maverick," a firm that has a greater incentive to keep prices low or otherwise deviate from the terms of coordination than its rivals, the acquisition of that maverick firm could make coordinated interaction more likely, more successful, or more complete. Indeed, one reason a firm may acquire a maverick is to facilitate coordination. Do or should the 2010 Merger Guidelines create a presumption that a merger involving a maverick harms competition? These issues are explored further in Sidebar 5–6, and were arguably an important part of the coordinated effects analysis in the next principal case, *H & R Block*.

UNITED STATES V. H & R BLOCK, INC.
United States District Court for the District of Columbia, 2011.
833 F. Supp. 2d 36.

[For the relevant excerpt, see *supra* Chapter 5, at 738. Eds.]

What evidence did the court rely upon to demonstrate the three elements of a coordinated effects case set forth above: (1) market concentration is high and increasing, (2) the market shows signs of vulnerability to coordinated conduct, and (3) the merger may enhance that vulnerability? To what extent did it rely on analyzing factors facilitating or frustrating coordination to show market vulnerability to coordination? Did it consider similar factors to those relied upon in *Hospital Corp. of America*?

The court asserted that it did not find the argument over whether TaxACT is a "maverick" helpful to its analysis. It nevertheless found that TaxACT played a "special role" in the DDIY market that constrained prices, and that the merged firm would have different incentives in setting prices than those of TaxACT premerger. Is this conclusion tantamount to viewing TaxACT as a maverick firm, and treating the loss of a maverick through merger as a basis for concluding that the merger would make coordination more likely or more effective? If the government had been unable to show that TaxACT played a special role in constraining prices, could the government have prevailed by relying solely on the change in market structure—the loss of one of three significant rivals and the resulting increase in market concentration—as the basis for concluding that the merger would make a difference, enhancing the market's vulnerability to coordination? Was the record reviewed in *Hospital Corp. of America* sufficient to show that the merger would enhance the market's vulnerability to coordination under the approach to making that demonstration suggested by the Merger Guidelines now in effect or under the approach applied in *H & R Block*?

Note that throughout its opinion in *H & R Block*, the court relied on the Horizontal Merger Guidelines as persuasive authority. Yet it also said that the government "has not set out a clear standard, based on functional or economic considerations, to distinguish a maverick from any other aggressive competitor." 833 F. Supp. 2d at 79. What evidence does the court rely on to identify TaxACT's special role in the market that constrained prices? How does the court's approach compare with the methods of identifying a maverick firms set forth in Sidebar 5–6? Do you agree with the court that the Merger Guidelines do not provide a sufficiently clear standard for identifying a maverick?

The merging firms argued that the merger would not result in the loss of a maverick, but instead would create one—and thus that the transaction would enhance competition rather than lessen competition. An similar argument had succeeded in the district court in *Heinz*, but the appellate panel reversed that decision. *FTC v. H.J. Heinz Co.*, 116 F. Supp. 2d 190 (D.D.C. 2000), *rev'd* 246 F.3d 708 (D.C. Cir. 2001). *See generally* Jonathan B. Baker, *Efficiencies and High Concentration: Heinz Proposes to Acquire Beech-Nut*, *in* THE ANTITRUST REVOLUTION 151 (John E. Kwoka, Jr. & Lawrence J. White eds., 5th ed. 2008). The use of the maverick concept as shield as well as sword is discussed in Sidebar 5–6.

As we will see when studying unilateral competitive effects, economists have developed a number of approaches for quantifying the incentive to raise price when unilateral effects are the primary concern. By comparison, the use of mathematical tools and simulation methods for assessing coordinated effects has been limited. For a brief survey of the economic issues, sketching possible approaches and emphasizing the role of mavericks, see Jonathan B. Baker, *Merger Simulation in an Administrative Context*, 77 ANTITRUST L.J. 451, 465–70 (2011).

Sidebar 5–6:
Mavericks and the Coordinated
Competitive Effects of Mergers[a]

Maverick firms can play an important role in the analysis of the likely coordinated competitive effects of mergers. The Merger Guidelines observe that "a merger may lessen competition by eliminating a 'maverick' firm, *i.e.*, a firm that plays a disruptive role in the market to the benefit of customers." *Horizontal Merger Guidelines* § 2.1.5 (2010). This Sidebar explains first, why mavericks can constrain coordination; second, how mavericks can be identified; and third, the significance of mavericks for merger analysis. It concludes by asking what to do if the maverick cannot be identified reliably, or if the effect of the merger on the maverick's incentives cannot be determined with precision.

Incomplete Coordination and Mavericks

Although some commentators have argued that coordination among rivals is unlikely to be successful or last for long, modern economists generally accept that it can and does occur. When coordination does occur, moreover, it is likely to be imperfect and incomplete (relative to what a monopolist could achieve). This is because coordinating firms may have difficulty punishing cheating rivals severely, allocating joint profits in a way satisfactory to all without making "side payments" to

---

[a] This Sidebar has been adapted from Jonathan B. Baker, *Mavericks, Mergers, and Exclusion: Proving Coordinated Competitive Effects Under the Antitrust Laws*, 77 N.Y.U. L. REV. 135, 177–88 (2002).

recalcitrant rivals, detecting cheating when prices decline frequently for unrelated reasons like unexpected declines in demand, and identifying the joint-profit maximizing outcome when firms must coordinate pricing and output over multiple products or markets without communicating.

When coordination is imperfect or incomplete, it is likely that some firms would be nearly indifferent between coordination and cheating, while others strongly prefer the coordinated outcome. From this perspective, a "maverick" firm is one that is nearly indifferent between coordination and cheating, and in consequence, constrains coordination from becoming more effective. A maverick is likely to play a more significant role than its rivals in constraining the effectiveness of coordination. In theory, there could be more than one maverick in a market, particularly in markets where it is impossible for firms to reach consensus or deter cheating. But in the oligopoly markets in which most serious merger investigations arise, it is often plausible that firms can coordinate to some extent. If so, it is unlikely that there will be more than one maverick unless the maverick firms are nearly identical or unless different mavericks constrain coordination on different competitive dimensions.

The term "maverick" may mislead to the extent it suggests that the firm must be a price-cutter. The maverick could indeed be an observably disruptive force, taking the lead in starting price wars or sales. Moreover, "if one of the merging firms has a strong incumbency position and the other merging firm threatens to disrupt market conditions with a new technology or business model, their merger can involve the loss of actual or potential competition." *Horizontal Merger Guidelines* § 2.1.5 (2010). But the maverick also could keep price from rising merely by refusing to follow rival attempts to raise price. *See id.* ("[O]ne of the merging firms may have the incentive to take the lead in price-cutting or other competitive conduct or to resist increases in industry prices.") In fact, it is possible that the maverick would not be recognizable as a holdout to the outside observer, as rivals would be expected not to attempt to increase price unless they had reason to think that industry conditions had changed in a way that would lead the maverick to go along.

Identifying Mavericks

Three strategies are available to antitrust enforcers and courts for identifying the maverick in an industry in which firms are thought to be coordinating, though none is guaranteed to succeed. First, a maverick firm might be identified based on past conduct showing that the firm has actually constrained industry pricing. *See Horizontal Merger Guidelines* § 2.1.5 (2010) (a firm "that has often resisted otherwise prevailing industry norms to cooperate on price setting or other terms of competition" can be a maverick). This approach was arguably employed in *H & R Block*, in identifying TaxACT's "special role." The second approach looks for "natural experiments" that identify the firm that constrains industry pricing. These are events that would be expected to lead a maverick to alter price but not affect the pricing of non-maverick firms. For example, one natural experiment might involve changes in a firm's marginal costs related to the nature or location of its production processes but not paralleled by cost changes affecting its rivals. If that firm is a maverick, the market price will change; if another firm is the maverick, the market price will not.

The third approach looks for features of market structure that tend to suggest that a firm would prefer a lower coordinated price than would its rivals. *See Horizontal Merger Guidelines* § 2.1.5 (2010) ("A firm that may discipline prices based on its ability and incentive to expand production rapidly using available capacity . . . can be a maverick"). For example, documentary evidence cited by the district court in *FTC v. Cardinal Health, Inc.*, 12 F. Supp. 2d 34, 63–64 (D.D.C.1998), indicated that in the drug wholesaling industry, excess capacity creates price pressure. If this was indeed the driving force behind firm preferences as to the industry price in that industry, and the firms were coordinating, a firm with substantially greater excess capacity than most of its rivals (either absolutely or relative to sales) would likely have been the industry maverick. (But recall that excess capacity may be double-edged, used by non-maverick firms in some industries to discourage cheating by rivals on a cartel. See, for example, the discussion in the Kolasky speech excerpted in Sidebar 5–5 of the role of excess capacity in cartels.) A variety of structural characteristics might give a firm a greater economic incentive to prefer a lower coordinated price than do its rivals (or to otherwise deviate from terms of coordination when its rivals would not), such as low costs and excess capacity, a low market share, or an unusual ability to expand sales by increasing captive production for a downstream affiliate.

The Significance of Mavericks for Merger Analysis

A focus on identifying the maverick explains why the loss of a firm through merger or exclusion will improve coordination.

Moreover, the concept of a maverick can help to distinguish anticompetitive mergers from procompetitive ones.

Mergers Involving the Maverick

A merger involving the maverick may harm competition by removing the maverick from the marketplace. Absent cognizable efficiencies from the transaction, the merged firm would most likely prefer higher prices than the maverick. If so, the merger could remove a constraint on more effective coordination, and lead to higher prices in the market. *See, e.g., United States v. H & R Block,* 833 F.Supp. 2d 36 (D.D.C. 2011); *United States v. Premdor, Inc.,* 66 Fed. Reg. 45,326, 45,336–37 (Aug. 28, 2001) (competitive impact statement); *In re Mahle,* 62 Fed. Reg. 10,566, 10,567 (F.T.C. Mar. 7, 1997) (Analysis to Aid Public Comment); *In re B.F. Goodrich,* 110 F.T.C. 207, 329–85 (1988); *United States v. Aluminum Co. of America,* 377 U.S. 271, 281 (1964) (*Rome Cable*).

In these instances, the concept of a maverick helps to explain why the prospective increase in market concentration generated by merger is likely to lead to higher prices. Because the acquisition of a maverick appears substantially more likely to harm competition than to promote it, the courts might plausibly adopt a rebuttable presumption that such a transaction would harm competition. For commentary advocating doing so, see Jonathan B. Baker & Carl Shapiro, Reinvigorating Horizontal Merger Enforcement, *in* WHERE THE CHICAGO SCHOOL OVERSHOT THE MARK: EFFECT OF CONSERVATIVE ECONOMIC ANALYSIS ON U.S. ANTITRUST 235, 258–64 (Robert Pitofsky ed. 2008). How close do the 2010 Merger Guidelines come to adopting this recommendation?

Mergers Involving Non-Mavericks

In the most straightforward scenario involving a merger of non-mavericks, the transaction may have no effect on competition. The industry maverick may continue to constrain prices after the merger much as it did before. If so, the concept of a maverick would tend to undermine an antitrust challenge to a merger that increases market concentration. *See, e.g., New York v. Kraft General Foods, Inc.,* 926 F. Supp. 321, 364–65 (S.D.N.Y. 1995) (coordinated competitive effects allegation rejected on the ground that the acquired firm did not constrain more effective coordination); *FTC v. Arch Coal, Inc.,* 329 F. Supp. 2d 109 (D.D.C. 2004) (coordinated effects found unlikely, in part because the acquired firm was the high cost producer and likely to stay that way, so did not constrain coordination).

In order for the loss of a non-maverick firm to make coordination more effective, the merger must affect the maverick's incentives.[b] For example, a merger not involving the maverick could harm competition by excluding the maverick (as by raising its costs or reducing its access to customers), thus forcing the maverick to compete less aggressively. Moreover, a merger among non-mavericks could affect the severity of the punishment response the merged firm would be expected to employ in the event any rival, including the maverick, cheated on a coordinated outcome.

A merger involving non-mavericks could instead promote competition by creating a new industry maverick. In particular, the acquisition could confer such large efficiencies on the merging parties as to lead them to prefer a much lower price than either did before the transaction, and below the price desired by the current industry maverick. *Horizontal Merger Guidelines* § 10 (2010) ("In a coordinated effects context, incremental cost reductions may make coordination less likely or effective by enhancing the incentive of a maverick to lower price or by creating a new maverick firm"). This possibility was suggested by the district court's decision in *FTC v. H.J. Heinz Co.*, 116 F. Supp. 2d 190 (D.D.C. 2000), *rev'd* 246 F.3d 708 (D.C. Cir. 2001).

Coordinated Competitive Effects Analysis Without a Maverick

It will not always be possible to identify the maverick with precision or to determine with confidence how the loss of a firm through merger affects the maverick's incentives. For example, the difference between the district court and the appellate court in *Heinz* can be understood as a dispute about whether the record in that case reasonably permitted identification of a maverick.

When courts and enforcers cannot identify a maverick in a market conducive to coordination they tend to have difficulty explaining why the particular merger under review matters. After all, any merger raises concentration but not every increase in concentration from merger necessarily makes coordination more likely or more effective. Yet when a maverick cannot be identified (or the effect of the merger on the maverick's incentives cannot reliably be assessed), courts may rely on changes in market structure, particularly the structural

---

    [b]   Alternatively, there may be some chance that one of the non-maverick merged firms would become the industry maverick in the future. If the merger removes this possibility, it would, with probability, harm competition much as would the merger of a maverick.

presumption, to explain the incremental impact of a merger on coordinated conduct.

The maverick analysis helps justify that practice, as it provides a theoretical connection between market concentration and more effective coordination: In the absence of specific evidence identifying a maverick or tending to suggest that any particular firm is likely to play that role, the fewer the number of significant sellers, the more likely it will be that the loss of any one would involve the loss of a firm that constrains the effectiveness of coordinated conduct. If, in addition, the merger narrows differences in product attributes across firms or differences in seller costs, the odds that the merger involves a maverick will increase. From this perspective, changes in market structure, including increased market concentration, provide a basis for inferring that the merger makes a difference to the likelihood or effectiveness of coordinated conduct when they suggest that it is probable that the merger involves the loss of a maverick firm, even when a specific maverick cannot confidently be identified.

Conclusion

Increased awareness of the role of mavericks may offer important insights into the analysis of the expected coordinated effects of mergers. But can such awareness also be relevant in other areas of antitrust analysis? For example, should conduct excluding a maverick raise concerns regardless of other market features?

As was no doubt evident from reading *Hospital Corp. of America* and *H & R Block*, antitrust enforcers and courts reviewing their actions may rely on a wide variety of evidence in reaching their conclusions about a merger's likely effects, and that evidence may come from a variety of sources. Of course, in most instances the bulk of the evidence will come from the merging firms, themselves, through disclosures required through the HSR process and the formal discovery that follows in the form of Second Requests and other follow-on discovery. Two other critical sources of information, however, are rival firms and customers of the merging firms. Sidebar 5–7 evaluates the utility and issues that arise in connection with reliance on such information.

Sidebar 5–7:
Competitor vs. Customer Complaints

In *Hospital Corp. of America*, Judge Posner observed that the merging firms' "most telling point" was that the impetus for the government investigation came from a competitor. Judge Posner explained that the very fact of a competitor complaint was inconsistent with the government's anticompetitive theory. If the merger would facilitate tacit collusion, the competitor should expect to share in the gains from higher market prices, and thus would not be expected to object to the deal. Only if the merger would promote competition and lead to lower prices, would rivals lose profits and be expected to oppose the deal. Judge Posner suggested, therefore, that competitor complaints should be discounted or ignored.

On the other hand, customer views normally would be aligned with the public interest. If the merger would raise price, customers should object; if it would lower price, they should favor the transaction. When coordinated anticompetitive effects are alleged, Judge Posner implied, the enforcement agency should always do what the customers suggest, and the opposite of what competitors recommend! Judge Easterbrook similarly proposed that courts employ the identity of the plaintiff as a filter for screening out unpromising cases, and "dismiss outright" some lawsuits brought by rivals. Frank H. Easterbrook, *The Limits of Antitrust*, 63 TEX. L. REV. 1, 35 (1984). This way of thinking also underlies the "antitrust injury" doctrine, which we discussed in Chapter 1 in reading *Brunswick*.

This analysis helps explain why the antitrust enforcement agencies are often more interested in customer views than rival views when reviewing a horizontal merger. In investigating a transaction, the agencies routinely talk to rivals to learn about the industry and confirm factual assertions about the market made by the merging firms—but such information may be discounted to the extent the rivals are seen as interested parties, just as information provided by the merging firms is often not accepted without testing.

Customers and suppliers may be less informed about the market than rivals, but their interests may generally be more aligned with the public interest that the agency hopes to vindicate. "Customers" in this context need not be consumers. Many goods are "intermediate goods," sold by one set of firms to large and sophisticated businesses who use them in their own production. For example, automobile manufacturers are customers whose views might be consulted in the event of horizontal mergers in a wide range of supplier markets, including steel, car audio units, tires, and the like. In sum, the enforcement agencies are more likely to view information provided by customers as disinterested, and they are more likely to see customer complaints as a reason to launch an investigation. *But cf. United States v. Bazaarvoice, Inc.*, 2014 WL 203966, at 61 (N.D. Cal. 2014) (declining to rely upon customer testimony when customers were likely to be uninformed about the impact and likely effect of the merger).

It is one thing to approach the views of competitors with skepticism; it is another to draw the opposite inference—that the merger is likely pro-competitive—from their complaints, as would Judges Posner and Easterbrook. First, in some important respects, the enforcement agency is arguably in a better position to learn about competitive conditions in the market than is any firm involved in it, customer or competitor. No single firm will have access to the confidential marketing analyses and plans of every seller, for example, but the agency, with its subpoena power, does. Second, sometimes customers may be poor guides to the likely competitive effects of the transaction. Small customers may not understand the industry in which their sellers participate. If the product whose sellers are merging is an intermediate good, the immediate customers may not pay much attention to the price they are charged by some suppliers: the intermediate product may only account for a small share of the cost of the final downstream product (as the car audio unit is to the automobile), and if the downstream industry has a relatively inelastic demand, the sellers may be able to pass through most of any increase in the costs of inputs to end use consumers (such as the automobile buyer). Under such circumstances, moreover, the end use consumer may have little understanding of the upstream markets subject to merger, and thus little basis for providing an informed opinion to antitrust enforcers.

Third, the inference that a merger is procompetitive derived from rival complaints presumes that any anticompetitive harm is collusive, not exclusionary. While this is often the case, if the merger would harm competition by excluding competitors, the complaints of the excluded rivals are consistent with the anticompetitive theory, and so should be given some weight by antitrust enforcers. Should antitrust enforcers ignore this possibility on the view expressed by some that anticompetitive exclusionary conduct is either rare or difficult for enforcers to attack without chilling procompetitive conduct, or should they welcome competitor complaints about anticompetitive exclusionary conduct as a guide to identifying harmful mergers? *Cf.* Staff Analysis and Findings, Applications of AT&T Inc. and Deutsche Telekom AG For Consent To Assign or Transfer Control of Licenses and Authorizations, FCC WT Docket No. 11–65 at 44–45 n.255 (Nov. 29, 2011), http://hraun foss.fcc.gov/edocs_public/attachmatch/DA–11–1955A2.pdf (describing interests of merging firms and merger opponents and their possible alignment with the public interest). *See also Cargill, Inc. v. Monfort of Colorado, Inc.*, 479 U.S. 104 (1986) (implying that a firm targeted for exclusion as a consequence of a merger would suffer antitrust injury, but finding that the plaintiff had not adequately alleged likely post-merger exclusionary conduct).

Some of those who are most enthusiastic about making inferences about the likely competitive effects of a merger by evaluating its effect on rivals propose doing so based on the effect of merger announcements on share prices in the stock market. If the stock market price of rival firms rises upon the announcement of the merger (or falls when the investment community learns that antitrust enforcers have launched an investigation), some would infer that the transaction is likely to harm competition; if the stock market price of rival firms falls on the merger announcement (or rises in response to information about increased enforcer concern), the transaction is thought likely to promote competition. *See* Serdar Dalkir & Frederick R. Warren-Boulton, *Prices, Market Definition, and the Effects of Merger: Staples-Office Depot, in* THE ANTITRUST REVOLUTION 153 (John E. Kwoka, Jr. & Lawrence J. White eds., 3d ed. 1999) (discussing the application of this approach in connection with a litigated merger challenge). Because this methodology makes inferences from the stock market response to outside events, it is often termed an "event study" methodology. *See generally* A. Craig MacKinlay, *Event Studies in Economics and Finance*, 35 J. ECON. LIT. 13 (1997).

Critics of the use of the event study methodology to resolve individual cases make several points. First, they point to technical difficulties in identifying when the relevant "events" occurred (when did the news actually get out?) and controlling for other factors that might have affected share prices (like the general trend of the stock market as a whole). Second, they note that the key inference—lower stock market prices for rival shares suggesting that the merger creates efficiencies rather than anticompetitive harm—is only correct on its own terms if the anticompetitive theory involves collusive rather than exclusionary effects. Third, they suggest that notwithstanding the way that the stock market aggregates information from throughout the economy, antitrust enforcers may have more information in important respects than is reflected in share values. Unlike investors and Wall Street analysts, enforcers can read the marketing documents of all the firms. *But cf.* Justin Wolfers & Eric Zitzewitz, *Prediction Markets,* 18 J. ECON. PERSPECTIVES 107, 113 (2004) (examples showing that markets predict as well as experts). Fourth, they note that event studies may have little power when rival firms derive a small fraction of their revenues from the markets potentially affected by the merger. Finally, they point out that when investors forecast the likely financial consequences of a merger proposal, they must consider not only the competitive effects of the deal but also the likelihood that the transaction will be challenged by antitrust enforcers. If investors believe that the merger would likely harm competition by facilitating tacit collusion, they should bid up the stock market price of rival shares. But if the resulting increase in the stock market price would make a government challenge to the deal more likely, investors would not want to increase the stock price after all. Under such circumstances, it is far from clear what, if anything, the antitrust agencies could reliably infer by analyzing the stock market response to merger announcements. Similarly, if the stock price of rivals falls when an antitrust investigation begins or appears to reflect serious agency concern, that observation could reflect greater investor expectations that antitrust enforcement would prevent rivals from being acquired rather than a reduction in the likelihood of future coordination.

Similar issues about the trustworthiness of competitor or customer evidence arise when executives from those firms provide evidence as to likely buyer substitution in connection with market definition or assessing unilateral effects of a merger among sellers of differentiated products. Before trusting customer views, a fact-finder can be expected to assess whether those views are informed, representative, and reliable. In *United States v. Oracle Corp.*, 331 F. Supp. 2d 1098, 1131 (N.D. Cal. 2004), for example, the court declined to consider customer views it considered inadequately supported. Moreover, when the issue is not market definition or unilateral effects, but the likelihood of coordinated effects, a court may be even more inclined to question the reliability of customer views. After all, buyers are unlikely to have special expertise as to how *seller* behavior would change after a merger, which is the competitive effects issue in a coordinated effects case. *See FTC v. Arch Coal, Inc.*, 329 F. Supp. 2d 109 (D.D.C. 2004).

b.　Unilateral Competitive Effects

Traditionally, merger enforcement was focused on coordinated competitive effects. That theory was implicitly or explicitly behind the decisions in the major cases we have read to this point, from *Philadelphia National Bank* to *Hospital Corp. of America*. But mergers among rivals may diminish competition even if they do not make coordination among the market participants more likely or more successful; they may instead harm competition "unilaterally" by making it possible for the merged firm to raise price on its own, without consideration of the likely responses of non-merging rivals. This possibility is most clear in a "merger to monopoly," where the merger creates a firm with sufficient market power to raise price on its own. As we shall see, however, the Guidelines' concept of unilateral effects extends beyond the setting of mergers to monopoly.

The many unilateral competitive effects possibilities have long been known to industrial organization economists, but they have taken on increased importance in antitrust practice, particularly at the federal enforcement agencies, since economists developed ways to quantify the magnitude of the possible anticompetitive effects, beginning with the work of Jonathan B. Baker and Timothy F. Bresnahan in the mid-1980s, and the appearance of these theories in the 1992 revisions to the Merger Guidelines. *See* Jonathan B. Baker, *Why Did the Antitrust Agencies Embrace Unilateral Effects?* 12 GEO. MASON L. REV. 31 (2003).

The 2010 Merger Guidelines set forth four unilateral competitive effects theories: for markets in which products are differentiated (§ 6.1), for markets where sellers negotiate with buyers or prices are determined through auctions (§ 6.2), for markets in which products are homogeneous (§ 6.3), and for markets in which unilateral effects are likely to take the form of diminished innovation or product variety (§ 6.4). Our presentation will begin with and emphasize the first theory, the one that applies when products are differentiated, but it will discuss the other three as well.

Goods and services may differ along a wide range of physical and non-physical characteristics, including features, colors, styles, geographic location, point-of-sale or post-sale services (like demonstrations and warranties), seller reputations for quality, delivery time, defect rate, and non-physical attributes, such as "brand" recognition or an image related to lifestyle (like "cool," "young," or "cutting-edge"). *See* Thomas J. Campbell, *Predation and Competition in Antitrust: The Case of Nonfungible Goods*, 87 COLUM. L. REV. 1625 (1987). Differentiation is common in branded consumer products industries, such as soft drinks and breakfast cereals; in markets where buyers see important differences in the nature or quality of services offered by potential suppliers, such as automotive steel or the auditing services provided by accounting firms; and in industries where seller locations are important to buyers, such as supermarkets or hospitals.

In such markets, competition may be "localized," in the sense that buyers view some products within the market as closer substitutes to each other, and individual sellers compete more directly—more "head-to-head"—with those rivals selling the closest substitutes.

Although the analysis of unilateral effects among sellers of differentiated products was routine at the federal enforcement agencies by the early 1990s, the courts took longer to address the topic, in part because merger litigation is rare. One early judicial effort to consider unilateral effects was *New York v. Kraft General Foods, Inc.*, 926 F. Supp. 321 (S.D.N.Y 1995), which involved a challenge to an acquisition in the breakfast cereal industry. The challenge was initiated by the New York State Attorney General, who alleged both coordinated and unilateral competitive effects; here we focus on the unilateral competitive effects issue.

The case involved a November 1992 transaction in which Kraft, the owner of Post cereals, acquired the ready-to-eat ("RTE") cereal assets of Nabisco. The Federal Trade Commission reviewed the transaction and declined to challenge it. At that time, over 200 RTE cereal products were available for sale to consumers. RTE cereals differ from one another in important respects, including type of grain, degree of sweetness, product form (*e.g.*, flake, nugget, shredded, etc.), texture, flavor, complexity, type of additional ingredients (*e.g.*, nuts and fruit), and perceived health benefits. Even the most popular RTE cereals accounted for only a small percentage of total RTE cereal sales. The best-selling RTE cereal, Kellogg's Corn Flakes, had a share only slightly above 5%.

Kellogg and General Mills were the two largest manufacturers, together accounting for 60% of RTE cereal products sold in the United States. Kraft, the third largest manufacturer with about 12% of sales, produced and sold 28 RTE cereal products, most under the "Post" name. Grape Nuts was one of Post's most successful products. Nabisco, with a market share of less than 3%, was sixth largest. Its main strength was its shredded wheat line of cereals.

The district court rejected New York's unilateral effects claim because it concluded that "Grape Nuts and Nabisco Shredded Wheat compete with many other products and are not the first and second choices of a significant number of consumers." 926 F. Supp. at 352. One notable feature of the decision is the wide range of evidence the court relied upon in reaching this conclusion. At least five different types of evidence were analyzed.

First, the court looked at the extent to which the two brands had similar physical characteristics and images. It found that Grape Nuts and Nabisco Shredded Wheat differed in physical characteristics and that the two brands emphasized different attributes in their advertising. Grape

Nuts was marketed first as "healthy" and later as "energy sustaining;" Nabisco Shredded Wheat was marketed as "pure," with no added sugar or salt. Many other cereal brands were also promoted as healthy, plain cereals, such as Corn Flakes, Cheerios, Chex, Special K, Total, and Rice Krispies.

Second, the court also relied upon customer testimony about the extent of buyer substitution between the brands. It noted that executives of two large grocery retailers testified that they did not consider Grape Nuts and Nabisco Shredded Wheat to be particularly close competitors, and that they set the retail price for the two brands independently.

Third, the court relied upon marketing survey data about the characteristics of each brand's customers. It found that Grape Nuts consumers tended to be "upscale," younger, and more educated, while Nabisco Shredded Wheat consumers tended to be "downscale," older, and less educated.

Fourth, the district court examined the extent to which the merging firms monitored and responded to key marketing decisions of each other. The evidence in this category was mixed, according to the court. Some Post documents indicated that the two brands were viewed as at or near the top of each other's list of most direct competitors. But the evidence also showed that Post generally looked to Kellogg products, not Nabisco Shredded Wheat, as a benchmark in pricing Grape Nuts and that the evidence did not support plaintiff's assertion that Post tracked Nabisco Shredded Wheat's pricing, advertising, and promotional activities to determine expenditures for Grape Nuts.

Finally, the court relied upon an econometric study of buyer demand conducted by defendant's expert economist. The expert found low cross-price elasticities of demand between Grape Nuts and Nabisco Shredded Wheat, and that cross-price elasticities of demand were higher between Grape Nuts and a number of other cereals, including Cheerios, Kellogg's Raisin Bran, Kellogg's Frosted Mini-Wheats, the Kellogg's Nutri-Grain line, and Ralston Chex.

When turning to the law, the district court recognized that unilateral effects cases were at the time novel in the courts and relied upon the Merger Guidelines as persuasive authority. (At the time of the decision, the 1992 Merger Guidelines were in force.)

> The State contends that, even absent any consideration of coordinated effects, the Acquisition is unlawful because it promotes anticompetitive unilateral effects, i.e., by placing Shredded Wheat and Grape Nuts under one roof, the Acquisition diminishes the likelihood that there will be competition between the two brands, which the State contends are very close substitutes for one another. The Merger Guidelines recognize the

danger of anticompetitive unilateral effects, pointing out (put most simply) that a merged firm may be able to raise the price of one product and capture any sales lost due to that price rise, if buyers will switch to another product that is now sold by the merged firm. As the Merger Guidelines note, a firm can wield such power (i.e., achieve substantial unilateral price elevation) in a market for differentiated products only if there is "a significant share of sales in the market accounted for by consumers who regard the products of the merging firms as their first and second choices, and that repositioning of the non-parties' product lines to replace the localized competition lost through the merger [is] unlikely."

Although courts do not invariably concern themselves with unilateral effects in Section 7 cases, I will assume, arguendo, that the Merger Guidelines' concern for this effect is valid. * * *

* * *

The foregoing demonstrates that it would not be profitable for Kraft to raise the price of Grape Nuts in the expectation that a substantial portion of its lost sales would go to Nabisco Shredded Wheat, because it is likely that the lost sales would be dispersed among a wide variety of products, and that Nabisco Shredded Wheat would gain only a small percentage of those losses. The State has failed to prove its claim of adverse unilateral effects.

926 F. Supp. at 365–66.

Note that in analyzing unilateral effects, the *Kraft* court examined the same types of evidence that courts look to in defining markets under the Merger Guidelines. This is not a coincidence. Both market definition (under the Guidelines approach) and unilateral effects among sellers of differentiated products turn on the same economic force: demand (buyer) substitution. Would *Kraft* have come out differently had the plaintiff instead framed the unilateral effects allegation as a merger to monopoly within a narrow market or submarket (perhaps limited to "healthy" cereals)? After reading the Crunchies/Fruities illustration, which explicates the economic logic of unilateral effects among sellers of differentiated products, consider what, if anything, in the economics analysis turns on the scope of the product market, and whether market definition is necessary if unilateral effects between sellers of differentiated products can be demonstrated directly using evidence about buyer substitution.

NOTE ON THE ECONOMICS OF UNILATERAL EFFECTS IN DIFFERENTIATED-PRODUCT MARKETS: THE MERGER OF CRUNCHIES AND FRUITIES[23]

To understand the unilateral competitive effects theory analyzed in *Kraft*, consider a merger in a hypothetical, and much simplified, breakfast cereal industry. Suppose the Crunchy Cereal Co., which makes the Crunchies brand, seeks to acquire the Fruity Cereal Co., maker of Fruities. Assume further, at variance with the real breakfast cereal industry, that each firm sells only one brand and that firms promote their brands exclusively through national advertising, not by discounting prices at supermarkets. The example set forth in the following paragraphs is also summarized below in tables.

Before the merger, Crunchies sells its cereal to supermarkets for $2.00 per standard-sized box; this is the price that maximizes its profits. An additional cereal box costs $1.10 to produce and sell. Assume that if Crunchies were to raise the price of a box of its product by 5%, to $2.10, Crunchies would lose 10 out of every 100 unit sales, or 10% of its sales. (If a 5% price increase induces a 10% reduction in the quantity sold, the own-price elasticity of demand is –2.) Quantity sold declines because supermarkets pass along the entire price increase to their retail customers, leading some customers to buy fewer boxes of Crunchies than before, some to substitute other breakfast cereals, and some to do without cereal altogether, much as we saw in discussing the coffee hypothetical in Chapter 1.

With these assumptions, the manufacturer would not be able to increase profits by raising the Crunchies price. In making that determination, the company balances the projected costs of lost sales against the gain from higher price-cost margins. On the cost side, the company would lose a contribution margin (price less marginal cost) of $0.90 on the 10 out of every 100 premerger sales that it no longer makes, for a total loss of $9.00. Against that loss, Crunchies would gain an additional $0.10 profit on the 90 out of 100 sales it still makes at the higher price, for a gain of $9.00 per 100 units sold premerger. Because the gain from raising price ($9.00) does not exceed the cost (also $9.00), the firm will not attempt to increase its price.[24]

---

[23] This example is adapted from Jonathan B. Baker, *Unilateral Competitive Effects Theories in Merger Analysis*, ANTITRUST, Spring 1997, at 21, 23.

[24] Nothing of consequence in the example would change were the variable costs of production $1.099 per box, so that the price of $2.00 is strictly more profitable than the price of $2.10.

Figure 5–6:

A Price Increase Would Not Increase Crunchies Profits Pre-Merger

Types of Gains and Losses		Gain or Loss (per 100 buyers)
Gain from higher price-cost margin, per 100 customers	+$0.10 x 90 customers	+$9.00
Loss from losing contribution margin on sales, per 100 customers	–$0.90 x 10 customers	–$9.00
Net gain or loss		**$0**

The merger of Crunchies and Fruities can alter this calculus, making an increase in the price of Crunchies profitable. Three of the 10 unit sales lost (out of every 100 lost sales) represent customers switching from Crunchies to Fruities as a consequence of the Crunchies price increase. For those three lost customers, Fruities is the closest substitute for Crunchies at current prices. The Merger Guidelines term this figure—the three lost Crunchies customers out of every ten that go to Fruities—a *"diversion ratio."* The Guidelines observe that diversion ratios between products sold by the merging firms "can be very informative" for assessing unilateral price effects. Diversion ratios are mathematically related to the cross-price elasticity of demand between the brands.

To see why the merger makes it profitable to increase the price of Crunchies, suppose further that Fruities already sells for $2.10 and that the next box of Fruities would cost $1.30 to produce and distribute. If Crunchies acquires Fruities and then raises the price of Crunchies to $2.10, Crunchies will divert some Crunchies sales to what is now its other brand, Fruities, thereby avoiding some of the losses it would otherwise have sustained. On the three out of every 100 Crunchies units sold premerger that become Fruities sales, the merged firm earns a profit of $0.80 per unit ($2.10—$1.30), for a total gain of $2.40 per 100 Crunchies units sold premerger. That is, selling 90 units of Crunchies at $2.10 and 3 units of Fruities at $2.10 would be more profitable than selling 100 units of Crunchies alone at $2.00.[25] Accordingly, as a consequence of the merger, it is now profitable to increase the Crunchies price to $2.10.

---

[25] $90 \times (\$2.10–\$1.10) + 3 \times (\$2.10–\$1.30) = \$92.40$, whereas $100 \times (\$2.00–\$1.10) = \$90$.

Figure 5–7:

A Price Increase Would Increase Crunchies Profits Post-Merger

Types of Gains and Losses		Gain or Loss (per 100 buyers)
Gain from higher price-cost margin, per 100 customers	+$0.10 x 90 customers	+$9.00
Loss from losing contribution margin on sales, per 100 customers	−$0.90 x 10 customers	−$9.00
Gain in added profits to Fruities	+$0.80 x 3 customers	+$2.40
Net gain or loss		**+$2.40**

The profitability of a unilateral increase in the price of Crunchies may constitute a motive for merger. Before the merger, the Crunchies price was constrained by the collective presence of competition from rival brands, including Fruities, which were each the second choice for a significant fraction of consumers. But with the merger, Crunchies is no longer concerned about the diversion of some buyers to Fruities—it has recaptured those three buyers. Thus, the merger removes Fruities as a constraint on Crunchies pricing. For similar reasons, the merger may also give the merged firm an incentive to increase the price of Fruities.

Fruities need not be the *most* preferred alternative among the buyers who switch away from Crunchies in response to a price rise in order for the merger to create harmful unilateral effects, so long as Fruities is the preferred alternative for a substantial group of those buyers. To see this, note that it does not matter in the example which brand was chosen by the remaining seven of every 10 lost Crunchies customers that did not select Fruities as their second choice, or whether or not those lost customers continue to buy breakfast cereal. Perhaps, for example, six out of every 10 lost Crunchies customers switched to Oaties. So long as a substantial fraction of lost Crunchies customers (here three out every 10 lost customers) selected Fruities as their second choice, the merged firm will profit by raising the Crunchies price. In other words, Fruities must be the closest substitute for a substantial group of Crunchies buyers, but it is not necessary that Fruities be the closest substitute for the largest group of Crunchies buyers.

Moreover, the higher price of the merged firm's products may make it profitable for non-merging rivals like Oaties to raise the prices for their products. In this way, the adverse consequences of mergers creating unilateral effects may spread beyond the products of the merged firms.

The example also can be used to illustrate two kinds of defenses Crunchies and Fruities might offer to the claim that their merger will harm competition by reducing localized competition among sellers of differentiated products. The first involves expansion of output by rival suppliers, as through entry of new products (either by new or established firms), or the "repositioning" of existing products by competing firms (modifying product or brand attributes, or extending brands by adding variants to the product line). For example, Oaties, a third cereal brand, may respond to the Crunchies price increase by adding Crunchy Oaties and Fruity Oaties to its product line, or by stepping up promotion of these brands if they already exist. This repositioning response by Oaties might lead more than 10 out of 100 Crunchies customers to switch away in response to a Crunchies price increase and lead most of the switchers who formerly saw Fruities as their second choice to select an Oaties product instead. If so, it may no longer be profitable to increase the price of Crunchies after the merger. A second defense possibility is that efficiencies from the merger may counteract the incentive to raise price. For example, Crunchies and Fruities together may be able to achieve substantial cost savings from their increased scale of promotion and distribution. If the marginal cost of producing Crunchies were to decline sufficiently, the post-merger price could fall, notwithstanding the loss of direct competition between the two brands. Efficiencies are considered in more detail later in this Chapter.

What element of the unilateral competitive effects theory sketched in this note did the district court find lacking in rejecting New York's challenge to Kraft's acquisition of Nabisco? Would the court agree that "it is not necessary that Fruities be the most preferred alternative among the buyers who switch away from Crunchies in response to a price rise" in order for the merger of Crunchies and Fruities to harm competition?

Economists analyzing unilateral effects have developed a range of methods for quantifying the unilateral effects concern based on the kind of information used in the example in this Note. Some of these methods are referenced by the Merger Guidelines. They are surveyed in the next Sidebar.

Sidebar 5–8:
Methods of Quantifying Unilateral
Effects in the Merger Guidelines

The Merger Guidelines suggest two methods of quantifying the unilateral incentive to raise price post-merger: employing an indicator of *upward pricing pressure* ("UPP") and simulating the effects of the merger. First, the Guidelines look to the "value of diverted sales" from a product of one merging firm to products previously sold by the other merging firm as an "indicator of the upward pricing pressure" on the first firm's product. *Horizontal Merger Guidelines* § 6.1 (2010). The value is not evaluated in dollars, but "in proportion to the lost revenues attributable to the reduction in unit sales resulting from the price increase." *Id.* § 6.1 n.11. This indicator is called the GUPPI (an acronym for "Gross Upward Pricing Pressure Index") in the economics literature, though the Guidelines do not use the term. For a discussion with citations to the literature, see Carl Shapiro, *The 2010 Horizontal Merger Guidelines: From Hedgehog to Fox in Forty Years*, 77 ANTITRUST L.J. 49, 722–43 (2010).

UPP and GUPPI Scoring

The mechanics of computing this upward pricing pressure indicator can be clarified using the figures set forth in the previous note on the merger of Crunchies and Fruities. The Guidelines define the value of sales diverted to a product as equal to "the number of units diverted to that product multiplied by the [dollar] margin between price and incremental [variable] cost on that product." In the Crunchies-Fruites example, suppose that Crunchies sold 100 boxes pre-merger. If the price of a box of Crunchies were to rise by $0.10 before the merger, three pre-merger sales would be diverted to Fruities. Each of the sales diverted to Fruities is worth $0.80 (Fruities' contribution margin) to Fruities. Hence the total value of sales diverted to Fruities (*value of diverted sales*), which Crunchies would regain by acquiring Fruities, would be $2.40 (3 × $.80). This value is measured in proportion to lost revenues attributable to the loss in unit sales resulting from the price increase, which the Guidelines define as "the reduction in the number of units sold of that product multiplied by that product's price." In the example, Crunchies would lose a total of 10 boxes. At a premerger price of $2.00 per box, Crunchies' lost revenues amount to $20.00. Thus, the Crunchies GUPPI would equal 12% ($2.40/$20).[a]

The Guidelines do not indicate whether 12% should be viewed as a large number, indicative of a serious unilateral effects concern. However, according to a former senior agency official, a figure below 5% would suggest that adverse unilateral effects would be considered unlikely. Carl Shapiro, Deputy Assistant Attorney General for Economics, U.S. Dep't of

---

[a] The GUPPI can be calculated in another way, which may be simpler to apply. First, express the three units diverted to Fruities as a proportion of the 10 total lost Crunchies sales, *i.e.*, as a 30% diversion ratio for Crunchies. Second, express Fruities' contribution margin, which is $0.80 in the example, as a percentage of Fruities' price, which is $2.10 in the example, to compute a percentage contribution margin for Fruities of 38.1% ($0.80/$2.10). Third, calculate the ratio of Fruties' price to Crunchies' price, which is 1.05 ($2.10/$2.00 = 1.05). Fourth, multiply the Crunchies diversion ratio (30%) times the Fruities percentage contribution margin (38.1%) times the ratio of Fruities' price to Crunchies' price (1.05), to calculate a GUPPI for Crunchies of 12% (30% × 38.1% × 1.05). The calculation of the GUPPI for Fruities would be analogous.

Justice, Antitrust Division, *Update from the Antitrust Division*, Remarks as Prepared for the American Bar Association Section of Antitrust Law Fall Forum 24 (Nov. 18, 2010), http://www.justice.gov/atr/public/speeches/264295.pdf. Accordingly, the 5% figure can be interpreted as a "safe harbor." The GUPPI of 13.5% calculated for Crunchies exceeds this benchmark.

The higher the GUPPI score, the more significant are concerns about unilateral effects. In fact, under certain very limited conditions that simplify economic modeling, the merged firm would have the incentive to increase a product's price by half the GUPPI (6%, or $0.12, for Crunchies), holding the prices of the other products at their premerger levels.[b] However, the GUPPI score and this simple prediction do not take into account a number of factors relevant to evaluating unilateral competitive effects. First, and most importantly, the GUPPI score ignores the *downward pricing pressure* created by merger-specific cost-savings. A full unilateral effects analysis must net out the upward and downward pricing pressure. Second, the GUPPI score does not take into account certain factors that may enhance the upward pricing pressure. It ignores the impact of a price increase for one merging product on the simultaneous incentives to raise the price of the other merging products.[c] It also does not take into account that competitors typically also would have an incentive to raise their prices when the merging firm raises its prices. Third, the GUPPI score does not take into account supply responses that may mitigate the upward pricing pressure: the potential for entry and repositioning by non-merging firms. (Entry is discussed later in this Chapter; repositioning would be analyzed similarly.) Because the predicted price increase would likely change after these effects are taken into account, the economics literature (and the Guidelines) describe the GUPPI as a diagnostic screen and as one type of evidence that would be taken into account in a full unilateral effects analysis, rather than as a tool for predicting the post-merger price. Do the Guidelines implicitly suggest that a high GUPPI creates a presumption of unilateral

---

[b]   The technical conditions assume that the merger involves single product firms with constant marginal costs, and a particular type of interaction among firms called Bertrand-Nash conduct (which, among other things, rules out pricing coordination). They also assume that demand is linear and thus, for example, that a $10 rise in marginal cost by a firm would lead to a $5 price increase. In addition, they assume no variable cost savings from merger, no response by non-merging rivals, and no entry. Economists sometimes alter these assumptions where appropriate, thereby altering the relationship between the GUPPI and the predicted increase in price. Merger simulation approaches, discussed below in this note, can be understood as sophisticated ways of making those adjustments.

[c]   See Jerry Hausman, Serge Moresi & Mark Rainey, *Unilateral Effect of Mergers With General Linear Demand*, 111 ECON. LETTERS 119 (2011).

anticompetitive effects? If not, should they? For commentary advocating doing so, see Jonathan B. Baker & Carl Shapiro, *Reinvigorating Horizontal Merger Enforcement*, *in* WHERE THE CHICAGO SCHOOL OVERSHOT THE MARK: EFFECT OF CONSERVATIVE ECONOMIC ANALYSIS ON U.S. ANTITRUST 235, 264–66 (Robert Pitofsky ed., 2008); Steven C. Salop, *The Evolution and Vitality of Merger Presumptions: A Decision-Theoretic Approach*, 80 ANTITRUST L. J. 301 (2015).

When analyzing the unilateral effects of mergers between sellers of differentiated products, courts could establish a safe harbor for a low GUPPI or a presumption of competitive harm when the GUPPI is high. Would either or both presumptions be appropriate? If so, what are the best theoretical or empirical justifications?

If such presumptions were established, how strong should they be? That is, what factual showing by the party opposing the application of either presumption should be deemed sufficient to overcome the presumption? Professor Salop suggests that the strength should depend on the reliability of the facts creating the presumption as a predictor of competitive effects relative to the reliability of the additional evidence that is proffered. *Id*. If a presumption almost always leads to the correct inference, therefore, it should be difficult to rebut (*i.e.,* require a very strong showing to do so). Do you consider a low GUPPI to be a highly reliable indicator that unilateral effects are unlikely? Do you consider a high GUPPI to be a highly reliable indicator that unilateral effects are likely?

Note that similar questions could be asked about the bases for presumptions involving coordinated effects. How reliable are concentration levels and changes in market concentration as indicators that coordinated effects are likely or unlikely? How reliable is a presumption that a merger involving a maverick firm makes coordination more likely or more effective? What about a presumption that a merger involving non-maverick firms does not make coordination more likely or more effective?

Merger Simulation

The Merger Guidelines recognize merger simulation approaches as a second way to quantify unilateral effects. *Horizontal Merger Guidelines* § 6.1 (2010) ("When sufficient data are available, the Agencies may construct economic models designed to quantify the unilateral price effects resulting from the merger."). *Id*. The earlier observation that under specific conditions, the merged firm would raise the Crunchies price by

$0.14 can be thought of as the result of applying a very simple simulation model, though the merger simulation tools applied in practice are substantially more complex. These tools can be particularly valuable when the agency must assess the net effect of upward pricing pressure from the elimination of competition between the merging firms and downward pricing pressure from efficiencies. Simulations may also address limitations of the GUPPI score, as by incorporating parallel pricing responses by non-merging firms and feedbacks to the prices of the merging firms. Simulations also can take into account supply side responses. Expert economists also sometimes employ simulation modeling as a basis for the testimony in merger cases. *See, e.g.*, United States v. H & R *Block,* 833 F. Supp. 2d 36, 86–88 (D.D.C. 2011). For a technical survey of merger simulation methods, including methods for simulating the consequences of merger when other unilateral effects theories are employed, see Gregory J. Werden & Luke M. Froeb, *Unilateral Competitive Effects of Horizontal Mergers, in* HANDBOOK OF ANTITRUST ECONOMICS 43 (Paolo Buccirossi ed., 2008). The appropriate use of different types of merger simulations in various administrative contexts—as a screen enforcers can apply to identify mergers worth investigating, as a basis for agency decision-making, and a basis for expert testimony in litigation—is discussed in Jonathan B. Baker, *Merger Simulation in an Administrative Context*, 77 ANTITRUST L. J. 451 (2011).

Conclusion

These quantitative methods assume that it is possible to estimate diversion ratios and price-cost margins—the types of information important in the Crunchies-Fruities example. If the estimates cannot be made precise, that is not necessarily a bar to the use of quantitative tools. Rather, it suggests applying those tools using a range of alternative estimates. If the conclusions are robust to reasonable variation in the estimated values, they should be credited more than if the results are sensitive to those alternatives. Moreover, it may be possible to use additional information, possibly qualitative, to evaluate which alternatives should be preferred. For this reason, the Merger Guidelines emphasize that merger simulation evidence "is not conclusive in itself" and that a consistent prediction of substantial price increases using a range of plausible assumptions as to the parameters and the structure of the model is more convincing than the precise price increase implied by any single simulation.

The *Staples* case, which we will read next, involves an FTC challenge to a proposed merger of two of the three leading office supply superstore chains, Staples and Office Depot. As you read the case, consider how the economic principles explored in the previous Note on the Crunchies-Fruities merger could explain the FTC's theory of anticompetitive effects.

FEDERAL TRADE COMMISSION V. STAPLES, INC.

United States District Court for the District of Columbia, 1997.
970 F. Supp. 1066.

THOMAS F. HOGAN, DISTRICT JUDGE.

Plaintiff, the Federal Trade Commission ("FTC" or "Commission"), seeks a preliminary injunction pursuant to Section 13(b) of the Federal Trade Commission Act, 15 U.S.C. § 53(b), to enjoin the consummation of any acquisition by defendant Staples, Inc., of defendant Office Depot, Inc., pending final disposition before the Commission of administrative proceedings to determine whether such acquisition may substantially lessen competition in violation of Section 7 of the Clayton Act, 15 U.S.C. § 18, and Section 5 of the Federal Trade Commission Act, 15 U.S.C. § 45. The proposed acquisition has been postponed pending the Court's decision on the motion for a preliminary injunction, which is now before the Court for decision after a five-day evidentiary hearing and the filing of proposed findings of fact and conclusions of law. For the reasons set forth below, the Court will grant the plaintiff's motion. This Memorandum Opinion constitutes the Court's findings of fact and conclusions of law.

Background

* * *

Defendants are both corporations which sell office products—including office supplies, business machines, computers and furniture—through retail stores, commonly described as office supply superstores, as well as through direct mail delivery and contract stationer operations. Staples is the second largest office superstore chain in the United States with approximately 550 retail stores located in 28 states and the District of Columbia, primarily in the Northeast and California. In 1996 Staples' revenues from those stores were approximately $4 billion through all operations. Office Depot, the largest office superstore chain, operates over 500 retail office supply superstores that are located in 38 states and the District of Columbia, primarily in the South and Midwest. Office Depot's 1996 sales were approximately $6.1 billion. OfficeMax, Inc., is the only other office supply superstore firm in the United States.

* * *

Discussion

I.   Section 13(B) Standard for Preliminary Relief

* * *

In order to determine whether the Commission has met its burden with respect to showing its likelihood of success on the merits, that is, whether the FTC has raised questions going to the merits so serious, substantial, difficult and doubtful as to make them fair ground for thorough investigation, study, deliberation and determination by the FTC in the first instance and ultimately by the Court of Appeals and that there is a "reasonable probability" that the challenged transaction will substantially impair competition, the Court must consider the likely competitive effects of the merger, if any. Analysis of the likely competitive effects of a merger requires determinations of (1) the "line of commerce" or product market in which to assess the transaction, (2) the "section of the country" or geographic market in which to assess the transaction, and (3) the transaction's probable effect on competition in the product and geographic markets. * * *

II.   The Geographic Market

One of the few issue about which the parties to this case do not disagree is that metropolitan areas are the appropriate geographic markets for analyzing the competitive effects of the proposed merger. * * *

III.   The Relevant Product Market

In contrast to the parties' agreement with respect to the relevant geographic market, the Commission and the defendants sharply disagree with respect to the appropriate definition of the relevant product market or line of commerce. As with many antitrust cases, the definition of the relevant product market in this case is crucial. In fact, to a great extent, this case hinges on the proper definition of the relevant product market.

The Commission defines the relevant product market as "the sale of consumable office supplies through office superstores," * * * with "consumable" meaning products that consumers buy recurrently, i.e., items which "get used up" or discarded. For example, under the Commission's definition, "consumable office supplies" would not include capital goods such as computers, fax machines, and other business machines or office furniture, but does include such products as paper, pens, file folders, post-it notes, computer disks, and toner cartridges. The defendants characterize the FTC's product market definition as "contrived" with no basis in law or fact, and counter that the appropriate product market within which to assess the likely competitive consequences of a Staples-Office Depot combination is simply the overall sale of office products, of which a combined Staples-Office Depot accounted for 5.5% of total sales in North America in 1996. In addition, the defendants argue that the challenged combination is not likely "substantially to lessen competition" however the product market is defined. After considering the arguments on both sides and all of the evidence in this case and making evaluations of each witness's credibility as well as the weight that the Court should give certain evidence and testimony, the Court finds that the appropriate relevant product market definition in this case is, as the Commission has argued, the sale of consumable office supplies through office supply superstores.

* * *

The Court recognizes that it is difficult to overcome the first blush or initial gut reaction of many people to the definition of the relevant product market as the sale of consumable office supplies through office supply superstores. The products in question are undeniably the same no matter who sells them, and no one denies that many different types of retailers sell these products. After all, a combined Staples-Office Depot would only have a 5.5% share of the overall market in consumable office supplies. Therefore, it is logical to conclude that, of course, all these retailers compete, and that if a combined Staples-Office Depot raised prices after the merger, or at least did not lower them as much as they would have as separate companies, that consumers, with such a plethora of options, would shop elsewhere.

The Court acknowledges that there is, in fact, a broad market encompassing the sale of consumable office supplies by all sellers of such supplies, and that those sellers must, at some level, compete with one another. However, the mere fact that a firm may be termed a competitor in the overall marketplace does not necessarily require that it be included in the relevant product market for antitrust purposes. The Supreme Court has recognized that within a broad market, "well-defined submarkets may exist which, in themselves, constitute product markets for antitrust purposes." *Brown Shoe Co. v. United States*, 370 U.S. 294, 325, 82 S.Ct. 1502, 1524, 8 L.Ed.2d 510 (1962). * * * There is a possibility, therefore, that the sale of consumable office supplies by office superstores may qualify as a submarket within a larger market of retailers of office supplies in general.

The Court in *Brown Shoe* provided a series of factors or "practical indicia" for determining whether a submarket exists. * * *

* * * [T]he FTC focused on what it termed the "pricing evidence," which the Court finds corresponds with *Brown Shoe's* "sensitivity to price changes" factor. First, the FTC presented evidence comparing Staples' prices in geographic markets where Staples is the only office superstore, to markets where Staples competes with Office Depot or OfficeMax, or both. Based on the FTC's calculations, in markets where Staples faces no office superstore competition at all, something which was termed a one firm market during the hearing, prices are 13% higher than in three firm markets where it competes with both Office Depot and OfficeMax. * * * Similarly, the evidence showed that Office Depot's prices are significantly higher—well over 5% higher, in Depot-only markets than they are in three firm markets.

* * *

The FTC also pointed to internal Staples documents which present price comparisons between Staples' prices and Office Depot's prices and Staples' prices and OfficeMax's prices within different price zones.[9] * * * Using Staples' data, but organizing it differently to show which of those zones were one, two, or three firm markets, the FTC showed once again that Staples charges significantly higher prices, more than 5% higher, where it has no office superstore competition than where it competes with the two other superstores. * * *

This evidence all suggests that office superstore prices are affected primarily by other office superstores and not by non-superstore competitors such as mass merchandisers like Wal-Mart, Kmart, or Target, wholesale clubs such as BJ's, Sam's, and Price Costco, computer or electronic stores such as Computer City and Best Buy, independent retail office supply stores, mail orders firms like Quill and Viking, and contract stationers. Though the FTC did not present the Court with evidence regarding the precise amount of non-superstore competition in each of Staples' and Office Depot's one, two, and three firm markets, it is clear to the Court that these competitors, albeit in different combinations and concentrations, are present in every one of these markets. * * *

* * * Staples' own pricing information shows that warehouse clubs have very little effect on Staples' prices. For example, Staples' maintains a "warehouse club only" price zone, which indicates a zone where Staples exists with a warehouse club but without another office superstore. The data presented by the Commission on Staples' pricing shows only a slight variation in prices (1%–2%) between "warehouse club only" zones and one superstore markets without a warehouse club. * * *

There is also consistent evidence with respect to computer and/or consumer electronics stores such as Best Buy. For example, Office Depot maintains a separate price zone, which it calls "zone 30," for areas with Best Buy locations but no other office supply superstores. However, the FTC introduced evidence * * * that prices in Office Depot's "zone 30" price zone are almost as high as in its "non-competitive" price zone, the zone where it does not compete with another office superstore.

---

[9]   It was established at the hearing that Staples and Office Depot do not maintain nationally uniform prices in their stores. Instead, both companies currently organize their stores into price zones which are simply groups of one or more stores that have common prices.

There is similar evidence with respect to the defendants' behavior when faced with entry of another competitor. The evidence shows that the defendants change their price zones when faced with entry of another superstore, but do not do so for other retailers. * * * There are numerous additional examples of zones being changed and prices falling as a result of superstore entry. There is no evidence that zones change and prices fall when another non-superstore retailer enters a geographic market.

* * * [T]he Court finds this evidence a compelling showing that a small but significant increase in Staples' prices will not cause a significant number of consumers to turn to non-superstore alternatives for purchasing their consumable office supplies. * * *

Turning back to the other *Brown Shoe* "practical indicia" of submarkets that the Commission offered in this case, the Commission presented and the Court heard a great deal of testimony at the hearing and through declarations about the uniqueness of office superstores and the differences between the office superstores and other sellers of office supplies such as mass merchandisers, wholesale clubs, and mail order firms as well as the special characteristics of office superstore customers. In addition, the Court was asked to go and view many of the different types of retail formats. That evidence shows that office superstores are, in fact, very different in appearance, physical size, format, the number and variety of SKU's offered, and the type of customers targeted and served than other sellers of office supplies. * * * [SKUs, or stock-keeping units, are finely defined product categories, such as blue medium-point Bic pens. Eds.]

In addition to the differences in SKU numbers and variety, the superstores are different from many other sellers of office supplies due to the type of customer they target and attract. The superstores' customer base overwhelmingly consists of small businesses with fewer than 20 employees and consumers with home offices. * * *

* * * Based on the Court's observations, the Court finds that the unique combination of size, selection, depth and breadth of inventory offered by the superstores distinguishes them from other retailers. * * * No one entering Staples or Office Depot would mistakenly think he or she was in Best Buy or CompUSA. You certainly know an office superstore when you see one. * * *

Another of the "practical indicia" for determining the presence of a submarket suggested by *Brown Shoe* is "industry or public recognition of the submarket as a separate economic entity." * * * The Commission offered abundant evidence on this factor from Staples' and Office Depot's documents which shows that both Staples and Office Depot focus primarily on competition from other superstores. The documents reviewed by the Court show that the merging parties evaluate their "competition" as the other office superstore firms, without reference to other retailers, mail order firms, or independent stationers. In document after document, the parties refer to, discuss, and make business decisions based upon the assumption that "competition" refers to other office superstores only. * * *

* * * In a monthly report entitled "Competitor Store Opening/Closing Report" which Office Depot circulates to its Executive Committee, Office Depot notes all competitor store closings and openings, but the only competitors referred to for its United States stores are Staples and OfficeMax.

While it is clear to the Court that Staples and Office Depot do not ignore sellers such as warehouse clubs, Best Buy, or Wal-Mart, the evidence clearly shows that Staples and Office Depot each consider the other superstores as the primary competition. For example, Office Depot has a Best Buy zone and Staples has a warehouse club zone. However, each still refers to its one firm markets with no other office superstore as "non-competitive" zones or markets. In addition, it is clear from the evidence that Staples and Office Depot price check the other office superstores much more frequently and extensively than they price check other retailers such as BJ's or Best Buy, and that Staples and Office Depot are more concerned with keeping their prices in parity with the other office superstores in their geographic areas than in undercutting Best Buy or a warehouse club.

* * *

IV. Probable Effect on Competition

After accepting the Commission's definition of the relevant product market, the Court next must consider the probable effect of a merger between Staples and Office Depot in the geographic markets previously identified. One way to do this is to examine the concentration statistics and HHIs within the geographic markets. * * * If the relevant product market is defined as the sale of consumable office supplies through office supply superstores, the HHIs in many of the geographic markets are at problematic levels even before the merger. * * * The average increase in HHI caused by the merger would be 2,715 points. The concentration statistics show that a merged Staples-Office Depot would have a dominant market share in 42 geographic markets across the country. The combined shares of Staples and Office Depot in the office superstore market would be 100% in 15 metropolitan areas. It is in these markets the post-merger HHI would be 10,000. In 27 other metropolitan areas, where the number of office superstore competitors would drop from three to two, the post-merger market shares would range from 45% to 94%, with post-merger HHIs ranging from 5,003 to 9,049. Even the lowest of these HHIs indicates a "highly concentrated" market.

* * * With HHIs of this level, the Commission certainly has shown a "reasonable probability" that the proposed merger would have an anti-competitive effect. * * *

The HHI calculations and market concentration evidence, however, are not the only indications that a merger between Staples and Office Depot may substantially lessen competition. Much of the evidence already discussed with respect to defining the relevant product market also indicates that the merger would likely have an anti-competitive effect. The evidence of the defendants' own current pricing practices, for example, shows that an office superstore chain facing no competition from other superstores has the ability to profitably raise prices for consumable office supplies above competitive levels. The fact that Staples and Office Depot both charge higher prices where they face no superstore competition demonstrates that an office superstore can raise prices above competitive levels. The evidence also shows that defendants also change their price zones when faced with entry of another office superstore, but do not do so for other retailers. Since prices are significantly lower in markets where Staples and Office Depot compete, eliminating this competition with one another would free the parties to charge higher prices in those markets, especially those in which the combined entity would be the sole office superstore. In addition, allowing the defendants to merge would eliminate significant future competition. Absent the merger, the firms are likely, and in fact have planned, to enter more of each other's markets, leading to a deconcentration of the market and, therefore, increased competition between the superstores.

In addition, direct evidence shows that by eliminating Staples' most significant, and in many markets only, rival, this merger would allow Staples to increase prices or otherwise maintain prices at an anti-competitive level.[14] The merger would eliminate significant head-to-head competition between the two lowest cost and lowest priced firms in the superstore market. Thus, the merger would result in the elimination of a particularly aggressive competitor in a highly concentrated market, a factor which is certainly an important consideration when analyzing possible anti-competitive effects. * * * It is based on all of this evidence as well that the Court finds that the Commission has shown a likelihood of

---

[14] There has been tremendous argument regarding whether the FTC actually contends that prices will go up after the merger. The Court understands that is not precisely the Commission's contention. Rather, the Commission argues that the merger will have an anti-competitive effect such that the combined firm's prices will be higher after the merger than they would be absent the merger. This does not necessarily mean that prices would rise from the levels they are now. Instead, according to the Commission, prices would simply not decrease as much as they would have on their own absent the merger. It is only in this sense that the Commission has contended that prices would go up—prices would go up compared to where they would have been absent the merger. It is only in this sense that consumers would be faced with "higher" prices. Therefore, when the Court discusses "raising" prices it is also with respect to raising prices with respect to where prices would have been absent the merger, not actually an increase from present price levels. * * *

success on the merits and a "reasonable probability" that the proposed transaction will have an anti-competitive effect.

* * *

[The excerpt from *Staples* presented here includes the following section, which addresses the efficiency arguments urged on the court by the merging firms. Examination of this section of the decision can be delayed until later in this Chapter, when we more specifically explore efficiencies in merger analysis. Eds.]

VI. *Efficiencies*

Whether an efficiencies defense showing that the intended merger would create significant efficiencies in the relevant market, thereby offsetting any anti-competitive effects, may be used by a defendant to rebut the government's prima facie case is not entirely clear. The newly revised efficiencies section of the *Merger Guidelines* recognizes that, "mergers have the potential to generate significant efficiencies by permitting a better utilization of existing assets, enabling the combined firm to achieve lower costs in producing a given quality and quantity than either firm could have achieved without the proposed transaction." *See Merger Guidelines* § 4. This coincides with the view of some courts that "whether an acquisition would yield significant efficiencies in the relevant market is an important consideration in predicting whether the acquisition would substantially lessen competition. . . . [T]herefore, . . . an efficiency defense to the government's prima facie case in section 7 challenges is appropriate in certain circumstances." *FTC v. University Health*, 938 F.2d 1206, 1222 (11th Cir. 1991). The Supreme Court, however, in *FTC v. Procter & Gamble Co.*, 386 U.S. 568, 579, 87 S.Ct. 1224, 1230, 18 L.Ed.2d 303 (1967), stated that "[p]ossible economies cannot be used as a defense to illegality in section 7 merger cases." There has been great disagreement regarding the meaning of this precedent and whether an efficiencies defense is permitted. * * * Assuming that it is a viable defense, however, the Court cannot find in this case that the defendants' efficiencies evidence rebuts the presumption that the merger may substantially lessen competition or shows that the Commission's evidence gives an inaccurate prediction of the proposed acquisition's probable effect.

The Court agrees with the defendants that where, as here, the merger has not yet been consummated, it is impossible to quantify precisely the efficiencies that it will generate. In addition, the Court recognizes a difference between efficiencies which are merely speculative and those which are based on a prediction backed by sound business judgment. * * * [L]ike all rebuttal evidence in Section 7 cases, the defendants must simply rebut the presumption that the merger will substantially lessen competition by showing that the Commission's evidence gives an inaccurate prediction of the proposed acquisition's probable effect. * * *

Defendants, however, must do this with credible evidence, and the Court with respect to this issue did not find the defendants' evidence to be credible.

Defendants' submitted an "Efficiencies Analysis" which predicated that the combined company would achieve savings of between $4.9 and $6.5 billion over the next five years. In addition, the defendants argued that the merger would also generate dynamic efficiencies. For example, defendants argued that as suppliers become more efficient due to their increased sales volume to the combined Staples-Office Depot, they would be able to lower prices to their other retailers. Moreover, defendants argued that two-thirds of the savings realized by the combined company would be passed along to consumers.

Evaluating credibility, as the Court must do, the Court credits the testimony and Report of the Commission's expert, David Painter, over the testimony and Efficiencies Study of the defendants' efficiencies witness, * * * [the] Senior Vice President of Integration at Staples. Mr. Painter's testimony was compelling, and the Court finds, based primarily on Mr. Painter's testimony, that the defendants' cost savings estimates are unreliable. First, the Court notes that the cost savings estimate of $4.947 billion over five years which was submitted to the Court exceeds by almost 500% the figures presented to the two Boards of Directors in September 1996, when the Boards approved the transaction. The cost savings claims submitted to the Court are also substantially greater than those represented in the defendants' Joint Proxy Statement/Prospectus "reflecting the best currently available estimate of management," and filed with the Securities and Exchange Commission on January 23, 1997, or referenced in the "fairness opinions" rendered by the defendants' investment bankers which are contained in the Proxy Statement.

The Court also finds that the defendants' projected "Base Case" savings of $5 billion are in large part unverified, or at least the defendants failed to produce the necessary documentation for verification. One example of this is the estimated cost savings from the Goods and Services category which projects cost savings of $553 million, about 10% of the total cost savings attributed to the merger by the defendants. * * * [Staples' Vice President for Integration] admitted that the entire backup, source, and the calculations of the Goods and Services' cost savings were not included in the Efficiencies Analysis. In addition, * * * [she] was unable to explain the methods used to calculate many of the cost savings. Similarly, the projected distribution cost savings, $883 million or 17% of the projected total cost savings, are problematic. Defendants' consultant A.T. Kearney estimated the savings, and * * * [Staples' Vice President for Integration] admitted the Efficiency Analysis did not show that Kearney had deducted the projected Staples stand-alone savings from the new Hagerstown and Los Angeles full line distribution centers.

As with the failure to deduct the Staples stand-alone savings from the new Hagerstown and Los Angeles full line distribution centers from the projected distribution cost savings, the evidence shows that the defendants did not accurately calculate which projected cost savings were merger specific and which were, in fact, not related to the merger. For example, defendants' largest cost savings, over $2 billion or 40% of the total estimate, are projected as a result of their expectation of obtaining better prices from vendors. However, this figure was determined in relation to the cost savings enjoyed by Staples at the end of 1996 without considering the additional cost savings that Staples would have received in the future as a stand-alone company. Since Staples has continuously sought and achieved cost savings on its own, clearly the comparison that should have been made was between the projected future cost savings of Staples as a stand-alone company, not its past rate of savings, and the projected future cost savings of the combined company. Thus, the calculation in the Efficiencies Analysis included product cost savings that Staples and Office Depot would likely have realized without the merger. In fact, Mr. Painter testified that, by his calculation, 43% of the estimated savings are savings that Staples and Office Depot would likely have achieved as stand-alone entities. * * *

In addition to the problems that the Court has with the efficiencies estimates themselves, the Court also finds that the defendants' projected pass through rate—the amount of the projected savings that the combined company expects to pass on to customers in the form of lower prices—is unrealistic. The Court has no doubt that a portion of any efficiencies achieved through a merger of the defendants would be passed on to customers. Staples and Office Depot have a proven track record of achieving cost savings through efficiencies, and then passing those savings to customers in the form of lower prices. However, in this case the defendants have projected a pass through rate of two-thirds of the savings while the evidence shows that, historically, Staples has passed through only 15–17%. Based on the above evidence, the Court cannot find that the defendants have rebutted the presumption that the merger will substantially lessen competition by showing that, because of the efficiencies which will result from the merger, the Commission's evidence gives an inaccurate prediction of the proposed acquisition's probable effect. * * *

* * *

The merger analysis in *Staples* was framed by the district court judge as primarily a question of market definition. In particular, the court employed the *Brown Shoe* practical indicia to define a submarket consisting of the sale of consumable office supplies through superstores within a broader product market involving the sale of such products through all distribution methods (including stationary stores, mass merchandisers, warehouse club stores, mail order and contract vendors, and others). Within that narrow market, the merger meant that the number of sellers would fall from three to two in some metropolitan areas, and from two to one in others, if the merger was permitted. If the transaction can be characterized as a merger to monopoly, as the court concluded was true in a number of geographic markets, there is little need to engage in a detailed economic analysis of competitive effects.

But the court's narrow market definition can also be understood as an expositional tool for highlighting the potential loss of localized competition within the broader market (though this frame was not suggested by the district court judge). That is, the court in effect concluded that Staples and Office Depot were first and second choices for a substantial number of office supply customers, giving the merged firm an incentive to raise prices after the merger without regard to the presence of Wal-Mart and other non-superstore rivals in the market. One way a merged firm could exercise market power unilaterally under such circumstances is to do what the merged Crunchies/Fruities firm planned to do in the hypothetical breakfast cereal example: raise the price of one or both products. In some cases, a merged firm might do even better by altering some of the product or brand attributes. In *Staples*, the litigation proceeded under the assumption that post-merger, Staples would keep stores at the Office Depot locations, but change their name to Staples. Those locations would presumably remain the second choice for many shoppers who patronized the pre-merger Staples locations. If so, the competitive effects theory in the case can be understood as a variant of the unilateral effect theory for differentiated products set forth in the Merger Guidelines: by acquiring Office Depot, Staples could recapture many of the customers that would have been diverted by higher prices at its original stores to stores previously owned by Office Depot, thus making the increased prices more likely to be profitable.[26]

---

[26] In the Crunchies-Fruities example (as in *Kraft*), the merged firm kept the acquired brand. Doing so allowed it to recapture lost profits from raising the price of the acquiring firm's product. In *Staples,* by contrast, the merged firm planned to eliminate the Office Depot brand. This may not be as much of a difference as it appears, though, because the merged firm would likely have kept stores in most Office Depot locations, while changing the sign from Office Depot to Staples. To the extent customer loyalty to Office Depot was tied mainly to the location of the superstore facility rather than the Office Depot brand—that is, if differentiation among superstores was based largely on location—then the unilateral effects theory would be much like the theory set forth in the Crunchies-Fruities example. If it wished to, post-merger Staples could raise price at the former Staples locations (but not the Office Depot locations), and recapture some lost profits to the extent customers shifted to the former Office Depot locations. More likely, it would raise price at all locations, much as the merged Crunchies-Fruities firm would also have done. Complications to the analysis that arise when the merged firm intends to keep only one product, and the brand name is an important source of differentiation, are addressed in Staff Analysis and Findings, *Applications of AT&T Inc. and Deutsche Telekom AG For Consent To Assign or Transfer Control of Licenses and Authorizations*, FCC WT Docket No. 11–65 at 24–27 & 26 n.149 (Nov. 29, 2011), http://hraunfoss.fcc.gov/edocs_public/attachmatch/DA–11–1955A2.pdf.

As this discussion suggests, if the loss of head-to-head competition among merger partners would permit the firms to raise price regardless of the response by other sellers in the market, the competitive concern can be described equivalently as a unilateral competitive effect within a broad market, or as a merger to near monopoly within a narrow market. Framing the case in the latter terms may make it more appealing, at least if the narrow market definition can be simply stated, so as not to appear to reflect result-driven market gerrymandering. The lead attorney for the FTC when the case was tried, George Cary, has taken the view that *Staples* is best interpreted as a unilateral competitive effects case:

> I do think of *Staples* as a unilateral effects case. . . . Ultimately, I think it has to be viewed as a unilateral effects case because the proof that was put forward in defining the product market was the closeness of competition between Staples and Office Depot and the effect of that competition on prices, without regard to competition from other firms.

Roundtable Discussion: *Unilateral Effects Analysis After* Oracle, ANTITRUST, Spring 2005, at 8, 9. By contrast, another senior FTC insider, then-Chairman Robert Pitofsky, has emphasized the market definition interpretation of the decision. Robert Pitofsky, *Staples and Boeing: What They Say About Merger Enforcement at the FTC* (Sept. 23, 1997), http://www.ftc.gov/public-statements/1997/09/staples-and-boeing-what-they-say-about-merger-enforcement-ftc.

Which interpretation of *Staples* do you find more persuasive? What kind of evidence did the FTC and the court rely upon to demonstrate competitive effects? How (if at all) does that evidence differ from the evidence that the court relied upon to define the market?

In 2013, the FTC declined to challenge a merger between Office Depot and OfficeMax, two of the three largest office superstore chains. The FTC concluded that adverse competitive effects in the retail markets that were the subject of the 1997 case were no longer likely because non-superstore competition from Wal-Mart, Target, club stores like Costco and Sam's Club, and Internet retailers, particularly Amazon, had increased over the intervening sixteen years. The FTC also found that competition from non-superstore sellers would prevent competitive harm to large contract customers. *Statement of the Federal Trade Commission Concerning the Proposed Merger of Office Depot, Inc. and OfficeMax, Inc.,* No. 131–0104 (Nov. 1, 2013), https://www.ftc.gov/news-events/press-releases/2013/11/ftc-closes-seven-month-investigation-proposed-office. Staples and Office Depot again proposed to merge in 2015. The FTC successfully challenged the transaction, but not based on competitive harms in retail markets (the concern in the 1997 case). Instead, the court found that the merger would harm large business customers, which often contract for next-day delivery of office supplies to all of their locations nationwide. *FTC v. Staples, Inc.,* ___ F.Supp.3d ___, 2016 WL 2899222 (D.D.C. 2016). (The relevant unilateral effects theory, involving markets in which sellers negotiate with buyers, is discussed below in the *Note on Other Unilateral Effects Theories*.)

As noted above, we will return to *Staples* to consider the court's analysis of efficiencies later in this Chapter.

In the wake of the 1992 Merger Guidelines, the unilateral competitive effects analysis of mergers among sellers of differentiated products became more predominant, but some senior government antitrust enforcers began to question whether their agencies were relying too heavily on unilateral competitive effects analysis. These officials and other critics of over-reliance on the unilateral approach did not question its theoretical soundness. They instead raised several concerns about its practical implementation.

First, critics pointed out that the unilateral approach may render market definition unnecessary, as harm can be found without regard to whether market shares are large or small. Indeed, market definition may appear to be "reverse engineered," defined by the set of customers likely to be harmed by the merger. Yet the Clayton Act's "in any line of commerce" and "any section of the country" language appears to require market definition. In contrast, some defenders of the unilateral approach embrace this feature, arguing that indirect evidence of market power derived from market share should take a back seat to direct evidence of likely competitive effects in these cases, and that if harm to competition can be demonstrated directly, some market in which competition can be harmed must exist and it is not important to specify the bounds of that market with precision. Consider the decision in *Staples* in light of this criticism: Was the market definition reverse engineered? Did the court reach the right outcome?

Second, a number of econometric and conceptual issues may arise when attempting to assess quantitatively, through analysis of historical pricing data, the unilateral incentive to raise price arising from a given merger. Daniel Hosken, Daniel P. O'Brien, David Scheffman, & Michael Vita, *Demand System Estimation and its Application to Horizontal Merger Analysis*, FTC Working Paper No. 246 (April 2002), http://www.ftc.gov/be/workpapers/wp246.pdf.

Third, anticompetitive harm will always be found, to at least some degree, if efficiencies, repositioning, and entry cannot be taken explicitly into account. In practice, critics contend, this unilateral competitive effects approach may tend to make all mergers among sellers of differentiated products appear harmful, especially to the extent that the devaluation of market shares precludes appeal to the Guidelines' safe harbors, which are based on low concentration.

Do the results in *Staples* and *Kraft*—one a successful merger challenge, one an unsuccessful challenge—bear out these concerns? Or do they give you confidence that unilateral competitive effects analysis can successfully be employed to identify anticompetitive transactions without sweeping in procompetitive ones? Consider two subsequent efforts by the federal enforcement agencies to challenge mergers based on theories of anticompetitive unilateral effects in the next Note.

NOTE ON THE MERGER CHALLENGES IN *ORACLE* AND *H & R BLOCK*

Although the unilateral theory of competitive effects among sellers of differentiated products is well established at the federal enforcement agencies, merger litigation framed around this theory is infrequent and the judicial reaction has been mixed. In 2004, the Justice Department was unsuccessful in persuading a federal district court to block the merger of Oracle and PeopleSoft under a unilateral effects theory. *United States v. Oracle Corp.*, 331 F. Supp. 2d 1098 (N.D. Cal. 2004). In many respects, the district court sided with the critics of unilateral effects theory. *See generally* Roundtable Discussion: *Unilateral Effects Analysis After* Oracle, ANTITRUST, Spring 2005, at 8.

Oracle and PeopleSoft both produced enterprise resource planning software, packaged software used by large and complex enterprises to integrate data across most of the firm's activities. The Justice Department alleged that the merger harmed competition within a product market of "high function software used for financial management systems and human relations management." According to Justice, three firms dominated this category of business software: the merging firms and SAP. The government further claimed that Oracle and PeopleSoft were the leading choices for many customers. The merging firms argued for a broader market in which several other firms also participated, including Lawson, AMS, and Microsoft. The district court declined to enjoin the merger primarily on the ground that the Justice Department had failed to prove the product market it alleged.

In deciding the case for defendants, the district court stated a controversial legal standard for proving unilateral effects among sellers of differentiated products. The court held that "[t]o prevail on a differentiated products unilateral effects claim, a plaintiff must prove a relevant market in which the merging parties would have essentially a monopoly or dominant position." 331 F. Supp. 2d at 1123. Critics charged that this standard is inconsistent with the economic analysis of unilateral effects. Recall that in the Crunchies-Fruities example, it was neither necessary nor helpful to define a product market limited to the Crunchies and Fruities products. In that example, the products of the merging firms were the first and second choice for many customers, but more customers of each could have picked a different brand as their second choice. In consequence, Oaties could have been a closer substitute to both Crunchies and Fruities than those two products were to each other. After all, nothing in the example precludes the possibility that more lost

Crunchies customers could have switched to Oaties than to Fruities. Indeed, as previously noted, some economists have argued that market definition is unimportant or unnecessary in order to prove unilateral effects, as the same evidence about demand substitution would be analyzed in the same way regardless of how the claim is framed legally. Does any aspect of the economic logic demonstrating the harm to competition from the Crunchies-Fruities merger turn on whether the market is narrow or broad? What legal purpose might be served by the *Oracle* court's requirement that plaintiff prove a merger to monopoly or near monopoly in a challenge based on unilateral effects? Look again at the language of Section 7 of the Clayton Act.

Moreover, while insisting that the government prove a narrow market in order to prevail on a unilateral effects claim, the *Oracle* district court simultaneously expressed skepticism about whether narrow markets could ever be defined in a principled way. The court noted the difficulty of defining narrow markets when products are differentiated, because it may be hard to identify clear breaks in the chain of substitutes. The court also emphasized "the potential for 'localized competition' analysis to devolve into an unstructured submarket-type analysis" in which courts could improperly identify narrow groupings as markets on the basis of noneconomic criteria unrelated to the ability of firms to exercise market power. 331 F. Supp. 2d at 1119. In practical effect, critics said, the district court's approach would likely turn unilateral effects into a competitive effects possibility that plaintiffs can hardly ever prove, in which narrow markets have to be defined in theory but can rarely be defined in practice. Is the court's approach a sensible one for reining in the interventionist potential of unilateral effects analysis among sellers of differentiated products, or does it create a gap in the law by permitting mergers creating harmful unilateral effects to escape challenge except in the rare case that the government can prove a merger to monopoly or near-monopoly without defining a narrow market?

After *Oracle*, the Justice Department did not again litigate a merger challenge on a unilateral effects theory for nearly a decade, until *H & R Block* (which, as the earlier excerpt indicates, DOJ also challenged on a coordinated effects theory). The FTC brought unilateral effects challenges in the interim with only limited success. It lost a bid to enjoin a merger between organic supermarket chains in district court, and while that outcome was reversed on appeal, the splintered panel did not provide clear guidance for future litigation. *FTC v. Whole Foods Market, Inc.*, 502 F. Supp. 2d 1 (D.D.C.2007), *rev'd*, 548 F.3d 1028 (D.C. Cir. 2008). In another case, *FTC v. CCC Holdings, Inc.*, 605 F. Supp. 2d 26 (D.D.C. 2009), the FTC prevailed only on its coordinated effects theory, and not on its alternative unilateral effects claim. The *CCC Holdings* court applied a legal standard adapted from *Oracle*:

> Unilateral effects in a differentiated product market are likely to be profitable under the following conditions: (1) the products must be differentiated; (2) the products controlled by the *merging* firms must be close substitutes, *i.e.,* "a substantial number of the customers of one firm would turn to the other in response to a price increase"; (3)

other products must be sufficiently different from the products offered by the merging firms that a merger would make a small but significant and non-transitory price increase profitable for the merging firm; and (4) repositioning must be unlikely.

Id. at 68. Through its use of market definition language adapted from the Merger Guidelines, the third element incorporates the controversial idea from *Oracle* that the merging parties must have a dominant position in a relevant market.

H & R Block, decided in the wake of the 2010 Merger Guidelines, countered the efforts of the court in *Oracle* to cabin in unilateral effects theory. *United States v. H & R Block*, 833 F. Supp. 2d 36 (D.D.C. 2011). The *H & R Block* opinion quoted the legal standard relied upon in *CCC*, but the court explicitly rejected the merging firms' contention, based on *Oracle,* that unilateral effects cannot be demonstrated unless the combined firm's market share surpasses a given threshold—even if that threshold is set at 35%, far below a level consistent with a monopoly or dominant position. The *H & R Block* court defended its conclusion primarily on the basis that one of the opinions supporting the D.C. Circuit's judgment in *Whole Foods* implies that market definition may not be required for proving unilateral effects *Id.* at 84–85 (citing *Whole Foods,* 548 F.3d at 1036). This conclusion is tantamount to excising the third element from the legal standard adopted in *CCC Holdings.* The *H & R Block* decision also recognized, consistent with the economic analysis set forth above in the Crunchies-Fruities Note, that the merging firms' products do not need to be the closest substitutes for each other in order to satisfy the second element of the *CCC Holdings* legal standard. *Id.* at 83.

Which court's approach to evaluating unilateral effects is more consistent with the Merger Guidelines? Which is better policy? For commentary comparing the unilateral effects analysis in *Oracle* and *H & R Block,* see Scott A. Sher & Andrea Agathoklis Murino, *Unilateral Effects in Technology Markets:* Oracle, H & R Block, *and What it All Means*, ANTITRUST, Summer 2012, at 46; James A. Keyte, United States v. H & R Block: *The DOJ Invokes* Brown Shoe *to Shed the* Oracle *Albatross*, ANTITRUST, Spring 2012, at 32.

NOTE ON OTHER UNILATERAL EFFECTS THEORIES

As we noted at the outset of our discussion of unilateral effects, the Merger Guidelines recognize that adverse unilateral effects could arise in several settings other than differentiated product markets. In some markets—especially ones in which upstream firms sell to downstream producers, sellers negotiate with buyers, or prices are determined through auctions. Mergers in such markets are analyzed "using similar approaches" to those applied to mergers in differentiated product markets. *Horizontal Merger Guidelines* § 6.2 (2010). In markets where prices are determined through auctions or negotiation, as in differentiated product markets, unilateral effects arise when the merging firms' products are viewed by buyers as close substitutes. When bargaining determines prices and other terms of trade, buyers may have secured favorable terms before the merger by playing off the merging firms in negotiations—but would lose that ability as a result of the merger. To assess the extent of this concern, the Guidelines look in part to an analogue to diversion ratios: the frequency or probability with which, prior to the merger, one of the merging firms had been the runner-up when the other firm won the business. For an example of a case analyzed under this theory, see Competitive Impact Statement, *United States v. Baker Hughes Inc.*, No. 1:10–cv–00659 (D.D.C. April 27, 2010), http://www.justice.gov/atr/cases/f258200/258203.htm. *See also* Aviv Nevo, *Mergers That Increase Bargaining Leverage* (Jan. 22, 2014), https://www.justice.gov/atr/speech/mergers-increase-bargaining-leverage.

Adverse unilateral effects from merger may also arise in markets in which products are relatively undifferentiated. Under such circumstances, the merged firm may have an incentive to reduce what it sells in the market in order to reduce aggregate industry output, and thereby drive up the market price. *Id.* § 6.3. This strategy is more likely to be profitable the greater the merged firm's market share (and thus the greater the amount of sales on which the firm can profit from the price increase); the less that non-merging firms would respond to the merged firm's output reduction by increasing their output (as such a response would lessen the reduction in industry output, lessen the anticompetitive price increase, and thus reduce the profits the merged firm would obtain through this strategy); the less elastic industry demand (and thus the greater the industry price increase that would result from the merged firm's strategy); and the lower the price-cost margin on the sales the merged firm would have made had it not reduced its sales (and thus the lower the profits the merged firm must forgo in order to profit more on the sales it continues to make). For an example of a merger where the Justice Department was concerned about this unilateral effects possibility (and also concerned about coordinated effects from parallel accommodating conduct), see Competitive Impact Statement, *United States v. Int'l Paper Co.*, No. 1:12–cv–00227 (D.D.C. Feb. 10, 2012), http://www.justice.gov/atr/cases/f280100/280135.pdf. The Merger Guidelines highlight the possibility that this strategy might be profitable for a firm with a substantial market share if it can acquire a firm with significant excess capacity, even if the latter firm has a small share, as the smaller firm's ability to expand output may have prevented the larger firm from raising price pre-merger.

The fourth setting for unilateral effects discussed in the Guidelines applies when one merging firm is seeking to develop new products that would be close substitutes for what is sold by the other merging firm, and thus would capture substantial revenue from the merger partner, or at least when at least one merging firm has the capability to do so. *Id.* § 6.4. The merged firm would be less likely to pursue such innovations, so the merger may lead to the loss of that potential competition. For a similar reason, a merger could diminish innovation by combining two of a small number of firms with strong capabilities to innovate successfully in a specific direction. This section of the Guidelines also recognizes that the loss of product variety—withdrawing a product that many consumers would have strongly preferred remain available—could harm consumers over and above affects on price and quality of any product not withdrawn. For more discussion of the consequences of mergers for innovation and their significance for antitrust enforcement, see Michael L. Katz & Howard A. Shelanski, *Mergers and Innovation*, 74 ANTITRUST L.J. 1 (2007).

Sidebar 5–9:
Comparative Perspectives: Merger
Enforcement in the U.S. and E.U.[a]

Similarities Predominate

The European Commission ("EC"), the E.U.'s regulatory body, adopted its first Merger Regulation in 1989 and amended the regulation significantly in 2004. *See* Council Regulation (EC) No 139/2004 of 20 January 2004 on the control of concentrations between undertakings, O.J. L. 24, 29.01.2004, http://ec.europa.eu/comm/competition/mergers/legislation/regulations.html#merger_reg. Because the competition prohibitions of the original Treaty of Rome lacked a separate merger provision like Section 7 of the U.S. Clayton Act, the EC Merger Regulation is anchored to Article 102's prohibition of the abuse of dominant position. Soon after issuing its revised Merger Regulation, the EC adopted Horizontal Merger Guidelines. *See Guidelines on the assessment of horizontal mergers under the Council Regulation on the control of concentrations between undertakings*, O.J. L.C 31, 05.02.2004, http://europa.eu/legislation_summaries/competition/firms/l26107_en.htm. In 2007, the Commission also adopted guidelines for non-horizontal mergers. *See Guidelines on the assessment of non-horizontal mergers under the Council Regulation on the control of concentrations between undertakings*, O.J. L. C 265, 10.18.2008, http://eur-lex.europa.eu/legal-content/EN/TXT/PDF/?uri=CELEX:52008XC1018(03)&from=EN.

---

[a] The authors are grateful to Alison Jones and Richard Whish for many informative discussions about E.U. merger control. Excellent surveys of the E.U. merger control regime appear in ALISON JONES & BRENDA SUFRIN, EU COMPETITION LAW: TEXT CASES, AND MATERIALS 1084-1200 (6th ed. 2016) and RICHARD WHISH & DAVID BAILEY COMPETITION LAW 872-973 (8th ed. 2015). Parts of this sidebar are adapted from William E. Kovacic, Petros Mavroidis & Damien Neven, *Procedures and Institutions: A Comparison of EU and US Practice*, 59 ANTITRUST BULL. 55 (Mar. 2014).

Since the E.U. merger regulation entered into force in 1990, there have been occasional, widely studied episodes of disagreement. The two most notable disparate outcomes arose in mergers involving the aerospace sector transactions. In 1997, the FTC cleared the merger of Boeing and McDonnell Douglas. After threatening to block the deal outright, the E.U. cleared the transaction subject to a settlement by which Boeing agreed to release three U.S. airlines from exclusive contracts they had signed with the aircraft producer. *See* Case No. IV/M.877, *Boeing-McDonnell Douglas*, 1997 O.J. (L 336) 16. In 2001, the E.U.'s stated opposition led General Electric to abandon its efforts to purchase Honeywell; earlier in the year, the DOJ had cleared the proposed deal subject to the spin-off of one product line. In 2005, the Court of First Instance ("CFI"—now the "General Court") affirmed the Commission's conclusion that the GE/Honeywell merger would have created or strengthened a dominant position in specific markets and hence was properly blocked. However, the CFI also concluded that the EC committed "errors of assessment" in its analysis of conglomerate effects. According to the court, the evidence was insufficient to support the EC's conclusion that conglomerate effects from either vertical integration or product bundling would have harmed competition. *See* Case T–210/01, *General Electric Co. v. Commission*, 2005 WL 3429326, [2006] 4 C.M.L.R. 15 (Dec. 14, 2005).

Today horizontal merger policy in the E.U. and the U.S. share many significant features. In terms of process, both jurisdictions require pre-merger notifications of certain large transactions and impose mandatory waiting periods. In both jurisdictions, the enforcement agencies rely principally on information provided by the merging parties and by interested third parties, including customers and rivals. The informational demands imposed by the U.S. process through Hart-Scott-Rodino Second Requests tend to be more taxing than the information required by the EC. Unlike the U.S. system of dual enforcement, the EC has a single competition policy entity (the Directorate General for Competition—"DG Comp"), and there is no uncertainty about which instrumentality will review a deal with community-wide importance. Thus, parties in the E.U. need not await the results of a U.S.-style "clearance" process, and pre-filing discussions often provide a way for DG Comp and the parties to identify issues before the formal premerger notice (the "Form CO") is filed.

The elaboration and revision of merger guidelines in both jurisdictions since the early 1990s has yielded extensive convergence upon the analytical framework. In particular, the horizontal merger guidelines of the two jurisdictions share a largely common intellectual vision. Although the horizontal merger guidelines of the two systems are not identical, the merger teams of DG Comp, the DOJ, and the FTC use generally similar analytical methods. A substantial degree of osmosis, fostered by cooperation on dozens of individual cases, has taken place. Thus, for example, the E.U. Guidelines do not look to the "gross upward pricing pressure index" (GUPPI), a concept which appears in the U.S. 2010 Guidelines, though not by name (*see supra*, Sidebar 5–8), but E.U. merger analysts follow U.S. practice in taking it into account in assessing individual transactions.

Since 2000, judicial decisions in the E.U. and the U.S. have pressed both sets of public enforcement authorities to satisfy more demanding evidentiary standards and withstand closer judicial scrutiny of proof offered to demonstrate likely anticompetitive effects. *See* Case T–342/99, *Airtours plc v. Commission* [2002] E.C.R. II–2585, 5 C.M.L.R. 7, Case T–310/01, *Schneider Electric SA v. Commission*, [2002] E.C.R. II–4071, and Case T–5/02, *Tetra Laval BV v. Comm'n*, [2002] E.C.R. II–4381, *aff'd in part*, Cases C–12/03 P & C–13/03 P, *Comm'n v. Tetra Laval BV*, OJ 2005 C82/1 in the E.U. and *FTC v. Arch Coal*, 329 F. Supp. 2d 109 (D.D.C. 2004), *U.S. v. Oracle Corp.*, 331 F. Supp. 2d 1098 (N.D. Cal. 2004) in the U.S. Cases such as *AirTours* and *Arch Coal* are similar in their insistence that prosecutors show how the collaboration among firms in a coordinated effects case will unfold after the merger is completed.

The E.U. and U.S. enforcement agencies also have taken a number of steps in recent years to strengthen internal quality control mechanisms. For example, the 2002 "trilogy" of *Airtours*, *Schneider*, and *Tetra Laval* helped inspire major reforms inside DG Comp, including the establishment of a more robust process of peer review for individual cases and the creation of the position of Chief Economist, who reports to the Director General and to the Commissioner for Competition. *See* Jonathan B. Baker, *My Summer Vacation at the European Commission*, ANTITRUST SOURCE (Sept. 2005) (comparing merger enforcement in the U.S. and E.U.), http://www.americanbar.org/content/dam/aba/publishing/antitrust_source/Sep05_FullSource9_27.authcheckdam.pdf. The Chief Economist's Team now has more than twenty Ph.D. economists and has come to play an influential role in the examination of mergers.

Some Important Differences

Against a backdrop of substantial convergence, significant differences between the E.U. and U.S. systems are also apparent. Here we highlight three disparities.

First, compared to the U.S. regime, third parties have considerably stronger rights to challenge E.U. merger decisions. In Case No. T–464/04, *Independent Music Publishers and Labels Association v. Commission*, ECR II-2289 ("Impala"), the General Court annulled a DG Comp decision to clear a merger without conditions. The Court of Justice subsequently reversed the General Court's judgment. Case 413/06 P, *Bertelsmann AG v. Impala* [2008] ECR I-4951. In the U.S., a decision by the DOJ or the FTC not to challenge a transaction is not subject to judicial review, and private challenges to mergers are rare. By contrast, in transactions subject to review in the E.U., third parties can appeal a decision of the Commission not to intervene or to resolve competitive concerns with remedies that a third party believes to be inadequate.

Second, unlike U.S. practice, DG Comp is compelled to provide a written opinion explaining all decisions to intervene and not to intervene. In *Impala* the court agreed with third party complainants that the EC had provided an inadequate basis for deciding not to challenge the transaction in question (a merger of Sony and BMG's music businesses) and ordered the Commission to undertake a further review of the transaction. The Commission had to re-examine the case, and it issued a second clearance decision in 2007. The analysis of factors facilitating or frustrating tacit collusion played a prominent role in the court's decision. In recent years, the two U.S. agencies have resorted more often to issuing explanations of decisions not to prosecute, but they do not do so systematically and rarely provide supporting analyses when they do.

Third, the availability of judicial review for decisions not to prosecute has important implications for a competition agency. In merger control, for example, the U.S. agencies have greater latitude to rely on qualitative, subjective judgments about the strength of efficiency arguments that would weigh in favor of permitting a merger to take place. If it relies on efficiency arguments to withhold a challenge, the EC would be required to spell out those arguments and to offer evidence to substantiate them. This procedural requirement, coupled with the availability of judicial review for decisions not to prosecute, limits the freedom of EC decision makers to rely on relatively subjective considerations for which quantitative verification might be impractical if not impossible. By comparison, the U.S. agencies would have more leeway to give effect to such considerations.

As you have gathered from the examples discussed in this Sidebar, judicial oversight of EC merger decisions can be a powerful constraint on the EC's discretion. At the same time, it remains the case that the U.S. adversarial model continues to give the U.S. agencies comparatively less latitude to block mergers than the European Commission. This difference in process may continue, in occasional cases, to generate different outcomes. On the whole, however, merger analysis in the E.U. and the U.S. today shares a great deal of common ground and has been moving towards producing consistent results across jurisdictions.

3. SUPPLY SUBSTITUTION AND ENTRY

The Merger Guidelines consider more than whether market concentration exceeds safe harbor levels and whether a plausible threat of unilateral or coordinated competitive effects can be demonstrated; they also address three factors that can mitigate competitive concerns: powerful buyers, entry, and efficiencies. Powerful buyers were discussed in a Note earlier in this Chapter. This section looks at entry, and the following section considers efficiencies. These concepts are also applied outside of horizontal merger analysis.

During antitrust's structural era, around the time of *Philadelphia Nat'l Bank*, *Von's Grocery*, and *Pabst*, the Supreme Court issued a decision in *Rome Cable,* a merger case that seemed to foreclose the argument that a merger should be permitted on the ground that the prospect of new competition would prevent harm to competition. In that case, the Court placed insulated copper conductor and insulated aluminum conductor in separate markets, notwithstanding a strong dissent highlighting the extensive manufacturing interchangeability (supply substitution) between the two. *United States v. Aluminum Co. of Am.*, 377 U.S. 271 (1964) (*Rome Cable*). Nevertheless, in the wake of *General Dynamics*, and even before the adoption of the 1982 Merger Guidelines, lawyers considering the role of entry under Clayton Act § 7 began to ask how supply substitution and ease of entry can be used to rebut the inference of anticompetitive effect derived from high and increasing market concentration. There were two main possibilities: easy entry might merely dilute or weaken the inference of anticompetitive effect; or ease of entry might trump everything else.

Under the latter view, unless entry is *not easy*, the plaintiff must lose regardless of any other evidence including the level of market concentration. The "ease of entry is a trump" approach made sense as a matter of economics, but seemed hard to reconcile with *Rome Cable*. Could it be reconciled with the governing legal framework after *General Dynamics*?

A judicial response came during the mid-1980s. In 1984, the Second Circuit embraced the latter view, in the *Waste Management* decision, by deciding to treat ease of entry as a trump. In doing so the court relied on *General Dynamics*, and also asserted that it was merely holding the government to the terms of its own Merger Guidelines. The decision was quickly followed by a district court opinion and a Federal Trade Commission opinion taking a similar view. *See United States v. Calmar Inc.*, 612 F. Supp. 1298 (D.N.J. 1985); *In re Echlin Mfg. Co.*, 105 F.T.C. 410 (1985). This approach to adjudication is consistent with the economic perspective on market power: if the threat of entry would prevent price from rising after a merger, the merger would not make coordinated or unilateral price increases more likely or otherwise generate market power. In recent years the Federal Trade Commission has not challenged a merger when it determined that entry is easy. Federal Trade Commission, *Horizontal Merger Investigation Data, Fiscal Years 1996–2011* (Jan. 2013) (Table 10.1), http://www.ftc.gov/reports/horizontal-merger-investigation-data-fiscal-years–1996–2011. The evolution of economic thinking about entry and its influence on the courts in areas of antitrust analysis beyond mergers are discussed below in Sidebar 5–10.

UNITED STATES V. WASTE MANAGEMENT, INC.
United States Court of Appeals for the Second Circuit, 1984.
743 F.2d 976.

Before VAN GRAAFEILAND, WINTER and PRATT, CIRCUIT JUDGES.

WINTER, CIRCUIT JUDGE.

Appellants Waste Management, Inc. ("WMI") and EMW Ventures Incorporated ("EMW") appeal from Judge Griesa's decision, * * * after a bench trial, that WMI's acquisition of EMW violated section 7 of the Clayton Act * * *.

We reverse.

Background

* * *

We summarize those facts that are not in dispute. WMI is in the solid waste disposal business. It provides services in twenty-seven states and had revenues of approximately $442 million in 1980. At the time of the acquisition, EMW was a diversified holding company that owned a subsidiary by the name of Waste Resources, which was in the waste disposal business in ten states and had revenues of $54 million in 1980.

WMI and Waste Resources each had subsidiaries that operated in or near Dallas. WMI has one subsidiary, American Container Service ("ACS") in Dallas * * *. Waste Resources had a Dallas subsidiary called Texas Industrial Disposal, Inc. ("TIDI"). * * *

* * *

* * * The district court adopted a definition of the relevant product market that differed from the positions of both parties. Judge Griesa concluded that the product market included all trash collection, except for collection at single-family or at multiple family residences or small apartment complexes. Rejecting WMI's contentions as to the relevant geographic market, the district court excluded Tarrant County, which includes Fort Worth, thus limiting the market to Dallas County plus a small fringe area.

Based on revenue data, Judge Griesa found that the combined market share of TIDI and ACS was 48.8%. He viewed that market share as prima facie illegal under *United States v. Philadelphia National Bank*, 374 U.S. 321, 364–66, 83 S.Ct. 1715, 1742–43, 10 L.Ed.2d 915 (1963). Agreeing with appellants that entry into the product market is easy—indeed, individuals operating out of their homes can compete successfully "with any other company"—Judge Griesa nevertheless held that proof of ease of entry did not rebut the prima facie showing of illegality. The district court therefore ordered WMI to divest itself of TIDI. Because we conclude that potential entry into the relevant Dallas market by new firms or by firms now operating in Fort Worth is so easy as to constrain the prices charged by WMI's subs, we reverse on the grounds that the merged firm does not substantially lessen competition.

Discussion

* * *

B.   WMI's Rebuttal

A post-merger market share of 48.8% is sufficient to establish prima facie illegality under *United States v. Philadelphia National Bank*, 374 U.S. 321, 83 S.Ct. 1715, 10 L.Ed.2d 915 (1963), and its progeny.[27] That decision held that large market shares are a convenient proxy for appraising the danger of monopoly power resulting from a horizontal merger. Under its rationale, a merger resulting in a large market share is

---

[27] [Based on data reported in the district court opinion in this proceeding, the HHI for commercial trash collection in Dallas would have risen by 1184 points to 2678 as a result of the proposed transaction. *United States v. Waste Management, Inc.*, 588 F. Supp. 498, 512 (S.D.N.Y.1983). Eds.]

presumptively illegal, rebuttable only by a demonstration that the merger will not have anticompetitive effects. Thus in *United States v. General Dynamics Corp.*, 415 U.S. 486, 94 S.Ct. 1186, 39 L.Ed.2d 530 (1974), the Court upheld a merger of two leading coal producers because substantially all of the production of one firm was tied up in long-term contracts and its reserves were insubstantial. Since that firm's future ability to compete was negligible, the Court reasoned that its disappearance as an independent competitor could not affect the market.

WMI does not claim that 48.8% is too small a share to trigger the *Philadelphia National Bank* presumption. Rather, it argues that the presumption is rebutted by the fact that competitors can enter the Dallas waste hauling market with such ease that the finding of a 48.8% market share does not accurately reflect market power. WMI argues that it is unable to raise prices over the competitive level because new firms would quickly enter the market and undercut them.

* * *

The Supreme Court has never directly held that ease of entry may rebut a showing of *prima facie* illegality under *Philadelphia National Bank*. However, on several occasions it has held that appraisal of the impact of a proposed merger upon competition must take into account potential competition from firms not presently active in the relevant product and geographic markets. * * *

Moreover, under *General Dynamics*, a substantial existing market share is insufficient to void a merger where that share is misleading as to actual future competitive effect. * * * In the present case, a market definition artificially restricted to existing firms competing at one moment may yield market share statistics that are not an accurate proxy for market power when substantial potential competition able to respond quickly to price increases exists.

Finally, the Merger Guidelines issued by the government itself not only recognize the economic principle that ease of entry is relevant to appraising the impact upon competition of a merger but also state that it may override all other factors. * * * We conclude, therefore, that entry by potential competitors may be considered in appraising whether a merger will "substantially lessen competition."

Turning to the evidence in this case, we believe that entry into the relevant product and geographic market by new firms or by existing firms in the Fort Worth area is so easy that any anti-competitive impact of the merger before us would be eliminated more quickly by such competition than by litigation. * * * Judge Griesa specifically found that individuals operating out of their homes can acquire trucks and some containers and compete successfully "with any other company." The government's response to this factual finding is largely to the effect that economies of scale are more important than Judge Griesa believed. As with his other findings of fact, however, this one is not clearly erroneous, as there are examples in the record of such entrepreneurs entering and prospering.

In any event, entry by larger companies is also relatively easy. At existing prices most Fort Worth and Dallas haulers operate within their own cities, but it is clear from the record that Fort Worth haulers could easily establish themselves in Dallas if the price of trash collection rose above the competitive level. Although it may be true that daily travel from Fort Worth to Dallas and back is costly, there is no barrier to Fort Worth haulers' acquiring garage facilities in Dallas permitting them to station some of their trucks there permanently or for portions of each week. The risks of such a strategy are low since substantial business can be assured through bidding on contracts even before such garage facilities are acquired, as one Fort Worth firm demonstrated by winning such a contract and then opening a facility in a Dallas suburb. That example can hardly be ignored by WMI or other Dallas haulers (not to mention their customers) in arriving at contract bids. The existence of haulers in Fort Worth, therefore, constrains prices charged by Dallas haulers * * *.

The fact that such entry has not happened more frequently reflects only the existence of competitive, entry-forestalling prices * * *.

* * *

Judge Griesa's conclusion that "there is no showing of any circumstances, related to ease of entry or the trend of the business, which promises in and of itself to materially erode the competitive strength of [the merged firms]" is consistent with our decision. [The merged firms] may well retain their present market share. However, in view of the findings as to ease of entry, that share can be retained only by competitive pricing. Ease of entry constrains not only WMI, but every firm in the market. Should WMI attempt to exercise market power by raising prices, none of its smaller competitors would be able to follow the price increases because of the ease with which new competitors would appear. WMI would then face lower prices charged by all existing competitors as well as entry by new ones, a condition fatal to its economic prospects if not rectified.

The government argues that consumers may prefer WMI's services, even at a higher price, over those of a new entrant because of its "proven track record." We fail to see how the existence of good will achieved through effective service is an impediment to, rather than the natural result of, competition. The government also argues that existing contracts bind most customers to a particular hauler and thereby prevent new entrants from acquiring business. If so, they also prevent the price increases until new entrants can submit competitive bids.

Given Judge Griesa's factual findings, we conclude that the 48.8% market share attributed to WMI does not accurately reflect future market power. Since that power is in fact insubstantial, the merger does not, therefore, substantially lessen competition in the relevant market and does not violate Section 7.

Reversed.

————————

Waste Management drew a great deal of attention when it was decided. The case signaled that the government would be held to its own Merger Guidelines in court, and that the courts of appeals were willing to allow merger law to embrace modern economic thinking even without further guidance from the Supreme Court.

Do you agree with the court's rationale? What kind of evidence did the Second Circuit rely upon? Who had the burden of proof according to the court? Should the mere possibility of entry be enough to rebut the *Philadelphia Nat'l Bank* presumption? Is that what *Waste Management* holds, or does the decision depend on a more extensive factual showing by defendant?

In determining whether entry would deter or counteract competitive harm from merger, evidence of the history of entry, without further analysis, is double-edged. If entry occurred in the past, that fact is consistent both with low entry barriers in the past (which permitted the entry to occur) and with the exercise of market power in the past (which induced that entry). Similarly, if entry did not occur in the past, that fact is consistent both with a competitive market in the past (which made entry unattractive even though it was possible) or with the presence of entry barriers in the past (which made entry impractical or unprofitable).[28] On the other hand, past episodes of successful or unsuccessful entry may provide insight into the types of actions entrants must take and the problems that entrants must surmount for entry to succeed—which in turn may inform a judgment about the likelihood that entry after merger would address concerns about the exercise of market power. How was the history of entry employed by the court in *Waste Management*?

The role of entry also was at issue in the D.C. Circuit's 1990 decision in *United States v. Baker Hughes, Inc.*, 908 F.2d 981 (D.C. Cir. 1990), which we read earlier in this Chapter. As we saw, *Baker Hughes* set forth the modern interpretation of the *Philadelphia Nat'l Bank* presumption in light of *General Dynamics*, the Chicago School critique of structural merger

---

[28] When the 2010 Merger Guidelines explain that "Lack of successful and effective entry in the face of non-transitory increases in the margins earned on products in the relevant market tends to suggest that successful entry is slow or difficult," *Horizontal Merger Guidelines* § 9 (2010), they are supposing that information about the history of entry has been supplemented with information about price-cost margins.

policy, and contemporary developments in economics. As in *Waste Management*, the appeals court deciding *Baker Hughes* also concluded that the evidence of ease of entry was fatal to the Justice Department's efforts to challenge a proposed acquisition. The D.C. Circuit opinion is noteworthy for its strong rhetoric, suggesting that in bringing and litigating *Baker Hughes*, the Justice Department was willfully ignoring the teaching of *Waste Management*. Review that portion of the opinion now and consider whether, on the facts recounted in the opinion, this charge was warranted.

Recall that in concluding that evidence of ease of entry sufficiently rebutted the government's prima facie case, the court specifically rejected the government's position that the merging firms should have been required to "show clearly" that entry would be "quick and effective." The requirement in the current Merger Guidelines, discussed below, that entry be "timely, likely, and sufficient" in order to undermine inferences drawn from market concentration statistics, had not been developed when *Baker Hughes* was litigated. Why did the court reject application of the standard advocated by the Justice Department? Why did it conclude that entry would likely solve any competitive problem from the acquisition? Were similar facts demonstrated in *Waste Management*? Had the government's competitive effects theory in *Baker Hughes* been unilateral rather than coordinated anticompetitive effects, would entry analysis likely have proceeded differently?

In 1992, shortly after *Baker Hughes*, and *United States v. Syufy Enterprises*, 903 F.2d 659 (9th Cir. 1990), another appellate decision rejecting a Justice Department challenge to a merger in part on grounds of ease of entry, the Justice Department and Federal Trade Commission revised the Merger Guidelines to incorporate the "timely, likely, and sufficient" test. The section on entry, as further revised in 2010, is discussed in the following note.

NOTE ON ENTRY ANALYSIS IN THE MERGER GUIDELINES

The Merger Guidelines provide a more detailed explanation of the role of conditions of entry in horizontal merger analysis. First, they adopt a three part test, which, as noted above, requires that entry be "timely, likely, and sufficient" to solve any competitive harms of the merger, so that the merger will not substantially harm consumers. *Horizontal Merger Guidelines* § 9 (2010). In addition, the Guidelines draw a distinction that was not clear in the prior case law (including *Baker Hughes*) between entry and market participants not presently selling in the market that would likely respond by doing so in the event of a small price rise. The latter firms are termed "rapid entrants".[29] *Id.* § 5.1

---

[29] The 1992 Horizontal Merger Guidelines employed the term "uncommitted entry" to describe a similar concept.

The Merger Guidelines' concept of rapid entry, which was discussed earlier in this Chapter in connection with the identification of market participants, generalizes the idea of supply substitution. As we explained, rapid entrants can enter quickly and do so with little in the way of unrecoverable or "sunk" costs—expenditures that would be unrecoverable in the event the firm later chooses to exit the market. They take advantage of any short-run profit opportunities that anticompetitive behavior by incumbent firms might offer, and leave the market rapidly and inexpensively if those opportunities disappear. A metal stamping firm producing hubcaps, for example, might be a rapid entrant into the mailbox market. Or a firm producing no. 2 lead pencils might be a rapid entrant into the production of lead-based artists' sketching pencils.

In contrast, the entrants addressed by Guidelines § 9 are in for the long haul. Once they enter a market, they expect to stay, because to abandon the market would mean walking away from a substantial sunk investment. A firm that needs to build a new production facility to enter a market is likely an entrant, not a rapid entrant. In deciding whether it would be profitable to enter a market, a rapid entrant considers the current price in the market while other entrants instead consider what competition and prices will look like after they enter.

The latter point is important in the Merger Guidelines' approach to the analysis of "likelihood" (profitability) of entry. *Id.* § 9.2 In deciding whether to enter the market, a new competitor expecting to stay for the long term must consider the effect of its entry on the price it will receive and the profits it can expect to make. Entry may depress the market price for two reasons. First, the entrant adds output to the market, causing the industry outcome to move along the demand curve in the direction of a lower price. Second, incumbent firms may react to the competition from the new entrant with an aggressive competitive response (a price war) of their own. If that is likely, entry will be discouraged by the prospect of post-entry competition. The Merger Guidelines also recognize that the profitability of entry will be affected by the output the entrant is likely to obtain, accounting for obstacles facing new entrants, and the cost per unit the entrant would likely incur, which may depend on the scale of output at which it would operate. The Guidelines suggest that recent examples of entry, whether successful or unsuccessful, may provide information about the scale required for successful entry; the costs, risks, and timing of entry; the sales opportunities realistically available to entrants; and the presence or absence of entry barriers. If powerful buyers were to sponsor entry, that may also affect its profitability.

The Merger Guidelines also call for an analysis of whether entry would be "timely"—that is, whether it would achieve significant market impact in time to deter or counteract the competitive problem—and whether it would be "sufficient" in magnitude, character, and scope to solve the competitive problem. *Horizontal Merger Guidelines* §§ 9, 9.1, 9.3 (2010). Although the previous Guidelines had suggested evaluating timeliness with a two year horizon, the 2010 Guidelines decline to offer such a rule of thumb, and instead indicate that entry must be rapid enough to make unprofitable the anticompetitive acts of concern, or rapid enough to ensure that those acts do not impose significant harm on buyers. The sufficiency inquiry might consider, among other things, whether some potential entrants are better situated than others to solve the competitive problem, or whether entry into one niche of a market characterized by product differentiation would solve a competitive problem that arises largely in some other part of the market. It might also consider whether the increased capacity brought to the market by the most likely new entrants would be enough to offset the output-restricting result of a price increase by the merging firms. The Guidelines indicate that entry by a single firm that will replicate at least the scale and strength of one of the merging firms would be sufficient, and that entry by one or more firms operating at a smaller scale could be sufficient. Entry is considered easy, and thus likely to deter or counteract an anticompetitive problem from merger, only if that entry satisfies all three tests; that is, only if it is "timely, likely, and sufficient."

The Merger Guidelines also offer some practical guidance in conducting these inquiries. They give substantial weight to the actual history of entry into the relevant market. In particular, the Guidelines say, the lack of substantial and effective entry in the face of non-transitory increase in price-cost margins tends to suggest that entry is slow or difficult. The Guidelines also note that when firms have valuable intangible assets (such as goodwill or brand reputation)—as suggested by market values for firms greatly in excess of the replacement costs of their tangible assets—those assets may be difficult or time consuming for an entrant to replace, and thus raise the possibility that entry would not be timely or likely to solve the competitive problem. In addition, the Guidelines observe that some firms may be better situated than most to enter, for example because they have the necessary assets or incentives. In some cases, these might include firms operating in complementary or adjacent markets, or large customers themselves. If so, the analysis of entry may look first to those firms.

The Guidelines also indicate that possible "repositioning" responses to adverse unilateral effects in differentiated product markets—actions by non-merging firms to make them closer substitutes to the products of the merging firms, which may deter or counteract a competitive problem from merger—are evaluated "much like entry, with consideration given to timeliness, likelihood, and sufficiency." *Horizontal Merger Guidelines* § 6.1 (2010).

Does the Merger Guidelines framework differ from the approach set forth in *Waste Management* and *Baker Hughes*? Some have criticized the Guidelines for implicitly placing too great a burden of proof on defendants. Do you agree?

––––––––––

Are the Merger Guidelines consistent with what Clayton Act § 7 requires, according to the D.C. Circuit in *Baker Hughes*? Note that the D.C. Circuit rejected the government's argument that entry must be "quick and effective" in order to count as easy and thus be used to rebut the government's prima facie case based on market concentration. Yet just two years later, DOJ and the FTC published Merger Guidelines requiring that entry be something quite similar—"timely, likely, and sufficient"—in order to count, and that language remains in the current Guidelines. Did the agencies willfully ignore the dictates of the appellate court? Or did they view the entry possibilities in *Baker Hughes* as requiring sunk costs and delay while the D.C. Circuit instead saw the entry possibilities in that case as examples of rapid entry, and so viewed the DOJ's appeal as a misguided effort to overturn *Waste Management*?

District courts have not interpreted *Baker Hughes* as inconsistent with the entry framework of the Merger Guidelines. In *Staples*, the district court highlighted language from *Baker Hughes* indicating that defendants must show that entry into the market "would likely avert" anticompetitive effects in order to rebut the government's prima facie case with evidence about entry. *FTC v. Staples, Inc.*, 970 F. Supp. 1066, 1086 (D.D.C. 1997) (*quoting United States v. Baker Hughes Inc.*, 908 F.2d 981, 987 (D.C. Cir. 1990)). The *Staples* court relied in part on evidence of high sunk costs to conclude that the merging firms had failed to meet this standard, thus making clear that the court saw the relevant entry possibilities in that case as not rapid. Similarly, in *H & R Block* the district court directly applied the "timely, likely, and sufficient" framework of the Merger Guidelines for analyzing entry and treated its approach as consistent with *Baker Hughes*. *United States v. H & R Block,* 833 F. Supp. 2d 36, 73–77 (D.D.C. 2011). *See also United States v. Bazaarvoice, Inc.*, 2014 WL 203966 at 40 (N.D. Cal. 2014) ("The Court must determine whether entry or expansion would be timely, likely, and sufficient to replace the competitive constraint [the acquired firm] would have provided absent the acquisition.") (citing Merger Guidelines).

We conclude our discussion of entry with two sidebars that broaden our focus. Sidebar 5–10, on "Defining and Proving Entry Conditions," describes debates among economists and the courts about how to define the "entry barriers," in non-merger settings as well as in mergers, and identifies types of evidence relied upon in litigation to evaluate entry conditions. Sidebar 5–11, on "The Ethics of Taking Discovery From One Client in Connection With Another Client's Proposed Merger," considers some ethical issues that may arise when counsel for the merging firms also represent other firms that may have information relevant the merging firms' defense, including information about entry conditions.

Sidebar 5–10:
Defining and Proving Entry Conditions

Economists have long recognized that an attempt to exercise market power could be defeated or deterred by new supply entering the market. But antitrust law largely ignored this possibility until the mid-1970s, when two appeals courts rejected monopolization allegations by defining broad product markets to account for the possibility of supply substitution. *See Telex Corp. v. IBM Corp.*, 510 F.2d 894 (10th Cir. 1975); *Twin City Sportservice, Inc. v. Charles O. Finley & Co.*, 512 F.2d 1264 (9th Cir. 1975). When the courts began to take seriously the possibility that entry, or just the potential for entry, could prevent even so-called monopolists from exercising market power, they looked to the economic literature on entry for guidance. This Sidebar describes an economic debate over the appropriate definition of "entry barriers," looks at how the courts have reacted to that debate, and discusses types of evidence commonly relied upon in litigation for identifying and drawing conclusions about conditions of entry.

Economic Debates

The economic analysis of new competition before the mid-1970s was dominated by the contrasting views of two pioneering industrial organization economists, Joe S. Bain and George Stigler, on defining "barriers to entry." *See generally* Janusz A. Ordover & Daniel M. Wall, *Proving Entry Barriers: A Practical Guide to the Economics of New Entry*, ANTITRUST, Winter 1988, at 12 ("Proving Entry Barriers"); Gregory J. Werden, *Network Effects and Conditions of Entry: Lessons from the* Microsoft *Case*, 69 ANTITRUST L.J. 87, 97–100 (2001) (reviewing the economic literature on "barriers to entry"). Bain was interested in the effect of market structure on firm conduct and industry performance. He emphasized the way a range of structural factors created entry barriers, preventing new competition even when incumbents' prices exceeded competitive levels (which might be expected to attract entry). Bain's list of important entry barriers included absolute cost advantages of incumbents, product differentiation, and economies of scale (lower costs attributable to increases in output and sales). JOE S. BAIN, BARRIERS TO NEW COMPETITION (1956).

Stigler, too, was interested in the determinants of market concentration. But his approach to the question could be read as resisting the interventionist implications of Bain's analysis of entry barriers. Some of Stigler's fire was directed at the claim that high capital requirements could prevent new competition when incumbents were exercising market power. GEORGE STIGLER, THE ORGANIZATION OF INDUSTRY 113–22 (1968). He questioned the once common appeal to "imperfections-in-the-capital-market" by asking whether even large capital requirements would stand in the way of a firm seeking to finance a reasonable entry plan, given the wide range of well-funded participants in financial and credit markets.[a]

In analyzing entry, as elsewhere in Chicago School critiques of structural era antitrust, Stigler suggested that many practices previously thought harmful to competition in fact reflected healthy competition. He defined entry barriers as the *additional long-run costs that must be incurred by an entrant relative to the long-run costs faced by incumbent firms.* *Id.* at 67–70. This definition might include the possibility, of great concern to Chicago School antitrust commentators, that entry would be prevented by regulation, patents, tariffs or other government action. But if incumbents obtained an advantage over entrants by being first to make expenditures that entrants would need to replicate in order to compete, or if the market could not support multiple firms at the scale needed to achieve low costs, those advantages should merely be seen as an appropriate reward that competition provides to the incumbent, who had the foresight or luck to enter first.

Stigler's definition of entry barriers thus excluded multiple factors that Bain had suggested might inhibit new competition when incumbent firms were charging prices above the competitive level. Scale economies would not count when entrants could, in principle, achieve comparably low costs through internal growth. Product differentiation also would not count, unless the costs of advertising, product design or other means of achieving differentiation were higher for a new firm than for an incumbent firm. Accordingly, Stigler's perspective

---

[a] A number of modern commentators follow Stigler's lead in suggesting that capital markets generally work well enough so as to permit entrants to obtain financing for plausible entry plans without penalty relative to financing costs borne by incumbents. But others question whether financial markets invariably work this well, citing adverse selection and moral hazard problems endemic to capital markets that may limit the availability of capital and thus make it difficult for worthy firms to convince lenders of the promise of their entry plans. *See, e.g.,* Joseph E. Stiglitz & Andrew Weiss, *Credit Rationing in Markets with Imperfect Information*, 71 AM. ECON. REV. 912 (1983). Capital market imperfections could, for example, make predatory pricing a viable strategy. Patrick Bolton, et al., *Predatory Pricing: Strategic Theory and Legal Policy*, 88 GEO. L. J. 2239, 2285–99 (2000). It is also possible that discrimination by race and/or gender could create imperfections in capital markets, limiting the ability of some borrowers to obtain financing for promising projects. *Cf.* Ian Ayres, *Fair Driving: Gender and Race Discrimination in Retail Car Negotiations*, 104 HARV. L. REV. 817 (1991) (discussing possible discrimination in automobile retailing).

on entry barriers suggested more permissive antitrust standards than did Bain's.

During the 1970s, economists began to look at entry deterrence in strategic terms. *See generally* Steven C. Salop, *Strategic Entry Deterrence*, 69 AM. ECON. REV. 335 (1979) (Papers and Proceedings issue, May, 1979); Richard J. Gilbert, *Mobility Barriers and the Value of Incumbency*, *in* 1 HANDBOOK OF INDUSTRIAL ORGANIZATION 475 (Richard Schmalensee & Robert D. Willig eds., 1989). This work focused on the significance of "sunk" costs, that is expenditures by entrants that could not be recouped in the event the firm were to exit later. If the fixed costs of entry are not sunk, and entrants have variable costs comparable to those of incumbents, the market is "contestable" and performs competitively regardless of market concentration among incumbent sellers. WILLIAM J. BAUMOL, ET AL., CONTESTABLE MARKETS AND THE THEORY OF INDUSTRY STRUCTURE (1982). But if entry requires sunk expenditures (irreversible investments), and incumbents would be expected to react quickly to cut price in response to entry, entry may be deterred even if the pre-entry price exceeds competitive levels. This may occur because the prospective entrant, recognizing the prospect of post-entry competition, will not expect to earn a contribution margin (revenues less variable costs) adequate to cover its own sunk costs.

The strategic approach to understanding entry conditions offered industrial organization economists a way to transcend the old debate between Bain and Stigler. It explained that the need for high fixed expenditures by entrants could, under some circumstances, deter entry even if the expenditures merely mimicked costs previously borne by incumbents. That might occur if fixed expenditures would also be sunk. The categories of fixed expenditures highlighted by Bain—including the product design and advertising expenditures that often underlie product differentiation, and the up front costs of developing a large production facility—often are irreversible to a significant extent. That is, much of the brand reputation and product development costs may not be transferrable to another product if entry does not succeed. The plant and equipment used to produce a new product may have no other use, and would merely be sold as scrap in the event of exit. If so, the presence of these fixed (and sunk) expenditures may deter entry, as Bain supposed. But if the same fixed expenditures would not be sunk, entry would not be deterred, as those following Stigler suggested. The economic logic of strategic entry deterrence underlies the analysis of the "likelihood" of entry in the Horizontal Merger Guidelines.

Entry in the Courts

The courts have consistently recognized that markets with low entry barriers would be expected to perform competitively. *See e.g., United States v. Baker Hughes, Inc.*, 908 F.2d 98, 987 (D.C. Cir. 1990) ("In the absence of significant barriers, a company probably cannot maintain supra-competitive pricing for any length of time."). But the courts have followed the economists in disputing whether Bain or Stigler's definition of entry barriers should be preferred. In a merger case decided in 1985, the Federal Trade Commission formally adopted Stigler's definition, but nonetheless effectively accepted Bain's approach. Although the term "barrier to entry" was defined in terms of long run cost disadvantages of an entrant relative to incumbents, the FTC went on to agree with Bain by identifying an entry "impediment" as any condition that necessarily delays entry, allowing market power to be exercised in the interim. *In re Echlin Mfg. Co.*, 105 F.T.C. 479, 485–86 (1985).

Some circuit courts appear to follow Bain in focusing on the marketplace consequences of market structure rather than upon a comparison of entrant costs with incumbent costs. *See, e.g., Rebel Oil Co. v. Atlantic Richfield Co.*, 51 F.3d 1421, 1440 (9th Cir. 1995) (recognizing that entry, even if easy for some firms, may be insufficient to solve a competitive problem arising from monopolization "if the market is unable to correct itself despite the entry of small rivals"); *Colorado Interstate Gas v. Natural Gas Pipeline*, 885 F.2d 683, 695 n. 21 (10th Cir. 1989); *but see. Advo, Inc. v. Philadelphia Newspapers, Inc.*, 51 F.3d 1191, 1200–02 (3rd Cir. 1995) (rejecting high capital requirements and the need for sellers to develop a reputation for delivering a quality good or service as entry barriers). The Stigler-Bain debate also arose in *Microsoft*, which we read in Chapter 4. Inquiring whether "costs borne by all market participants should be considered entry barriers"—effectively, the choice between Bain and Stigler—the D.C. Circuit nevertheless side-stepped the issue, noting that although the question was "the subject of much debate," it "need not resolve" it in order to find entry barriers into the operating system market monopolized by Microsoft. *United States v. Microsoft Corp.*, 253 F.3d 34, 56 (D.C. Cir. 2001).

Entry Evidence

What evidence should count in favor or against the proposition that entry, or its threat, would prevent the exercise of market power? Entry has not been the subject of as much analysis in the courts outside the merger setting as it has been under Clayton Act § 7. One important potential difference is that the alleged competitive harm from a merger is typically evaluated prospectively—the question is whether entry in the future will solve a potential competitive problem. In contrast, the alleged competitive harm from Sherman Act violations, such as monopolization, is more often evaluated retrospectively—here the question is whether entry (or its threat) in fact prevented the alleged harm from occurring. Entry evidence thus cannot be assessed in a vacuum (as "barriers" with "height" analyzed in the abstract); entry conditions are relevant only to the extent that new competition would cure the competitive problem at issue, so entry evidence must be analyzed with reference to the allegations before the court.

Some courts that find for defendants in monopolization cases have inferred that entry is easy based upon evidence that firms have actually entered the market with seemingly little difficulty. *See, e.g., Tops Markets, Inc. v. Quality Markets, Inc.*, 142 F.3d 90, 99 (2d Cir. 1998). Such evidence must be analyzed with care to ensure that it is probative. For example, before accepting such evidence in a case where the alleged harm is retrospective and defendants claim entry cured the competitive problem, a court could look at, among other things, the price effects of entry, the success or difficulties entrants faced in capturing business, whether successful entrants were limited in their number or ability to expand once in the market by a scarcity of critical competitive assets (such as a substantial presence in adjacent markets or the reputational benefits of prior customer relationships), and whether changes in the market made entry less attractive over time. Where the alleged harm would be prospective, a court could reasonably ask whether entrants today can employ the same approaches as were successful in the past, whether they could do so as cheaply as did their predecessors, and whether entrants today could reasonably expect to receive as high a price as did their predecessors (who may have entered when there was less post-entry competition or when the market was larger).

Two commentators have explained that evidence of past entry may be "double-edged," consistent with either low entry barriers in the past or the past exercise of market power. Ordover & Wall, *Proving Entry Barriers, supra* at 13 (if the market has experienced "a reasonable amount" of entry and exit in response to market signals like price fluctuations or changes in cost, then "the plausible inference can usually be made that conditions of entry and exit do not unduly favor incumbent firms over potential entrants," but entry under such conditions "does not necessarily prove the absence of barriers" because the market may not be behaving competitively, "thus creating opportunities for entrants that should not be there"). Similarly, the absence of past entry could be consistent either with a competitive market or entry barriers. *Id.* at 13–14.

Particularly when the alleged harm is prospective, courts have identified a likely entry plan, perhaps modeling that plan on recent examples of successful and unsuccessful entry. They may then evaluate whether the inputs that an entrant must assemble to succeed can be obtained quickly and easily. *See, e.g., Advo, Inc. v. Philadelphia Newspapers, Inc.*, 51 F.3d 1191, 1200–02 (3d Cir. 1995) (recoupment of losses from below-cost pricing unlikely because entry would prevent price increases). By contrast, if even the best-situated potential entrants could not surmount the difficulties of doing so rapidly, entry may be found insufficient to solve the competitive problem. *See, e.g., United States v. Microsoft Corp.*, 253 F.3d 34, 56 (D.C. Cir. 2001); *United States v. United Tote, Inc.*, 768 F. Supp. 1064 (D. Del. 1991) (entry would not prevent harm from merger). Even if such inputs can be assembled easily, a court could reasonably go on to ask whether, considering additional factors such as the size of the market and the likely extent of post-entry competition, entry would be profitable, and thus likely to counteract or deter the exercise of market power. Ordover & Wall, *Proving Entry Barriers, supra* at 14. By framing the question this way, the courts would focus on whether entry *would* be likely to solve the competitive problem, not merely on whether new competition *could* in theory do so, in harmony with the way entry likelihood is analyzed under the Merger Guidelines.

Sidebar 5–11:
The Ethics of Taking Discovery from One Client in Connection with Another Client's Proposed Merger[a]

[Thus far we have examined cases involving proof of market concentration, competitive effects and conditions of entry. Typically, at least some of the evidence necessary to

---

[a]   This Sidebar was prepared by Kathryn M. Fenton, and is adapted from *Ask the Ethics Experts*, ANTITRUST, Summer 2000, at 50.

establish each of these elements of merger analysis—and often some of the crucial evidence—comes not from the merging parties, but from other firms in the industry, such as suppliers, customers, and rivals of the merging firms. This Sidebar considers some of the ethical issues that can arise when counsel defending a merger for one of the merging firms uses civil discovery techniques to obtain information from other industry participants—and she represents those parties in other, unrelated matters. Eds.]

In defending your corporate client in a federal district court lawsuit brought by the U.S. Department of Justice seeking to block the client's proposed merger, you conclude that it is necessary for the client's defense to seek third-party discovery from a number of other companies that compete with your client. It turns out that your law firm represents at least two of these companies on matters completely unrelated to the relevant product or issues raised by the DOJ merger challenge. Do you face any ethical issues if you file discovery demands seeking deposition testimony and the production of documents from these current clients on behalf of the client you represent in the DOJ merger case? What if you need to file motions to compel to enforce the subpoenas?

Under many circumstances, seeking discovery from a firm client to benefit another client may create a situation in which client interests are "directly adverse," thus triggering a conflict of interest that requires the consent of both clients for the law firm to proceed. Merely sending a civil subpoena for documents or information, on its own, may not create direct adversity. But once a discovery recipient has indicated an objection to the discovery or expressed concerns with its burden, it is hard to characterize the situation as anything but directly adverse. Thus, a lawyer's examining a client as a hostile witness or seeking to enforce third-party discovery demands of a client ordinarily will present a conflict of interest.

ABA Formal Opinion 92–367 succinctly captures the ethical concerns presented in seeking discovery or testimony from a current client:

> [A]s a general matter examining one's own client as an adverse witness on behalf of another client, or conducting third party discovery of one client on behalf of another client, is likely (1) to pit the duty of loyalty to each client against the duty of loyalty to the other; (2) to risk breaching the duty of confidentiality to the client-witness; and (3) to present a tension between

the lawyer's own pecuniary interest in continued employment by the client-witness and the lawyer's ability to effectively represent the litigation client.

While emphasizing that the degree of direct adversity presented will depend on the particular circumstances in which the question arises, the ABA Formal Opinion concluded that the specifics of the inquiry prompting its opinion—cross-examination of a doctor client as an adversary's expert witness—was directly adverse and thus disqualifying under ABA Model Rule 1.7(a).

Similarly, once the recipient of the discovery demand manifests an unwillingness to comply, and it becomes necessary to resort to a motion to compel or other means to enforce compliance with the subpoena, the threshold of direct adversity is likely to be crossed. Certainly a motion for sanctions against a current client because of a discovery dispute would likely be found directly adverse. *See In re Suard Barge Services, Inc.*, 1997 WL 703000 (E.D. La. 1997) (law firm disqualified from pursuing motions to compel and for discovery sanctions against current firm client). In most instances, however, reviewing courts have limited conflicts arising out of discovery matters to the discovery dispute only, and not granted disqualification motions with respect to the underlying litigation. *See Sykes v. Matter*, 316 F. Supp. 630 (M.D. Tenn. 2004) (law firm may not cross-examine expert who was longtime client; rather than granting motion to disqualify, separate counsel should be retained to conduct cross-examination).

Making appropriate disclosures and obtaining the consent of both clients to waive the conflict and allow the law firm to proceed with discovery is one way to address this conflict. Such consent is often obtained based on the law firm's commitment to implement screening procedures and similar measures to preserve client confidences. In the absence of such consent, another way of resolving such conflicts is to have a separate law firm (co-defendant's counsel, local counsel, or a law firm retained particularly for this purpose) initiate and pursue discovery against or examination of the firm client. *See, e.g.*, ABA Comm. on Ethics & Professional Responsibility, Formal Opin. 92–367 (1992) ("[A] satisfactory solution may be the retention of another lawyer solely for the purpose of examining the principal lawyer's client."). The general rule is that a co-counsel relationship generally does not, in and of itself, result in any imputed disqualification, and so the separate law firm is

> free to seek discovery without triggering conflict of interest concerns.
>
> Are all forms of discovery from the existing client likely to be viewed as directly adverse to the client? What ethical issues, if any, are posed by seeking discovery from a former client? Can you deal with concerns about possible misuse of client confidences or secrets by having another firm attorney conduct the discovery and by implementing an ethical screen? If your firm represents a party in underlying litigation, but a separate law firm is conducting third party discovery, can your firm then represent another firm client receives a third party discovery demand in the litigation?

4. EFFICIENCIES

Mergers and other cooperative relationships, such as joint ventures, can benefit the economy by allowing firms to reduce costs and prices, develop new or better products, or improve service. As one court has observed, "Cooperation is the basis of productivity. It is necessary for people to cooperate in some respects before they may compete in others, and cooperation facilitates efficient production." *Polk Bros., Inc. v. Forest City Enters., Inc.*, 776 F.2d 185, 188 (7th Cir. 1985). A merger or joint venture that harms competition can deprive the market of the efficiencies. Because "[c]ompetition usually spurs firms to achieve efficiencies internally," *Horizontal Merger Guidelines* § 10 (2010), a loss of competition in a market may lessen the incentive of the remaining firms, merged and non-merging alike, to achieve cost savings or other efficiencies. But efficiencies generated by merger can enhance competition if the combination of complementary assets permits the merged firm to form a more effective competitor. Such a merger may confer a unilateral incentive to reduce price or improve products, or undermine coordination by creating a maverick firm or by enhancing the incentives of an existing maverick to limit the adverse effects of coordinated conduct. Recall Figure 5–1, the Williamson diagram, which describes merger analysis as evaluating both harms and benefits to competition.

Supreme Court merger cases from antitrust's structural era questioned whether cost savings or other efficiencies from merger should ever count in favor of a transaction that increased market concentration substantially. For example, in *FTC v. Procter & Gamble Co.*, 386 U.S. 568, 580 (1967), the Court stated that "[p]ossible economies cannot be used as a defense to illegality." Recall as well the Court's observation in *Philadelphia Nat'l Bank*, that an otherwise anticompetitive merger "is not saved because, on some ultimate reckoning of social or economic debits and credits, it may be deemed beneficial." *United States v. Philadelphia Nat'l Bank*, 374 U.S. 321, 370–71 (1963). The Court explained that "[a] value choice of such magnitude is beyond the ordinary limits of judicial competence, and in any event has been made for us already, by Congress. * * * " *Id. See also Brown Shoe*, 370 U.S. at 344 ("Congress appreciated that occasional higher costs and prices might result from the maintenance of fragmented industries and markets. It resolved these competing considerations in favor of decentralization. We must give effect to that decision.").

Although these older decisions remain formally controlling, they have not been interpreted as foreclosing all consideration of efficiencies in the analysis of horizontal mergers. Decades ago, Professors Areeda and Turner observed that in *Procter & Gamble* "the court referred only to 'possible' economies and to economies that 'may' result from mergers that lessen competition. To reject an economies defense based on mere possibilities does not mean that one should reject such a defense based on more convincing proof." 4 PHILLIP AREEDA & DONALD TURNER, ANTITRUST LAW ¶ 941b, at 154 (1980). Moreover, *Procter & Gamble* was decided during an era in which merger law was thought to vindicate non-economic concerns such as halting trends toward market concentration in their incipiency and protecting small business, as well as preventing the exercise of market power. Consideration of efficiencies from merger may have been inconsistent with advancing these non-economic goals. Indeed, some older decisions could be read to create an "efficiency offense," by which efficiencies from merger would count against the deal because the creation of a large firm with low costs would accelerate the demise of small business rivals.[30] But the judicial hostility to efficiencies has steadily decreased as such concerns have come to take a back seat to economic concerns across much of antitrust.

Accordingly, beginning in the early 1990s, some lower courts indicated that efficiencies are a relevant consideration in merger analysis. In 1991, an appeals court cited efficiencies as one factor that may be used to rebut the plaintiff's prima facie case based on market concentration. *FTC v. University Health, Inc.*, 938 F.2d 1206 (11th Cir. 1991). Efficiencies from merger also have played a role in successful defenses by the merging firms against government challenges to two hospital mergers, although they were not the primary reason for the failure of the government's cases. *FTC v. Butterworth Health Corp.*, 946 F. Supp. 1285 (W.D. Mich. 1996), *aff'd*, 121 F.3d 708 (6th Cir. 1997); *United States v. Long Island Jewish Med. Ctr.*, 983 F. Supp. 121 (E.D.N.Y. 1997). More generally, the D.C. Circuit

---

[30] Suppose that a merger among non-maverick firms lowers their costs, and in consequence deters price-cuts by an existing maverick that fears a deeper price war, making coordination more effective and leading to higher prices. (See the discussion of mergers involving non-mavericks in Sidebar 5–6.) For a possible example, see *United States v. Premdor, Inc.*, 66 Fed. Reg. 45,326 (Aug. 28, 2001) (competitive impact statement) (closer alignment of merging firm cost structures would decrease the incentive of a non-merging firm to build market share by cutting prices and increasing that firm's incentive to coordinate with the merged firm).Would this theory of anticompetitive harm amount to finding an "efficiency offense"?

observed that "the trend among lower courts is to recognize the [efficiencies] defense." *FTC v. H.J. Heinz Co.*, 246 F.3d 708, 720 (D.C. Cir. 2001).

In 1991, when *University Health* was decided, the then-current Merger Guidelines recognized an efficiencies defense but made clear that it would rarely succeed. Those Guidelines required that the merging firms establish "by clear and convincing evidence" that their merger was "reasonably necessary to achieve significant net efficiencies," and indicated that the necessary level of expected net efficiencies would be greater, the more significant the competitive risks arising from the transaction. In 1997, the government's Merger Guidelines were revised to articulate an approach for taking efficiencies into account in evaluating the likely competitive effects of a merger. The revisions were prompted by a Federal Trade Commission staff report, issued in 1996, that discussed whether and how competition policy should be modified to account for the "new high-tech, global marketplace." The 2010 Guidelines refined the framework set forth in 1997.

Under the Guidelines now in force, efficiencies can be the basis for allowing a merger to go forward even though it otherwise appears likely to be anticompetitive. Such efficiencies must be "cognizable" as that term is defined in the Guidelines. Efficiencies are not "cognizable" unless they are (1) verified, (2) merger-specific, *i.e.*, they could not practically be achieved through some reasonable alternative that presents less risk to competition, and (3) do not arise from anticompetitive reductions in output or service. *Horizontal Merger Guidelines* § 10 (2010). The Guidelines charge the merging firms with substantiating efficiency claims to permit their verification, as through analogy to past experience. Efficiencies are assessed net of costs produced by the merger or incurred in achieving the efficiencies.

The Guidelines go on to suggest that certain types of efficiencies are more likely to be cognizable and substantial than others. For example, "efficiencies resulting from shifting production among facilities formerly owned separately, which enable the merging firms to reduce the incremental cost of production" are said to have promise; efficiencies relating to research and development are considered potentially substantial, but less susceptible to verification; and efficiencies relating to procurement, management, or capital cost are questioned as less likely to be cognizable or substantial. *Id.* If a merger affects not whether, but only when, an efficiency would be achieved, only the timing advantage is a merger-specific efficiency. *Id.* § 10 n. 13. For a summary of the efficiencies that are more or less likely to be deemed cognizable under the Guidelines, see Figure 5–7, *infra*.

The Guidelines indicate that a merger will not be challenged if the cognizable efficiencies are of a character and magnitude such that the merger is not likely to be anticompetitive in any relevant market. The efficiencies must reverse the merger's potential to harm competition, as by preventing price increases in that market. The *Note on Efficiencies and Consumer Welfare* that follows the discussion of *Staples* below relates this standard to measures of economic welfare and discusses the sliding scale the Merger Guidelines employ to weigh anticompetitive harms against efficiency benefits.

The approach to analyzing efficiencies introduced into the Merger Guidelines in 1997 and revised in 2010 was used as the template for the Antitrust Guidelines for Collaborations Among Competitors, issued jointly by the FTC and Justice Department in 2000. *Collaboration Guidelines*, § 3.36. Perhaps surprisingly, neither the Merger Guidelines nor the Collaboration Guidelines ever actually define "efficiency." In place of a definition, they offer examples of efficiencies and point to their beneficial consequences. The Merger Guidelines indicate that efficiencies may "result in lower prices, improved quality, enhanced service, or new products," permit "two ineffective competitors to form a more effective competitor," "reduce or reverse" the merged firm's unilateral incentive to raise price, or destabilize coordination "by enhancing the incentive of a maverick to lower price or by creating a new maverick firm."

Recall that efficiencies were asserted by the merging parties in Staples as a basis for rebutting the government's case. Review now that portion of the opinion that addressed, and rejected, the merging firms' effort to assert an efficiency defense.

FEDERAL TRADE COMMISSION V. STAPLES, INC.

United States District Court for the District of Columbia, 1997.
970 F. Supp. 1066.

[For the relevant excerpt, *see supra* Chapter 5, at 811. Eds.]

The discussion of efficiencies from *Staples* further illustrates the influence of the Merger Guidelines on the federal courts and provides an example of how the cognizability criteria are applied in practice. The Guidelines do not discuss how courts should allocate the relevant burdens of production and persuasion; they are intended as a guide for enforcement decisions. To the extent they do suggest an allocation of burdens, however, they are ambiguous. On the one hand, the Guidelines ask whether cognizable efficiencies "likely would be sufficient to reverse the merger's potential to harm consumers in the relevant market, *e.g.*, by preventing price increases in that market." *Horizontal Merger Guidelines* § 10. The emphasis here on rebutting the case for anticompetitive effects recalls the shifting burden of production concept associated procedurally with "defenses." On the other hand, the requirement that firms substantiate efficiency claims, along with the statement that "[e]fficiency claims will not be considered if they are vague, speculative, or otherwise cannot be verified by reasonable means," suggests that the firms asserting efficiencies bear a burden of proof, not merely one of production, and thus that efficiencies should be understood as providing an "affirmative defense" to an otherwise unlawful merger. *Id.* This effort to speak with two procedural voices may create confusion for those courts that look to the Guidelines for guidance in analyzing efficiencies. Should courts analyze efficiencies as an "affirmative defense" (carrying with it a burden of proof) or as a "defense" (requiring the merging firms to meet only a burden of production)? Which approach did the court take in *Staples*? The distinction also has implications for the choice of welfare standard, as is explored in the next Note.

NOTE ON EFFICIENCIES AND CONSUMER WELFARE

Under the Merger Guidelines, if a merger creates cognizable efficiencies, the agency then asks whether they "likely would be sufficient to reverse the merger's potential to harm consumers in the relevant market, *e.g.*, by preventing price increases in that market." *Horizontal Merger Guidelines* § 10. Moreover, the enforcement agencies "are mindful that the antitrust laws give competition, not internal operational efficiency primacy in protecting customers." *Id.* As these quotations suggest, the Merger Guidelines are generally read as concerned primarily with an anticompetitive merger's potential to harm competition by shifting wealth from sellers to buyers (the "transfer" in the Williamson diagram, Figure 5–1) within a market, not with efficiency losses to the economy. If so, the Guidelines' focus on consumer welfare rather than aggregate economic welfare, as these terms were used in the discussion of the goals of antitrust in Chapter 1.

The primary focus of the Merger Guidelines on consumer welfare arguably makes consideration of efficiencies part of the competitive effects analysis—part of the determination of whether the merger will likely raise price—rather than an analysis conducted in defense of an otherwise anticompetitive acquisition. Under such circumstances, whether and how the efficiencies will "reverse" the merger's potential to harm competition will depend on the nature of the harm alleged, *i.e.*, whether the concern is with coordinated interaction or some type of unilateral competitive effects. In a coordinated effects case, for example, the Guidelines suggest that the merger might promote competition by creating a maverick firm with an incentive to expand output and lower price. In a unilateral effects case, the merger might reduce the merged firm's variable costs, giving it an incentive to lower price that outweighs any incentive to increase price resulting from the loss of localized competition. Moreover, a focus on competitive effects means that variable cost savings matter more than reductions in fixed costs, as only the former have the potential to provide incentives for the merged firm to lower price in the relevant market. Fixed cost savings do not affect a firm's pricing decisions directly in any particular market. If they lead to higher than competitive profits and entry is easy, however, they may be competed away through reductions in the price of some or all of the full line of firm products. On the distinction between fixed and variable costs, see the Appendix to Chapter 1 on Cost Concepts.

Although the Guidelines emphasize a concern with the welfare of buyers, this is not their exclusive concern. The Guidelines do not insist that cost savings or other efficiencies be passed through to consumers in order to count, although that requirement is to some extent implicit in the suggestion that efficiencies must prevent price increases or otherwise reverse a merger's anticompetitive potential. One footnote to the Guidelines' efficiency section permits consideration of cost savings "with no short-term, direct effect on prices in the relevant market"—that is, fixed cost reductions that represent real resource savings—though it suggests giving those efficiencies less weight. *Horizontal Merger Guidelines* § 10, n. 15. In addition, the Guidelines indicate in another footnote that efficiencies from the merger accruing in *other* relevant markets might save a merger likely to raise price in a given market, if the two effects are "so inextricably linked * * * that a partial divestiture or other remedy could not feasibly eliminate the anticompetitive effect in the relevant market without sacrificing the efficiencies in the other market(s)." *Horizontal Merger Guidelines* § 10, n. 14. To the extent these footnotes allow consideration of fixed cost savings and efficiencies outside the relevant market along with variable cost savings within the relevant market, they could effectively convert what is said to be a consumer welfare analysis within the market where anticompetitive effects are alleged into an economy-wide aggregate economic welfare analysis. In addition, if agencies and courts define markets narrowly, that would tend to increase the likelihood that any efficiencies defendants proffer will accrue outside the relevant market in which harm is found, and thus increase the likelihood that cross-market balancing would be required if the efficiencies are credited (regardless of whether a consumer welfare standard or aggregate welfare standard is employed). *But cf.* Judd E. Stone & Joshua D. Wright, *The Sound of One Hand Clapping: The 2010 Merger Guidelines and the Challenge of Judicial Adoption*, 39 REV. INDUS. ORG. 145 (2011) (criticizing the Guidelines' treatment of out-of-market efficiencies and fixed costs savings as unlikely to maximize aggregate economic welfare, particularly when markets are defined narrowly).

In practice, the agencies have usually viewed their charge as focusing on the welfare of consumers rather than aggregate welfare. They do not commonly refrain from challenging a merger likely to raise price to consumers in one market on the ground that consumers in some other market would benefit, or refrain from challenging a merger likely to raise price on the ground that the transaction also produces large fixed cost savings, unlikely to benefit consumers in the relevant market.

The U.S. is not the only jurisdiction that has grappled with the question of the goals of the antitrust laws in connection with determining the proper role of efficiencies in merger analysis. *See, e.g.,* Canada (Comm'r of Competition) v. Superior Propane Inc., [2002] 18 C.P.R. (4th) 417 (Comp. Trib.), *aff'd,* [2003] 3 F.C. 529 (Fed. Ct. App.). Moreover, the competition policy adopted by countries with small economies is often more accommodating to efficiencies than the approach adopted by large economies. Michal S. Gal, *Size Does Matter: The Effects of Market Size on Optimal Competition Policy,* 74 S. CAL. L. REV. 1437, 1459–60 (2001).

The efficiency revisions to the Merger Guidelines explain that "[t]he greater the potential adverse competitive effect of a merger, the greater must be the cognizable efficiencies, and the more they must be passed through to customers" in order to conclude that the merger will not harm competition. *Horizontal Merger Guidelines* § 10. (Cost pass-through is discussed in the next *Note.*) A similar approach was adopted by the D. C. Circuit in *FTC v. H.J. Heinz Co.,* 246 F.3d 708, 720–21 (D.C. Cir. 2001). *See also Baker Hughes,* 908 F.2d at 991 ("The more compelling the prima facie case, the more evidence the defendant must present to rebut it successfully."). Is this "sliding scale" approach an unreasonable interpretation of the *Philadelphia Nat'l Bank* presumption, inconsistent with the outcome in *Baker Hughes* and likely to discourage procompetitive acquisitions? Or is it a sensible acknowledgment of the weight of evidence about market concentration, properly recognizing that buyers are unlikely to see lower prices from a merger to near-monopoly even if the merged firm obtains substantial cognizable variable cost reductions from the integration?

Efficiencies have at times persuaded the enforcement agencies not to bring a case. Moreover, notwithstanding the "sliding scale" approach of the Merger Guidelines, and the Guidelines statement that "[e]fficiencies almost never justify a merger to monopoly or near-monopoly," *Horizontal Merger Guidelines* § 10, efficiency arguments have occasionally been successful before the agencies in support of mergers in highly-concentrated markets. Indeed, on rare occasions, the agencies have refrained from challenging a merger among the only two firms participating in a market on efficiency grounds (as in some defense industry cases).

But efficiencies have historically had a less friendly reception in the courts, as is suggested by comparing the results in the entry and efficiencies cases. While efficiencies have played a role in successfully defending against merger challenges in some cases, they have not yet been the sole reason for a successful judicial defense to a government merger challenge. In contrast, as we observed in *Waste Management,* defendants have at times been successful in overcoming the government's prima facie case with proof that entry would solve the competitive problem. What accounts for these different litigation results?

The answer is probably not to be found in differences in the level of post-merger concentration in the cases. For example, the concentration levels in

Heinz, where the defendant's rebuttal based on efficiencies failed to overcome the government's prima facie case, were not much higher than those found in *Baker Hughes*, where the government's prima facie case was successfully rebutted on ease of entry grounds. One explanation relates the difference in the outcomes of the cases to differences in the defenses emphasized by the merging firms. When *Baker Hughes* was decided, proof of ease of entry, the main defense in that case, was a well-established route to rebutting the prima facie case based on concentration. In contrast, the merging firms in *Heinz* raised a less established rebuttal, relying primarily on evidence of efficiencies to explain why the merger would not harm competition. *See generally* Jonathan B. Baker, *Efficiencies and High Concentration: Heinz Proposes to Acquire Beech-Nut, in* THE ANTITRUST REVOLUTION 157 (John E. Kwoka, Jr. & Lawrence J. White eds., 5th ed. 2008). Once the appeals court concluded that the district court's acceptance of that defense was unwarranted, it was left with the unrebutted inference of harm to competition arising from the reduction in the number of sellers. Under this interpretation of the decisions, the focus on concentration in *Heinz* is more related to the continuing development of doctrinal standards related to the efficiency defense than to any rethinking of the totality-of-the-circumstances approach to merger analysis set forth in *Baker Hughes*.

It may be appropriate for courts to be more skeptical of an efficiencies defense than an entry defense. As previously noted, the modern trend may be for courts to analyze efficiencies as a defense—that is, to view them as offered to defeat the government's proof of higher prices or other competitive harm rather than as an affirmative defense that would excuse higher prices. This would mean that the defendants must meet a burden of production to raise efficiencies, but that the government would have the burden of persuasion to show that efficiencies do not undermine its showing of harm to competition. In practice, however, regardless of the formal allocation of the burdens of production and persuasion, defendants typically are expected to prove efficiencies because the relevant evidence is more likely under their control. In contrast, the government may more often be able to test entry claims by developing evidence from other sources, such as the experience of other firms considering entry under pre-merger conditions, which may be similar to some extent to entry conditions after the merger. In addition, some suggest that efficiency claims are generally more prospective and more speculative than entry claims, consistent with studies showing that mergers often turn out not to be profitable for the acquiring firm. But others may disagree, highlighting the key role of efficiencies as a motive for merger.

Do factors like these explain why courts appear to make it more difficult for a rebuttal to succeed if based on efficiencies? Should the courts treat entry arguments as a "defense" on which the defendant has a burden of production but plaintiff retains a burden of proof, or treat efficiency arguments as an "affirmative defense" on which defendant bears both burdens? Should efficiencies be treated differently in cases of coordinated as opposed to unilateral competitive effects?

NOTE ON CREDITING EFFICIENCIES IN THE FACE OF
ANTICOMPETITIVE HARM: VERIFICATION,
RELATEDNESS, AND PASS-THROUGH

Verification and Relatedness

The Horizontal Merger Guidelines define "cognizable" efficiencies as those that are both "merger-specific" and "verifiable." They maintain:

> Efficiencies are difficult to verify and quantify, in part because much of the information relating to efficiencies is uniquely in the possession of the merging firms. Moreover, efficiencies projected reasonably and in good faith by the merging firms may not be realized. Therefore, it is incumbent upon the merging firms to substantiate efficiency claims so that the Agencies can verify by reasonable means the likelihood and magnitude of each asserted efficiency, how and when each would be achieved (and any costs of doing so), how each would enhance the merged firm's ability and incentive to compete, and why each would be merger-specific.

> Efficiency claims will not be considered if they are vague or speculative or otherwise cannot be verified by reasonable means. Projections of efficiencies may be viewed with skepticism, particularly when generated outside of the usual business planning process. By contrast, efficiency claims substantiated by analogous past experience are those most likely to be credited.

Horizontal Merger Guidelines, § 10 (2010). The Merger Guidelines also provide some examples of efficiencies that are more or less likely to be verifiable (*see* Figure 5–8).

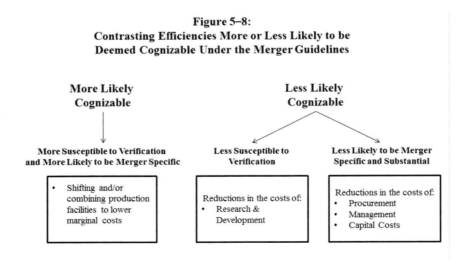

Figure 5–8:
Contrasting Efficiencies More or Less Likely to be
Deemed Cognizable Under the Merger Guidelines

How much and what kind of efficiency should be sufficient enough to offset how much and what kind of anticompetitive effect? Must the efficiency and the anticompetitive effect be specifically quantifiable? If so, would it be sufficient that the absolute amount of efficiency is greater than the amount of anticompetitive harm? Or would the efficiency need to be causally connected to the harm, so it is likely to keep it from occurring? Can the efficiency be largely theoretical? Although it may be easy to resolve issues in lopsided cases—lots of harm and only little in the way of efficiencies, or conversely, lots of efficiencies and little in the way of harm—closer cases will present greater challenges. Indeed, the assessment of how much harm and how much efficiency will result from certain conduct often may be dependent upon the quality of the evidence, may require predicting the way the merger changes the merging firms' competitive incentives, and may even require credibility assessments typically of the sort left to the fact-finder, including juries.

Contrast, for example, the treatment of efficiencies in two cases we have studied: *Staples* and *Broadcast Music* (Chapter 2). How would you characterize the treatment of efficiencies in each? Which involved relatively stronger evidence of efficiencies? Of anticompetitive effects? What form did the evidence of efficiencies and anticompetitive effects respectively take? How did the strength of the evidence on each side affect the courts' analysis?

The Merger Guidelines suggest a "sliding scale" approach when they state:

> The greater the potential adverse competitive effect of a merger, the greater must be the cognizable efficiencies, and the more they must be passed through to customers, for the Agencies to conclude that the merger will not have an anticompetitive effect in the relevant market. When the potential adverse competitive effect of a merger is likely to be particularly substantial, extraordinarily great cognizable efficiencies would be necessary to prevent the merger from being anticompetitive.

Horizontal Merger Guidelines, § 10 (2010). How would such a sliding scale work? What factors might cause the scale to tilt in favor of efficiencies or harm? Could such a scale be used effectively in an administrative or judicial setting, or is its utility limited to the agency setting? Was it used implicitly or explicitly in *Staples* or any of our other cases?

Economics of Cost Pass-Through

According to the Merger Guidelines, the enforcement agencies consider whether efficiencies might reverse a merger's potential to harm customers in the relevant market, as by preventing price increases in that market. The Guidelines identify the extent to which efficiencies would be passed through to buyers as a relevant consideration in that analysis. *Horizontal Merger Guidelines*, § 10 (2010). Recall that the *Staples* court cited a pass-through rate of 15%–17% as one reason not to accept the merging firms' efficiencies defense.

We have already seen, in the discussion of the Coffee Shop hypothetical case in Chapter 1, that any firm, including a monopolist or other firm exercising market power, has an incentive to respond to a reduction in marginal cost by reducing price and increasing output. The Coffee Shop hypothetical also made clear that whether a firm (or group of firms collectively) can exercise market power depends on the elasticity of the demand curve that firm (or those firms) face. The extent to which a firm passes through a reduction in marginal cost in the form of a lower price—whether, in response to, say, a $1 reduction in marginal cost, it lowers price by, for example, ten cents (a 10% pass through rate), 50 cents (a 50% pass-through rate), or $1 (a 100% pass-through rate)—depends not on the elasticity of demand but on the way that demand and marginal cost change as output increases. When marginal cost is constant, the pass-through rate is 50% if the demand curve is a straight line, and for other demand curve shapes it depends on how the slope or elasticity of demand changes as output rises. [31] In the *Heinz* case, defendants' expert economist testified that firm demand would likely grow substantially more elastic as price falls, giving Heinz an incentive to pass through to its buyers as much as 100% of any marginal cost reduction. Jonathan B. Baker, *Efficiencies and High Concentration: Heinz Proposes to Acquire Beech-Nut, in* THE ANTITRUST REVOLUTION 151, 169–71 (John E. Kwoka, Jr. & Lawrence J. White eds., 5th ed. 2008).

---

5. FAILING FIRMS

The Merger Guidelines' analysis of horizontal mergers also considers the special status of "failing firms." The Supreme Court created a narrow "failing company" defense to Clayton Act § 7 in *International Shoe Co. v. FTC*, 280 U.S. 291 (1930). The Guidelines incorporate failing firms considerations as a defense, and allow the acquisition of a firm notwithstanding possible harm to competition if the assets of the failing firm would exit the relevant market absent the merger, and three other conditions are met: (1) the firm would be unable to meet its financial obligations in the near future; (2) it would be unable to reorganize successfully; and (3) it has made unsuccessful good-faith efforts to sell its assets to a buyer who would keep its assets in the relevant market and pose a less severe danger to competition than the proposed merger. *Horizontal Merger Guidelines* § 11(2010). The Merger Guidelines also allow an analogous defense, not found in the case law, for a "failing division" of an otherwise healthy firm. *Id.*

---

[31]   Recall from the Coffee Shop example in Chapter 1 that when marginal cost declines, a firm with market power lowers price because it has an incentive to produce more in order to capture the now-higher profit-margin on additional sales. As the firm lowers price, though, its profit margin falls, which limits its price-cutting incentive. The greater the reduction in the profit margin relative to the increase in sales, the less profitable additional price reductions become. The magnitude of the profit reduction, and thus the extent to which the firm chooses to lower price in response to a decrease in marginal cost, is related mathematically to the way that the slope or elasticity of demand changes as output increases.

These requirements are construed strictly. *See FTC v. Harbour Group Investments*, 1990–2 TRADE CAS. (CCH) ¶ 69,247 (D.D.C. 1990). For example, a footnote to the Merger Guidelines notes that "[a]ny offer to purchase the assets of the failing firm for a price above the liquidation value of those assets"—defined as the highest value the assets could command for use outside the relevant market—"will be regarded a reasonable alternative offer." *Id.* n.16. This provision suggests why conflict may arise over the requirement that the failing firm seek multiple alternative purchasers. The shareholders can be expected to favor a buyer who will pay a premium over the liquidation value of the assets. Having found such a buyer, the company has little incentive to seek out a less anticompetitive purchaser, who might make a lower offer that the agencies may insist it take instead.

A weakened or "flailing" firm, in financial trouble but not close to bankruptcy, will not satisfy the strict tests for application of the failing firm defense when it seeks to merge with a rival. The merger partners may, however, argue that their transaction is unlikely to harm competition because the acquired firm, as a result of its financial distress, is unlikely to be a significant competitive force in the future, absent the merger. This argument is sometimes termed a *General Dynamics* defense. *See United States v. General Dynamics Corp.*, 415 U.S. 486, 506–08 (1974). In 1997, the FTC relied upon a *General Dynamics* argument to conclude that Boeing's acquisition of McDonnell Douglas did not violate Clayton Act § 7. The Merger Guidelines describe the failing firm provision as consistent with *General Dynamics*, terming it "an extreme instance of the more general circumstance in which the competitive significance of one of the merging firms is declining: the projected market share and significance of the exiting firm is zero." *Horizontal Merger Guidelines* § 11 (2010).

The next two sidebars raise issues that may arise in horizontal merger analysis that are not discussed in the Horizontal Merger Guidelines. Sidebar 5–12, entitled "Beyond Horizontal and Vertical: Conglomerate Mergers and Potential Competition," addresses the concern that competition could be harmed if a firm acquires a potential horizontal rival with which it is not now presently competing. Sidebar 5–13 is concerned with "Merger Remedies."

Sidebar 5–12:
Beyond Horizontal and Vertical: Conglomerate
Mergers and Potential Competition

Conglomerate and Market Extension
Mergers—Traditional Treatment

Conglomerate mergers—which involve firms not related either horizontally or vertically—were a significant enforcement concern at the height of antitrust's structural era.

These then-frequent transactions attracted a great deal of attention during the late 1960s, the heyday of businesses like Gulf & Western Industries, Ling-Temco-Vought (LTV), and International Telephone & Telegraph (ITT), which grew through conglomerate acquisitions to be among the largest industrial corporations in the nation. "Although they added little to horizontal concentration, these transactions produced large conglomerate enterprises whose existence suggested that antitrust policy was seriously deficient in dealing with sheer corporate size." William E. Kovacic, *Failed Expectations: The Troubled Past and Uncertain Future of the Sherman Act as a Tool for Deconcentration*, 74 IOWA L. REV. 1105, 1122–23 (1989).

Conglomerate merger enforcement played a role in the Watergate scandal during the administration of President Richard M. Nixon. The Antitrust Division of the Justice Department brought several conglomerate merger cases during the first two years of the Administration, in 1969 and 1970, including four against ITT. These enforcement actions—and the Justice Department's determination to pursue an expedited appeal of a district court loss to the Supreme Court—led to a furious lobbying effort by ITT to persuade Congress to repeal the Expediting Act (currently 15 U.S.C. § 29), which would have aided ITT by helping it delay or possibly avoid Supreme Court review. ITT also attempted to persuade the Nixon White House to instruct the Department of Justice to drop the appeal or settle the case. Evidence from that period established that President Nixon called Deputy Attorney General Richard Kleindienst and ordered the Justice Department to back off from pursuing conglomerate merger challenges. ITT's case was eventually settled.

A connection between that settlement and ITT's contemporaneous offer to help finance the 1972 Republican convention was alleged and given credence by some because of the overlap in the officials involved. Although a link was not conclusively demonstrated, the antitrust dispute became enmeshed in scandal. A cover-up of White House contacts with Justice Department officials over the disposition of the case led to one of the Watergate-related impeachment counts against President Nixon and the conviction of Kleindienst after his elevation to Attorney General for false testimony before a congressional committee.[a] *See generally* ROBERT M. GOOLRICK, PUBLIC POLICY TOWARD CORPORATE GROWTH: THE ITT MERGER

---

[a]   The congressional and criminal investigations focused on whether the settlement of ITT's antitrust case was connected to its offer to finance the Republican convention and on whether senior government officials lied under oath about President Nixon's role.

CASES (1978); FRANK MANKEWICZ, U.S. V. RICHARD M. NIXON: THE FINAL CRISIS 47–49, 70–72, 161–63, 207, 261 (1975); J. ANTHONY LUKAS, NIGHTMARE: THE UNDERSIDE OF THE NIXON YEARS 130–34, 182–85 (1976).

Historically, the Supreme Court distinguished a fourth category of mergers that are "neither horizontal, vertical nor conglomerate" involving what is termed a product or market extension. *FTC v. Procter & Gamble Co.*, 386 U.S. 568, 578 (1967). In that case, a laundry detergent's acquisition of a producer of bleach was considered a "product extension merger" because the two products are "complementary:" they may be produced in the same facilities, distributed through the same channels, advertised by the same media, and marketed to the same ultimate consumer. A "market extension merger" occurs when the merging firms sell the same product in different geographic markets.

Conglomerate and Market Extension Mergers Today

From a more contemporary perspective, market and product extension mergers generate a potential for collusive competitive effects similar to the traditional concern about horizontal mergers. To the extent either firm is a potential competitor in the market in which its merger partner participates, as may be plausible given that its involvement in complementary activities may give it a "leg up" on entry unavailable to other potential entrants, the merger may harm competition. These transactions may also give rise to exclusionary competitive effects similar to the traditional concern about vertical mergers. To the extent the merged firm can exploit its control of complementary products to impair or eliminate access to those complements by an unintegrated rival or the rival's customers, the merger may lessen competition. In addition, these types of mergers create the potential for cost savings similar to the efficiencies often available from vertical integration. Product and market extension mergers have nevertheless historically been viewed as closer to conglomerate mergers than to horizontal and vertical acquisitions.

Since the 1970s, government challenges to conglomerate mergers and product or market extension mergers have become rare. Still the legal theories that were important historically in the review of conglomerate mergers have some resonance today. The major themes in this area of antitrust jurisprudence are sketched below. The emphasis is on potential competition theories, which generate the most current attention, most likely because they are closely related to horizontal merger analysis.

Potential Competition Theories

The acquisition of a potential horizontal rival could harm competition in much the same way as could the acquisition of an actual horizontal rival.[b] Potential competition cases are divided into two categories. Under the "perceived potential competition" theory, the perceived threat of entry by a firm not now in the market limits anticompetitive behavior by incumbent sellers, so the acquisition of that outsider by an incumbent might harm competition because it relaxes that constraint. *Cf. United States v. Baker Hughes, Inc.,* 908 F.2d 981, 988 (D.C. Cir. 1990) ("[A] firm that *never* enters a given market can nevertheless exert significant pressure on that market.") (emphasis in original). Under the "actual potential competition" or "actual potential entrant" theory, the acquisition involves a firm that would otherwise have entered and made the market more competitive. The categories differ in their evidentiary focus: perceived potential competition is concerned with the incumbent's expectations, while the actual potential competition theory is concerned with the entrant's actual plans.

The "perceived potential competition" theory was endorsed by the Supreme Court during the late 1960s and early 1970s. *United States v. Marine Bancorporation,* 418 U.S. 602, 639–40 (1974); *United States v. Falstaff Brewing Corp.,* 410 U.S. 526, 532–34 & n. 13 (1973); *FTC v. Procter & Gamble Co.,* 386 U.S. 568, 581 (1967). While the Supreme Court reserved judgment on the "actual potential competition" theory, *see Marine Bancorporation*, 418 U.S. at 625, 639; *Falstaff*, 410 U.S. at 537–38, some lower courts and the FTC accepted that theory in principle, at least if stringent factual predicates for its application are satisfied.

Potential competition theories are recognized by the 2010 Horizontal Merger Guidelines to the extent the potential competitor is a "rapid entrant," able to come into a market in response to a price increase quickly and with little sunk costs. As discussed previously, such a firm is treated as a market participant—and thus effectively presumed to constrain existing rivalry—and assigned a market share based upon its likely future competitive significance. *Horizontal Merger Guidelines* §§ 5.1, 5.2, 9 (2010). Courts also apply the actual competition label generously, including to firms that have taken steps to compete but have not yet produced. *See Polypore Int'l, Inc. v. FTC,* 686 F.3d. 1208 (11th Cir. 2012) (acquired firm beginning to market its product and bidding for customer accounts but not yet producing deemed an actual competitor).

Although the 2010 Guidelines do not recognize potential competition theories involving entrants more generally, such possibilities are incorporated in the non-horizontal sections of the 1984 Department of Justice Merger Guidelines, which remain in force; only the horizontal merger standards of the 1984 Guidelines were superseded by later Horizontal Merger Guidelines. In general, the 1984 Guidelines limit the application of the potential competition theory to concentrated markets where no more than two other outside firms have an entry advantage comparable to that ascribed to the potential competitor involved in a merger. They indicate that a challenge is more likely the greater the increase in market concentration and the fewer the number of other potential entrants with comparable entry advantages as the acquired firm. In recent years, government enforcers have occasionally mounted investigations of mergers involving a potential competition theory, but such cases are rare. In *Polypore,* the Eleventh Circuit declined to decide whether the *Philadelphia National Bank* presumption would apply to the acquisition of a potential rival that was not yet an actual competitor, on the ground that the acquisition before it involved an actual rival. *Id.* In *FTC v. Steris Corp.*, 133 F. Supp.3d 962–(N.D. Ohio 2015), a federal district court denied the FTC's request for a preliminary injunction on the ground that the agency failed to make a sufficient showing that the acquired firm would have entered the relevant market absent the merger, and thus was unlikely to succeed in an administrative trial.

Other Theories

Conglomerate mergers have been attacked on a variety of grounds other than potential competition. One such ground is that the transaction would allow the merged firm to coerce suppliers or customers, as by facilitating tying, *see In re Heublein, Inc.*, 96 F.T.C. 385, 597–98 (1980), or reciprocal buying, *FTC v. Consolidated Foods Corp.*, 380 U.S. 592 (1965). Reciprocal buying occurs when a firm purchases only from other firms that buy from it. A computer manufacturer, for example, may purchase components only from firms that use its

---

[b]   If the merging firms are not actual rivals, but are likely future rivals in a market that has not yet developed, their merger would be seen as a horizontal acquisition within a future market, not as a potential competition merger between an incumbent and a potential entrant. *See Statement of the Federal Trade Commission In the Matter of Nielsen Holdings N.V. and Arbitron Inc.,* No. 131–0058 (Sept. 20, 2013), https://www.ftc.gov/enforcement/cases-proceedings/131–0058/nielsen-holdings-nv-arbitron-inc-matter.

computers in their offices. A related concern, termed "entrenchment," is that a firm, dominant in its market, could obtain significant competitive advantages through merger with a large acquiring firm, because the transaction may raise entry barriers and disadvantage small rivals. *See In re Heublein, Inc.,* 96 F.T.C. 385, 593–96 (1980); *Emhart Corp. v. USM Corp.,* 527 F.2d 177, 181 (1st Cir. 1975). Today, it is likely that these possibilities would be analyzed similarly to other potential exclusionary effects of mergers, as will be discussed later in this Chapter in connection with vertical mergers.

A final concern about conglomerate mergers in the case law relates to their potential for facilitating oligopolistic coordination through multimarket contact. For example, the government unsuccessfully argued in a 1974 bank merger case that the acquisition, and others it would likely trigger, would result in a market structure in which a few large statewide banks would face each other in a network of local, oligopolistic banking markets, and that this market structure would enhance the possibility of supra-competitive pricing through parallel, standardized conduct. *United States v. Marine Bancorporation,* 418 U.S. 602, 620, 623 (1974). This collusive theory would likely be analyzed today as a possible instance of coordinated competitive effects of horizontal mergers.

Acquisitions by Private Equity Firms—
The New "Conglomerates"

During the first decade of the 21st century, private equity firms grew in size and importance as financial market participants. These firms often purchase, in whole or part, businesses in many industries. Many of their investments are more than passive financial interests; the private equity buyer may appoint management to run the firm with the hope of improving operations or cutting costs, then seek to sell the business at a profit.

These financial entities can be thought of as conglomerates. Their acquisitions have only rarely drawn scrutiny from the antitrust enforcement agencies. They are most likely to draw such attention when the private equity buyer already owns or controls a rival firm. *See, e.g., In re TC Group,* File No. 061 0197; Docket No. C-4183 (F.T.C. Jan. 27, 2007), http://www.ftc.gov/os/caselist/0610197/index.shtm (analysis of proposed agreement containing consent orders to aid public comment) (acquisition of interests in Kinder Morgan by private equity funds managed and controlled by The Carlyle Group and Riverside Holdings). To similar effect, competition may be harmed when multiple large financial investors (such as Fidelity or Vanguard) own shares of the stock of competing firms (such as rival airlines or banks). For discussion of the potential scope of this problem and possible antitrust enforcement responses, see Einer Elhauge, *Horizontal Shareholding*, 129 HARV. L. REV. 1267 (2016); Jonathan B. Baker, *Overlapping Financial Investor Ownership, Market Power, and Antitrust Enforcement: My Qualified Agreement with Professor Elhauge*, 129 HARV. L. REV. F. 212 (2016).

Sidebar 5–13:
Merger Remedies

When confronted with a merger that poses anticompetitive hazards, a government enforcement agency can pursue one of two remedial paths. It can seek to prohibit the merger outright, or it can negotiate a settlement that permits the transaction to proceed only if the merging parties take measures to resolve the competitive problem. It may be possible to cure a competitive overlap by compelling the parties to divest assets or take other steps to transfer some of the competitive capacity that the merger would have created to a third party.

Merger policy today features substantial reliance on settlements. The adoption of pre-merger notification systems, such as the Hart-Scott-Rodino Antitrust Improvements Act (*see* Sidebar 5–3), has played an important role in this development by giving the U.S. government the right to review transactions before they are completed. The mandatory waiting periods of many merger notification mechanisms worldwide create a natural opportunity for negotiation as the government identifies possible problems and brings them to the attention of the merging parties. In a number of instances, the parties are fully aware of a competitive problem and will approach the government with a proposed solution even before filing the required pre-merger notification.

In cases involving anything less than a simple condemnation of the entire proposed merger, the design of merger remedies, whether by settlement or in litigation, can pose a number of challenges. One task is to identify the assets to be divested. What collection of human capital, physical facilities, and intellectual property is necessary to put the buyer of divested assets in a position to exert a strong competitive influence in the market? If the merging parties own several plants in the relevant market, which plant or plants should be divested? Are there trademarks, patents, or copyrights that the prospective buyer must obtain in order to operate successfully? If the divestiture does not encompass the right combination of assets, the buyer may not be able to replicate the competitive presence that the seller previously exerted. As you might imagine, the merging parties generally would prefer to satisfy a demand for divestitures by selling off what they believe to be their weakest assets.

A second challenge that arises in the course of negotiated settlements is to determine the timing of the execution of the remedy. Sometimes the government will explain its concerns, and encourage the merging firms to restructure their transaction ("fix-it-first") in order to obviate the need for a court or Federal Trade Commission order. Another approach is for the government simply to obtain the defendant's promise to carry out the required remedy, such as a divestiture, by some time certain in the future. To ensure that such promises are fulfilled, the government might also insist that the merging parties agree to alienate other valued assets—sometimes called "crown jewels"—if the parties fail to meet the deadlines specified in the settlement. A more ironclad way for the government to assure itself that the remedy will be executed properly is to demand that the parties identify and gain the government's approval for the prospective buyer before the settlement is entered. A "buyer-up-front" provision gives the government greater assurance that the divestiture will be carried out in a timely manner, that a suitable purchaser will obtain the assets, and that the package of assets (as evaluated by the prospective buyer) is sufficient to transfer the relevant competitive capability. But such a provision can delay consummation of the transaction—and achievement of the efficiencies from merger—while the parties find, and obtain approval for, a buyer. A monitor may be appointed to oversee the divestiture, for example, to prevent the seller from mismanaging assets during the divesture period or to ensure that the seller complies with any associated conduct obligations (such as a requirement to supply the buyer with a key input).

A third challenge, determining the capability of the buyer of divested assets, is closely related to the second. The government would prefer a purchaser that is both experienced in the relevant market and will be able to use the assets in a manner that exerts a competitive influence in the market. The merging parties, by contrast, may prefer to divest the assets to a buyer that is likely to be a comparatively ineffective or submissive market participant. The government agencies do not insist that the prospective buyer be the "best" from a competitive standpoint, but they do ask that a prospective purchaser satisfy certain basic standards of capability in order to be confident that the divestiture will solve the competitive problem otherwise created by the merger. In some cases, the merging parties may offer to improve the buyer's capability by assisting the buyer after assets are divested—for example, by offering to manage a divested factory until the buyer becomes familiar with the industry. But these and other forms of "continuing entanglements" raise questions about the buyer's incentives and ability to compete effectively in the relevant market. To avoid such entanglements, the government may seek to guarantee commercial viability of the carved-out assets by insisting upon a broader divestiture than might strictly be suggested by focusing on the threatened harm to competition— for example, to include production facilities for key inputs or additional products necessary to preserve economies in joint production and distribution. But broadening the required divestiture may deprive the merging firms of some of the desired efficiency benefits of their transaction.

The actual negotiation of settlement terms can be a contentious process, as each side measures the wisdom of making specific concessions against the risks associated with litigating the government's request for an injunction in court. A district court's issuance of an injunction, whether preliminary or permanent, is likely to kill a transaction, as few companies are willing to cope with the uncertainty and delay of pursuing a full trial on the merits (after a preliminary injunction) or seeking vindication before a court of appeals (after a permanent injunction).

In some recent cases, the inadequacy of the merging firms' remedial proposal has been an issue in the preliminary injunction action. *See, e.g., FTC v. Sysco Corp.*, 133 F. Supp. 3d. 1, at 48–53 (D.D.C. 2015); *FTC v. CCC Holdings Inc.*, 605 F. Supp. 2d 26, 56–59 (D.D.C. 2009); *United States v. Franklin Elec. Co.*, 130 F. Supp. 2d 1025 (W.D. Wis. 2000). *See generally* Howard Morse & Megan Browdie, *Proposing a Fix? Ready to Litigate the Fix? Recent Cases Should Guide Strategy*, 15 THE THRESHOLD 10 (Summer 2015), http://www.cooley.com/71950. When the Justice Department (but not the FTC) reaches a civil settlement with an antitrust defendant, and asks a court to enter the settlement as a final judgment, the court is obliged, under the Tunney Act, to review whether the settlement is in the public interest. The court generally defers to the government. *See, e.g., U.S. v. US Airways Group, Inc.*, 38 F. Supp.3d 69 (D.D.C. 2014).

In the many instances in which the merging parties and the government achieve a settlement, does the chosen remedy ensure that competition is preserved? In the typical settlement, it is difficult for those other than the parties to the negotiations and their rivals to answer this question. But neither the industry participants nor the government has an incentive to depict the settlement as anything other than a successful resolution of the competition policy issues.

A 1999 FTC study examined the efficacy of merger remedies. STAFF OF THE BUREAU OF COMPETITION OF THE FEDERAL TRADE COMMISSION, A STUDY OF THE COMMISSION'S DIVESTITURE PROCESS (1999). Though not attempting to assess the impact of the remedies in a comprehensive manner, the FTC study raised concerns about the ability of settling firms to limit the effectiveness of the relief in protecting post-merger competition by manipulating the settlement process, and led the Commission to insist more frequently upon the use of "crown jewel" and "buyer-up-front" measures, discussed above, in negotiating remedies. The government also may employ operating, monitoring, or selling trustees to safeguard the effective implementation of the remedy.

The most recent government policy statement as to merger remedies, from the Justice Department, also discusses remedying vertical mergers. ANTITRUST DIVISION POLICY GUIDE TO MERGER REMEDIES (2011), http://www.justice.gov/atr/public/guidelines/272350.pdf. The statement generally calls for divestitures to remedy problems with horizontal mergers, but is more sympathetic to relying on conduct remedies—such as firewalls, non-discrimination provisions, mandatory licensing, transparency, and anti-retaliation provisions—for addressing problems with vertical mergers. For a critical analysis of conduct remedies and their effectiveness, see JOHN KWOKA, MERGERS, MERGER CONTROL, AND REMEDIES: A RETROSPECTVE ANALYSIS OF U.S. POLICY (2014).

D. VERTICAL MERGERS

So far in this Chapter, we have examined horizontal mergers. When horizontal mergers raise competitive concerns, those concerns typically involve the threat of *collusive* effects—either the post-merger ability of the merged firms to raise price unilaterally, or the post-merger ability of the merged firms to coordinate their pricing or other competitive conduct with their remaining rivals.

This section addresses *vertical* mergers—mergers that involve firms at different levels of a chain of production or distribution. Vertical mergers more often raise competitive concerns when they threaten *exclusionary* anticompetitive effects. If so, the analysis of vertical mergers proceeds much like the analysis of other exclusionary conduct, which we first met in Chapter 1, examined in Chapter 4, and will study further in Chapter 6.

Antitrust law's approach to the analysis of vertical mergers has evolved over time in parallel to the way horizontal merger law has developed, but with even less input from the courts. As with horizontal merger analysis, a Supreme Court decision from antitrust's structural era remains formally controlling precedent, but is no longer closely tied to enforcement agency practice or the likely decisions of the courts today.

1. VERTICAL MERGER ANALYSIS BEFORE 1980

We will begin by reading an excerpt from the Supreme Court's decision in that case, *Brown Shoe*, which we reviewed earlier in connection with horizontal merger analysis and the "submarket" approach to market definition. Consistent with those excerpts, which questioned relatively small reductions in horizontal competition, the Court here highlights a competitive concern that arises from small amounts of foreclosure by contemporary standards: "Brown's avowed policy of forcing its own shoes upon its retail subsidiaries" meant that other shoe manufacturers were denied access to Kinney retail outlets, which accounted for only 1.2% of shoes sold.

BROWN SHOE CO. v. UNITED STATES

Supreme Court of the United States, 1962.
370 U.S. 294, 82 S.Ct. 1502, 8 L.Ed.2d 510.

[The Court's analysis of the legislative history of the Clayton Act and its analysis of the horizontal aspects of the merger were highlighted in an excerpt from this decision set forth earlier in this Chapter. An introductory note to the earlier excerpt sketches the facts, some of which are repeated here.

Brown was the fourth largest shoe manufacturer in the country, accounting for about 4% of total domestic production and 6% of wholesale shoes sold nationally. It was also the nation's third largest shoe retailer, controlling 1,230 retail shoe outlets. Of these, 470 were company owned and operated, and the rest were mainly independently-owned stores operating under the Brown franchise program. Most retail shoe stores were independent of any manufacturer: the 1230 retail shoe outlets controlled by Brown accounted for only 20% of the firm's approximately 6000 retail customers.

Kinney was primarily in the retail business, though it also was the twelfth largest domestic shoe manufacturer, with about a 0.5% share. It was the country's eighth largest retailer, with over 350 retail outlets, accounting for 1.2% of shoes sold (and 2% of children's shoes sold). Kinney-manufactured products accounted for about one fifth of the company's retail sales. Brown was the largest outside supplier of the shoes sold in Kinney's retail outlets, supplying nearly 8% of those products. Eds.]

* * *

IV.

THE VERTICAL ASPECTS OF THE MERGER

Economic arrangements between companies standing in a supplier-customer relationship are characterized as 'vertical.' The primary vice of a vertical merger or other arrangement tying a customer to a supplier is that, by foreclosing the competitors of either party from a segment of the market otherwise open to them, the arrangement may act as a 'clog on competition,' which 'deprive(s) * * * rivals of a fair opportunity to compete.'[40] Every extended vertical arrangement by its very nature, for at least a time, denies to competitors of the supplier the opportunity to compete for part or all of the trade of the customer-party to the vertical arrangement. However, the Clayton Act does not render unlawful all such vertical arrangements, but forbids only those whose effect 'may be substantially to lessen competition, or to tend to create a monopoly' 'in any line of commerce in any section of the country.' * * *

* * *

The Probable Effect of the Merger.

* * *

Since the diminution of the vigor of competition which may stem from a vertical arrangement results primarily from a foreclosure of a share of the market otherwise open to competitors, an important consideration in determining whether the effect of a vertical arrangement 'may be substantially to lessen competition, or to tend to create a monopoly' is the size of the share of the market foreclosed. However, this factor will seldom be determinative. If the share of the market foreclosed is so large that it approaches monopoly proportions, the Clayton Act will, of course, have been violated. * * * On the other hand, foreclosure of a *de minimis* share of the market will not tend 'substantially to lessen competition.'

---

[40] In addition, a vertical merger may disrupt and injure competition when those independent customers of the supplier who are in competition with the merging customer, are forced either to stop handling the supplier's lines, thereby jeopardizing the goodwill they have developed, or to retain the supplier's lines, thereby forcing them into competition with their own supplier.

Between these extremes, in cases such as the one before us, in which the foreclosure is neither of monopoly nor *de minimis* proportions, the percentage of the market foreclosed by the vertical arrangement cannot itself be decisive. In such cases, it becomes necessary to undertake an examination of various economic and historical factors in order to determine whether the arrangement under review is of the type Congress sought to proscribe.

A most important such factor to examine is the very nature and purpose of the arrangement. Congress not only indicated that 'the tests of illegality (under § 7) are intended to be similar to those which the courts have applied in interpreting the same language as used in other sections of the Clayton Act,' but also chose for § 7 language virtually identical to that of § 3 of the Clayton Act, which had been interpreted by this Court to require an examination of the interdependence of the market share foreclosed by, and the economic purpose of, the vertical arrangement. Thus, for example, if a particular vertical arrangement, considered under § 3, appears to be a limited term exclusive-dealing contract, the market foreclosure must generally be significantly greater than if the arrangement is a tying contract before the arrangement will be held to have violated the Act. The reason for this is readily discernible. The usual tying contract forces the customer to take a product or brand he does not necessarily want in order to secure one which he does desire. Because such an arrangement is inherently anticompetitive, we have held that its use by an established company is likely 'substantially to lessen competition' although only a relatively small amount of commerce is affected. Thus, unless the tying device is employed by a small company in an attempt to break into a market, the use of a tying device can rarely be harmonized with the strictures of the antitrust laws, which are intended primarily to preserve and stimulate competition. On the other hand, requirement contracts are frequently negotiated at the behest of the customer who has chosen the particular supplier and his product upon the basis of competitive merit. Of course, the fact that requirement contracts are not inherently anticompetitive will not save a particular agreement if, in fact, it is likely 'substantially to lessen competition, or to tend to create a monopoly.' Yet a requirement contract may escape censure if only a small share of the market is involved, if the purpose of the agreement is to insure to the customer a sufficient supply of a commodity vital to the customer's trade or to insure to the supplier a market for his output and if there is no trend toward concentration in the industry. Similar considerations are pertinent to a judgment under § 7 of the Act.

* * *

* * * In 1955, the date of this merger, Brown was the fourth largest manufacturer in the shoe industry. * * * Not only was Brown one of the leading manufacturers of men's, women's, and children's shoes, but

Kinney, with over 350 retail outlets, owned and operated the largest independent chain of family shoe stores in the Nation. Thus, in this industry, no merger between a manufacturer and an independent retailer could involve a larger potential market foreclosure. Moreover, it is apparent both from past behavior of Brown and from the testimony of Brown's President, that Brown would use its ownership of Kinney to force Brown shoes into Kinney stores. Thus, in operation this vertical arrangement would be quite analogous to one involving a tying clause.[55]

* * *

The existence of a trend toward vertical integration, which the District Court found, is well substantiated by the record. Moreover, the court found a tendency of the acquiring manufacturers to become increasingly important sources of supply for their acquired outlets. The necessary corollary of these trends is the foreclosure of independent manufacturers from markets otherwise open to them. And because these trends are not the product of accident but are rather the result of deliberate policies of Brown and other leading shoe manufacturers, account must be taken of these facts in order to predict the probable future consequences of this merger. It is against this background of continuing concentration that the present merger must be viewed.

Brown argues, however, that the shoe industry is at present composed of a large number of manufacturers and retailers, and that the industry is dynamically competitive. But remaining vigor cannot immunize a merger if the trend in that industry is toward oligopoly. It is the probable effect of the merger upon the future as well as the present which the Clayton Act commands the courts and the Commission to examine.

Moreover, as we have remarked above, not only must we consider the probable effects of the merger upon the economics of the particular markets affected but also we must consider its probable effects upon the economic way of life sought to be preserved by Congress. Congress was desirous of preventing the formation of further oligopolies with their attendant adverse effects upon local control of industry and upon small business. Where an industry was composed of numerous independent units, Congress appeared anxious to preserve this structure. * * *

The District Court's findings, and the record facts * * * convince us that the shoe industry is being subjected to just such a cumulative series of vertical mergers which, if left unchecked, will be likely 'substantially to lessen competition.'

We reach this conclusion because the trend toward vertical integration in the shoe industry, when combined with Brown's avowed policy of forcing

---

[55] Moreover, ownership integration is a more permanent and irreversible tie than is contract integration.

its own shoes upon its retail subsidiaries, may foreclose competition from a substantial share of the markets for men's, women's, and children's shoes, without producing any countervailing competitive, economic, or social advantages.

* * *

———————

In analyzing this vertical merger, *Brown Shoe* examined more than the extent of the market foreclosed to rivals; it also considered the purpose of the acquisition and whether there was a trend toward vertical integration in the industry. But foreclosure is termed a vertical merger's "primary vice" and the percentage of the market foreclosed to rivals became the central issue for analyzing vertical mergers in the wake of this decision. Throughout antitrust's structural era, in parallel with antitrust's concern about small increases in horizontal concentration, vertical mergers were barred when they denied rivals access to small parts of the market, particularly in concentrated markets. This parallels the treatment of early exclusive dealing cases, especially *Standard Stations*, which we will discuss in Chapter 6.

In *Brown Shoe*, the Court appears concerned primarily with the prospect that "Brown would use its ownership of Kinney to force Brown shoes into Kinney stores" thereby "foreclos[ing] competition from a substantial share of the markets for men's, women's, and children's shoes." 370 U.S. at 334. The foreclosed rivals would appear to be other shoe manufacturers, who would be denied access to Kinney's retail outlets. As with vertical exclusion cases generally, a vertical merger can, in principle, harm competition by denying horizontal rivals access either to upstream inputs or as in this case, downstream customers. The same merger can do both: the Court could have chosen also to analyze the transaction as harming *Kinney*'s rivals by foreclosing them from access to a key input, namely Brown's shoes.

The note at the start of the case indicates, however, that Kinney sold only 1.2% of all shoes (and 2% of children's shoes). If rival shoe manufacturers are kept from retail outlets accounting for no more than 2% of the market, is it likely that the price of shoes will rise? Does it matter to the analysis that the shoe industry was relatively unconcentrated by modern standards? If higher prices are not the problem, what problem is the Supreme Court trying to solve by upholding the government's challenge to this shoe industry merger?

Finally, after reading about exclusive dealing in Chapter 6, return to this case to consider how it might have been decided if instead of acquiring Kinney, Brown Shoe had entered into an exclusive dealing agreement with it. Would the Court's analysis have been different? Its conclusion? *See FTC v. Brown Shoe Co.*, 384 U.S. 316 (1966).

NOTE ON *FORD MOTOR CO. V. UNITED STATES (AUTOLITE)*

The Supreme Court reaffirmed *Brown Shoe*'s concern with the anticompetitive potential of vertical mergers foreclosing rivals from small portions of a market toward the end of antitrust's structural era in its only other (and still most recent) substantive vertical merger decision, *Ford Motor Co. v. United States*, 405 U.S. 562 (1972) (*Autolite*). However, the upstream and downstream markets in *Autolite* were substantially more concentrated than their counterparts in *Brown Shoe*.

In *Autolite*, the Court upheld a district court's decision prohibiting Ford's acquisition of a leading manufacturer of original equipment spark plugs that "marked 'the foreclosure of Ford as a purchaser of about ten per cent of total [spark plug] industry output." *Id.* at 568. The upstream (spark plug) and downstream (automobile) markets were both concentrated: "Prior to the acquisition * * * there were only two major independent producers and only two significant purchasers of original equipment spark plugs." *Id.* at 570. In addition, as Justice Stewart emphasized in a concurring opinion, the transaction "eliminated one of the only two independent producers with a sufficient share of the aftermarket [replacement spark plugs] to give it a chance to compete effectively without an OE [original equipment] tie," and thus "had the probable effect of indefinitely postponing the day when existing market forces" could undermine the oligopoly market structure. *Id.* at 581 (Stewart, J., concurring). The Court also followed *Philadelphia National Bank* in refusing to consider the defense "that the acquisition had some beneficial effect" in making the merged firm a more effective competitor with automobile and spark plug manufacturers. *Id.* at 569.

The lower courts took their lead from the Supreme Court in *Brown Shoe* and *Autolite*, and upheld challenges to vertical mergers excluding rivals from small portions of a market. An instructive and not atypical example comes from a 1975 decision by the Federal Trade Commission, later affirmed by the Ninth Circuit, challenging two vertical acquisitions in the cement industry. The acquiring firm was Ash Grove, a manufacturer of portland cement accounting for 13% to 18% of total annual sales of portland in the Kansas City area. The acquired firms were downstream buyers of portland: two ready-mix cement producers.

One of the acquired firms, Fordyce, produced 14% of the local output, purchased 10% of the cement shipped into Kansas City, and was the largest independent ready-mix manufacturer in town. Two larger firms had previously been acquired by other portland manufacturers. The other, Lee, was the seventh largest Kansas City ready-mixer. Lee accounted for 4.3%

of ready-mix market sales and purchased 3.1% of all shipments of portland cement into the market area. The challenge to the smaller of these acquisitions was too much for a dissenting Commissioner to accept, but even he did not question the FTC's opposition to the larger acquisition, notwithstanding the small foreclosure percentages it presented, thus suggesting how lines were drawn during antitrust's structural era:

> One can hardly deny that, if each of the 4 largest cement firms doing business in a given city is allowed to buy a customer holding 10 percent of the local concrete market, other cement producers are going to be foreclosed from at least 40 percent of the total business in town and hence that one of the major arteries feeding into the competitive life-line of that particular market might well suffer some significant amount of clogging. Those are the kinds of numbers that can leave the competition gasping for breath.

> My Brethren lose their grip on the realities of the competitive arena, however, when they let their justifiable concern with the probable effects of such a substantial merger [the acquisition of Fordyce] spill over onto * * * Ash Grove's acquisition of a small ready mixer [Lee]. * * *

> * * * To be sure, this market is already concentrated and the law is reasonably intended to deal not just with the kind of monopolization that leaps upon us in great bounds but the kind that enters in small increments and sneaks in on little cat feet in the middle of the night. But 3.1 percent of a market?

In re Ash Grove Cement Co., 85 F.T.C. 1123, 1154 (1975) (dissenting statement of Commissioner Thompson), *aff'd sub nom.*, *Ash Grove Cement Co. v. FTC*, 577 F.2d 1368 (9th Cir. 1978).

Sidebar 5–14:
Vertical Integration and Transaction Cost Economics

Suppliers and their customers may take many different approaches to structuring their distribution systems. A firm might decide to acquire all or many of its inputs from various suppliers, act largely as an "assembler" of those inputs, and sell its assembled and finished product either directly or through a network of independent wholesalers and/or retail dealers. A personal computer manufacturer, for example, might elect to purchase processors, hard drives, wireless communication devices, and flat panel displays from various suppliers, rather than manufacture them itself. It then would assemble those various inputs into a finished product—a PC—which it would in turn sell through direct sales or through dealers.

In the alternative, a firm might elect to *vertically integrate* backwards or forwards. With *backward integration*, a firm will decide to assume responsibility for producing one of its inputs. An automobile manufacturer, for example, might decide to produce its own tires rather than purchase them from independent tire manufacturers, or a PC manufacturer might decide to produce some of its own circuit boards. *Forward integration* might involve a movement down the distribution chain, such as when an automobile manufacturer or gasoline producer decides to own and operate its own retail dealership, or, in our PC example, when a company decides to sell directly to consumers through Internet sites and catalogue sales, rather than by using independent retail dealers.

Vertical integration can be accomplished in a number of ways. The automobile manufacturer in our example might decide to expand into tire manufacturing by building its own facility. In the alternative, it might acquire an existing tire manufacturer. Finally, it might in effect vertically integrate with a tire manufacturer, at least to a substantial extent, by entering into an exclusive dealing, output, or requirements contract that binds the two links in the distribution chain more closely together. What factors might motivate firms to choose a particular strategy?

Whether or not a firm integrates vertically by owning and operating assets in two or more stages of production or levels of distribution usually turns on relative operating costs or efficiencies. If internal integration is more cost-effective, the firm will tend to integrate and operate at both the manufacturing and retailing levels; on the other hand, the firm will operate at only one level and will not expand vertically if utilizing unaffiliated suppliers and dealers is less costly. *See* OLIVER E. WILLIAMSON, *Transaction Cost Economics*, *in* 1 HANDBOOK OF INDUSTRIAL ORGANIZATION 136, 150–59 (Richard Schmalensee & Robert D. Willig Eds., 1989). Vertical integration in this view usually results from the firm's effort to achieve efficiencies—i.e. lower costs—not available to it with other market arrangements such as contracts. *See generally* TIMOTHY BRESNAHAN & JONATHAN LEVIN, *Vertical Integration and Market Structure*, *in* THE HANDBOOK OF ORGANIZATIONAL ECONOMICS 853 (Robert Gibbons & John Roberts eds., 2013).

Similar transactional savings frequently are sought by firms that integrate vertically on a less formal basis—that is, through contracts. A firm may seek a stable supply or output by arranging a long-term exclusive dealing agreement or by requiring that dealers buying its product for resale concentrate sales and advertising efforts within assigned territories. In some cases, however, such restraints may merely mask efforts by manufacturers or dealers to fix prices horizontally, as can be the case with resale price maintenance. Or the producer may attempt to extract a monopoly price at retail when it cannot do so at the manufacturing point.

Vertical contractual restraints and vertical integration by ownership thus may often be substitutes for one another. In organizing production and distribution, the firm must decide which activities it can best conduct internally and which functions are best contracted out to separate business entities. In recognition of their common economic justifications and limited anticompetitive potential, these approaches arguably should be treated consistently under the antitrust laws to permit firms to choose the mix of strategies that minimizes transaction costs. As Michael Katz observes, however, modern antitrust doctrine falls short of this goal:

> * * * [T]here is one particularly striking incongruity in U.S. antitrust policy. Integrated firms are allowed to implement almost any contract internally. Thus, antitrust laws that restrict independent firms' writing of arm's length contracts may have the effect of encouraging vertical integration even in cases in which this form of business organization is not the most efficient one. For this reason, a public policy that prevents pernicious vertical practices by unintegrated firms may actually be worse than a policy that allows these practices. * * *

MICHAEL KATZ, *Vertical Contractual Relations*, in 1 HANDBOOK OF INDUSTRIAL ORGANIZATION 715 (Richard Schmalensee & Robert D. Willig eds., 1989).

As you learn more in Chapter 6 about the various kinds of distribution agreements used by firms with their suppliers and customers, consider how similar or different is the courts' treatment of vertical integration through merger and vertical integration by contract. Would you agree with Katz's conclusion that by being more restrictive the law of exclusive dealing might have inadvertently been encouraging inefficient levels of vertical integration? Could the converse be true, i.e., could a hostile attitude towards vertical mergers encourage inefficient levels of exclusive contracting? Why might it be important to ensure, as Katz suggests, that antitrust doctrine remains "neutral," i.e. that it creates neither incentives nor disincentives for firms choose one distribution strategy over another?

2. VERTICAL MERGER ANALYSIS SINCE 1980

Chicago School commentators proffered two main criticisms of the structural era's case law. First, they emphasized that foreclosure of rivals does not necessarily harm competition. After all, all vertical agreements foreclose someone. As Judge Bork explained in analyzing "the series of vertical mergers that spurred the Federal Trade Commission to intervene in the cement industry," "[f]oreclosure may occasionally be a threat to individual firms. It is never a threat to competition." ROBERT H. BORK, THE ANTITRUST PARADOX 244 (1978) (citing cases prior to *Ash Grove*). This criticism called into question whether small amounts of foreclosure could harm competition. Under such circumstances, it may be plausible that the foreclosed rivals could merely find other supply or distribution relationships, at little or no cost penalty. Judge Bork made this point while ridiculing another vertical merger government case: If "eager suppliers and hungry customers" find themselves "unable to find each other, forever foreclosed and left to languish," then the FTC "could have cured this aspect of the situation by throwing an industry social mixer." *Id.* at 232.

Second, Chicago School critics emphasized that vertical integration was often procompetitive, for much the same reasons that other vertical practices could often be efficient. With specific reference to *Autolite*, Judge Bork asserted that "The structure of an industry * * * will be whatever is most efficient for [that industry] * * *. The decision to make oneself or buy from others is always made on the basis of the difference in cost and effectiveness, criteria the law should permit the manufacturer to apply without interference." ROBERT H. BORK, THE ANTITRUST PARADOX 236 (1978).

Although the Supreme Court has not revisited vertical merger analysis since the 1970s, as is also true in the area of horizontal mergers, it is likely that today's Supreme Court would take these criticisms seriously and would not still agree with its older decisions in *Brown Shoe* and *Autolite*. Indeed, the Chicago School's powerful criticism of prior vertical merger enforcement set the stage for a retrenchment by the federal enforcement agencies and courts during the 1980s. The 1982 Merger Guidelines, amended in 1984, reframed vertical merger analysis around the question of whether such transactions would harm horizontal competition in either upstream or downstream markets. The section on "Horizontal Effects from Non-Horizontal Mergers" in the 1984 Merger Guidelines (§ 4) formally remains in force as a statement of Justice Department enforcement policy.[32]

---

[32] The 1992, 1997, and 2010 merger guidelines revisions were limited to horizontal mergers.

The 1984 Guidelines set forth three theories by which a vertical merger could harm competition. The first, commonly described as raising "two-level entry" barriers, requires extensive integration between the upstream and downstream markets, such that a new entrant to one level also must enter the other level simultaneously. Under such circumstances, the Guidelines indicate, additional vertical integration may increase the difficulty of simultaneous entry. This could harm competition either upstream or downstream, if market concentration and other characteristics at one market level suggest that the increased difficulty of entry is likely to affect market performance. *1984 Merger Guidelines* § 4.21. From a contemporary perspective, this theory can be thought of as one example of the way that exclusionary conduct can harm competition. If the agencies were to update their vertical merger guidelines, they would likely broaden their discussion to reflect the modern economics of exclusion, discussed in Chapter 4.

The second theory is that vertical integration could facilitate horizontal collusion. *1984 Merger Guidelines* § 4.22. For example, the Guidelines suggest that the acquisition of retailers by manufacturers may make it easier for the manufacturers to detect cheating by monitoring the retail price, thereby facilitating manufacturer-level coordination. Or the vertical merger may facilitate collusion by eliminating a particularly disruptive buyer, which is sufficiently important to sellers as to be in a position to induce seller cheating.

Finally, the 1984 Guidelines explain that a vertical merger can be used by monopoly public utilities subject to rate regulation as a tool for evading that regulation. *1984 Merger Guidelines* § 4.23. Integration may allow the merged firm to shift costs from unregulated to regulated activities undetected by the regulatory agency. The result might be higher prices for the regulated service (which is permitted by the regulator to pass through costs) and, perhaps also, distorted competition in the unregulated market (where the merged firm's activities would now effectively be subsidized).

The 1984 Merger Guidelines also were more sympathetic to the efficiency defense in vertical merger analysis than in analyzing horizontal mergers:

> An extensive pattern of vertical integration may constitute evidence that substantial economies are afforded by vertical integration. Therefore, the Department will give relatively more weight to expected efficiencies in determining whether to challenge a vertical merger than in determining whether to challenge a horizontal merger.

1984 Merger Guidelines § 4.24

How closely do these guidelines for the exercise of prosecutorial discretion comport with Supreme Court vertical merger decisions like

Brown Shoe and *Autolite*? Can either case be interpreted as examples of any of these three theories of anticompetitive vertical integration, or are the 1984 Guidelines better understood as rooted in an economic approach to antitrust divorced from the social and political goals that animated antitrust enforcement in antitrust's pre-Chicago structural era?

As was true in the area of horizontal mergers, the lower courts were quick to follow the lead of the enforcement agencies and recede from the prior judicial hostility to vertical mergers. By 1989, a district court could write: "vertical integration is not an unlawful or even suspect category under the antitrust laws." *Reazin v. Blue Cross and Blue Shield of Kan., Inc.*, 663 F. Supp. 1360, 1489 (D. Kan. 1987), *aff'd*, 899 F.2d 951 (10th Cir. 1990). The *O'Neill v. Coca-Cola* case excerpt that follows illustrates how far the judicial analysis of vertical mergers moved in the dozen years that followed the FTC's decision in *Ash Grove*. Notice also how that movement toward a focus on the question of whether competition was harmed in any narrow economic sense was facilitated by the introduction of a robust inquiry into "antitrust injury," which we first explored in Chapter 1.

O'NEILL V. COCA-COLA CO.

United States District Court for the Northern District of Illinois, 1987.
669 F. Supp. 217.

BUA, DISTRICT JUDGE.

Before this court are the motions of defendants, The Coca-Cola Company, Inc. and PepsiCo, Inc., to dismiss plaintiff Dixie O'Neill's claims for declaratory and injunctive relief for alleged antitrust injury she, and the class she seeks to represent, will suffer from alleged antitrust violations resulting from defendants' vertical acquisitions of certain bottling facilities. * * * For the reasons stated herein, both defendants' motions are granted and plaintiff's claims are dismissed in their entirety.

* * *

II. *Facts*

A. *Acquisitions of Bottling Concerns*

Coca-Cola and PepsiCo dominate the highly concentrated United States soft drink industry with 37.4% and 28.9% respective national market shares of all carbonated soft drink products. Coca-Cola and PepsiCo produce syrups and concentrates which are sold to bottlers who add carbonated water, bottle, and sell the resulting carbonated soft drinks. Coca-Cola and PepsiCo both grant exclusive territorial marketing areas to their respective trademark licensee bottlers and prohibit them from distributing competing flavors of other companies.

On May 30, 1986, PepsiCo announced its purchase of MEI Corporation ("MEI"), the third largest independent bottler of PepsiCo carbonated soft drink products. * * * [Also in 1986, Coca-Cola acquired the soft drink bottling assets of BCI Holding Corporation ("Beatrice") and JTL Corporation ("JTL"), and merged them. Later that year, Coke transferred all its bottling operations to its Coca-Cola Enterprises ("CCE") subsidiary, and sold 51% of CCE stock to the public (while continuing to hold the remaining 49%).—Eds.]

* * *

B.   Transshipment Restrictions

PepsiCo grants each of its licensed bottlers an exclusive territory in which to produce and market PepsiCo products. To protect the exclusivity of these territories, PepsiCo forbids its bottlers to supply retailers who buy or sell outside their territories, buy from or sell to other retailers within their territories, or facilitate transshipment by selling to intermediaries. PepsiCo enforces this policy by firing, boycotting, or otherwise punishing those who violate the noted prohibitions.

III. *Discussion*

O'Neill brings this action individually as a purchaser of Coca-Cola and PepsiCo carbonated soft drink products, and as a representative of a class of all purchasers of Coca-Cola and PepsiCo carbonated soft drinks, pursuant to Rule 23 of the Federal Rules of Civil Procedure. O'Neill's complaint sets forth two claims. In Count I, O'Neill complains that defendants, with their respective acquisitions of JTL, Beatrice, and MEI bottlers, have violated the antitrust laws. Specifically, O'Neill alleges that these acquisitions effectively reduce competition in the soft drink industry, thereby increasing prices for herself and all consumers of Coca-Cola and PepsiCo soft drinks. O'Neill asserts that PepsiCo's acquisition of MEI provides PepsiCo with ownership of bottlers that produce approximately 33% of all PepsiCo brand carbonated soft drinks in the United States. O'Neill similarly asserts that Coca-Cola's retention of the largest single interest in CCE stock permits it to control, through CCE, ownership of bottlers that produce approximately 31% of all Coca-Cola brand carbonated soft drinks in the United States.

* * *

B.   Standing to Assert Claims Under Count I

O'Neill, as a consumer, alleges higher prices as her antitrust injury resulting from Coca-Cola's and PepsiCo's vertical acquisitions. Higher prices, as well as lower output, are "the principal vices proscribed by the antitrust laws." Although higher prices are specifically recognized as an antitrust injury, the question in this case is whether the alleged antitrust violation proximately threatens plaintiff with such an injury.

* * *

O'Neill argues that PepsiCo's and Coca-Cola's acquisitions of MEI, JTL, and Beatrice will have the following anticompetitive effects: increasing barriers to entry and mobility in the carbonated soft drink market; reducing or eliminating existing suppliers, customers, distributors and retailers of all three bottlers; increasing interdependent pricing practices between PepsiCo and Coca-Cola; reducing or eliminating preexisting competition between defendants and the bottlers; and increasing concentration of distribution channels and the industry in general. O'Neill claims that the vertical acquisitions violate antitrust laws and that these mergers, producing the aforementioned results, will increase the price of PepsiCo and Coca-Cola soft drink products, thereby causing her to suffer pocketbook injury.

O'Neill does not specifically allege how higher prices will result from these alleged consequences of the vertical acquisitions. Nor does O'Neill show that higher prices are likely to result from the vertical acquisitions. Indeed, O'Neill burdens this court to provide the causal links between what she alleges to be the consequences of the vertical acquisitions and how those consequences result in higher prices.

Accepting O'Neill's allegations of the consequences of vertical acquisitions to be true, higher prices could theoretically result from either of two ways. The reduced competition between the bottlers and manufacturers may allow for an increase in prices by the manufacturer who now owns and controls the bottler's operation and resale prices to the wholesaler. If the wholesaler faces a higher purchasing price from the manufacturer/bottler, the wholesaler could theoretically pass any additional costs on to the retailer who may in turn pass on the increase in price to the consumer. Alternatively, or additionally, O'Neill implies that the vertical acquisitions will increase the potential for interdependent pricing practices between PepsiCo and Coca-Cola. Presumably, O'Neill wishes the court to infer that such potential for interdependent pricing will result in price-fixing, yielding higher prices for the consumer. However, as the following discussion details, O'Neill fails to show that either of these paths to higher consumer prices are probable or proximately threaten her with antitrust injury.

If O'Neill seeks to show higher prices resulting from the elimination or reduction of any preexisting competition between the manufacturer and bottler, her approach fails in two manners. First, O'Neill is unable to show any indication that such elimination of any preexisting competition between bottlers and manufacturers will have any perceivable effect on price. It is not any more self-evident that the elimination of such competition will result in higher prices as opposed to lower prices. For example, the vertical acquisitions may just as likely lead to economies in scale that could reduce prices to consumers as they could theoretically lead to increased prices from manufacturers who now control the bottlers' resale price to wholesalers. O'Neill offers no proof that the elimination of competition will more likely lead to the detrimental consequence of higher prices as opposed to the beneficial consequence of lower prices.

Second, even if this court were to assume that higher prices would naturally result from the elimination of any preexisting competition between the manufacturers and the bottlers, O'Neill does not show that she purchases any of the products of either defendant in any of the areas serviced by the JTL, Beatrice, or MEI acquisitions. Even if this court were to assume that higher prices threatened a consumer serviced by these bottlers and that higher prices were proximately related to the vertical acquisitions, absent evidence that she resides in an area serviced by or regularly purchases from retailers receiving carbonated beverages from these bottlers, O'Neill cannot be considered to suffer any injury.

* * *

* * * O'Neill's implied claim that vertical acquisitions will result in interdependent pricing that will yield higher consumer prices is fatally speculative. O'Neill offers no indication that vertical acquisitions have any rational nexus to the potential for interdependent pricing practices between the defendants. Again, even if this court were to assume true that interdependent pricing was a natural consequence of such vertical acquisitions, O'Neill does not claim she purchases products from any of the retailers serviced by the acquired bottlers. What Coca-Cola and PepsiCo acquire within their respective vertical chains of production, distribution, and sales has no self-evident, logical relationship to how they may behave outside of their individual vertical chains toward each other and ultimately toward the consumer. Acquiring independent bottlers may have serious ramifications for other independent bottlers who do business with these defendants within their respective vertical markets. It does not, however, dictate how PepsiCo and Coca-Cola will behave toward each other or whether such acquisitions are more likely to lead to collusive pricing as opposed to predatory pricing. Pure speculation, or vaguely defined links are not sufficient to establish a chain of causation that demonstrates a threat of antitrust injury. Mere opinion or conclusory statements of what may happen when three bottlers are purchased by two dominant concentrate manufacturers are not sufficient to establish price-fixing as a threatened antitrust injury.

* * * Because O'Neill fails to assert any logical connection between vertical acquisitions and how they ultimately affect the regional or national pricing policies of PepsiCo and Coca-Cola, O'Neill is unable to establish that she is proximately threatened by an antitrust injury. As such, O'Neill is without standing and defendants' motions to dismiss Count I of the amended complaint are granted.

What fraction of which markets was foreclosed to whom by the acquisition of soft drink bottlers by the leading manufacturers of soft drink concentrate (Coke and Pepsi)?

During the mid-1980s, the FTC challenged two horizontal mergers among soft drink manufacturers (the concentrate firms, which owned the brands), blocking Coca-Cola's proposed acquisition of Dr Pepper and PepsiCo's proposed acquisition of Seven-Up. Around the same time, the FTC allowed Coke and Pepsi to buy up many of their bottlers without challenging those vertical transactions, and allowed consolidation among the so-called "third bottlers" that served Dr Pepper or Seven-Up rather than Coke or Pepsi, but challenged some horizontal bottler transactions between the Coke or Pepsi bottler and third bottlers. A study by FTC economists found, among other things, that the vertical integration which took place during the 1980s and 1990s tended to lower consumer prices in this industry. Harold Saltzman, Roy Levy & John C. Hilke, *Transformation and Continuity: The U.S. Carbonated Soft Drink Bottling Industry and Antitrust Policy Since 1980* (FTC Bureau of Economics Report Nov. 1999).

After the 1980s, the federal enforcement agencies demonstrated a renewed interest in vertical merger analysis. In part, this reflected the influence of modern thinking about exclusionary conduct under the "raising rivals' costs" framework we have discussed at the beginning of Chapter 4. As a methodology for vertical merger analysis, raising rivals costs can be understood as a more general description of the concern with two-level entry set forth in the 1984 Merger Guidelines. This new framework for analyzing vertical mergers was developed by Michael Riordan and Steven Salop. *See* Michael H. Riordan & Steven C. Salop, *Evaluating Vertical Mergers: A Post-Chicago Approach*, 63 ANTITRUST L.J. 513, 520–22 (1995). As with former Judge Robert Bork, Riordan & Salop undertake an economic analysis of vertical mergers, unconcerned with other goals that might have been important to the Supreme Court in 1972. *Compare* ROBERT H. BORK, THE ANTITRUST PARADOX 225–45 (1978).

During the 1990s, the federal enforcement agencies questioned some vertical mergers—small in absolute number or relative to the number of horizontal mergers subject to equally close scrutiny, but more than had generated enforcement attention during the previous decade. All were settled by consent. For example, the Justice Department's complaint against Lockheed Martin's acquisition of Northrop Grumman—which was abandoned by the parties after the government announced its challenge— was a vertical merger case. Lockheed Martin produced platforms for fighter aircraft and integrated the electronics systems for various military projects including ships, submarines and satellites. Northrop produced a number of electronic subsystems such as radar and sonar that were inputs into Lockheed's stage of production. Similarly, the FTC's investigation of Time Warner's acquisition of Turner Broadcasting did not just focus on the horizontal aspect of the deal arising out of the combination of the cable programming assets of the firms (Time Warner owned HBO; Turner owned CNN, Turner Classic Movies, and the WTBS cable superstation). The consent settlement also addressed vertical issues that arose because Time Warner operated cable systems covering 17 percent of cable households, which meant it was both a programming provider and a cable service provider.

The renewed federal enforcement attention to vertical mergers has continued. One notable example involved the acquisition by Comcast, a major cable system operator, of General Electric's NBC Universal programming assets, which included a number of broadcast and cable networks. The transaction was primarily vertical, but it also had a horizontal component because Comcast had some programming assets of its own. The Justice Department reached a consent settlement, and the Federal Communications Commission simultaneously issued an order permitting the transaction to proceed subject to conditions that tracked and augmented those required by the Justice Department. *See generally,* Jonathan B. Baker, *Comcast/NBCU: The FCC Provides a Roadmap for Vertical Merger Analysis*, ANTITRUST, Spring 2011, at 36 (describing the FCC as providing a contemporary model for vertical merger analysis). For a detailed discussion of vertical merger analysis that assimilates the modern economic learning and antitrust commentary on exclusionary conduct, see Steven C. Salop & Daniel P. Culley, *Revising the U.S. Vertical Merger Guidelines: Policy Issues and an Interim Guide for Practitioners*, 4 J. ANTITRUST ENFORCEMENT 1 (2016).

A modern economic analysis of the exclusionary effects of vertical merger would consider both input foreclosure and customer foreclosure. In either case, as with exclusionary conduct generally, it would be necessary to explain how the merger would give the merged firm an ability or incentive to exclude at least some rivals (actual or potential), why their exclusion would permit the merged firm to raise price (or harm competition on some other dimension), and why efficiency benefits from the vertical merger would not make the merger pro-competitive overall. Moreover, a vertical merger could allow the merged firm to employ both input foreclosure and customer foreclosure strategies.

Input foreclosure arises where the merger is likely to raise the costs of downstream rivals by restricting their access to an important input. The merged entity may do so by restricting access to the products that it otherwise would supply to its unaffiliated downstream rivals, thereby raising their costs. For example, a decision of the merged firm to restrict access to its inputs could reduce the competitive pressure exercised on remaining input suppliers, which may allow them to raise the input price they charge to nonintegrated downstream competitors. If rivals lack cost-effective substitutes, their costs will rise. Rivals' higher input costs may give the merged firm the ability and incentive to profitably increase its price to consumers. That may happen, for example, if the merged firm raises costs for all its downstream rivals; or if it targets a downstream maverick, allowing the remaining firms to coordinate more effectively. If downstream buyers lack effective substitutes, downstream prices will rise.

Customer foreclosure arises where the firm forecloses upstream rivals by restricting their access to a sufficient customer base, as by integrating with an important customer in the downstream market. If actual or potential rivals in the upstream market (the input market) lose access to a sufficient customer base, without the ability to reach customers cost-effectively in other ways, their ability or incentive to compete may be reduced. This in turn may raise downstream rivals' costs, as by making it harder for them to obtain input supplies at similar prices as absent the merger, or, by reducing their sales, lessening their ability to obtain scale economies. As a result, the excluded rivals may be led to compete less aggressively, as by reducing output or raising price, or even exiting altogether. If so, the merged entity may be able profitably to establish higher prices in the downstream market.

With respect to both input foreclosure and customer foreclosure, the excluded firms could be incumbents or potential entrants. The 1984 Merger Guidelines discussion of raising two-level entry barriers is concerned with the latter possibility.

With the modern economic understanding of exclusionary conduct set forth in Chapter 4 in mind, should the *O'Neill* court have allowed the plaintiff to obtain discovery on either an input foreclosure or customer foreclosure theory by which the merger could have harmed competition, as suggested below?

> (1) *Input foreclosure.* Coke and Pepsi could use the vertical acquisitions of bottlers to cut off or limit the access of rival soft drink concentrate manufacturers from access to the best (most efficient) bottlers. Or, even if the unaffiliated bottlers are not more efficient than the ones that Coke and Pepsi acquired, the unaffiliated bottlers might recognize that they no longer need fear competition from those affiliated with Coke and Pepsi when rival soft drink manufacturers are looking for bottlers, and, consequently, charge higher prices for bottling services. Either way, the merger would raise distribution costs for those rivals and create "two-level" entry barriers for potential entrants at the concentrate manufacturing level, thereby reducing the competition that Coke and Pepsi face and allowing Coke and Pepsi to raise the price of soft drinks sold at retail.

> (2) *Customer foreclosure.* The vertical mergers could lead Coke and Pepsi to shift their bottling business from those independent

bottlers they previously employed to bottlers affiliated with Coke and Pepsi. The unaffiliated bottlers could, in consequence, have higher costs (because they operate at lower scale) or even exit from the market, thereby raising the bottling and distribution costs facing fringe soft drink concentrate manufacturers. This would reduce the competition that Coke and Pepsi face, allowing them to raise the price of soft drinks sold at retail.

The 1984 Merger Guidelines point out that a vertical merger can harm competition by facilitating tacit or express coordination, not just through foreclosure. A vertical merger may do so, for example, by eliminating or impeding a maverick competitor, by increasing the degree of symmetry among competitors, by increasing the ability of coordinating firms to detect deviations and more effectively punishing companies that deviate from the coordinated outcome, or by eliminating disruptive buyers that significantly tempt such deviations. Does the *O'Neill* decision fully capture the following three ways that a vertical merger could facilitate coordination between Coke and Pepsi?

(3) *Facilitate coordination through the elimination of a disruptive buyer.* Coke and Pepsi could acquire bottlers that were instrumental in preventing them from successful tacit collusion in the sale of concentrate to bottlers. The result could be higher concentrate prices to bottlers.

(4) *Facilitate coordination through information exchange.* The vertical mergers could give Coke and Pepsi access to sensitive competitive information about each other obtained by buyers in the normal course of business (such as planned introduction of new products or reduced soft drink concentrate prices), thereby making it easier for the two to reach consensus on terms of coordination or to detect and police cheating. The result could be tacit collusion among soft drink concentrate manufacturers.

(5) *Facilitate coordination by impeding a maverick competitor.* The vertical mergers could give Coke and Pepsi the ability to raise bottling costs for manufacturers of rival brands such as RC cola and Seven-Up. If either of these firms is a "maverick" competitor in the soft drink market, the merger could reduce the maverick's incentive to limit coordination between Coke and Pepsi, leading to higher soft drink prices.

On the other hand, how could vertical integration in the soft drink bottling industry benefit competition? Are efficiency explanations for the vertical mergers more plausible than anticompetitive ones? Will the mergers reduce concentrate distribution costs, and make Coke and Pepsi lower cost competitors, as by (1) allowing the bottlers to achieve greater economies of scale? (2) assuring the manufacturers that they will have more reliable bottlers? (3) better aligning the incentives of the manufacturer and bottler, eliminating bottler free riding in promotion? (4) increasing investment incentives upstream or downstream?, (5) eliminating "double marginalization" (*see infra Note on Eliminating Double Marginalization*), or (6) enhancing the ability or incentive of the merged firm to innovate in bottle design or the bottling process?

How well do the 1984 Merger Guidelines capture the modern approach to vertical merger analysis? Should the agencies promulgate revised guidelines incorporating an updated analysis, as the European Union did in 2007? The pros and cons are discussed in Deborah L. Feinstein, *Are the Vertical Merger Guidelines Ripe for Revision?* ANTITRUST, Summer 2010, at 5.[33]

NOTE ON ELIMINATING DOUBLE MARGINALIZATION

One of the potential efficiency benefits of vertical integration comes from the elimination of double marginalization (or successive markups). To see why, suppose an upstream firm, say a television manufacturer, has a (marginal) cost of $70 and transfers its product to retailers at a wholesale price of $100. Suppose the retailers have (marginal) distribution costs of their own of $10, so their total cost is $110. With a cost of $110, the retailers' profit-maximizing decision is to add a further markup of $30 to generate a retail price of $140.

What would happen to the retail price if the upstream producer and downstream distributor merged? The merged firm no longer has to set a wholesale price. In selecting its retail price, it would recognize that its costs are $80 ($70 in manufacturing plus $10 in retailing), which is less than the cost of $110 that the stand-alone retailer faced. With a lower cost than the stand-alone retailer, the merged firm has an incentive to lower price below what the stand-alone retailer charged, say to $110, and in consequence to expand output.[34] Doing so simultaneously benefits consumers and increases

---

[33] In 2007, the European Commission adopted guidelines for non-horizontal mergers. See Guidelines on the Assessment of Non-Horizontal Mergers Under the Council Regulation on the Control of Concentrations Between Undertakings, http://ec.europa.eu/comm/competition/mergers/legislation/nonhorizontalguidelines.pdf. The European Guidelines take a modern approach to the analysis of exclusionary effects, distinguishing between input and customer foreclosure. They also recognize that for foreclosure to lead to consumer harm, it is not necessary that the rivals exit the market. The relevant benchmark instead is whether the merger would lead to higher prices for consumers. In addition, the Guidelines recognize that vertical mergers and mergers involving complementary products often are procompetitive because they can provide substantial scope for efficiencies, including better coordination of product design and the organization of the production process and incentives for lower prices from the elimination of "double-marginalization", discussed in the next Note.

[34] This example assumes that a firm with a marginal cost of 110 (the former retailer) maximizes profits by charging a price of 140. If it lowers price to 139, its gain (a price-cost margin of 29 on the next unit it sells) is slightly less than its loss (a reduction of 1 in the margin it earns on all other units sold, which means it was selling slightly more than 29 units). A firm with a marginal cost of 80 (the merged firm) will find it profitable to lower price: the cost (a lost margin of 1 on the first 29+ units sold) does not change but it recognizes that its gain from a small price

the merged firm's profits. Both are possible because buyers and the seller share in the efficiency gains that come from reducing the allocative efficiency loss. Although the merged firm continues to price in excess of the social cost of production and distribution, here $80, the retail price falls closer to the social cost, generating efficiencies that sellers and buyers can share.

It is possible that the firms could reach the same outcome through vertical contract, short of merger. The agreement would require the manufacturer to set a wholesale price of $70, its cost, leading the retailer to lower the price to consumers to the same lower level that the vertically integrated firm would charge. To make this deal profitable for the manufacturer, the retailer would need to pay the manufacturer a fixed sum (one that does not vary with the amount sold, and hence would not affect the retailer's marginal cost). The fixed sum would need to equal the lost manufacturer profits resulting from lowering the wholesale price plus a share of the increased profits that accrue from increasing output. This kind of contract is called a "two-part tariff" because the manufacturer and retailer negotiate both a (lower) wholesale price and a fixed "franchise fee." But it may be impractical for the manufacturer and retailer to negotiate such a complex contract, particularly when consumer demand is not stable or the retailers compete.

The efficiency benefits of eliminating double marginalization can appear in contexts beyond the manufacturer/retailer relationship, whenever complementary products are sold at separate markups. For example, if hotels buy lift tickets from a nearby ski resort and sell ski packages, and both the lodging and the lift tickets are sold above cost, a similar inefficiency results that could be eliminated by merger or contract.

―――――――――

Although the principal focus of agency and judicial scrutiny has been and is very likely to remain on horizontal mergers, it appears that vertical mergers that raise significant concerns will continue to arise, as well, particularly in industries facing significant competitive pressures to vertically integrate. Like horizontal mergers, however, vertical mergers will be analyzed primarily with reference to government guidelines, more recent lower court decisions, and economic commentary, as the influence of Supreme Court decisions from the structural era continues to wane.

―――――――――

cut is 59 (the sum of the previous wholesale margin (30) and previous retail margin (30) less the reduction in price (1)), which exceeds the cost of 29+. The example also supposes that it would be profitable for the merged firm to keep reducing price to 110, but no farther. The figure 110 was arbitrarily chosen to literally eliminate one of the two pre-merger margins (each 30); the actual retail price could be higher or lower, but must be below the pre-merger retail price of 140. (If the retail demand function has a constant demand elasticity, the pre-merger and post-merger markups will be the same in percentage terms; this would imply a post-merger retail price of $101.82.)

E. CONCLUSION

In this Chapter, we have seen how the courts and federal enforcement agencies analyze horizontal and vertical mergers. Horizontal merger analysis today is conducted within a traditional doctrinal framework that relies on a structural presumption of harm from high and increasing market concentration. But as that presumption has eroded over time, consistent with antitrust law's shift to focus on core economic concepts, a broader economic analysis, guided by the government's Horizontal Merger Guidelines, has become the rule in the federal enforcement agencies and the courts. Vertical merger analysis is not as well developed because the enforcement agencies have not litigated any vertical merger challenges in decades, but would likely also be subject to a broader analysis today than was undertaken in Supreme Court decisions from the 1960s and early 1970s.

F. PROBLEMS AND EXERCISES

Problem 5–1:
Spotless

Most American households have dishwashers. Four firms sell dishwashers for residential use in the U.S. Their names and shares of U.S. sales revenue are set forth in the following table.

Firm	Share
Whirly	60%
Spotless	20%
Dishwasher Corp. of America (DCA)	10%
Brite	10%

Spotless proposes to acquire DCA. If "residential dishwashers sold in the U.S." are an appropriate market, the proposed transaction would raise the HHI by 400 points to 4600.

Dishwashers are not sold directly by these manufacturers to homeowners or to the contractors that build houses or renovate kitchens. Rather they are sold through three kinds of distributors: national retail chains, local appliance stores, and wholesale building supply firms that sell to contractors. There are three national retail chains, dozens of building supply firms, and hundreds of appliance stores selling dishwashers in the U.S. The three national retail chains collectively account for half of all retail dishwasher sales.

The distributors are the direct customers of the dishwasher manufacturers: the manufacturers set the wholesale price, and the distributors pick the retail price. The manufacturers set wholesale list prices for sales to appliance stores, but negotiate a percentage discount off those standard prices in their distribution agreements with national retail chains and building supply firms. Wholesale price lists are distributed widely but wholesale discounts are not made public. The ultimate consumers are usually individual homeowners, or contractors building or renovating individual homes or apartments, but some of the contractors purchase in bulk for new subdivisions or apartment buildings.

Each firm sells a wide range of dishwasher models that vary in size, features, and price. To economize on floor space and inventory costs, the three national retail chains each carry only two manufacturers' product lines. Whirly products are offered by all three chains, Spotless by two chains, and Brite by one chain. Local appliance stores typically carry as many brands as wish to do business with them. The appliance stores display only a few of the models they sell. When a customer orders from an appliance store, the store arranges for the product to be shipped to it by manufacturer, and the store delivers the dishwasher to the customer. As a result, an appliance store customer typically receives its dishwasher several days after the appliance is purchased. Because the national chains keep their own inventory, they are able to offer next day delivery. But appliance stores typically offer a wider range of models, have more informed sales personnel, and provide better repair services than the national chains.

Whirly and Brite dishwashers are known for reliability and are premium-priced. Spotless's dishwashers also sell for premium prices. Spotless is known for introducing innovative features. For example, Spotless was the first to offer programmable dishwashers, water-saving dishwashers, reconfigurable racks, and other product improvements. DCA is known as the value brand, and its dishwashers typically sell at a discount relative to the prices of similar dishwashers produced by the other manufacturers. DCA markets its products mainly to contractors rather than consumers, and most of its sales are made through building supply wholesalers.

Executives from all four firms say that the dishwasher market is highly competitive. Marketing documents indicate that each firm pays close attention to the retail prices that its rivals' dishwashers sell for at the national chains and at appliance stores, and each makes estimates of rivals' wholesale prices based on fragmentary information they learn from their customers. Financial reports suggest that dishwashers sell at a high price-cost margin.

What are the most plausible coordinated and unilateral competitive effects theories that might be used in opposition to Spotless's proposed acquisition of DCA? What are the most plausible product and geographic market definitions? Assume that entry would not solve a competitive problem and that efficiencies would not defeat any competitive harm.

Problem 5–2:
Chic Shampoo

Chic Shampoo, Inc. is considering an acquisition of Stellar Shampoo Corp. Chic and Stellar are two of only six firms that sell shampoo in the U.S.

Each of the six firms in the shampoo industry sells one brand, except that both Chic and Stellar also sell an anti-dandruff variant. (Thus, Chic sells "Chic Regular" and "Chic Dandruff," but each rival other than Stellar sells only a regular shampoo.) Annual sales revenues by brand and firm are indicated in the following table:

Brand	Annual Revenue ($millions)
Chic Regular	$1.0
Chic Dandruff	1.0
Stellar Regular	1.0
Stellar Dandruff	1.0
Forest Regular	1.0
Newport Regular	1.0
Plymouth Regular	1.0
Sudbury Regular	3.0
Total (all brands)	$10.0

Shampoo brands differ in their chemical composition and on many dimensions apparent to consumers, such as like texture, color, scent, and lather. The regular shampoo products all clean hair equally well. Five of the six brands (all but Plymouth) have developed product images and reputations for quality through extensive national television and magazine advertising. Drug stores, supermarkets, and convenience stores will not stock any shampoo that lacks a national reputation. Plymouth differs from the others in that it is distributed through salons. All brands are offered for sale throughout the U.S., with similar market shares in all regions of the country. The leading national producer of soap and detergent, the

Sparkling division of Rainbow, a large consumer products company, says it could quickly and easily produce a high quality regular shampoo, but that its existing brand names may not convey an image appropriate for the sale of shampoo. Dandruff shampoo is more difficult to formulate and manufacture than regular shampoo, and only Chic and Stellar have been able to produce a high-quality anti-dandruff product.

According to Chic's CEO, the proposed merger of Chic and Stellar would help Chic in three main ways: by allowing Chic to use Stellar's high speed bottling equipment to lower the unit costs of producing additional units of the Chic product, by giving Chic the ability to obtain more and better shelf space from supermarkets than either company would get on its own, and by allowing Chic to consolidate duplicative management activities.

What are the most plausible coordinated and unilateral competitive effects theories that might be used in opposition to Chic's proposed acquisition of Stellar? What are the most plausible product and geographic market definitions? What arguments are Chic most likely to make in response to any government challenge?

How might your analysis change if Sudbury is a dandruff shampoo rather than a regular shampoo? What if regular shampoo manufacturers could easily formulate a dandruff shampoo (though Sparkling could not), but that successful marketing of a dandruff shampoo would require substantial advertising expenditures?

Problem 5–3:
Super Propane

Super Propane ("Super") is one of only five major marketers of propane in the State of Tazland. Propane is a chemical by-product of the extraction of natural gas, and is produced in Canada and some regions of the United States. It is thereafter transported by pipelines and tankers throughout North America, and sold to local or regional marketers, like Super. Super engages in the retailing and wholesaling of propane, as well as the sale of various products that use propane, such as propane heating equipment, cooking equipment, and forklifts.

Super proposes to acquire one of its rivals, GKBW Propane ("GKBW"). Like Super, GKBW retails and wholesales propane in Tazland, but it does not sell any propane-using products. GKBW also owns and operates a propane storage facility in Sun City, the capital of Tazland, that is the largest on the Eastern seaboard of the United States. The facility has the added advantage of being located at an access point to one of few supply pipelines that pass through Tazland. With direct pipeline access, GKBW avoids the additional costs associated with transporting propane from the pipeline to its storage facility, a cost that its rivals must incur. Obtaining direct pipeline access has become quite difficult for several reasons. First, physical access to the pipeline is limited, and is only available at two or three locations in Tazland. Second, building propane storage facilities requires local zoning and regulatory approvals that are only infrequently granted by local authorities.

In the last decade, two other wholesaler/retailers have succeeded in securing the approvals necessary to construct storage facilities. The approval process took 12–18 months in each case. The actual construction followed and was completed in both instances within twelve months after that. One of those wholesaler/retailers had previously operated solely in the neighboring State of Currland, and had never before sold propane in Tazland.

The combination of GKBW's direct access to the pipeline and significant storage capacity permit GKBW to alter its inventory substantially, which in turn allows it to "stock up" when prices are most favorable from its suppliers. It can then sell the propane through its retail and wholesale business as needed, frequently at a cost advantage over its rivals. It also permits GKBW to bid for long-term supply contracts that are currently beyond Super's reach due to its limited storage capacity and consequent dependence on spot market prices. To bid effectively on long-term contracts, a supplier must have predictable and adequate long-term sources of supply—something GKBW has and Super does not. At the present time, however, GKBW's storage facility is only operating at about 60% of its design capacity. At full capacity, propane costs could be even lower.

Super and GKBW currently account for 35% and 20% respectively of total propane sales in Tazland. Their two principal rivals account for 25% and 10%. Although their combination will mean they will account for 55% of total propane sales in Tazland, Super and GKBW contend that it will lower their joint operating costs, lower their joint production costs, allow for more complete utilization of GKBW's storage facility, and facilitate long-overdue reductions in their respective work forces. These combined effects, they argue, will better enable them jointly to bid for long-term contracts in Tazland as well as in several neighboring states.

What are the best arguments the State of Tazland could make to support its challenge of the proposed transaction? What is the likelihood that the challenge will succeed at least at the preliminary injunction stage?

CHAPTER 6

ANTICOMPETITIVE DISTRIBUTION PRACTICES

■ ■ ■

INTRODUCTION

We began our study of antitrust law in Chapter 1 by noting how conduct can usefully be classified based on the nature of its anticompetitive effect: collusive and exclusionary. Chapters 2 and 3 more closely examined how coordination by competitors may lead to collusive effects, whereas Chapter 4 explored the economics of exclusion, focusing largely on unilateral conduct by dominant firms.

As in Chapter 2, in this Chapter we will be looking mostly at examples of concerted action—agreements between two or more firms. Chapter 2, however, considered such agreements among or between competing firms, which traditionally have been referred to as "horizontal" restraints to emphasize the fact that the firms involved provide *substitute* products or services. This Chapter focuses on coordination between firms that do not directly compete, but that nevertheless choose to cooperate in order to bring a product or service to market. Typically, these firms perform distinct functions at different stages of a chain or channel of distribution. Coordination agreements between such firms traditionally have been referred to as "vertical" to emphasize the fact that they involve *complementary* products or services. Much of the case law addressed in this Chapter, therefore, is concerned with agreements between manufacturers and distributors or retailers, but the principles explored apply more generally to agreements between sellers of any complementary products. For example, these principles would likely apply to the review of a hypothetical agreement between Microsoft (personal computer operating system software) and Intel (central processing units), or one between Ford (an automaker) and an independent provider of automobile repair services.

Figure 6–1:
Horizontal and Vertical Relationships Compared

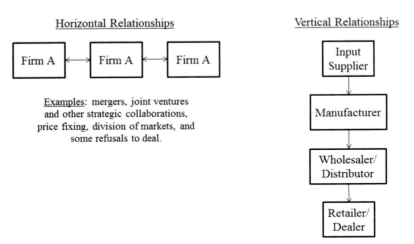

Horizontal Relationships

Vertical Relationships

Examples: mergers, joint ventures and other strategic collaborations, price fixing, division of markets, and some refusals to deal.

Examples: exclusive distributorships and dealerships, resale price maintenance, territorial and customer restrictions.

As was true of horizontal agreements and mergers, vertical restraints can have collusive or exclusionary anticompetitive effects, but traditionally they have not been grouped by type of effect. Instead, they have been divided into two principal categories based on the kind of competition they affect: "int*ra*brand" or "int*er*brand."

Intrabrand restraints affect competition between sellers of the same supplier or brand—such as rival Chevrolet automobile dealers, ExxonMobil gasoline stations, or Burger King franchises. Often, these single brand sellers are authorized to sell only from specified locations, or within a specific geographic area, which may tend to diminish competition between them. But as we will learn, restricting intrabrand competition can at the same time intensify interbrand competition—competition between rival sellers of *different* brands. Figure 6–2, for example, illustrates the use by a supplier of an exclusive distributor at the wholesale level and restricted territories at the dealer level. The supplier has elected to distribute its product exclusively through one wholesaler and only authorizes its dealers to sell in specified territories. Why might the supplier choose to structure its distribution network in this way? As we will learn, so long as interbrand competition is robust, these kinds of restrictions on intrabrand competition are unlikely to raise significant antitrust concerns and are generally viewed as benign or procompetitive.

Figure 6–2:
Vertical Intrabrand Restraints—Examples

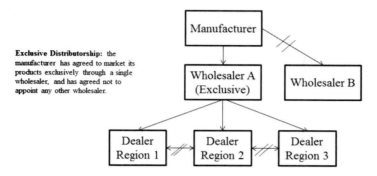

Exclusive Distributorship: the manufacturer has agreed to market its products exclusively through a single wholesaler, and has agreed not to appoint any other wholesaler.

Territorial Restrictions (with or without exclusive distributorships): Each dealer has agreed to concentrate its sales efforts within an assigned region (or group of customers), and each is prohibited from selling the wholesaler's products outside of that region to customers or another dealer. The wholesaler may appoint additional dealers in each region, depending upon whether it has also agreed to make each dealer an exclusive distributor. Restrictions might also apply to customers, products, or sales locations.

However, vertical intrabrand agreements are not always procompetitive or competitively neutral. They can be used by a group of competing dealers or manufacturers to help facilitate price coordination—*collusive* effects. They could also be used to facilitate efforts by a dominant dealer or a dominant manufacturer to exclude their respective rivals—*exclusionary* effects. Less clear today is whether a dominant manufacturer or supplier could use vertical intrabrand restraints to protect or enhance its own market power simply by reducing intrabrand competition, a possible *collusive* effect.

In contrast to intrabrand restraints, interbrand restraints limit competition between competing brands, such as Chevrolet and Ford, ExxonMobil and Shell, or Burger King and McDonald's. Often, the distributors or retailers that sell these kinds of single brands are prohibited by their suppliers from carrying competing brands, perhaps through "*exclusive dealing*" provisions in their dealer or franchise agreements. As a consequence, Ford dealers do not sell Chevrolet automobiles, Shell gasoline is not offered for sale at an ExxonMobil station, and a McDonald's franchise does not sell Burger King "Whoppers." Why might the supplier choose to structure its distribution network in this way? As is true of intrabrand restraints, we shall learn that interbrand restraints are often procompetitive or competitively neutral. But they can also raise concerns about anticompetitive *exclusion* that could lead to higher prices or other anticompetitive effects.

Exclusivity in distribution can take a variety of forms, some of which have been historically treated differently, even though they often share common economic characteristics. This can complicate the analysis of their legality under the antitrust laws. Another example is a practice labelled "tying," which requires a dealer or consumer to purchase a second, generally unwanted product or service (the "tied" product) as a condition of purchasing a desired item (the "tying" product). Examples could include a manufacturer of laser printers requiring that its customers purchase toner as a condition of sale of the printer, or a photocopier manufacturer only offering its photocopiers for sale on the condition that the customer purchase all of its photocopier paper from the manufacturer. Recall that in the *Microsoft* case, which we studied in Chapter 4, Microsoft integrated its Internet Explorer web browser into its Windows operating system, a practice that was viewed by some as tying.

Like exclusive dealing, tying can raise concerns about *exclusion* that can lead to higher prices or other anticompetitive harms. Most recently, enforcement attention has focused on the treatment of "conditional pricing practices," a label used to describe a variety of practices that involve the adjustment of prices by a supplier in return for some degree of exclusivity by its dealers.

Figure 6–3:
Vertical Interbrand Restraints—Examples

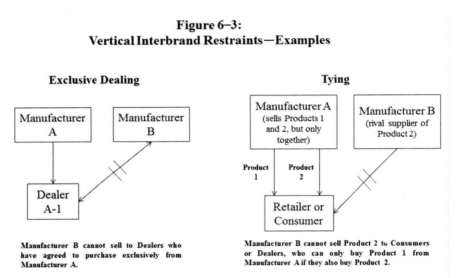

Addressing the competitive issues posed by these various types of arrangements demands a discriminating eye. First, as we have noted, they can take many forms. Indeed, they may not be obvious—they can be embedded within more detailed contractual arrangements and thus require interpretation. Also, vertical and horizontal restraints traditionally have been distinguished and analyzed under different legal standards. Third, once a restraint has been characterized as "vertical," assessing its economic effects can range from being a rather simple matter to being extremely complex. Intrabrand restraints rarely raise serious competitive concerns, but when they do those concerns can relate to collusive or exclusionary effects, or both, and may require careful analysis. Interbrand restraints also raise concerns about collusive or exclusionary effects and likewise can require thoughtful and detailed analysis to differentiate pro- from anticompetitive uses.

Further complexity can arise because of the scope of the Sherman and Clayton Acts. Vertical intrabrand restraints are generally addressed under Section 1 of the Sherman Act, whereas vertical interbrand restraints can be addressed under Section 1 and/or Section 3 of the Clayton Act, which has distinct standards of proof. Because interbrand restraints pose the threat of exclusionary effects, they can also be relevant to claims of monopolization or attempted monopolization under Section 2 of the Sherman Act, as we saw in the *Microsoft* case in Chapter 4. Finally, tying has historically been associated with per se analysis, whereas all others have always been judged under a more comprehensive rule of reason. As we shall see, however, there has been a sea change of attitudes about the antitrust treatment of vertical distribution restraints generally, and some, like tying, may remain in a state of transition.

Our exploration of vertical restraints in this Chapter moves beyond the traditional. As we look towards integrating our understanding of vertical restraints into the broader picture of modern antitrust, it is necessary to take from the cases an understanding of when and how vertical restraints can be efficient, and when they can lead to collusive or exclusionary anticompetitive effects. Antitrust lawyers advising clients today about their distribution practices are likely to be considering a variety of such restraints alone or in combination. To avoid any artificial separation based solely on tradition, therefore, we have combined consideration of all such restraints into this single Chapter.

It is important to realize at the outset that vertical restraints—both intra-and interbrand—are ubiquitous in the United States, owing in part to a pronounced trend in antitrust law towards increased acceptance of their economic utility. Vertical restraints can provide solutions for many of the practical problems that arise in the course of producing, distributing, and selling products and frequently present the parties to the restraint with a more flexible and cost effective alternative to vertical integration through expansion, merger, or acquisition. As in Chapters 2, 4 and 5, therefore, the principal challenge we face is to develop legal standards that can effectively distinguish between efficient and anticompetitive distribution strategies, examining their potential for collusive or exclusionary effects.

A. SINGLE BRAND PRICE AND NON-PRICE RESTRAINTS

1. HISTORICAL FOUNDATIONS AND DEVELOPMENT

The antitrust treatment of vertical intrabrand restraints has varied significantly over the past century. At times, such practices have faced very harsh treatment, even per se illegality. Today, by contrast, they are seen as largely benign and far more likely to promote than restrict competition. In this introductory note we outline some of the critical case developments that provide the historical foundation for the two modern pillars in this area, the Supreme Court's 1977 decision in *Sylvania* and its 2007 decision in *Leegin*, which follow.

Vertical restraint doctrine began to develop with the Supreme Court's 1911 decision in *Dr. Miles Medical Co. v. John D. Park & Sons Co.*, 220 U.S. 373 (1911), which addressed "minimum resale price maintenance," (RPM) whereby a manufacturer or supplier specifies the minimum price at which its product can be resold by a downstream firm. Although *Dr. Miles* did not itself use the "per se" label, the practice of minimum RPM was treated as per se unlawful just like price fixing by competitors after *Dr. Miles*—at least until the 1930s.

Although *Dr. Miles* likened minimum RPM to price fixing by competitors, its condemnation of minimum RPM was largely rooted in two other considerations. First, it followed from the Court's conclusion that the restraints were not "fairly necessary" to "the protection of the covenantee," and were therefore "unreasonable." Its reasoning thus echoed the ancillary restraint analysis developed in *Addyston Pipe* (*supra*, Chapter 2), which the Court cited in its opinion. The per se ban of minimum RPM, often referred to as the "rule of *Dr. Miles*," therefore, derived from the absence of any underlying legitimate purpose, rather than from a conclusion about likely competitive effects. The Court also referred to traditional principles of property law, relying upon the common law's prohibition of general restraints on alienation—once a supplier parted title with its goods, it could no longer restrict the purchaser's "right" to dispose of it on its own terms. The Court's approach prompted Justice Oliver Wendell Holmes' dissent, in which he took the majority to task for failing to focus on the competitive impact of RPM. Hinting at a possible justification that the majority failed to credit, he criticized the Court for protecting "knaves" (discounting dealers) who would be free to cut retail prices even if the manufacturer or supplier would prefer otherwise.

To the extent the Court provided any competition-related rationale for using a per se rule in such cases, it suggested that RPM could be used to facilitate either a dealer-organized or manufacturer-organized cartel. In today's economic terms, explored in Chapter 3, RPM could be used to help solve cartel problems of reaching consensus and detecting cheating, either among dealers or among manufacturers, most importantly because it makes it easier for industry participants to coordinate and reach a consensus to set retail prices and to identify price-cutting (cheating).

The seeds of the contemporary debate over the scope and wisdom of *Dr. Miles's* per se rule were sown soon afterward. Eight years after *Dr. Miles*, the Supreme Court generated a tension in the case law when it held in *United States v. Colgate & Co.*, 250 U.S. 300 (1919) that a firm was free to impose minimum RPM on its distributors or retailers "unilaterally," provided it was not a monopolist:

> The purpose of the Sherman Act is to prohibit monopolies, contracts and combinations which probably would unduly interfere with the free exercise of their rights by those engaged, or who wish to engage, in trade or commerce—in a word to preserve the right of freedom of trade. In the absence of any purpose to create or maintain a monopoly, the act does not restrict the long recognized right of trader or manufacturer engaged in an entirely private business, freely to exercise his own independent discretion as to parties with whom he will deal; and, of course, he may announce in advance the circumstances under which he will refuse to sell. * * *

Id. at 307. The Court's conclusion was grounded in two factors: Section 1's requirement of "agreement" and a presumption of manufacturer "freedom of contract," similar to the property rights concepts at work in *Dr. Miles.* The "*Colgate* Doctrine," as it later became known, led RPM litigation to focus on the first element of a Section 1 Sherman Act charge based on RPM—evidence of agreement—usually between a manufacturer or supplier and its dealer. RPM was illegal per se, but a manufacturer could accomplish a similar end by avoiding an "agreement." It could in theory do so by "announcing" that it would not sell to price-cutting dealers, selling its products, and then terminating its relationship with discounters. This in effect was viewed as "*unilateral* resale price maintenance," outside the scope of Sherman Act Section 1. But *Colgate* did not delve deeply into the question of how much and what kind of evidence of supplier coercion and dealer accession is necessary to establish proof of agreement.

Bolstered by the Court's later harsh pronouncements on price fixing generally, as in horizontal cases like *Trenton Potteries*, the per se prohibition on RPM established by *Dr. Miles* remained the law until the late 1930s. But, in response to the economic strain of the Great Depression, many believed that permitting firms to place a floor under resale prices would help to stabilize the economy by providing a remedy for rapid deflation. It was also believed that enforceable price floors would help small businesses in their struggle to compete with large discounting retailers, who were just starting to emerge. As a consequence, Congress passed the Miller-Tydings Fair Trade Amendments in 1937, ch. 690, 50 Stat. 693 (1937), which authorized states, in their own discretion, to establish "fair trade" pricing, *i.e.*, RPM agreements, on an industry by industry basis.

In response to the Supreme Court's narrow reading of Miller-Tydings in *Schwegmann Bros. v. Calvert Distillers Corp.*, 341 U.S. 384 (1951), Congress broadened the states' authority to authorize RPM in the McGuire Act of 1952, ch. 745, 66 Stat. 632 (1952). The combination of the Miller-Tydings Amendment and the McGuire Act significantly limited the impact of *Dr. Miles* through the mid-1970s. In 1975, however, Congress restored the per se ban on RPM from *Dr. Miles* when it repealed Miller-Tydings and the McGuire Act in the Consumer Goods Pricing Act, Pub. L. No. 94–145, 89 Stat. 80 (1975). In the interim, the Supreme Court had extended per se analysis to cover vertical intrabrand *non*-price restraints in *United States v. Arnold, Schwinn & Co.*, 388 U.S. 365 (1967) and to *maximum* RPM in *Albrecht v. Herald Co.*, 390 U.S. 145 (1968). As we shall see when we read the Court's 1977 *Sylvania* decision, the Court would later observe that *Schwinn* represented something of an unexplained departure from earlier Supreme Court treatments of vertical non-price agreements, particularly *White Motor Co. v. United States*, 372 U.S. 253 (1963), which had applied a rule of reason analysis. But *Schwinn* was consistent with the Court's increased reliance on per se analysis from 1940 to 1972.

Almost immediately after *Dr. Miles* was fully restored in 1975, however, a second tension developed in the law. Whereas *Dr. Miles* and *Colgate* led to a "unilateral-concerted" axis of tension that placed a premium on the importance of evidence of "agreement" in analyzing vertical conduct, the Supreme Court's 1977 decision in *Continental T.V., Inc. v. GTE Sylvania Inc.*, 433 U.S. 36 (1977), our next principle case, added another tension by treating vertical non-price agreements differently from vertical price agreements. The tension created by a difference in the legal rule governing vertical agreements that depended on whether the agreement concerned price persisted for thirty years until it was resolved in *Leegin*, which we will read after *Sylvania*.

2. ABANDONING PER SE ANALYSIS: *SYLVANIA* AND *LEEGIN*

Sylvania involved a challenge to the provisions of a consumer electronics manufacturer's dealer agreements that limited the locations from which its dealers were authorized to resell its televisions. Location restraints are *non*-price restrictions, a variant of exclusive territories such as those at issue in cases like *Schwinn*. As we have noted, by 1977, when *Sylvania* came before the Court, virtually all vertical intrabrand restraints were treated as per se unlawful under *Dr. Miles*, *Albrecht*, and *Schwinn*, and as we discussed in Chapter 2, horizontal territorial allocations had been declared per se unlawful in *Topco* (1972). To abandon the per se rule for vertical intrabrand non-price restraints, therefore, the Court in *Sylvania* had to distinguish vertical from horizontal agreements to allocate territories (*i.e.,* distinguish *Sylvania* from *Topco*), and vertical agreements involving non-price from price restraints (*i.e.,* distinguish *Sylvania* from *Dr. Miles*). It also had to decide whether *Schwinn* should be reaffirmed, distinguished, or overruled.

As you read the case, focus on how those distinctions were made. Are the Court's reasons for abandoning per se analysis of vertical intrabrand non-price restraints persuasive? Are they economic? Are they legal? If they are persuasive, are the reasons for distinguishing vertical non-price from vertical price and horizontal territorial allocations also persuasive? Finally, consider the implications of *Sylvania* for cases like *Dr. Miles* and *Topco*—did it undermine the rationale for maintaining their per se approach?

CONTINENTAL T.V., INC. v. GTE SYLVANIA INCORPORATED

United States Supreme Court, 1977.
433 U.S. 36, 97 S.Ct. 2549, 53 L.Ed.2d 568.

MR. JUSTICE POWELL delivered the opinion of the Court.

Franchise agreements between manufacturers and retailers frequently include provisions barring the retailers from selling franchised products from locations other than those specified in the agreements. This case presents important questions concerning the appropriate antitrust analysis of these restrictions under § 1 of the Sherman Act and the Court's decision in *United States v. Arnold, Schwinn & Co.*, 388 U.S. 365 (1967).

I

Respondent GTE Sylvania Inc. (Sylvania) manufactures and sells television sets. * * * Prior to 1962, like most other television manufacturers, Sylvania sold its televisions to independent or company-owned distributors who in turn resold to a large and diverse group of retailers. Prompted by a decline in its market share to a relatively insignificant 1% to 2% of national television sales,[1] Sylvania conducted an intensive reassessment of its marketing strategy, and in 1962 adopted the franchise plan challenged here. Sylvania phased out its wholesale distributors and began to sell its televisions directly to a smaller and more select group of franchised retailers. An acknowledged purpose of the change was to decrease the number of competing Sylvania retailers in the hope of attracting the more aggressive and competent retailers thought necessary to the improvement of the company's market position. To this

---

[1]   RCA at that time was the dominant firm with as much as 60% to 70% of national television sales in an industry with more than 100 manufacturers.

end, Sylvania limited the number of franchises granted for any given area and required each franchisee to sell his Sylvania products only from the location or locations at which he was franchised. * * * The revised marketing strategy appears to have been successful during the period at issue here, for by 1965 Sylvania's share of national television sales had increased to approximately 5%, and the company ranked as the Nation's eighth largest manufacturer of color television sets.

This suit is the result of the rupture of a franchiser-franchisee relationship that had previously prospered under the revised Sylvania plan. Dissatisfied with its sales in the city of San Francisco,[4] Sylvania decided in the spring of 1965 to franchise Young Brothers, an established San Francisco retailer of televisions, as an additional San Francisco retailer. The proposed location of the new franchise was approximately a mile from a retail outlet operated by petitioner Continental T. V., Inc. (Continental), one of the most successful Sylvania franchisees. Continental protested that the location of the new franchise violated Sylvania's marketing policy, but Sylvania persisted in its plans. Continental then canceled a large Sylvania order and placed a large order with Phillips, one of Sylvania's competitors.

During this same period, Continental expressed a desire to open a store in Sacramento, Cal., a desire Sylvania attributed at least in part to Continental's displeasure over the Young Brothers decision. Sylvania believed that the Sacramento market was adequately served by the existing Sylvania retailers and denied the request.[6] In the face of this denial, Continental advised Sylvania in early September 1965, that it was in the process of moving Sylvania merchandise from its San Jose, Cal., warehouse to a new retail location that it had leased in Sacramento. Two weeks later, allegedly for unrelated reasons, Sylvania's credit department reduced Continental's credit line from $300,000 to $50,000. In response to the reduction in credit and the generally deteriorating relations with Sylvania, Continental withheld all payments owed to * * * Sylvania. * * * Shortly thereafter, Sylvania terminated Continental's franchises. * * *

The antitrust issues before us originated in cross-claims brought by Continental against Sylvania. * * * Most important for our purposes was the claim that Sylvania had violated § 1 of the Sherman Act by entering into and enforcing franchise agreements that prohibited the sale of Sylvania products other than from specified locations.[8] At the close of evidence in the jury trial of Continental's claims, Sylvania requested the

---

[4] Sylvania's market share in San Francisco was approximately 2.5%, half its national and northern California average.

[6] Sylvania had achieved exceptional results in Sacramento, where its market share exceeded 15% in 1965.

[8] Although Sylvania contended in the District Court that its policy was unilaterally enforced, it now concedes that its location restriction involved understandings or agreements with the retailers.

District Court to instruct the jury that its location restriction was illegal only if it unreasonably restrained or suppressed competition. Relying on this Court's decision in *United States v. Arnold, Schwinn & Co.* * * * the District Court rejected the proffered instruction.* * *

In answers to special interrogatories, the jury found that Sylvania had engaged "in a contract, combination or conspiracy in restraint of trade in violation of the antitrust laws with respect to location restrictions alone," and assessed Continental's damages at $591,505, which was trebled pursuant to 15 U.S.C. § 15 to produce an award of $1,774,515.

On appeal, the Court of Appeals for the Ninth Circuit, sitting en banc, reversed by a divided vote. The court acknowledged that there is language in *Schwinn* that could be read to support the District Court's instruction but concluded that *Schwinn* was distinguishable on several grounds.* * *

We granted Continental's petition for certiorari to resolve this important question of antitrust law. * * *

II

We turn first to Continental's contention that Sylvania's restriction on retail locations is a *per se* violation of § 1 of the Sherman Act as interpreted in *Schwinn*. The restrictions at issue in *Schwinn* were part of a three-tier distribution system comprising, in addition to Arnold, Schwinn & Co. (Schwinn), 22 intermediate distributors and a network of franchised retailers. Each distributor had a defined geographic area in which it had the exclusive right to supply franchised retailers. Sales to the public were made only through franchised retailers, who were authorized to sell Schwinn bicycles only from specified locations. In support of this limitation, Schwinn prohibited both distributors and retailers from selling Schwinn bicycles to nonfranchised retailers. At the retail level, therefore, Schwinn was able to control the number of retailers of its bicycles in any given area according to its view of the needs of that market.

* * *

Schwinn came to this Court on appeal by the United States from the District Court's decision. Abandoning its per se theories, the Government argued that Schwinn's prohibition against distributors' and retailers' selling Schwinn bicycles to nonfranchised retailers was unreasonable under § 1. * * *

The Court acknowledged the Government's abandonment of its *per se* theories and stated that the resolution of the case would require an examination of "the specifics of the challenged practices and their impact upon the marketplace in order to make a judgment as to whether the restraint is or is not 'reasonable' in the special sense in which § 1 of the Sherman Act must be read for purposes of this type of inquiry." Despite this description of its task, the Court proceeded to articulate the following "bright line" *per se* rule of illegality for vertical restrictions: "Under the Sherman Act, it is unreasonable without more for a manufacturer to seek to restrict and confine areas or persons with whom an article may be traded after the manufacturer has parted with dominion over it." * * *

* * *

In the present case * * * the *Schwinn per se* rule applies unless Sylvania's restriction on locations falls outside Schwinn's prohibition against a manufacturer's attempting to restrict a "retailer's freedom as to where and to whom it will resell the products." As the Court of Appeals conceded, the language of *Schwinn* is clearly broad enough to apply to the present case. Unlike the Court of Appeals, however, we are unable to find a principled basis for distinguishing *Schwinn* from the case now before us.

Both Schwinn and Sylvania sought to reduce but not to eliminate competition among their respective retailers through the adoption of a franchise system. * * * [The location] restrictions [adopted by both] allowed Schwinn and Sylvania to regulate the amount of competition among their retailers by preventing a franchisee from selling franchised products from outlets other than the one covered by the franchise agreement. To exactly the same end, the Schwinn franchise plan included a companion restriction, apparently not found in the Sylvania plan, that prohibited franchised retailers from selling Schwinn products to nonfranchised retailers. In *Schwinn* the Court expressly held that this restriction was impermissible under the broad principle stated there. In intent and competitive impact, the retail-customer restriction in *Schwinn* is indistinguishable from the location restriction in the present case. In both cases the restrictions limited the freedom of the retailer to dispose of the purchased products as he desired. The fact that one restriction was addressed to territory and the other to customers is irrelevant to functional anti-trust analysis, and indeed, to the language and broad thrust of the opinion in *Schwinn*. * * *

III

Sylvania argues that if *Schwinn* cannot be distinguished, it should be reconsidered. Although *Schwinn* is supported by the principle of *stare decisis*, we are convinced that the need for clarification of the law in this area justifies reconsideration. *Schwinn* itself was an abrupt and largely unexplained departure from *White Motor Co. v. United States*, 372 U.S. 253 (1963), where only four years earlier the Court had refused to endorse a *per se* rule for vertical restrictions. Since its announcement, *Schwinn* has been the subject of continuing controversy and confusion, both in the scholarly journals and in the federal courts. The great weight of scholarly opinion has been critical of the decision, and a number of the federal courts confronted with analogous vertical restrictions have sought to limit its reach.[14] In our view, the experience of the past 10 years should be brought to bear on this subject of considerable commercial importance.

The traditional framework of analysis under § 1 of the Sherman Act is familiar and does not require extended discussion. Section 1 prohibits "[e]very contract, combination . . . , or conspiracy, in restraint of trade or commerce." Since the early years of this century a judicial gloss on this statutory language has established the "rule of reason" as the prevailing standard of analysis. Under this rule, the factfinder weighs all of the circumstances of a case in deciding whether a restrictive practice should be prohibited as imposing an unreasonable restraint on competition. *Per se* rules of illegality are appropriate only when they relate to conduct that is manifestly anticompetitive. As the Court explained in *Northern Pac. R. Co. v. United States*, 356 U.S. 1, 5 (1958), "there are certain agreements or practices which because of their pernicious effect on competition and lack of any redeeming virtue are conclusively presumed to be unreasonable and therefore illegal without elaborate inquiry as to the precise harm they have caused or the business excuse for their use."[16]

In essence, the issue before us is whether *Schwinn's* per se rule can be justified under the demanding standards of *Northern Pac.* * * * The Court's refusal to endorse a per se rule in *White Motor Co.* was based on its uncertainty as to whether vertical restrictions satisfied those standards. * * *

The market impact of vertical restrictions[18] is complex because of their potential for a simultaneous reduction of intrabrand competition and

---

[14] Indeed, as one commentator has observed, many courts "have struggled to distinguish or limit *Schwinn* in ways that are a tribute to judicial ingenuity." * * *

[16] *Per se* rules thus require the Court to make broad generalizations about the social utility of particular commercial practices. The probability that anticompetitive consequences will result from a practice and the severity of those consequences must be balanced against its pro-competitive consequences. Cases that do not fit the generalization may arise, but a *per se* rule reflects the judgment that such cases are not sufficiently common or important to justify the time and expense necessary to identify them. Once established, *per se* rules tend to provide guidance to the business community and to minimize the burdens on litigants and the judicial system of the more complex rule-of-reason trials but those advantages are not sufficient in themselves to justify the creation of *per se* rules. If it were otherwise, all of antitrust law would be reduced to *per se* rules, thus introducing an unintended and undesirable rigidity in the law.

[18] As in *Schwinn*, we are concerned here only with nonprice vertical restrictions. The *per se* illegality of price restrictions has been established firmly for many years and involves significantly different questions of analysis and policy. * * * [S]ome commentators have argued that the manufacture's motivation for imposing vertical price restrictions may be the same as for nonprice restrictions. There are, however, significant differences that could easily justify different treatment. * * * [U]nlike nonprice restrictions, "[r]esale price maintenance is not only designed to, but almost invariably does in fact, reduce price competition not only *among* sellers of the affected product, but quite as much *between* that product and competing brands." * * * Professor Posner also recognized that "industry-wide resale price maintenance might facilitate cartelizing." * * * Furthermore, Congress recently has expressed its approval of a *per se* analysis of vertical price restrictions by repealing those provisions of the Miller-Tydings and McGuire Acts allowing fair trade pricing at the option of the individual States. Consumer Goods Pricing Act of 1975, 89 Stat.

stimulation of interbrand competition.[19] Significantly, the Court in *Schwinn* did not distinguish among the challenged restrictions on the basis of their individual potential for intrabrand harm or interbrand benefit. Restrictions that completely eliminated intrabrand competition among Schwinn distributors were analyzed no differently from those that merely moderated intrabrand competition among retailers. The pivotal factor was the passage of title: All restrictions were held to be per se illegal where title had passed, and all were evaluated and sustained under the rule of reason where it had not. The location restriction at issue here would be subject to the same pattern of analysis under *Schwinn*.

It appears that this distinction between sale and nonsale transactions resulted from the Court's effort to accommodate perceived intrabrand harm and interbrand benefit of vertical restrictions. The *per se* rule for sale transactions reflected the view that vertical restrictions are "so obviously destructive" to intrabrand competition that their use would "open the door to exclusivity of outlets and limitation of territory further than prudence permits."[21] Conversely, the continued adherence to the traditional rule of reason for nonsale transactions reflected the view that the restrictions have too great a potential for promotion of interbrand competition to justify complete prohibition. The Court's opinion provides no analytical support for these contrasting positions. Nor is there even an assertion in the opinion that the competitive impact of vertical restrictions is significantly affected by the form of the transaction. Non-sale transactions appear to be excluded from the *per se* rule, not because of a greater danger of intrabrand harm or a greater promise of interbrand benefit, but rather because of the

---

801, amending 15 U.S.C. §§ 1, 45(a). No similar expression of congressional intent exists for nonprice restrictions.

[19] Interbrand competition is the competition among the manufacturers of the same generic product, television sets in this case, and is the primary concern of antitrust law. The extreme example of a deficiency of interbrand competition is monopoly, where there is only one manufacturer. In contrast, intrabrand competition is the competition between the distributors, wholesale or retail, of the product of a particular manufacturer.

The degree of intrabrand competition is wholly independent of the level of interbrand competition confronting the manufacturer. Thus, there may be fierce intrabrand competition among the distributors of a product produced by a monopolist and no intrabrand competition among the distributors of a product produced by a firm in a highly competitive industry. But when interbrand competition exists, as it does among television manufacturers, it provides a significant check on the exploitation of intrabrand market power because of the ability of consumers to substitute a different brand of the same product.

[21] The Court also stated that to impose vertical restrictions in sale transactions would "violate the ancient rule against restraints on alienation." The isolated reference has provoked sharp criticism from virtually all of the commentators on the decision, most of whom have regarded the Court's apparent reliance on the "ancient rule" as both a misreading of legal history and a perversion of antitrust analysis. We quite agree with Mr. Justice Stewart's dissenting comment in *Schwinn* that "the state of the common law 400 or even 100 years ago is irrelevant to the issue before us: the effect of the antitrust laws upon vertical distributional restraints in the American economy today." * * * Competitive economies have social and political as well as economic advantages, but an antitrust policy divorced from market considerations would lack any objective benchmarks. * * *

Court's unexplained belief that a complete *per se* prohibition would be too "inflexibl[e]."

Vertical restrictions reduce intrabrand competition by limiting the number of sellers of a particular product competing for the business of a given group of buyers. Location restrictions have this effect because of practical constraints on the effective marketing area of retail outlets. Although intrabrand competition may be reduced, the ability of retailers to exploit the resulting market may be limited both by the ability of consumers to travel to other franchised locations and, perhaps more importantly, to purchase the competing products of other manufacturers. None of these key variables, however, is affected by the form of the transaction by which a manufacturer conveys his products to the retailers.

Vertical restrictions promote interbrand competition by allowing the manufacturer to achieve certain efficiencies in the distribution of his products. These "redeeming virtues" are implicit in every decision sustaining vertical restrictions under the rule of reason. Economists have identified a number of ways in which manufacturers can use such restrictions to compete more effectively against other manufacturers.[23] For example, new manufacturers and manufacturers entering new markets can use the restrictions in order to induce competent and aggressive retailers to make the kind of investment of capital and labor that is often required in the distribution of products unknown to the consumer. Established manufacturers can use them to induce retailers to engage in promotional activities or to provide service and repair facilities necessary to the efficient marketing of their products. Service and repair are vital for many products, such as automobiles and major household appliances. The availability and quality of such services affect a manufacturer's goodwill and the competitiveness of his product. Because of market imperfections such as the so-called "free rider" effect, these services might not be provided by retailers in a purely competitive situation, despite the fact that each retailer's benefit would be greater if all provided the services than if none did.

Economists also have argued that manufacturers have an economic interest in maintaining as much intrabrand competition as is consistent with the efficient distribution of their products. Although the view that the manufacturer's interest necessarily corresponds with that of the public is not universally shared, even the leading critic of vertical restrictions concedes that *Schwinn's* distinction between sale and nonsale transactions is essentially unrelated to any relevant economic impact. Indeed, to the

---

[23] Marketing efficiency is not the only legitimate reason for a manufacturer's desire to exert control over the manner in which his products are sold and serviced. As a result of statutory and common-law developments, society increasingly demands that manufacturers assume direct responsibility for the safety and quality of their products. * * *

extent that the form of the transaction is related to interbrand benefits, the Court's distinction is inconsistent with its articulated concern for the ability of smaller firms to compete effectively with larger ones. Capital requirements and administrative expenses may prevent smaller firms from using the exception for nonsale transactions.[24] Although the view that the manufacturer's interest necessarily corresponds with that of the public is not universally shared, even the leading critic of vertical restrictions concedes that *Schwinn's* distinction between sale and nonsale transactions is essentially unrelated to any relevant economic impact. Indeed, to the extent that the form of the transaction is related to interbrand benefits, the Court's distinction is inconsistent with its articulated concern for the ability of smaller firms to compete effectively with larger ones. Capital requirements and administrative expenses may prevent smaller firms from using the exception for nonsale transactions.[26]

We conclude that the distinction drawn in *Schwinn* between sale and nonsale transactions is not sufficient to justify the application of a *per se* rule in one situation and a rule of reason in the other. The question remains whether the *per se* rule stated in *Schwinn* should be expanded to include non-sale transactions or abandoned in favor of a return to the rule of reason. We have found no persuasive support for expanding the *per se* rule.
* * *

We revert to the standard articulated in *Northern Pac. R. Co.*, and reiterated in *White Motor*, for determining whether vertical restrictions must be "conclusively presumed to be unreasonable and therefore illegal without elaborate inquiry as to the precise harm they have caused or the business excuse for their use." Such restrictions, in varying forms, are widely used in our free market economy. As indicated above, there is substantial scholarly and judicial authority supporting their economic utility. There is relatively little authority to the contrary. Certainly, there has been no showing in this case, either generally or with respect to Sylvania's agreements, that vertical restrictions have or are likely to have a "pernicious effect on competition" or that they "lack . . . any redeeming virtue."[29] Accordingly, we conclude that the *per se* rule stated in *Schwinn*

---

[24] "Generally a manufacturer would prefer the lowest retail price possible, once its price to dealers has been set, because a lower retail price means increased sales and higher manufacturer revenues." Note, 88 HARV. L. REV. 636, 641 (1975). In this context, a manufacturer is likely to view the difference between the price at which it sells to its retailers and their price to the consumer as his "cost of distribution," which it would prefer to minimize.

[26] We also note that *per se* rules in this area may work to the ultimate detriment of the small businessmen who operate as franchisees. To the extent that a *per se* rule prevents a firm from using the franchise system to achieve efficiencies that it perceives as important to its successful operation, the rule creates an incentive for vertical integration into the distribution system, thereby eliminating to that extent the role of independent businessmen.

[29] The location restriction used by Sylvania was neither the least nor the most restrictive provision that it could have used. But we agree with the implicit judgment in *Schwinn* that a per se rule based on the nature of the restriction is, in general, undesirable. Although distinctions can

must be overruled. In so holding we do not foreclose the possibility that particular applications of vertical restrictions might justify *per se* prohibition under *Northern Pac. R. Co.* But we do make clear that departure from the rule-of-reason standard must be based upon demonstrable economic effect rather than—as in *Schwinn*—upon formalistic line drawing.

* * * When anticompetitive effects are shown to result from particular vertical restrictions they can be adequately policed under the rule of reason, the standard traditionally applied for the majority of anticompetitive practices challenged under § 1 of the Act. * * *

[JUSTICE REHNQUIST did not take part in the consideration or decision of the case. JUSTICE WHITE's concurring opinion is omitted. Eds.]

Sylvania's significance cannot be over-emphasized. On its most narrow terms, *Sylvania* initiated a major change of course for the law of vertical restraints, overruling *Schwinn* and with it per se treatment of vertical, intrabrand, non-price restraints. Moreover, the Supreme Court embraced the proposition that interbrand competition was the "primary concern of antitrust law" (footnote 19) and asserted that "an antitrust policy divorced from market considerations would lack any objective benchmarks" (footnote 21). That represented a remarkable turnabout from the position taken by the Court just five years earlier in *Topco*, where the majority refused in the horizontal context to "ramble through the wilds of economic theory" by entertaining the assertion that reductions in intrabrand competition might be reasonable if they benefitted interbrand competition. (*See supra* Chapter 2).

The decision also ushered in a period of far more lenient treatment of distribution restraints that provided suppliers with significantly greater discretion in structuring their distribution practices. It also endorsed the view that manufacturer's and consumer interests are generally aligned when it comes to maximizing the efficiency of distribution systems. What factors did it find so persuasive? And how might those factors guide firms considering the use of vertical restraints? Consider Figure 6–4.

---

be drawn among the frequently used restrictions, we are inclined to view them as differences of degree and form. We are unable to perceive significant social gain from channeling transactions into one form or another. Finally, we agree with the Court in *Schwinn* that the advantages of vertical restrictions should not be limited to the categories of new entrants and failing firms. Sylvania was faltering, if not failing, and we think it would be unduly artificial to deny it the use of valuable competitive tools.

Figure 6–4:

Justifications for Vertical Non-Price Intrabrand Restrictions Recognized in *Sylvania*

- Induce competent retailers to carry new products

- Induce retailers to promote existing products

- Defeat market imperfections, such as free riding

- Insulate manufacturer from product liability exposure by ensuring safety

- Protect manufacturer's reputation by assuring quality

More broadly, despite fifty years of almost uninterrupted expansion in its reliance on per se analysis, the *Sylvania* Court declared that the rule of reason was "the rule," and that per se analysis was "the exception" under Section 1 of the Sherman Act. "Departure from the rule of reason," it declared, could only be justified by "demonstrable economic effects." In doing so, it implicitly rejected reliance on non-economic goals as a guide to antitrust analysis, especially the kinds of concerns for protecting property rights and dealer autonomy that had animated *Schwinn*, *Colgate*, and *Dr. Miles*. Justice White took note of this change of direction in his concurring opinion:

> After summarily rejecting this concern, reflected in our interpretations of the Sherman Act, for "the autonomy of independent businessmen," [*Sylvania, supra*, at n.21], the majority not surprisingly finds "no justification" for *Schwinn's* distinction between sale and nonsale transactions because the distinction is "essentially unrelated to any relevant economic impact." But while according some weight to the businessman's interest in controlling the terms on which he trades in his own goods may be anathema to those who view the Sherman Act as directed solely to economic efficiency, this principle is without question more deeply embedded in our cases than the notions of "free rider" effects and distributional efficiencies borrowed by the majority from the "new economics of vertical relationships."

Sylvania, 433 U.S. at 68–69 (WHITE, J., concurring).

Sylvania's seemingly abrupt turn towards more economic analysis, particularly the preservation and promotion of economically efficient business practices, ushered in a period of rapid evolution for all antitrust doctrine. Thereafter, the Court systematically revisited its reliance on per se analysis in a number of cases decided in the previous fifty years, and increasingly turned to modern economic theory to inform its interpretation and application of the Sherman Act. The trend was evident two years after *Sylvania* in *Broadcast Music* (1979) (*See supra* Chapter 2), and in many other subsequent cases. For an examination of the behind-the scenes thinking of the Court in Sylvania through the private papers of Justice Lewis Powell, who authored the decision, see Andrew I. Gavil, *Sylvania and the Process of Change in the Supreme Court: A First Look at the Powell Papers*, ANTITRUST, FALL 2002, at 9.

The decision also marked the re-emergence of the rule of reason as the guiding force of antitrust law. As we discussed in Chapter 2, the rule of reason had been largely dormant from its origins in *Standard Oil* and *Chicago Board of Trade*. It began to evolve again in the courts in both vertical cases owing to *Sylvania*, and horizontal cases because of *Broadcast Music*, decided two years later. Perhaps more so than in its original form, however, the Court emphasized that the rule of reason had to be grounded in economic principles. Sylvania's location clauses had no doubt reduced intrabrand competition—they literally "restrained trade." But the evidence indicated that they also helped Sylvania expand its output by reducing its distribution costs, attracting aggressive retailers, and strengthening its ability to compete on the interbrand level with other, more successful television brands. In short, the object and effect of its marketing plan was to abate impediments to its entry and expansion by reducing costs and inducing product promotion—hallmarks of economic efficiency. Again, in decided contrast with the views expressed in *Topco* just five years earlier, the Court's rationale implicitly acknowledged that courts applying the Sherman Act must indeed be willing and able to "ramble through the wilds of economic theory" in order to identify and protect such arrangements from successful challenge under rigid, formalistic, and economically unsophisticated analysis. Similar themes were evident in *National Society of Professional Engineers* (1978) and *Broadcast Music* (1979), which followed.

Sylvania introduced two critical distinctions in antitrust law—one that has now been abandoned and one that continues to challenge courts and legal counselors. First, because it left *Dr. Miles* undisturbed, the Court drew a distinction between vertical, intrabrand *price* restraints, which remained per se unlawful, and vertical, intrabrand, *non*-price restraints, like the location clauses at issue in *Sylvania*, which were thereafter to be judged under a more comprehensive application of the rule of reason. The distinction between price and non-price vertical restraints led to persistent controversy, owing in large part to the fact that the effects of price and non-price vertical intrabrand restraints, and the justifications for their use, can be so alike. This was almost immediately apparent as the lower courts began to grapple with *Sylvania's* meaning. To appreciate the tension, consider a manufacturer that leaves its dealer free to establish its resale prices within an assigned territory, but requires it to sell at the manufacturer's list price if it sells outside of its assigned area. Viewed as an agreement on resale price, this agreement would be illegal per se under

Dr. Miles. But it can also be viewed as a non-price agreement, subject to the rule of reason after *Sylvania*. After all, it is less restrictive than an exclusive territories requirement, as the dealer is permitted to sell outside its territory so long as it does not discount. In a case decided shortly after *Sylvania*, an appellate court took the latter view on similar facts, thereby demarcating a line between price and non-price restraints in a manner that would help to protect *Sylvania* from erosion. *See, e.g., Eastern Scientific Co. v. Wild Heerbrugg Instruments, Inc.*, 572 F.2d 883, 885–86 (1st Cir. 1978).

Noting this tension in his concurring opinion, Justice White predicted that *Sylvania* would increase pressure on the Court to overrule *Dr. Miles*:

> * * * It is common ground among the leading advocates of a purely economic approach to the question of distribution restraints that the economic arguments in favor of allowing vertical nonprice restraints generally apply to vertical price restraints as well.[10] Although the majority asserts that "the per se illegality of price restrictions ... involves significantly different questions of analysis and policy," [*Sylvania, supra* n.18], I suspect this purported distinction may be as difficult to justify as that of *Schwinn* under the terms of the majority's analysis. Thus Professor Posner, in an article cited five times by the majority, concludes: "I believe that the law should treat price and nonprice restrictions the same and that it should make no distinction between the imposition of restrictions in a sale contract and their imposition in an agency contract." Indeed, the Court has already recognized that resale price maintenance may increase output by inducing "demand-creating activity" by dealers (such as additional retail outlets, advertising and promotion, and product servicing) that outweighs the additional sales that would result from lower prices brought about by dealer price competition. These same output-enhancing possibilities of nonprice vertical restraints are relied upon by the majority as evidence of their social utility and economic soundness, and as a justification for judging them under the rule of reason. The effect, if not the intention, of the Court's opinion is necessarily to call into question the firmly established *per se* rule against price restraints.

---

[10] Professor Posner writes, for example:

"There is no basis for choosing between (price fixing and market division) on social grounds. If resale price maintenance is like dealer price fixing, and therefore bad, a manufacturer's assignment of exclusive territories is like market division, and therefore bad too. . . .

"(If helping new entrants break into a market) is a good justification for exclusive territories, it is an equally good justification for resale price maintenance, which as we have seen is simply another method of dealing with the free-rider problem. . . .

In fact, any argument that can also be made on behalf of exclusive territories can also be made on behalf of resale price maintenance."

Sylvania, 433 U.S. at 69–70 (White, J., concurring). Do you agree with the Court's stated assumption that price restraints are more inherently anticompetitive than non-price restraints? Do you think Justice White's concerns are well-taken? Could non-price restraints actually be more anticompetitive in practice than price restraints, for example, because they can eliminate all forms of intrabrand competition, not just price? As we shall see in our next case, *Leegin*, Justice White's prediction has come true, although it took longer than he perhaps would have predicted at the time.

Finally, *Sylvania* also perpetuated a distinction between *vertical* and *horizontal* non-price restrictions. *Vertical* restrictions—supplier limitations on the geographic areas or classes of customers to which a downstream supplier is authorized to sell, or, as in *Sylvania*, the locations from which it is authorized to sell, were to be evaluated under a comprehensive application of the rule of reason. Yet *horizontal* non-price restrictions remained per se unlawful under *Topco*. As a consequence, in cases where the restraints were deemed vertical, the reduction of intrabrand competition could be weighed against enhanced interbrand competition. But the same would not be permitted if the restraints were deemed horizontal. Whereas before *Sylvania* all such distribution restraints, price and non-price, vertical and horizontal, were condemned as per se unreasonable, afterwards the characterization of a restraint had grave consequences. Only vertical intrabrand, non-price restraints would receive full rule of reason analysis. Vertical price restraints, and horizontal territorial, customer or location restraints, all remained per se unlawful. Other vertical/horizontal disparities also developed.

The next Sidebar looks at the practical consequences of the *Sylvania* decision for supplier-dealer relations.

Sidebar 6–1:
Dealer Relations After *Sylvania*

The most critical unanswered question of *Sylvania* was "how would the rule of reason apply to *Sylvania*-type restraints"? Although Sylvania had rejected reliance on per se analysis, it left the application of the rule of reason for the lower courts. *See Continental T.V., Inc. v. G.T.E. Sylvania Inc.*, 694 F.2d 1132 (9th Cir. 1982) (on remand from the Supreme Court, district court upheld Sylvania's restrictions as reasonable and court of appeals affirmed). What would make vertical intrabrand non-price restraints "unreasonable"? Although the decision expounded upon the reasons why vertical restraints might be reasonable, it offered little guidance for identifying those that would not.

Since *Sylvania*, there have been only two or three instances in which the plaintiff has prevailed in attacking such arrangements, and virtually no government enforcement actions have been brought. In one plaintiff's victory, *Graphic Products Distributors, Inc. v. ITEK Corp.*, 717 F.2d 1560 (11th Cir. 1983), the court found that the defendant had a market share of over 70%. With a market share of 70% the defendant in *Graphic Products* arguably faced little significant interbrand competition. Building on the Supreme Court's reasoning in *Sylvania*, the court of appeals in *Graphic Products* concluded that, because interbrand competition was largely absent, intrabrand competition served as the only significant source of downward pressure on price. One answer to the question left unanswered by *Sylvania*, "when can vertical, intrabrand, non-price restraints be unreasonable," therefore, may be "when intrabrand competition represents a substantial source of downward pressure on price, *i.e.*, when the firm imposing the restraint has interbrand market power." But that general proposition provides little guidance as to difficult questions of degree and, as we shall see, may have been implicitly rejected by the Supreme Court in our next case, the Court's 2007 decision in *Leegin*.

In another early case, *Eiberger v. Sony Corp. of Am.*, 622 F.2d 1068 (2d Cir. 1980), the defendants adopted vertical, intrabrand, non-price restraints and enforced them rather brutally. Although there was little evidence that the defendant possessed interbrand market power, there was almost no apparent evidence that the defendant had any of the kinds of procompetitive purposes cited in *Sylvania* as justifications for its actions. There were, in effect, no procompetitive, interbrand effects that mitigated the restraining effect of the arrangements on intrabrand competition. One explanation for the decision, therefore, is that even small negative effects on intrabrand competition may be unreasonable if there is no justification for the restraint and no apparent benefits to interbrand competition.

Since *Sylvania*, vertical, intrabrand, non-price restraints have become even more common for firms engaged in multi-level distribution, particularly franchising. In large part, the paucity of successful challenges to these common arrangements may reflect what critics of *Schwinn* had asserted—that vertical, intrabrand, non-price restraints are almost always procompetitive in the interbrand market. As a practical matter, therefore, they have become almost per se *lawful*. See, e.g., Douglas H. Ginsburg, *Vertical Restraints: De Facto Legality Under the Rule of Reason*, 60 ANTITRUST L.J. 67 (1991). This was a specific goal of commentators that heralded *Sylvania*, but urged the Court to go even further in authorizing all vertical restraints. *See, e.g.,* Richard A. Posner, *The Next Step in the Antitrust Treatment of Restricted Distribution: Per Se Legality,* 48 U. CHI. L. REV. 6 (1981). They provide manufacturers with valuable flexibility in shaping their distribution systems, and a potentially cost-effective alternative to vertical integration.

That is not to say, however, that *Sylvania* is without critics. The "free rider" rationale so important to the Court's reasoning in *Sylvania* may simply be inapplicable to many products that involve no significant point of sale services or promotional activities. This is an argument that the dissenting Justices will make in our next principal case, *Leegin.* And as one court has observed, compensation from the supplier to dealers that supply services can neutralize the negative effect of "free riding" dealers who do not receive any payments because they do not supply the services. *See Toys "R" Us, Inc. v. FTC,* 221 F.3d 928, 937–38 (7th Cir. 2000). We will return to a discussion of the economics of the free rider argument in Sidebar 6–2.

After *Sylvania,* the Supreme Court continued to erode the rule of *Dr. Miles* both directly and indirectly by addressing the remaining tension between *Dr. Miles* and *Colgate* (the standards governing proof of *concerted* RPM) and the tension newly created by *Sylvania* (the different standards governing price and non-price vertical agreements).

Before *Sylvania,* the Court had consistently sought to protect *Colgate's* core holding that a manufacturer can decline to sell to a dealer that refuses to adhere to the manufacturer's specified resale prices, provided that its policy is truly unilateral, *i.e.,* in the absence of evidence of "agreement." In deference to *Dr. Miles,* however, the Court had also recognized that *Colgate's* protections could be forfeited if the manufacturer undertakes efforts to cajole or coerce a resisting dealer to adhere to the specified prices through, for example, threats to terminate sales. Such "negotiations" between the supplier and dealer—dealer discounting, followed by supplier threats of termination and dealer adherence—could establish "agreement." *See, e.g., United States v. Parke, Davis & Co.,* 362 U.S. 29 (1960). Trying to toe this line between *Colgate* and *Dr. Miles* highlighted the tension between them. *See generally* Edward H. Levi, *The Parke, Davis-Colgate Doctrine: The Ban on Resale Price Maintenance,* 1960 SUP. CT. REV. 258.

To appreciate this tension, consider the following distinction, which *Colgate* and *Parke, Davis* endorsed:

(1) A manufacturer who announces to its dealer: "I only sell to dealers who resell at the prices I determine in advance," and then asks "will you agree to my terms?," has invited a resale price maintenance agreement. If the dealer responds "yes, I accept your

terms," the dealer and the manufacturer have entered into an agreement to fix minimum resale prices.

(2) On the other hand, if the manufacturer announces: "I only sell to dealers that resell at the prices I determine in advance," but then asks only "would you like to place an order?," it can arguably assert that no "agreement" has been reached, even if the sale is made, and even if the evidence discloses that the dealer thereafter adhered to the announced price.

This technical and artificial legal fiction is unrelated to economic analysis. If minimum RPM is economically objectionable in the first example, shouldn't it be equally objectionable in the second? To what extent should the "agreement" requirement of Section 1 of the Sherman Act alter that consequence? And isn't it reasonable to infer that the dealer who places an order following a recitation of the supplier's terms of dealing has "agreed" to them?

In 1984, the Court appeared poised to overrule *Dr. Miles* when it granted review in *Monsanto Co. v. Spray-Rite Service Corp.*, 465 U.S. 752 (1984). The narrow question presented in the case was whether a terminated discounting dealer could establish an unlawful RPM agreement if it alleged and proved only that rival dealers complained about its discounting to their common supplier and the supplier responded by terminating all sales to the dealer. Because of the per se rule of *Dr. Miles*, the answer to this question could be outcome determinative: if an agreement was found, a per se unlawful violation had occurred. Both the Department of Justice and *Monsanto* urged the Court to use the case to overrule *Dr. Miles* and thus harmonize the treatment of price and non-price vertical restraints under the rule of reason.

The Court declined this invitation, instead confining itself to the narrow question presented, *i.e.*, whether the plaintiff had introduced sufficient evidence of "agreement." To formally preserve *Dr. Miles*, but protect *Sylvania* by narrowing the practical application of per se analysis, the Court elevated the burden of proving an RPM "agreement":

> Thus, something more than evidence of complaints is needed. There must be evidence that tends to exclude the possibility that the manufacturer and nonterminated distributors were acting independently. * * * [T]he antitrust plaintiff should present direct or circumstantial evidence that reasonably tends to prove that the manufacturer and others "had a conscious commitment to a common scheme designed to achieve an unlawful objective."

Monsanto, 465 U.S. at 764. It then went on to hold that the evidence was sufficient under its newly announced and heightened standard to support the jury's verdict against *Monsanto*. *Id.* at 765–68.[1]

Four years after *Monsanto*, the Court again visited the burden of proof for dealers alleging they were terminated for failure to adhere to minimum RPM requirements imposed by their supplier. In *Business Electronics Corp. v. Sharp Electronics Corp.*, 485 U.S. 717 (1988), the Court reaffirmed *Monsanto's* holding that dealer complaints about a rival dealer's low prices, followed by termination of the price cutting dealer, were alone insufficient to establish a per se unlawful vertical price maintenance agreement. An elevated standard of proof was necessary, the Court maintained, to prevent *Dr. Miles* from encroaching upon *Sylvania* and *Colgate*. 485 U.S. at 724–26. But the Court went further, arguably adding yet another requirement:

> Our approach to the question presented in the present case is guided by the premises of *GTE Sylvania* and *Monsanto*: that there is a presumption in favor of a rule-of-reason standard; that departure from that standard must be justified by demonstrable economic effect, such as the facilitation of cartelizing, rather than formalistic distinctions; that interbrand competition is the primary concern of the antitrust laws; and that rules in this area should be formulated with a view towards protecting the doctrine of *GTE Sylvania*. * * *

> There has been no showing here that an agreement between a manufacturer and a dealer to terminate a "price cutter," *without a further agreement on the price or price levels to be charged by the remaining dealer*, almost always tends to restrict competition and reduce output. Any assistance to cartelizing that such an agreement might provide cannot be distinguished from the sort of minimal assistance that might be provided by vertical nonprice agreements like the exclusive territory agreement in *GTE Sylvania*, and is insufficient to justify a *per se* rule. Cartels are neither easy to form nor easy to maintain. Uncertainty over the terms of the cartel, particularly the prices to be charged in the future, obstructs both formation and adherence by making cheating easier. Without an agreement with the remaining dealer on price, the manufacturer both retains its incentive to cheat on any manufacturer-level cartel (since lower prices can still be passed on to consumers) and cannot as easily be used to organize and hold together a retailer-level cartel.

---

[1] You may recall from Chapter 3 that two years after *Monsanto*, the Court imported this "tends to exclude the possibility" standard to *Matsushita*, thus applying it to certain horizontal conspiracies, as well.

* * * Any agreement between a manufacturer and a dealer to terminate another dealer who happens to have charged lower prices can be alleged to have been directed against the terminated dealer's "price cutting." In the vast majority of cases, it will be extremely difficult for the manufacturer to convince a jury that its motivation was to ensure adequate services, since price cutting and some measure of service cutting usually go hand in hand. * * *

We cannot avoid this difficulty by invalidating as illegal *per se* only those agreements imposing vertical restraints that contain the word "price," or that affect the "prices" charged by dealers. Such formalism was explicitly rejected in *GTE Sylvania*. As the above discussion indicates, all vertical restraints, including the exclusive territory agreement held not to be *per se* illegal in *GTE Sylvania*, have the potential to allow dealers to increase "prices" and can be characterized as intended to achieve just that. In fact, vertical nonprice restraints only accomplish the benefits identified in *GTE Sylvania* because they reduce intrabrand price competition to the point where the dealer's profit margin permits provision of the desired services. * * *

Id. at 726–28 (emphasis added). The combination of *Colgate, Monsanto* and *Business Electronics* made it very difficult for terminated discounters to prove that their termination was pursuant to an agreement to fix minimum resale prices. *See, e.g., Miles Distributors, Inc. v. Specialty Const. Brands, Inc.*, 476 F.3d 442 (7th Cir. 2007).

What does the emphasized language in the excerpt from *Business Electronics* add to the test set forth in *Monsanto*? Did *Monsanto* and *Business Electronics* modify and narrow the per se rule against minimum RPM as conceived in *Dr. Miles*? If so, how? Why does the Court refer to the fear of "cartelization"? Would you agree or disagree with the proposition that *Business Electronics* attempted to limit reliance on per se analysis to those circumstances where minimum RPM is most likely to prove unreasonably anticompetitive? If that is true, is such an approach fairly characterized as "per se" analysis?

Although the Court in *Monsanto* and *Business Electronics* remained formally respectful of *Dr. Miles*, the respect was grudging. Indeed, the papers of Justice Lewis Powell, the author of the Court's opinions in *Sylvania* and *Monsanto*, indicate that he was inclined to overrule *Dr. Miles* in *Monsanto*, but ultimately felt constrained from doing so because the issue had not been preserved by the parties and Congress had expressed its continuing support for *Dr. Miles* while *Monsanto* was pending before the Court. In a perhaps unique incident in the history of public antitrust enforcement, after the Department of Justice had filed an amicus brief urging the Court to overrule *Dr. Miles*, Congress intervened with a bill that precluded the Justice Department from expending any of its appropriation to argue its position before the Court. Although the brief was not formally withdrawn, at oral argument the spokesperson for the Justice Department could say only that the Department stood by its brief. *See Monsanto*, 465 U.S. at 761 n.7. *See* Andrew I. Gavil, *Sylvania and the Process of Change in the Supreme Court: A First Look at the Powell Papers*, ANTITRUST, FALL 2002, at 9, 10) (quoting Powell's hand-written notes from the December 7, 1983 conference, which stated: "I'd like to over-rule Dr. Miles & perhaps construe others—but not before us.").

In our next case, *Leegin Creative Leather Products, Inc. v. PSKS, Inc.*, 551 U.S. 877, 127 S.Ct. 2705 (2007), the Court completed the work it had begun in *Sylvania* thirty years earlier and overruled *Dr. Miles*. As we have explained, by this time, the Court had elevated the burden of proving minimum RPM agreements in *Monsanto* and *Business Electronics*. It also had abandoned per se analysis for *maximum* RPM in *State Oil Co. v. Khan*, 522 U.S. 3, 118 S.Ct. 275 (1997). Given this history of erosion of *Dr. Miles*, perhaps the biggest surprise when *Leegin* was announced was how close the vote was. As you read the decision, consider what prompted the dissenters to mount a defense of *Dr. Miles* despite these other developments.

LEEGIN CREATIVE LEATHER PRODUCTS, INC. V. PSKS, INC.

United States Supreme Court, 2007.
551 U.S. 877, 127 S.Ct. 2705, 168 L.Ed.2d 623.

JUSTICE KENNEDY delivered the opinion of the Court.

* * *

I

Petitioner, Leegin Creative Leather Products, Inc. (Leegin), designs, manufactures, and distributes leather goods and accessories. In 1991, Leegin began to sell belts under the brand name "Brighton." The Brighton brand has now expanded into a variety of women's fashion accessories. It is sold across the United States in over 5,000 retail establishments, for the most part independent, small boutiques and specialty stores. Leegin's president, Jerry Kohl, also has an interest in about 70 stores that sell Brighton products. Leegin asserts that, at least for its products, small retailers treat customers better, provide customers more services, and make their shopping experience more satisfactory than do larger, often impersonal retailers. Kohl explained: "[W]e want the consumers to get a different experience than they get in Sam's Club or in Wal-Mart. And you can't get that kind of experience or support or customer service from a store like Wal-Mart."

Respondent, PSKS, Inc. (PSKS), operates Kay's Kloset, a women's apparel store in Lewisville, Texas. Kay's Kloset buys from about 75 different manufacturers and at one time sold the Brighton brand. It first started purchasing Brighton goods from Leegin in 1995. Once it began selling the brand, the store promoted Brighton. For example, it ran Brighton advertisements and had Brighton days in the store. Kay's Kloset became the destination retailer in the area to buy Brighton products. Brighton was the store's most important brand and once accounted for 40 to 50 percent of its profits.

In 1997, Leegin instituted the "Brighton Retail Pricing and Promotion Policy." Following the policy, Leegin refused to sell to retailers that discounted Brighton goods below suggested prices. The policy contained an exception for products not selling well that the retailer did not plan on reordering. * * * Leegin adopted the policy to give its retailers sufficient margins to provide customers the service central to its distribution strategy. It also expressed concern that discounting harmed Brighton's brand image and reputation.

A year after instituting the pricing policy Leegin introduced a marketing strategy known as the "Heart Store Program." It offered retailers incentives to become Heart Stores, and, in exchange, retailers pledged, among other things, to sell at Leegin's suggested prices. Kay's Kloset became a Heart Store soon after Leegin created the program. After a Leegin employee visited the store and found it unattractive, the parties appear to have agreed that Kay's Kloset would not be a Heart Store beyond 1998. Despite losing this status, Kay's Kloset continued to increase its Brighton sales.

In December 2002, Leegin discovered Kay's Kloset had been marking down Brighton's entire line by 20 percent. Kay's Kloset contended it placed Brighton products on sale to compete with nearby retailers who also were undercutting Leegin's suggested prices. Leegin, nonetheless, requested that Kay's Kloset cease discounting. Its request refused, Leegin stopped selling to the store. The loss of the Brighton brand had a considerable negative impact on the store's revenue from sales.

PSKS sued Leegin * * * [alleging] that Leegin had violated the antitrust laws by "enter[ing] into agreements with retailers to charge only those prices fixed by Leegin." Leegin planned to introduce expert testimony describing the procompetitive effects of its pricing policy. The District Court excluded the testimony, relying on the *per se* rule established by *Dr. Miles*. At trial PSKS argued that the Heart Store program, among other things, demonstrated Leegin and its retailers had agreed to fix prices. Leegin responded that it had established a unilateral pricing policy lawful under § 1, which applies only to concerted action. See *United States v. Colgate & Co.,* 250 U.S. 300, 307, 39 S.Ct. 465, 63 L.Ed. 992 (1919). The jury agreed with PSKS and awarded it $1.2 million. Pursuant to 15 U.S.C. § 15(a), the District Court trebled the damages and reimbursed PSKS for its attorney's fees and costs. It entered judgment against Leegin in the amount of $3,975,000.80.

The Court of Appeals for the Fifth Circuit affirmed. On appeal Leegin did not dispute that it had entered into vertical price-fixing agreements with its retailers. Rather, it contended that the rule of reason should have applied to those agreements. The Court of Appeals rejected this argument. It was correct to explain that it remained bound by *Dr. Miles* "[b]ecause [the Supreme] Court has consistently applied the *per se* rule to [vertical minimum price-fixing] agreements." On this premise the Court of Appeals held that the District Court did not abuse its discretion in excluding the testimony of Leegin's economic expert, for the *per se* rule rendered irrelevant any procompetitive justifications for Leegin's pricing policy. We granted certiorari to determine whether vertical minimum resale price maintenance agreements should continue to be treated as *per se* unlawful.

II

[In part II of its opinion, the Court reiterated that Section 1 only prohibits unreasonable restraints of trade and that the rule of reason is the "accepted standard for testing whether a practice restrains trade in violation of § 1." The inquiry under the rule of reason requires an evaluation of "all of the circumstances of a case," such as the history, nature, and effect of the restraint, as well as industry structure and the defendant's market power. In the Court's view, "[i]n its design and function the rule [of reason] distinguishes between restraints with anticompetitive effect that are harmful to the consumer and restraints stimulating competition that are in the consumer's best interest."

Per se analysis provides more clear guidance and "eliminates the need to study the reasonableness of an individual restraint in light of the real market forces at work," but [r]esort to *per se* rules is confined to restraints * * * "that would always or almost always tend to restrict competition and decrease output." Such restraints must be "manifestly anticompetitive" and "lack any redeeming virtue." Quoting *Sylvania*, the Court emphasized that a "departure from the rule-of-reason standard must be based upon demonstrable economic effect rather than . . . upon formalistic line drawing." Eds.]

* * *

III

The Court has interpreted *Dr. Miles Medical Co. v. John D. Park & Sons Co.*, 220 U.S. 373, 31 S.Ct. 376, 55 L.Ed. 502 (1911), as establishing a *per se* rule against a vertical agreement between a manufacturer and its distributor to set minimum resale prices. In *Dr. Miles* the plaintiff, a manufacturer of medicines, sold its products only to distributors who agreed to resell them at set prices. The Court found the manufacturer's control of resale prices to be unlawful. It relied on the common-law rule that "a general restraint upon alienation is ordinarily invalid." The Court then explained that the agreements would advantage the distributors, not the manufacturer, and were analogous to a combination among competing distributors, which the law treated as void.

The reasoning of the Court's more recent jurisprudence has rejected the rationales on which *Dr. Miles* was based. By relying on the common-law rule against restraints on alienation, the Court justified its decision based on "formalistic" legal doctrine rather than "demonstrable economic effect," *GTE Sylvania, supra,* at 58–59, 97 S.Ct. 2549. The Court in *Dr. Miles* relied on a treatise published in 1628, but failed to discuss in detail the business reasons that would motivate a manufacturer situated in 1911 to make use of vertical price restraints. Yet the Sherman Act's use of "restraint of trade" "invokes the common law itself, . . . not merely the static content that the common law had assigned to the term in 1890." * * * We reaffirm that "the state of the common law 400 or even 100 years ago is irrelevant to the issue before us: the effect of the antitrust laws upon vertical distributional restraints in the American economy today." *GTE Sylvania,* 433 U.S., at 53 n. 21, 97 S.Ct. 2549 (internal quotation marks omitted).

Dr. Miles, furthermore, treated vertical agreements a manufacturer makes with its distributors as analogous to a horizontal combination among competing distributors. In later cases, however, the Court rejected the approach of reliance on rules governing horizontal restraints when defining rules applicable to vertical ones. Our recent cases formulate antitrust principles in accordance with the appreciated differences in economic effect between vertical and horizontal agreements, differences the *Dr. Miles* Court failed to consider.

The reasons upon which *Dr. Miles* relied do not justify a *per se* rule. As a consequence, it is necessary to examine, in the first instance, the economic effects of vertical agreements to fix minimum resale prices, and to determine whether the *per se* rule is nonetheless appropriate.

A

Though each side of the debate can find sources to support its position, it suffices to say here that economics literature is replete with procompetitive justifications for a manufacturer's use of resale price maintenance. Even those more skeptical of resale price maintenance acknowledge it can have procompetitive effects.

The few recent studies documenting the competitive effects of resale price maintenance also cast doubt on the conclusion that the practice meets the criteria for a *per se* rule.

The justifications for vertical price restraints are similar to those for other vertical restraints. Minimum resale price maintenance can stimulate interbrand competition—the competition among manufacturers selling different brands of the same type of product—by reducing intrabrand competition-the competition among retailers selling the same brand. The promotion of interbrand competition is important because "the primary purpose of the antitrust laws is to protect [this type of] competition." A single manufacturer's use of vertical price restraints tends to eliminate intrabrand price competition; this in turn encourages retailers to invest in tangible or intangible services or promotional efforts that aid the manufacturer's position as against rival manufacturers. Resale price maintenance also has the potential to give consumers more options so that they can choose among low-price, low-service brands; high-price, high-service brands; and brands that fall in between.

Absent vertical price restraints, the retail services that enhance interbrand competition might be underprovided. This is because discounting retailers can free ride on retailers who furnish services and then capture some of the increased demand those services generate. Consumers might learn, for example, about the benefits of a manufacturer's product from a retailer that invests in fine showrooms, offers product demonstrations, or hires and trains knowledgeable employees. Or consumers might decide to buy the product because they see it in a retail establishment that has a reputation for selling high-quality merchandise. If the consumer can then buy the product from a retailer that discounts because it has not spent capital providing services or developing a quality reputation, the high-service retailer will lose sales to the discounter, forcing it to cut back its services to a level lower than consumers would otherwise prefer. Minimum resale price maintenance alleviates the problem because it prevents the discounter from undercutting the service provider. With price competition decreased, the manufacturer's retailers compete among themselves over services.

Resale price maintenance, in addition, can increase interbrand competition by facilitating market entry for new firms and brands. "[N]ew manufacturers and manufacturers entering new markets can use the restrictions in order to induce competent and aggressive retailers to make the kind of investment of capital and labor that is often required in the distribution of products unknown to the consumer." New products and new brands are essential to a dynamic economy, and if markets can be penetrated by using resale price maintenance there is a procompetitive effect.

Resale price maintenance can also increase interbrand competition by encouraging retailer services that would not be provided even absent free riding. It may be difficult and inefficient for a manufacturer to make and enforce a contract with a retailer specifying the different services the retailer must perform. Offering the retailer a guaranteed margin and threatening termination if it does not live up to expectations may be the most efficient way to expand the manufacturer's market share by inducing the retailer's performance and allowing it to use its own initiative and experience in providing valuable services.

B

While vertical agreements setting minimum resale prices can have procompetitive justifications, they may have anticompetitive effects in other cases; and unlawful price fixing, designed solely to obtain monopoly profits, is an ever present temptation. Resale price maintenance may, for example, facilitate a manufacturer cartel. An unlawful cartel will seek to discover if some manufacturers are undercutting the cartel's fixed prices. Resale price maintenance could assist the cartel in identifying price-cutting manufacturers who benefit from the lower prices they offer. Resale price maintenance, furthermore, could discourage a manufacturer from cutting prices to retailers with the concomitant benefit of cheaper prices to consumers.

Vertical price restraints also "might be used to organize cartels at the retailer level." A group of retailers might collude to fix prices to consumers and then compel a manufacturer to aid the unlawful arrangement with resale price maintenance. In that instance the manufacturer does not establish the practice to stimulate services or to promote its brand but to give inefficient retailers higher profits. Retailers with better distribution systems and lower cost structures would be prevented from charging lower prices by the agreement.

A horizontal cartel among competing manufacturers or competing retailers that decreases output or reduces competition in order to increase price is, and ought to be, *per se* unlawful. To the extent a vertical agreement setting minimum resale prices is entered upon to facilitate either type of cartel, it, too, would need to be held unlawful under the rule of reason. This type of agreement may also be useful evidence for a plaintiff attempting to prove the existence of a horizontal cartel.

Resale price maintenance, furthermore, can be abused by a powerful manufacturer or retailer. A dominant retailer, for example, might request resale price maintenance to forestall innovation in distribution that decreases costs. A manufacturer might consider it has little choice but to accommodate the retailer's demands for vertical price restraints if the manufacturer believes it needs access to the retailer's distribution network. A manufacturer with market power, by comparison, might use resale price maintenance to give retailers an incentive not to sell the products of smaller rivals or new entrants. As should be evident, the potential anticompetitive consequences of vertical price restraints must not be ignored or underestimated.

C

Notwithstanding the risks of unlawful conduct, it cannot be stated with any degree of confidence that resale price maintenance "always or almost always tend[s] to restrict competition and decrease output." Vertical agreements establishing minimum resale prices can have either procompetitive or anticompetitive effects, depending upon the circumstances in which they are formed. And although the empirical evidence on the topic is limited, it does not suggest efficient uses of the agreements are infrequent or hypothetical. As the rule would proscribe a significant amount of procompetitive conduct, these agreements appear ill suited for *per se* condemnation.

Respondent contends, nonetheless, that vertical price restraints should be *per se* unlawful because of the administrative convenience of *per se* rules. That argument suggests *per se* illegality is the rule rather than the exception. This misinterprets our antitrust law. *Per se* rules may decrease administrative costs, but that is only part of the equation. Those rules can be counterproductive. They can increase the total cost of the antitrust system by prohibiting procompetitive conduct the antitrust laws should encourage. They also may increase litigation costs by promoting frivolous suits against legitimate practices. The Court has thus explained that administrative "advantages are not sufficient in themselves to justify the creation of *per se* rules," and has relegated their use to restraints that are "manifestly anticompetitive." Were the Court now to conclude that vertical price restraints should be *per se* illegal based on administrative costs, we would undermine, if not overrule, the traditional "demanding standards" for adopting *per se* rules. Any possible reduction in administrative costs cannot alone justify the *Dr. Miles* rule.

Respondent also argues the *per se* rule is justified because a vertical price restraint can lead to higher prices for the manufacturer's goods. Respondent is mistaken in relying on pricing effects absent a further showing of anticompetitive conduct. For, as has been indicated already, the antitrust laws are designed primarily to protect interbrand competition, from which lower prices can later result. The Court, moreover, has evaluated other vertical restraints under the rule of reason even though prices can be increased in the course of promoting procompetitive effects. And resale price maintenance may reduce prices if manufacturers have resorted to costlier alternatives of controlling resale prices that are not *per se* unlawful.

Respondent's argument, furthermore, overlooks that, in general, the interests of manufacturers and consumers are aligned with respect to retailer profit margins. The difference between the price a manufacturer charges retailers and the price retailers charge consumers represents part of the manufacturer's cost of distribution, which, like any other cost, the manufacturer usually desires to minimize. A manufacturer has no incentive to overcompensate retailers with unjustified margins. The retailers, not the manufacturer, gain from higher retail prices. The manufacturer often loses; interbrand competition reduces its competitiveness and market share because consumers will "substitute a different brand of the same product." As a general matter, therefore, a single manufacturer will desire to set minimum resale prices only if the "increase in demand resulting from enhanced service . . . will more than offset a negative impact on demand of a higher retail price."

The implications of respondent's position are far reaching. Many decisions a manufacturer makes and carries out through concerted action can lead to higher prices. A manufacturer might, for example, contract with different suppliers to obtain better inputs that improve product quality. Or it might hire an advertising agency to promote awareness of its goods. Yet no one would think these actions violate the Sherman Act because they lead to higher prices. The antitrust laws do not require manufacturers to produce generic goods that consumers do not know about or want. The manufacturer strives to improve its product quality or to promote its brand because it believes this conduct will lead to increased demand despite higher prices. The same can hold true for resale price maintenance.

Resale price maintenance, it is true, does have economic dangers. If the rule of reason were to apply to vertical price restraints, courts would have to be diligent in eliminating their anticompetitive uses from the market. This is a realistic objective, and certain factors are relevant to the inquiry. For example, the number of manufacturers that make use of the practice in a given industry can provide important instruction. When only a few manufacturers lacking market power adopt the practice, there is little likelihood it is facilitating a manufacturer cartel, for a cartel then can be undercut by rival manufacturers. Likewise, a retailer cartel is unlikely when only a single manufacturer in a competitive market uses resale price maintenance. Interbrand competition would divert consumers to lower priced substitutes and eliminate any gains to retailers from their price-fixing agreement over a single brand. Resale price maintenance should be subject to more careful scrutiny, by contrast, if many competing manufacturers adopt the practice.

The source of the restraint may also be an important consideration. If there is evidence retailers were the impetus for a vertical price restraint, there is a greater likelihood that the restraint facilitates a retailer cartel or supports a dominant, inefficient retailer. If, by contrast, a manufacturer adopted the policy independent of retailer pressure, the restraint is less likely to promote anticompetitive conduct. A manufacturer also has an incentive to protest inefficient retailer-induced price restraints because they can harm its competitive position.

As a final matter, that a dominant manufacturer or retailer can abuse resale price maintenance for anticompetitive purposes may not be a serious concern unless the relevant entity has market power. If a retailer lacks market power, manufacturers likely can sell their goods through rival retailers. And if a manufacturer lacks market power, there is less likelihood it can use the practice to keep competitors away from distribution outlets.

The rule of reason is designed and used to eliminate anticompetitive transactions from the market. This standard principle applies to vertical price restraints. A party alleging injury from a vertical agreement setting minimum resale prices will have, as a general matter, the information and resources available to show the existence of the agreement and its scope of operation. As courts gain experience considering the effects of these restraints by applying the rule of reason over the course of decisions, they can establish the litigation structure to ensure the rule operates to eliminate anticompetitive restraints from the market and to provide more guidance to businesses. Courts can, for example, devise rules over time for offering proof, or even presumptions where justified, to make the rule of reason a fair and efficient way to prohibit anticompetitive restraints and to promote procompetitive ones.

For all of the foregoing reasons, we think that were the Court considering the issue as an original matter, the rule of reason, not a *per se* rule of unlawfulness, would be the appropriate standard to judge vertical price restraints.

IV

We do not write on a clean slate, for the decision in *Dr. Miles* is almost a century old. So there is an argument for its retention on the basis of *stare decisis* alone. Even if *Dr. Miles* established an erroneous rule, "[s]tare decisis reflects a policy judgment that in most matters it is more important that the applicable rule of law be settled than that it be settled right." And concerns about maintaining settled law are strong when the question is one of statutory interpretation.

Stare decisis is not as significant in this case, however, because the issue before us is the scope of the Sherman Act. From the beginning the Court has treated the Sherman Act as a common-law statute. Just as the common law adapts to modern understanding and greater experience, so too does the Sherman Act's prohibition on "restraint[s] of trade" evolve to meet the dynamics of present economic conditions. The case-by-case adjudication contemplated by the rule of reason has implemented this common-law approach. Likewise, the boundaries of the doctrine of *per se* illegality should not be immovable. For "[i]t would make no sense to create out of the single term 'restraint of trade' a chronologically schizoid statute, in which a 'rule of reason' evolves with new circumstance and new wisdom, but a line of *per se* illegality remains forever fixed where it was."

A

Stare decisis, we conclude, does not compel our continued adherence to the *per se* rule against vertical price restraints. As discussed earlier, respected authorities in the economics literature suggest the *per se* rule is inappropriate, and there is now widespread agreement that resale price maintenance can have procompetitive effects. It is also significant that both the Department of Justice and the Federal Trade Commission—the antitrust enforcement agencies with the ability to assess the long-term impacts of resale price maintenance—have recommended that this Court replace the *per se* rule with the traditional rule of reason. In the antitrust context the fact that a decision has been "called into serious question" justifies our reevaluation of it.

Other considerations reinforce the conclusion that *Dr. Miles* should be overturned. Of most relevance, "we have overruled our precedents when subsequent cases have undermined their doctrinal underpinnings." The Court's treatment of vertical restraints has progressed away from *Dr. Miles'* strict approach. We have distanced ourselves from the opinion's rationales. This is unsurprising, for the case was decided not long after enactment of the Sherman Act when the Court had little experience with antitrust analysis. Only eight years after *Dr. Miles,* moreover, the Court reined in the decision [in *Colgate*] by holding that a manufacturer can announce suggested resale prices and refuse to deal with distributors who do not follow them.

In more recent cases the Court, following a common-law approach, has continued to temper, limit, or overrule once strict prohibitions on vertical restraints. [Here the Court discussed its subsequent decisions in *Sylvania, Monsanto, Business Electronics,* and *Khan,* which it characterized as collectively "limiting of the reach of" *Dr. Miles.* Eds.]

The *Dr. Miles* rule is also inconsistent with a principled framework, for it makes little economic sense when analyzed with our other cases on vertical restraints. If we were to decide the procompetitive effects of resale price maintenance were insufficient to overrule *Dr. Miles,* then cases such as *Colgate* and *GTE Sylvania* themselves would be called into question. These later decisions, while they may result in less intrabrand competition, can be justified because they permit manufacturers to secure the procompetitive benefits associated with vertical price restraints through other methods. The other methods, however, could be less efficient for a particular manufacturer to establish and sustain. The end result hinders competition and consumer welfare because manufacturers are forced to engage in second-best alternatives and because consumers are required to shoulder the increased expense of the inferior practices.

The manufacturer has a number of legitimate options to achieve benefits similar to those provided by vertical price restraints. A manufacturer can exercise its *Colgate* right to refuse to deal with retailers that do not follow its suggested prices. The economic effects of unilateral and concerted price setting are in general the same. The problem for the manufacturer is that a jury might conclude its unilateral policy was really a vertical agreement, subjecting it to treble damages and potential criminal liability. The increased costs these burdensome measures generate flow to consumers in the form of higher prices.

Furthermore, depending on the type of product it sells, a manufacturer might be able to achieve the procompetitive benefits of resale price maintenance by integrating downstream and selling its products directly to consumers. *Dr. Miles* tilts the relative costs of vertical integration and vertical agreement by making the former more attractive based on the *per se* rule, not on real market conditions. This distortion might lead to inefficient integration that would not otherwise take place, so that consumers must again suffer the consequences of the suboptimal distribution strategy. And integration, unlike vertical price restraints, eliminates all intrabrand competition.

There is yet another consideration. A manufacturer can impose territorial restrictions on distributors and allow only one distributor to sell its goods in a given region. Our cases have recognized, and the economics literature confirms, that these vertical nonprice restraints have impacts similar to those of vertical price restraints; both reduce intrabrand competition and can stimulate retailer services. The same legal standard (*per se* unlawfulness) applies to horizontal market division and horizontal price fixing because both have similar economic effect. There is likewise little economic justification for the current differential treatment of vertical price and nonprice restraints. Furthermore, vertical nonprice restraints may prove less efficient for inducing desired services, and they reduce intrabrand competition more than vertical price restraints by eliminating both price and service competition.

In sum, it is a flawed antitrust doctrine that serves the interests of lawyers—by creating legal distinctions that operate as traps for the unwary-more than the interests of consumers—by requiring manufacturers to choose second-best options to achieve sound business objectives.

B

[In the final portion of the majority opinion, the Court rejected several additional arguments urged by the respondent in support of *stare decisis*. First, the Court rejected the argument that Congress over time had approved of the per se rule in several previous acts. In the Court's view, none of the cited acts specifically approved of *Dr. Miles*. And it reiterated its view that Congress gave the Court wide discretion in interpreting the Sherman Act so it might evolve over time to reflect economic learning. Second, the Court rejected the argument that reliance interests justified continued adherence to the *per se* rule of *Dr. Miles*, asserting that "reliance interests * * * cannot justify an inefficient rule." Finally, the Court noted that even when resale price maintenance was specifically authorized for a time, few manufacturers embraced it as a regular practice. Hence overruling *Dr. Miles* would not result in any major disruption of most manufacturers' distribution practices. Eds.]

* * *

For these reasons the Court's decision in *Dr. Miles Medical Co. v. John D. Park & Sons Co.*, 220 U.S. 373, 31 S.Ct. 376, 55 L.Ed. 502 (1911), is now overruled. Vertical price restraints are to be judged according to the rule of reason.

* * *

———————

Justice Stephen Breyer authored a lengthy dissent that was joined by Justices Stevens, Souter, and Ginsburg. The dissenters did not take issue with the principal thrust of the majority: that minimum RPM might be anti-or procompetitive depending on the circumstances and, therefore, that if the practice were being considered as a matter of first impression, the Court would not likely subject it to per se analysis. They were more skeptical that minimum RPM would be used predominantly for procompetitive purposes, however, and questioned the adequacy of the Court's arguments for abandoning the century old rule of *Dr. Miles*:

> The Court justifies its departure from ordinary considerations of *stare decisis* by pointing to a set of arguments well known in the antitrust literature for close to half a century. Congress has repeatedly found in these arguments insufficient grounds for overturning the *per se* rule. And, in my view, they do not warrant the Court's now overturning so well-established a legal precedent.

551 U.S. at 908–09. Like the majority, the dissent evaluated the historical evidence and economic literature relating to the likely competitive effects of minimum RPM, but it found the evidence to be more equivocal:

> The upshot is, as many economists suggest, sometimes resale price maintenance can prove harmful; sometimes it can bring benefits. But before concluding that courts should consequently apply a rule of reason, I would ask such questions as, how often are harms or benefits likely to occur? How easy is it to separate the beneficial sheep from the antitrust goats?

Id. at 914. As a consequence, the dissent emphasized the implications of imposing the added administrative burden on parties and courts of shifting from a bright line per se approach to a more complete rule of reason analysis:

> Economic discussion, such as the studies the Court relies upon, can *help* provide answers to these questions, and in doing so, economics can, and should, inform antitrust law. But antitrust law cannot, and should not, precisely replicate economists' (sometimes conflicting) views. That is because law, unlike economics, is an administrative system the effects of which depend upon the content of rules and precedents only as they are applied by judges and juries in courts and by lawyers advising their clients. And that fact means that courts will often bring their own administrative judgment to bear, sometimes applying rules of *per se* unlawfulness to business practices even when those practices sometimes produce benefits.

Id. at 914–15. He later asked: "Are there special advantages to a bright-line rule?" And expressed his concern that "[w]ithout such a rule" the level of enforcement would necessarily diminish, which might "tempt some producers or dealers to enter into agreements that are, on balance, anticompetitive." *Id.* at 917.

On the merits, the dissent questioned, in particular, the argument that minimum RPM can lead to competitive benefits, especially the elimination of "free-riding," a rationale that persuaded the Court in both *Sylvania* and *Leegin.* Justice Breyer asked: "[h]ow often, for example, will the benefits to which the Court points occur in practice? I can find no economic consensus on this point. There is a consensus in the literature that 'free riding' takes place. But 'free riding' often takes place in the economy without any legal effort to stop it. * * * The question is how often the 'free riding' problem is serious enough significantly to deter dealer investment." *Id.* at 915. He also questioned "[h]ow easily * * * courts [can] identify instances in which the benefits are likely to outweigh potential harms?" His answer: "*not very easily.*" *Id.* at 916 (emphasis original). Breyer also singled out the Court's identification of market power as an important factor to consider in a rule of reason analysis, questioning the practical implications of relying on it as a factor relevant to full rule of reason analysis:

> The Court's invitation to consider the existence of "market power," for example, invites lengthy time-consuming argument among competing experts, as they seek to apply abstract, highly technical, criteria to often ill-defined markets. And resale price maintenance cases, unlike a major merger or monopoly case, are likely to prove numerous and involve only private parties. One cannot fairly expect judges and juries in such cases to apply

complex economic criteria without making a considerable number of mistakes, which themselves may impose serious costs.

Id. at 917.

Justice Breyer's concern for the burdens of administering full rule of reason analysis for minimum RPM, however, returned his discussion to *stare decisis*:

> Given the uncertainties that surround key items in the overall balance sheet, particularly in respect to the 'administrative' questions, I can concede to the majority that the problem is difficult. And, if forced to decide now, at most I might agree that the *per se* rule should be slightly modified to allow an exception for the more easily identifiable and temporary condition of 'new entry.' But I am not now forced to decide this question. The question before us is not what should be the rule, starting from scratch. We here must decide whether to change a clear and simple price-related antitrust rule that the courts have applied for nearly a century.

Id. at 917–18. Arguing that "[t]hose who wish this Court to change so well-established a legal precedent bear a heavy burden of proof" he concluded that the case had not been made, again alluding to his obvious concerns that RPM would not be confined to its procompetitive uses:

> No one claims that the American economy has changed in ways that might support the majority. Concentration in retailing has increased. That change, other things being equal, may enable (and motivate) more retailers, accounting for a greater percentage of total retail sales volume, to seek resale price maintenance, thereby making it more difficult for price-cutting competitors (perhaps internet retailers) to obtain market share.

Id. at 921. In closing, he again expressed his twin concerns about the likely consequences of a more tolerant approach to RPM and abandonment of long-settled precedent:

> The only safe predictions to make about today's decision are that it will likely raise the price of goods at retail and that it will create considerable legal turbulence as lower courts seek to develop workable principles. I do not believe that the majority has shown new or changed conditions sufficient to warrant overruling a decision of such long standing. All ordinary *stare decisis* considerations indicate the contrary. For these reasons, with respect, I dissent.

Id. at 929.

Recall that from 1967–77 the treatment of vertical price and non-price restraints was aligned under *Dr. Miles* and *Schwinn*: all vertical intrabrand restraints, price and non-price, were per se unlawful. *Sylvania* created disequilibrium and tension by differentiating vertical intrabrand non-price from price restraints. *Leegin* reestablished an equilibrium, but it was one far more tolerant of all vertical intrabrand restraints. What arguments persuaded the majority that it was time to abandon *Dr. Miles* despite its near-century reign?

Why was the Court divided 5–4, given the Justices' apparently unanimous view that minimum RPM, if judged anew, would not warrant per se treatment? To what degree was the dissent influenced by its skepticism of the purported procompetitive uses of minimum RPM? To what degree was it also concerned about the cost/benefit calculus of moving from a bright line approach to one that would require deeper analysis? Embedded in its arguments, is there a broader skepticism about the ability of courts to fairly and consistently apply full rule of reason analysis? How persuasive a case do the dissenters make for invoking *stare decisis* to retain *Dr. Miles*? At the time, some commentators also suggested that *Leegin* may have been a proxy fight for other controversial issues facing the Court at the time. They noted, in particular, the selection of cases cited by the dissenting Justices in support of their plea for *stare decisis*, which revealed their concern for non-antitrust precedent, especially a woman's right to choose under *Roe v. Wade*, 410 U.S. 113 (1973). *See* 551 U.S. at 918 (BREYER, J., dissenting).

In *Leegin,* the Supreme Court observes that minimum RPM may promote competition by stimulating interbrand competition or by facilitating entry. It also notes that minimum RPM may harm competition by facilitating a manufacturers' cartel or a retailers' cartel. Some of these economic arguments were also noted in *Sylvania*. *Leegin* extends the Court's prior economic analysis by also recognizing two exclusionary anticompetitive theories: minimum RPM may allow a powerful manufacturer or retailer to obtain or maintain market power by excluding rivals. In the next Sidebar, we consider these economic theories in more detail. We also discuss some of the ramifications of *Leegin* and subsequent developments.

Sidebar 6–2:
After *Leegin*: The Law and Economics of RPM

Leegin harmonized the treatment of minimum RPM with the treatment of intrabrand non-price restraints under *Sylvania*, but appeared to recognize that additional guidance in the application of the rule of reason to vertical restraints was needed and sought to supply it in a number of ways. First, it described four situations in which minimum RPM is more likely to be anticompetitive. Second, it also listed three factors that could aid in identifying those situations. Expanding on *Sylvania*, it also discussed how minimum RPM might be procompetitive or competitively neutral. Finally, echoing the development of the law of horizontal restraints (as we learned in Chapter 2), it invited lower courts to consider ways to allocate burdens and structure the rule of reason inquiry—likely a response to the concerns expressed by the dissent. This Sidebar examines each of these sources of guidance in greater depth, as well as some other issues that follow from the holding in *Leegin*.

Anticompetitive Uses of RPM

Leegin identified four ways in which minimum RPM might be anticompetitive. It could (1) facilitate a manufacturer's cartel; (2) facilitate a dealer cartel; (3) be used by a manufacturer with market power to protect that power by providing its dealers with an incentive not to sell the products of the manufacturer's smaller rivals or new entrants; and (4) be used by a dealer with market power to forestall innovation in lower cost methods of distribution. 551 U.S. at 892–94. Note that the first two scenarios involve *collusive* effects, so you will find parallels with the material we learned in Chapter 3 on cartel formation; the second two involve *exclusionary* effects, so you will find parallels with the material in Chapter 4 on the economics of exclusion.

Manufacturers' Cartel

As we learned in Chapter 3, for a cartel to form and remain stable, the cartel members must reach consensus and then be able to detect and deter cheating by its participants. Since *Dr. Miles*, courts and commentators have expressed the concern that RPM can serve that function by making it easier to police agreed upon prices. With minimum RPM, it will be easier to identify cartel members who cut their price to dealers, because those dealers will in turn promote the product by lowering the retail price. Maintaining resale prices thus provides a more transparent method for policing cheating, and, in doing so, neutralizes the incentive to cheat in the first place. *Sylvania* recognized this theory when it sought to distinguish RPM from non-price restraints. *See Sylvania*, 433 U.S. at 51 n.18.

For this theory to make sense, however, other factors must also be present that make the market conducive to coordination. The tacitly colluding firms must be capable of exercising market power by reducing output collectively in a relevant market protected against entry. In addition, all the competing manufacturers must employ RPM, or those that do not must otherwise be free from the temptation or ability to cheat through alternate means, perhaps because they cannot easily expand their production capacity, a necessity to meet increased demand for their product if they cheat on the cartel by cutting price. And RPM would be expected to be a cost-effective way to stop cartel cheating by those firms that employ it relative to other available alternatives. For example, RPM may be a good tool to detect and deter cheating if rival manufacturers find it difficult to observe reductions in each other's wholesale price directly or to infer them from fluctuations in the retail price, which may arise from shifts in retailing costs. In addition, the dealers must not be able to substitute non-price promotions that are as attractive to customers but more difficult for rival manufacturers to observe.

Dealers' Cartel

Second, as arguably suggested by *Dr. Miles* and emphasized in *Business Electronics*, minimum RPM can be used to police and enforce a horizontal price fixing agreement by a group of colluding dealers. As with any cartel, a successful cartel of dealers would need a means to detect and deter cheating. One or more manufacturers could help make such dealer collusion successful, and make price-cutting impossible, by insisting upon a resale price and threatening to reduce the quantity of product they will ship to discounting retailers. They could even threaten to cut off discounting dealers from access to their products altogether.

The simple-sounding "dealers' cartel" theory appears more complex upon analysis, however, although there are indeed circumstances under which such an arrangement could work. To begin with, the goods over which the dealers would like to collude must themselves be sufficiently free of competition to make a dealer cartel profitable. Collusion could probably not be limited to some models of a product, for example, if most buyers would respond by substituting other models.[a] In addition, entry into retailing of the product cannot be easy; otherwise some or all of the manufacturers who would not benefit from a dealers' cartel would avoid selling through the colluding dealers merely by shifting their distribution to new retailers coming into the market.

---

[a] On the other hand, it may not be necessary for all manufacturers to employ RPM in order for dealer cheating to be deterred. For example, those manufacturers that do not employ RPM may be limited in their ability to expand output or attract the customers of those that do so through lower prices, or those that employ RPM may be willing to terminate dealers who cut the prices of goods produced by manufacturers who do not impose RPM.

Finally, the theory must explain why a manufacturer would be willing to police the dealer cartel. If a manufacturer were a monopolist, it could earn greater profits by setting a monopoly wholesale price and allowing retailers to compete than by enforcing a dealer cartel. Enforcing the cartel would require the monopolist to share some of its market power gains with the retailers. If there are multiple, competing manufacturers of the product, and the manufacturers are not colluding themselves, the colluding dealers are likely extending their cartel to multiple, competing products. Doing so would permit the dealers collectively to earn monopoly profits in the retailing of the products generally if they can convince enough of the manufacturers to impose RPM, and thus perform the "service" of making the cartel viable by preventing dealer cheating.

If manufacturers do not have an interest in facilitating such a dealer cartel, the issue becomes how the dealers can persuade them to do so. The dealers can induce the manufacturers to impose RPM with either a carrot or a stick. The carrot would be compensation to the manufacturers, for example if the dealers were to accede to a higher wholesale price or accept lower manufacturer payments into a cooperative advertising fund. The stick would involve a threat to harm the manufacturer, as by denying the manufacturer access to the retail market through a "group boycott." The latter possibility presumes significant dealer market power. Moreover, for the latter alternative to make sense, it must be easier for the dealers to police cheating on a group boycott than to police cheating on collusion in retail sales. Finally, for a dealers' cartel to succeed, the costs of using the carrot or stick must not exceed the monopoly profits earned by the dealer cartel.

Exclusionary Strategies by a Manufacturer or Dealer with Market Power

Whereas the first two anticompetitive scenarios described by the Court in *Leegin* focused on the role RPM can play in facilitating cartel behavior, the third and fourth relate to exclusionary conduct.

First, the Court posits that a *manufacturer with market power* might adopt minimum RPM to impair its rivals' access to dealers. For this strategy to work, several conditions would have to be satisfied. For the dealer, RPM must result in higher profits than would obtain if it agreed to carry the products of the manufacturer's rivals. The manufacturer would in effect use RPM to pay the dealer for its agreement not to carry the products of the manufacturer's rivals, creating a larger margin between the wholesale price and the manufacturer's required resale price. One way to view this scenario is as a form of compensated exclusive dealing. (Exclusive dealing is examined later in this Chapter.) For the manufacturer, the exclusionary benefits of the strategy must outweigh its costs. The manufacturer would have to believe, therefore, that impairing its rivals' access to dealers will raise their costs and thereby confer, or insulate from erosion, its own market power. *Cf.* John Asker & Heski Bar-Issac, *Raising Retailers' Profits: On Vertical Practices and the Exclusion of Rivals*, 104 AM. ECON. REV. 672 (2014) (model in which a monopolist manufacturer uses RPM or other exclusionary practices to induce retailers to prevent entry in manufacturing, to the benefit of both the manufacturer and the retailers).

Second, the Court suggested that a *dealer with market power* might induce minimum RPM to forestall innovation in distribution that could reduce costs. In this scenario, a dominant dealer fearful that it might lose significant sales to an innovative dealer with lower costs might solicit minimum RPM from a common supplier. RPM could reduce the incentive of the rival dealer to develop more efficient distribution strategies because it will prevent it from fully exploiting those strategies by reducing prices in an effort to compete with the dominant dealer. Although its own greater efficiency might still increase its profitability, minimum RPM would prevent the rival dealer from expanding its market share through lower prices. Normally, one would presume that the manufacturer has an interest in promoting more efficient methods of distribution and therefore would resist the use of RPM under these circumstances. So the dominant dealer's ability to induce the RPM is a critical assumption of this scenario.

The Court in *Leegin* did not address two additional situations in which RPM could be anticompetitive. Because they are not discussed at all, it is difficult to say whether the Court would recognize them if they arose.

Dampening Competition

The Court in *Leegin* did not discuss a fifth anticompetitive possibility, which is suggested by some contemporary economic models of strategic interaction among firms that are *not* coordinating (tacitly colluding). Under some circumstances, manufacturers may impose RPM on dealers as a way of making a commitment to compete less aggressively with each other. This would lead to higher retail prices in settings in which rivals would be expected to respond by becoming less aggressive as well. *See* Daniel P. O'Brien & Greg Shaffer, *Vertical Control with Bilateral Contracts*, 23 RAND J. ECON. 299 (1992); Greg Shaffer, *Slotting Allowances and Resale Price Maintenance: A Comparison of Facilitating Practices*, 22 RAND J. ECON. 120 (1991). RPM is likely to have more power in generating higher prices through this mechanism if adopted by multiple, competing manufacturers. The dampening competition theory is well established in economics, but its practical relevance for antitrust enforcement has been questioned and enforcers and courts have yet to confront the litigation challenges that might arise in demonstrating that a commitment to less-aggressive behavior has led, or likely will lead, rivals to act likewise. The theory was acknowledged by the European Commission in its Guidelines on Vertical Restraints. *See* European Commission Notice, *Guidelines on Vertical Restraints* C(2010) 2365, at 63 (2010), http://ec.europa.eu/competition/antitrust/legislation/guidelines_vertical_en.pdf.

Monopoly Pricing

Leegin did not discuss the possibility that by limiting intrabrand competition RPM could enhance a dominant manufacturer's ability to exercise its own market power, even though this was the principal theory of anticompetitive harm implicit in *Sylvania*. In declaring interbrand competition to be the "primary concern of antitrust law," the *Sylvania* Court seemed to imply that in the absence of significant interbrand competition, antitrust law might intervene to protect against a dominant firm's exercise of "intrabrand market power." *See Sylvania*, 433 U.S. at 52 n.19 (interbrand competition "provides a significant check on the exploitation of intrabrand market power because of the ability of consumers to substitute a different brand of the same product."). Under this view, absent interbrand competition, intrabrand competition might provide the only source of downward pressure on price. *Accord Business Electronics*, 485 U.S. at 748–49 (Stevens, J., dissenting)("Not a word in the *Sylvania* opinion implied that the elimination of intrabrand competition could be justified as reasonable without any evidence of a purpose to improve interbrand competition."). *See also Graphic Products Distributors, Inc. v. ITEK Corp.*, 717 F.2d 1560 (11th Cir. 1983) (discussed *supra* in Sidebar 6–1).

This notion of competitive harm, however, requires a response to the "single monopoly profit" theory—an explanation as to how a dominant firm can extract more monopoly profits from consumers by imposing minimum RPM on its dealers than it could obtain merely by charging an appropriate (high) wholesale price, or by charging a high lump-sum "franchise" fee, or both. As we shall see later in this Chapter in *E & L Consulting, Ltd. v. Doman Indus. Ltd.*, 472 F.3d 23 (2d Cir. 2006), acceptance of the single monopoly profit theory can lead to the conclusion that interbrand competition is not merely the "primary" concern of antitrust law, as the Court held in *Sylvania*, but the *only* concern of antitrust law. Under this view, neither RPM nor any non-price restraint can enhance that power by eliminating intrabrand competition. The Supreme Court seemed implicitly to reject the single monopoly profit idea in *Sylvania*, but perhaps to embrace it in *Leegin*, although neither case directly addresses it. The *Note on Intrabrand Competition and the "Single Monopoly Profit" Theory*, which appears later in this Chapter after *E & L Consulting*, provides an example in which a reduction in intrabrand competition could allow a monopolist to increase its market power.

Figure 6–5 summarizes the anticompetitive theories discussed in *Sylvania* and *Leegin*.

Figure 6–5:

Anticompetitive Theories Associated with Vertical Intrabrand Restraints Recognized by the Supreme Court in *Sylvania* and *Leegin*

Sylvania

Collusive Effects

- Facilitate exercise of market power by a dominant firm by eliminating the downward pressure on price created by intrabrand competition
  - *Criticism*: Single Monopoly Profit Theory
- RPM could facilitate cartel formation (fn. 18)

Leegin

Collusive Effects

- Facilitate manufacturer cartel
- Facilitate retailer cartel

Exclusionary Effects

- Facilitate exclusion of rivals of dominant firm
- Facilitate exclusion of rivals of dominant retailer

Excess Services

Finally, not all consumers will need or want to pay for the same services, yet under a system of RPM they will all be treated alike. The studious consumer, for example, who researches major purchases and obtains information that is publicly available, may be ready to purchase when she enters the retailer. She neither needs nor wants to pay for all the point-of-sale services it offers. Yet, under a system of RPM, she is forced to do so, because all consumers pay the same price. This can lead to a diminution in consumer welfare, especially when the manufacturer over-estimates the actual consumer demand for point-of-sale services.[b]

Three Factors Relevant to Identifying Anticompetitive RPM

In addition to identifying four anticompetitive uses of minimum RPM, the *Leegin* Court described three factors that would be relevant to a rule of reason analysis of the practice: (1) the scope of use of minimum RPM in a market; (2) the source of the restraint, *i.e.*, whether it originated with the supplier or its dealers; and (3) the market power of the supplier and the dealer. 551 U.S. at 897–98. In the Court's view, each of these factors might help to identify instances of minimum RPM that are more likely to be anticompetitive. For a manufacturer cartel scenario, for example, one would expect to see widespread adoption of RPM by rival suppliers. And if the evidence suggests that dealers have sought RPM, it might make a dealer cartel scenario more likely. Finally, absent market power at at least one level, none of the four scenarios are probable.

On the other hand, these factors can be difficult to interpret and apply. For example, although widespread use of minimum RPM could suggest that the practice has anticompetitive potential by facilitating a dealer or manufacturer cartel, it also could suggest that it is widely perceived to be an efficient marketing practice by many firms in an industry. Second, while it may be easy to discern in some cases whether the idea for the practice originated with dealers as opposed to suppliers, in others the evidence may be more ambiguous. Litigating the question of "whose idea was it" might well divert attention and litigation resources from the more central question of evaluating the competitive effects of the practice and might not be necessarily probative of the practice's anti-or procompetitive effects. Finally, market power can be an enticing screening device: if the supplier (or retailer demanding RPM) lacks it, the case can be terminated; but if the supplier (or retailer demanding RPM) possesses it, the potential for anticompetitive

---

[b] For a discussion of these arguments, see William S. Comanor, *Vertical Price-Fixing, Vertical Market Restrictions, and the New Antitrust Policy*, 98 HARV. L. REV. 983 (1985). In evaluating these arguments, it is worth noting that even in competitive markets, product variety may be limited and, in consequence, some customers may be forced to accept undesirable features in a similar sense.

harm increases and the burden of production should shift to the defendants to justify its use. But as Justice Breyer argued in his dissent, market power assessments can themselves be subtle and require extensive discovery and expert elucidation before a reliable judgment can be reached.

Procompetitive Justifications for RPM

Criticism of the per se rule of *Dr. Miles* was long-standing and rooted in some specific scholarship associated with the Chicago School. Justice Breyer's dissent, however, gave voice to some responses to that criticism that have also developed over time. In considering these justifications, it is important to appreciate the paradox of RPM. All of the justifications for its use—both pro-and anticompetitive—lead to higher absolute prices. What arguably differentiates them is that the procompetitive instances provide value to consumers that can justify the higher price. The challenge for critics of *Dr. Miles* was to identify and evaluate that value.

In addition to canvassing the possible anticompetitive uses of minimum RPM, the Court reviewed possible procompetitive uses. Drawing from and further elaborating on the arguments accepted in *Sylvania*, it observed that these uses were "similar to those for other vertical restraints." Their shared characteristic was their ability to stimulate interbrand competition, even though they restrict intrabrand competition, such as by: (1) encouraging dealers to invest in tangible and intangible services or promotional efforts, as by offering dealers a high price-cost margin or limiting competition among dealers; (2) preventing free riding, which might lead to the under-provision of retail services that enhance interbrand competition; (3) facilitating efforts by new firms to enter or expand into a market, as by inducing retailers to invest in promoting and distributing a new product; and (4) providing consumers with more competitive alternatives, such as goods that are low price/low service, high price/high service, or a range of options in between. 551 U.S. at 890–92.

The "free-rider" justification for intrabrand restraints that persuaded the Court in both *Sylvania* and *Leegin* was developed in Lester G. Telser, *Why Should Manufacturers Want Fair Trade*, 3 J. L. & ECON. 86 (1960). Telser challenged the "monopoly prices" hypothesis of *Dr. Miles*, doubted the plausibility of dealer cartels, and, perhaps most importantly, suggested that the prevention of free riding was the most plausible (and procompetitive) explanation of RPM, making per se analysis ill-suited for use with RPM.[c] Indeed, a free rider problem was evident in the record of *Dr. Miles*. *See* 221 U.S. at 374 (Statement by Mr. Justice Hughes). It was also the argument advocated by Leegin's economic consultant. *See* Kenneth G. Elzinga & David E. Mills, Leegin *and Procompetitive Resale Price Maintenance*, 55 ANTITRUST BULL. 349, 349 (2010) ("[t]he most compelling explanation for Leegin's conduct is that it sought to induce efficient retail services to support Leegin's product line and to increase interbrand competition between the company and its many competitors.").

Telser observed that a product sold at retail can usefully be viewed in two component parts: (1) the actual product; and (2) the point-of-sale services associated with the product, such as product information, promotion, and instructions on its use. A manufacturer can provide the dealers with an incentive to undertake such services by lowering its price or otherwise "compensating" the dealers for the services. If the strategy proves successful, the dealers and the manufacturer will be rewarded through higher output. In this respect, Telser observed, the manufacturer's desire to profit through expanded output was consistent with the consumers' interest, as reflected in increased demand for its products. Deferring to the manufacturer's wishes was for Telser presumptively likely to best serve consumers. Consider how well this explanation must have resonated with the Court in *Sylvania* given the facts related to Sylvania's efforts to promote its televisions against the industry leaders of the day.

A full-service dealer's incentive to supply output-expanding services can be undermined, however, if rival dealers are able to avoid the costs of promotion yet divert its customers at low cost. Telser posited that minimum RPM could be a solution for the manufacturer. By being able to set minimum resale prices, the manufacturer can eliminate the free riding dealer's advantage in selling to consumers. To increase sales, it too must now offer services—and it can afford to do so because its price-cost margins are now guaranteed to be higher. In fact, as *Leegin* acknowledged, the two dealers may compete with each other to provide the best services, which could result in increased sales for the manufacturer.

The free rider scenario, however, may be something of a caricature. Recall that in his dissent in *Leegin*, Justice Breyer

---

c   Telser's arguments were later elaborated by other Chicago School proponents. *See, e.g.,* Robert H. Bork, *The Rule of Reason and the Per Se Concept: Price Fixing and Market Division*, 75 YALE L.J. 373 (1966).

questioned whether free riding happens often and, if it does happen, whether it will frequently eliminate the full-service dealer's incentive to continue its promotional efforts. Many products simply do not require much in the way of point-of-sale information or services. They are sold off the shelf, frequently contain all the information the consumer needs either on or in the packaging, and rarely require post-sale service. For other products, the manufacturer pays the retailer to perform point-of-sale services, so there is no possibility of one dealer free riding off another dealer's expenditures. Moreover, the "no frills" store may be a very innovative, lower cost (*i.e.*, more efficient) retailer, not a "free rider." It may offer all of the services consumers need, but at lower cost. The full-service store may simply represent a more expensive method for selling a product given the tastes and needs of consumers. If so, RPM can stifle innovative, discount retailing and lead to higher prices, as noted above. The dissent in *Leegin* also questioned the ability of courts to easily differentiate reasonable from unreasonable instances of RPM purportedly used to eliminate free riding.

Economists writing after Telser have provided additional efficiency explanations for RPM, some of which were also discussed in *Leegin*. *See, e.g.*, Pauline M. Ippolito, *Resale Price Maintenance: Economic Evidence From Litigation* 18 (FTC, April 1986). These go beyond preventing free riding on point-of-sale services to include preventing free riding on post-sale services that influence product quality, such as rapid, high quality repairs or advice on product upgrades, or inducing greater dealer inventory holdings through shifting risk of overstocking from the dealers to the manufacturer. A related issue can arise in markets where consumers infer high quality from a good's high relative price. Some clothing manufacturers, for example, may sell through upscale department stores, but not through discount chains, in order to protect their quality image against price-cutting. RPM could allow such manufactures to expand their distribution and sales without undermining consumer perceptions of product quality. This issue has become more prominent in the age of Internet retailing. Moreover, manufacturers may be able to use RPM procompetitively even absent free riding to provide a financial incentive for retailers to identify and implement strategies for promoting the manufacturer's product. *See* Benjamin Klein, *Competitive Resale Price Maintenance in the Absence of Free Riding*, 76 ANTITRUST L.J. 431 (2009); Benjamin Klein & Kevin M. Murphy, *Vertical Restraints as Contract Enforcement*

Mechanisms, 31 J. L. & ECON. 265 (1988). The *Leegin* dissent noted this possibility but questioned it. *Leegin*, 551 U.S. at 921 (Breyer, J., dissenting).

This overview of *Leegin's* roots returns us to a basic question about its meaning: can *Leegin* fairly be characterized as holding that vertical price and non-price restraints should both be treated under the rule of reason because they are competitively *identical*? Or would it be more accurate to say that whereas all vertical intrabrand restraints share common justifications, minimum RPM still presents some distinct possibilities for anti-competitive results, but that those possibilities can be adequately policed, in the Court's view, under the rule of reason?

RPM and the Rule of Reason: Is There a Structured Approach?

Recall that in Chapter 2 we observed how courts over time have developed a structured, burden-shifting approach to applying the rule of reason to competitor agreements, one that embraces, where appropriate, abbreviated forms of analysis. Although it rejected per se treatment for minimum RPM, the Court in *Leegin* seemed to invite courts and the government enforcement agencies to develop similar approaches for efficiently applying the rule of reason to RPM cases:

> As courts gain experience considering the effects of these restraints by applying the rule of reason over the course of decisions, they can establish the litigation structure to ensure the rule operates to eliminate anticompetitive restraints from the market and to provide more guidance to businesses. Courts can, for example, devise rules over time for offering proof, or even presumptions where justified, to make the rule of reason a fair and efficient way to prohibit anticompetitive restraints and to promote procompetitive ones.

551 U.S. at 898–99. Perhaps the Court hoped that over time the lower courts would develop approaches that would truncate rule of reason analysis, such as burden-shifting presumptions based on evidence that suggests a high probability of anticompetitive effects, inferences of harm to competition from the absence of a legitimate business justification, and reasons for more easily screening out cases in which anticompetitive harm is unlikely. Or maybe the Court majority simply believed that it *should* be difficult to allege and prove anticompetitive RPM, because such cases in actuality will be rare because the practice is so likely

to be procompetitive or benign. The experience since *Sylvania* strongly suggested, perhaps, that successful challenges to vertical restraints would become rare under the full rule of reason. Thus far, that has also been the case under *Leegin*, starting with the remand of the decision. *See, e.g., PSKS, Inc. v. Leegin Creative Leather Prods., Inc.*, 615 F.3d 412 (5th Cir. 2010) (complaint dismissed for failure to allege a plausible relevant product market, a theory of anticompetitive effect within the boundaries of the Supreme Court's decision, or a basis for a horizontal conspiracy); *Jacobs v. Tempur-Pedic Int'l, Inc.*, 626 F.3d 1327, 1340 (11th Cir. 2010) (dismissing challenge to minimum RPM for failure to allege a plausible relevant market or any harm to interbrand competition, as with "marketwide increased prices or reduced output"). *But see Toledo Mack Sales & Service, Inc. v. Mack Trucks, Inc.*, 530 F.3d 204 (3d Cir. 2008) (reversing grant of summary judgment for defendant and concluding that plaintiff had sufficient evidence to warrant a jury trial on its allegations that RPM was being used to facilitate a dealer cartel).

Consider how you might construct a "continuum" approach based on the guidance set forth in *Leegin*. To establish harm to competition, you might start by examining the available evidence to see if it tends to support any of the four anticompetitive scenarios acknowledged by the Court, taking into account its three guiding factors. And if the evidence of harm was sufficient to shift a burden to the defendants, you would next consider whether any of the procompetitive justifications noted by the Court, such as a demonstrable free rider problem, might be the basis for shifting a burden back to the plaintiff. For two proposals of ways to structure the rule of reason analysis of RPM, see *In the Matter of Nine West Group Inc.*, File No. 981 0386, Docket No. C-3937, Order Granting In Part Petition To Reopen and Modify Order Issued April 11, 2000, May 6, 2008, http://www.ftc.gov/os/caselist/9810386/080506order.pdf (suggesting structured approaches to applying *Leegin*); Christine A. Varney, *A Post-*Leegin *Approach to Resale Price Maintenance Using a Structured Rule of Reason*, 24 ANTITRUST 22 (2009). *See also* Andrew I. Gavil, *Resale Price Maintenance in the Post-*Leegin *World: A Comparative Look at Recent Developments in the United States and European Union*, CPI ANTITRUST J., Summer 2010, Vol. 6, No. 2, https://www.competitionpolicyinternational.com/resale-price-maintenance-in-the-post-leegin-world-a-comparative-look-at-recent-developments-in-the-united-states-and-european-union/.

Ramifications of Leegin for Proving RPM "Agreement"

At one point the *Leegin* majority acknowledged that in order to accommodate the interests expressed in *Colgate* and *Sylvania*, *Monsanto* and *Business Electronics* had "limit[ed] the reach" of *Dr. Miles* by raising the burden of proving RPM agreements. 551 U.S. at 901–02. But the Court stopped short of overruling those decisions as no longer necessary in light of its decision to abandon per se analysis for RPM. If they remain good law, do they now serve to "limit the reach" of *Leegin* instead of *Dr. Miles*? Both the majority and the dissent seem to presume that at the very least *Colgate*—which allows a manufacturer to refuse to deal with retailers that do not follow its suggested prices—would now excuse even a demonstrably unreasonable use of RPM. *Id.* at 901; *see also id.* at 924 (BREYER, J., dissenting). Similarly, one circuit court concluded that the rule that a manufacturer may lawfully set minimum prices for its products when there is a genuine principal-agent relationship between the manufacturer and its distributors survives *Leegin*. *Valuepest.com of Charlotte, Inc. v. Bayer Corp.*, 561 F.3d 282 (4th Cir. 2009). Will these decisions, which may have been motivated by judicial efforts to ameliorate the force of *Dr. Miles*, eventually be called into question?

Before *Leegin*, several pricing strategies that tested the limits of *Dr. Miles* had been deemed "reasonable" despite *Dr. Miles'* seeming inflexibility: (1) *cooperative advertising programs*, which typically condition manufacturer financial support for advertising on the dealers' agreement not to advertise discounted prices; (2) *minimum advertised pricing programs* ("MAP"), which similarly restricted a dealer's ability to advertise discounted prices; and (3) *discount pass through programs*, whereby manufacturers agreed to specific discounts to dealers on the condition that the dealer pass-on the discount to its customers. In addition, many firms utilized "manufacturer's *suggested* retail prices" ("MSRP") in an effort to avoid allegations of "agreement," or use of "consignment" sales, which do not involve passage of title or risk from the manufacturer to the consignee. To the extent these practices were adopted by firms that would have preferred to implement RPM, the fact that RPM too will now be reviewed under the rule of reason may lead manufacturers to employ RPM instead of employing these workarounds.

RPM and State Antitrust Enforcement

Since *Leegin*, a number of states have expressed their continued interest in challenging RPM as per se unlawful under state antitrust laws and at least one, Maryland, has amended its antitrust laws to specifically reject *Leegin* and codify per se treatment. *See* MD. CODE ANN., COM. LAW § 11–204(a)(1), (b) (West 2013). In a follow-on case directed at the same defendant, at least one state high court has expressly rejected *Leegin*, retaining per se treatment for RPM under state law. *See O'Brien v. Leegin Creative Leather Prods.*, Inc., 294 Kan. 318, 277 P.3d 1062 (2012). For a state-by-state survey, see Michael A. Lindsay, *Overview of State RPM*, ANTITRUST SOURCE (Oct. 2014), http://www.americanbar.org/content/dam/aba/publishing/antitrust_source/lindsay_chart.authcheckdam.pdf.

Few cases have been brought, however, and many other states have elected to follow *Leegin*. A recent study compared prices and output for selected goods in states that maintain a per se prohibition with those in states that have followed *Leegin* and found prices higher and output lower in *Leegin* states. *See* Alexander MacKay & David Aron Smith, *The Empirical Effects of Resale Price Maintenance on Prices and Output* (Working Paper, Apr. 29, 2013), http://home.uchicago.edu/mackay/files/The%20Empirical%20Effects%20of%20MRPM.pdf. *But see* Thomas A. Lambert & Michael Sykuta, *Why the New Evidence on Minimum Resale Price Maintenance Does Not Justify a* Per Se *or "Quick Look" Approach*, CPI ANTITRUST CHRON., Winter 2013, Vol. 11, No. 1, at 6–8 (questioning the probative value of MacKay & Smith's study).

Conclusion

Leegin illustrates some of the core concerns that currently motivate the Court in establishing antitrust rules. First, the Court has progressively moved away from reliance on per se analysis when it appeared to be a poor fit for practices that have possible procompetitive uses. In doing so, the Court has observed that "stare decisis is not an inexorable command" in antitrust cases interpreting the restraint of trade language of Section 1 of the Sherman Act. *State Oil Co. v. Khan,* 522 U.S. 3, 20 (1997). That recognition provides a degree of flexibility that allows for the integration of new learning in the formulation of antitrust standards. In addition, although it has expressed its concern with the costs and risks of private treble damage antitrust actions, the Court remains committed to the rule of reason as the principal standard for evaluating practices. As in *Leegin*, it has encouraged the lower courts to develop more

> structured, effective, and efficient ways to apply it without relying on per se analysis except when warranted.

3. EXCLUSIVE DISTRIBUTORS AND SUPPLIERS

To this point, our discussion of vertical, intrabrand non-price restraints has focused exclusively on *Sylvania*-style restraints that limit the discretion of the dealer or downstream firm by, for example, limiting the territory in which it can sell, the customers to whom it can sell, or the locations from which it can sell. But there are economically related kinds of vertical intrabrand non-price restraints that constrain the upstream firm.

The most typical example is the "exclusive distributorship." Exclusive distributorships take the form of commitments by a supplier to limit its distribution, as by agreeing that it will not appoint more than one or some limited number of dealers within a certain geographic area or to sell to a specified class or classes of customers. By limiting the number of dealers that might directly compete with each other in the sale of the same brand or line of products, exclusive distributorships limit intrabrand competition, just like territorial and customer restraints. Why would a dealer want such protections? Why would a supplier agree to provide them?

The economic justification for exclusive distributorships is indistinguishable from that identified in *Sylvania* to justify vertical intrabrand non-price restraints generally: to entice a dealer to undertake its best efforts to promote the supplier's brand of product. For example, a manufacturer may appoint an exclusive distributor in each of various regions to ensure that its dealers not face free riding dealers who will refrain from promoting the product, thereby minimizing their own costs, and then steal away customers persuaded to buy the product by the dealer's promotional efforts. In fact, it is likely that Sylvania objected to Continental T.V.'s efforts to expand into Sacramento because it had another dealer already serving that area successfully.

Exclusive distributorships are ubiquitous and rarely present any serious antitrust concerns. Examples include gasoline retailers, automobile dealerships, and many kinds of restaurant franchises. Indeed, recognition of their utility and legality under the Sherman Act long pre-dates *Sylvania*, and they never underwent a period of harsh treatment as did *Sylvania* type restraints. *See, e.g., Packard Motor Car Co. v. Webster Motor Car Co.*, 243 F.2d 418 (D.C. Cir.), *cert. denied*, 355 U.S. 822 (1957); *United States v. Bausch & Lomb Optical Co.*, 45 F. Supp. 387 (S.D.N.Y. 1942), *aff'd by an equally divided court*, 321 U.S. 707 (1944). Even *Schwinn* singled them out as warranting less harsh treatment. *Schwinn*, 388 U.S. at 376.

Exclusive distributorships operate differently, however, than "exclusive dealing," which we will discuss later in this Chapter. An exclusive distributorship typically limits the upstream supplier's discretion to appoint other competing distributors or to distribute its own products in competition with its dealers. In contrast, exclusive dealing involves commitments by the dealer not to carry the products of its supplier's rivals. Whereas exclusive distributorships thus limit int*ra*brand competition, exclusive dealing restricts int*er*brand competition by limiting the dealer's access to rival supplies and rival suppliers' access to dealers. Although some supplier-dealer arrangements can include both kinds of restraints, as we shall learn, the economic analysis of these two kinds of restraints is different because they involve different kinds of competitive effects and justifications.

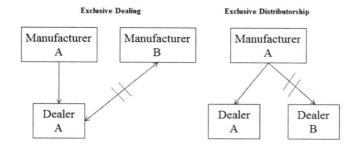

Figure 6–6:
Exclusive Dealing and Exclusive Distributorship Compared

In *E & L Consulting*, which follows, we look at a modern example of the practice. As you read *E & L Consulting*, note the impact of *Sylvania* on the court's analysis. Also consider the role that economic analysis plays today in evaluating the anticompetitive potential of vertical restraints. Consider whether that analysis is focused on the threat of collusive or exclusionary anticompetitive effects.

E & L CONSULTING, LTD. V. DOMAN INDUSTRIES LTD.

United States Court of Appeals for the Second Circuit, 2006.
472 F.3d 23.

Before WINTER, POOLER, and SOTOMAYOR, CIRCUIT JUDGES.

WINTER, CIRCUIT JUDGE.

E & L Consulting, Ltd. ("E & L"), which does business under the name C.B.C. Lumber, Co., and C.B.C. Wood Products, Inc. appeal from [the district court's] * * * dismissal of their complaint against a Canadian lumber company and its exclusive distributor. The complaint asserts, among other things, that a distribution agreement between appellees violates Section 1 of the Sherman Act * * *. We affirm principally because appellants have failed to allege facts that, if proven, would demonstrate harm to competition.

Background

* * *

From 1990 until 2004, E & L was the distributor of green hem-fir lumber in New York, New Jersey, and Pennsylvania for appellees Doman Industries Limited ("Doman") and Eacom Timber Sales Ltd., a Doman subsidiary. The termination of that distribution arrangement gave rise to the present dispute.

Green hem-fir lumber is an inexpensive, durable wood that is "often utilized for homebuilding," particularly in the northeast. There is no hem-fir or green hem-fir tree; the product is a manufactured combination of different woods. Doman and Eacom together supply 95 percent of the green hem-fir lumber sold in New York, New Jersey, Connecticut, Rhode Island, Maryland, Delaware, and Pennsylvania.

Beginning in 1990, E & L had an arrangement with Doman under which E & L "would take delivery, but not ownership, of the green hem-fir lumber products at its port facility in Red Hook, Brooklyn, New York." E & L sold the lumber on Doman's behalf at prices set by Doman, and Doman provided E & L with set monthly payments and commissions. E & L had arrangements with two other green hem-fir distributors, Atlantic Coast Lumber Co. in Rhode Island and Futter Lumber in Delaware.

By 1998, Doman had severed its relationship with Atlantic Coast Lumber. To replace Atlantic Coast, Doman contracted with appellee Sherwood Lumber Corp., a New York corporation that sells lumber-including green hem-fir-and finished wood products. Under its agreement with Doman, Sherwood purchased green hem-fir lumber from Doman and resold it out of the port in New London, Connecticut. Doman prohibited E & L from selling lumber in the area served by Sherwood.

In 2003, Doman cancelled its agreement with Futter Lumber and replaced it with Sherwood. Doman continued to prohibit E & L from selling green hem-fir lumber in states served by Sherwood.

* * *

On January 30, 2004, Doman terminated its distribution agreement with E & L. On February 1, 2004, Doman notified its customers that Sherwood had become the exclusive distributor of Doman green hem-fir lumber in areas previously served by E & L, Futter, and Atlantic Coast.

E & L alleges that there are no commercially feasible alternative sources of green hem-fir lumber. Only one other company beside Doman supplies green hem-fir lumber—Timber West—and it supplies very little. Furthermore, no shipping carriers operate a route from the western United States to Brooklyn, and, consequently, the only way to get lumber from Timber West is by rail. This increases the cost of the lumber by "more than

10 percent," rendering it "uncompetitive for resale." In addition, the only ocean shipping line transporting lumber from Canada to New York told E & L that "no shipments [of non-Doman lumber products] could be made for an indefinite period of time." E & L alleges that Doman's reservation of all potential shipping methods was intended to prevent E & L and other distributors from obtaining an alternative source of supply.

E & L asserts that only a handful of other types of lumber are suitable for the framing of homes, and they cost 25 percent more than green hem-fir, which "precludes these products from being adequate substitutions." Once Sherwood obtained exclusive distribution rights in the northeast, it raised the price of green hem-fir lumber by, in some cases, "over 20 percent."

* * *

The district court concluded that plaintiffs' federal antitrust claims failed because the complaint did not adequately allege a relevant product market, or injury cognizable under the antitrust laws. With no remaining federal questions, [the district court] * * * declined to exercise supplemental jurisdiction over the state law claims. The present appeal ensued.

Discussion

a)   *Standard of Review*

We review a district court's grant of a motion to dismiss under Rule 12(b)(6) de novo. For purposes of such a review, we accept as true all allegations in the complaint and draw all reasonable inferences in favor of the non-moving party.[2] * * *

* * *

b)   *Section 1 Claim*

Appellants' Sherman Act Section 1 claim, based on the Doman-Sherwood distribution agreement, fails because they have not alleged an injury to competition, an element of a *prima facie* Section 1 claim.[3]

---

[2]   We indulge in this assumption despite seeming anomalies in some factual allegations. For example, the complaint alleges that a 10% increase in transportation costs when rail is used renders green hem-fir lumber from another producer "uncompetitive for resale" because of the elasticity of demand for the product while also alleging that Sherwood has raised prices by over 20% and that alternative kinds of suitable lumber sell for 25% more than green hem-fir. Moreover, the complaint alleges that Doman has sold green hem-fir lumber at a discount to Sherwood to allow the latter to sell green hem-fir lumber at lower prices than E & L and to tie the sale of that product to Sherwood's sale of finished wood products, conduct that hardly benefits Doman.

[3]   One basis on which the district court dismissed the complaint was its conclusion that plaintiffs had not alleged "antitrust injury," because they had failed to "allege some type of harm to competition market-wide." We agree with the district court that the plaintiffs' failure to proffer allegations of harm to competition is fatal to their antitrust claims. However, the failure to allege harm to competition is analytically distinct from failure to plead antitrust injury. Antitrust injury

* * *

The complaint alleges a vertical restraint between a supplier (Doman) and a distributor (Sherwood).[4] The agreement between Doman and Sherwood designating the latter as the exclusive distributor of Doman green hem-fir in the northeast, like any commercial agreement, restrains trade. But, critically, nothing in the complaint suggests that this agreement results in either a "predictable and pernicious" (*per se* violation) or "unreasonable" (rule of reason violation) effect on competition. It is not "a violation of the antitrust laws, without a showing of actual adverse effect on competition market-wide, for a manufacturer to terminate a distributor . . . and to appoint an exclusive distributor."

Doman is alleged to have a market share in green hem-fir lumber amounting to 95% in the northeastern United States. Appellants do not assert that Doman's market share is somehow an illegal monopoly and seek no relief on that ground. But, they allege, the exclusive distributorship with Sherwood further harms competition. However, appellants' hypothesizing of an unreasonable effect on competition fails because such a vertical arrangement provides no monopolistic benefit to Doman that it does not already enjoy and would not continue to enjoy if the exclusive distributorship were enjoined. To put it another way, had Doman established its own in-house distribution system with the same monopoly that Sherwood is alleged to possess, there would have been no increase in the restriction of output of green hem-fir lumber and in the resultant misallocation of resources.

Indeed, an exclusive distributorship would be counterproductive so far as any monopolization goal of Doman is concerned. A monopolist manufacturer of a product restricts output of the product in order to maximize its profits. The power to restrict output to maximize profit is complete in the manufacturing monopoly, and there is no additional monopoly profit to be made by creating a monopoly in the retail distribution of the product. On the contrary, a firm with a monopoly at the retail distribution level will further reduce output to maximize *its* profits, thereby reducing the sales and profit of the monopoly manufacturer. *See Cont'l T.V., Inc. v. GTE Sylvania Inc.,* 433 U.S. 36, 56 (1977) * * *. Like any seller of a product, a monopolist would prefer multiple competing buyers unless

---

is "injury of the type the antitrust laws were intended to prevent and that flows from that which makes defendants' acts unlawful." *Brunswick Corp. v. Pueblo Bowl-O-Mat, Inc.,* 429 U.S. 477, 489 (1977). An antitrust plaintiff "must show not only injury-in-fact, but also that [the injury] constitutes . . . the kind that the antitrust laws are designed to prevent and that [is] congruent with the rationale for finding an antitrust violation in the first place." It should go without saying, therefore, that a party cannot establish antitrust injury without establishing a violation of the antitrust laws, which, under Section 1, must involve an injury to competition.

4   "Restraints imposed by agreement between competitors have traditionally been denominated as horizontal restraints, and those imposed by agreement between firms at different levels of distribution as vertical restraints." *Business Elecs. Corp. v. Sharp Elecs. Corp.,* 485 U.S. 717, 730 (1988).

an exclusive distributorship arrangement provides other benefits in the way of, for example, product promotion or distribution. *See Cont'l T.V.*, 433 U.S. at 54–56. In fact, we have explicitly noted that "a vertically structured monopoly can take only one monopoly profit."

The only detriment to competition alleged to result from the Doman-Sherwood agreement is that "end-users of lumber and finished wood products have fewer options to purchase their required supplies and are now required to pay artificially inflated prices." This, by itself, is not a sufficient allegation of harm to competition caused by the exclusive distributorship, again, because the alleged single source and price increase, even if monopolistic, is something Doman can achieve without the aid of a distributor.

Thus, we have noted that "exclusive distributorship arrangements are presumptively legal." To be sure, we have never held that all exclusive arrangements are reasonable as a matter of law. In *Geneva Pharmaceuticals*, for example, we vacated a grant of summary judgment on a Section 1 claim that was based on an exclusive supply agreement between a drug-maker and a supplier of the active ingredient in the drug. *Geneva Pharms. Tech. Corp. v. Barr Labs. Inc.,* 386 F.3d 485 (2d Cir. 2004). We acknowledged the general rule that "it usually does not further harm competition for a monopolist in one market to leverage its advantage into a monopoly in a downstream market." However, in that case there was a "window of monopoly opportunity [that] is unique." *Geneva* involved an allegation of two temporary, related monopolies in different products, a drug and its active ingredient. Moreover, the two firms, which had overlapping ownership, were jointly involved in predatory practices designed to extend their respective temporary monopolies by deterring entry by competitors. * * *

The facts in *Geneva*, therefore, were quite different from the claim in a typical exclusive distribution case, like the present one, where it is alleged only that a monopolist manufacturer is trying to extend its monopoly into the distribution or sale of its product. Unlike *Geneva*, the present case is a "run-of-the-mill exclusive distributorship controversy, where a former exclusive distributor is attempting to protect its competitive position vis a vis its supplier." The complaint simply does not allege, therefore, "that the challenged action has had an *actual* adverse effect on competition as a whole in the relevant market."

* * *

Note that E & L, as the plaintiff, bore the burden of showing that Doman's switch from several to a single exclusive distributor was anticompetitive. What was its theory of competitive harm? Did it allege collusive or exclusionary anticompetitive effects? What evidence did it point to? Was E & L attempting to make the argument alluded to in *Sylvania* and discussed above, that in a highly concentrated market intrabrand competition provides the only downward pressure on price, and hence its elimination through exclusive territories, customers, or, as in this case, through an exclusive distributorship, unreasonably restrained trade?

Given the procedural posture of the case, the court presumes that green hem-fir lumber is a product market. Why, in the court's view, was the combination of a very high market share and an apparent increase in price following the change in distribution insufficient to state a claim? Did it doubt the economic basis of the alleged relevant market, and hence the alleged inference that Doman had market power? Why was it also insufficient to allege that "end-users of lumber and finished wood products have fewer options to purchase their required supplies and are now required to pay artificially inflated prices"? Under the court's reasoning, when, if ever, could an exclusive distributorship—or any other vertical intrabrand restraint—raise any significant antitrust concerns? *See also Paddock Publ'ns, Inc. v. Chicago Tribune Co.*, 103 F.3d 42, 45, 47 (7th Cir. 1996) (noting in the context of an antitrust challenge to the selection of exclusive distributors of news content that "[c]ompetition-for-the-contract is a form of competition that antitrust laws protect rather than proscribe, and it is common" and encouraging the displaced distributor to "outbid" its rival distributors in the marketplace rather than trying to "outmaneuver them in court").

Because in the court's view E & L failed to establish anticompetitive effect, Doman was not required to offer any evidence of a procompetitive justification for the switch—there was no burden shift. Does the court nevertheless assume one, based on the arguments developed in *Sylvania*? Note that it alludes to improving promotional efforts and to free riding by its citation to *Sylvania*. Was there any evidence that those were in fact the reasons for Doman's change of distribution? Was E & L a "discounter"? When the court reaffirms its view that exclusive distributorships are "presumptively legal," is it assuming that they are most likely to be procompetitive? Is that what *Sylvania* held?

What might be the remedy if the court had reached a different result? What would have been E & L's theory of damages? Would they have been related to sales lost because of diminished competition, as required by the antitrust injury doctrine and noted by the court? Would E & L have dropped the suit if Doman had offered to substitute it for Sherwood as its exclusive distributor? That would have been a better result for E & L, but would it have been any better for competition and consumers? What kind of injunctive relief might the court have considered? Would it have ordered Doman to create additional intrabrand competition by appointing more dealers? Would Doman have likely done so, or would it, as the court intimates, vertically integrated, either on its own or by acquiring one of its distributors? After *Leegin*, if it chose the route of selling to more dealers, might it also consider using minimum RPM to defeat discounting, if that was a concern? Could it lawfully do so under *Leegin*?

The court's principal economic argument is what economists refer to as the "single monopoly profit" theory. What is that theory, and is it supported by *Sylvania*, as the court appears to suggest? We will examine it in depth in the next Note.

Finally, there are two additional and interesting facts noted by the court in its description of the case's background. First, under its distribution arrangement with Doman, note that E & L would "take delivery, but not ownership, of the green hem-fir lumber products" and "E & L sold the lumber on Doman's behalf at prices set by Doman, and Doman provided E & L with set monthly payments and commissions." Was this Doman's effort to comply with *Colgate* and utilize unilateral RPM? If so, is there any suggestion that it used RPM in any of the four anticompetitive ways outlined by the Court in *Leegin*? Is it more likely, as the court here appeared to assume, that, consistent with its reliance on exclusive distribution, it was an effort to secure promotional allegiance? Second, the court recounts E & L's allegation that "the only ocean shipping line transporting lumber from Canada to New York told E & L that 'no shipments [of non-Doman lumber products] could be made for an indefinite period of time.'" And that "E & L alleges that Doman's reservation of all potential shipping methods was intended to prevent E & L and other distributors from obtaining an alternative source of supply." Could this have constituted a second, distinct practice that E & L could have challenged? Does it sound more like exclusive distributing, which it challenged, or exclusive *dealing*?

NOTE ON THE "SINGLE MONOPOLY PROFIT" THEORY

Some antitrust commentators have suggested that competition cannot be harmed when a monopolist adopts vertical restraints (e.g., vertical mergers, exclusive dealing contracts, tying, and price or non-price restrictions imposed on distributors), because there is only a "single monopoly profit" and the monopolist cannot profitably expand or extend that power through vertical practices. Judge Bork described antitrust enforcement under such circumstances as making "the simple arithmetical error of counting the same market power twice." ROBERT BORK, THE ANTITRUST PARADOX 137–38 (1978); *see also id.* at 140, 372. If accepted, the single monopoly profit theory could exempt from antitrust scrutiny many kinds of vertical restraints, regardless of their potential exclusionary effects.

Some courts have cited this theory as reason to reject antitrust challenges to vertical agreements by monopolists. We have just discussed *E & L Consulting,* and later in the Chapter we will see the theory invoked by the

Supreme Court in *NYNEX Corp. v. Discon, Inc.*, 525 U.S. 128 (1998) and the Ninth Circuit in *Brantley v. NBC Universal, Inc.*, 675 F.3d 1192 (9th Cir. 2012). *See also G.K.A. Beverage Corp. v. Honickman*, 55 F.3d 762, 767 (2d Cir. 1995) ("a vertically structured monopoly can take only one monopoly profit"); *Jefferson Parish Hosp. Dist. No. 2 v. Hyde*, 466 U.S. 2, 36–37, 104 S. Ct. 1551, 1570–71 (1984) (O'Connor, J., concurring) ("A seller with a monopoly on flour . . . cannot increase the profit it can extract from flour consumers simply by forcing them to buy sugar along with their flour," though it may be possible for the flour monopolist "to use its market power to acquire additional power in the sugar market, perhaps by driving out competing sellers of sugar . . ."); *Town of Concord v. Boston Edison Co.*, 915 F.2d 17, 23, 32 (1st Cir. 1990) (Breyer, C.J.) ("the extension of monopoly power from one to two levels does not *necessarily*, nor in an *obvious* way, give a firm added power to raise prices").

Yet it has long been recognized, even by advocates of the single monopoly theory, that the theory is not generally applicable to most antitrust allegations. For example, in discussing vertical mergers, Robert Bork observed that cases in which one key assumption underlying the single monopoly profit theory does not hold "are quite common," ROBERT H. BORK, THE ANTITRUST PARADOX 229 (1978) (referring to the assumption of fixed proportions, which is discussed below), and Richard Posner was *more* concerned about the exclusionary potential of vertical mergers when one of the parties was a monopolist than otherwise. RICHARD A. POSNER, ANTITRUST LAW 226 (2d ed. 2001); *see also id.* at 228 (describing the possible competitive harm from a vertical merger involving a monopoly input supplier when the input is used in variable proportions in producing the final product).[2] Critics contend that the single monopoly profit theory also is based on other assumptions that are not "realistic," and conclude that it should not be credited as a basis for presuming that vertical mergers or other exclusionary conduct are neutral or procompetitive.

The single monopoly profit theory is logically valid as a matter of economic theory only in one extreme case: when buyers have literally no alternatives to the monopolist's product and prohibitively high entry barriers prevent any future competition. *See* Jonathan B. Baker, *Taking the Error Out of "Error Cost" Analysis: What's Wrong with Antitrust's Right*, 80 ANTITRUST L. J. 1, 16–17 (2015). This extreme case relies on a much more narrow and literal definition of the term "monopolist" than is typically used in antitrust law. The dispute between supporters and critics of the theory can be understood as focused on its practical significance in situations that do not satisfy the extreme case. Advocates of the theory would justify imposing a high bar for plaintiffs seeking to demonstrate harm to competition from certain types of dominant firm conduct on the grounds that exceptions to the single monopoly profit theory are rare or implausible; critics contend that the exceptions are

---

[2]   Both Bork and Posner recommended caution in vertical merger enforcement, mainly to permit firms to achieve efficiencies. ROBERT H. BORK, THE ANTITRUST PARADOX 230 (1978); RICHARD A. POSNER, ANTITRUST LAW 224–29 (2d ed. 2001).

common and important, and the conditions under which the single monopoly profit theory itself should be applied are rare or implausible.

This Note presents four scenarios in which the single monopoly profit theory would not prevent an antitrust monopolist (or any firm with market power) from enhancing or maintaining its market power through use of vertical restraints. In the first three examples, the monopolist uses exclusionary conduct to prevent some form of buyer substitution to the products of actual or potential rivals.[3] (Of course, a full analysis of the competitive effects of the conduct would also need to account for any efficiencies that the business practices confer.) As you review the examples, consider whether the possibility of competitive harm is sufficiently insubstantial as to justify courts *presuming* that the alleged exclusionary conduct is highly unlikely to harm competition, as some courts have done when they have relied on the single monopoly profit theory.

Exclusion of Actual or Potential Rivals to a Dominant Firm

Suppose that water heaters are manufactured by national firms and distributed in metropolitan area markets by plumbing supply houses. Heatco is the dominant manufacturer of water heaters, with a 90% share in the typical city, and its products are carried by all the plumbing supply houses (distributors). If charged with monopolization, Heatco likely would be found to have monopoly power in a market for water heaters. But it is not a literal monopolist in that it has some actual manufacturing rivals, which collectively account for a 10% share, and there could be potential entrants as well.

The typical city has three plumbing supply houses, for whom the cost of holding inventory is a major concern. That cost varies with the level of a distributor's sales: it is low if the distributor has a high volume of water heater business, but high otherwise. (The cost functions for plumbing supply houses thus exhibit scale economies, as discussed in the Appendix to Chapter 1 on Cost Concepts.)

Suppose Heatco selects one of the distributors, Plumbhouse, as its exclusive distributor in a city. Now Heatco's fringe rivals and potential manufacturing entrants would be forced to distribute through the remaining two distributors only. But, without Heatco's business, suppose that the other two distributors will have high inventory costs and, as these are variable costs, they will have to charge higher retail prices for water heaters. As a result, Plumbhouse will also be able to charge a higher retail price.[4]

---

[3] The fourth example involves the evasion of rate regulation. In addition to the mechanisms by which vertical restraints could increase the dominant firm's monopoly profits set forth in these examples, such restraints could do so by allowing a dominant firm to price discriminate more effectively or by facilitating coordination.

[4] Even if Heatco's manufacturing rivals do not exit the market, the higher retail price will generate enough additional revenues for Plumbhouse on sales of Heatco water heaters to allow Heatco to profit even after compensating Plumbhouse for lost retail profits on sales of the rival products. Also, as noted in the text, the example treats the increase in inventory costs as a higher marginal cost; if instead the higher inventory costs were solely increased fixed costs, competition would still be harmed if the other distributors were forced to exit the sale of water heaters.

Rival water heater manufacturers will also be placed at a distribution cost disadvantage relative to Heatco. As a result, one or more of the other manufacturers may go out of business, and potential manufacturers may decide not to enter, thereby allowing Heatco to maintain or even enhance its market power. In a more extreme case, if the other two distributors do not sell enough units, one or both of them may be forced to stop selling water heaters. If that were to happen, it would end competition to Heatco.

In this example, Heatco's exclusive distribution contract allows it to prevent the erosion of or enhance its market power. The exclusive arrangement raises its rivals' distribution costs and creates barriers to entry and rival expansion. Heatco could achieve a similar anticompetitive outcome with other types of exclusionary practices, most obviously by acquiring a distributor in each city (vertical mergers).

Did the court in *E & L Consulting* consider possibilities like these? Recall the Ninth Circuit's decision in *Microsoft* (*see supra* Chapter 4). Why didn't the single monopoly profit theory prevent the D.C. Circuit from upholding the district court's conclusion that a monopolist of operating systems for Intel-compatible personal computers could maintain its market power, harming competition, through exclusionary conduct that inhibited the development of complementary products that rival operating systems could use to compete more effectively? How is the economic theory accepted in *Microsoft* similar to the hypothetical Heatco example?

Leveraging Market Power to a Complementary Market[5]

Suppose that a small resort island has a single very large hotel, and also numerous villas that are rented out by independent owners. Hotel guests, villa renters and local residents can eat at the hotel restaurant or at local restaurants that are not affiliated with the hotel. Suppose further that the island is a unique place and the hotel is a monopolist in that distinct geographic market.

The hotel recently decided to require that its guests eat all their meals at the hotel—that is, it began to bundle (tie) hotel rooms with meals at its restaurant. This bundling will cause the island's local restaurants to lose customers. If most or all of the restaurants fail as a result, local residents and villa renters, too, will lose a substitution opportunity. That may give the hotel restaurant the ability to charge higher prices to the villa renters and local residents, even though they do not stay at the hotel.[6] Thus, the hotel

---

[5]   The example is adapted from Dennis W. Carlton & Michael Waldman, *The Strategic Use of Tying to Preserve and Create Market Power in Evolving Industries*, 33 RAND J. ECON. 194 (2002), where it is attributed to Robert Gertner. The procompetitive and anticompetitive uses of tying, which go beyond the exclusionary possibility described in this example and the regulatory evasion possibility described in the last example, are surveyed in Sidebar 6–5, *infra*.

[6]   If the hotel restaurant must charge the same price to guests and local residents, then the hotel would raise restaurant prices and lower room prices to fully offset the higher cost of meals for hotel guests in the hotel package. Local residents would pay more for meals, but hotel guests would not pay more for their island visits.

monopolist uses tying literally to extend its market power into a separate market for restaurants. It can, in consequence, earn more than its single monopoly profit on hotel rooms.[7]

As this example suggests, many allegations of anticompetitive exclusion through tying or bundling involve products that are complements. These are typically goods that buyers use together, like an operating system and a browser, or a printer and ink.[8] (Vertically-related sellers, like manufacturers and dealers, produce complements in a special sense: the buyer purchases both the product and distribution services.)

Preventing Buyers from Economizing On Products They Can Use in Variable Proportions

Suppose that refrigerators are produced in a competitive industry, the cooling system is a costly part of refrigerator manufacturing, and refrigerant chemicals are the most costly part of the cooling system. Suppose further that when filling their systems with refrigerants, refrigerator manufacturers can use either Freezon or Iceon exclusively, or can use a mix of the two. Freezon and Iceon have different chemical compositions.

Chempont is the monopoly producer of Freezon, while Iceon is produced and sold by many competing firms. Given the properties of the chemicals and the prices at which Freezon and Iceon are sold, home kitchen refrigerator manufacturers find that their most cost-effective option is to use a particular combination of the two mixed together: 70% Freezon and 30% Iceon. Chempont's Freezon price is constrained because refrigerator manufacturers would respond to a higher Freezon price by changing their refrigerant mix to substitute to more Iceon and less Freezon. Thus, the production process here involves *variable proportions* rather than a rigid ratio (i.e., *fixed proportions*).

Instead of simply setting its Freezon price and having customers choose their preferred mix, suppose that Chempont now insists that its refrigerator manufacturer customers use a mix of at least 90% Freezon. The refrigerator manufacturers may be unable to resist Chempont's demand: for each, the alternative of using 100% Iceon would be even costlier. By restricting customer substitution with this (nearly) all-or-nothing offer, Chempont may be able to charge a higher price for Freezon even though Iceon continues to be available in the marketplace. In addition, if Iceon cannot cover its fixed costs when

---

[7]   In this example, the hotel guests use hotel rooms and meals in fixed proportions so it might seem that the single monopoly profit theory could apply. But, non-hotel guests do not buy in fixed proportions from the tying product monopolist. They buy the tied product (restaurant meals), but not the tying product (hotel rooms). The tie thus permits the monopolist of the tying product to exercise market power over a new group of customers (non-hotel guests). *Cf.* Ward S. Bowman, Jr., *Tying Arrangements and the Leverage Problem*, 67 YALE L.J. 19, 25–27 (1957) (a monopolist can use tying to leverage its monopoly power into the market for a complementary product used by buyers in variable proportions with the monopolized product). Fixed and variable proportions are discussed in the next example in this Note.

[8]   More technically, if the price of a product increases, buyers will purchase less of it, more of its demand substitutes, and less of its demand complements. Products do not have to be consumed together to be complements in demand. Baseball tickets and football tickets might be complements, for example, for sports fans that like to attend games year-round.

manufacturers adopt a 90–10 mix, Freezon may drive Iceon out of business. If so, Chempoint would achieve a monopoly in the refrigerant market.

Chempont may also be able to reach a similar result through a "two-way" exclusive dealing agreement with the leading manufacturer of home kitchen refrigerators, Chillaire. Chempont would agree not to sell Freezon to any refrigerator manufacturer other than Chillaire, and Chillaire would agree to pay a higher price for the Freezon it uses. The exclusive dealing agreement would force Chillaire's rivals to use Iceon alone, which is more expensive, or else to exit. Either way, Chillaire would face less aggressive competition than before, allowing it to raise the price of refrigerators. This outcome could be profitable for both Chillaire and Chempont. [9] As another alternative, Chempont and Chillaire might (vertically) merge to achieve the same outcome.

Evasion of Rate Regulation

Suppose that Powerco sells two products to households: electricity and light bulbs. It is the only firm with electric wires running to houses, most likely because electric power is a natural monopoly (*i.e.*, substantial scale economies in electricity distribution that mean that only one firm would survive in an unregulated market). The state public utilities commission regulates Powerco's electric rates. Its rates are set well below the monopoly price, at a level that provides Powerco with only slightly more than the competitive rate of return.

Powerco also sells light bulbs, but so do several other firms and the market price of light bulbs is set by competition—it is not regulated. If Powerco institutes a policy that forces its electricity customers to use only Powerco's light bulbs (and if it can enforce that requirement, which may not be easy), then it may be able to exercise market power in the light bulb market, when it could not do so before. Powerco would continue to charge the regulated price for electricity, but it would raise the price of light bulbs above the competitive level. Households would be forced to pay the higher price for bulbs in order to obtain electricity to use the bulbs.

In this example, Powerco, the electricity monopolist, uses tying to exercise market power in light bulbs because its regulators are preventing it from charging the monopoly price for electricity. Should Powerco's behavior be treated as an antitrust concern for the courts, or should it be treated solely as a regulatory problem for the public utility commission to remedy? The significance of regulation for judicial willingness to consider antitrust claims is discussed in our next Note.

Concluding Comment

In the four scenarios set forth in this Note, the single monopoly profit theory would not prevent a firm with market power, including an antitrust monopolist, from using vertical restraints to enhance or maintain its market

---

[9]   This is likely to be most profitable if the demand for refrigerators is relatively inelastic (so the total profits in the downstream market rise substantially) and if substitution to 100% Iceon is much more expensive.

power. What efficiencies might those vertical arrangements also confer? Are the harms sufficiently implausible and the efficiencies sufficiently plausible to justify a presumption that a vertical restraint employed by a monopolist is highly unlikely to harm competition, as some courts do when they rely on the single monopoly profit theory?

B. EXCLUSIVE DEALING, TYING AND RELATED PRACTICES

Thus far in this Chapter we have been considering how distribution arrangements between suppliers and their customers that affect in*tra*brand competition are analyzed under the antitrust laws. Recall that a principal justification for permitting intrabrand restraints is their ability to enhance in*ter*brand competition, which, according to the Supreme Court, "is the primary concern of antitrust law." *Sylvania*, 433 U.S. at 52 n.19. In *Leegin*, the Court further explained that intrabrand restraints only pose a significant anticompetitive risk when: (1) they are being used to facilitate a dealer or manufacturer cartel; or (2) when the dealer or manufacturer has market power and the intrabrand restraint is being used to implement an exclusionary strategy. In other words, intrabrand restraints were of concern when they adversely affected interbrand competition.

Now we turn to distribution restraints that are directed at in*ter*brand competition. As with restraints on intrabrand competition, interbrand restrictions can be anticompetitive because they have collusive or exclusionary effects, but they frequently can be an integral part of a distribution strategy that promotes competition. In lieu of the traditional approach that differentiates distribution-related restraints based on whether they affect intrabrand or interbrand competition, therefore, we focus on the analysis of competitive effects, including potential justifications. In doing so, we will be drawing upon the law and economics of exclusion, which we examined in Chapter 4 and the material already covered in this Chapter.

As was illustrated in Figure 6–3, interbrand restraints can take a number of forms, such as "exclusive dealing" and "tying" arrangements, although there are other variations. In exclusive dealing arrangements, a supplier and its customer, such as a retail dealer, agree that the dealer will buy exclusively from the supplier. Similarly, "output" or "requirements" contracts can make such supply arrangements effectively exclusive. Under an output contract, a buyer agrees to purchase all of a supplier's output of a specified good or service. Conversely, under a requirements contract a buyer agrees to purchase all of its requirements for a certain product or service from a specified supplier. In the output context the supplier is effectively precluded from selling to any other buyers, which makes it similar to an exclusive distributorship arrangement; in the requirements context, the buyer is effectively precluded from buying from other suppliers, which makes it similar to an exclusive dealing arrangement. Because the typical exclusive dealing arrangement limits the dealer's discretion to buy from rival suppliers, by implication it also limits those suppliers' access to the dealer and any others that might also be subject to exclusivity. As we shall see, although exclusive dealing, output and requirements contracts, and tying all involve interbrand exclusion to some degree, they also can have many procompetitive justifications and are very common.

As has been true in each of the previous Chapters, the challenge is to develop a legal and economic framework for distinguishing reasonable restraints from unreasonably exclusionary ones—those whose actual or probable exclusionary effects are so significant, or which are so lacking in business justifications, that they warrant prohibition under the antitrust laws. As a consequence, the analysis of interbrand restraints has grown increasingly similar to that used to evaluate other exclusionary arrangements, such as exclusion by a dominant firm and exclusionary group boycotts, which we studied in Chapter 4.

The study of vertical interbrand restraints is complicated by two other factors: one economic and the other legal. First, even more so than was true in the case of intrabrand vertical restraints, the economic analysis of interbrand restraints can be complex. Especially when a firm with market power implements such restraints, they can have mixed results: they may have the potential to harm, but also to benefit competition. As has been true throughout our study thus far, these kinds of mixed-result cases present the greatest challenges to antitrust enforcers and courts.

Second, and again somewhat similarly to the history of intrabrand restraints, the law of interbrand restraints has been characterized by intense academic and legal debate for decades and the courts have developed distinct and still evolving legal rules for some categories of agreements. For example, although exclusive dealing has always been examined under some version of a reasonableness test, tying has for a long time been labeled "per se" unlawful when certain conditions are present. But, as we shall see, the current status of the per se treatment of tying is at best uncertain, in part due to years of criticism. As we will learn later in this Chapter, in the *Microsoft* litigation the D.C. Circuit refused to apply per se analysis to "technological tying," the integration of seemingly separable software programs, such as Internet browsers, media players, and a computer operating system, on the ground that the approach was ill-suited to the analysis of platform software.

Finally, although tying and exclusive dealing can be evaluated under Section 1 of the Sherman Act as "contracts in restraint of trade," they also can be the focus of allegations of unilateral exclusionary conduct by a single firm under Section 2 of the Sherman Act, and are most specifically addressed under Section 3 of the Clayton Act. We will consider the role of Section 3 of the Clayton Act later in this Chapter. We have already examined dominant firm exclusionary conduct in Chapter 4.

These factors—complex economic analysis, the presence of some history of per se treatment, and the applicability of multiple statutory prohibitions—all make for a complicated picture. We begin with an overview of the historical development that concludes with an examination of the Supreme Court's last consideration of these kinds of arrangements in *Jefferson Parish Hospital District No. 2 v. Hyde*, 466 U.S. 2, 104 S.Ct. 1551, 80 L.Ed.2d 2 (1984).

1. HISTORICAL FOUNDATIONS AND DEVELOPMENT

Tying

Tying has a long and distinct history of treatment under the antitrust laws that pre-dates the adoption of the Clayton Act in 1914, Section 3 of which includes a specific prohibition of tying and exclusive dealing agreements when their effect "may be to substantially lessen competition or tend to create a monopoly." *See infra* Appendix A. The provision was adopted in part as a response to *Henry v. A.B. Dick Co.*, 224 U.S. 1 (1912) and the then still pending *United States v. United Shoe Mach. Co.*, 247 U.S. 32 (1918). *See Int'l Bus. Machs. Corp. v. United States*, 298 U.S. 131, 137–38 (1936) (discussing the origins of the Clayton Act's prohibition of tying). Note that Section 3 does not refer to and therefore does not apply to services.

Like RPM, an important component of tying's unique legacy is its treatment as a per se offense. Three early cases provided the foundation for the later treatment of tying as per se unlawful—*United Shoe Mach. Corp. v. United States*, 258 U.S. 451 (1922), *Int'l Bus. Machs. Corp. v. United States*, 298 U.S. 131 (1936) ("*IBM*"), and *Int'l Salt Co. v. United States*, 332 U.S. 392 (1947). *United Shoe* and *IBM* both arose under Section 3 of the Clayton Act, whereas *International Salt* was brought under both Section 3 of the Clayton Act and Section 1 of the Sherman Act. All three cases involved allegations that the defendants had conditioned the leasing of one product on the purchaser's agreement to buy, or in the case of *United Shoe* lease, another, unwanted product; in all three cases the defendants asserted that the tying arrangement was protected by patent rights in the tying product; and in all three cases the Supreme Court condemned the practice as unlawful.

IBM is representative of the Court's thinking. IBM conditioned the leasing of its mechanical tabulation machines on the lessee's agreement to purchase and use only IBM punch cards in the machines. It argued that, unless the cards were produced to conform to "minute tolerances," the machines could produce inaccurate results which would damage IBM's reputation. The Court responded:

> There is no contention that others than appellant cannot meet these requirements. It affirmatively appears, by stipulation, that others are capable of manufacturing cards suitable for use in appellant's machines, and that paper required for that purpose may be obtained from the manufacturers who supply appellant. * * * The suggestion that without the tying clause an adequate supply of cards would not be forthcoming from competitive sources is not supported by the evidence. * * *

298 U.S. at 139. After noting that IBM could protect its good will by touting the "virtues of its own cards" and warning its customers of the risk of using punch cards that did not conform to its specifications, the Court concluded that the tying arrangement was greater than necessary to achieve its goals and hence violated the Clayton Act:

> The Clayton Act names no exception to its prohibition of monopolistic tying clauses. Even if we are free to make an exception to its unambiguous command, we can perceive no tenable basis for an exception in favor of a condition whose substantial benefit to the lessor is the elimination of business competition and the creation of monopoly, rather than the protection of its good will, and where it does not appear that the latter can not be achieved by methods which do not tend to monopoly and are not otherwise unlawful.

298 U.S. at 140 (citations omitted). *IBM* illustrates the earliest and most rudimentary features of the "tying" arrangement: (1) the presence of two products, one desired by buyers, the other not; (2) a degree of "forcing," in the sense that the purchaser has no choice but to take the second product to get the first; and (3) a legal inference that the effects of such forcing can be "monopolistic." Note that *IBM*, however, did not unambiguously identify tying as per se unlawful. Although reasoning that the "Clayton Act names no exception," it went on to consider IBM's proffered justifications, that tying was necessary to guarantee the proper functioning of its machines and to maintain its good will. The Court did not decline to consider these arguments, as might be expected with a true per se approach, but rather rejected them because they were not supported by the evidence and because in the Court's view there were less "monopolistic" methods available for realizing those goals.

The Court explicitly applied per se analysis to tying a decade later in *International Salt*, where the defendant required lessees of its patented salt dispensing machines also to acquire all of their salt needs from the lessor:

> The appellant's patents confer a limited monopoly of the invention they reward. From them appellant derives a right to restrain others from making, vending or using the patented machines. But the patents confer no right to restrain use of, or trade in, unpatented salt. By contracting to close this market for salt against competition, International has engaged in a restraint of trade for which its patents afford no immunity from the anti-trust laws.
>
> Appellant contends, however, that summary judgment was unauthorized because it precluded trial of alleged issues of fact as to whether the restraint was unreasonable within the Sherman Act or substantially lessened competition or tended to create a monopoly in salt within the Clayton Act. We think the admitted facts left no genuine issue. Not only is price-fixing unreasonable, *per se*, United States v. Socony-Vacuum Oil Co., 310 U.S. 150; United States v. Trenton Potteries Co., 273 U.S. 392, but also it is unreasonable, *per se*, to foreclose competitors from any substantial market. Fashion Originators' Guild of America v. Federal Trade Commission, 312 U.S. 457. The volume of business affected by these contracts cannot be said to be insignificant or insubstantial and the tendency of the arrangement to accomplishment of monopoly seems obvious. Under the law, agreements are forbidden which "tend to create a monopoly," and it is immaterial that the tendency is a creeping one rather than one that proceeds at full gallop; nor does the law await arrival at the goal before condemning the direction of the movement.

332 U.S. at 395–96. As had IBM, International Salt argued that the conditioned sale was necessary to guarantee the proper operation if its machines and to protect its good will, but again the Court rejected these arguments. *Id.* at 397.

Note the significance that the Court assigns to the defendant's patents, and its view that patent law is qualified by antitrust law. We will consider the interaction between intellectual property rights and antitrust law further in Chapter 7.

Do you find persuasive the Court's suggestion that patent rights afford some degree of monopoly power? We will examine that question in greater depth in our next case, *Jefferson Parish Hosp. Dist. No. 2 v. Hyde* and in the notes that follow. Do you find persuasive the Court's association of tying with the kinds of practices condemned in the three cases it cites? Recall that *Socony-Vaccum Oil* and *Trenton Potteries* involved price-fixing and hence collusive effects. *Fashion Originators' Guild* is an early example of an exclusionary group boycott. Is tying likely to have the same kind of anticompetitive effects as all three cases? Does the answer to that question depend on whether it is asked from the perspective of the buyer or the rival producer of the tied product?

Taken together, *United Shoe, IBM,* and *International Salt* laid the foundation for the definition of tying and its historically harsh treatment under federal antitrust laws. Tying entered its second principal phase of development, however, with a series of cases from *Times-Picayune Pub. Co. v. United States*, 345 U.S. 594 (1953) to the Supreme Court's decision in *U.S. Steel Corp. v. Fortner Enters., Inc.*, 429 U.S. 610 (1977) ("*Fortner II*"), the last significant tying case to be decided by the Court until we enter the modern period with *Jefferson Parish* (1984), our next case. These cases progressively refined the definition of tying, and the conditions under which it could be condemned under the per se rule, until a four-part test emerged:

- There must be *two distinct products* or services;

- There must be a *conditioned sale, i.e.*, the tying product must be available only on the condition that the second, tied product also be purchased;

- The seller must have "*appreciable economic power*" in the tying product, such that "forcing" is likely, *i.e.*, it appears that the second product would either not be purchased at all, or would not be purchased from the seller of the tying product, but for the seller's market power; and

- The arrangement must affect a "*substantial volume of commerce* in the tied market."

Fortner Enters., Inc. v. United States Steel Corp., 394 U.S. 495, 503 (1969) ("*Fortner I*"). *See also Northern Pac. Ry. Co. v. United States*, 356 U.S. 1, 5–6 (1958); *United States v. Loew's, Inc.*, 371 U.S. 38 (1962); *Fortner II*, 429 U.S. at 613–16. A great deal of case law developed over the years addressing each of the four requirements. Does this four-part framework warrant labeling as a "per se" approach? Is it more like a modified application of the rule of reason? What elements of comprehensive rule of reason analysis do not appear to be included?

As we shall see in *Jefferson Parish*, however, differentiating tying from exclusive dealing can be difficult. Consider, for example, whether it would aid the analysis to consider IBM and International Salt's lease arrangements as imposing exclusive dealing arrangements, as opposed to tying arrangements. Would it alter the economic analysis? Indeed, in *Jefferson Parish*, the Court considered the same agreements as both tying and exclusive dealing. Before reading the case, therefore, we need to consider the somewhat separate history and development of the law of exclusive dealing.

Exclusive Dealing

In contrast to tying, the economic utility of exclusive dealing has long been recognized, even though both practices are covered by Section 1 of the Sherman Act and Section 3 of the Clayton Act. Nevertheless, some hostility to exclusive dealing was evident in the early cases, although it was manifest in the form of relatively minimal requirements for proving the requisite anticompetitive effect, not per se condemnation. Two such cases are particularly worth noting before we look at the more contemporary authorities.

The law of exclusive dealing began to develop in *Standard Oil Co. v. United States*, 337 U.S. 293 (1949) ("*Standard Stations*"), where the government challenged exclusive supply contracts between Standard's wholly owned subsidiary, Standard Stations, and its independent dealers under both Section 1 of the Sherman Act and Section 3 of the Clayton Act. The contracts prohibited the retailers from selling any brand of gasoline other than Standard.

According to the Court, Standard accounted for 23% of all gasoline sales to consumers in what was described as "the Western area," comprising Arizona, California, Idaho, Nevada, Oregon, Utah and Washington, making it the largest seller of automotive petroleum products in the region. It sold gasoline through company-owned retail service stations, independent stations, and to industrial users. Retail service-station sales by Standard's six leading competitors accounted for 42.5% and the remaining retail sales were divided among more than seventy small companies. Of the total amount of gasoline sold in the Western area, 6.8% was sold through Standard's company-owned stations, and 6.7% was sold to independent dealers subject to the exclusive contracts. It was also "undisputed that Standard's major competitors employ[ed] similar exclusive dealing arrangements" and that only 1.6% of retail outlets in the Western area were "split-pump" stations that sold gasoline from more than one supplier. Exclusive dealing agreements thus could be understood as a feature of competition, coexisting with a competitive market in which suppliers went head to head through company-owned stations and directly vied to "sign up" exclusive dealers. *Id.* at 295.

By a 5–4 margin, the Court condemned the exclusive agreements and enjoined their enforcement. First, however, it distinguished them from tying, recognizing their potential economic utility to buyers and sellers. The following excerpt illustrates both the Court's traditional hostility to tying and its recognition of economic justifications for exclusive dealing:

> In favor of confining the standard laid down by the *International Salt* case to tying agreements, important economic differences

may be noted. Tying agreements serve hardly any purpose beyond the suppression of competition. The justification most often advanced in their defense—the protection of the good will of the manufacturer of the tying device—fails in the usual situation because specification of the type and quality of the product to be used in connection with the tying device is protection enough. If the manufacturer's brand of the tied product is in fact superior to that of competitors, the buyer will presumably choose it anyway. The only situation, indeed, in which the protection of good will may necessitate the use of tying clauses is where specifications for a substitute would be so detailed that they could not practicably be supplied. In the usual case only the prospect of reducing competition would persuade a seller to adopt such a contract and only his control of the supply of the tying device, whether conferred by patent monopoly or otherwise obtained, could induce a buyer to enter one. The existence of market control of the tying device, therefore, affords a strong foundation for the presumption that it has been or probably will be used to limit competition in the tied product also.

Requirements contracts, on the other hand, may well be of economic advantage to buyers as well as to sellers, and thus indirectly of advantage to the consuming public. In the case of the buyer, they may assure supply, afford protection against rises in price, enable long-term planning on the basis of known costs, and obviate the expense and risk of storage in the quantity necessary for a commodity having a fluctuating demand. From the seller's point of view, requirements contracts may make possible the substantial reduction of selling expenses, give protection against price fluctuations, and—of particular advantage to a newcomer to the field to whom it is important to know what capital expenditures are justified—offer the possibility of a predictable market. They may be useful, moreover, to a seller trying to establish a foothold against the counterattacks of entrenched competitors. Since these advantages of requirements contracts may often be sufficient to account for their use, the coverage by such contracts of a substantial amount of business affords a weaker basis for the inference that competition may be lessened than would similar coverage by tying clauses, especially where use of the latter is combined with market control of the tying device.

337 U.S. at 305–07.

The Court nevertheless condemned the challenged agreements, citing the broad sweep of Section 3 of the Clayton Act and the lack of evidence of procompetitive justifications. Interpreting the legislative history of the Act, the Court reasoned that evidence of general injury to competition of the sort expected under a rule of reason analysis under Section 1 of the Sherman Act was not required to establish a violation of Section 3. Instead, all that was necessary was "proof that competition has been foreclosed in a substantial share of the line of commerce affected." *Id.* at 314. The Court concluded that the 6.7% foreclosure that resulted from Standard's contracts met this standard of "substantiality." *Id.*

A little more than a decade later, the Court appeared to change course in *Tampa Elec. Co. v. Nashville Coal Co.*, 365 U.S. 320 (1961). *Tampa* tested the legality under the Clayton Act of a 20 year requirements agreement entered into between Tampa, a Florida electric utility, and Nashville, a coal supplier. The agreement was reached before Tampa began construction of two new coal-fired power plants. After the plants were completed, but before any coal had actually been delivered under the contract, Nashville notified Tampa that it would not honor the agreement because in its view it was void and unenforceable under the Clayton Act. Tampa initiated the declaratory judgment action, alleging that between the time the contract was concluded and the completion of the plants, the price of coal rose unexpectedly. In its view, therefore, Nashville was invoking antitrust to relieve itself of the contract's obligations to sell coal to Tampa at the previously negotiated prices, which had become unfavorable for Nashville.

The case turned in large part on a debate about the definition of the relevant geographic market for purposes of assessing the impact of the agreements. That debate was resolved when the Supreme Court defined the market broadly and found that it "foreclosed" less than 1% of coal supplies in the defined Southeast region. Distinguishing but not overruling *Standard Stations*, the Court appeared to raise the burden of proving the requisite anticompetitive effect, describing its approach in terms akin to a rule of reason analysis under Section 1:

> * * * [T]he competition foreclosed by the contract must be found to constitute a substantial share of the relevant market. That is to say, the opportunities for other traders to enter into or remain in that market must be significantly limited as was pointed out in *Standard Oil Co. v. United States* * * *.

> To determine substantiality in a given case, it is necessary to weigh the probable effect of the contract on the relevant area of effective competition, taking into account the relative strength of the parties, the proportionate volume of commerce involved in relation to the total volume of commerce in the relevant market area, and the probable immediate and future effects which pre-emption of that share of the market might have on effective competition therein. It follows that a mere showing that the

contract itself involves a substantial number of dollars is ordinarily of little consequence.

365 U.S. at 328–29.

Five years after *Tampa*, the Supreme Court arguably returned to the approach taken in *Standard Stations*, scrutinizing even very low levels of market foreclosure. In *FTC v. Brown Shoe Co.*, 384 U.S. 316 (1966), the Court upheld an FTC decision under Section 5 of the FTC Act (*see infra* Appendix A), objecting to exclusive dealing contracts by a shoe manufacturer that accounted for less than 1% of national shoe sales. As we shall see, the foreclosure levels that concerned the Court in *Standard Stations* and *Brown Shoe* would raise little or no concern under contemporary standards. Our task is to explain why, and to understand the methodology that informs the modern analysis of exclusive dealing.

Note how Section 3 of the Clayton Act figured prominently in some of these foundation cases. Before we move on to our next principal case, therefore, we consider the role of the Clayton Act and its seemingly unique concern with exclusionary distribution practices.

Sidebar 6–3:
Section 3 of the Clayton Act
and the Role of "Incipiency"

In 1914, almost a quarter century after the passage of the Sherman Act, Congress acted to augment and strengthen it by adopting the Federal Trade Commission Act and the Clayton Act. In contrast to the broadly worded prohibitions of the Sherman Act, the Clayton Act more particularly identified and prohibited certain categories of conduct—*e.g.*, price discrimination (Section 2), vertical exclusionary practices such as tying and exclusive dealing (Section 3), and mergers (Section 7). The Clayton Act also contains the modern remedial provisions of the federal antitrust laws, authorizing private treble damage actions by injured persons or firms (Section 4), as well as suits by the United States (Section 4A) and the States (Section 4C).

One of the principal textual features of the Clayton Act, found in Sections 2, 3, and 7, is what is commonly referred to as the "incipiency" standard: each of its prohibitions reaches conduct that "may" substantially lessen competition or tend to monopoly. Congress viewed the incipiency standard as a means of expanding the Sherman Act as it had been interpreted at the time, providing that conduct falling within the scope of the Clayton Act could be challenged "before the harm to competition is effected." *See Standard Fashion Co. v. Magrane-Houston Co.*,

258 U.S. 346, 356–57 (1922). *See also Brown Shoe Co. v. United States*, 370 U.S. 294, 317–18 & n. 32–33 (1962) (citing and discussing the Clayton Act's legislative history); *Fashion Originators' Guild of America v. FTC*, 312 U.S. 457, 466 (1941) (similarly noting that "it was the object of the Federal Trade Commission Act to reach not merely in their fruition but also in their incipiency combinations which could lead to these and other trade restraints and practices deemed undesirable.").[a] The Supreme Court differentiated, however, between the "mere possibility" that an agreement falling within its terms would "substantially lessen competition or tend to create a monopoly" and the probability that it would do so, noting that Section 3 could reach the latter, though not the former. *See Standard Fashion*, 258 U.S. at 356–57. As the Court would later observe, however, *Standard Fashion* "did not draw the line where 'remote' ended and 'substantial' began." *Tampa Elec. Co. v. Nashville Coal Co.*, 365 U.S. 320, 325–27 (1961).

Perceptions of "probability" have evolved over time, however, and, as we observed in Chapter 5 in considering the evolution of merger control law, it is unlikely today that some of the cases that satisfied the incipiency standard in the past would do so in light of contemporary approaches to probability. On the other hand, to any degree that the Sherman Act was read as requiring evidence of actual effects prior to 1914, as we learned in Chapter 2 today, it is well-settled that a violation of the Act can rest on evidence of actual *or* probable effects. Although parties, courts, and commentators can still differ on the kind and quantity of evidence of probable harm that is sufficient to shift a burden to a defendant to offer procompetitive justifications for its conduct, in application, therefore, the Clayton Act's "substantial lessening of competition" standard is often indistinguishable from the rule of reason under the Sherman Act. The Court has, however, preserved the possibility that in some circumstances the evidentiary demands of the Clayton Act might still be distinguished and less demanding. *See, e.g., Brooke Group Ltd v. Brown & Williamson Tobacco Corp.*, 509 U.S. 209, 222 (1993) (noting that whereas proof of a violation of Section 2 of the Sherman Act requires "probability" of competitive harm, a violation of the price discrimination provisions of Section 2(a) of the Clayton Act only requires a "possibility" of harm).

---

[a]   In other ways, however, the Clayton Act is narrower than the Sherman Act. For example, Sections 2 (price discrimination) and 3 (exclusive dealing and tying), are limited in scope to sales of goods and exclude services.

These two lines of cases, those dealing with tying and those dealing with exclusive dealing, intersected in our next case, *Jefferson Parish*. As you read *Jefferson Parish*, consider carefully how the Court approaches and interprets each element of a traditional tying offense. What test does the Court employ to define the "two product" requirement? When is a sale "conditional," *i.e.*, a tie-in? What does the Court mean by "economic power"? How much "economic power" is needed to justify invocation of per se analysis? Is "economic power" the same as "market power"? Is there any room in this framework to argue that the tie-in is efficient in some way? Consider, too, the concurring Justices' arguments for abandoning the per se rubric altogether, and the majority's response.

In addition, note how the characterization of the conduct as "tying" or "exclusive dealing" illustrates how closely related these two types of distribution restraints can be as a matter of economics. Are you persuaded by the distinction drawn by the Court in its footnote 28? Does it make legal or economic sense to analyze the practices differently? Does the distinction relate to the nature of the anticompetitive effect identified by the Court, one collusive and the other exclusionary? How does the concurring opinion differentiate them and how does it analyze the concept of "foreclosure" for purposes of the exclusive contract?

JEFFERSON PARISH HOSPITAL DISTRICT. NO. 2 V. HYDE
Supreme Court of the United States, 1984.
466 U.S. 2, 104 S.Ct. 1551, 80 L.Ed.2d 2.

JUSTICE STEVENS delivered the opinion of the Court.

At issue in this case is the validity of an exclusive contract between a hospital and a firm of anesthesiologists. We must decide whether the contract gives rise to a *per se* violation of § 1 of the Sherman Act because every patient undergoing surgery at the hospital must use the services of one firm of anesthesiologists, and, if not, whether the contract is nevertheless illegal because it unreasonably restrains competition among anesthesiologists.

In July 1977, respondent Edwin G. Hyde, a board certified anesthesiologist, applied for admission to the medical staff of East Jefferson Hospital. The credentials committee and the medical staff executive committee recommended approval, but the hospital board denied the application because the hospital was a party to a contract providing that all anesthesiological services required by the hospital's patients would be performed by Roux & Associates. * * * Respondent then commenced this action seeking a declaratory judgment that the contract is unlawful and an injunction ordering petitioners to appoint him to the hospital staff. After trial, the District Court denied relief, finding that the anticompetitive consequences of the Roux contract were minimal and outweighed by benefits in the form of improved patient care. The Court of Appeals reversed because it was persuaded that the contract was illegal *"per se."* We granted certiorari and now reverse.

I

In February 1971, shortly before East Jefferson Hospital opened, it entered into an "Anesthesiology Agreement" with Roux & Associates ("Roux"). * * * The contract provided that any anesthesiologist designated by Roux would be admitted to the hospital's medical staff. The hospital agreed to provide the space, equipment, maintenance, and other supporting services necessary to operate the anesthesiology department. It also agreed to purchase all necessary drugs and other supplies. All nursing personnel required by the anesthesia department were to be supplied by the hospital, but Roux had the right to approve their selection and retention.[3] The hospital agreed to "restrict the use of its anesthesia department to Roux & Associates and [that] no other persons, parties or entities shall perform such services within the Hospital for the ter[m] of this contract."[4]

The 1971 contract provided for a one-year term automatically renewable for successive one-year periods unless either party elected to terminate. In 1976, a second written contract was executed containing most of the provisions of the 1971 agreement. Its term was five years and the clause excluding other anesthesiologists from the hospital was deleted; the hospital nevertheless continued to regard itself as committed to a closed anesthesiology department. Only Roux was permitted to practice anesthesiology at the hospital. * * *

The exclusive contract had an impact on two different segments of the economy: consumers of medical services, and providers of anesthesiological services. Any consumer of medical services who elects to have an operation performed at East Jefferson Hospital may not employ any anesthesiologist not associated with Roux. No anesthesiologists except those employed by Roux may practice at East Jefferson.

There are at least 20 hospitals in the New Orleans metropolitan area and about 70 per cent of the patients living in Jefferson Parish go to hospitals other than East Jefferson. Because it regarded the entire New Orleans metropolitan area as the relevant geographic market in which

---

[3] The contract required all of the physicians employed by Roux to confine their practice of anesthesiology to East Jefferson.

[4] Originally Roux agreed to provide at least two full time anesthesiologists acceptable to the hospital's credentials committee. Roux agreed to furnish additional anesthesiologists as necessary. The contract also provided that Roux would designate one of its qualified anesthesiologists to serve as the head of the hospital's department of anesthesia.

The fees for anesthesiological services are billed separately to the patients by the hospital. They cover the hospital's costs and the professional services provided by Roux. After a deduction of eight percent to provide a reserve for uncollectible accounts, the fees are divided equally between Roux and the hospital.

hospitals compete, this evidence convinced the District Court that East Jefferson does not possess any significant "market power"; therefore it concluded that petitioners could not use the Roux contract to anticompetitive ends. The same evidence led the Court of Appeals to draw a different conclusion. Noting that 30 percent of the residents of the Parish go to East Jefferson Hospital, and that in fact "patients tend to choose hospitals by location rather than price or quality," the Court of Appeals concluded that the relevant geographic market was the East Bank of Jefferson Parish. The conclusion that East Jefferson Hospital possessed market power in that area was buttressed by the facts that the prevalence of health insurance eliminates a patient's incentive to compare costs, that the patient is not sufficiently informed to compare quality, and that family convenience tends to magnify the importance of location.[8]

The Court of Appeals held that the case involves a "tying arrangement" because the "users of the hospital's operating rooms (the tying product) are also compelled to purchase the hospital's chosen anesthesia service (the tied product)." Having defined the relevant geographic market for the tying product as the East Bank of Jefferson Parish, the court held that the hospital possessed "sufficient market power in the tying market to coerce purchasers of the tied product." Since the purchase of the tied product constituted a "not insubstantial amount of interstate commerce," under the Court of Appeals' reading of our decision in *Northern Pacific R. Co. v. United States*, 356 U.S. 1 (1957) the tying arrangement was therefore illegal "*per se.*"

II

Certain types of contractual arrangements are deemed unreasonable as a matter of law. The character of the restraint produced by such an arrangement is considered a sufficient basis for presuming unreasonableness without the necessity of any analysis of the market context in which the arrangement may be found. A price fixing agreement between competitors is the classic example of such an arrangement. It is far too late in the history of our antitrust jurisprudence to question the proposition that certain tying arrangements pose an unacceptable risk of stifling competition and therefore are unreasonable "*per se.*" The rule was first enunciated in *International Salt Co. v. United States*, 332 U.S. 392 (1947) and has been endorsed by this Court many times since. The rule also

---

[8] While the Court of Appeals did discuss the impact of the contract upon patients, it did not discuss its impact upon anesthesiologists. The District Court had referred to evidence that in the entire State of Louisiana there are 156 anesthesiologists and 345 hospitals with operating rooms. The record does not tell us how many of the hospitals in the New Orleans metropolitan area have "open" anesthesiology departments and how many have closed departments. Respondent, for example, practices with two other anesthesiologists at a hospital which has an open department; he previously practiced for several years in a different New Orleans hospital and, prior to that, had practiced in Florida. The record does not tell us whether there is a shortage or a surplus of anesthesiologists in any part of the country, or whether they are thriving or starving.

reflects congressional policies underlying the antitrust laws. In enacting § 3 of the Clayton Act Congress expressed great concern about the anticompetitive character of tying arrangements. While this case does not arise under the Clayton Act,[10] the congressional finding made therein concerning the competitive consequences of tying is illuminating, and must be respected.

It is clear, however, that every refusal to sell two products separately cannot be said to restrain competition. If each of the products may be purchased separately in a competitive market, one seller's decision to sell the two in a single package imposes no unreasonable restraint on either market, particularly if competing suppliers are free to sell either the entire package or its several parts. * * * Buyers often find package sales attractive; a seller's decision to offer such packages can merely be an attempt to compete effectively—conduct that is entirely consistent with the Sherman Act.

Our cases have concluded that the essential characteristic of an invalid tying arrangement lies in the seller's exploitation of its control over the tying product to force the buyer into the purchase of a tied product that the buyer either did not want at all, or might have preferred to purchase elsewhere on different terms. When such "forcing" is present, competition on the merits in the market for the tied item is restrained and the Sherman Act is violated. * * *

Accordingly, we have condemned tying arrangements when the seller has some special ability—usually called "market power"—to force a purchaser to do something that he would not do in a competitive market. * * *[20] When "forcing" occurs, our cases have found the tying arrangement to be unlawful.

Thus, the law draws a distinction between the exploitation of market power by merely enhancing the price of the tying product, on the one hand, and by attempting to impose restraints on competition in the market for a tied product, on the other. When the seller's power is just used to maximize its return in the tying product market, where presumably its product enjoys some justifiable advantage over its competitors, the competitive ideal of the Sherman Act is not necessarily compromised. But if that power is used to impair competition on the merits in another market, a potentially inferior product may be insulated from competitive pressures. This impairment could either harm existing competitors or create barriers to

---

[10] [By its express terms, the Clayton Act does not apply to services, and hence was not at issue in the case. Eds.]

[20] This type of market power has sometimes been referred to as "leverage." Professors Areeda and Turner provide a definition that suits present purposes. " 'Leverage' is loosely defined here as a supplier's ability to induce his customer for one product to buy a second product from him that would not otherwise be purchased solely on the merit of that second product." V. P. Areeda & D. Turner, Antitrust Law ¶ 1134a, at 202 (1980).

entry of new competitors in the market for the tied product and can increase the social costs of market power by facilitating price discrimination, thereby increasing monopoly profits over what they would be absent the tie.[23] And from the standpoint of the consumer—whose interests the statute was especially intended to serve—the freedom to select the best bargain in the second market is impaired by his need to purchase the tying product, and perhaps by an inability to evaluate the true cost of either product when they are available only as a package.[24] In sum, to permit restraint of competition on the merits through tying arrangements would be * * * to condone "the existence of power that a free market would not tolerate."

Per se condemnation—condemnation without inquiry into actual market conditions—is only appropriate if the existence of forcing is probable.[25] Thus, application of the *per se* rule focuses on the probability of anticompetitive consequences. Of course, as a threshold matter there must be a substantial potential for impact on competition in order to justify *per se* condemnation. If only a single purchaser were "forced" with respect to the purchase of a tied item, the resultant impact on competition would not be sufficient to warrant the concern of antitrust law. * * * Similarly, when a purchaser is "forced" to buy a product he would not have otherwise bought even from another seller in the tied product market, there can be no adverse impact on competition because no portion of the market which would otherwise have been available to other sellers has been foreclosed.

Once this threshold is surmounted, *per se* prohibition is appropriate if anticompetitive forcing is likely. For example, if the government has granted the seller a patent or similar monopoly over a product, it is fair to presume that the inability to buy the product elsewhere gives the seller market power. Any effort to enlarge the scope of the patent monopoly by using the market power it confers to restrain competition in the market for a second product will undermine competition on the merits in that second market. Thus, the sale or lease of a patented item on condition that the buyer make all his purchases of a separate tied product from the patentee is unlawful.

The same strict rule is appropriate in other situations in which the existence of market power is probable. When the seller's share of the

---

[23] Sales of the tied item can be used to measure demand for the tying item; purchasers with greater needs for the tied item make larger purchases and in effect must pay a higher price to obtain the tying item.

[24] Especially where market imperfections exist, purchasers may not be fully sensitive to the price or quality implications of a tying arrangement, and hence it may impede competition on the merits.

[25] The rationale for *per se* rules in part is to avoid a burdensome inquiry into actual market conditions in situations where the likelihood of anticompetitive conduct is so great as to render unjustified the costs of determining whether the particular case at bar involves anticompetitive conduct.

market is high, or when the seller offers a unique product that competitors are not able to offer, the Court has held that the likelihood that market power exists and is being used to restrain competition in a separate market is sufficient to make *per se* condemnation appropriate. * * * When, however, the seller does not have either the degree or the kind of market power that enables him to force customers to purchase a second, unwanted product in order to obtain the tying product, an antitrust violation can be established only by evidence of an unreasonable restraint on competition in the relevant market.

In sum, any inquiry into the validity of a tying arrangement must focus on the market or markets in which the two products are sold, for that is where the anticompetitive forcing has its impact. Thus, in this case our analysis of the tying issue must focus on the hospital's sale of services to its patients, rather than its contractual arrangements with the providers of anesthesiological services. In making that analysis, we must consider whether petitioners are selling two separate products that may be tied together, and, if so, whether they have used their market power to force their patients to accept the tying arrangement.

III

The hospital has provided its patients with a package that includes the range of facilities and services required for a variety of surgical operations.[27] At East Jefferson Hospital the package includes the services of the anesthesiologist.[28] Petitioners argue that the package does not involve a tying arrangement at all—that they are merely providing a functionally integrated package of services. * * *

Our cases indicate, however, that the answer to the question whether one or two products are involved turns not on the functional relation between them, but rather on the character of the demand for the two items.[30] * * * [A] tying arrangement cannot exist unless two separate product markets have been linked.

---

[27] The physical facilities include the operating room, the recovery room, and the hospital room where the patient stays before and after the operation. The services include those provided by staff physicians, such as radiologists or pathologists, and interns, nurses, dietitians, pharmacists and laboratory technicians.

[28] It is essential to differentiate between the Roux contract and the legality of the contract between the hospital and its patients. The Roux contract is nothing more than an arrangement whereby Roux supplies all of the hospital's needs for anesthesiological services. That contract raises only an exclusive dealing question. The issue here is whether the hospital's insistence that its patients purchase anesthesiological services from Roux creates a tying arrangement.

[30] The fact that anesthesiological services are functionally linked to the other services provided by the hospital is not in itself sufficient to remove the Roux contract from the realm of tying arrangements. We have often found arrangements involving functionally linked products at least one of which is useless without the other to be prohibited tying devices. In fact, in some situations the functional link between the two items may enable the seller to maximize its monopoly return on the tying item as a means of charging a higher rent or purchase price to a larger user of the tying item. See n. 23, *supra*.

The requirement that two distinguishable product markets be involved follows from the underlying rationale of the rule against tying. The definitional question depends on whether the arrangement may have the type of competitive consequences addressed by the rule. The answer to the question whether petitioners have utilized a tying arrangement must be based on whether there is a possibility that the economic effect of the arrangement is that condemned by the rule against tying—that petitioners have foreclosed competition on the merits in a product market distinct from the market for the tying item.[34] Thus, in this case no tying arrangement can exist unless there is a sufficient demand for the purchase of anesthesiological services separate from hospital services to identify a distinct product market in which it is efficient to offer anesthesiological services separately from hospital services.

Unquestionably, the anesthesiological component of the package offered by the hospital could be provided separately and could be selected either by the individual patient or by one of the patient's doctors if the hospital did not insist on including anesthesiological services in the package it offers to its customers. As a matter of actual practice, anesthesiological services are billed separately from the hospital services petitioners provide. There was ample and uncontroverted testimony that patients or surgeons often request specific anesthesiologists to come to a hospital and provide anesthesia, and that the choice of an individual anesthesiologist separate from the choice of a hospital is particularly frequent in respondent's specialty, obstetric anesthesiology. * * * The record amply supports the conclusion that consumers differentiate between anesthesiological services and the other hospital services provided by petitioners.[39]

---

[34] Of course, the Sherman Act does not prohibit "tying," it prohibits "contract[s] . . . in restraint of trade." Thus, in a sense the question whether this case involves "tying" is beside the point. The legality of petitioners' conduct depends on its competitive consequences, not whether it can be labeled "tying." If the competitive consequences of this arrangement are not those to which the *per se* rule is addressed, then it should not be condemned irrespective of its label.

[39] One of the most frequently cited statements on this subject was made by Judge Van Dusen in *United States v. Jerrold Electronics Corp.*, 187 F.Supp. 545 (E.D.Pa.1960), aff'd, 365 U.S. 567, 81 S.Ct. 755, 5 L.Ed.2d 806 (1961) (*per curiam*). * * *

"There are several facts presented in this record which tend to show that a community television antenna system cannot properly be characterized as a single product. Others who entered the community antenna field offered all the equipment necessary for a complete system, but none of them sold their gear exclusively as a single package as did Jerrold. The record also establishes that the number of pieces in each system varied considerably so that hardly any two versions of the alleged product were the same. Furthermore, the customer was charged for each item of equipment and not a lump sum for total payment. Finally, while Jerrold had cable and antennas to sell which were manufactured by other concerns, it required that the electronic equipment in the system be bought from it." 187 F.Supp., at 559.

The record here shows that other hospitals often permit anesthesiological services to be purchased separately, that anesthesiologists are not fungible in that the services provided by each are not precisely the same, that anesthesiological services are billed separately, and that the hospital

Thus, the hospital's requirement that its patients obtain necessary anesthesiological services from Roux combined the purchase of two distinguishable services in a single transaction. Nevertheless, the fact that this case involves a required purchase of two services that would otherwise be purchased separately does not make the Roux contract illegal. * * * Only if patients are forced to purchase Roux's services as a result of the hospital's market power would the arrangement have anticompetitive consequences. If no forcing is present, patients are free to enter a competing hospital and to use another anesthesiologist instead of Roux. The fact that petitioners' patients are required to purchase two separate items is only the beginning of the appropriate inquiry.[42]

IV

The question remains whether this arrangement involves the use of market power to force patients to buy services they would not otherwise purchase. Respondent's only basis for invoking the *per se* rule against tying and thereby avoiding analysis of actual market conditions is by relying on the preference of persons residing in Jefferson Parish to go to East Jefferson, the closest hospital. A preference of this kind, however, is not necessarily probative of significant market power.

Seventy per cent of the patients residing in Jefferson Parish enter hospitals other than East Jefferson. Thus East Jefferson's "dominance" over persons residing in Jefferson Parish is far from overwhelming.[43] The fact that a substantial majority of the parish's residents elect not to enter

---

required purchases from Roux even though other anesthesiologists were available and Roux had no objection to their receiving staff privileges at East Jefferson. Therefore, the *Jerrold* analysis indicates that there was a tying arrangement here. *Jerrold* also indicates that tying may be permissible when necessary to enable a new business to break into the market. See *id.*, at 555–558. Assuming this defense exists, and assuming it justified the 1971 Roux contract in order to give Roux an incentive to go to work at a new hospital with an uncertain future, that justification is inapplicable to the 1976 contract, since by then Roux was willing to continue to service the hospital without a tying arrangement.

    [42] Petitioners argue and the District Court found that the exclusive contract had what it characterized as procompetitive justifications in that an exclusive contract ensures 24-hour anesthesiology coverage, enables flexible scheduling, and facilitates work routine, professional standards and maintenance of equipment. The Court of Appeals held these findings to be clearly erroneous since the exclusive contract was not necessary to achieve these ends. * * * In the past, we have refused to tolerate manifestly anticompetitive conduct simply because the health care industry is involved. * * * We have also uniformly rejected similar "goodwill" defenses for tying arrangements, finding that the use of contractual quality specifications are generally sufficient to protect quality without the use of a tying arrangement. Since the District Court made no finding as to why contractual quality specifications would not protect the hospital, there is no basis for departing from our prior cases here.

    [43] In fact its position in this market is not dissimilar from the market share at issue in *Times-Picayune*, which the Court found insufficient as a basis for inferring market power. See 345 U.S., at 611–613, 73 S.Ct., at 881–883. Moreover, in other antitrust contexts this Court has found that market shares comparable to that present here do not create an unacceptable likelihood of anticompetitive conduct. See *United States v. Connecticut National Bank*, 418 U.S. 656, 94 S.Ct. 2788, 41 L.Ed.2d 1016 (1974); *United States v. du Pont & Co.*, 351 U.S. 377, 76 S.Ct. 994, 100 L.Ed. 1264 (1956).

East Jefferson means that the geographic data does not establish the kind of dominant market position that obviates the need for further inquiry into actual competitive conditions. The Court of Appeals acknowledged as much; it recognized that East Jefferson's market share alone was insufficient as a basis to infer market power, and buttressed its conclusion by relying on "market imperfections" that permit petitioners to charge noncompetitive prices for hospital services: the prevalence of third party payment for health care costs reduces price competition, and a lack of adequate information renders consumers unable to evaluate the quality of the medical care provided by competing hospitals. While these factors may generate "market power" in some abstract sense,[46] they do not generate the kind of market power that justifies condemnation of tying.

Tying arrangements need only be condemned if they restrain competition on the merits by forcing purchases that would not otherwise be made. A lack of price or quality competition does not create this type of forcing. If consumers lack price consciousness, that fact will not force them to take an anesthesiologist whose services they do not want—their indifference to price will have no impact on their willingness or ability to go to another hospital where they can utilize the services of the anesthesiologist of their choice. Similarly, if consumers cannot evaluate the quality of anesthesiological services, it follows that they are indifferent between certified anesthesiologists even in the absence of a tying arrangement—such an arrangement cannot be said to have foreclosed a choice that would have otherwise been made "on the merits."

Thus, neither of the "market imperfections" relied upon by the Court of Appeals forces consumers to take anesthesiological services they would not select in the absence of a tie. It is safe to assume that every patient undergoing a surgical operation needs the services of an anesthesiologist; at least this record contains no evidence that the hospital "forced" any such services on unwilling patients.[47] The record therefore does not provide a basis for applying the *per se* rule against tying to this arrangement.

---

[46] As an economic matter, market power exists whenever prices can be raised above the levels that would be charged in a competitive market.

[47] Nor is there an indication in the record that petitioner's practices have increased the social costs of its market power. Since patients' anesthesiological needs are fixed by medical judgment, respondent does not argue that the tying arrangement facilitates price discrimination. Where variable-quantity purchasing is unavailable as a means to enable price discrimination, commentators have seen less justification for condemning tying. While tying arrangements like the one at issue here are unlikely to be used to facilitate price discrimination, they could have the similar effect of enabling hospitals "to evade price control in the tying product through clandestine transfer of the profit to the tied product. . . ." Insurance companies are the principal source of price restraint in the hospital industry; they place some limitations on the ability of hospitals to exploit their market power. Through this arrangement, petitioners may be able to evade that restraint by obtaining a portion of the anesthesiologists' fees and therefore realize a greater return than they could in the absence of the arrangement. This could also have an adverse effect on the anesthesiology market since it is possible that only less able anesthesiologists would be willing to give up part of their fees in return for the security of an exclusive contract. However, there are no

V

In order to prevail in the absence of *per se* liability, respondent has the burden of proving that the Roux contract violated the Sherman Act because it unreasonably restrained competition. That burden necessarily involves an inquiry into the actual effect of the exclusive contract on competition among anesthesiologists. This competition takes place in a market that has not been defined. The market is not necessarily the same as the market in which hospitals compete in offering services to patients; it may encompass competition among anesthesiologists for exclusive contracts such as the Roux contract and might be statewide or merely local.[48] There is, however, insufficient evidence in this record to provide a basis for finding that the Roux contract, as it actually operates in the market, has unreasonably restrained competition. The record sheds little light on how this arrangement affected consumer demand for separate arrangements with a specific anesthesiologist.[49] * * *

In sum, all that the record establishes is that the choice of anesthesiologists at East Jefferson has been limited to one of the four doctors who are associated with Roux and therefore have staff privileges.[51] Even if Roux did not have an exclusive contract, the range of alternatives open to the patient would be severely limited by the nature of the transaction and the hospital's unquestioned right to exercise some control over the identity and the number of doctors to whom it accords staff privileges. If respondent is admitted to the staff of East Jefferson, the range of choice will be enlarged from four to five doctors, but the most significant restraints on the patient's freedom to select a specific anesthesiologist will nevertheless remain.[52] Without a showing of actual adverse effect on

findings of either the District Court or the Court of Appeals which indicate that this type of exploitation of market power has occurred here. * * * Moreover, there is nothing in the record which details whether this arrangement has enhanced the value of East Jefferson's market power or harmed quality competition in the anesthesiology market.

[48] While there was some rather impressionistic testimony that the prevalence of exclusive contracts tended to discourage young doctors from entering the market, the evidence was equivocal and neither the District Court nor the Court of Appeals made any findings concerning the contract's effect on entry barriers. * * * It is possible that under some circumstances an exclusive contract could raise entry barriers since anesthesiologists could not compete for the contract without raising the capital necessary to run a hospital-wide operation.* * *

[49] While it is true that purchasers may not be fully sensitive to the price or quality implications of a tying arrangement, so that competition may be impeded, this depends on an empirical demonstration concerning the effect of the arrangement on price or quality, and the record reveals little if anything about the effect of this arrangement on the market for anesthesiological services.

[51] The effect of the contract has, of course, been to remove the East Jefferson Hospital from the market open to Roux's competitors. Like any exclusive requirements contract, this contract could be unlawful if it foreclosed so much of the market from penetration by Roux's competitors as to unreasonably restrain competition in the affected market, the market for anesthesiological services. However, respondent has not attempted to make this showing.

[52] The record simply tells us little if anything about the effect of this arrangement on price or quality of anesthesiological services. As to price, the arrangement did not lead to an increase in the price charged to the patient. As to quality, the record indicates little more than that there have

competition, respondent cannot make out a case under the antitrust laws, and no such showing has been made.

* * *

[The Concurring Opinion of MR. JUSTICE BRENNAN, with who MR. JUSTICE MARSHALL joined, has been omitted. Eds.]

* * *

JUSTICE O'CONNOR, with whom the CHIEF JUSTICE, JUSTICE POWELL, and JUSTICE REHNQUIST join, concurring in the judgment.

* * * I concur in the Court's decision * * * but write separately to explain why I believe the Hospital-Roux contract, whether treated as effecting a tie between services provided to patients, or as an exclusive dealing arrangement between the Hospital and certain anesthesiologists, is properly analyzed under the Rule of Reason.

I

Tying is a form of marketing in which a seller insists on selling two distinct products or services as a package. * * * In this case the allegation is that East Jefferson Hospital has unlawfully tied the sale of general hospital services and operating room facilities (the tying service) to the sale of anesthesiologists' services (the tied services). The Court has on occasion applied a *per se* rule of illegality in actions alleging tying in violation of § 1 of the Sherman Act.

Under the usual logic of the *per se* rule, a restraint on trade that rarely serves any purposes other than to restrain competition is illegal without proof of market power or anti-competitive effect. In deciding whether an economic restraint should be declared illegal *per se*, "[t]he probability that anticompetitive consequences will result from a practice and the severity of those consequences [is] balanced against its pro-competitive consequences. Cases that do not fit the generalization may arise, but a *per se* rule reflects the judgment that such cases are not sufficiently common or important to justify the time and expense necessary to identify them." Only when there is very little loss to society from banning a restraint altogether is an inquiry into its costs in the individual case considered to be unnecessary.

Some of our earlier cases did indeed declare that tying arrangements serve "hardly any purpose beyond the suppression of competition." However, this declaration was not taken literally even by the cases that purported to rely upon it. In practice, a tie has been illegal only if the seller

---

never been any complaints about the quality of Roux's services, and no contention that his services are in any respect inferior to those of respondent. Moreover, the self interest of the hospital, as well as the ethical and professional norms under which it operates, presumably protect the quality of anesthesiological services.

is shown to have "sufficient economic power with respect to the tying product to appreciably restrain free competition in the market for the tied product. . . ." Without "control or dominance over the tying product," the seller could not use the tying product as "an effectual weapon to pressure buyers into taking the tied item," so that any restraint of trade would be "insignificant." The Court has never been willing to say of tying arrangements, as it has of price-fixing, division of markets and other agreements subject to *per se* analysis, that they are always illegal, without proof of market power or anticompetitive effect.

The "*per se*" doctrine in tying cases has thus always required an elaborate inquiry into the economic effects of the tying arrangement.[1] As a result, tying doctrine incurs the costs of a rule of reason approach without achieving its benefits: the doctrine calls for the extensive and time-consuming economic analysis characteristic of the rule of reason, but then may be interpreted to prohibit arrangements that economic analysis would show to be beneficial. Moreover, the *per se* label in the tying context has generated more confusion than coherent law because it appears to invite lower courts to omit the analysis of economic circumstances of the tie that has always been an necessary element of tying analysis.

The time has therefore come to abandon the "*per se*" label and refocus the inquiry on the adverse economic effects, and the potential economic benefits, that the tie may have. The law of tie-ins will thus be brought into accord with the law applicable to all other allegedly anticompetitive economic arrangements, except those few horizontal or quasi-horizontal restraints that can be said to have no economic justification whatsoever.[2] This change will rationalize rather than abandon tie-in doctrine as it is already applied.

II

Our prior opinions indicate that the purpose of tying law has been to identify and control those tie-ins that have a demonstrable exclusionary impact in the tied product market, or that abet the harmful exercise of market power that the seller possesses in the tying product market. Under

---

[1] This inquiry has been required in analyzing both the prima facie case and affirmative defenses. Most notably, *United States v. Jerrold Electronics Corp.*, 187 F. Supp. 545, 559–560 (E.D. Pa.1960), aff'd *per curiam*, 365 U.S. 567, 81 S.Ct. 755, 5 L.Ed.2d 806 (1961), upheld a requirement that buyers of television systems purchase the complete system, as well as installation and repair service, on the grounds that the tie assured that the systems would operate and thereby protected the seller's business reputation.

[2] Tying law is particularly anomalous in this respect because arrangements largely indistinguishable from tie-ins are generally analyzed under the rule of reason. For example, the "*per se*" analysis of tie-ins subjects restrictions on a franchisee's freedom to purchase supplies to a more searching scrutiny than restrictions on his freedom to sell his products. And exclusive contracts, that, like tie-ins, require the buyer to purchase a product from one seller, are subject only to the rule of reason.

the rule of reason tying arrangements should be disapproved only in such instances.

Market power in the *tying* product may be acquired legitimately (*e.g.*, through the grant of a patent) or illegitimately (*e.g.*, as a result of unlawful monopolization). In either event, exploitation of consumers in the market for the tying product is a possibility that exists and that may be regulated under § 2 of the Sherman Act without reference to any tying arrangements that the seller may have developed. The existence of a tied product normally does not increase the profit that the seller with market power can extract from sales of the *tying* product. A seller with a monopoly on flour, for example, cannot increase the profit it can extract from flour consumers simply by forcing them to buy sugar along with their flour. Counterintuitive though that assertion may seem, it is easily demonstrated and widely accepted. *See, e.g.*, R. Bork, The Antitrust Paradox 372–374 (1978); P. Areeda, Antitrust Analysis 735 (3d ed. 1981).

Tying may be economically harmful primarily in the rare cases where power in the market for the tying product is used to create *additional* market power in the market for the tied product.[4] The antitrust law is properly concerned with tying when, for example, the flour monopolist threatens to use its market power to acquire additional power in the sugar market, perhaps by driving out competing sellers of sugar, or by making it more difficult for new sellers to enter the sugar market. But such extension of market power is unlikely, or poses no threat of economic harm, unless the two markets in question and the nature of the two products tied satisfy three threshold criteria.

First, the seller must have power in the tying product market.[6] Absent such power tying cannot conceivably have any adverse impact in the tied-product market, and can be only procompetitive in the tying product market.[7] * * *

---

[4] Tying might be undesirable in two other instances, but the Hospital-Roux arrangement involves neither one.

In a regulated industry a firm with market power may be unable to extract a supercompetitive profit because it lacks control over the prices it charges for regulated products or services. Tying may then be used to extract that profit from sale of the unregulated, tied products or services.

Tying may also help the seller engage in price discrimination by "metering" the buyer's use of the tying product. Price discrimination may be independently unlawful. Price discrimination may, however, *decrease* rather than increase the economic costs of a seller's market power. * * *

[6] The Court has failed in the past to define how much market power is necessary, but in the context of this case it is inappropriate to attempt to resolve that question.* * *

[7] A common misconception has been that a patent or copyright, a high market share, or a unique product that competitors are not able to offer suffices to demonstrate market power. While each of these three factors might help to give market power to a seller, it is also possible that a seller in these situations will have no market power: for example, a patent holder has no market power in any relevant sense if there are close substitutes for the patented product. Similarly, a high market share indicates market power only if the market is properly defined to include all reasonable substitutes for the product.* * *

Second, there must be a substantial threat that the tying seller will acquire market power in the tied-product market. No such threat exists if the tied-product market is occupied by many stable sellers who are not likely to be driven out by the tying, or if entry barriers in the tied product market are low. * * * If, on the other hand, the tying arrangement is likely to erect significant barriers to entry into the tied-product market, the tie remains suspect.

Third, there must be a coherent economic basis for treating the tying and tied products as distinct. All but the simplest products can be broken down into two or more components that are "tied together" in the final sale. Unless it is to be illegal to sell cars with engines or cameras with lenses, this analysis must be guided by some limiting principle. For products to be treated as distinct, the tied product must, at a minimum, be one that some consumers might wish to purchase separately *without also purchasing the tying product*.[8] When the tied product has no use other than in conjunction with the tying product, a seller of the tying product can acquire no *additional* market power by selling the two products together. * * *

Even when the tied product does have a use separate from the tying product, it makes little sense to label a package as two products without also considering the economic justifications for the sale of the package as a unit. When the economic advantages of joint packaging are substantial the package is not appropriately viewed as two products, and that should be the end of the tying inquiry. * * *[10]

These three conditions—market power in the tying product, a substantial threat of market power in the tied product, and a coherent economic basis for treating the products as distinct—are only threshold requirements. Under the rule of reason a tie-in may prove acceptable even when all three are met. Tie-ins may entail economic benefits as well as economic harms, and if the threshold requirements are met these benefits should enter the rule-of-reason balance.

> "Tie-ins . . . may facilitate new entry into fields where established sellers have wedded their customers to them by ties of habit and custom. * * * They may permit clandestine price cutting in products which otherwise would have no price competition at all because of fear of retaliation from the few other producers dealing in the market. They may protect the reputation of the tying product if failure to use the tied product in conjunction with it may

---

[8] Whether the tying product is one that consumers might wish to purchase without the tied product should be irrelevant. Once it is conceded that the seller has market power over the tying product it follows that the seller can sell the tying product on noncompetitive terms. The injury to consumers does not depend on whether the seller chooses to charge a supercompetitive price, or charges a competitive price but insists that consumers also buy a product that they do not want.

[10] The examination of the economic advantages of tying may properly be conducted as part of the rule-of-reason analysis, rather than at the threshold of the tying inquiry. * * *

cause it to misfunction. * * * And, if the tied and tying products are functionally related, they may reduce costs through economies of joint production and distribution." *Fortner I*, 394 U.S., at 514 n. 9, 89 S.Ct., at 1264 n. 9 (Justice WHITE, dissenting).

The ultimate decision whether a tie-in is illegal under the antitrust laws should depend upon the demonstrated economic effects of the challenged agreement. It may, for example, be entirely innocuous that the seller exploits its control over the tying-product to "force" the buyer to purchase the tied product. For when the seller exerts market power only in the tying product market, it makes no difference to him or his customers whether he exploits that power by raising the price of the tying product or by "forcing" customers to buy a tied product. On the other hand, tying may make the provision of packages of goods and services more efficient. A tie-in should be condemned only when its anticompetitive impact outweighs its contribution to efficiency.

III

Application of these criteria to the case at hand is straightforward.

Although the issue is in doubt, we may assume that the hospital does have market power in the provision of hospital services in its area. * * *

Second, in light of the hospital's presumed market power, we may also assume that there is a substantial threat that East Jefferson will acquire market power over the provision of anesthesiological services in its market. By tying the sale of anesthesia to the sale of other hospital services the hospital can drive out other sellers of those services who might otherwise operate in the local market. * * *

But the third threshold condition for giving closer scrutiny to a tying arrangement is not satisfied here: there is no sound economic reason for treating surgery and anesthesia as separate services. Patients are interested in purchasing anesthesia only in conjunction with hospital services, so the hospital can acquire no *additional* market power by selling the two services together. Accordingly, the link between the hospital's services and anesthesia administered by Roux will affect neither the amount of anesthesia provided nor the combined price of anesthesia and surgery for those who choose to become the hospital's patients. In these circumstances, anesthesia and surgical services should probably not be characterized as distinct products for tying purposes.

Even if they are, the tying should not be considered a violation of § 1 of the Sherman Act because tying here cannot increase the seller's already absolute power over the volume of production of the tied product, which is an inevitable consequence of the fact that very few patients will choose to undergo surgery without receiving anesthesia. The hospital-Roux contract therefore has little potential to harm the patients. On the other side of the balance, * * * the tie-in conferred significant benefits upon the hospital and the patients that it served.

The tie-in improves patient care and permits more efficient hospital operation in a number of ways. From the viewpoint of hospital management, the tie-in ensures 24 hour anesthesiology coverage, aids in standardization of procedures and efficient use of equipment, facilitates flexible scheduling of operations, and permits the hospital more effectively to monitor the quality of anesthesiological services. Further, the tying arrangement is advantageous to patients because * * * the closed anesthesiology department places upon the hospital, rather than the individual patient, responsibility to select the physician who is to provide anesthesiological services. The hospital also assumes the responsibility that the anesthesiologist will be available, will be acceptable to the surgeon, and will provide suitable care to the patient. * * * Such an arrangement, which has little anticompetitive effect and achieves substantial benefits in the provision of care to patients, is hardly one that the antitrust law should condemn.[13] * * *

* * *

IV

Whether or not the hospital-Roux contract is characterized as a tie between distinct products, the contract unquestionably does constitute exclusive dealing. Exclusive-dealing arrangements are independently subject to scrutiny under § 1 of the Sherman Act, and are also analyzed under the rule of reason.

The hospital-Roux arrangement could conceivably have an adverse effect on horizontal competition among anesthesiologists, or among hospitals. Dr. Hyde * * * may have grounds to complain that the exclusive contract stifles horizontal competition and therefore has an adverse, albeit indirect, impact on consumer welfare even if it is not a tie.

Exclusive-dealing arrangements may, in some circumstances, create or extend market power of a supplier or the purchaser party to the exclusive-dealing arrangement, and may thus restrain horizontal competition. Exclusive dealing can have adverse economic consequences by allowing one supplier of goods or services unreasonably to deprive other suppliers of a market for their goods, or by allowing one buyer of goods unreasonably to deprive other buyers of a needed source of supply. In determining whether an exclusive-dealing contract is unreasonable, the proper focus is on the structure of the market for the products or services in question—the number of sellers and buyers in the market, the volume

---

[13] The Court of Appeals disregarded the benefits of the tie because it found that there were less restrictive means of achieving them. In the absence of an adequate basis to expect any harm to competition from the tie-in, this objection is simply irrelevant.

of their business, and the ease with which buyers and sellers can redirect their purchases or sales to others. Exclusive dealing is an unreasonable restraint on trade only when a significant fraction of buyers or sellers are frozen out of a market by the exclusive deal. When the sellers of services are numerous and mobile, and the number of buyers is large, exclusive-dealing arrangements of narrow scope pose no threat of adverse economic consequences. To the contrary, they may be substantially procompetitive by ensuring stable markets and encouraging long term, mutually advantageous business relationships.

At issue here is an exclusive dealing arrangement between a firm of four anesthesiologists and one relatively small hospital. There is no suggestion that East Jefferson Hospital is likely to create a "bottleneck" in the availability of anesthesiologists that might deprive other hospitals of access to needed anesthesiological services, or that the Roux associates have unreasonably narrowed the range of choices available to other anesthesiologists in search of a hospital or patients that will buy their services. * * * Even without engaging in a detailed analysis of the size of the relevant markets we may readily conclude that there is no likelihood that the exclusive dealing arrangement challenged here will either unreasonably enhance the hospital's market position relative to other hospitals, or unreasonably permit Roux to acquire power relative to other anesthesiologists. Accordingly, this exclusive-dealing arrangement must be sustained under the rule of reason.

* * *

A critical issue in *Jefferson Parish* with respect to the tying claim was the analysis of the "two product" requirement dictated by previous Supreme Court tying decisions. Why was the two product requirement adopted in those cases? What function does it serve in the analysis of tying? What specific test did the majority embrace for satisfying the two product requirement? Did you find the majority's conclusion persuasive that surgery and anesthesia are two distinct services? What was the concurring Justices' view? What did they mean when they asserted that "there is no sound economic reason for treating surgery and anesthesia as separate services?" For a later discussion of the two market issue by the Supreme Court, see *Eastman Kodak Co. v. Image Tech. Servs., Inc.*, 504 U.S. 451, 462–63 (1992) (concluding that defendant was not entitled to summary judgment on the question whether replacement parts and service for a manufacturer's photocopying machines constituted two products for purposes of tying).

How truly "per se" was the analysis applied by the majority? Note that the Court considered a great deal of evidence about the alleged conduct and the market, including Jefferson Parish Hospital's market share. Is the approach fairly characterized as "per se"? Does it illustrate a point the Court made in *NCAA* (*see supra* Chapter 2) that even per se analysis may in some cases require a degree of inquiry beyond facial evaluation of the conduct? Note, too, that in Part V of its opinion, once the majority had concluded that the plaintiff had not presented enough evidence to justify reliance on per se analysis, it considered the conduct under the Rule of Reason in Part V. There the Court concluded that even if there was a tie (forcing), the evidence of adverse competitive effect was insufficient to establish a violation.

How persuasive a case do the concurring Justices in *Jefferson Parish* make for abandoning use of per se analysis for tying? We will return to the arguments of the concurring Justices after we more closely examine the Court's decision-making process in the case with the aid of the papers of Justice Thurgood Marshall in Sidebar 6–4.

Both the *Jefferson Parish* majority and dissent appeared to agree that tying cannot be anticompetitive absent market power in the tying product. But what degree of market power should be necessary, and how should it be established? Should it be inferred from market shares calculated in a relevant market? Recall that the district court viewed the entire New Orleans metropolitan area as the relevant geographic market, but the court of appeals viewed it solely as the East Bank of Jefferson Parish. Did the Supreme Court agree with the district court or the court of appeals? Why? How did it affect the Court's analysis of market power?

Traditionally, the courts presumed that a patent conferred market power. If the tying product was patented, therefore, tying was frequently condemned. *See, e.g, United States v. Loew's, Inc.*, 371 U.S. 38 (1962). Note that the majority and the concurrence differ as to the propriety of this assumption. Citing *Loew's* and several other previous decisions of the Court, Justice Stevens writes: "if the government has granted the seller a patent or similar monopoly over a product, it is fair to presume that the inability to buy the product elsewhere gives the seller market power." *Jefferson Parish*, 466 U.S. at 16. In contrast, Justice O'Connor terms this presumption a "common misperception." *Id.* at 37 n.7 (O'Connor, J., concurring). In her view, "a patent holder has no market power in any relevant sense if there are close substitutes for the patented product." *Id.* Who has the better argument? Does a patent necessarily convey some degree of market power? If so, will it always be sufficient to threaten competition for the tied product? The Supreme Court has since endorsed Justice O'Connor's view, rejecting the notion that market power can be presumed in a tying case based on the fact that the tying product is patented. *See Illinois Tool Works Inc. v. Indep. Ink, Inc.*, 547 U.S. 28 (2006).

Justice O'Connor clearly doubted whether the Roux contract should even be treated as a tying arrangement. She preferred to analyze it as exclusive dealing. What difference did this characterization make in her analysis? Would it eliminate any concern about application of the per se rule? According to the *Jefferson Parish* concurrence, under what circumstances could an exclusive dealing arrangement be anticompetitive? What factors would have to be evaluated in order to reach that conclusion? What factors would tend to mitigate any such effects? Why did the concurring Justices conclude that the facts in *Jefferson Parish* did not present an anticompetitive example of exclusive dealing?

Jefferson Parish is the last decision of the Supreme Court addressing tying or exclusive dealing, but the analysis of both kinds of distribution restrictions has continued to evolve in the lower courts and been the focus of a great deal of commentary. Before we turn to more recent examples, however, consider the following Sidebar, which more closely examines *Jefferson Parish* from inside the Court.

Sidebar 6–4:
The Per Se Rule, the Rule of Reason, and Tying—
A View from the Marshall Papers[a]

Justice Thurgood Marshall's papers reveal that the Supreme Court's deliberations leading to the issuance of the *Jefferson Parish* decision featured a robust debate over the desirability of maintaining a per se rule against tying. Justice Sandra Day O'Connor corresponded extensively with Justice John Paul Stevens, who eventually wrote for the majority in the case. Justice O'Connor unsuccessfully urged Justice Stevens to abandon the per se standard of earlier Supreme Court tying decisions in favor of a more comprehensive rule of reason analytical framework. In a memorandum dated February 27, 1984, O'Connor summarized her proposed standard:

> I must emphasize that I would not apply a "per se" approach in any circumstances. If that does not come through in my draft, I will offer appropriate changes. I have tried to make clear that the three conditions I describe are merely threshold conditions, necessary, but not sufficient, to establish harmful economic effects from the tie. It is only when the three conditions are met that a further inquiry into economic impacts is required under the Rule of Reason. My "different label," in other words, is intended to go with a different

---

[a]   This Sidebar is adapted from William E. Kovacic, *Antitrust Decision Making and the Supreme Court: Perspectives from the Thurgood Marshall Papers*, 42 ANTITRUST BULL. 93, 97–99 (1997).

mode of analysis. The purpose of the threshold conditions is to avoid the lengthy and cumbersome processes of a trial if it is unnecessary.

Several of O'Connor's colleagues also wrote letters stating their opposition to the continued application of a per se rule to tying. In a letter dated December 28, 1983, Justice Lewis Powell gave Justice Stevens his reactions to an initial draft of the *Jefferson Parish* opinion:

> As you know, I have thought—both when practicing law and since coming to the Court—that the *per se* rule has been unwisely expanded. At least for me, the rule of reason—enabling judgments to be made on the basis of economic effects—is a far more sensible application of the Sherman Act in our free enterprise system. I therefore would be reluctant to join much of your opinion.

In the same vein, in a January 4, 1984 letter to Justice Stevens, then Associate Justice William Rehnquist said "I think this case offers an opportunity to cut back on the broad sweep of the *per se* prohibition against tying, and I am reluctant to join an opinion which passes up that opportunity, to say nothing of one which may broaden its sweep."

Justice Stevens considered but rejected these recommendations, often emphasizing (as his majority opinion ultimately did) fidelity to past Supreme Court decisions that had used the per se nomenclature for tying. As we saw, Justice O'Connor offered her views in a concurring opinion that called for replacing the per se analytical framework with a structured rule of reason approach. Her approach attracted the votes of Chief Justice Warren Burger and Justices Powell and Rehnquist.

None of the members of the Court in *Jefferson Parish* remain on the Court today. Given the Court's willingness today to abandon reliance on per se analysis in other long-standing cases, such as *Leegin's* decision to overrule *Dr. Miles* with respect to minimum RPM, it seems unlikely that if faced with a tying case in the future a majority of the Court will feel as strongly as Justice Stevens did about standing by the label the Court has applied to tying in the past. In the next section, we will explore more of the critique of the per se approach, which had developed over time and likely influenced the views of Justice O'Connor and the other concurring Justices.

2. THE MODERN LAW AND ECONOMICS OF TYING AND EXCLUSIVE DEALING

a. Tying

In Chapter 4, we studied portions of the D.C. Circuit's opinion in the government's case against Microsoft. Our earlier excerpt did not include the court's discussion of one of the most challenging issues in the case, the district court's finding that Microsoft had violated Section 1 of the Sherman Act by unlawfully tying Internet Explorer, its Internet browser, to its Windows operating system. *See United States v. Microsoft Corp.*, 87 F. Supp. 2d 30, 47–51 (D.D.C. 2000). Microsoft successfully challenged that finding in the court of appeals, at least as it related to Section 1 as a stand-alone offense.

As you read the excerpt below, consider everything we have read so far about tying, including the discussion in Sidebar 6–4. What was the government and district court's anticompetitive theory with regard to Microsoft's tying? Did the court of appeals reject that theory, or just the district court's use of the per se rule? What were Microsoft's responses and proffered justifications? On what basis did the D.C. Circuit conclude that the per se rule should not be applied? In doing so, how did it account for the majority's decision in *Jefferson Parish*?

UNITED STATES V. MICROSOFT CORP.

United States Court of Appeals for the District of Columbia Circuit, 2001.
253 F.3d 34.

PER CURIAM.

* * *

IV. Tying

* * * The District Court concluded that Microsoft's contractual and technological bundling of the IE [Internet Explorer] web browser (the "tied" product) with its Windows operating system ("OS") (the "tying" product) resulted in a tying arrangement that was per se unlawful. We hold that the rule of reason, rather than per se analysis, should govern the legality of tying arrangements involving platform software products. The Supreme Court has warned that " '[i]t is only after considerable experience with certain business relationships that courts classify them as *per se* violations. . . .' " *Broad. Music, Inc. v. CBS*, 441 U.S. 1, 9, 99 S.Ct. 1551, 60 L.Ed.2d 1 (1979) (quoting *United States v. Topco Assocs.*, 405 U.S. 596, 607–08, 92 S.Ct. 1126, 31 L.Ed.2d 515 (1972)). While every "business relationship" will in some sense have unique features, some represent entire, novel categories of dealings. As we shall explain, the arrangement before us is an example of the latter, offering the first up-close look at the technological integration of added functionality into software that serves as a platform for third-party applications. There being no close parallel in prior antitrust cases, simplistic application of per se tying rules carries a serious risk of harm. Accordingly, we vacate the District Court's finding of a per se tying violation and remand the case. Plaintiffs may on remand pursue their tying claim under the rule of reason.

The facts underlying the tying allegation substantially overlap with those set forth in Section II.B in connection with the § 2 monopoly maintenance claim. The key District Court findings are that (1) Microsoft required licensees of Windows 95 and 98 also to license IE as a bundle at a single price; (2) Microsoft refused to allow OEMs to uninstall or remove IE from the Windows desktop; (3) Microsoft designed Windows 98 in a way that withheld from consumers the ability to remove IE by use of the Add/Remove Programs utility; and (4) Microsoft designed Windows 98 to override the user's choice of default web browser in certain circumstances. The court found that these acts constituted a per se tying violation. * * *

There are four elements to a per se tying violation: (1) the tying and tied goods are two separate products; (2) the defendant has market power in the tying product market; (3) the defendant affords consumers no choice but to purchase the tied product from it; and (4) the tying arrangement forecloses a substantial volume of commerce. *See Eastman Kodak Co. v. Image Tech. Servs., Inc.,* 504 U.S. 451, 461–62, 112 S.Ct. 2072, 119 L.Ed.2d 265 (1992); *Jefferson Parish Hosp. Dist. No. 2 v. Hyde,* 466 U.S. 2, 12–18, 104 S.Ct. 1551, 80 L.Ed.2d 2 (1984).

Microsoft does not dispute that it bound Windows and IE in the four ways the District Court cited. Instead it argues that Windows (the tying good) and IE browsers (the tied good) are not "separate products," and that it did not substantially foreclose competing browsers from the tied product market. (Microsoft also contends that it does not have monopoly power in the tying product market, but * * * we uphold the District Court's finding to the contrary.)

We first address the separate-products inquiry, a source of much argument between the parties and of confusion in the cases. Our purpose is to highlight the poor fit between the separate-products test and the facts of this case. We then offer further reasons for carving an exception to the per se rule when the tying product is platform software. * * *

A. *Separate-Products Inquiry Under the Per Se Test*

The requirement that a practice involve two separate products before being condemned as an illegal tie started as a purely linguistic requirement: unless products are separate, one cannot be "tied" to the other. Indeed, the nature of the products involved in early tying cases * * * led courts either to disregard the separate-products question, or to discuss it only in passing. * * *

The first case to give content to the separate-products test was *Jefferson Parish*. That case addressed a tying arrangement in which a hospital conditioned surgical care at its facility on the purchase of anesthesiological services from an affiliated medical group. The facts were a challenge for casual separate-products analysis because the tied service—anesthesia—was neither intuitively distinct from nor intuitively contained within the tying service—surgical care. A further complication was that, soon after the Court enunciated the per se rule for tying liability in *International Salt Co.* and *Northern Pacific Railway Co.*, new economic research began to cast doubt on the assumption, voiced by the Court when it established the rule, that " 'tying agreements serve hardly any purpose beyond the suppression of competition.' "

The *Jefferson Parish* Court resolved the matter in two steps. First, it clarified that "the answer to the question whether one or two products are involved" does not turn "on the functional relation between them. . . ." In other words, the mere fact that two items are complements, that "one . . . is useless without the other," does not make them a single "product" for purposes of tying law. Second, reasoning that the "definitional question [whether two distinguishable products are involved] depends on whether the arrangement may have the type of competitive consequences addressed by the rule [against tying]," the Court decreed that "no tying arrangement can exist unless there is a sufficient *demand* for the purchase of anesthesiological services separate from hospital services to identify a distinct product market in which it is *efficient* to offer anesthesiological services separately from hospital service."

The Court proceeded to examine direct and indirect evidence of consumer demand for the tied product separate from the tying product. Direct evidence addresses the question whether, when given a choice, consumers purchase the tied good from the tying good maker, or from other firms. * * * Indirect evidence includes the behavior of firms without market power in the tying good market, presumably on the notion that (competitive) supply follows demand. If competitive firms always bundle the tying and tied goods, then they are a single product. Here the Court noted that only 27% of anesthesiologists in markets other than the defendant's had financial relationships with hospitals, and that, unlike radiologists and pathologists, anesthesiologists were not usually employed by hospitals, *i.e.*, bundled with hospital services. With both direct and indirect evidence concurring, the Court determined that hospital surgery and anesthesiological services were distinct goods.

To understand the logic behind the Court's consumer demand test, consider first the postulated harms from tying. The core concern is that tying prevents goods from competing directly for consumer choice on their merits, *i.e.*, being selected as a result of "buyers' independent judgment." With a tie, a buyer's "freedom to select the best bargain in the second market [could be] impaired by his need to purchase the tying product, and perhaps by an inability to evaluate the true cost of either product. . . ." Direct competition on the merits of the tied product is foreclosed when the tying product either is sold only in a bundle with the tied product or, though offered separately, is sold at a bundled price, so that the buyer pays the same price whether he takes the tied product or not. In both cases, a consumer buying the tying product becomes entitled to the tied product; he will therefore likely be unwilling to buy a competitor's version of the tied product even if, making his own price/quality assessment, that is what he would prefer.

But not all ties are bad. Bundling obviously saves distribution and consumer transaction costs. This is likely to be true, to take some examples from the computer industry, with the integration of math co-processors and memory into microprocessor chips and the inclusion of spell checkers in word processors. Bundling can also capitalize on certain economies of scope. A possible example is the "shared" library files that perform OS and browser functions with the very same lines of code and thus may save drive space from the clutter of redundant routines and memory when consumers use both the OS and browser simultaneously. Indeed, if there were no efficiencies from a tie (including economizing on consumer transaction costs such as the time and effort involved in choice), we would expect distinct consumer demand for each individual component of every good. In a competitive market with zero transaction costs, the computers on which this opinion was written would only be sold piecemeal—keyboard, monitor, mouse, central processing unit, disk drive, and memory all sold in separate transactions and likely by different manufacturers.

Recognizing the potential benefits from tying, the Court in *Jefferson Parish* forged a separate-products test that, like those of market power and substantial foreclosure, attempts to screen out false positives under per se analysis. The consumer demand test is a rough proxy for whether a tying arrangement may, on balance, be welfare-enhancing, and unsuited to per se condemnation. In the abstract, of course, there is always direct separate demand for products: assuming choice is available at zero cost, consumers will prefer it to no choice. Only when the efficiencies from bundling are dominated by the benefits to choice for enough consumers, however, will we actually observe consumers making independent purchases. In other words, perceptible separate demand is inversely proportional to net efficiencies. On the supply side, firms without market power will bundle two goods only when the cost savings from joint sale outweigh the value consumers place on separate choice. So bundling by all competitive firms implies strong net efficiencies. If a court finds either that there is no noticeable separate demand for the tied product or, there being no convincing direct evidence of separate demand, that the entire "competitive fringe" engages in the same behavior as the defendant, then the tying and tied products should be declared one product and per se liability should be rejected.

Before concluding our exegesis of *Jefferson Parish*'s separate-products test, we should clarify two things. First, *Jefferson Parish* does not endorse a direct inquiry into the efficiencies of a bundle. Rather, it proposes easy-to-administer proxies for net efficiency. In describing the separate-products test we discuss efficiencies only to explain the rationale behind the consumer demand inquiry. To allow the separate-products test to become a detailed inquiry into possible welfare consequences would turn a screening test into the very process it is expected to render unnecessary.

Second, the separate-products test is not a one-sided inquiry into the cost savings from a bundle. Although *Jefferson Parish* acknowledged that prior lower court cases looked at cost-savings to decide separate products, the Court conspicuously did not adopt that approach in its disposition of the tying arrangement before it. Instead it chose proxies that balance costs savings against reduction in consumer choice.

With this background, we now turn to the separate products inquiry before us. The District Court found that many consumers, if given the option, would choose their browser separately from the OS. Turning to industry custom, the court found that, although all major OS vendors bundled browsers with their OSs, these companies either sold versions without a browser, or allowed OEMs or end-users either not to install the bundled browser or in any event to "uninstall" it. The court did not discuss the record evidence as to whether OS vendors other than Microsoft sold at a bundled price, with no discount for a browserless OS, perhaps because the record evidence on the issue was in conflict.

Microsoft does not dispute that many consumers demand alternative browsers. But on industry custom Microsoft contends that no other firm requires non-removal because no other firm has invested the resources to integrate web browsing as deeply into its OS as Microsoft has. (We here use the term "integrate" in the rather simple sense of converting individual goods into components of a single physical object (*e.g.*, a computer as it leaves the OEM, or a disk or sets of disks), without any normative implication that such integration is desirable or achieves special advantages.) Microsoft contends not only that its integration of IE into Windows is innovative and beneficial but also that it requires non-removal of IE. In our discussion of monopoly maintenance we find that these claims fail the efficiency balancing applicable in that context. But the separate-products analysis is supposed to perform its function as a proxy *without* embarking on any direct analysis of efficiency. Accordingly, Microsoft's implicit argument—that in this case looking to a competitive fringe is inadequate to evaluate fully its potentially innovative technological integration, that such a comparison is between apples and oranges—poses a legitimate objection to the operation of *Jefferson Parish's* separate-products test for the per se rule.

In fact there is merit to Microsoft's broader argument that *Jefferson Parish's* consumer demand test would "chill innovation to the detriment of consumers by preventing firms from integrating into their products new functionality previously provided by standalone products—and hence, by definition, subject to separate consumer demand." The per se rule's direct consumer demand and indirect industry custom inquiries are, as a general matter, backward-looking and therefore systematically poor proxies for overall efficiency in the presence of new and innovative integration. The direct consumer demand test focuses on historic consumer behavior, likely before integration, and the indirect industry custom test looks at firms that, unlike the defendant, may not have integrated the tying and tied goods. Both tests compare incomparables—the defendant's decision to bundle in the presence of integration, on the one hand, and consumer and competitor calculations in its absence, on the other. If integration has efficiency benefits, these may be ignored by the *Jefferson Parish* proxies. Because one cannot be sure beneficial integration will be protected by the other elements of the per se rule, simple application of that rule's separate-products test may make consumers worse off.

In light of the monopoly maintenance section, obviously, we do not find that Microsoft's integration is welfare-enhancing or that it should be absolved of tying liability. Rather, we heed Microsoft's warning that the separate-products element of the per se rule may not give newly integrated products a fair shake.

B.   *Per Se Analysis Inappropriate for this Case.*

We now address directly the larger question as we see it: whether standard per se analysis should be applied "off the shelf" to evaluate the defendant's tying arrangement, one which involves software that serves as a platform for third-party applications. There is no doubt that "[i]t is far too late in the history of our antitrust jurisprudence to question the proposition that *certain* tying arrangements pose an unacceptable risk of stifling competition and therefore are unreasonable 'per se.'" *Jefferson Parish*, 466 U.S. at 9, 104 S.Ct. 1551 (emphasis added). But there are strong reasons to doubt that the integration of additional software functionality into an OS falls among these arrangements. Applying per se analysis to such an amalgamation creates undue risks of error and of deterring welfare-enhancing innovation.

* * *

In none of these [previous Supreme Court tying] cases was the tied good physically and technologically integrated with the tying good. Nor did the defendants ever argue that their tie improved the value of the tying product to users *and* to makers of complementary goods. In those cases where the defendant claimed that use of the tied good made the tying good more valuable to users, the Court ruled that the same result could be achieved via quality standards for substitutes of the tied good. Here Microsoft argues that IE and Windows are an integrated physical product and that the bundling of IE APIs[11] with Windows makes the latter a better applications platform for third-party software. It is unclear how the benefits from IE APIs could be achieved by quality standards for different browser manufacturers. We do not pass judgment on Microsoft's claims regarding the benefits from integration of its APIs. We merely note that these and other novel, purported efficiencies suggest that judicial "experience" provides little basis for believing that, "because of their pernicious effect on competition and lack of *any* redeeming virtue," a software firm's decisions to sell multiple functionalities as a package should be "conclusively presumed to be unreasonable and therefore illegal without elaborate inquiry as to the precise harm they have caused or the business excuse for their use."

* * *

While the paucity of cases examining software bundling suggests a high risk that per se analysis may produce inaccurate results, the nature of the platform software market affirmatively suggests that per se rules might stunt valuable innovation. We have in mind two reasons.

First, as we explained in the previous section, the separate-products test is a poor proxy for net efficiency from newly integrated products. Under per se analysis the first firm to merge previously distinct functionalities (*e.g.*, the inclusion of starter motors in automobiles) or to eliminate entirely the need for a second function (*e.g.*, the invention of the stain-resistant carpet) risks being condemned as having tied two separate products because at the moment of integration there will appear to be a robust "distinct" market for the tied product. Rule of reason analysis, however, affords the first mover an opportunity to demonstrate that an efficiency gain from its "tie" adequately offsets any distortion of consumer choice.

The failure of the separate-products test to screen out certain cases of productive integration is particularly troubling in platform software markets such as that in which the defendant competes. Not only is integration common in such markets, but it is common among firms without market power. We have already reviewed evidence that nearly all competitive OS vendors also bundle browsers. Moreover, plaintiffs do not dispute that OS vendors can and do incorporate basic internet plumbing and other useful functionality into their OSs. Firms without market power have no incentive to package different pieces of software together unless

---

[11] ["API" stands for "Application Programming Interface," and is explained by the court in the excerpt from its opinion that appears in Chapter 4. Eds.]

there are efficiency gains from doing so. The ubiquity of bundling in competitive platform software markets should give courts reason to pause before condemning such behavior in less competitive markets.

Second, because of the pervasively innovative character of platform software markets, tying in such markets may produce efficiencies that courts have not previously encountered and thus the Supreme Court had not factored into the per se rule as originally conceived. For example, the bundling of a browser with OSs enables an independent software developer to count on the presence of the browser's APIs, if any, on consumers' machines and thus to omit them from its own package. It is true that software developers can bundle the browser APIs they need with their own products, but that may force consumers to pay twice for the same API if it is bundled with two different software programs. It is also true that OEMs can include APIs with the computers they sell, but diffusion of uniform APIs by that route may be inferior. * * * [O]ur qualms about redefining the boundaries of a defendant's product and the possibility of consumer gains from simplifying the work of applications developers makes us question any hard and fast approach to tying in OS software markets.

There may also be a number of efficiencies that, although very real, have been ignored in the calculations underlying the adoption of a per se rule for tying. We fear that these efficiencies are common in technologically dynamic markets where product development is especially unlikely to follow an easily foreseen linear pattern. * * *

These arguments all point to one conclusion: we cannot comfortably say that bundling in platform software markets has so little "redeeming virtue," and that there would be so "very little loss to society" from its ban, that "an inquiry into its costs in the individual case [can be] considered [ ] unnecessary." *Jefferson Parish,* 466 U.S. at 33–34, 104 S.Ct. 1551 (O'Connor, J., concurring). We do not have enough empirical evidence regarding the effect of Microsoft's practice on the amount of consumer surplus created or consumer choice foreclosed by the integration of added functionality into platform software to exercise sensible judgment regarding that entire class of behavior. (For some issues we have no data.) * * * We remand the case for evaluation of Microsoft's tying arrangements under the rule of reason. That rule more freely permits consideration of the benefits of bundling in software markets, particularly those for OSs, and a balancing of these benefits against the costs to consumers whose ability to make direct price/quality tradeoffs in the tied market may have been impaired.

Our judgment regarding the comparative merits of the per se rule and the rule of reason is confined to the tying arrangement before us, where the tying product is software whose major purpose is to serve as a platform for third-party applications and the tied product is complementary software functionality. While our reasoning may at times appear to have broader force, we do not have the confidence to speak to facts outside the record, which contains scant discussion of software integration generally. Microsoft's primary justification for bundling IE APIs is that their inclusion with Windows increases the value of third-party software (and Windows) to consumers. Because this claim applies with distinct force when the tying product is *platform* software, we have no present basis for finding the per se rule inapplicable to software markets generally. Nor should we be interpreted as setting a precedent for switching to the rule of reason every time a court identifies an efficiency justification for a tying arrangement. Our reading of the record suggests merely that integration of new functionality into platform software is a common practice and that wooden application of per se rules in this litigation may cast a cloud over platform innovation in the market for PCs, network computers and information appliances.

* * *

The D.C. Circuit's treatment of tying in *Microsoft* is noteworthy in a number of ways. First, the court appears to carve out an exception to per se analysis of tying for "platform software." Whereas the district court viewed itself as bound to apply per se analysis, 87 F. Supp. 2d at 51 ("To the extent that the Supreme Court has spoken authoritatively on these issues * * * this Court is bound to follow its guidance and is not at liberty to extrapolate a new rule governing the tying of software products."), the court of appeals concluded that it was at least free enough to distinguish the case. Why? How persuasive are its arguments for doing so? Is the court's insistence that the exception be limited to "platform software" persuasive? Is it likely that others will cite the case to support further erosion of per se analysis of tying? Was the D.C. Circuit inviting the Supreme Court to recognize an efficiency defense when it next considers the tying per se rule?

What role did the court's perception of possible efficiencies play in its decision not to utilize per se analysis? How can its willingness to entertain Microsoft's assertions of efficiencies be squared with its conclusion in its Section 2 analysis (*see supra* Chapter 4) that Microsoft's election to bundle IE and Windows had an anticompetitive effect and *no* justifications? If that was true for purposes of Section 2, why didn't the court proceed to decide the Section 1 claim under the rule of reason and similarly conclude that Microsoft's integration strategy was unreasonably anticompetitive? Also recall from our discussion of the *Microsoft* court's analysis of monopolization claims in Chapter 4 that a practice can support monopolization in conjunction with other bad acts even if it doesn't harm competition looked at on its own (as the tying analysis requires). Should that also affect the analysis of tying under the rule of reason? How?

Second, do you agree with the court's interpretation and application of *Jefferson Parish's* "two product" test? What did the court of appeals mean when it said that test was fashioned to "screen out false positives under per se analysis"? The court reasoned: "The consumer demand test is a rough proxy for whether a tying arrangement may, on balance, be welfare-enhancing, and unsuited to per se condemnation." Do you agree? How could the consumer demand test accomplish this goal?

In a portion of the opinion not excerpted here, the court provided some specific guidelines for the district court to follow when the case resumed in district court. *See* 253 F.3d at 95–97. On remand, however, the federal government and the states concluded that they would not pursue the tying claim. Why might they have reached that decision?

Sidebar 6–5:
The Economics of Tying

As the foregoing material reveals, tying was for a long time treated very simply and harshly under both the Clayton and Sherman Acts. A fundamental economic assumption of that harsh treatment was that a firm engaged in tying was trying to expand or "leverage" its monopoly from one product market, the tying product market, to another market, that of the tied product. In the Supreme Court's view, this injured buyers of the tied products and excluded rivals from the sale of the tied product.

In this Sidebar, we discuss how these traditional assumptions were questioned over time and have eroded as a consequence, leaving tying doctrine in a somewhat uncertain state.

The Chicago School Critique

The assumption that tying is almost always anticompetitive came under pointed attack from Chicago School proponents in the late 1950s. *See* Ward S. Bowman, Jr., *Tying Arrangements and the Leverage Problem*, 67 YALE L.J. 19 (1957). Bowman responded in two ways. First, he argued that tying could have procompetitive uses. He also asserted that the "leverage" idea was largely implausible absent an independent reason to believe that the seller could monopolize the tied product market. If the seller were in fact a monopolist of the tying product, it could maximize its profits by charging the monopolist's price for the tying product, and "tying" could add nothing to that profit. Some explanation other than "leverage" would have to be found. This became known as the "single monopoly profit" theory, which we discussed earlier in the *Note on the "Single Monopoly Profit" Theory.*

Bowman's critique of tying doctrine has not gone entirely unchallenged, *see, e.g.,* Louis Kaplow, *Extension of Monopoly Power Through Leverage*, 85 COLUM. L. REV. 515 (1985), but it had a lasting impact on the economic analysis of tying. It also has eroded support for use of any version of per se analysis, and later commentators, not limited to the Chicago School, who agreed with and built upon his views were cited with approval by the concurring Justices in *Jefferson Parish*. 466 U.S. at 36 (O'Connor, J., concurring), *citing* ROBERT H. BORK, THE ANTITRUST PARADOX 372–74 (1978); PHILLIP AREEDA, ANTITRUST ANALYSIS 735 (3d ed. 1981).

Many tying or bundling examples involve product complements. These are goods that buyers use together, like a computer and a printer, or a printer and ink.[a] As is explained above in the *Note on the "Single Monopoly Profit" Theory*, the single monopoly profit issue is raised by any type of exclusivity in the sale of product complements, not simply tying and manufacturer-dealer relationships. (Vertically related sellers produce complements in a special sense: the buyer purchases both the product and distribution services.)

Pro and Anti-Competitive Uses of Tying

As we have already observed, courts traditionally have condemned tying arrangements on the theory that they can harm competition by having collusive or exclusionary effects, and they did so by invoking variants of per se analysis. Although a slim majority of the Supreme Court clung to the per se approach in *Jefferson Parish*, it is more widely accepted today that tying may have an unusually wide range of economic explanations, some anticompetitive, some procompetitive, and one (price discrimination) with ambiguous economic consequences. As a consequence, its status as a "per se violation" remains unstable, and some have seriously questioned how often tying is likely to lead to anticompetitive effects at all.

Anticompetitive Effects of Tying. Because purchasers from the tying seller must buy both the tying and the tied product, even though they might have preferred to buy only the tying product, or to have purchased the tied product from another supplier, courts concluded that tying can lead to collusive

---

[a]   More technically, if the price of a product increases, buyers will purchase less of it, more of its demand substitutes, and less of its demand complements.

anticompetitive effects. Having to purchase a second, unwanted product is the economic equivalent of being charged a higher price. Likewise, having to forego choice also may be viewed as a collusive effect, when it is tantamount to an increase in the quality-adjusted price. These theories of anticompetitive harm, however, were the target of the Chicago School critique of tying—how could such "forcing" actually benefit the seller of the tying and tied products? If it was in a position to "force," why not simply charge a higher price for the tying product? In raising these questions, the Chicago School's "single monopoly profit" theory cast doubt on the validity of the collusive effects view of tying, and invited debate about other possible explanations for the selling firm's use of tying. *See Jefferson Parish Hosp. Dist. No. 2 v. Hyde*, 466 U.S. 2, 36, 104 S.Ct. 1551, 1570–71 (1984) (O'CONNOR, J., concurring) (observing that any anticompetitive explanation must overcome the single monopoly profit theory). This is also discussed further in the following *Note on Brantley and the Continued Viability of Exploitative Theories of Competitive Harm for Tying.*

As is discussed in the *Note on the Single Monopoly Profit Theory* (discussion of "Leveraging Market Power to a Complementary Market"), the "single monopoly profit" critique of the collusive effects theory of tying does not necessarily address the possibility that tying can harm competition as a method of *exclusion* (or, more generally, raising rival's costs), which protects or confers market power.

As we just read, the government's case against Microsoft included a claim that Microsoft violated Section 1 of the Sherman Act when it tied its Internet Explorer browser to the Windows operating system, excluding Netscape's competing browser. That claim can be understood in this framework. The possibility that computer users could one day employ Netscape's browser (along with Sun's Java programming language) to run applications programs on all computer operating systems (not just Windows) means that in the future, a new group of browser users could arise that would use an Internet browser while sidestepping Microsoft's operating system monopoly. By tying its own browser to Windows, Microsoft could exclude Netscape from the current market (in which Windows has a monopoly) and, in consequence, from the nascent future market, in which other operating systems would compete with Windows using the browser as a platform on which to run applications programs.[b] *See generally* Dennis W. Carlton & Michael Waldman, *The Strategic Use of Tying to Preserve and Create Market Power in Evolving Industries*, 33 RAND J. ECON. 194, 209–12 (2002).

Much of the case law has focused on the possible exclusionary harm of tying. By effectively cutting off rival suppliers of the tied product from some or all of their potential customers, tying can reduce competition in the *market for the tied product*. The firm engaged in tying might thereby obtain or maintain power over price with respect to the tied product, as in the resort example. Note, however, that in the Microsoft example, the government successfully argued that tying might also be a method of perpetuating a dominant position in the *market for the tying product*. By tying Internet Explorer, its Internet browser, to its dominant Windows operating system, Microsoft snuffed out the possibility that competing browsers could evolve from being merely Internet browsers into an alternative operating system to Windows. Even though the court of appeals reversed the government's claim that Microsoft attempted to monopolize the alleged browser market, and reversed and remanded the specific tying claim for a variety of reasons, it affirmed the district court's conclusion that the tying arrangement constituted unjustified exclusionary conduct for purposes of the government's Section 2 Sherman Act monopolization claim. *United States v. Microsoft Corp.*, 253 F.3d 34 (D.C. Cir. 2001) (*see supra* Chapter 4).

Tying also may harm competition if it is used as a method of *evading rate regulation*. *See, e.g., Jefferson Parish*, 466 U.S. at 36 n.4 (O'Connor, J., concurring). A regulated firm that sells both a regulated and an unregulated product can effectively raise the price of the regulated good by tying its sale to that of an unregulated product and charging a high price for the unregulated good (and thus for the bundle). *See Note on the "Single Monopoly Profit" Theory* (discussion of "Evasion of Rate Regulation"). In the usual situation of public utility regulation, we assume that the unregulated firm would charge too high a price by reducing output too much. Regulation then expands output by forcing down the price. If so, evading regulation would lead to an allocative efficiency loss.

---

[b] Another possibility by which tying the browser to Windows could increase Microsoft's market power, one not raised in the case, would arise if browsers can be used in computers without Windows. (In an anachronistic example, browsers today can also be used with mobile telephones that do not run on the Windows operating system.) Then it might be possible for Microsoft to exclude Netscape from both markets by excluding it from selling browsers to personal computer users.

Procompetitive Uses of Tying. Tying also can promote competition in a number of ways. For example, through tying, a seller can make sure that its product is used with other products that do not degrade the first good's performance. This practice could allow the seller to protect its reputation through *assuring product quality.* This argument was asserted, but seemingly unsupported by the evidence, even in very early cases, such as *IBM* and *International Salt*, discussed earlier in this Chapter, but has on occasion proven effective. *See, e.g., Dehydrating Process Co. v. A.O. Smith Corp.*, 292 F.2d 653 (1st Cir. 1961). Also, *compare Mozart Co. v. Mercedes-Benz of North America, Inc.*, 833 F.2d 1342, 1348–51 (9th Cir. 1987) (accepting "quality control defense" to tying), *with Metrix Warehouse, Inc. v. Daimler-Benz Aktiengesellschaft*, 828 F.2d 1033, 1040–42 (4th Cir. 1987) (rejecting the same defense in connection with the same parties and practices). Relatedly, tying may provide an incentive for the seller to invest in product quality. *See* James D. Dana, Jr. & Kathryn E. Spier, *Do Tying, Bundling, and Other Purchase Restraints Increase Product Quality?* 43 J. INDUS. ORG. 142 (2015).

Tying also may reduce production or distribution costs when sellers experience economies of joint production, distribution, and marketing. Related buyer-side economies sometimes arise in the development of a new industry, when it is expensive for buyers to learn how to integrate components. *See, e.g., United States v. Jerrold Elecs. Corp.*, 187 F. Supp. 545 (E.D. Pa. 1960), *aff'd per curiam*, 365 U.S. 567 (1961). Tying can also promote the sale of a system of related products by preventing excessive markups by the seller of complementary goods. This procompetitive benefit is closely related to the possible benefit of vertical integration in avoiding double marginalization (transferring inputs at marginal cost). *See Note on Eliminating Double Marginalization, supra* Chapter 5. Tying may also undermine a seller cartel by *facilitating secret price-cutting.*

Ambiguous Competitive Effects—Price Discrimination

Tying can be a means of price discrimination, where the term is used here in its economic sense of charging different markups over marginal cost to different customers. If the marginal cost of producing and selling the good to those customers is identical, then price discrimination would occur when those customers are charged different prices. Buyers willing to pay more without cutting back markedly on their purchases are charged a higher markup than buyers unwilling to do so. For price discrimination to be successful, the seller must be able to sort buyers into different groups based on their willingness to pay, and prevent arbitrage, that is, prevent those buyers able to purchase the product at a low price from reselling it to those forced by the seller to purchase at a higher price.

For example, tying can create price discrimination through metering. *See, e.g., Jefferson Parish*, 466 U.S. at 15 n.23, 19 n.30. *See also id.* at 36 n.4 (O'Connor, J., concurring). Some commentators have suggested that Xerox adopted such a policy in the early days of the photocopier, when copiers required special paper. At that time, Xerox leased its copier machines at a low rental and charged a price for copier paper well in excess of the marginal cost of that paper, arguably tying the two products together by forcing copier users to purchase paper at a high price through Xerox. This policy could be understood as metering. Intensive copier users were likely willing to pay more for a copier than more casual users; if so, Xerox was effectively able to extract a higher price for the copier from intensive users by requiring those buyers to purchase the high volumes of paper they required at a substantial premium relative to the cost of paper.[c] A more contemporary example might involve the pricing of printers and toner cartridges. The potential anticompetitive effects of metering are highlighted in Einer Elhague & Barry J. Nalebuff, *The Welfare Effects of Metering Ties* (April 2015), http://ssrn.com/abstract=2591577. The economics of price discrimination was discussed in greater detail in Sidebar 5–4.

Figure 6–7:

Summary of Potential Pro- and Anti-Competitive Effects of Tying

Anti-Competitive Effects of Tying	Pro-Competitive Effects of Tying
• Raise prices to consumers or limit their choices (collusive effects) • Exclude or impair rival by raising costs, leading to higher consumer prices (exclusionary effects)	• Assure product quality • Achieve economies through joint production, distribution or marketing • Undermine seller cartel by facilitating secret price-cutting

---

[c] If the buyer is risk-averse and unsure whether its business will succeed, while the seller is risk neutral, metering could also be a pro-competitive method of allocating risk between the parties.

- Evade rate regulation
- Facilitate price discrimination (as through metering)

- Prevent excessive mark-ups by the seller of complementary goods or services
- Avoid double marginalization
- Facilitate price discrimination (as through metering)

Conclusion

In this Sidebar we have canvassed some of the most prevalent arguments for and against maintaining a per se rule against tying.[d] In doing so, we also examined the variety of pro- and anticompetitive uses of tying arrangements. As should be evident, the issue is complex, both legally and economically. On the other hand, the trend has been fairly consistent in recent years, pointing towards greater tolerance for tying arrangements. That trend will likely continue, given the variety of economic justifications for tying arrangements, and the combined impact of the views of the concurring Justices in *Jefferson Parish*, the D.C. Circuit in *Microsoft*, and commentators who have advocated abandonment of per se analysis for tying may lead the Supreme Court in an appropriate case to overrule the various cases endorsing some form of per se analysis for the practice . . .

NOTE ON *BRANTLEY* AND THE CONTINUED VIABILITY OF EXPLOITATIVE THEORIES OF COMPETITIVE HARM FOR TYING

Courts traditionally viewed tying as anticompetitive in two ways because of its potential to produce both collusive and exclusionary effects. A consumer "forced" to purchase a second, unwanted product was effectively being charged a higher price and was being deprived of the choice to forego purchasing the tied product or to purchase it from another seller. As the Supreme Court majority in *Jefferson Parish* reasoned:

> Our cases have concluded that the essential characteristic of an invalid tying arrangement lies in the seller's exploitation of its control over the tying product to force the buyer into the purchase of a tied product that the buyer either did not want at all, or might have preferred to purchase elsewhere on different terms. When such

---

d   For an interesting discussion of consumer protection issues raised by tying, see Richard Craswell, *Tying Requirements in Competitive Markets: The Consumer Protection Issues*, 62 B.U. L. REV. 661 (1982).

"forcing" is present, competition on the merits in the market for the tied item is restrained and the Sherman Act is violated.

Jefferson Parish, 466 U.S. at 12. That view of "exploitative" harm, however, was subjected to criticism, discussed in the *Jefferson Parish* concurrence, *id.* at 36–38 (O'Connor, J., concurring) and in Sidebar 6–5, on the ground that tying could not add to a firm's market power unless it had exclusionary effects. One response to that criticism was to better explain how tying could have exclusionary effects. But to some degree, that response may have implicitly conceded the point that tying may not have any significant "collusive effects."

The continued viability of a collusive effects-based objection to tying appears to have been at issue in *Brantley v. NBC Universal, Inc.*, 675 F.3d 1192 (9th Cir. 2012). There a putative class of retail cable and satellite television subscribers alleged that television programmers and their distributors (cable and satellite television service providers) violated Section 1 of the Sherman Act by selling cable channels exclusively in packages rather than on an a la carte basis; that is, programmers contractually limited distributors from offering subscribers "must have" channels unless they also agreed to purchase "low-demand" channels. After initially contending that the channel-bundling practice prevented independent programmers from entering and competing in the upstream programming channel market (a traditional foreclosure-based theory of anticompetitive harm), plaintiffs amended their complaint to abandon their foreclosure theory, asserting instead that the relevant antitrust harm derived exclusively from three sources: (1) limitations upon distributors' method of doing business; (2) reductions in consumer choice; and (3) increases in price. *Id.* at 1201. Plaintiffs did not argue that the bundling was subject to per se analysis, *id.* at 1197 n.7, so their antitrust claims were evaluated under the rule of reason. The critical inquiry, therefore, focused on the plaintiffs' ability to allege harm to competition. That in turn promoted consideration of the anticompetitive theories that support claims of tying. *Id.* at 1199.

As quoted above, *Jefferson Parish* had appeared to endorse the idea that "forcing" compromised the competitive process. The Ninth Circuit found support for a contrary view, however, both in *Jefferson Parish* and in its own prior decisions. Quoting from *Jefferson Parish*, the court sought to define the nature of competitive injuries that can flow from tying:

> ... [C]ourts distinguish between tying arrangements in which a company exploits its market power by attempting "to impose restraints on competition in the market for a tied product" (which may threaten an injury to competition) and arrangements that let a company exploit its market power "by merely enhancing the price of the tying product" (which does not).

Id. at 1199 (*quoting Jefferson Parish*, 466 U.S. at 14). It also quoted *Jefferson Parish* for the proposition that:

> ... when a purchaser is 'forced' to buy a product he would not have otherwise bought even from another seller in the tied product market,

there can be no adverse impact on competition because no portion of the market which would otherwise have been available to other sellers has been foreclosed.

Id. (*quoting Jefferson Parish*, 466 U.S. at 16). This reasoning seems to beg the question whether such competition would have emerged absent the bundling practice.

Then turning to *Sylvania* and *Leegin*, the court concluded that "allegations that an agreement has the effect of reducing consumers' choices or increasing prices to consumers does not sufficiently allege an injury to competition. Both effects are fully consistent with a free, competitive market." *Id.* at 1202. Because the plaintiffs' claims thus no longer included allegations either of substantial foreclosure or of collusion among the programmers or the distributors, the Ninth Circuit found that the plaintiffs had failed to allege injury to competition and ordered the complaint dismissed. *Id.* at 1200–04. Having concluded that the plaintiffs' allegations of harm were insufficient, the court did not consider the possible efficiency arguments of the defendants. What kinds of justifications might the programmers and distributors have had for their use of tying? Can *Brantley's* dismissal of the plaintiffs' case be defended on the ground that the harms to consumers from cable channel packaging are so unlikely absent some evidence of exclusion or industry collusion, and the efficiency justifications for the practice so likely to be substantial, that permitting the case to proceed to discovery and possibly protracted litigation was unwarranted? *Cf.* Gregory S. Crawford & Ali Yurukoglu, *The Welfare Effects of Bundling in Multichannel Television Markets,* 102 AM. ECON. REV. 643 (2012) (empirical economic study finds that if distributors were forced to offer cable channels to subscribers on an a la carte basis, consumers would be harmed but aggregate economic welfare would increase).

Brantley thus raises important, and heavily debated, questions about the nature of antitrust injury in a purely vertical tying case, and perhaps more broadly in cases involving vertical restraints. First, the court rejected the adequacy of the plaintiffs' allegation that the tying diminished competition among the distributors, concluding that "limitations on the manner in which Distributors compete with one another do not, without more, constitute a cognizable injury to competition." *Id.* at 1201–02.

Second, the court also rejected the plaintiffs' allegations that reduced consumer choice attributable to tying, without more, constitutes antitrust injury. Scholars have debated whether "consumer choice" should be incorporated into antitrust law's conception of competitive harm. Proponents of the "consumer choice" standard contend that antitrust violations are rightly defined as activities "that unreasonably restrict[ ] the totality of price and nonprice choices that would otherwise have been available." Neil W. Averitt & Robert H. Lande, *Using the "Consumer Choice" Approach to Antitrust Law,* 74 ANTITRUST L.J. 175, 183 (2007). Fundamentally, the consumer choice theory asserts that any reduction in "choice," even if accompanied by reduced prices or increased output, constitutes a cognizable antitrust harm, a view that appears to be supported by at least some language in the *Jefferson Parish* majority. Proponents of this framework accordingly argue that tying arrangements can have anticompetitive results even when they do not occasion serious market foreclosure. *See* Einer Elhauge, *Tying, Bundled Discounts, and the Death of the Single Monopoly Profit Theory*, 123 HARV. L. REV. 397, 400 (2009).

Critics find the consumer choice framework to be over-inclusive. Some point out that it lacks any limiting principle and others emphasize that it is untethered to any welfare analysis. In their view, condemnation of practices resulting in a loss of consumer choice, without regard to whether that conduct is tantamount to an increase in quality-adjusted prices, is likely to deter business conduct that increases consumer welfare. For example, if applied without limitation, the consumer choice standard might prohibit many kinds of legitimate and pro-consumer uses of exclusive dealing arrangements, exclusive territories, or other vertical restraints. *See* Joshua D. Wright & Douglas H. Ginsburg, *The Goals of Antitrust: Welfare Trumps Choice*, 81 FORDHAM L. REV. 2405 (2013). In holding that the plaintiffs' allegations failed to state a claim under Section 1 of the Sherman Act, the Ninth Circuit appears to have come down against consumer choice as an independent basis of injury to competition.

More broadly, should the prohibition of tying be confined to instances of exclusionary effects, as *Brantley* seems to suggest? Doing so would appear to be at odds with decades of tying law, which emphasized the adverse effect of "forcing" on consumers, which could be interpreted as supporting an inference that competition likely will be harmed. Yet it would also appear to be consistent with a great weight of economic commentary on tying, which views tying as objectionable when it is exclusionary, although its exclusionary effects can affect either the market for the tied product, or, as in *Microsoft*, the market for the tying product.

---

b. Exclusive Dealing

The categorization of an exclusionary vertical interbrand restraint as "tying" often is a matter of perspective, and the perspective can have an important impact on the analysis of its effects. The law of tying, as we saw in *Jefferson Parish*, can be read to emphasize the effects of the restraint on consumers: those who purchase the tying product are "forced" to also purchase the tied product. So the anticompetitive effect of tying on consumers can be perceived as *collusive*, taking the form of diminished choice or higher prices, since being coerced into buying an unwanted product or service is essentially the same as paying more than you otherwise would have. This was the issue being debated in *Brantley*.

But tying also can be viewed as *exclusionary* from the perspective of rival suppliers of the tied product, whose potential customers may dwindle in number if the tying arrangement is successful. From their perspective, the tying arrangement is indistinguishable from an "exclusive dealing" arrangement, because for all intents and purposes, its customers, actual or potential, must agree to buy exclusively from the dominant firm engaged in tying. So tying can be viewed as "exclusive dealing" as it was in *Jefferson Parish*.

As we have already noted, however, the history of exclusive dealing was not encumbered by debates over reliance on per se analysis. To the contrary, as we observed as early as *Standard Stations*, the Supreme Court recognized that they could have legitimate and procompetitive uses. However, as has been true of tying, attitudes about exclusive dealing have significantly evolved even further in the direction of accepting their utility. Since *Standard Stations* and *Tampa Electric*, therefore, few cases have been successful in demonstrating that the probable effects of the practice will be unreasonably anticompetitive. In addition to *Microsoft*, which we read in Chapter 4, other examples include *United States v. Dentsply Int'l, Inc.*, 399 F.3d 181 (3d Cir. 2005) and *ZF Meritor, LLC v. Eaton Corp.*, 696 F.3d 254 (3d Cir. 2012). All three cases were influential in persuading the FTC and the Eleventh Circuit to condemn the exclusive dealing arrangement challenged in our next case, *McWane*. As you read the decision, note how similar the court's analytical framework is to cases we studied applying the modern rule of reason, such as *RealComp II* (*see supra* Chapter 2), and the economic analysis to cases like the D.C. Circuit's *Microsoft* decision and the Supreme Court's decision in *Lorain Journal* (*see supra* Chapter 4).

MCWANE, INC. V. FEDERAL TRADE COMMISSION
United States Court of Appeals for the Eleventh Circuit, 2015.
783 F.3d 814.

Before MARCUS, and JILL PRYOR, CIRCUIT JUDGES, and HINKLE,* DISTRICT JUDGE.

MARCUS, CIRCUIT JUDGE.

This antitrust case involves allegedly anticompetitive conduct in the ductile iron pipe fittings ("DIPF") market by McWane, Inc., a family-run company headquartered in Birmingham, Alabama. In 2009, following the passage of federal legislation that provided a large infusion of money for waterworks projects that required domestic pipe fittings, Star Pipe Products entered the domestic fittings market. In response, McWane, the dominant producer of domestic pipe fittings, announced to its distributors

---

*   Honorable Robert L. Hinkle, United States District Judge for the Northern District of Florida, sitting by designation.

that (with limited exceptions) unless they bought all of their domestic fittings from McWane, they would lose their rebates and be cut off from purchases for 12 weeks. The Federal Trade Commission ("FTC") investigated and brought an enforcement action under Section 5 of the Federal Trade Commission Act, 15 U.S.C. § 45. The Administrative Law Judge ("ALJ"), after a two-month trial, and then a divided Commission, found that McWane's actions constituted an illegal exclusive dealing policy used to maintain McWane's monopoly power in the domestic fittings market. The Commission issued an order directing McWane to stop requiring exclusivity from distributors. McWane appealed, challenging nearly every aspect of the Commission's ruling.

After thorough review, we affirm the Commission's order. The Commission's factual and economic conclusions—identifying the relevant product market for domestic fittings produced for domestic-only projects, finding that McWane had monopoly power in that market, and determining that McWane's exclusivity program harmed competition—are supported by substantial evidence in the record, as required by our deferential standard of review, and their legal conclusions are supported by the governing law.

I.

A.

* * * Pipe fittings join together pipes and help direct the flow of pressurized water in pipeline systems. They are sold primarily to municipal water authorities and their contractors. Although there are several thousand unique configurations of fittings (different shapes, sizes, coatings, etc.), approximately 80% of the demand is for about 100 commonly used fittings.

Fittings are commodity products produced to American Water Works Association ("AWWA") standards, and any fitting that meets AWWA specifications is interchangeable, regardless of the country of origin. Ductile iron pipe fittings manufacturers rarely sell fittings directly to end users; instead, they sell them to middleman distributors, who in turn sell them to end users. An end user (e.g., a municipal water authority) will issue a "specification" for its project, detailing the pipes, fittings, and other products required. Competing contractors solicit bids for the specified products from distributors, who in turn seek quotes from various manufacturers like McWane.

End users issue either "open specifications," permitting the use of fittings manufactured anywhere in the world, or "domestic specifications," requiring the use of fittings made in the United States. An end user might issue a domestic specification either because of its preference or due to legal procurement requirements: certain municipal, state, and federal laws require waterworks projects to use domestic-only fittings.[1] Domestic fittings sold for use in projects with domestic-only specifications command higher prices than imported fittings or domestic fittings sold for use in projects with open specifications. The majority of specifications are open, and the majority of fittings sold (approximately 80–85%) are imported.

* * *

Today, the overall market for fittings sold in the United States—whether manufactured domestically or abroad, sold into both open-specification and domestic-only projects—is an oligopoly with three major suppliers: McWane, Star [Pipe Fittings], and Sigma [Corporation]. Together they account for approximately 90% of the fittings sold in the United States. There are two national distributors, HD Supply and Ferguson, which together account for approximately 60% of the overall waterworks distribution market.

* * *

In [June] 2009, looking to take advantage of the increased demand for domestic fittings prompted by ARRA * * * Star publicly announced at an industry conference and in a letter to customers that it would offer domestic fittings starting in September 2009. Star became a "virtual manufacturer" of domestic fittings, contracting with six third-party foundries in the U.S. to produce fittings to Star's specifications. Star also investigated acquiring its own U.S. foundry, which the Commission found would have been a decidedly less costly and more efficient way to produce domestic fittings.

In response to Star's forthcoming entry into the domestic DIPF market, McWane implemented its "Full Support Program" in order "[t]o protect [its] domestic brands and market position." This program was announced in a September 22, 2009 letter to distributors. McWane informed customers that if they did not "fully support McWane branded products for their domestic fitting and accessory requirements," they "may forgo participation in any unpaid rebates [they had accrued] for domestic fittings and accessories or shipment of their domestic fitting and accessory orders of [McWane] products for up to 12 weeks." In other words, distributors who bought domestic fittings from other companies (such as Star) might lose their rebates or be cut off from purchasing McWane's domestic fittings for up to three months.[2] * * *

---

[1]   In particular, the American Recovery and Reinvestment Act of 2009 ("ARRA") * * * provided more than $6 billion to fund water infrastructure projects, all with domestic-only specifications. Pennsylvania and New Jersey state laws also require domestic materials in public projects, as do Air Force bases, certain federal programs, and various municipalities. * * *

[2]   McWane emphasizes that the policy deliberately used the words "may" and "or" to convey "a weak stance." However, McWane's Vice President and General Manager Richard Tatman recognized that "[a]lthough the words 'may' and 'or' were specifically used, the market has interpreted the communication in the more hard line 'will' sense."

Internal documents reveal that McWane's express purpose was to raise Star's costs and impede it from becoming a viable competitor. McWane executive Richard Tatman wrote, "We need to make sure that they [Star] don't reach any critical market mass that will allow them to continue to invest and receive a profitable return." In another document, he "observed that 'any competitor' seeking to enter the domestic fittings market could face 'significant blocking issues' if they are not a 'full line' domestic supplier." In yet another, McWane employees described the nascent Full Support Program as a strategy to "[f]orce [d]istribution to [p]ick their [h]orse," which would "[f]orce[ ] Star[ ] to absorb the costs associated with having a more full line before they can secure major distribution." Mr. Tatman was concerned about the "[e]rosion of domestic pricing if Star emerges as a legitimate competitor," and another McWane executive wrote that his "chief concern is that the domestic market [might] get[ ] creamed from a pricing standpoint" should Star become a "domestic supplier."

Initially, the Full Support Program was enforced as threatened. Thus, for example, when the Tulsa, Oklahoma branch of distributor Hajoca Corporation purchased Star domestic fittings, McWane cut off sales of its domestic fittings to all Hajoca branches and withheld its rebates.[3] Other distributors testified to abiding by the Full Support Program in order to avoid the devastating result of being cut off from all McWane domestic fittings. * * * Indeed, the Commission found that "Star was rebuffed by some distributors even after offering a more generous rebate than McWane." However, some distributors also identified other factors that contributed to their decision not to purchase from Star, including "concerns about Star's inventory, the quality of fittings produced at several different foundries, . . . the timeliness of delivery," and negative past business dealings with Star.

Despite McWane's Full Support Program, Star entered the domestic fittings market and made sales to various distributors. From 2006 until Star's entry in 2009, McWane was the only manufacturer of domestic fittings, with 100% of the market for domestic-only projects. By 2010, Star had gained approximately 5% of the domestic fittings market, while McWane captured the remaining 95%. Star grew to just under 10% market share in 2011, leaving the remaining 90% for McWane, and Star was "on pace, at the time of trial, to have its best year ever for [d]omestic [f]ittings sales in 2012." The Commission noted that "many distributors made purchases under the exceptions allowed by the Full Support Program," but that Star's sales in total "were small compared to the overall size of the

---

[3] McWane maintains that this was the only example of the Full Support Program's enforcement: "McWane never enforced the rebate program against any other distributor." Of course, the goal of the program was not necessarily to enforce the punishments but to dissuade customers from leaving McWane in the first place.

market." Star estimated that if the Full Support Program had not been in place, its sales would have been greater by a multiple of 2.5 in 2010 and by a multiple of three in 2011.

Star never ended up building or buying a domestic foundry of its own. The Commission found that this was because Star "believed its sales level was insufficient to justify running its own foundry." Star estimated that the cost of producing fittings at its own domestic foundry would have been significantly lower than the cost of contracting with independent foundries, and that operating its own foundry would have allowed it to appreciably reduce its domestic fittings prices. * * * The Commission and the ALJ also found that the Full Support Program was a "significant reason" that another distributor, Serampore Industries Private, decided not to enter the domestic fittings market.

During 2009–2010, following Star's entry into the market and the Full Support Program's implementation, McWane's production costs for domestic fittings remained flat, but it raised its prices for domestic fittings and increased its gross profits. These prices were relatively consistent across all states, regardless of whether Star had entered the domestic fittings market as a rival; Star's presence in various states did not result in lower prices. McWane "continued to sell its domestic fittings into domestic-only specifications at prices that earned significantly higher gross profits than for non-domestic fittings, which faced greater competition." Star's average prices, however, were higher than McWane's in several states.

The duration of the Full Support Program is a matter of some dispute. McWane contends that it ended the Full Support Program in early 2010, eliminating the provision that customers might forego shipments for up to 12 weeks. But the Commission found that McWane had never "publicly withdrawn the policy or notified distributors of any changes," and that some distributors believed that the policy was "still in effect." There is also evidence that some distributors started to ignore the Full Support Program in 2010 after they learned of the FTC's investigation into McWane's practices.

* * *

II.

* * *

We review *de novo* the Commission's legal conclusions and the application of the facts to the law. * * * However, "we afford the FTC some deference as to its informed judgment that a particular commercial practice violates the Federal Trade Commission Act." * * *

* * *

III.

The Commission found that McWane adopted an exclusionary distribution policy that maintained its monopoly power in the domestic fittings market in violation of Section 5 of the Federal Trade Commission Act, which prohibits "[u]nfair methods of competition in or affecting commerce." 15 U.S.C. § 45.[10] Although exclusive dealing arrangements are common and can be procompetitive, particularly in competitive markets, these arrangements can harm competition in certain circumstances, *see Jefferson Parish Hosp. Dist. No. 2 v. Hyde,* 466 U.S. 2, 45, 104 S.Ct. 1551, 80 L.Ed.2d 2 (1984) (O'CONNOR, J., concurring) ("Exclusive dealing can have adverse economic consequences by allowing one supplier of goods or services unreasonably to deprive other suppliers of a market for their goods . . .") * * *. When a market is competitive, the "competition for the [exclusive] contract is a vital form of rivalry" that can induce the offering firm to provide price reductions or improved services to buyers, to the ultimate benefit of consumers. But, notably, in the absence of such competition, a dominant firm can impose exclusive deals on downstream dealers to "strengthen[ ] or prolong[ ] [its] market position." IIIB Philip E. Areeda & Herbert Hovenkamp, *Antitrust Law* ¶ 760b7, at 54 (3d ed.2008). Thus, while such arrangements are "not illegal in themselves," they can run afoul of antitrust laws as "an improper means of maintaining a monopoly." *United States v. Dentsply Int'l, Inc.,* 399 F.3d 181, 187 (3d Cir. 2005).

A violation of Section 5 of the Federal Trade Commission Act premised on monopolization requires proof of "(1) the possession of monopoly power in the relevant market and (2) the willful acquisition or maintenance of that power as distinguished from growth or development as a consequence of a superior product, business acumen, or historic accident." * * * Thus, for the Commission's conclusion that McWane violated the Federal Trade Commission Act to stand, it must have successfully defined the relevant market, demonstrated that McWane had monopoly power in that market, and showed that McWane's Full Support Program constituted the illegal maintenance of that monopoly power. McWane challenges all three of the Commission's determinations, and we address each of them in turn.

A. *Monopoly Power in the Relevant Market*

1. *Market Definition*

[The court observed that "Defining the market is a necessary step in any analysis of market power and thus an indispensable element in the consideration of any monopolization . . . case arising under section 2." Citing the Supreme Court's decision in *DuPont* (*see supra* Chapter 4), the

---

[10] The Commission acknowledged that violations of Section 2 of the Sherman Act (monopolization) also constitute "unfair methods of competition" under Section 5 of the Federal Trade Commission Act, and therefore relied on Section 2 caselaw in its analysis. * * *

court noted that a relevant product market consists of "products that have reasonable interchangeability for the purposes for which they are produced" and that "reasonable interchangeability of use or the cross-elasticity of demand between a product and its substitutes constitutes the outer boundaries of a product market for antitrust purposes." It noted that neither party contested the ALJ's and Commission's finding that the relevant geographic market was the United States. The issue on appeal was whether the relevant product market was properly limited to domestically-produced ductile iron pipe fittings. Eds.]

As for the product market, the Commission, agreeing with the ALJ, found that the relevant market was one "for the supply of domestically-manufactured fittings for use in . . . projects with domestic-only specifications." It noted that various laws and end-user preferences requiring projects to use domestic fittings precluded imported fittings from being "reasonable substitutes" for those projects, even though the fittings themselves are functionally identical. The Commission also noted that McWane charged higher prices for (and reaped greater profits from) domestic fittings in domestic-only projects: the ALJ found that McWane charged approximately 20%–95% more for its domestic fittings for domestic-only projects than for open-specification projects. This price differentiation reflected McWane's ability to target customers with domestic-only project specifications who could not avoid the higher prices by substituting imported fittings. * * *

McWane contends, however, that domestic and imported fittings are, in fact, interchangeable, because some customers (those whose projects' specifications are not dictated by law) can "flip" their projects from domestic-only to open, thereby turning imported fittings into a reasonable substitute. However, the Commission found, based on testimony in the record, that "flipping typically only occurs when domestic fittings are unavailable, rather than as a result of competition between domestic and imported fittings." This is consonant with the ALJ's finding that end users with domestic-only preferences "are aware of, but not sensitive to, the price differential between domestic fittings and import fittings."

McWane also alleges that the Commission's definition was insufficient as a matter of law because it "was unsupported by an expert economic test," which McWane claims is a requirement under Eleventh Circuit caselaw. It is true that in some circumstances we have said that a market definition "must be based on expert testimony." * * * Such testimony can be insufficient when "conclusory" or "based upon insufficient economic analysis." * * *

But in this case, the Commission did rely in part on the complaint counsel's expert witness, Dr. Laurence Schumann, who considered a hypothetical monopolist test and the lack of interchangeability between domestic and imported fittings in domestic-only projects. Nevertheless, McWane claims that the expert's analysis was insufficient because it did not involve an econometric analysis, such as a cross-elasticity of demand study. However, there appears to be no support in the caselaw for McWane's claim that such a technical analysis is always required. Indeed, as the Commission correctly noted, "[c]ourts routinely rely on qualitative economic evidence to define relevant markets." * * * Given the identification of persistent price differences between domestic fittings and imported fittings, the distinct customers, and the lack of reasonable substitutes in this case, there was sufficient evidence to support the Commission's market definition.

2.   *Monopoly Power*

"As a legal matter, Sherman Act § 2 requires that the defendant either have monopoly power or a dangerous probability of achieving it . . . " * * * Monopoly power is the ability "to control prices or exclude competition." However, "[b]ecause . . . direct proof [of the ability to profitably raise prices substantially above the competitive level] is only rarely available, courts more typically examine market structure in search of circumstantial evidence of monopoly power." *United States v. Microsoft Corp.*, 253 F.3d 34, 51 (D.C.Cir. 2001) (en banc) (per curiam). Courts regularly ask whether the firm has a predominant market share, * * * and look to other circumstantial factors such as "the size and strength of competing firms, freedom of entry, pricing trends and practices in the industry, ability of consumers to substitute comparable goods, and consumer demand," * * *

In determining that McWane had monopoly power, the Commission found that McWane's market share of the domestic fittings market had been 100% from 2006 until Star's entry into the market in 2009. McWane's market share was then approximately 95% in 2010 and approximately 90% in 2011, "far exceed [ing] the levels that courts typically require to support a *prima facie* showing of monopoly power." It also observed that there were "substantial barriers to entry in the domestic fittings market" both for brand new entrants and for those who already supply imported fittings. Although Star was able to enter the market, the Commission noted that its share remained below 10% in 2010 and 2011, and, notably, its entry had no effect on McWane's prices. The Commission reasoned that McWane's "ability to control prices" in the market "provide[d] direct evidence of [its] monopoly power."

The difficulty in this case is that the circumstantial evidence does not all point in the same direction. McWane's market share during the relevant time period is plainly high enough to be considered predominant. * * * Standing alone, this would seem to be sufficient evidence to support the Commission's conclusion that McWane had monopoly power in the domestic fittings market.

However, there is also evidence that, despite the presence of the Full Support Program, Star was still able to enter the domestic fittings market and expand its market share from 0% in 2009 to approximately 5% in 2010 to approximately 10% in 2011, while McWane's market share correspondingly declined. McWane contends that this "clear and successful entry" and growth by a competitor precludes a finding of monopoly power by demonstrating a lack of barriers to entry in the market. The Commission disagreed, finding that, despite Star's entry and growth, substantial barriers to entry existed in both the overall fittings market and the domestic fittings market. The ALJ found (and the Commission agreed) that "a significant capital investment" is required to enter the overall fittings market, as "new entrant[s] must overcome existing relationships between existing manufacturers[,] and the [d]istributors[,] and [e]nd [u]sers," in addition to "develop[ing] hundreds of patterns and moldings." All told, the Commission agreed with the ALJ that a *de novo* entrant would need approximately three to five years to enter the fittings market. Star, as an established player in the overall fittings market, did not face all of these obstacles in entering the domestic fittings market. (For example, it had pre-existing relationships with some distributors and did not need to alter its sales team.) Nevertheless, the Commission found that significant barriers to entry existed in the domestic market, as Star still needed to purchase its own foundry or contract with third-party domestic foundries. * * * Moreover, the Commission found that the Full Support Program itself posed a barrier to entry by shrinking the number of available distributors. In support of this argument, the Commission observed that two other suppliers of imported fittings, Sigma Corporation and Serampore Industries Private, considered entering the domestic fittings market but ultimately concluded that the costs and challenges were too high.

[Here the court noted that "[s]ome caselaw from other circuits appears to support" McWane's argument about the significance of evidence of successful entry, but that "not all courts agree." Others had concluded that evidence of some entry does not "necessarily preclude" a finding that significant barriers to entry exist. This could be true, for example if the manufacturing capacity or output of a new entrant is insufficient to take significant business away from the monopolist. Similarly, another court had observed that although a "declining market share may reflect an absence of market power . . . it does not foreclose a finding of such power." Eds.]

In addition to McWane's overwhelming (albeit declining) market share, the Commission cited the particular importance of Star's inability to constrain McWane's pricing for domestic fittings. After Star's entry, McWane continued to sell domestic fittings for domestic-only products at prices that "earned significantly higher gross profits than for non-domestic fittings, which faced greater competition." Indeed, McWane's prices and profits for domestic fittings rose in 2010, the year after Star's entry.

On this record, we are unprepared to say that Star's entry and growth foreclose a finding that McWane possessed monopoly power in the relevant market. Although the limited entry and expansion of a competitor sometimes may cut against such a finding, the evidence of McWane's overwhelming market share (90%), the large capital outlays required to enter the domestic fittings market, and McWane's undeniable continued power over domestic fittings prices amount to sufficient evidence that "a reasonable mind might accept as adequate to support" the Commission's conclusion.

B. *Monopoly Maintenance*

Having established that McWane "possess[es] . . . monopoly power in the relevant market," we turn to the question of whether the government proved that McWane engaged in "the willful . . . maintenance of that power as distinguished from growth or development as a consequence of a superior product, business acumen, or historic accident."

As we've observed, exclusive dealing arrangements are not per se unlawful, but they can run afoul of the antitrust laws when used by a dominant firm to maintain its monopoly. Of particular relevance to this case, an exclusive dealing arrangement can be harmful when it allows a monopolist to maintain its monopoly power by raising its rivals' costs sufficiently to prevent them from growing into effective competitors. *See* XI [Philip E. Areeda & Herbert Hovenkamp, *Antitrust Law]* * * *, ¶ 1804a, at 116–17 (describing how exclusive contracts can raise rivals' costs and harm competition); *see generally* Thomas G. Krattenmaker & Steven C. Salop, *Anticompetitive Exclusion: Raising Rivals' Costs to Achieve Power Over Price,* 96 Yale L.J. 209 (1986). The following description seems particularly appropriate here:

> [S]uppose an established manufacturer has long held a dominant position but is starting to lose market share to an aggressive young rival. A set of strategically planned exclusive-dealing contracts may slow the rival's expansion by requiring it to develop alternative outlets for its product, or rely at least temporarily on inferior or more expensive outlets. Consumer injury results from the delay that the dominant firm imposes on the smaller rival's growth.

XI Areeda & Hovenkamp, *supra,* ¶ 1802c, at 76. * * *

Tracking this economic argument, the Commission's theory is that McWane's Full Support Program was an exclusive dealing policy designed specifically to maintain its monopoly power "by impairing the ability of rivals to grow into effective competitors that might erode the firm's dominant position." To prevail, the FTC must establish that McWane "has engaged in anti-competitive conduct that reasonably appears to be a significant contribution to maintaining monopoly power." * * *

Neither the Supreme Court nor this Circuit has provided a clear formula with which to evaluate an exclusive dealing monopoly maintenance claim, but the D.C. Circuit has synthesized a structured, "rule of reason"-style approach to monopolization cases that has been cited with approval. * * * First, the government must show that the monopolist's conduct had the "anticompetitive effect" of "harm[ing] competition, not just a competitor." *Microsoft,* 253 F.3d at 58–59. If the government succeeds in demonstrating this anticompetitive harm, the burden then shifts to the defendant to present procompetitive justifications for the exclusive conduct, which the government can refute. *Microsoft,* 253 F.3d at 59; *Dentsply* 399 F.3d at 196; *see Eastman Kodak,* 504 U.S. at 482–84, 112 S.Ct. 2072 (describing defendant's proffered "valid business reasons" for its actions and plaintiff's rebuttal). If the court accepts the defendant's proffered justifications, it must then decide whether the conduct's procompetitive effects outweigh its anticompetitive effects. *Microsoft,* 253 F.3d at 59. This approach mirrors rule of reason analysis. * * *

The Commission followed this approach. It found that McWane's Full Support Program was an exclusive dealing policy that harmed competition by foreclosing Star's access to necessary distributors and contributed significantly to Star's lost sales and subsequent inability to purchase its own foundry and expand output. It considered McWane's procompetitive justifications but ultimately found them unpersuasive.

McWane challenges each aspect of the Commission's ruling: first, it says that its Full Support Program was "presumptively legal" because it was nonbinding and short-term; second, it contends that the government failed to carry its burden of establishing harm to competition; third, it argues that the Commission wrongly rejected its proffered procompetitive justifications. We address each claim in turn.

1. *Presumptive Legality*

McWane suggests that the Full Support Program lacked the characteristics of anticompetitive exclusive dealing arrangements. Specifically, it urges that the Full Support Program was "presumptively legal" and "[could not] harm competition" because it was short-term and voluntary (rather than a binding contract of a longer term). No binding precedent from the Supreme Court or this Court speaks specifically to this issue, but McWane hangs its hat on caselaw from other circuits.

But not all courts agree. The Third Circuit * * * [has] held that where exclusive deals were "technically only a series of independent sales," they nevertheless constituted antitrust violations because "the economic elements involved—the large share of the market held by [the defendant] and its conduct excluding competing manufacturers—realistically ma[d]e the arrangements . . . as effective as those in written contracts." The * * * court noted that "in spite of the legal ease with which the relationship can be terminated, the [distributors] have a strong economic incentive to continue [buying defendant's product]." * * * Likewise, in the case at hand, both the Commission and the ALJ found that distributors were essential to the domestic fittings market: "No evidence supports the existence of viable alternate distribution channels, including direct sales to end users."

This approach is consistent with the Supreme Court's instruction to look at the "practical effect" of exclusive dealing arrangements. *Tampa Elec. Co. v. Nashville Coal Co.,* 365 U.S. 320, 326–28, 81 S.Ct. 623, 5 L.Ed.2d 580 (1961). * * * The Commission adopted this approach, looking to "the reality of [the] marketplace" and finding that "the practical effect of McWane's program was to make it economically infeasible for distributors to . . . switch to Star." * * * So do we.

Moreover, the nature of the Full Support Program arguably posed a greater threat to competition than a conventional exclusive dealing contract, as it lacked the traditional procompetitive benefits of such contracts. As we've noted, courts often take a permissive view of such contracts on the grounds that firms compete for exclusivity by offering procompetitive inducements (e.g., lower prices, better service). But not here. The Full Support Program was "unilaterally imposed" by fiat upon all distributors, and the ALJ found that it resulted in "no competition to become the exclusive supplier" and no "discount, rebate, or other consideration" offered in exchange for exclusivity. This is consistent with evidence that McWane's prices rose, rather than fell, in the wake of the program.

* * *

2.   *Harm to Competition*

* * *

As with many areas of antitrust law, the federal judiciary's approach to evaluating exclusive dealing has undergone significant evolution over the past century. Under the approach laid out by the Supreme Court in *Standard Oil Co. of California and Standard Stations, Inc. v. United States (Standard Stations),* 337 U.S. 293, 69 S.Ct. 1051, 93 L.Ed. 1371 (1949), all that was required for an exclusive deal to violate the Clayton Act was proof of substantial foreclosure—"proof that competition ha[d] been foreclosed in a substantial share of the line of commerce affected." The Supreme Court amended that approach in *Tampa Electric,* in which it continued to emphasize the importance of substantial foreclosure, but opened the door to a broader analysis.

Lower federal courts have burst through that door over the past 50 years, interpreting *Tampa Electric* as authorizing a rule of reason approach to exclusive dealing cases. * * * This Court, without specifically citing *Tampa Electric*, has joined the consensus that exclusive dealing arrangements are "reviewed under the rule of reason."

The difference between the traditional rule of reason and the rule of reason for exclusive dealing is that in the exclusive dealing context, courts are bound by *Tampa Electric's* requirement to consider substantial foreclosure. But foreclosure is usually no longer sufficient by itself; rather, it "serves a useful screening function" as a proxy for anticompetitive harm. Thus, foreclosure is one of several factors we now examine in determining whether the conduct harmed competition. * * * We will also look for direct evidence that the challenged conduct has affected price or output, along with other indirect evidence, such as the degree of rivals' exclusion, the duration of the exclusive deals, and the existence of alternative channels of distribution. * * * The ultimate question remains whether the defendant's conduct harmed competition.

To effect anticompetitive harm, a defendant "must harm the competitive *process,* and thereby harm consumers. In contrast, harm to one or more *competitors* will not suffice." This distinction makes good sense, particularly in a competitive market where injury to a single competitor may not have a significant effect on overall competition due to the persistence of other rivals. However, competitors and competition are linked, particularly in the right market settings: "in a concentrated market with very high barriers to entry, competition will not exist without competitors." *Spirit Airlines, Inc. v. Nw. Airlines, Inc.,* 431 F.3d 917, 951 (6th Cir. 2005). Indeed, this is one reason that the behavior of monopolists faces more exacting scrutiny under the antitrust statutes. * * *

Before we proceed, we address a point of disagreement between the Commission, the dissenting commissioner, and the amici: the government's burden of proof in demonstrating harm to competition. The dissenting commissioner[12] insisted that, given the high likelihood that an exclusive dealing arrangement is actually procompetitive, a plaintiff alleging illegal exclusive dealing must show "clear evidence of anticompetitive effect." Applying that standard, Commissioner Wright concluded that the government had not met its burden for several reasons, including that it had not sufficiently established that the Full Support Program caused the observed price effects. The Commission countered that Commissioner Wright sought "a new, heightened standard of proof for exclusive dealing cases" that had "no legal support." Although McWane does not articulate its proposed burden of proof using the dissenting commissioner's language,

---

12 [The Commission voted 3–1 to affirm the ALJ's finding of liability with respect to the exclusive dealing claim, with then Commissioner Joshua D. Wright, now a co-author of this Casebook, dissenting. Eds.]

it agrees in substance that the Commission did not prove harm to competition with sufficient certainty.

We agree with the Commission. Putting aside the possible economic merits of raising the standard of proof for exclusive dealing cases, we can find no foundation for this conclusion in the caselaw. The governing Supreme Court precedent speaks not of "clear evidence" or definitive proof of anticompetitive harm, but of "probable effect." * * * Indeed, this Court has often articulated the rule of reason—the governing standard for evaluating exclusive dealing claims—by quoting the Supreme Court's instruction in *Board of Trade of Chicago v. United States,* 246 U.S. 231, 238, 38 S.Ct. 242, 62 L.Ed. 683 (1918), to analyze the effects of the challenged conduct, "actual or probable."

Of course, the FTC's allegation is not merely that McWane engaged in exclusive dealing, but that it used exclusive dealing to maintain its monopoly power. In the monopolization context, courts have articulated the government's burden in terms of the causality that must be shown between the defendant's conduct and the anticompetitive harm. These formulations, too, are framed in terms of probability: "unlawful maintenance of a monopoly is demonstrated by proof that a defendant has engaged in anti-competitive conduct that *reasonably appears* to be a *significant contribution* to maintaining monopoly power." In *Microsoft,* the D.C. Circuit found no case supporting the proposition that Sherman Act § 2 liability requires plaintiffs to "present direct proof that a defendant's continued monopoly power is precisely attributable to its anticompetitive conduct." *Microsoft,* 253 F.3d at 79. It noted that "[t]o require that § 2 liability turn on a plaintiff's ability or inability to reconstruct the hypothetical marketplace absent a defendant's anticompetitive conduct would only encourage monopolists to take more and earlier anticompetitive action." * * *

We agree with the Commission and our sister circuits that in these circumstances the government must show that the defendant engaged in anticompetitive conduct that reasonably appears to significantly contribute to maintaining monopoly power. As we've already discussed, because this determination is an economic conclusion, the Commission's finding on this count must be supported by substantial evidence.

a) *Substantial Foreclosure*

"Substantial foreclosure" continues to be a requirement for exclusive dealing to run afoul of the antitrust statutes. Foreclosure occurs when "the opportunities for other traders to enter into or remain in [the] market [are] significantly limited" by the exclusive dealing arrangements. Traditionally a foreclosure percentage of at least 40% has been a threshold for liability in exclusive dealing cases. However, some courts have found that a lesser degree of foreclosure is required when the defendant is a monopolist. * * *

In this case, both the Commission and the ALJ found that the Full Support Program foreclosed Star from a substantial share of the market. Although the Commission did not quantify a percentage, it did note that the two largest distributors, who together controlled approximately 50–60% of distribution, prohibited their branches from purchasing from Star (except through the Full Support Program exceptions) following the announcement of the Full Support Program. Indeed, HD Supply went so far as to cancel pending orders for domestic fittings that it had placed with Star. The Commission also observed that the third-largest distributor was initially interested in purchasing domestic fittings from Star, but followed suit soon after the Full Support Program was announced. Testimony in the record supports the Commission's conclusion that this pattern recurred with other dealers, even when Star promised lower prices than McWane. * * * Although the Commission did not place an exact number on the percentage foreclosed, it found that the Full Support Program "tie[d] up the key dealers" and that the foreclosure was "substantial and problematic."

These factual findings are all consistent with the ALJ's determinations, and all pass our deferential review. Nevertheless, McWane challenges the Commission's conclusion by arguing that Star's entry and growth in the market demonstrate that, as a matter of law, the Full Support Program did not cause substantial foreclosure. As before, when McWane raised a substantially similar claim to rebut the Commission's finding of monopoly power, this argument is ultimately unpersuasive. Again, "[t]he test is not total foreclosure, but whether the challenged practices bar a substantial number of rivals or severely restrict the market's ambit." Our sister circuits have found monopolists liable for anticompetitive conduct where, as here, the targeted rival gained market share—but less than it likely would have absent the conduct. As noted above, exclusive dealing measures that slow a rival's expansion can still produce consumer injury. Given the ample evidence in the record that the Full Support Program significantly contributed to key dealers freezing out Star, the Commission's foreclosure determination is supported by substantial evidence and sufficient as a matter of law.

b)   *Evidence of Harm to Competition*

* * * The Commission found that McWane's program "deprived its rivals . . . of distribution sufficient to achieve efficient scale, thereby raising costs and slowing or preventing effective entry." It found that the Full Support Program made it infeasible for distributors to drop the monopolist McWane and switch to Star. This, the Commission found, deprived Star of the revenue needed to purchase its own domestic foundry, forcing it to rely on inefficient outsourcing arrangements and preventing it from providing meaningful price competition with McWane.

Perhaps the Commission's most powerful evidence of anticompetitive harm was direct pricing evidence. It noted that McWane's prices and profit margins for domestic fittings were notably higher than prices for imported fittings, which faced greater competition. Thus, these prices appeared to be supracompetitive. Yet in states where Star entered as a competitor, notably there was no effect on McWane's prices. Indeed, soon after Star entered the market, McWane raised prices and increased its gross profits—despite its flat production costs and its own internal projections that Star's unencumbered entry into the market would cause prices to fall. Since McWane was an incumbent monopolist already charging supracompetitive prices (as demonstrated by the difference in price and profit margin between domestic and imported fittings), evidence that McWane's prices did not fall is consistent with a reasonable inference that the Full Support Program significantly contributed to maintaining McWane's monopoly power.

McWane claims, however, that the government did not adequately prove that the Full Support Program was responsible for this price behavior. But as we've noted, McWane demands too high a bar for causation. While it is true that there could have been other causes for the price behavior, the government need not demonstrate that the Full Support Program was the sole cause—only that the program "reasonably appear[ed] to be a significant contribution to maintaining [McWane's] monopoly power." * * *

The Commission also drew on testimony from Star executives that the Full Support Program deprived Star of the sales and revenue needed to invest in a domestic foundry of its own. These estimates were based in part on distributors' withdrawn requests for quotes or orders in the wake of the Full Support Program. Indeed, Star had identified a specific foundry to acquire and had entered negotiations to purchase it, but after the announcement of the Full Support Program, decided not to move forward with the purchase. Without a foundry of its own with which to manufacture fittings, Star was forced to contract with six third-party domestic foundries to produce raw casings—a "more costly and less efficient" arrangement on account of higher shipping, labor, and logistical costs; smaller batch sizes; less specialized equipment; and various other factors. Star estimated that with its own foundry, it could have reduced costs and substantially lowered its domestic fittings prices.

Moreover, as the ALJ found, some customers, including HD Supply and Ferguson, were reluctant to purchase from a supplier that lacked its own foundry, thereby further inhibiting any challenge to McWane's market dominance. Thus, the record evidence suggests that the Full Support Program stunted the growth of Star—McWane's only rival in the domestic fittings market—and prevented it from emerging as an effective competitor who could challenge McWane's supracompetitive prices.

We also consider it significant that alternative channels of distribution were unavailable to Star. In cases where exclusive dealing arrangements tie up distributors in a market, courts will often consider whether alternative channels of distribution exist. If firms can use other means of distribution, or sell directly to consumers, then it is less likely that their foreclosure from distributors will harm competition. * * * The Commission found * * * [that alternate means of distribution, such as direct dales, were not feasible and that as a consequence] Star's foreclosure from the major distributors was particularly likely to harm competition in this market.

Finally, the clear anticompetitive intent behind the Full Support Program also supports the inference that it harmed competition. Anticompetitive intent alone, no matter how virulent, is insufficient to give rise to an antitrust violation. But, as this Court has said, "[e]vidence of intent is highly probative 'not because a good intention will save an otherwise objectionable regulation or the reverse; but because knowledge of intent may help the court to interpret facts and to predict consequences.'" * * *

In this case, the evidence of anticompetitive intent is particularly powerful. Testimony from McWane executives leaves little doubt that the Full Support Program was a deliberate plan to prevent Star from "reach[ing] any critical market mass that will allow them to continue to invest and receive a profitable return" by "[f]orc[ing] Star[ ] to absorb the costs associated with having a more full line before they can secure major distribution." Indeed, the plan was implemented as a reaction to concerns about the "[e]rosion of domestic pricing if Star emerges as a legitimate competitor." Although such intent alone is not illegal, it could reasonably help the Commission draw the inference that the witnessed price behavior was the (intended) result of the Full Support Program.

Not all of the evidence adduced in this case uniformly points against McWane. For example, as we've previously noted, Star was not completely excluded from the domestic fittings market; it was able to enter and grow despite the presence of the Full Support Program. However, it is still perfectly plausible to conclude on this record that Star's growth was meaningfully (and deliberately) slowed and its development into a rival that could constrain McWane's monopoly power was stunted. * * *

3.   *Procompetitive Justifications*

Having established that the defendant's conduct harmed competition, the burden shifts to the defendant to offer procompetitive justifications for its conduct. As the Commission explained, "[c]ognizable justifications are typically those that reduce cost, increase output or improve product quality, service, or innovation." * * * Such justifications, however, cannot be "merely pretextual."

McWane offers two; neither is persuasive. First, McWane says that the Full Support Program was necessary to retain enough sales to keep its domestic foundry afloat. The Commission rightly rejected this argument; as other courts have recognized, such a goal is "not an unlawful end, but neither is it a procompetitive justification." And as the Commission noted, the steps McWane took to preserve its sales volume "were not the type of steps, such as a price reduction, that typically promote consumer welfare by increasing overall market output." McWane's sales "did not result from lower prices, improved service or quality, or other consumer benefits," but rather from reducing the output of its only rival.

Second, McWane offers the more sophisticated argument that the Full Support Program was needed to keep Star from " 'cherrypick[ing]' the core of [the] domestic fittings business by making only the top few dozen fittings that account for roughly 80% of all fittings sold," while leaving McWane alone to sell the remaining 20%. But even if McWane had good business reasons to adopt such a strategy, and such conduct could result in increased efficiency in the right market conditions, McWane offers no reasons to think that such conditions exist in this case. As the Commission noted, a full-line supplier like McWane could instead compete "by lowering its price for [the more common] products and increasing its price for the less common products." Again, McWane has not explained why such a strategy would not work, how the collapse of the full line of products would harm consumers, or why full-line forcing was instead necessary. Thus, this argument is also unpersuasive.

Moreover, McWane's internal documents belie the notion that the Full Support Program was designed for any procompetitive benefit. As the Commission noted, McWane executives discussed the Full Support Program in terms of maintaining domestic prices and profitability by preventing Star from becoming an effective competitor. For example, McWane executive Richard Tatman said that his "chief concern" with Star becoming a domestic fittings supplier was that "the domestic market [might] get[ ] creamed from a pricing standpoint," and identified the biggest risk factor of Star's entry as the "[e]rosion of domestic pricing if Star emerged as a legitimate competitor." In a document encouraging the adoption of an exclusive dealing arrangement, Tatman opined that not doing so would allow Star to "drive profitability out of our business." And in an e-mail, he stated, with regard to Star, "we need to make sure that they don't reach any critical mass that will allow them to continue to invest and receive a profitable return." The Supreme Court has looked to evidence that proffered justifications for conduct "are merely . . . an excuse to cover up different and anticompetitive reasons." McWane's damning internal documents seem to be powerful evidence that its procompetitive justifications are "merely pretextual."

IV.

All told, the Commission's factual and economic conclusions are supported by substantial evidence and its legal conclusions comport with the governing law. The Commission's determination of the relevant market and its findings of monopoly power and anticompetitive harm pass our deferential review, and we agree that the conduct amounts to a violation of Section 5 of the Federal Trade Commission Act.

Accordingly, we AFFIRM.

––––––––––

What were the FTC's theories of competitive harm in *McWane*? On what basis did the court conclude that the FTC had presented evidence sufficient to establish such harm? Was there direct evidence of harm, such as higher market prices or reduced output (relative to what prices or output would have been absent defendant's conduct)? Did the FTC and the court rely on inferences drawn from other, indirect evidence (including McWane's intent) to establish competitive harm? If the latter, what was the basis for those inferences, and were they consistent with other exclusion cases we have read, such as *Microsoft*?

What was the role of "foreclosure" in the FTC's analysis and how in the court's view did it support the conclusion that competition was harmed by McWane's Full Support Program? Can it be related to the raising rival's costs framework we studied in Chapter 4? How? Was there evidence that the Full Support Program raised Star's costs of distribution, or prevented Star from lowering its distribution costs (as by denying it growth opportunities that might have led to the construction of its own domestic foundry), making it a less effective competitor to McWane? The role of foreclosure evidence is further discussed below in Sidebar 6–6: The Contemporary Economics of Exclusive Dealing.

After concluding that the FTC had successfully shifted the burden of production to McWane, the court turned to defendant's procompetitive justifications. Why did the court conclude that those arguments were unpersuasive? Should the court have undertaken a more searching examination of the justifications evidence?

McWane presented an argument commonly advocated by defendants in many kinds of antitrust cases, i.e., that the antitrust laws protect "competition, not competitors," and that the evidence presented by the FTC only indicated harm to a competitor, Star, and therefore was insufficient. How should courts evaluate such an argument in monopolization cases, when a dominant firm is accused of impeding one or more of its very few rivals? *See, e.g., Spirit Airlines, Inc. v. Northwest Airlines, Inc.*, 431 F.3d 917 (6th Cir. 2005) ("in a concentrated market with very high barriers to entry, competition will not exist without competitors."). Should a court demand less evidence of anticompetitive effect from exclusive dealing before shifting the burden of production to defendants the fewer the number and size of unexcluded rivals? *See* Jonathan B. Baker, *Exclusion as a Core Competition Concern*, 78 ANTITRUST L.J. 527, 548 (2013) (finding that courts condemn exclusionary conduct without undertaking a comprehensive reasonableness analysis when all actual or potential rivals other than insignificant competitors have been excluded through conduct lacking a plausible efficiency justification).

As is noted by the *McWane* court, the Commission vote in the case was 3–1 on the exclusive dealing claim, with then Commissioner Wright (now a co-author of this book) dissenting. In his view, it was wrong for the FTC and the court to conclude that the FTC satisfied its burden of production without any direct evidence of price or output effects, without evidence that foreclosure was substantial in the sense that it was likely to lead to competitive harm, and in the face of evidence to the contrary that the allegedly excluded rival, Star, grew at the same rate before and after the restraint was imposed. *See* Dissenting Statement of Commissioner Joshua D. Wright, *In re McWane, Inc.*, Dkt. No. 9351 (FTC Feb. 6, 2014), https:// www.ftc.gov/system/files/documents/public_statements/202211/140206 mcwanestatement.pdf. What reasons did the court give for rejecting his arguments? Are his arguments limited to the interpretation of the record in *McWane*, or do they perhaps suggest a more general critique of the treatment of exclusive dealing by the courts? For a further response to his dissent, see Steven C. Salop, et. al, *The Appropriate Legal Standard and Sufficient Economic Evidence for Exclusive Dealing Under Section 2: The FTC's* McWane *Case* (Aug. 7, 2014), http://ssrn.com/abstract=2477448.

NOTE ON THE TREATMENT OF EXCLUSIVE DEALING IN GILBARCO

The Eleventh Circuit in *McWane* relied in significant part on *United States v. Dentsply, Int'l, Inc.*, 399 F.3d 181 (3d Cir. 2005) and *United States v. Microsoft Corp.*, 253 F.3d 34, 70 (D.C. Cir. 2001), two previous cases brought by the Justice Department to challenge exclusive dealing. These three cases are relatively rare examples of successful modern challenges to exclusive dealing. Most such claims fail, most typically because of the insufficiency of the plaintiff's allegations or proof of competitive harm. This Note examines *Omega Envt'l, Inc. v. Gilbarco, Inc.*, 127 F.3d 1157 (9th Cir. 1997), an earlier case, in which the court rejected an antitrust challenge to exclusive dealing. The case was distinguished in *Microsoft*, *Dentsply*, and *McWane*, providing a valuable opportunity to compare and contrast the cases as a group.

Gilbarco involved a challenge under Section 3 of the Clayton Act to the exclusive dealing practices of the leading manufacturer of petroleum dispensing equipment used at retail gasoline stations, including pumps, vapor recovery systems, and canopies that protect motorists from the rain. With 55%

of the domestic market for dispensers, Gilbarco was the leading manufacturer among five firms that competed for sales in the United States. Its next closest competitor accounted for 18% of sales in the agreed-upon relevant market. The manufacturers sold their equipment both directly to their largest customers and through a network of authorized dispenser distributors. Gilbarco had 120 such distributors, who accounted for just over two-thirds of its sales; the remaining one-third of its business involved sales made directly to larger customers, such as major oil companies and national convenience store chains. 127 F.3d at 1160.

The plaintiff, Omega Environmental, was not itself a manufacturer. Instead, through the acquisition of existing distributors, it planned to establish a distribution network that would consolidate purchasing from the manufacturers and provide "one-stop shopping" to dispenser customers that would include multiple product lines. In response to Omega's acquisition of two of Gilbarco's authorized distributors, Gilbarco notified all of its distributors that it would only sell to those who sold the Gilbarco line of dispensing equipment exclusively. It also notified the acquired distributors that their distribution agreements with Gilbarco would not be renewed. *Id.* at 1160–61.

Gilbarco appealed the district court's denial of its motion for judgment as a matter of law following a jury verdict for Omega. A divided court of appeals reversed. In the court's view, the "foreclosure effect" of the agreements was not substantial and hence the plaintiff had not satisfied the standards of Section 3. The court reasoned that although 38% of relevant market sales were potentially foreclosed by Gilbarco's exclusive dealing, [13] a seemingly "substantial" percentage, the figure overstated the magnitude of the foreclosure and its likely anticompetitive effects. *Id.* at 1162. In the court's view, alternative channels of distribution "eliminate[d] substantially any foreclosure effect Gilbarco's policy might have." *Id.* at 1163. Gilbarco's competitors were "free to sell directly" and, because of the "short duration and easy terminability" of the agreements, "to develop alternative distributors, or to compete for services of the existing distributors." *Id.* at 1163–64. Current competitors, for example, could sign up experienced distributors and new entrants offering a superior product could recruit distributors. It also found no "credible evidence" that Gilbarco's policy "actually deterred entry," noting that there was some evidence of actual past entry. *Id.* at 1164. The court rejected the plaintiff's claim that exclusive dealing facilitated coordination among the manufacturers and concluded by asserting: "[n]or are we persuaded that a jury could reasonably infer probable injury to competition even in this highly concentrated market where the undisputed evidence shows increasing output, decreasing prices, and significantly fluctuating market shares among the major manufacturers." *Id.* at 1164–65. Although it noted that there are "well-recognized economic benefits to exclusive dealing," *id.* at 1162, the majority did

---

[13] Recall that Gilbarco accounted for 55% of the overall market and 70% of its sales were made through its authorized distributors, who were subject to its exclusive dealing policy. The court reasoned, therefore, that 38% of the market (70% of 55%) was foreclosed from its rivals as a result of its policy.

not discuss whether there were any efficiencies associated with Gilbarco's conduct.

Circuit Judge Pregerson dissented, focusing in particular on the probable foreclosure of new dispensing equipment manufacturers, prospective entrants, and consequent competitive harm. In his view, the majority "shortchanged" the required analysis by adopting a blanket presumption that restrictions on distributors should be treated more leniently from end-users, and that short contract length and easy terminability mitigate any potential anticompetitive effects of exclusive dealing. *Id.* at 1170–71. He emphasized Gilbraco's dominant position in the relevant market and argued that the relevant standard under Section 3 is "probable" not "actual" effect, accusing the majority of demanding proof of actual entry deterrence. *Id.* at 1176. Under the appropriate standard, in his view, the evidence supported the conclusion that Gilbarco's conduct probably raised entry barriers and deterred entry into the market. Challenging the majority's observations with respect to output and pricing, he pointed to contrary evidence in the record from which a reasonable jury could have concluded that (1) Gilbarco's conduct allowed the manufacturers to "avoid intense price competition," (2) although there was some evidence of price decreases, there was also evidence of price stagnation; and that (3) Gilbarco's conduct prevented "the prices of retail petroleum dispensers from falling as much as they would have" absent the exclusive dealing agreements. *Id.* at 1175–77. Moreover, he reasoned that, notwithstanding the short duration of the agreements, direct distribution was not a "realistic possibility" for sales to independent buyers because there were high costs associated with a distributor switching brands. *Id.* at 1177–78. Finally, he noted that Gilbarco had failed to rebut Omega's expert, who testified that although exclusive dealing can have procompetitive effects, there was no evidence that Gilbarco's use of it had such effects. *Id.* at 1176.

Does the split in the panel in Gilbarco appear to be driven by the judges' differing views of the law, the facts, or the economics of exclusive dealing? What was the basis for the majority's theory that the evidence was insufficient to establish harm to competition? The dissent concludes that Gilbarco's use of exclusive dealing agreements could raise barriers to entry for manufacturers of retail petroleum dispensers and that the result was increased prices (or at least that prices were prevented from falling as much as they otherwise would have). Did the dissenting judge think that the exclusive dealing raised the distribution costs of rival manufacturers and thus allowed Gilbarco to exercise some power over price? Did he think the agreements facilitated better tacit coordination among the manufacturers?

The dissent accused the majority of elevating the standard of proof of harm on the plaintiff from probable to actual harm. How relevant should evidence of actual anticompetitive effect be in exclusive dealing cases, as opposed to evidence of "foreclosure" and predictive or "probable" effect? Is substantial foreclosure a sufficient basis for inferring anticompetitive effects, such as higher prices? Would the incipiency standard of Section 3 of the Clayton Act justify making such an inference? Should the absence of any evidence of actual anticompetitive effects be sufficient to defeat such an inference drawn from some percentage of foreclosure? What evidence is cited in the opinions on this point and to what end?

McWane and *Gilbarco* provide an interesting contrast in the treatment of exclusive dealing in the courts. Note how several common elements appeared in both cases and influenced the courts' resolution of the cases: (1) the burden on the plaintiff of demonstrating competitive harm, including reliance on "foreclosure" theory, evidence of market power, evidence that the conduct raised rivals' costs and facilitated higher prices (or kept prices from decreasing as much as they would), and some tension about assessing "probability"; (2) the significance and efficiency of alternative channels of distribution; (3) the significance, if any, that should be assigned to short duration exclusive dealing contracts; and (4) the burden of coming forward with evidence of procompetitive justifications. Can the two cases be reconciled? Are there parallels in the approach to these issues taken in *McWane* and in the dissent in *Gilbarco*? Between the dissent of one FTC Commissioner in *McWane* (which was rejected by the court in *McWane*) and the majority in *Gilbarco*?

In Sidebar 6–7, The Economics of Exclusive Dealing, which follows, we will more closely examine the theories of competitive harm that were at stake in these cases. Here we consider some of the other specific arguments that were made by the parties.

As in *McWane* and *Gilbarco*, the defendants in *Microsoft and Dentsply* argued that their exclusive dealing could not have been anticompetitive because their competitors had access to alternative channels of distribution. For example, Microsoft sought to undermine the government's argument that its exclusive dealing agreements with personal computer ("PC") manufacturers and Internet access providers ("IAPs") were anticompetitive by arguing that there were alternate channels of distribution available to its principal Internet browser rival. The government responded that Microsoft had restricted its rival's access to the most cost-effective channel of distribution, which raised its costs and impaired competition. The district court accepted Microsoft's argument, observing that "[w]here courts have found that the agreements in question failed to foreclose absolutely outlets that together accounted for a substantial percentage of the total distribution of the relevant products, they have consistently declined to assign liability." *United States v. Microsoft Corp.*, 87 F. Supp. 2d 30, 52 (D.D.C. 2000). Citing *Gilbarco*, the district court further observed that "[o]ther courts in similar contexts have declined to find liability where alternative channels of distribution are available to the competitor, even if those channels are not as efficient or reliable as the channels foreclosed by the defendant." *Id.* at 54.

Although the government did not appeal its loss on the stand-alone exclusive dealing claim, the court of appeals nevertheless appeared to cast doubt on the district court's reading of *Gilbarco* and the other exclusive dealing cases it had relied upon: "The District Court appears to have based its holding with respect to § 1 upon a 'total exclusion test' rather than the 40% standard drawn from the caselaw. Even assuming the holding is correct, however, we nonetheless reject Microsoft's contention." *United States v. Microsoft Corp.*, 253 F.3d 34, 70 (D.C. Cir. 2001). Citing *Tampa Electric* and other authorities, the D.C. Circuit concluded that the evidence was sufficient to support the district court's findings that Microsoft's exclusive dealing agreements had harmed competition, and that it had failed to establish any procompetitive justifications for their use. *Id.* at 70–71. Similarly, in *United States v. Dentsply, Int'l, Inc.*, 399 F.3d 181 (3d Cir. 2005), in concluding that exclusive supply contracts between a dominant manufacturer of prefabricated artificial teeth and its dealers violated Section 2 of the Sherman Act, the court of appeals rejected the district court's attribution of great competitive significance to the presence of alternate channels of distribution, especially direct sales. Such alternatives simply were not economically equivalent to the dealers, and barring rivals from dealers impaired Dentsply's rivals and created barriers to entry. *Id.* at 191–96.

Gilbarco, *Dentsply*, and *McWane* also addressed arguments by defendants that contracts of short term duration should be viewed as presumptively unlikely to result in substantial competitive harm. As in *McWane*, and in contrast with *Gilbarco*, the Third Circuit in *Dentsply* found that Dentsply's rivals were foreclosed from access to dealers even though Dentsply's associations with those dealers were "essentially terminable at will." *Id.* at 185. "Although its rivals could theoretically convince a dealer to buy their products and drop Dentsply's line, that has not occurred." *Id.* at 189. The appeals court concluded that the dealers "acceded to heavy economic pressure" in sticking with Dentsply. *Id.* at 196. *See also McWane*, 783 F.3d at 833–35 (agreeing with *Dentsply* and rejecting *Gilbarco* and another appellate decision, *Roland Machinery*, discussed below).

This argument can be traced to Judge Richard A. Posner, who took the position in his 1976 monograph that exclusive dealing agreements of short duration or that can readily be canceled cannot have any significant exclusionary effect. RICHARD A. POSNER, ANTITRUST LAW: AN ECONOMIC PERSPECTIVE 201–02 (1976) ("Whether . . . [an exclusive dealing] contract will have any exclusionary effect depends on its duration."). After his appointment to the Seventh Circuit, he wrote that position into the law of exclusive dealing in *Roland Mach. Co. v. Dresser Indus., Inc.*, 749 F.2d 380, 394 (7th Cir. 1984), which the majority cited and relied upon in *Gilbarco*, 127 F.3d at 1163. *See also Allied Orthopedic Appliances, Inc. v. Tyco Health Care Grp.*, 592 F.3d 991, 997 (9th Cir. 2010) (quoting *Gilbarco* with approval for the proposition that exclusive dealing agreements that are easily terminable are unlikely to foreclose competition); *Concord Boat Corp. v. Brunswick Corp.*, 207 F.3d. 1039, 1059 (8th Cir. 2000) (citing *Roland Machinery* for the proposition that agreements that neither appeared to be exclusive nor specified any term were inconsistent with a finding of competitive harm); *Thompson Everett, Inc. v. National Cable Advertising, L.P.*, 57 F.3d 1317, 1326 (4th Cir. 1995) (holding exclusive dealing agreements of a one year duration to be presumptively lawful); *U.S. Healthcare, Inc. v. Healthsource, Inc.*, 986 F.2d 589, 596 (1st Cir.

1993) (where exclusive dealing contracts could be terminated on 30 days' notice, any constraint on competition was minimal). *But see ZF Meritor, LLC v. Eaton Corp.*, 696 F.3d 254, 286–87 (3d Cir. 2012) (distinguishing *Roland Machinery* and *Gilbarco* and concluding that the combination of breadth of market coverage and five year duration of exclusive contracts made them more probably anticompetitive).

Although a number of courts have accepted this simple "short duration" presumption, Professor Herbert Hovenkamp would qualify it by also requiring that there be no impediments to switching. 11 PHILLIP AREEDA & HERBERT HOVENKAMP, ANTITRUST LAW ¶ 1821d3, at 200 (3d ed. 2011) ("[E]ven a high foreclosure percentage will not exclude competition if the period covered by the exclusive-dealing arrangement is short *and* there are no other impediments to switching.") (emphasis in original). Yet other courts, including those deciding *McWane* and *Dentsply*, as well as the dissent in *Gilbarco*, take a view similar to Professor Hovenkamp. They have concluded that Posner's view must be tempered by a case-by case assessment of market realities in light of switching costs, which may substantially lengthen the effective duration of contracts that appear to be contestable.

Finally, note the operation of shifting burdens of production in each of these cases. In *McWane* and *Dentsply*, once the courts concluded that the plaintiffs had produced sufficient evidence of competitive harm, the burden of coming forward with evidence of procompetitive effect shifted to the defendant—and in both cases the defendant failed to meet that burden. As we have noted, the *Gilbarco* majority did not consider possible efficiencies once it concluded that the plaintiff failed to provide sufficient evidence of harm. Because the dissenting judge concluded that the burden should have shifted, he looked to the trial record for evidence of an efficiency justification and found it wanting. How should courts considering exclusive dealing claims approach efficiency evidence? Should courts considering exclusive dealing claims in close cases routinely consider whether the defendant has offered any evidence of a procompetitive justification? Or should courts raise the initial burden on plaintiffs, on the view that exclusive dealing is most likely to be procompetitive? Would doing so be warranted in cases involving either firms with evident market power, when harm may be more likely, or cases with evidence of actual anticompetitive effects, when harm has already occurred? Should courts presume that exclusive dealing and other vertical restraints are procompetitive, absent strong evidence otherwise? *Compare* James C. Cooper, Luke M. Froeb, Dan O'Brien & Michael G. Vita, *Vertical Antitrust Policy as a Problem of Inference,* 23 INT'L J. INDUS. ORG. 639, 648, 662 (2005) (empirical studies of vertical restraints favor procompetitive theories, so courts should abandon aggressive enforcement against vertical restraints unless the loss from false negative is relatively large) *with* Jonathan B. Baker, *Taking the Error Out of "Error Cost" Analysis: What's Wrong with Antitrust's Right*, 80 ANTITRUST L.J. 1, 17–23 (2015) (empirical studies do not support creating a high bar to proving that exclusionary vertical restraints harm competition).

In the next Sidebar, we explore these issues and the continuing and lively debate about the economic and legal analysis of exclusive dealing.

Sidebar 6–6:
The Contemporary Economics of Exclusive Dealing
Efficiencies

As we have seen, exclusive dealing was never accorded the same harsh treatment as tying. Largely, this is because the efficient uses of exclusive dealing arrangements have long been acknowledged, *see, e.g.*, *Standard Stations*, 337 U.S. at 306–07 (discussing potential competitive benefits of exclusive dealing arrangements), and are now widely accepted. These may include prevention of interbrand free riding, providing an alternative to more costly vertical integration by sellers, facilitating expansion or entry by a new firm, or improving the efficacy of intrabrand restraints. *See generally* 11 PHILLIP AREEDA & HERBERT HOVENKAMP, ANTITRUST LAW ¶¶ 1810–14 (3d ed. 2011) (discussing economic benefits of exclusive dealing).

Most of these advantages are associated with the manufacturer, but there are also pro-competitive reasons that dealers might seek to enter exclusive dealing arrangements with their suppliers. Dealers who seek exclusivity are unlikely to be motivated by a desire to limit their supply options, but could be seeking better pricing, a reliable and uninterrupted stream of supply, better quality and product uniformity, or other cost-related efficiencies. *See, e.g.*, Richard M. Steuer, *Customer-Instigated Exclusive Dealing*, 68 ANTITRUST L.J. 239 (2000).

Figure 6–8:
Summary of Potential Effects of Exclusive Dealing

Potential Anticompetitive Effects of Exclusive Dealing	Potential Justifications for Exclusive Dealing
• Exclude or impair access of rivals to most cost-effective distribution channels (downstream dealers), or most cost-effective input sources (upstream suppliers), leading to: • higher prices	• Reduce transaction costs • Secure dealer loyalty • Prevent interbrand free riding • Competition for exclusive contracts

• reduced consumer choice	And in the case of output and requirements variants:
• In addition, cost of vertical integration could be forced on rivals and/or potential entrants (two-level entry).	• Protect buyers and sellers from price fluctuations • Ensure long term supply/customer stability • Ensure consistent operation at efficient scale

Note the similarity between some of these justifications for exclusive dealing and the justifications we discussed earlier in this Chapter in connection with *Sylvania*. (*See supra* Figure 6–4). For example, recall that the prevention of intrabrand free riding is a recognized procompetitive justification for the use of vertical intrabrand restraints such as territorial, location, and customer restrictions, as well as for resale price maintenance. Similarly, the prevention of interbrand free riding is a recognized justification for permitting exclusive dealing. *See, e.g.*, Howard Marvel, *Exclusive Dealing*, 25 J.L. & ECON. 1 (1982). The incentive for a manufacturer to undertake substantial promotional efforts, such as advertising, would be dissipated if those efforts succeeded in attracting a customer only to have it "switch brands" at the point-of-sale.

Recall as well from earlier in this Chapter, that intrabrand restraints can be used to induce retailers to carry and promote the product of a particular manufacturer. Again, exclusive dealing can be justified on the same grounds. By limiting a dealer to the sale of a single brand, the supplier can enhance the dealer's incentive to promote the supplier's product. Exclusive distributing and exclusive dealing often go hand in hand: to provide sufficient incentives for the dealer to carry only the supplier's product, the supplier may need to agree not to appoint any other competing dealer within a specified territory. By insulating the dealer from intrabrand competition, the supplier can secure the dealer's commitment to focus its marketing energies on interbrand competition. Protecting quality and reputation may also justify either intrabrand or interbrand restraints. *See generally* Benjamin Klein & Andres V. Lerner, *The Expanded Economics of Free-Riding: How Exclusive Dealing Prevents Free Riding and Creates Undivided Loyalty*, 74 ANTITRUST L.J. 473 (2007).

The typical franchise agreement provides an example. As an inducement to franchisees, franchisors often grant exclusive territories that insulate franchisees from intrabrand competition. This is designed to enhance the franchisee's incentive to promote the franchisor's product or service, as well as to alleviate any intrabrand free riding problems. A franchisor also typically prohibits its franchisees from selling the goods of the franchisor's competitors. We would not expect to find Burger King's signature foods for sale at a McDonald's restaurant. Exclusive dealing also may be prompted by a dealer's interest in securing lower wholesale prices. By promising to be exclusive, it can increase competition among the manufacturers. This may be why fast food chains typically offer only one brand of soft drink.

When procompetitive benefits like these are salient, exclusive dealing may reflect competition *for* distribution (often termed "competition for exclusives"). Manufacturers may be willing to compensate dealers in order to secure their services exclusively as part of a competitive strategy, not an anticompetitive one. Even if such payments raise the costs of distribution, competition among dealers may lead those payments to get passed on to consumers. *See* Benjamin Klein, *Exclusive Dealing as Competition for Distribution "On the Merits,"* 12 GEO. MASON L. REV. 119 (2003).

Anticompetitive Concerns

Since the Supreme Court's decision in *Standard Stations*, courts have traditionally looked to the concept of "foreclosure" in assessing the anticompetitive potential of exclusive dealing arrangements. A manufacturer may use exclusive dealing to prevent rival sellers from marketing to some fraction of distributors or other intermediate buyers (*e.g.,* firms that use the good to produce their own product for sale downstream). A distributor or other intermediate buyer may use exclusive dealing to prevent its rivals from obtaining access to the products of some fraction of manufacturers or input producers. As the concurring opinion in *Jefferson Parish* asserted:

> In determining whether an exclusive-dealing contract is unreasonable, the proper focus is on the structure of the market for the products or services in question— the number of sellers and buyers in the market, the volume of their business, and the ease with which buyers and sellers can redirect their purchases or sales to others. Exclusive dealing is an unreasonable restraint on trade only when a significant fraction of buyers or sellers are frozen out of a market by the exclusive deal.

466 U.S. at 45 (O'CONNOR, J., concurring).

As we discussed at the outset of Chapter 4, The Economics of Exclusion, the anticompetitive potential of foreclosure depends on whether it excludes rivals in the sense of input foreclosure (raising rival's costs) or customer foreclosure (reducing rival's access to buyers and markets), and whether doing so permits the excluding firm or firms to achieve, enhance, or maintain market power. The strategy must also be profitable for the excluding firms, or expected to be profitable. Finally, whether competition is harmed also depends on an assessment of the resulting harm to competition from the exclusion and any cognizable procompetitive benefits.

Suppose, for example, that a manufacturer can distribute its product through either of two alternate channels, but one is decidedly more effective and less costly. By securing exclusive contracts with distributors in the more cost-effective channel, the supplier can force its rivals to rely on the costlier distribution channel. By doing so the predator "raises its rival's costs." Such a strategy might result in the rival's exit from the market, or the rival may remain, but be forced to raise its prices in light of its higher costs. Or, it may be unable to expand because it lacks sufficient distribution or loses economies of scale. Even if the rival can obtain equally efficient distribution from some other firms, it may be unable to reach the entire market. In all these illustrations, if there is not sufficient competition from other non-excluded firms, the excluding firm may be able to obtain "power over price," the power to raise or maintain supracompetitive prices. *See generally* Thomas G. Krattenmaker and Steven C. Salop, *Anticompetitive Exclusion: Raising Rivals' Costs to Achieve Power over Price*, 96 YALE L.J. 209 (1986).

Whether exclusive dealing arrangements are effective may be related to the percentage of distributors that were foreclosed, the "foreclosure percentage" (fraction of customers or suppliers unavailable to excluded firms) that was the historical focus of the courts. But it need not be. In the above example, rivals must pay a cost penalty regardless of the fraction of the market accounted for by the less costly distribution channel, which the excluding supplier locked up. If the foreclosure percentage is stated as a fraction of total distribution, the percentage could be small. But the foreclosure percentage would capture the competitive problem in the example if distributors are described as foreclosed from the more efficient distribution channel. Issues in the measurement of foreclosure rates in exclusive dealing cases are examined in Joshua D. Wright, *Moving Beyond Naïve Foreclosure Analysis*, 19 GEO. MASON L. REV. 1163 (2012).

The inquiry into whether rivals are excluded will often focus on whether the excluded rivals can obtain equally cost-effective distribution (as in the example) or other critical inputs, or whether their costs will be materially raised. When Robert Bork suggested (in the context of vertical merger analysis) that the FTC could remedy exclusion "by throwing an industry social mixer," he was implicitly assuming that when the excluding firm restricted its number of distributors or suppliers, a foreclosed firm could simply switch to another distributor or supplier at little or no cost penalty. ROBERT H. BORK, THE ANTITRUST PARADOX 232 (1978). Whether an efficient alternative means of distribution is available also may depend on the extent to which ultimate consumers would bear the costs of switching to an alternative distributor to purchase the products of the foreclosed rivals.

When a firm enters into exclusive dealing arrangements, it can obtain market power if the excluded rivals were constraining its ability to raise or maintain a supracompetitive price. For this reason, the market power inquiry may focus on whether other rivals that are not excluded (perhaps because they have exclusive dealing arrangements of their own) are sufficient to preserve competition in the market as a whole. If multiple suppliers adopt exclusive dealing contracts with distributors, collectively foreclosing rival suppliers that do not have similar arrangements, the suppliers engaging in the practice may prevent one another from raising prices and may even force prices to fall if the exclusives promote competition. But the suppliers adopting exclusive dealing also might obtain market power collectively if the excluded rivals had previously constrained their pricing.

An exclusionary strategy would be profitable so long as the increased profits from higher prices or market share exceed the costs of securing the exclusive dealing contracts (such as payments or some other form of consideration made to distributors in exchange for exclusivity). The defendant firm may have to compensate its supplier or customer to induce that firm not to deal with the defendant's rivals or to outbid rivals seeking to avoid exclusion. Anticompetitive exclusive dealing would not make economic sense unless the excluding firm or firms expected it to be profitable.

In a case in which the effects of exclusive dealing have already been realized, some would argue that proof of the profitability of an anticompetitive strategy should be a required showing for antitrust liability. Others would argue that proof of anticompetitive effects should be sufficient to establish liability, regardless of whether the defendant's conduct turned out to be profitable. That is, one may infer from proof of anticompetitive effects that the strategy was expected to be profitable when it was adopted. In a case in which exclusive dealing is attacked at the time it is introduced, however, the latter inference may be unavailable. Relevant considerations in evaluating the strategy's prospective profitability may include the likely cost of the strategy to the defendant, the likely increase in profits from gaining the ability to raise or maintain its prices or market share, and whether suppliers or customers who agree to exclusivity with the defendant expect that the strategy will harm rivals to the excluding firm and allow the defendant to obtain or maintain supracompetitive prices. *See generally* Jonathan B. Baker, *Exclusion as a Core Competition Concern*, 78 ANTITRUST L.J. 527, 566–72 (2013).

An anticompetitive exclusive dealing strategy that is profitable for a defendant manufacturer may or may not be profitable for the dealers that agree to the arrangement. As Judge Posner explained in *JTC Petroleum*, which we read in Chapter 1, the dealers may be compensated for doing so with a share of the profits from the exercise of market power, or coerced into accepting exclusivity. In addition, an economics literature on "naked" exclusion explains why all the dealers of a product might agree to work exclusively with one manufacturer, even though doing so would allow the dominant manufacturer to obtain market power to the disadvantage of all the dealers. Each dealer would decide to accept exclusivity with the dominant supplier if each dealer expects the other dealers to work exclusively with that firm. Under such circumstances, no individual dealer would believe that shifting business to a rival manufacturer would do much to help the rival succeed, so the dealers have little to lose by accepting an exclusive arrangement with the monopolist. *See* Eric B. Rasmussen, et al., *Naked Exclusion*, 81 AM. ECON. REV. 1137 (1991); Ilya R. Segal & Michael D. Whinston, *Naked Exclusion: Comment*, 90 AM. ECON. REV. 296 (2000). Some commentators and government officials have referred to *Dentsply* as an example of "naked" exclusion.

Conclusion

The economic analysis of exclusive dealing has become virtually indistinguishable from the analysis of other forms of exclusionary conduct. Driven by the importance of core economic concepts, the legal analysis of exclusion today is arguably also converging with the structured rule of reason analysis developed for other exclusionary conduct, in which likely anticompetitive exclusion, market power, and efficiency play critical roles.

NOTE ON THE ECONOMIC EFFECTS OF "MOST FAVORED NATION" PROVISIONS

A most-favored-nation (MFN) clause, also called an "antidiscrimination" or "most-favored-customer" provision, is a promise by one party, often a supplier, to treat a buyer as well as the supplier treats its best, "most-favored" customer. A bottle maker might promise a brewer, for example, not to sell bottles at a lower price for some period of time to any other brewer, or perhaps more broadly, to any other bottle buyer (also including soft drink producers).

MFNs can have anticompetitive or procompetitive effects. For a more extensive survey of economic effects, see Jonathan B. Baker & Judith A. Chevalier, *The Competitive Consequences of Most-Favored-Nation Provisions*, ANTITRUST, Spring 2013, at 20. *See also* Steven C. Salop & Fiona Scott Morton, *Developing an Administrable MFN Enforcement Policy*, ANTITRUST, Spring 2013, at 15 (highlighting antitrust applications).

Background

Some MFNs appear as express provisions in a supply contract. In other cases a seller will establish a most-favored-customer policy for all its buyers across-the-board. These provisions can be retroactive (a commitment to treat a buyer as well as the supplier treated its best customer in the recent past) or contemporaneous (a commitment to treat a buyer as well as the supplier treats its best customer today). Sometimes a seller will commit to give a particular buyer a better price than it charges any other buyer; this type of contractual provision has been termed an "MFN plus" clause.

Most MFNs that have been scrutinized under the antitrust laws have involved the sale of intermediate goods—products or services sold to other firms that use them as an input in their own production—as with the bottle maker's hypothetical commitment to a brewer. In addition, retailers may use MFNs when selling to final consumers. MFNs often involve commitments by sellers, but not necessarily: a buyer may agree with a particular seller not to pay a higher price to any other seller.

Anticompetitive Effects

Facilitating Coordination. MFNs, when employed by sellers that might otherwise have an incentive to cheat on a coordinated arrangement, may facilitate tacit collusion by deterring price discounting. With an MFN in place, a firm that offers a lower price to a single customer—as it might do if it wished to "cheat" on the cartel price—will be compelled to offer that discount to all customers, making it more expensive for the seller to offer any customer a discount. At the same time, a buyer will see less benefit from attempting to drive a hard bargain when negotiating price with a seller that will find it expensive to discount. The use of MFNs may also facilitate coordination by making it easier for rivals to detect cheating, if selective discounting is more difficult to identify than across-the-board discounting.

To have these anticompetitive effects, it may be enough for a firm to offer most-favored-customer protection only to major customers, or even to a single large customer. Concern for the coordination-facilitating effects of most-favored customer clauses was one subject of the FTC's unsuccessful *Ethyl* litigation, discussed in Chapter 3. *In re Ethyl Corp.*, 101 F.T.C. 425, 628–32 (1983), *vacated sub nom. E.I. du Pont de Nemours & Co. v. FTC*, 729 F.2d 128 (2d Cir. 1984). *See also United States v. Gen. Elec. Co.*, No. 28228, 1977 WL 1474, at*1 (E.D. Pa. Sept. 16, 1977) (modifying consent decree prohibiting firms previously convicted of price-fixing from employing price protection provisions that discouraged discounting); *United States v. Eli Lilly & Co.*, 1959 TRADE CAS. (CCH) ¶ 69,536, at 76,152–53 (D.N.J. 1959).

The economic literature also recognizes the potential of MFN's to facilitate coordination through what the 2010 Horizontal Merger Guidelines refer to as "parallel accommodating conduct." (*See supra* Chapter 5.) As explained above, a seller that adopts an MFN is committing to compete less aggressively. If rival sellers respond by competing less aggressively, as they might, the firms may reach a comfortable détente in which prices rise. Manufacturers might use MFNs similarly to dampen retail competition, as a manufacturer's commitment to dealers not to give other dealers better terms may make it worthwhile for the dealers to agree to charge a high price to consumers. Dampening competition is discussed further in connection with resale price maintenance in Sidebar 6–2, *supra*.

Exclusion. Most-favored-customer provisions can also harm competition by helping firms exclude their rivals. Firms that demand and obtain most-favored-customer treatment from important input suppliers are assured that new entrants and existing competitors will not be able to secure lower costs by getting better prices from those suppliers. By reducing the ability of entrants or rivals to lower their costs, firms can discourage entry, expansion, and aggressive price competition, and thereby achieve or maintain prices above competitive levels.

A number of antitrust cases have identified this competitive concern in the context of large health insurance plans contracting with hospitals or doctors. Suppose, for example, that the contract between a dominant insurance plan and a group of its affiliated doctors provides that they will charge competing insurance plans at least as much as they do the dominant firm for their services, i.e., they will not agree to any lower reimbursement rates. Perhaps the contract goes further and mandates that they charge any other insurance firm more (an example of an "MFN plus" agreement). These MFNs may harm competition by making it uneconomic for an entrant to contract selectively with a limited panel of doctors. The entrant would be unable to adopt a business model by which it promises to direct patients to doctors on its panel in exchange for giving those doctors a lower per-patient reimbursement rate, and then pass through some of its lower costs to the employers that purchase health plans in the form of lower insurance premiums. Had this occurred, competition from the entrant would have put pressure on the dominant insurer to lower what it charges employers. But MFN provisions could prevent this form of entry, and thereby help protect from erosion the high rates the dominant insurer charges employers. *See, e.g., United States v. Blue Cross Blue Shield of Mich.*, 809 F. Supp. 2d 665 (E.D. Mich. 2011) (denying insurer motion to dismiss complaint); *United States v. Delta Dental of R.I.*, 943 F. Supp. 172 (D.R.I. 1996) (denying insurer motion for summary judgment).

MFNs have also been found to facilitate coordination by firms that were simultaneously colluding to raise price and colluding to exclude discounting rivals or other firms that would undermine coordination. *See, e.g., In re RxCare of Tenn., Inc.*, 121 F.T.C. 762 (1996) (consent order prohibiting MFNs imposed by pharmacist-owned pharmacy network); *United States v. Apple, Inc.*, 791 F.3d 290 (2d Cir. 2015) (MFN between colluding ebook publishers and one ebook retailer enhanced the incentive of the publishers to follow through on their agreement to exclude a second retailer that was inhibiting publisher coordination by discounting).

Procompetitive Effects

Preventing "Hold-Up" Problems. MFNs may encourage suppliers and buyers to make investments that benefit both, by limiting the incentive for one of the firms to "hold up" its vertically-related partner after the latter has made costly and irreversible (sunk) investments. For example, a brewer may want to work with a bottle manufacturer to develop an improved bottle. To make it profitable for the brewer to undertake those investments and convert its bottling line to work with the new product, the brewer may require a long term contract with the bottle maker. Once the two firms sign a long contract and the brewer makes its investments, though, the brewer is committed to the new bottled design. If the bottle maker then were to sell bottles with the improved design to the brewer's rivals at a lower price, the brewer's investment in the new bottle might no longer prove profitable. If so, the brewer must foreclose this possibility; it could do so through an MFN (or, alternatively, by requiring the bottle maker to deal with it exclusively).

Similarly, suppose that a natural gas well owner must contract with a pipeline without knowing the future demand for gas. A long-term fixed-price contract may be unattractive for both parties because it could discourage production from responding efficiently to changes in demand. Yet, the well owner would not be willing to agree to renegotiate the price every year because doing so puts it in a difficult bargaining position: once it drills, it would find itself at the mercy of a single pipeline buyer in future years, and have no alternative but to accede to buyer demands for discounts. One contractual solution that would make it profitable for the well owner to drill and contract with the pipeline, is for the parties to sign a long-term contract that contemplates annual price changes and employs an MFN to constrain the pipeline's ability to exploit individual well owners.

Reducing Delays. MFNs may benefit competition by reducing delays in transacting that may arise when some sellers or buyers have incentives to hold out in order to improve their bargaining position. For example, if a land developer needs a number of small parcels of land for a project, it may promise early sellers that it will pay them the difference if it offers a higher price to later sellers in order to reduce or eliminate seller incentives to hold out until they are the last to bargain. Similarly, if many customers decline to purchase theater tickets in the hope of buying unsold tickets cheaply from a discounter at the last minute, the theater owner can encourage more early ticket sales—which may help it make an early decision whether demand will be high enough to produce the show—by promising a partial refund in the event tickets are discounted later.

Reducing Transaction and Negotiation Costs. A contracting party may use an MFN to reduce its transaction and negotiation costs. *See, e.g., Blue Cross & Blue Shield United of Wisconsin v. Marshfield Clinic*, 65 F.3d 1406, 1415 (7th Cir. 1995) (Posner, C.J.) (describing MFNs as "standard devices by which buyers try to bargain for low prices). For example, a new Internet music service seeking to assemble a broad range of content may find that some small record labels, concerned about the new firm's long term prospects for success in competing with existing services even if it signs up most record labels, may not be willing to expend the effort to negotiate a deal; its transaction costs would swamp the expected benefit. But the small label may be willing to do so if it is guaranteed terms equivalent to those the music startup agrees to with major record labels. These transaction cost savings may be enhanced if the MFN allows the supplier to avoid repeated negotiations as demand and supply conditions change (as with the natural gas well owner contracting with the pipeline discussed above). Transaction cost savings from MFNs have been found to lower prices for widely-advertised consumer products sold at retail, where consumers likely differ substantially in what they know about the distribution of retail prices and in their costs of obtaining that information.

There are limits to the resulting efficiency gains, however. In the Internet music example, the small record label will not succeed in keeping transaction costs low if it is expensive for it to determine later the price that the major labels are paying to the startup; this could be the case if contracts are complex and auditing is costly. In addition, a large customer may reasonably expect to do better negotiating on its own than by signing an MFN and then relying on smaller customers' negotiating efforts. This possibility could call into question whether the large customer benefits more from the MFN's anticompetitive effects than from any reduction of transaction costs.

Even when buyers desire MFNs, moreover, and regard them as a way to negotiate lower prices, buyers may not actually receive lower prices. A large buyer may seek an MFN to assure itself of a cost advantage over its rivals; so long as it accomplishes that goal, the buyer may not be concerned about an increase in the seller's absolute price. To similar effect, if many or most buyers obtain MFNs, the seller will have little incentive to offer discounts to the buyers still trying to negotiate, in which case no buyer may receive a cost advantage.

Either Procompetitive or Anticompetitive Effects

Prevent Price Discrimination. Suppose a monopolist sells to two buyers that do not compete, as with a bottle maker that sells the same product to both a beer brewer and a soft drink producer, and charges a higher price to (say) the brewer. Suppose too that the brewer negotiates an MFN. If the monopoly bottle maker prefers to sell to both customers rather than to cut off the soft drink firm, then the MFN would lead to a lower price for the brewer and a higher price for the soft drink producer, with ambiguous effects on economic welfare. (Price discrimination is discussed in Sidebar 5–4.)

The economic effects of an MFN used to prevent price discrimination would be complicated further if the buyers are competing. That might happen, for example, if a monopolist seller supplied a small buyer at a discount in order to make use of what otherwise would be excess capacity. Under such circumstances, if a large buyer negotiates an MFN, that may lead the seller simply to eliminate the small buyer's discount. Doing so could raise the small buyer's costs, which could lead both buyers to increase the retail price they charge to final consumers.

To the extent a privately-negotiated MFN that prevents seller price discrimination would be justified as enhancing economic efficiency, would a government-imposed ban on seller price discrimination in the same industry also enhance efficiency? The Robinson-Patman Act, which prevents certain types of price discrimination, is discussed later in this Chapter.

Conditional Pricing Practices

MFNs are one type of what have been termed "conditional pricing practices." Sellers engage in conditional pricing when the price that a buyer pays depends on the prices paid by its rivals (as with an MFN) or on the other purchases it makes (as with loyalty discounts). The economic literature on loyalty discounts makes clear that, as with MFNs, they too can have collusive or exclusionary anticompetitive effects, or create efficiencies. But the economic literature on loyalty discounts is less well developed than the literature on MFNs. We now turn to a more in-depth examination of conditional pricing practices.

c. Conditional Pricing Practices

One type of exclusionary distribution, "conditional pricing practices" ("CPPs"), has been the subject of modern controversy. CPPs can take a variety of forms, but typically involve a combination of price and a condition: in order to receive a specified price, the buyer must agree to a condition that commits it to purchase a degree of its supplies from the seller. To illustrate, in what are commonly referred to as "loyalty" (or "share") discounts, a seller offers its customers a better price if the customer purchases a specified percentage of its sales from the seller, *e.g.*, "if you purchase 70% of your requirements from me, I will give you a 10% discount on all of your purchases." Multi-line sellers sometimes use "bundled rebates," whereby they offer special pricing to customers that purchase a specified "bundle" of products, such as multiple lines, *e.g.*, "if you purchase products A, B, and C from me, I will give you a 10% discount on all of your purchases."

CPPs thus share characteristics with the kinds of exclusionary distribution practices we have been studying in this Chapter, especially exclusive dealing, but also predatory pricing, which we studied in Chapter 4. Recall that under the Supreme Court's decisions in *Matsushita*, which we read in Chapter 3, *and Brooke Group*, which we read in Chapter 4, to be deemed "predatory," pricing must be (1) below some appropriate measure of cost, and (2) it must be probable that the alleged predator will be able to recoup its losses through the later exercise of market power. (*See supra* Chapter 4.) Implementation of a *Brooke Group*-influenced the price-cost test has raised additional issues in the context of bundled pricing. In the typical context, bundled pricing has been challenged by a competitor who sells a subset of the bundle, perhaps just one product. In such cases, the courts have faced the question of how to allocate the "discount"—across all of the products in the bundle or just the ones facing competition. See *Cascade Health Solutions v. Peacehealth*, 515 F.3d 883 (9th Cir. 2008) (endorsing use of a "discount attribution" test, which measures price-cost by allocating the discount to the competitive product in the bundle).

Some courts and commentators have argued that because CPPs involve "discounts" or "rebates," they should be analyzed like predatory pricing and upheld as a form of price competition unless they are below cost. Others point out that the labels "discount" and "rebate" should not be given so much weight given that CPPs can take many forms and can be easily manipulated to appear to be "discounts." However fashioned, in contractual terms the price adjustment can be thought of as consideration for the condition, perhaps a sharing of the benefits of market power that are derived from the arrangement when it is anticompetitive. For example, if a CPP results in different prices being paid by a seller's customers, is it accurate to characterize the better price paid by those who satisfy the condition as a "discount," or are the customers paying the higher price paying a "penalty"? Critics of reliance on the price-cost test also argue that the mechanism of exclusion in cases involving CPPs—that which can lead to exclusion of rivals—is the condition, not the price, which draws CPPs closer to exclusive dealing. The important antitrust question, therefore, should be whether the CPP impedes a rival's ability to compete for sales in a way that might facilitate the seller's exercise of market power, or perpetuate or protect it from erosion. As the debate has evolved, there have also been arguments made to the effect that not all CPPs should be treated alike—that perhaps loyalty-type CPPs should be evaluated like exclusive dealing, but bundled pricing-type CPPs would be best addressed like predatory pricing. Or perhaps the choice of approach should be a choice left to the individual plaintiff based on the evidence available.

Courts and commentators tend to divide over whether CPPs should be analyzed in an exclusive dealing framework or a predatory pricing framework. Proponents of the predatory pricing model argue that CPPs are a form of price competition that should be protected. Some of those who believe that the framework used to judge exclusive dealing should be used to evaluate the effects of CPPs, nevertheless advocate for use of the predatory pricing approach out of concern for the increased incidence of litigation, coerced settlements, and false positives that could arise from reliance on the exclusive dealing approach, which they argue will be easier to satisfy than the predatory pricing standard. Combined with their view that exclusive dealing generally can serve many procompetitive purposes, these commentators worry that the relative leniency of the exclusive dealing approach compared to the predatory pricing approach might lead to false positives and the consequent deterrence of efficient distribution practices. Critics, however, respond that very few exclusive dealing challenges have been successful, so concern about the application of that approach is being overstated. In addition, they worry about false negatives under the predatory pricing approach, because it imposes a demanding burden of proof on plaintiffs. No plaintiff, public or private, has prevailed on the merits in a predatory pricing case since *Matsushita* was decided in 1986. Hence a court's decision to proceed under one or the other standard can be outcome determinative.

A complete canvassing of the debate is beyond the scope of this Chapter. Here, we will focus on one court's approach to evaluating a CPP and its reasoning for making the choice of approach. The papers and presentations made at a 2014 joint workshop conducted by the Federal Trade Commission and the Department of Justice offer a more in-depth examination of the competing views and other relevant cases. *See* Conditional Pricing Practices: Economic Analysis & Policy Implications, https://www.ftc.gov/news-events/events-calendar/2014/06/conditional-pricing-practices-economic-analysis-legal-policy (including a complete transcript and many of the papers and presentations).

ZF MERITOR, LLC v. EATON CORPORATION

United States Court of Appeals for the Third Circuit, 2012.
696 F.3d 254.

Before: FISHER and GREENBERG, CIRCUIT JUDGES, and OLIVER,* DISTRICT
JUDGE.

FISHER, CIRCUIT JUDGE.

This case arises from an antitrust action brought by ZF Meritor, LLC ("ZF Meritor") and Meritor Transmission Corporation ("Meritor") (collectively, "Plaintiffs") against Eaton Corporation ("Eaton") for allegedly anticompetitive practices in the heavy-duty truck transmissions market. The practices at issue are embodied in long-term agreements between Eaton, the leading supplier of heavy-duty truck transmissions in North America, and every direct purchaser of such transmissions. Following a four-week trial, a jury found that Eaton's conduct violated Section 1 and Section 2 of the Sherman Act, and Section 3 of the Clayton Act. Eaton filed a renewed motion for judgment as a matter of law, arguing that its conduct was *per se* lawful because it priced its products above-cost. The District Court disagreed, reasoning that notwithstanding Eaton's above-cost prices, there was sufficient evidence in the record to establish that Eaton engaged in anticompetitive conduct—specifically that Eaton entered into long-term *de facto* exclusive dealing arrangements—which foreclosed a substantial share of the market and, as a result, harmed competition. We agree with the District Court and will affirm the District Court's denial of Eaton's renewed motion for judgment as a matter of law.

* * *

I. BACKGROUND

A. Factual Background

1. *Market Background*

The parties agree that the relevant market in this case is heavy-duty "Class 8" truck transmissions ("HD transmissions") in North America. Heavy-duty trucks include 18-wheeler "linehaul" trucks, which are used to travel long distances on highways, and "performance" vehicles, such as cement mixers, garbage trucks, and dump trucks. * * * Linehaul and performance transmissions, which comprise over 90% of the market, typically use manual or automated mechanical transmissions.

There are only four direct purchasers of HD transmissions in North America: Freightliner, LLC ("Freightliner"), International Truck and Engine Corporation ("International"), PACCAR, Inc. ("PACCAR"), and Volvo Group ("Volvo"). These companies are referred to as the Original Equipment Manufacturers ("OEMs"). The ultimate consumers of HD transmissions, truck buyers, purchase trucks from the OEMs. Truck buyers have the ability to select many of the components used in their trucks, including the transmissions, from OEM catalogues called "data books." Data books list the alternative component choices, and include a price for each option relative to the "standard" or "preferred" offerings. The "standard" offering is the component that is provided to the customer unless the customer expressly designates another supplier's product, while the "preferred" or "preferentially-priced" offering is the lowest priced component in data book among comparable products. Data book positioning is a form of advertising, and standard or preferred positioning generally means that customers are more likely to purchase that supplier's components. Although customers may, and sometimes do, request components that are not published in a data book, doing so is often cumbersome and increases the cost of the component. Thus, data book positioning is essential in the industry.

Eaton has long been a monopolist in the market for HD transmissions in North America.[2] It began making HD transmissions in the 1950s, and was the only significant manufacturer until Meritor entered the market in 1989 and began offering manual transmissions primarily for linehaul trucks. By 1999, Meritor had obtained approximately 17% of the market for sales of HD transmissions, including 30% for linehaul transmissions. In mid-1999, Meritor and ZF Friedrichshafen ("ZF AG"), a leading supplier of HD transmissions in Europe, formed the joint venture ZF Meritor, and Meritor transferred its transmissions business into the joint venture. Aside from Meritor, and then ZF Meritor, no significant external supplier of HD transmissions has entered the market in the past 20 years.[4]

One purpose of the ZF Meritor joint venture was to adapt ZF AG's two-pedal automated mechanical transmission, ASTronic, which was used exclusively in Europe, for the North American market. The redesign and testing took 18 months, and ZF Meritor introduced the adapted ASTronic model into the North American market in 2001 under the new name FreedomLine. FreedomLine was the first two-pedal automated mechanical transmission to be sold in North America.[5] When FreedomLine was released, Eaton projected that automated mechanical transmissions would account for 30–50% of the market for all HD transmission sales by 2004 or 2005.

2. Eaton's Long-Term Agreements

In late 1999 through early 2000, the trucking industry experienced a 40–50% decline in demand for new heavy-duty trucks. Shortly thereafter,

---

[2]   At trial, Eaton disputed that it was a monopolist, but on appeal, does not challenge the jury's finding that it possessed monopoly power in the HD transmissions market in North America.

[4]   "External" transmission sales do not include transmissions manufactured by Volvo Group for use in its own trucks.

[5]   Eaton did not produce a two-pedal automated mechanical transmission at the time, and would not fully release one until 2004.

Eaton entered into new long-term agreements ("LTAs") with each OEM. Although long-term supply contracts were not uncommon in the industry, and were also utilized by Meritor in the 1990s, Eaton's new LTAs were unprecedented in terms of their length and coverage of the market. Eaton signed LTAs with every OEM, and each LTA was for a term of at least five years.

Although the LTAs' terms varied somewhat, the key provisions were similar. Each LTA included a conditional rebate provision, under which an OEM would only receive rebates if it purchased a specified percentage of its requirements from Eaton.[6] Eaton's LTA with Freightliner, the largest OEM, provided for rebates if Freightliner purchased 92% or more of its requirements from Eaton. Under Eaton's LTA with International, Eaton agreed to make an up-front payment of $2.5 million, and any additional rebates were conditioned on International purchasing 87% to 97.5% of its requirements from Eaton. The PACCAR LTA provided for an up-front payment of $1 million, and conditioned rebates on PACCAR meeting a 90% to 95% market-share penetration target. Finally, Eaton's LTA with Volvo provided for discounts if Volvo reached a market-share penetration level of 70% to 78%.[8] The LTAs were not true requirements contracts because they did not expressly require the OEMs to purchase a specified percentage of their needs from Eaton. However, the Freightliner and Volvo LTAs gave Eaton the right to terminate the agreements if the share penetration goals were not met. Additionally, if an OEM did not meet its market-share penetration target for one year, Eaton could require repayment of all contractual savings.

Each LTA also required the OEM to publish Eaton as the standard offering in its data book, and under two of the four LTAs, the OEM was required to remove competitors' products from its data book entirely. * * * In the 1990s, Meritor's products were listed in all OEM component data books, and in some cases, had preferred positioning.

The LTAs also required the OEMs to "preferential price" Eaton transmissions against competitors' equivalent transmissions. Eaton claims that it sought preferential pricing to ensure that its low prices were passed on to truck buyers. However, there were no express requirements in the LTAs that savings be passed on to truck buyers (i.e., that Eaton's prices be reduced) and there is evidence that the "preferential pricing" was achieved

---

[6]   We will refer to these as "market-share" discounts or "market-penetration" discounts. It is important to distinguish such discounts from quantity or volume discounts. Quantity discounts provide the buyer with a lower price for purchasing a specified minimum quantity or volume from the seller. In contrast, market-share discounts grant the buyer a lower price for taking a specified minimum percentage of its purchases from the seller.

[8]   The share penetration targets in the Volvo LTA were lower because Volvo also manufactured transmissions for use in its own trucks. The commitment to Eaton, plus Volvo's own manufactured products, accounted for more than 85% of Volvo's needs.

by both lowering the prices of Eaton's products and raising the prices of competitors' products. * * *

Finally, each LTA contained a "competitiveness" clause, which permitted the OEM to purchase transmissions from another supplier if that supplier offered the OEM a lower price or a better product, the OEM notified Eaton of the competitor's offer, and Eaton could not match the price or quality of the product after good faith efforts. The parties dispute the significance of the "competitiveness" clauses. Eaton maintains that Plaintiffs were free to win the OEMs' business simply by offering a better product or a lower price, while Plaintiffs argue and presented testimony from OEM officials that, due to Eaton's status as a dominant supplier, the competitiveness clauses were effectively meaningless.

3. Competition under the LTAs and Plaintiffs' Exit from the Market

After Eaton entered into its LTAs with the OEMs, ZF Meritor shifted its marketing focus from the OEM level to a strategy targeted at truck buyers. Also during this time period, both ZF Meritor and Eaton experienced quality and performance issues with their transmissions. For example, Eaton's Lightning transmission, which was an initial attempt by Eaton to compete with FreedomLine, was "not perceived as a good [product]" and was ultimately taken off the market. ZF Meritor's FreedomLine and "G Platform" transmissions required frequent repairs, and in 2002 and 2003, ZF Meritor faced millions of dollars in warranty claims.

During the life of the LTAs, the OEMs worked with Eaton to develop a strategy to combat ZF Meritor's growth. On Eaton's urging, the OEMs imposed additional price penalties on customers that selected ZF Meritor products, "force fed" Eaton products to customers, and sought to persuade truck fleets using ZF Meritor transmissions to shift to Eaton transmissions. At all times relevant to this case, Eaton's average prices were lower than Plaintiffs' average prices, and on several occasions, Plaintiffs declined to grant price concessions requested by OEMs. Although Eaton's prices were generally lower than Plaintiffs' prices, Eaton never priced at a level below its costs.

By 2003, ZF Meritor determined that it was limited by the LTAs to no more than 8% of the market, far less than the 30% that it had projected at the beginning of the joint venture. ZF Meritor officials concluded that the company could not remain viable with a market share below 10% and therefore decided to dissolve the joint venture. After ZF Meritor's departure, Meritor remained a supplier of HD transmissions and became a sales agent for ZF AG to ensure continued customer access to the FreedomLine. However, Meritor's market share dropped to 4% by the end of fiscal year 2005, and Meritor exited the business in January 2007.

B. Procedural History

* * * [In a complaint filed in 2006], Plaintiffs alleged that Eaton "used its dominant position to induce all heavy duty truck manufacturers to enter into *de facto* exclusive dealing contracts with Eaton," and that such agreements foreclosed Plaintiffs from over 90% of the market for HD transmission sales. Plaintiffs sought treble damages, pursuant to Section 4 of the Clayton Act and injunctive relief, pursuant to Section 16 of the Clayton Act.

* * *

The parties proceeded to trial on liability. On October 8, 2009, after a four-week trial, the jury returned a complete verdict for Plaintiffs, finding that Eaton had violated Sections 1 and 2 of the Sherman Act, and Section 3 of the Clayton Act. * * *

On November 3, 2009, Eaton filed a renewed motion for judgment as a matter of law, or in the alternative, for a new trial. Eaton's principal argument was that Plaintiffs failed to establish that Eaton engaged in anticompetitive conduct because Plaintiffs did not show, nor did they attempt to show, that Eaton priced its transmissions below its costs. Sixteen months later, on March 10, 2011, the District Court denied Eaton's motion, reasoning that Eaton's prices were not dispositive, and that there was sufficient evidence for a jury to conclude that Eaton's conduct unlawfully foreclosed competition in a substantial portion of the HD transmissions market.

On August 4, 2011, * * * the District Court entered an order awarding Plaintiffs $0 in damages. On August 19, 2011, the District Court entered an injunction prohibiting Eaton from "linking discounts and other benefits to market penetration targets," but stayed the injunction pending appeal. Eaton filed a timely notice of appeal and Plaintiffs filed a timely cross-appeal.

II. JURISDICTION AND STANDARD OF REVIEW

* * * A motion for judgment as a matter of law should be granted "only if, viewing the evidence in the light most favorable to the nonmovant and giving it the advantage of every fair and reasonable inference, there is insufficient evidence from which a jury reasonably could find liability." * * * Underlying legal questions aside, "[a] jury verdict will not be overturned unless the record is critically deficient of that quantum of evidence from which a jury could have rationally reached its verdict."

* * *

III. DISCUSSION

A. Effect of the Price-Cost Test

The most significant issue in this case is whether Plaintiffs' allegations under Sections 1 and 2 of the Sherman Act and Section 3 of the Clayton Act are subject to the price-cost test or the "rule of reason" applicable to exclusive dealing claims. Under the rule of reason, an exclusive dealing arrangement will be unlawful only if its "probable effect" is to substantially lessen competition in the relevant market. In contrast, under the price-cost test, to succeed on a challenge to the defendant's pricing practices, a plaintiff must prove "that the [defendant's] prices are below an appropriate measure of [the defendant's] costs."[9]

Eaton urges us to apply the price-cost test, arguing that Plaintiffs failed to establish that Eaton engaged in anticompetitive conduct or that Plaintiffs suffered an antitrust injury because Plaintiffs did not prove—or even attempt to prove—that Eaton priced its transmissions below an appropriate measure of its costs. We decline to adopt Eaton's unduly narrow characterization of this case as a "pricing practices" case, i.e., a case in which price is the clearly predominant mechanism of exclusion. Plaintiffs consistently argued that the LTAs, in their entirety, constituted *de facto* exclusive dealing contracts, which improperly foreclosed a substantial share of the market, and thereby harmed competition. Accordingly, as we will discuss below, we must evaluate the legality of Eaton's conduct under the rule of reason to determine whether the "probable effect" of such conduct was to substantially lessen competition in the HD transmissions market in North America. The price-cost test is not dispositive.

1. Law of Exclusive Dealing

An exclusive dealing arrangement is an agreement in which a buyer agrees to purchase certain goods or services only from a particular seller for a certain period of time. The primary antitrust concern with exclusive dealing arrangements is that they may be used by a monopolist to strengthen its position, which may ultimately harm competition. Generally, a prerequisite to any exclusive dealing claim is an agreement to

---

[9] Although Plaintiffs brought claims under three statutes (Sections 1 and 2 of the Sherman Act and Section 3 of the Clayton Act), our analysis regarding the applicability of the price-cost test is the same for all of Plaintiffs' claims. In order to establish an actionable antitrust violation, a plaintiff must show both that the defendant engaged in anticompetitive conduct and that the plaintiff suffered antitrust injury as a result. Because a lack of anticompetitive conduct precludes a finding of antitrust injury, the key question for us is whether Eaton engaged in anticompetitive conduct.

Sections 1 and 2 of the Sherman Act and Section 3 of the Clayton Act each include an anticompetitive conduct element, although each statute articulates that element in a slightly different way. * * * Thus, regardless of which test applies, that test is applicable to each of Plaintiffs' claims.

deal exclusively.[10] An express exclusivity requirement, however, is not necessary, because we look past the terms of the contract to ascertain the relationship between the parties and the effect of the agreement "in the real world." Thus, *de facto* exclusive dealing claims are cognizable under the antitrust laws.

Exclusive dealing agreements are often entered into for entirely procompetitive reasons, and generally pose little threat to competition. For example, "[i]n the case of the buyer, they may assure supply, afford protection against rises in price, enable long-term planning on the basis of known costs, and obviate the expense and risk of storage in the quantity necessary for a commodity having a fluctuating demand." From the seller's perspective, an exclusive dealing arrangement with customers may reduce expenses, provide protection against price fluctuations, and offer the possibility of a predictable market. *see also Ryko Mfg. Co. v. Eden Servs* (explaining that exclusive dealing contracts can help prevent dealer free riding on manufacturer-supplied investments to promote rival's products). As such, competition to be an exclusive supplier may constitute "a vital form of rivalry," which the antitrust laws should encourage. However, "[e]xclusive dealing can have adverse economic consequences by allowing one supplier of goods or services unreasonably to deprive other suppliers of a market for their goods[.]" Exclusive dealing arrangements are of special concern when imposed by a monopolist. For example:

> [S]uppose an established manufacturer has long held a dominant position but is starting to lose market share to an aggressive young rival. A set of strategically planned exclusive-dealing contracts may slow the rival's expansion by requiring it to develop alternative outlets for its product, or rely at least temporarily on inferior or more expensive outlets. Consumer injury results from the delay that the dominant firm imposes on the smaller rival's growth.

Phillip Areeda & Herbert Hovenkamp, *Antitrust Law* ¶ 1802c, at 64 (2d ed. 2002). In some cases, a dominant firm may be able to foreclose rival suppliers from a large enough portion of the market to deprive such rivals of the opportunity to achieve the minimum economies of scale necessary to compete.

Due to the potentially procompetitive benefits of exclusive dealing agreements, their legality is judged under the rule of reason. The legality of an exclusive dealing arrangement depends on whether it will foreclose competition in such a substantial share of the relevant market so as to adversely affect competition. In conducting this analysis, courts consider

---

[10] Evidence of an agreement is expressly required under Section 1 of the Sherman Act and Section 3 of the Clayton Act. However, an agreement is not necessarily required under Section 2 of the Sherman Act, which can provide a vehicle for challenging a dominant firm's unilateral imposition of exclusive dealing on customers.

not only the percentage of the market foreclosed, but also take into account "the restrictiveness and the economic usefulness of the challenged practice in relation to the business factors extant in the market." * * * In other words, an exclusive dealing arrangement is unlawful only if the "probable effect" of the arrangement is to substantially lessen competition, rather than merely disadvantage rivals.

There is no set formula for evaluating the legality of an exclusive dealing agreement, but modern antitrust law generally requires a showing of significant market power by the defendant, substantial foreclosure, contracts of sufficient duration to prevent meaningful competition by rivals, and an analysis of likely or actual anticompetitive effects considered in light of any procompetitive effects. Courts will also consider whether there is evidence that the dominant firm engaged in coercive behavior, and the ability of customers to terminate the agreements. The use of exclusive dealing by competitors of the defendant is also sometimes considered.

2.   Brooke Group *and the Price-Cost test*

[Here the court reviewed the principles and rationale developed by the Supreme Court in *Brooke Group Ltd. v. Brown & Williamson Tobacco Corp.* It noted that the Court was skeptical of predatory pricing claims and explained that, as a result, it adopted a two-part test that requires proof of both below-cost pricing and a "dangerous probability" of recoupment. It observed that the Supreme Court "rejected the notion that above-cost prices that are below general market levels or below the costs of a firm's competitors are actionable under the antitrust laws," because low prices generally benefit consumers and "so long as they are above predatory levels [i.e., above-cost], they do not threaten competition." For an excerpt of the relevant portions of *Brooke Group* and further discussion of the case, see *supra* Chapter 4. Eds]

3.   *Effect of the Price-Cost Test on Plaintiffs' Exclusive Dealing Claims*

Eaton argues that principles from the predatory pricing case law apply in this case because Plaintiffs' claims are, at their core, no more than objections to Eaton offering prices, through its rebate program, which Plaintiffs were unable to match. Eaton contends that Plaintiffs have identified nothing, other than Eaton's pricing practices, that incentivized the OEMs to enter into the LTAs, and because price was the incentive, we must apply the price-cost test. We acknowledge that even if a plaintiff frames its claim as one of exclusive dealing, the price-cost test may be dispositive. Implicit in the Supreme Court's creation of the price-cost test was a balancing of the procompetitive justifications of above-cost pricing against its anticompetitive effects (as well as the anticompetitive effects of allowing judicial inquiry into above-cost pricing), and a conclusion that the balance always tips in favor of allowing above-cost pricing practices to stand. Thus, in the context of exclusive dealing, the price-cost test may be utilized as a specific application of the "rule of reason" when the plaintiff alleges that price is the vehicle of exclusion.

Here, Eaton argues that the price-cost test is dispositive, and therefore that Plaintiffs' claims must fail because Plaintiffs failed to show that the market-share rebates offered by Eaton pursuant to the LTAs resulted in below-cost prices. We do not disagree that predatory pricing principles, including the price-cost test, would control if this case presented solely a challenge to Eaton's pricing practices.[11] The lesson of the predatory pricing case law is that, generally, above-cost prices are not anticompetitive, and although there may be rare cases where above-cost prices are anticompetitive in the long run, it is "beyond the practical ability" of courts to identify those rare cases without creating an impermissibly high risk of deterring legitimate procompetitive behavior (i.e., price-cutting). These principles extend to above-cost discounting or rebate programs, which condition the discounts or rebates on the customer's purchasing of a specified volume or a specified percentage of its requirements from the seller.

Moreover, a plaintiff's characterization of its claim as an exclusive dealing claim does not take the price-cost test off the table. Indeed, contracts in which discounts are linked to purchase (volume or market share) targets are frequently challenged as *de facto* exclusive dealing arrangements on the grounds that the discounts induce customers to deal exclusively with the firm offering the rebates. However, when price is the clearly predominant mechanism of exclusion, the price-cost test tells us that, so long as the price is above-cost, the procompetitive justifications for, and the benefits of, lowering prices far outweigh any potential anticompetitive effects.

In each of the cases relied upon by Eaton, the Supreme Court applied the price-cost test, regardless of the way in which the plaintiff cast its grievance, because pricing itself operated as the exclusionary tool. * * *

---

[11] * * * [O]ur decision in * * * [*LePage's Inc. v. 3M*, 324 F.3d 141 (3d Cir. 2003)] does not indicate otherwise. In *LePage's,* we declined to apply the price-cost test to a challenge to a bundled rebate scheme, reasoning that such a scheme was better analogized to unlawful tying than to predatory pricing. * * *

For several reasons, we interpret *LePage's* narrowly. Most important, in light of the analogy drawn in *LePage's* between bundled rebates and unlawful tying, which "cannot exist unless two separate product markets have been linked," * * * *LePage's* is inapplicable where, as here, only one product is at issue and the plaintiffs have not made any allegations of bundling or tying. The reasoning of *LePage's* is limited to cases in which a single-product producer is excluded through a bundled rebate program offered by a producer of multiple products, which conditions the rebates on purchases across multiple different product lines. Accordingly, we join our sister circuits in holding that the price-cost test applies to market-share or volume rebates offered by suppliers within a single-product market. * * *

Additionally, several of the bases on which we distinguished *Brooke Group* have been undermined by intervening Supreme Court precedent, which counsels caution in extending *LePage's*. * * *

Here, in contrast to * * * [*Cargill, Inc. v. Monfort of Colorado*, 479 U.S. 104 (1986), *Atlantic Richfield Co. v. USA Petroleum Co.*, 495 U.S. 328 (1990)] and *Brooke Group,* Plaintiffs did not rely solely on the exclusionary effect of Eaton's prices, and instead highlighted a number of anticompetitive provisions in the LTAs. Plaintiffs alleged that Eaton used its position as a supplier of necessary products to persuade OEMs to enter into agreements imposing *de facto* purchase requirements of roughly 90% for at least five years, and that Eaton worked in concert with the OEMs to block customer access to Plaintiffs' products, thereby ensuring that Plaintiffs would be unable to build enough market share to pose any threat to Eaton's monopoly. Therefore, because price itself was not the clearly predominant mechanism of exclusion, the price-cost test cases are inapposite, and the rule of reason is the proper framework within which to evaluate Plaintiffs' claims.

We recognize that Eaton's rebates were part of Plaintiffs' case. * * * That fact is not irrelevant, as it may help explain why the OEMs agreed to otherwise unfavorable terms and it may help to rebut an argument that the agreements were inefficient. However, contrary to Eaton's assertions, that fact is not dispositive.

Plaintiffs presented considerable evidence that Eaton was a monopolist in the industry and that it wielded its monopoly power to effectively force every direct purchaser of HD transmissions to enter into restrictive long-term agreements, despite the inclusion in such agreements of terms unfavorable to the OEMs and their customers. Significantly, there was considerable testimony that the OEMs did not want to remove ZF Meritor's transmissions from their data books, but that they were essentially forced to do so or risk financial penalties or supply shortages. Several OEM officials testified that exclusive data book listing was not a common practice in the industry and, in fact, it was probably detrimental to customers. * * *

Plaintiffs also introduced evidence that not only were the rebates conditioned on the OEMs meeting the market penetration targets, but so too was Eaton's continued compliance with the agreements. As one OEM executive testified, if the market penetration targets were not met, the OEMs "would have a big risk of cancellation of the contract, price increases, and shortages if the market [was] difficult." Eaton was a monopolist in the HD transmissions market, and even if an OEM decided to forgo the rebates and purchase a significant portion of its requirements from another supplier, there would still have been a significant demand from truck buyers for Eaton products. Therefore, losing Eaton as a supplier was not an option.

Accordingly, this is not a case in which the defendant's low price was the clear driving force behind the customer's compliance with purchase targets, and the customers were free to walk away if a competitor offered a better price. Rather, Plaintiffs introduced evidence that compliance with the market penetration targets was mandatory because failing to meet such targets would jeopardize the OEMs' relationships with the dominant manufacturer of transmissions in the market.

* * * Nothing in the case law suggests, nor would it be sound policy to hold, that above-cost prices render an otherwise unlawful exclusive dealing agreement lawful. We decline to impose such an unduly simplistic and mechanical rule because to do so would place a significant portion of anticompetitive conduct outside the reach of the antitrust laws without adequate justification.

* * *

In contrast to the price-cost test line of cases, here, Plaintiffs do not allege that price itself functioned as the exclusionary tool. As such, we conclude that the price-cost test is not adequate to judge the legality of Eaton's conduct. Although prices are unlikely to exclude equally efficient rivals unless they are below-cost, exclusive dealing arrangements can exclude equally efficient (or potentially equally efficient) rivals, and thereby harm competition, irrespective of below-cost pricing. Where, as here, a dominant supplier enters into *de facto* exclusive dealing arrangements with every customer in the market, other firms may be driven out not because they cannot compete on a price basis, but because they are never given an opportunity to compete, despite their ability to offer products with significant customer demand. Therefore, Eaton's attempt to characterize this case as a pricing practices case, subject to the price-cost test, is unavailing. We hold that, instead, the rule of reason from *Tampa Electric* and its progeny must be applied to evaluate Plaintiffs' claims.

B. Proof of Anticompetitive Conduct and Antitrust Injury

We turn now to Eaton's contention that even leaving aside the price-cost test, Plaintiffs failed to prove that Eaton's LTAs were anticompetitive or that they caused antitrust injury to Plaintiffs. * * *

Our inquiry on appeal has several components. First, we examine whether the LTAs could reasonably be viewed as exclusive dealing arrangements, despite the fact that the LTAs covered less than 100% of the OEMs' purchase requirements and contained no express exclusivity provisions. Second, because the unique characteristics of the HD transmissions market bear heavily on our inquiry, we review Eaton's monopoly power, the concentrated nature of the market, and the ability of a monopolist in Eaton's position to engage in coercive conduct. Third, we discuss the anticompetitive effects of the various provisions in the LTAs, and consider Eaton's procompetitive justifications for the agreements.

Finally, we consider whether Plaintiffs established that they suffered antitrust injury as a result of Eaton's conduct.

1.   De Facto *Partial Exclusive Dealing*

* * * Eaton argues that Plaintiffs' claims must fail because the LTAs were not "true" exclusive dealing arrangements in that they did not contain express exclusivity requirements, nor did they cover 100% of the OEMs' purchases. Neither contention is persuasive because *de facto* partial exclusive dealing arrangements may, under certain circumstances, be actionable under the antitrust laws.

* * *

Here, there was sufficient evidence from which a jury could infer that, although the LTAs did not expressly require the OEMs to meet the market penetration targets, the targets were as effective as mandatory purchase requirements. Evidence presented at trial indicated that not only were lower prices (rebates) conditioned on the OEMs meeting the market-share targets, but so too was Eaton's continued compliance with the LTAs. For example, Eaton's LTAs with Freightliner, the largest OEM, and Volvo explicitly gave Eaton the right to terminate the agreements if the market-share targets were not met. And despite the fact that Eaton did not actually terminate the agreements on the rare occasion when an OEM failed to meet its target, the OEMs believed that it might. Critically, due to Eaton's position as the dominant supplier, no OEM could satisfy customer demand without at least some Eaton products, and therefore no OEM could afford to lose Eaton as a supplier. Accordingly, we agree with the District Court that a jury could have concluded that, under the circumstances, the market penetration targets were as effective as express purchase requirements "because no risk averse business would jeopardize its relationship with the largest manufacturer of transmissions in the market."

Second, an agreement does not need to be 100% exclusive in order to meet the legal requirements of exclusive dealing. We acknowledge that "partial" exclusive dealing is rarely a valid antitrust theory. Partial exclusive dealing agreements such as partial requirements contracts and contracts stipulating a fixed dollar or quantity amount are generally lawful because market foreclosure is only partial, and competing sellers are not prevented from selling to the buyer.

However, we decline to adopt Eaton's view that a requirements contract covering less than 100% of the buyer's needs can *never* be an unlawful exclusive dealing arrangement. * * * Therefore, just as "total foreclosure" is not required for an exclusive dealing arrangement to be unlawful, nor is complete exclusivity required with each customer. The legality of such an arrangement ultimately depends on whether the agreement foreclosed a substantial share of the relevant market such that competition was harmed.

In our case, although the market-share targets covered less than 100% of the OEMs' needs, a jury could nevertheless find that the LTAs unlawfully foreclosed competition in a substantial share of the HD transmissions market. There are only four direct purchasers of HD transmissions in North America, and Eaton, long the dominant supplier in the industry, entered into long-term agreements with each of them. Each LTA imposed a market-penetration target of roughly 90% (with the exception of Volvo, which manufactured some of its own transmissions for use in its own trucks), which we explained above, could be viewed as a requirement that the OEM purchase that percentage of its requirements from Eaton. Although no agreement was completely exclusive, the foreclosure that resulted was no different than it would be in a market with many customers where a dominant supplier enters into complete exclusive dealing arrangements with 90% of the customer base. Under such circumstances, the lack of complete exclusivity in each contract does not preclude Plaintiffs' *de facto* exclusive dealing claim.

2. *Market Conditions in HD Transmissions Market*

Exclusive dealing will generally only be unlawful where the market is highly concentrated, the defendant possesses significant market power, and there is some element of coercion present. For example, if the defendant occupies a dominant position in the market, its exclusive dealing arrangements invariably have the power to exclude rivals. Here, the jury found that Eaton possessed monopoly power in the HD transmissions market, and Eaton does not contest that finding on appeal.

A hard look at the nature of the market in which the parties compete is equally important. An exclusive dealing arrangement is most likely to present a threat to competition in a situation in which the market is highly concentrated, such that long-term contracts operate to "foreclose so large a percentage of the available supply or outlets that entry" or continued operation in "the concentrated market is unreasonably constricted." Here, the HD transmissions market had long been dominated by Eaton. Except for Meritor's production of manual transmissions in the 1990s and the ZF Meritor joint venture, no significant external supplier has entered the market for the last twenty years. A jury could certainly infer that Eaton's dominance over the OEMs created a barrier to entry that any potential rival manufacturer would have to confront. The record shows that the barriers to entry in the North American HD transmission market are especially high: HD transmissions are expensive to produce; transmissions developed for other geographic markets must be substantially modified for the North American market; and all HD transmission sales must pass through the highly concentrated intermediate market in which the OEMs operate. Eaton's theory that ZF Meritor or any new HD transmissions manufacturer would be able to "steal" an Eaton customer by offering a superior product at a lower price "simply has not proved to be realistic." * * * "The paltry penetration in the market by competitors over the years has been a refutation of [Eaton's] theory by tangible and measurable results in the real world."

Although we generally "assume that a customer will make [its] decision only on the merits," a monopolist may use its power to break the competitive mechanism and deprive customers of the ability to make a meaningful choice. A highly concentrated market, in which there is one (or a few) dominant supplier(s), creates the possibility for such coercion. And here, there was evidence that Eaton leveraged its position as a supplier of necessary products to coerce the OEMs into entering into the LTAs. Plaintiffs presented testimony from OEM officials that many of the terms of the LTAs were unfavorable to the OEMs and their customers, but that the OEMs agreed to such terms because without Eaton's transmissions, the OEMs would be unable to satisfy customer demand.

Accordingly, this case involves precisely the combination of factors that we explained would be present in the rare case in which exclusive dealing would pose a threat to competition.

3.   Sufficiency of the Evidence: Anticompetitive Conduct

We turn now to a discussion of whether there was sufficient evidence for a jury to conclude that Eaton engaged in anticompetitive conduct. * * *

i.   Extent of Foreclosure

First, the extent of the market foreclosure in this case was significant. "The share of the market foreclosed is important because, for the contract to have an adverse effect upon competition, 'the opportunities for other[s] . . . to enter into or remain in that market must be significantly limited.'" Substantial foreclosure allows the dominant firm to prevent potential rivals from ever reaching "the critical level necessary" to pose a real threat to the defendant's business. Here, Eaton entered into long-term agreements with every direct purchaser in the market, and under each agreement, imposed what could be viewed as mandatory purchase requirements of at least 80%, and up to 97.5%. The OEMs generally met these targets, which, as Plaintiffs' expert testified, resulted in approximately 15% of the market remaining open to Eaton's competitors by 2003. From 2000 through 2003, Plaintiffs' overall market share ranged from 8–14%, and by 2005, Plaintiffs' market share had dropped to 4%.

ii.   Duration of LTAs

Second, the LTAs were not short-term agreements, which would present little threat to competition. Rather, each LTA was for a term of at least five years, and the PACCAR LTA was for a seven-year term. Although long exclusive dealing contracts are not *per se* unlawful, "[t]he significance of any particular contract duration is a function of both the number of such contracts and market share covered by the exclusive-dealing contracts." Here, Eaton entered into long-term contracts with *every* direct purchaser in the market, which locked up over 85% of the market for at least five years. Although long-term agreements had previously been used in the HD transmissions industry, it was unprecedented for a supplier to enter into contracts of such duration with the entire customer base.

Eaton acknowledges, as it must, the unprecedented length of the LTAs, but maintains that the LTAs were not anticompetitive because they were easily terminable. Each LTA included a "competitiveness" clause, which permitted the OEM to purchase from another supplier or terminate the agreement if another supplier offered a better product or a lower price. However, Plaintiffs presented evidence that any language giving OEMs the right to terminate the agreements was essentially meaningless because Eaton had assured that there would be no other supplier that could fulfill the OEMs' needs or offer a lower price. Thus, a jury could very well conclude that "in spite of the legal ease with which the relationship c[ould] be terminated," the OEMs had a strong economic incentive to adhere to the terms of the LTAs, and therefore were not free to walk away from the agreements and purchase products from the supplier of their choice.

iii. Additional Anticompetitive Provisions in LTAs

Third, the LTAs were replete with provisions that a reasonable jury could find anticompetitive. To begin, a jury could have found that the data book provisions were anticompetitive in that they limited the ability of ZF Meritor to effectively market its products, and limited the ability of truck buyers to choose from a full menu of available transmissions. Eaton downplays the significance of the data book provisions, arguing that truck buyers always remained free to request unlisted transmissions, and ZF Meritor remained free to market directly to truck buyers. However, the mere existence of potential alternative avenues of distribution, without "an assessment of their overall significance to the market," is insufficient to demonstrate that Plaintiffs' opportunities to compete were not foreclosed. An OEM's data book was the "most important tool" that any buyer selecting component parts for a truck would use. If a product was not listed in a data book, it was "a disaster for the supplier." Although truck buyers could request unpublished components, doing so involved additional transaction costs, and in practice, meant that truck buyers were far more likely to select a product listed in the data book. Additionally, prior to the LTAs, it was not common practice for one supplier to be given exclusive data book listing. Historically, data books had included all product offerings, including Meritor transmissions, and the OEMs acknowledged that removing ZF Meritor products, especially FreedomLine, from the data books was "from a customer perspective," the wrong thing to do so because they were "good product[s] with considerable demand in the marketplace."

A jury could also have found that the "preferential pricing" provisions in the LTAs were anticompetitive. Although it was "common" for price savings to be passed down to truck buyers in the form of lower prices, and there are indications that at least some of the savings from Eaton transmissions were indeed passed down, there is also evidence that the preferential prices were achieved by artificially increasing the prices of Plaintiffs' products.

Additionally, the jury could have determined that the "competitiveness" clauses were of little practical import because Eaton's conduct ensured that no rival would be able to offer a comparable deal. There was also evidence that the competitiveness clauses were met with stiff resistance by Eaton.

iv. Anticompetitive Effects vs. Procompetitive Effects

Finally, the only procompetitive justification offered by Eaton on appeal is that the LTAs were crafted to meet customer demand to reduce prices, as well as engineering and support costs. In response to the economic downturn in the heavy-duty trucking industry in the late 1990s and early 2000s, each OEM sought to negotiate lower prices, and some sought to reduce the number of suppliers. During this time, oversupply was a problem, as were low truck prices, and an unavailability of drivers. It appears that Eaton responded well to the downturn; despite persistent quality control problems and a relatively late introduction of two-pedal automated mechanical transmissions, the company cut costs and increased market share.

However, no OEM ever asked Eaton to be a sole supplier, and there was considerable testimony from OEM officials that it was in an OEM's interest to have multiple suppliers. Although long-term agreements offering market-share or volume discounts had been used in the industry in the past (for transmissions and for other truck components), OEM executives consistently testified that Eaton's new LTAs represented a substantial departure from past practice. For example, the longest supply agreements Freightliner and Volvo had ever signed previously were for two-year terms. Likewise, OEM officials testified that the provisions in the LTAs requiring exclusive data book listing and "preferential pricing" were not common. Critically, there was considerable evidence from which a jury could infer that the primary purpose of the LTAs was not to meet customer demand, but to take preemptive steps to block potential competition from the new ZF Meritor joint venture. Eaton devised the unprecedented LTAs only after Meritor formed the joint venture with ZF AG, which Eaton viewed as a "serious competitor." Eaton feared that the ZF Meritor joint venture would put Eaton's "[North American] position at risk" by introducing a new product (FreedomLine) for which there was significant customer demand, but for which Eaton did not produce a comparable alternative.

In sum, the LTAs included numerous provisions raising anticompetitive concerns and there was evidence that Eaton sought to aggressively enforce the agreements, even when OEMs voiced objections. Accordingly, we hold that there was more than sufficient evidence for a jury to conclude that the cumulative effect of Eaton's conduct was to adversely affect competition.[21]

4.   Sufficiency of the Evidence: Antitrust Injury

Having concluded that there was sufficient evidence from which a jury could determine that the LTAs functioned as unlawful exclusive dealing agreements, we have no difficulty concluding that there was likewise sufficient evidence that Plaintiffs suffered antitrust injury. Eaton's conduct unlawfully foreclosed a substantial share of the HD transmissions market, which would otherwise have been available for rivals, including Plaintiffs. ZF Meritor exited the market in 2003, followed by Meritor in 2006, because they could not maintain high enough market shares to remain viable. A jury could certainly conclude that Plaintiffs' inability to grow was a direct result of Eaton's exclusionary conduct.

* * *

[Here the court undertook an extensive review of the district court's rulings on the admissibility of the plaintiff's expert's testimony on liability and damages. It affirmed the district court's decision to admit the testimony on liability, but reversed its decision not to permit the plaintiff to submit alternative damage calculations. Eds.]

GREENBERG, CIRCUIT JUDGE, dissenting.

Notwithstanding the majority's thoughtful and well-crafted opinion, I respectfully dissent as I would reverse the District Court's order that it entered * * * denying Eaton's motion for judgment as a matter of law. * * *

* * *

---

[21] It is worth noting that despite Eaton's contention that Plaintiffs' higher prices and quality problems led to their decline in market share, the OEMs felt differently. In 2002, a Freightliner executive wrote: "[t]his is a dangerous situation. We have already killed Meritor's transmission business. It is just a matter of time before they close their doors." Likewise, a 2006 Volvo presentation states: "With all its OEM customers, Eaton has established long term supply contracts . . . [which] ha[ve] led to . . . Eaton's only North American competitor, Meritor, [being] gradually marginalized to its current market position with a 10% market share."

II. ANALYSIS

* * *

The majority appears to split the difference between the parties' two positions. The majority concludes that the *Brooke Group* price-cost test may be dispositive in a case where a plaintiff brings a claim challenging a defendant's pricing practices[11] and alleges that price itself functioned as the exclusionary tool. I agree completely with the majority's conclusion in this regard. Thereafter, however, our paths diverge because the majority appears to conclude that where a plaintiff brings a claim of unlawful exclusive dealing against a defendant's pricing practices but does not contend that the defendant's prices operated as the exclusionary tool, the price-cost test is irrelevant and has neither dispositive nor persuasive effect.[12]

As I explain further below, while I do not believe that the Supreme Court has held that the inferior courts must impose and give dispositive effect to the *Brooke Group* price-cost test in every claim challenging a defendant's pricing practices, the Court's unwavering adherence to the general principle that above-cost pricing practices are not anticompetitive and its justifications for that position lead me to conclude that this principle is a cornerstone of antitrust jurisprudence that applies regardless of whether the plaintiff focuses its claim on the price or non-price aspects of the defendant's pricing program. Thus, although the price-cost test may not bar a claim of exclusive dealing challenging a defendant's above-cost pricing practices, regardless of how a plaintiff casts its claim or the non-price elements of the pricing practices that the plaintiff identifies as the exclusionary conduct, where a plaintiff attacks a defendant's pricing practices—and to be clear that is what the market-share rebate programs at issue here are—the fact that defendant's prices were above-cost must be a high barrier to the plaintiff's success. Accordingly, I believe that we must apply the *Brooke Group* price-cost test to the present case and give that test persuasive effect in the context of our broader analysis under the antitrust laws at issue.

Allowing appellees that opportunity, the majority concludes that the plaintiffs adduced sufficient evidence at trial from which a jury reasonably could infer that the LTAs represented unlawful "de facto partial exclusive dealing." In doing so, the majority concludes that despite the fact that the

---

[11] Throughout this opinion I use the term "pricing practices" to encompass the variety of ways in which a firm may set its prices, including but not limited to, straightforward price cuts and conditional rebates or discounts.

[12] I recognize that the majority states that Eaton's low prices are not irrelevant to the extent they may help explain why the OEMs entered the LTAs even though the LTAs allegedly included terms that were unfavorable to the OEMs and to rebut an argument that the agreements were inefficient but the majority does not factor the circumstance that Eaton's prices were above cost into its analysis of whether the LTAs were exclusionary and anticompetitive, and I believe its failure to do so is error.

LTAs by their terms were not exclusive nor mandatory and despite the fact that the prices offered under them were at all times above-cost such that an equally-efficient competitor could have matched them, they were de facto partial exclusive dealing contracts because Eaton was a dominant supplier, the OEMs could not have afforded to lose Eaton as a supplier, and thus, the majority reasons, the OEMs were compelled to enter the LTAs and meet their market-share targets. The majority reaches its conclusion despite the absence of evidence in the record suggesting that Eaton would have refused to supply transmissions to the OEMs had the OEMs failed to meet the LTAs' market-share targets or that Eaton at any point coerced the OEMs into entering the LTAs or meeting the targets. * * * I cannot join my colleagues in this judicial reworking of the LTAs and the unbridled speculation the majority's reasoning requires to convert the LTAs into exclusive dealing contracts. Even analyzing appellees' claims under the rule of reason and the principles used to ascertain whether an exclusive-dealing arrangement is lawful and employing the deferential standard of review to which we subject jury verdicts, it is plain that the agreements could not have been and in fact were not anticompetitive.

* * *

B. Clayton Act Section 3 and Sherman Act Section 1 Claims

* * *

As was true of the contracts at issue in . . . [*Allied Orthopedic Appliances Inc. v. Tyco Health Group LP*, 592 F.3d 991 (9th Cir. 2010)] and . . . [*Concord Boat Corp. v. Brunswick Corp.*, 207 F.3d 1039 (8th Cir. 2000)] with respect to what are suggested to be, wrongly in my view, mandatory purchase obligations, the LTAs did not obligate the OEMs to purchase anything from Eaton, much less 100% of their transmission needs, nor did they preclude the OEMs from purchasing transmissions from any other manufacturer. Rather, the agreements provided for increasing rebates and thus lower prices based on the percentage of an OEM's transmission needs that it purchased from Eaton. In such a circumstance, the LTAs did not foreclose competition in *any* share of the market because Eaton's competitors were able to compete for this business as the OEMs were at liberty to walk away from the LTAs at any time.

Indeed, this point is precisely where the *Brooke Group* price-cost test comes into play. In a situation such as this one, where the contract in terms is not exclusive and merely provides discounted but above-cost prices conditioned upon a market-share target, any equally efficient competitor, including ZFM, if it was an equally efficient competitor, had an ongoing opportunity to offer competitive discounts to capture the OEMs' business. If Eaton's discounts had resulted in prices that were below-cost, a charge that appellees do not make, then even an equally-efficient competitor might not have the opportunity to compete for the business the LTAs covered and thus it could be said that competition was foreclosed in that share of the market notwithstanding the non-obligatory and non-exclusive nature of the LTAs. But we do not need to address that unlikely circumstance because Eaton's discounts resulted in prices that were above-cost and thus the LTAs "left ample room" for ZFM or new competitors to enter the market and "to lure customers away by offering superior discounts." Absent evidence that notwithstanding the above-cost prices of the LTAs the non-price aspects of the LTAs rendered them anticompetitive, we should conclude that as a matter of law Eaton's LTAs were not anticompetitive.

The majority dismisses as inapplicable the reasoning of *Allied Orthopedic* and *Concord Boat* by stating that "this is not a case in which the defendant's low price was the clear driving force behind the customer's compliance with purchase targets, and the customers were free to walk away if a competitor offered a better price." But the reality is to the contrary as the testimony I have summarized establishes it is precisely the case that Eaton's low prices led the OEMs to enter the LTAs and to strive to meet the market-share targets. Likewise, it is clearly the case that the OEMs were free to walk away from the market-share rebates the LTAs offered at any time. In attempting to overcome this crucial defect in appellees' claim and concluding that notwithstanding the LTAs' terms the LTAs were in fact mandatory agreements to which the OEMs were beholden against their will the majority sets forth two justifications.

First, the majority downplays the possibility that ZFM could "steal" Eaton's customers by offering a superior product or lower price because that possibility did not "prove[ ] to be realistic.". In other words, the majority appears to assume that because ZFM did not lure away Eaton's customers through offering superior products or lower prices, it could not have done so and the reason for its inability to do so was the LTAs. I find the majority's treatment of this point to be an unpersuasive answer to the logic of *Allied Orthopedic* and *Concord Boat*.

I hardly need make the logical point that one cannot assume that because an event *did* not happen it *could* not have happened. It appears that ZFM did not lure away Eaton's customers. That does not mean, however, that ZFM was incapable of doing so. It is beyond dispute and indeed a central point to this case that ZFM did not offer lower prices than Eaton's prices and ZFM did not develop a full product line as it knew it had to do in order to compete effectively with Eaton.[36] In other words, ZFM did

---

[36] The majority states, without elaboration, that Eaton assured that there would be no other supplier that could fulfill the OEMs' needs or offer a lower price. I note first that it is an undisputed fact that when Meritor entered into the joint venture with ZF AG at a time prior to any allegation of anticompetitive conduct by Eaton, Meritor did not offer a full product line of HD truck transmissions. Thereafter, ZFM explicitly identified its lack of a full product line as a barrier to its market success and yet it did not develop a full product line. There is no evidence that Eaton

not even engage in the type of competitive conduct that potentially could have lured away Eaton's customers. Thus, we cannot say that it is not realistic to think that if it had engaged in that competition conduct ZFM could have been successful.

Second, the majority attempts to overcome this absolutely fundamental defect in appellees' case by concluding that notwithstanding the fact that the LTAs were not by their terms mandatory and the fact that Eaton's prices after consideration of the rebates were at all times above-cost such that appellees, were they equally efficient competitors, could have matched them, there nevertheless was sufficient evidence that the LTAs foreclosed competition in a substantial share of the HD truck transmission market because "the targets were as effective as mandatory purchase requirements." In this regard, the majority reasons that "[c]ritically, due to Eaton's position as the dominant supplier no OEM could satisfy customer demand without at least some Eaton products, and therefore no OEM could afford to lose Eaton as a supplier." Therefore, the majority reasons, "a jury could have concluded that, under the circumstances, the market penetration targets were as effective as express purchase requirements because no risk averse business would jeopardize its relationship with the largest manufacturer of transmissions in the market."

Undoubtedly, there is evidence in the record that the OEMs required Eaton's products, to the end that an OEM could not have afforded to lose Eaton as a supplier. However, there is not a scintilla of evidence that if an OEM did not meet its LTA's market-share target Eaton would have refused to supply it with transmissions. * * *

Nevertheless, regardless of whether the LTAs granted Eaton a right of termination, the majority's suggestion that the OEMs faced losing Eaton as a supplier if they failed to meet the market-share targets is contradicted by the market reality that while Eaton was the largest manufacturer of transmissions in the market there were only four OEMs that bought Eaton's transmissions. Accordingly, the idea that Eaton could or would have refused to deal with one of the OEMs in addition to being unsupported by the record is irrational from an economic viewpoint for if Eaton had done so it would have turned its back on a significant purchaser of its products measured in sales volume. The notion is completely unjustified.

* * *

I must address also an aspect of the majority's reasoning on this point that I find to suffer from a serious flaw with dangerous implications for antitrust jurisprudence. Perhaps the majority does not believe that any

---

somehow prevented either Meritor or later ZFM from developing a full product line. Furthermore, there is no evidence in the record indicating that Eaton prevented ZFM from offering more attractive discounts to capture Eaton's business and there is no evidence that other firms tried to enter the HD truck transmission market but were thwarted by Eaton.

evidence was required to rebut the reality that even though the market-share targets were facially voluntary, the mere circumstances that Eaton was the dominant supplier in the market and that no OEM could afford to lose it as a supplier sufficed to render the LTAs mandatory. The majority's reasoning in this regard literally would mean that had Eaton not been the dominant supplier of HD truck transmissions in the NAFTA market, there would not have been sufficient evidence for the jury to conclude that the LTAs were de facto exclusive. While I realize that monopolists may face more constraints on their conduct under the antitrust laws than less dominant firms, it is an unfair and unwarranted leap to create the specter of coercion out of reference to Eaton's market dominance, In sum, I cannot ascribe to the view that a non-mandatory, non-exclusive contract is transformed magically into a mandatory, exclusive contract by virtue of reference to the firm's market position alone such that dominant firms must be wary when they enter voluntary contracts that offer rebates or discounts lest a court later permit a jury to interpret those contracts as mandatory simply due to that firm's dominant position.

* * *

In point of fact, there is not a trace of evidence beyond appellees' own baseless accusations and the majority does not bring our attention to any such evidence supporting its rather serious accusation that Eaton leveraged its position as a monopolist to force the OEMs to enter into agreements that the OEMs did not want to enter. Eaton's offer of lower prices to the OEMs in the form of rebates and direct payments in an effort to gain their business is hardly coercion. Rather, it is nothing more than legitimate good business

Likewise, there is no evidence that the LTAs represented unfavorable arrangements for the OEMs such that the OEMs only agreed to enter the contracts out of fear of losing Eaton as a supplier. Indeed, to the extent one may be tempted to infer that the market-share targets were so high as to be unfavorable to the OEMs I note that the targets were actually very close to or in fact below Eaton's preexisting market share at three out of the four OEMs measured at a time before the adoption of the LTAs during which appellees do not claim that Eaton was violating any law. The reality that the market share levels that Eaton reached prior to the adoption of the LTAs makes it, in a word I do not like using but fits perfectly here, ridiculous to conclude that the LTAs had a coercive effect on the OEMs.

After studying the majority's treatment of the LTAs I am left with the impression that it pictures Eaton representatives as using coercion when they handed the OEM representatives the LTAs. Yet the reality is that there is absolutely no evidence in the record suggesting that Eaton compelled the OEMs by the threat of punishment to agree to the LTAs or compelled them to meet the share targets. Quite to the contrary, the record is replete with evidence, as I have summarized above, that shows that far from cowering under Eaton's "threats," the OEMs entered into the LTAs in furtherance of their own economic self-interests and because those agreements provided the best possible prices and assurance of a full product line supply. They worked to meet the market-share targets because by achieving those targets they received discounted prices.

* * *

* * * In sum, because appellees failed to produce evidence to show that the LTAs and their voluntary, above-cost market-share target rebates could have or did foreclose competition in any, much less a substantial, share of the market, notwithstanding the jury's verdict it is obvious that appellees' claims must fail under *Tampa Electric*.

* * *

III. CONCLUSION

I offer a few final thoughts on this important case, which, though seemingly complicated, should have an obvious result. It is axiomatic that "[t]he antitrust laws . . . were enacted for 'the protection of *competition* not *competitors*.' " Yet as often as this refrain is repeated throughout antitrust jurisprudence, it appears increasingly that disappointed competitors, on the assumption that their deficient performances must be attributable to their competitors' anticompetitive conduct rather than their own errors in judgment or shortcomings or their competitors' more desirable products or business decisions, or on the assumption that they can convince a jury of that view, turn to the antitrust laws when they have been outperformed in the marketplace. Of course, competitors can be and sometimes are harmed by their peers' anticompetitive conduct and when they show that is what happened they may have viable antitrust claims. Yet often it is the case that a defeated competitor falls back on the antitrust laws in an attempt to achieve in the courts the goal that it could not reach in the properly-functioning competitive marketplace. This case is a classic demonstration of that process, which so far with respect to liability even if not damages has been successful. Indeed, I find it remarkable that appellees' case that is predicated on nothing more than smoke and mirrors has gotten so far.

But the basic facts are clear. Appellees do not bring a predatory pricing claim because they cannot do so as Eaton's prices were above cost. Instead, they seek refuge in the law of exclusive dealing to challenge the LTAs, which based on the record could not be found to be either facially or de facto exclusive or mandatory. After stripping this case of appellees' baseless insinuations that Eaton engaged in coercive or threatening conduct in regards to the LTAs, it becomes apparent that the core of appellees' claim really is their belief they had a superior product in the FreedomLine and the disappointing sales of that product relative to their expectations must have been attributable to Eaton's anticompetitive conduct. Appellees thus "appear[ ] to be assuming that if [Eaton's] product was not objectively superior, then its victories were not on the merits."

* * * The truth is that neither judges nor juries have expertise in determining the best transmission to buy. Certainly, the purchasers of trucks and transmissions should make transmission decisions for themselves and so long as appellees manufactured their transmissions they had a chance to be their supplier.

I recognize that the record could support a finding that the FreedomLine was a technological innovation for which Eaton did not offer a technically comparable product, and I further recognize that Eaton engaged in vigorous competition through aggressive but above-cost methods to compensate for the possible deficiency of their transmission offerings in that regard. But in the absence of anticompetitive conduct, the antitrust laws do not forbid Eaton's response. In reality, however, the record compels that the conclusion that Eaton was able to maintain its dominant market position in the face of the availability of the FreedomLine for myriad reasons, including its capability of offering the OEMs a full product line, favorable pricing, its long-standing, positive reputation, and various market forces that favored an established market player such as Eaton. And it is also evident from the record, especially from ZFM's internal documents, that there were numerous intervening factors, such as ZFM's precipitously falling market share, which tellingly predated the adoption of the LTAs, the market's drive towards full-product line manufacturers, the OEMs' hesitancy to purchase new products, and the severe market downturn, that disfavored ZFM. In the difficult market it faced, Meritor entered into a joint venture that needed to achieve an almost one-third market share within approximately four years of the venture's formation to maintain a viable business, an obviously ambitious goal indeed even when one overlooks the fact that the joint venture offered a limited product line and a flagship transmission that cost far more than other transmissions in the market.

I note finally that courts' erroneous judgments in cases such as this one do not come without a cost to the economy as a whole. Discounts of all varieties, whether tied to the purchase of multiple products, exclusivity, volume, or market-share, are ubiquitous in our society. "Discounts are the age-old way that merchants induce customers to purchase from them and not from someone else or to purchase more than they otherwise would." Indeed, market-share discounts can be particularly pro-competitive because they can result in lower prices for a broader range of customers as they extend to smaller purchasers discounts typically reserved for the largest of purchasers under more common volume-discount programs. The competitive marketplace that the antitrust laws encourage and protect is characterized by firms willing and able to cut prices in order to take customers from their rivals." Accordingly, "mistaken inferences in cases such as this one are especially costly, because they chill the very conduct the antitrust laws are designed to protect."

Thus, as the Supreme Court has stressed, courts do not issue these decisions in a vacuum: once we file our opinion in this case firms that engage in price competition but seek to stay within the confines of the antitrust laws must attempt to use the precedent that we establish as a guide for their conduct, at least if they are subject to the law of this Circuit. This is serious business indeed. For this reason, the Supreme Court has "repeatedly emphasized the importance of clear rules in antitrust law." I confess I can glean no such clear rule from the majority's opinion. I do not know how corporate counsel presented with a firm's business plan at least if it is a dominant supplier that seeks to expand sales through a discount program that might be challenged by competitors as providing for a de facto exclusive dealing program and asked if the plan is lawful under the Sherman and Clayton Acts will be able to advise the management. The sad truth is that the counsel only will be able to tell management that it will have to take a chance in the courtroom casino at some then uncertain future date to find out.

If Eaton's above-cost market-share rebate program memorialized in the LTAs, which were neither explicitly nor de facto exclusive or mandatory, can be condemned as unlawful de facto partial exclusive dealing on the basis of literally a handful of disjointed statements that amount at most to unsupported speculation as to the possibility that Eaton may have stopped supplying its transmissions if the OEMs did not meet the targets, firms face a difficult task indeed in structuring lawful discount programs. "Perhaps most troubling, firms that seek to avoid . . . liability [for market-share rebate programs] will have no safe harbor for their pricing practices." What I find most troubling is that firms will play it safe by not formulating discount programs and that the result of this case will be an increase of prices to purchasers and the stifling of competition, surely a perverse outcome. It is ironical that the very circumstance that the majority's opinion is so thoughtful and well crafted that the risk that it poses is so great. On the other hand, the approach I believe the Supreme Court's precedent compels—applying and giving persuasive effect to the *Brooke Group* price-cost test and granting a presumption of lawfulness to pricing practices that result in above-cost prices—provides clear direction to firms engaging in price competition but still allows for an antitrust plaintiff to allege that a defendant has engaged in attendant anticompetitive conduct that renders its practices unlawful.

* * *

ZF Meritor illustrates the continuing debate about how best to evaluate conditional pricing practices. What led the court to conclude that the exclusive dealing, not the price-cost test, was the most appropriate way to analyze the practices challenged by ZF Meritor? What was the dissent's principal objection to use of an exclusive dealing approach? What did the court mean when it reasoned that the "mechanism of exclusion" was not the price, as such, but the related conditions, which were akin to exclusive dealing? Note, too, that the "exclusive dealing framework," is essentially a rule of reason-type analysis. How did the court structure that analysis? Which of the opinions in ZF Meritor did you find most persuasive? Why? The Third Circuit again faced a choice between application of the rule of reason and a price-cost test in *Eisai, Inc. v. Sanofi Aventis U.S., LLC*, 821 F.3d 394 (3d Cir. 2016). The district court applied a price-cost test and granted the defendant's motion for summary judgment. The court of appeals declined to apply a price-cost test, however, noting that it was "not persuaded that Eisai's claims fundamentally relate to pricing practices." *Id.* at 408. Nevertheless, it affirmed summary judgment, concluding that under a rule of reason analysis the plaintiff had failed to meet its burden of production with respect to adverse competitive effects.

CPPs continue to challenge the courts and to be the focus of extensive commentary. *See, e.g.*, Derek W. Moore & Joshua D. Wright, *Conditional Discounts and the Law of Exclusive Dealing*, 22 GEO. MASON L. REV. 1205 (2015); Einer Elhauge & Abraham L. Wickelgren, *Robust Exclusion and Market Division Through Loyalty Discounts*, 43 INT'L J. INDUS. ORG. 111 (2015); Daniel A. Crane, *Bargaining over Loyalty*, 92 TEXAS L. REV. 253 (2014); Abraham L. Wickelgren, *Detailed Analysis, Not Catechism: A Comment on Crane's "Bargaining over Loyalty"*, 92 TEXAS L. REV. 1 (2014); *see also* Sean P. Gates, *Antitrust By Analogy: Developing Rules for Loyalty Rebates and Bundled Discounts*, 79 ANTITRUST L.J. 99 (2013). It has also been a focus of interest in the European Union, which has sought to integrate the two approaches. *See* Commission Notice: Guidelines on Vertical Restraints § 2.1 (2010), http://ec.europa.eu/competition/antitrust/legislation/guidelines_vertical_en.pdf. *See also* Case T-286/09, *Intel v. Commission* (Jun 12, 2014), http://curia.europa.eu/juris/liste.jsf?num=T–286/09 (EC prevailed in challenging Intel's exclusive loyalty rebates) (an appeal to the European Court of Justice is pending).

C. PRICE DISCRIMINATION AND THE ROBINSON-PATMAN ACT

INTRODUCTION: THE ROBINSON PATMAN ACT—AN OVERVIEW

Section 2 of the Clayton Act, as originally signed into law in 1914, included a prohibition of "price discrimination," where the effect "may be substantially to lessen competition or tend to create a monopoly in any line of commerce." Price discrimination, literally charging different prices to at least two different customers, was viewed at the time as a serious weapon of the trusts, which were wielding it to discipline and destroy their rivals. By selectively reducing prices, often to predatory or "below cost" levels, it was believed that the trusts could impede entry by would-be rivals or drive existing rivals from the market. Price discriminations used in this fashion were characterized as "primary line"—its competitive effects occurred at the same functional level of the market, *i.e.*, rivals of the discriminating seller.

But price discrimination might also arise in the context of competitive struggles between two competing purchasers from a common supplier. In that context, one of the purchasers might seek favorable treatment from the supplier in the form of better pricing, conditions of sale or allowances not made available to its rival, a fellow purchaser. In these instances, the price discrimination was categorized as "secondary line." Although the discrimination originated with an upstream seller, as in the case of primary line discrimination, its effects were felt at the "secondary" or dealer level, one step removed. The discrimination would not injure one of the discriminator's rivals, but instead the "disfavored purchaser," a competitor of the favored purchaser and customer of the discriminating seller.

Two issues arose under the original language of Section 2 of the Clayton Act. First, courts and commentators questioned whether it condemned both primary and secondary line price discrimination, or was limited in scope to just primary line injury. The question was answered in *George Van Camp & Sons Co. v. Am. Can Co.*, 278 U.S. 245 (1929), where the Supreme Court held that the Act covered both types of injury. The second issue concerned the nature and extent of the competitive effects required to make out a violation of Section 2 of the Clayton Act. From 1914 to 1936 the provision was consistently read as limiting the Act to discriminations that resulted in *generalized competitive injury*.

In 1936, in the wake of the Great Depression, the law of price discrimination underwent a major revision in the form of the Robinson-Patman Act, which amended Section 2 of the Clayton Act. (*See infra* Appendix A). Concerned about the rapid growth of large chain stores, particularly their emergence in the grocery retailing business and their impact on smaller, "mom-and-pop" grocery stores, Congress acted to strengthen the provisions of the original Clayton Act, particularly as it applied to secondary line injury occasioned by the presence of "power buyers." Many in the Congress firmly believed that such power buyers, like large supermarket chains, were systematically extracting favorable terms from their suppliers, which in turn facilitated their ascendance over equally efficient, but disfavored smaller-scale merchants.

To strengthen the Clayton Act's prohibition of price discrimination, Congress added a conjunctive, alternative standard of injury to the "substantially to lessen competition or tend to create a monopoly" formula of the original Section 2. As amended, the prohibition also condemned price discrimination where the effect may be "to injure, destroy, or prevent *competition with any person* who either grants or knowingly receives the benefit of such discrimination, *or with customers of either of them.* . . ." 15 U.S.C. § 13(a) (emphasis added). Although not expressly limited, this amended competitive effects language of the Robinson-Patman Act was incorporated to enhance the Clayton Act's prohibition of secondary line price discrimination so it might more effectively outlaw successful efforts by powerful buyers to secure price concessions to the detriment of their smaller rivals. As the Supreme Court later held in *FTC v. Morton Salt Co.*, 334 U.S. 37 (1948), this "new provision * * * was intended to justify a finding of injury to competition by a showing of 'injury to a competitor victimized by the discrimination.'" *Id.* at 49. Evidence of generalized competitive injury, such as higher prices, lower output or other manifestations of anticompetitive effects, was no longer required of secondary line claimants.

It is important to note, too, that Section 2 of the Clayton Act goes beyond simple price discrimination by a seller. Section 2(f) of the Act makes it unlawful to knowingly solicit and receive a price discrimination that violates Section 2(a)—the flip side of offering one. Potentially less obvious forms of price discrimination are also addressed. Section 2(c) prohibits the granting of phantom brokerage allowances, and has been invoked even in cases of commercial bribery. Sections 2(d) and (e) extend the prohibitions of Section 2(a) to discriminatory promotional allowances and services, which can mask price discriminations, and require that such allowances and services be made available to all customers on "proportionately equal terms." Implementing these standards has proved to be a long-standing challenge. *See FTC v. Fred Meyer, Inc.*, 390 U.S. 341 (1968); *see also* FTC GUIDES FOR ADVERTISING ALLOWANCES AND OTHER MERCHANDISING PAYMENTS AND SERVICES, 16 C.F.R. § 240 (Sept. 29, 2014) ("*Fred Meyer* Guides"); *Woodman's Food Market, Inc. v. Clorox Co.*, 833 F.3d 743 (7th Cir. 2016)(unique packaging size alone was not enough to run afoul of Section 2(e)). Significantly, neither Section 2(d) nor 2(e) contain any competitive injury language such as that found in Section 2(a), making them broader in scope than Section 2(a).

Also significant are the Act's two affirmative defenses. The "cost justification" defense contained in Section 2(a) permits the seller to lower its price to a customer in recognition of efficiencies, *i.e.*, lower costs it incurs in selling to that customer, but is not available as a defense to a Section 2(d) or (e) violation. The "meeting competition" defense of Section 2(b) allows a seller to lower its prices selectively if necessary to meet (not beat) the price of one of its rivals, and can be used to defend alleged violations of Sections 2(a), as well as 2(d) and (e). *See generally Falls City Indus., Inc. v. Vanco Beverage, Inc.*, 460 U.S. 428 (1983). There are also some "non-statutory" defenses that have been recognized by the courts over the years, such as the defense for "functional discounts." *See Texaco Inc. v. Hasbrouck*, 496 U.S. 543 (1990).

A complete discussion of the law and economics of price discrimination is beyond the scope of this Casebook. For more comprehensive treatments of the history and development of the traditional law on price discrimination, see RICHARD A. POSNER, THE ROBINSON PATMAN ACT: FEDERAL REGULATION OF PRICE DIFFERENCES (1976); FREDERICK ROWE, PRICE DISCRIMINATION UNDER THE ROBINSON-PATMAN ACT (1962); HARRY L. SHNIDERMAN & BINGHAM B. LEVERICH, PRICE DISCRIMINATION IN PERSPECTIVE (2d ed. 1987).

In Chapter 4, in *Brooke Group* we considered the treatment of *primary line price discrimination*, which is analyzed today largely as an instance of unilateral, predatory conduct, akin to "predatory pricing." In this section, we address *secondary line price discrimination* as an additional example of exclusionary vertical agreements. In particular, we will examine the controversy that has surrounded the Act's diminished injury standard as interpreted in *Morton Salt*. Before doing so, however, you might want to review Sidebar 5–4, which expands upon the economics of price discrimination.

————————

The Supreme Court's first opportunity to interpret the impact of the Robinson-Patman amendments on secondary line price discrimination came in *FTC v. Morton Salt Co.*, 334 U.S. 37 (1948). *Morton Salt* involved a challenge to the quantity discount practices of the leading manufacturer of table salt. In the FTC's view, those discounts, which were only offered to Morton Salt's larger customers, illustrated the kind of secondary line injury the Robinson-Patman Act was designed to redress.

One of the critical issues in the case concerned the competitive effects standard applicable in a secondary line injury case. Morton Salt argued unsuccessfully that in order to prevail, the FTC was required to demonstrate generalized injury to competition. The Court unequivocally rejected this view, relying on the Act's incipiency "may" language, and the Robinson-Patman Act's legislative history:

> The statute requires no more than that the effect of the prohibited price discriminations "may be substantially to lessen competition * * * or to injure, destroy, or prevent competition." After a careful consideration of this provision of the Robinson-Patman Act, we have said that "the statute does not require that the

discriminations must in fact have harmed competition, but only that there is a reasonable possibility that they 'may' have such an effect." *Corn Products Co. v. Federal Trade Comm'n*, 324 U.S. 726, 742. Here the Commission found what would appear to be obvious, that the competitive opportunities of certain merchants were injured when they had to pay respondent substantially more for their goods than their competitors had to pay. The findings are adequate.

* * *

Furthermore, in enacting the Robinson-Patman Act, Congress was especially concerned with protecting small businesses which were unable to buy in quantities, such as the merchants here who purchased in less-than-carload lots. To this end it undertook to strengthen this very phase of the old Clayton Act. The committee reports on the Robinson-Patman Act emphasized a belief that § 2 of the Clayton Act had "been too restrictive, in requiring a showing of general injury to competitive conditions. . . ." *The new provision, here controlling, was intended to justify a finding of injury to competition by a showing of "injury to the competitor victimized by the discrimination."*

334 U.S. at 46–47, 49 (footnotes omitted; emphasis added).

The final, italicized phrase became critical: injury to generalized competition could be inferred from injury to a single disfavored purchaser. But all the Court required in order to establish injury to a competitor was evidence of a difference in price over time. Combined, these two inferences became known as the *"Morton Salt inference"*—from a persistent difference in price over time one could infer injury to a competitor, and from injury to a competitor, one could further infer injury to competition. The Court stated the modern formulation in *Vanco Beverage*: "injury to competition is established prima facie by proof of a substantial price discrimination between competing purchasers over time." *Falls City Indus., Inc. v. Vanco Beverage, Inc.*, 460 U.S. 428, 435 (1983).

Morton Salt's minimal standard of proof, coupled with more recent cases in the primary line area that mandate more substantial evidence of injury to competition, have led to continuing controversy. In fact, no U.S. antitrust statute has been subjected to as much harsh criticism and repeated calls for reform or repeal as the Robinson-Patman Act. For one of the classic Chicago School criticisms of the statute, see Edward H. Levi, *The Robinson-Patman Act—Is It in the Public Interest?*, 1 ABA ANTITRUST SECTION 60 (1952); *see also* RICHARD A. POSNER, THE ROBINSON-PATMAN ACT: FEDERAL REGULATION OF PRICE DIFFERENCES (1976). In April 2007, the Antitrust Modernization Commission called for its repeal in its final Report. *See* Antitrust Modernization Commission, *Report and*

Recommendations 312 (Apr. 2007), http://govinfo.library.unt.edu/amc/report_recommendation/amc_final_report.pdf.

Since the Supreme Court's 1992 decision in *Brooke Group*, defendants in secondary line price discrimination cases have argued that like *Brooke Group*, which harmonized the law of *primary* line price discrimination with the law of predatory pricing by applying the same standard of competitive harm, courts should harmonize *secondary* line injury with more contemporary notions of competitive harm. All of the courts of appeals to face that specific argument have rejected it, however, in light of the unambiguous language and history of the Robinson-Patman Act's injury requirement for secondary line cases, as it was interpreted in *Morton Salt. See, e.g., Chroma Lighting v. GTE Prods. Corp.*, 111 F.3d 653 (9th Cir. 1997). *But see Boise Cascade Corp. v. FTC*, 837 F.2d 1127, 1144 (D.C. Cir. 1988) (imposing higher competitive injury standard before *Brooke Group*). For a further discussion of these cases and a proposal for harmonizing *Morton Salt* with more contemporary notions of competitive injury, see Andrew I. Gavil, *Secondary Line Price Discrimination and the Fate of* Morton Salt: *To Save it Let it Go*, 48 EMORY L.J. 1057 (1999).

As a consequence of persistent doubts about the wisdom and efficacy of the Robinson-Patman Act, particularly as it concerns secondary line price discrimination, enforcement of its provisions has evolved largely into a private affair. Whereas private treble damage actions by disfavored purchasers continue to be filed, the FTC has largely exited from the field of enforcement. In the 1960s the FTC filed a minimum of ten Robinson-Patman Act cases per year and in some years issued substantially more. In 1966, for example, the Commission issued 73 Robinson-Patman complaints, with most being consent orders involving small clothing manufacturers. But in the early 1970s the average number of FTC complaints fell to four per year, and by the late 1970s had dropped to an average of two per year. In the complete decade of the 1980s the FTC initiated a total of only five Robinson-Patman matters, including but a single new case from 1982 through 1989. The FTC issued no Robinson-Patman complaints in the 1990s and has issued a single case—*McCormick*—since January 1, 2000. *In the Matter of McCormick & Co., Inc.*, No. C-3939, 2000 WL 521741 (F.T.C. Apr. 27, 2000).

The tension between *Morton Salt* and *Brooke Group* has still not been resolved, but in our next case, the Supreme Court came as close as it has ever come to suggesting that a more substantial competitive injury standard should be implied in secondary line price discrimination cases. As you read the case, note how it reads and interprets these two cases.

VOLVO TRUCKS NORTH AMERICA, INC. v. REEDER-SIMCO GMC, INC.

Supreme Court of the United States, 2006.
546 U.S. 164, 126 S.Ct. 860, 163 L.Ed.2d 663.

GINSBURG, J., delivered the opinion of the Court, in which ROBERTS, C. J., and O'CONNOR, SCALIA, KENNEDY, SOUTER, and BREYER, JJ., joined. STEVENS, J., filed a dissenting opinion, in which THOMAS, J., joined.

JUSTICE GINSBURG delivered the opinion of the Court.

* * *

I

Volvo manufactures heavy-duty trucks. Reeder sells new and used trucks, including heavy-duty trucks. * * * Reeder generally sold Volvo's trucks through a competitive bidding process. In this process, the retail customer describes its specific product requirements and invites bids from several dealers it selects. The customer's "decision to request a bid from a particular dealer or to allow a particular dealer to bid is controlled by such factors as an existing relationship, geography, reputation, and cold calling or other marketing strategies initiated by individual dealers."

Once a Volvo dealer receives the customer's specifications, it turns to Volvo and requests a discount or "concession" off the wholesale price (set at 80% of the published retail price). It is common practice in the industry for manufacturers to offer customer-specific discounts to their dealers. Volvo decides on a case-by-case basis whether to offer a discount and, if so, what the discount rate will be, taking account of such factors as industry-wide demand and whether the retail customer has, historically, purchased a different brand of trucks. The dealer then uses the discount offered by Volvo in preparing its bid; it purchases trucks from Volvo only if and when the retail customer accepts its bid.

Reeder was one of many Volvo dealers, each assigned by Volvo to a geographic territory. Reeder's territory encompassed ten counties in Arkansas and two in Oklahoma. Although nothing prohibits a Volvo dealer from bidding outside its territory, Reeder rarely bid against another Volvo dealer. In the atypical event that the same retail customer solicited a bid from more than one Volvo dealer, Volvo's stated policy was to provide the same price concession to each dealer competing head to head for the same sale.

In 1997, Volvo announced a program it called "Volvo Vision," in which the company addressed problems it faced in the market for heavy trucks, among them, the company's assessment that it had too many dealers. Volvo projected enlarging the size of its dealers' markets and reducing the number of dealers from 146 to 75. Coincidentally, Reeder learned that Volvo had given another dealer a price concession greater than the concessions Reeder typically received, and "Reeder came to suspect it was one of the dealers Volvo sought to eliminate." Reeder filed suit against Volvo in February 2000, alleging losses attributable to Volvo's violation of the Arkansas Franchise Practices Act and the Robinson-Patman Act.

* * *

II

Section 2, "when originally enacted as part of the Clayton Act in 1914, was born of a desire by Congress to curb the use by financially powerful corporations of localized price-cutting tactics which had gravely impaired the competitive position of other sellers." *FTC v. Anheuser-Busch, Inc.,* 363 U.S. 536, 543, and n. 6, 80 S.Ct. 1267, 4 L.Ed.2d 1385 (1960). Augmenting that provision in 1936 with the Robinson-Patman Act, Congress sought to target the perceived harm to competition occasioned by powerful buyers, rather than sellers; specifically, Congress responded to the advent of large chainstores, enterprises with the clout to obtain lower prices for goods than smaller buyers could demand. * * *

Pursuant to § 4 of the Clayton Act, a private plaintiff may recover threefold for actual injury sustained as a result of a violation of the Robinson-Patman Act. See 15 U.S.C. § 15(a); *J. Truett Payne Co. v. Chrysler Motors Corp.,* 451 U.S. 557, 562, 101 S.Ct. 1923, 68 L.Ed.2d 442 (1981).

Mindful of the purposes of the Act and of the antitrust laws generally, we have explained that Robinson-Patman does not "ban all price differences charged to different purchasers of commodities of like grade and quality," *Brooke Group Ltd. v. Brown & Williamson Tobacco Corp.,* 509 U.S. 209, 220, 113 S.Ct. 2578, 125 L.Ed.2d 168 (1993); rather, the Act proscribes "price discrimination only to the extent that it threatens to injure competition," Our decisions describe three categories of competitive injury that may give rise to a Robinson-Patman Act claim: primary-line, secondary-line, and tertiary-line. Primary-line cases entail conduct—most conspicuously, predatory pricing—that injures competition at the level of the discriminating seller and its direct competitors. Secondary-line cases, of which this is one, involve price discrimination that injures competition among the discriminating seller's customers (here, Volvo's dealerships); cases in this category typically refer to "favored" and "disfavored" purchasers. Tertiary-line cases involve injury to competition at the level of the purchaser's customers.

To establish the secondary-line injury of which it complains, Reeder had to show that (1) the relevant Volvo truck sales were made in interstate commerce; (2) the trucks were of "like grade and quality"; (3) Volvo "discriminate[d] in price between" Reeder and another purchaser of Volvo trucks; and (4) "the effect of such discrimination may be . . . to injure, destroy, or prevent competition" to the advantage of a favored purchaser, *i.e.*, one who "receive[d] the benefit of such discrimination." 15 U.S.C. § 13(a). It is undisputed that Reeder has satisfied the first and second requirements. Volvo and the United States, as *amicus curiae,* maintain that Reeder cannot satisfy the third and fourth requirements, because Reeder has not identified any differentially-priced transaction in which it was both a "purchaser" under the Act and "in actual competition" with a favored purchaser for the same customer.

A hallmark of the requisite competitive injury, our decisions indicate, is the diversion of sales or profits from a disfavored purchaser to a favored purchaser. *FTC v. Sun Oil Co.,* 371 U.S. 505, 518–519, 83 S.Ct. 358, 9 L.Ed.2d 466 (1963) (evidence showed patronage shifted from disfavored dealers to favored dealers); *Falls City Industries, Inc. v. Vanco Beverage, Inc.,* 460 U.S. 428, 437–438, and n. 8, 103 S.Ct. 1282, 75 L.Ed.2d 174 (1983) (complaint "supported by direct evidence of diverted sales"). We have also recognized that a permissible inference of competitive injury may arise from evidence that a favored competitor received a significant price reduction over a substantial period of time. See *FTC v. Morton Salt Co.,* 334 U.S. 37, 49–51, 68 S.Ct. 822, 92 L.Ed. 1196 (1948); *Falls City Industries,* 460 U.S., at 435, 103 S.Ct. 1282. Absent actual competition with a favored Volvo dealer, however, Reeder cannot establish the competitive injury required under the Act.

III

The evidence Reeder offered at trial falls into three categories: (1) comparisons of concessions Reeder received for four successful bids against *non-Volvo* dealers, with larger concessions other successful Volvo dealers received for *different sales* on which Reeder did not bid (purchase-to-purchase comparisons); (2) comparisons of concessions offered to Reeder in connection with several unsuccessful bids against *non-Volvo* dealers, with greater concessions accorded other Volvo dealers who competed successfully for *different sales* on which Reeder did not bid (offer-to-purchase comparisons); and (3) evidence of two occasions on which Reeder bid against another Volvo dealer (head-to-head comparisons). The Court of Appeals concluded that Reeder demonstrated competitive injury under the Act because Reeder competed with favored purchasers "at the same functional level . . . and within the same geographic market." As we see it, however, selective comparisons of the kind Reeder presented do not show the injury to competition targeted by the Robinson-Patman Act.

A

Both the purchase-to-purchase and the offer-to-purchase comparisons fall short, for in none of the discrete instances on which Reeder relied did Reeder compete with beneficiaries of the alleged discrimination *for the same customer.* Nor did Reeder even attempt to show that the compared dealers were consistently favored vis-à-vis Reeder. Reeder simply paired occasions on which it competed with *non-Volvo* dealers for a sale to Customer A with instances in which other Volvo dealers competed with *non-Volvo* dealers for a sale to Customer B. The compared incidents were tied to no systematic study and were separated in time by as many as seven months.

We decline to permit an inference of competitive injury from evidence of such a mix-and-match, manipulable quality. No similar risk of manipulation occurs in cases kin to the chain-store paradigm. Here, there is no discrete "favored" dealer comparable to a chain store or a large independent department store-at least, Reeder's evidence is insufficient to support an inference of such a dealer or set of dealers. For all we know, Reeder, on occasion, might have gotten a better deal vis-à-vis one or more of the dealers in its comparisons.

* * *

B

Reeder did offer evidence of two instances in which it competed head to head with another Volvo dealer. When multiple dealers bid for the business of the *same* customer, only one dealer will win the business and thereafter purchase the supplier's product to fulfill its contractual commitment. Because Robinson-Patman "prohibits only discrimination 'between different *purchasers*,' " Volvo and the United States argue, the Act does not reach markets characterized by competitive bidding and special-order sales, as opposed to sales from inventory. We need not decide that question today. Assuming the Act applies to the head-to-head transactions, Reeder did not establish that it was *disfavored* vis-à-vis other Volvo dealers in the rare instances in which they competed for the same sale-let alone that the alleged discrimination was substantial. See 1 ABA Section of Antitrust Law, Antitrust Law Developments 478–479 (5th ed. 2002) ("No inference of injury to competition is permitted when the discrimination is not substantial."(collecting cases)).

Reeder's evidence showed loss of only one sale to another Volvo dealer, a sale of 12 trucks that would have generated $30,000 in gross profits for Reeder. Per its policy, Volvo initially offered Reeder and the other dealer the same concession. Volvo ultimately granted a larger concession to the other dealer, but only after it had won the bid. In the only other instance of head-to-head competition Reeder identified, Volvo increased Reeder's initial 17% discount to 18.9%, to match the discount offered to the other competing Volvo dealer; neither dealer won the bid. In short, if price discrimination between two purchasers existed at all, it was not of such magnitude as to affect substantially competition between Reeder and the "favored" Volvo dealer.

IV

Interbrand competition, our opinions affirm, is the "primary concern of antitrust law." *Continental T. V., Inc. v. GTE Sylvania, Inc.,* 433 U.S. 36, 51–52 n. 19, 97 S.Ct. 2549, 53 L.Ed.2d 568 (1977). The Robinson-Patman Act signals no large departure from that main concern. Even if the Act's text could be construed in the manner urged by Reeder and embraced by the Court of Appeals, we would resist interpretation geared more to the protection of existing *competitors* than to the stimulation of *competition*.[4] In the case before us, there is no evidence that any favored purchaser possesses market power, the allegedly favored purchasers are dealers with little resemblance to large independent department stores or chain operations, and the supplier's selective price discounting fosters competition among suppliers of different brands. See *id.,* at 51–52, 97 S.Ct. 2549 (observing that the market impact of a vertical practice, such as a change in a supplier's distribution system, may be a "simultaneous reduction of intrabrand competition and stimulation of interbrand competition"). By declining to extend Robinson-Patman's governance to such cases, we continue to construe the Act "consistently with broader policies of the antitrust laws." *Brooke Group,* 509 U.S., at 220, 113 S.Ct. 2578 (quoting *Great Atlantic & Pacific Tea Co. v. FTC,* 440 U.S. 69, 80 n. 13, 99 S.Ct. 925, 59 L.Ed.2d 153 (1979)); see *Automatic Canteen Co. of America v. FTC,* 346 U.S. 61, 63, 73 S.Ct. 1017, 97 L.Ed. 1454 (1953) (cautioning against Robinson-Patman constructions that "extend beyond the prohibitions of the Act and, in doing so, help give rise to a price uniformity and rigidity in open conflict with the purposes of other antitrust legislation").

* * *

For the reasons stated, the judgment of the Court of Appeals for the Eighth Circuit is reversed, and the case is remanded for further proceedings consistent with this opinion.

It is so ordered.

[The dissenting opinion of Mr. JUSTICE STEVENS, with whom Mr. JUSTICE THOMAS joined, has been omitted. Eds.]

Volvo Trucks is an illuminating study in the nuances of antitrust decision-making at the Supreme Court. As it once was with other, older and criticized antitrust precedent, the Court is formally respectful of

---

[4]   The dissent assails Volvo's decision to reduce the number of its dealers. But Robinson-Patman does not bar a manufacturer from restructuring its distribution networks to improve the efficiency of its operations. If Volvo did not honor its obligations to Reeder as its franchisee, "[a]ny remedy . . . lies in state laws addressing unfair competition and the rights of franchisees, not in the Robinson-Patman Act." Brief for United States as *Amicus Curiae* 28.

Morton Salt, acknowledging its holding and its long history. Yet the Court's narrow reading of the Robinson-Patman Act as it applied to bidding situations was hardly compelled. *Volvo Trucks* can fairly be read therefore, as grudgingly acknowledging the lenient competitive injury standard of the Robinson-Patman Act, but limiting the scope of its application.

The final section of its opinion, however, may have signaled a more radical departure from *Morton Salt*. There the Court stated that the Robinson-Patman Act signals no large departure from antitrust law's primary concern, interbrand competition. Drawing from precedent under the Sherman Act, especially *Brooke Group* and *Sylvania*, two of the pillars of modern antitrust analysis at the Court, it further cautioned that it would resist any interpretation of the Act geared more to the protection of existing competitors than to the stimulation of competition. It observed that in the instant case there was no evidence that any favored purchaser possesses market power. Moreover, it appeared that the supplier's selective price discounting fosters competition among suppliers of different brands. By declining to extend the Robinson-Patman Act to such cases, the Court reasoned, it aims to construe the Act consistently with the procompetitive polices of other antitrust laws. 546 U.S. at 180–81.

Dissenting, Justice Stevens, joined by Justice Thomas, argued that the Court's reading of the Act ignored decades of precedent—including *Morton Salt*—as well as the plain language of the statute. *Id.* at 873–76. Concluding, Stevens openly concedes that the Act may not make economic sense, yet he also argues that it is inappropriate for the Court to ignore its language and history simply because it may disagree with the Act's policy. *Id.* (Stevens, J., dissenting).

The decision, therefore, can be viewed both narrowly and broadly. Narrowly, the case holds that competitive bidding generally falls outside of the reach of the Robinson-Patman Act because it never involves two competing sales—just one. As the dissent points out, this was not a necessary reading of the Act. However, it is perhaps a reasonable one. More broadly, the decision seems intended to signal that a clear majority of the Court is willing to stretch the Act's language—and discount its origins and legislative history—in order to harmonize it with other antitrust laws, *i.e.*, to read it far more narrowly in order to dissipate its arguably unique purposes and potentially *anti*-competitive application. It remains to be seen how far the Court is willing to push its desire to harmonize the Robinson-Patman Act with other antitrust laws and whether it would do so in a more traditional secondary line case.

D. CONCLUSION

In this Chapter we have explored a range of distributional arrangements and relationships that can under some circumstances produce collusive or exclusionary anticompetitive effects. For the most part today, such relationships are treated leniently in recognition of their procompetitive potential. Although the categorization scheme that evolved over time generated a variety of fault lines that complicated the analysis of these kinds of arrangements and triggered disputes, the more recent cases have alleviated many of those tensions and moved the law towards a more uniformly economic approach. Greater reliance on economic concepts has brought greater clarity, but also some continuing challenges for the contemporary antitrust counselor.

E. PROBLEMS AND EXERCISES

Problem 6–1:
Pomegranate Apparel

Pomegranate Apparel Company of Oak Park, Illinois ("Pomegranate") sells sports apparel from several retail stores in and around Chicago, Illinois. One of its principal suppliers is M. Scott Reubens Sportswear, Inc. ("Reubens"), one of only three apparel manufacturers in the United States licensed by the Federal Football League ("FFL") to manufacture and sell clothing bearing the official colors, emblems and logos of FFL member teams. Total sales of authorized FFL clothing in the United States totaled $100 million in 2006, and Reubens' annual sales exceeded $50 million.

Reubens is the FFL's exclusive authorized distributor in seven Midwestern states, including Illinois and Wisconsin, where it distributes the apparel through a small group of hand-picked dealers, such as Pomegranate. All of Reubens's dealers sign written dealer agreements with Reubens. Those agreements provide, in pertinent part:

Uniform Dealership Agreement

* * *

15. Dealer agrees that it shall not, without the prior written consent of Reubens, sell authentic FFL satin jackets (hereafter "the licensed goods") from any location other than that specified in paragraph 29 of this Agreement;

16. Reubens agrees that it will not appoint any other dealer of the licensed goods within a five (5) mile radius of the location specified in paragraph 29 of this agreement;

17. Dealer also agrees:

(a) to maintain adequate displays of the licensed goods at the specified location;

(b) to hire sales personnel that are knowledgeable of the licensed goods and adequately trained in the fitting of the licensed goods at the specified location; and

(c) to advertise and promote said goods through local media including, but not limited to, newspapers, radio and television.

18. Dealer agrees that it will not sell the licensed goods to any person other than a retail customer.

19. Dealer agrees that it will promptly report the appearance in its assigned territory of any unlicensed, pirated or copied version of the licensed goods to Reubens.

* * *

Paragraph 29 of Pomegranate's agreement reads:

29. The authorized location for purposes of this agreement shall be: Pomegranate Apparel Company, 112 Jenny Place, Oak, Park, Illinois.

Reubens now believes that Pomegranate may be in violation of paragraphs 15 and 18 of the Uniform Dealership Agreement. That view is based on correspondence Reubens has received from two of its other authorized FFL apparel dealers, one in downtown Chicago, the other in nearby Milwaukee, Wisconsin. The letter from the Chicago dealer accused Pomegranate of selling satin jackets bearing FFL logos from Pomegranate's downtown Chicago store, which was located across the street from another Reubens dealer. A complaint from Reubens's licensed dealer in Wisconsin accuses Pomegranate of transhipping satin jackets from Illinois to an unlicensed retailer in Milwaukee, Wisconsin, where they were sold in direct competition with Reubens's licensed dealer.

Although Pomegranate does not contest Reubens's accusations, it asserts that the real reason for the complaints from the Chicago and Milwaukee dealers is the prices it charged, which were significantly below Reubens's suggested retail prices. According to Pomegranate, since it refurbished and expanded its two stores and installed a state of the art computerized inventory control and accounting system, its costs decreased by almost 20%, allowing it to reduce its prices on all of its apparel, including the satin jackets. Pomegranate also maintains that none of the twelve other Reubens dealers it contacted in the midwest since its termination would agree to sell officially licensed satin jackets to it. A random investigation of Reubens's dealers in three metropolitan areas in the midwest finds that, during the football season, the satin jackets typically sell at a price equal to or greater than the manufacturer's suggested retail price approximately 85% of the time.

Reubens has provided you with two letters, one from its Chicago dealer and one from its Milwaukee dealer, complaining about competition from Pomegranate. Both letters comment at length on the "low prices" at which the jackets were being sold. They also question whether the jackets are "authentic." One is captioned "Notice of Incident of Design Piracy Pursuant to Paragraph 19 of the Uniform Dealership Agreement." Both dealers assert they assumed that Pomegranate was selling unlicensed merchandise, because each was "the only dealer authorized to sell the jackets" in its specified territories. Reubens also mentions that Pomegranate's stores never lived up to paragraph 17 of the Uniform Dealer Agreement. The letters also state, in almost identical language, that "these problems could be eliminated if you would just set the minimum prices for all of us."

How would you assess the antitrust risks associated with: (1) terminating Pomegranate as a Reubens dealer; and/or (2) adopting a uniform set of resale prices for all FFL merchandise sold by Reubens to its Midwestern dealers, including Pomegranate?

Problem 6–2:
Printing Products Corporation

Printing Products Corp. ("PPC") is a U.S. manufacturer of computer printers, facsimile machines, scanners, and photocopying equipment and is about to introduce it's a new line of combination printer/copier/facsimile machines. At one time, PPC was a dominant player in the market for photocopying machines, and later expanded its operations into printers and ultimately scanners and facsimile machines. It also competes in the sale of combination machines, which are popular with more cost-conscious purchasers, such as small businesses and individuals. These devices combine the capabilities of printers, copiers, scanners, and facsimile machines into a single machine, generally at a much lower cost to the purchaser than two or three separate machines. The profitability of sales of combination machines, however, is very limited. Given the intense competition PPC faces from several other domestic and foreign brands, the machines themselves are sold at prices very close to their costs.

Like dedicated machines, each combination machine is sold with one installed toner cartridge, which permits the actual printing. The ink supply in those toner cartridges is finite, and once it has been exhausted the cartridge must be replaced. Replacement cartridges must be of the design specified for each particular model of machine, and can cost as much as 25% of the price of the machine, itself. PPC sells replacement cartridges. It also has a recycling program, whereby used cartridges can be returned to PPC for refurbishing and reloading. They are thereafter sold as a slightly less expensive alternative to new replacement cartridges. As a general rule, sales of recycled and replacement cartridges are very profitable for PPC and others.

In recent years, several firms have begun to compete with PPC and the other manufacturers in the sale of replacement and recycled cartridges. Typically, like the machine manufacturers, these firms do not fabricate cartridges themselves, but purchase them from cartridge manufacturers, often the very same suppliers used by the machine manufacturers, and offer free shipping to consumers willing to return empty cartridges for recycling.

PPC has designed a new toner cartridge to accompany its latest combination machine model. More ink efficient and less costly to produce, the new cartridge will be produced for PPC by Machine Cartridge Corp. ("MCC"), a manufacturer of original equipment and replacement cartridges. In connection with the planned introduction of the new machine and cartridge, PPC is considering the following new distribution strategies.

First, PPC is currently negotiating a contract with MCC, pursuant to which MCC would supply all of PPC's requirements of new, recycled, and replacement cartridges for the next three years. In addition, the contract would prohibit MCC from selling recycled or replacement cartridges for the new machines to any other manufacturer or cartridge supplier for the duration of the contract. The contract cannot be cancelled in its first year. It can be cancelled thereafter by either party, but only for "good cause shown" and only with six (6) months prior written notice.

Second, PPC proposes that the three-year warranty to customers of the new PPC combination model include the following provision:

C. VOIDING OF WARRANTY. If, at any time during the warranty period, customer uses a toner cartridge other than an unmodified new, replacement or recycled cartridge purchased from PPC, or if it uses a toner cartridge that has been modified in any way from its original configuration, THIS WARRANTY SHALL BE VOID.

What antitrust issues, if any, are posed by each aspect of PPC's proposed distribution strategy?

CHAPTER 7

INNOVATION, INTELLECTUAL PROPERTY, AND THE "NEW ECONOMY"

■ ■ ■

INTRODUCTION

Antitrust doctrine is to a significant extent a product of its times—and times change. Industries and industry practices change, economic learning changes, and attitudes about government regulation change. Such changes can spark antitrust scrutiny, particularly when they affect consumers and rivals, which they often do. It is no accident, for example, that in its formative years, antitrust enforcement focused on industries such as steel, oil, tobacco, and railroads—the high-tech markets of the nineteenth century—whereas attention now has turned to industries such as health care and the information and other technology industries of today's "New Economy." The development of competition law has generally corresponded with advances in our economic understanding. This relationship has also influenced the antitrust analysis of high-tech markets and business practices involving intellectual property.

This Chapter explores the relationship between antitrust and the New Economy. Although when we speak of today's New Economy we refer broadly to the information-age typified by the rise of computers, telecommunications, and the Internet, in truth, today's New Economy is but one example of a broader phenomenon. At least since the dawn of the industrial age, some sectors of the economy are almost always undergoing significant change as a consequence of technological evolution and revolution. "New" economies are almost always being created and destroyed in various industries at various times.

The birth of new economies is triggered by "innovation." Innovation can take the form of new products and services, new processes for producing products, new methods of assembling and distributing those products, and new business models, sometimes facilitated by technology. It can lead to the emergence of entirely new industries and to the demise of others. Innovation can also take the form of new relationships among rivals and can spawn new strategies by entrants and incumbents alike. Finally, innovation can take the form of "intellectual property" ("IP")—patents, copyrights, know-how, and to a lesser extent, trademarks and trade names. Indeed, IP laws exist to reward innovation, thereby creating an incentive to its creation. They reflect a philosophy that associates innovation through the creation of IP with progress and the public good. IP laws confer on the owners of IP certain "intellectual property rights" ("IPRs"), the most critical of which is the right to exclude others from using the IP for some period of time.

Dynamic economies demand adaptable principles and rules of competition and intellectual property. The constant clash of old and new has persistently triggered antitrust challenges and ensured that antitrust plays a critical role in protecting the process of innovation. But has antitrust proved adaptable enough to changing times? Today, the information age challenges antitrust doctrine and institutions to adapt to the hastening pace of change.

A comprehensive examination of the interaction of antitrust and innovation, technology, and intellectual property, however, could fill an entire volume. Our goal in this Chapter is more modest: to use a limited selection of illustrative issues and topics to introduce some of the many ways in which antitrust laws and institutions have adapted to change. We begin in Sidebar 7–1 with an overview of the economic principles that distinguish today's New Economy. Consistent with the general approach of the Casebook, we will then turn to an examination of the various types of both collusive and exclusionary conduct that may involve intellectual property and the suppression of innovation.

Sidebar 7–1:
Antitrust Principles and the "New Economy"[a]

The term "New Economy" lost some of its cachet after the boom years of the 1990s ended with a technology bust. Still, one can point to a number of distinct features common to many high-technology markets in the information age. In short, new economies can be characterized by new economics. These features affect how virtually all of the core concepts of antitrust, including market power, entry, efficiency, and anti-competitive effects, apply in information-based sectors of the economy. Moreover, as this Sidebar will explain, the application of antitrust to high-technology markets today can be rationalized around a handful of core principles.

What Makes the "New Economy" New?

Relationship of Marginal and Fixed Costs. First, marginal costs are often low relative to fixed costs of production (in the sense that most of the costs of production are fixed and marginal costs are not increasing with output). A new software

---

[a] This Sidebar was adapted in part from Jonathan B. Baker, *Can Antitrust Keep Up?: Competition Policy in High-Tech Markets*, BROOKINGS REV. 16 (Winter 2001), http://www. brookings.edu/research/articles/2001/12/winter-regulation-baker

product may cost millions of dollars to develop, but each additional unit sold may cost only pennies to produce if distributed by disk, and even less if distributed via the Internet. And software is not the sole example—digital media, including books, music, and video, is also nearly costless to distribute online, especially given the proliferation of websites such as Amazon, Netflix, and YouTube. In such industries, firms would lose money if they were led by rivalry to reduce prices across-the-board and permanently to marginal cost—they would never recover their fixed costs. Accordingly, marginal cost pricing cannot be the competitive equilibrium in such markets—the competitive price must be higher—if firms are to be induced to enter and remain in the industry. In contrast, perfect competition leads to marginal cost pricing when marginal costs are increasing with output and variable costs are substantial relative to fixed costs.[b]

As you will recall, "market power" is the power to profitably raise or maintain the market price above the competitive level for a significant period of time. Often, as we have generally assumed in this Casebook, "the competitive level" is best understood as referring to the marginal cost of expanding output by industry participants. To facilitate the evaluation of allegedly anticompetitive conduct in information industries, however, it is necessary to recognize that in such settings, "competitive price" must be defined differently.

What should we think of as the "competitive price" in a high-fixed cost, low-marginal cost industry? Economists most often suggest thinking of competition in such settings as a hypothetical market with "free entry," by which a new rival would enter so long as price exceeds its *average* cost.[c] From this perspective, the competitive price in a high fixed cost, low marginal cost industry may be equated with *entrant average cost* for an entrant with a reasonable and practical entry plan, which is likely to be sufficient to keep price from rising. With free entry, after all, price could not rise above the entrant's

---

[b] New Economy industries are not unique in having this type of cost structure. The cost of filling an otherwise empty seat in a movie theater may be very small, and the cost of adding a passenger to an aircraft to fill a seat that would otherwise go empty might literally be peanuts. But low marginal costs of expanding output are a particularly distinctive feature of information industries, which are mainstays of the high-technology sector today.

[c] Under the free entry assumption, the entrant does not worry about the issues raised by the entry "likelihood" analysis in the merger setting. It does not fear that its additional output will depress the market price, making it unable to recover its sunk expenditures, nor worry that aggressive incumbent reactions to its entry might depress price further.

average cost without attracting new competition.[d] Entrant average cost will generally exceed incumbent firm marginal cost in industries in which firms experience high fixed costs and low marginal costs.

Of course, many firms sell multiple products, charge different prices to different customers, or allow prices to vary over time. In markets where these practices are common, it is difficult to speak of a single competitive "price." Firms cover the fixed costs for their operations as a whole, but do so with high prices to some customers, on some products or at some times, and low prices in other cases. The definition of competition set forth above naturally generalizes. Under such circumstances— high fixed-cost, low marginal cost sellers in industries with multi-product sellers, firms that discriminate in price, or price promotions—prices can be thought of as competitive if *on average* they do not exceed entrant average cost. We employed a similar analysis in describing what market power might mean among firms that discriminate on price in Chapter 4. (*See supra* Sidebar 4–5.)

Shifting Market Boundaries. The second feature common to many high-technology industries is that product boundaries change rapidly. Product upgrades may be common, both to improve quality and to add features, and new generations of a product may be sold before old generations have been withdrawn. These settings may well add complexity to market definition in practice, but they do not change the conceptual task: to identify a collection of products and locations that would constitute a valuable monopoly, notwithstanding buyer incentives to substitute alternatives in the event price were to rise. Moreover, innovation may come from unlikely sources. For example, which telephone wire manufacturers would have predicted that their product would be challenged by new fiber optic lines developed by the glass industry? Possibilities such as these may make entry analysis less certain, but courts are unlikely to presume that entry is easy in high-technology markets without analysis of the best available evidence.

Rapid product and process innovation creates another dilemma for antitrust enforcement: high-technology industries can be highly innovative sectors important to economic growth. As we will see later in this Chapter, courts have often been reluctant to interfere with markets that are producing new and

---

[d]   The entrant's average cost can be understood as the industry's marginal cost of expanding output when the industry performs competitively by virtue of free entry. In this sense, "the competitive price" defined for a high-fixed cost, low-marginal cost industry continues to be a form of marginal cost pricing.

better products, even when confronted by serious arguments that the dominant firms have improperly acted to exclude rivals that seek to supplant the leading firm with better products. Might this attitude explain the deference often given by the courts to firms said to have harmed competition through exclusionary new product design?

Network Externalities. Third, many high-technology markets are characterized by *network externalities* (also termed "demand-side scale economies"). When a product or service exhibits network externalities, its value to a buyer is greater when some other buyer also purchases the product or service—and the more buyers there are, the more significant the network externality. If these network externalities are not internalized by market participants, such as consumers or network owners, they are often termed "network effects."[e] Network externalities and effects are often especially important in communications or computer operating system software. The value of a particular cell phone service, for example, would be very limited if it only facilitated calls to other subscribers of the same service. But, as the number of subscribers increases, the value of the service to *all* subscribers increases. The more subscribers there are on the "network," the more valuable it becomes to join, and the more likely it is that others will subscribe as well. Network effects can also be indirect. The value of particular software programs for word processing or spreadsheets, for example, increases for a firm if its suppliers and customers use similar software, making it easier to share information and for new employees to be trained to use it. Both direct and indirect network effects are positive demand-side externalities that, when internalized, benefit buyers. Though, as we shall see, direct and indirect networks can also give rise to competitive concerns.

Markets with strong network effects are frequently characterized by "tipping." A firm that is expected to become dominant, perhaps after it achieves a small advantage in early competition, may find that new buyers disproportionately select its product. The market may quickly establish such a firm as the winner of what is effectively a standard-setting competition. Such competition is typically winner-take-most or winner-take-all, and for good reason: buyers benefit from joining the network of buyers patronizing the winner.

---

[e] On the distinction between network externalities and network effects, see S.J. Liebowitz & Stephen E. Margolis, *Network Externality: An Uncommon Tragedy*, 8 J. Econ. Persp. 133 (1994).

Once a market tips, however, it becomes harder for a rival to compete, even with a better product. Some losers nevertheless may remain in the market, profitably serving small groups of buyers whose preferences for variety or the rival's unique features are so strong as to justify the sacrifice of not joining the network. To dislodge an industry leader in a market with strong network effects, however, the entrant may need to develop a dramatically improved new product that "leapfrogs" the market leader's technology. Recognizing this, firms often compete very aggressively to become the winner— even giving away their products. Recall from our discussion of the *Microsoft* case in Chapter 4 that Microsoft and Netscape were led to do so with their Internet browsers in the 1990s.

The possibility that a market may quickly tip, and the difficulty of dislodging a winner once it does so, creates special problems for antitrust enforcement. Anticompetitive practices during the period in which firms are competing aggressively to become the winner may lead the market to tip to the violator, not because it has better or cheaper products, but because it found a way to significantly impair or exclude its rivals through exclusionary conduct. By the time a court reaches a verdict, however, it may be too late to restore the lost competition. Buyers have selected a dominant product or standard and have made investments to join the winner's installed base that may be costly and difficult to dislodge. It may be especially challenging to design a remedy that restores competition to its pre-tipping state without harming the buyers the remedy aims to help and because the rivals may have exited the market.

Five Antitrust Principles for Addressing Competition in High-Technology Markets

Antitrust's contemporary engagement with high-technology markets is best understood as based upon five core principles that arguably define an emerging intellectual consensus. As you read the materials in this Chapter, consider whether these five principles are reflected in the modern cases, and whether they are (or should be) more contested than the claim of intellectual consensus we make here would suggest.

1. Intellectual Property is Property. The first principle is that for antitrust purposes, intellectual property is just another form of property. A high-technology firm's patents and copyrights are no different from its physical property, its plants and equipment. That it may be easier to misappropriate many forms of intellectual property than to steal physical products is no reason to make intellectual property more or less suspect under the antitrust laws than any other form of property.

Mergers provide an example. If Coke were to acquire Pepsi, or United Airlines were to acquire Delta, the transaction would surely trigger an antitrust investigation, because the products and services sold by the acquired firm are likely important substitutes to customers of the acquiring firm. The analysis is similar when the key assets of the firms are intellectual property rights. Antitrust enforcers would also be skeptical if a firm that owns the rights to one drug for treating a disease were to acquire a firm with the rights to the only other drug with a similar use, for example, or if the merging firms were among a small number of rivals in a technology market. Moreover, as this Chapter makes clear, the examples extend throughout antitrust law. The Justice Department's analysis of a "patent pool" among owners of competing patents follows the general template for the antitrust analysis of collaboration among competitors. And the D.C. Circuit's analysis in *Microsoft* of exclusionary conduct involving high-technology products like Internet browsers resembled the Supreme Court's analysis of exclusionary conduct involving lower-tech advertising in *Lorain Journal* (*See supra* Chapter 4).

2. Competition Promotes Innovation. The second principle, that competition promotes innovation, recognizes that firms have a powerful incentive to gain an advantage over their rivals by cutting costs or by being first with new products or product improvements. Just as competition encourages firms to increase output and lower prices, it also leads firms to improve product quality and service, develop new products, and introduce new methods of production and distribution that lower cost. For example, in many of the leading oligopolistic sectors of the economy, including the computer industry, innovation competition, not price competition, is the "prime competitive weapon" and that competition is an enormous engine for economic-growth. WILLIAM J. BAUMOL, THE FREE-MARKET INNOVATION MACHINE: ANALYZING THE GROWTH MIRACLE OF CAPITALISM 4 (2002).

An important question these observations raise asks whether, and if so how, different market structures may affect innovation—whether certain market structures are more likely to foster or to hinder innovation. The extensive economic literature relating market structure to investments in research and development and the prospects for innovation is arguably consistent with the view that competition promotes innovation, but it also suggests ways in which non-competitive market structures can also do so.

The question related to the importance of competition for innovation most studied by economists asks whether innovation tends to increase or decrease as the number of firms in the market declines. On the one hand, a monopolist may have less incentive to innovate than would competitors, because the monopolist may have little to gain and more to lose—innovating could be quite costly, and a monopolist, by definition, already has most of the business there is to get. *See* Kenneth J. Arrow, *Economic Welfare and the Allocation of Resources for Innovation*, *in* THE RATE AND DIRECTION OF INVENTIVE ACTIVITY 609–25 (Nat'l Bureau of Econ. Research ed., 1962). Put differently, competition encourages innovation because firms have a strong incentive to develop new, better, or less expensive products in order to escape competition, i.e. to succeed and perhaps surmount their rivals. Monopoly may also discourage innovation because a monopolist might not want to risk undermining the success of its own products, and because its employees may resist innovations that would threaten the existing organizational structure.

On the other hand, some argue that monopoly may instead encourage innovation, as a monopolist may have greater access to low-cost internal finance and may be better able to take advantage of scale economies in research and development and to appropriate the full value of its new ideas. *See* JOSEPH SCHUMPETER, CAPITALISM, SOCIALISM, AND DEMOCRACY 81–106 (1942); Morton I. Kamien, *Market Structure and Innovation Revisited*, 1 JAPAN & WORLD ECON. 331 (1989). One way to harmonize a monopolist's incentive to innovate with the monopolist's disincentive to innovate resulting from its pre-innovation profits is to suppose that many industries exhibit a form of Schumpeterian "creative destruction," by which a temporary monopolist is supplanted by another that has developed an improved product or production process. LUÍS M.B. CABRAL, INTRODUCTION TO INDUSTRIAL ORGANIZATION 295 (2000). The credible threat of being supplanted—leapfrogged— may provide a monopolist with an incentive to innovate. The Schumpeterian concern for appropriability recognizes that the prospect of post-innovation competition discourages innovation. Antitrust law asks whether or when allowing a pre-innovation monopoly is the best way to alleviate that disincentive. *See* Jonathan B. Baker, *Evaluating Appropriability Defenses for the*

*Exclusionary Conduct of Dominant Firms in Innovative
Industries*, 80 ANTITRUST L.J. 431 (2016).

Consensus on which of these competing theories is better
supported by data has not been reached. Some recent evidence
is arguably consistent with the view that competition promotes
innovation once the degree of appropriability across industries
is controlled for.[f]

Recent theoretical work about the determinants of
innovative effort and the prospects for innovation success has
begun to consider the significance of strategic behavior in
market structures not at the extremes of monopoly or
competition. From this work, a number of important concepts
relating competition and innovation have emerged.

- **Competition in innovation itself**—that is,
  competition among firms seeking to develop the
  same new product or process—**encourages
  innovation**.

- **Competition among rivals producing an
  existing product encourages those firms to
  find ways to lower costs, improve quality, or
  develop better products**. Firms engage in R &
  D because innovation may allow them to escape
  competition, and thus earn greater profits. By
  contrast, a firm that faces less competition has
  less need to work hard to escape competition.

- **Firms that expect to face more product
  market competition after innovating have
  less incentive to invest in R & D**. A firm has
  less incentive to innovate in the first place if doing
  so would not allow it to profit by escaping
  competition, but would instead be expected to
  throw it into a pool with sharks, causing it to
  profit less from R & D. This incentive may
  encourage firms introducing new products to seek
  to differentiate them from those of their rivals, as
  differentiated products often face less post-
  innovation product market competition than do
  products similar to those sold by other firms.

---

[f]   For further discussion of this evidence, see Jonathan B. Baker, *Beyond Schumpeter vs.
Arrow: How Antitrust Fosters Innovation*, 74 ANTITRUST L.J. 575 (2007); Carl Shapiro, *Competition
and Innovation: Did Arrow Hit the Bull's Eye?*, in THE RATE AND DIRECTION OF INVENTIVE
ACTIVITY REVISITED 361 (Josh Lerner & Scott Stern, eds. 2012). *But see* Philippe Aghion et al.,
Competition and Innovation: An Inverted-U Relationship, 120 Q.J. ECON. 701 (2005) (providing
evidence that oligopoly market structures maximize innovation).

- **A firm will have an extra incentive to innovate if in doing so it can discourage potential rivals from investing in R & D.** This preemption incentive arises because an innovating firm may be able to benefit from its investments in R & D not simply through its ability to offer buyers better or cheaper products, but also by discouraging potential rivals from innovating.
- **Firms may enhance their innovation capabilities by combining complementary assets, as through merger, joint venture, or contract.**

Accordingly, looking solely to economic theory and without regard to the facts of any specific industry, antitrust enforcement that would restrict the conduct of a dominant firm could, on balance, enhance or reduce aggregate industry innovation in general. The most direct effects likely pull in opposite ways: decreasing the incentive of the dominant firm to innovate, while increasing the incentive of fringe firms to innovate. However, it has been suggested that when innovation competition is winner-take-most or winner-take-all, as when network effects are important or the first to invent obtains broad intellectual property protection, the dominant firm's innovation incentives are unlikely to decline substantially because of antitrust intervention against the dominant firm. This is because the prize to innovation, from the point of view of the dominant firm, is likely to be large whether or not the antitrust laws prohibit monopolization. If so, antitrust enforcement could, on balance, promote industry innovation in the aggregate in winner-take-most markets characterized by a dominant firm and competitive fringe. For an argument that antitrust rules and enforcement today are appropriately focused to promote innovation, see Jonathan B. Baker, *Beyond Schumpeter vs. Arrow: How Antitrust Fosters Innovation*, 74 ANTITRUST L.J. 575 (2007).

Moreover, broad IPRs can offer rich rewards to initial innovation, but they may also impede follow-on innovation. For this reason, some might seek to justify a policy of fostering competition among owners of intellectual property solely in terms of its benefits in encouraging innovation, even ignoring consumer benefits from limiting the exercise of monopoly power.

3. *Network Effects Heighten the Concern with Exclusion.* The third core principle is that network effects increase the antitrust concern with anticompetitive exclusion. As already noted in our discussion above of network externalities, when network effects are important, the market may quickly tip to select a winner of what is effectively a winner-take-most or winner-take-all standard-setting competition, and that winner may be difficult to dislodge. If competition problems are not identified until after buyers have committed to the winning standard, it may be difficult to restore competition through an antitrust remedy. Accordingly, in markets with network effects, antitrust enforcers may believe they need to move rapidly once they identify a competitive problem in order to make relief meaningful.

But enforcement agencies, cognizant of this difficulty, may be led to take action before all the facts are clear, raising the risks of error. Firms that initially obtain very high market shares in a market characterized by network effects do not necessarily obtain durable monopolies—for example, Yahoo was the leading internet search engine over a decade ago, but far from becoming dominant, it was quickly surpassed by Google. For an argument that antitrust enforcement is unnecessary in markets where network externalities are important because they are likely to be internalized by consumers or network owners, see Daniel F. Spulber, *Consumer Coordination in the Small and in the Large: Implications for Antitrust in Markets with Network Effects*, 4 J. COMPETITION L. & ECON. 207 (2008).

4. *Rapid Information Exchange Could Benefit or Harm Competition.* The fourth key principle underlying contemporary antitrust enforcement in high-technology markets is that rapid information exchange need not create a perfectly competitive market. The vision of "frictionless competition" from rapid information exchange is a powerful one. What could be more procompetitive than the instant and universal exchange of enormous amounts of market and product information? Information exchange can dramatically reduce a buyer's transactions costs of search and help firms make better production and pricing decisions. In addition, Internet access and advertising could reduce the sunk costs of entry, also making markets more competitive. For these reasons, the rapid information exchange made possible by the Internet is likely, in general, a strongly procompetitive force, helping buyers obtain better and cheaper products.

But not always. Entry in the world of electronic commerce is not necessarily as easy as going online to create a website. The entrant must establish a reputation, both for high-quality products and for fair business practices. Furthermore, rapid information exchange could lead to higher-than competitive prices if it gives sellers a better way to reach an anticompetitive consensus on prices and market shares, or if it makes it easy for price-fixing rivals to detect cheating on that consensus. *See* Jonathan B. Baker, *Identifying Horizontal Price Fixing in the Electronic Marketplace*, 65 ANTITRUST L.J. 41 (1996); Ariel Ezrachi & Maurice E. Stucke, *Artificial Intelligence & Collusion: When Computers Inhibit Competition* (Apr. 8, 2015), http://ssrn.com/abstract=2591874.

5.   *Most Business Conduct Involving Innovation Does Not Harm Competition.* The final core principle shaping antitrust's perspective on competition in the high-technology sector is that most business conduct involving innovation by high-technology firms is procompetitive or competitively benign. To be sure, antitrust enforcers pay attention to emerging markets. When today's "Old Economy" industries like oil refining, steelmaking, and aluminum production were high-technology, they too were an appropriate focus for federal antitrust activity. But relative to the scope of high-technology markets in the economy, both yesterday and today, antitrust enforcement in the high-technology sector has been both measured and infrequent. Indeed, the antitrust enforcement agencies and the courts have long recognized the importance of innovation, the procompetitive benefits of most R & D collaborations, and the strong innovation record of many firms with large market shares. There are many market leaders whose market conduct does not seem to attract antitrust litigation.

In summary, under the contemporary perspective on competition and antitrust enforcement in high-technology markets—the five principles highlighted above—antitrust enforcement does not supplant the market. The principles support the market by enlisting competition in the service of promoting innovation. Under this view, antitrust is far from irrelevant to high-technology industries. Competition is vital to ensuring the continued rapid pace of innovation, and antitrust remains as essential as it always has been to preserving competition.

How did the issues raised in this Sidebar play out in the *Microsoft* litigation, which we studied in Chapter 4? Is platform software (computer operating systems) a high-fixed cost, low-marginal cost industry? If so, did the nature of the industry make it difficult for the economic experts and the court to identify the competitive price and determine whether Microsoft exercised market power? Did the speed of product upgrades and innovations in the software industry make it hard for the experts and the court to define the boundaries of the product market? Were the software products at issue in the case, including computer operating systems and Internet browsers, characterized by strong network effects? If so, did the network effects increase the antitrust concern with exclusion? Make relief more difficult? Did the outcome in *Microsoft* suggest that courts and antitrust enforcers will scrutinize business conduct involving innovation closely in the future, or that antitrust's engagement with the high-technology sector will continue to be both measured and infrequent? What lessons might we draw from that case, and the issues raised in this Sidebar, that will help us to understand and analyze competition issues that may arise in the context of today's mobile device operating systems and Internet search engines?

A. ANTITRUST AND INNOVATION

Competition in most product markets is rarely static. Even in markets featuring products with relatively stable designs and quality characteristics, existing producers continue to offer refinements to the state of the art, and other firms attempt to devise new approaches to satisfying the same consumer needs. Innovation in developing and improving products supplies an unequaled source of vitality to the market system. In 1942, in perhaps the most famous statement of this view, Joseph Schumpeter declared that the "competition that counts" is "the competition from the new commodity, the new technology, the new source of supply, the new type of organization * * *—competition which commands a decisive cost or quality advantage and which strikes not at the margins of the profits and the outputs of the existing firms but at their foundations and their very lives." To survive in a capitalist system, he argued, incumbent firms must withstand a "perennial gale of competition" in the form of "the new consumers' goods, the new methods of production or transportation, the new markets, the new forms of industrial organization." JOSEPH A. SCHUMPETER, CAPITALISM, SOCIALISM AND DEMOCRACY 83–84 (1942).

We focus here upon the antitrust analysis of business practices that may suppress innovation. An important question this discussion raises is how antitrust enforcement can be used as a tool to foster innovation in dynamic high-tech markets, without unduly impeding it. As Schumpeter observed, "innovation," whether in products, services, or processes of production and distribution, can itself be a substantial source of competitive vigor. Current markets for research and development, for instance, can be vital and characterized by intense rivalry. Conduct that impairs or compromises that rivalry, therefore, can pose a significant competitive threat to current markets. For example, some empirical research indicates research joint ventures may be used to facilitate collusion. *See* Michelle Goeree & Eric Helland, *Do Research Joint Ventures Serve a Collusive Function?*, TWELFTH CEPR/JIE CONF. APPLIED INDUS. ORG. (2011). What is the appropriate role of antitrust in restoring or maintaining this form of competition without threatening rapid innovation?

Not all innovation, however, concerns current markets. Some innovation will be directed at developing future products or processes in either existing markets or markets yet to emerge. As one court has observed:

> When an established producer of conventional products enters into a conspiracy to suppress a competitor's new and innovative product, that conspiracy will give rise to liability under sections 1 and 2 [of the Sherman Act]—assuming all of the other elements of the causes of action under those sections are present.

Impro Products, Inc. v. Herrick, 715 F.2d 1267, 1273 (8th Cir. 1983). *See also SD3, LLC v. Black & Decker, Inc.*, 801 F.3d 412 (4th Cir. 2015) (plaintiff adequately stated a claim that manufacturers conspired to boycott new technology). Note the court's qualification, however, that prohibition of efforts to suppress innovation assumes that "all of the other elements of the causes of action under those sections are present." Traditional approaches to antitrust analysis may make it difficult to do so, however, in the case of emerging or developing markets. For example, it can be difficult to predict the future effects of innovation-inhibiting conduct on these kinds of potential or nascent markets for several reasons. Innovation often represents future competitive potential only. Some, perhaps most, innovations fail or have little competitive effect. If development of a future product is somehow suppressed before those effects can be observed, how can courts or agencies accurately predict whether the product would have succeeded, or even have made it to the market at all? On the other hand, as the D.C. Circuit observed in the *Microsoft* case: "it would be inimical to the purpose of the Sherman Act to allow monopolists free reign to squash nascent, albeit unproven, competitors at will—particularly in industries marked by rapid technological advance and frequent paradigm shifts." *Microsoft*, 253 F.3d at 375.

Moreover, private plaintiffs may be hard-pressed to establish antitrust injury when the threat to competition is deemed speculative. Although that might portend a greater role for government enforcement, the government too can face difficult questions of proof when it seeks to demonstrate that consumers have been deprived of the possibility of future products never born due to allegedly anticompetitive conduct. How certain must the prediction be that the suppressed or impaired new technology would have overtaken the old before this standard can be satisfied?

Although there are a number of cases involving alleged efforts by a firm or firms to suppress innovation, comprehensive discussions of it are notably lacking. We will explore the phenomenon, therefore, by looking at several areas of concern suggested by the cases. Later in this Chapter, we will look more specifically at the relationship between IPRs, such as patents and copyrights, which often embody innovation and antitrust. Before proceeding, however, we need to more carefully consider the relationship of innovation to competition and to IP.

NOTE ON INNOVATION AND THE SCOPE OF INTELLECTUAL PROPERTY PROTECTION

As should already be apparent, innovation is an extremely important economic activity. Because of new products and improvements to production processes and product design, many people in the most developed nations of the world are dramatically healthier and wealthier than their ancestors. Think, for example, of auto and air travel; consumer electronics; air conditioning and refrigeration; the food for sale year round in the supermarket; antibiotics and medical imaging; and the goods and services available in department stores, catalogs, and on the Internet. All these are the product of innovation over time. If anything, innovation likely occurs less frequently than would be socially optimal given its costs and the opportunities for doing so. Studies of the return to research and development find that the return to society is more than double the return to the firms making the investment, suggesting that private markets provide less than the optimal incentive to innovate.

From an economic perspective, the benefits of intellectual property protection result from their tendency to generate incentives to innovate. Absent IPRs, a free rider problem would inhibit much innovative effort. An inventor or firm would not be expected to put much effort into R & D if rivals could quickly and inexpensively copy new ideas. Intellectual property rights, including patents and trade secrets, address this possible market failure, and so enhance incentives to innovate by protecting the inventor's ability to appropriate the benefits of new inventions. Clear intellectual property rights also encourage economic exchange in the form of commercialization innovation and facilitating its dispersion across the economy.

Intellectual property rights are not the only way to ensure that an innovator can appropriate the benefits of its new ideas, however. When intellectual property protections are imperfect, a firm with a monopoly in existing products may be able to exploit that position to protect its gains from innovation. In particular, intellectual property laws do not directly protect knowledge—meaning that valuable information relating to the benefits of an innovation may be diffused to rivals. Accordingly, a monopolist may more fully appropriate the benefits of its innovative investments than could a smaller firm, because its large market share necessarily reduces the opportunities for information to flow to competitors. *See* Richard J. Gilbert & Steven C. Sunshine, *Incorporating Dynamic Efficiency Concerns in Merger Analysis: The Use of Innovation Markets*, 63 ANTITRUST L.J. 569 (1995).

Moreover, even when intellectual property protections are critical for protecting an innovator's ability to profit from its new ideas, more extensive intellectual property rights would not necessarily generate more new products or other innovation. A potential problem arises because much, if not all, innovation is cumulative. Policies that broaden intellectual property protections might enhance the incentives for initial innovation, but in doing so, they may discourage follow-on innovation. When intellectual property protections are broad, an owner of the IPRs may have strong incentives to develop product improvements, but others may not. For anyone else, the only way to profit from a product enhancement is to sell it to a single buyer, the initial innovator. In order to avoid placing themselves in a disadvantageous bargaining situation, third parties may prefer to channel their innovation efforts elsewhere.

The resulting tradeoff has been described succinctly in testimony by Nobel Prize-winning economist Joseph E. Stiglitz, then a member of President Bill Clinton's Council of Economic Advisers:

> We often talk about how important patents are to promote innovation, because without patents, people don't appropriate the returns to their innovation activity, and I certainly very strongly subscribe to that. The key importance of intellectual property rights is [that they are] part of the mechanism that the market economy has to stimulate [innovation]. * * * On the other hand, some people jump from that to the conclusion that the broader the patent rights are, the better it is for innovation, and that isn't always correct, because we have an innovation system in which one innovation builds on another. If you get monopoly rights down at the bottom, you may stifle competition that uses those patents later on, and so * * * the breadth and utilization of patent rights can be used not only to stifle competition, but also have adverse effects in the long run on innovation. We have to strike a balance.

FTC Hearings on Global and Innovation-Based Competition, Day 1, at 11 (Oct. 12, 1995).

Striking the right balance is in part an issue for the intellectual property system. But it is also an issue for antitrust, as we discussed in Sidebar 7–1. *See, e.g., FTC v. Actavis, Inc.*, 133 S.Ct. 2223, 2230–31 (2013) (discussed *infra*). Intellectual property rights may be "too broad" for any number of reasons—for example, they may be too permissive or endure too long. Such overly broad patent rights might provide too much incentive to innovate. And overly-broad intellectual property rights discourage innovation because they dissuade successive innovators from improving, and seeking the returns from supplanting, existing approaches. Moreover, intellectual property rights, however valuable in providing incentives to create new ideas, limit the use of those innovations by allowing rights owners to set a price for their use. Once new ideas arise, after all, their public goods nature (use by one person does not prevent others from also using the idea) means that society benefits most if they are widely adopted. Accordingly, the social benefit of intellectual property rights in providing incentives to innovate must be balanced against the social costs they present of limiting the use of innovations once created. Limitations on the scope and duration of intellectual property rights attempt to strike the best balance, as can targeted antitrust enforcement with respect to IP-related conduct.

The tradeoff between incentives for use and creation may be most acute when intellectual property rights confer significant market power on the holder of those rights. In other words, the problem for antitrust law is that the exclusionary right specified by intellectual property law may be too large. The prospect of a large future prize for successful innovation—in the form of the profits that arise from the intellectual property rights owner's ability to exclude others—is undoubtedly a spur to innovation. However, granting exclusionary rights is not the sole method of fostering innovation—competition also promotes innovation. Firms have a powerful incentive to beat their rivals by cutting cost or being first with new products or product improvements. This innovation-driving incentive should be factored into the calculus when determining whether the exclusionary right is larger than it needs to be. Further, intellectual property rights can function to facilitate transactions by lowering transaction and information costs, thereby promoting the commercialization of new products, processes, and services. Well-defined intellectual property rights facilitate both the licensing and sale of intellectual property rights, which can, in turn, increase incentives to innovate.

As we shall see in this Chapter, antitrust rules have, to varying degrees in different eras, restricted what an intellectual property owner can do with its intellectual property rights. In this broad sense, therefore, the antitrust rules operate as another limit on the scope of intellectual property rights, just as they limit the use of any other kind of property if it would significantly harm competition.

1. HISTORY

a. The Rise and Fall of the "Nine No-Nos"

Today's tensions arise after a century of evolution in attitudes about the competitive consequences of various practices associated with the exercise of intellectual property rights. Perhaps best illustrated by some of the early tying cases, the Supreme Court associated IPRs with "monopoly." *See, e.g., Int'l Bus. Machs. Corp. v. United States*, 298 U.S. 131 (1936); *Int'l Salt Co. v. United States*, 332 U.S. 392 (1947); *United States v. Loew's, Inc.*, 371 U.S. 38 (1962). Indeed, as recently as 1984, the Court continued to rely on these and other cases for the proposition that patents confer market power. *See Jefferson Parish Hosp. Dist. No. 2 v. Hyde*, 466 U.S. 2, 16–17 (1984). The coupling of the presumption of market power with the right to exclude inherent in IP rights led the Court to view with great suspicion a variety of practices that went beyond the mere act of licensing or refusing to license IP rights. That view formally ended in 2006, when the Supreme Court expressly rejected the long-standing presumption that patent rights confer market power. *See Ill. Tool Works Inc. v. Indep. Ink, Inc.*, 547 U.S. 28 (2006).

Antitrust's hostility to intellectual property rights, in particular to patent rights, eventually coalesced into what became known as the the "Nine No-Nos." In an address delivered by a former official of the Antitrust Division in 1970,[1] the Justice Department articulated nine practices associated with the exercise of intellectual property that the Division would view not only as suspect, but as per se violations of the Sherman Act.

Figure 7–1:

The Now Outmoded Nine No-Nos

(1) Tying of unpatented to patented products;

(2) Mandatory know-how grantbacks from the patent licensee to the patent licensor;

(3) Post-sale resale restrictions on purchasers of patented products;

(4) "Tie-out" agreements, whereby the purchase of a patented product was conditioned on the purchaser's agreement not to purchase another product not covered by the patent, typically one supplied by the patent holder's rivals;

(5) Exclusive licensing—particularly, a guarantee by the licensor that it will not grant any other licenses without the consent of the licensee;

(6) Mandatory package licensing;

(7) Compulsory payment of royalties in amounts not reasonably related to sales of the patented product;

(8) Restrictions on sales of unpatented products made by a patented process; and

(9) Utilizing resale price maintenance in connection with the licensing of patented products.

---

[1] Bruce B. Wilson, *Patent and Know-How License Agreements: Field of Use, Territorial, Price and Quantity Restrictions*, Address Before the Fourth New England Antitrust Conference (Nov. 6, 1970).

In large part, these restrictions reflected the state of antitrust law that prevailed at the time. Recall from Chapter 6 that in 1970, all vertical intrabrand agreements and many kinds of horizontal agreements were more readily condemned as per se unlawful until *Sylvania* (and later *Leegin*) and *Broadcast Music* established the modern trend. But the Nine No-Nos were also rooted in a long line of Supreme Court and lower court decisions that evidenced great suspicion of the impact intellectual property could have on competition. Consider each in turn. What would the rationale be for prohibiting them? For making them per se unlawful? What assumptions are they based upon, particularly with respect to the market power associated with intellectual property? Can you imagine pro-competitive benefits of any of them? Consider these questions in reviewing the following excerpt from the complaint and consent order entered in 1975 by the FTC and Xerox Corporation.

IN THE MATTER OF XEROX CORPORATION

Federal Trade Commission, 1975.
86 F.T.C. 364.

COMPLAINT

* * *

IV. NATURE OF TRADE AND COMMERCE

PAR. 8. The relevant market is the sale and lease of office copiers in the United States, hereinafter referred to as the office copier market. This market includes as a relevant submarket the sale and lease of plain paper office copiers in the United States, hereinafter referred to as the plain paper submarket. The office copier market is dominated by the plain paper submarket and Xerox dominates the plain paper submarket.

PAR. 9. (a) In 1971, revenues from the sale and lease of office copiers were approximately $1.1 billion and total revenues from the sale and lease of office copiers and supplies were approximately $1.7 billion; Xerox accounted for approximately 86 percent of the former and 60 percent of the latter. In 1971, revenues from the sale and lease of plain paper copiers and supplies were approximately $1.0 billion; Xerox accounted for approximately 95 percent of said revenues.

(b) Approximately 25 firms are presently engaged in the office copier market. Of these 23 sell or otherwise distribute coated paper copiers and three sell or otherwise distribute plain paper copiers. After Xerox, the next largest firm in the office copier market accounted for approximately 10 percent of 1971 revenues from the sale or lease of office copiers and the sale of supplies therefor.

PAR. 10. The office copier market has had and continues to have high barriers to entry and barriers to effective competition among existing competitors.

* * *

VI. VIOLATIONS

PAR. 12. (a) Xerox has monopoly power in the relevant market and submarket.

(b) Xerox has the power to inhibit, frustrate, and hinder effective competition among firms participating in the relevant market and submarket.

* * *

PAR. 14. Xerox has engaged in acts, practices and methods of competition relating to patents including, but not limited to,

(a) monopolizing and attempting to monopolize patents applicable to office copiers,

(b) maintaining a patent barrier to competition by attempting to recreate a patent structure which would be equivalent in scope to expired patents,

(c) developing and maintaining a patent structure of great size, complexity, and obscurity of boundaries,

(d) using its patent position to obtain access to technology owned by actual or potential competitors,

(e) entering into cross-license arrangements with actual or potential competitors,

(f) including in licenses under United States Patent Number 3,121,006 provisions having the effect of limiting licensees to the manufacture and sale of only coated paper copiers,

(g) offering patent licenses applicable to plain paper copiers with provisions which, in effect, limit the licensee to the manufacture or sale of low speed copiers,

(h) including in patent licenses provisions having the effect of precluding the licensee from utilizing Xerox patents in the office copier market,

(i) entering into and maintaining agreements with Battelle Memorial Institute, Inc. and Battelle Development Corporation, Delaware corporations with principal offices at Columbus, Ohio, hereinafter referred to collectively as Battelle, pursuant to which Battelle is required to convey to Xerox all patents, patent applications, and know-how coming into its possession relative to xerography.

(j)   preventing actual and potential competitors from developing plain paper copiers while permitting them to develop coated paper copiers.

* * *

The influence of the Nine No-Nos is of course evident in the list of violations alleged by the Federal Trade Commission in the *Xerox* complaint, which included pricing, licensing, grantback, and acquisition practices. It was also evident in the elaborate remedial order that followed, which, in addition to prohibiting the alleged practices, compelled Xerox to license its patents at what was arguably a minimal royalty. The breadth of the prohibitions and remedies in *Xerox* is extraordinary by contemporary standards, but it reflected the law and attitudes of the time about dominant firm conduct, particularly with respect to patents.

Nevertheless, evaluating Xerox with the benefit of hindsight is not a simple matter. As one commentator has written:

> At the most superficial level, the *Xerox* case fascinates in the way that a previously undiscovered ancient culture would draw the attention of an anthropologist, or a car crash would attract that of a rubbernecker. This is so, first, because so many of the practices alleged in the complaint or prohibited by the order seem innocuous to modern eyes and thus suggest an entirely foreign way of looking at the world, and second, because the subsequent judicial backlash in *SCM Corp. v. Xerox Corp.* [the next case in this Chapter] led to contortions in reasoning that were unnecessary and could impede appropriate antitrust enforcement. More deeply, the case is unsettling because, for all the case's flaws, the FTC's remedy actually seems to have done quite a bit of good, by breaking up a "killer patent portfolio" that threatened to insulate Xerox from competition, not for seventeen years, but forever, bringing with it the sluggish unimaginativeness long thought characteristic of a monopoly. In this respect, *Xerox* provides a window into some tensions—not yet resolved and perhaps unresolvable by antitrust principles—between the reward system created by the intellectual property laws and the very innovation those laws are intended to foster. The extent to which any progress can be made in reducing those tensions is one of the more interesting issues to be addressed in the coming years.

Willard K. Tom, *The 1975* Xerox *Consent Decree: Ancient Artifacts and Current Tensions*, 68 ANTITRUST L.J. 967 (2001). *See also* Timothy F. Bresnahan, *Post-Entry Competition in the Plain Paper Copier Market, in* ISSUES IN THE ECONOMICS OF R & D, 75 AM. ECON. REV. 15 (1985) (Papers and Proceedings).

The core concern in *Xerox* was the firm's ability to assemble what has been termed a "killer patent portfolio." Tom argues, however, that just as we distinguish between monopoly achieved through skill, industry, and foresight, on the one hand, and exclusionary practices on the other, there may be grounds to distinguish between the internally generated "killer portfolio," which may cause "no concern at all," and the portfolio assembled through other, externally directed and more debatable means, such as:

Conduct/Effects Involving Substitutes:

- acquisitions of emergent substitutes, by assignment, license, or purchase

- "predatory patenting," a kind of patent proliferation strategy designed more to block others from entering a market than to develop new products or processes

Conduct/Effects Involving Complements:

- creating bottlenecks through acquisition

- network effects and the extension of monopoly power across generations

- incomplete information about the scope of patents as an entry barrier

Tom, *The 1975* Xerox *Consent Decree*, 68 ANTITRUST L.J. at 981–89. Tom does not suggest that each of these scenarios should necessarily be regulated by antitrust remedies, but he does point out through these examples how *Xerox* can be used to inform a more contemporary perspective.

As we move forward in this Section of the Chapter, consider the reasons why the attitude about intellectual property that is reflected in *Xerox* might lead to inadequate protections for IPRs, even though in *Xerox*, itself, they perhaps led to a more competitive market.

As we noted earlier in the Chapter, economists have long recognized that innovation is critical to growth in productivity and ultimately to economic progress. But what kind of economic ordering is most conducive to innovation? Will competition maximize innovation? Will a monopoly? Will small or large firms prove more adept at innovation?

In addition to these basic choices of how economic decisions are to be made in a society and within firms, IPRs greatly impact the course of innovation. If antitrust imposes extensive constraints on intellectual property rights, it may fail to generate adequate incentives to innovate. If antitrust intervention reduces substantially the promise of reward to innovation, some innovators will focus their creative energies elsewhere. On the other hand, if IPRs are defined too broadly, some initial innovators may be over-compensated at the expense of subsequent innovators, who may suffer exclusion. Because striking that balance may prove difficult and may vary by industry and innovation, the convention of using unitary statutory rules to define the scope of IPRs necessarily risks instances of over-and under-protection—of too much and too little innovation.

Whether antitrust laws can serve as an effective method for identifying and correcting instances of "over-protection" is at the heart of current debates over the relationship of antitrust and intellectual property. If innovation is a critical dimension of competition that drives economic progress—especially in the New Economy—then antitrust would seem a natural policing device for attempts to exclude competition that cannot be justified in terms of the incentive to innovate. Critics argue, however, that striking the balance should be accomplished within the parameters of intellectual property laws themselves, and not by subjecting IP owners to the vagaries of antitrust regulation.

Note how these issues were framed by the court in the following excerpt from a private challenge against Xerox that followed on the heels of the government's 1975 prosecution.

SCM CORPORATION V. XEROX CORP.
United States Court of Appeals for the Second Circuit, 1981.
645 F.2d 1195.

[SCM accused Xerox of acquiring, then refusing to license, patents relating to plain paper copying machines. According to SCM's complaint, Xerox's refusal to license precluded SCM from "competing effectively" in the market for plain paper copiers and constituted violations of Sections 1 and 2 of the Sherman Act as well as Section 7 of the Clayton Act. The district court had set aside the jury's treble damage verdict of $111.3 million holding that monetary damages under the antitrust laws could not be recovered for Xerox's patent related conduct. Eds.]

Before WATERMAN, FRIENDLY and MESKILL, CIRCUIT JUDGES.

MESKILL, CIRCUIT JUDGE.

* * *

I

The patent laws were enacted pursuant to Congress' authority to "promote the Progress of Science and useful Arts, by securing for limited Times to Inventors the exclusive Right to their Discoveries." U.S. Const., Art. I, § 8, cl. 8. That the first patent laws were enacted at the second session of our first Congress manifests the importance our founding fathers attached to encouraging inventive genius, a resource that proved to be bountiful throughout this nation's history. The patent laws reward the inventor with the power to exclude others from exploiting his invention for a period of seventeen years. 35 U.S.C. § 154 (1976). In return, the public benefits from the disclosure of inventions, the entrance into the market of valuable products whose invention might have been delayed but for the incentives provided by the patent laws, and the increased competition the patented product creates in the marketplace. The antitrust laws, on the other hand, were enacted to protect competition in the market. The antitrust laws are based upon the fundamental premise that the public benefits most from a competitive marketplace. *Standard Oil Co. v. United States*, 221 U.S. 1, 58, 31 S.Ct. 502, 515, 55 L.Ed. 619 (1911); *United States v. Aluminum Co. of America*, 148 F.2d 416, 428–29 (2d Cir. 1945).

The conflict between the antitrust and patent laws arises in the methods they embrace that were designed to achieve reciprocal goals. While the antitrust laws proscribe unreasonable restraints of competition, the patent laws reward the inventor with a temporary monopoly that insulates him from competitive exploitation of his patented art. When the patented product, as is often the case, represents merely one of many products that effectively compete in a given product market, few antitrust problems arise. When, however, the patented product is so successful that it evolves into its own economic market, as was the case here, or succeeds in engulfing a large section of a preexisting product market, the patent and antitrust laws necessarily clash. In such cases the primary purpose of the antitrust laws to preserve competition can be frustrated, albeit temporarily, by a holder's exercise of the patent's inherent exclusionary power during its term.

II

The law is unsettled concerning the effect under the antitrust laws, if any, that the evolution of a patent monopoly into an economic monopoly might have upon a patent holder's right to exercise the exclusionary power ordinarily inherent in a patent. Indeed, implicit in Judge Newman's decision below is a deep concern over the uncertain antitrust law implications just such an event might have had in this case. His thoughtful analysis of the relationship between the patent and antitrust laws led him to conclude that "the need to accommodate the patent laws with the antitrust laws precludes the imposition of damage liability for a unilateral refusal to license valid patents." 463 F.Supp. at 1012–13. * * *

SCM has contended that a unilateral refusal to license a patent should be treated like any other refusal to deal by a monopolist, *see generally Otter Tail Power Co. v. United States*, 410 U.S. 366, 93 S.Ct. 1022, 35 L.Ed.2d 359 (1973); *Lorain Journal Co. v. United States*, 342 U.S. 143, 72 S.Ct. 181, 96 L.Ed. 162 (1951); *Eastman Kodak Co. v. S. Photo Materials Co.*, 273 U.S. 359, 47 S.Ct. 400, 71 L.Ed. 684 (1927), where the patent has afforded its holder monopoly power over an economic market. While, as SCM suggests, a concerted refusal to license patents is no less unlawful than other concerted refusals to deal, in such cases the patent holder abuses his patent by attempting to enlarge his monopoly beyond the scope of the patent granted him. Where a patent holder, however, merely exercises his "right to exclude others from making, using, or selling the invention," 35 U.S.C. § 154 (1976), by refusing unilaterally to license his patent for its seventeen-year term, such conduct is expressly permitted by the patent laws. * * * Simply stated, a patent holder is permitted to maintain his patent monopoly through conduct permissible under the patent laws.

No court has ever held that the antitrust laws require a patent holder to forfeit the exclusionary power inherent in his patent the instant his patent monopoly affords him monopoly power over a relevant product market. In *Alcoa* this Court never questioned the legality of the economic monopoly *Alcoa* maintained by virtue of the two successive patents it had acquired. Indeed, Judge Learned Hand termed Alcoa's economic monopoly during the terms of those patents "lawful." We do not interpret Judge Wyzanski's decision in *United States v. United Shoe Machinery Corp.*, 110 F.Supp. 295 (D.Mass.1953), *aff'd per curiam*, 347 U.S. 521, 74 S.Ct. 699, 98 L.Ed. 910 (1954), as supporting SCM's argument to the contrary. In *United Shoe*, the primary vehicle found to have been employed by United Shoe in achieving and maintaining its monopoly was its lease-only system of distributing its machines. The patent acquisitions scrutinized by Judge Wyzanski occurred after United Shoe possessed substantial market power and were not "one of the principal factors enabling (United Shoe) to achieve and hold its share of the market." 110 F.Supp. at 312. Thus, contrary to appellant's contention, the *United Shoe* case stands in stark contrast to the one at bar where the patents were acquired prior to the appearance of the relevant product market and where the patents themselves afforded Xerox the power to achieve eventual market dominance.

In *Alcoa* Judge Learned Hand stated that the "successful competitor, having been urged to compete, must not be turned upon when he wins." 148 F.2d at 430. And while that statement was made in regard to a hypothetical situation where only one of a group of competitors ultimately survives, it at least indicates a concern Judge Hand had for preserving those economic incentives that provide the primary impetus for competition. * * *

* * *

The tension between the objectives of preserving economic incentives to enhance competition while at the same time trying to contain the power a successful competitor acquires is heightened tremendously when the patent laws come into play. As the facts of this case demonstrate, the acquisition of a patent can create the potential for tremendous market power.

III

Patent acquisitions are not immune from the antitrust laws. Surely, a [Section] 2 violation will have occurred where, for example, the dominant competitor in a market acquires a patent covering a substantial share of the same market that he knows when added to his existing share will afford him monopoly power. That the asset acquired is a patent is irrelevant; in such a case the patented invention already has been commercialized successfully, and the magnitude of the transgression of the antitrust laws' proscription against willful aggregations of market power outweighs substantially the negative effect that the elimination of that class of purchasers for commercialized patents places upon the patent system.

The patent system would be seriously undermined, however, were the threat of potential antitrust liability to attach upon the acquisition of a patent at a time prior to the existence of the relevant market and, even more disconcerting, at a time prior to the commercialization of the patented art. As SCM itself admits, the procurement of a patent by the inventor will not violate § 2 even where it is likely that the patent monopoly will evolve into an economic monopoly; yet SCM would deny the same reward to anyone but the patentee.

If the antitrust laws were interpreted to proscribe the natural evolution of a patent monopoly into an economic monopoly, then Judge Newman's concern would be well founded. If the threat of treble damage liability for refusing to license were imbedded in the minds of potential patent holders as a likely prospect incident to every successful commercial exploitation of a patented invention, the efficacy of the economic incentives afforded by our patent system might be severely diminished.

Nevertheless, it is especially clear that the economic incentives provided by the patent laws were intended to benefit only those persons who lawfully acquire the rights granted under our patent system. *Cf. Walker Process Equipment, Inc. v. Food Mach. & Chem. Corp.*, 382 U.S. 172, 86 S.Ct. 347, 15 L.Ed.2d 247 (1965) (patent obtained by fraud on Patent Office as basis for monopolization claim). Where a patent in the first instance has been lawfully acquired, a patent holder ordinarily should be allowed to exercise the patent's exclusionary power even after achieving commercial success; to allow the imposition of treble damages based on what a reviewing court might later consider, with the benefit of hindsight, to be too much success would seriously threaten the integrity of the patent system. Where, however, the acquisition itself is unlawful, the subsequent exercise of the ordinarily lawful exclusionary power inherent in the patent would be a continuing wrong, a continuing unlawful exclusion of potential competitors.

Without passing upon the validity of Judge Newman's theory to preclude antitrust damage liability in all cases where the injury is predicated upon a patent holder's refusal to license, we hold that where a patent has been lawfully acquired, subsequent conduct permissible under the patent laws cannot trigger any liability under the antitrust laws.[10] This holding, we believe, strikes an adequate balance between the patent and antitrust laws. * * *

* * *

Do you agree with the Second Circuit's premise that the patent laws and the antitrust laws serve different goals and are in "conflict"? If they are, how can a court know whether in any given case the policies of the antitrust or patent laws should be given precedence? Does the court suggest any guidelines for making that choice?

One traditional method of resolving conflicts arising between the antitrust and patent laws has been antitrust counterclaims to patent infringement suits. An infringement suit asserting a fraudulent patent against the defendant can be sufficient to establish an antitrust counterclaim. *See Walker Process Equipment, Inc. v. Food Mach. & Chem. Corp.*, 382 U.S. 172 (1965). The Federal Circuit has interpreted *Walker Process* to require proof of materiality and intent to deceive the patent examiner. *Nobelpharma AB v. Implant Innovations, Inc.*, 141 F.3d 1059, 1070 (Fed. Cir. 1998). A defendant to a patent infringement claim may also bring an antitrust countersuit on the grounds that the patent litigation itself violates the antitrust laws, but it "must prove that the suit was both objectively baseless and subjectively motivated by a desire to impose collateral, anti-competitive injury rather than to obtain a justifiable legal remedy." *Nobelpharma*, 141 F.3d at 1071 (citing *Prof'l Real Estate Investors, Inc. v. Columbia Pictures Indus., Inc.*, 508 U.S. 49, 60–61 (1993). Such antitrust counterclaims are commonly dismissed on the grounds that the original suit is not objectively baseless. *See, e.g., ERBE Elektromedizin GmbH v. Canady Tech. LLC,* 629 F.3d 1278 (Fed. Cir. 2010); *Honeywell Intern'l. Inc. v. Universal Avionics Sys. Corp.*, 488 F.3d 982 (Fed. Cir. 2007); *Q-Pharma, Inc. v. Andrew Jergens Co.*, 360 F.3d 1295 (Fed. Cir. 2004); *ESCO Corp. v. Cashman Equip. Co.*, No. 2:12–cv–01545–RCJ–CWH, 2016 WL 320113 (D. Nev. Jan. 26, 2016); *Pactiv, LLC v. Multisorb Techs., LLC*, 63 F. Supp. 3d 832 (N.D. Ill. 2015).One commentator describes the high standard for successful antitrust counterclaims as necessary to strike an appropriate balance between antitrust and IP law because "[t]oo expansive a conception of baselessness could turn many infringement actions into antitrust claims against the infringement plaintiff, thus putting the patent owner at peril even in defending its own property rights." *See* Herbert J.

---

[10] We leave for an appropriate case the resolution of the question whether damage liability can accrue to a holder for refusing to license patents that he subsequently abuses through pooling or otherwise.

Hovenkamp, *The Walker Process Doctrine: Infringement Lawsuits as Antitrust Violations* 14 (U. of Iowa Legal Studies, Research Paper No. 36, 2008), http://papers.ssrn.com/sol3/papers.cfm?abstract_id=1259877. Do you agree the doctrines in *Walker Process* and *Professional Real Estate Investors* appropriately resolve the conflict between antitrust and the patent laws?

b. Changing Times, Changing Attitudes: The Intellectual Property Guidelines (1995)[2]

By the early 1980s, government attitudes, building on the sea-change in the case law, specifically disavowed the Nine No-Nos in favor of a decidedly more permissive attitude towards intellectual property licensing and sales practices. That new attitude recognized the complex nature and pro-competitive potential of IPRs and conduct related to the exercise of those rights.[3] These changes in enforcement policy paralleled a similar evolution in the courts, reflected in cases like *SCM* and *Dawson Chem. Co. v. Rohm & Haas Co.*, 448 U.S. 176 (1980).

Movement away from the Nine No-Nos continued for more than a decade. At the enforcement agencies, it culminated in the 1995 adoption of *Antitrust Guidelines for the Licensing of Intellectual Property. See* U.S. DEPT'T OF JUSTICE & FED. TRADE COMM'N, ANTITRUST GUIDELINES FOR THE LICENSING OF INTELLECTUAL PROPERTY 28 (1995), http://www.ftc.gov/bc/0558.pdf [hereinafter *IP Guidelines*]. Much as did the court in *SCM*, the Guidelines opened with a discussion of the characteristics of antitrust and IPRs. After briefly summarizing the "right to exclude" provided by both the patent and copyright laws, however, they offer the following observation, which is suggestive of quite a different philosophy from that embraced in *SCM*:

> The intellectual property laws and the antitrust laws share the common purpose of promoting innovation and enhancing consumer welfare. [4] The intellectual property laws provide incentives for innovation and its dissemination and commercialization by establishing enforceable property rights for the creators of new and useful products, more efficient processes,

---

[2] As this Casebook was going to press, the U.S. Department of Justice and the Federal Trade Commission issued a proposed update to their Antitrust Guidelines for the Licensing of Intlellectual Property that would alter some of the language quoted in this Section and in later portions of this Chapter. When those Guidelines become final, we will revise the Chapter as needed.

[3] *See* Abbott B. Lipsky, Deputy Assistant Attorney General, Antitrust Division, Remarks before the American Bar Association, Antitrust Section (Nov. 5, 1981), reprinted in 4 Trade Reg. Rep. (CCH) ¶ 13, 129.

[4] "[T]he aims and objectives of patent and antitrust laws may seem, at first glance, wholly at odds. However, the two bodies of law are actually complementary, as both are aimed at encouraging innovation, industry and competition." *Atari Games Corp. v. Nintendo of America, Inc.*, 897 F.2d 1572, 1576 (Fed. Cir. 1990).

and original works of expression. In the absence of intellectual property rights, imitators could more rapidly exploit the efforts of innovators and investors without compensation. Rapid imitation would reduce the commercial value of innovation and erode incentives to invest, ultimately to the detriment of consumers. The antitrust laws promote innovation and consumer welfare by prohibiting certain actions that may harm competition with respect to either existing or new ways of serving consumers.

IP Guidelines, § 1.0. Note how the Guidelines thus appear to propose that the promotion of "innovation" can serve as the unitary and harmonizing goal for both antitrust and IP. Why might that be so? How might it operate in practice? How might it have affected the court's analysis in *SCM*?

The Guidelines then proceed to state three baseline principles for implementing that goal:

2.0 These Guidelines embody three general principles:

a.   for the purpose of antitrust analysis, the Agencies regard intellectual property as being essentially comparable to any other form of property;

b.   the Agencies do not presume that intellectual property creates market power in the antitrust context; and

c.   the Agencies recognize that intellectual property licensing allows firms to combine complementary factors of production and is generally procompetitive.

What is the significance of these three principles? What is the *antitrust* significance of the Guidelines' assertion that IP is "essentially comparable to any other form of property"? How is it related to the second assertion, that IP rights do not necessarily confer market power? Of course, that assertion, which was at the time contrary to a long line of Supreme Court cases, is pivotal in terms of re-connecting the analysis of conduct involving IP to the analysis of any allegedly anticompetitive conduct.

To illustrate the third, and also critical principle, the Guidelines offer the following hypothetical:

EXAMPLE 1

Situation:

ComputerCo develops a new, copyrighted software program for inventory management. The program has wide application in the health field. ComputerCo licenses the program in an arrangement that imposes both field of use and territorial limitations. Some of ComputerCo's licenses permit use only in hospitals; others permit use only in group medical practices. ComputerCo charges different royalties for the different uses. All of ComputerCo's licenses permit use only in specified portions of the United States and in specified foreign countries. The licenses contain no provisions that would prevent or discourage licensees from developing, using, or selling any other program, or from competing in any other good or service other than in the use of the licensed program. None of the licensees are actual or likely potential competitors of ComputerCo in the sale of inventory management programs.

How would you go about analyzing this problem in the absence of the Guidelines' three stated principles? How would that analysis change once those principles are taken into account? How would you go about analyzing Example 1 based on what we have learned in the course, taking into account the issues raised in this Chapter concerning the need to accommodate intellectual property rights and the Guidelines' premise that we should interpret IP and antitrust law as to promote innovation? Here's an excerpt from the Guidelines' discussion:

Discussion:

The key competitive issue raised by the licensing arrangement is whether it harms competition among entities that would have been actual or likely potential competitors in the absence of the arrangement. Such harm could occur if, for example, the licenses anticompetitively foreclose access to competing technologies (in this case, most likely competing computer programs), prevent licensees from developing their own competing technologies (again, in this case, most likely computer programs), or facilitate market allocation or price-fixing for any product or service supplied by the licensees. * * * If the license agreements contained such provisions, the Agency evaluating the arrangement would analyze its likely competitive effects as described in parts 3–5 of these Guidelines. In this hypothetical, there are no such provisions and thus the arrangement is merely a subdivision of the licensor's intellectual property among different fields of use and territories. The licensing arrangement does not appear likely to harm competition among entities that would have been actual or likely potential competitors if ComputerCo had chosen not to license the software program. The Agency therefore would be unlikely to object to this arrangement. Based on these facts, the result of the antitrust analysis would be the same whether the technology was protected by patent, copyright, or trade secret. The Agency's conclusion as to likely competitive effects could differ if, for example, the license barred licensees from using any other inventory management program.

After discussing these three foundational principles, the IP Guidelines go on to address the kinds of markets that can be affected by intellectual property licenses, and the framework for analysis that the agency will use in evaluating the anticompetitive potential of particular licenses. At this point, you should review Sections 3 and 4 of the Guidelines. As you do so, consider the extent, if any, to which the conceptual framework we have discussed throughout the Casebook, which focuses on the need to identify a theory of anticompetitive effects—collusive and/or exclusionary—as a prerequisite to any antitrust challenge is imbedded in the IP Guidelines.

With basic principles set, and a framework for analysis in place, the IP Guidelines establish a "Safety Zone" or safe harbor for IP licensing arrangements that (1) are not facially anticompetitive, and (2) involve a licensor and licensees who together account for "no more than twenty percent of each relevant market significantly affected by the restraint." *IP Guidelines*, § 4.3. They then turn to seven particular categories of conduct that have traditionally given rise to antitrust concerns: (1) horizontal restraints, (2) resale price maintenance,[5] (3) tying, (4) exclusive dealing, (5) cross-licensing and pooling arrangements, (6) grantbacks, and (7) acquisition of intellectual property rights. Note how many of these also were addressed—albeit far more harshly—by the Nine No-Nos, and surfaced in *Xerox*.

Many of these same issues have garnered attention in the European Union. To address them and to update previous regulations, the EU adopted a revised block exemption pursuant to Article 101(3), as well as its own set of Guidelines. *See* Commission Regulation (EC) No 316/2014 of 21 March 2014 on the application of Article 101(3) of the Treaty on the Functioning of the European Union to categories of technology transfer agreements, OJ L 123, 27.04.2004, http://eur-lex.europa.eu/legal-content/EN/TXT/PDF/?uri=CELEX:32014R0316&from=EN; *Guidelines on the application of Article 101 of the Treaty on the Functioning of the European Union to technology transfer agreements*, http://eur-lex.europa.eu/legal-content/EN/TXT/PDF/?uri=CELEX:52014XC0328(01)&from=EN.

Antitrust agencies have examined the interplay of innovation and antitrust, attempting to develop a more comprehensive understanding of the performance and capabilities of antitrust institutions in dynamic industries. The FTC and DOJ released a joint report in 2007 that conducts an in-depth analysis of emerging issues affecting antitrust, intellectual property, and innovation. *See* U.S. DEP'T OF JUSTICE & FED. TRADE COMM'N, ANTITRUST ENFORCEMENT AND INTELLECTUAL PROPERTY RIGHTS: PROMOTING INNOVATION AND COMPETITION (2007), http://www.justice.gov/atr/public/hearings/ip/222655.pdf [hereinafter IP REPORT]. This report

---

[5] The Guidelines' discussion of resale price maintenance pre-dates and therefore does not reflect the Supreme Court's decision in *Leegin Creative Leather Prods., Inc. v. PSKS, Inc.*, 551 U.S. 877 (2007) (*see supra* Chapter 4).

largely affirmed that the foundation laid by the 1995 Guidelines continues to guide the agencies' analyses of licensing arrangements. It goes on to both reexamine complex issues at the interface of antitrust and intellectual property law in light of case law developments, such as the Federal Circuit's 2000 *CSU, L.L.C. v. Xerox Corp.* decision (discussed *infra* Section C), and present the agencies' views on newer issues, including the interactions between standard setting organizations and patent holders.

Scholarly work, as well, has continued to enhance antitrust's understanding of innovative industries. One author, for instance, identifies several lessons antitrust has learned over the last few years, including that antitrust does not have a monopoly on protecting competition in high-tech industries—indeed, he argues intellectual property statutes may more effectively address some of these concerns—and that simply because conduct is lawful under intellectual property regimes does not imply that conduct also incentivizes innovation. Herbert Hovenkamp, *Antitrust and Innovation: Where We Are and Where We Should Be Going*, 77 ANTITRUST L.J. 749 (2011). Another scholar argues that the current U.S. legal system threatens innovation—and places part of the blame with antitrust law, which he argues fails to appreciate the value of innovation. MICHAEL A. CARRIER, INNOVATION FOR THE 21ST CENTURY: HARNESSING THE POWER OF INTELLECTUAL PROPERTY AND ANTITRUST LAW (2009).

Throughout the rest of the Chapter, we examine some specific practices addressed in the U.S. IP Guidelines, which have continued to attract significant attention from commentators, government enforcement agencies and the courts. In each instance consider two issues: (1) how does each court approach the problem of defining the scope of IP rights through its relationship to competition law principles?; and (2) to what extent might the decision-makers be utilizing distinct institutional perspectives in answering that question?

2. CHANGING TECHNOLOGIES AND ANTITRUST INSTITUTIONS

Before we examine some of the specific types of innovation-related conduct that have been evaluated for their collusive or exclusionary effects on competition, it is worth pausing to consider the challenges to antitrust institutions of assessing competitive effects in high-technology industries. Not only do the "perennial gales" of which Schumpeter spoke greatly complicate the processes of defining relevant markets, measuring market power, and analyzing the effects upon competition as a whole, but the intricate intertwining of competition and innovation (as discussed in Sidebar 7–1) renders antitrust analysis significantly more complex.

Dynamic competition models entail the prediction of future competitive outcomes. Those competitive outcomes include considerations of entry, investment, innovation, price, output, and quality. Some scholars have questioned the capabilities of courts and antitrust agencies to fully incorporate dynamic considerations into antitrust analysis on the grounds that economic theory does not yet provide a reliable foundation upon which to base presumptions about the relationships between market structure, competition, and innovation. For a recent example of this critique, see Douglas H. Ginsburg & Joshua D. Wright, *Dynamic Analysis and the Limits of Antitrust Institutions*, 78 ANTITRUST L.J. 1 (2012). *But see* Jonathan B. Baker, *Evaluating Appropriability Defenses for the Exclusionary Conduct of Dominant Firms in Innovative Industries*, 80 ANTITRUST L. J. 431 (2016) (proposing a framework for taking innovation incentives into account in the antitrust analysis of monopolization claims); Michael L. Katz & Howard A. Shelanski, *Mergers and Innovation*, 74 ANTITRUST L.J. 1 (2007) (proposing a framework for taking innovation incentives into account in the antitrust analysis of mergers).

These challenges to antitrust institutions are not new or novel. Indeed, the petroleum industry provided an important early test of the judiciary's ability to respond to these challenges. In 1924, the Justice Department sued 50 petroleum companies for illegally combining to create a monopoly in a new technology for refining crude petroleum. The principal defendants were four petroleum refiners, Standard Oil Company of Indiana (a remnant of the original Standard Oil trust that was later known as Amoco), the Texas Company (later known as Texaco), Standard Oil Company of New Jersey (also a remnant of the Standard Oil trust, later known as Exxon), and the Gasoline Products Company. These four refiners held patents for extracting gasoline from crude oil by the process of "cracking." Developed in 1913 by Standard of Indiana, cracking enabled refiners to extract a larger amount of gasoline (a higher valued product) from each barrel of crude oil.

The government alleged that the defendants violated Sections 1 and 2 of the Sherman Act by creating a patent pool to share and license rights to use cracking technology that each company had developed. The companies argued that the pool was necessary to avoid infringement actions that would impede any one firm's use of cracking technology. The focus of the government's concerns was a provision in the pooling agreements by which the firms collectively set the royalties that each could charge for licensing patents covered by the pool and created a formula for distributing royalty payments among themselves.

The district court sustained the government's complaint against the defendants, but the Supreme Court reversed in a unanimous opinion by Justice Louis Brandeis. Crucial to the Court's assessment of the challenged pooling arrangement was its evaluation of the primary defendants' collective position in the market for petroleum refining.

STANDARD OIL COMPANY (INDIANA) V. UNITED STATES

United States Supreme Court, 1931.
283 U.S. 163, 51 S.Ct. 421, 75 L.Ed. 926.

MR. JUSTICE BRANDEIS delivered the opinion of the Court.

* * *

* * * The main contention of the Government is that even if the exchange of patent rights and division of royalties are not necessarily improper and the royalties are not oppressive, the three contracts are still obnoxious to the Sherman Act because specific clauses enable the primary defendants to maintain existing royalties and thereby to restrain interstate commerce. The provisions which constitute the basis for this charge are these. The first contract specifies that the Texas Company shall get from the Indiana Company one-fourth of all royalties thereafter collected under the latter's existing license agreements; and that all royalties received under licenses thereafter issued by either company shall be equally divided. Licenses granting rights under the patents of both are to be issued at a fixed royalty—approximately that charged by the Indiana Company when its process was alone in the field. By the second contract, the Texas Company is entitled to receive one-half of the royalties thereafter collected by the Gasoline Products Company from its existing licensees, and a minimum sum per barrel for all oil cracked by its future licensees. The third contract gives to the Indiana Company one-half of all royalties thereafter paid by existing licensees of the New Jersey Company, and a similar minimum sum for each barrel treated by its future licensees,—subject in the latter case to reduction if the royalties charged by the Indiana and Texas companies for their processes should be reduced. The alleged effect of these provisions is to enable the primary defendants, because of their monopoly of patented cracking processes, to maintain royalty rates at the level established originally for the Indiana process.

The rate of royalties may, of course be a decisive factor in the cost of production. If combining patent owners effectively dominate an industry, the power to fix and maintain royalties is tantamount to the power to fix prices. Where domination exists, a pooling of competing process patents, or an exchange of licenses for the purpose of curtailing the manufacture and supply of an unpatented product, is beyond the privileges conferred by the patents and constitutes a violation of the Sherman Act. The lawful individual monopolies granted by the patent statutes cannot be unitedly exercised to restrain. But an agreement for cross-licensing and division of royalties violates the Act only when used to effect a monopoly, or to fix prices, or to impose otherwise an unreasonable restraint upon interstate commerce. In the case at bar, the primary defendants own competing patented processes for manufacturing an unpatented product which is sold in interstate commerce; and agreements concerning such processes are likely to engender the evils to which the Sherman Act was directed. We must, therefore, examine the evidence to ascertain the operation and effect of the challenged contracts.

No monopoly, or restriction of competition, in the business of licensing patented cracking processes resulted from the execution of these agreements. Up to 1920 all cracking plants in the United States were either owned by the Indiana Company alone, or were operated under licenses from it. In 1924 and 1925, after the cross-licensing arrangements were in effect, the four primary defendants owned or licensed, in the aggregate, only 55 percent of the total cracking capacity, and the remainder was distributed among twenty-one independently owned cracking processes. This development and commercial expansion of competing processes is clear evidence that the contracts did not concentrate in the hands of the four primary defendants the licensing of patented processes for the production of cracked gasoline. Moreover, the record does not show that after the execution of the agreements there was a decrease of competition among them in licensing other refiners to use their respective processes.

No monopoly, or restriction of competition, in the production of either ordinary or cracked gasoline has been proved. The output of cracked gasoline in the years in question was about 26 percent of the total gasoline production. Ordinary or straight run gasoline is indistinguishable from cracked gasoline and the two are either mixed or sold interchangeably. Under these circumstances the primary defendants could not effectively control the supply or fix the price of cracked gasoline by virtue of their alleged monopoly of the cracking processes, unless they could control, through some means, the remainder of the total gasoline production from all sources. Proof of such control is lacking. Evidence of the total gasoline production by all methods, of each of the primary defendants and their licensees is either missing or unsatisfactory in character. The record does not accurately show even the total amount of cracked gasoline produced, or the production of each of the licensees, or competing refiners. Widely variant estimates of such production figures have been submitted. These were not accepted by the master and there is no evidence which would justify our doing so.

No monopoly, or restriction of competition, in the sale of gasoline has been proved. On the basis of testimony relating to the marketing of both cracked and ordinary gasoline, the master found that the defendants were in active competition among themselves and with other refiners; that both kinds of gasoline were refined and sold in large quantities by other companies; and that the primary defendants and their licensees neither individually or collectively controlled the market price or supply of any gasoline moving in interstate commerce. There is ample evidence to support these findings.

Thus it appears that no monopoly of any kind, or restraint of interstate commerce, has been effected either by means of the contracts or in some other way. In the absence of proof that the primary defendants had such control of the entire industry as would make effective the alleged domination of a part, it is difficult to see how they could by agreeing upon royalty rates control either the price or the supply of gasoline, or otherwise restrain competition. By virtue of their patents they had individually the right to determine who should use their respective processes or inventions and what the royalties for such use should be. To warrant an injunction which would invalidate the contracts here in question, and require either new arrangements or settlement of the conflicting claims by litigation, there must be a definite factual showing of illegality. Chicago Board of Trade v. United States, 246 U.S. 231, 238, 38 S.Ct. 242.

* * *

* * * The District Court accepted the Government's estimates of cracked gasoline production; found that the primary defendants were able to control both supply and price by virtue of their control of the cracking patents; held that although these patents were valid consideration for the cross-licenses, the agreement to maintain royalties was in effect a method for fixing the price of cracked gasoline; and concluded that a monopoly existed as a result of such agreements. This appears to be the only basis for the relief granted. But the widely varying estimates, relied upon to establish dominant control of the production of cracked gasoline were insufficient for that purpose. And the court entirely disregarded not only the fact that the manufacture of gasoline by the cracking process constituted only a part of the total gasoline production, but also the evidence showing active competition among the defendants themselves and with others. Its findings are without adequate support in the evidence. The bill should have been dismissed.

* * *

The Supreme Court's evaluation of the patent pooling arrangement in *Standard Oil (Cracking)* rested heavily upon whether the principal defendants had substantial market power. If the relevant market consisted of the output of gasoline from cracking technology, the principal defendants' market share was 55 percent. If the relevant market included gasoline produced from both cracking technology and the older distillation method of refining, their share was 26 percent. By choosing to treat cracking technology and distillation technology as fungible, *i.e.*, as part of an indivisible product market, the Court decided that the firms controlled only 26 percent of total gasoline output. They therefore did not threaten to suppress competition unduly by jointly setting the royalties to be charged for patents included in the pooling arrangement.

As the New Economy becomes increasingly reliant upon industries dominated by patented technologies, questions revolving around the existence and appropriate uses of patents gain prominence. For example, when does combining several allegedly "weak" patents add to their potential exclusionary capacity? Should the combination of separately valid patents trigger greater antitrust scrutiny? Another significant concern is that if building one's "patent arsenal" becomes a common industry practice, rivals are less likely to sue each other—for fear that mutual suits will reveal the invalidity of both their competitors' and their own patents. Incumbents may then be able to stand upon powerful—but questionable—patent portfolios, preventing newcomers (whose resources are far more limited) or rivals outside the pool from entering or competing effectively. Accordingly, combining patents in a common owner or pool may increase their exclusionary potential. On the other hand, it may also create substantial integrative efficiencies by reducing transaction costs, clearing blocking positions, and integrating complementary technologies.

Some commentators argue this effect may be especially profound when a firm is acquiring "blocking" patents, that is, patents that are so comprehensive or so crucial to the underlying product that other firms simply cannot manufacture the product without infringing upon the patent. Yet note that when a firm acquires so-called blocking patents, it does so only with probability, not certainty. While a firm may believe it is gaining a blocking patent, the patent may later be found invalid or it may be that other firms are not, in fact, infringing. Building one's patent portfolio, then, may reflect an endeavor to engage in a valuable competitive strategy. Gideon Parchomovsky & R. Polk Wagner, *Patent Portfolios*, 154 U. PA. L. REV. 1, 29 (2005).

Although the question of how combining patents alters a firm's exclusionary capacity exists in contemporary antitrust analysis, it is by no means a new one. In the 1963 case *United States v. Singer Manufacturing, Co.*, the Supreme Court analyzed claims that Singer had entered into various cross-licensing and assignment agreements with two other European sewing machine manufacturers in order to bolster its own patent portfolio, and thereby to exclude competition from a Japanese manufacturer.

UNITED STATES V. SINGER MANUFACTURING CO.

Supreme Court of the United States, 1963.
374 U.S. 174, 83 S.Ct. 1773, 10 L.Ed.2d 823.

MR. JUSTICE CLARK delivered the opinion of the Court.

This is a direct appeal from the judgment of the United States District Court for the Southern District of New York, dismissing a civil antitrust action brought by the United States against the Singer Manufacturing Company to prevent and restrain alleged violations of §§ 1 and 2 of the Sherman Act. The complaint alleged that Singer combined and conspired with two competitors, Gegauf of Switzerland and Vigorelli of Italy, to restrain and monopolize and that Singer unilaterally attempted to monopolize interstate and foreign trade in the importation, sale and distribution of household zigzag sewing machines. The District Court dismissed after an extended trial, concluding that the charges were without merit. * * * We have examined the record * * * [and] have concluded that there was a conspiracy to exclude Japanese competitors in household zigzag sewing machines and that the judgment must be reversed.

I

* * *

C.   It appears that Singer by April 29, 1953, through its experimental department, had completed a design of a multiple cam zigzag mechanism in what it calls the Singer '401' machine. It is disclosed in Singer's Johnson Patent. In 1953 Singer was also developing its Perla Patent as used in its '306' replaceable cam machine and in 1954 its '319' machine-carried multiple cam machine. In September of 1953 Vigorelli, an Italian corporation, introduced in the United States a sewing machine incorporating a stack of cams with a single follower. Singer concluded that Vigorelli had on file applications covering its machine in the various patent offices in the world and that the Singer design would infringe. On June 10, 1955, Singer bought for $8,000 a patent disclosing a plurality of cams with a single cam follower from Carl Harris, a Canadian. It was believed that this patent, filed June 9, 1952, might be reissued with claims covering the Singer 401 as well as its 319 machine, and that the reissued patent would dominate the Vigorelli machine as well as a Japanese one introduced into the United States in September 1954 by Brother International Corporation. Thereafter Singer concluded that litigation would result between it and Vigorelli unless a cross-licensing agreement could be made, and this was effected on November 17, 1955. The license was nonexclusive, world-wide and royalty free. * * * The agreement also contained provisions by which each of the parties agreed not to bring any infringement action against the other 'in any country' or institute against the other any opposition, nullity or invalidation proceedings in any country. In accordance with this agreement Singer withdrew its opposition to Vigorelli's patent application in Brazil and Vigorelli later (1958) abandoned a United States interference to the Johnson application which cleared the way for the Johnson Patent to issue on December 2 of that year.

D.   While Singer was negotiating the cross-license agreement with Vigorelli it learned that Gegauf, a Swiss corporation, had a patent covering a multiple cam mechanism. This placed an additional cloud over Singer's Harris reissue plan because the Gegauf patent enjoyed an effective priority date in Italy of May 31, 1952. This was nine days earlier than Singer's Harris patent filing date in the United States. In December 1955 Singer learned that Gegauf and Vigorelli had entered a cross-licensing agreement covering their multiple cam patents similar to the Vigorelli-Singer agreement. In January 1956 Singer found that Gegauf had pending an application in the United States Patent Office and assumed that it was based on the same priority date, i.e., May 31, 1952. If this was true Singer could use its Harris reissue patent only to oppose through interference the allowance of broad claims to Gegauf. It therefore made preparation to negotiate with Gegauf, first approaching Vigorelli in order to ascertain how the latter had induced Gegauf to grant him a royalty-free license and drop any claim of infringement. Singer made direct arrangements for a conference with Gegauf for April 12, 1956, and the license agreement was made April 14, 1956.

* * * Gegauf felt secure in his patent claims but insecure with reference to the inroads the Japanese machines were making on the United States market. It was this 'lever' which Singer used to secure the license, pointing out that without an agreement Gegauf and Singer might litigate for a protracted period; that they should not be fighting each other as that would only delay the issue of their respective patents; and, finally, that they should license each other and get their respective patents 'so they could be enforced by whoever would own the particular patent.' * * *

The license agreement covered (1) the Singer-Harris patent and its reissue application in the United States and nine corresponding foreign ones, and (2) the Gegauf Swiss, Italian and German patents, as well as the United States and German applications covering the same. The parties agreed in the first paragraph of the agreement 'not to do anything, either directly or indirectly and in any country, the result of which might restrict the scope of the claims of the other party relating to the subject matter of the above mentioned patents and patent applications.' In addition 'each undertakes, in accordance with the laws and regulations of the Patent Office concerned, to facilitate the allowance in any country of claims as broad as possible, as regards the subject matter of the patents and patent applications referred to above.' The parties also agreed not to sue one another on the basis of any of the patents or applications. * * *

* * *

[Later,] Gegauf assigned to Singer its application and all rights in the invention claimed and to all United States patents which might be granted under it for $90,000. The accompanying agreement provided that (1) Singer would grant Gegauf a nonexclusive royalty-free license to sell in the United States sewing machines made in Gegauf's factory in Switzerland; (2) Singer would not institute, without the consent of Gegauf, legal proceedings asserting the patents when issued against Pfaff in Germany or Vigorelli in Italy with respect to machines manufactured in their home factories; and (3) Singer would not make a 'slavish' copy of Gegauf's Bernina machine.

F. The Gegauf patent issued on April 29, 1958, and Singer filed two infringement suits against Brother, the largest domestic importer of Japanese machines. It also sued two other distributors of multicam machines, those actions terminating in consent decrees. * * *

* * *

II

First it may be helpful to set out what is not involved in this case. There is no claim by the Government that it is illegal for one merely to acquire a patent in order to exclude his competitors; or that the owner of a lawfully acquired patent cannot use the patent laws to exclude all infringers of the patent; or that a licensee cannot lawfully acquire the covering patent in order better to enforce it on his own account, even when the patent dominates an industry in which the licensee is the dominant firm. Therefore, we put all these matters aside without discussion.

What is claimed here is that Singer engaged in a series of transactions with Gegauf and Vigorelli for an illegal purpose, i.e., to rid itself and Gegauf, together, perhaps, with Vigorelli, of infringements by their common competitors, the Japanese manufacturers. The Government claims that in this respect there were an identity of purpose among the parties and actions pursuant thereto that in law amount to a combination or conspiracy violative of the Sherman Act. * * *

* * * [T]he fact that the cross-license agreement provided that Singer and Gegauf would facilitate the allowance to each other of claims 'as broad as possible' indicates a desire to secure as broad coverage for the patent as possible, the more effectively to stifle competition, the overwhelming percentage of which was Japanese. This effect was accomplished, for when the Patent Office placed the Harris (Singer) and Gegauf patents in interference, Singer abandoned the proceeding, thus facilitating the issuance of broad claims to Gegauf.

We now come to the assignment of the Gegauf patent to Singer. The trial court found: * * * Singer proposed to Vigorelli that it could prosecute the Gegauf patent in the United States better than Gegauf and, after Vigorelli agreed, solicited his help in getting Gegauf to agree to assign the patent. * * * Gegauf told Singer that he had no objection 'to making an agreement with Singer, in order to stop as far as possible Japanese competitors in the United States market.' * * * Gegauf ultimately assigned the patent for only $90,000, much less than its original asking price and much less than Gegauf believed it would realize annually from a license grant. Gegauf's beliefs as to the inadequacy of the monetary consideration were well founded, since Singer received more than twice that amount in a two-year period from the one license it granted under the Gegauf patent. * * *

III

* * *

* * * [B]y entwining itself with Gegauf and Vigorelli in such a program Singer went far beyond its claimed purpose of merely protecting its own 401 machine—it was protecting Gegauf and Vigorelli, the sole licensees under the patent at the time, under the same umbrella. This the Sherman Act will not permit. * * * [T]he facts as found by the trial court indicate a common purpose to suppress the Japanese machine competition in the United States through the use of the patent, which was secured by Singer on the assurances to Gegauf and its colicensee, Vigorelli, that such would certainly be the result. Singer cannot, of course, contend that it sought the assignment of the patent merely to assure that it could produce and sell its machines, since the preceding cross-license agreement had assured that right. The fact that the enforcement plan likewise served Singer is of no consequence, the controlling factor being the overall common design, i.e., to destroy the Japanese sale of infringing machines in the United States by placing the patent in Singer's hands the better to achieve this result. It is this concerted action to restrain trade, clearly established by the course of dealings, that condemns the transactions under the Sherman Act. * * *

* * *

* * * It is well settled that 'beyond the limited monopoly which is granted, the arrangements by which the patent is utilized are subject to the general law,' and it 'is equally well settled that the possession of a valid patent or patents does not give the patentee any exemption from the provisions of the Sherman Act beyond the limits of the patent monopoly. By aggregating patents in one control, the holder of the patents cannot escape the prohibitions of the Sherman Act.' That Act imposes strict limitations on the concerted activities in which patent owners may lawfully engage, and those limitations have been exceeded in this case.

The judgment of the District Court is reversed and the case is remanded for the entry of an appropriate decree in accordance with this opinion. It is so ordered.

Reversed and remanded.

MR. JUSTICE WHITE, concurring.

* * *

More must be said about the interference settlement. In 1956, Singer's 'Harris' multicam zigzag reissue-patent application was pending in the United States Patent Office; Gegauf had an application pending at the same time covering substantially the same subject matter, but enjoying a nine-day earlier priority date. In the circumstances, it appeared to Singer that, between Singer and Gegauf, Gegauf would have a better claim to a patent on the multicam zigzag, at least on the broad and thus more valuable claims. But it was by no means certain that either of them would get the patent. In cases where several applicants claim the same subject matter, the Patent Office declares an 'interference.' This is an adversary proceeding between the rival applicants, primarily for the purpose of determining relative priority. But a party to an interference also can, by drawing additional prior art to the attention of the Patent Office which will require the Office to issue no patent at all to anyone, prevent his rival from securing a patent which if granted might exclude him from the manufacture of the subject matter. Gegauf, after Singer approached it to negotiate an agreement before the Office declared an interference, feared that Singer might in self-defense draw to the attention of the Patent Office certain earlier patents the Office was unaware of, and which might cause the Gegauf claims to be limited or invalidated; Singer 'let them know that we thought we could knock out their claims but that in so doing we were probably going to hurt both of us.'

The result was that in April 1956 Singer and Gegauf entered a general cross-licensing agreement providing that the parties were not to attack one another's patent applications 'directly or indirectly,' not to do anything to restrict one another's claims in patents or applications, and to facilitate the allowance to one another of 'claims as broad as possible.' In August 1956 the Patent Office declared the anticipated interference. Singer and Gegauf settled the interference pursuant to their prior agreement: Singer withdrew its interfering claims and in April 1957 the Patent Office dissolved the interference proceeding before it had ever reached the litigation stage. Eventually the Gegauf patent issued and was sold to Singer as part of the concerted action to exclude the Japanese which is involved in the first branch of the case.

In itself the desire to secure broad claims in a patent may well be unexceptionable—when purely unilateral action is involved. And the settlement of an interference in which the only interests at stake are those of the adversaries, as in the case of a dispute over relative priority only and where possible invalidity, because of known prior art, is not involved, may well be consistent with the general policy favoring settlement of litigation. But the present case involves a less innocuous setting. Singer and Gegauf agreed to settle an interference, at least in part, to prevent an open fight over validity. There is a public interest here, which the parties have subordinated to their private ends-the public interest in granting patent monopolies only when the progress of the useful arts and of science will be furthered because as the consideration for its grant the public is given a novel and useful invention. When there is no novelty and the public parts with the monopoly grant for no return, the public has been imposed upon and the patent clause subverted. Whatever may be the duty of a single party to draw the prior art to the Office's attention, clearly collusion among applicants to prevent prior art from coming to or being drawn to the Office's attention is an inequitable imposition on the Office and on the public. In my view, such collusion to secure a monopoly grant runs afoul of the Sherman Act's prohibitions against conspiracies in restraint of trade-if not bad per se, then such agreements are at least presumptively bad. The patent laws do not authorize, and the Sherman Act does not permit, such agreements between business rivals to encroach upon the public domain and usurp it to themselves.

Both the *Singer* and the *Standard Oil (Cracking)* cases raise important issues concerning the application of antitrust laws to patent-related conduct associated with advancing industries. *Singer* highlights whether pooling patents can magnify their exclusionary capacity. Note that Justice White's concurrence condemns Singer for evading the typical patent interference proceeding. In particular, he points out that neither Singer nor Gegauf were certain *ex ante* that their patents would be granted. How important is this fact to the analysis? If Singer and Gegauf had entered into their agreements after each had been granted its own patents, would the court have reached the same conclusion? Does the answer depend upon the strength of the individual patents? What might make a patent "strong" or "weak" and how might that be relevant to the antitrust analysis?

How should antitrust institutions respond when the extent to which conduct is exclusionary depends on patent validity and strength? Many commentators argue that the Patent & Trademark Office (PTO) grants patents too readily and liberally in its endeavor to keep up with the recent explosion of patent applications and grants. On the other hand, even if this were true, some would argue that, as in the case of other property rights, a patent should be presumed valid absent a judicial determination that it is invalid or was obtained through fraud. Antitrust enforcers' inquiries into the "strength" of particular patents, which is generally outside their area of expertise, raise potential problems of error costs and second-guessing decisions properly within PTO's purview. If so, is there a greater need for antitrust to consider patent strength? Does this make it more likely patent holders are pooling their patents to enhance their exclusionary capacity? Antitrust largely operates by taking the patent system as given. Is it correct, then, for antitrust to take into consideration the fact that if certain patents under common ownership were to be challenged, they might be found invalid or not infringed? If yes, how large a role in the antitrust analysis should this consideration play—can (or should) it create a presumption that the pool was created for exclusionary purposes, or does it have a less determinative function?

The *Standard Oil (Cracking)* case also revolved around a patent pool, but focused upon how to define the market of which the pool was a part. Was the Court correct in combining in a single product market the old and new technologies? The argument against such an approach is that by doing so the Court underestimated the significance of cracking technology. By allowing refiners to extract a greater amount of gasoline from each barrel of crude oil, cracking conferred a significant cost advantage upon its users. Broad application of cracking technology throughout the industry promised to reduce the industry's cost of producing gasoline, and the pooling arrangement at issue in *Standard Oil (Cracking)*, by raising the price that companies had to pay to license the cracking patents, may have retarded that development.

As we have observed at many points in the Casebook, the reliability of market shares as a proxy for market power largely depends on the accuracy of the relevant market definition. In the case of industries that involve competing production processes, defining a product market may require difficult judgments about which industrial processes to include and which to leave out. By declining to identify control of cracking technology as its own relevant product market, the Court generated a market share for the defendants (26 percent) that may have obscured the true significance of a new process in petroleum refining.

It is also apparent that a court cannot calculate market shares accurately without sound data. The Supreme Court's reluctance to accept the government's suggested approach to defining the relevant market in terms of cracking technology seems to have stemmed partly from its concerns about the reliability of the prosecution's data on gasoline production. This underscores an additional basic point about the use of market shares as proxies for market power: the reliability of market shares as measures of market power is largely a function of the quality of data concerning the industry activity to be analyzed.

But is there an argument to be made that *Standard Oil (Cracking)* could have been decided in favor of the government even with a broad market definition? If the defendants' practices prevented prices from falling, *i.e.*, had actual anticompetitive effects, should the choice of market definition be outcome determinative? Recall cases like *NCAA* from Chapter 2 and *Staples* from Chapter 5. What importance should be assigned to such actual effects evidence and how might it affect the role of market definition?

Standard Oil and *Singer* serve as reminders that "new economies" are a persistent feature of markets over time. Although the locus of innovation may change, its power to transform industries has remained constant. In the 1920s, the emergence of cracking technology was transforming oil refining.

What factors should influence the decision to isolate "new" technologies as a distinct relevant market? The idea that current research and development efforts could constitute a distinct relevant market for antitrust purposes—even though they have yet to produce a marketable product—began to take hold in the early 1990s, and it has engendered a great deal of discussion at the enforcement agencies and in the literature. Consider the implications of the following scenarios, some of which we have already observed:

- A merger is proposed between two firms that are both leaders in R & D for a particular *future* product or process.

- A dominant firm undertakes conduct that delays or otherwise impairs the emergence of a new product or technology that may in the *future* develop into a serious challenge to its own, currently dominant product or process.

- A group of rivals agrees to limit the access of another one of their rivals to a product or process necessary to the development of "next generation" products.

The next Sidebar explores some of the commentary that has focused on the pluses and minuses of seeking to protect "innovation" markets in these sorts of circumstances and others.

Sidebar 7–2:
Innovation, Technology, and Future Product Markets

As highlighted in the *Singer* and *Cracking* cases, high-tech, dynamic industries can challenge antitrust's ability to make accurate predictions regarding innovation markets and markets for future products. Consider, for example, the Federal Trade Commission's acceptance of a final consent order growing out of its review of the merger of Ciba-Geigy and Sandoz, two pharmaceutical firms that combined to create Novartis. *In re Ciba-Geigy*, 123 F.T.C. 842 (1997). *See generally* Richard J. Gilbert & Willard K. Tom, *Is Innovation King at the Antitrust Agencies? The Intellectual Property Guidelines Five Years Later*, 69 ANTITRUST L.J. 43, 55–58 (2001). The settlement addressed several FTC concerns involving gene therapy treatments for medical conditions, which would work by modifying the genes in patients' cells. At the time of the merger, this industry did not actually exist—no gene therapy product had been marketed or even approved by the Food and Drug Administration—but some such products were in clinical trials and pharmaceutical firms were investing heavily in their development and commercialization.

The FTC's complaint alleged harmful competitive effects in markets for the "research, development, manufacture and sale" of gene therapy products for treating various diseases, including cancer. *In re Ciba-Geigy*, 123 F.T.C. at 844. According to the Commission, only the merging firms and one other, Chiron, controlled the substantial property rights necessary to commercialize gene therapy products. The adverse competitive effects would include:

> (1) a reduction in innovation competition among firms developing gene therapy products, resulting in delay or redirection of R & D tracks;
>
> (2) market power in various gene therapy markets, exercised either unilaterally or through coordinated interaction with Chiron;
>
> (3) a reduction in potential competition by prospective entrants, who would be required to invent around a broader portfolio of patents in order to succeed; and
>
> (4) a disincentive for the merged firm to license intellectual property rights or collaborate with other firms as compared with premerger incentives. *Id.* at 851–52.

The fourth allegation involves harm to competition in markets for the sale of *current* products, namely various intellectual property rights. This kind of product market is termed a "technology market" in the Intellectual Property Guidelines. U.S. Dep't of Justice and Fed. Trade Comm'n, *Antitrust Guidelines for the Licensing of Intellectual Property* § 3.2.2 (April 6, 1995) (hereinafter "*IP Guidelines*"). But the second and third allege harm to competition in markets for the sale of *future* products, involving collusive and exclusionary effects respectively. The first allegation involves the loss of competition in what the IP Guidelines term an "innovation market"—a market for research and development directed to particular new or improved goods or processes, and the close substitutes for that research and development. *IP Guidelines*, § 3.2.3. Innovation markets may be defined not only for merger analysis, but also to analyze the full range of possible antitrust offenses, including licensing of intellectual property (the subject of the Intellectual Property Guidelines), collaborations among rivals, and alleged monopolization.

Why do the enforcement agencies seek to define innovation markets and future product markets? Why not merely plead harmful competitive effects involving innovation in existing product markets? One reason is that many forms of conduct under review, especially mergers, are analyzed prospectively, before the possible harms appear. If, as a result, the competitive harms would arise in future product markets, or through a reduction in the prospects for innovation that would lead to new products, they would not necessarily fall on the customers of current products. *See generally* Richard J. Gilbert & Steven C. Sunshine, *Incorporating Dynamic Efficiency Concerns in Merger Analysis: The Use of Innovation Markets*, 63 ANTITRUST L.J. 569 (1995); Richard J. Gilbert & Steven C. Sunshine, *The Use of Innovation Markets: A Reply to Hay, Rapp, and Hoerner*, 64 ANTITRUST L.J. 75, 80–82 (1995).

A key problem for defining innovation markets is that new products and processes that supplant existing goods and methods can be developed in unrelated industries. As one critic put it, "the capacity to innovate is hard to monopolize." Richard T. Rapp, *The Misapplication of the Innovation Market Approach to Merger Analysis*, 64 ANTITRUST L.J. 19, 36–37 (1995). The IP Guidelines anticipate this criticism, and explain that "[t]he Agencies will delineate an innovation market only when the capabilities to engage in the relevant research and development can be associated with specialized assets or characteristics of specific firms." *IP Guidelines*, § 3.2.3. Under such circumstances, the enforcement agencies contend, they can identify the particular research and development tracks directed at a particular new product or process, and in competition. Thus, many of the FTC's innovation market cases have involved the development of new pharmaceuticals; for these products, it may be easy to determine how far along each firm has come in the Food & Drug Administration approval process. Perhaps because of this limitation, innovation markets are not commonly defined. In other words, these innovation cases may really involve "highly likely" future product markets, rather than "markets for innovation."

Buyers or excluded rivals who allege that they are victims of anticompetitive conduct in innovation markets may face an additional hurdle: proving injury and causation sufficient to ground standing to sue. *See generally* 1 HERBERT HOVENKAMP, MARK D. JANIS & MARK A. LEMLEY, IP AND ANTITRUST: AN ANALYSIS OF ANTITRUST PRINCIPLES APPLIED TO INTELLECTUAL PROPERTY LAW ¶ 4.3d (2011). Should that also be a concern in a government prosecution?

The analysis of firm conduct within future product markets or innovation markets does not end at market definition— rather, it requires antitrust institutions to make further predictions as to the competitive effects likely to arise in these dynamic markets. Firms merging their research and development activities, or collaborating in R & D, for example, may often achieve substantial efficiencies by doing so, and these efficiencies should be accounted for in assessing the reasonableness of the practice. The firms may be able to achieve scale economies in R & D, for example, or improve their prospects for innovation success by pooling complementary knowledge or skills. Here, as elsewhere in antitrust, indirect evidence of market power, derived from market definition and market shares, may not capture all aspects of competitive harm that might be relevant under the rule of reason. Reconsider the *Standard Oil (Cracking)* case from this perspective. Would the Court's analysis have differed if the product market had been limited to production (or innovation) using the new technology? Should the market definition matter to the competitive effects analysis?

The definition and competitive significance of innovation markets has continued to spawn differences of opinion and debate. In January 2004, by a divided vote, the FTC closed its investigation into the 2001 acquisition by Genzyme Corporation of Novazyme Pharmaceuticals, Inc. Novazyme was engaged primarily in conducting early pre-clinical studies relating to enzyme-replacement treatment (ERT) for Pompe disease, a rare and often fatal early childhood disease. Genzyme was also engaged in preclinical animal testing of ERTs. The Commission's investigation focused on the transaction's potential impact on the pace and scope of research into the development of a treatment for Pompe disease, given that the two firms appeared to be the only active sources of R & D into therapies for Pompe disease.

The Commission voted 3–1–1 to close the investigation. Three separate statements were filed, one by then Chairman Muris for the majority, a dissenting statement by Commissioner Thompson, and a separate statement by Commissioner Harbour. All focused on and discussed the analysis of innovation markets in the context of mergers. *See* http://www.ftc.gov/opa/2004/01/genzyme.htm.

Future product markets have also continued to be a topic of discussion and debate. In September 2013, the FTC authorized a complaint and entered into a consent order with Nielsen Holdings N.V. ("Nielsen") to remedy the allegedly anticompetitive effects of Nielsen's proposed acquisition of Arbitron Inc. ("Arbitron"). The complaint alleged that Nielsen's proposed acquisition would substantially lessen competition in the future market for national syndicated cross-platform audience measurement services in violation of Section 7 of the Clayton Act. Nielsen entered into a consent agreement to license Arbitron's television audience measurement service to a third party in order to restore any future competition lost as a result of the transaction.

The Commission voted 3–1 to authorize the complaint and approve the consent order. Commissioner Wright issued a dissenting statement emphasizing the limits of predicting competitive effects in future markets, especially, as was the case in the Nielsen transaction, when the allegation involves products that do not exist today. *See* http://www.ftc.gov/enforcement/cases-proceedings/131–0058/nielsen-holdings-nv-arbitron-inc-matter.

As you continue with your readings in this Chapter, consider how the use of "innovation markets" and future markets might enhance understanding of the competitive effects of the conduct being challenged. *See* U.S. DEP'T OF JUSTICE & FED. TRADE COMM'N, HORIZONTAL MERGER GUIDELINES (2010), http://www.justice.gov/atr/public/guidelines/hmg–2010.pdf.

B. COLLUSIVE AGREEMENTS

In Section A we examined courts' and antitrust enforcement agencies' initial efforts to reconcile a desire for vigorous innovation with concerns about potentially anticompetitive conduct in novel high-tech environments, as well as how those efforts related to the intellectual property laws historically. Notice how the attitudes reflected in these cases and enforcement principles have evolved over time, reflecting increased learning and familiarity with business behavior in these contexts.

We shift and narrow the focus now to investigate how antitrust doctrine has developed with respect to conduct having collusive effects in settings that relate to technology and innovation, especially industries in which tensions arose due to the clash between old and new technologies. Some also involve standard setting organizations and IPRs. Given the proliferation of IP rights in the New Economy—and the fact that these rights can be both overlapping and dispersed among multiple owners—cooperation among rivals can be not only desirable from the firms' viewpoint, but necessary in order for these firms to operate and produce their respective products or services at all. Analyzing the competitive effects of collaboration among competitors in these settings, therefore, can be an intricate endeavor. And importantly, it is one that arises under a variety of antitrust provisions—Section 7 of the Clayton Act in the merger and acquisition cases, and Section 1 of the Sherman Act and Section 5 of the FTC Act in standard setting cases. We examine several of these iterations and intricacies below.

1. MANIPULATION OF PRODUCT STANDARDS AND CERTIFICATIONS

Standards are used in many industries to certify products as safe and effective for specified uses. For example, local building codes normally specify in great detail the kind of plumbing, electrical, and general material requirements of residential and commercial construction. Often these codes are the product of efforts by industries to develop codes themselves through trade associations. Independent testing labs such as Underwriters Laboratories and the National Science Foundation also test and certify products. States, counties, and municipalities adopt these codes as public law.

Products and safety standards evolve over time, which necessitates a continual process of reevaluating codes. New products that could not have even been imagined at the time a code was drafted may necessitate redrafting or amending the code to account for new technology and new designs. Safety may dictate use of a certain material today, but the advent of a different, safer material may lead to changes in code. Asbestos insulation, for example, may at one time have been viewed as "state of the art" and approved by many building codes, but that is clearly no longer the case.

A supplier of a product that "does not meet code" will at best have a difficult time selling the product. For example, if a building code specifies that only steel electrical conduit can be used for certain purposes, the use of polyvinyl chloride ("PVC") conduit will, in effect, be prohibited, and suppliers of PVC conduit may find that there is no market for their product in a particular locale. *See, e.g., Allied Tube & Conduit Corp. v. Indian Head, Inc.*, 486 U.S. 492 (1988). This possibility—that a code or industry standard could in effect bar a substitute product—may in some circumstances create an incentive for a firm to attempt to influence the drafting of the code or standard in a way that will disadvantage its rivals. This incentive may be heightened when a new, innovative product threatens to displace an old one. Producers of the incumbent technology may try to delay or even totally preclude the emergence of the new technology by maintaining outdated codes, or advocating for more restrictive ones. In doing so, they may prevent price erosion and/or forestall improvements in product quality or choice—all to the detriment of consumers.

Our next case, *Am. Soc'y of Mech. Eng'rs, Inc. v. Hydrolevel, Corp.*, 456 U.S. 556 (1982), illustrates such a scenario. The narrow legal issue in the case concerned the Society's vicarious liability for the acts of its agent—an industry participant that had used its role as an ASME member to interpret an ASME-promulgated code to exclude the product of one of its nascent rivals. Note that the Court assumed that the activities described in the following excerpt violated the Sherman Act.

AMERICAN SOCIETY OF MECHANICAL ENGINEERS, INC. V. HYDROLEVEL CORP.

Supreme Court of the United States, 1982.
456 U.S. 556, 102 S. Ct. 1935, 72 L. Ed. 2d 330.

JUSTICE BLACKMUN delivered the opinion of the Court.

Petitioner, the American Society of Mechanical Engineers, Inc. (ASME), is a nonprofit membership corporation organized in 1880 under the laws of the State of New York. This case presents the important issue of the Society's civil liability under the antitrust laws for acts of its agents performed with apparent authority. Because the judgment of the Court of Appeals upholding civil liability is consistent with the central purposes of the antitrust laws, we affirm that judgment.

I

ASME has over 90,000 members drawn from all fields of mechanical engineering.* * * It employs a full-time staff, but much of its work is done through volunteers from industry and government. * * *

* * * ASME promulgates and publishes over 400 separate codes and standards for areas of engineering and industry. These codes, while only advisory, have a powerful influence: federal regulations have incorporated many of them by reference, as have the laws of most States, the ordinances of major cities, and the laws of all the Provinces of Canada. Obviously, if a manufacturer's product cannot satisfy the applicable ASME code, it is at a great disadvantage in the marketplace.

Among ASME's many sets of standards is its Boiler and Pressure Vessel Code. This set, like ASME's other codes, is very important in the affected industry; it has been adopted by 46 States and all but one of the Canadian Provinces. Section IV of the code sets forth standards for components of heating boilers, including "low-water fuel cutoffs." If the water in a boiler drops below a level sufficient to moderate the boiler's temperature, the boiler can "dry fire" or even explode. A low-water fuel cutoff does what its name implies: when the water in the boiler falls below a certain level, the device blocks the flow of fuel to the boiler before the water level reaches a dangerously low point. To prevent dry firing and boiler explosions, ¶ HG-605 of Section IV provides that each boiler "shall have an automatic low-water fuel cutoff so located as to automatically cut off the fuel supply when the surface of the water falls to the lowest visible part of the water gage glass."

For some decades, McDonnell & Miller, Inc. (M & M), has dominated the market for low-water fuel cutoffs. But in the mid-1960's, respondent Hydrolevel Corporation entered the low-water fuel cutoff market with a different version of this device. The relevant distinction, for the purposes of this case, was that Hydrolevel's fuel cutoff, unlike M & M's, included a time delay.

In early 1971, Hydrolevel secured an important customer. Brooklyn Union Gas Company, which had purchased M & M's product for several years, decided to switch to Hydrolevel's probe. Not surprisingly, M & M was concerned.

Because of its involvement in ASME, M & M was in an advantageous position to react to Hydrolevel's challenge. ASME's governing body had delegated the interpretation, formulation, and revision of the Boiler and Pressure Vessel Code to a Boiler and Pressure Vessel Committee. That committee in turn had authorized subcommittees to respond to public inquiries about the interpretation of the code. An M & M vice president, John W. James, was vice chairman of the subcommittee which drafted, revised, and interpreted Section IV, the segment of the Boiler and Pressure Vessel Code governing low-water fuel cutoffs.

After Hydrolevel obtained the Brooklyn Union Gas account, James and other M & M officials met with T. R. Hardin, the chairman of the Section IV subcommittee. The participants at the meeting planned a course of action. They decided to send an inquiry to ASME's Boiler and Pressure Vessel Committee asking whether a fuel cutoff with a time delay would satisfy the requirements of ¶ HG-605 of Section IV. James and Hardin, as vice chairman and chairman, respectively, of the relevant subcommittee, cooperated in drafting a letter, one they thought would elicit a negative response.

The letter was mailed over the name of Eugene Mitchell, an M & M vice president, to W. Bradford Hoyt, secretary of the Boiler and Pressure Vessel Committee and a full-time ASME employee. Following ASME's standard routine, Hoyt referred the letter to Hardin, as chairman of the subcommittee. Under the procedures of the Boiler and Pressure Vessel Committee, the subcommittee chairman—Hardin—could draft a response to a public inquiry without referring it to the entire subcommittee if he treated it as an "unofficial communication."

As a result, Hardin, one of the very authors of the inquiry, prepared the response. Although he retained control over the inquiry by treating the response as "unofficial," the response was signed by Hoyt, secretary of the Boiler and Pressure Vessel Committee, and it was sent out on April 29, 1971, on ASME stationery. Predictably, Hardin's prepared answer, utilized verbatim in the Hoyt letter, condemned fuel cutoffs that incorporated a time delay * * *.

* * *

As anticipated, M & M seized upon this interpretation of Section IV to discourage customers from buying Hydrolevel's product. It instructed its salesmen to tell potential customers that Hydrolevel's fuel cutoff failed to satisfy ASME's code. And M & M's employees did in fact carry the message of the subcommittee's response to customers interested in buying fuel cutoffs. Thus, M & M successfully used its position within ASME in an effort to thwart Hydrolevel's competitive challenge.

* * *

What was the nature of the anticompetitive effect being alleged in *Hydrolevel*? Are there predictable dangers to providing industry-run trade or membership organizations the authority to establish industry product standards? What might the advantages be? How would you counsel a client interested in participating in an industry-run standard-setting effort based on what you just learned in *Hydrolevel*? For another illustration of the threat to research, development, and innovation that can arise when rivals cooperate in the context of product development, see *United States v. Auto. Mfrs. Ass'n*, 307 F. Supp. 617 (C.D. Cal.1969) (approving a consent decree where automobile manufacturers were accused of conspiring to suppress research and development of automotive air pollution control equipment). An anticompetitive manipulation of standard setting also can arise in the context of intellectual property, which we will discuss in greater depth later in this Chapter. For an unsuccessful attempt to allege a concerted effort by industry members to exclude a new technology through a standards-setting organization, see *SD3, LLC v. Black & Decker, Inc.*, 801 F.3d 412 (4th Cir. 2015) (allegation of conspiracy insufficient).

2. PATENT POOLS AND CROSS LICENSING

As was evident from the underlying conduct in *Singer* and *Standard Oil* (*Cracking*), "patent pooling," or the licensing of patent portfolios, is not a particularly new category of conduct in the IP area. But in contrast to the time of the *Cracking* case, today the enforcement agencies recognize the potential procompetitive benefits of such agreements. As noted in § 5.5 of the IP Guidelines:

> Cross-licensing and pooling arrangements are agreements of two or more owners of different items of intellectual property to license one another or third parties. These arrangements may provide procompetitive benefits by integrating complementary technologies, reducing transaction costs, clearing blocking positions, and avoiding costly infringement litigation. By promoting the dissemination of technology, cross-licensing and pooling arrangements are often procompetitive.

But patent pools and cross licensing also can have collusive or exclusionary anticompetitive consequences.

In our next reading, we will examine the response of the Antitrust Division of the Justice Department to a request for a Business Review Letter regarding a proposed patent pooling and licensing arrangement relating to digital audio and visual compression technology. Under 28 C.F.R. § 50.6, the parties to a proposed transaction that raises antitrust concerns can request a statement of the Department's current "enforcement intention" with respect to the transaction. Although a positive response neither permanently binds the agency nor any private party, it generally does indicate that the practice can proceed without fear of government challenge in the near term. It also serves as a useful source of guidance for the immediate parties, as well as the members of the antitrust bar and their clients.

In this instance, nine companies and one university make the request, seeking to create a "one-stop-shopping" clearinghouse by pooling all of their patents. Firms interested in manufacturing equipment that stores or transmits compressed video technology could not do so without infringing one or more of the many patents that covered the compression technology, which would require individual negotiations and potentially prohibitive royalties. The pool was intended to solve those problems and permit cost-effective, widespread exploitation of the technology.

PATENTS FOR MPEG-2 TECHNOLOGY

United States Department of Justice, 1997.
1997 WL 356954 (D.O.J.).

VIA FAX
GERRARD R. BEENEY, ESQ.
SULLIVAN & CROMWELL
125 BROAD STREET
NEW YORK, NY 10004–2498

Dear Mr. Beeney:

This is in response to your request on behalf of the Trustees of Columbia University, Fujitsu Limited, General Instrument Corp., Lucent Technologies Inc., Matsushita Electric Industrial Co., Ltd., Mitsubishi Electric Corp., Philips Electronics N.V., Scientific-Atlanta, Inc., and Sony Corp. (collectively the "Licensors"), Cable Television Laboratories, Inc. ("CableLabs"), MPEG LA, L.L.C. ("MPEG LA"), and their affiliates for the issuance of a business review letter pursuant to the Department of Justice's Business Review Procedure, 28 C.F.R. § 50.6. You have requested a statement of the Department of Justice's antitrust enforcement intentions with respect to a proposed arrangement pursuant to which MPEG LA will offer a package license under the Licensors' patents that are essential to compliance with the MPEG-2 compression technology standard, and distribute royalty income among the Licensors.

I.   THE PROPOSED ARRANGEMENT

A.   *The MPEG-2 Standard*

The MPEG-2 standard has been approved as an international standard by the Motion Picture Experts Group of the International organization for Standards (ISO) and the International Electrotechnical Commission (IEC) and by the International Telecommunication Union Telecommunication Standardization Sector ("ITU-T"). It contains nine operative parts. Only Parts 1 (ISO/IEC 13818–1) and 2 (ISO/IEC 13818–2), which deal with systems and video, are relevant to the proposed activity. * * *6

The video and systems parts of the MPEG-2 standard will be applied in many different products and services in which video information is stored and/or transmitted, including cable, satellite and broadcast television, digital video disks, and telecommunications. However, compliance with the standards will infringe on numerous patents owned by many different entities. Consequently, a number of firms that

---

6   Notably, neither Part 1 nor Part 2 dictates a particular method for encoding video or programs into the specified syntax and semantics. Users of the standard are thus free to develop and use the encoding method they find most advantageous, while preserving the compatibility necessary to the integrity of the standard.

participated in the development of the standard formed the MPEG-2 Intellectual Property Working Group ("IP Working Group") to address intellectual property issues raised by the proposed standard. Among other things, the IP Working Group sponsored a search for the patents that covered the technology essential to compliance with the proposed standard and explored the creation of a mechanism to convey those essential intellectual property rights to MPEG-2 users. That exploration led ultimately to an agreement among the Licensors, CableLabs and Baryn S. Futa establishing MPEG LA as a Delaware Limited Liability Company.

Each of the Licensors owns at least one patent that the IP Working Group's patent search identified as essential to compliance with the video and/or systems parts of the MPEG-2 standard (hereinafter "MPEG-2 Essential Patent" or "Essential Patent"). Among them, they account for a total of 27 Essential Patents, which are most, but not all, of the Essential Patents. Pursuant to a series of four proposed agreements, the Licensors will combine their Essential Patents into a single portfolio (the "Portfolio") in the hands of a common licensing administrator that would grant licenses under the Portfolio on a nondiscriminatory basis, collect royalties, and distribute them among the Licensors pursuant to a pro-rata allocation based on each Licensor's proportionate share of the total number of Portfolio patents in the countries in which a particular royalty-bearing product is made and sold.

* * *

B. MPEG LA

* * * MPEG LA will: (1) grant a worldwide, nonexclusive sublicense under the Portfolio to make, use and sell MPEG-2 products "to each and every potential Licensee who requests an MPEG-2 Patent Portfolio License and shall not discriminate among potential licensees"; (2) solicit Portfolio licensees; (3) enforce and terminate Portfolio license agreements; and (4) collect and distribute royalties. For this purpose, each MPEG-2 Licensor will grant MPEG LA a nonexclusive license under its Essential Patents, while retaining the right to license them independently for any purpose, including for making MPEG-2-compliant products.

The Licensing Administrator Agreement places the day-to-day conduct of MPEG LA's business, including its licensing activities, under the sole control of Futa and his staff. The other owners retain some control, however, over "major decisions," including approval of budgets and annual financial statements, extraordinary expenditures, entry into new businesses, mergers and acquisitions, and the sale or dissolution of the corporation.

C. The MPEG-2 Portfolio

As noted above, the Portfolio initially will consist of 27 patents, which constitute most, but not all, Essential Patents. These 27 patents were identified in a search carried out by an independent patent expert under the sponsorship of the IP Working Group. Once the MPEG-2 standard was largely in place, the IP working Group issued a public call for the submission of patents that might be infringed by compliance with the MPEG-2 standard. CableLabs, whose COO Futa was an active participant in the IP Working Group, retained an independent patent expert familiar with the standard and the relevant technology to review the submissions. In all, the expert and his assistant reviewed approximately 8000 United States patent abstracts and studied about 800 patents belonging to over 100 different patentees or assignees. No submission was refused, and no entity or person that was identified as having an essential patent was in any way excluded from the effort in forming the proposed joint licensing program.

The proposed agreement among the Licensors creates a continuing role for an independent expert as an arbiter of essentiality. It requires the retention of an independent expert to review patents submitted to any of the Licensors for inclusion in the Portfolio and to review any Portfolio patent which an MPEG-2 Licensor has concluded is not essential or as to which anyone has claimed a good-faith belief of non-essentiality. In both cases, the Licensors are bound by the expert's opinion.

* * *

D. The Portfolio License

The planned license from MPEG LA to users of the MPEG-2 standards is a worldwide, nonexclusive, nonsublicensable license under the Portfolio patents for the manufacture, sale, and in most cases, use of: (1) products and software designed to encode and/or decode video information in accordance with the MPEG-2 standard; (2) products and software designed to generate MPEG-2 program and transport bitstreams; and (3) so-called "intermediate products," such as integrated circuit chips, used in the aforementioned products and software. The license grant to use encoding-related products and software for recording video information on a "packaged medium," e.g., encoding a motion picture for copying on digital video disks, is separate from the other grants for the same products and software.

The Portfolio license expires January 1, 2000, but is renewable at the licensee's option for a period of not less than five years, subject to "reasonable amendment of its terms and conditions." That "reasonable amendment" may not, however, increase royalties by more than 25%. Each Portfolio licensee may terminate its license on 30 days' written notice. The per-unit royalties are those agreed upon in the Agreement Among Licensors, but they are subject to reduction pursuant to a "most-favored-nation" clause. The royalty obligations are predicated on actual use of one or more of the licensed patents in the unit for which the royalty is assessed. The Portfolio license imposes no obligation on the licensee to use only the licensed patents and explicitly leaves the licensee free independently to develop "competitive video products or video services which do not comply with the MPEG-2 Standard."[25]

The Portfolio license will list the Portfolio patents in an attachment. It also explicitly addresses the licensee's ability, and possible need, to obtain Essential Patent rights elsewhere. The Portfolio license states that each Portfolio patent is also available for licensing independently from the MPEG-2 Licensor that had licensed it to MPEG LA and that the license may not convey rights to all Essential Patents.

The license's grantback provision requires the licensee to grant any of the Licensors and other Portfolio licensees a nonexclusive worldwide license or sublicense, on fair and reasonable terms and conditions, on any Essential Patent that it has the right to license or sublicense. The Licensors' per-patent share of royalties is the basis for determining a fair and reasonable royalty for the grantback. Alternatively, a licensee that controls an Essential Patent may choose to become an MPEG-2 licensor and add its patent to the Portfolio. * * *

A separate provision allows for partial termination of a licensee's Portfolio license as to a particular MPEG-2 Licensor's patents. Pursuant to Section 6.3, an MPEG-2 Licensor may direct MPEG LA to withdraw its patents from the Portfolio license if the licensee has (a) brought a lawsuit or other proceeding against the MPEG-2 Licensor for infringement of an Essential Patent or an MPEG-2 Related Patent ("Related Patent") and (b) refused to grant the MPEG-2 Licensor a license under the Essential Patent or MPEG-2 Related Patent on fair and reasonable terms and conditions.[33]

---

[25] * * * We understand this to mean that licensees are free also to develop technological alternatives to the MPEG-2 compression standard.

[33] * * * The Portfolio license, like several of the relevant documents, defines "MPEG-2-Related Patent" as "any Patent which is not an MPEG-2 Essential Patent but which has one or more claims directed to an apparatus or a method that may be used in the implementation of a product or a service designed in whole or in part to exploit the MPEG-2 Standard under the laws of the country which issued or published the Patent." Read literally, this definition could encompass any patent capable of being employed in a product or service that exploits the MPEG-2 standard. At the extreme, it would take in any patent relevant not only to MPEG-2 applications but also to unrelated products, as well as patents on products or services that someone might build into an MPEG-2 Royalty Product—for example, a patented informational display on a DVD player. You have informed the Department, however, that such a broad, literal interpretation was not the intent of the drafters of the Patent Portfolio License and that your clients would construe the term "MPEG-2 Related Patents" to encompass only patents which, as applied, constitute implementations of the MPEG-2 standard. Further, you have told the Department that it is exceedingly unlikely that any Related Patent would have any utility for any application other than MPEG-2.

As with the grantback, the per-patent share of Portfolio license royalties is the basis for determining a fair and reasonable royalty for the licensee's patent. * * *

II. ANALYSIS

A. The Patent Pool in General

* * *

A starting point for an antitrust analysis of any patent pool is an inquiry into the validity of the patents and their relationship to each other. A licensing scheme premised on invalid or expired intellectual property rights will not withstand antitrust scrutiny.[39] And a patent pool that aggregates competitive technologies and sets a single price for them would raise serious competitive concerns. On the other hand, a combination of complementary intellectual property rights, especially ones that block the application for which they are jointly licensed, can be an efficient and procompetitive method of disseminating those rights to would-be users.

Based on your representations to us about the complementary nature of the patents to be included in the Portfolio, it appears that the Portfolio is a procompetitive aggregation of intellectual property. The Portfolio combines patents that an independent expert has determined to be essential to compliance with the MPEG-2 standard; there is no technical alternative to any of the Portfolio patents within the standard. Moreover, each Portfolio patent is useful for MPEG-2 products only in conjunction with the others.[40] The limitation of the Portfolio to technically essential patents, as opposed to merely advantageous ones, helps ensure that the Portfolio patents are not competitive with each other and that the Portfolio license does not, by bundling in non-essential patents, foreclose the competitive implementation options that the MPEG-2 standard has expressly left open.

The continuing role of an independent expert to assess essentiality is an especially effective guarantor that the Portfolio patents are complements, not substitutes. The relevant provisions of the Agreement Among Licensors appear well designed to ensure that the expert will be called in whenever a legitimate question is raised about whether or not a particular patent belongs in the Portfolio; in particular, they seem designed to reduce the likelihood that the Licensors might act concertedly to keep

---

[39] See, e.g., United States v. Pilkington Plc, 1994–2 Trade Cas. (CCH) ¶ 70,842 (D.Ariz.1994) (consent decree resolving antitrust suit against exclusive licenses premised on technology covered by expired patents).

[40] The Department presumes from the information you have provided us that the Portfolio patents are valid. Should this prove not to be so, the Department's analysis and enforcement intentions would likely be very different. As noted above, the Agreement Among Licensors provides for the deletion from the Portfolio of licenses held invalid or unenforceable.

invalid or non-essential patents in the Portfolio or to exclude other essential patents from admission to the Portfolio.

B.   Specific Terms of the Agreements

Despite the potential procompetitive effects of the Portfolio license, we would be concerned if any specific terms of any of the contemplated agreements seemed likely to restrain competition. Such possible concerns might include the likelihood that the Licensors could use the Portfolio license as a vehicle to disadvantage competitors in downstream product markets; to collude on prices outside the scope of the Portfolio license, such as downstream MPEG-2 products; or to impair technology or innovation competition, either within the MPEG-2 standard or from rival compression technologies. It appears, however, that the proposed arrangement will not raise any significant competitive concerns.

1.   Effect on Rivals

There does not appear to be any potential for use of the Portfolio license to disadvantage particular licensees. The Agreement Among Licensors commits the Licensors to nondiscriminatory Portfolio licensing, and the Licensing Administrator agreement both vests sole licensing authority in MPEG LA and explicitly requires MPEG LA to offer the Portfolio license on the same terms and conditions to all would-be licensees. Thus, maverick competitors and upstart industries will have access to the Portfolio on the same terms as all other licensees. The Portfolio license's "most-favored-nation" clause ensures further against any attempt to discriminate on royalty rates.

Although it offers the Portfolio patents only as a package, the Portfolio license does not appear to be an illegal tying agreement. The conditioning of a license for one intellectual property right on the license of a second such right could be a concern where its effect was to foreclose competition from technological alternatives to the second. In this instance, however, the essentiality of the patents—determined by the independent expert— means that there is no technological alternative to any of them and that the Portfolio license will not require licensees to accept or use any patent that is merely one way of implementing the MPEG-2 standard, to the detriment of competition. Moreover, although a licensee cannot obtain fewer than all the Portfolio patents from MPEG LA, the Portfolio license informs potential licensees that licenses on all the Portfolio patents are available individually from their owners or assignees. While the independent expert mechanism should ensure that the Portfolio will never contain any unnecessary patents, the independent availability of each Portfolio patent is a valuable failsafe. The list of Portfolio patents attached to the Portfolio license will provide licensees with information they need to assess the merits of the Portfolio license.

2. *Facilitation of Collusion*

From what you have told us, there does not appear to be anything in the proposed agreements that is likely to facilitate collusion among Licensors or licensees in any market. Although MPEG LA is authorized to audit licensees, 42 confidentiality provisions prohibit it from transmitting competitively sensitive information among the Licensors or other licensees. Further, since the contemplated royalty rates are likely to constitute a tiny fraction of MPEG-2 products' prices, at least in the near term, it appears highly unlikely that the royalty rate could be used during that period as a device to coordinate the prices of downstream products.

3. *Effect on Innovation*

It further appears that nothing in the arrangement imposes any anticompetitive restraint, either explicitly or implicitly, on the development of rival products and technologies. Nothing in the Agreement Among Licensors discourages, either through outright prohibition or economic incentives, any Licensor from developing or supporting a rival standard. As noted above, the Portfolio license explicitly leaves licensees free independently to make products that do not comply with the MPEG-2 standard and premises royalty obligations on actual use of at least one Portfolio patent.[44] Since the Portfolio includes only Essential Patents, the licensee's manufacture, use or sale of MPEG-2 products will necessarily infringe the Portfolio patents. By weeding out non-essential patents from the Portfolio, the independent-expert mechanism helps ensure that the licensees will not have to pay royalties for making MPEG-2 products that do not employ the licensed patents.

The license's initial duration, to January 1, 2000, does not present any competitive concern. While the open-ended renewal term of "no less than five years" holds open the possibility of a perpetual license, its competitive impact will depend substantially on whether any of the "reasonable amendments" made at that time increase the license's exclusionary impact. While the term "reasonable" is the Portfolio license's only limitation on the Licensors' ability to impose onerous non-royalty terms on licensees at renewal time, the 25% cap on royalty increases and the "most-favored-nation" clause appear to constrain the Licensors' ability to use royalties to exploit any locked-in installed base among its licensees.

Nor does the Portfolio license's grantback clause appear anticompetitive. Its scope, like that of the license itself, is limited to Essential Patents. It does not extend to mere implementations of the

---

[44] *Cf. United States v. Microsoft Corp.*, 1995–2 Trade Cas. (CCH) ¶ 71,096 (D.D.C.1995) (consent decree resolving suit against, among other things, use of per-processor royalty for license of dominant operating system).

standard or even to improvements on the essential patents.[45] Rather, the grantback simply obliges licensees that control an Essential Patent to make it available to all, on a nonexclusive basis, at a fair and reasonable royalty, just like the Portfolio patents. This will mean that any firm that wishes to take advantage of the cost savings afforded by the Portfolio license cannot hold its own essential patents back from other would-be manufacturers of MPEG-2 products. While easing, though not altogether clearing up, the holdout problem,[46] the grantback should not create any disincentive among licensees to innovate. Since the grantback extends only to MPEG-2 Essential Patents, it is unlikely that there is any significant innovation left to be done that the grantback could discourage.[47] The grantback provision is likely simply to bring other Essential Patents into the Portfolio, thereby limiting holdouts' ability to exact a supracompetitive toll from Portfolio licensees and further lowering licensees' costs in assembling the patent rights essential to their compliance with the MPEG-2 standard.

In different circumstances, the right of partial termination set forth in Section 6.3 of the Portfolio license could raise difficult competition issues. That section provides that, on instruction from any Licensor, MPEG LA, pursuant to its obligations under the Licensing Administrator Agreement, shall withdraw from a particular licensee's portfolio license that Licensor's patent or patents if the licensee has sued the Licensor for infringement of an Essential Patent or a Related Patent and refused to grant a license on the allegedly infringed patent on "fair and reasonable terms."

Of course, a licensee's refusal to license an Essential Patent on fair and reasonable terms, as required by Section 7.3 of the Portfolio License, is grounds for termination of the Portfolio license altogether. Even though MPEG LA may choose not to exercise its right to terminate, a Licensor that has been denied a license may invoke the less drastic partial termination provision, which is mandatory on MPEG LA. Partial termination would force the licensee to negotiate with the Licensor as if the pool had never existed. Thus, while the partial termination right leaves the licensee no worse off than it was in the absence of the pool, it enforces the Essential Patent grantback, which, as discussed above, appears procompetitive.

The right of partial termination could have a very different impact on a Portfolio licensee that owns a Related Patent. No matter how attractive

---

[45] Consequently, much of the section on grantbacks in the IP Guidelines is not directly applicable to this provision. The ultimate question, though, is the same: whether, by reducing licensees' incentives to innovate, the grantback causes competitive harm that outweighs its procompetitive effects. *See* IP Guidelines, § 5.6.

[46] Any non-manufacturing owner of an Essential Patent, in contrast, can still be a holdout, having no need for the Portfolio license.

[47] Improvements on MPEG-2 Essential Patents and technological alternatives to the Essential Patents would not be Essential Patents themselves and would not be subject to the grantback. Therefore, the grantback should not discourage their development.

the licensee's patented implementation of the MPEG-2 standard may be, by definition the Related Patent will not be essential to compliance with the standard. And, not being essential, the patent is not subject to the Section 7.3 grantback. If the Portfolio licensee that owns a Related Patent chooses not to license others to use its technology, those others may still have alternatives to choose from. But if a Licensor chooses to infringe the Portfolio licensee's Related Patent after having been denied a license, the Portfolio licensee's decision to sue for infringement could cause it to become unable, at least temporarily, to comply with the MPEG-2 standard.[48]

The MPEG-2 Licensor is not entirely unconstrained: Importantly, as you have pointed out, its undertakings to the ISO and/or the ITU-T obligate it to license on fair and reasonable terms. However, it is not clear that this general commitment alone deprives the Licensor of the ability to impair competition. The partial termination right may enable Licensors to obtain licenses on Related Patents at royalty levels below what they would have been in a competitive market. Consequently, the partial termination right may dampen licensees' incentives to invest in research and development of MPEG-2 implementations, undercutting somewhat the benefits of the openness of the MPEG-2 standard and the prospects for improvements on the Essential Patents.

This impact on the incentive to innovate within the MPEG-2 standard would be of particular concern were the partial termination right designed to benefit all portfolio licensees. In that event, the partial termination right would function much like a compulsory grantback into the Portfolio. Licensees that owned Related Patents would not be able to choose among and negotiate freely with potential users of their inventions. The licensees' potential return from their R & D investments could be curtailed drastically, and the corresponding impact on their incentive to innovate could be significant.

Here, however, the partial termination right, unlike the grantback, protects only the Licensors. Other portfolio licensees have no right under the pool license to practice fellow licensees' inventions. And the Licensors are likely to be restrained in exercising their partial termination rights because the development of Related Patents will enhance MPEG-2 and, thus, the value of the Portfolio. The long-term interest of the Licensors is generally to encourage innovation in Related Patents, not to stifle it.

Moreover, the partial termination right may have procompetitive effects to the extent that it functions as a nonexclusive grantback

---

[48] Since, as noted in note 33 above, it is exceedingly unlikely that a Related Patent would ever have any utility outside the MPEG-2 standard, it is correspondingly unlikely that an owner of a Related Patent would ever have cause to sue an MPEG-2 Licensor for infringement of that patent in connection with the manufacture, use or sale of anything other than MPEG-2-related products or services. If Section 6.3 were used in response to such an infringement action, we could have serious concerns.

requirement on licensees' Related Patents. It could allow Licensors and licensees to share the risk and rewards of supporting and improving the MPEG-2 standard by enabling Licensors to capture some of the value they have added to licensees' Related Patents by creating and licensing the Portfolio. In effect, the partial termination right may enable Licensors to realize greater returns on the Portfolio license from the licensees that enjoy greater benefits from the license, while maintaining the Portfolio royalty at a level low enough to attract licensees that may value it less. This in turn could lead to more efficient exploitation of the Portfolio technology.

Therefore, in light of both its potentially significant procompetitive effects and the limited potential harm it poses to Portfolio licensees' incentives to innovate, the partial-termination clause appears on balance unlikely to be anticompetitive.

III. CONCLUSION

Like many joint licensing arrangements, the agreements you have described for the licensing of MPEG-2 Essential Patents are likely to provide significant cost savings to Licensors and licensees alike, substantially reducing the time and expense that would otherwise be required to disseminate the rights to each MPEG-2 Essential Patent to each would-be licensee. Moreover, the proposed agreements that will govern the licensing arrangement have features designed to enhance the usual procompetitive effects and mitigate potential anticompetitive dangers. The limitation of the Portfolio to technically essential patents and the use of an independent expert to be the arbiter of that limitation reduces the risk that the patent pool will be used to eliminate rivalry between potentially competing technologies. Potential licensees will be aided by the provision of a clear list of the Portfolio patents, the availability of the Portfolio patents independent of the Portfolio, and the warning that the Portfolio may not contain all Essential Patents. The conditioning of licensee royalty liability on actual use of the Portfolio patents, the clearly stated freedom of licensees to develop and use alternative technologies, and the imposition of obligations on licensees' own patent rights that do not vitiate licensees' incentives to innovate, all serve to protect competition in the development and use of both improvements on, and alternatives to, MPEG-2 technology.

For these reasons, the Department is not presently inclined to initiate antitrust enforcement action against the conduct you have described. This letter, however, expresses the Department's current enforcement intention. In accordance with our normal practices, the Department reserves the right to bring an enforcement action in the future if the actual operation of the proposed conduct proves to be anticompetitive in purpose or effect.

This statement is made in accordance with the Department's Business Review Procedure, 28 C.F.R. § 50.6. Pursuant to its terms, your business review request and this letter will be made publicly available immediately, and any supporting data will be made publicly available within 30 days of the date of this letter, unless you request that part of the material be withheld in accordance with Paragraph 10(c) of the Business Review Procedure.

SINCERELY,

JOEL I. KLEIN*

[* Then Assistant Attorney General, Antitrust Division, Department of Justice. Eds.]

There are many important aspects to the DOJ's 1997 Business Review letter in *MPEG*. On a basic level, first note how the Department used the IP Guidelines to shape its analysis. Note, too, that as we have emphasized throughout the book, its inquiry focused on the arrangement's potential to lead to collusive or exclusionary anticompetitive effects. But it devoted a considerable portion of its analysis to whether the arrangement would more particularly have a negative effect on *innovation*. What explains that emphasis?

MPEG-2 also illustrates the many kinds of antitrust issues that can arise in the context of patent pooling or cross-licensing. Note how the DOJ touched upon and evaluated the possibility that the pooling plan would lead to horizontal price fixing, exclusionary boycotts, exclusive dealing, and tying. What elements of its analysis could you tie to cases we have studied? Consider how cases like *Broadcast Music*, *Visa*, and *Jefferson Parish* provide a backdrop for the Department's analysis.

The key distinctions *MPEG* recognizes, namely those regarding essential patents and the effects of complements versus substitutes, continue to guide the DOJ's analysis in modern patent pooling cases. *See* IP REPORT, ch. 3; Letter from Thomas Barnett, Assistant Att'y Gen., Antitrust Div., Dep't of Justice, to William Dolan, Esq., and Geoffrey Oliver, Esq., Jones Day (Oct. 21, 2008), http://www.justice.gov/atr/public/busreview/238429.pdf; *Request for Business Review Letter Regarding the Licensing of Patents for DVD Technology*, 1999 WL 392163 (D.O.J. 1999); *Business Review Letter Regarding the Licensing of Patents Essential to DVD-Video and DVD-Rom*, 1998 WL 890334 (D.O.J. 1998). *See also U.S. IP Guidelines*, § 5.5; Competition Bureau of Canada, *Enforcement Guidelines Intellectual Property* Ex. 6 (Mar. 31, 2016), http://www.competitionbureau.gc.ca/eic/site/cb-bc.nsf/vwapj/cb-IPEG-e.pdf/$file/cb-IPEG-e.pdf.

Consider the conduct from the perspective of the parties. What was the "problem" the *MPEG* parties were trying to solve? How did cross-licensing and pooling patents provide an efficient resolution of their problem? What were the specific features and characteristics of the agreements that were negotiated by the *MPEG* parties? How clear of a road map does the government's analysis provide to others who might want to propose similar arrangements? Were there features that were indispensable from the DOJ's view, in terms of ensuring that the pooling arrangement would not be anticompetitive?

What might have caused "the problem"? How could there have been 8000 related patents? Twenty-seven that were "essential"? One commentator has termed this issue the "patent thicket"—"an overlapping set of patent rights requiring that those seeking to commercialize new technology obtain licenses from multiple patentees." Carl Shapiro, *Navigating the Patent Thicket: Cross-Licenses, Patent Pools, and Standard Setting, in* 1 INNOVATION POLICY AND THE ECONOMY 119 (Adam Jaffe, Joshua Lerner & Scott Stern eds., 2001).

NOTE ON THE ROLE OF THE PTO IN DEFINING THE SCOPE OF PATENT PROTECTION

As we discussed at the outset of our treatment of IPRs, their essential characteristic is the "right to exclude." That right to exclude, of course, generates both the incentive to innovate that is the point of IPRs, as well as concern for their possible negative impact on competition. As a general matter, the more broadly the Patent & Trademark Office ("PTO") defines IPRs, and the more applications the PTO grants, the greater the possibility that the IPRs system will (1) confer greater power to exclude than is necessary to spur innovation, and (2) diminish competition for innovation by facilitating unjustifiable and unnecessary exclusion. The equilibrium of the IP rights system can also be disrupted by granting IP rights that endure longer than is necessary to attract the investment and effort to innovate. These issues— patent scope, proliferation, and duration—and how to calibrate competition policy to take them into account, have been the focus of a great deal of study. *See, e.g.*, Fed. Trade Comm'n & Dep't of Justice, Antitrust Div., *Antitrust Enforcement and Intellectual Property Rights: Promoting Innovation and Competition* (Apr. 2007), https://www.ftc.gov/sites/default/files/documents/ reports/antitrust-enforcement-and-intellectual-property-rights-promoting- innovation-and-competition-report.s.department-justice-and-federal-trade- commission/p040101promotinginnovationandcompetitionrpt0704.pdf; Fed. Trade Comm'n, *To Promote Innovation: The Proper Balance of Competititon and Patent Law and Policy* (Oct. 2003), https://www.ftc.gov/sites/default/files/ documents/reports/promote-innovation-proper-balance-competition-and- patent-law-and-policy/innovationrpt.pdf. *See also* Fed. Trade Comm'n Report, *The Evolving IP Marketplace: Aligning Patent Notice and Remedies with Competition* (2011), https://www.ftc.gov/sites/default/files/documents/reports/

evolving-ip-marketplace-aligning-patent-notice-and-remedies-competition-report-federal-trade/110307patentreport.pdf.

The America Invents Act of 2011 represented the first significant changes to the U.S. patent system since 1952. *Leahy-Smith America Invents Act, Pub. L. No. 112–29, § 16(b)(4)* (2011). The Act establishes a first-to-file standard for patent approval, replacing the first-to-invent standard. Additionally, it implements a post-grant review system and establishes processes to assist the PTO in addressing the backlog of patent applications. This final aspect may be particularly useful, given the proliferation of patent applications in recent decades—the total number of patents granted by the PTO increased from approximately 67,000 per year in 1980 to more than 325,000 in 2015. *See* U.S. Patent Statistics Chart, Calendar Years 1963–2015, http://www.uspto.gov/web/offices/ac/ido/oeip/taf/us_stat.htm. As in *MPEG*, this proliferation of patents may necessitate greater degrees of cooperation among rivals, who may find themselves unable to utilize a process or produce a product because of the presence of multiple patents and the threat of infringement actions, and consequently higher risks of anticompetitive coordination. *See* Carl Shapiro, *Navigating the Patent Thicket: Cross-Licenses, Patent Pools, and Standard Setting, in* 1 INNOVATION POLICY AND THE ECONOMY (Adam Jaffe, Joshua Lerner & Scott Stern eds., 2001), http://faculty.haas.berkeley.edu/shapiro/thicket.pdf.

Understanding the factors driving patent scope, proliferation, and quality is important to understanding the interplay of the patent and antitrust laws. For instance, if patent thickets exist and the predominant method for navigating these thickets involves cross-licensing, patent pooling, or standard setting, antitrust analysis should account for this reality and its analysis of competitive effects. On the other hand, if such arrangements are symptoms of a broken patent system that grants patents too frequently and easily, and hence may lead to unwarranted collusion or exclusion, in addition to continued patent reforms measured antitrust enforcement may be a necessary corrective to forestall competitive harm. Indeed, resolving many of the issues this Chapter poses may turn on the answers to these questions. In short, the antitrust response to IP rights will ultimately be a function of the scope of those rights, themselves, how they are used, and how their use affects both competition and incentives for innovation.

3. PATENT SETTLEMENTS IN THE PHARMACEUTICAL INDUSTRY

An especially thorny issue that has arisen in the context of patent licensing concerns the ability of rivals to settle patent infringement actions, either through cross-licensing of patents, or through payments designed to keep a competing, and allegedly infringing product, from being marketed. As we will see in our next *Note*, these issues have arisen primarily in the pharmaceutical industry, owing, at least in the United States, to some industry-specific legislation, and arise in disputes between branded and generic pharmaceutical firms.

These kinds of settlements are sometimes referred to as "reverse payment" settlements or "pay-for-delay," because instead of the compensation flowing from the alleged infringer (the generic producer) to the patent holder (the branded pharmaceutical firm), it flows from the patent holder to the alleged infringer. A group of such cases has arisen in the prescription drug industry, where competition from generic versions of popular prescription drugs poses a competitive threat to the branded and patented drug as its patent life comes to an end. While patent settlement issues can arise outside the pharmaceutical context, most involve prescription drugs and involve the intricacies of the Hatch-Waxman Act.

NOTE ON THE HATCH-WAXMAN ACT AND EARLY PAY-FOR-DELAY CASES

To encourage the production of generic pharmaceutical drugs, Congress enacted the Hatch-Waxman Amendments in 1984. *See* Drug Price Competition & Patent Term Restoration Act of 1984, Pub. L. No. 98–417, 98 Stat. 1585 (1984), to the Federal Food, Drug, and Cosmetic Act, 21 U.S.C. §§ 301–399. Hatch-Waxman allows a generic producer of a patented pioneer drug to file an Abbreviated New Drug Application ("ANDA") with the Food and Drug Administration ("FDA"). In turn, the ANDA allows a generic manufacturer to rely upon the FDA's prior determination that the pioneer drug is safe and effective, rather than requiring the generic to follow the often costly and time-consuming process of conducting and submitting for approval its own studies proving the efficacy of the drug. *Id.* § 355(j)(2)(A). Each ANDA must include a "certification that, in the opinion of the applicant and to the best of his knowledge, the proposed generic drug does not infringe any patent listed with the FDA as covering the pioneer drug." *Id.* § 355(j)(2)(A)(vii).

This certification may take several forms. Recent antitrust litigation has been most concerned with the "paragraph IV" certification. Under paragraph IV, the ANDA filer certifies that any relevant patent "is invalid or will not be infringed by the manufacture, use, or sale of the new drug for which the application is submitted." *Id.* § 355(j)(2)(A)(vii)(IV). The filer must further give notice to the patent holder, *id.* § 355(j)(2)(B), who then has forty-five days to file an infringement action. *Id.* § 355(j)(5)(B)(iii). The patent-holder's filing of suit initiates a stay that precludes the FDA from granting approval to the generic for thirty months, unless a court makes a determination as to infringement or to the patent's validity in the interim. *Id.* § 355(j)(5)(B)(iii)(I). Paragraph IV certification is particularly appealing to potential generic manufacturers because the first approved paragraph IV filer receives a 180 day period of exclusive marketing rights. During this period, the FDA will not approve any other ANDA application; accordingly, although the first filer will likely face competition from the patent holder, it faces no other generic competition during this time period—meaning that the drug price does not immediately plummet (or, at least, declines only slightly) as it would were all generics to enter at once. This 180 day period begins either when (1) the first ANDA filer starts to commercially market its generic product (marketing trigger), or (2) a court rules that the patent is invalid or not infringed (court decision trigger), whichever comes first. *Id.*

Antitrust litigation has brought to bear the arguments on both sides and endeavored to determine the proper standards for evaluating these arrangements. *See, e.g., In re Cardizem CD Antitrust Litigation*, 332 F.3d 896 (6th Cir. 2003) (holding that defendants' reverse-payment agreement was a per se violation of the antitrust laws). However, other appellate courts to subsequently address reverse payment settlements rejected the per se approach. See, e.g., *In re Schering-Plough Corp.*, 136 F.T.C. 956, 970, 991 (2003); *Schering-Plough Corp. v. FTC*, 402 F.3d 1056, 1072–76 (11th Cir. 2005); *In re Ciprofloxacin Hydrochloride Antitrust Litigation*, 544 F.3d 1323, 1341 (2008).

In 2013, the Supreme Court granted a petition for a writ of certiorari in a reverse payment case and resolved the emerging circuit split by adopting a rule of reason analysis. Is the Court's case for a rule of reason analysis applied to reverse payment cases more compelling than the arguments in favor of the per se approach?

FEDERAL TRADE COMMISSION V. ACTAVIS, INC.

Supreme Court of the United States, 2013.
133 S.Ct. 2223.

BREYER, J., delivered the opinion of the Court.

Company A sues Company B for patent infringement. The two companies settle under terms that require (1) Company B, the claimed infringer, not to produce the patented product until the patent's term expires, and (2) Company A, the patentee, to pay B many millions of dollars. Because the settlement requires the patentee to pay the alleged infringer, rather than the other way around, this kind of settlement agreement is often called a "reverse payment" settlement agreement. And the basic question here is whether such an agreement can sometimes unreasonably diminish competition in violation of the antitrust laws.

In this case, the Eleventh Circuit dismissed a Federal Trade Commission (FTC) complaint claiming that a particular reverse payment settlement agreement violated the antitrust laws. In doing so, the Circuit stated that a reverse payment settlement agreement generally is "immune from antitrust attack so long as its anticompetitive effects fall within the scope of the exclusionary potential of the patent." And since the alleged infringer's promise not to enter the patentee's market expired before the patent's term ended, the Circuit found the agreement legal and dismissed the FTC complaint. In our view, however, reverse payment settlements such as the agreement alleged in the complaint before us can sometimes violate the antitrust laws. We consequently hold that the Eleventh Circuit should have allowed the FTC's lawsuit to proceed.

I

A

Apparently most if not all reverse payment settlement agreements arise in the context of pharmaceutical drug regulation, and specifically in the context of suits brought under statutory provisions allowing a generic drug manufacturer (seeking speedy marketing approval) to challenge the validity of a patent owned by an already-approved brand-name drug owner. We consequently describe four key features of the relevant drug-regulatory framework established by the Drug Price Competition and Patent Term Restoration Act of 1984. That Act is commonly known as the Hatch-Waxman Act.

First, a drug manufacturer, wishing to market a new prescription drug, must submit a New Drug Application to the federal Food and Drug Administration (FDA) and undergo a long, comprehensive, and costly testing process, after which, if successful, the manufacturer will receive marketing approval from the FDA.

Second, once the FDA has approved a brand-name drug for marketing, a manufacturer of a generic drug can obtain similar marketing approval through use of abbreviated procedures. The Hatch-Waxman Act permits a generic manufacturer to file an Abbreviated New Drug Application specifying that the generic has the "same active ingredients as," and is "biologically equivalent" to, the already-approved brand-name drug. In this way the generic manufacturer can obtain approval while avoiding the "costly and time-consuming studies" needed to obtain approval "for a pioneer drug." The Hatch-Waxman process, by allowing the generic to piggy-back on the pioneer's approval efforts, "speed[s] the introduction of low-cost generic drugs to market," thereby furthering drug competition.

Third, the Hatch-Waxman Act sets forth special procedures for identifying, and resolving, related patent disputes. It requires the pioneer brand-name manufacturer to list in its New Drug Application the "number and the expiration date" of any relevant patent. And it requires the generic manufacturer in its Abbreviated New Drug Application to "assure the FDA" that the generic "will not infringe" the brand-name's patents.

The generic can provide this assurance in one of several ways. It can certify that the brand-name manufacturer has not listed any relevant patents. It can certify that any relevant patents have expired. It can request approval to market beginning when any still-in-force patents expire. Or, it can certify that any listed, relevant patent "is invalid or will not be infringed by the manufacture, use, or sale" of the drug described in the Abbreviated New Drug Application. Taking this last-mentioned route (called the "paragraph IV" route), automatically counts as patent infringement, and often "means provoking litigation." If the brand-name patentee brings an infringement suit within 45 days, the FDA then must withhold approving the generic, usually for a 30-month period, while the parties litigate patent validity (or infringement) in court. If the courts decide the matter within that period, the FDA follows that determination; if they do not, the FDA may go forward and give approval to market the generic product.

Fourth, Hatch-Waxman provides a special incentive for a generic to be the first to file an Abbreviated New Drug Application taking the paragraph IV route. That applicant will enjoy a period of 180 days of exclusivity (from the first commercial marketing of its drug). During that period of exclusivity no other generic can compete with the brand-name drug. If the first-to-file generic manufacturer can overcome any patent obstacle and bring the generic to market, this 180-day period of exclusivity can prove valuable, possibly "worth several hundred million dollars." Indeed, the Generic Pharmaceutical Association said in 2006 that the " 'vast majority of potential profits for a generic drug manufacturer materialize during the 180-day exclusivity period.' " The 180-day exclusivity period, however, can belong only to the first generic to file. Should that first-to-file generic forfeit the exclusivity right in one of the ways specified by statute, no other generic can obtain it.

B

1

In 1999, Solvay Pharmaceuticals, a respondent here, filed a New Drug Application for a brand-name drug called AndroGel. The FDA approved the application in 2000. In 2003, Solvay obtained a relevant patent and disclosed that fact to the FDA, as Hatch-Waxman requires.

Later the same year another respondent, Actavis, Inc. (then known as Watson Pharmaceuticals), filed an Abbreviated New Drug Application for a generic drug modeled after AndroGel. Subsequently, Paddock Laboratories, also a respondent, separately filed an Abbreviated New Drug Application for its own generic product. Both Actavis and Paddock certified under paragraph IV that Solvay's listed patent was invalid and their drugs did not infringe it. A fourth manufacturer, Par Pharmaceutical, likewise a respondent, did not file an application of its own but joined forces with Paddock, agreeing to share the patent litigation costs in return for a share of profits if Paddock obtained approval for its generic drug.

Solvay initiated paragraph IV patent litigation against Actavis and Paddock. Thirty months later the FDA approved Actavis' first-to-file generic product, but, in 2006, the patent-litigation parties all settled. Under the terms of the settlement Actavis agreed that it would not bring its generic to market until August 31, 2015, 65 months before Solvay's patent expired (unless someone else marketed a generic sooner). Actavis also agreed to promote AndroGel to urologists. The other generic manufacturers made roughly similar promises. And Solvay agreed to pay millions of dollars to each generic—$12 million in total to Paddock; $60 million in total to Par; and an estimated $19–$30 million annually, for nine years, to Actavis. The companies described these payments as compensation for other services the generics promised to perform, but the FTC contends the other services had little value. According to the FTC the true point of the payments was to compensate the generics for agreeing not to compete against AndroGel until 2015.

2

On January 29, 2009, the FTC filed this lawsuit against all the settling parties, namely, Solvay, Actavis, Paddock, and Par. The FTC's complaint (as since amended) alleged that respondents violated § 5 of the Federal Trade Commission Act by unlawfully agreeing "to share in Solvay's monopoly profits, abandon their patent challenges, and refrain from launching their low-cost generic products to compete with AndroGel for nine years." The District Court held that these allegations did not set forth an antitrust law violation. * * *

The Court of Appeals for the Eleventh Circuit affirmed the District Court. It wrote that "absent sham litigation or fraud in obtaining the patent, a reverse payment settlement is immune from antitrust attack so long as its anticompetitive effects fall within the scope of the exclusionary potential of the patent." The court recognized that "antitrust laws typically prohibit agreements where one company pays a potential competitor not to enter the market." But, the court found that "reverse payment settlements of patent litigation presen[t] atypical cases because one of the parties owns a patent." Patent holders have a "lawful right to exclude others from the market,"; thus a patent "conveys the right to cripple competition." The court recognized that, if the parties to this sort of case do not settle, a court might declare the patent invalid. But, in light of the public policy favoring settlement of disputes (among other considerations) it held that the courts could not require the parties to continue to litigate in order to avoid antitrust liability. * * *

* * *

II

A

Solvay's patent, if valid and infringed, might have permitted it to charge drug prices sufficient to recoup the reverse settlement payments it agreed to make to its potential generic competitors. And we are willing to take this fact as evidence that the agreement's "anticompetitive effects fall within the scope of the exclusionary potential of the patent." But we do not agree that that fact, or characterization, can immunize the agreement from antitrust attack.

For one thing, to refer, as the Circuit referred, simply to what the holder of a valid patent could do does not by itself answer the antitrust question. The patent here may or may not be valid, and may or may not be infringed. "[A] *valid* patent excludes all except its owner from the use of the protected process or product." And that exclusion may permit the patent owner to charge a higher-than-competitive price for the patented product. But an *invalidated* patent carries with it no such right. And even a valid patent confers no right to exclude products or processes that do not actually infringe. The paragraph IV litigation in this case put the patent's validity at issue, as well as its actual preclusive scope. The parties' settlement ended that litigation. The FTC alleges that in substance, the plaintiff agreed to pay the defendants many millions of dollars to stay out of its market, even though the defendants did not have any claim that the plaintiff was liable to them for damages. That form of settlement is unusual. And, for reasons discussed in Part II–B, there is reason for concern that settlements taking this form tend to have significant adverse effects on competition.

Given these factors, it would be incongruous to determine antitrust legality by measuring the settlement's anticompetitive effects solely against patent law policy, rather than by measuring them against procompetitive antitrust policies as well. And indeed, contrary to the Circuit's view that the only pertinent question is whether "the settlement agreement . . . fall[s] within" the legitimate "scope" of the patent's "exclusionary potential," this Court has indicated that patent and antitrust policies are both relevant in determining the "scope of the patent monopoly"—and consequently antitrust law immunity—that is conferred by a patent.

* * *

Thus, contrary to the dissent's suggestion, there is nothing novel about our approach. What *does* appear novel are the dissent's suggestions that a patent holder may simply "pa[y] a competitor to respect its patent" and quit its patent invalidity or noninfringement claim without any antitrust scrutiny whatever, and that "such settlements . . . are a well-known feature of intellectual property litigation." Closer examination casts doubt on these claims. The dissent does not identify any patent statute that it understands to grant such a right to a patentee, whether expressly or by fair implication. It would be difficult to reconcile the proposed right with the patent-related policy of eliminating unwarranted patent grants so the public will not "continually be required to pay tribute to would-be monopolists without need or justification." And the authorities cited for this proposition (none from this Court, and none an antitrust case) are not on point. * * * In the traditional examples cited above, a party with a claim (or counterclaim) for damages receives a sum equal to or less than the value of its claim. In reverse payment settlements, in contrast, a party with no claim for damages (something that is usually true of a paragraph IV litigation defendant) walks away with money simply so it will stay away from the patentee's market. That, we think, is something quite different.

Finally, the Hatch-Waxman Act itself does not embody a statutory policy that supports the Eleventh Circuit's view. Rather, the general procompetitive thrust of the statute, its specific provisions facilitating challenges to a patent's validity, and its later-added provisions requiring parties to a patent dispute triggered by a paragraph IV filing to report settlement terms to the FTC and the Antitrust Division of the Department of Justice, all suggest the contrary. * * *

B

The Eleventh Circuit's conclusion finds some degree of support in a general legal policy favoring the settlement of disputes. The Circuit's related underlying practical concern consists of its fear that antitrust scrutiny of a reverse payment agreement would require the parties to litigate the validity of the patent in order to demonstrate what would have happened to competition in the absence of the settlement. Any such litigation will prove time consuming, complex, and expensive. The antitrust game, the Circuit may believe, would not be worth that litigation candle.

We recognize the value of settlements and the patent litigation problem. But we nonetheless conclude that this patent-related factor should not determine the result here. Rather, five sets of considerations lead us to conclude that the FTC should have been given the opportunity to prove its antitrust claim.

First, the specific restraint at issue has the "potential for genuine adverse effects on competition." The payment in effect amounts to a purchase by the patentee of the exclusive right to sell its product, a right it already claims but would lose if the patent litigation were to continue and the patent were held invalid or not infringed by the generic product. Suppose, for example, that the exclusive right to sell produces $50 million in supracompetitive profits per year for the patentee. And suppose further that the patent has 10 more years to run. Continued litigation, if it results in patent invalidation or a finding of noninfringement, could cost the patentee $500 million in lost revenues, a sum that then would flow in large part to consumers in the form of lower prices.

We concede that settlement on terms permitting the patent challenger to enter the market before the patent expires would also bring about competition, again to the consumer's benefit. But settlement on the terms said by the FTC to be at issue here—payment in return for staying out of the market—simply keeps prices at patentee-set levels, potentially producing the full patent-related $500 million monopoly return while dividing that return between the challenged patentee and the patent challenger. The patentee and the challenger gain; the consumer loses. Indeed, there are indications that patentees sometimes pay a generic challenger a sum even larger than what the generic would gain in profits if it won the paragraph IV litigation and entered the market. The rationale behind a payment of this size cannot in every case be supported by traditional settlement considerations. The payment may instead provide strong evidence that the patentee seeks to induce the generic challenger to abandon its claim with a share of its monopoly profits that would otherwise be lost in the competitive market.

But, one might ask, as a practical matter would the parties be able to enter into such an anticompetitive agreement? Would not a high reverse payment signal to other potential challengers that the patentee lacks confidence in its patent, thereby provoking additional challenges, perhaps too many for the patentee to "buy off?" Two special features of Hatch-Waxman mean that the answer to this question is "not necessarily so." First, under Hatch-Waxman only the first challenger gains the special advantage of 180 days of an exclusive right to sell a generic version of the brand-name product. And as noted, that right has proved valuable—indeed, it can be worth several hundred million dollars. Subsequent challengers cannot secure that exclusivity period, and thus stand to win significantly less than the first if they bring a successful paragraph IV challenge. That is, if subsequent litigation results in invalidation of the patent, or a ruling that the patent is not infringed, that litigation victory will free not just the challenger to compete, but all other potential competitors too (once they obtain FDA approval). The potential reward available to a subsequent challenger being significantly less, the patentee's payment to the initial challenger (in return for not pressing the patent challenge) will not necessarily provoke subsequent challenges. Second, a generic that files a paragraph IV after learning that the first filer has settled will (if sued by the brand-name) have to wait out a stay period of (roughly) 30 months before the FDA may approve its application, just as the first filer did. These features together mean that a reverse payment settlement with the first filer (or, as in this case, *all* of the initial filers) "removes from consideration the most motivated challenger, and the one closest to introducing competition." The dissent may doubt these provisions matter, but scholars in the field tell us that "where only one party owns a patent, it is virtually unheard of outside of pharmaceuticals for that party to pay an accused infringer to settle the lawsuit." It may well be that Hatch-Waxman's unique regulatory framework, including the special advantage that the 180-day exclusivity period gives to first filers, does much to explain why in this context, but not others, the patentee's ordinary incentives to resist paying off challengers (*i.e.,* the fear of provoking myriad other challengers) appear to be more frequently overcome.

Second, these anticompetitive consequences will at least sometimes prove unjustified. As the FTC admits, offsetting or redeeming virtues are sometimes present. The reverse payment, for example, may amount to no more than a rough approximation of the litigation expenses saved through the settlement. That payment may reflect compensation for other services that the generic has promised to perform—such as distributing the patented item or helping to develop a market for that item. There may be other justifications. Where a reverse payment reflects traditional settlement considerations, such as avoided litigation costs or fair value for services, there is not the same concern that a patentee is using its monopoly profits to avoid the risk of patent invalidation or a finding of noninfringement. In such cases, the parties may have provided for a reverse payment without having sought or brought about the anticompetitive consequences we mentioned above. But that possibility does not justify dismissing the FTC's complaint. An antitrust defendant may show in the antitrust proceeding that legitimate justifications are present, thereby explaining the presence of the challenged term and showing the lawfulness of that term under the rule of reason.

Third, where a reverse payment threatens to work unjustified anticompetitive harm, the patentee likely possesses the power to bring that harm about in practice. * * *

Fourth, an antitrust action is likely to prove more feasible administratively than the Eleventh Circuit believed. The Circuit's holding does avoid the need to litigate the patent's validity (and also, any question of infringement). But to do so, it throws the baby out with the bath water, and there is no need to take that drastic step. That is because it is normally not necessary to litigate patent validity to answer the antitrust question (unless, perhaps, to determine whether the patent litigation is a sham). An unexplained large reverse payment itself would normally suggest that the patentee has serious doubts about the patent's survival. And that fact, in turn, suggests that the payment's objective is to maintain supracompetitive prices to be shared among the patentee and the challenger rather than face what might have been a competitive market— the very anticompetitive consequence that underlies the claim of antitrust unlawfulness. The owner of a particularly valuable patent might contend, of course, that even a small risk of invalidity justifies a large payment. But, be that as it may, the payment (if otherwise unexplained) likely seeks to prevent the risk of competition. And, as we have said, that consequence constitutes the relevant anticompetitive harm. In a word, the size of the unexplained reverse payment can provide a workable surrogate for a patent's weakness, all without forcing a court to conduct a detailed exploration of the validity of the patent itself.

Fifth, the fact that a large, unjustified reverse payment risks antitrust liability does not prevent litigating parties from settling their lawsuit. They may, as in other industries, settle in other ways, for example, by allowing the generic manufacturer to enter the patentee's market prior to the patent's expiration, without the patentee paying the challenger to stay out prior to that point. * * *

In sum, a reverse payment, where large and unjustified, can bring with it the risk of significant anticompetitive effects; one who makes such a payment may be unable to explain and to justify it; such a firm or individual may well possess market power derived from the patent; a court, by examining the size of the payment, may well be able to assess its likely anticompetitive effects along with its potential justifications without litigating the validity of the patent; and parties may well find ways to settle patent disputes without the use of reverse payments. In our view, these considerations, taken together, outweigh the single strong consideration—the desirability of settlements—that led the Eleventh Circuit to provide near-automatic antitrust immunity to reverse payment settlements.

III

The FTC urges us to hold that reverse payment settlement agreements are presumptively unlawful and that courts reviewing such agreements should proceed via a "quick look" approach, rather than applying a "rule of reason." We decline to do so. In *California Dental,* we held (unanimously) that abandonment of the "rule of reason" in favor of presumptive rules (or a "quick-look" approach) is appropriate only where "an observer with even a rudimentary understanding of economics could conclude that the arrangements in question would have an anticompetitive effect on customers and markets." We do not believe that reverse payment settlements, in the context we here discuss, meet this criterion.

That is because the likelihood of a reverse payment bringing about anticompetitive effects depends upon its size, its scale in relation to the payor's anticipated future litigation costs, its independence from other services for which it might represent payment, and the lack of any other convincing justification. The existence and degree of any anticompetitive consequence may also vary as among industries. These complexities lead us to conclude that the FTC must prove its case as in other rule-of-reason cases.

To say this is not to require the courts to insist, contrary to what we have said, that the Commission need litigate the patent's validity, empirically demonstrate the virtues or vices of the patent system, present every possible supporting fact or refute every possible pro-defense theory. As a leading antitrust scholar has pointed out, " '[t]here is always something of a sliding scale in appraising reasonableness,' " and as such " 'the quality of proof required should vary with the circumstances.' "

As in other areas of law, trial courts can structure antitrust litigation so as to avoid, on the one hand, the use of antitrust theories too abbreviated to permit proper analysis, and, on the other, consideration of every possible fact or theory irrespective of the minimal light it may shed on the basic question—that of the presence of significant unjustified anticompetitive consequences. We therefore leave to the lower courts the structuring of the present rule-of-reason antitrust litigation. * * *

CHIEF JUSTICE ROBERTS, with whom JUSTICE SCALIA and JUSTICE THOMAS join, dissenting.

* * *

A patent carves out an exception to the applicability of antitrust laws. The correct approach should therefore be to ask whether the settlement gives Solvay monopoly power beyond what the patent already gave it. The Court, however, departs from this approach, and would instead use antitrust law's amorphous rule of reason to inquire into the anticompetitive effects of such settlements. This novel approach is without support in any statute, and will discourage the settlement of patent litigation. * * *

I

* * *

* * * [U]nder our precedent, this is a fairly straight-forward case. Solvay paid a competitor to respect its patent—conduct which did not exceed the scope of its patent. No one alleges that there was sham litigation, or that Solvay's patent was obtained through fraud on the PTO. As in any settlement, Solvay gave its competitors something of value (money) and, in exchange, its competitors gave it something of value (dropping their legal claims). In doing so, they put an end to litigation that had been dragging on for three years. Ordinarily, we would think this a good thing.

II

Today, however, the Court announces a new rule. It is willing to accept that Solvay's actions did not exceed the scope of its patent. But it does not agree that this is enough to "immunize the agreement from antitrust attack." According to the majority, if a patent holder settles litigation by paying an alleged infringer a "large and unjustified" payment, in exchange for having the alleged infringer honor the patent, a court should employ the antitrust rule of reason to determine whether the settlement violates antitrust law.

* * * [A] patent holder acting within the scope of its patent has an obvious defense to any antitrust suit: that its patent allows it to engage in conduct that would otherwise violate the antitrust laws. But again, that's the whole point of a patent: to confer a limited monopoly. The problem, as the Court correctly recognizes, is that we're not quite certain if the patent

is actually valid, or if the competitor is infringing it. But that is always the case, and is plainly a question of patent law.

* * *

The majority suggests that "[w]hether a particular restraint lies 'beyond the limits of the patent monopoly' is a *conclusion* that flows from" applying traditional antitrust principles. It seems to have in mind a regime where courts ignore the patent, and simply conduct an antitrust analysis of the settlement without regard to the validity of the patent. But a patent holder acting within the scope of its patent does not engage in any unlawful anticompetitive behavior; it is simply exercising the monopoly rights granted to it by the Government. Its behavior would be unlawful only if its patent were invalid or not infringed. And the scope of the patent—i.e., what rights are conferred by the *patent*—should be determined by reference to *patent law*. While it is conceivable to set up a legal system where you assess the validity of patents or questions of infringement by bringing an antitrust suit, neither the majority nor the Government suggests that Congress has done so.

* * *

* * * [P]atent settlements—and for that matter, any agreements relating to patents—are subject to antitrust scrutiny if they confer benefits beyond the scope of the patent. This makes sense. A patent exempts its holder from the antitrust laws only insofar as the holder operates within the scope of the patent. When the holder steps outside the scope of the patent, he can no longer use the patent as his defense. The majority points to *no* case where a patent settlement was subject to antitrust scrutiny merely because the validity of the patent was uncertain. Not one. It is remarkable, and surely worth something, that in the 123 years since the Sherman Act was passed, we have never let antitrust law cross that Rubicon.

* * *

* * * I fear the Court's attempt to limit its holding to the context of patent settlements under Hatch-Waxman will not long hold.

III

The majority's rule will discourage settlement of patent litigation. Simply put, there would be no incentive to settle if, immediately after settling, the parties would have to litigate the same issue—the question of patent validity—as part of a defense against an antitrust suit. In that suit, the alleged infringer would be in the especially awkward position of being for the patent after being against it.

This is unfortunate because patent litigation is particularly complex, and particularly costly. * * *

* * *

* * * [S]ettling a patent claim *cannot possibly* impose unlawful anticompetitive harm if the patent holder is acting within the scope of a valid patent and therefore permitted to do precisely what the antitrust suit claims is unlawful. This means that in any such antitrust suit, the defendant (patent holder) will want to use the validity of his patent as a defense—in other words, he'll want to say "I can do this because I have a valid patent that lets me do this." I therefore don't see how the majority can conclude that it won't normally be "necessary to litigate patent validity to answer the antitrust question," unless it means to suggest that the defendant (patent holder) cannot raise his patent as a defense in an antitrust suit. But depriving him of such a defense—if that's what the majority means to do—defeats the point of the patent, which is to confer a *lawful* monopoly on its holder.

The majority seems to think that *even if* the patent is valid, a patent holder violates the antitrust laws merely because the settlement took away some chance that his patent would be declared invalid by a court. This is flawed for several reasons.

First, a patent is either valid or invalid. The parties of course don't know the answer with certainty at the outset of litigation; hence the litigation. But the same is true of any hard legal question that is yet to be adjudicated. Just because people don't know the answer doesn't mean there is no answer until a court declares one. Yet the majority would impose antitrust liability based on the parties' subjective uncertainty about that legal conclusion.

The Court does so on the assumption that offering a "large" sum is reliable evidence that the patent holder has serious doubts about the patent. Not true. A patent holder may be 95% sure about the validity of its patent, but particularly risk averse or litigation averse, and willing to pay a good deal of money to rid itself of the 5% chance of a finding of invalidity. What is actually motivating a patent holder is apparently a question district courts will have to resolve on a case-by-case basis. The task of trying to discern whether a patent holder is motivated by uncertainty about its patent, or other legitimate factors like risk aversion, will be made all the more difficult by the fact that much of the evidence about the party's motivation may be embedded in legal advice from its attorney, which would presumably be shielded from discovery.

* * *

Thus, although the question posed by this case is fundamentally a question of patent law—*i.e.*, whether Solvay's patent was valid and therefore permitted Solvay to pay competitors to honor the scope of its patent—the majority declares that such questions should henceforth be scrutinized by antitrust law's unruly rule of reason. Good luck to the district courts that must, when faced with a patent settlement, weigh the "likely anticompetitive effects, redeeming virtues, market power, and potentially offsetting legal considerations present in the circumstances."

IV

The majority invokes "procompetitive antitrust policies," but misses the basic point that patent laws promote consumer interests in a different way, by providing protection against competition. As one treatise explains:

> "The purpose of the rule of reason is to determine whether, on balance, a practice is reasonably likely to be anticompetitive or competitively harmless—that is, whether it yields lower or higher marketwide output. By contrast, patent policy encompasses a set of judgments about the proper tradeoff between competition and the incentive to innovate over the *long* run. Antitrust's rule of reason was not designed for such judgments and is not adept at making them."

* * *

V

The majority today departs from the settled approach separating patent and antitrust law, weakens the protections afforded to innovators by patents, frustrates the public policy in favor of settling, and likely undermines the very policy it seeks to promote by forcing generics who step into the litigation ring to do so without the prospect of cash settlements. I would keep things as they were and not subject basic questions of patent law to an unbounded inquiry under antitrust law, with its treble damages and famously burdensome discovery.

NOTE ON RULE OF REASON ANALYSIS OF REVERSE PAYMENT SETTLEMENTS AFTER ACTAVIS

The Supreme Court ruled in *Actavis* that reverse-payment settlement agreements between branded and generic pharmaceutical companies are subject to antitrust scrutiny and should be analyzed under the traditional, but not necessarily comprehensive, rule of reason. The Court's decision in *Actavis* makes clear that the rule of reason is the appropriate analytical approach to apply to reverse-payment settlements, rejecting both the scope of the patent test and a rule of per se illegality. However, the Court did not fully define the contours of the rule of reason analysis to be applied in future reverse-payment cases, and instead largely delegated that task to lower courts. Recall from Chapter 6 that in *Leegin* the Court similarly left further refinement of the rule of reason in cases of resale price maintenance for the lower courts to develop, inviting them in that case, as well, to develop structured approaches based on an identified list of particularly relevant factors.

Central to the Supreme Court's decision in *Actavis* was the recognition that "there is reason for concern that [reverse-payment] settlements . . . tend to have significant adverse effects on competition." The core concern with these agreements, and what the Court termed "the relevant anticompetitive harm," is that they may allow the brand to "prevent the risk of competition" by splitting monopoly profits with the prospective entrant. As a result, the Court recognized these agreements may lead to higher prices for pharmaceuticals by deterring generic entry and contribute to increased health care costs that consumers, employers, and federal and state governments are struggling to contain.

The Court outlined five considerations that will likely be central to lower courts' rule of reason analysis:

First, the Court held that reverse-payment settlements have the potential for "genuine adverse effects on competition" by removing the manufacturer most likely to introduce competition.

Second, the Court explained that the anticompetitive harm created by a reverse payment "will at least sometimes prove unjustified." The Court observed that "[w]here a reverse payment reflects traditional settlement considerations, such as avoided litigation costs or fair value for services, there is not the same concern that a patentee is using its monopoly profits to avoid the risk of patent invalidation or a finding of noninfringement."

Third, the Court recognized that a brand-name drug manufacturer that makes a reverse payment likely has the power to bring about anticompetitive harm. As the Court explained, "a firm without that power" is unlikely "to pay 'large sums' to induce 'others to stay out of its market.' "

Fourth, the Court found that "it is normally not necessary to litigate patent validity" to determine the anticompetitive effects of the settlement, and thus that antitrust claims are feasible to administer without a detailed inquiry into the strength of the patent. According to the Court, "prevent[ing] the risk of competition"—even where the patentee's risk of losing the patent suit may be small—is "the relevant anticompetitive harm." As a result, companies cannot defend their agreements by merely arguing that the brand-name drug company would have likely prevailed had the patent case been fully litigated or that the settlement provided for entry prior to patent expiration.

Finally, the Court recognized that parties in the pharmaceutical industry can, and do, settle patent litigation without reverse payments, specifically rejecting the defendants' argument that such payments are necessary for settlement.

Within those general parameters, however, the Court left considerable room for lower courts to structure the contours of the analysis. Further, although the Court identified a number of potentially relevant factors for determining whether a reverse payment is likely to result in anticompetitive effects—in particular, payment size—the Court did not purport to offer an exhaustive list of such factors, and thus courts appear to be free to weigh other considerations within the traditional antitrust rule of reason framework.

A number of important questions remain concerning how the rule of reason will be applied in reverse-payment cases. Perhaps the most critical question for lower courts to address is how to determine the size of any reverse payment sufficient to establish that the settlement is likely anticompetitive.

Another issue raised in post-*Actavis* litigation is whether non-cash payments, including "no-authorized generic" agreements and marketing commitments from the brand-name manufacturer, can constitute a reverse-payment. (A "no-authorized generic" agreement refers to a brand-name manufacturer's agreement not to introduce an authorized generic in competition with the generic manufacturer in exchange for the generic's agreement to delay its own entry.) The majority view is that non-cash payments can constitute a reverse payment. *See, e.g., In re Loestrin 24 Fe Antitrust Litig.*, 814 F.3d 538 (1st Cir. 2016) (holding that *Actavis* applies to non-monetary payments such as no-authorized generic agreements and acceleration clauses, explaining that *Actavis* itself involved non-cash "side deals in which the generic manufacturers agreed to promote the brand name drug at issue in exchange for multi-million dollar payments from the brand manufacturer"); *King Drug Co. of Florence, Inc. v. Smithkline Beecham Corp.*, 791 F.3d 388, 394 (3d Cir. 2015) ("We believe this no-AG agreement falls under *Actavis*'s rule because it may represent an unusual, unexplained reverse transfer of considerable value from the patentee to the alleged infringer and may therefore give rise to the inference that it is a payment to eliminate the risk of competition."). *See also* Brief of Federal Trade Commission as Amicus Curiae in Support of Plaintiffs-Appellants, *In re Lamictal Direct Purchaser Antitrust Litig.*, at 23 (3d Cir. Apr. 28, 2014) ("Substituting one form of consideration for another does not protect consumers from the harms of anticompetitive agreements between competitors, nor does it alter the antitrust analysis."), https://www.ftc.gov/system/files/documents/amicus_ briefs/re-lamictal-direct-purchaser-antitrust-litigation/140428lamictalbrief. pdf. At least one district court has taken a qualified view, requiring that non-monetary payments be "converted to a reliable estimate of its monetary value." *In re Lipitor Antitrust Litig.*, 46 F. Supp. 3d 523, 543 (D.N.J. 2014).

Some commentators argue the Supreme Court *implicitly* endorsed a "quick-look" treatment for such agreements. *See* Aaron Edlin, Scott Hemphill, Herbert Hovenkamp & Carl Shapiro, *Activating* Actavis, ANTITRUST, Fall 2013, at 16, 17. *See also* Robert A. Skitol & Kenneth M. Vorrasi, FTC v. Actavis: *Inviting A More Nimble Rule of Reason*, ANTITRUST, Fall 2013, at 51, 53. These commentators argue that the Court's emphasis on the size of the reverse payment as a proxy for market power and the likelihood of anticompetitive effects will, for all practical purposes, truncate the rule of reason analysis. They argue that, because the size of payment is a reliable predictor of anticompetitive effects arising from reverse payment settlements, a showing of a large payment should, without more, allow plaintiffs to successfully shift the burden of production to defendants. *See, e.g.*, Thomas F. Cotter, FTC v. Actavis: *When is the Rule of Reason Not the Rule of Reason?* 15 MINN. J.L. SCI. & TECH. 41 (2014). Others read the Court's decision as requiring more than evidence of a large reverse payment to satisfy the plaintiff's burden of demonstrating competitive harm under a rule of reason analysis. *See, e.g.*, Ian Simmons, Kenneth R. O'Rourke & Scott Schaeffer, *Viewing* FTC v. Actavis *Through the Lens of the Clayton Act Section 4*, ANTITRUST, Fall 2013, at 24. These commentators point to the Court's rejection of a general presumption that reverse payments, which are generally quite large, are per se unlawful.

Regardless, there is consensus that the antitrust relevance of a large reverse payment turns upon its relationship to the likelihood a particular settlement harms competition. The Court viewed the size of payment as a "strong indicator" of anticompetitive effects, and went on to explain that "the likelihood of a reverse payment bringing about anticompetitive effects depends upon its size, its scale in relation to the payor's anticipated future litigation costs, its independence from other services for which it might represent payment, and the lack of any other convincing justification." The Court also observed that the risk of anticompetitive effects is especially significant where the reverse payment is "large and unjustified."

A critical and unsettled question is how lower courts should go about identifying the "large and unjustified" payments the Court has singled out as most likely to generate anticompetitive effects and to violate Section 1 of the Sherman Act. How should lower courts identify large payments? What benchmark should be used to assess payment magnitude? Several options have been suggested. The Court itself suggested that at least one relevant inquiry is the size of the payment relative to the sum of expected litigation costs and the value of any services provided by the generic. One group of academics proposes a rule stating a payment is "otherwise unexplained" if the "net payment"—that is, the reverse payment minus the patent holder's avoided litigation costs minus the value of services provided by the generic—is positive. *See* Aaron Edlin, Scott Hemphill, Herbert Hovenkamp & Carl Shapiro, *Activating* Actavis, ANTITRUST, Fall 2013, at 16, 18. If that difference is positive, the authors argue the anticompetitive effect is likely to occur due to an unreasonably prolonged lack of price competition between the brand and the generic.

Another approach would be to analyze the size of the payment relative to other factors including the risk preferences of the branded manufacturer and the relative strength of the patent at issue. Economists favoring this approach argue that a rule narrowly focused on a comparison of payment size to anticipated litigation costs and any services provided by the generic to the brand will deter some settlements that increase consumer welfare. *See* Barry C. Harris, Kevin M. Murphy, Robert D. Willig & Matthew B. Wright, *Activating* Actavis: *A More Complete Story*, ANTITRUST, Spring 2014, at 83, 83. For example, a brand's risk aversion might cause the generic's settled-upon entry date to be sooner than the generic's expected entry date under litigation. *But see* Aaron Edlin, Scott Hemphill, Herbert Hovenkamp & Carl Shapiro,

Actavis *and Error Costs: A Reply to Critics*, THE ANTITRUST SOURCE (Oct. 2014), at 1.

And yet another set of commentators suggest that regulating the size of a patent settlement will be ineffective and potentially adverse to consumer welfare. *See* Bruce H. Kobayashi, Joshua D. Wright, Douglas H. Ginsburg, and Joanna Tsai, Actavis *and Multiple ANDA Entrants: Beyond the Temporary Duopoly*, ANTITRUST, Spring 2015, at 89. The authors argue that when analyzing anticompetitive effects of the payment size, considering the possibility of entry by multiple generics under the Hatch-Waxman regime rather than assuming the brand and generic will enjoy duopoly profits after a successful challenge by the generic, actually yields a broader range of settlement payments under "which a brand and generic entrant have legitimate incentives to settle the case other than 'to prevent the risk of competition.'" *Id.* This suggests the size of the reverse payment is not a useful proxy for the likely anticompetitive effects of a settlement.

Sidebar 7–3:
Product Hopping and Other Conduct
That May Delay Generic Entry

Product Hopping

Reverse-payment settlements are not the only strategy allowing patent holders to evade the effects of simplified generic entry under the Hatch-Waxman Act. "Product hopping" is another strategy, which involves a patentee making changes to a branded drug for the purpose of obtaining a new patent covering the drug and thereby extending the patentee's exclusivity period. Drug modifications can delay generic entry because generic manufacturers rely upon the branded manufacturer's original NDA when submitting ANDAs. The generic manufacturers must show their proposed generic is bioequivalent to the branded drug. A simple change to a branded drug's strength, dosage, or form of delivery combined with removal of the original drug from the market may prevent generic entry because state substitution laws prohibit pharmacists from substituting generic drugs for branded drugs that are not therapeutically equivalent.

Although product hopping is not a new practice, there have thus far been a small number of cases that have fully litigated the practice on the merits, as it only began appearing in courts in the past decade. Antitrust issues potentially arise when product hopping involves product design changes that are alleged to provide little or no benefit to consumers, but that impede generic competition and maintain pharmaceutical prices at monopoly levels. While antitrust law is generally reluctant to impose limits on product design decisions or to ask courts or regulators to second-guess those decisions, district and circuit courts have made it clear that product hopping is subject to antitrust scrutiny. *See, e.g., Abbott Labs. v. Teva Pharm.*, USA Inc., 432 F. Supp. 2d 408 (D. Del. 2006) (holding that a complaint alleging repeated changes to a drug formulation to prevent generic entry and subsequent removal of the older formulations from the market is sufficient to plead a violation of antitrust laws).

In 2015, the Second Circuit ruled a district court did not abuse its discretion when it granted a motion for a preliminary injunction against a pharmaceutical company engaged in alleged product hopping. *New York v. Actavis plc*, 787 F.3d 638 (2d Cir. 2015). The State of New York sought a preliminary injunction from the district court against Actavis and its wholly owned subsidiary, Forest Laboratories LLC (collectively, Actavis), which manufactured a branded drug designed to treat moderate-to-severe Alzheimer's disease. *Id.* at 642. The original formulation, Namenda IR, was a twice-daily, immediate-release drug protected by patent until 2015. *Id.* at 646–47. In 2013, Actavis introduced the second formulation, Namenda XR, a once-daily, extended-release drug with exclusivity under its patent until 2029. *Id.* at 646–47. Actavis then began taking steps to convert patients from Namenda IR to Namenda XR and to withdraw Namenda IR from the market within a year. *Id.* at 647–48. In February 2014, Actavis announced its intent to withdraw Namenda IR, effective August 2014. *Id.* at 648. Pursuant to this plan, Namenda patients would need to switch to Namenda XR, at least in the interim between removal of Namenda IR and introduction of its generic in 2015. Pharmaceutical companies that had developed generic twice-daily, immediate-release formulations that were therapeutically equivalent to Namenda IR asserted this was problematic: state substitution laws would prohibit pharmacists from substituting their generic products for Namenda XR, which would comprise the vast majority, if not all, Namenda prescriptions. *Id.* at 647. Furthermore, they argued, once patients switched from Namenda IR to Namenda XR, it would be nearly impossible to switch them back to the original formulation.

New York filed an antitrust complaint against Actavis on the theory that the company anticompetitively forced consumers to switch from Namenda IR to Namenda XR, depriving them of their ability to freely choose between the two formulations, thwarting generic entry of competition to Namenda, and unlawfully extending its monopoly over the drug. The district court granted New York's motion for a preliminary injunction and prohibited Actavis from withdrawing Namenda IR from the market until 30 days after generic manufactures could enter the market. *See id.* at 649–50. The Second Circuit affirmed the district court's ruling and held that "New York ha[d] demonstrated a substantial likelihood of success on the merits of its claim under the Sherman Act and has made a strong showing of irreparable harm to competition and consumers in the absence of a preliminary injunction." *Id.* at 643 (internal citation omitted).

Since product innovation typically benefits consumers, "[a]s a general rule, courts are properly very skeptical about claims that competition has been harmed by a dominant firm's product design changes." *Id.* at 652 (internal quotation marks omitted) (quoting *United States v. Microsoft Corp.*, 253 F.3d 34, 65 (D.C. Cir. 2001)). In determining whether Actavis's conduct was anticompetitive, the court found that "[c]ertainly, neither product withdrawal nor product improvement alone is anticompetitive"; rather, "when a monopolist *combines* product withdrawal with some other conduct, the overall effect of which is to coerce consumers rather than persuade them on the merits, and to impede competition, its actions are anticompetitive under the Sherman Act." *Id.* at 654 (internal citations omitted).

Importantly, the court emphasized and relied upon the distinction between a "hard switch" and a "soft switch" in reaching its conclusion. Both involve a seller's attempt to transition consumers from one product to a new product. A hard switch requires removal of the original product from the market to effectively force the switch, and a soft switch allows the original product to remain on the market, though it can involve the seller offering discounts or other incentives to facilitate consumer switching to the new product. A soft switch thus relies on competition and market forces, not coercion, to persuade customers to make the change.[a] The court relied upon *Berkey Photo, Inc. v. Eastman Kodak Co.*, 603 F.2d 263 (2d Cir. 1979), the leading case in the Second Circuit regarding antitrust liability for product redesign, and held that Actavis's hard switch from Namenda IR to Namenda XR "crosse[d] the line from persuasion to coercion and [wa]s anticompetitive." *Id.* at 654. Courts evaluating product redesign must distinguish between actions taken by branded companies that defeat

---

[a] Canada's 2016 IP Guidelines explicitly recognize the difference between hard and soft switches, taking the position that the latter is unlikely to raise antitrust issues. *See Canada IP Guidelines*, Ex. 9B.

generic competition because of efficiency and consumer satisfaction and actions that impede competition through means other than competition on the merits. *Id.* at 652. The Second Circuit reasoned that Actavis's hard switch forced patients to the new formulation and likely would impede generic competition by preventing generic substitution under state drug substitution laws. *Id.* at 655–56.

As the first court of appeals to resolve a claim of product hopping, the Second Circuit's decision in *New York v. Actavis* is likely to be influential, as it provides some general guidance for product hopping litigation. Because it was decided on a motion for preliminary injunction, however, questions remain regarding when it is appropriate for courts to find antitrust liability for product redesign. For example, will the court's reasoning be limited to cases of hard switching, or are there circumstances under which a soft switch strategy might also give rise to an antitrust violation? The court did not purport to evaluate whether the dosage change involved constituted a true "innovation," but how will future courts treat instances of changes that have obvious patient benefits? Will any consumer benefit be sufficient to defeat an antitrust claim, regardless of the anticompetitive consequences? Will courts want to debate the genuine value of an alteration in drug dosage or other reformulation? What are the implications of a court sitting in judgment on an antirust claim concluding that a validly issued patent nevertheless involves only a superficial innovation? Some scholars have recommended that, considering the potential for significant consumer benefits from even small changes in product design, coupled with antitrust agencies and courts being ill-equipped to displace the judgments of consumers (and, with regard to drugs, their doctors) about the value of a new product design, product hopping should be per se lawful absent objective evidence that Product B is a sham innovation with zero or negative consumer welfare effects. *See* Douglas H. Ginsburg, Koren W. Wong-Ervin, & Joshua D. Wright, *Product Hopping and the Limits of Antitrust: The Danger of Micromanaging Innovation,* COMPETITION POLICY INTERNATIONAL ANTITRUST CHRONICLE Vol. 12 No. 1 (Dec. 14, 2015). Will courts in the pharmaceutical context, despite the general unwillingness to do so in other settings, weigh the costs and benefits of particular product design changes? What is the optimal rule for courts to apply that would simultaneously encourage innovation and condemn anticompetitive product modifications? For a later decision rejecting a product hopping claim at the summary judgment stage of the litigation, see

Mylan Pharm. Inc. v. Warner Chilcott Public Ltd. Co., ___ F.3d
___, 2016 WL 5403626 (3d Cir. 2016).

Risk Evaluation and Mitigation Strategies

Risk Evaluation and Mitigation Strategies (REMS)
programs may also delay generic entry into the market. The
FDA is authorized to mandate REMS programs for certain
high-risk pharmaceuticals that raise significant safety
concerns. If a REMS program prevents distribution of a drug
through customary channels, a brand-name drug manufacturer
has the ability to essentially foreclose generic competition by
refusing to sell a limited quantity of the drug to potential
generic rivals, frustrating efforts to conduct necessary
bioequivalency tests.

The practice has been challenged as an anticompetitive
"refusal to deal" that violates Section 2 of the Sherman Act. *See,
e.g., In re Thalomid and Revlimid Antitrust Litigation*, 2015 WL
9589217 (D.N.J. 2015) (denying motion to dismiss Section 2
claim based on a refusal to deal). *See also* Fed. Trade Comm'n,
Brief as Amicus Curiae, *Mylan Pharms., Inc. v. Celgene Corp.*,
Case No. 2:14–CV–2094–ES–MAH (D.N.J. 2014) (supporting
plaintiffs' claim of unlawful refusal to deal), https://www.ftc.
gov/system/files/documents/amicus_briefs/mylan-pharma
ceuticals-inc.v.celgene-corporation/140617celgeneamicusbrief.
pdf. As we observed in Chapter 4 in connection with our
discussion of concerted and unilateral refusals to deal, however,
there is continuing debate regarding the circumstances under
which a unilateral refusal to deal can be the basis for a violation
of Section 2. Recall that in *Verizon Commc'ns, Inc. v. Law
Offices of Curtis v. Trinko*, 540 U.S. 398 (2004), the Court
cautioned against too easily concluding that a refusal to deal
could do so, and although reaffirming the conclusion of the
Court in *Aspen Skiing Co. v. Aspen Highlands Skiing Corp.*, 472
U.S. 585 (1985), *Trinko* observed that *Aspen* was "at or near the
outer boundary" of any possible violation. *See also Pac. Bell Tel
Co. v. LinkLine Commc'ns, Inc.*, 555 U.S. 438, 448 (2009)("[a]s
a general rule, businesses are free to choose the parties with
whom they will deal. . . ").

Although some have read *Trinko* as confining claims to the
facts of *Aspen Skiing*, which involved discontinuation of a prior
course of dealing, *Trinko* did not suggest that a prior course of
dealing was a prerequisite to a claim for unlawful refusal to
deal. Under such a narrow view of *Trinko*, a brand-name drug
manufacturer might not be viewed as violating Section 2 by
choosing not to provide samples of a REMS-restricted drug

unless it terminated an existing supply contract for a REMS-restricted drug. As noted above, the FTC weighed in on *Celgene* to support the plaintiff's statement of a claim. Others suggest the relevant inquiry is whether the defendant's refusal can only be explained by its negative impact on the rival and the resulting harm to competition. *See* Susan A. Creighton & Jonathan M. Jacobson, *Twenty-Five Years of Access Denials*, ANTITRUST, Fall 2012, at 50, 53 (relevant inquiry is whether the defendant's refusal can only be explained by its negative impact on the rival and the resulting harm to competition). For several discussions of the REMS-specific issues posed by such claims, see Jan M. Rybnicek, *When Does Sharing Make Sense?: Antitrust & Risk Evaluation and Mitigation Strategies*, CPI ANTITRUST CHRONICLE, April 2014 (2), at 6 (advocating use of a "no economic sense" test that would permit liability "only in those rare circumstances where the sole justification for the refusal is the negative impact the conduct could have on the rival and the benefits conferred by eliminating competition."); Darren S. Tucker, et. al, *REMS: The Next Pharmaceutical Enforcement Priority?*, ANTITRUST, Spring 2014, at 74 (providing an overview of REMS and the various competition theories that have arisen).

Conclusion

Somewhat in contrast to pay-for delay agreements, product hopping and REMS each involve unilateral conduct rather than collusion between rival firms. The former generally involves collusion in order to exclude potential generic entrants; the latter involves only exclusionary conduct by the branded pharmaceutical firm. Note the relationship between collusive and exclusionary effects in this setting. Is the treatment of Section 2 monopolization claims involving unilateral conduct in the pharmaceutical industry—such as product hopping and REMS—consistent with antitrust treatment of product design and refusal to deal in non-pharmaceutical settings? With the messages of *Actavis*? Should it be?

4. MERGERS AND JOINT VENTURES

a. Acquisition of Intellectual Property Rights ("IPRs") and the Role of "Blocking Patents"

Although many IP related practices are policed under Sections 1 and 2 of the Sherman Act, the acquisition of IP rights, like the acquisition of any "asset," also can be analyzed under the provisions of Section 7 of the Clayton Act. As we note within this Chapter, innovation can be suppressed through acquisition. In the case of IPRs, acquisitions could lead to exclusionary or collusive anticompetitive effects. Acquisitions could be exclusionary, for example, if the acquired technology is completely suppressed, if its introduction to the market is delayed, or if the acquiring firm makes access to the technology more expensive or unavailable to a downstream rival that relies on it. Acquisitions can also lead to coordinated or unilateral collusive effects, such as restricted output and higher prices. Examples might include the merger of two firms that own competing IPRs, or the acquisition by one firm of the IPRs of another. Section 5.7 of the IP Guidelines declares the government's intention to examine IPR acquisitions under all of the relevant antitrust provisions, including Section 7, and to analyze a merger or acquisition under the Merger Guidelines, when appropriate.

One of the issues garnering significant attention in recent years is the role in merger review of "blocking patents." A blocking patent is typically one so broad in scope that no potential rival can compete in the relevant market without infringing the patent. A blocking patent also, however, may cover a narrow technological feature that is necessary for producing a particular downstream product (for example, a technology covering a specific feature of a semiconductor chip that is required by an industry standard). Blocking positions are most often asserted in merger analysis by an acquiring firm, which asserts that its IPRs are broad enough to block competition from any rival, including the acquired firm. Hence, the acquisition cannot substantially lessen competition. The acquired firm poses no threat to competition owing to the fact that the acquired firm could only compete with it by infringing its IPRs.

If it is true that the acquired firm can only compete by infringing on the blocking patents, the argument may hold some merit. However, the assertion of a blocking position may depend upon the validity of and broad scope of the patents—either or both of which may be contestable. Moreover, there may be evidence that the acquiring firm faces competition, either from the acquired firm, or other firms, that has not led to infringement. Does that necessarily defeat the claim of a blocking position? How should the agencies evaluate entry if the threat of an infringement action is genuine? In such circumstances, the agencies can be faced with difficult choices between the acquiring firm's assertion of patent validity and broad scope, and an alternative view that competition without infringement is possible. If the latter is true, the acquisition might indeed prove anticompetitive and might pose serious threats to innovation. Recall our earlier discussion, regarding the *Singer* case, which questioned the competitive effects of pooling weak patents and of obtaining blocking patents with probability, not certainty. *See* Gideon Parchomovsky & R. Polk Wagner, *Patent Portfolios*, 154 U. PA. L. REV. 1, 29 (2005).

NOTE ON ACQUISITIONS OF IPRS
BY PATENT ASSERTION ENTITIES

One current antitrust controversy involves the appropriate role of competition law and policy, if any, in regulating the conduct of patent assertion entities (PAEs). The FTC defines PAEs as companies that "purchas[e] and assert[ ] patents against manufacturers already using the technology, rather than developing and transferring technology [themselves]." FED. TRADE COMM'N, THE EVOLVING IP MARKETPLACE: ALIGNING PATENT NOTICE AND REMEDIES WITH COMPETITION 8 (2011), http://www.ftc.gov/os/2011/03/110307patentreport.pdf. According to some, PAEs typically do not engage in any R & D themselves; rather they specialize in monetizing patents, often by obtaining licensing agreements in settlement of patent infringement litigation. They then identify firms that may already be using technology covered by the patents, and seek to extract royalty payments from them through threats of "patent assertion," *i.e.* law suits for patent infringement. Critics label these entities "patent trolls," claiming that the PAE business model constitutes a "tax" on innovation. On the other hand, defenders of these entities argue that they are efficient intermediaries that yield a more robust secondary market for patents and that allow small inventors to obtain a return on their activities, thus incentivizing further innovation. Should the aggregation of patents, which contain exclusion rights, raise antitrust concerns? When does PAE behavior harm competition and violate the antitrust laws? Is the harm to competition outweighed by countervailing benefits provided by PAEs?

In contrast to PAEs, operating companies may fear countersuit when contemplating whether to bring an infringement lawsuit, which frequently results in a détente—encouraging cross-licensing agreements and "a high level of non-enforcement." Erica S. Mintzer & Suzanne Munck, *The Joint U.S. Department of Justice and Federal Trade Commission Workshop on Patent Assertion Entity Activities—"Follow the Money*," 79 ANTITRUST L.J. 423, 426 (2014). PAEs change that calculus. Because they do not manufacture or sell products, PAEs are immune to infringement countersuits. Perhaps for this reason, patent lawsuits, in addition to PAEs' share of total infringement cases, have skyrocketed in recent years. On the other hand, certain commentators argue that the increase in litigation may be largely attributable to procedural changes in 2011 patent legislation and that, in any event, claims of a "litigation explosion" are overblown. Critics contend that PAEs impose direct costs to operating firms as time and resources are detracted from innovative efforts. This argument is complicated by the fact that some large operating firms also purchase patents and arguably engage in some "troll-like" activity. Some scholars, businesses, policy makers, and the White House have argued that PAE activity negatively impacts competition, innovation, and consumer welfare. But even PAE critics often appear to agree that a categorical ban on PAEs or their business model of mass aggregation and patent enforcement would be inappropriate and contrary to the goals of antitrust law.

Should the antitrust laws prohibit the transfer of IPRs to PAEs? Proponents of applying or extending the antitrust laws to reach PAE activities identify two forms of PAE conduct that, they say, might give rise to antitrust liability. The first is PAE acquisition of IPRs that cover substitute technologies. Professors Fiona M. Scott Morton and Carl Shapiro describe the acquisition of substitute patents as "effectively horizontal mergers in the technology markets," which could create monopoly power for the PAE. Fiona M. Scott Morton & Carl Shapiro, *Strategic Patent Acquisitions*, 79 ANTITRUST L.J. 463, 487 (2014). They contend that horizontal mergers involving IPRs are especially suspect because IPRs involve "exclusion rights" that make it easier to acquire market power. *See id.* at 464. The success of such claims may depend on judicial willingness to define "technology markets" when reviewing PAE transactions (*see supra* Sidebar 7–2). *See Intellectual Ventures I LLC v. Capital One Fin. Corp.*, 2013 WL 6682981 (E.D. Va. Dec. 18, 2013) (dismissing antitrust claims against a PAE because, among other things, plaintiff did not properly define a relevant market). A second PAE practice that may attract antitrust scrutiny is "privateering." Privateering occurs when a patent holder sells its patents to a PAE with an expressed or implied understanding that it will target the firm's rivals with patent assertion claims.

When the antitrust laws do apply to PAE activity, efficiencies must be considered. PAEs may improve the functioning of technology markets by consolidating patent ownership. For example, prospective licensees may benefit if fewer patent holders mean decreased search and negotiation costs. Revenue-sharing agreements between original patent holders and PAEs can help innovators receive royalties while continuing to innovate. These royalties can be reinvested in R & D efforts. PAEs, because of their expertise, may be more efficient than original patent holders in negotiating licensing agreements. Furthermore, the existence of this secondary patent market also allows innovators to quickly sell failed or weak patents to PAEs and "exit." The ability to do so may decrease innovators' risk and thereby encourage future R & D. Following on a workshop held in 2012, the FTC, using its Section 6(b) authority to collect data from PAEs and other non-manufacturing firms, conducted an empirical study on PAE assertion and licensing activities that was followed by an extensive report. *See* PATENT ASSERTION ENTITY ACTIVITY: AN FTC STUDY (Oct. 2016), https://www.ftc.gov/system/files/documents /reports/patent-assertion-entity-activity-ftc-study/p131203_patent_assertion _entity_activity_an_ftc_study.pdf.

b. Suppression of Rival Innovation Through Acquisition

Another scenario concerns the acquisition and subsequent suppression of an innovative rival, or perhaps of its intellectual property. Intellectual property, of course, is an "asset," and so acquisitions of intellectual property can be subject to scrutiny under Section 7 of the Clayton Act. What if the acquisition itself appears lawful, but the acquiring firm's sole purpose is to acquire the new technology for the purpose of suppressing it?

Those were the allegations in *McDonald v. Johnson & Johnson*, 722 F.2d 1370 (8th Cir. 1983), a case brought under Sections 1 and 2 of the Sherman Act, as well as Section 7 of the Clayton Act, by the former shareholders of an electronic pain-relieving device called "TENS" ("transcutaneous electronic nerve stimulator"). The plaintiffs had sold their interests in their firm to Johnson & Johnson, a pharmaceutical company, and alleged that in violation of the sale agreement, Johnson & Johnson suppressed rather than promoted their TENS device in order to protect its popular pain-relieving pharmaceuticals from competition.

The case proceeded on fraud and breach of contract grounds, but the antitrust claims were dismissed for lack of antitrust injury, with the court relying on *Brunswick*. Why would the court so hold? Could former shareholders suffer injury of the kind the antitrust laws were designed to prevent? According to the Eighth Circuit, because the plaintiffs had sold their interests *in toto*, voluntarily withdrawing from the TENS market, they were no longer competitors of Johnson & Johnson, hence they could not have suffered the effects of any exclusionary conduct. Moreover, since they were not consumers of TENS either, they were not damaged by any collusive effects of Johnson & Johnson's conduct. Their injuries though real were contractual, not competitive in nature. 722 F.2d at 1374–79.

But the underlying scenario may nevertheless raise legitimate antitrust concerns. Under what circumstances should the acquisition for purposes of suppression of new emerging technologies constitute an antitrust violation? Should it matter that the technology is intellectual property? Should the new owner of property be free to decide not to exploit the technology? What problems can you foresee in trying to remedy a failure adequately to promote acquired technology? Could such a remedy undermine the essential right, applicable to patents as to other forms of property, not to utilize or exploit the property one owns?

Litigation involving claims like those in *Johnson & Johnson* are relatively rare. An obvious intent to *suppress* innovation through acquisition makes it akin to other exclusionary effects cases, such as a firm's efforts to manipulate standards or to preclude entry by a new rival. Acquisitions can also have collusive anticompetitive effects (either unilateral or coordinated), by reducing competition for innovation. (*See Note on Other Unilateral Effects Theories*, *supra* Chapter 5, which discusses unilateral effects theories regarding innovation in the 2010 Merger Guidelines.)

As we learned in Chapter 5, however, to complete that analysis, in many cases it will first be necessary to define a relevant market. A number of issues, some quite controversial, have arisen in that regard, as discussed above.

One final point worth noting here is that the 2010 Horizontal Merger Guidelines added a paragraph on the role of innovation in merger efficiency analysis:

[T]he Agencies consider the ability of the merged firm to conduct research or development more effectively. Such efficiencies may spur innovation but not affect short-term pricing. The Agencies also consider the ability of the merged firm to appropriate a greater fraction of the benefits resulting from its innovations. Licensing and intellectual property conditions may be important to this enquiry, as they affect the ability of a firm to appropriate the benefits of its innovation. Research and development cost savings may be substantial and yet not be cognizable efficiencies because they are difficult to verify or result from anticompetitive reductions in innovative activities.

Horizontal Merger Guidelines § 10. The agencies accordingly seem to acknowledge that mergers may produce dynamic efficiencies, by stimulating innovation, but to discount these efficiencies because they do not affect the short-term pricing or production upon which the agencies focus their analysis. Note, moreover, the agencies' concern with a firm's ability to appropriate the benefits of its innovations. Recall the institutional capacity question we have raised throughout this Chapter. How does this new section reflect upon the agencies' ability to comprehend and incorporate into their analyses competitive effects in dynamic markets? What if evidence suggests that long-term innovation in a particular market holds the potential for huge dynamic welfare gains that would swamp short-term static welfare losses?

Figure 7–2 summarizes some of the theories of collusive behavior potentially harmful to innovation that we have just reviewed. In evaluating the list, also consider: (1) the statutory basis most likely to be invoked to challenge the conduct in each instance, (2) the traditional elements required to establish each such offense, (3) the proof problems likely to arise in each case, and (4) whether rivals or consumers could adequately demonstrate antitrust injury in challenging conduct falling into any of the categories.

Figure 7–2:
Some Antitrust Theories for Challenging Collusive Agreements That Restrict Innovation

- Manipulation of product standards or certifications
- Pooling or cross-licensing substitute patents
- Reverse payment settlements restricting entry
- Suppression of rival innovation through acquisition

The scenarios discussed in this section are just a sampling of the kinds of innovation-suppressing conduct courts have examined. While there appears to be a consensus that the successful suppression of a new product or innovation should constitute an "anticompetitive effect" cognizable under the antitrust laws, as you can see, there may be challenging questions of fit and proof in such cases.

C. EXCLUSIONARY CONDUCT

We turn now from a discussion of how firms may use tactics to inflict collusive competitive harms to an examination of possible exclusionary strategies. The New Economy raises myriad opportunities for firms to engage in traditional, well-understood exclusionary behavior, while simultaneously seeking out new methods for excluding rivals. Accordingly, the antitrust analysis invokes both traditional antitrust economic learning and examinations of previously undiagnosed conduct. Recall the discussion at the beginning of the Chapter outlining economic principles that make the New Economy new (relationship of marginal and fixed costs, shifting market boundaries, and network effects)—these factors may affect the incentives to engage in various forms of exclusionary conduct. Notice the interplay of old and new theories of exclusionary harm. As we proceed through the Chapter, notice also how well-existing antitrust understanding does or does not capture the effects of dominant firms operating in high-tech—and often highly dynamic—environments.

1. SUPPRESSION OF RIVAL INNOVATION BY A DOMINANT FIRM OR FIRMS

Dominant firms may use a variety of strategies to impede or forestall competition from new and innovative products. One such strategy involves product design, which we noted in the previous section in Sidebar 7–3: Product Hopping and Other Conduct that May Delay Generic Entry. In *Berkey Photo, Inc. v. Eastman Kodak, Co.*, 603 F.2d 263 (2d Cir. 1979), the Second Circuit analyzed Kodak's conduct in designing new varieties of amateur film and cameras. Conceded to hold a monopoly in the film market, Kodak introduced a new type of amateur film and made it available in a configuration compatible only with one of Kodak's cameras. The plaintiff was Berkey Photo, which produced its own line of cameras and offered photograph finishing services in competition with Kodak. Berkey alleged that Kodak, by reason of its monopoly power in the film industry, had an obligation under Section 2 to give competing camera makers and photograph finishers advance notice of its new film designs.

In responding to Berkey, Kodak executives may have experienced some ambivalence as they observed other companies developing goods that complemented their own. On the one hand, firms typically see the development of complementary goods as a benefit, because the emergence of such goods can increase the attractiveness of (and demand for) the original product. At the same time, the producer of the original good would like to obtain some of the revenues generated by sales of the complementary products. The producer is likely to view the creation of complements as, in some sense, the result of its own labors and will desire to receive some of the gains. The original producer also may realize that the creator of complements may be best positioned to challenge the producer in the market for the original product itself.

At trial, the jury found that Kodak's conduct was unreasonably exclusionary and awarded Berkey treble damages, costs, and attorneys' fees totaling nearly $100 million. The Second Circuit reversed and vacated all but $1 million of the damage award. In refusing to require Kodak to provide Berkey advance notice of its product design choices, the court said that "any firm, even a monopolist, may generally bring its products to market whenever and however it chooses," without regard to the impact on its rivals. 603 F.2d at 286. The court emphasized that requiring pre-disclosure by a dominant firm, by enabling its rivals to free-ride on its research and development activities, would reduce the incumbent's incentive to innovate:

> Kodak did not have a duty to predisclose information about the 110 camera system to competing camera manufacturers. * * * [A] firm may normally keep its innovations secret from its rivals as long as it wishes, forcing them to catch up on the strength of their own efforts after the new product is introduced. It is the possibility of success in the marketplace, attributable to superior performance, that provides the incentives on which the proper functioning of our competitive economy rests. If a firm that has engaged in the risks and expenses of research and development were required in all circumstances to share with its rivals the benefits of those endeavors, this incentive would very likely be vitiated.

603 F.2d at 281. The court also noted the severe administrative difficulty of "discerning workable guidelines" for courts and companies to follow in deciding when pre-disclosure was required.

Subsequent appellate decisions have adopted a similarly permissive philosophy. In the late 1970s and early 1980s, IBM defeated many challenges from companies that produced tape drives or disk drives that were compatible with IBM's mainframe computers. Some plaintiffs alleged that IBM deliberately reconfigured its mainframe computers to impair compatibility with their products and to ensure that IBM alone would be the supplier of "peripheral devices" that operated with its mainframe computers. Courts typically rejected these claims where IBM provided evidence that its design choice in some way improved the quality of its machines, even though one aim of the design choice was to frustrate compatibility. *See, e.g., Memorex Corp. v. IBM Corp.*, 636 F.2d 1188 (9th Cir. 1980). In another category of cases, plaintiffs unsuccessfully insisted that IBM had a duty to reveal new interface designs in advance of their introduction. In *Cal. Computer Prods., Inc. v. IBM Corp.*, 613 F.2d 727, 744 (9th Cir. 1979), the Ninth Circuit explained that IBM "need not have provided its rivals with disk products to examine and copy nor have constricted its product development so as to facilitate the sales of rival products."

Although courts have accorded dominant firms extensive latitude in making product design choices, they also have indicated that such freedom has limits. In *Berkey*, the Second Circuit explained that "[i]f a monopolist's products gain acceptance in the market, * * * it is of no importance that a judge or jury may later regard them as inferior, so long as that success was not based on any form of coercion." 603 F.2d at 287. The court of appeals also found that Berkey might have been entitled to recover for Kodak's refusal to package its new film in formats compatible to Berkey's designs if Berkey had shown that it suffered damages as a result. The Second Circuit concluded that Berkey had presented no evidence of such harm. *Id.* at 290. Several cases have said that deliberate efforts to create incompatibility with a rival's products without achieving any improvement in quality or reduction in cost could be illegal. *See Transamerica Computer Co. v. IBM Corp.*, 698 F.2d 1377, 1383 (9th Cir. 1983); *Northeastern Tel. Co. v. AT & T Co.*, 651 F.2d 76, 94–96 (2d Cir. 1981). *See generally* John M. Newman, *Anticompetitive Product Design in the New Economy*, 39 FLA. ST. U. L. REV. 1 (2013).

More broadly, *Berkey* suggests standards for judging whether and when a dominant firm's investment in new products might be scrutinized as an instrument of strategic entry deterrence. Antitrust's fundamental task here is to find ways to challenge those R & D and marketing strategies involving new products that deter competition by rivals without producing benefits to buyers, and it is a tough assignment. One approach to this task was suggested by *Berkey*, which explained that Kodak's introduction of a new film format and simultaneous withdrawal of an old format, forcing photographers to buy photofinishing from Kodak rather than Berkey, could have supplied the "bad act" necessary to support a charge of monopolization—but only if the new format had not been better or cheaper than the old. *Berkey Photo*, 603 F.2d at 287 n.39.

The use of strategies targeted at impeding competition from new and innovative products was at the heart of the 1998 prosecution of Microsoft for monopolization, which we studied in Chapter 4. As we learned, the federal government and a group of states alleged that Microsoft, perceiving a threat to its monopoly in Intel-compatible PC desktop operating systems, set out to impede competition from what was termed "middleware," such as Netscape's Navigator Internet browser and Sun Microsystems' Java programming language. Although middleware did not itself constitute an alternative to Intel-compatible PC desktop operating systems, such as Microsoft's Windows and Apple's Mac OS, the prosecution's theory— ultimately endorsed by both the district and the court of appeals—was that middleware had the potential either to become an operating system alternative itself, or spur the creation of competing operating systems by others. Microsoft was accused of attempting to quell that threat through a range of exclusionary conduct, including exclusive dealing arrangements, tying, pricing, and other anticompetitive strategies.

The competitive threat of middleware as an operating system substitute, however, was at best nascent—it had yet to coalesce into a true alternative to Windows. Relying on that fact, Microsoft maintained that the government had failed to demonstrate any causal link between Microsoft's allegedly anticompetitive conduct and its maintenance of monopoly power—the emerging technologies never coalesced into a true threat to its monopoly. According to Microsoft, the elimination of Netscape and Sun, therefore, was competitively inconsequential. In the following brief excerpt from the case, the court responded in strong terms.

UNITED STATES v. MICROSOFT CORP.

United States Court of Appeals for the District of Columbia Circuit, 2001.
253 F.3d 34.

PER CURIAM.

* * *

II

* * *

* * * To require that § 2 liability turn on a plaintiff's ability or inability to reconstruct the hypothetical marketplace absent a defendant's anticompetitive conduct would only encourage monopolists to take more and earlier anticompetitive action.

We may infer causation where exclusionary conduct is aimed at producers of nascent competitive technologies as well as when it is aimed at producers of established substitutes. Admittedly, in the former case there is added uncertainty, inasmuch as nascent threats are merely *potential* substitutes. But the underlying proof problem is the same— neither plaintiffs nor the court can confidently reconstruct a product's hypothetical technological development in a world absent the defendant's exclusionary conduct. To some degree, "the defendant is made to suffer the uncertain consequences of its own undesirable conduct." 3 AREEDA & HOVENKAMP, ANTITRUST LAW ¶ 651c, at 78.

Given this rather edentulous test for causation, the question in this case is not whether Java or Navigator would actually have developed into viable platform substitutes, but (1) whether as a general matter the exclusion of nascent threats is the type of conduct that is reasonably capable of contributing significantly to a defendant's continued monopoly power and (2) whether Java and Navigator reasonably constituted nascent threats at the time Microsoft engaged in the anticompetitive conduct at issue. As to the first, suffice it to say that it would be inimical to the purpose of the Sherman Act to allow monopolists free reign to squash nascent, albeit unproven, competitors at will—particularly in industries marked by rapid technological advance and frequent paradigm shifts. As to the second, the District Court made ample findings that both Navigator and Java showed potential as middleware platform threats.

* * *

The D.C. Circuit was unequivocal in its conclusion that the antitrust laws should be able to reach conduct that threatens to forestall or completely to impede emerging competitive threats. But how developed and concrete must those threats be? Would the court's conclusion have been altered had Navigator and Java never actually made it to market? In other words, how "nascent" and how "imminent" must the competitive threat be before the plaintiff can satisfy the Sherman Act's threshold requirements of substantiality?

More broadly, what are the permissible boundaries of a dominant firm's responses to new competition? Must it sit back and avoid aggressive responses for fear that it will cross the line of legality? Will the cost in terms of diminished competitive vigor outweigh the value of too strict a standard? Given what we have read about Microsoft's conduct, would you agree with Microsoft's position that its hands were being tied unfairly by the court, impeding Microsoft's own ability to innovate without promoting innovation by its rivals?

In the following case, the Ninth Circuit analyzes these boundaries in a different setting. Notice the delineations the court makes between those behaviors related to innovation and product improvement that are acceptable and how it distinguishes these from potentially impermissible acts of monopolization. What is the standard it sets? Does it strike the right balance between fostering innovation and preventing competitive harm?

ALLIED ORTHOPEDIC APPLIANCES, INC.
v. TYCO HEALTHCARE GROUP LP

United States Court of Appeals for the Ninth Circuit, 2010.
592 F.3d 991.

SILVERMAN, CIRCUIT JUDGE.

Plaintiffs in this antitrust suit are a group of hospitals and other health care providers that purchased pulse oximetry sensors from Tyco Healthcare Group LP after November 2003. They * * * allege that by introducing OxiMax, a patented pulse oximetry system that is incompatible with generic sensors, Tyco unlawfully maintained its monopoly over the sensor market in violation of Section 2 of the Sherman Act, 15 U.S.C. § 2.

The district court * * * granted Tyco's motion for summary judgment on the Section * * * 2 claim[ ]. * * * We [ ] agree that there is no Section 2 violation; the undisputed evidence shows that the patented OxiMax design is an improvement over the previous design. Innovation does not violate the antitrust laws on its own, and there is no evidence that Tyco used its monopoly power to force customers to adopt its new product. Accordingly, we affirm the district court's judgment on the merits. * * *

BACKGROUND

The pulse oximetry products at issue in this litigation include sensors and monitors. Sensors attach to a patient's body. A monitor receives and interprets the signal from a sensor and then displays the patient's level of blood oxygenation. Stand-alone monitors measure only blood oxygenation. Multi-parameter monitors measure various patient diagnostics in addition to blood oxygenation. Monitors are more expensive than sensors on a unit basis, but the volume of sensor sales is much larger than the volume of monitor sales.

Tyco was an early entrant in the pulse oximetry market and was able to establish an installed base of monitors greatly exceeding that of its competitors. Its technology was initially protected by its "R-Cal" patent, which prevented competitors from selling sensors compatible with its installed base of monitors. Tyco anticipated that upon expiration of the R-Cal patent in November 2003, competitors would begin to produce generic sensors compatible with its installed base of monitors. It thus set about creating a new proprietary oximetry technology.

Tyco's plan matured into what became known as the "OxiMax Strategy." Tyco created a new patented sensor design that contained a writable memory chip. Moving the digital memory chip from the monitor to the sensor allowed Tyco to add new features to the OxiMax sensors, such as the ability to store the patient's oxygen saturation history in the sensor itself (the "sensor event reporting" feature) and the ability to inform a physician of possible causes of and solutions for signal interruption (the "sensor messaging" feature).

The digital memory chip also allowed Tyco to move essential calibration coefficients from the monitors into the sensors themselves. Because the new OxiMax monitors do not contain any calibration coefficients, they are incompatible with generic sensors. However, OxiMax monitors are compatible with new types of sensors that Tyco develops. Previously, when Tyco introduced a new sensor, customers either had to buy a new monitor or reprogram their entire installed base of stand-alone and multiparameter monitors with the appropriate calibration coefficients. With the OxiMax system, customers can adopt new types of sensors without affecting their installed base of monitors because the necessary coefficients are contained in the sensors themselves. This reduces costs for customers and frees sensor designers from having to use the predefined coefficients programmed into the installed base of monitors. Moving the calibration coefficients into the sensors therefore facilitates the development and introduction of new types of sensors.

For example, Tyco developed the Max-Fast Adhesive Forehead Sensor for use with the OxiMax system. According to Tyco, the Max-Fast sensor "has a more efficient and spectrally different [Light Emitting Diode]" than previous versions of the sensor. "Because the MAX-FAST sensor is calibrated specifically for use on the forehead, its calibration differs from the existing RCAL curve set," and consequently it can only be used with the new OxiMax system.

Tyco launched OxiMax in March 2002 and notified equipment manufacturers that all remaining R-Cal boards were being discontinued in February 2003. * * *

After expiration of Tyco's R-Cal patent in November 2003, a number of companies, including Masimo and GE, began manufacturing generic R-Cal sensors. Masimo planned to price its generic sensors between $5.75 and $7.50 each. GE priced its sensors at $6.50. In contrast, the average price for Tyco's branded sensors was just over $10. By March of 2004, Tyco estimated that 44% of the installed base of stand-alone monitors and 24% of the installed base of multiparameter monitors used OxiMax technology. From 2002 to 2005, Tyco's share of stand-alone pulse oximetry monitor sales in the U.S. was between 62% and 64%. In 2006, its market share dropped to 35%. In October 2007, Masimo estimated that its share of new monitor sales in the U.S. was roughly 40% to 45%.

DISCUSSION

* * *

II. TYCO'S INTRODUCTION OF OXIMAX DID NOT VIOLATE SECTION 2 OF THE SHERMAN ACT

* * * For purposes of Tyco's motion and this appeal, the parties agree that Tyco is a monopolist in the U.S. pulse oximetry sensor market. The focus of the dispute is whether Tyco unlawfully maintained its monopoly power in that market by introducing OxiMax.

Plaintiffs contend that Tyco maintained its monopoly by (1) designing its new patent-protected OxiMax sensors to be compatible with its new OxiMax monitors and the installed base of R-Cal monitors, but designing its new OxiMax monitors to be incompatible with the old R-Cal sensors; and (2) allegedly forcing customers and OEMs to adopt the new OxiMax monitors by discontinuing its R-Cal monitors and implementing other exclusionary business practices. Plaintiffs argue that the district court erred in rejecting these arguments because it did not balance the benefits of Tyco's alleged product improvement against its anticompetitive effects. They further argue that the district court impermissibly decided disputed issues of material fact regarding the sufficiency of Tyco's innovation and the competitive effect of its overall OxiMax strategy. We agree with the district court.

A. Product Improvement Alone Does Not Violate Section 2

"Section 2 of the Sherman Act proscribes 'monopolization'; it does not render unlawful all monopolies." "A monopolist, no less than any other competitor, is permitted and indeed encouraged to compete aggressively on the merits, and any success it may achieve solely through 'the process of invention and innovation' is necessarily tolerated by the antitrust laws." Accordingly, "[a]s a general rule, courts are properly very skeptical about claims that competition has been harmed by a dominant firm's product design changes."

However, changes in product design are not immune from antitrust scrutiny and in certain cases may constitute an unlawful means of maintaining a monopoly under Section 2. For example, in *United States v. Microsoft*, the plaintiffs showed that Microsoft harmed competition by integrating its Web browser, Internet Explorer, into the Windows 98 operating system. Microsoft provided no "procompetitive justification," for having integrated Internet Explorer into Windows. Having failed to show "that its conduct serve[d] a purpose other than protecting its operating system monopoly," the D.C. Circuit held that Microsoft had violated Section 2 of the Sherman Act.

In contrast, a design change that improves a product by providing a new benefit to consumers does not violate Section 2 absent some associated anticompetitive conduct. In *Calcomp*, a manufacturer of peripheral computer devices argued that "IBM made design changes on certain of its CPUs, disk drives and controllers of no technological advantage and solely for the purpose of frustrating competition" from peripheral device manufacturers. However, there was uncontroverted evidence that IBM's changes allowed it to reduce manufacturing costs and prices to the consumer and also improved performance of the product. We thus held:

> IBM, assuming it was a monopolist, had the right to redesign its products to make them more attractive to buyers whether by reason of lower manufacturing cost and price or improved performance. It was under no duty to help CalComp or other peripheral equipment manufacturers survive or expand. IBM need not have provided its rivals with disk products to examine and copy, nor have constricted its product development so as to facilitate sales of rival products. The reasonableness of IBM's conduct in this regard did not present a jury issue.

Following *CalComp*, we decided *Foremost Pro Color, Inc. v. Eastman Kodak, Co.*, 703 F.2d 534 (9th Cir. 1983). Kodak, a monopolist in photographic film and amateur still cameras, had introduced a new line of smaller cameras and related film products. The new film could not be processed with previously used photographic paper and chemicals, so photofinishers had to buy all new paper and chemicals from Kodak. One such photofinisher, Foremost, brought suit alleging that Kodak had introduced its new system to maintain its monopoly in violation of Section 2.

Foremost made no allegation that Kodak's new film was not an improvement over previous films. Rather, it simply alleged that Kodak had unlawfully maintained its monopoly by "continually researching and developing new photographic products . . . that are incompatible with then existing photographic products and photofinishing equipment" and then introducing those products "in such a manner that [Foremost] was required to purchase new paper, chemistry and photofinishing equipment."

We held that such an allegation does not state a claim for relief under Section 2. It was "of no legal import" that Foremost had characterized Kodak's activities "as a form of technological predation" because a monopolist has "the right to redesign its products to make them more attractive to buyers." We acknowledged, however, that introduction of a new and improved product design could constitute a violation of Section 2 where "some associated conduct . . . supplies the violation." Specifically, we held that to state a claim for relief under Section 2,

> product introduction must be alleged to involve some associated conduct which constitutes an anticompetitive abuse or leverage of monopoly power, or a predatory or exclusionary means of

attempting to monopolize the relevant market, rather than aggressive competition on the merits.

CalComp and *Foremost* therefore stand for the uncontroversial proposition that product improvement by itself does not violate Section 2, even if it is performed by a monopolist and harms competitors as a result. There is no violation of Section 2 unless plaintiff proves that some conduct of the monopolist associated with its introduction of a new and improved product design "constitutes an anticompetitive abuse or leverage of monopoly power, or a predatory or exclusionary means of attempting to monopolize the relevant market."

There is no room in this analysis for balancing the benefits or worth of a product improvement against its anticompetitive effects. If a monopolist's design change is an improvement, it is "necessarily tolerated by the antitrust laws," unless the monopolist abuses or leverages its monopoly power in some other way when introducing the product. To hold otherwise "would be contrary to the very purpose of the antitrust laws, which is, after all, to foster and ensure competition on the merits." "Antitrust scholars have long recognized the undesirability of having courts oversee product design, and any dampening of technological innovation would be at cross-purposes with antitrust law." *United States v. Microsoft Corp.*, 147 F.3d 935, 948 (1998).

To weigh the benefits of an improved product design against the resulting injuries to competitors is not just unwise, it is unadministrable. There are no criteria that courts can use to calculate the "right" amount of innovation, which would maximize social gains and minimize competitive injury. A seemingly minor technological improvement today can lead to much greater advances in the future. The balancing test proposed by plaintiffs would therefore require courts to weigh as-yet-unknown benefits against current competitive injuries. Our precedents and the precedents we have relied upon strongly counsel against such a test. Although one federal court of appeals has nominally included a balancing component in its test, it has not yet attempted to apply it. *See United States v. Microsoft Corp.*, 253 F.3d 34, 59, 66–67 (D.C. Cir. 2001) (including balancing as the last step of its test but not applying that step, either because the defendant had provided no justification for its product change or because the plaintiff had not rebutted the justification provided). Absent some form of coercive conduct by the monopolist, the ultimate worth of a genuine product improvement can be adequately judged only by the market itself.

B.   Undisputed Evidence that OxiMax Was an Improvement

In this case, it is undisputed that by placing a digital memory chip in the sensor and moving the calibration coefficients from the monitor to the sensor, Tyco made its new OxiMax system incompatible with generic sensors and harmed generic sensor manufacturers. We must therefore decide whether there remains a genuine issue that the OxiMax sensor design provided some new benefit to consumers and thus constituted an improvement.

First, the United States Patent and Trademark Office found the OxiMax sensor design to be sufficiently innovative over the prior art to deserve a patent, and there is no allegation, much less proof, that the patent is invalid. Although, as the district court properly noted, there is not a per se rule barring Section 2 liability on patented product innovation, the existence of a patent on a new product design is some evidence that the change is an improvement over previous designs. After all, "the proper amount of gains to innovation are left to Congress, who has the authority to vary the terms of patent protections, the point in time from which the protections run, or the scope of patentable innovations."

Second, it is undisputed that Tyco's new sensor design allows it to introduce new types of sensors without requiring its customers to purchase new monitors or reprogram their installed base of monitors. This added flexibility promotes the introduction of new types of sensors, such as Max-Fast, and reduces costs for consumers of pulse oximetry equipment. It also allows new functions, such as sensor event reporting and sensor messaging, to be included in the sensors themselves. Plaintiffs have provided evidence that Max-Fast is no more accurate than previous forehead sensors and that physicians have not found the sensor event reporting or messaging features very useful. But even if Tyco has not yet been able to successfully utilize the new flexibility provided by the OxiMax platform, that in no way contradicts that the platform facilitates the introduction of new types of sensors and sensor functions and will reduce costs for consumers in the long run.

Tyco's internal documents show that from the very earliest stages of its development of OxiMax, it aimed to produce a new technology that both served as "a new, flexible platform for future oximetry innovation" and added customer value by improving performance. To ensure that the new feature set enabled by OxiMax would help to differentiate its new sensors from generics, Tyco surveyed clinicians and initially received positive feedback. Plaintiffs focus on statements showing that Tyco hoped its new technology would constitute a barrier to entry for generic sensor manufacturers. However, even legitimate product improvement can have the effect of harming or even destroying competitors. Statements of an innovator's intent to harm a competitor through genuine product improvement are insufficient by themselves to create a jury question under Section 2.

Likewise, Plaintiffs mistakenly focus on documents showing that, sometime in 2001, Tyco began to realize that the sensor messaging and sensor event reporting features were less valuable than it initially believed and worried that the market would perceive its new technology as nothing more than a way to lock out generics. These documents do not create a genuine issue of material fact about whether OxiMax represented an improvement over previous sensor designs. Since technological innovation "is accompanied by tremendous uncertainty as to cost, technical success, and eventual market success . . . *ex post* realizations are rarely a useful indicator of *ex ante* expectations." Evidence of an innovator's initial intent may be helpful to the extent that it shows that the innovator knew all along that the new design was no better than the old design, and thus introduced the design solely to eliminate competition. But the documents here show that Tyco initially believed that clinicians would value the new feature set. Moreover, the documents show that Tyco continued to believe that the flexibility of the new OxiMax platform would appeal to consumers at the point that it introduced OxiMax.

In sum, Plaintiffs have presented no evidence to refute that the patented OxiMax sensor design facilitates the introduction of new types of sensors with added capabilities at less cost to consumers. The district court properly concluded that Plaintiffs had not created a genuine issue of material fact on whether OxiMax was a genuine improvement.

C.   *Tyco Did Not Use Its Market Power to Force Adoption of OxiMax*

Although it is undisputed that the OxiMax sensor design is an improvement over previous designs, Tyco may still have violated Section 2 if any of its other conduct "constitutes an anticompetitive abuse or leverage of monopoly power, or a predatory or exclusionary means of attempting to monopolize the relevant market."

Plaintiffs argue that Tyco forced consumers to adopt OxiMax by discontinuing the older R-Cal technology. A monopolist's discontinuation of its old technology may violate Section 2 if it effectively forces consumers to adopt its new technology. *Berkey Photo*, 603 F.2d at 287 n.39. Here, however, there was uncontroverted evidence that Masimo was effectively competing for pulse oximetry monitor sales during the relevant time period. By 2006, Tyco's share of new monitor sales in the U.S. had dropped to 35%, and by 2007, Masimo's share had grown to 40% to 45%. Masimo and GE were also selling generic sensors compatible with Tyco's R-Cal monitors, and Masimo was able to make its own proprietary sensors compatible with Tyco's R-Cal monitors by employing a simple cable. Given all these alternatives, Tyco did not force consumers to purchase its OxiMax monitors simply by discontinuing its support of the R-Cal technology.

Plaintiffs' argument that Tyco could have made its monitors compatible with the old sensors also fails. Our precedents make clear that a monopolist has no duty to help its competitors survive or expand when introducing an improved product design. The evidence shows that the OxiMax monitors' incompatibility with R-Cal sensors was the necessary consequence of moving the calibration coefficients from the monitor into the sensor. Thus, the product improvement at issue in this case, not some associated conduct by Tyco, caused the incompatibility.

* * *

In sum, Plaintiffs have provided no evidence that Tyco used its monopoly power to force consumers of pulse oximetry products to adopt its new OxiMax technology. Absent evidence of such compulsion, the only rational inference that can be drawn from some consumers' adoption of OxiMax is that they regarded it to be a superior product. The district court therefore properly concluded that Plaintiffs had failed to create a genuine issue of material fact regarding Tyco's introduction of OxiMax and properly granted summary judgment on the Section 2 claim.

CONCLUSION

Plaintiffs have presented no evidence to refute Tyco's evidence that its OxiMax sensor design facilitates the introduction of new types of sensors with added capabilities at less cost to consumers. Nor have Plaintiffs presented any evidence that Tyco used its monopoly power to coerce adoption of OxiMax. Tyco's market-share discount agreements and sole-source agreements did not prevent consumers from choosing to purchase the less expensive generic sensors that existed in the market. The district court therefore properly granted Tyco summary judgment on the claim[ ] under Section[ ] * * * 2 of the Sherman Act.

AFFIRMED.

* * *

———————

Why does the Ninth Circuit conclude that OxiMax's conduct did not violate Section 2 even though it excluded generic sensor manufacturers? Was the court's decision correct from a consumer welfare standpoint? Why or why not?

Note the role patents play in this case. In determining there was no genuine issue as to whether the OxiMax sensor design was an improvement, how much significance does the court place upon the PTO's finding that the technology was sufficiently innovative to deserve a patent? Does the court view this finding as dispositive? Should it? Could the court have found that, despite being awarded a patent, the OxiMax sensor was not a significant enough improvement to avoid antitrust liability? Would that determination be different from or at odds with the PTO's? Could that determination inject uncertainty into future business decisions regarding new products? Might such uncertainty chill the incentives of a dominant firm to innovate? Or, on the other hand, might the imposition of liability in cases involving "weak" patents, patents that involve little or no genuine innovation, promote innovation by channeling creative efforts into more substantial patents?

Fashioning remedies in cases involving innovation presents another challenge to courts and antitrust institutions. One of the most notable proceedings to yield restrictions upon a dominant firm's innovation-related activities is *In re Xerox Corp.*, 86 F.T.C. 364 (1975), discussed *supra* Section A. Recall that in that case the FTC alleged that Xerox had violated Section 5 of the FTC Act by maintaining a non-competitive market structure in the market for plain-paper photocopiers. With a market share of over 90 percent in plain-paper copiers, Xerox was alleged to have (a) built a "patent thicket" around the company's pathbreaking, dry paper, copier technology and (b) aggressively pursued patent infringement claims against any company that drew near to the thicket with its own copier design. The parties reached a settlement by which Xerox, among other requirements, agreed to make any three patents in its intellectual property portfolio available to competitors without charge. The settlement spurred new entry into the photocopier industry and dramatically reduced the market share of Xerox. For a thought-provoking analysis of the long-term impact of the case, see Willard K. Tom, *The 1975* Xerox *Consent Decree: Ancient Artifacts and Current Tensions*, 68 ANTITRUST L.J. 967 (2001).

To remedy the conduct in the Microsoft case, the Consent Decree negotiated between Microsoft and the government mandates certain changes in Microsoft's contractual policies and requires it to disclose certain information to facilitate the interoperability of rival middleware with Windows. Does it also explicitly or implicitly mandate design changes? Consider the following excerpt.

IN THE UNITED STATES DISTRICT COURT
FOR THE DISTRICT OF COLUMBIA

Civil Action No. 98–1232 (CKK)

UNITED STATES OF AMERICA,

Plaintiff

v.

MICROSOFT CORPORATION,

Defendant.

MODIFIED FINAL JUDGMENT

Originally Entered November 12, 2002;
Modified *September 7*, 2006

* * *

C.   Microsoft shall not restrict by agreement any OEM licensee from exercising any of the following options or alternatives:

1.   Installing, and displaying icons, shortcuts, or menu entries for, any Non-Microsoft Middleware or any product or service (including but not limited to IAP products or services) that distributes, uses, promotes, or supports any Non-Microsoft Middleware, on the desktop or Start menu, or anywhere else in a Windows Operating System Product where a list of icons, shortcuts, or menu entries for applications are generally displayed, except that Microsoft may restrict an OEM from displaying icons, shortcuts and menu entries for any product in any list of such icons, shortcuts, or menu entries specified in the Windows documentation as being limited to products that provide particular types of functionality, provided that the restrictions are non-discriminatory with respect to non-Microsoft and Microsoft products.

2.   Distributing or promoting Non-Microsoft Middleware by installing and displaying on the desktop shortcuts of any size or shape so long as such shortcuts do not impair the functionality of the user interface.

3.   Launching automatically, at the conclusion of the initial boot sequence or subsequent boot sequences, or upon connections to or disconnections from the Internet, any Non-Microsoft Middleware if a Microsoft Middleware Product that provides similar functionality would otherwise be launched automatically at that time, provided that any such Non-Microsoft Middleware displays on the desktop no user interface or a user interface of similar size and shape to the user interface displayed by the corresponding Microsoft Middleware Product.

4.   Offering users the option of launching other Operating Systems from the Basic Input/Output System or a non-Microsoft boot-loader or similar program that launches prior to the start of the Windows Operating System Product.

5. Presenting in the initial boot sequence its own IAP offer provided that the OEM complies with reasonable technical specifications established by Microsoft, including a requirement that the end user be returned to the initial boot sequence upon the conclusion of any such offer.

6. Exercising any of the options provided in Section III.H of this Final Judgment.

D. Starting at the earlier of the release of Service Pack 1 for Windows XP or 12 months after the submission of this Final Judgment to the Court, Microsoft shall disclose to ISVs, IHVs, IAPs, ICPs, and OEMs, for the sole purpose of interoperating with a Windows Operating System Product, via the Microsoft Developer Network ("MSDN") or similar mechanisms, the APIs and related Documentation that are used by Microsoft Middleware to interoperate with a Windows Operating System Product. For purposes of this Section III.D, the term APIs means the interfaces, including any associated callback interfaces, that Microsoft Middleware running on a Windows Operating System Product uses to call upon that Windows Operating System Product in order to obtain any services from that Windows Operating System Product. In the case of a new major version of Microsoft Middleware, the disclosures required by this Section III.D shall occur no later than the last major beta test release of that Microsoft Middleware. In the case of a new version of a Windows Operating System Product, the obligations imposed by this Section III.D shall occur in a Timely Manner.

E. Starting nine months after the submission of this proposed Final Judgment to the Court, Microsoft shall make available for use by third parties, for the sole purpose of interoperating or communicating with a Windows Operating System Product, on reasonable and non-discriminatory terms (consistent with Section III.I), any Communications Protocol that is, on or after the date this Final Judgment is submitted to the Court, (i) implemented in a Windows Operating System Product installed on a client computer, and (ii) used to interoperate, or communicate, natively (*i.e.*, without the addition of software code to the client operating system product) with a Microsoft server operating system product.

* * *

H. Starting at the earlier of the release of Service Pack 1 for Windows XP or 12 months after the submission of this Final Judgment to the Court, Microsoft shall:

1. Allow end users (via a mechanism readily accessible from the desktop or Start menu such as an Add/Remove icon) and OEMs (via standard preinstallation kits) to enable or remove

access to each Microsoft Middleware Product or Non-Microsoft Middleware Product by (a) displaying or removing icons, shortcuts, or menu entries on the desktop or Start menu, or anywhere else in a Windows Operating System Product where a list of icons, shortcuts, or menu entries for applications are generally displayed, except that Microsoft may restrict the display of icons, shortcuts, or menu entries for any product in any list of such icons, shortcuts, or menu entries specified in the Windows documentation as being limited to products that provide particular types of functionality, provided that the restrictions are non-discriminatory with respect to non-Microsoft and Microsoft products; and (b) enabling or disabling automatic invocations pursuant to Section III.C.3 of this Final Judgment that are used to launch Non-Microsoft Middleware Products or Microsoft Middleware Products. The mechanism shall offer the end user a separate and unbiased choice with respect to enabling or removing access (as described in this subsection III.H.1) and altering default invocations (as described in the following subsection III.H.2) with regard to each such Microsoft Middleware Product or Non-Microsoft Middleware Product and may offer the end-user a separate and unbiased choice of enabling or removing access and altering default configurations as to all Microsoft Middleware Products as a group or all Non-Microsoft Middleware Products as a group.

2. Allow end users (via an unbiased mechanism readily available from the desktop or Start menu), OEMs (via standard OEM preinstallation kits), and Non-Microsoft Middleware Products (via a mechanism which may, at Microsoft's option, require confirmation from the end user in an unbiased manner) to designate a Non-Microsoft Middleware Product to be invoked in place of that Microsoft Middleware Product (or vice versa) in any case where the Windows Operating System Product would otherwise launch the Microsoft Middleware Product in a separate Top-Level Window and display either (i) all of the user interface elements or (ii) the Trademark of the Microsoft Middleware Product.

Notwithstanding the foregoing Section III.H.2, the Windows Operating System Product may invoke a Microsoft Middleware Product in any instance in which:

    (a)   that Microsoft Middleware Product would be invoked solely for use in interoperating with a server maintained by Microsoft (outside the context of general Web browsing), or

    (b)   that designated Non-Microsoft Middleware Product fails to implement a reasonable technical requirement (*e.g.*, a requirement to be able to host a particular ActiveX control) that is necessary for valid technical reasons to supply the end user with functionality consistent with a Windows Operating System Product, provided that the technical reasons are described in a reasonably prompt manner to any ISV that requests them.

3.   Ensure that a Windows Operating System Product does not (a) automatically alter an OEM's configuration of icons, shortcuts or menu entries installed or displayed by the OEM pursuant to Section III.C of this Final Judgment without first seeking confirmation from the user and (b) seek such confirmation from the end user for an automatic (as opposed to user-initiated) alteration of the OEM's configuration until 14 days after the initial boot up of a new Personal Computer. Any such automatic alteration and confirmation shall be unbiased with respect to Microsoft Middleware Products and Non-Microsoft Middleware. Microsoft shall not alter the manner in which a Windows Operating System Product automatically alters an OEM's configuration of icons, shortcuts or menu entries other than in a new version of a Windows Operating System Product.

* * *

———————

Remedies, by necessity, are attempts to solve a problem observed at a given point in time. If markets are advancing quickly, that may require courts and enforcers to consider remedies that include periodic review, relatively short duration, and the possibility of revision in light of changed circumstances. Similarly, courts and enforcers ought to evaluate the potential impact of remedies on the innovation incentives of both the dominant firm and its rivals. Particularly invasive remedies may force dominant firms to take approaches or make considerations they otherwise would not have, potentially impeding the rate at which dominant firms develop better or cheaper products. On the other hand, particularly weak or ineffective remedies may inhibit the innovation incentives of fringe rivals that might otherwise have challenged the dominant firm.

How does the *Microsoft* court attempt to fashion a remedy that will alleviate Microsoft's anticompetitive behavior, restore the innovation incentives of its rivals, and allow it to continue to be adequately innovative? Do you think the court's remedy is successful at striking this balance?

Although the Final Consent Decree clearly appears to mandate design changes as a remedy for Microsoft's anticompetitive conduct, the leadership of the U.S. Department of Justice was quick to lash out at other antitrust enforcement jurisdictions, especially the European Commission and the Korean Fair Trade Commission, when they sought to impose additional restrictions on Microsoft's design autonomy. Why might the Antitrust Division have been concerned about other enforcers imposing more demanding restrictions than those included in the U.S. Consent Decree? Why might those other enforcers have been inclined to do so? Why might antitrust enforcement agencies generally need to be sensitive to the implications of antitrust remedies that impose conditions or restrictions on a dominant firm's design autonomy? Are firms in innovative markets particularly sensitive to the possibility of conflicting restrictions across nations? Why or why not? For a further discussion of these issues in the *Microsoft* cases, see ANDREW I. GAVIL & HARRY FIRST, THE MICROSOFT ANTITRUST CASES: COMPETITION POLICY FOR THE TWENTY-FIRST CENTURY 235–79 (2014) (discussing the full range of remedies that were imposed on, or agreed to by, Microsoft in the public and private cases brought against it following the 1998 case in the U.S.).

2. SINGLE FIRM LICENSING PRACTICES

Perhaps the most common practice associated with patents and copyrights is "licensing." Although patent owners utilize many patents, many more are licensed to others, be they process or product patents. Copyrights, of course, by their nature are almost all the subject of licensing.

Anticompetitive issues associated with licensing practices parallel to a degree the full range of horizontal and vertical relationships we have studied. A critical threshold issue, therefore, is whether the patent holder and the licensee produce substitutable products. If not, the license will be analyzed as "vertical." *See Antitrust Guidelines for the Licensing of Intellectual Property*, § 3.3 & accompanying problem. "Cross-licensing" and "patent pooling," two kinds of licensing that often involve rival patent holders, are discussed above.

Many typical patent and copyright licensing practices, however, are "vertical"—the IP owner and the licensee do not compete, at least not in the market for the IP protected product. Vertical IP licensing can mirror virtually all of the vertical intrabrand and interbrand restrictions we studied in Chapter 6. For example, a patent holder might negotiate territorial, customer, or "field of use" restrictions with its licensees in order to best develop and exploit its IP rights, or seek to use minimum or maximum resale price restrictions. Similarly, it might agree to grant the equivalent of an exclusive distributorship to a single licensee. The patent holder might also seek to limit its licensees through exclusive dealing, as well as bundling or tying either multiple patented products or a mix of patented and unpatented ones.

The IP Guidelines focus their attention upon four vertical licensing practices: (1) resale price maintenance ("RPM") (§ 5.2); (2) tying (§ 5.3); (3) exclusive dealing (§ 5.4); and (4) grantbacks (§ 5.6). We describe each here only briefly. For a more in-depth treatment, see the respective sections of the IP Guidelines.

RPM. At the time the IP Guidelines were issued, both minimum and maximum RPM were still per se illegal. As we learned in Chapter 6, however, since that time the Supreme Court has reversed course and abandoned per se analysis in *Leegin* (minimum RPM) and *Khan* (maximum RPM). Although the IP Guidelines still discuss minimum RPM as per se illegal, the agencies and the courts would likely take those newer decisions into account and analyze any use of RPM under the rule of reason.

Tying. As we noted at the beginning of our discussion of IP rights, tying was among the earliest of IP practices to command severe antitrust scrutiny. That level of scrutiny followed largely from the Supreme Court's assumption that IP rights conferred market power. Recall, however, that one of the IP Guidelines' first principles is that such a presumption is unwarranted (and the Supreme Court endorsed that view in *Ill. Tool Works Inc. v. Indep. Ink, Inc.*, 547 U.S. 28 (2006)).

Hence, the Guidelines, without focusing upon the past per se prohibition of tying, indicate that tying would only be challenged in the context of IP licensing if (1) the seller (whether licensor or licensee) has market power; (2) the arrangement will have an adverse effect on competition in a relevant market; and (3) "efficiency justifications * * * do not outweigh the anticompetitive effects." *IP Guidelines*, § 5.3.

Section 5.3 of the Guidelines also discusses "package licensing," that is, "the licensing of multiple items of intellectual property in a single license or in a group of related licenses." Noting their efficiency potential, the IP Guidelines indicate that package licenses will be evaluated by their anticompetitive effects and efficiencies, like all other tying arrangements.

Exclusive Dealing. Tracking traditional case law, the IP Guidelines' discussion of exclusive dealing notes that it has been evaluated under a rule of reason analysis. Two steps are set forth as critical:

> In determining whether an exclusive dealing arrangement is likely to reduce competition in a relevant market, the Agencies will take into account the extent to which the arrangement (1)

promotes the exploitation and development of the licensor's
technology and (2) anticompetitively forecloses the exploitation
and development of, or otherwise constrains competition among,
competing technologies.

IP Guidelines, § 5.4. Relevant factors include:

> * * * the degree of foreclosure in the relevant market, the duration
> of the exclusive dealing arrangement, and other characteristics of
> the input and output markets, such as concentration, difficulty of
> entry, and the responsiveness of supply and demand to changes
> in price in the relevant markets.

Id. Note that the approach reflects some of the uncertainty in this area that
we explored in Chapter 6, by combining consideration for "foreclosure" with
consideration of other factors that might constrain competition.

Grantbacks. Grantbacks can arise in the context of horizontal or
vertical licensing. According to the *Guidelines*, a grantback is "an
arrangement under which a licensee agrees to extend to the licensor of
intellectual property the right to use the licensee's improvements to the
licensed technology." *IP Guidelines*, § 5.6. The IP Guidelines recognize that
grantbacks can have procompetitive effects, "especially if they are
nonexclusive. Such arrangements provide a means for the licensee and the
licensor to share risks and reward the licensor for making possible further
innovation based on or informed by the licensed technology, and both
promote innovation in the first place and promote the subsequent licensing
of the results of the innovation." Grantbacks can also pose competitive
risks, however, "if they substantially reduce the licensee's incentives to
engage in research and development and thereby limit rivalry in
innovation markets."

Because grantbacks can diminish the incentive to innovate, the
analysis of grantbacks can be linked to an evaluation of innovation and
technology markets. (*See supra* Sidebar 7–2). Hence, an "important factor
in the Agencies' analysis of a grantback will be whether the licensor has
market power in a relevant technology or innovation market." *IP
Guidelines*, § 5.6. The Guidelines continue:

> If the Agencies determine that a particular grantback provision is
> likely to reduce significantly licensees' incentives to invest in
> improving the licensed technology, the Agencies will consider the
> extent to which the grantback provision has offsetting
> procompetitive effects, such as (1) promoting dissemination of
> licensees' improvements to the licensed technology, (2) increasing
> the licensors' incentives to disseminate the licensed technology, or
> (3) otherwise increasing competition and output in a relevant
> technology or innovation market. *See* section 4.2. In addition, the
> Agencies will consider the extent to which grantback provisions in

the relevant markets generally increase licensors' incentives to innovate in the first place.

Id.

NOTE ON *KODAK* AND REFUSALS TO LICENSE INTELLECTUAL PROPERTY RIGHTS

In the early 1990s Kodak faced a significant challenge from a group of "Independent Service Organizations" ("ISOs"), who provided replacement parts and repair services for Kodak photocopying machines. (The case was discussed in Chapter 4). After the Supreme Court decided that summary judgment for Kodak was unwarranted, it remanded the case for a trial, at which the ISOs prevailed. On appeal from its loss at trial, Kodak continued to assert its IPRs as a defense for its refusal to deal with the ISOs, arguing that the district court erred when it failed to properly instruct the jury as to the legal import of its patented parts and copyrighted software. More specifically, it argued that the presence of such IPRs affects the analysis of a refusal to deal when it takes the form of a refusal to license intellectual property.

In *Image Tech. Servs., Inc. v. Eastman Kodak, Co.*, 125 F.3d 1195 (9th Cir. 1997), the Ninth Circuit agreed, viewing Kodak's assertion of IPRs as a "presumptively legitimate business justification." *Id.* at 1219. But it nevertheless affirmed the district court's finding of liability against Kodak, concluding that the district court's failure to so instruct the jury was a harmless error because Kodak's defense based on IPRs was pretext. In support of this conclusion, the Ninth Circuit observed that although Kodak held 220 patents covering 65 parts for its high volume photocopiers and micrographics equipment, its refusal to deal also covered thousands of unpatented parts. *Id.* Moreover, it concluded that evidence of Kodak's subjective intent in refusing to deal with the ISOs also supported the view that its defense based on IP rights was pretext. *Id.* ("Evidence regarding the state of mind of Kodak employees may show pretext, when such evidence suggests that the proffered business justification played no part in the decision to act.").

Kodak triggered a still robust controversy about the appropriate treatment of refusals to license intellectual property as a basis for antitrust liability, in part because the decision included arguably contradictory themes. The court observed that "[c]ase law * * * supports the right of a patent or copyright holder to refuse to sell or license protected work," *id.* at 1215, and that "patent and copyright holders may refuse to sell or license protected work." *Id.* It also concluded that there was "no reported case in which a court has imposed antitrust liability for a unilateral refusal to sell or license a patent or copyright" and that "[c]ourts do not generally view a monopolist's unilateral refusal to license a patent as 'exclusionary conduct.'" *Id.* at 1216. As already noted above, it concluded that IPRs provide a "presumptively legitimate business justification" for a refusal to license. *Id.* at 1219.

Yet the court also held that "neither patent nor copyright holders are immune from antitrust liability." *Id.* at 1215. In the court's view, "the presumption of legitimacy can be rebutted by evidence that the monopolist acquired the protection of the intellectual property laws in an unlawful manner. The presumption may also be rebutted by evidence of pretext." *Id.* at 1219. And, also as previously noted, subjective evidence could be used to establish pretext.

Despite its mixed messages, critics viewed *Kodak* as an assault on IPRs. In their view, it leaned too strongly in favor of antitrust rights and against IPRs, which, they feared, could undermine the incentives for dominant firms to innovate. They also complained of the unreliability of evidence of subjective intent and of the remedial problems associated with a court-imposed system of compulsory IP licensing.

Two years after the *Kodak* remand, the Federal Circuit, which exercises exclusive jurisdiction over the appeals of patent and copyright disputes, took issue with *Kodak* in a high profile case involving Intel Corporation, the largest manufacturer of high performance computer microprocessors in the world. *See Intergraph Corp. v. Intel Corp.*, 195 F.3d 1346 (Fed. Cir. 1999). *See also In the Matter of Intel Corp.*, Dkt. No. 9288, Decision and Order, https://www.ftc.gov /sites/default/files/documents/cases/1999/08/intel.do__0.htm (FTC 1999) (a related case that was settled by the FTC and Intel). *Intergraph* can be seen as favoring IPRs, in contrast to *Kodak*, which was widely perceived as favoring antitrust.

Shortly after the Federal Circuit's decision in *Intergraph*, the court again found itself at the center of a controversy that pitted intellectual property rights against antitrust law. Like Kodak, it pitted ISOs against a well-known equipment supplier, Xerox. Matching the principles set forth in *Intergraph* against those articulated in the various opinions in *Kodak*, the court again appeared to reject antitrust as an effective means of policing exercises of intellectual property rights.

CSU, L.L.C. v. XEROX CORP.

United States Court of Appeals for the Federal Circuit, 2000.
203 F.3d 1322.

Before MAYER, CHIEF JUDGE, ARCHER, SENIOR CIRCUIT JUDGE, and PLAGER, CIRCUIT JUDGE.

MAYER, CHIEF JUDGE.

CSU, L.L.C. appeals the judgment of the United States District Court for the District of Kansas, dismissing on summary judgment CSU's claims that Xerox's refusal to sell patented parts and copyrighted manuals and to license copyrighted software violate the antitrust laws. Because we agree with the district court that CSU has not raised a genuine issue as to any material fact and that Xerox is entitled to judgment as a matter of law, we affirm.

BACKGROUND

Xerox manufactures, sells, and services high-volume copiers. Beginning in 1984, it established a policy of not selling parts unique to its series 10 copiers to independent service organizations ("ISOs"), including CSU, unless they were also end-users of the copiers. In 1987, the policy was expanded to include all new products as well as existing series 9 copiers. Enforcement of this policy was tightened in 1989, and Xerox cut off CSU's direct purchase of restricted parts. Xerox also implemented an "on-site end-user verification" procedure to confirm that the parts ordered by certain ISOs or their customers were actually for their end-user use. Initially this procedure applied to only the six most successful ISOs, which included CSU.

To maintain its existing business of servicing Xerox equipment, CSU used parts cannibalized from used Xerox equipment, parts obtained from other ISOs, and parts purchased through a limited number of its customers. For approximately one year, CSU also obtained parts from Rank Xerox, a majority-owned European affiliate of Xerox, until Xerox forced Rank Xerox to stop selling parts to CSU and other ISOs. In 1994, Xerox settled an antitrust lawsuit with a class of ISOs by which it agreed to suspend its restrictive parts policy for six and one-half years and to license its diagnostic software for four and one-half years. CSU opted out of that settlement and filed this suit alleging that Xerox violated the Sherman Act by setting the prices on its patented parts much higher for ISOs than for end-users to force ISOs to raise their prices. This would eliminate ISOs in general and CSU in particular as competitors in the relevant service markets for high speed copiers and printers.

Xerox counterclaimed for patent and copyright infringement and contested CSU's antitrust claims as relying on injury solely caused by Xerox's lawful refusal to sell or license patented parts and copyrighted software. Xerox also claimed that CSU could not assert a patent or copyright misuse defense to Xerox's infringement counterclaims based on Xerox's refusal to deal.

The district court granted summary judgment to Xerox dismissing CSU's antitrust claims and holding that if a patent or copyright is lawfully acquired, the patent or copyright holder's unilateral refusal to sell or license its patented invention or copyrighted expression is not unlawful exclusionary conduct under the antitrust laws, even if the refusal to deal impacts competition in more than one market. The court also held, in both the patent and copyright contexts, that the right holder's intent in refusing to deal and any other alleged exclusionary acts committed by the right holder are irrelevant to antitrust law. This appeal followed.

DISCUSSION

* * *

As a general proposition, when reviewing a district court's judgment involving federal antitrust law, we are guided by the law of the regional circuit in which that district court sits, in this case the Tenth Circuit. We apply our own law, not regional circuit law, to resolve issues that clearly involve our exclusive jurisdiction. * * * The district court's grant of summary judgment as to CSU's antitrust claims arising from Xerox's refusal to sell its patented parts is therefore reviewed as a matter of Federal Circuit law, while consideration of the antitrust claim based on Xerox's refusal to sell or license its copyrighted manuals and software is under Tenth Circuit law.

A.

Intellectual property rights do not confer a privilege to violate the antitrust laws. *See Intergraph Corp. v. Intel Corp.*, 195 F.3d 1346, 1362, 52 USPQ2d 1641, 1652 (Fed.Cir. 1999). "But it is also correct that the antitrust laws do not negate the patentee's right to exclude others from patent property." *Id.* (citation omitted). "The commercial advantage gained by new technology and its statutory protection by patent do not convert the possessor thereof into a prohibited monopolist." "The patent right must be 'coupled with violations of § 2', and the elements of violation of 15 U.S.C. § 2 must be met." * * *

A patent alone does not demonstrate market power. The United States Department of Justice and Federal Trade Commission have issued guidance that, even where it exists, such "market power does not 'impose on the intellectual property owner an obligation to license the use of that property to others.'" *Intergraph*, 195 F.3d at 1362, 52 USPQ2d at 1652 (citing United States Department of Justice and Federal Trade Comm'n Antitrust Guidelines for the Licensing of Intellectual Property 4 (1995)).[7] There is "no reported case in which a court ha[s] imposed antitrust liability for a unilateral refusal to sell or license a patent. . . ." *Id.* The patentee's right to exclude is further supported by section 271(d) of the Patent Act which states, in pertinent part, that "[n]o patent owner otherwise entitled to relief . . . shall be denied relief or deemed guilty of misuse or *illegal extension of the patent right* by reason of his having . . . (4) refused to license or use any rights to the patent . . . " 35 U.S.C. § 271(d) (1999) (emphasis added).

* * *

To support its argument that Xerox illegally sought to leverage its presumably legitimate dominance in the equipment and parts market into

---

[7] [This proposition has now been endorsed by the Supreme Court. *See Illinois Tool Works Inc. v. Independent Ink, Inc.*, 547 U.S. 28 (2006). Eds.]

dominance in the service market, CSU relies on a footnote in *Eastman Kodak Co. v. Image Technical Services, Inc.*, 504 U.S. 451, 480 n. 29, 112 S.Ct. 2072, 2089 n. 29, 119 L.Ed.2d 265 (1992), that "[t]he Court has held many times that power gained through some natural and legal advantage such as a patent, . . . can give rise to liability if 'a seller exploits his dominant position in one market to expand his empire into the next.'" Notably, *Kodak* was a tying case when it came before the Supreme Court, and no patents had been asserted in defense of the antitrust claims against Kodak. Conversely, there are no claims in this case of illegally tying the sale of Xerox's patented parts to unpatented products. Therefore, the issue was not resolved by the *Kodak* language cited by CSU. Properly viewed within the framework of a tying case, the footnote can be interpreted as restating the undisputed premise that the patent holder cannot use his statutory right to refuse to sell patented parts to gain a monopoly in a market *beyond the scope of the patent.* * * *

The cited language from *Kodak* does nothing to limit the right of the patentee to refuse to sell or license in markets within the scope of the statutory patent grant. In fact, we have expressly held that, absent exceptional circumstances, a patent may confer the right to exclude competition altogether in more than one antitrust market. * * *

CSU further relies on the Ninth Circuit's holding on remand in *Image Technical Services* that "'while exclusionary conduct can include a monopolist's unilateral refusal to license a [patent] or to sell its patented . . . work, a monopolist's desire to exclude others from its [protected] work is a presumptively valid business justification for any immediate harm to consumers.'" 125 F.3d at 1218, 44 USPQ2d at 1081 (citing *Data General Corp. v. Grumman Sys. Support Corp.*, 36 F.3d 1147, 1187, 32 USPQ2d 1385, 1417 (1st Cir. 1994)). By that case, the Ninth Circuit adopted a rebuttable presumption that the exercise of the statutory right to exclude provides a valid business justification for consumer harm, but then excused as harmless the district court's error in failing to give any instruction on the effect of intellectual property rights on the application of the antitrust laws. It concluded that the jury must have rejected the presumptively valid business justification as pretextual. This logic requires an evaluation of the patentee's subjective motivation for refusing to sell or license its patented products for pretext. We decline to follow *Image Technical Services.*

We have held that "if a [patent infringement] suit is not objectively baseless, an antitrust defendant's subjective motivation is immaterial." We see no more reason to inquire into the subjective motivation of Xerox in refusing to sell or license its patented works than we found in evaluating the subjective motivation of a patentee in bringing suit to enforce that same right. In the absence of any indication of illegal tying, fraud in the Patent and Trademark Office, or sham litigation, the patent holder may enforce the statutory right to exclude others from making, using, or selling the claimed invention free from liability under the antitrust laws. We therefore will not inquire into his subjective motivation for exerting his statutory rights, even though his refusal to sell or license his patented invention may have an anticompetitive effect, so long as that anticompetitive effect is not illegally extended beyond the statutory patent grant. It is the infringement defendant and not the patentee that bears the burden to show that one of these exceptional situations exists and, in the absence of such proof, we will not inquire into the patentee's motivations for asserting his statutory right to exclude. Even in cases where the infringement defendant has met this burden, which CSU has not, he must then also prove the elements of the Sherman Act violation.

We answer the threshold question of whether Xerox's refusal to sell its patented parts exceeds the scope of the patent grant in the negative.[2] Therefore, our inquiry is at an end. Xerox was under no obligation to sell or license its patented parts and did not violate the antitrust laws by refusing to do so.

B.

The Copyright Act expressly grants a copyright owner the exclusive right to distribute the protected work by "transfer of ownership, or by rental, lease, or lending." 17 U.S.C. § 106(3) (1996). "[T]he owner of the copyright, if [it] pleases, may refrain from vending or licensing and content [itself] with simply exercising the right to exclude others from using [its] property."

The Supreme Court has made clear that the property right granted by copyright law cannot be used with impunity to extend power in the marketplace beyond what Congress intended. *See United States v. Loew's, Inc.*, 371 U.S. 38, 47–48, 83 S.Ct. 97, 103–04, 9 L.Ed.2d 11 (1962) (block booking of copyrighted motion pictures is illegal tying in violation of Sherman Act). The Court has not, however, directly addressed the antitrust implications of a unilateral refusal to sell or license copyrighted expression.

* * *

Perhaps the most extensive analysis of the effect of a unilateral refusal to license copyrighted expression was conducted by the First Circuit in *Data General Corp. v. Grumman Systems Support Corp.*, 36 F.3d 1147, 32 USPQ2d 1385. There, the court noted that the limited copyright monopoly is based on Congress' empirical assumption that the right to "exclude others from using their works creates a system of incentives that promotes consumer welfare in the long term by encouraging investment in the creation of desirable artistic and functional works of expression. . . . We

---

[2]   Having concluded that Xerox's actions fell within the statutory patent grant, we need not separately consider CSU's allegations of patent misuse and they are rejected.

cannot require antitrust defendants to prove and reprove the merits of this legislative assumption in every case where a refusal to license a copyrighted work comes under attack." The court went on to establish as a legal standard that "while exclusionary conduct can include a monopolist's unilateral refusal to license a copyright, an author's desire to exclude others from use of its copyrighted work is a presumptively valid business justification for any immediate harm to consumers." The burden to overcome this presumption was firmly placed on the antitrust plaintiff. The court gave no weight to evidence showing knowledge that developing a proprietary position would help to maintain a monopoly in the service market in the face of contrary evidence of the defendant's desire to develop state-of-the-art diagnostic software to enhance its service and consumer benefit.

As discussed above, the Ninth Circuit adopted a modified version of this *Data General* standard. Both courts agreed that the presumption could be rebutted by evidence that "the monopolist acquired the protection of the intellectual property laws in an unlawful manner." *Image Technical Servs.*, 125 F.3d at 1219, 44 USPQ2d at 1082 (citing *Data General*, 36 F.3d at 1188, 32 USPQ2d at 1418). The Ninth Circuit, however, extended the possible means of rebutting the presumption to include evidence that the defense and exploitation of the copyright grant was merely a pretextual business justification to mask anticompetitive conduct. The hazards of this approach are evident in both the path taken and the outcome reached. The jury in that case was instructed to examine each proffered business justification for pretext, and no weight was given to the intellectual property rights in the instructions. This permitted the jury to second guess the subjective motivation of the copyright holder in asserting its statutory rights to exclude under the copyright laws without properly weighing the presumption of legitimacy in asserting its rights under the copyright laws. While concluding that the failure to weigh the intellectual property rights was an abuse of discretion, the Ninth Circuit nevertheless held the error harmless because it thought the jury must have rejected the presumptive validity of asserting the copyrights as pretextual. This is in reality a significant departure from the First Circuit's central premise that rebutting the presumption would be an uphill battle and would only be appropriate in those rare cases in which imposing antitrust liability is unlikely to frustrate the objectives of the Copyright Act.

We believe the First Circuit's approach is more consistent with both the antitrust and the copyright laws and is the standard that would most likely be followed by the Tenth Circuit in considering the effect of Xerox's unilateral right to refuse to license or sell copyrighted manuals and diagnostic software on liability under the antitrust laws. We therefore reject CSU's invitation to examine Xerox's subjective motivation in asserting its right to exclude under the copyright laws for pretext, in the absence of any evidence that the copyrights were obtained by unlawful means or were used to gain monopoly power beyond the statutory copyright granted by Congress. In the absence of such definitive rebuttal evidence, Xerox's refusal to sell or license its copyrighted works was squarely within the rights granted by Congress to the copyright holder and did not constitute a violation of the antitrust laws.

* * *

———————

What explains the different outcomes in *Kodak* and *Xerox*? Do they agree on the general rule that IPRs can provide a presumptively legitimate defense to a refusal to deal? If so, what "exceptions" did each court recognize? Are there any differences? Did the Ninth and Federal Circuits merely disagree about the propriety of considering "pretext" as a defense? About using pretext as a defense when it is invoked based on subjective evidence? Is it true, as *Xerox* appears to assume, that the Ninth Circuit relied solely on subjective evidence in rejecting Kodak's purported business justification? Do the two decisions evidence a more fundamental disagreement about the relative balance to be struck between antitrust laws and intellectual property laws? Is one more consistent with the foundation laid in the IP Guidelines?

The debate about the relative merits of *Kodak* and *Xerox* has continued and in some quarters has become quite heated. The question of whether, and under what conditions, antitrust liability can be based on a dominant firm's unilateral refusal to license has also spread to other jurisdictions around the world, including the European Union and Asia. In the Sidebar that follows, we explore some of these contemporary developments.

Sidebar 7–4:
Antitrust Liability for Unilateral Refusals to License Intellectual Property Rights
Reactions to Kodak, Intergraph, and Xerox

Kodak, *Intergraph*, and *Xerox* garnered a great deal of attention. In responding directly and critically to *Kodak*, and in appearing to favor the protection of intellectual property rights over principles of competition under the antitrust laws, *Intergraph* and *Xerox* arguably sought to diminish the role antitrust could play in policing exclusionary conduct effectuated through the exercise of intellectual property rights. The decisions also appeared to signal an institutional shift in responsibility away from federal antitrust enforcement agencies and into the hands of the Federal Circuit. The Federal Circuit might now have a major role to play in striking the

---

balance between antitrust and intellectual property. *See Symposium: The Federal Circuit and Antitrust*, 69 ANTITRUST L.J. 627 (2002).[a]

Intergraph and *Xerox* also sounded alarms with those who cautioned of the danger of permitting intellectual property rights too readily to trump antitrust policies, especially because IPRs are so prevalent in high-technology industries. A former chair of the Federal Trade Commission argued, for example, that "[b]eyond the matter of result, the court [in *Xerox*] reached its decision in sweeping language that exalts patent and copyright rights over other considerations and throws into doubt the validity of previous lines of authority that attempted to strike a balance between intellectual property and antitrust." Robert Pitofsky, *Challenges of the New Economy: Issues at the Intersection Of Antitrust And Intellectual Property*, 68 ANTITRUST L.J. 913, 920 (2001) ("*Challenges of the New Economy*").[b] Pitofsky also viewed *Xerox's* three exceptions for fraud, sham litigation, and efforts to extend the patent as through tying as "extremely narrow limits on a virtually unfettered right of a patent holder to refuse to deal in order to achieve an anticompetitive objective." *Id.* at 921. For a response to Pitofsky that defends *Xerox* and challenges his reading of the case as "overly expansive," see R. Hewitt Pate, *Refusals to Deal and Intellectual Property Rights*, 10 GEO. MASON L. REV. 429, 431 & n.10 (2002). Other scholars argue the apparent conflict between *Xerox* and *Kodak* "results from a failure to recognize the differences in the scope of the refusals to deal." Michelle M. Burtis & Bruce H. Kobayashi, *Why an Original can be Better than a Copy: Intellectual Property, the Antitrust Refusal to Deal, and ISO Antitrust Litigation*, 9 S. CT. ECON. REV. 143, 145, 151 (2001).

The doctrinal and economic issues raised by *Kodak, Intergraph*, and *Xerox* continue to garner serious attention in

---

[a] It is arguable that today the Federal Circuit would not have jurisdiction to hear a case like *Xerox*. In *Holmes Grp., Inc. v. Vornado Air Circulation Sys., Inc.*, 535 U.S. 826 (2002), the Supreme Court held that the Federal Circuit's appellate jurisdiction is limited to cases initiated under the patent laws and does not include patent counterclaims filed in response to non-patent claims. Recall that CSU initiated its antitrust claims against Xerox and Xerox responded with a patent infringement counterclaim, which at that time provided the basis for an appeal to the Federal Circuit. In light of *Vornado*, the case could no longer be appealed to the Federal Circuit and would instead go to the Tenth Circuit, where the complaint was originally filed. Might *Vornado* prompt a race to the courthouse by patent holders who anticipate antitrust claims and wish to insure that their appeals, if any, will be heard by the Federal Circuit?

[b] Pitofsky cited two other explications of this traditional balance. *See* Willard K. Tom & Joshua A. Newberg, *Antitrust and Intellectual Property: From Separate Spheres to Unified Field*, 66 ANTITRUST L.J. 167 (1998); and Louis Kaplow, *The Patent Antitrust Intersection: A Reappraisal*, 97 HARV. L. REV. 1815 (1984).

the antitrust community both in the U.S. and in Europe. Despite that attention, however, they are far from resolved and have illuminated some fairly fundamental points of difference among antitrust commentators and enforcers.[c]

The 2007 FTC/DOJ IP Report

Following extensive hearings, the FTC and the Department of Justice issued a joint report in April 2007 on the interface of antitrust and intellectual property rights. *See* U.S. Dep't of Justice and Fed. Trade Comm'n, *Antitrust Enforcement and Intellectual Property Rights: Promoting Innovation and Competititon* (Apr. 2007) (IP REPORT), https://www.ftc.gov/sites/default/files/documents/reports/antitrust-enforcement-and-intellectual-property-rights-promoting-innovation-and-competition-report.s.department-justice-and-federal-trade-commission/p040101promotinginnovationandcompetition rpt0704.pdf.

After summarizing the arguments for and against *Kodak* and *Xerox*, the Report identifies four policy issues that relate to the question whether antitrust liability should attach to a refusal to license: (1) Should antitrust law accord special treatment to patents, or is conventional antitrust analysis sufficiently sensitive to the issues raised by patents? (2) Should a patent holder be presumed to possess market power? (3) Is compulsory licensing a workable remedy for a unilateral refusal to license patents? (4) And would prohibiting unilateral refusals to license have a significant ill effect on incentives to invest in innovation?

In addressing these issues, largely by summarizing the testimony of the various speakers who testified at the government's hearings, the Report considers the two critical economic issues in the debate: (1) the likely impact of a regime of compulsory licensing on incentives to innovate; and (2) whether and under what circumstances refusals to license can produce significant anticompetitive effects.

The Report concludes on an indeterminate note: "The Agencies * * * conclude that antitrust liability for mere

---

[c] The literature is extensive. For a sampling, see Joseph P. Bauer, *Refusals to Deal with Competitors by Owners of Patents and Copyrights: Reflections on the* Image Technical *and* Xerox *Decisions*, 55 DEPAUL L. REV. 1211 (2006); Michael A. Carrier, *Refusals to License Intellectual Property after* Trinko, 55 DEPAUL L. REV. 1191 (2006); Herbert Hovenkamp, et al., *Unilateral Refusals to License*, 2 J. COMP. L. & ECON. 1 (2006); A. Douglas Melamed & Ali M. Stoeppelwerth, *The* CSU *Case: Facts, Formalism and the Intersection of Antitrust and Intellectual Property Law*, 10 GEO. MASON L. REV. 407 (2002); Jonathan I. Gleklen, *The ISO Litigation Legacy of Eastman Kodak Co. v. Image Technical Services: Twenty Years and Not Much to Show for It*, ANTITRUST, Fall 2012, at 56; Thomas Cheng, *Putting the Innovation Incentives Back in the Patent-Antitrust Interface*, 11 NW. J. TECH & INTELL. PROP. 385 (2013).

unilateral, unconditional refusals to license patents will not play a meaningful part in the interface between patent rights and antitrust protections." The Report's penultimate conclusion—likely the product of compromise between the two federal agencies—thus failed to take a firm position in favor of *Kodak* or *Xerox*, although it was strongly suggestive of a very limited view of the role of antitrust laws in policing refusals to deal. It also invites additional questions: When is a refusal to license wholly "unilateral"? When is it "conditional," and why should conditionality, however it is defined, tip the implicit balance from IPRs to antitrust, which presumably would in any case be guided by a concern for significant anticompetitive effects?[d] These issues will likely produce additional debate and ultimately will have to be resolved in future cases in the U.S.

Treatment in the European Union

The standards for evaluating the competitive consequences of unilateral refusals to license were developed in the E.U. primarily in two decisions of the European Court of Justice ("ECJ"), *Volvo v. Veng*, Case 238/87, [1988] ECR 6211 and *RTE and ITP v. Commission*, Case C-241/91P, [1995] ECR I 743 ("*Magill*"). These decisions established the broad principal that unilateral refusals to license will only be deemed anticompetitive, and a violation of Article 82 of the Treaty as an "abuse of dominant position," under "exceptional circumstances." Much of the commentary and decisional law, therefore, has focused on defining these "exceptional circumstances," a debate that has become the focal point of European efforts to strike a balance between the protections accorded IP rights and the interests of competition laws.

The European Court of Justice again explored refusals to license as a basis for violation of Art. 102 in Case C-418/01, *IMS Health GmbH & Co. OHG* v. *NDC Health GmbH & Co. KG*, [2004] ECR I5039, a private action in which the German national court referred the case to the ECJ under European procedures seeking a clarification of "exceptional circumstances." The Court of Justice reaffirmed its general view that a refusal to license cannot alone constitute an abuse of dominant position under Article 102, except under

---

[d] For a further discussion of the IP Report's distinction between conditional and unconditional refusals to license, see Willard K. Tom, *The DOJ/FTC Report on Antitrust Enforcement and Intellectual Property Rights*, ANTITRUST, Summer 2007, at 35, 37.

"exceptional circumstances." To establish such circumstances, it held, three conditions must be met:

(1)   the undertaking which requested the license must intend to offer new products or services not offered by the owner of the copyright and for which there is potential consumer demand;

(2)   the refusal cannot be justified by objective considerations; and

(3)   the refusal is such as to reserve to the undertaking which owns the copyright the relevant market, by eliminating all competition on that market.

See also Note on Microsoft Prosecutions in the European Union, supra Chapter 4. For an additional comparative perspective, see Competititon Bureau of Canada, *Intellectual Property Enforcement Guidelines*, Example 8 ("Refusal to License Intellectual Property") (Mar. 31, 2016), http://www.competition bureau.gc.ca/eic/site/cb-bc.nsf/vwapj/cb-IPEG-e.pdf/$file/cb-IPEG-e.pdf.

Conclusion

Every authority to consider the question explored in this Sidebar—whether a refusal to license patents or copyrights can provide the basis for antitrust liability—has concurred that if the answer is ever "yes," it will be in limited circumstances. There is widespread consensus that IPRs can promote innovation and that the right to exclude others from using the IP is fundamental to the idea of IPRs.

All authorities also appear to agree that there can be limited exceptions to this general principle. The differences surface in the degree to which the law should recognize those exceptions, the specific conditions that justify them, and their likely consequences for both competition and the incentives to innovate. How those questions are resolved can have very significant implications for the legal standards used to judge refusals to license, specifically whether they will be weighted in favor of IPRs or antitrust enforcement. The critical policy question is how can intellectual property law's desire to promote competition by rewarding innovation and the antitrust law's concern that competition can sometimes suffer at the hand of intellectual property owners be harmonized.

3. CONCERNS ABOUT PATENT HOLDUP AND HOLDOUT

The New Economy's increasing reliance upon patented technologies has given rise to some complicated questions for antitrust law. One example is what has been labelled "patent holdup." The potential for patent holdup (by either patent holders or implementers) arises after one party makes *ex ante*, relationship-specific investments that either the patent holder or the implementer has the incentive to exploit *ex post*. A typical example of holdup by patent holders involves the inclusion of a patented technology in an industry "standard" that is adopted by a standard-development or standard setting organization ("SDO" or "SSO"). Such patents are then referred to as "standard-essential patents" ("SEPs"), because an adopter of the standard cannot produce products under the standard without utilizing the included IP. SSOs create significant value by fostering interoperability across various products—especially within network technologies—and, as such, their actions are typically analyzed under the rule of reason despite the coordination between rivals that they necessarily entail. *See* U.S. DEP'T OF JUSTICE & FED. TRADE COMM'N, ANTITRUST ENFORCEMENT AND INTELLECTUAL PROPERTY RIGHTS: PROMOTING INNOVATION AND COMPETITION (2007) ("IP REPORT"), at 37 http://www.justice.gov/atr/public/hearings/ip/222655.pdf.

Once producers begin to utilize the standard in their products, the patent holder may have the incentive to "holdup" potential licensees by demanding a higher royalty rate than would have prevailed in a competitive process. Standard-implementing companies with asset-specific investments can be locked in to the technologies that define the standard once they begin producing products in compliance with the standard. *See generally* Mark A. Lemley & Carl Shapiro, *Patent Holdup and Royalty Stacking*, 85 TEXAS L. REV. 1991 (2007). On the other hand, patent holders who contribute their technology to a standard in order to commercialize the patent and promote its widespread use can also be locked-in if their technologies have a market only within the standard. Thus, incentives for opportunism might run in both directions. Whereas patent holders might seek to holdup those who practice the standard, those who practice the standard might seek to holdup the patent holder or engage in "holdout." "Holdup" by implementers refers to the situation when licensees seek to obtain rates and terms greater than "fair, reasonable and nondiscriminatory" ("FRAND") terms; "holdout" refers to licensees either refusing to take a FRAND license or delaying doing so, perhaps to avoid paying licensing fees altogether or to drive down the cost. In these cases, SEP holders may seek to enjoin their continued use of the patented technologies. Holdup by patent holders can also occur if a patent holder fails to disclose the fact that its technology is patented (also commonly referred to as "patent ambush"), or if an *ex post* dispute arises with respect to the negotiation of FRAND terms.

To mitigate the risk of holdup, many SSOs have policies that require patent holders who submit their technologies for use in a standard to: (1) disclose the fact of the patent; and (2) commit to license their technology on Reasonable and Non-Discriminatory Terms ("RAND") or Fair, Reasonable and Non-Discriminatory terms ("FRAND"). SEPS that are included in standards based on FRAND commitments are referred to as "FRAND-encumbered" or "FRAND-assured" SEPs. *See, e.g.*, Joanna Tsai & Joshua D. Wright, *Standard Setting, Intellectual Property Rights, and the Role of Antitrust in Regulating Incomplete Contracts*, 80 ANTITRUST L. J. 157 (2015). *See also* Mark A. Lemley, *Intellectual Property Rights and Standard Setting Organizations*, 90 CALIF. L. REV. (online) 1889 (2002), http://scholarship.law.berkeley.edu/californialawreview/vol90/iss6/3.

As the U.S. Federal Trade Commission has explained, market mechanisms impose a number of constraints that militate against acting on the opportunity for holdup. For example, reputational and business costs may deter repeat players from engaging in holdup and "patent holders that have broad cross-licensing agreements with the SEP-owner may be protected from hold-up."[8] In addition, patent holders often enjoy a first-mover advantage if their technology is adopted as the standard. "As a result, patent holders who manufacture products using the standardized technology 'may find it more profitable to offer attractive licensing terms in order to promote the adoption of the product using the standard, increasing demand for its product rather than extracting high royalties.' "

In addition, numerous mechanisms exist for solving the patent holdup problem, each of which falls into the traditional categories of ownership or contractual solutions. For example, patent pools and cross-licensing arrangements may alleviate some issues associated with patent holdup. Another very important contractual option—which has raised issues for antitrust law—is to establish an SSO or SDO. SSOs solicit patent holders to bid for inclusion within the industry standard. As noted above, prior to accepting any given technology as part of the standard, many SSOs require patent holders to disclose certain rights and to agree to license these rights on FRAND or RAND terms. Predecessors of FRAND terms frequently appeared in antitrust patent licensing remedies from the 1940s through the 1970s, but only began to garner serious attention in the early 2000s with the rise of SSOs. *See* Jorge L. Contreras, *A Brief History of FRAND:*

---

[8]   *See, e.g.*, Prepared Statement of the Federal Trade Commission Before the U.S. Senate Committee on the Judiciary Subcommittee on Antitrust, Competition Policy and Consumer Rights Concerning "Standard Essential Patent Disputes and Antitrust Law" at 6 (July 30, 2013), https://www.ftc.gov/sites/default/files/documents/public_statements/prepared-statement-federal-trade-commission-concerning-standard-essential-patent-disputes-and/130730standardessentialpatents.pdf.

Analyzing Current Debates in Standard Setting and Antitrust Through a Historical Lens, 80 ANTITRUST L.J. 39 (2015).

While SSOs may mitigate *ex post* opportunistic behavior by patent holders, the potential and incentive for *ex post* exploitation persist due to problems of incomplete contracting and of relationship-specific investments, as well as asymmetric information. Given the sometimes vague *ex ante* disclosure requirements and terms to which patent holders acquiesce, they may deceptively withhold information regarding their IPRs and seek to exploit these rights after becoming part of the standard. A patent holder may then gain significant market power by virtue of its deceptively obtained inclusion within a standard technology. Such behavior portends serious welfare losses. The FTC and DOJ describe the patent holdup problem in the SSO context as follows:

> A holder of IP incorporated into a standard can exploit its position if it is costly for users of the standard to switch to a different technology after the standard is set. Making such a change would require abandoning that standard and developing a new one, but developing an alternative standard could be costly and may delay the introduction of a new product. The profits lost by such a delay may represent a significant portion of the cost of developing the alternative standard. In addition, to implement an alternative standard for an existing product that requires compatibility and interoperability, the SSO members might incur switching costs in redesigning components that had been based on the old standard and might have to subsidize customers' migration from a standard based on one technology to a standard based on another technology. Generally, the greater the cost of the switching to an alternative standard, the more an IP holder can charge for a license.

IP REPORT, *supra*, at 38. *See also* George S. Cary, et. al, *The Case for Antitrust Law to Police the Patent Holdup Problem in Standard Setting*, 77 ANTITRUST L.J. 913 (2011); Joseph Farrell, et. al, *Standard Setting, Patents, and Hold-Up*, 74 ANTITRUST L.J. 603 (2007). *But see* Bruce H. Kobayashi and Joshua D. Wright, *The Limits of Antitrust and Patent Holdup: A Reply to Cary et al.*, 78 ANTITRUST L. J. 505 (2012).

As should be evident, the issues posed by patent holdup are complex. For our purposes, the relevant question is whether antitrust is a possible mechanism for disciplining holdup behavior, given the potential for market power deriving from these deceptive actions. Our next two principal cases illustrate how U.S. courts have grappled with delineating the boundaries of antitrust liability in the SSO patent holdup context.

BROADCOM CORP. V. QUALCOMM INC.

United States Court of Appeals for the Third Circuit, 2007.
501 F.3d 297.

BARRY, CIRCUIT JUDGE.

This appeal presents important questions regarding whether a patent holder's deceptive conduct before a private standards-determining organization may be condemned under antitrust laws and, if so, what facts must be pled to survive a motion to dismiss. Broadcom Corporation ("Broadcom") alleged that Qualcomm Inc. ("Qualcomm"), by its intentional deception of private standards-determining organizations and its predatory acquisition of a potential rival, has monopolized certain markets for cellular telephone technology and components, primarily in violation of Sections 1 and 2 of the Sherman Act. * * * The District Court dismissed the Complaint, and Broadcom appeals. For the reasons that follow, we conclude that Broadcom has stated [a] claim[ ] for monopolization under § 2 of the Sherman Act. * * *

I.   BACKGROUND

A.   Mobile Wireless Telephony and the UMTS Standard

Mobile wireless telephony is the general term for describing the technology and equipment used in the operation of cellular telephones. A cellular telephone contains one or more computer "chipsets"—the core electronics that allow it to transmit and receive information, either telephone calls or data, to and from the wireless network. Chipsets transmit information, via radio waves, to cellular base stations. Base stations, in turn, transmit information to and from telephone and computer networks. It is essential that all components involved in this transmission of information be able to communicate seamlessly with one another. Because multiple vendors manufacture these components, industry-wide standards are necessary to ensure their interoperability. In mobile wireless telephony, standards are determined privately by industry groups known as standards-determining organizations ("SDOs").

Two technology paths, or families of standards, are in widespread use today: "CDMA," which stands for "code division multiple access"; and "GSM," which stands for "global system for mobility." Cellular telephone service providers operate under one or the other path, with, for example, Verizon Wireless and Sprint Communications operating CDMA-path networks, and Cingular (now AT & T) and T-Mobile operating GSM-path networks. The CDMA and GSM technology paths are not interoperable; equipment and technologies used in one cannot be used in the other. For this reason, each technology path has its own standard or set of standards. The standard used in current generation GSM-path networks is the third generation ("3G") standard created for the GSM path, and is known as the Universal Mobile Telecommunications System ("UMTS") standard.

The UMTS standard was created by the European Telecommunications Standards Institute ("ETSI") and its SDO counterparts in the United States and elsewhere after a lengthy evaluation of available alternative equipment and technologies. Qualcomm supplies some of the essential technology that the ETSI ultimately included in the UMTS standard, and holds intellectual property rights ("IPRs"), such as patents, in this technology. Given the potential for owners of IPRs, through the exercise of their rights, to exert undue control over the implementation of industry-wide standards, the ETSI requires a commitment from vendors whose technologies are included in standards to license their technologies on fair, reasonable, and non-discriminatory ("FRAND") terms. Neither the ETSI nor the other relevant SDOs further define FRAND.

Broadcom alleged that Qualcomm was a member of the ETSI, among other SDOs, and committed to abide by its IPR policy. Specifically, Broadcom alleged, the ETSI included Qualcomm's proprietary technology in the UMTS standard only after, and in reliance on, Qualcomm's commitment to license that technology on FRAND terms. The technology in question is called Wideband CDMA ("WCDMA"), not to be confused with the CDMA technology path. Although it represents only a small component of the technologies that collectively comprise the UMTS standard, WCDMA technology is said to be essential to the practice of the standard.

B. Broadcom's Complaint

[Broadcom's] Complaint alleged that Qualcomm induced the ETSI and other SDOs to include its proprietary technology in the UMTS standard by falsely agreeing to abide by the SDOs' policies on IPRs, but then breached those agreements by licensing its technology on non-FRAND terms. The intentional acquisition of monopoly power through deception of an SDO, Broadcom posits, violates antitrust law.

The Complaint also alleged that Qualcomm ignored its FRAND commitment to the ETSI and other SDOs by demanding discriminatorily higher (i.e., non-FRAND) royalties from competitors and customers using chipsets not manufactured by Qualcomm. Qualcomm, the Complaint continued, has a 90% share in the market for CDMA-path chipsets, and by withholding favorable pricing in that market, coerced cellular telephone manufacturers to purchase only Qualcomm-manufactured UMTS-path chipsets. These actions are alleged to be part of Qualcomm's effort to obtain a monopoly in the UMTS chipset market because it views competition in that market as a long-term threat to its existing monopolies in CDMA technology.

Broadcom claims to have been preparing to enter the UMTS chipset market for several years prior to its filing of the Complaint. After Broadcom purchased Zyray Wireless, Inc., a developer of UMTS chipsets, Qualcomm allegedly demanded that Broadcom license Qualcomm's UMTS technology on non-FRAND terms. Broadcom refused, and commenced this action. Qualcomm also allegedly acquired Flarion Technologies, a competitor in the development of technologies for inclusion in the forthcoming B3G and 4G standards, in an effort to extend Qualcomm's monopolies into future generations of standards.

C. The District Court's Opinion

Qualcomm moved to dismiss the Complaint under Federal Rule of Civil Procedure 12(b)(6) for failure to state a claim. * * * [T]he District Court granted the motion. In dismissing Broadcom's claim of monopolization in the WCDMA technology markets, the Court reasoned that Qualcomm enjoyed a legally-sanctioned monopoly in its patented technology, and that this monopoly conferred the right to exclude competition and set the terms by which that technology was distributed. Acknowledging that industry-wide standards merit "additional antitrust scrutiny," the Court nevertheless quickly concluded that the inclusion of Qualcomm's WCDMA technology in the UMTS standard did not harm competition because an absence of competition was the inevitable result of any standard-setting process. That inclusion of Qualcomm's technology may have been the product of deception was of no moment under antitrust law, the Court continued, because no matter which company's patented technology ultimately was chosen, the adoption of a standard would have eliminated competition. The Court did not discuss the possibility that the FRAND commitments that SDOs required of vendors were intended as a bulwark against unlawful monopoly, nor did it consider the possibility that the SDOs might have chosen nonproprietary technologies for inclusion in the standard.

* * *

III. DISCUSSION

A. The District Court erred in dismissing Claim 1—the monopolization claim—on the ground that abuse of a private standard-setting process does not state a claim under antitrust law.

Claim 1 of the Complaint alleged that Qualcomm monopolized markets for WCDMA technology by inducing the relevant SDOs to include Qualcomm's patented technology as an essential element of the UMTS standard. Qualcomm did this by falsely promising to license its patents on FRAND terms, and then reneging on those promises after it succeeded in having its technology included in the standard. These actions, the Complaint alleged, violated § 2 of the Sherman Act, 15 U.S.C. § 2.

1. Unlawful Monopolization Under § 2: Monopoly Power

Section 2 of the Sherman Act, in what we have called "sweeping language," makes it unlawful to monopolize, attempt to monopolize, or conspire to monopolize, interstate or international commerce. It is, we have observed, "the provision of the antitrust laws designed to curb the excesses of monopolists and near-monopolists." Liability under § 2 requires "(1) the possession of monopoly power in the relevant market and (2) the willful acquisition or maintenance of that power as distinguished from growth or development as a consequence of a superior product, business acumen, or historic accident." Monopoly power is the ability to control prices and exclude competition in a given market. If a firm can profitably raise prices without causing competing firms to expand output and drive down prices, that firm has monopoly power.

The existence of monopoly power may be proven through direct evidence of supracompetitive prices and restricted output. It may also be inferred from the structure and composition of the relevant market. To support an inference of monopoly power, a plaintiff typically must plead and prove that a firm has a dominant share in a relevant market, and that significant "entry barriers" protect that market. Barriers to entry are factors, such as regulatory requirements, high capital costs, or technological obstacles, that prevent new competition from entering a market in response to a monopolist's supracompetitive prices.

Proving the existence of monopoly power through indirect evidence requires a definition of the relevant market. Competing products are in the same market if they are readily substitutable for one another; a market's outer boundaries are determined by the reasonable interchangeability of use between a product and its substitute, or by their cross-elasticity of demand. Failure to define the proposed relevant market in these terms may result in dismissal of the complaint.

2. Unlawful Monopolization Under § 2: Anticompetitive Conduct

The second element of a monopolization claim under § 2 requires the willful acquisition or maintenance of monopoly power. As this element makes clear, the acquisition or possession of monopoly power must be accompanied by some anticompetitive conduct on the part of the possessor. Anticompetitive conduct may take a variety of forms, but it is generally defined as conduct to obtain or maintain monopoly power as a result of competition on some basis other than the merits. Conduct that impairs the opportunities of rivals and either does not further competition on the merits or does so in an unnecessarily restrictive way may be deemed anticompetitive. Conduct that merely harms competitors, however, while not harming the competitive process itself, is not anticompetitive.

* * *

The primary goal of antitrust law is to maximize consumer welfare by promoting competition among firms. Private standard setting advances this goal on several levels. In the end-consumer market, standards that ensure the interoperability of products facilitate the sharing of information among purchasers of products from competing manufacturers, thereby enhancing the utility of all products and enlarging the overall consumer market. This, in turn, permits firms to spread the costs of research and development across a greater number of consumers, resulting in lower per-unit prices. Industry-wide standards may also lower the cost to consumers of switching between competing products and services, thereby enhancing competition among suppliers.

Standards enhance competition in upstream markets, as well. One consequence of the standard-setting process is that SDOs may more readily make an objective comparison between competing technologies, patent positions, and licensing terms before an industry becomes locked in to a standard. Standard setting also reduces the risk to producers (and end consumers) of investing scarce resources in a technology that ultimately may not gain widespread acceptance. The adoption of a standard does not eliminate competition among producers but, rather, moves the focus away from the development of potential standards and toward the development of means for implementing the chosen standard.

Each of these efficiencies enhances consumer welfare and competition in the marketplace and is, therefore, consistent with the procompetitive aspirations of antitrust law. Thus, private standard setting—which might otherwise be viewed as a naked agreement among competitors not to manufacture, distribute, or purchase certain types of products—need not, in fact, violate antitrust law.

This is not to say, however, that acceptance, including judicial acceptance, of private standard setting is without limits. Indeed, that "private standard-setting by associations comprising firms with horizontal and vertical business relations is permitted at all under the antitrust laws [is] only on the understanding that it will be conducted in a nonpartisan manner offering procompetitive benefits," and in the presence of "meaningful safeguards" that "prevent the standard-setting process from being biased by members with economic interests in stifling product competition." As the Supreme Court acknowledged in *Allied Tube,* and as administrative tribunals, law enforcement authorities, and some courts have recognized, conduct that undermines the procompetitive benefits of private standard setting may, at least in some circumstances, be deemed anticompetitive under antitrust law.

a. Patent Hold-Up

Inefficiency may be injected into the standard-setting process by what is known as "patent hold-up." An SDO may complete its lengthy process of evaluating technologies and adopting a new standard, only to discover that certain technologies essential to implementing the standard are patented. When this occurs, the patent holder is in a position to "hold up" industry participants from implementing the standard. Industry participants who have invested significant resources developing products and technologies that conform to the standard will find it prohibitively expensive to abandon their investment and switch to another standard. They will have become "locked in" to the standard. In this unique position of bargaining power, the patent holder may be able to extract supracompetitive royalties from the industry participants.

In actions brought before the Federal Trade Commission ("FTC"), patent holders have faced antitrust liability for misrepresenting to an SDO that they did not hold IPRs in essential technologies, and then, after a standard had been adopted, seeking to enforce those IPRs. In 1996, the FTC entered into a consent order with Dell Computer Corporation. The complaint issued in conjunction therewith alleged that Dell participated in an SDO's adoption of a design standard for a computer bus (i.e., an information-carrying conduit), but failed to disclose that it owned a patent for a key design feature of the standard, and even certified to the SDO that the proposed standard did not infringe any of Dell's IPRs. After the design standard proved successful, Dell attempted to assert its IPRs, prompting the FTC to commence an enforcement action under § 5 of the FTC Act, for unfair methods of competition in or affecting commerce. Dell's actions, it was alleged, created uncertainty that hindered industry acceptance of the standard, increased the costs of implementing the standard, and chilled the willingness of industry participants to engage in the standard-setting process.

The consent order required, among other things, that Dell cease and desist from asserting that the use or implementation of the standard violated its IPRs. Significantly, the FTC's announcement that accompanied the order stated that in the "limited circumstances . . . where there is evidence that the [SDO] would have implemented a different non-proprietary design had it been informed of the patent conflict during the certification process, and where Dell failed to act in good faith to identify and disclose patent conflicts . . . enforcement action is appropriate to prevent harm to competition and consumers." It also noted that once the standard had gained widespread acceptance, "the standard effectively conferred market power upon Dell as the patent holder. This market power was not inevitable: had [the SDO] known of the Dell patent, it could have chosen an equally effective, non-proprietary standard." One Commissioner, writing in dissent, conceded that "[i]f Dell had obtained market power by knowingly or intentionally misleading a standards-setting organization, it would require no stretch of established monopolization theory to condemn that conduct." She objected, nevertheless, to imposing antitrust liability on Dell absent specific allegations in the proposed complaint that Dell misled the SDO intentionally or knowingly, and that it obtained market power as a result of its misleading statements.

In 2005, the FTC entered into a consent order resolving allegations that Union Oil Company of California ("Unocal") made deceptive and bad-faith misrepresentations to a state standards-determining board concerning the status of Unocal's IPRs. The administrative complaint had alleged that the board relied on these misrepresentations in promulgating new standards governing low-emissions gasoline, and that Unocal's misrepresentations led directly to its acquisition of monopoly power and harmed competition after refiners became locked in to regulations that required the use of Unocal's proprietary technology. Unocal's anticompetitive conduct was alleged to have violated § 5 of the FTC Act. The consent order required Unocal, among other things, to cease and desist from all efforts to enforce its relevant patents.

Most recently, a landmark, 120-page opinion in *In re Rambus, Inc.*, was entered on the docket on August 2, 2006 by a unanimous FTC. Rambus, a developer of computer memory technologies, was found to have deceived an SDO by failing to disclose its IPRs in technology that was essential to the implementation of now-ubiquitous computer memory standards, by misleading other members of the SDO into believing that Rambus was not seeking any new patents relevant to the standard then under consideration, and by using information that it gained from its participation in the standard-setting process to amend its pending patent applications so that they would cover the ultimate standard. Noting that such conduct "has grave implications for competition," the FTC found that Rambus had distorted the standard-setting process and engaged in anticompetitive hold-up. For the first time, the FTC held that deceptive conduct of the type alleged in *Dell Computer* and *Union Oil* constituted "exclusionary conduct" under § 2 of the Sherman Act, as well as unlawful monopolization under § 5 of the FTC Act.

Rambus is particularly noteworthy for its extensive discussion of deceptive conduct in the standard-setting context and the factors that make such conduct anticompetitive under § 2 of the Sherman Act. The FTC likened the deception of an SDO to the type of deceptive conduct that the D.C. Circuit found to violate § 2 of the Sherman Act in *Microsoft*. There, the Court found that Microsoft had marketed software-development tools that would permit software developers to create programs that, ostensibly, did not need to run on Microsoft's ubiquitous operating system, but that, in fact, could operate properly *only* on Microsoft's operating system. The Court found that in an environment in which software developers reasonably expected Microsoft not to mislead them, Microsoft's deceptive conduct was anticompetitive. Analogizing to *Microsoft*, the FTC found that Rambus's deception occurred in an environment-the standard-setting process-in which participants "expected each other to act cooperatively."

The FTC discussed at length the unique dangers of deception in the standard-setting context. Private standard setting occurs in a consensus-oriented environment, where participants rely on structural protections, such as rules requiring the disclosure of IPRs, to facilitate competition and constrain the exercise of monopoly power. In such an environment, participants are less likely to be wary of deception and may not detect such conduct and take measures to counteract it until after lock-in has occurred. At that point, the resulting harm to competition may be very difficult to correct.

These decisions reflect a growing awareness of the risks associated with deceptive conduct in the private standard-setting process. The Supreme Court acknowledged these risks in *Allied Tube*, and the FTC has found deception of an SDO to constitute anticompetitive conduct in violation of § 2 of the Sherman Act. Recent statements by Department of Justice officials support this trend.

b. FRAND Commitments

Against this backdrop, we must determine whether Broadcom has stated actionable anticompetitive conduct with allegations that Qualcomm deceived relevant SDOs into adopting the UMTS standard by committing to license its WCDMA technology on FRAND terms and, later, after lock-in occurred, demanding non-FRAND royalties. As Qualcomm is at pains to point out, no court, nor agency, has decided this *precise* question and, in that sense, our decision will break new ground. The authorities we have cited in our lengthy discussion that has preceded this point, however, decidedly favor a finding that Broadcom's allegations, if accepted as true, describe actionable anticompetitive conduct.

To guard against anticompetitive patent hold-up, most SDOs require firms supplying essential technologies for inclusion in a prospective standard to commit to licensing their technologies on FRAND terms. A firm's FRAND commitment, therefore, is a factor—and an important factor—that the SDO will consider in evaluating the suitability of a given proprietary technology vis-à-vis competing technologies.

The FRAND commitment, or lack thereof, is, moreover, a key indicator of the cost of implementing a potential technology. During the critical competitive period that precedes adoption of a standard, technologies compete in discrete areas, such as cost and performance characteristics. Misrepresentations concerning the cost of implementing a given technology may confer an unfair advantage and bias the competitive process in favor of that technology's inclusion in the standard.

A standard, by definition, eliminates alternative technologies. When a patented technology is incorporated in a standard, adoption of the standard eliminates alternatives to the patented technology. Although a patent confers a lawful monopoly over the claimed invention, its value is limited when alternative technologies exist. That value becomes significantly enhanced, however, after the patent is incorporated in a standard. Firms may become locked in to a standard requiring the use of a competitor's patented technology. The patent holder's IPRs, if unconstrained, may permit it to demand supracompetitive royalties. It is in such circumstances that measures such as FRAND commitments become important safeguards against monopoly power.

We hold that (1) in a consensus-oriented private standard-setting environment, (2) a patent holder's intentionally false promise to license essential proprietary technology on FRAND terms, (3) coupled with an SDO's reliance on that promise when including the technology in a standard, and (4) the patent holder's subsequent breach of that promise, is actionable anticompetitive conduct. This holding follows directly from established principles of antitrust law and represents the emerging view of enforcement authorities and commentators, alike. Deception in a consensus-driven private standard-setting environment harms the competitive process by obscuring the costs of including proprietary technology in a standard and increasing the likelihood that patent rights will confer monopoly power on the patent holder. Deceptive FRAND commitments, no less than deceptive nondisclosure of IPRs, may result in such harm.

3. Claim 1 States a Claim for Monopolization of WCDMA Technology Markets

The District Court's only stated reason for dismissing Broadcom's Claim 1 was that it did not plead an antitrust cause of action. Having now held that a firm's deceptive FRAND commitment to an SDO may constitute actionable anticompetitive conduct, we conclude quickly and easily that Claim 1 states a claim for monopolization under § 2 of the Sherman Act.

First, the Complaint adequately alleged that Qualcomm possessed monopoly power in the relevant market. The Complaint defined the relevant market as the market for Qualcomm's proprietary WCDMA technology, a technology essential to the implementation of the UMTS standard. This technology was not interchangeable with or substitutable for other technologies, and adherents to the UMTS standard have become locked in. With respect to monopoly power, Qualcomm had the power to extract supracompetitive prices, it possessed a dominant market share, and the market had entry barriers. These allegations satisfied the first element of a § 2 monopolization claim.

Qualcomm objects to a relevant market definition that is congruent with the scope of its WCDMA patents, arguing that such a definition would result in every patent holder being condemned as a monopolist. This objection misconstrues Broadcom's theory. It is the incorporation of a patent into a standard—not the mere issuance of a patent—that makes the scope of the relevant market congruent with that of the patent.

Second, the Complaint also adequately alleged that Qualcomm obtained and maintained its market power willfully, and not as a consequence of a superior product, business acumen, or historic accident. Qualcomm excluded competition and refused to compete on the merits. As discussed above, the alleged anticompetitive conduct was the intentional false promise that Qualcomm would license its WCDMA technology on FRAND terms, on which promise the relevant SDOs relied in choosing the WCDMA technology for inclusion in the UMTS standard, followed by Qualcomm's insistence on non-FRAND licensing terms. Qualcomm's deceptive conduct induced relevant SDOs to incorporate a technology into the UMTS standard that they would not have considered absent a FRAND commitment. Although the Complaint did not specifically allege that Qualcomm made its false statements in a consensus-oriented environment of the type discussed in *Microsoft* and *Rambus*, this omission is not fatal in light of allegations that FRAND assurances were required, as well as allegations concerning the SDOs' reliance on Qualcomm's assurances. Together, these allegations satisfy the second element of a § 2 claim.

Qualcomm makes much of the Complaint's failure to allege that there were viable technologies competing with WCDMA for inclusion in the UMTS standard. As Qualcomm concedes, however, the Complaint does allege that an SDO's adoption of a standard eliminates competing technologies. The District Court also inferred that the relevant SDOs selected Qualcomm's WCDMA technology "to the detriment of those patent-holders competing to have their patents incorporated into the standard." This inference was reasonable, particularly because even if Qualcomm's WCDMA technology was the only candidate for inclusion in the standard, it still would not have been selected by the relevant SDOs absent a FRAND commitment. Thus, the allegations of the Complaint foreclose the possibility that WCDMA's inclusion in the standard was inevitable.

* * *

We also agree with *Amici* that the District Court erred when it concluded that Qualcomm's alleged inducement of an SDO did not harm competition, as is required for a § 2 claim, because "it is the SDO's decision to set a standard for WCDMA technology, not Qualcomm's 'inducement,' that results in the absence of competing WCDMA technologies." This conclusion failed to recognize that Qualcomm's FRAND commitment was an essential part of its competitive effort to win inclusion of its patented technology in the UMTS standard. The Court also failed to recognize that even if adoption of the UMTS standard did not expand Qualcomm's exclusionary rights as a patent holder, it nevertheless significantly expanded Qualcomm's market power by eliminating alternatives to its patented technology. Finally, the Court erroneously assumed that monopoly is the "natural consequence of the standard-setting process," an unsupported factual finding that ignores the possibility of a standard comprised of nonproprietary technologies.

IV. CONCLUSION

For the reasons discussed, we will affirm in part and reverse in part, and remand for further proceedings consistent with this Opinion.

* * *

———————

Before turning to our next U.S. case, we turn to the following *Note*, which discusses some of these issues as they have arisen in other jurisdictions.

NOTE ON THE TREATMENT OF FRAND-SEP ISSUES IN OTHER JURISDICTIONS

A number of foreign courts and competition enforcers, including in the European Union, Brazil, China, India, and Korea, have issued decisions and guidelines on the role of competition law in governing conduct involving SEPs. The decisions mainly address seeking injunctive relief to enforce a FRAND-encumbered SEP. In addition, unlike U.S. antitrust law, which does not regulate price, many foreign competition laws (including in the European Union and many Asian countries), explicitly prohibit "excessive" or "unfairly high or low" pricing. Thus, many of the foreign decisions focus on whether a particular royalty rate or calculation methodology is "excessive."

Courts and agencies in the European Union, China, and Korea have taken the position that a patent holder who seeks injunctive relief on its FRAND-encumbered SEPs may be subject to a competition law sanction, whereas Brazil's competition agency has declined to adopt such a position.

European Union. In July 2015, the European Court of Justice ("ECJ") held that seeking injunctive relief on a FRAND-encumbered SEP may constitute a violation of Article 102 of the Treaty on the Functioning of the European Union ("TFEU").[9] However, the court created a safe harbor from Article 102 liability for a SEP holder who: first, prior to initiating an infringement action, alerts the alleged infringer of the complained infringement specifying the way in which the patent has been infringed; and second, after the alleged infringer has expressed its willingness to conclude a license agreement on FRAND terms, presents to the infringer a specific, written offer for a license on such terms, specifying the royalty and calculation methodology. The ECJ then put the burden on the alleged infringer to "diligently respond" to that offer, "in accordance with recognized commercial practices in the field and in good faith," including by promptly providing a

———————

[9]   Case C-170/13, *Huawei Technologies Co. v. ZTE Corp.* (July 16, 2015), http://curia.europa. eu/juris/document/document.jsf?text=&docid=165911&pageIndex=0&doclang=EN&mode=lst& dir=&occ=first&part=1&cid=603775.

specific written counter-offer that corresponds to FRAND terms, and by providing appropriate security (e.g., a bond or funds in escrow) from the point at which the counter-offer is rejected and prior to using the teachings of the SEP.

Prior to the ECJ's decision in *Huawei v. ZTE*, the European Commission adopted two decisions, one involving Samsung Electronics Co., Ltd. and the other involving Motorola Mobility Inc., holding that seeking injunctive relief on a FRAND-encumbered SEP against a "willing licensee" may constitute a violation of Article 102. The decisions also created a safe harbor from injunctive relief, under which implementers can demonstrate that they are a "willing licensee" by agreeing that a court or a mutually agreed upon arbitrator shall adjudicate the FRAND terms in the event that negotiations fail. The decisions do not preclude injunctive relief for FRAND-encumbered SEPs per se, nor do they make findings on the definition of a "willing licensee" outside the safe harbor.

China. In April 2014, the Guangdong People's Court issued two related decisions involving Huawei and InterDigital, affirming the lower court's FRAND royalty determination of 0.019 percent of the sales price for each Huawei product for InterDigital, Inc.'s 2G, 3G, and 4G Chinese essential patents, and holding that InterDigital violated China's Anti-Monopoly Law (AML) by, among other things, seeking an exclusion order in the U.S. International Trade Commission against Huawei while negotiations were still in progress regarding InterDigital's Chinese SEPs. Following this decision, China's National Development and Reform Commission ("NDRC") (one of China's three Anti-Monopoly Law agencies) entered into a consent agreement with InterDigital that prohibits the company from seeking injunctive relief against any Chinese manufacturer that agrees to resolve the licensing dispute through binding arbitration.

In February of 2015, NDRC issued a penalty decision against Qualcomm, imposing a $975 million fine. NDRC concluded that the company had a dominant market position in the market for licensing SEPs involving CDMA, WCDMA, and LTE, and that it abused its dominance by: (1) charging excessive or unreasonably high royalties by refusing to provide the patent list and charging royalties for expired patents, requiring royalty-free grantbacks of relevant patents, bundling SEPs and non-SEPs, and charging "relatively high royalty rate[s] based on the wholesale net selling price of devices"; (2) bundling SEPs and non-SEPs "without justification"; and (3) imposing other "unreasonable conditions" on the sale of baseband chips, including waiving the right to challenge the agreement.

Korea. In February 2014, the Korea Fair Trade Commission ("KFTC") issued its first decision on the issue of whether seeking injunctive relief on a FRAND-encumbered SEP constitutes a violation of Korea's Fair Trade Law. The KFTC concluded that, because Apple Inc. failed to engage in good faith negotiations, Samsung's injunction claims against Apple on SEPs related to 3G mobile communication technology do not constitute an abuse of dominance or unfair trade practice. The KFTC also rejected Apple's contention that such conduct constitutes a refusal of access to essential facilities, concluding that FRAND-encumbered SEPs do not constitute essential facilities.

In December 2014, the KFTC amended its "Review Guidelines on Unfair Exercise of Intellectual Property Rights," specifying that, prior to seeking injunctive relief, an SEP holder must first negotiate in "good faith" or its conduct will likely be deemed a violation of the Fair Trade Law. The Guidelines further specify that, in determining whether an SEP holder has fulfilled its obligation to negotiate in good faith, the following factors may be considered: (1) whether the SEP holder has formally proposed a negotiation to the potential licensee; (2) whether the negotiation period with the potential licensee was reasonable; (3) whether the license terms proposed to the potential licensee were reasonable and non-discriminatory; and (4) whether it was agreed that upon failure to agree on licensing terms, the matter be submitted to a court or arbitral institution. The Guidelines explicitly recognize that prohibiting injunctive relief may result in "reverse hold up," specifying that seeking injunctive relief is "less likely" to be deemed unlawful when an accused infringer refuses to comply with the decision of a neutral third party or is unable to pay monetary damages due to bankruptcy or otherwise. The Guideline also specify that certain other conduct, such as tying SEPs and "unnecessary" non-SEPs, "runs a high risk" of constituting an unfair act.

Brazil. In June 2015, the Administrative Council for Economic Defense ("CADE") issued a decision recommending the closing of its investigation of Ericsson, concluding that any harm suffered by the accused infringer as a result of Ericsson's claims for injunctive relief resulted from a reasonable commercial dispute and did not result in market effects.

India. In November 2013 and January 2014, the Competition Commission of India ("CCI") issued two orders in related investigations against Ericsson, alleging that the company violated its FRAND commitments by imposing discriminatory and "excessive" royalty rates and using Non-Disclosure Agreements ("NDAs"). According to CCI, "forcing a party to execute [an] NDA" and "imposing excessive and unfair royalty rates" constitutes "prima facie" abuse of dominance and a violation of Section 4 of the India Competition Act, as does "[i]mposing a jurisdiction clause debarring [licensees] from getting disputes adjudicated in the country where both parties were in business." The investigations alleged that Ericsson "seem[ed] to be acting contrary to the FRAND terms by imposing royalties linked with cost of product of user for its patents." Thus, "[f]or the use of GSM chip in a phone costing Rs 100, royalty would be Rs. 1.25 but if this GSM chip is used in a phone of Rs. 1000, royalty would be Rs. 12.5." According to the CCI, "[c]harging of two different license fees per unit phone for use of the same technology *prima facie* is discriminatory and also reflects excessive pricing vis-à-vis high cost phones."

Following the issuance of these two orders, the High Court of Delhi questioned CCI's jurisdiction over FRAND-related issues, stating that it was "prima facie of the view that a substantial question of jurisdiction" is at issue based on Ericsson's argument that the Patent Act provides an adequate mechanism to balance the rights of the patentee and other stakeholders. In March of 2015, the Delhi High Court issued an interim injunction in Ericsson's favor on certain of its FRAND-encumbered SEPs, further concluding that executing an NDA is a legitimate "sin qua non in every licensing deal, particularly in patent licensing negotiations," and rejecting the accused infringer's argument that the royalty should be based on the chipset as opposed to handset price.

Conclusion

Antitrust agencies and courts around the world have begun to weigh in on conduct involving SEPs, including bringing investigations and issuing guidelines. Most have agreed that some SEP-related conduct can violate competititon laws. Some have also sought to prohibit "excessive" or "unfairly high" royalty rates, conduct that is not regulated by the U.S. antitrust agencies and which raises important questions on how to calculate FRAND royalties.

In *Broadcom*, the Third Circuit relied heavily upon the FTC's opinion in our next principal case, *Rambus* in concluding that patent holders violate antitrust laws when they intentionally enter into deceptive FRAND commitments while simultaneously and deceptively failing to disclose their IPRs. However, the D.C. Circuit set aside the FTC's findings against *Rambus* on appeal. We turn now to the D.C. Circuit's opinion. Note the distinctions the *Rambus* court draws between the underlying facts of *Rambus* and *Broadcom*. Which seem to drive the court's analysis? Are any of them outcome determinative? If yes, why?

RAMBUS INC. V. FEDERAL TRADE COMMISSION

United States Court of Appeals for the District of Columbia, 2008.
522 F.3d 456.

WILLIAMS, SENIOR CIRCUIT JUDGE.

Rambus Inc. develops computer memory technologies, secures intellectual property rights over them, and then licenses them to manufacturers in exchange for royalty payments. In 1990, Rambus's founders filed a patent application claiming the invention of a faster architecture for dynamic random access memory ("DRAM"). In recent years, Rambus has asserted that patents issued to protect its invention cover four technologies that a private standard-setting organization ("SSO") included in DRAM industry standards.

Before an SSO adopts a standard, there is often vigorous competition among different technologies for incorporation into that standard. After standardization, however, the dynamic typically shifts, as industry members begin adhering to the standard and the standardized features start to dominate. In this case, 90% of DRAM production is compliant with the standards at issue, and therefore the technologies adopted in those standards-including those over which Rambus claims patent rights-enjoy a similar level of dominance over their alternatives.

After lengthy proceedings, the Federal Trade Commission determined that Rambus, while participating in the standard-setting process, deceptively failed to disclose to the SSO the patent interests it held in four technologies that were standardized. Those interests ranged from issued patents, to pending patent applications, to plans to amend those patent applications to add new claims; Rambus's patent rights in all these interests are said to be sufficiently connected to the invention described in Rambus's original 1990 application that its rights would relate back to its date. Finding this conduct monopolistic and in violation of § 2 of the Sherman Act, 15 U.S.C. § 2, the Commission went on to hold that Rambus had engaged in an unfair method of competition and unfair or deceptive acts or practices prohibited by § 5(a) of the Federal Trade Commission Act ("FTC Act").

Rambus petitions for review. We grant the petition, holding that the Commission failed to sustain its allegation of monopolization. Its factual conclusion was that Rambus's alleged deception enabled it *either* to acquire a monopoly through the standardization of its patented technologies rather than possible alternatives, *or* to avoid limits on its patent licensing fees that the SSO would have imposed as part of its normal process of standardizing patented technologies. But the latter-deceit merely enabling a monopolist to charge higher prices than it otherwise could have charged-would not in itself constitute monopolization. We also address whether there is substantial evidence that Rambus engaged in deceptive conduct at all, and express our serious concerns about the sufficiency of the evidence on two particular points.

* * *

During the early 1990s, the computer hardware industry faced a "memory bottleneck": the development of faster memory lagged behind the development of faster central processing units, and this risked limiting future gains in overall computer performance. To address this problem, Michael Farmwald and Mark Horowitz began collaborating during the late 1980s and invented a higher-performance DRAM architecture. Together, they founded Rambus in March 1990 and filed Patent Application No. 07/510,898 ("the 898 application") on April 18, 1990.

As originally filed, the 898 application included a 62-page written description of Farmwald and Horowitz's invention, 150 claims, and 15 technical drawings. Under the direction of the Patent Office, acting pursuant to 35 U.S.C. § 121, Rambus effectively split the application into several (the original one and 10 "divisionals"). Thereafter, Rambus amended some of these applications and filed additional continuation and divisional applications.

While Rambus was developing a patent portfolio based on its founders' inventions, the computer memory industry was at work standardizing DRAM technologies. The locus of those efforts was the Joint Electron Device Engineering Council ("JEDEC")—then an "activity" of what is now called the Electronics Industries Alliance ("EIA") and, since 2000, a trade association affiliated with EIA and known as the JEDEC Solid State Technology Association. Any company involved in the solid state products industry could join JEDEC by submitting an application and paying annual dues, and members could receive JEDEC mailings, participate in JEDEC committees, and vote on pending matters.

One JEDEC committee, JC 42.3, developed standards for computer memory products. Rambus attended its first JC 42.3 meeting as a guest in December 1991 and began formally participating when it joined JEDEC in February 1992. At the time, JC 42.3 was at work on what became JEDEC's synchronous DRAM ("SDRAM") standard. The committee voted to approve the completed standard in March 1993, and JEDEC's governing body gave its final approval on May 24, 1993. The SDRAM standard includes two of the four technologies over which Rambus asserts patent rights-programmable CAS latency and programmable burst length.

Despite SDRAM's standardization, its manufacture increased very slowly and asynchronous DRAM continued to dominate the computer memory market, so JC 42.3 began to consider a number of possible responses-among them specifications it could include in a next-generation SDRAM standard. As part of that process, JC 42.3 members received a survey ballot in October 1995 soliciting their opinions on features of an advanced SDRAM-which ultimately emerged as the double data rate ("DDR") SDRAM standard. Among the features voted on were the other two technologies at issue here: on-chip phase lock and delay lock loops ("on-chip PLL/DLL") and dual-edge clocking. The Committee tallied and discussed the survey results at its December 1995 meeting, which was Rambus's last as a JEDEC member. Rambus formally withdrew from JEDEC by letter dated June 17, 1996, saying (among other things) that the terms on which it proposed to license its proprietary technology "may not be consistent with the terms set by standards bodies, including JEDEC."

JC 42.3's work continued after Rambus's departure. In March 1998 the committee adopted the DDR SDRAM standard, and the JEDEC Board of Directors approved it in 1999. This standard retained SDRAM features including programmable CAS latency and programmable burst length, and it added on-chip PLL/DLL and dual-edge clocking; DDR SDRAM, therefore, included all four of the technologies at issue here.

Starting in 1999, Rambus informed major DRAM and chipset manufacturers that it held patent rights over technologies included in JEDEC's SDRAM and DDR SDRAM standards, and that the continued manufacture, sale, or use of products compliant with those standards infringed its rights. It invited the manufacturers to resolve the alleged infringement through licensing negotiations. A number of manufacturers agreed to licenses; others did not, and litigation ensued.

On June 18, 2002, the Federal Trade Commission filed a complaint under § 5(b) of the FTC Act, 15 U.S.C. § 45(b), charging that Rambus engaged in unfair methods of competition and unfair or deceptive acts or practices in violation of the Act. Specifically, the Commission alleged that Rambus breached JEDEC policies requiring it to disclose patent interests related to standardization efforts and that the disclosures it did make were misleading. By this deceptive conduct, it said, Rambus unlawfully monopolized four technology markets in which its patented technologies compete with alternative innovations to address technical issues relating to DRAM design-markets for latency, burst length, data acceleration, and clock synchronization technologies.

Proceedings began before an administrative law judge, who in due course dismissed the Complaint in its entirety. He concluded that Rambus did not impermissibly withhold material information about its intellectual property, and that, in any event, there was insufficient evidence that, if Rambus had disclosed all the information allegedly required of it, JEDEC would have standardized an alternative technology.

Complaint Counsel appealed the ALJ's Initial Decision to the Commission. * * * [T]he Commission vacated the ALJ's decision and set aside his findings of fact and conclusions of law. The Commission found that while JEDEC's patent disclosure policies were "not a model of clarity," members expected one another to disclose patents and patent applications that were relevant to technologies being considered for standardization, *plus* (though the Commission was far less clear on these latter items) planned amendments to pending applications or "anything they're working on that they potentially wanted to protect with patents down the road." Based on this interpretation of JEDEC's disclosure requirements, the Commission held that Rambus willfully and intentionally engaged in misrepresentations, omissions, and other practices that misled JEDEC members about intellectual property information "highly material" to the standard-setting process.

The Commission focused entirely on the allegation of monopolization. In particular, the Commission held that the evidence and inferences from Rambus's purpose demonstrated that "but for Rambus's deceptive course of conduct, JEDEC either would have excluded Rambus's patented technologies from the JEDEC DRAM standards, or would have demanded

RAND assurances [*i.e.,* assurances of 'reasonable and nondiscriminatory' license fees], with an opportunity for *ex ante* licensing negotiations." Rejecting Rambus's argument that factors other than JEDEC's standards allowed Rambus's technologies to dominate their respective markets, the Commission concluded that Rambus's deception of JEDEC "significantly contributed to its acquisition of monopoly power."

* * *

Rambus challenges the Commission's determination that it engaged in unlawful monopolization—and thereby violated § 5 of the FTC Act—on a variety of grounds, of which two are most prominent. First, it argues that the Commission erred in finding that it violated any JEDEC patent disclosure rules and thus that it breached any antitrust duty to provide information to its rivals. Second, it asserts that even if its nondisclosure contravened JEDEC's policies, the Commission found the consequences of such nondisclosure only in the alternative: that it prevented JEDEC *either* from adopting a non-proprietary standard, *or* from extracting a RAND commitment from Rambus when standardizing its technology. As the latter would not involve an antitrust violation, says Rambus, there is an insufficient basis for liability.

We find the second of these arguments to be persuasive, and conclude that the Commission failed to demonstrate that Rambus's conduct was exclusionary under settled principles of antitrust law. Given that conclusion, we need not dwell very long on the substantiality of the evidence, which we address only to express our serious concerns about the breadth the Commission ascribed to JEDEC's disclosure policies and their relation to what Rambus did or did not disclose.

* * *

In this case under § 5 of the FTC Act, the Commission expressly limited its theory of liability to Rambus's unlawful monopolization of four markets in violation of § 2 of the Sherman Act, 15 U.S.C. § 2. Therefore, we apply principles of antitrust law developed under the Sherman Act, and we review the Commission's construction and application of the antitrust laws *de novo.*

It is settled law that the mere existence of a monopoly does not violate the Sherman Act. In addition to "the possession of monopoly power in the relevant market," the offense of monopolization requires " 'the willful acquisition or maintenance of that power as distinguished from growth or development as a consequence of a superior product, business acumen, or historical accident.' " In this case, Rambus does not dispute the nature of the relevant markets or that its patent rights in the four relevant technologies give it monopoly power in each of those markets. The critical question is whether Rambus engaged in exclusionary conduct, and thereby acquired its monopoly power in the relevant markets unlawfully.

To answer that question, we adhere to two antitrust principles that guided us in *Microsoft*. First, "to be condemned as exclusionary, a monopolist's act must have 'anticompetitive effect.' That is, it must harm the competitive *process* and thereby harm consumers. In contrast, harm to one or more *competitors* will not suffice." Second, it is the antitrust plaintiff-including the Government as plaintiff-that bears the burden of proving the anticompetitive effect of the monopolist's conduct.

The Commission held that Rambus engaged in exclusionary conduct consisting of misrepresentations, omissions, and other practices that deceived JEDEC about the nature and scope of its patent interests while the organization standardized technologies covered by those interests. Had Rambus fully disclosed its intellectual property, "JEDEC either would have excluded Rambus's patented technologies from the JEDEC DRAM standards, or would have demanded RAND assurances, with an opportunity for *ex ante* licensing negotiations." But the Commission did not determine that one or the other of these two possible outcomes was the more likely. The Commission's conclusion that Rambus's conduct was exclusionary depends, therefore, on a syllogism: Rambus avoided one of two outcomes by not disclosing its patent interests; the avoidance of either of those outcomes was anticompetitive; therefore Rambus's nondisclosure was anticompetitive.

We assume without deciding that avoidance of the first of these possible outcomes was indeed anticompetitive; that is, that if Rambus's more complete disclosure would have caused JEDEC to adopt a different (open, non-proprietary) standard, then its failure to disclose harmed competition and would support a monopolization claim. But while we can assume that Rambus's nondisclosure made the adoption of its technologies somewhat more likely than broad disclosure would have, the Commission made clear in its remedial opinion that there was insufficient evidence that JEDEC would have standardized other technologies had it known the full scope of Rambus's intellectual property. Therefore, for the Commission's syllogism to survive—and for the Commission to have carried its burden of proving that Rambus's conduct had an anticompetitive effect—we must also be convinced that if Rambus's conduct merely enabled it to avoid the other possible outcome, namely JEDEC's obtaining assurances from Rambus of RAND licensing terms, such conduct, alone, could be said to harm competition. We are not convinced.

Deceptive conduct—like any other kind—must have an anticompetitive effect in order to form the basis of a monopolization claim. "Even an act of pure malice by one business competitor against another does not, without more, state a claim under the federal antitrust laws," without proof of "a dangerous probability that [the defendant] would monopolize a particular market." Even if deception raises the price secured by a seller, but does so without harming competition, it is beyond the antitrust laws' reach. Cases that recognize deception as exclusionary hinge, therefore, on whether the conduct impaired rivals in a manner tending to bring about or protect a defendant's monopoly power. In *Microsoft*, for example, we found Microsoft engaged in anticompetitive conduct when it tricked independent software developers into believing that its software development tools could be used to design cross-platform Java applications when, in fact, they produced Windows-specific ones. The deceit had caused "developers who were opting for portability over performance . . . unwittingly [to write] Java applications that [ran] only on Windows." The focus of our antitrust scrutiny, therefore, was properly placed on the resulting harms to competition rather than the deception itself.

Another case of deception with an anticompetitive dimension is *Conwood Co. v. U.S. Tobacco Co.*, 290 F.3d 768 (6th Cir. 2002), where the Sixth Circuit found that U.S. Tobacco's dominance of the moist snuff market caused retailers to rely on it as a "category manager" that would provide trusted guidance on the sales strategy and in-store display for all moist snuff products. Under those circumstances, the court held that its misrepresentations to retailers about the sales strength of its products versus its competitors' strength reduced competition in the monopolized market by increasing the display space devoted to U.S. Tobacco's products and decreasing that allotted to competing products.

But an otherwise lawful monopolist's use of deception simply to obtain higher prices normally has no particular tendency to exclude rivals and thus to diminish competition. Consider, for example, *NYNEX Corp. v. Discon, Inc.*, 525 U.S. 128, 119 S.Ct. 493 (1998), in which the Court addressed the antitrust implications of allegations that NYNEX's subsidiary, New York Telephone Company, a lawful monopoly provider of local telephone services, charged its customers higher prices as result of fraudulent conduct in the market for the service of removing outdated telephone switching equipment (called "removal services"). Discon had alleged that New York Telephone (through its corporate affiliate, Materiel Enterprises) switched its purchases of removal services from Discon to a higher-priced independent firm (AT & T Technologies). Materiel Enterprises would pass the higher fees on to New York Telephone, which in turn passed them on to customers through higher rates approved by regulators. The nub of the deception, Discon alleged, was that AT & T Technologies would provide Materiel Enterprises with a special rebate at year's end, which it would then share with NYNEX. By thus hoodwinking the regulators, the scam raised prices for consumers; Discon, which refused to play the rebate game, was driven out of business. Discon alleged that this arrangement was anticompetitive and constituted both an agreement in restraint of trade in violation of § 1 of the Sherman Act and a conspiracy to monopolize the market for removal services in violation of § 2.

As to Discon's § 1 claim, the Court held that where a single buyer favors one supplier over another for an improper reason, the plaintiff must "allege and prove harm, not just to a single competitor, but to the competitive process." Nor, as Justice Breyer wrote for a unanimous Court, would harm to the consumers in the form of higher prices change the matter: "We concede Discon's claim that the [defendants'] behavior hurt consumers by raising telephone service rates. But that consumer injury naturally flowed not so much from a less competitive market for removal services, as from the exercise of market power that is *lawfully* in the hands of a monopolist, namely, New York Telephone, combined with a deception worked upon the regulatory agency that prevented the agency from controlling New York Telephone's exercise of its monopoly power."

Because Discon based its § 2 claim on the very same allegations of fraud, the Court vacated the appellate court's decision to uphold that claim because "[u]nless those agreements harmed the competitive process, they did not amount to a conspiracy to monopolize."

While the Commission's brief does not mention *NYNEX*, much less try to distinguish it, it does cite *Broadcom Corp. v. Qualcomm Inc.*, 501 F.3d 297 (3d Cir. 2007), which in turn had cited the Commission's own "landmark" decision in the case under review here. There the court held that a patent holder's intentionally false promise to a standard-setting organization that it would license its technology on RAND terms, "coupled with [the organization's] reliance on that promise when including the technology in a standard," was anticompetitive conduct, on the ground that it increased "the likelihood that patent rights will confer monopoly power on the patent holder." To the extent that the ruling (which simply reversed a grant of dismissal) rested on the argument that deceit lured the SSO away from non-proprietary technology, it cannot help the Commission in view of its inability to find that Rambus's behavior caused JEDEC's choice; to the extent that it may have rested on a supposition that there is a cognizable violation of the Sherman Act when a lawful monopolist's deceit has the effect of raising prices (without an effect on competitive structure), it conflicts with *NYNEX*.

Here, the Commission expressly left open the likelihood that JEDEC would have standardized Rambus's technologies *even if Rambus had disclosed* its intellectual property. Under this hypothesis, JEDEC lost only an opportunity to secure a RAND commitment from Rambus. But loss of such a commitment is not a harm to competition from alternative technologies in the relevant markets. Indeed, had JEDEC limited Rambus to reasonable royalties and required it to provide licenses on a nondiscriminatory basis, we would expect *less* competition from alternative technologies, not more; high prices and constrained output tend to attract competitors, not to repel them.

Scholars in the field have urged that if nondisclosure to an SSO enables a participant to obtain higher royalties than would otherwise have been attainable, the "overcharge can properly constitute competitive harm attributable to the nondisclosure," as the overcharge "will distort competition in the downstream market." The contention that price-raising deception has downstream effects is surely correct, but that consequence was equally surely true in *NYNEX* (though perhaps on a smaller scale) and equally obvious to the Court. The Commission makes the related contention that because the ability to profitably restrict output and set supracompetitive prices is the *sine qua non* of monopoly power, any conduct that permits a monopolist to avoid constraints on the exercise of that power must be anticompetitive. But again, as in *NYNEX*, an otherwise lawful monopolist's end-run around price constraints, even when deceptive or fraudulent, does not alone present a harm to competition in the monopolized market.

Thus, if JEDEC, in the world that would have existed but for Rambus's deception, would have standardized the very same technologies, Rambus's alleged deception cannot be said to have had an effect on competition in violation of the antitrust laws; JEDEC's loss of an opportunity to seek favorable licensing terms is not as such an antitrust harm. Yet the Commission did not reject this as being a possible-perhaps even the more probable-effect of Rambus's conduct. We hold, therefore, that the Commission failed to demonstrate that Rambus's conduct was exclusionary, and thus to establish its claim that Rambus unlawfully monopolized the relevant markets.

* * *

Our conclusion that the Commission failed to demonstrate that Rambus inflicted any harm on competition requires vacatur of the Commission's orders. But the original complaint also included a count charging Rambus with other unfair methods of competition in violation of § 5(a) of the FTC Act, 15 U.S.C. § 45(a). While the Commission dropped this aspect of its case and focused on a theory of liability premised on unlawful monopolization, at least one Commissioner suggested that a "stand-alone" § 5 action would have had a "broader province" than a Sherman Act case. Because of the chance of further proceedings on remand, we express briefly our serious concerns about strength of the evidence relied on to support some of the Commission's crucial findings regarding the scope of JEDEC's patent disclosure policies and Rambus's alleged violation of those policies.

In noting our concerns, we recognize, of course, that the Commission's findings are conclusive so long as they are supported by substantial evidence. The Commission's findings are murky on both the relevant margins: what JEDEC's disclosure policies were, and what, within those mandates, Rambus failed to disclose.

First, the Commission evidently could find that Rambus violated JEDEC's disclosure policies only by relying quite significantly on participants' having been obliged to disclose their work in progress on *potential* amendments to pending applications, as that work became pertinent. The Commission's counsel confirmed as much at oral argument. Indeed, the parties stipulated that as of Rambus's last JEDEC meeting it held no patents that were essential to the manufacture or use of devices complying with any JEDEC standard, and that when JEDEC issued the SDRAM standard Rambus had no pending patent claims that would necessarily have been infringed by a device compliant with that standard.

The case *appears* (and we emphasize *appears,* as the Commission's opinion leaves us uncertain of its real view) to turn on the idea that JEDEC participants were obliged to disclose not merely relevant patents and patent applications, but also their work in progress on amendments to pending applications that included new patent claims. We do not see in the record any formal finding that the policies were so broad, but the Commission's opinion points to testimony of witnesses that might be the basis of such a finding. Five former JC 42.3 participants testified (in some cases ambiguously) that they understood JEDEC's written policies, requiring the disclosure of *pending* applications, to also include a duty to disclose work in progress on *unfiled* amendments to those applications, and JEDEC's general counsel testified that he believed a firm was required to disclose *plans* to amend if supported by the firm's current interpretation of an extant application. JEDEC participants did not have unanimous recollections on this point, however, and the Commission noted that another JC 42.3 member testified that there was no duty to disclose work on future filings.

Reading these statements as interpretations of JEDEC's written policies seems to significantly stretch the policies' language. The most disclosure-friendly of those policies is JEDEC Manual No. 21–I, published in October 1993, which refers to "the obligation of all participants to inform the meeting of any knowledge they may have of any patents, or pending patents, that might be involved in the work they are undertaking." This language speaks fairly clearly of disclosure obligations related to patents and pending patent applications, but says nothing of unfiled work in progress on potential amendments to patent applications. We don't see how a few strands of trial testimony would persuade the Commission to read this language more broadly, especially as at least two of the five participants cited merely stated that disclosure obligations reached anything in the patent "process"—which leaves open the question of when that "process" can be said to begin.

Alternatively, to the extent the Commission reads this testimony not to broaden the interpretation of Manual 21–I, but rather to provide evidence of disclosure expectations that extended beyond those incorporated into written policies, a different problem may arise. As the Federal Circuit has said, JEDEC's patent disclosure policies suffered from "a staggering lack of defining details." Even assuming that any evidence of unwritten disclosure expectations would survive a possible narrowing effect based upon the written directive of Manual 21–I, the vagueness of any such expectations would nonetheless remain an obstacle. One would expect that disclosure expectations ostensibly requiring competitors to share information that they would otherwise vigorously protect as trade secrets would provide "clear guidance" and "define clearly what, when, how, and to whom the members must disclose." This need for clarity seems especially acute where disclosure of those trade secrets itself implicates antitrust concerns; JEDEC involved, after all, collaboration by *competitors*. In any event, the more vague and muddled a particular expectation of disclosure, the more difficult it should be for the Commission to ascribe competitive harm to its breach.

The Commission's conclusion that Rambus engaged in deceptive conduct affecting the inclusion of on-chip PLL/DLL and dual-edge clocking in the DDR SDRAM standard, which JEDEC adopted more than two years after Rambus's last JC 42.3 meeting, presents an additional, independent concern. To support this conclusion, the Commission looked to a technical presentation made to JC 42.3 in September 1994, and the survey balloting of that committee in October 1995 on whether to proceed with the consideration of particular features (including the two Rambus technologies ultimately adopted), finding that Rambus deliberately failed to disclose patent interests in any of the named technologies. This finding is evidently the basis, so far as DDR SDRAM is concerned, of its conclusion that Rambus breached a duty to disclose.

Once again, the Commission has taken an aggressive interpretation of rather weak evidence. For example, the October 1995 survey ballot gauged participant interest in a range of technologies and did not ask those surveyed about their intellectual property (as did the more formal ballots on proposed standards). The Commission nonetheless believes that every member of JC 42.3—membership that included most of the DRAM industry—was duty-bound to disclose *any* potential patents they were working on that related to *any* of the questions posed by the survey. The record shows, however, that the only company that made a disclosure at the next meeting was the one that formally presented the survey results. For reasons similar to those that make vague but broad disclosure obligations among competitors unlikely, it seems to us unlikely that JEDEC participants placed themselves under such a sweeping and early duty to disclose, triggered by the mere chance that a technology might someday (in this case, more than two years later) be formally proposed for standardization.

* * *

We set aside the Commission's orders and remand for further proceedings consistent with this opinion.

So ordered.

* * *

———————

Notice the crucial role of timing in both *Broadcom* and *Rambus*. *Broadcom* involves deceptive conduct that allegedly occurred prior to the defendant's acquisition of monopoly power—indeed, Broadcom alleged that Qualcomm acquired its market power by virtue of its deceptive conduct. In *Rambus*, however, the order of the allegedly deceptive act and the defendant's acquisition of monopoly power is less clear. Specifically, if Rambus' technologies and patents were strong relative to alternative technologies under consideration by the standard-setting body, then it would have likely been selected for the standard (or allowed to become the *de facto* standard) regardless of Rambus' behavior. If true, one could argue that the deceptive act did not "cause" Rambus' acquisition of market power. Rather, Rambus' conduct merely allowed it to evade the pricing constraints imposed upon it by its RAND commitment.

As we learned in Chapter 4, Section 2 of the Sherman Act reaches conduct that results in the acquisition or maintenance of monopoly power, but does not condemn the mere exercise of it, if it is lawfully obtained. The case law under Sherman Act Section 2 therefore distinguishes conduct that allows a firm to acquire monopoly power and reduce competition from the exercise of lawfully acquired monopoly power—arguably including when the exercise of lawfully acquired monopoly power involves an act evading pricing constraints imposed by regulation. The D.C. Circuit reasoned that under the Supreme Court's decision in *NYNEX Corp. v. Discon, Inc.*, 525 U.S. 128 (1998), the plaintiff must demonstrate that the price-increasing deception caused the acquisition of market power rather than merely allowing the exercise of previously and lawfully acquired monopoly power. It concluded that the Commission had not met the *NYNEX* causation standard because it left open the possibility that Rambus lawfully acquired market power by virtue of a superior patented product, *i.e.* that even had Rambus disclosed its patent, JEDEC might still have included it in the relevant standard owing to a lack of alternative, competitive technologies. For a discussion of the role of *NYNEX* in understanding patent holdup antitrust claims, see Joshua D. Wright, *Why the Supreme Court Was Correct to Deny Certiorari in* FTC v. Rambus, GCP: ONLINE MAG. GLOBAL

COMPETITION POL'Y 16 (March 2009). Does the timing of the deceptive act fully explain the different outcomes in *Broadcom* and *Rambus*? What other important substantive or procedural differences between the two cases might explain the potentially divergent outcomes?

Broadcom and *Rambus* each highlight various challenges presented in applying antitrust analysis in the SSO patent holdup context. One such complication is that SSOs routinely establish disclosure rules and FRAND terms that are not highly specified, perhaps at times deliberately. Both patent holders and SSO members may derive value from ambiguous IP policies because they offer some flexibility with respect to licensing terms. However, contractual ambiguity may also facilitate later opportunistic holdup behavior—the concern of antitrust enforcers in the U.S. and Europe. Contractual ambiguity may also complicate antitrust analysis when an SSO participant or licensee alleges the firm violated its F/RAND commitment. What factors help to distinguish cases in which patent holders engage in opportunistic behavior that give rise to antitrust concerns from those contract changes that arise naturally out of the flexibility of F/RAND commitments? Another difficulty in analyzing FRAND commitments in the antitrust context is calculating royalty rates. Ambiguity in a FRAND agreement can create the potential for a significant divide between what the patent holder and what the SSO each perceive as fair and reasonable. Accordingly, the question of what constitutes an appropriate royalty looms large not only for damages calculations, but also for liability if deviations from FRAND commitments give rise to antitrust violations.

NOTE ON *N-DATA, GOOGLE,* AND *PATENT HOLDUP* AS AN *UNFAIR METHOD* OF *COMPETITION*

The SSO patent holdup cases we have covered so far involve allegations of deceptive conduct by an alleged monopolist. In a second line of cases, the FTC alleged violations of Section 5 of the FTC Act—but not Section 2 of the Sherman Act—in the SSO context even in the absence of deception. This extension involves challenging instances in which the patent holder seeks to renegotiate or otherwise to deviate from an original FRAND agreement made in good faith and absent any allegation of deceptive conduct.

In re Negotiated Data Solutions LLC (*N-Data*), No. 051–0094, 2008 WL 258308 (F.T.C. Jan. 23, 2008), is a recent application of patent holdup without alleged deception. Vertical Networks, Inc., N-Data's predecessor, had rights to an SEP for an Ethernet auto-negotiation technology for the Institute of Electrical and Electronics Engineers' ("IEEE") 802.3u standard. The original agreement pledged royalty-free licenses for $1,000 to those utilizing the standard, but Vertical renegotiated the original agreement with IEEE— deviating from the $1,000 commitment—before transferring its rights to N-Data.

The FTC brought stand-alone Section 5 claims against N-Data, alleging its conduct constituted both an unfair method of competition and an unfair act or practice. After settling with N-Data, the FTC Majority Statement read, "[N]o doubt that the type of behavior engaged in by N-Data harms consumers. . . . [B]ad faith or deceptive behavior that undermines the [standard setting] process may also undermine competition in an entire industry, raise prices to consumers, and reduce choices." *Id.* at *30. Chairman Majoras, writing in dissent, first questioned whether N-Data in fact held antitrust relevant market power, given that it was merely an optional component of the standard. Further, Chairman Majoras noted there was little evidence of competitive harm because, despite Vertical's and N-Data's licensing efforts, just one company paid significantly more for the NWay technology than the original $1,000 commitment. Majoras also objected that N-Data had not engaged in deception, and thus that this case "departs materially from the prior line . . . in that there is no allegation that National engaged in improper or exclusionary conduct" to gain inclusion within the standard, and worried that the "majority has not identified a meaningful limiting principle that indicates when an action—taken in the standard-setting context or otherwise—will be considered an 'unfair method of competition.' " *Id.* at 27.

What did Chairman Majoras mean by her reference to "limiting principles"? Was she correct that *N-Data* fails to establish any meaningful limiting principles to the application of antitrust liability under Section 5 in the SSO context? What, if any, limits could be set that would establish the appropriate contours of liability? Recall the D.C. Circuit's wariness of utilizing a "stand alone" Section 5 claim in *Rambus*. Given its expressed skepticism of such claims, do you think the D.C. Circuit would have affirmed the FTC's theories in *N-Data*, had the case gone before it? Why or why not?

Before we conclude our discussion of patent holdup, a final issue regarding the role of injunctions in FRAND negotiations bears mention. In early 2012, the DOJ released a statement closing its investigation of Google Inc.'s acquisition of Motorola Mobility as well as the acquisitions of certain patents by Apple Inc., Microsoft Corp., and Research in Motion Ltd. *See* Press Release, U.S. Dep't of Justice, Statement of the Department of Justice's Antitrust Division on Its Decision to Close Its Investigations of Google Inc.'s Acquisition of Motorola Mobility Holdings Inc. and the Acquisitions of Certain Patents by Apple Inc., Microsoft Corp. and Research in Motion Ltd. (Feb. 13, 2012), http://www.justice.gov/opa/pr/2012/February/12–at–210.html. In its statement, the DOJ approved of Apple's policy that "[s]eeking an injunction would be a violation of the party's commitment to FRAND licensing," and of Microsoft's statement that it would "not seek an injunction or exclusion order against any firm on the basis of" SEPs. *Id.* However, the DOJ expressed serious skepticism regarding Google's policy, which did not entirely preclude the possibility of an injunctive action.

The FTC has also taken the position that a patent holder violates a FRAND commitment if it seeks or uses the threat of an injunction (or an exclusion order from the International Trade Commission) to enhance its bargaining position and extract higher royalties from potential licensees, and that breach of a FRAND commitment in turn, constitutes an unfair method of competition under Section 5 of the FTC Act. The Commission recently entered into two consents based upon the theory that breaching a FRAND commitment by seeking an injunction violates Section 5 of the FTC Act as an unfair method of competition. *See In re Robert Bosch GmbH*, File No. 121–0081, 2012 WL 5944820 (F.T.C. Nov. 21, 2012); *In re Motorola Mobility LLC, a limited liability company, and Google, Inc.*, File No. 121–0120, 2013 WL 124100 (F.T.C. Jan. 3, 2013). In *Bosch*, the FTC challenged Bosch's acquisition of SPX Service Solutions and also alleged that SPX breached its licensing commitments seeking injunctions against willing licensees. In *Google*, the FTC reached a settlement with Google and its subsidiary, Motorola, Inc., after alleging that it violated Section 5 of the FTC Act when it sought injunctions on various SEPs. Some scholars have argued that the FTC's enforcement actions in *Bosch* and *Google* rely upon the asymmetric view of IPRs and real property rights and are in tension with the symmetry principle outlined in the 1995 Antitrust-IP Guidelines. *See* Joshua D. Wright & Douglas H. Ginsburg, *Whither Symmetry? Antitrust Analysis of Intellectual Property Rights at the FTC and DOJ*, 9 COMPETITION POL'Y INT'L 41, 45 (2013).

D. CONCLUSION

In this Chapter we have explored a sampling of some of the competitive ramifications of innovation, in its various forms, and how antitrust has adapted to them. As we observed, enforcement agencies, commentators, and courts increasingly recognize that innovation may often be a critical source of competitive vigor that requires protection under competition laws.

Particularly difficult issues emerged, however, in connection with innovation that takes the form of intellectual property rights. These issues are likely to continue to spur economic thought and doctrinal development, as well as debates over the efficacy of antitrust institutions.

E. PROBLEMS AND EXERCISES

In each of the Problems below, consider how you would approach the analysis. What cases, principles, and policies would be relevant? What accommodation, if any, would you have to make to non-IP precedent to apply it to these situations? What questions would you ask?

Problem 7–1:
In re Union Oil Co. of Cal. ("Unocal")

In a March 4, 2003 administrative complaint, the FTC accused Unocal of making false and misleading statements to a state regulatory body—the California Air Resources Board ("CARB")—for the purpose of inducing it to

. . .

issue regulatory standards incorporating Unocal's patented technology. Specifically, Unocal allegedly failed to disclose its patent rights in certain reformulated gasoline standards, which it was urging CARB to adopt. According to the complaint, Unocal (1) induced CARB to adopt reformulated gasoline standards that substantially overlapped Unocal's patent claims and (2) induced other refiners to reconfigure their refineries in ways that subsequently exposed them to Unocal's patent claims. Unocal claimed it was entitled to hundreds of millions of dollars in royalties.

What is the theory of antitrust harm in this case? Are the facts here most like those in *Broadcom*, *Rambus*, or *N-DATA*? How would the FTC resolve this case if it arose today? Note that Unocal and CARB did not enter into a F/RAND agreement. Does this affect the analysis?

See In re Union Oil Co. of Cal., Dkt No. 9305 (July 6, 2004), http://www.ftc.gov/enforcement/cases-proceedings/0110214/union-oil-company-california-matter.

The last two problems are taken from the IP Guidelines. After initially working through each problem, consult the discussions of each that can be found in the corresponding section of the relevant Guidelines. The U.S. IP Guidelines can be accessed on the internet at http://www.justice.gov/atr/public/guidelines/0558.pdf. Additional problems are analyzed in the Canadian IP Guidelines at http://www.competitionbureau.gc.ca/eic/site/cb-bc.nsf/vwapj/cb-IPEG-e.pdf/$file/cb-IPEG-e.pdf. Do there appear to be differences in the competition statutes of the two jurisdictions? Do those differences appear to affect the analysis of the problems? Are the differences, if any, a function of differing enforcement philosophies? Other factors?

Problem 7–2:
U.S. IP Guidelines Problem 9
("Horizontal Restraints")

EXAMPLE 9

Situation:

Two of the leading manufacturers of a consumer electronic product hold patents that cover alternative circuit designs for the product. The manufacturers assign their patents to a separate corporation wholly owned by the two firms. That corporation licenses the right to use the circuit designs to other consumer product manufacturers and establishes the license royalties. None of the patents is blocking; that is, each of the patents can be used without infringing a patent owned by the other firm. The different circuit designs are substitutable in that each permits the manufacture at a comparable cost to consumers of products that consumers consider interchangeable. One of the Agencies is analyzing the licensing arrangement.

Problem 7–3:
U.S. IP Guidelines Problem 11
("Acquisitions of Intellectual Property Rights")

EXAMPLE 11

Situation:

Omega develops a new, patented pharmaceutical for the treatment of a particular disease. The only drug on the market approved for the treatment of this disease is sold by Delta. Omega's patented drug has almost completed regulatory approval by the Food and Drug Administration. Omega has invested considerable sums in product development and market testing, and initial results show that Omega's drug would be a significant competitor to Delta's. However, rather than enter the market as a direct competitor of Delta, Omega licenses to Delta the right to manufacture and sell Omega's patented drug. The license agreement with Delta is nominally nonexclusive. However, Omega has rejected all requests by other firms to obtain a license to manufacture and sell Omega's patented drug, despite offers by those firms of terms that are reasonable in relation to those in Delta's license.

CHAPTER 8

IMPLEMENTING COMPETITION POLICY RULES: THE STRUCTURE OF ANTITRUST ENFORCEMENT

■ ■ ■

INTRODUCTION

In previous chapters we have examined how competition law draws the line between lawful and unlawful behavior, *i.e.*, on the *substance* of antitrust rules. The impact of competition laws, however, derives not solely from the content of their substantive commands, but also from the effectiveness of the institutions entrusted with *implementing* them, which occupies our attention in this Chapter.

A. DEFINING THE BOUNDARIES OF NATIONAL JURISDICTION

The U.S. federal antitrust statutes are grounded in the constitutional power of Congress to regulate interstate or foreign trade or commerce. The Sherman Act governs conduct "in restraint of trade or commerce among the several States, or with foreign nations" and reaches restraints that are "in" interstate commerce *or* that have a substantial "effect" on such commerce. 15 U.S.C. §§ 1–2. *See Mandeville Island Farms, Inc. v. Am. Crystal Sugar Co.*, 334 U.S. 219 (1948). In general, the Sherman Act has been read as co-extensive with the scope of the federal commerce power, although as we shall see, more recently some defendants have sought to narrow its jurisdictional reach.

The Clayton Act as it currently is constituted, has a narrower jurisdictional scope and applies only to persons operating "in" interstate commerce. *See Gulf Oil Corp. v. Copp Paving, Inc.*, 419 U.S. 186 (1974). This "in commerce" requirement has been interpreted as requiring more than a mere effect on commerce, but rather actual movement of commerce across state lines. It thereby constrains the reach of Section 2 of the Clayton Act, as amended by the Robinson-Patman Act (price discrimination), and Section 3 of the Clayton Act (exclusionary vertical agreements).

An important exception is the Clayton Act's merger provision (Section 7, 15 U.S.C. § 18). In response to *United States v. Am. Bldg. Maint. Indus.*, 422 U.S. 271 (1975), which read Section 7's jurisdictional reach narrowly to keep it consistent with the provisions of Sections 2 and 3 of the Act, Congress amended Section 7 in 1980 to permit jurisdiction over persons "engaged in commerce *or in any activity affecting commerce*." (emphasis added) The amendment was designed to and has had the effect of making antitrust jurisdiction over mergers and acquisitions co-extensive with the reach of the Sherman Act under its more lenient "effects" test. Similarly, to alter a narrow reading of the FTC's jurisdiction in *FTC v. Bunte Bros.*, 312 U.S. 349 (1941), Section 5 of the FTC Act was amended in 1975 to authorize jurisdiction over unfair methods of competition or deceptive acts or practices "in or affecting commerce." 15 U.S.C. § 45(a)(2). Since that time, the FTC's jurisdiction under Section 5 has resembled that of the Sherman Act.

1. INTERSTATE COMMERCE REQUIREMENT

The Sherman Act's interstate commerce requirement is easily satisfied today. Plaintiffs can establish this jurisdictional element by showing that the challenged conduct: (a) directly interfered with the flow of goods in commerce (the "in commerce" test), or (b) substantially affected interstate commerce (the "effect on commerce" test). As the following case demonstrates, the Sherman Act's "effect on commerce" test can reach a wide range of seemingly local behavior, but defining that reach has generated significant disagreement within the Court.

SUMMIT HEALTH, LTD. v. PINHAS

Supreme Court of the United States, 1991.
500 U.S. 322, 111 S.Ct. 1842, 114 L.Ed.2d 366.

MR. JUSTICE STEVENS delivered the opinion of the Court.

The question presented is whether the interstate commerce requirement of antitrust jurisdiction is satisfied by allegations that petitioners conspired to exclude respondent, a duly licensed and practicing physician and surgeon, from the market for ophthalmological services in Los Angeles because he refused to follow an unnecessarily costly surgical procedure.

In 1987, respondent Dr. Simon J. Pinhas filed a complaint in District Court alleging that petitioners Summit Health, Ltd. (Summit), Midway Hospital Medical Center (Midway), its medical staff, and others had entered into a conspiracy to drive him out of business "so that other ophthalmologists and eye physicians [including four of the petitioners] will have a greater share of the eye care and ophthalmic surgery in Los Angeles." Among his allegations was a claim that the conspiracy violated § 1 of the Sherman Act. The District Court granted defendants' (now petitioners') motion to dismiss the First Amended Complaint (complaint) without leave to amend, but the United States Court of Appeals for the

Ninth Circuit reinstated the antitrust claim. We granted certiorari to consider petitioners' contention that the complaint fails to satisfy the jurisdictional requirements of the Sherman Act, as interpreted in *McLain v. Real Estate Bd. of New Orleans, Inc.*, 444 U.S. 232, 100 S.Ct. 502 (1980), because it does not describe a factual nexus between the alleged boycott and interstate commerce.

* * *

II

Congress enacted the Sherman Act in 1890. During the past century, as the dimensions and complexity of our economy have grown, the federal power over commerce, and the concomitant coverage of the Sherman Act, have experienced similar expansion. * * *

We therefore begin by noting certain propositions that are undisputed in this case. Petitioner Summit, the parent of Midway as well as of several other general hospitals, is unquestionably engaged in interstate commerce. Moreover, although Midway's primary activity is the provision of health care services in a local market, it also engages in interstate commerce. A conspiracy to prevent Midway from expanding would be covered by the Sherman Act, even though any actual impact on interstate commerce would be " 'indirect' " and " 'fortuitous.' " *Hospital Building Co. v. Rex Hospital Trustees*, 425 U.S. 738, 744, 96 S.Ct. 1848, 1852 (1976). No specific purpose to restrain interstate commerce is required. *Id.,* at 745, 96 S.Ct., at 1852. As a "matter of practical economics," *ibid.,* the effect of such a conspiracy on the hospital's "purchases of out-of-state medicines and supplies as well as its revenues from out-of-state insurance companies," *id.,* at 744, 96 S.Ct., at 1852, would establish the necessary interstate nexus.

This case does not involve the full range of activities conducted at a general hospital. Rather, this case involves the provision of ophthalmological services. It seems clear, however, that these services are regularly performed for out-of-state patients and generate revenues from out-of-state sources; their importance as part of the entire operation of the hospital is evident from the allegations of the complaint. A conspiracy to eliminate the entire ophthalmological department of the hospital, like a conspiracy to destroy the hospital itself, would unquestionably affect interstate commerce. Petitioners contend, however, that a boycott of a single surgeon has no such obvious effect because the complaint does not deny the existence of an adequate supply of other surgeons to perform all of the services that respondent's current and future patients may ever require. Petitioners argue that respondent's complaint is insufficient because there is no factual nexus between the restraint on this one surgeon's practice and interstate commerce.

There are two flaws in petitioners' argument. First, because the essence of any violation of § 1 is the illegal agreement itself—rather than the overt acts performed in furtherance of it—proper analysis focuses, not upon actual consequences, but rather upon the potential harm that would ensue if the conspiracy were successful. * * * Thus, respondent need not allege, or prove, an actual effect on interstate commerce to support federal jurisdiction.

Second, if the conspiracy alleged in the complaint is successful, " 'as a matter of practical economics' " there will be a reduction in the provision of ophthalmological services in the Los Angeles market. *McLain,* 444 U.S., at 246, 100 S.Ct., at 511 (quoting *Hospital Building Co. v. Rex Hospital Trustees,* 425 U.S., at 745, 96 S.Ct., at 1852). In cases involving horizontal agreements to fix prices or allocate territories within a single State, we have based jurisdiction on a general conclusion that the defendants' agreement "almost surely" had a marketwide impact and therefore an effect on interstate commerce, *Burke v. Ford,* 389 U.S. 320, 322, 88 S.Ct. 443, 444 (1967) (*per curiam*), or that the agreement "necessarily affect[ed]" the volume of residential sales and therefore the demand for financing and title insurance provided by out-of-state concerns. *McLain,* 444 U.S., at 246, 100 S.Ct., at 511. In the latter case, we explained:

> "To establish the jurisdictional element of a Sherman Act violation it would be sufficient for petitioners to demonstrate a substantial effect on interstate commerce generated by respondents' bokerage activity. Petitioners need not make the more particularized showing of an effect on interstate commerce caused by the alleged conspiracy to fix commission rates, or by those other aspects of respondents' activity that are alleged to be unlawful." *Id.,* at 242–243, 100 S.Ct., at 509.

Although plaintiffs in *McLain* were consumers of the conspirators' real estate brokerage services, and plaintiff in this case is a competing surgeon whose complaint identifies only himself as the victim of the alleged boycott, the same analysis applies. For if a violation of the Sherman Act occurred, the case is necessarily more significant than the fate of "just one merchant whose business is so small that his destruction makes little difference to the economy." *Klor's, Inc. v. Broadway-Hale Stores, Inc.,* 359 U.S. 207, 213, 79 S.Ct. 705, 710 (1959) (footnote omitted). The case involves an alleged restraint on the practice of ophthalmological services. The restraint was accomplished by an alleged misuse of a congressionally regulated peer review process, which respondent characterizes as the gateway that controls access to the market for his services. The gateway was closed to respondent, both at Midway and at other hospitals, because petitioners insisted upon adhering to an unnecessarily costly procedure. The competitive significance of respondent's exclusion from the market must be measured, not just by a particularized evaluation of his own practice, but rather, by a general evaluation of the impact of the restraint on other participants and potential participants in the market from which he has been excluded.

We have no doubt concerning the power of Congress to regulate a peer review process controlling access to the market for ophthalmological surgery in Los Angeles. Thus, respondent's claim that members of the peer review committee conspired with others to abuse that process and thereby deny respondent access to the market for ophthalmological services provided by general hospitals in Los Angeles has a sufficient nexus with interstate commerce to support federal jurisdiction.

The judgment of the Court of Appeals is affirmed.

[Dissenting opinion by JUSTICE SCALIA, with whom JUSTICE O'CONNOR, JUSTICE KENNEDY, and JUSTICE SOUTER join, omitted. Eds.]

The *Summit* majority emphasized that if the alleged conspiracy succeeded, the plaintiff's exclusion would have curtailed ophthalmology services in Los Angeles, which attracted out-of-state patients and generated revenues from out-of-state sources. In response, the *Summit* dissenting justices argued that the majority's rationale left few matters outside the Sherman Act's reach. Justice Scalia's dissent observed: "Federal courts are an attractive forum, and the treble damages of the Clayton Act an attractive remedy. We have today made them available for routine business torts, needlessly destroying a sensible statutory allocation of federal-state responsibility and contributing to the trivialization of the federal courts." 500 U.S. at 343 (Scalia, J., dissenting). The modest residuum of commerce that remains purely intrastate after *Summit* ordinarily is subject to scrutiny under state antitrust laws.

Perhaps the biggest surprise in *Summit Health* was that the defendant's argument for a more circumspect view of Sherman Act jurisdiction garnered the votes of four of the Justices, which may suggest that the expansive reading of the Sherman Act's jurisdiction that has endured since *Mandeville Island Farms* might still be subject to challenge in an appropriate case. What is the point of difference between the majority and dissent? One explanation may lie in their differing views of the relevant "jurisdictional nexus"—the relationship between the challenged conduct and interstate commerce. Should the "nexus" issue be answered through reference to the general activities of the defendants, or solely through reference to the anticompetitive consequences of the unlawful conduct? Which approach did the majority use? Would use of a different approach have resulted in a different outcome? *See generally* Andrew I. Gavil, *Reconstructing the Jurisdictional Foundation of Antitrust Federalism*, 61 GEO. WASH. L. REV. 657 (1993) (discussing *Summit Health*).

More broadly, what are Justice Scalia's concerns, reflected in his assertion that federal courts are "an attractive forum," that treble damages is "an attractive remedy," and that federal courts should not be available for the prosecution of "routine business torts"? Is he concerned that broad jurisdictional principles invite the filing of anemic antitrust claims and increase the chance of false positives? Did the Court majority express similar concerns in *Trinko* (Chapter 4) and *Twombly* (Chapters 1 and 3)?

2.   FOREIGN JURISDICTIONAL BARRIERS

With increasing frequency, antitrust disputes involve the extraterritorial reach of the U.S. antitrust statutes. The Sherman Act applies to conduct that restrains trade or commerce "among the several States, or with foreign nations." Cases interpreting this limitation generally have concluded that the antitrust laws ordinarily do not apply to conduct by U.S. companies or foreign firms outside the United States, when such conduct neither affects consumers or markets in the United States nor restricts export opportunities for U.S. firms.

The current state of extraterritorial jurisdiction, however, developed over the course of much of the twentieth century. In its first consideration of the issue in *American Banana Co. v. United Fruit Co.*, 213 U.S. 347 (1909), the Supreme Court embraced a very narrow, territorial view of the Sherman Act's jurisdiction over foreign conduct: "[T]he general and almost universal rule is that the character of an act as lawful or unlawful must be determined wholly by the law of the country where the act was done." *Id.* at 356. In so holding, the Court, consistent with the then contemporary views of the limits of subject matter and personal jurisdiction, did not admit of the possibility that conduct outside U.S. borders that causes ill effects within its borders could give rise to jurisdiction.

With the expansion of international commerce and the erosion of territorial notions of jurisdiction domestically, *cf. International Shoe Co. v. Washington*, 326 U.S. 310 (1945) (adopting "minimum contacts" test for personal jurisdiction), the courts began to move away from the doctrine of *American Banana*. In what became the most significant symbol of that movement, the now familiar "effects doctrine" emerged in *United States v. Aluminum Co. of Am.*, 148 F.2d 416 (2d Cir. 1945) ("*Alcoa*"). Rejecting the rule of territoriality that controlled in *American Banana*, *Alcoa* instead held that foreign conduct having effects on U.S. import commerce indeed fell within the reach of the Sherman Act: "any state may impose liabilities, even upon persons not within its allegiance, for conduct outside its borders that has consequences within its borders which the state reprehends." *Id.* at 443. *See also* U.S. Dep't of Justice and Federal Trade Comm'n, *Antitrust Enforcement Guidelines for International Operations* § 3.1 (1995) (endorsing effects doctrine).

As we shall see in *Hartford Fire*, *Alcoa's* "effects doctrine" is now more generally accepted. But for a time it triggered a great deal of controversy internationally. Some of that controversy stemmed from foreign reactions to the substance of U.S. antitrust prohibitions, especially the notion that some Sherman Act violations might be prosecuted criminally. Foreign authorities also reacted with hostility to the liberal scope of U.S. discovery, the availability of class actions, the prospect of large scale treble damages, and the notion that recovery of attorney's fees could be limited to prevailing plaintiffs. As we shall see immediately below in connection with *Hartford Fire*, these tensions led to calls for the recognition by U.S. courts of principles of "comity" to moderate the impact of U.S. antitrust jurisdiction over extraterritorial conduct. Today, however, the effects doctrine is more widely recognized and has been endorsed by the EU. *See, e.g.*, Cases 89/85, *A. Ahlstrom Osakeyhtio v. Commission*, 1988 E.C.R. 5193 ("*Wood Pulp*").

After decades of heightening controversy over the operation of *Alcoa's* effects test, Congress acted in 1982 to codify U.S. antitrust jurisdictional principles in the Foreign Trade Antitrust Improvements Act of 1982 ("FTAIA"), 15 U.S.C. § 6a. The FTAIA excluded from the jurisdiction of the U.S. antitrust laws conduct "involving trade or commerce (other than import trade or import commerce) with foreign nations unless (1) such conduct has a direct, substantial and reasonably foreseeable effect (A) on [domestic or import commerce], or (B) on export trade or export commerce * * * of a person engaged in such commerce in the United States." 15 U.S.C. § 6a. Claimants who base jurisdiction on subclause (B) must show that the conduct involves "injury to export business in the United States." As we shall see in the three cases that follow, however, the full meaning of the FTAIA's convoluted language remains a source of some uncertainty in the courts. The language and the legislative history of the Act strongly suggest that it was intended to promote U.S. exports by precluding the exercise of U.S. jurisdiction over U.S. firms engaged in foreign commerce when the only injured parties are foreign firms or consumers. But other significant issues of interpretation have arisen.

a. Comity

Several judge-made doctrines limit the application of the U.S. antitrust statutes to transnational business activity. Since the mid-1970s, American courts sometimes have used the doctrine of *comity* in determining whether to apply the antitrust laws extraterritorially where doing so might damage relations between the United States and foreign governments. Where the law of the defendant's home country conflicts with the U.S. antitrust laws, courts will balance foreign interests against U.S. interests in deciding whether to exercise jurisdiction. *See, e.g., Timberlane Lumber Co. v. Bank of America*, 549 F.2d 597 (9th Cir. 1976).

In *Hartford Fire Ins. Co. v. California*, 509 U.S. 764, 113 S.Ct. 2891 (1993), the Supreme Court considered whether principles of international comity should preclude the exercise of jurisdiction over British reinsurance companies who were alleged to have conspired with American insurance companies to limit certain forms of insurance coverage. It also considered the relationship between the "substantial effects" doctrine of *Alcoa* and the "direct, substantial and reasonably foreseeable effects" standard of the FTAIA.

HARTFORD FIRE INSURANCE CO. V. CALIFORNIA

Supreme Court of the United States, 1993.
509 U.S. 764, 113 S.Ct. 2891, 125 L.Ed.2d 612.

SOUTER, J., announced the judgment of the Court and delivered the opinion for a unanimous Court with respect to Parts I and II–A, the opinion of the Court with respect to Parts III and IV, in which REHNQUIST, C.J., and WHITE, BLACKMUN, and STEVENS, JJ., joined, and an opinion concurring in the judgment with respect to Part II–B, in which WHITE, BLACKMUN, and STEVENS, JJ., joined. SCALIA, J., delivered the opinion of the Court with respect to Part I, in which REHNQUIST, C.J., and O'CONNOR, KENNEDY, and THOMAS, JJ., joined, and a dissenting opinion with respect to Part II, in which O'CONNOR, KENNEDY, and THOMAS, JJ., joined.

The Sherman Act makes every contract, combination, or conspiracy in unreasonable restraint of interstate or foreign commerce illegal. These consolidated cases present questions about the application of that Act to the insurance industry, both here and abroad. The plaintiffs (respondents here) allege that both domestic and foreign defendants (petitioners here) violated the Sherman Act by engaging in various conspiracies to affect the American insurance market. A group of domestic defendants argues that the McCarran-Ferguson Act, 59 Stat. 33, as amended, 15 U.S.C. § 1011 *et seq.*, precludes application of the Sherman Act to the conduct alleged; a group of foreign defendants argues that the principle of international comity requires the District Court to refrain from exercising jurisdiction over certain claims against it. We hold that most of the domestic defendants' alleged conduct is not immunized from antitrust liability by the McCarran-Ferguson Act, and that, even assuming it applies, the principle of international comity does not preclude District Court jurisdiction over the foreign conduct alleged.

I

The two petitions before us stem from consolidated litigation comprising the complaints of 19 States and many private plaintiffs alleging that the defendants, members of the insurance industry, conspired in violation of § 1 of the Sherman Act to restrict the terms of coverage of commercial general liability (CGL) insurance available in the United

States. Because the cases come to us on motions to dismiss, we take the allegations of the complaints as true.

According to the complaints, the object of the conspiracies was to force certain primary insurers (insurers who sell insurance directly to consumers) to change the terms of their standard CGL insurance policies to conform with the policies the defendant insurers wanted to sell. The defendants wanted four changes.

First, CGL insurance has traditionally been sold in the United States on an "occurrence" basis, through a policy obligating the insurer "to pay or defend claims, whenever made, resulting from an accident or 'injurious exposure to conditions' that occurred during the [specific time] period the policy was in effect." In place of this traditional "occurrence" trigger of coverage, the defendants wanted a "claims-made" trigger, obligating the insurer to pay or defend only those claims made during the policy period. Such a policy has the distinct advantage for the insurer that when the policy period ends without a claim having been made, the insurer can be certain that the policy will not expose it to any further liability. Second, the defendants wanted the "claims-made" policy to have a "retroactive date" provision, which would further restrict coverage to claims based on incidents that occurred after a certain date. Such a provision eliminates the risk that an insurer, by issuing a claims-made policy, would assume liability arising from incidents that occurred before the policy's effective date, but remained undiscovered or caused no immediate harm. Third, CGL insurance has traditionally covered "sudden and accidental" pollution; the defendants wanted to eliminate that coverage. Finally, CGL insurance has traditionally provided that the insurer would bear the legal costs of defending covered claims against the insured without regard to the policy's stated limits of coverage; the defendants wanted legal defense costs to be counted against the stated limits (providing a "legal defense cost cap").

To understand how the defendants are alleged to have pressured the targeted primary insurers to make these changes, one must be aware of two important features of the insurance industry. First, most primary insurers rely on certain outside support services for the type of insurance coverage they wish to sell. Defendant Insurance Services Office, Inc. (ISO), an association of approximately 1,400 domestic property and casualty insurers (including the primary insurer defendants, Hartford Fire Insurance Company, Allstate Insurance Company, CIGNA Corporation, and Aetna Casualty and Surety Company), is the almost exclusive source of support services in this country for CGL insurance. ISO develops standard policy forms and files or lodges them with each State's insurance regulators; most CGL insurance written in the United States is written on these forms. All of the "traditional" features of CGL insurance relevant to this litigation were embodied in the ISO standard CGL insurance form that had been in use since 1973 (1973 ISO CGL form). For each of its standard policy forms, ISO also supplies actuarial and rating information: it collects, aggregates, interprets, and distributes data on the premiums charged, claims filed and paid, and defense costs expended with respect to each form, and on the basis of this data it predicts future loss trends and calculates advisory premium rates. Most ISO members cannot afford to continue to use a form if ISO withdraws these support services.

Second, primary insurers themselves usually purchase insurance to cover a portion of the risk they assume from the consumer. This so-called "reinsurance" may serve at least two purposes, protecting the primary insurer from catastrophic loss, and allowing the primary insurer to sell more insurance than its own financial capacity might otherwise permit. Thus, "[t]he availability of reinsurance affects the ability and willingness of primary insurers to provide insurance to their customers." Insurers who sell reinsurance themselves often purchase insurance to cover part of the risk they assume from the primary insurer; such "retrocessional reinsurance" does for reinsurers what reinsurance does for primary insurers. Many of the defendants here are reinsurers or reinsurance brokers, or play some other specialized role in the reinsurance business; defendant Reinsurance Association of America (RAA) is a trade association of domestic reinsurers.

The prehistory of events claimed to give rise to liability starts in 1977, when ISO began the process of revising its 1973 CGL form. For the first time, it proposed two CGL forms (1984 ISO CGL forms), one the traditional "occurrence" type, the other "with a new 'claims-made' trigger." The "claims-made" form did not have a retroactive date provision, however, and both 1984 forms covered " 'sudden and accidental pollution' " damage and provided for unlimited coverage of legal defense costs by the insurer. Within the ISO, defendant Hartford Fire Insurance Company objected to the proposed 1984 forms; it desired elimination of the "occurrence" form, a retroactive date provision on the "claims-made" form, elimination of sudden and accidental pollution coverage, and a legal defense cost cap. Defendant Allstate Insurance Company also expressed its desire for a retroactive date provision on the "claims-made" form. Majorities in the relevant ISO committees, however, supported the proposed 1984 CGL forms and rejected the changes proposed by Hartford and Allstate. In December 1983, the ISO Board of Directors approved the proposed 1984 forms, and ISO filed or lodged the forms with state regulators in March 1984.

Dissatisfied with this state of affairs, the defendants began to take other steps to force a change in the terms of coverage of CGL insurance generally available, steps that, the plaintiffs allege, implemented a series of conspiracies in violation of § 1 of the Sherman Act. * * *

* * *

II

* * *

[The Court concluded that the McCarran-Ferguson Act did not confer antitrust immunity upon the insurance-related activities at issue in the plaintiffs' claims. Eds.]

III

* * * [W]e take up the question * * * whether certain claims against the London reinsurers should have been dismissed as improper applications of the Sherman Act to foreign conduct. The Fifth Claim for Relief in the California Complaint alleges a violation of § 1 of the Sherman Act by certain London reinsurers who conspired to coerce primary insurers in the United States to offer CGL coverage on a claims-made basis, thereby making "occurrence CGL coverage * * * unavailable in the State of California for many risks." The Sixth Claim for Relief in the California Complaint alleges that the London reinsurers violated § 1 by a conspiracy to limit coverage of pollution risks in North America, thereby rendering "pollution liability coverage * * * almost entirely unavailable for the vast majority of casualty insurance purchasers in the State of California." The Eighth Claim for Relief in the California Complaint alleges a further § 1 violation by the London reinsurers who, along with domestic retrocessional reinsurers, conspired to limit coverage of seepage, pollution, and property contamination risks in North America, thereby eliminating such coverage in the State of California.

At the outset, we note that the District Court undoubtedly had jurisdiction of these Sherman Act claims, as the London reinsurers apparently concede. * * * Although the proposition was perhaps not always free from doubt, [citing *American Banana*], it is well established by now that the Sherman Act applies to foreign conduct that was meant to produce and did in fact produce some substantial effect in the United States [citing *Alcoa*, *Matsushita* and other authorities]. Such is the conduct alleged here: that the London reinsurers engaged in unlawful conspiracies to affect the market for insurance in the United States and that their conduct in fact produced substantial effect.[1]

---

[1]   Under § 402 of the Foreign Trade Antitrust Improvements Act of 1982 (FTAIA), the Sherman Act does not apply to conduct involving foreign trade or commerce, other than import trade or import commerce, unless "such conduct has a direct, substantial, and reasonably foreseeable effect" on domestic or import commerce. The FTAIA was intended to exempt from the Sherman Act export transactions that did not injure the United States economy, and it is unclear how it might apply to the conduct alleged here. Also unclear is whether the Act's "direct, substantial, and reasonably foreseeable effect" standard amends existing law or merely codifies it. We need not address these questions here. Assuming that the FTAIA's standard affects this litigation, and assuming further that that standard differs from the prior law, the conduct alleged plainly meets its requirements.

According to the London reinsurers, the District Court should have declined to exercise such jurisdiction under the principle of international comity. The Court of Appeals agreed that courts should look to that principle in deciding whether to exercise jurisdiction under the Sherman Act. This availed the London reinsurers nothing, however. To be sure, the Court of Appeals believed that "application of [American] antitrust laws to the London reinsurance market 'would lead to significant conflict with English law and policy,'" and that "[s]uch a conflict, unless outweighed by other factors, would by itself be reason to decline exercise of jurisdiction." But other factors, in the court's view, including the London reinsurers' express purpose to affect United States commerce and the substantial nature of the effect produced, outweighed the supposed conflict and required the exercise of jurisdiction in this litigation.

When it enacted the FTAIA, Congress expressed no view on the question whether a court with Sherman Act jurisdiction should ever decline to exercise such jurisdiction on grounds of international comity. See H.R. Rep. No. 97–686, p. 13 (1982) ("If a court determines that the requirements for subject matter jurisdiction are met, [the FTAIA] would have no effect on the court['s] ability to employ notions of comity * * * or otherwise to take account of the international character of the transaction") (citing *Timberlane* [*Timberlane Lumber Co. v. Bank of America, N.T. & S.A.*, 549 F.2d 597 (1976). Eds.]). We need not decide that question here, however, for even assuming that in a proper case a court may decline to exercise Sherman Act jurisdiction over foreign conduct (or, as Justice Scalia would put it, may conclude by the employment of comity analysis in the first instance that there is no jurisdiction), international comity would not counsel against exercising jurisdiction in the circumstances alleged here.

The only substantial question in this litigation is whether "there is in fact a true conflict between domestic and foreign law." The London reinsurers contend that applying the Act to their conduct would conflict significantly with British law, and the British Government, appearing before us as *amicus curiae,* concurs. They assert that Parliament has established a comprehensive regulatory regime over the London reinsurance market and that the conduct alleged here was perfectly consistent with British law and policy. But this is not to state a conflict. "[T]he fact that conduct is lawful in the state in which it took place will not, of itself, bar application of the United States antitrust laws," even where the foreign state has a strong policy to permit or encourage such conduct. Restatement (Third) Foreign Relations Law § 415, Comment *j*. No conflict exists, for these purposes, "where a person subject to regulation by two states can comply with the laws of both." Restatement (Third) Foreign Relations Law § 403, Comment *e*. Since the London reinsurers do not argue that British law requires them to act in some fashion prohibited by the law of the United States * * * or claim that their compliance with the laws of both countries is otherwise impossible, we see no conflict with British law. See Restatement (Third) Foreign Relations Law § 403, Comment *e*, § 415, Comment *j*. We have no need in this litigation to address other considerations that might inform a decision to refrain from the exercise of jurisdiction on grounds of international comity.

* * *

Although the Court notes that in adopting the FTAIA Congress expressed no view about whether an American court should decline to exercise Sherman Act jurisdiction on comity grounds, *Hartford* said American courts should consider doing so only where American law and foreign law truly *conflict*. The British reinsurance firms argued that such a conflict existed because their activities were legal under British law. Stating that "[n]o conflict exists 'where a person subject to regulation by two states can comply with the laws of both,'" the Court ruled that a conflict would exist only if the British law compelled the behavior in question. Without a conflict, there was "no need to address other considerations that might inform a decision to refrain from the exercise of jurisdiction on grounds of international comity." What is the impact of this approach on the role of comity?

As early as the late 1950s, noted commentator Kingman Brewster, Jr. advocated a greater role for comity in the form of a "jurisdictional rule of reason" that could serve as an antidote to the broad assertion by U.S. courts of effects-based antitrust jurisdiction. *See* KINGMAN BREWSTER, JR., ANTITRUST AND AMERICAN BUSINESS ABROAD 446 (1958). One commentator has observed, however, that Brewster, and later courts such as the Ninth Circuit in *Timberlane*, were responding in part to the perceived hostility of foreign nations unaccustomed to and unaccepting of U.S. antitrust laws. Today antitrust laws—and the effects doctrine—are more widely accepted, and national antitrust prosecutors are more sensitive to the international ramifications of their enforcement decisions. These and other factors suggest that *Hartford Fire's* decision to limit the role of comity may in part be a function of changing times, in which more energy has been turned to convergence and harmonization than comity. *See* Spencer Weber Waller, *The Twilight of Comity*, 38 COLUM. J. TRANSNAT'L L. 563 (2000). *See also* Eleanor Fox, *National Law, Global Markets, and* Hartford: *Eyes Wide Shut*, 68 ANTITRUST L.J. 73 (2000) (arguing that *Hartford Fire*, the U.S. Guidelines for International Operations, and the relevant EU authorities all suffer from an insufficiently global perspective).

On the other hand, *Hartford* may also reflect a more basic and traditional competing line of thought: that once a court determines that

Congress has granted it jurisdiction to entertain an antitrust controversy, it lacks the authority to decline to exercise that jurisdiction on grounds of "comity." *See, e.g., Laker Airways Ltd. v. Sabena, Belgian World Airlines*, 731 F.2d 909 (D.C. Cir. 1984):

> [B]oth institutional limitations on the judicial process and Constitutional restrictions on the exercise of judicial power make it unacceptable for the Judiciary to seize the political initiative and determine that legitimate application of American laws must evaporate when challenged by a foreign jurisdiction.

731 F.2d at 954. *See generally* Michael Sennett & Andrew I. Gavil, *Antitrust Jurisdiction, Extraterritorial Conduct and Interest-Balancing*, 19 INT'L LAW. 1185 (1985) (discussing conflict between *Timberlane* and *Laker Airways*). By focusing on "conflict" as a prerequisite to any discussion of comity, *Hartford Fire* left this more structural question for another day. Arguably, by acting through FTAIA to define more specifically U.S. court jurisdiction over extraterritorial conduct, and by doing so without directing courts to moderate their exercise of the jurisdiction granted through the discretionary exercise of comity analysis, Congress has implicitly rejected such a role for courts.

b. The Substantial Effects Test: Sorting out the Relationship Between *Hartford Fire* and the FTAIA

As we learned in the previous section, under *McLain* and *Summit Health*, the jurisdictional threshold for domestic antitrust violations is relatively minimal—all that need be alleged is that the challenged conduct *affected* interstate commerce. Although cases like *Alcoa* were perceived as expanding U.S. antitrust jurisdiction through the effects doctrine, they imposed a more elevated jurisdictional standard on foreign conduct than did the domestic cases like *McLain*. As *Hartford Fire* formulated the standard, in order to assert U.S. antitrust jurisdiction over foreign conduct, that conduct must "produce some substantial effect in the United States." Other lower courts argued that general effects on domestic commerce alone would not suffice—the illegal conduct itself had to produce substantial domestic *anticompetitive* effects. *See Nat'l Bank of Canada v. Interbank Card Ass'n*, 666 F.2d 6, 8 (2d Cir. 1981). FTAIA selected yet a different formulation, but as the Court in *Hartford Fire* observed, it was not clear whether FTAIA simply codified prior case law or sought to change it. *Hartford Fire*, 509 U.S. at 796 n.23.

The international vitamin cartel, first discussed early in Chapter 1, led to a significant number of private class actions, including actions brought on behalf of foreign plaintiffs allegedly injured by the cartel's price-fixing activities. In one of those cases, the Supreme Court appeared to resolve a conflict in the circuits that had developed regarding the ability of foreign plaintiffs to sue in U.S. courts under the Sherman Act for injuries suffered abroad. In doing so, it provided additional guidance on the interpretation of FTAIA.

F. HOFFMANN-LA ROCHE LTD. V. EMPAGRAN S.A.

Supreme Court of the United States, 2004.
542 U.S. 155, 124 S.Ct. 2359, 159 L.Ed.2d 226.

JUSTICE BREYER delivered the opinion of the Court.

* * *

We here focus upon anticompetitive price-fixing activity that is in significant part foreign, that causes some domestic antitrust injury, and that independently causes separate foreign injury. We ask two questions about the price-fixing conduct and the foreign injury that it causes. First, does that conduct fall within the FTAIA's general rule excluding the Sherman Act's application? That is to say, does the price-fixing activity constitute "conduct involving trade or commerce . . . with foreign nations"? We conclude that it does.

Second, we ask whether the conduct nonetheless falls within a domestic-injury exception to the general rule, an exception that applies (and makes the Sherman Act nonetheless applicable) where the conduct (1) has a "direct, substantial, and reasonably foreseeable effect" on domestic commerce, and (2) "such effect gives rise to a [Sherman Act] claim." §§ 6a(1)(A), (2). We conclude that the exception does not apply where the plaintiff's claim rests solely on the independent foreign harm.

* * *

I

The plaintiffs in this case originally filed a class-action suit on behalf of foreign and domestic purchasers of vitamins under, *inter alia,* § 1 of the Sherman Act and §§ 4 and 16 of the Clayton Act. The complaint alleged that petitioners, foreign and domestic vitamin manufacturers and distributors, had engaged in a price-fixing conspiracy, raising the price of vitamin products to customers in the United States and to customers in foreign countries.

As relevant here, petitioners moved to dismiss the suit as to the *foreign* purchasers (the respondents here), five foreign vitamin distributors located in Ukraine, Australia, Ecuador, and Panama, each of which bought vitamins from petitioners for delivery outside the United States. * * * Respondents have never asserted that they purchased any vitamins in the United States or in transactions in United States commerce, and the question presented assumes that the relevant "transactions occurr[ed] entirely outside U.S. commerce." The District Court dismissed their claims.

It applied the FTAIA and found none of the exceptions applicable. Thereafter, the *domestic* purchasers transferred their claims to another pending suit and did not take part in the subsequent appeal.

A divided panel of the Court of Appeals reversed. The panel concluded that the FTAIA's general exclusionary rule applied to the case, but that its domestic-injury exception also applied. It basically read the plaintiffs' complaint to allege that the vitamin manufacturers' price-fixing conspiracy (1) had "a direct, substantial, and reasonably foreseeable effect" on ordinary domestic trade or commerce, *i.e.*, the conspiracy brought about higher domestic vitamin prices, and (2) "such effect" gave "rise to a [Sherman Act] claim," *i.e.*, an injured *domestic* customer could have brought a Sherman Act suit. Those allegations, the court held, are sufficient to meet the exception's requirements.

The court assumed that the foreign effect, *i.e.*, higher prices in Ukraine, Panama, Australia, and Ecuador, was independent of the domestic effect, *i.e.*, higher domestic prices. But it concluded that, in light of the FTAIA's text, legislative history, and the policy goal of deterring harmful price-fixing activity, this lack of connection does not matter. * * *

We granted certiorari to resolve a split among the Courts of Appeals about the exception's application. Compare *Den Norske Stats Oljeselskap As v. HeereMac Vof*, 241 F.3d 420, 427 (C.A.5 2001) (exception does not apply where foreign injury independent of domestic harm), with *Kruman v. Christie's Int'l PLC*, 284 F.3d 384, 400 (C.A.2 2002) (exception does apply even where foreign injury independent) * * *.

II

The FTAIA seeks to make clear to American exporters (and to firms doing business abroad) that the Sherman Act does not prevent them from entering into business arrangements (say, joint-selling arrangements), however anticompetitive, as long as those arrangements adversely affect only foreign markets. See H.R.Rep. No. 97–686, pp. 1–3, 9–10 (1982), U.S.Code Cong. & Admin.News 1982, 2487, 2487–2488, 2494–2495 (hereinafter House Report). It does so by removing from the Sherman Act's reach, (1) export activities and (2) other commercial activities taking place abroad, *unless* those activities adversely affect domestic commerce, imports to the United States, or exporting activities of one engaged in such activities within the United States.

* * *

[The FTAIA's] * * * technical language initially lays down a general rule placing *all* (non-import) activity involving foreign commerce outside the Sherman Act's reach. It then brings such conduct back within the Sherman Act's reach *provided that* the conduct *both* (1) sufficiently affects American commerce, *i.e.*, it has a "direct, substantial, and reasonably foreseeable effect" on American domestic, import, or (certain) export commerce, *and* (2) has an effect of a kind that antitrust law considers harmful, *i.e.*, the "effect" must "giv[e] rise to a [Sherman Act] claim."

We ask here how this language applies to price-fixing activity that is in significant part foreign, that has the requisite domestic effect, and that also has independent foreign effects giving rise to the plaintiff's claim.

III

Respondents make a threshold argument. They say that the transactions here at issue fall outside the FTAIA because the FTAIA's general exclusionary rule applies only to conduct involving exports. The rule says that the Sherman Act "shall not apply to conduct involving trade or commerce (other than import trade or import commerce) *with* foreign nations." § 6a (emphasis added). The word "with" means *between* the United States and foreign nations. And, they contend, commerce between the United States and foreign nations that is not import commerce must consist of export commerce—a kind of commerce irrelevant to the case at hand.

The difficulty with respondents' argument is that the FTAIA originated in a bill that initially referred only to "export trade or export commerce." But the House Judiciary Committee subsequently changed that language to "trade or commerce (other than import trade or import commerce)." And it did so deliberately to include commerce that did not involve American exports but which was wholly foreign. * * *

For those who find legislative history useful, the House Report's account should end the matter. Others, by considering carefully the amendment itself and the lack of any other plausible purpose, may reach the same conclusion, namely that the FTAIA's general rule applies where the anticompetitive conduct at issue is foreign.

IV

We turn now to the basic question presented, that of the exception's application. Because the underlying antitrust action is complex, potentially raising questions not directly at issue here, we reemphasize that we base our decision upon the following: The price-fixing conduct significantly and adversely affects both customers outside the United States and customers within the United States, but the adverse foreign effect is independent of any adverse domestic effect. In these circumstances, we find that the FTAIA exception does not apply (and thus the Sherman Act does not apply) for two main reasons.

First, this Court ordinarily construes ambiguous statutes to avoid unreasonable interference with the sovereign authority of other nations. This rule of construction reflects principles of customary international law—law that (we must assume) Congress ordinarily seeks to follow.

This rule of statutory construction cautions courts to assume that legislators take account of the legitimate sovereign interests of other nations when they write American laws. It thereby helps the potentially conflicting laws of different nations work together in harmony—a harmony particularly needed in today's highly interdependent commercial world.

No one denies that America's antitrust laws, when applied to foreign conduct, can interfere with a foreign nation's ability independently to regulate its own commercial affairs. But our courts have long held that application of our antitrust laws to foreign anticompetitive conduct is nonetheless reasonable, and hence consistent with principles of prescriptive comity, insofar as they reflect a legislative effort to redress *domestic* antitrust injury that foreign anticompetitive conduct has caused.

But why is it reasonable to apply those laws to foreign conduct *insofar as that conduct causes independent foreign harm and that foreign harm alone gives rise to the plaintiff's claim?* Like the former case, application of those laws creates a serious risk of interference with a foreign nation's ability independently to regulate its own commercial affairs. But, unlike the former case, the justification for that interference seems insubstantial. Why should American law supplant, for example, Canada's or Great Britain's or Japan's own determination about how best to protect Canadian or British or Japanese customers from anticompetitive conduct engaged in significant part by Canadian or British or Japanese or other foreign companies?

We recognize that principles of comity provide Congress greater leeway when it seeks to control through legislation the actions of *American* companies, and some of the anticompetitive price-fixing conduct alleged here took place in *America*. But the higher foreign prices of which the foreign plaintiffs here complain are not the consequence of any domestic anticompetitive conduct *that Congress sought to forbid,* for Congress did not seek to forbid any such conduct insofar as it is here relevant, *i.e.,* insofar as it is intertwined with foreign conduct that causes independent foreign harm. Rather Congress sought to *release* domestic (and foreign) anticompetitive conduct from Sherman Act constraints when that conduct causes foreign harm. Congress, of course, did make an exception where that conduct also causes domestic harm. But any independent domestic harm the foreign conduct causes here has, by definition, little or nothing to do with the matter.

We thus repeat the basic question: Why is it reasonable to apply this law to conduct that is significantly foreign *insofar as that conduct causes independent foreign harm and that foreign harm alone gives rise to the plaintiff's claim?* We can find no good answer to the question.

The Areeda and Hovenkamp treatise notes that under the Court of Appeals' interpretation of the statute "a Malaysian customer could . . . maintain an action under United States law in a United States court against its own Malaysian supplier, another cartel member, simply by noting that unnamed third parties injured [in the United States] by the American [cartel member's] conduct would also have a cause of action. Effectively, the United States courts would provide worldwide subject matter jurisdiction to any foreign suitor wishing to sue its own local supplier, but unhappy with its own sovereign's provisions for private antitrust enforcement, provided that a different plaintiff had a cause of action against a different firm for injuries that were within U.S. [other-than-import] commerce. It does not seem excessively rigid to infer that Congress would not have intended that result." P. Areeda & H. Hovenkamp, Antitrust Law ¶ 273, pp. 51–52 (Supp.2003).

We agree with the comment. We can find no convincing justification for the extension of the Sherman Act's scope that it describes.

Respondents reply that many nations have adopted antitrust laws similar to our own, to the point where the practical likelihood of interference with the relevant interests of other nations is minimal. Leaving price fixing to the side, however, this Court has found to the contrary. [citing *Hartford Fire*.]

Regardless, even where nations agree about primary conduct, say price fixing, they disagree dramatically about appropriate remedies. The application, for example, of American private treble-damages remedies to anticompetitive conduct taking place abroad has generated considerable controversy. And several foreign nations have filed briefs here arguing that to apply our remedies would unjustifiably permit their citizens to bypass their own less generous remedial schemes, thereby upsetting a balance of competing considerations that their own domestic antitrust laws embody.

These briefs add that a decision permitting independently injured foreign plaintiffs to pursue private treble-damages remedies would undermine foreign nations' own antitrust enforcement policies by diminishing foreign firms' incentive to cooperate with antitrust authorities in return for prosecutorial amnesty.

Respondents alternatively argue that comity does not demand an interpretation of the FTAIA that would exclude independent foreign injury cases *across the board*. Rather, courts can take (and sometimes have taken) account of comity considerations case by case, abstaining where comity considerations so dictate.

In our view, however, this approach is too complex to prove workable. The Sherman Act covers many different kinds of anticompetitive agreements. Courts would have to examine how foreign law, compared with American law, treats not only price fixing but also, say, information-sharing agreements, patent-licensing price conditions, territorial product resale limitations, and various forms of joint venture, in respect to both primary conduct and remedy. The legally and economically technical nature of that enterprise means lengthier proceedings, appeals, and more proceedings—to the point where procedural costs and delays could themselves threaten interference with a foreign nation's ability to maintain the integrity of its own antitrust enforcement system. Even in this relatively simple price-fixing case, for example, competing briefs tell us (1) that potential treble-damage liability would help enforce widespread anti-price-fixing norms (through added deterrence) and (2) the opposite, namely that such liability would hinder antitrust enforcement (by reducing incentives to enter amnesty programs). How could a court seriously interested in resolving so empirical a matter—a matter potentially related to impact on foreign interests—do so simply and expeditiously?

We conclude that principles of prescriptive comity counsel against the Court of Appeals' interpretation of the FTAIA. Where foreign anticompetitive conduct plays a significant role and where foreign injury is independent of domestic effects, Congress might have hoped that America's antitrust laws, so fundamental a component of our own economic system, would commend themselves to other nations as well. But, if America's antitrust policies could not win their own way in the international marketplace for such ideas, Congress, we must assume, would not have tried to impose them, in an act of legal imperialism, through legislative fiat.

Second, the FTAIA's language and history suggest that Congress designed the FTAIA to clarify, perhaps to limit, but not *to expand* in any significant way, the Sherman Act's scope as applied to foreign commerce. And we have found no significant indication that at the time Congress wrote this statute courts would have thought the Sherman Act applicable in these circumstances.

[Here the Court first noted that "the Solicitor General and petitioners tell us that they have found no case in which any court applied the Sherman Act to redress foreign injury in such circumstances," and then discussed and distinguished six cases cited by respondents in reply. First, the Court deemed it significant that the U.S. government was the plaintiff in three of the cited decisions—previous opinions of the Supreme Court—noting that "A Government plaintiff, unlike a private plaintiff, must seek to obtain the relief necessary to protect the public from further anticompetitive conduct and to redress anticompetitive harm. And a Government plaintiff has legal authority broad enough to allow it to carry out this mission." In such cases, the government obtained relief that "might have helped to protect those injured abroad." But, according to the Court, that "tells us little or nothing about whether this Court would have awarded similar relief at the request of private plaintiffs." Moreover, the

Court argued, "[n]either did the Court focus explicitly in its opinions on a claim that the remedies sought to cure only independently caused foreign harm. Thus the three cases tell us even less about whether this Court then thought that foreign private plaintiffs could have obtained foreign relief based solely upon such independently caused foreign injury."

The Court distinguished the other three cases cited—all lower court cases—on the grounds that they either involved mixed domestic and foreign harm, and not solely "independent" foreign harm, or simply did not squarely address the issue of jurisdiction over solely foreign harm. The Court concluded, therefore, that "no pre-1982 case provides significant authority for application of the Sherman Act in the circumstances we here assume." Eds.]

Taken together, these two sets of considerations, the one derived from comity and the other reflecting history, convince us that Congress would not have intended the FTAIA's exception to bring independently caused foreign injury within the Sherman Act's reach.

V

Respondents point to several considerations that point the other way. For one thing, the FTAIA's language speaks in terms of the Sherman Act's *applicability* to certain kinds of *conduct*. The FTAIA says that the Sherman Act applies to foreign "conduct" with a certain kind of harmful domestic effect. Why isn't that the end of the matter? How can the Sherman Act both *apply to the conduct* when one person sues but *not apply to the same conduct* when another person sues? The question of who can or cannot sue is a matter for other statutes (namely, the Clayton Act) to determine.

Moreover, the exception says that it applies if the conduct's domestic effect gives rise to "*a claim*," not to "*the plaintiff's claim*" or "*the claim at issue.*" The alleged conduct here did have domestic effects, and those effects were harmful enough to give rise to "a" claim. Respondents concede that this claim is not their own claim; it is someone else's claim. But, linguistically speaking, they say, that is beside the point. Nor did Congress place the relevant words "gives rise to a claim" in the FTAIA to suggest any geographical limitation; rather it did so for a here neutral reason, namely, in order to make clear that the domestic effect must be an *adverse* (as opposed to a beneficial) effect.

Despite their linguistic logic, these arguments are not convincing. Linguistically speaking, a statute can apply and not apply to the same conduct, depending upon other circumstances; and those other circumstances may include the nature of the lawsuit (or of the related underlying harm). It also makes linguistic sense to read the words "a claim" as if they refer to the "plaintiff's claim" or "the claim at issue."

At most, respondents' linguistic arguments might show that respondents' reading is the more natural reading of the statutory language. But those arguments do not show that we *must* accept that reading. And that is the critical point. The considerations previously mentioned—those of comity and history—make clear that the respondents' reading is not consistent with the FTAIA's basic intent. If the statute's language reasonably permits an interpretation consistent with that intent, we should adopt it. And, for the reasons stated, we believe that the statute's language permits the reading that we give it.

Finally, respondents point to policy considerations that we have previously discussed, namely, that application of the Sherman Act in present circumstances will (through increased deterrence) help protect Americans against foreign-caused anticompetitive injury. As we have explained, however, the plaintiffs and supporting enforcement-agency *amici* have made important experience-backed arguments (based upon amnesty-seeking incentives) to the contrary. We cannot say whether, on balance, respondents' side of this empirically based argument or the enforcement agencies' side is correct. But we can say that the answer to the dispute is neither clear enough, nor of such likely empirical significance, that it could overcome the considerations we have previously discussed and change our conclusion.

* * *

VI

We have assumed that the anticompetitive conduct here independently caused foreign injury; that is, the conduct's domestic effects did not help to bring about that foreign injury. Respondents argue, in the alternative, that the foreign injury was not independent. Rather, they say, the anticompetitive conduct's domestic effects were linked to that foreign harm. Respondents contend that, because vitamins are fungible and readily transportable, without an adverse domestic effect (*i.e.*, higher prices in the United States), the sellers could not have maintained their international price-fixing arrangement and respondents would not have suffered their foreign injury. They add that this "but for" condition is sufficient to bring the price-fixing conduct within the scope of the FTAIA's exception.

The Court of Appeals, however, did not address this argument, and, for that reason, neither shall we. Respondents remain free to ask the Court of Appeals to consider the claim. The Court of Appeals may determine whether respondents properly preserved the argument, and, if so, it may consider it and decide the related claim.

For these reasons, the judgment of the Court of Appeals is vacated, and the case is remanded for further proceedings consistent with this opinion.

It is so ordered.

JUSTICE O'CONNOR took no part in the consideration or decision of this case.

JUSTICE SCALIA, with whom JUSTICE THOMAS joins, concurring in the judgment.

I concur in the judgment of the Court because the language of the statute is readily susceptible of the interpretation the Court provides and because only that interpretation is consistent with the principle that statutes should be read in accord with the customary deference to the application of foreign countries' laws within their own territories.

<hr />

As a consequence of *Empagran*, it is now settled that foreign plaintiffs may not sue in U.S. courts under the Sherman Act for foreign injuries from international cartels—provided those injuries are "independent" of any domestic U.S. harms caused by the cartel. But what does the Court mean by "independent" foreign effect? Given the possibility of arbitrage, can a world-wide cartel ever be maintained absent the agreement of sellers in other geographic areas? In other words, don't higher prices in the United States always make possible higher prices abroad, and vice versa, *i.e.*, aren't the effects of a cartel necessarily *interdependent*? The plaintiffs, of course, made that very argument to the Court. Was the Court simply evading the real question of the case, therefore, by remanding the case to the court of appeals? What argument could the plaintiffs make on remand? How could the defendants respond? If the lower courts find that the foreign effects of the international vitamin cartel were indeed intertwined with domestic U.S. effects, might *Empagran* prove to be a very narrow precedent?

On remand, the D.C. Circuit resolved that issue, again concluding that the federal courts were without jurisdiction under the FTAIA to hear the foreign plaintiffs' claims. *Empagran S.A. v. F. Hoffmann-LaRoche, Ltd.*, 417 F.3d 1267 (D.C. Cir. 2005). While conceding that "[t]he appellants paint a plausible scenario under which maintaining super-competitive prices in the United States might well have been a 'but-for' cause of the appellants' foreign injury," the court nevertheless concluded that the FTAIA requires "a direct causal relationship, that is, proximate causation." In its view, the "but for" scenario did not satisfy that standard. *See also In re Monosodium Glutamate Antitrust Litigation*, 477 F.3d 535 (8th Cir. 2007) (following *Empagran*).

Congress clearly intended, of course, to place some limitations on U.S. antitrust jurisdiction over wholly foreign conduct. In the late 1970s and early 1980s, when the FTAIA was adopted, Congress concluded in response to arguments from the private sector that the threat of U.S. Sherman Act liability was inhibiting U.S. exporters from engaging in cooperative activities that would promote U.S. exports. The FTAIA, which included the Export Trading Company Act, was arguably designed, therefore, to promote exports by providing something of a safe harbor for exporters. Congress did not have international cartels in mind when it enacted FTAIA and the Export Trading Company Act. In light of these facts, was there an alternative interpretation of the FTAIA that was available to the Court in *Empagran*?

What is the relationship, if any, between the foreign conduct issues being posed in cases like *Hartford Fire* and *Empagran* and the split in the Supreme Court in *Summit Health*? What are the policy implications, in terms of effective enforcement, compensation, and deterrence, of restrictive jurisdictional rules?

Why would foreign plaintiffs pursue antitrust claims in U.S. courts when so many nations have their own competition laws? A variety of factors may be at work.

First, relatively few foreign antitrust laws grant private rights of action, and nations that allow private suits typically permit recovery for actual damages only, not treble damages. Also, when attorney's fee shifting exists overseas, it is usually symmetric: although a prevailing plaintiff may recover fees as under U.S. law, a prevailing defendant also will have the right to recover fees—i.e., the loser pays the winner's attorney's fees regardless of who is the plaintiff and the defendant. As we have seen, Section 4 of the Clayton Act allows only a prevailing plaintiff to recover treble damages, attorney's fees, and costs of suit. 15 U.S.C. § 15. Moreover, contingency fee and other flexible funding arrangements, which are common in the U.S., are often prohibited by other jurisdictions, making it far more difficult for a plaintiff or class of plaintiffs to retain counsel to pursue antitrust claims.

Other less obvious factors may also be at work. U.S. federal courts authorize far more extensive discovery than do their foreign counterpart jurisdictions. The Federal Rules of Civil Procedure also provide for the use of class actions, a device not commonly available in other jurisdictions. The combination of class actions, treble damages, discovery, and attorney's fees can facilitate very substantial potential recoveries. Indeed, the possibility of such recoveries has spawned an active class action bar in the United States, the availability of which may itself be a factor that facilitates the initiation of U.S. antitrust claims by foreign plaintiffs.

The greater attractiveness of the U.S. private enforcement system has led foreign firms to sue in the United States for damages suffered offshore due to illegal behavior that occurs, at least in part, within the United States. When should the U.S. courts be available to foreign claimants—and perhaps allow recovery by large classes of foreign companies and individuals? What policy reasons might be urged in favor of and against permitting such suits to proceed? Would liberal recourse by foreign parties to the U.S. courts raise the potential cost to defendants of participation in hard core cartels and help deter misconduct?

For an additional application of the FTAIA, see *In re Dynamic Random Access Memory (DRAM) Antitrust Litigation*, 546 F.3d 981 (9th Cir. 2008) (British computer manufacturer failed to show proximate cause between its alleged injuries and domestic U.S. effects of alleged cartel). Most recently, in a controversial decision, the Seventh Circuit held that sales of priced-fixed LCD panels to foreign manufacturers of cellular phones that were subsequently sold in the U.S. fell outside the scope of the FTAIA. *See Motorola Mobility LLC v. AU Optronics Corp.*, 746 F.3d 842 (7th Cir. 2014). On rehearing the Seventh Circuit amended, but affirmed, its decision. *See Motorola Mobility LLC v. AU Optronics Corp.*, 775 F.3d 816 (7th Cir. 2014). In *AU Optronics Corp.*, the LCD panels were purchased and integrated into cellphones by Motorola's foreign subsidiaries. Some of these cellphones were later shipped and sold abroad while others were sent to Motorola for the purpose of being sold in the United States. The court emphasized that while the foreign subsidiaries may have been directly harmed by purchasing the LCD panels, it could not treat foreign corporations and Motorola as a single entity. Having established that Motorola may have only been indirectly injured as a subsequent buyer of the integrated LCD panels, the court held that this type of "derivative injury rarely gives rise to a claim under antitrust law."

Questions about the applicability of the FTAIA to import commerce also remain. In *United States v. Hui Hsiung*, 778 F.3d 738 (9th Cir. 2015), the Ninth Circuit held that import commerce falls within the scope of the Sherman Act and therefore outside the scope of the type of conduct the FTAIA was designed to affect. The court further clarified that non-import trade could be brought as a Sherman Act claim as long as the domestic effects requirement within the FTAIA is met. What qualifies as import commerce? In *Minn-Chem, Inc. v. Agrium Inc.*, 683 F.3d 845 (7th Cir. 2012), the court held that direct purchases of products from foreign entities by U.S. buyers qualifies as import commerce that is exempt from the FTAIA. But there is no unified interpretation of import trade among the Circuits and questions remain about the application of the import commerce exception. *See* Andre Fiebig, *Import Commerce and the Foreign Trade Antitrust Improvements Act*, 35 NW. J. INT'L L. & BUS. AMBASSADOR

1A (2015); Ellen Meriwether, *Motorola Mobility and the FTAIA: If Not Here, Then Where?*, ANTITRUST, Spring 2015, at 8.

Should motions to dismiss under FTAIA be treated as jurisdictional (Federal Rule of Civil Procedure 12(b)(1)) or as relating to the elements of an offense (12(b)(6))? The Seventh Circuit recently reversed course on this issue, concluding that the FTAIA is not a jurisdictional limit on the power of the federal courts, but rather a limitation on the substantive prohibitions of the Sherman Act. It went on to conclude that the allegations set forth by the direct purchaser plaintiffs in the case were sufficient to state a claim. *See Minn-Chem, Inc. v. Agrium Inc.*, 683 F.3d 845 (7th Cir. 2012). The decision also sheds light on how the pleading requirements of *Twombly* should be applied.

c.   Act of State Doctrine

A second limit on extraterritoriality is the act of state doctrine, which bars U.S. courts from considering the validity of sovereign acts by foreign governments where such acts occur in the foreign state. In most cases, the act of state doctrine is invoked by a private party defendant who argues that injuries asserted to arise from misconduct in a foreign jurisdiction resulted from intervention by a foreign government. In *W.S. Kirkpatrick & Co. v. Environmental Tectonics Corp.*, 493 U.S. 400, 110 S. Ct. 701 (1990), the Supreme Court refused to ban the application of the Robinson-Patman Act to the alleged payment of bribes to government officials in Nigeria to obtain a government contract. The Court ruled that act of state issues "only arise when a court must decide—that is, when the outcome of the case turns upon—the effect of official action by a foreign sovereign." The doctrine allows the U.S. antitrust laws to be applied if judicial inquiry "involves only the 'motivation' for, rather than the 'validity' of, a foreign sovereign act." Here the act of state doctrine did not apply because the plaintiff did not contest the validity of the contract issued by the Nigerian Government, but only questioned the motive (a possible bribe) for the agreement.

d.   Foreign Sovereign Immunity

A further jurisdictional limitation involves the potential antitrust liability of foreign governments for their own sovereign acts. The Foreign Sovereign Immunities Act, 28 U.S.C. § 1602, immunizes foreign governments from suits challenging the acts of the sovereign. Such immunity may be lost when the sovereign's acts are purely "commercial" in nature. *See Alfred Dunhill of London v. Republic of Cuba*, 425 U.S. 682 (1976). Courts also will not impose antitrust liability on private parties for conduct that otherwise would constitute an antitrust violation, if it was a consequence of compulsion by a foreign government. *See Interamerican Ref. Corp. v. Texaco Maracaibo, Inc.*, 307 F.Supp. 1291, 1297–98 (D. Del. 1970).

In March 2013, however, a jury found that various Chinese companies had conspired to fix the prices of vitamin C. As trebled, the civil damages exceeded $150 million. *In re: Vitamin C Antitrust Litigation*, Case No. 1:06–md–01738. At an earlier stage of the proceedings, the district court had rejected arguments by the defendants that they acted pursuant to compulsion by the government of the People's Republic of China, and that sovereign compulsion shielded them from liability under the U.S. antitrust laws. *See* Jonathan Randles, *Jury Finds Chinese Vitamin C Makers Fixed Prices*, LAW 360 (Mar. 13, 2013). The case is currently on appeal in the Second Circuit.

Sidebar 8–1:
Suing OPEC[a]

The Organization of Petroleum Exporting Countries ("OPEC") was formed in the early 1960s by many of the major oil producing nations. OPEC is an express cartel: it sets prices and assigns production levels to its members at face-to-face meetings. Shortly after OPEC's formation, the price of oil rose dramatically. The resulting transfer of resources to oil producers from oil buyers made many oil producing nations, particularly the Persian Gulf States, wealthy and caused some of the economic malaise experienced by the United States and other industrial nations during the mid- and late-1970s.

Suing either OPEC or its member nations offers a useful way to think about the myriad special defenses and immunities that potentially apply in the foreign commerce area when sovereign nations participate in anticompetitive activity. While there are older decisions rejecting suit against OPEC on two different grounds, a close examination of more recent developments suggests that OPEC's conduct may some day be judged on the merits.

Foreign Sovereign Immunity

The Foreign Sovereign Immunities Act ("FSIA"), 28 U.S.C. § 1602 et seq., bars all suits against foreign states and their instrumentalities unless one of the Act's exceptions apply. For antitrust purposes, the most important exception is for "commercial activities." Foreign states are not immune from a suit:

in which the action is based upon a commercial activity carried on in the United States by the foreign state; or

---

[a]   This Sidebar was prepared by Professor Spencer Weber Waller, Loyola University Chicago School of Law, and is adapted from Spencer Weber Waller, *Suing OPEC*, 64 U. PITT. L. REV. 105 (2002) and SPENCER WEBER WALLER & ANDRE FIEBIG, ANTITRUST AND AMERICAN BUSINESS ABROAD (4th ed. 2016 & supp.).

upon an act performed in the United States in connection with a commercial activity of the foreign state elsewhere; or upon an act outside the territory of the United States in connection with a commercial activity of the foreign state elsewhere and that act causes a direct effect in the United States. * * *

28 U.S.C. § 1605(a)(2). There is also this additional key sentence: "The commercial character of an activity shall be determined by reference to the nature of the course of conduct or particular transaction or act, rather than by reference to its purpose." 28 U.S.C. § 1603(d).

The legislative history of these provisions suggests that state conduct normally performed by private persons should be regarded as commercial, even where the object of the activity is to fulfill a governmental purpose. For example, contracting to buy provisions for the armed services or to repair an embassy building are to be treated as commercial, since private parties normally negotiate and sign contracts. On the other hand, if the activity is normally done only by governments—such as imposing a tariff or issuing export licenses—immunity is available even if there are important business or commercial motivations behind the government action.

Characterizing the conduct of the OPEC nations is difficult. A district court in the late 1970s undertook its own study of OPEC's price-setting efforts and concluded that they were accomplished through (1) taxation of private companies, (2) production controls administered by "conservation" laws, and (3) direct price quotations on government-owned oil. The first two functions were deemed clearly governmental in nature. The third, while commercial at first blush, was merely a different "medium" by which the OPEC governments were performing sovereign acts. The court noted considerable acceptance within the United Nations, and indeed by the United States, of the sovereign right of states to exercise control over the extraction and exploitation of their natural resources. Thus:

> The control over a nation's natural resources stems from the nature of sovereignty. By necessity and by traditional recognition, each nation is its own master in respect to its physical attributes. The defendants' control over their oil resources is an especially sovereign function because oil, as their primary, if not sole, revenue-producing resource, is crucial to the welfare of their nations' peoples.

> *International Ass'n of Machinists v. Organization of Petroleum Exporting Countries*, 477 F. Supp. 553, 568 (C.D. Cal. 1979), *aff'd on other grounds*, 649 F.2d 1354 (9th Cir. 1981), *cert. denied*, 454 U.S. 1163 (1982) ("*OPEC*").

The district court's analysis of sovereign immunity was understandable—but arguably wrong, even in 1979 under the "nature not purpose" standard for the commercial activity exception of the FSIA. It is more likely in error today.

The first *OPEC* decision came at the high water mark of state involvement in natural resources markets. Since that time, most nations have privatized key aspects of their extractive industries, making it more clear that the activities of the OPEC nations are the kinds of activities customarily engaged in by private firms, and hence not immune under the FSIA. On appeal, the Ninth Circuit admitted this flaw in the district court's opinion, but found a way around it to nonetheless avoid adjudicating the merits of the case. While questioning the district court's sovereign immunity analysis, the court of appeals affirmed the dismissal of the first *OPEC* decision on act of state grounds.[b]

Act of State

The Supreme Court subsequently clarified the scope of the act of state doctrine in *W.S. Kirkpatrick & Co. v. Environmental Tectonics Corp., Int'l,* 493 U.S. 400 (1990), a unanimous decision. At issue in *Kirkpatrick* was whether the act of state doctrine barred a United States court from entertaining a cause of action that did not rest upon the asserted invalidity of an official act of a foreign sovereign, but required imputing to foreign officials an unlawful motivation in the performance of such an official act.

Environmental Tectonics was an unsuccessful bidder on a military procurement contract awarded by the Republic of Nigeria. The successful bidder, Kirkpatrick & Co., had made arrangements with a Nigerian citizen, whereby the citizen would endeavor to secure the contract for Kirkpatrick. The Nigerian citizen and Kirkpatrick agreed that, in the event the contract was awarded to Kirkpatrick, Kirkpatrick would pay two Panamanian entities controlled by the Nigerian citizen a "commission" equal to 20 per cent of the contract price, which would, in turn, be given as a bribe to officials of the Nigerian

---

[b] On a related issue, in *Prewitt Enters. v. OPEC*, 353 F.3d 916 (11th Cir. 2003), the Eleventh Circuit held that OPEC as an organization could not be validly served with process because of an agreement between OPEC and the Austrian Government granting it immunity from service of process. The Eleventh Circuit noted, however, that in its view OPEC would not qualify for immunity under the FSIA as a result of its commercial activities.

government. Nigerian law prohibited both the payment and the receipt of bribes in connection with the award of government contracts.

The Supreme Court held that the act of state doctrine was inapplicable because nothing in the case required the Court to declare invalid the official act of a foreign sovereign. Under *Kirkpatrick*, act of state issues only arise when the outcome of the case turns upon the effect of official action by a foreign sovereign. *Kirkpatrick* thus overruled a line of lower court cases which had applied the act of state doctrine to dismiss claims that called for examination of the *motives* of a foreign government in taking action. The Court noted that, in every case in which the Supreme Court has held the act of state doctrine applicable, the relief sought or the defense interposed would have required a United States court to declare invalid the official act of a foreign sovereign performed in its own territory.

Because the legality of the Nigerian contract itself was not a question before the Court in *Kirkpatrick*, there was no occasion to apply the act of state doctrine at all. The Court emphasized that the act of state doctrine does not establish an exception to the court's power to decide cases and controversies properly presented to it merely because judicial review in a United States court might embarrass a foreign government. It merely requires that, in the process of deciding such cases, the acts of foreign sovereigns within their own jurisdictions shall be deemed valid. *Kirkpatrick* thus further weakened the key portion of the original *OPEC* Ninth Circuit decision, which sought to justify the application of the act of state doctrine based on the potential for embarrassing the executive branch by drawing an analogy to the domestic political question doctrine. *But see Spectrum Stores, Inc. v. Citgo Petroleum Corp.*, 632 F. 3d 938 (5th Cir. 2011) (dismissing antitrust claim against foreign owned U.S. petroleum refiners connected to OPEC under political question doctrine).

Foreign Sovereign Compulsion

The OPEC defendants would not be able to take advantage of another frequently discussed, but seldom litigated, special defense in international antitrust litigation. The foreign sovereign compulsion defense may provide a safe harbor for a private defendant who has been compelled to engage in conduct which violates United States antitrust law. While the contours and exceptions of the defense are hotly debated, the defense has only been successful on two occasions, and has been otherwise rejected because the court determined that the defendants had acted pursuant to the advice, encouragement, or prodding of a foreign government, but had not been subject to outright compulsion. *See* Spencer Weber Waller, *Redefining the Foreign Compulsion Defense: The Japanese Automobile Restraints and Beyond*, 14 LAW & POL'Y INT'L BUS. 747 (1982). Whatever comfort this defense may provide to private firms acting under the directions of a state, therefore, it has no application in the OPEC context, where the behavior of the foreign governments themselves are at issue. This defense has also been raised in recent antitrust litigation involving Chinese export cartels for minerals and rare earths where the defendants and the Chinese government have asserted that the conduct was compelled.

Comity

The OPEC defendants undoubtedly also would raise issues of comity. Whether comity provides a separate basis for dismissing such a suit depends on the reading of *Hartford Fire Ins. Co. v. California*, 509 U.S. 764 (1993) *(See supra* Chapter 8). Recall that in *Hartford* the Court, by a 5–4 vote, appeared to limit comity to those few situations akin to foreign compulsion where the foreign law required a violation of the Sherman Act. In the event of such a "true conflict," the Court appeared willing to permit the balancing of United States and foreign interests to determine whether jurisdiction should be exercised or declined. Thus, the Court seems to have both transformed foreign compulsion into a balancing test rather than a complete defense and virtually eliminated another potential defense for OPEC nations in future litigation.

Conclusion

A case against OPEC is thus a perfect exercise to analyze the various special defenses and immunities in foreign commerce antitrust cases and to contemplate whether such a suit would be successful and whether even a "successful" antitrust suit against OPEC (by the federal agencies, state attorneys general, or private parties) would be in the overall interests of the United States.

If an antitrust violation was found, what would constitute an effective remedy in light of the remedial goals of deterrence, compensation, and punishment? What practical hurdles might lie in its path? Could a U.S. court effectively enjoin OPEC? How would it enforce its orders against OPEC member countries and their officials? Could private parties, perhaps organized into a class, establish their injury and accurately prove their damages? Could they collect those damages? Who would be the "best" plaintiff—the federal government? a group of states? a private class action? And finally, consider the institutional ramifications for the U.S. antitrust enforcement system if a violation was established, but no effective remedy was possible. Does that prospect help to explain the development of doctrines like act of state and foreign sovereign compulsion?

Sidebar 8–2:
Paths to International Convergence

As we first noted in Chapter 1, concerns about the costs associated with the proliferation of competition policy systems have inspired considerable discussion about approaches for promoting acceptance of common procedural and substantive norms.[a] The perceived urgency to promote competition policy convergence increased with the expansion in the number of competition policy regimes following the dissolution in late 1991 of the Soviet Union and, from the perspective of the United States, in 2001 following the European Union's decision to block General Electric's acquisition of Honeywell. In that instance, the U.S. Department of Justice had approved the transaction with relatively minor modifications, and the EU's intervention triggered a sharp exchange of words between top officials at the DOJ and the Competition Directorate.

Modern efforts to reconcile disparate legal regimes, including competition policy systems, have two basic elements. The first is *establishing an intellectual consensus* about what constitutes superior norms. The ingredients of consensus-building often include the identification of possible substantive and procedural standards, experimentation by one or more jurisdictions, and debate—for example, in conferences or in professional journals—about the conceptual merits and practical results of specific approaches. The second element of convergence is a *process of acceptance* by which individual jurisdictions embrace common procedural or substantive norms.

The process of acceptance can proceed in at least two ways. One method is for two or more jurisdictions to adopt common approaches voluntarily and unilaterally. This method sometimes is called *soft convergence*. Without the benefit of a treaty or other formal agreement, different countries might

---

[a] For one of the most influential early expressions of such concerns, see *International Competition Policy Advisory Committee to the Attorney General and Assistant Attorney General for Antitrust*, FINAL REPORT (2000) ("ICPAC Report"), https://www.justice.gov/atr/final-report.

choose to emulate procedures or substantive rules that the experience of another jurisdiction has proven to be successful. The 1982 U.S. Department of Justice Merger Guidelines provide an example. As amended in 1984 by the DOJ and reissued jointly with the FTC with modifications in 1992, 1997, and 2010, the Merger Guidelines have influenced many jurisdictions (including the European Union) in formulating their own merger control regimes. The analytical quality of and practical experience with the U.S. Guidelines, rather than any binding international agreement, have motivated their emulation by jurisdictions outside the United States. A second path of acceptance, sometimes called *hard convergence*, is a formal agreement by which nations commit themselves to abide by common principles. Soft and hard convergence are not mutually exclusive techniques, as progress through soft convergence sometimes serves as a precursor to formulating binding agreements on international norms.

Modern initiatives concerning competition policy convergence generally seek to encourage the formulation of an intellectual consensus and to facilitate acceptance of superior norms either by a voluntary process of opting-in or through participation in binding international agreements. Convergence-related activities have taken essentially three paths.

Bilateral agreements. Bilateral agreements usually commit the participants to cooperate in executing enforcement initiatives, to take measures to avoid or manage disputes, and to develop collaborative working groups to address issues of common substantive and procedural interest. The United States has established bilateral accords with a number of other jurisdictions, including the European Union. For a current compilation, see https://www.ftc.gov/policy/international/international-cooperation-agreements. In 1994, Congress passed the International Antitrust Enforcement Assistance Act (IAEAA), 15 U.S.C. §§ 6200–12, which authorized the U.S. to enter into Antitrust Mutual Assistance Agreements ("AMAAs") with foreign antitrust enforcement agencies, which facilitate the exchange of confidential information with foreign governments. Owing to some of IAEAA's requirements, however, foreign jurisdictions have been reluctant to enter into formal AMAAs, however, and since the law's passage, the United States has entered into only one such agreement—with Australia.

Regional agreements. A number of regional organizations have created competition policy initiatives that directly or indirectly promise to promote convergence. Some arrangements, such as the Asia-Pacific Economic Cooperation and Mercosur, have focused mainly on consensus-building by holding regular conferences and workshops on competition policy. Other agreements contain rudimentary competition policy commitments (such as the North American Free Trade Agreement) or, in the case of the Andean Pact and the Caribbean Community, create a system of binding competition policy commands and a common mechanism for enforcement involving cross-border matters within the region. Other regional undertakings—such as the Free Trade Agreement of the Americas and the Common Market of Eastern and Southern Africa—are engaged in negotiations to establish binding regional standards for the establishment of national competition policy systems.

Global networks. Several institutions with broad international representation have established programs to facilitate the identification and adoption of best practices in competition policy. Two of the oldest institutions are the Organization for Economic Cooperation and Development (OECD) and the United Nations Conference on Trade and Development (UNCTAD). The OECD operates a Competition Law and Policy Committee that meets four times annually and whose secretariat has produced a number of studies and recommendations concerning international competition policy. The OECD's membership consists mainly of developed market economies, but the organization in 2001 began a Global Competition Forum to engage transition economies in discussions about competition policy. UNCTAD's chief constituency has consisted of developing nations, and its programs have focused chiefly on providing technical assistance and other policy guidance to countries with new competition policy regimes.

Both OECD and UNCTAD have served to encourage the development of an intellectual consensus and to facilitate soft convergence by offering models of procedure and substantive rules that nations might emulate unilaterally. The framework for broad international hard convergence began to emerge in 1996 when the World Trade Organization (WTO) announced the formation of a Trade and Competition Policy Working Group. The WTO initiative may foreshadow development of binding principles that would be applied and enforced through the WTO's existing apparatus of trade dispute institutions. In

2001, the WTO's ministerial meeting in Doha, Qatar announced that the Working Group would focus on gaining acceptance for general principles concerning transparency, non-discriminatory treatment, and capacity building.

A number of countries saw limits to the ability of the OECD, UNCTAD, or WTO to serve as platforms for achieving international competition policy convergence. OECD's membership, emphasizing well-established industrialized states, might be ill-suited to promote broad agreement among older and newer market economies. UNCTAD's focus on emerging markets could slight the interests and experience of older competition regimes, and some feared that WTO's trade-related orientation would unduly subordinate competition policy concerns.

These and other impulses stimulated the formation in 2001 of the International Competition Network (ICN). *See* http://www.internationalcompetitionnetwork.org/. ICN membership is limited to nations with competition policy systems, but there are now more than 100 members, including a significant number of emerging market economies. ICN has established working groups on cartels, competition policy implementation, merger control, and unilateral conduct, with the aim of identifying best practices for adoption by its members and promoting soft convergence. ICN intends to work extensively with the private sector, academic groups, and other non-government organizations to formulate policy proposals. For additional information, see http://www.international competitionnetwork.org/. *See also* William E. Kovacic, *Extraterritoriality, Institutions, and Convergence in International Competition Policy*, 97 AM. SOC'Y OF INT'L L. PROC. 309 (2003).

B. AN OVERVIEW OF THE AMERICAN SYSTEM FOR PROSECUTING AND ADJUDICATING ANTITRUST VIOLATIONS

1. NATIONAL PROSECUTORS: THE DEPARTMENT OF JUSTICE AND THE FEDERAL TRADE COMMISSION

In the United States, two major federal government agencies—the Justice Department's Antitrust Division and the Federal Trade Commission—share enforcement responsibility for the Nation's antitrust laws. The Justice Department enforces the Sherman and Clayton Acts. The Antitrust Division is headed by an Assistant Attorney General, who is nominated by the President and confirmed by the Senate. The Department exercises its enforcement authority through civil and criminal actions. The DOJ brings all of its lawsuits in the federal courts. When it files civil suits, the Department can obtain equitable relief (*e.g.*, an injunction forbidding specific conduct) or collect treble damages when it sues on behalf of the United States as a purchaser of goods and services. Section 4B of the Clayton Act creates a four-year statute of limitations from the time the claim for relief "accrues." No statute of limitations governs suits for injunctive relief, and (unlike private parties) neither the Justice Department nor the FTC are constrained by the equitable doctrine of laches.

The Justice Department alone can prosecute federal antitrust crimes. DOJ usually seeks criminal sanctions when direct rivals covertly engage in naked output restraints and realize the likely anticompetitive effects of their conduct. The Department must commence its criminal antitrust suits within five years of the offense, 18 U.S.C. § 3282. Where an illegal conspiracy is continuing in nature, the limitations period begins to run only from the "last act" in furtherance of the conspiracy. Nearly all DOJ criminal suits have consisted of Sherman Act Section 1 cases against hard core horizontal restraints such as price-fixing, bid-rigging, and market division schemes. Since the 1980s the Department often has pursued multi-count indictments that charge defendants with Sherman Act violations and other offenses concerning conduct providing the basis for antitrust prosecution. Commonly alleged collateral offenses include conspiracy to defraud the government, mail fraud, wire fraud, and making false statements to government officials.

The FTC shares responsibility with the Justice Department for civil enforcement of the Clayton Act, but also enforces various consumer protection laws. The FTC is headed by five commissioners appointed by the President and confirmed by the Senate. Commissioners serve seven-year terms, and no more than three commissioners may belong to the same political party. Antitrust cases are developed by the agency's Bureau of Competition, with assistance from the Bureau of Economics. There is also a Bureau of Consumer Protection. The FTC exercises its enforcement authority through administrative adjudication and uses Section 13(b) of the FTC Act to file civil suits in federal district court for injunctive relief to preserve the status quo pending the conclusion of an administrative proceeding. To avoid redundant investigations and prosecutions, the FTC and Justice Department use a "clearance" procedure to notify each other before commencing investigations and to decide which agency will handle specific matters.

The FTC alone may enforce Section 5 of the FTC Act and its prohibition of unfair methods of competition. Courts have interpreted Section 5 as enabling the FTC to prosecute conduct that violates the letter of the antitrust statutes (including the Sherman Act) and to proscribe behavior that contradicts their spirit. The FTC's remedial authority is limited to issuing equitable decrees such as cease and desist orders and restitution. The FTC's history, operations, and programs are the subject of an extensive set of papers collected in *Federal Trade Commission 90th Anniversary Symposium*, 72 ANTITRUST L.J. 745 (2005).

The FTC and the Justice Department use policymaking tools other than litigation. Both agencies influence counseling and adjudication by promulgating enforcement guidelines such as the Horizontal Merger Guidelines discussed at length in Chapter 1. Each agency also gives business officials guidance about the antitrust consequences of proposed conduct. The Antitrust Division issues "business review letters," 28 C.F.R. § 50.6, and the FTC issues "advisory opinions," 16 C.F.R. § 1.1. These procedures can be time-consuming and do not preclude subsequent changes in the government's enforcement posture. Both agencies also advise other government bodies such as regulatory commissions and legislative committees about the competitive effects of existing or proposed regulations and statutes. Under Section 6 of the FTC Act, the FTC also has unique authority to use compulsory process to study industry trends and conduct. Section 6 also provides support for the FTC's competition advocacy program, pursuant to which it regularly submits comments to federal, state, and local legislators and regulators urging them to consider the competition consequences of their actions. *See generally* Andrew I. Gavil, *The FTC's Study and Advocacy Authority in Its Second Century: A Look Ahead*, 83 GEO. WASH. L. REV. 1902 (2015). Figure 8–1 depicts the relative allocation of authority between the DOJ and FTC.

Figure 8–1:
FTC & DOJ: Exclusive & Shared Jurisdiction

Sidebar 8–3:
Detecting Antitrust Violations:
The Role of Information Gathering

No system of antitrust rules can succeed unless prosecutors can obtain information that illuminates the purpose and effect of specific business practices and identifies possible violations of the law. Antitrust prosecutors tend to rely on six basic sources of information to identify and prove violations of the law.

Publicly available information. In market economies, business actors voluntarily disclose substantial information about themselves to the public. To attract investors and employees, companies frequently reveal their business plans, including product development strategies and intentions to acquire or spin-off assets. A wide range of company outsiders— business journalists, securities analysts, and debt ratings services—press company managers to provide information about the firm's operations. Many countries have adopted securities laws that compel firms to disclose a wide range of information to the investing public about events or trends that promise to have a material impact on firm performance. These public sources of information frequently supply antitrust enforcers with data needed to develop an investigation plan and perform research tasks (such as identifying industry participants and calculating market shares) central to analyzing possible violations.

Voluntary disclosures of information to antitrust enforcers. Antitrust officials obtain substantial amounts of valuable data from industry insiders. A disaffected employee may provide information about her employer that identifies a price-fixing cartel. Individual consumers may submit complaints about suspicious sales practices to an enforcement agency. Firms sometimes provide complaints, in conversations or in "white papers," to enforcement agencies concerning business phenomena, such as a merger involving a company's suppliers or competitors. The volume of information obtained through voluntary disclosures depends partly on the enforcement agency's success in publicizing its interest in receiving information about potential antitrust violations and its willingness, at least in some circumstances, to preserve the confidentiality of its sources.

Mandatory Disclosures. As we discussed in Chapter 5, the Hart-Scott Rodino pre-merger notification system can also be understood as a mechanism for informing the government of potential antitrust violations. Firms subject to the HSR size thresholds must share certain basic information in connection with their initial filing. If the government concludes that further investigation is warranted, they may also be compelled to respond to a "second request," although the compulsion will hold only if the parties wish to pursue the merger. *See* Sidebar 5–3.

Civil compulsory process. Antitrust agencies rely heavily upon legally enforceable demands that individuals or institutions provide testimony or written information in investigations and, when necessary, civil cases. Compulsory civil process is crucial, for example, in forcing the defendant in a monopolization case to provide business records that reveal its assessment of its own market power and shed light on the legitimacy of justifications asserted for challenged conduct. Compulsory civil process also may be necessary to induce reluctant third parties, often including firms that have continuing business relationships with the target, to supply information.

In the United States, the DOJ and the FTC routinely use pre-filing civil investigative demands (essentially, subpoenas) to collect documents and compel individuals to provide testimony. Once a complaint is filed, private plaintiffs also may use compulsory discovery techniques (depositions, interrogatories, and document requests) to build the factual foundation for antitrust cases. Some jurisdictions, such as the European Union, that enforce their laws only through civil sanctions allow the competition authority to conduct surprise inspections of business offices, sometimes referred to as "dawn raids." In recent years, the U.S. and the Competition Directorate of the EC have coordinated joint efforts to exercise their respective authority to gather information on potential antitrust law violations that affect both jurisdictions.

Criminal compulsory process and covert surveillance. To collect information concerning possible antitrust crimes such as horizontal price-fixing, the DOJ empanels grand juries that issue subpoenas to compel the appearance of witnesses and the presentation of documents. In cooperation with the Federal Bureau of Investigation, the DOJ also may obtain warrants to search business offices and the homes of employees suspected of participating in criminal antitrust conspiracies; use wire taps to monitor telephone conversations; secretly photograph and record suspected cartel meetings; and enlist informants to wear listening devices to monitor conversations involving cartel members. The United States and other countries that use criminal investigative techniques typically subject their application to strict control by a judicial officer who is independent of the prosecutor.

Rewards for information. In the early 1990s, the DOJ broadened the availability of immunity from criminal prosecution for companies that disclose their participation in illegal cartel activities. The DOJ leniency program, described in Sidebar 3–1, provides complete criminal immunity for the first violator to reveal the scheme, so long as the informing party has not orchestrated the illegal arrangement. In recent years, some governments have begun considering whether to provide bounties to individuals who provide information that facilitates the successful prosecution of hard core antitrust violations.

Data from other government agencies. Antitrust agencies often use information routinely collected and maintained by other government bodies. A major example involves government procurement authorities, which frequently are targets of bid-rigging schemes. Competition policy agencies in many countries have created close working relationships with government purchasing units to identify suspicious bidding patterns and to cooperate in prosecuting violators.

2. STATE PROSECUTORS: STATE ATTORNEYS GENERAL AND THE MULTISTATE ANTITRUST TASK FORCE OF THE NATIONAL ASSOCIATION OF ATTORNEYS GENERAL

The Sherman Act was not America's first antitrust experiment. At least 26 states had adopted constitutional or statutory "antimonopoly" measures by 1890. *See* David Millon, *The First Antitrust Statute*, 29 WASHBURN L.J. 141 (1990) (reporting that 12 states had adopted general antitrust statutes prior to enactment of the Sherman Act). From 1890 until 1920, the states used their antitrust statutes to achieve significant victories. Measured by the number of cases filed and the amount of fines recovered, state enforcement rivaled the Justice Department's early accomplishments in applying the Sherman Act. *See, e.g.,* James May, *Antitrust Practice and Procedure in the Formative Era: The Constitutional and Conceptual Reach of State Antitrust Law, 1880–1918*, 135 U. PA. L. REV. 495, 497–507 (1987).

For the half-century following the end of World War I, state antitrust enforcement lapsed. Resource constraints, doubts about the constitutional reach of state antitrust statutes, and the emergence of sustained federal enforcement stifled state antitrust activity. But the seeds of a major revival were planted in the 1970s, as over 20 states enacted new antitrust statutes, and federal grants enabled the states to create new, or expand existing, antitrust offices. Through the 1970s, the states prosecuted local horizontal output restraints and filed federal antitrust suits on behalf of state and local bodies who had been victimized by bid-rigging. Until that time, however, the idea that states might play a major part in merger enforcement was alien to state authorities.

State enforcement today proceeds along two paths. One is to apply state antitrust and related laws. Many states have "baby FTC Acts," which mirror Section 5 of the FTC Act and authorize state challenges to unfair and deceptive trade practices. Most states also have antitrust statutes that contain close analogues to Sections 1 and 2 of the Sherman Act, and the courts of many states rely on federal antitrust jurisprudence to construe these provisions. Over twenty states also have enacted antimerger provisions. *See* ANTITRUST LAW SECTION, ABA, STATE ANTITRUST PRACTICE AND STATUTES (3d ed. 2004).

The second path for state enforcement is to file federal antitrust suits. Like any private person injured or threatened with injury by reason of antitrust violations, states and their political subdivisions may sue under Sections 4 and 16 of the Clayton Act to obtain damages and injunctive relief, respectively. *See Chattanooga Foundry & Pipe Works v. City of Atlanta*, 203 U.S. 390 (1906) (states and subdivisions, like municipalities, are "persons" for purposes of private right of action). However, in *Hawaii v. Standard Oil of California*, 405 U.S. 251 (1972), the Supreme Court concluded that Section 4 of the Clayton Act did not entitle states to sue in their sovereign capacity as *parens patriae* to recover damages for injury to their economies.

Congress sought to overcome this restriction through the Hart-Scott-Rodino Antitrust Improvements Act of 1976, which added Sections 4C through 4H to the Clayton Act. These provisions enabled states to seek treble damages as *parens patriae* for injuries to natural persons within their borders and sought to provide an alternative to class actions where many individuals each had suffered relatively small monetary harm. The Supreme Court severely limited the effect of this reform in *Illinois Brick Co. v. Illinois*, 431 U.S. 720 (1977), however, which we examine later in this Chapter. *Illinois Brick* held that states could not invoke the *parens patriae* mechanism to sue on behalf of consumers who were not "direct purchasers" of the product affected by anticompetitive conduct. *Illinois Brick*'s impact has been attenuated significantly by state statutes (called "*Illinois Brick* repealers") that allow indirect purchasers in state antitrust cases to recover damages as a matter of state law. In *California v. ARC America Corp.*, 490 U.S. 93 (1989), the Supreme Court ruled that the federal antitrust laws do not preempt such state statutes which allow recovery by indirect purchasers.

States face fewer curbs when they seek injunctions under Section 16 of the Clayton Act. In *California v. American Stores Co.*, 495 U.S. 271 (1990), the Supreme Court reversed the Ninth Circuit's conclusion that Section 16 of the Clayton Act did not authorize states to obtain injunctive relief as *parens patriae* for actual or threatened harm to their economy.

American Stores involved a challenge by the State of California under Section 7 of the Clayton Act to the merger of two competing supermarket chains. The FTC had already reviewed the transaction and reached an agreement with American requiring certain divestitures, but California deemed the settlement inadequate to preserve competition in 62 California cities. The specific issue before the Court was whether California had the right to seek divestiture pursuant to Section 16 for a violation of Section 7 of the Clayton Act. Based on its interpretation of the relevant statutes, as well as the legislative history, the Court concluded that indeed California could seek divestiture, reasoning that:

> Section 16, construed to authorize a private divestiture remedy when appropriate in light of equitable principles, fits well in a statutory scheme that favors private enforcement, subjects mergers to searching scrutiny, and regards divestiture as the remedy best suited to redress the ills of an anticompetitive merger.

495 U.S. at 284.

As noted above, before the State of California had begun its suit, the merging parties had agreed to an FTC consent order forcing divestiture of some retail outlets. When the state proceeded successfully with its own action seeking additional divestitures it became evident to the U.S. antitrust community that state governments had become partners of the DOJ and FTC in public enforcement of the Clayton Act's antimerger provision. By elevating the states' role in the public enforcement arena, *American Stores* also may have helped lay the foundation for the more active role that the state governments have played in nonmerger matters, including the *Microsoft* monopolization case, which was initiated in 1998. But *American Stores* creates possibilities for inconsistency in public enforcement of Section 7. Moreover, some states have been challenged due to lack of resources to mount major antitrust cases on their own, particularly in the case of mergers. This has led to instances of cooperation between federal and state enforcers. *See, e.g., Saint Alphonsus Medical Cntr. v. St. Luke's Health System, Ltd.*, 778 F.3d 775 (9th Cir. 2015) (hospital merger jointly challenged by FTC, State of Idaho and rival hospital). Some states, however, have continued to be able to mount independent antitrust challenges. *See, e.g., New York v. Actavis PLC*, 787 F.3d 638 (2d Cir. 2015) (condemning practice of "product hopping" by branded pharmaceutical companies); *California v. Safeway, Inc.*, 651 F.3d

1118 (9th Cir. 2011) (unsuccessful challenge to alleged conspiracy among supermarkets to restrain competition to defeat union tactics—discussed in Chapter 2).

What are the costs and benefits of maintaining an antitrust enforcement system with multiple enforcers? What particular costs and benefits are associated with having two federal enforcement agencies? With having both federal and state public enforcement agencies? *Contrast* Richard A. Posner, *Antitrust in the New Economy,* 68 ANTITRUST L.J. 925, 940–42 (2001) (arguing that states should be stripped of their authority to enforce federal antitrust laws), *with* Harry First, *Delivering Remedies: The Role of the States in Antitrust Enforcement,* 69 GEO. WASH. L. REV. 1004 (2001) (responding to Judge Posner). *See also* ANDREW I. GAVIL & HARRY FIRST, THE MICROSOFT ANTITRUST CASES: COMPETITION POLICY FOR THE TWENTY-FIRST CENTURY 281–308 (2014) (discussing arguments in favor of institutional diversity).

3. ADJUDICATION: THE ROLE OF THE COURTS

The federal antitrust system gives federal judges—and particularly Supreme Court justices—considerable discretion to interpret the antitrust laws and regulations. Judges exercise this discretion in three principal ways. First, they play a pivotal role in defining liability standards. Antitrust liability standards have changed over time, often in response to new economic learning and to shifting views about antitrust's goals. The adoption of price-cost relationships and recoupment tests to evaluate predatory pricing claims (*see supra* Chapter 4) and the movement from per se condemnation to rule of reason treatment for vertical restraints (*see supra* Chapter 6) are two noteworthy examples of judicial modifications of liability rules.

Second, judges have defined which "persons" qualify to press claims for relief under the Clayton Act. As we will see in Section E below, the requirements that the plaintiff establish injury to her business or property, antitrust injury, standing, and directness are largely the products of judicial construction.

Third, judges define procedural and evidentiary requirements that plaintiffs must satisfy to establish liability. The non-interventionist leaning of Supreme Court antitrust jurisprudence since *Sylvania* sometimes has taken the form of elevated burdens of pleading (*e.g., Twombly*), more ready access to summary judgment (*e.g., Matsushita*), and more formidable burdens of proof. Throughout the Casebook we have seen many examples of how the courts, especially the Supreme Court, have become increasingly demanding of antitrust plaintiffs, public and private. Establishing violations today under the rule of reason, for monopolization, and for anticompetitive mergers can be difficult as a consequence.

Judges do not consider issues of standing/injury, substantive liability standards, evidentiary requirements, and remedies in isolation. These considerations are closely interrelated, as the court can adjust its treatment of any single factor to offset the perceived inadequacies of another factor. Judges can neutralize expansive per se liability rules, for example, by imposing antitrust injury requirements that effectively preclude damage recoveries by private plaintiffs or by defining evidentiary standards in ways that ensure that violations of nominally draconian conduct standards rarely will be proven. One commentator has described these as "equilibrating" tendencies. *See* Stephen Calkins, *Summary Judgment, Motions to Dismiss, and Other Examples of Equilibrating Tendencies in the Antitrust System*, 74 GEO. L.J. 1065 (1986).

Sidebar 8–4:
Antitrust and Arbitration

For much of the Casebook thus far, we have focused on two ways to resolve antitrust disputes—litigation and negotiation. Here we examine alternate dispute resolution, especially arbitration, which has often been used to address manufacturer-dealer tensions. The debate has recently spread, however, to encompass arbitration of antitrust class actions pursuant to contractual waiver clauses.

The American Safety Doctrine

For nearly twenty years, from 1968 to 1985, the courts expressed a decided hostility towards the use of arbitration in antitrust cases. That hostility can be traced *to American Safety Equip. Corp. v. J.P. Maguire & Co.*, 391 F.2d 821 (2d Cir. 1968), where the court refused to enforce an arbitration clause in connection with an antitrust dispute between a trademark licensor and licensee, concluding that "the issues in antitrust cases are prone to be complicated, and the evidence extensive and diverse, far better suited to judicial than to arbitration procedures." 391 F.2d at 826–27. *American Safety* proved to be influential and was quickly followed by other circuits. Contractual arbitration clauses were thereafter viewed as void as against public policy. Over time, however, the Second Circuit's arguments in favor of refusing to enforce arbitration clauses were questioned and undermined.

Mitsubishi Motors Corp. v. Soler Chrysler-Plymouth

Mitsubishi Motors Corp. v. Soler Chrysler-Plymouth, 473 U.S. 614 (1985) squarely placed the arbitrability of antitrust claims before the Supreme Court—but solely in the context of international transactions. The district court ordered the parties to arbitration, reasoning that the international context of the case distinguished it from *American Safety*. After rejecting several other points raised by Soler, the Supreme Court agreed. 473 U.S. at 628–40, reserving the question of *American Safety's* vitality in the purely domestic context.

The Revitalization of Arbitration of Domestic Antitrust Disputes

Manufacturers and suppliers who perceived arbitration as a more desirable method of resolving dealer disputes than litigation viewed *Soler* as an invitation to provide for arbitration of all dealer disputes. Arbitration clauses became more common as a "forum selection" device, and the inevitable question was put to the courts: should *Soler* be extended to the domestic context and *American Safety* abandoned? A number of courts of appeals answered that question in the affirmative. *See, e.g., Seacoast Motors of Salisbury, Inc. v. DaimlerChrysler Motors Corp.*, 271 F.3d 6 (1st Cir. 2001); *Kotam Electronics, Inc. v. JBL Consumer Products, Inc.*, 93 F.3d 724 (11th Cir. 1996) (abandoning *American Safety* doctrine in domestic context in light of *Soler*); *Nghiem v. NEC Electronic, Inc.*, 25 F.3d 1437 (9th Cir. 1994) (*American Safety* doctrine did not preclude arbitration of antitrust dispute between employer and employee). The First Circuit's reasoning in *Seacoast* is typical:

> *American Safety* rested on the basic premise that the public interest in antitrust enforcement, the complexity of the antitrust laws, and the inadequacy of arbitral tribunals make arbitration of private antitrust claims inappropriate. This premise has since been rejected by the Supreme Court with respect to a variety of other statutory claims no less important or complex.
>
> There is no question here of an advance waiver of antitrust claims; arbitration clauses do not eliminate substantive rights but submit them for resolution in an arbitral, rather than a judicial forum. *Mitsubishi*, 473 U.S. at 628, 105 S.Ct. 3346. And while some antitrust cases do involve large issues in which the public has an interest, others are essentially business quarrels peculiar to the parties. For those in the former category, government agencies remain free to pursue the defendant regardless of private actions, whether before courts or arbitrators. We think time has passed by the *American Safety* doctrine and so hold.

271 F.3d at 10–11.

Arbitration of Antitrust Class Action Claims

The Supreme Court addressed the validity of arbitration clauses covering antitrust class actions in *Stolt-Nielsen S.A. v. AnimalFeeds Int'l Corp.*, 559 U.S. 662, 130 S.Ct. 1758 (2010) and *American Express Co. v. Italian Colors Restaurant*, 570 U.S. ___, 133 S.Ct. 2304 (2013). In *Stolt-Nielsen*, the Court held that a panel of arbitrators exceeded its authority under the Federal Arbitration Act ("FAA") when it concluded that an antitrust class action was subject to arbitration. It reasoned that although the contracts between the parties provided for arbitration of claims, including antitrust claims, they were silent as to the intentions of the parties regarding arbitration of class claims. Yet in *American Express*, the Court, by a 5–3 vote, invoked the FAA to enforce a contractual class action waiver clause in American Express' merchant agreement to bar an antitrust class action. Citing *Mitsubishi*, the Court held that "The antitrust laws do not 'evinc[e] an intention to preclude a waiver' of class action procedure." *Id.* at 2309. *Cf. AT & T Mobility, LLC v. Concepcion*, 131 S.Ct. 1740 (2011) (holding the Federal Arbitration Act preempted state law of unconscionability as applied to consumer class action waivers). For a critique of *Italian Colors*, see Einer Elhauge, *How* Italian Colors *Guts Private Antitrust Enforcement by replacing it With Ineffective forms of Arbitration*, 38 FORDHAM IN'L L.J. 771 (2015).

How should courts respond when class waivers appear in consumer product contracts or licenses? In *Kristian v. Comcast Corp.*, 446 F.3d 25 (1st Cir. 2006), the court reversed a district court's conclusion that an arbitration clause in a cable provider's customer contract could not be enforced retroactively, but it went on to invalidate provisions of the arbitration agreement that purported to bar antitrust class actions as well as the recovery of treble damages and attorney's fees. Could the case be decided the same way after *Italian Colors*?

Conclusion

The trend in the courts suggests that forum choice clauses providing for the arbitration of antitrust claims, including class action claims, are increasingly likely to be used in a variety of contracts, both business-to-business and business-to-consumer. Do you view that as a positive or negative development? Is it a matter of perspective? Why in each of the cases just discussed were the dealers, consumers, and customers all resisting and the suppliers pressing for arbitration? Finally, should the courts be as willing to uphold waiver of antitrust claims clauses

> when they are included in the fine print of consumer products
> packaging or inserted into software licenses for popular
> computer programs? What public policy arguments from
> *American Safety* might resurface in these two examples? What
> exceptions alluded to by the Court in *Mitsubishi*? What if the
> waiver limits a consumer's remedies to bilateral arbitration and
> precludes any form of class-wide relief, either through a class
> action or arbitration?

C. ANTITRUST ENFORCEMENT UNDER THE U.S. CONSTITUTIONAL SCHEME: ANTITRUST FEDERALISM AND ANTITRUST'S RELATIONSHIP WITH THE FIRST AMENDMENT

As we observed in Chapter 1, antitrust is only one of many forms of government intervention in the economy. "Competition policy," broadly conceived, can be implemented by more than one federal entity, and in the U.S.'s federal system, state and local public entities, as well. Whereas some such regulatory measure may seek to cure market failures, others may reflect successful efforts by private interests to enlist the state in restricting output or otherwise reducing competition.

This poses a dilemma for competition policy. First, firms know that government controls can encumber rivals more effectively than private trade restraints. Manipulating the machinery of government—for example, by filing baseless patent infringement lawsuits, by lobbying for public adoption of exclusionary standards, or otherwise engaging in conduct that may impose significant costs on rivals as a consequence of subsequent government action—can impede entry and hinder competition. And it may do so with less risk of incurring the kind of costs associated with exclusionary strategies such as below-cost pricing. Compared to private output restriction agreements, which may be difficult to reach and enforce, government bodies have superior tools for reaching consensus in the form of legislation, policing violations of that legislation, and punishing deviations, even through criminal sanctions. *See* Andrew I. Gavil & Tara Isa Koslov, *A Flexible Health Care Workforce Requires A Flexible Regulatory Environment: Promoting Health Care Competition Through Regulatory Reform*, 91 WASH. L. REV. 147 (2016) (discussing adverse competitive consequences of state regulation of nursing practice).

Moreover, First Amendment guarantees of free speech and petitioning contemplate few limits on the ability of citizens or firms to urge public officials to adopt favored policies, including measures that may favor some rivals over others and reduce competition. These protections may encourage private firms to seek public assistance in achieving anticompetitive goals, safe in the knowledge that in the asking they will retain constitutionally conferred immunity from prosecution.

Finally, the backdrop of federalism preserves a substantial economic policymaking role to state governments—at least for activities occurring largely within their own boundaries, and sovereign immunity under the Eleventh Amendment may insulate states from suits under federal law by injured persons.

In this section we will examine the principles adopted by the courts to manage these conflicts between federal antitrust laws and competition-suppressing government regulation. Their task in doing so has been to reconcile conflicting approaches for organizing the economy. These principles have emerged mainly in the context of antitrust litigation that attacks:

- anticompetitive action undertaken by states and their subdivisions (*e.g.*, counties, municipalities);

- anticompetitive action undertaken by private parties acting with the apparent approval of a public entity, typically pursuant to a publicly adopted regulatory scheme; and

- private efforts to elicit anticompetitive government regulation or intervention.

1. FEDERAL REGULATION

Antitrust exemptions that result from federal intervention in the market arise in two basic ways—by express directive or by implication. Express directives can take two basic forms. First, Congress may expressly declare that the antitrust laws do not apply to a particular industry or set of industry practices. *See* Figure 8–2, *infra* (listing principal federal statutory exemptions). In other instances, Congress has expressly committed the task of evaluating competition in an industry to just one federal antitrust enforcer. For example, common carriers are outside the jurisdiction of the FTC Act, but are subject to antitrust oversight by the DOJ.

In a second (and small) set of cases, immunity arises by implication. Where Congress creates a pervasive regulatory scheme, courts sometimes have implied antitrust immunity for the activity of regulated firms if application of the antitrust laws would disrupt the operation of the regulatory plan. In *Credit Suisse Securities (USA) LLC v. Billing*, 551 U.S. 264, 127 S. Ct. 2383 (2007), the Court ruled that there was a "plain repugnancy" between the plaintiffs' antitrust claims and federal securities laws, and that permitting private antitrust suits directed at conduct also regulated by federal securities laws would be "clearly incompatible" with the federal regulatory scheme, which already prohibited the practices. *See also Elec. Trading Grp., LLC v. Banc of Am. Sec. LLC*, 588 F.3d 128 (2d Cir. 2009) (short seller's antitrust claim against prime brokers was implicitly precluded by securities laws because "all four [*Credit Suisse*] considerations weigh[ed] in favor of implied preclusion."). *Credit Suisse* built upon the Court's earlier decision in *Verizon Commc'ns, Inc. v. Trinko*, 540 U.S. 398 (2004), which we read in Chapter 4. In *Trinko*, the fact that a dominant firm's duty to deal with rivals was the subject of federal regulation under the 1996 Telecommunications Act was among the factors that persuaded the Court to establish narrow rules of antitrust liability for refusals to deal.

Regulatory complexity alone does not establish immunity. The Supreme Court has warned that "[r]epeals of the antitrust laws by implication from a regulatory statute are strongly disfavored, and have only been found in cases of plain repugnancy between the antitrust and regulatory provisions." *United States v. Philadelphia Nat'l Bank*, 374 U.S. 321, 350–51 (1963). *See also National Gerimedical Hosp. & Gerontology Ctr. v. Blue Cross*, 452 U.S. 378, 389–90 (1981). *Cf. Ricci v. Chicago Mercantile Exchange*, 409 U.S. 289 (1973) (even if immunity is not warranted, agency may have primary jurisdiction over competition matters).

The Court also has held that the power to exempt conduct from antitrust attack resides with Congress—not individual federal officials. *See Otter Tail Power Co. v. United States*, 410 U.S. 366 (1973). Moreover, firms usually cannot avoid antitrust liability by arguing that federal officials endorsed conduct that otherwise violated the antitrust laws unless the federal officials had actual authority to immunize the behavior. Recall that in *Socony Vacuum Oil* in Chapter 2 the Supreme Court refused to entertain the defendants' argument that Department of Interior officials privately had encouraged them to engage in the concerted action at issue. *Accord Office of Personnel Mgmt. v. Richmond*, 496 U.S. 414 (1990) (officials lacking actual authority cannot bind the government). Nevertheless, one can imagine that a defendant's reasonable, good faith reliance on the approval of a federal official might weigh against a finding of criminal intent in an antitrust case or could count in favor of applying a rule of reason (rather than a per se test) in a civil action.

Private plaintiffs sometimes have argued that cooperation between agencies of the federal government or combinations by federal officials and private actors constituted antitrust violations. But courts consistently have refused to apply the antitrust statutes to the acts of federal agencies or individual federal officials acting within their official capacity. *See Rex Sys., Inc. v. Holiday*, 814 F.2d 994 (4th Cir. 1987) (military procurement decisions immune).

The presence of federal regulation also can limit the remedies available in an antitrust case. The Supreme Court held, for example, that treble damages are unavailable for private shippers who challenge, on antitrust grounds, the reasonableness of rates submitted to and approved by the now abolished Interstate Commerce Commission ("ICC"). *See Keogh v. Chicago & N.W. Ry.*, 260 U.S. 156 (1922). Despite some misgivings, the Supreme Court has endorsed the vitality of the "filed rate" doctrine, stating that *Keogh* does not create general antitrust immunity, but only bars the recovery of treble damages in actions involving ICC-approved rates. *See Square D Co. v. Niagara Frontier Tariff Bureau*, 476 U.S. 409 (1986).

Nevertheless, the "filed rate doctrine" has been expanded by some courts beyond its original ICC context outside of the antitrust area. *See, e.g., Montana-Dakota Util. Co. v. Northwestern Pub. Serv. Co.*, 341 U.S. 246, 71 S.Ct. 692, 95 L.Ed. 912 (1951) (electric utility rates approved by the Federal Power Commission challenged as fraudulent); and *Wegoland Ltd. v. NYNEX Corp.*, 27 F.3d 17 (2d Cir. 1994) (RICO-based challenge to utility rates that had been approved by the FCC). It has also been extended to various types of state regulation. *See id.* at 20. But there is an apparent split among courts on whether it should apply in the face of allegations that the filed rate was set pursuant to improper conduct, such as fraud or conspiracy. For a general discussion of the current reach of the filed rate doctrine, see *Blaylock v. First Am. Title Ins. Co.*, 504 F. Supp. 2d 1091, 1100–01 (W.D. Wash. 2007) (collecting and discussing cases).

Finally, extensive federal regulation that fails to provide immunity nonetheless can give rise to a "regulatory justification defense" to antitrust liability. *See Phonetele, Inc. v. AT & T Co.*, 664 F.2d 716 (9th Cir. 1981) ("[i]f a defendant can establish that, at the time the various anticompetitive acts alleged here were taken, it had a reasonable basis to conclude that its actions were necessitated by concrete factual imperatives recognized as legitimate by the regulatory authority, then its actions did not violate the antitrust laws.") Other tribunals have relied on extensive government rate regulation to reject antitrust claims against public utilities. *See Town of Concord v. Boston Edison Co.*, 915 F.2d 17 (1st Cir. 1990) (Breyer, C.J.). These decisions are important, because the deregulation of industries once subject to complete regulation of rates, service, and entry (*e.g.*, airlines and telecommunications) has increased the number of antitrust disputes that arise where antitrust and other federal regulatory regimes intersect.

2.   STATE REGULATION

State governments can limit competition by adopting legislation that sets prices, limits output, or restricts entry into a market. At first glance, such measures might appear to encroach upon the pro-competition policy of the national antitrust laws. How are the interests of national economic integration and state sovereignty to be reconciled? The Supreme Court first tackled this question in the early 1940s in *Parker v. Brown*, 371 U.S. 341, 63 S. Ct. 307 (1943). *Parker* was decided following years of economic turmoil brought about by the Great Depression in which the respective roles of competition and regulation dominated debates about economic policy. The Court considered whether a program that created a proration system for raisins violated the Sherman Act. The proration system was a marketing program implemented under the authority of the California Agricultural Prorate Act. Under the program, raisins would be classified into three different categories. Different rules were established for each category, affecting the purposes for which, and through what channels, the raisins could be sold. The system in effect governed the price of raisins. The Court found that the prorate program was not prohibited by the Sherman Act, characterizing it as a matter of state concern. Grounded in principles of federalism, *Parker* rested on the assumptions that neither the language nor the legislative history of the Sherman Act suggested any intention on the part of Congress that its provisions should apply to states.

Notice the impact of the regulatory regime at issue in *Parker*. California raisin growers produced virtually all the raisins that were consumed in the United States. The proration system governed the price of raisins sold throughout the country. By refusing to allow antitrust oversight to interfere with the state's output restrictions, the Supreme Court in effect permitted California—the growers' state—to determine the nationwide price of raisins, noting however, that Congress could legislate otherwise. Why might Congress want to do so?

Elaboration of *Parker* was confined to the lower courts until 1975, when *Goldfarb v. Virginia State Bar*, 421 U.S. 773, 95 S.Ct. 2004 (1975), signaled the Court's willingness to narrow *Parker's* broad scope. In *Goldfarb* the Court declined to apply *Parker* to minimum fee schedules set by a county bar association and enforcement of the schedules in disciplinary proceedings conducted by the state bar. The Court termed this conduct "essentially a private anticompetitive activity," as neither Virginia's laws nor the rules of its supreme court required the minimum fees. However, in *Bates v. State Bar of Arizona*, 433 U.S. 350, 97 S.Ct. 2691, 53 L.Ed.2d 810 (1977), the Court again declared that the legislative actions of the state—in that case the state supreme court's prohibition of attorney advertising—were actions of "the state" that were exempt from the coverage of the Sherman Act. *See also Hoover v. Ronwin*, 466 U.S. 558, 104 S.Ct. 1989, 80 L.Ed.2d 590 (1984).

Two other issues have arisen in connection with defining the scope of the state action doctrine. First, whether *Parker* extends to the political subdivisions of the state, and second, whether there is a "conspiracy exception" to *Parker*, *i.e.*, whether misconduct by government officials, such as colluding with private parties to the detriment of competition, falls outside the scope of *Parker's* protection.

Both issues were addressed in *City of Columbia v. Omni Outdoor Advertising, Inc.*, 499 U.S. 365, 111 S.Ct. 1344, 113 L.Ed.2d 382 (1991). As a general matter, the Court observed, *Parker* does not apply directly to local governments, citing *Town of Hallie v. Eau Claire*, 471 U.S. 34, 38, 105 S.Ct. 1713, 1716 (1985); *Community Commc'ns Co. v. Boulder*, 455 U.S. 40, 50–51, 102 S.Ct. 835, 840–841 (1982); and *Lafayette v. Louisiana Power & Light Co.*, 435 U.S. 389, 412–413, 98 S.Ct. 1123, 1136–1137 (1978) (plurality opinion). The state action doctrine may be available, however, when a municipality's restriction of competition is an authorized implementation of state policy. We will discuss the issues related to municipal liability in the next section of the Chapter.

City of Columbia involved a challenge by an outdoor advertising company to the city's decisions on the placement of billboards, which, it argued, had favored its rivals. State statutes authorized municipalities to adopt zoning and land use regulations affecting construction within their boundaries, including the placement of billboards. The first issue was whether the fact that state law clearly authorized regulation of billboards was enough to invoke the state action doctrine, as the defendants argued. The Court concluded "such an expansive interpretation of the *Parker*-defense authorization requirement would have unacceptable consequences." 499 U.S. at 371. In the Court's view, "in order to prevent *Parker* from undermining the very interests of federalism it is designed to protect, it is necessary to adopt a concept of authority broader than what is applied to determine the legality of the municipality's action under state law. * * * " *Id.* at 372. However, it also concluded that "here no more is needed to establish, for *Parker* purposes, the city's authority to regulate than its unquestioned zoning power over the size, location, and spacing of billboards." *Id.*

Authority to regulate alone, however, is insufficient to trigger *Parker*. According to the Court, the "*Parker* defense also requires authority to suppress competition—more specifically, 'clear articulation of a state policy to authorize anticompetitive conduct' by the municipality in connection with its regulation." *Id., quoting Town of Hallie*, 471 U.S., at 40, 105 S.Ct., at 1717 (internal quotation omitted). To satisfy that requirement, however, it is not necessary that the statute delegating authority to the municipality "explicitly permits the displacement of competition. It is enough, we have held, if suppression of competition is the 'foreseeable result' of what the statute authorizes." *Id.* at 372–73. The Court concluded that this condition was "amply met here." *Id.* at 373. *But see Southern Motor Carriers Rate Conference, Inc. v. United States*, 471 U.S. 48 (1985) (no mention of "foreseeable result" standard).

The Court also resolved a second issue: whether there was a "conspiracy exception" to *Parker*:

> There is no such conspiracy exception. The rationale of *Parker* was that, in light of our national commitment to federalism, the general language of the Sherman Act should not be interpreted to prohibit anticompetitive actions by the States in their governmental capacities as sovereign regulators. * * * The impracticality of such a principle is evident if, for purposes of the exception, "conspiracy" means nothing more than an agreement to impose the regulation in question. Since it is both inevitable and desirable that public officials often agree to do what one or another group of private citizens urges upon them, such an exception would virtually swallow up the *Parker* rule * * *.

Id. at 374–75.

City of Columbia also hinted at a third possible exception to *Parker* that would permit the antitrust laws to apply to a municipality when it acts as a "market participant" rather than as a regulator. *Id.* at 379. This passing reference has not been clarified by the Supreme Court and, although it has been discussed in some lower court decisions, has not coalesced into a firm exception to *Parker*. *See generally* ABA ANTITRUST SECTION, ANTITRUST LAW DEVELOPMENTS 1282–83 (6th ed. 2007). *See also* ANTITRUST MODERNIZATION COMMISSION, FINAL REPORT AND RECOMMENDATIONS 375–77 (2007) (endorsing market participant exception), http://govinfo.library.unt.edu/amc/report_recommendation /amc_final_report.pdf.

On September 23, 2003, the State Action Task Force at the Federal Trade Commission, which had been established in the summer of 2001, issued a comprehensive Staff Report urging clarifications of the State Action Doctrine. The Report identifies a variety of ways in which the Task Force believed the State Action doctrine is being read too broadly to the detriment of competition, and urges that it be constrained, particularly through refinement of the definition of "the State," and interpretation of both "clear articulation" and "active supervision." *See* FTC, Office of Policy Planning, *Report of the State Action Task Force* (Sept. 2003), http://www. ftc.gov/os/2003/09/stateactionreport.pdf.

Parker and later cases established that the legislative acts of the state (including those of a state supreme court acting in a legislative capacity) are acts of the sovereign that are exempt from the reach of the Sherman Act. But they also recognized that states can implement their policies indirectly in many different ways, as through commissions, boards, and other instrumentalities, and that the justification for the *Parker* exemption might become attenuated as the challenged conduct becomes increasingly removed from the state. Tension developed around a key issue: to what extent, if any, should the acts of these kinds of bodies be deemed acts of "the state" for purposes of extending the *Parker* exemption?

The Court first answered that question in *California Retail Liquor Dealers Ass'n v. Midcal Aluminum, Inc.*, 445 U.S. 97, 100 S.Ct. 937 (1980). *Midcal* involved a California statute that regulated wine pricing through fair trade contracts or price schedules. If a producer chose not to use a fair trade contract, it had to adhere to price schedules, posted by wholesalers, for its brands. These price schedules affected merchants, who had to follow the pricing in either the fair trade contract or, if there was no contract, the schedule posted by wholesalers when selling wines to retailers. The Court provided a two-pronged framework for answering whether this pricing regime sufficiently constituted an act "of the state" to allow for a *Parker* exemption. The first prong of *Midcal's* test for application of the state action doctrine to the acts of private parties—the "clear articulation" requirement—asks whether the state has clearly chosen to displace competition. For example, in *Southern Motor Carriers Rate Conference, Inc. v. United States*, 471 U.S. 48 (1985), the Supreme Court ruled that "a state policy that expressly *permits,* but does not compel, anticompetitive behavior may be 'clearly articulated' within the meaning of *Midcal.*" Thus, it is enough that the state policy merely authorizes (but does not command) departures from competition. The Supreme Court had occasion to examine the "clear articulation" standard in *FTC v. Phoebe Putney Health System, Inc.*, a case brought by the Federal Trade Commission to challenge a hospital acquisition in Albany, Georgia.

FEDERAL TRADE COMMISSION V. PHOEBE PUTNEY HEALTH SYSTEM, INC.

Supreme Court of the United States, 2013.
___ U.S. ___, 133 S.Ct. 1003, 185 L.Ed.2d 43.

SOTOMAYOR, J., delivered the opinion for a unanimous Court.

Under this Court's state-action immunity doctrine, when a local governmental entity acts pursuant to a clearly articulated and affirmatively expressed state policy to displace competition, it is exempt from scrutiny under the federal antitrust laws. In this case, we must decide whether a Georgia law that creates special-purpose public entities called hospital authorities and gives those entities general corporate powers, including the power to acquire hospitals, clearly articulates and affirmatively expresses a state policy to permit acquisitions that substantially lessen competition. Because Georgia's grant of general corporate powers to hospital authorities does not include permission to use those powers anticompetitively, we hold that the clear-articulation test is not satisfied and state-action immunity does not apply.

I

A

In 1941, the State of Georgia amended its Constitution to allow political subdivisions to provide health care services. The State concurrently enacted the Hospital Authorities Law (Law), "to provide a mechanism for the operation and maintenance of needed health care facilities in the several counties and municipalities of th[e] state." "The purpose of the constitutional provision and the statute based thereon was to . . . create an organization which could carry out and make more workable the duty which the State owed to its indigent sick." As amended, the Law authorizes each county and municipality, and certain combinations of counties or municipalities, to create "a public body corporate and politic" called a "hospital authority." Hospital authorities are governed by 5-to 9-member boards that are appointed by the governing body of the county or municipality in their area of operation.

Under the Law, a hospital authority "exercise[s] public and essential governmental functions" and is delegated "all the powers necessary or convenient to carry out and effectuate" the Law's purposes. Giving more content to that general delegation, the Law enumerates 27 powers conferred upon hospital authorities, including the power "[t]o acquire by purchase, lease, or otherwise and to operate projects, which are defined to include hospitals and other public health facilities;" "[t]o construct, reconstruct, improve, alter, and repair projects;" "[t]o lease . . . for operation by others any project" provided certain conditions are satisfied; and "[t]o establish rates and charges for the services and use of the facilities of the authority." Hospital authorities may not operate or construct any project for profit, and accordingly they must set rates so as only to cover operating expenses and create reasonable reserves.

B

[The Court explained that when the Law was adopted, the city of Albany and Dougherty County established the Hospital Authority of Albany-Dougherty County (Authority). The Authority then acquired Phoebe Putney Memorial Hospital (Memorial). In 1990, the Authority restructured its operations by forming two private nonprofit corporations to manage Memorial: Phoebe Putney Health System, Inc. (PPHS), and its subsidiary, Phoebe Putney Memorial Hospital, Inc. (PPMH).-Eds.]

Memorial is one of two hospitals in Dougherty County. The second, Palmyra Medical Center (Palmyra), was established in Albany in 1971 and is located just two miles from Memorial. At the time suit was brought in this case, Palmyra was operated by a national for-profit hospital network, HCA, Inc. (HCA). Together, Memorial and Palmyra account for 86 percent of the market for acute-care hospital services provided to commercial health care plans and their customers in the six counties surrounding Albany. Memorial accounts for 75 percent of that market on its own.

In 2010, PPHS began discussions with HCA about acquiring Palmyra. Following negotiations, PPHS presented the Authority with a plan under which the Authority would purchase Palmyra with PPHS controlled funds and then lease Palmyra to a PPHS subsidiary for $1 per year under the Memorial lease agreement. The Authority unanimously approved the transaction.

The Federal Trade Commission (FTC) shortly thereafter issued an administrative complaint alleging that the proposed purchase-and-lease transaction would create a virtual monopoly and would substantially reduce competition in the market for acute-care hospital services, in violation of § 5 of the Federal Trade Commission Act and § 7 of the Clayton Act. The FTC, along with the State of Georgia,[1] subsequently filed suit against the Authority, HCA, Palmyra, PPHS, PPMH, and the new PPHS subsidiary created to manage Palmyra (collectively respondents), seeking to enjoin the transaction pending administrative proceedings.

* * *

We granted certiorari on two questions: whether the Georgia Legislature, through the powers it vested in hospital authorities, clearly articulated and affirmatively expressed a state policy to displace competition in the market for hospital services; and if so, whether state-action immunity is nonetheless inapplicable as a result of the Authority's minimal participation in negotiating the terms of the sale of Palmyra and the Authority's limited supervision of the two hospitals' operations. Concluding that the answer to the first question is "no," we reverse without reaching the second question.

II

In *Parker v. Brown*, this Court held that because "nothing in the language of the Sherman Act or in its history" suggested that Congress intended to restrict the sovereign capacity of the States to regulate their economies, the Act should not be read to bar States from imposing market restraints "as an act of government." Following *Parker,* we have held that under certain circumstances, immunity from the federal antitrust laws may extend to nonstate actors carrying out the State's regulatory program.

But given the fundamental national values of free enterprise and economic competition that are embodied in the federal antitrust laws, "state-action immunity is disfavored, much as are repeals by implication." Consistent with this preference, we recognize state-action immunity only when it is clear that the challenged anticompetitive conduct is undertaken

---

[1] Georgia did not join the notice of appeal filed by the FTC and is no longer a party in the case.

pursuant to a regulatory scheme that "is the State's own." Accordingly, "[c]loser analysis is required when the activity at issue is not directly that of" the State itself, but rather "is carried out by others pursuant to state authorization." When determining whether the anticompetitive acts of private parties are entitled to immunity, we employ a two-part test, requiring first that "the challenged restraint . . . be one clearly articulated and affirmatively expressed as state policy," and second that "the policy . . . be actively supervised by the State."

This case involves allegedly anticompetitive conduct undertaken by a substate governmental entity. Because municipalities and other political subdivisions are not themselves sovereign, state-action immunity under *Parker* does not apply to them directly. At the same time, however, substate governmental entities do receive immunity from antitrust scrutiny when they act "pursuant to state policy to displace competition with regulation or monopoly public service." This rule "preserves to the States their freedom . . . to use their municipalities to administer state regulatory policies free of the inhibitions of the federal antitrust laws without at the same time permitting purely parochial interests to disrupt the Nation's free-market goals."

As with private parties, immunity will only attach to the activities of local governmental entities if they are undertaken pursuant to a "clearly articulated and affirmatively expressed" state policy to displace competition. But unlike private parties, such entities are not subject to the "active state supervision requirement" because they have less of an incentive to pursue their own self-interest under the guise of implementing state policies.[5]

"[T]o pass the 'clear articulation' test," a state legislature need not "expressly state in a statute or its legislative history that the legislature intends for the delegated action to have anticompetitive effects." Rather, * * * state-action immunity applies if the anticompetitive effect was the "foreseeable result" of what the State authorized. * * *

III

A

Applying the clear-articulation test to the Law before us, we conclude that respondents' claim for state-action immunity fails because there is no evidence the State affirmatively contemplated that hospital authorities would displace competition by consolidating hospital ownership. The

---

[5] The Eleventh Circuit has held that while Georgia's hospital authorities are "unique entities" that lie "somewhere between a local, general-purpose governing body (such as a city or county) and a corporation," they qualify as "an instrumentality, agency, or 'political subdivision' of Georgia for purposes of state action immunity." The FTC has not challenged that characterization of Georgia's hospital authorities, and we accordingly operate from the assumption that hospital authorities are akin to political subdivisions.

acquisition and leasing powers exercised by the Authority in the challenged transaction, which were the principal powers relied upon by the Court of Appeals in finding state-action immunity, mirror general powers routinely conferred by state law upon private corporations. Other powers possessed by hospital authorities that the Court of Appeals characterized as having "impressive breadth," also fit this pattern, including the ability to make and execute contracts, to set rates for services, to sue and be sued, to borrow money, and the residual authority to exercise any or all powers possessed by private corporations.

Our case law makes clear that state-law authority to act is insufficient to establish state-action immunity; the substate governmental entity must also show that it has been delegated authority to act or regulate anticompetitively. In [*Community Communications Co. v. City of Boulder*, 455 U.S. 40 (1982)], we held that Colorado's Home Rule Amendment allowing municipalities to govern local affairs did not satisfy the clear-articulation test. There was no doubt in that case that the city had authority as a matter of state law to pass an ordinance imposing a moratorium on a cable provider's expansion of service. But we rejected the proposition that "the general grant of power to enact ordinances necessarily implies state authorization to enact specific anticompetitive ordinances" because such an approach "would wholly eviscerate the concepts of 'clear articulation and affirmative expression' that our precedents require." We explained that when a State's position "is one of mere *neutrality* respecting the municipal actions challenged as anticompetitive," the State cannot be said to have " 'contemplated' " those anticompetitive actions.

The principle articulated in *Boulder* controls this case. Grants of general corporate power that allow substate governmental entities to participate in a competitive marketplace should be, can be, and typically are used in ways that raise no federal antitrust concerns. As a result, a State that has delegated such general powers "can hardly be said to have 'contemplated' " that they will be used anticompetitively. *See also* 1A P. Areeda & H. Hovenkamp, Antitrust Law ¶ 225a, p. 131 (3d ed.2006) (hereinafter Areeda & Hovenkamp) ("When a state grants power to an inferior entity, it presumably grants the power to do the thing contemplated, but not to do so anticompetitively"). Thus, while the Law does allow the Authority to acquire hospitals, it does not clearly articulate and affirmatively express a state policy empowering the Authority to make acquisitions of existing hospitals that will substantially lessen competition.

B

In concluding otherwise, and specifically in reasoning that the Georgia Legislature "must have anticipated" that acquisitions by hospital authorities "would produce anticompetitive effects," the Court of Appeals applied the concept of "foreseeability" from our clear-articulation test too loosely.

In [*Town of Hallie v. City of Eau Claire*, 471 U.S. 34 (1985)], we recognized that it would "embod[y] an unrealistic view of how legislatures work and of how statutes are written" to require state legislatures to explicitly authorize specific anticompetitive effects before state-action immunity could apply. "No legislature," we explained, "can be expected to catalog all of the anticipated effects" of a statute delegating authority to a substate governmental entity. Instead, we have approached the clear-articulation inquiry more practically, but without diluting the ultimate requirement that the State must have affirmatively contemplated the displacement of competition such that the challenged anticompetitive effects can be attributed to the "state itself." Thus, we have concluded that a state policy to displace federal antitrust law was sufficiently expressed where the displacement of competition was the inherent, logical, or ordinary result of the exercise of authority delegated by the state legislature. In that scenario, the State must have foreseen and implicitly endorsed the anticompetitive effects as consistent with its policy goals.

* * *

By contrast, "simple permission to play in a market" does not "foreseeably entail permission to roughhouse in that market unlawfully." When a State grants some entity general power to act, whether it is a private corporation or a public entity like the Authority, it does so against the backdrop of federal antitrust law. Of course, both private parties and local governmental entities conceivably may transgress antitrust requirements by exercising their general powers in anticompetitive ways. But a reasonable legislature's ability to anticipate that (potentially undesirable) possibility falls well short of clearly articulating an affirmative state policy to displace competition with a regulatory alternative.

* * * [T]he Court of Appeals stated that "[i]t defies imagination to suppose the [state] legislature could have believed that every geographic market in Georgia was so replete with hospitals that authorizing acquisitions by the authorities could have no serious anticompetitive consequences." Respondents echo this argument, noting that each of Georgia's 159 counties covers a small geographical area and that most of them are sparsely populated, with nearly three-quarters having fewer than 50,000 residents as of the 2010 Census.

Even accepting, *arguendo,* the premise that facts about a market could make the anticompetitive use of general corporate powers "foreseeable," we reject the Court of Appeals' and respondents' conclusion because only a relatively small subset of the conduct permitted as a matter of state law by [Georgia] has the potential to negatively affect competition. * * * [T]he power to acquire hospitals still does not ordinarily produce anticompetitive effects. * * * While subsequent acquisitions by authorities have the potential to reduce competition, they will raise federal antitrust concerns only in markets that are large enough to support more than one hospital but sufficiently small that the merger of competitors would lead to a significant increase in market concentration. This is too slender a reed to support the Court of Appeals' and respondents' inference.

IV

A

Taking a somewhat different approach than the Court of Appeals, respondents insist that the Law should not be read as a mere authorization for hospital authorities to participate in the hospital-services market and exercise general corporate powers. Rather, they contend that hospital authorities are granted unique powers and responsibilities to fulfill the State's objective of providing all residents with access to adequate and affordable health and hospital care. Respondents argue that in view of hospital authorities' statutory objective, their specific attributes, and the regulatory context in which they operate, it was foreseeable that authorities facing capacity constraints would decide they could best serve their communities' needs by acquiring an existing local hospital rather than incur the additional expense and regulatory burden of expanding a facility or constructing a new one.

In support of this argument, respondents observe that hospital authorities are simultaneously empowered to act in ways private entities cannot while also being subject to significant regulatory constraints. On the power side, as the Court of Appeals noted, hospital authorities may acquire through eminent domain property that is "essential to the [authority's] purposes." On the restraint side, hospital authorities are managed by a publicly accountable board, they must operate on a nonprofit basis, and they may only lease a project for others to operate after determining that doing so will promote the community's public health needs and that the lessee will not receive more than a reasonable rate of return on its investment. Moreover, hospital authorities operate within a broader regulatory context in which Georgia requires any party seeking to establish or significantly expand certain medical facilities, including hospitals, to obtain a certificate of need from state regulators.

We have no doubt that Georgia's hospital authorities differ materially from private corporations that offer hospital services. But nothing in the Law or any other provision of Georgia law clearly articulates a state policy to allow authorities to exercise their general corporate powers, including their acquisition power, without regard to negative effects on competition. The state legislature's objective of improving access to affordable health care does not logically suggest that the State intended that hospital authorities pursue that end through mergers that create monopolies. Nor do the restrictions imposed on hospital authorities, including the requirement that they operate on a nonprofit basis, reveal such a policy. Particularly in light of our national policy favoring competition, these restrictions should be read to reflect more modest aims. The legislature may have viewed profit generation as incompatible with its goal of providing care for the indigent sick. In addition, the legislature may have believed that some hospital authorities would operate in markets with characteristics of natural monopolies, in which case the legislature could not rely on competition to control prices.

We recognize that Georgia, particularly through its certificate of need requirement, does limit competition in the market for hospital services in some respects. But regulation of an industry, and even the authorization of discrete forms of anticompetitive conduct pursuant to a regulatory structure, does not establish that the State has affirmatively contemplated other forms of anticompetitive conduct that are only tangentially related. * * *

In this case, the fact that Georgia imposes limits on entry into the market for medical services, which apply to both hospital authorities and private corporations, does not clearly articulate a policy favoring the consolidation of existing hospitals that are engaged in active competition. As to the Authority's eminent domain power, it was not exercised here and we do not find it relevant to the question whether the State authorized hospital authorities to consolidate market power through potentially anticompetitive acquisitions of existing hospitals.

B

Finally, respondents contend that to the extent there is any doubt about whether the clear-articulation test is satisfied in this context, federal courts should err on the side of recognizing immunity to avoid improper interference with state policy choices. But we do not find the Law ambiguous on the question whether it clearly articulates a policy authorizing anticompetitive acquisitions; it does not.

More fundamentally, respondents' suggestion is inconsistent with the principle that "state-action immunity is disfavored." *Parker* and its progeny are premised on an understanding that respect for the States' coordinate role in government counsels against reading the federal antitrust laws to restrict the States' sovereign capacity to regulate their economies and provide services to their citizens. But federalism and state sovereignty are poorly served by a rule of construction that would allow "essential national policies" embodied in the antitrust laws to be displaced by state delegations of authority "intended to achieve more limited ends." As an *amici* brief filed by 20 States in support of the FTC contends, loose application of the clear-articulation test would attach significant unintended consequences to

States' frequent delegations of corporate authority to local bodies, effectively requiring States to disclaim any intent to displace competition to avoid inadvertently authorizing anticompetitive conduct. We decline to set such a trap for unwary state legislatures.

———————

As noted, above, *Midcal* established a two-prong test. *Phoebe Putney* clarified the meaning and application of the first prong, "clear articulation." *Midcal's* second prong—"active state supervision"—seeks to ensure that *Parker* "will shelter only the particular anticompetitive acts of private parties that, in the judgment of the State, actually further state regulatory policies." In *Patrick v. Burget*, 486 U.S. 94 (1988), for example, the Court found that Oregon had exercised insufficient oversight of a peer review mechanism by which physicians determined whether to grant a rival doctor hospital privileges. For state oversight to constitute active supervision, state officials must "have and exercise power to review particular anticompetitive acts of private parties and disapprove those that fail to accord with state policy." Such scrutiny serves to ensure that states do not simply repeal fundamental elements of national competition policy without installing alternative, operational public oversight machinery. *See also 324 Liquor Corp. v. Duffy*, 479 U.S. 335 (1987) (state action doctrine inapplicable to state liquor pricing regulations absent state supervision).

The Supreme Court revisited the active supervision issue in *FTC v. Ticor Title Ins. Co.*, 504 U.S. 621 (1992), where it again withheld application of the state action doctrine, in that case from title insurance companies that jointly set fees for title searches and examinations through rate bureaus subject to state regulation. The defendants' proposed rates took effect unless state regulators exercised a "negative option" to veto the rates. The Supreme Court said that the active supervision test requires an inquiry into "whether the State has exercised sufficient independent judgment and control so that the details of the rates or prices have been established as a product of deliberate state intervention, not simply by agreement among private parties." Several features of the regulatory oversight process belied the existence of adequate "independent judgment and control." In two states, the regulators examined rate filings for "mathematical accuracy" alone or left filings "unchecked altogether." In other states, the regulators failed to press private rate bureaus to comply with requests for information.

Ticor sought to define when nominal state oversight might fall short of active supervision. The Court said an "infrequent lapse of state supervision" might not preclude application of the state action doctrine; oversight tools such as "sampling techniques or a specified rate of return" might provide the requisite "comprehensive supervision without complete control." Moreover, the Court said *Ticor* "should be read in light of the gravity of the antitrust offense [horizontal price-fixing], the involvement of private actors throughout, and the clear absence of state supervision." Despite these attempts at limitation, *Ticor* left some degree of uncertainty for firms attempting to predict the effect of state oversight on their exposure to federal antitrust liability.

Less than two years after *Phoebe Putney*, the Supreme Court had the occasion to again consider the second *Midcal* prong, active state supervision, in another case brought by the FTC, and again it ruled in favor of the Commission's position.

NORTH CAROLINA STATE BOARD OF DENTAL EXAMINERS V. FTC

Supreme Court of the United States, 2015.
___ U.S. ___, 135 S.Ct. 1101, 191 L.Ed.2d 35.

JUSTICE KENNEDY delivered the opinion of the Court.

This case arises from an antitrust challenge to the actions of a state regulatory board. A majority of the board's members are engaged in the active practice of the profession it regulates. The question is whether the board's actions are protected from Sherman Act regulation under the doctrine of state-action antitrust immunity, as defined and applied in this Court's decisions beginning with *Parker v. Brown,* 317 U.S. 341, 63 S.Ct. 307, 87 L.Ed. 315 (1943).

I

A

In its Dental Practice Act (Act), North Carolina has declared the practice of dentistry to be a matter of public concern requiring regulation. Under the Act, the North Carolina State Board of Dental Examiners (Board) is "the agency of the State for the regulation of the practice of dentistry."

The Board's principal duty is to create, administer, and enforce a licensing system for dentists. To perform that function it has broad authority over licensees. The Board's authority with respect to unlicensed persons, however, is more restricted: like "any resident citizen," the Board may file suit to "perpetually enjoin any person from . . . unlawfully practicing dentistry."

The Act provides that six of the Board's eight members must be licensed dentists engaged in the active practice of dentistry. They are elected by other licensed dentists in North Carolina, who cast their ballots in elections conducted by the Board. The seventh member must be a licensed and practicing dental hygienist, and he or she is elected by other licensed hygienists. The final member is referred to by the Act as a "consumer" and is appointed by the Governor. * * *

Board members swear an oath of office, and the Board must comply with the State's Administrative Procedure Act, and open-meetings law. The Board may promulgate rules and regulations governing the practice of dentistry within the State, provided those mandates are not inconsistent with the Act and are approved by the North Carolina Rules Review Commission, whose members are appointed by the state legislature.

B

In the 1990's, dentists in North Carolina started whitening teeth. Many of those who did so, including 8 of the Board's 10 members during the period at issue in this case, earned substantial fees for that service. By 2003, nondentists arrived on the scene. They charged lower prices for their services than the dentists did. Dentists soon began to complain to the Board about their new competitors. Few complaints warned of possible harm to consumers. Most expressed a principal concern with the low prices charged by nondentists.

Responding to these filings, the Board opened an investigation into nondentist teeth whitening. A dentist member was placed in charge of the inquiry. Neither the Board's hygienist member nor its consumer member participated in this undertaking. The Board's chief operations officer remarked that the Board was "going forth to do battle" with nondentists. The Board's concern did not result in a formal rule or regulation reviewable by the independent Rules Review Commission, even though the Act does not, by its terms, specify that teeth whitening is "the practice of dentistry."

Starting in 2006, the Board issued at least 47 cease-and-desist letters on its official letterhead to nondentist teeth whitening service providers and product manufacturers. Many of those letters directed the recipient to cease "all activity constituting the practice of dentistry"; warned that the unlicensed practice of dentistry is a crime; and strongly implied (or expressly stated) that teeth whitening constitutes "the practice of dentistry." In early 2007, the Board persuaded the North Carolina Board of Cosmetic Art Examiners to warn cosmetologists against providing teeth whitening services. Later that year, the Board sent letters to mall operators, stating that kiosk teeth whiteners were violating the Dental Practice Act and advising that the malls consider expelling violators from their premises.

These actions had the intended result. Nondentists ceased offering teeth whitening services in North Carolina.

C

In 2010, the Federal Trade Commission (FTC) filed an administrative complaint charging the Board with violating § 5 of the Federal Trade Commission Act. The FTC alleged that the Board's concerted action to exclude nondentists from the market for teeth whitening services in North

Carolina constituted an anticompetitive and unfair method of competition. The Board moved to dismiss, alleging state-action immunity. An Administrative Law Judge (ALJ) denied the motion. On appeal, the FTC sustained the ALJ's ruling. It reasoned that, even assuming the Board had acted pursuant to a clearly articulated state policy to displace competition, the Board is a "public/private hybrid" that must be actively supervised by the State to claim immunity. The FTC further concluded the Board could not make that showing.

Following other proceedings not relevant here, the ALJ conducted a hearing on the merits and determined the Board had unreasonably restrained trade in violation of antitrust law. On appeal, the FTC again sustained the ALJ. The FTC rejected the Board's public safety justification, noting, *inter alia,* "a wealth of evidence . . . suggesting that non-dentist provided teeth whitening is a safe cosmetic procedure."

The FTC ordered the Board to stop sending the cease-and-desist letters or other communications that stated nondentists may not offer teeth whitening services and products. It further ordered the Board to issue notices to all earlier recipients of the Board's cease-and-desist orders advising them of the Board's proper sphere of authority and saying, among other options, that the notice recipients had a right to seek declaratory rulings in state court.

On petition for review, the Court of Appeals for the Fourth Circuit affirmed the FTC in all respects. * * *

II

Federal antitrust law is a central safeguard for the Nation's free market structures. In this regard it is "as important to the preservation of economic freedom and our free-enterprise system as the Bill of Rights is to the protection of our fundamental personal freedoms." The antitrust laws declare a considered and decisive prohibition by the Federal Government of cartels, price fixing, and other combinations or practices that undermine the free market.

The Sherman Act serves to promote robust competition, which in turn empowers the States and provides their citizens with opportunities to pursue their own and the public's welfare. See *FTC v. Ticor Title Ins. Co.,* 504 U.S. 621, 632, 112 S.Ct. 2169, 119 L.Ed.2d 410 (1992). The States, however, when acting in their respective realm, need not adhere in all contexts to a model of unfettered competition. While "the States regulate their economies in many ways not inconsistent with the antitrust laws," in some spheres they impose restrictions on occupations, confer exclusive or shared rights to dominate a market, or otherwise limit competition to achieve public objectives. If every duly enacted state law or policy were required to conform to the mandates of the Sherman Act, thus promoting competition at the expense of other values a State may deem fundamental, federal antitrust law would impose an impermissible burden on the States' power to regulate.

For these reasons, the Court in *Parker v. Brown* interpreted the antitrust laws to confer immunity on anticompetitive conduct by the States when acting in their sovereign capacity. That ruling recognized Congress' purpose to respect the federal balance and to "embody in the Sherman Act the federalism principle that the States possess a significant measure of sovereignty under our Constitution." *Community Communications Co. v. Boulder,* 455 U.S. 40, 53, 102 S.Ct. 835, 70 L.Ed.2d 810 (1982). Since 1943, the Court has reaffirmed the importance of *Parker*'s central holding.

III

In this case the Board argues its members were invested by North Carolina with the power of the State and that, as a result, the Board's actions are cloaked with *Parker* immunity. This argument fails, however. A nonsovereign actor controlled by active market participants—such as the Board—enjoys *Parker* immunity only if it satisfies two requirements: "first that 'the challenged restraint . . . be one clearly articulated and affirmatively expressed as state policy,' and second that 'the policy . . . be actively supervised by the State.' " *FTC v. Phoebe Putney Health System, Inc.,* 568 U.S. ___, ___, 133 S.Ct. 1003, 1010, 185 L.Ed.2d 43 (2013) (quoting *California Retail Liquor Dealers Assn. v. Midcal Aluminum, Inc.,* 445 U.S. 97, 105, 100 S.Ct. 937, 63 L.Ed.2d 233 (1980)). The parties have assumed that the clear articulation requirement is satisfied, and we do the same. While North Carolina prohibits the unauthorized practice of dentistry, however, its Act is silent on whether that broad prohibition covers teeth whitening. Here, the Board did not receive active supervision by the State when it interpreted the Act as addressing teeth whitening and when it enforced that policy by issuing cease-and-desist letters to nondentist teeth whiteners.

A

Although state-action immunity exists to avoid conflicts between state sovereignty and the Nation's commitment to a policy of robust competition, *Parker* immunity is not unbounded. "[G]iven the fundamental national values of free enterprise and economic competition that are embodied in the federal antitrust laws, 'state action immunity is disfavored, much as are repeals by implication.' " *Phoebe Putney, supra,* at ___, 133 S.Ct., at 1010. * * *

An entity may not invoke *Parker* immunity unless the actions in question are an exercise of the State's sovereign power. State legislation and "decision[s] of a state supreme court, acting legislatively rather than judicially," will satisfy this standard, and "*ipso facto* are exempt from the operation of the antitrust laws" because they are an undoubted exercise of state sovereign authority.

But while the Sherman Act confers immunity on the States' own anticompetitive policies out of respect for federalism, it does not always confer immunity where, as here, a State delegates control over a market to a non-sovereign actor. See *Parker, supra,* at 351, 63 S.Ct. 307 ("[A] state does not give immunity to those who violate the Sherman Act by authorizing them to violate it, or by declaring that their action is lawful"). For purposes of *Parker,* a nonsovereign actor is one whose conduct does not automatically qualify as that of the sovereign State itself. State agencies are not simply by their governmental character sovereign actors for purposes of state-action immunity. * * * Immunity for state agencies, therefore, requires more than a mere facade of state involvement, for it is necessary in light of *Parker*'s rationale to ensure the States accept political accountability for anticompetitive conduct they permit and control.

Limits on state-action immunity are most essential when the State seeks to delegate its regulatory power to active market participants, for established ethical standards may blend with private anticompetitive motives in a way difficult even for market participants to discern. Dual allegiances are not always apparent to an actor. In consequence, active market participants cannot be allowed to regulate their own markets free from antitrust accountability. See *Midcal, supra,* at 106, 100 S.Ct. 937 ("The national policy in favor of competition cannot be thwarted by casting [a] gauzy cloak of state involvement over what is essentially a private price-fixing arrangement"). Indeed, prohibitions against anticompetitive self-regulation by active market participants are an axiom of federal antitrust policy. * * * So it follows that, under *Parker* and the Supremacy Clause, the States' greater power to attain an end does not include the lesser power to negate the congressional judgment embodied in the Sherman Act through unsupervised delegations to active market participants. * * *

Parker immunity requires that the anticompetitive conduct of nonsovereign actors, especially those authorized by the State to regulate their own profession, result from procedures that suffice to make it the State's own. * * * The question is not whether the challenged conduct is efficient, well-functioning, or wise. Rather, it is "whether anticompetitive conduct engaged in by [nonsovereign actors] should be deemed state action and thus shielded from the antitrust laws." * * *

To answer this question, the Court applies the two-part test set forth in *California Retail Liquor Dealers Assn. v. Midcal Aluminum, Inc.,* 445 U.S. 97, 100 S.Ct. 937, 63 L.Ed.2d 233, a case arising from California's delegation of price-fixing authority to wine merchants. Under *Midcal,* "[a] state law or regulatory scheme cannot be the basis for antitrust immunity unless, first, the State has articulated a clear policy to allow the anticompetitive conduct, and second, the State provides active supervision of [the] anticompetitive conduct."

Midcal's clear articulation requirement is satisfied "where the displacement of competition [is] the inherent, logical, or ordinary result of the exercise of authority delegated by the state legislature. In that scenario, the State must have foreseen and implicitly endorsed the anticompetitive effects as consistent with its policy goals." *Phoebe Putney,* 568 U.S., at ___, 133 S.Ct., at 1013. The active supervision requirement demands, *inter alia,* "that state officials have and exercise power to review particular anticompetitive acts of private parties and disapprove those that fail to accord with state policy." * * *

The two requirements set forth in *Midcal* provide a proper analytical framework to resolve the ultimate question whether an anticompetitive policy is indeed the policy of a State. The first requirement—clear articulation—rarely will achieve that goal by itself, for a policy may satisfy this test yet still be defined at so high a level of generality as to leave open critical questions about how and to what extent the market should be regulated. Entities purporting to act under state authority might diverge from the State's considered definition of the public good. The resulting asymmetry between a state policy and its implementation can invite private self-dealing. The second *Midcal* requirement—active supervision— seeks to avoid this harm by requiring the State to review and approve interstitial policies made by the entity claiming immunity.

Midcal's supervision rule "stems from the recognition that '[w]here a private party is engaging in anticompetitive activity, there is a real danger that he is acting to further his own interests, rather than the governmental interests of the State.'" Concern about the private incentives of active market participants animates *Midcal's* supervision mandate, which demands "realistic assurance that a private party's anticompetitive conduct promotes state policy, rather than merely the party's individual interests."

B

In determining whether anticompetitive policies and conduct are indeed the action of a State in its sovereign capacity, there are instances in which an actor can be excused from *Midcal's* active supervision requirement. In *Hallie v. Eau Claire,* 471 U.S. 34, 45, 105 S.Ct. 1713, 85 L.Ed.2d 24 (1985), the Court held municipalities are subject exclusively to *Midcal's* " 'clear articulation' " requirement. That rule, the Court observed, is consistent with the objective of ensuring that the policy at issue be one enacted by the State itself. *Hallie* explained that "[w]here the actor is a municipality, there is little or no danger that it is involved in a private price-fixing arrangement. The only real danger is that it will seek to further purely parochial public interests at the expense of more overriding state goals." *Hallie* further observed that municipalities are electorally accountable and lack the kind of private incentives characteristic of active participants in the market. Critically, the municipality in *Hallie* exercised a wide range of governmental powers across different economic spheres, substantially reducing the risk that it would pursue private interests while regulating any single field. That *Hallie* excused municipalities from *Midcal's* supervision rule for these reasons all but confirms the rule's applicability to actors controlled by active market participants, who ordinarily have none of the features justifying the narrow exception *Hallie* identified.

* * * [T]he Court in *Columbia v. Omni Outdoor Advertising, Inc.,* 499 U.S. 365, 111 S.Ct. 1344, 113 L.Ed.2d 382, addressed whether an otherwise immune entity could lose immunity for conspiring with private parties. In *Omni,* an aspiring billboard merchant argued that the city of Columbia, South Carolina, had violated the Sherman Act—and forfeited its *Parker* immunity—by anticompetitively conspiring with an established local company in passing an ordinance restricting new billboard construction. The Court disagreed, holding there is no "conspiracy exception" to *Parker*.

Omni, like the cases before it, recognized the importance of drawing a line "relevant to the purposes of the Sherman Act and of *Parker*: prohibiting the restriction of competition for private gain but permitting the restriction of competition in the public interest." In the context of a municipal actor which, as in *Hallie,* exercised substantial governmental powers, *Omni* rejected a conspiracy exception for "corruption" as vague and unworkable, since "virtually all regulation benefits some segments of the society and harms others" and may in that sense be seen as " 'corrupt.' " *Omni* also rejected subjective tests for corruption that would force a "deconstruction of the governmental process and probing of the official 'intent' that we have consistently sought to avoid." Thus, whereas the cases preceding it addressed the preconditions of *Parker* immunity and engaged in an objective, *ex ante* inquiry into nonsovereign actors' structure and incentives, *Omni* made clear that recipients of immunity will not lose it on the basis of ad hoc and *ex post* questioning of their motives for making particular decisions.

Omnis' holding makes it all the more necessary to ensure the conditions for granting immunity are met in the first place. The Court's two state-action immunity cases decided after *Omni* reinforce this point. * * * The lesson is clear: *Midcal's* active supervision test is an essential prerequisite of *Parker* immunity for any nonsovereign entity—public or private—controlled by active market participants.

C

The Board argues entities designated by the States as agencies are exempt from *Midcal's* second requirement. That premise, however, cannot be reconciled with the Court's repeated conclusion that the need for supervision turns not on the formal designation given by States to regulators but on the risk that active market participants will pursue private interests in restraining trade.

State agencies controlled by active market participants, who possess singularly strong private interests, pose the very risk of self-dealing *Midcal*'s supervision requirement was created to address. This conclusion does not question the good faith of state officers but rather is an assessment of the structural risk of market participants' confusing their own interests with the State's policy goals.

* * *

* * * In important regards, agencies controlled by market participants are more similar to private trade associations vested by States with regulatory authority than to the agencies *Hallie* considered. And as the Court observed three years after *Hallie,* "[t]here is no doubt that the members of such associations often have economic incentives to restrain competition and that the product standards set by such associations have a serious potential for anticompetitive harm." For that reason, those associations must satisfy *Midcal*'s active supervision standard.

The similarities between agencies controlled by active market participants and private trade associations are not eliminated simply because the former are given a formal designation by the State, vested with a measure of government power, and required to follow some procedural rules. * * * *Parker* immunity does not derive from nomenclature alone. When a State empowers a group of active market participants to decide who can participate in its market, and on what terms, the need for supervision is manifest. * * * The Court holds today that a state board on which a controlling number of decisionmakers are active market participants in the occupation the board regulates must satisfy *Midcal*'s active supervision requirement in order to invoke state-action antitrust immunity.

D

The State argues that allowing this FTC order to stand will discourage dedicated citizens from serving on state agencies that regulate their own occupation. If this were so—and, for reasons to be noted, it need not be so—there would be some cause for concern. The States have a sovereign interest in structuring their governments, * * * and may conclude there are substantial benefits to staffing their agencies with experts in complex and technical subjects * * *. There is, moreover, a long tradition of citizens esteemed by their professional colleagues devoting time, energy, and talent to enhancing the dignity of their calling.

* * * In the United States, there is a strong tradition of professional self-regulation, particularly with respect to the development of ethical rules. Dentists are no exception. The American Dental Association, for example, in an exercise of "the privilege and obligation of self-government," has "call[ed] upon dentists to follow high ethical standards," including "honesty, compassion, kindness, integrity, fairness and charity." State laws and institutions are sustained by this tradition when they draw upon the expertise and commitment of professionals.

Today's holding is not inconsistent with that idea. The Board argues, however, that the potential for money damages will discourage members of regulated occupations from participating in state government. * * * But this case, which does not present a claim for money damages, does not offer occasion to address the question whether agency officials, including board members, may, under some circumstances, enjoy immunity from damages liability. * * * And, of course, the States may provide for the defense and indemnification of agency members in the event of litigation.

States, furthermore, can ensure *Parker* immunity is available to agencies by adopting clear policies to displace competition; and, if agencies controlled by active market participants interpret or enforce those policies, the States may provide active supervision. Precedent confirms this principle. The Court has rejected the argument that it would be unwise to apply the antitrust laws to professional regulation absent compliance with the prerequisites for invoking *Parker* immunity * * *.

E

The Board does not contend in this Court that its anticompetitive conduct was actively supervised by the State or that it should receive *Parker* immunity on that basis.

By statute, North Carolina delegates control over the practice of dentistry to the Board. The Act, however, says nothing about teeth whitening, a practice that did not exist when it was passed. After receiving complaints from other dentists about the nondentists' cheaper services, the Board's dentist members—some of whom offered whitening services— acted to expel the dentists' competitors from the market. In so doing the Board relied upon cease-and-desist letters threatening criminal liability, rather than any of the powers at its disposal that would invoke oversight by a politically accountable official. With no active supervision by the State, North Carolina officials may well have been unaware that the Board had decided teeth whitening constitutes "the practice of dentistry" and sought to prohibit those who competed against dentists from participating in the teeth whitening market. Whether or not the Board exceeded its powers under North Carolina law, * * * there is no evidence here of any decision by the State to initiate or concur with the Board's actions against the nondentists.

IV

The Board does not claim that the State exercised active, or indeed any, supervision over its conduct regarding nondentist teeth whiteners; and, as a result, no specific supervisory systems can be reviewed here. It suffices to note that the inquiry regarding active supervision is flexible and context-dependent. Active supervision need not entail day-to-day involvement in an agency's operations or micromanagement of its every decision. Rather, the question is whether the State's review mechanisms provide "realistic assurance" that a nonsovereign actor's anticompetitive conduct "promotes state policy, rather than merely the party's individual interests." * * *

The Court has identified only a few constant requirements of active supervision: The supervisor must review the substance of the anticompetitive decision, not merely the procedures followed to produce it; the supervisor must have the power to veto or modify particular decisions to ensure they accord with state policy; and the "mere potential for state supervision is not an adequate substitute for a decision by the State," * * *. Further, the state supervisor may not itself be an active market participant. In general, however, the adequacy of supervision otherwise will depend on all the circumstances of a case.

The Sherman Act protects competition while also respecting federalism. It does not authorize the States to abandon markets to the unsupervised control of active market participants, whether trade associations or hybrid agencies. If a State wants to rely on active market participants as regulators, it must provide active supervision if state-action immunity under *Parker* is to be invoked.

The judgment of the Court of Appeals for the Fourth Circuit is affirmed.

It is so ordered.

Justice Samuel Alito dissented in an opinion joined by Justices Antonin Scalia and Clarence Thomas. He argued that, as an agency of the state, the Board should have been viewed as immune under *Parker*:

> Today * * * the Court takes the unprecedented step of holding that *Parker* does not apply to the North Carolina Board because the Board is not structured in a way that merits a good-government seal of approval; that is, it is made up of practicing dentists who have a financial incentive to use the licensing laws to further the financial interests of the State's dentists. There is nothing new about the structure of the North Carolina Board. When the States first created medical and dental boards, well before the Sherman Act was enacted, they began to staff them in this way. Nor is there

anything new about the suspicion that the North Carolina Board—in attempting to prevent persons other than dentists from performing teeth-whitening procedures—was serving the interests of dentists and not the public. Professional and occupational licensing requirements have often been used in such a way. But that is not what *Parker* immunity is about. Indeed, the very state program involved in that case was unquestionably designed to benefit the regulated entities, California raisin growers.

The question before us is not whether such programs serve the public interest. The question, instead, is whether this case is controlled by *Parker,* and the answer to that question is clear. Under *Parker,* the Sherman Act (and the Federal Trade Commission Act, see *FTC v. Ticor Title Ins. Co.,* 504 U.S. 621, 635, 112 S.Ct. 2169, 119 L.Ed.2d 410 (1992)) do not apply to state agencies; the North Carolina Board of Dental Examiners is a state agency; and that is the end of the matter. By straying from this simple path, the Court has not only distorted *Parker*; it has headed into a morass. Determining whether a state agency is structured in a way that militates against regulatory capture is no easy task, and there is reason to fear that today's decision will spawn confusion. The Court has veered off course, and therefore I cannot go along.

135 S.Ct. at 1117 (ALITO, J., dissenting).

NOTE ON SEMINOLE TRIBE, SOVEREIGN IMMUNITY AND THE CONTINUED VITALITY OF THE PARKER FRAMEWORK

As we have seen, *Parker* spawned a long line of cases, which, over time, have sought to establish a line between permissible and impermissible state action under the Sherman Act. The Court has consistently adhered, however, to the basic premise of *Parker*: that *state* action is outside the purview of the Sherman Act. The more difficult issues have arisen in the context of anticompetitive conduct undertaken by subdivisions of the state, or by private parties purporting to act pursuant to state regulatory schemes.

It is questionable, however, whether the Supreme Court will continue to analyze state action in the same way. Recall that in *Parker* the Supreme Court's decision rested on two observations about the Sherman Act: (1) that nothing in its *language* suggested coverage of state action; and (2) that similarly, nothing in its *legislative history* indicated a Congressional intent to authorize application of the Sherman Act to state conduct. The Court assumed, however, that "Congress could, in the exercise of its commerce power, prohibit a state from maintaining a stabilization program like the present because of its effect on interstate commerce." The state action doctrine, therefore, applied as a matter of statutory interpretation, not constitutional infirmity. Indeed, in observing that the commerce power was adequate to reach the anticompetitive activities of states, the Court left the impression that Congress could, if it wanted to, amend the statute to extend to anticompetitive state action. But who could enforce such an expanded Sherman Act? The Court had no occasion to evaluate the implications of Congress' authorizing public versus private rights of action for a broader Sherman Act.

Any implication that Congress could not only expand coverage of the Act to reach state action, but that it also could permit private suits to challenge state action, appears to be at odds with *Seminole Tribe of Florida v. Florida*, 517 U.S. 44 (1996), in which the Court by a 5–4 vote held that the commerce clause does not provide Congress with authority to abrogate the states' Eleventh Amendment sovereign immunity. Subsequent decisions of the Court have further entrenched that view, maintaining that sovereign immunity is a feature of the Constitution as a whole, not simply a function of the Eleventh Amendment. *See Federal Maritime Comm'n v. South Carolina State Ports Auth.*, 535 U.S. 743, 122 S.Ct. 1864 (2002). It is arguable, therefore, that the question whether a private party can sue a state for alleged violations of the Sherman Act would today have to take account of both *Parker* and *Seminole Tribe*. *See generally* Susan Beth Farmer, *Balancing State Sovereignty and Competition: An Analysis of the Impact of* Seminole Tribe *on the Antitrust State Action Immunity Doctrine*, 42 VILL. L. REV. 111 (1997).

Seminole Tribe adopted a two-part test for assessing a private party's right to sue a state for damages. The test asks: (1) has Congress expressed an unequivocal intention to abrogate the State's sovereign immunity?; and (2) if it has, has it done so pursuant to a valid exercise of constitutional power? 517 U.S. at 44. This framework would appear to supersede *Parker*, at least with respect to private plaintiffs, even though the answers to the questions it poses can still be found there. According to the Court in *Parker*, the answer to the first question would be an unequivocal "no"—there is no evidence in either the language or legislative history of the Sherman Act that Congress intended for the Act to cover the anticompetitive conduct of states, whether the allegation is pursued by public or private plaintiffs. Hence, there is no evidence of an intention to abrogate sovereign immunity.

Even if Congress were to seek to alter that scheme—as *Parker* assumed it could—the second hurdle erected by *Seminole Tribe* could not be surmounted, at least with respect to private suits for damages. *Parker* acknowledges, as have other cases, that the Sherman Act was adopted pursuant to the commerce clause, and *Seminole Tribe* clearly holds that the commerce clause is an insufficient source of authority to abrogate state sovereign immunity with respect to private suits for damages. Hence, Congress's authority to alter state action immunity as it developed under *Parker* probably has been limited by *Seminole Tribe*.

There are, however, two important exceptions to the rule of *Seminole Tribe*. First, it does not preclude the long recognized right of private parties to vindicate their federal rights by seeking *prospective injunctive relief* against state officials. *See Ex Parte Young*, 209 U.S. 123 (1908). Second, it does not limit Congress's power to authorize suits by the *federal government* against states for violations of federal law. It is here, however, that *Parker* may continue to play a vital role. To the extent the Eleventh Amendment may not bar either private suits against the states for injunctive relief or public suits against the states for damages, *Parker* may, due to its holding that the Sherman Act does not reach state action (assuming that the requirements for establishing state action, currently set forth under the *Midcal* test, are satisfied).

The courts are still in the process of trying to synthesize and integrate these three complex lines of cases—*Parker*, *Seminole Tribe*, and *Ex Parte Young*. *See, e.g., TFWS, Inc. v. Schaefer*, 242 F.3d 198 (4th Cir. 2001); *Neo Gen Screening, Inc. v. New England Newborn Screening Program*, 187 F.3d 24 (1st Cir. 1999). It appears likely, however, that *Parker's* role has been fundamentally altered. One set of possible post-*Seminole Tribe* rules might be:

- any suit under the Sherman Act initiated by a private party against a state and seeking damages would be barred—under the analysis required in *Seminole Tribe*, not *Parker*—although *Parker would* provide the answers to *Seminole's* two part test;

- any suit under the Sherman Act initiated by a private party against a state seeking prospective injunctive relief also would be barred—but under the analysis of *Parker* (*i.e., Ex Parte Young* would be irrelevant);

- any suit by the federal government against a state for damages or injunctive relief would continue to be barred—not by *Seminole Tribe* or *Young*, but by *Parker*; and

- if Congress deemed it appropriate to amend the Sherman Act to prohibit the anticompetitive acts of states, it could do so under the authority of *Parker*; however, establishing permissible rights of relief to enforce such an expanded Sherman Act would have to be carefully delineated under *Seminole Tribe* and *Young*: (1) Congress could grant the federal government a right to relief against the states for damages and/or injunctive relief, but (2) *private parties* could only be authorized to seek prospective injunctive relief as permitted by *Young*.

Even if these rules were to come to fruition, important unanswered questions remain. Paramount among them is whether the concepts of sovereign immunity established by *Parker* and *Seminole Tribe* are co-extensive. For example, if *Parker* reaches deeper into the subdivisions of state government than does *Seminole Tribe*, *Parker* will retain a relatively more vital role in assessing the scope of a state's potential liability. Under such circumstances, even when immunity is found unavailable under *Seminole Tribe* as a constitutional matter, it might still be urged as a matter of the state action doctrine under *Parker*. On the other hand, if the scope of *Seminole Tribe's* immunity is read more broadly than *Parker*, *Parker's* role will further diminish.

A second and related question concerns the continued role of the *Midcal* active state supervision test. As Professor Beth Farmer has recognized, *Midcal's* analysis is an attempt to balance the competition policy concerns of the Sherman Act with the sovereign immunity concerns recognized in *Parker*. Requiring "active state supervision" of private conduct is one way to insure that the balance is being properly struck. But it is possible to posit a reading of *Seminole Tribe* so broad that *Midcal's* analysis would be unnecessary. With significantly greater deference to sovereign immunity might come diminished judicial authority to balance competition policy concerns and far broader antitrust immunity, even for essentially private, anticompetitive schemes. If *Seminole Tribe* were to be read that broadly, therefore, the incentive for private firms to secure anticompetitive state action surely would increase.

The courts have been struggling with many of these issues. For example, at various times, the Court itself has referred to *Parker* as an "immunity" and as a "defense". In *South Carolina State Bd. of Dentistry v. FTC*, 455 F.3d 436 (4th Cir. 2006), the Fourth Circuit recently held that the FTC's refusal to apply *Parker* in a pending administrative proceeding was not a collateral order subject to immediate review. In so holding, the court argued that *Parker* and Eleventh Amendment immunity are not co-extensive, and hence *Parker* does not provide "immunity from suit," just a "defense to liability." What is the significance of viewing *Parker* as an "immunity," like sovereign immunity, as opposed to a "defense" to an otherwise potentially valid antitrust claim? Are the interests protected by immunities and defenses the same? Do they procedurally operate in the same way? Note that in *North Carolina State Board of Dental Examiners*, the Supreme Court referred to "state action antitrust immunity." Does this phrasing clarify the status of *Parker* or leave it uncertain?

3. INTERVENTION BY MUNICIPAL AND OTHER LOCAL AUTHORITIES

As was noted in *City of Columbia v. Omni Outdoor Advertising, Inc.*, 499 U.S. 365, 111 S.Ct. 1344, 113 L.Ed.2d 382 (1991), discussed *supra*, under the current state of the law the decisions of political subdivisions such as cities, counties, and townships are not entitled to the same protections as the decisions of the state itself. *City of Lafayette v. Louisiana Power & Light Co.*, 435 U.S. 389 (1978). Application of the state action doctrine based on the acts of a political subdivision exists only if the subdivision acts pursuant to a mandate from the state itself. *See Hertz Corp. v. City of New York*, 1 F.3d 121 (2d Cir. 1993) (exercise of city's home-rule authority deemed not to immunize city law that barred rental car firms from imposing certain fees).

In *Town of Hallie v. City of Eau Claire*, 471 U.S. 34 (1985), discussed in *City of Columbia*, the Supreme Court considered how the *Midcal* test applies to anticompetitive conduct by political subdivisions. *Hallie* involved a city's refusal to provide sewage treatment services to neighboring unincorporated townships unless landowners in those areas agreed to have their properties annexed. *Midcal's* clear articulation standard was met if "it was clear that anticompetitive effects logically would result from this broad authority to regulate." *Id.* at 42. The defendant city's behavior was "a foreseeable result of empowering the City to refuse to serve unannexed areas." *Id.* As you saw in the discussion of *City of Columbia*, the Supreme Court concluded that the challenged zoning regulation satisfied *Hallie's* "foreseeable result" test because "[t]he very purpose of zoning regulation is to displace unfettered business freedom in a manner that regularly has the effect of preventing normal acts of competition." 499 U.S. at 373.

In contrast, in *FTC v. Phoebe Putney Health Sys. Inc.*, 133 S.Ct. 1003 (2013), the Court rejected the lower court's reliance on a loose concept of foreseeability and held that the power granted to a hospital authority to acquire hospitals was too general to be construed as having the reasonably foreseeable result of displacing competition. *Id.* at 1013–15. That is, the displacement of competition was not the "inherent, logical, or ordinary result of the exercise of authority delegated by the state legislature." *Id.* at 1013. The Court rejected the defendants' claims, "because only a relatively small subset of the conduct permitted as a matter of state law . . . ha[d] the potential to negatively affect competition." *Id.* at 1014. Even in the context of the hospital authority's power to acquire hospitals, the Court concluded "the power to acquire hospitals still does not ordinarily produce anticompetitive effects." *Id.* Thus, the connection between the authority's power to acquire hospitals and the effect of that power was too tenuous to render foreseeable any anticompetitive effects resulting from the exercise of that power.

Hallie also held that states need not supervise their subdivisions' exercise of authority for state action immunity to apply: "Once it is clear that state authorization exists, there is no need to require the State to actively supervise the municipality's execution of what is a properly delegated function." *Town of Hallie*, 471 U.S. at 47. In a footnote, the Court also suggested without deciding that the same would be true if the actor is a state agency other than a municipality, but it distinguished cases brought against private parties:

> In cases in which the actor is a state agency, it is likely that active state supervision would also not be required, although we do not here decide that issue. Where state or municipal regulation by a private party is involved, however, active state supervision must be shown, even where a clearly articulated state policy exists.

Id. at 46 n.10. *See also Benton, Benton & Benton v. Louisiana Pub. Facilities Auth.*, 897 F.2d 198 (5th Cir. 1990) (relying on footnote 10 to conclude that *Hallie* obviates the need for states to actively supervise state agencies to create immunity). Would the analysis be different taking into account the Supreme Court's later decisions in *Phoebe Putney* and *North Carolina State Board of Dental Examiners*?

The application of the antitrust laws to local governments in *Lafayette* and cases such as *Community Commc's, Co., Inc. v. City of Boulder*, 455 U.S. 40 (1982), which held that Colorado's home rule statute did not immunize the City of Boulder from antitrust liability for its regulation of cable television, raised fears that cities might be exposed to the risk of treble damage liability. Through the Local Government Antitrust Act of 1984 "LGAA", 15 U.S.C. §§ 34–36, Congress responded, barring antitrust damage suits against local governments and against private parties acting under their direction. The LGAA permits suits for equitable relief under Section 16 of the Clayton Act and allows the recovery of attorneys' fees for plaintiffs who substantially prevail in such suits.

4. PREEMPTION

State regulation must withstand scrutiny under the Supremacy Clause of the Constitution, which preempts state laws that are inconsistent with federal legislation. The preemption inquiry in antitrust cases has focused on whether state regulation clashes so substantially with the federal antitrust statutes that the two regimes cannot coexist. Preemption occurs only in cases of acute conflict and is a weak check on state regulation that displaces competition.

In *Rice v. Norman Williams Co.*, 458 U.S. 654 (1982), the Supreme Court refused to enjoin enforcement of a California statute that allowed liquor importers to buy liquor outside California only if the liquor was consigned to a licensed importer. The Court held that preemption would occur only if the statute "necessarily constitutes a violation of the antitrust laws in all cases, or if it places irresistible pressure on a private party to violate the antitrust laws in order to comply with the [state] statute." The Court indicated that a facial inconsistency would exist only if conduct compelled by the state law is illegal per se—a condition found lacking in *Rice. See also Fisher v. City of Berkeley*, 475 U.S. 260 (1986) (municipal rent control ordinance held not to be facially preempted by Section 1 of the Sherman Act; ordinance did not necessarily violate Section 1 "in all cases," mainly because the city unilaterally imposed the rent control ordinance and the concerted action needed under Section 1 was lacking). Significant preemption arguments have been made to attack the "master settlement agreement" reached between a number of states and the tobacco industry, with mixed results. *Contrast Sanders v. Brown*, 504 F.3d 903 (9th Cir. 2007) (state statutes implementing "master settlement agreement" with tobacco industry were not preempted by federal antitrust laws) *with Freedom Holdings, Inc. v. Spitzer*, 357 F.3d 205 (2d Cir. 2004) (reaching opposite conclusion).

Sidebar 8–5:
Revisiting Immunities Based on Government Intervention—U.S. and Comparative Perspectives[a]

As can be seen from the cases and materials presented above, government action can have a substantial impact on competition. *See* JEAN-JACQUES LAFFONT & JEAN TIROLE, A THEORY OF INCENTIVES IN PROCUREMENT AND REGULATION 538–57 (1993); DANIEL F. SPULBER, REGULATION AND MARKETS 21–109 (1989); W. KIP VISCUSI, ET AL., ECONOMICS OF REGULATION AND ANTITRUST 295–329 (1992). In some instances, government dispensations from competition serve to correct market failures. *See* MICHAEL A. CREW & PAUL R. KLEINDORFER, THE ECONOMICS OF PUBLIC UTILITY REGULATION 3–30 (1986) (describing rationale for public intervention to regulate natural monopolies). Whereas in many others regulation that restricts business rivalry by limiting entry into the market, authorizing producers to cooperate in setting prices or other terms of commerce, or granting exclusive privileges to selected entrepreneurs may enable an individual firm or group of firms to gain monopoly rents. *See* Paul L. Joskow & Nancy L. Rose, *The Effects of Economic Regulation, in* II HANDBOOK OF INDUSTRIAL ORGANIZATION 1451, 1469–72 (Richard Schmalensee & Robert Willig eds., 1989). Government-imposed restraints on competition can be even more powerful and effective than private restraints, owing to the government's ability to enforce its will by using the machinery of the state to punish transgressors with civil sanctions or criminal penalties. It can also invite efforts by incumbent firms to use the regulatory process to exclude would be rivals and new business models. As the scope of government measures to restrict competition grows, the vitality of a market system can suffer significantly.

For these and other reasons, transition economies—those nations in the process of converting from a high degree of state control to a more market-driven economy—often are encouraged to empower their competition policy authorities to engage in "competition advocacy" or enforcement functions to curb state efforts to suppress competition. *See* WORLD BANK &

---

[a] Parts of this Sidebar are adapted from William E. Kovacic, *Lessons of Competition Policy Reform in Transition Economies for U.S. Antitrust Policy*, 74 ST. JOHN'S L. REV. 361 (2000).

ORGANIZATION FOR ECONOMIC COOPERATION AND DEVELOPMENT, A FRAMEWORK FOR THE DESIGN AND IMPLEMENTATION OF COMPETITION LAW AND POLICY 93–100 (1999); Craig W. Conrath & Barry T. Freeman, *A Response to "The Effectiveness of Proposed Antitrust Programs for Developing Countries,"* 19 N.C. J. INT'L L. & COM. 233, 243–35 (1994). Many transition economies have taken this advice to heart, perhaps out of their own keen awareness of the dangers of government intervention born from decades of intrusive central economic controls. *See* William E. Kovacic, *Antitrust and Competition Policy in Transition Economies: A Preliminary Assessment,* 2000 FORDHAM CORP. L. INST. 513, 525–26 (B. Hawk, ed. 2000).

Competition authorities in transition economies have developed a variety of tools for restricting the role of the state, including (1) subjecting state-owned enterprises to the same competition policy commands that govern private enterprises, and (2) permitting competition authorities to veto government action that restricts competition, unless such restrictions have been expressly approved by the national legislature. *See* Ben Slay, *Industrial De-monopolization and Competition Policy in Poland, in* DE-MONOPOLIZATION AND COMPETITION POLICY IN POST-COMMUNIST ECONOMIES 123, 143 (Ben Slay ed., 1996); William E. Kovacic & Ben Slay, *Perilous Beginnings: The Establishment of Antimonopoly and Consumer Protection Programs in the Republic of Georgia,* 43 ANTITRUST BULL. 15, 39 (1998).

Even as Western consultants counsel transition economies to resist government intervention to suppress business rivalry, however, the United States tolerates large-scale government incursions into the economy that appear to be inconsistent with the pro-competition goals of the federal antitrust laws. At the federal level, for example, Congress continues to embrace measures, in areas such as agriculture, that encourage or mandate cooperation by producers to restrict output and raise prices. *See generally* ABA SECTION OF ANTITRUST LAW, ANTITRUST LAW DEVELOPMENTS 1306–10 (6th ed. 2007). And as we have seen in this Chapter, by displacing the operation of the federal antitrust laws, the judicially-created state action doctrine creates incentives for producer groups to elicit government intervention at the state and local level to forestall competition. *See* John Shepard Wiley, *A Capture Theory of Antitrust Federalism,* 99 HARV. L. REV. 713, 714–15 (1986). For a description of the FTC's role in competition advocacy, see Andrew I. Gavil, *The FTC's Study and Advocacy Authority in its Second Century: A Look Ahead*, 83 GEO. WASH. L. REV. 1902 (2015).

One might accept state measures to suppress rivalry that inflicts harm solely or chiefly on the citizens of the jurisdiction adopting the measures. But in such circumstances, at least in theory, the state's voters have electoral tools to change the policies. The modern state action doctrine is not so discriminating, for it confers immunity without accounting for whether the intervention of one state imposes significant, adverse economic spillovers on the citizens of other states—a fact that was evident in *Parker*, itself, which allowed California raisin growers to in effect set nation-wide raisin prices. *See* Robert P. Inman & Daniel L. Rubinfeld, *Making Sense of the Antitrust State-Action Doctrine: Balancing Political Participation and Economic Efficiency in Regulatory Federalism*, 75 TEX. L. REV. 1203 (1997).

On the other hand, a number of American commentators have suggested that state action immunity can be viewed as a source of desirable experimentation in economic regulation by state governments. *See* Jean Wegman Burns, *Embracing Both Faces of Antitrust Federalism: Parker and ARC America Corp.*, 68 ANTITRUST L.J. 29, 44 (2000). State antitrust officials devote comparatively few resources to opposing measures by state instrumentalities that restrict competition. The acceptance of intervention by state governments also finds support in Supreme Court jurisprudence that applies the commerce clause as a relatively weak limit on state economic regulation and suggests that congressional efforts to abolish or circumscribe the state action doctrine might constitute impermissible infringements of state sovereignty. *See* Inman & Rubinfeld, *supra*, at 1272–73 & n.228; Burns, *supra*, at 38.

Competition-suppressing government intervention at the national or regional levels arguably is more inimical to economic growth in transition economies than in mature Western market countries. The United States is a prosperous nation and has more margin for error in pursuing policies that allow producers to reallocate, rather than pressing them to expand, society's total wealth. Yet regulatory limits on entry by new entrepreneurs or expansion by existing firms also can impose important social costs even in a wealthy country by raising prices and retarding innovation.

Heeding the message conveyed to transition economies would induce American antitrust institutions to devote more energy to resisting government policies at all levels that suppress competition. At the national level, this might entail greater efforts to publicize the harmful effects of federal programs that curb rivalry. One might even consider adopting the practice of the European Union competition regime, embodied in Article 86, to subject government efforts to limit competition to close scrutiny.

At the state level, if the existing dimensions of state action immunity are politically or constitutionally immutable, state antitrust bureaus might assume more responsibility for opposing measures by state governments and their political subdivisions to restrict competition. This would require some reorientation of state antitrust priorities that moves at least some resources now dedicated to pursuing matters treated by federal enforcement agencies toward efforts to oppose state legislative or regulatory encroachments on the competitive process. The urgency for state antitrust officials to undertake a robust advocacy role becomes all the more important if the Supreme Court remains indifferent to state measures that restrict competition and impede the functioning of a national economic union by imposing serious adverse spillovers upon other jurisdictions.

5. PETITIONING

Antitrust challenges to anticompetitive government action often include claims directed at private parties who have succeeded in soliciting government action that reduces competition. Although the government entity may not be subject to antitrust liability by virtue of the state action doctrine or some other exemption, such claims pose a distinct question: should that insulation from liability extend to the private parties that have actively sought the anticompetitive state action? The actions of such parties frequently are challenged as monopolization or attempts to monopolize under Section 2 of the Sherman Act, although there have also been claims asserted under Section 1.

The analysis of efforts to secure anticompetitive state action is complicated by the First Amendment, which provides in part that "Congress shall make no law * * * abridging * * * the right of the people * * * to petition the Government for a redress of grievances." U.S. Const., amend. I. Such petitioning may include lobbying officers of the legislative or executive branches, initiating lawsuits, and lobbying administrative agencies and other regulators. Guided mainly by concerns for the protection of First Amendment rights, the Supreme Court has limited the application of the Sherman Act to these kinds of petitioning activities, regardless of their anticompetitive intentions or effects. Regulating abuses of those processes instead falls to other laws designed to safeguard the integrity of the policymaking process. Thus, criminal laws seek to stop bribery. And other anti-corruption, lobbying, and campaign finance laws—along with public discussion and publicity—serve to promote the aspiration that official actions reflect the public interest.

These limitations on the applicability of the Sherman Act took shape in three Supreme Court decisions issued in the 1960s and early 1970s. In *Eastern R.R. Presidents Conference v. Noerr Motor Freight, Inc.*, 365 U.S. 127 (1961), the Court concluded that the Sherman Act could not reach joint efforts by 24 railroads and an association of railroad presidents to obtain legislative and executive action unfavorable to competing trucking firms. The Court emphasized that condemning the railroads' lobbying campaign "would impute to the Sherman Act a purpose to regulate, not business activity, but political activity, a purpose which would have no basis whatever in the legislative history of that Act." A finding of Sherman Act liability also "would raise important constitutional questions" concerning the right to petition under the First Amendment. *Noerr* was later extended to efforts to solicit anticompetitive actions from administrative agencies in *United Mine Workers v. Pennington*, 381 U.S. 657 (1965), and to the initiation of litigation in *California Motor Transp. Co. v. Trucking Unlimited*, 404 U.S. 508 (1972). The resulting principles are collectively referred to as "the *Noerr-Pennington* Doctrine."

Noerr cautioned, however, that its protections might be withheld when petitioning activity "ostensibly directed toward influencing governmental action, is a mere sham to cover * * * an attempt to interfere directly" with a rival's business relationships. 365 U.S. at 144. That admonition took on greater significance after *California Motor Transport*, where the Court ruled that the First Amendment does not protect sham conduct. In so holding, the Court suggested that the Sherman Act can reach misrepresentation or other unethical conduct directed at subverting judicial processes, such as the initiation of baseless lawsuits designed to injure rivals. It reasoned that, in contrast to legislative, executive and administrative processes, the courts are less able to protect themselves from being used for anticompetitive purposes. Moreover, it noted that judicial process involves competing constitutional values, especially due process. The sham exception, therefore, requires courts to weigh the value of the alleged offender's First Amendment rights against the potential Fifth Amendment due process interests of the party seeking redress. With understatement, the Court said the boundary between legitimate petitioning and sham behavior might prove to be "a difficult line to discern and draw."

Subsequent cases have focused on (1) defining the appropriate targets of petitioning activity, and (2) describing the contours of the sham exception.

For example, in *Allied Tube & Conduit Corp. v. Indian Head, Inc.*, 486 U.S. 492 (1988), the Supreme Court refused to apply *Noerr's* protections to private efforts to influence the standard-setting activities of a private trade association. The Court added, however, that *Noerr* might apply if the defendants' conduct, though directed at a private body, was mainly "political" rather than "commercial." In *FTC v. Superior Court Trial Lawyers' Ass'n* (*See supra* Chapter 2), the Court withheld petitioning protection from attorneys who collectively refused to represent indigent criminal defendants unless the District of Columbia government raised the fees for such work. In so holding, the Court emphasized that the higher fees ultimately secured were the product of private restraint—the attorneys' collusive group boycott—not simple lobbying for government action, which would have been eligible for *Noerr-Pennington* protection.

Refining the definition of the sham exception in *City of Columbia*, discussed *supra* in connection with the scope of *Parker* and the state action doctrine, the Supreme Court conferred state action protection on a zoning measure and concluded that *Noerr* protected the defendant's efforts to persuade the city to adopt the ordinance. In rejecting the plaintiff's assertion that the defendant's petitioning efforts fell within the "sham exception" to *Noerr*, the Court defined sham conduct as involving "activities [that] are 'not genuinely aimed at procuring favorable government action.' " *City of Columbia*, 499 U.S. at 380. Although the *Omni* defendant clearly wished to exclude the plaintiff, "it sought to do so not through the very process of lobbying, or of causing the city council to consider zoning measures, but rather through the ultimate *product* of that lobbying and consideration, viz., the zoning ordinances." *Id.* at 381 (emphasis original). In drawing this distinction between the petitioning efforts themselves and the ultimate ends sought, the Court limited the sham exception to "a context in which the conspirators' participation in the governmental process was itself claimed to be a 'sham,' employed as a means of imposing cost and delay." *Id.* at 381–82.

When should a firm's initiation of proceedings before a court or administrative tribunal be deemed a "sham," such that it will fall outside the protections of the *Noerr-Pennington* doctrine? The Supreme Court sought to better define the contours of the *Noerr-Pennington* and to provide added guidance on the scope of the sham exception in our next case.

PROFESSIONAL REAL ESTATE INVESTORS, INC. V. COLUMBIA PICTURES INDUSTRIES, INC.

Supreme Court of the United States, 1993.
508 U.S. 49, 113 S.Ct. 1920, 123 L.Ed.2d 611.

JUSTICE THOMAS delivered the opinion of the Court.

This case requires us to define the "sham" exception to the doctrine of antitrust immunity first identified in *Eastern Railroad Presidents Conference v. Noerr Motor Freight, Inc.*, 365 U.S. 127, 81 S.Ct. 523 (1961), as that doctrine applies in the litigation context. Under the sham exception, activity "ostensibly directed toward influencing governmental action" does not qualify for *Noerr* immunity if it "is a mere sham to cover . . . an attempt to interfere directly with the business relationships of a competitor." *Id.*, at 144, 81 S.Ct., at 533. We hold that litigation cannot be deprived of immunity as a sham unless the litigation is objectively baseless. * * *

I

Petitioners Professional Real Estate Investors, Inc., and Kenneth F. Irwin (collectively, PRE) operated La Mancha Private Club and Villas, a resort hotel in Palm Springs, California. Having installed videodisc players in the resort's hotel rooms and assembled a library of more than 200 motion picture titles, PRE rented videodiscs to guests for in-room viewing. PRE also sought to develop a market for the sale of videodisc players to other hotels wishing to offer in-room viewing of prerecorded material. Respondents, Columbia Pictures Industries, Inc., and seven other major motion picture studios (collectively, Columbia), held copyrights to the motion pictures recorded on the videodiscs that PRE purchased. Columbia also licensed the transmission of copyrighted motion pictures to hotel rooms through a wired cable system called Spectradyne. PRE therefore competed with Columbia not only for the viewing market at La Mancha but also for the broader market for in-room entertainment services in hotels.

In 1983, Columbia sued PRE for alleged copyright infringement through the rental of videodiscs for viewing in hotel rooms. PRE counterclaimed, charging Columbia with violations of §§ 1 and 2 of the Sherman Act * * *. In particular, PRE alleged that Columbia's copyright action was a mere sham that cloaked underlying acts of monopolization and conspiracy to restrain trade.

* * *

II

PRE contends that "the Ninth Circuit erred in holding that an antitrust plaintiff must, as a threshold prerequisite . . ., establish that a sham lawsuit is baseless as a matter of law." It invites us to adopt an approach under which either "indifference to . . . outcome," or failure to prove that a petition for redress of grievances "would . . . have been brought but for [a] predatory motive," would expose a defendant to antitrust liability under the sham exception. We decline PRE's invitation.

* * *

Our original formulation of antitrust petitioning immunity required that unprotected activity lack objective reasonableness. *Noerr* rejected the contention that an attempt "to influence the passage and enforcement of laws" might lose immunity merely because the lobbyists' "sole purpose . . . was to destroy [their] competitors." 365 U.S., at 138, 81 S.Ct., at 530. Nor were we persuaded by a showing that a publicity campaign "was intended to and did in fact injure [competitors] in their relationships with the public and with their customers," since such "direct injury" was merely "an incidental effect of the . . . campaign to influence governmental action." *Id.*, at 143, 81 S.Ct., at 532. We reasoned that "[t]he right of the people to inform their representatives in government of their desires with respect to the passage or enforcement of laws cannot properly be made to depend upon their intent in doing so." *Id.*, at 139, 81 S.Ct., at 530. In short, "*Noerr* shields from the Sherman Act a concerted effort to influence public officials regardless of intent or purpose." *Pennington*, 381 U.S., at 670, 85 S.Ct., at 1593.

Nothing in *California Motor Transport* [*Co. v. Trucking Unlimited*, 404 U.S. 508, 92 S.Ct. 609 (1972)], retreated from these principles. Indeed, we recognized that recourse to agencies and courts should not be condemned as sham until a reviewing court has "discern[ed] and draw[n]" the "difficult line" separating objectively reasonable claims from "a pattern of baseless, repetitive claims . . . which leads the factfinder to conclude that the administrative and judicial processes have been abused." 404 U.S., at 513, 92 S.Ct., at 613. Our recognition of a sham in that case signifies that the institution of legal proceedings "without probable cause" will give rise to a sham if such activity effectively "bar[s] . . . competitors from meaningful access to adjudicatory tribunals and so . . . usurp[s] th[e] decisionmaking process." *Id.*, at 512, 92 S.Ct., at 612.

Since *California Motor Transport*, we have consistently assumed that the sham exception contains an indispensable objective component. We have described a sham as "evidenced by repetitive lawsuits carrying the hallmark of *insubstantial* claims." We regard as sham "private action that is not genuinely aimed at procuring favorable government action," as opposed to "a valid effort to influence government action." And we have explicitly observed that a successful "effort to influence governmental action . . . certainly cannot be characterized as a sham." Whether applying *Noerr* as an antitrust doctrine or invoking it in other contexts, we have repeatedly reaffirmed that evidence of anticompetitive intent or purpose alone cannot transform otherwise legitimate activity into a sham.

* * *

In sum, fidelity to precedent compels us to reject a purely subjective definition of "sham." The sham exception so construed would undermine, if not vitiate, *Noerr*. And despite whatever "superficial certainty" it might provide, a subjective standard would utterly fail to supply "real 'intelligible guidance.' "

III

We now outline a two-part definition of "sham" litigation. First, the lawsuit must be objectively baseless in the sense that no reasonable litigant could realistically expect success on the merits. If an objective litigant could conclude that the suit is reasonably calculated to elicit a favorable outcome, the suit is immunized under *Noerr*, and an antitrust claim premised on the sham exception must fail.[5] Only if challenged litigation is objectively meritless may a court examine the litigant's subjective motivation. Under this second part of our definition of sham, the court should focus on whether the baseless lawsuit conceals "an attempt to interfere directly with the business relationships of a competitor," through the "use [of] the governmental *process*—as opposed to the *outcome* of that process—as an anticompetitive weapon." This two-tiered process requires the plaintiff to disprove the challenged lawsuit's *legal* viability before the court will entertain evidence of the suit's *economic* viability. Of course, even a plaintiff who defeats the defendant's claim to *Noerr* immunity by demonstrating both the objective and the subjective components of a sham must still prove a substantive antitrust violation. Proof of a sham merely deprives the defendant of immunity; it does not relieve the plaintiff of the obligation to establish all other elements of his claim.

Some of the apparent confusion over the meaning of "sham" may stem from our use of the word "genuine" to denote the opposite of "sham." The word "genuine" has both objective and subjective connotations. On one hand, "genuine" means "actually having the reputed or apparent qualities or character." "Genuine" in this sense governs Federal Rule of Civil Procedure 56, under which a "genuine issue" is one "that properly can be resolved only by a finder of fact because [it] may *reasonably* be resolved in favor of either party." On the other hand, "genuine" also means "sincerely and honestly felt or experienced." To be sham, therefore, litigation must fail to be "genuine" in both senses of the word.[6]

---

[5]   A winning lawsuit is by definition a reasonable effort at petitioning for redress and therefore not a sham. On the other hand, when the antitrust defendant has lost the underlying litigation, a court must "resist the understandable temptation to engage in *post hoc* reasoning by concluding" that an ultimately unsuccessful "action must have been unreasonable or without foundation." The court must remember that "[e]ven when the law or the facts appear questionable or unfavorable at the outset, a party may have an entirely reasonable ground for bringing suit."

[6]   In surveying the "forms of illegal and reprehensible practice which may corrupt the administrative or judicial processes and which may result in antitrust violations," we have noted that "unethical conduct in the setting of the adjudicatory process often results in sanctions" and that "[m]isrepresentations, condoned in the political arena, are not immunized when used in the

IV

We conclude that the Court of Appeals properly affirmed summary judgment for Columbia on PRE's antitrust counterclaim. Under the objective prong of the sham exception, the Court of Appeals correctly held that sham litigation must constitute the pursuit of claims so baseless that no reasonable litigant could realistically expect to secure favorable relief.

The existence of probable cause to institute legal proceedings precludes a finding that an antitrust defendant has engaged in sham litigation. The notion of probable cause, as understood and applied in the common law tort of wrongful civil proceedings, requires the plaintiff to prove that the defendant lacked probable cause to institute an unsuccessful civil lawsuit and that the defendant pressed the action for an improper, malicious purpose. Probable cause to institute civil proceedings requires no more than a "reasonabl[e] belie[f] that there is a chance that [a] claim may be held valid upon adjudication." Because the absence of probable cause is an essential element of the tort, the existence of probable cause is an absolute defense. Just as evidence of anticompetitive intent cannot affect the objective prong of *Noerr*'s sham exception, a showing of malice alone will neither entitle the wrongful civil proceedings plaintiff to prevail nor permit the factfinder to infer the absence of probable cause. When a court has found that an antitrust defendant claiming *Noerr* immunity had probable cause to sue, that finding compels the conclusion that a reasonable litigant in the defendant's position could realistically expect success on the merits of the challenged lawsuit. Under our decision today, therefore, a proper probable cause determination irrefutably demonstrates that an antitrust plaintiff has not proved the objective prong of the sham exception and that the defendant is accordingly entitled to *Noerr* immunity.

* * *

[Concurring Opinion of MR. JUSTICE SOUTER, omitted. Eds.]

JUSTICE STEVENS, with whom JUSTICE O'CONNOR joins, concurring in the judgment.

While I agree with the Court's disposition of this case and with its holding that "an objectively reasonable effort to litigate cannot be sham regardless of subjective intent," I write separately to disassociate myself from some of the unnecessarily broad dicta in the Court's opinion. Specifically, I disagree with the Court's equation of "objectively baseless" with the answer to the question whether any "reasonable litigant could realistically expect success on the merits." There might well be lawsuits that fit the latter definition but can be shown to be objectively

---

adjudicatory process." We need not decide here whether and, if so, to what extent *Noerr* permits the imposition of antitrust liability for a litigant's fraud or other misrepresentations.

unreasonable, and thus shams. It might not be objectively reasonable to bring a lawsuit just because some form of success on the merits—no matter how insignificant—could be expected. With that possibility in mind, the Court should avoid an unnecessarily broad holding that it might regret when confronted with a more complicated case.

* * *

One can ask at least two questions about how future litigants will be able to satisfy the demanding conditions that the *PRE* majority imposes on those who seek to limit *Noerr's* scope by invoking the sham exception. First, what volume of "objectively baseless" activity constitutes sham behavior? For example, in the context of patent infringement litigation, could the initiation of a single baseless infringement suit by a dominant incumbent firm supply the element of improper conduct that establishes illegal monopolization? The bare terms of *PRE* do not seem to demand the barrage of filings featured in *California Motor Transport.* Second, by what evidentiary means should the court decide whether a suit is "objectively baseless"? Do attorney-client communications, which may be shielded by privilege, inevitably become the focal point of attempts by plaintiffs to determine the defendant's expectation of success in suing? To be a "sham," must a complaint violate the provisions of Rule 11 of the Federal Rules of Civil Procedure, which requires that allegations be well-grounded in law and fact based on an inquiry reasonable under the circumstances?

As noted above, the FTC has focused a great deal of attention on the contours of the State Action doctrine, evaluating whether it has been too permissive to the detriment of competition. Similarly, it studied the application of the *Noerr-Pennington* doctrine, pursuing several enforcement actions directed at anticompetitive petitioning activities. *See* FTC, Office of Policy Planning, *Enforcement Perspectives on the Noerr-Pennington Doctrine* (Oct. 2006), http://www.ftc.gov/reports/P013518enf perspectNoerr-Penningtondoctrine.pdf.

D. THE LIMITED ROLE OF STATUTORY EXEMPTIONS

Do you think that competition should be mandated for all industries under the federal antitrust laws? Although a comprehensive treatment is beyond the scope of this Casebook, note that Congressionally created, industry-wide exemptions exist for certain labor union activities, 29 U.S.C. § 105 (Norris-LaGuardia Act), the business of insurance, 15 U.S.C. §§ 1011–13 (McCarran-Ferguson Act), for certain agricultural cooperatives, 7 U.S.C. §§ 291–92 (Capper-Volstead Act), for certain newspaper joint ventures, 15 U.S.C. §§ 1801–04 (Newspaper Preservation

Act) and for medical peer review proceedings that meet certain guidelines, 42 U.S.C. §§ 11101, 11111–15 (Health Care Quality Improvements Act). There are also long-standing non-statutory exemptions for labor, *Brown v. Pro Football*, 518 U.S. 231 (1996), and baseball. *See Fed'l Baseball Club of Baltimore, Inc. v. Nat'l League of Prof. Baseball Clubs*, 259 U.S. 200 (1922); *Flood v. Kuhn*, 407 U.S. 258 (1972). For additional discussions of exemptions under U.S. antitrust law, see ABA SECTION OF ANTITRUST LAW, ANTITRUST LAW DEVELOPMENTS 1305–1500 (6th ed. 2007); ANTITRUST MODERNIZATION COMMISSION, FINAL REPORT AND RECOMMENDATIONS 333–78 (2007), http://govinfo.library.unt.edu/amc/report_recommendation /toc.htm.

Figure 8–2:

Major U.S. Antitrust Exemptions[2]

Statutory Exemptions from the Antitrust Laws

Agricultural Marketing Agreement Act, 7 U.S.C. §§ 608b–608c

Anti-Hog-Cholera Serum and Hog-Cholera Virus Act, 7 U.S.C. § 852

Capper-Volstead Act, 7 U.S.C. §§ 291–92

Charitable Donation Antitrust Immunity Act, 15 U.S.C. §§ 37–37a

Defense Production Act exemption, 50 U.S.C. app. § 2158

Export Trading Company Act, 15 U.S.C. §§ 4001–21

Fishermen's Collective Marketing Act, 15 U.S.C. §§ 521–22

Health Care Quality Improvement Act, 42 U.S.C. §§ 11101–52

Labor exemptions (statutory and non-statutory), 15 U.S.C. § 17; 29 U.S.C. §§ 52, 101–15,151–69; (and common law)

Local Government Antitrust Act, 15 U.S.C. §§ 34–36

Medical resident matching program exemption, 15 U.S.C. § 37b

National Cooperative Research and Production Act, 15 U.S.C. §§ 4301–06

Need-Based Educational Aid Act, 15 U.S.C. § 1 note

Newspaper Preservation Act, 15 U.S.C. §§ 1801–04

Non-profit agricultural cooperatives exemption, 15 U.S.C. § 17

Small Business Act exemption, 15 U.S.C. §§ 638(d), 640

Soft Drink Interbrand Competition Act, 15 U.S.C. §§ 3501–03

Sports Broadcasting Act, 15 U.S.C. §§ 1291–95

---

[2]   Source: ANTITRUST MODERNIZATION COMMISSION, REPORT AND RECOMMENDATIONS, at 378 (2007), *http://govinfo.library.unt.edu/amc/report_recommendation/toc.htm.*

Standard Setting Development Organization Advancement Act, 15 U.S.C. §§ 4301–05, 4301 note

Webb-Pomerene Export Act, 15 U.S.C. §§ 61–66

Statutory Exemptions Created as Part of a Regulatory Regime

Air transportation exemption, 49 U.S.C. §§ 41308–09, 42111

McCarran-Ferguson Act, 15 U.S.C. §§ 1011–15

Motor transportation exemption, 49 U.S.C. §§ 13703, 14302–03

Natural Gas Policy Act exemption, 15 U.S.C. § 3364(e)

Railroad transportation exemption, 49 U.S.C. §§ 10706, 11321(a)

Shipping Act, 46 U.S.C. app. §§ 1701–19

Judicially Created Exemptions

Baseball exemption

Filed-rate/*Keogh* doctrine

Noerr-Pennington Immunity

State Action Doctrine

Various implied immunities created in specific regulatory settings

---

Would you support legislative exemptions for any industries? Why might some industries seek exemptions? Why might some succeed in getting them?

In the U.S., only Congress can create exemptions to the antitrust laws. In contrast, Article 101(3) of the E.U. Treaty authorizes the European Commission to create firm and industry specific exemptions, and exempt specific agreements or categories of agreements that might otherwise violate Article 101(1), provided they contribute to "improving the production or distribution of goods" or promote "technical or economic progress." *See* Article 101(3) of the Treaty on the Functioning of the European Union (Appendix A). Since 1962, the EC often has invoked these provisions, which can be read as permitting exemptions based on goals other than economic efficiency, such as promoting more general economic progress. What are the advantages and disadvantages of such a process? Would you favor such an approach over the U.S., which leaves such decisions solely to Congress?

E. PRIVATE RIGHTS OF ACTION

Section 4 of the Clayton Act authorizes private parties injured by an antitrust violation to sue for treble damages. 15 U.S.C. § 15. Section 16 also authorizes suits for injunctions against "threatened loss or damage" to remedy actual or imminent federal antitrust violations. 15 U.S.C. § 26. Successful private plaintiffs are also entitled to recover reasonable attorneys' fees and costs. Section 4A authorizes very limited recovery of pre-judgment interest. 15 U.S.C. § 15A, and post judgment interest is available as in non-antitrust cases. 28 U.S.C. § 1961.

Section 4B of the Clayton Act creates a four-year statute of limitations for private antitrust actions. The limitations period generally runs from the time the plaintiff suffers injury. *Zenith Radio Corp. v. Hazeltine Research, Inc.*, 401 U.S. 321, 338–39 (1971). If the plaintiff alleges concerted anticompetitive behavior, a new claim may arise from subsequent acts in furtherance of a challenged conspiracy.

Section 5(i) of the Clayton Act, 15 U.S.C. § 16, provides that the statute of limitations for private suits may be suspended while certain federal government antitrust suits are pending and for one year thereafter. This suspension facilitates the operation of Section 5(a), whereby private plaintiffs may use judgments or decrees entered against a defendant in a government antitrust suit as "prima facie evidence against such defendant * * * as to all matters respecting which said judgment or decree would be an estoppel as between the parties." This form of statutory preclusion is distinct from common law claim and issue preclusion, which may also be available. *See, e.g., Parklane Hosiery Co. v. Shore*, 439 U.S. 322 (1979).

The effective scope of Section 5 preclusion, however, may be limited. First, few government cases are litigated through to conclusion, so opportunities to invoke Section 5 are infrequent. Moreover, the provision has been read narrowly. For example, in *In re Microsoft Corp. Antitrust Litig.*, 355 F.3d 322 (4th Cir. 2004), the Fourth Circuit reversed the district court's order of preclusion in a private case brought by Sun Microsystems following the conclusion of the government's prosecution of Microsoft. The issue was how courts should interpret the "critical and necessary" requirement for collateral estoppel. The Fourth Circuit rejected as too broad the district court's interpretation of "critical and necessary" facts as facts "supportive of" the district court's conclusions, favoring "essential":

> Because a fact that is "supportive of" a judgment may be consistent with it but not necessary or essential to it, the term "supportive of" is a broader term than "critical and necessary." The term "supportive of" sweeps so broadly that it might lead to inclusion of all facts that may have been "relevant" to the prior judgment. Such a broad application of offensive collateral estoppel risks the very unfairness about which the Supreme Court was concerned in *Parklane*, and we conclude therefore that it is inappropriate.

Id. at 327.

Treble damages and attorney's fees have made private enforcement an important antitrust enforcement tool. Although government enforcement actions are influential in setting policy priorities, typically there are far more private than public actions filed each year in the federal courts. These cases can be initiated in the absence of any government interest or prosecution, or, owing to the preclusion provisions of the Clayton Act, they may constitute "follow-on" or complementary private actions that follow on the heels of federal investigations or prosecutions.

According to government figures, in the five year period from 2010–2014 an average of 75 civil and criminal antitrust cases were filed each year by the U.S. Department of Justice. For its fiscal years 2011–2015, the Bureau of Competition at the FTC reported an annual average of 38 civil enforcement matters initiated, which includes merger consent orders, filed merger cases, abandoned transactions, non-merger actions, and civil penalty actions. During roughly the same period, 633 civil antitrust cases (public and private) were filed each year in the federal courts. That figure is roughly forty percent of the number of civil antitrust cases that were being filed in the 1970s, although today's cases tend to be larger and more complex.

This decrease in case filings was no doubt in part a reflection of Supreme Court imposed restrictions on the private treble damage remedy, such as *Brunswick*, which we first studied in Chapter 1, and *Illinois Brick* and *Associated General Contractors*, which we will study shortly, as well as enhanced burdens of proof. Nevertheless, as we have seen throughout the Casebook, private cases have been and remain the source of important doctrinal developments that have been crucial to the evolution of antitrust law.

Antitrust is one of several federal statutory regimes that give private parties the power to prosecute. The wisdom of using private rights of action to supplement government enforcement is a matter of extensive scholarly debate. Four basic arguments support enforcement by "private attorneys general." First, private enforcement promotes deterrence, because it enlists the help of parties closest to information about violations. For example, a commercial buyer of raw materials may best be able to detect suspicious, cartelistic bidding by suppliers. Second, private suits provide a means for compensation of the victims of antitrust violations, something that public enforcement actions may not be able to do or will only partially do. Third, they afford a safeguard against lax public enforcement that results from neglect, limited resources, or corruption. Fourth, a private right of action can increase overall levels of enforcement without expanding public enforcement bureaus.

For many of these reasons, as part of its efforts to modernize its antitrust system, the European Commission has for some time been encouraging the expansion of private rights of action at the member state level, while at the same time venturing to avoid what are viewed as the excesses of the U.S. antitrust system. The Commission has stated that its goal is to promote a "culture of competition" in Europe, not a "culture of litigation," a not-so-subtle observation about the perceived excesses of the U.S. system. These efforts have included consideration of "group actions," a variation on class actions, which might facilitate more private actions on behalf of consumer interests.

Despite their potential benefits, private enforcement schemes (including private antitrust enforcement) also can have adverse consequences. Private enforcement can generate questionable claims, and can enable firms to use the courts to impede efficient behavior by their rivals. Although private enforcement reduces the need to enlarge public enforcement bodies, private suits can consume substantial social resources in the form of costs incurred to prosecute and defend such cases.

Perhaps recognizing these adverse possibilities, courts have established limits on the ability of private plaintiffs to obtain relief under the Clayton Act. One group of restrictions, treated immediately below, narrows the set of plaintiffs who may challenge antitrust violations. These devices screen claims according to the type of injury alleged (requirements that the plaintiff suffer harm to its "business or property" and allege "antitrust injury") and the plaintiff's proximity to the source of harm (limits on standing and recovery by indirect purchasers). A second group of restrictions increases the evidentiary burden that plaintiffs must satisfy to establish liability. The evidentiary limits apply to public and private antitrust plaintiffs, alike, and are addressed below in connection with the role of the federal courts in the antitrust system.

1.   INJURY TO BUSINESS OR PROPERTY

To obtain damages under Section 4 of the Clayton Act, 15 U.S.C. § 15, the plaintiff must show that the defendant's conduct harmed its "business or property." The term "business" broadly encompasses "commercial interests or enterprises." See *Hawaii v. Standard Oil Co.*, 405 U.S. 251, 264 (1972). "Property" includes any legally-protected property interest. In an important recognition of the centrality of consumer harm to antitrust enforcement, in *Reiter v. Sonotone*, 442 U.S. 330, 339 (1979), the Supreme Court held that consumers who pay more for goods acquired for personal use are injured in their "property" under Section 4.

2.   ANTITRUST INJURY

As we observed in Chapter 1, the Supreme Court's 1977 decision in *Brunswick Corp. v. Pueblo Bowl-O-Mat, Inc.*, 429 U.S. 477 (1977), established the requirement that the private plaintiff in a treble damage action show that its injury resulted from the anticompetitive effects of the defendant's conduct. As we have discussed, this "antitrust injury" requirement has helped to rationalize antitrust private actions by requiring courts to consider carefully the economic basis for alleged violations and injuries of the antitrust laws. When antitrust proof standards were more lax, it provided courts with a mechanism to mitigate the impact of liability standards perceived as excessively harsh, or of the automatic trebling of damages, or both. As such, it has been a screen that helps to diminish the likely incidence of false positives. On the other hand, antitrust injury has been criticized, because especially in the hands of over-zealous judges, it creates an unjustified obstacle to the resolution of some potentially legitimate antitrust claims. By placing artificial limits on who may sue, it creates the possibility of under-deterrence and false negatives. You might want to re-read this important decision, which is excerpted in Chapter 1.

3.   DIRECT PURCHASERS

The same term as *Brunswick*, the Supreme Court expressed concern about the ability of courts to identify damages flowing from the defendant's conduct and to apportion them to differently situated victims. This concern relates to a distinct requirement that considers the plaintiff's proximity to the defendant in the distribution chain through which the defendants goods or services reach end users. The Court relied on the concept of directness first articulated in the late 1960s and reaffirmed in 1977 in the case presented below.

ILLINOIS BRICK CO. V. ILLINOIS
Supreme Court of the United States, 1977.
431 U.S. 720, 97 S.Ct. 2061, 52 L.Ed.2d 707.

MR. JUSTICE WHITE delivered the opinion of the Court.

Hanover Shoe, Inc. v. United Shoe Machinery Corp., 392 U.S. 481, 88 S.Ct. 2224 (1968), involved an antitrust treble-damages action brought under § 4 of the Clayton Act against a manufacturer of shoe machinery by one of its customers, a manufacturer of shoes. In defense, the shoe machinery manufacturer sought to show that the plaintiff had not been injured in its business as required by § 4 because it had passed on the claimed illegal overcharge to those who bought shoes from it. Under the defendant's theory, the illegal overcharge was absorbed by the plaintiff's customers indirect purchasers of the defendant's shoe machinery who were the persons actually injured by the antitrust violation.

In Hanover Shoe this Court rejected as a matter of law this defense that indirect rather than direct purchasers were the parties injured by the antitrust violation. The Court held that except in certain limited circumstances,[2] a direct purchaser suing for treble damages under § 4 of the Clayton Act is injured within the meaning of § 4 by the full amount of the overcharge paid by it and that the antitrust defendant is not permitted to introduce evidence that indirect purchasers were in fact injured by the illegal overcharge. The first reason for the Court's rejection of this offer of proof was an unwillingness to complicate treble-damages actions with attempts to trace the effects of the overcharge on the purchaser's prices, sales, costs, and profits, and of showing that these variables would have behaved differently without the overcharge. A second reason for barring the pass-on defense was the Court's concern that unless direct purchasers were allowed to sue for the portion of the overcharge arguably passed on to indirect purchasers, antitrust violators "would retain the fruits of their illegality" because indirect purchasers "would have only a tiny stake in the lawsuit" and hence little incentive to sue.

In this case we once again confront the question whether the overcharged direct purchaser should be deemed for purposes of § 4 to have suffered the full injury from the overcharge; but the issue is presented in the context of a suit in which the plaintiff, an indirect purchaser, seeks to show its injury by establishing pass-on by the direct purchaser and in which the antitrust defendants rely on Hanover Shoe's rejection of the pass-on theory. Having decided that in general a pass-on theory may not be used defensively by an antitrust violator against a direct purchaser plaintiff, we must now decide whether that theory may be used offensively by an indirect purchaser plaintiff against an alleged violator.

I

Petitioners manufacture and distribute concrete block in the Greater Chicago area. They sell the block primarily to masonry contractors, who submit bids to general contractors for the masonry portions of construction projects. The general contractors in turn submit bids for these projects to customers such as the respondents in this case, the State of Illinois and 700 local governmental entities in the Greater Chicago area* * *. Respondents are thus indirect purchasers of concrete block, which passes through two separate levels in the chain of distribution before reaching respondents. * * *

Respondent State of Illinois, on behalf of itself and respondent local governmental entities, brought this antitrust treble-damages action under § 4 of the Clayton Act, alleging that petitioners had engaged in a combination and conspiracy to fix the prices of concrete block in violation of § 1 of the Sherman Act. * * * The only way in which the antitrust violation alleged could have injured respondents is if all or part of the

---

[2]   The Court cited, as an example of when a pass-on defense might be permitted, the situation where "an overcharged buyer has a pre-existing 'cost-plus' contract, thus making it easy to prove that he has not been damaged. . . ." 392 U.S., at 494, 88 S.Ct., at 2232.

overcharge was passed on by the masonry and general contractors to respondents, rather than being absorbed at the first two levels of distribution.

* * *

We granted certiorari, to resolve a conflict among the Courts of Appeals on the question whether the offensive use of pass-on authorized by the decision below is consistent with Hanover Shoe's restrictions on the defensive use of pass-on. We hold that it is not, and we reverse. We reach this result in two steps. First, we conclude that whatever rule is to be adopted regarding pass-on in antitrust damages actions, it must apply equally to plaintiffs and defendants. Because Hanover Shoe would bar petitioners from using respondents' pass-on theory as a defense to a treble-damages suit by the direct purchasers (the masonry contractors), we are faced with the choice of overruling (or narrowly limiting) Hanover Shoe or of applying it to bar respondents' attempt to use this pass-on theory offensively. Second, we decline to abandon the construction given § 4 in Hanover Shoe that the overcharged direct purchaser, and not others in the chain of manufacture or distribution, is the party "injured in his business or property" within the meaning of the section in the absence of a convincing demonstration that the Court was wrong in Hanover Shoe to think that the effectiveness of the antitrust treble-damages action would be substantially reduced by adopting a rule that any party in the chain may sue to recover the fraction of the overcharge allegedly absorbed by it.

II

* * *

First, allowing offensive but not defensive use of pass-on would create a serious risk of multiple liability for defendants. Even though an indirect purchaser had already recovered for all or part of an overcharge passed on to it, the direct purchaser would still recover automatically the full amount of the overcharge that the indirect purchaser had shown to be passed on; similarly, following an automatic recovery of the full overcharge by the direct purchaser, the indirect purchaser could sue to recover the same amount. * * * [W]e are unwilling to "open the door to duplicative recoveries" under § 4.[11]

---

[11] In recognition of the need to avoid duplicative recoveries, courts adopting the view that pass-on theories should not be equally available to plaintiffs and defendants have agreed that defendants should be allowed to assert a pass-on defense against a direct purchaser if an indirect purchaser is also attempting to recover on a pass-on theory in the same lawsuit. Various procedural devices, such as the Multidistrict Litigation Act, 28 U.S.C. § 1407, and statutory interpleader, 28 U.S.C. § 1335, are relied upon to bring indirect and direct purchasers together in one action in order to apportion damages among them and thereby reduce the risk of duplicative recovery. These procedural devices cannot protect against multiple liability where the direct purchasers have already recovered by obtaining a judgment or by settling, as is more likely (and as occurred here); acknowledging that the risk of multiple recoveries is inevitably increased by

Second, the reasoning of Hanover Shoe cannot justify unequal treatment of plaintiffs and defendants with respect to the permissibility of pass-on arguments. The principal basis for the decision in Hanover Shoe was the Court's perception of the uncertainties and difficulties in analyzing price and out-put decisions "in the real economic world rather than an economist's hypothetical model," and of the costs to the judicial system and the efficient enforcement of the antitrust laws of attempting to reconstruct those decisions in the courtroom. This perception that the attempt to trace the complex economic adjustments to a change in the cost of a particular factor of production would greatly complicate and reduce the effectiveness of already protracted treble-damages proceedings applies with no less force to the assertion of pass-on theories by plaintiffs than it does to the assertion by defendants. * * *

It is argued, however, that Hanover Shoe rests on a policy of ensuring that a treble-damages plaintiff is available to deprive antitrust violators of "the fruits of their illegality," a policy that would be furthered by allowing plaintiffs but not defendants to use pass-on theories. We do not read the Court's concern in Hanover Shoe for the effectiveness of the treble-damages remedy as countenancing unequal application of the Court's pass-on rule. Rather, we understand Hanover Shoe as resting on the judgment that the antitrust laws will be more effectively enforced by concentrating the full recovery for the overcharge in the direct purchasers rather than by allowing every plaintiff potentially affected by the overcharge to sue only for the amount it could show was absorbed by it.

We thus decline to construe § 4 to permit offensive use of a pass-on theory against an alleged violator that could not use the same theory as a defense in an action by direct purchasers. In this case, respondents seek to demonstrate that masonry contractors, who incorporated petitioners' block into walls and other masonry structures, passed on the alleged overcharge on the block to general contractors, who incorporated the masonry structures into entire buildings, and that the general contractors in turn passed on the overcharge to respondents in the bids submitted for those buildings. We think it clear that under a fair reading of Hanover Shoe petitioners would be barred from asserting this theory in a suit by the masonry contractors.

* * *

We are left, then, with two alternatives: either we must overrule Hanover Shoe (or at least narrowly confine it to its facts), or we must

---

allowing offensive but not defensive use of pass-on, proponents of this approach ultimately fall back on the argument that it is better for the defendant to pay sixfold or more damages than for an injured party to go uncompensated. We do not find this risk acceptable. Moreover, even if ways could be found to bring all potential plaintiffs together in one huge action, the complexity thereby introduced into treble-damages proceedings argues strongly for retaining the Hanover Shoe rule.

preclude respondents from seeking to recover on their pass-on theory. We choose the latter course.

III

* * *

Permitting the use of pass-on theories under § 4 essentially would transform treble-damages actions into massive efforts to apportion the recovery among all potential plaintiffs that could have absorbed part of the overcharge from direct purchasers to middlemen to ultimate consumers. However appealing this attempt to allocate the overcharge might seem in theory, it would add whole new dimensions of complexity to treble-damages suits and seriously undermine their effectiveness.

As we have indicated, potential plaintiffs at each level in the distribution chain are in a position to assert conflicting claims to a common fund the amount of the alleged overcharge by contending that the entire overcharge was absorbed at that particular level in the chain. A treble-damages action brought by one of these potential plaintiffs (or one class of potential plaintiffs) to recover the overcharge implicates all three of the interests that have traditionally been thought to support compulsory joinder of absent and potentially adverse claimants * * *.

* * *

It is unlikely, of course, that all potential plaintiffs could or would be joined. Some may not wish to assert claims to the overcharge; others may be unmanageable as a class; and still others may be beyond the personal jurisdiction of the court. We can assume that ordinarily the action would still proceed, the absent parties not being deemed "indispensable" under Fed. Rule Civ. Proc. 19(b). But allowing indirect purchasers to recover using pass-on theories, even under the optimistic assumption that joinder of potential plaintiffs will deal satisfactorily with problems of multiple litigation and liability, would transform treble-damages actions into massive multiparty litigations involving many levels of distribution and including large classes of ultimate consumers remote from the defendant. In treble-damages actions by ultimate consumers, the overcharge would have to be apportioned among the relevant wholesalers, retailers, and other middlemen, whose representatives presumably should be joined. And in suits by direct purchasers or middlemen, the interests of ultimate consumers are similarly implicated.

There is thus a strong possibility that indirect purchasers remote from the defendant would be parties to virtually every treble-damages action (apart from those brought against defendants at the retail level). * * * We are no more inclined than we were in Hanover Shoe to ignore the burdens that such an attempt would impose on the effective enforcement of the antitrust laws.

Under an array of simplifying assumptions, economic theory provides a precise formula for calculating how the overcharge is distributed between the overcharged party (passer) and its customers (passees). If the market for the passer's product is perfectly competitive; if the overcharge is imposed equally on all of the passer's competitors; and if the passer maximizes its profits, then the ratio of the shares of the overcharge borne by passee and passer will equal the ratio of the elasticities of supply and demand in the market for the passer's product. Even if these assumptions are accepted, there remains a serious problem of measuring the relevant elasticities—the percentage change in the quantities of the passer's product demanded and supplied in response to a one percent change in price. In view of the difficulties that have been encountered, even in informal adversary proceedings, with the statistical techniques used to estimate these concepts, it is unrealistic to think that elasticity studies introduced by expert witnesses will resolve the pass-on issue. * * *

More important, as the Hanover Shoe Court observed, "in the real economic world rather than an economist's hypothetical model," the latter's drastic simplifications generally must be abandoned. Overcharged direct purchasers often sell in imperfectly competitive markets. They often compete with other sellers that have not been subject to the overcharge; and their pricing policies often cannot be explained solely by the convenient assumption of profit maximization. As we concluded in Hanover Shoe, attention to "sound laws of economics" can only heighten the awareness of the difficulties and uncertainties involved in determining how the relevant market variables would have behaved had there been no overcharge.

* * *

We think the longstanding policy of encouraging vigorous private enforcement of the antitrust laws, supports our adherence to the Hanover Shoe rule, under which direct purchasers are not only spared the burden of litigating the intricacies of pass-on but also are permitted to recover the full amount of the overcharge. We recognize that direct purchasers sometimes may refrain from bringing a treble-damages suit for fear of disrupting relations with their suppliers. But on balance, and until there are clear directions from Congress to the contrary, we conclude that the legislative purpose in creating a group of " 'private attorneys general' " to enforce the antitrust laws under § 4, is better served by holding direct purchasers to be injured to the full extent of the overcharge paid by them than by attempting to apportion the overcharge among all that may have absorbed a part of it.

It is true that, in elevating direct purchasers to a preferred position as private attorneys general, the Hanover Shoe rule denies recovery to those indirect purchasers who may have been actually injured by antitrust violations. Of course, as Mr. Justice Brennan points out in dissent, "from the deterrence standpoint, it is irrelevant to whom damages are paid, so long as some one redresses the violation. But § 4 has another purpose in addition to deterring violators and depriving them of "the fruits of their illegality," it is also designed to compensate victims of antitrust violations for their injuries. Hanover Shoe does further the goal of compensation to the extent that the direct purchaser absorbs at least some and often most of the overcharge. In view of the considerations supporting the Hanover Shoe rule, we are unwilling to carry the compensation principle to its logical extreme by attempting to allocate damages among all "those within the defendant's chain of distribution," especially because we question the extent to which such an attempt would make individual victims whole for actual injuries suffered rather than simply depleting the overall recovery in litigation over pass-on issues. Many of the indirect purchasers barred from asserting pass-on claims under the Hanover Shoe rule have such a small stake in the lawsuit that even if they were to recover as part of a class, only a small fraction would be likely to come forward to collect their damages. And given the difficulty of ascertaining the amount absorbed by any particular indirect purchaser, there is little basis for believing that the amount of the recovery would reflect the actual injury suffered.

For the reasons stated, the judgment is reversed, and the case is remanded for further proceedings consistent with this opinion.

So ordered.

[Dissenting opinions of MR. JUSTICE BRENNAN, with whom MR. JUSTICE MARSHALL and MR. JUSTICE BLACKMUN join, omitted. Eds.]

For almost thirty years after it was decided, little was known about the internal process at the Supreme Court that produced the *Illinois Brick* decision. With the release of the papers of several Supreme Court justices who participated in the deliberations of *Illinois Brick*, new light was shed on that process. One notable discovery is that the Court initially voted to uphold indirect purchaser rights, but that after additional internal debate several justices changed their votes to produce the result you have just read. For a more comprehensive discussion of the Supreme Court debates in *Illinois Brick*, see Andrew I. Gavil, *Antitrust Remedy Wars Episode I:* Illinois Brick *from Inside the Supreme Court*, 79 ST. JOHN'S L. REV. 553 (2005). Sidebar 8–6 further examines the rationale and consequences of *Illinois Brick*, as well as the generation of controversy it triggered.

Sidebar 8–6:
The Aftermath of *Illinois Brick*: *ARC America*
and the Emergence of Multi-Jurisdictional
Antitrust Litigation[a]

Illinois Brick ruled that the Clayton Act generally does not permit damage suits for illegal overcharges when the plaintiff does not buy the product directly from one of the violators. In so holding, it established a strong presumption that the Clayton Act's remedial goals are best advanced by allowing direct purchasers to recover all overcharges. The Court feared that permitting indirect purchasers to sue would create intolerable administrative difficulties as courts sought to trace the amount and locus of harm throughout the distribution chain and to apportion damages to each claimant. Uncertainty about the amount of overcharge owing to each plaintiff might "reduce the incentive to sue," and the complexity of tracing and apportionment could lead to duplicative recoveries, thus over-deterring various business practices. As a consequence, indirect purchasers typically have failed in their attempts to recover damages under Section 4 by arguing that the direct purchasers "passed on" the overcharges to them.

Nevertheless, the *Hanover Shoe-Illinois Brick* presumption is not absolute. The Supreme Court indicated that indirect purchasers might be allowed to recover: (1) where fixed quantity, pre-existing cost-plus contracts enable the direct purchaser to pass on overcharges while being "insulated from any decrease in its sales * * * because its customer is committed to buying a fixed quantity regardless of price"; or (2) where the customer owns or controls the direct purchaser. A third exception has been recognized when the direct purchaser is a party to the conspiracy. However, these exceptions have proven extremely difficult to establish in practice. *See, e.g., Kansas v. UtiliCorp United, Inc.*, 497 U.S. 199 (1990).

As a general matter, therefore, *Illinois Brick* bars indirect purchasers from pursuing private treble damage antitrust actions in the federal courts to recover overcharges from members of cartels or monopolists. The right of action in such circumstances is limited to the parties who first purchased from the defendant. For example, if a group of tire manufacturers entered into a cartel to fix the price of original equipment tires sold on automobiles, only the automobile manufacturers, who purchased the price-fixed tires, would be allowed to sue for damages. Retail auto dealers, or consumers, for that matter, would not. They would be "indirect purchasers."

Of course, consumers are frequently "indirect purchasers," so *Illinois Brick* was perceived by some to be in conflict with the avowed pro-consumer purposes of the Sherman and Clayton Acts, most particularly the private right of action. As a consequence, in the years immediately following *Illinois Brick*, a number of states responded to it by adopting "*Illinois Brick* repealers." These statutes purported to remove the bar of *Illinois Brick* for purposes of state antitrust law. These repealers were challenged on preemption grounds, but ultimately approved by the Supreme Court in 1989 in *California v. ARC America Corp.*, 490 U.S. 93 (1989), which saw no conflict in the co-existence of differing and complementary state and federal remedies for antitrust violations.

Since that time, an impressive divide has opened between the scope of federal and state antitrust remedies. Even as indirect purchasers have been barred from seeking antitrust remedies in federal court, they have been welcomed in the courts of many states. Ironically, state remedies, which were once viewed as so inadequate as to require federal antitrust legislation, are now preferred, particularly for consumer class actions on behalf of indirect purchasers, who would be barred from federal court by *Illinois Brick*.

The movement to compensate for *Illinois Brick* by expanding state antitrust rights of action, combined with a spate of highly visible federal price-fixing and monopolization prosecutions in the 1990s, combined to amplify that divide. Owing in part to the preclusive provisions of Section 5(a) of the Clayton Act, successful government prosecutions have been followed by the institution of sometimes scores of private treble damage actions. In the past, such cases would almost invariably have been filed exclusively in federal courts. Even if they were initiated in multiple federal venues, or within the same venue, such cases could later be transferred under 28 U.S.C. §§ 1404 and 1406, and/or consolidated pursuant to Rule 42 of the Federal Rules of Civil Procedure. Another alternative was transfer and consolidation under the authority of the Judicial Panel on Multi-District Litigation, 28 U.S.C. § 1407.

Today, however, such follow-on cases are far more likely to be initiated in both federal and state courts—and the direct/indirect purchaser issue is often the divining rod that leads plaintiffs to one or the other. Direct purchaser actions

---

ᵃ   Portions of this Sidebar are adapted from Andrew I. Gavil, *Federal Judicial Power and the Challenges of Multi-Jurisdictional Direct and Indirect Purchaser Antitrust Litigation*, 69 GEO. WASH. L. REV. 860 (2001) and Andrew I. Gavil, *Thinking Outside the* Illinois Brick *Box: A Proposal for Reform*, 76 ANTITRUST L.J. 167 (2009).

more often are filed in federal courts; state courts are the repository of indirect purchaser actions. Traditionally, efforts to remove state court indirect purchaser actions under 28 U.S.C. § 1441 were met with significant resistance. By definition, indirect purchaser actions do not present any "federal question" because they are barred in federal court due to *Illinois Brick*. And for many years, the Supreme Court limited diversity class actions, and hence diversity removal, to actions where each and every member of the class meets the minimum jurisdictional amount in controversy, currently $75,000. *See Zahn v. International Paper Co.*, 414 U.S. 291 (1973). Two developments have significantly eroded these previous impairments to removal of state antitrust law indirect purchaser cases: (1) In *Exxon Mobil Corp. v. Allapattah Servs., Inc.*, 545 U.S. 546 (2005), the Supreme Court held that *Zahn* had been effectively overruled by the Supplemental Jurisdiction statute, 28 U.S.C. § 1367; and (2) the Class Action Fairness Act of 2004, codified at 28 U.S.C. § 1332(d), expanded removal authority in certain types of large class actions filed in state courts. Taken together, these two developments have increased the possibilities for removal, transfer, and consolidation, at least for pre-trial purposes, of state indirect purchaser actions. But they were not a complete fix for the challenge of multi-forum, multi-jurisdictional direct and indirect purchaser actions arising out of the same conduct.

Multi-*district* litigation, therefore, has become more multi-*jurisdictional*, and the procedural means for capturing the efficiencies to be gained through coordination are far less certain. *See, e.g., In re Microsoft Corp. Antitrust Litig.*, 127 F. Supp. 2d 702 (D. Md. 2001). Achieving procedural efficiency is sometimes left to informal efforts by courts and counsel, not formal means of transfer, consolidation, and coordination. Ironically, this remedial divergence comes at a time when in most other ways, state and federal antitrust laws have converged around common concepts and common standards for liability. Many states today, either by statute or judicial decree, require their courts to follow federal precedent in interpreting and applying their state antitrust laws. Convergence of substantive antitrust liability standards at the state and federal levels thus is becoming an increasing reality for American antitrust, and it increases the likelihood that coordination of state and federal antitrust litigation— particularly on common questions of liability—could yield significant economies. Yet those economies go unrealized as debate continues about the wisdom of the multi-jurisdictional antitrust model.

Critics of the current state of affairs argue that it over-deters anticompetitive conduct and unnecessarily tasks both state and federal courts. Echoing some of the concerns embraced by the Court in *Illinois Brick*, they argue that concurrent prosecution by direct and indirect purchasers of civil actions in state and federal courts substantially increases the likelihood of duplicative and multiple damages. The inadequacy of removal also means that defendants can find themselves responding to multiple class actions in different states, as well as different federal courts. And even when the federal cases can be combined for pre-trial purposes under Section 1407 MDL procedures, current law requires remand for trial. *See Lexecon Inc. v. Milberg Weiss Bershad Hynes & Lerach*, 523 U.S. 26 (1998).

Supporters of remedial diversity respond, however, that such cases are rare and generally involve fairly egregious conduct, such as price fixing. Paralleling the policy arguments we saw urged in connection with interpretation of FTAIA, they assert that the threat of multi-jurisdictional litigation may add significantly to the deterrent value of the private right of action. They also point to various examples of successful informal efforts to coordinate cases by parties and courts. Finally, citing the Supreme Court's rationale in *ARC America*, they point out that the co-existence of direct and indirect purchaser litigation is simply a function of the federal nature of U.S. government, and that no conflict can arise from the mere fact that the federal government and the states have defined the scope of their antitrust remedial rights differently.

Ironically, this divided system may well have produced many of the problems the Supreme Court sought to avoid in *Illinois Brick*. Many cases can easily lose sight of the central concern with overcharges and get bogged down in litigation over "actual injury" to various levels of direct and indirect purchasers. These tensions play out in battles over class certification and the admissibility of expert economic reports seeking to establish class-wide harm at each level. The result may be an admixture of under-deterrence and under-compensation. For a proposal to overrule *Illinois Brick* and replace it with a legislatively created presumptive allocation scheme for damages, see Andrew I. Gavil, *Thinking Outside the* Illinois Brick *Box: A Proposal for Reform*, 76 ANTITRUST L.J. 167 (2009).

4. STANDING

Five years after *Brunswick* and *Illinois Brick*, the Court imposed additional restrictions on the rights of plaintiffs to sue in federal court for antitrust violations. "Standing" focuses on the plaintiff's proximity to the alleged harm. In *Blue Shield of Virginia v. McCready*, 457 U.S. 465 (1982), the Supreme Court held that Section 4 of the Clayton Act gave standing to a health insurance policyholder (McCready) to sue her insurance company for allegedly conspiring with physicians to refuse to deal with a psychologist whose services the plaintiff wanted the insurer to reimburse. The Court observed that "Congress did not intend to allow every person tangentially affected by an antitrust violation" to maintain a treble damage action. To determine standing, it is necessary to examine "the physical and economic nexus between the alleged violation and the harm to the plaintiff." 457 U.S. at 478. The Court rejected the defendants' argument that, because the concerted refusal to deal targeted the psychologists, McCready's injury was "too 'fortuitous' 'incidental' . . . and 'remote'" to confer standing. Instead, McCready fell "within the area of the economy . . . endangered by the breakdown of competitive conditions, resulting from Blue Shield's selective refusal to reimburse." The Court tightened standing requirements the next year in the case that follows.

ASSOCIATED GENERAL CONTRACTORS OF CALIFORNIA INC. v. CALIFORNIA STATE COUNCIL OF CARPENTERS

United States Supreme Court, 1983.
459 U.S. 519, 103 S.Ct. 897, 74 L.Ed.2d 723.

JUSTICE STEVENS delivered the opinion of the Court.

This case arises out of a dispute between parties to a multiemployer collective bargaining agreement. The plaintiff unions allege that, in violation of the antitrust laws, the multiemployer association and its members coerced certain third parties, as well as some of the association's members, to enter into business relationships with nonunion firms. This coercion, according to the complaint, adversely affected the trade of certain unionized firms and thereby restrained the business activities of the unions. The question presented is whether the complaint sufficiently alleges that the unions have been "injured in [their] business or property by reason of anything forbidden in the antitrust laws" and may therefore recover treble damages under § 4 of the Clayton Act. 15 U.S.C. § 15. Unlike the majority of the Court of Appeals for the Ninth Circuit, we agree with the District Court's conclusion that the complaint is insufficient.

* * *

II

* * *

The Union's antitrust claims arise from alleged restraints caused by defendants in the market for construction contracting and subcontracting.[14] The complaint alleges that defendants "coerced" two classes of persons: (1) landowners and others who let construction contracts, *i.e.*, the defendants' customers and potential customers; and (2) general contractors, *i.e.*, defendants' competitors and defendants themselves. Coercion against the members of both classes was designed to induce them to give some of their business—but not necessarily all of it—to nonunion firms.[16] Although the pleading does not allege that the coercive conduct increased the aggregate share of nonunion firms in the market, it does allege that defendants' activities weakened and restrained the trade "of certain contractors." Thus, particular victims of coercion may have diverted particular contracts to nonunion firms and thereby caused certain unionized subcontractors to lose some business.

We think the Court of Appeals properly assumed that such coercion might violate the antitrust laws. An agreement to restrain trade may be unlawful even though it does not entirely exclude its victims from the market. Coercive activity that prevents its victims from making free choices between market alternatives is inherently destructive of competitive conditions and may be condemned even without proof of its actual market effect.[18]

Even though coercion directed by defendants at third parties in order to restrain the trade of "certain" contractors and subcontractors may have been unlawful, it does not, of course, necessarily follow that still another party—the Union—is a person injured by reason of a violation of the antitrust laws within the meaning of § 4 of the Clayton Act.

III

We first consider the language in the controlling statute. The class of persons who may maintain a private damage action under the antitrust laws is broadly defined in § 4 of the Clayton Act. 15 U.S.C. § 15. That section provides:

---

[14] There is no allegation of wrongful conduct directed at nonunion subcontracting firms. * * * The amended complaint also does not allege any restraint on competition in the market for labor union services. * * *

[16] There is no allegation that any person subjected to coercion was required to deal exclusively with nonunion firms.

[18] Although we do not know what kind of coercion defendants allegedly employed, we assume for purposes of decision that it had a predatory "nature or character," *Klors, Inc. v. Broadway-Hale Stores, Inc.*, 359 U.S. 207, 211, 79 S.Ct. 705, 709, 3 L.Ed.2d 741 (1959), and that it would "cripple the freedom of traders and thereby restrain their ability to sell in accordance with their own judgment." *Kiefer-Stewart Co. v. Seagram & Sons*, 340 U.S. 211, 213, 71 S.Ct. 259, 260, 95 L.Ed. 219 (1951).

"Any person who shall be injured in his business or property by reason of anything forbidden in the antitrust laws may sue therefor in any district court of the United States in the district in which the defendant resides or is found or has an agent, without respect to the amount in controversy, and shall recover threefold the damages by him sustained, and the cost of suit, including a reasonable attorney's fee."

A literal reading of the statute is broad enough to encompass every harm that can be attributed directly or indirectly to the consequences of an antitrust violation. Some of our prior cases have paraphrased the statute in an equally expansive way. But before we hold that the statute is as broad as its words suggest, we must consider whether Congress intended such an open-ended meaning.

The critical statutory language was originally enacted in 1890 as § 7 of the Sherman Act. The legislative history of the section shows that Congress was primarily interested in creating an effective remedy for consumers who were forced to pay excessive prices by the giant trusts and combinations that dominated certain interstate markets.[20] That history supports a broad construction of this remedial provision. A proper interpretation of the section cannot, however, ignore the larger context in which the entire statute was debated.

* * *

Just as the substantive content of the Sherman Act draws meaning from its common-law antecedents, so must we consider the contemporary legal context in which Congress acted when we try to ascertain the intended scope of the private remedy created by § 7.

In 1890, notwithstanding general language in many state constitutions providing in substance that "every wrong shall have a remedy," a number of judge-made rules circumscribed the availability of damages recoveries in both tort and contract litigation—doctrines such as foreseeability and proximate cause, directness of injury, certainty of damages, and privity of contract. Although particular common-law limitations were not debated in Congress, the frequent references to common-law principles imply that Congress simply assumed that antitrust

---

[20] The original proposal, which merely allowed recovery of the amount of actual enhancement in price, was successively amended to authorize double damages and then treble-damages recoveries, in order to provide otherwise remediless small consumers with an adequate incentive to bring suit. The same purpose was served by the special venue provisions, the provision for the recovery of attorneys' fees, and the elimination of any requirement that the amount in controversy exceed the jurisdictional threshold applicable in other federal litigation. * * *

damages litigation would be subject to constraints comparable to well-accepted common-law rules applied in comparable litigation.[28]

* * *

As this Court has observed, the lower federal courts have been "virtually unanimous in concluding that Congress did not intend the antitrust laws to provide a remedy in damages for all injuries that might conceivably be traced to an antitrust violation." Hawaii v. Standard Oil Co., 405 U.S. 251, 263 n. 14, 92 S.Ct. 885, 891 n. 14 (1972). Just last Term we stated:

> "An antitrust violation may be expected to cause ripples of harm to flow through the Nation's economy; but 'despite the broad wording of § 4 there is a point beyond which the wrongdoer should not be held liable.' Id., [Illinois Brick Co. v. Illinois, 431 U.S. 720] at 760 [97 S.Ct. 2061 at 2082] (Brennan, J., dissenting) [citing Illinois Brick v. Illinois, 431 U.S. 720, 97 S.Ct. 2061 (1977)]. It is reasonable to assume that Congress did not intend to allow every person tangentially affected by an antitrust violation to maintain an action to recover threefold damages for the injury to his business or property." Blue Shield of Virginia, Inc. v. McCready, 457 U.S. 465, 476–77, 102 S.Ct. 2540, 2547 (1982).

It is plain, therefore, that the question whether the Union may recover for the injury it allegedly suffered by reason of the defendants' coercion against certain third parties cannot be answered simply by reference to the broad language of § 4. Instead, as was required in common-law damages litigation in 1890, the question requires us to evaluate the plaintiff's harm, the alleged wrongdoing by the defendants, and the relationship between them.[31]

IV

There is a similarity between the struggle of common-law judges to articulate a precise definition of the concept of "proximate cause," and the struggle of federal judges to articulate a precise test to determine whether a party injured by an antitrust violation may recover treble damages.[33] It

---

[28] The common law, of course, is an evolving body of law. We do not mean to intimate that the limitations on damages recoveries found in common-law actions in 1890 were intended to serve permanently as limits on Sherman Act recoveries. But legislators familiar with these limits could hardly have intended the language of § 7 to be taken literally.

[31] The label "antitrust standing" has traditionally been applied to some of the elements of this inquiry. As commentators have observed, the focus of the doctrine of "antitrust standing" is somewhat different from that of standing as a constitutional doctrine. Harm to the antitrust plaintiff is sufficient to satisfy the constitutional standing requirement of injury in fact, but the court must make a further determination whether the plaintiff is a proper party to bring a private antitrust action.

[33] Some courts have focused on the directness of the injury. Others have applied the requirement that the plaintiff must be in the "target area" of the antitrust conspiracy, that is, the

is common ground that the judicial remedy cannot encompass every conceivable harm that can be traced to alleged wrongdoing. In both situations the infinite variety of claims that may arise make it virtually impossible to announce a black-letter rule that will dictate the result in every case. Instead, previously decided cases identify factors that circumscribe and guide the exercise of judgment in deciding whether the law affords a remedy in specific circumstances.

The factors that favor judicial recognition of the Union's antitrust claim are easily stated. The complaint does allege a causal connection between an antitrust violation and harm to the Union and further alleges that the defendants intended to cause that harm. As we have indicated, however, the mere fact that the claim is literally encompassed by the Clayton Act does not end the inquiry. We are also satisfied that an allegation of improper motive, although it may support a plaintiff's damages claim under § 4, is not a panacea that will enable any complaint to withstand a motion to dismiss. * * *

A number of other factors may be controlling. In this case it is appropriate to focus on the nature of the plaintiff's alleged injury. As the legislative history shows, the Sherman Act was enacted to assure customers the benefits of price competition, and our prior cases have emphasized the central interest in protecting the economic freedom of participants in the relevant market. Last Term in *Blue Shield of Virginia v. McCready, supra,* we identified the relevance of this central policy to a determination of the plaintiff's right to maintain an action under § 4. McCready alleged that she was a consumer of psychotherapeutic services and that she had been injured by the defendants' conspiracy to restrain competition in the market for such services. The Court stressed the fact that "McCready's injury was of a type that Congress sought to redress in providing a private remedy for violations of the antitrust laws." [C]*iting Brunswick Corp. v. Pueblo Bowl-O-Mat, Inc.,* 429 U.S. 477, 487–489, 97 S.Ct. 690, 697, 50 L.Ed.2d 701 (1977). After noting that her injury "was inextricably intertwined with the injury the conspirators sought to inflict on psychologists and the psychotherapy market," the Court concluded that such an injury "falls squarely within the area of congressional concern."

In this case, however, the Union was neither a consumer nor a competitor in the market in which trade was restrained.[40] It is not clear whether the Union's interests would be served or disserved by enhanced

---

area of the economy which is endangered by a breakdown of competitive conditions in a particular industry. Another court of appeals has asked whether the injury is "arguably within the zone of interests protected by the antitrust laws." As a number of commentators have observed, these labels may lead to contradictory and inconsistent results. In our view, courts should analyze each situation in light of the factors set forth in the text *infra.*

[40] Moreover, it has not even alleged any marketwide restraint of trade. The allegedly unlawful conduct involves predatory behavior directed at "certain" parties, rather than a claim that output has been curtailed or prices enhanced throughout an entire competitive market.

competition in the market. As a general matter, a union's primary goal is to enhance the earnings and improve the working conditions of its membership; that goal is not necessarily served, and indeed may actually be harmed, by uninhibited competition among employers striving to reduce costs in order to obtain a competitive advantage over their rivals. At common law—as well as in the early days of administration of the federal antitrust laws—the collective activities of labor unions were regarded as a form of conspiracy in restraint of trade. Federal policy has since developed not only a broad labor exemption from the antitrust laws, but also a separate body of labor law specifically designed to protect and encourage the organizational and representational activities of labor unions. Set against this background, a union, in its capacity as bargaining representative, will frequently not be part of the class the Sherman Act was designed to protect, especially in disputes with employers with whom it bargains. In each case its alleged injury must be analyzed to determine whether it is of the type that the antitrust statute was intended to forestall. In this case, particularly in light of the longstanding collective bargaining relationship between the parties, the Union's labor-market interests seem to predominate, and the *Brunswick* test is not satisfied.

An additional factor is the directness or indirectness of the asserted injury. In this case, the chain of causation between the Union's injury and the alleged restraint in the market for construction subcontracts contains several somewhat vaguely defined links. According to the complaint, defendants applied coercion against certain landowners and other contracting parties in order to cause them to divert business from certain union contractors to nonunion contractors. As a result, the Union's complaint alleges, the Union suffered unspecified injuries in its "business activities." It is obvious that any such injuries were only an indirect result of whatever harm may have been suffered by "certain" construction contractors and subcontractors.

If either these firms, or the immediate victims of coercion by defendants, have been injured by an antitrust violation, their injuries would be direct and, as we held in *McCready, supra,* they would have a right to maintain their own treble damages actions against the defendants. An action on their behalf would encounter none of the conceptual difficulties that encumber the Union's claim.[47] The existence of an identifiable class of persons whose self-interest would normally motivate them to vindicate the public interest in antitrust enforcement diminishes the justification for allowing a more remote party such as the Union to perform the office of a private attorney general. Denying the Union a remedy on the basis of its allegations in this case is not likely to leave a significant antitrust violation undetected or unremedied.

---

[47] Indeed, if there is substance to the Union's claim, it is difficult to understand why these direct victims of the conspiracy have not asserted any claim in their own right. * * *

Partly because it is indirect, and partly because the alleged effects on the Union may have been produced by independent factors, the Union's damages claim is also highly speculative. There is, for example, no allegation that any collective bargaining agreement was terminated as a result of the coercion, no allegation that the aggregate share of the contracting market controlled by union firms has diminished, no allegation that the number of employed union members has declined, and no allegation that the Union's revenues in the form of dues or initiation fees have decreased. Moreover, although coercion against certain firms is alleged, there is no assertion that any such firm was prevented from doing business with any union firms or that any firm or group of firms was subjected to a complete boycott. Other than the alleged injuries flowing from breaches of the collective bargaining agreements—injuries that would be remediable under other laws—nothing but speculation informs the Union's claim of injury by reason of the alleged unlawful coercion. Yet, as we have recently reiterated, it is appropriate for § 4 purposes "to consider whether a claim rests at bottom on some abstract conception or speculative measure of harm." *Blue Shield of Virginia v. McCready, supra.*

The indirectness of the alleged injury also implicates the strong interest, identified in our prior cases, in keeping the scope of complex antitrust trials within judicially manageable limits. These cases have stressed the importance of avoiding either the risk of duplicate recoveries on the one hand, or the danger of complex apportionment of damages on the other. [Citing *Hanover Shoe, Inc. v. United Shoe Machinery Corp.*, 392 U.S. 481, 88 S.Ct. 2224, 20 L.Ed.2d 1231 (1968), and *Illinois Brick Co. v. Illinois*, 431 U.S. 720, 97 S.Ct. 2061, 52 L.Ed.2d 707 (1977).] * * *

The same concerns should guide us in determining whether the Union is a proper plaintiff under § 4 of the Clayton Act. As the Court wrote in *Illinois Brick,* massive and complex damages litigation not only burdens the courts, but also undermines the effectiveness of treble-damages suits. In this case, if the Union's complaint asserts a claim for damages under § 4, the District Court would face problems of identifying damages and apportioning them among directly victimized contractors and subcontractors and indirectly affected employees and union entities. It would be necessary to determine to what extent the coerced firms diverted business away from union subcontractors, and then to what extent those subcontractors absorbed the damage to their businesses or passed it on to employees by reducing the workforce or cutting hours or wages. In turn it would be necessary to ascertain the extent to which the affected employees absorbed their losses and continued to pay union dues.

We conclude, therefore, that the Union's allegations of consequential harm resulting from a violation of the antitrust laws, although buttressed by an allegation of intent to harm the Union, are insufficient as a matter of law. Other relevant factors—the nature of the Union's injury, the tenuous and speculative character of the relationship between the alleged antitrust violation and the Union's alleged injury, the potential for duplicative recovery or complex apportionment of damages, and the existence of more direct victims of the alleged conspiracy—weigh heavily against judicial enforcement of the Union's antitrust claim. Accordingly, we hold that, based on the allegations of this complaint, the District Court was correct in concluding that the Union is not a person injured by reason of a violation of the antitrust laws within the meaning of § 4 of the Clayton Act. The judgment of the Court of Appeals is reversed.

It is so ordered.

[The Dissenting opinion of MR. JUSTICE MARSHALL has been omitted. Eds.]

Associated General directed lower courts to analyze standing in light of five factors:

- the causal connection between the antitrust violation and injury to the plaintiff, and whether the injury was intended;

- the nature of the injury, including whether the plaintiff is a consumer or competitor in the relevant market;

- the directness of the injury and whether claimed damages are too speculative;

- the potential for duplicative recovery and whether apportioning damages would be too complex; and

- the existence of more direct victims.

Are these factors distinct from the "antitrust injury" requirements of *Brunswick*? From the concerns expressed in *Illinois Brick* about indirect purchasers? Are they related? Do they overlap in any significant way? Should they be viewed as independent screens, *i.e.*, a direct purchaser might still be barred under *Associated General* if the causal connection between its harm and the challenged conduct is attenuated? What effects will screening private plaintiffs under *Brunswick* and *Associated General* have on the incidence of private antitrust litigation? Finally, consider the policy arguments for and against the tests for statutory standing set forth in *Brunswick* and *Associated General*. Do you find the case for developing distinct standing requirements for antitrust persuasive? How often are these requirements likely to prove determinative?

5. DEFENSES BASED ON *IN PARI DELICTO* AND UNCLEAN HANDS

Although the Supreme Court has embraced a variety of limitations on the scope of the private right of action, it has rejected for the most part efforts to defend antitrust cases on the ground that the plaintiff either (1) was a participant in the challenged conduct ("*in pari delicto*"—meaning "of equal fault"); or (2) was otherwise an antitrust scofflaw, itself ("unclean hands").

In *Kiefer-Stewart Co. v. Joseph E. Seagram & Sons, Inc.*, 340 U.S. 211, 214 (1951) (unclean hands) and *Perma Life Mufflers, Inc. v. International Parts Corp.*, 392 U.S. 134, 138–39 (1968) (*in pari delicto*), the Court refused to endorse blanket defenses based on either unclean hands or *in pari delicto*, respectively. In *Perma Life* the Court concluded: "[t]here is nothing in the language of the antitrust acts which indicates that Congress wanted to make the common-law *in pari delicto* doctrine a defense to treble damage actions." *Id.* at 138. Referring more broadly to both the unclean hands defense raised in *Kiefer-Stewart*, and the *in pari delicto* defense urged in *Perma Life*, the Court reasoned:

> * * * [T]he purposes of the antitrust laws are best served by insuring that the private action will be an ever-present threat to deter anyone contemplating business behavior in violation of the antitrust laws. The plaintiff who reaps the reward of treble damages may be no less morally reprehensible than the defendant, but the law encourages his suit to further the overriding public policy in favor of competition. A more fastidious regard for the relative moral worth of the parties would only result in seriously undermining the usefulness of the private action as a bulwark of antitrust enforcement. And permitting the plaintiff to recover a windfall gain does not encourage continued violations by those in his position since they remain fully subject to civil and criminal penalties for their own illegal conduct.

Id. at 139. Some exceptions, first hinted at in *Perma Life*, have emerged, however, and under very limited circumstances these sorts of defenses can be significant. *See generally* ABA SECTION OF ANTITRUST LAW, ANTITRUST LAW DEVELOPMENTS 876–80 (6th ed. 2007).

F. REMEDIES FOR ANTITRUST VIOLATIONS

In this section we take a closer look at several key elements of the competition policy remedial scheme, including the application of criminal penalties for certain antitrust violations, the role of injunctive relief, including divestiture, and finally the U.S. treble damage remedy.

1. CRIMINAL SANCTIONS

Criminal sanctions for antitrust violations have increased substantially since 1970 as a consequence of both changes in the relevant legal provisions as well as experience with global cartels such as those we studied in Chapter 1. Today, the Sherman Act sets a maximum fine of $100 million for corporate defendants. Individuals may be punished by fines of up to $1 million and by jail sentences as long as ten years. 15 U.S.C. §§ 1–2. Under 18 U.S.C. § 3571(d), fines may also be "not more than the greater of twice the gross gain or twice the gross loss, unless imposition of a fine under this subsection would unduly complicate or prolong the sentencing process." In addition, in 2006, Congress added antitrust offenses to the list of crimes that can be investigated using court-ordered wiretaps, enhancing the Antitrust Division's investigatory authority. 18 U.S.C. § 2516.

Criminal antitrust sentencing also is addressed by the federal Sentencing Guidelines promulgated by the U.S. Sentencing Commission. *See* U.S. SENTENCING COMMISSION, GUIDELINES MANUAL § 2R1.1 (2015). Under the Guidelines, which are not binding, judges have been more likely to impose substantial fines and prison terms upon entities or individuals convicted of bid-rigging, price-fixing, and market allocation schemes. General controversy over the constitutionality of judicial procedures under the Guidelines has injected some uncertainty into this area for antitrust, as well. Nevertheless, according to the Department of Justice, criminal fines and jail time for criminal antitrust offenders has risen and defendants today are more likely to receive jail time and longer sentences than ever before. For the most recent statistics on criminal fines and jail sentences, see U.S. Dep't of Justice, Antirust Division, *Criminal Enforcement Trends Charts*, https://www.justice.gov/atr/criminal-enforcement-fine-and-jail-charts.

––––––––––

The following example reveals how the Department of Justice proposed to set the sanction for several key participants in the Vitamins, Inc. cartel, which we introduced in Chapter 1. Reprinted below is the sentencing statement that the DOJ entered to settle criminal charges against the conspiracy's ringleader, Hoffmann-La Roche, and Kuno Sommer, the executive who orchestrated the cartel. To date, the $500 million fine imposed on Hoffman-La Roche remains the largest criminal antitrust fine ever imposed in the U.S.

UNITED STATES V. F. HOFFMANN-LA ROCHE LTD.

United States District Court, N.D. Texas.
May 1999.

Sentencing Statement for the United States

Had this case gone to trial, the United States would have presented evidence to establish the following facts:

* * *

From at least January 1990 until February 1999, Roche, and other worldwide manufacturers of vitamins engaged in an illegal conspiracy, the primary purpose of which was to fix, increase, and maintain the prices and allocate the volume of certain vitamins sold in the United States and worldwide. Initially, this conspiracy focused on vitamins A and E and it quickly evolved into an extremely well organized operation. Throughout the world, on a country and regional level, Roche and other conspirator companies tasked their lower level employees and managers to forward pricing and market share information to higher level management. On a quarterly basis, regional and world marketing managers from the conspirator companies would meet to exchange pricing and sales information in order to have an accurate picture of the overall global demand and price for the vitamins. Once a year, the global marketing directors for each of the conspirator companies, in concert with the various product managers for the companies, would conduct a "budget" meeting. During this meeting, the overall global sales volume for the vitamins would be determined for the current year, and based on agreed-upon projected growth rates, the global sales volume for the coming year would be determined. Next, each company would be allocated a percentage of this projected global market demand as its "budget target" for the following year which it would then implement on a regional or country basis. Finally, vitamin pricing would be reviewed and, if price increases were needed to either account for currency discrepancies or to raise profit levels, new pricing would be agreed upon, to include the timing of the price increases and designation of which company would lead the price increase.

To implement the budgeted amounts of vitamins A and E in the United States, Roche and another coconspirator found it necessary to allocate between themselves various vitamin premix accounts in the U.S. To do this, representatives from the two companies would meet on a quarterly basis to review bid requests that were sent out by the major food and animal feed premix customers in the country. Meeting in private homes to avoid detection, these representatives would determine which customer would "belong" to Roche and which customer would "belong" to the other conspirator company. The representatives would then determine what the winning bid price would be for each company, fill out the bids to either "win" or "lose" the bid, and then mail the bids back to the customers.

Over time, the scope of the conspiracy was adjusted, usually with Roche as the instigator of activity, to either include or exclude additional vitamins and vitamin manufacturers involved in the conspiracy. Over the course of the conspiracy vitamins A, B2 (riboflavin), B5 (Calpan), C, Beta Carotene, and various vitamin premixes were all subject to collusive and illegal agreements and sold to a wide array of customers in America, many with household names such as General Mills, Kelloggs, Coca-Cola, Tyson Foods, and Proctor and Gamble.

Roche and its coconspirators were very concerned with maintaining the secrecy of their cartel activity. It was expressly understood by conspiracy meeting participants that documents were to be kept to a minimum and destroyed after each meeting. Internally, Roche personnel were continually instructed to destroy all documents that might be evidence of illegal agreements with competitors. In those instances where it was necessary to generate spreadsheets to show each conspirator's current market share, companies were never listed by name; instead they were allocated a code number that was used on the spreadsheet to conceal their true identities.

Throughout the course of the conspiracy, Roche sold to U.S. customers over 3.2 billion dollars of vitamins and vitamin premixes that were the subject of and affected by this illegal cartel activity.

WITH RESPECT TO SENTENCING:

The jointly recommended criminal fine of 500 million dollars is an appropriate punishment for Roche in this case. If the court accepts the joint sentencing recommendation, Roche will pay the largest criminal fine ever imposed, not only for an antitrust offense, but the largest fine ever imposed for any criminal offense. From an antitrust perspective, a 500 million dollar fine is 365 million dollars more that the previous record antitrust fine. Overall, a 500 million dollar fine is 140 million dollars more than any criminal fine ever imposed in DOJ history. In this respect, a 500 million dollar fine recognizes the seriousness of the offense, the role played by Roche in the offense, the impact of the offense on American consumers, the fact that Roche is a repeat offender, and the attempts by Roche to obstruct the Antitrust Division's investigation in this matter. Because the obstructive efforts of Roche are relevant for sentencing, let me take a moment to detail these activities.

Roche's quest to maintain the secrecy of its collusive activities led it to actions which obstructed the Government's investigative efforts. Dr. Kuno Sommer, Roche's Worldwide Marketing Director, was interviewed by Department of Justice, Antitrust Division attorneys on March 12, 1997 in connection with a plea agreement reached between the United States and Roche concerning criminal antitrust violations committed by Roche in the sale and production of citric acid. Prior to his interview, Sommer was advised by Antitrust Division enforcement officials that he would also be asked questions about possible criminal antitrust violations concerning other food and animal feed additives, particularly vitamins.

From 1994 to 1997, Dr. Kuno Sommer was the key executive at Roche responsible for the day-to-day supervision and administration of the vitamins cartel. He was not only the senior executive to whom Roche regional managers and global product managers reported, but he was also the senior point of contact between Roche and other conspirator companies.

In order to conceal from Antitrust investigators the existence of collusive agreements and activities between Roche and its vitamin manufacturing competitors, Sommer met separately with at least two other high level Roche executives. At the end of those meetings, it was understood by these individuals that if Sommer was asked about Roche's participation in a vitamins cartel, Sommer would lie and deny that such a cartel existed. At subsequent preparation meetings between Sommer and one or more of the individuals, Sommer's "cover story" denying any cartel activity affecting vitamins was rehearsed. When, on March 12, 1997, Antitrust Division enforcement officials ultimately questioned Sommer about the existence of a vitamins cartel, Sommer lied by stating that there was no conspiracy among the world's leading vitamins manufacturers, including Roche; that he had never participated in meetings, conversations, or agreements to fix, increase, and maintain prices, or allocate sales volumes of, or customers for, certain vitamins with any representative of any other manufacturer of vitamins; and that he was not aware of any meetings or conversations among other representatives of Roche and any other vitamin manufacturer relating to any agreements of conspiracy to fix, increase, or maintain prices, or allocate sales volumes and customers in the vitamin industry.

Sommer's efforts to cover up the conspiracy were successful in delaying and obstructing the Division's vitamins investigation. With renewed confidence in the secrecy of the cartel's activity, Roche and its high level executives continued to participate in the vitamins cartel even while a court was taking Roche's citric acid plea, and even while Roche was cooperating in the citric acid investigation as required by its plea agreement.

Given these circumstances, it is clear that a fine of this magnitude is particularly necessary as a means to deter future international cartel activity. As Roche's conduct has demonstrated, significantly lesser fines are not of sufficient deterrent value to curtail large-scale international collusion. It is important to note that the vitamins cartel was in full swing in October of 1996 when Archer Daniels Midland was assessed a 100 million dollar fine for its role in two international cartels in the food and feed additives industry. Despite this enormous fine, Roche and its coconspirators did not miss a beat in continuing to fix prices and allocate global market share for the vitamins industry.

Of equal importance with the need to properly punish the offender, a 500 million dollar fine, when compared to the possible exposure Roche faces under the Federal Sentencing Guidelines, properly recognizes and rewards the exemplary cooperation Roche has provided to the Antitrust Division. Beginning on March 2, 1999, Roche, through counsel, informed Antitrust Division attorneys that it had colluded with competitors on at least some vitamins and that it was in the process of determining the full extent of Roche's involvement in the illegal activity. From that moment on, the speed, nature, and spirit of Roche's cooperation was unprecedented and a model of what full cooperation should be.

Within a matter of weeks, Roche made available in the United States over a half dozen current and former foreign-based employees that were intimately involved in the day-to-day operations of Roche's conspiracy activities. These witnesses gave candid, complete, and detailed information concerning their participation in the charged conspiracy and that of other companies and individuals involved. This information concerning other corporate and individual coconspirators significantly enhanced the quantity and quality of evidence respecting those coconspirators and has increased the likelihood of expeditious, successful prosecutions of such corporations and individuals. These witnesses also brought forward documents that had not been destroyed during the course of the conspiracy which clearly detailed the extent of information sharing and global market allocation that occurred during the course of the conspiracy. Additionally, these witnesses have provided valuable information concerning a collusive agreement between Roche and other coconspirators on another nonvitamin product which will likely lead to additional prosecutions involving the product.

Roche, through counsel, also informed some of its corporate coconspirators that it was cooperating with the Antitrust Division in this investigation. Consequently, some of these corporate coconspirators have initiated discussions with Division prosecutors to resolve their criminal liability for vitamin price fixing and market allocation conduct. Without this assistance, such corporate coconspirators would likely not be at the negotiating table at this time and the Division's investigation would not be progressing as significantly as it is in terms of additional prospective prosecutions.

The information provided by Roche, through its current and former employees, increased our knowledge of the conspiracy. Roche has committed to, and we fully anticipate and expect that Roche will continue to provide valuable information and assistance as the investigation of criminal cartel activity in the vitamins industry continues, including grand jury appearances and possible testimony at any eventual trial involving such violations. Given all of these circumstances, a 500 million dollar fine not only recognizes the extraordinary cooperation that Roche has and will continue to provide, given the potential liability Roche faces in terms of its Guidelines fine range, such a significant departure from the Guidelines fine range offers a clear incentive to future defendants to provide quick and complete cooperation.

The sentencing statement for Roche and Sommer reveals several factors at work. The conspirators fully understood that U.S. antitrust law deemed their conduct to be criminal. In carrying out their scheme, the violators focused on whether they would be apprehended and prosecuted, and how they might be punished. "Vitamins, Inc." exercised caution to hold its meetings and orchestrate most of its affairs outside the United States—expecting, perhaps, that the cartel could exploit gaps in the capacity of the U.S. laws to reach their offshore arrangements and to obtain jurisdiction over culpable individuals. The cartel also strove to conceal the arrangement and avoid detection. The extraordinary size of the fine imposed on HLR—$500 million, the largest criminal fine obtained by DOJ in any matter—reflected a desire to deter similar misconduct by other firms.

Recall, too from our discussion of the *ADM* in Chapter 1 ("Lysine"), that in addition to fines, individuals who commit criminal violations of the Sherman Act can be punished with prison sentences. What factors might lead the Justice Department to seek prison time for violators? What factors might lead a court to impose prison time, and how much time is appropriate for individuals who play leading roles in orchestrating the conspiracy? At this point, you may want to review the excerpt from the Seventh Circuit's decision in *ADM* to enhance the prison sentences of the "ring-leaders" of the Lysine cartel, which we read in Chapter 1. *See also United States v. A. Alfred Taubman*, 297 F.3d 161 (2d Cir. 2002) (affirming criminal conviction of individual in price fixing case).

2. CIVIL REMEDIES

Civil remedies for antitrust law violations generally take two basic forms: the chastening effect on the defendant of the lawsuit itself and judicially-imposed remedies. Remedies fall into one of two categories: (1) equitable relief, such as injunctions or divestiture orders, and (2) damages. After briefly considering the role that the mere threat of litigation can play, we turn to judicial treatment of equitable relief and damages.

a. Lawsuits as Remedies

The mere filing and prosecution of an antitrust case sometimes alters the defendant's conduct. Prosecuting a group of conspirators under Section 1, or a dominant firm under Section 2, for example, can have two effects. The first is what might be called the *inhibition* effect. The lawsuit itself can give consumers and/or rivals breathing room by inhibiting the defendant from engaging in overly aggressive commercial moves. Under scrutiny from the court, the prosecutor, and the press, the dominant firm, for example, might hesitate to employ tactics that strengthen its position in the relevant market or extend its preeminence into another market. The firms' internal business decisions may be subject to more exacting review by in-house and external legal advisors, instilling greater caution throughout the firm.

For a dominant firm, a diminished ability to make swift, decisive commercial adjustments can be significant in highly dynamic industries, where even slight hesitation can be punished by a dramatic loss in sales. Emboldened competitors may perceive how the lawsuit's inhibition effect robs the defendant of some adroitness and may try more aggressive measures with confidence that the defendant will not strike back as forcefully or ruthlessly as it has in the past. The opportunity created by the pendency of the case may help fringe firms to expand operations or allow entrants to gain competitive footholds. Similarly, the pendency of a suit against an alleged cartel might encourage members of the cartel to cheat, and others to compete more aggressively, particularly on price, with less concern that the cartel will be able to execute any effective punishment under the watchful eyes of courts or investigators.

A second lawsuit-generated remedial consequence is the *distraction* effect. To fully respond to a lawsuit, an antitrust defendant must devote a formidable amount of the time of its own employees to support the preparation and presentation of the defense. This distraction can have significant but under-appreciated costs to the company. The diversion of firm personnel to support the case, as well as the time employees spend in casual conversation or mental speculation about the status of the case, may diminish the company's creative resources and impair its competitive vision. Every minute that firm's employees spend in assisting with the case is a minute that will not be devoted to developing new products, improving existing services, or seeking new sales. Where the lawsuit and proposed remedies strike at the heart of what the company believes to be indispensable elements of its culture and strategy, a spare-no-cost defense usually results. The firm's employees may come to believe that their chief goal is to vanquish the government plaintiff rather than surpassing competitors.

Experience with abuse of dominance cases indicates the importance of the inhibition and distraction effects. DOJ's case against IBM for monopolizing the mainframe computer sector provides an important illustration. The IBM case is routinely depicted as a singular example of prosecutorial failure. From the filing of the case on the last day of Lyndon Johnson's presidency in January 1969, until the dismissal of the matter at DOJ's request in 1982, the IBM case consumed vast resources of the government and IBM, alike. The government's case triggered the filing of over 40 private treble damage lawsuits. As it did with DOJ, IBM crushed nearly all of the private plaintiffs—but arguably at a great price in terms of its standing in the very markets that were the subject of the suit. Along with the private lawsuits, the DOJ case caused IBM to elevate the role of lawyers in shaping commercial strategy and led the firm to pull its competitive punches. To help IBM repel its antitrust adversaries, the firm's employees spent countless hours in tasks having nothing to do with designing new products and increasing sales. Once thought to be invincible, an inhibited and distracted IBM failed to grasp the significance of new industry developments, such as the ascent of the personal computer, that propelled an upstart software firm named Microsoft to the fore and opened opportunities for other hardware manufacturers.

Consider how these "remedial" effects of antitrust suits might be considered laudatory or as a basis for criticism of the antitrust system. The difference depends in part on how the firm responds and whether the allegations turn out in fact to be well-founded. Depending on the firm's culture and the advice it receives, it may have a less dramatic, more measured response to the claims, which may in turn diminish any distraction effect. And if the allegations turn out to have merit, the distraction effect of antitrust lawsuits can arrest unlawful behavior and add to deterrence. Antitrust suits have been faulted, however, for causing all the same distraction effects in weak or meritless antitrust claims. In those instances, the lawsuits themselves can have ironically anti-competitive consequences on the performance of a firm or industry. The difference also depends on precisely what form the inhibition or distraction takes—that is, whether the conduct the firm does not undertake would have been beneficial or harmful.

b. Judicially-Imposed Remedies

Although litigation effects are not insignificant, the principal measure of any successful antitrust prosecution is the remedy secured by the plaintiffs. Courts in civil antitrust cases have the authority to impose equitable, as well as legal remedies. Equitable remedies can include negative and mandatory injunctions that can be directed at both conduct and industry structure. This broad authority provides them with discretion to terminate unlawful conduct, impose measures to correct improper accumulations of market power, and to diminish the defendant's capacity to suppress rivalry in the future. Collectively, courts in civil cases thus can fashion remedies to deter, to compensate, and to remediate—to repair the market. As we have learned, although the Sherman Act treats antitrust offenses as crimes, few contemporary cases alleging misconduct other than hard core collusion have resulted in criminal charges. For purposes of modern policy, therefore, the central issue for the court is what collection of civil remedies will correct the effects of improper conduct and reinvigorate competition in the future.

Perhaps surprisingly, the challenges of remedying antitrust violations have proved to be formidable and remain a frequent topic of controversy. Courts can bifurcate the trial of liability and remedies, addressing the remedy phase only after liability has been found. These follow-on hearings can be substantial trials in themselves, and frequently require the courts to evaluate competing expert testimony. As you read the cases and materials that follow, assemble a list of issues that might influence a district judge's final remedy decision.

The most common remedy in civil prosecutions is termination of the unlawful conduct. But simply terminating the conduct would do little to compensate, punish or deter. As a consequence, the typical equitable remedy also includes restrictions on the conduct of the defendants intended to both prevent the conduct from re-occurring and to restore competitive conditions that may have been altered by the conduct. In a Section 2 prosecution, for example, conduct-related controls often take the form of an injunction prohibiting the specific behavior that the trial established to be improper, but may also involve divestiture, or some other kind of "structural" relief designed to deconcentrate the market.

Our next case excerpt is taken from a case we have already studied—*National Society of Professional Engineers*. Recall from Chapter 2 that the Society's code of ethics banned competitive bidding by its members. The Supreme Court concluded that such a ban was a violation of the Sherman Act. It then reviewed the district court's remedial order, which went well beyond simply enjoining the ban.

NATIONAL SOCIETY OF PROFESSIONAL ENGINEERS V. UNITED STATES

Supreme Court of the United States, 1978.
435 U.S. 679, 98 S.Ct. 1355, 55 L.Ed.2d 637.

MR. JUSTICE STEVENS delivered the opinion of the Court.

[For the facts and liability discussion, *see supra* Chapter 2, Eds.]

* * *

III

The judgment entered by the District Court, as modified by the Court of Appeals, prohibits the Society from adopting any official opinion, policy statement, or guideline stating or implying that competitive bidding is unethical. Petitioner argues that this judgment abridges its First Amendment rights. We find no merit in this contention.

Having found the Society guilty of a violation of the Sherman Act, the District Court was empowered to fashion appropriate restraints on the Society's future activities both to avoid a recurrence of the violation and to eliminate its consequences. *See, e.g., International Salt Co.* v. *United States*, 332 U.S. 392, 400–401; *United States v. Glaxo Group, Ltd.*, 410 U.S. 52, 64. While the resulting order may curtail the exercise of liberties that the Society might otherwise enjoy, that is a necessary and, in cases such as this, unavoidable consequence of the violation. Just as an injunction against price fixing abridges the freedom of businessmen to talk to one another about prices, so too the injunction in this case must restrict the Society's range of expression on the ethics of competitive bidding.[26] The First Amendment does not "make it . . . impossible ever to enforce laws against agreements in restraint of trade . . . ." In fashioning a remedy, the District Court may, of course, consider the fact that its injunction may impinge upon rights that would otherwise be constitutionally protected, but those protections do not prevent it from remedying the antitrust violations.

The standard against which the order must be judged is whether the relief represents a reasonable method of eliminating the *consequences* of the illegal conduct. We agree with the Court of Appeals that the injunction, as modified, meets this standard. While it goes beyond a simple proscription against the precise conduct previously pursued, that is entirely appropriate.

---

[26] Thus, in *Goldfarb*, although the bar association believed that its fee schedule accurately reflected ethical price levels, it was nonetheless enjoined "from adopting, publishing, or distributing any future schedules of minimum or suggested fees." *Goldfarb v. Virginia State Bar*, 355 F. Supp. 491, 495–496 (E.D. Va.1973). *See also United States v. National Assn. of Real Estate Boards*, 339 U.S. 485 (1950).

"The District Court is not obliged to assume, contrary to common experience, that a violator of the antitrust laws will relinquish the fruits of his violation more completely than the court requires him to do. And advantages already in hand may be held by methods more subtle and informed, and more difficult to prove, than those which, in the first place, win a market. When the purpose to restrain trade appears from a clear violation of law, it is not necessary that all of the untraveled roads to that end be left open and that only the worn one be closed." *International Salt Co., supra*, at 400.

The Society apparently fears that the District Court's injunction, if broadly read, will block legitimate paths of expression on all ethical matters relating to bidding. But the answer to these fears is, as the Court held in *International Salt*, that the burden is upon the proved transgressor "to bring any proper claims for relief to the court's attention." *Ibid.* In this case, the Court of Appeals specifically stated that "[if] the Society wishes to adopt some other ethical guideline more closely confined to the legitimate objective of preventing deceptively low bids, it may move the district court for modification of the decree." 181 U. S. App. D. C., at 46, 555 F.2d, at 983. This is, we believe, a proper approach, adequately protecting the Society's interests. We therefore reject petitioner's attack on the District Court's order.

* * *

National Society of Professional Engineers leaves little doubt that a district court has discretion to go beyond simply prohibiting the illegal conduct. Why? What does the Court mean when it asks whether the remedy chosen by the district court is a "reasonable method of eliminating the *consequences* of the illegal conduct"? What factors might a court want to consider in making that judgment? Consider the following list of possibilities:

- The scope and duration of the violation;

- The defendant's past history of anticompetitive acts;

- The anticompetitive effects of the conduct that constituted a violation, *i.e.*, were they collusive, exclusionary, or both?;

- The victims of the violation, *i.e.*, were they rivals, consumers or both?;

- The expected benefits to competition of the proposed remedy;

- The expected costs of adopting and implementing the remedy;

- The practicality of the remedy, *i.e.*, how feasible and readily administrable is it?;

- The duration of the remedy; and

- The likely efficacy of the enforcement procedures proposed for implementing the remedy.

Note how most of these factors will be matters of degree. It is not surprising, therefore, that the Court's approach leaves the district court considerable discretion. Evaluating and balancing these factors may turn on factors such as the credibility of witnesses that are uniquely within the purview of the district court.

Recall from Chapter 4 (our discussion of *Microsoft*), and Chapter 5 (*Mergers*) that remedies might also include the divestiture of assets. It might be appropriate at this point to review those materials again.

* * *

Sidebar 8–7:
Federal Settlements, the Tunney Act and Statutory Preclusion Under Section 5 of the Clayton Act

The Justice Department and the FTC rely extensively on consent decrees and orders to redress antitrust violations. These measures memorialize settlements of threatened or actual litigation between the government and the defendants. Typically, DOJ consent decrees are filed with the court along with a complaint, fully resolve the litigation, and are thereafter as enforceable as any other court or agency order. It should also be noted, however, that as compromises, consent decrees do not have precedential value and do not necessarily reflect the state of the law.

A special set of procedures applies to the settlement of litigation by the Antitrust Division of the Department of Justice. The Antitrust Procedures and Penalties Act of 1974 (also known as the "Tunney Act") requires the Justice Department to give public notice of proposed settlements 60 days before the entry of a consent decree and to solicit public comments. The Department also must file a "competitive impact statement" with the court, which may enter the consent decree as a judgment only if it finds that the decree is in the "public interest." 15 U.S.C. § 16(a). The FTC typically issues an Analysis to Aid Public Comment along with its consent orders, which must be published in the Federal Register for sixty days to obtain public comments, but it is not required to file its

---

consent decrees with the court and to seek judicial approval. 16 C.F.R. § 16.

The Tunney Act was drafted in response to the alleged misuse of political influence by the White House during the administration of President Richard M. Nixon to induce the settlement of an antitrust action by the Department of Justice. It functions in part as a "sunshine law" by requiring that government settlements be scrutinized on the public record. But by assigning the district court the role of evaluating whether the settlement is in the "public interest," a term the Act did not originally define, the Act also contemplates a more substantive review of proposed settlements. The Act's provisions were amended in 2004, in theory to permit a more searching review by the district court. *See* Title II, Subtitle B of Pub. L. No. 108–237, "Tunney Act Reform," codified at 15 U.S.C. §§ 16 (e)-(f). The amendments appeared to expand upon the definition of the district court's "public interest" charge, but were read narrowly by the first court to evaluate their import. *See United States v. SBC Communications, Inc.*, 489 F. Supp. 2d 1 (D.D.C. 2007). For two reviews of the history of the Tunney Act and analyses of the amendments, see Lloyd C. Anderson, *Mocking the Public Interest: Congress Restores Meaningful Judicial Review of Government Antitrust Decrees*, 31 VT. L. REV. 593 (2007); Lawrence M. Frankel, *Rethinking the Tunney Act: A Model for Judicial Review of Antitrust Consent Decrees*, 75 ANTITRUST L.J. 549 (2008).

The court's mandated role in approving settlements under the Tunney Act, however, has given rise to some significant controversy over the years. That controversy has focused on the scope of the court's independent authority to evaluate such settlements and the degree of deference it owes to the Justice Department when a settlement is submitted for approval. Like any decision to settle a civil action, the government's decision to do so may turn on many factors, such as the perceived strength of the case, the likely outcome of trial, the resources it will take to pursue the case, budgetary constraints, enforcement priorities, and the perceived effectiveness of the settlement.

That a district court might second guess the Department of Justice's evaluation of these factors—especially prior to the taking of any evidence and in the absence of any finding of illegality—could give rise to substantial separation of powers concerns. *See United States v. AT & T Co.*, 552 F.Supp. 131 (D.D.C. 1982), *aff'd mem., Maryland v. United States*, 460 U.S.

1001 (1983) (Rehnquist, J., dissenting from Court's per curiam approval of *AT & T* consent decree); *United States v. Microsoft Corp.*, 56 F.3d 1448 (D.C. Cir. 1995). Moreover, it is unclear what would in fact happen if a settlement was rejected—how could a court compel the Justice Department to continue prosecuting a case that it prefers to settle? On the other hand, it is clear from both the language and legislative history of the Tunney Act that Congress did not intend for the court to merely "rubber stamp" federal settlements. *Id.* at 1458.

On two occasions, government litigation with Microsoft produced important decisions interpreting the Tunney Act. In the mid-1990s the Department of Justice sought to resolve its first dispute with Microsoft with a consent decree, which was filed with the U.S. District Court in Washington, D.C. In response to the filing, Judge Stanley Sporkin demanded extensive additional information from the parties on Microsoft's allegedly ongoing anticompetitive acts. He also sought to assess the government's internal decision-making process in reaching the settlement and ultimately rejected the decree as inadequate—only to be soundly reversed for abuse of discretion by the D.C. Circuit Court of Appeals. *United States v. Microsoft Corp.*, 56 F.3d 1448 (D.C. Cir. 1995).

In the court's view, the district court had no authority to in effect conduct its own investigation of Microsoft's conduct, pursuant to which it implicitly and explicitly sought to expand the scope of the government's case. Moreover, it was error to inquire into the internal decision-making processes of the DOJ in the absence of evidence of bad faith or improper behavior. The scope of the relevant Tunney Act inquiry, the court held, is limited to an evaluation of the decree itself, not the actions or behavior of the Department. Finally, the court could not demand remedies based on violations that were not alleged by the government. *Id.* at 1459–60.

Even as it chastised Judge Sporkin, however, the D.C. Circuit instructed district courts applying the Tunney Act to "pay special attention" to the settlement's "clarity," to "pay close attention" to its compliance mechanisms, and to "inquire" into its "purpose, meaning, and efficacy." *Id.* at 1461–62. The appeals court further declared: "[i]f the decree is ambiguous, or the district judge can foresee difficulties in implementation, we would expect the court to insist that these matters are attended to." *Id.* It emphasized that "certainly, if third parties contend that they would be positively injured by the decree, a district judge might well hesitate before assuming that the decree is appropriate." *Id.*

Critics of probing Tunney Act review tend to emphasize the first portion of the D.C. Circuit's opinion, and have contended that the Tunney Act review process should be narrowly construed lest the federal courts invade the province of prosecutorial discretion, posing serious separation of powers problems under the Constitution. They also caution that any other approach may undermine defendants' incentives to reach settlements and hence the Justice Department's ability to secure them. Yet, without exception, the judicial decisions supporting a constrained view of the Act are confined to the most typical Tunney Act situation—settlement achieved before trial. Those same courts, including the D.C. Circuit in the first *Microsoft* proceeding, have made clear that the judge's authority to scrutinize the settlement is more extensive when it follows evidentiary proceedings. *Id.* at 1461. *See also United States v. AT&T*, 552 F. Supp. at 152. Nevertheless, in the second Microsoft proceeding, the court of appeals approved the district court's limited review and approval of the decree. *See Massachusetts v. Microsoft Corp.*, 373 F.3d 1199 (D.C. Cir. 2004) ("*Microsoft II*").

Another issue that has arisen in connection with consent decrees concerns their impact on subsequent private litigation. As we noted earlier in the Chapter, Section 5(a) of the Clayton Act permits private plaintiffs to use "a final judgment or decree * * * rendered in any civil or criminal proceeding brought by or on behalf of the United States under the antitrust laws" as "prima facie evidence" against the same defendant "as to all matters respecting which said judgment or decree would be an estoppel between" the parties to the original action. But the Act also includes the following proviso: "That this section shall not apply to consent judgments or decrees entered before any testimony has been taken."

If the language of the proviso is read literally, there can be no estoppel when the government reaches settlement with a defendant prior to trial, but there *will* be estoppel once evidence is taken, even though a final decision by the court has yet to be rendered. This makes the proviso a bit more expansive on its face than common law estoppel, which generally is only available once an issue has been "fully litigated," is "necessary to" a prior judgment, and has been "finally decided." What policy reasons might there be for Section 5's estoppel provisions? For its limiting proviso?

First, Section 5 creates potentially valuable incentive for follow-on private litigants, who need not shoulder the significant burden of reestablishing the defendant's antitrust violation. If the government frequently litigated its civil cases through to final judgment, this advantage might lead to more follow-on litigation than might otherwise be the case—and it would provide a significant tool of deterrence. Of course, it also affects the litigation strategy of the defendant faced with civil or criminal prosecution by the DOJ. By limiting the preclusive effects of the Act prior to the taking of evidence, and giving full preclusive effect after evidence is taken, it provides a powerful incentive for such defendants to settle before any evidence is taken. By doing so, the defendant disarms the would-be future follow-on suit by forcing future private plaintiffs likely to be seeking treble damages to have to fully litigate and prove liability. This is the far more common result.

What then should be the effect of a consent judgment entered *after* evidence has been taken, or even after a trial on the merits has concluded, as was the case in *Microsoft II*? One would assume that to preserve the statute's balance of incentives, the answer would be that it has full preclusive effects, but the courts have demonstrated surprising flexibility on the issue.

One solution to the problems posed under Section 5 and the common law has been for settling parties to condition their settlements on the district court's agreement to withdraw any findings it has made and expressly to indicate that no conclusion as to liability under the antitrust laws was reached by the court. Some courts have generally endorsed the practice, even when settlement comes after the hearing of evidence. In such circumstances, the court has taken the position that the parties and the district court should be given significant leeway in stating their intentions with respect to the predictable consequences of settlement, lest settlement be discouraged. *See, e.g., S. Pac. Commc'n Co. v. AT & T Co.*, 740 F.2d 1011, 1020–22 (D.C. Cir. 1984); *United States v. Nat'l Ass'n of Broadcasters*, 553 F.Supp. 621, 623 (D.D.C. 1982).

Novel issues occasionally still arise under the Tunney Act. In a case of first impression, the court in *United States v. Blavatnik*, 2016 WL 593449 (D.D.C. 2016), held that the Tunney Act applied to a consent judgment that imposed penalties on a party for the defendant's alleged violation of the Hart-Scott-Rodino Act's pre-merger notification requirements. The DOJ, with the agreement of the defendant, argued that the

> Tunney Act did not apply because the proposed judgment sought only monetary penalties, and did not require any injunctive relief. The court rejected that position, however, relying on the language of the Act, which applies to "any proposal for a consent judgment," as well as the Act's legislative history, which did not appear to support the government's position.

3. THE PRIVATE TREBLE DAMAGES REMEDY

Incorporated in Section 7 of the original Sherman Act, today's private right of action is contained in Section 4 of the Clayton Act, 15 U.S.C. § 15, which provides:

> * * * [A]ny person who shall be injured in his business or property by reason of anything forbidden in the antitrust laws may sue therefor in any district court of the United States . . . and shall recover threefold the damages by him sustained, and the cost of suit, including a reasonable attorney's fee.

In this Section of the Chapter we consider several aspects of the private treble damage remedy. First, we briefly survey the policy arguments for and against maintaining the treble damage remedy. Second, we will look at the practical evidentiary question of how a party goes about proving its actual damages, a prerequisite to recovery of treble damages.

a. Why "Treble" Damages?

Much of the debate concerning the private right of action has focused on its authorization of "treble damages." Whereas it is relatively easier to argue in favor of some kind of private right of action that permits recovery of actual damages sustained, it is more challenging to ask, "why treble damages"? Indeed, early versions of the Sherman Act proposed only double damages. According to an ABA Antitrust Section survey, the traditional justifications most often cited by the Supreme Court include:

- to provide private relief or compensation;
- to encourage private enforcement of the antitrust laws;
- to deter violations;
- to deprive antitrust violators of the fruits of their illegal acts; and
- to punish violators.

See ABA ANTITRUST SECTION, MONOGRAPH NO. 13, TREBLE-DAMAGES REMEDY 16–21 (1986) ("Treble Damages Monograph"). Clearly an assumption was made in 1890 and since that authorizing recovery of mere actual damages would be inadequate to achieve these basic goals. For additional comprehensive studies, see WILLIAM BREIT & KENNETH G. ELZINGA, ANTITRUST PENALTY REFORM: AN ECONOMIC ANALYSIS (1986); LAWRENCE J. WHITE, ED., PRIVATE ANTITRUST LITIGATION: NEW EVIDENCE, NEW LEARNING (1988) (hereafter "Georgetown Study").

As with many of the other issues we have studied in this Chapter, debates over the wisdom and efficacy of the treble damage remedy often turn on perceptions about the relative tendency of antitrust prohibitions to under or overdeter anticompetitive conduct. Critics argue that the possibility of treble damages unduly encourages parties and their counsel to initiate and pursue civil antitrust actions, and might lead defendants to settle less than fully meritorious cases for fear of treble damage exposure. These arguments have intensified due to the increase in multi-jurisdictional federal and state antitrust litigation owing in part to *Illinois Brick* and *ARC America* (*see supra* Sidebar 8–6), with some critics asserting that, more than ever, defendants face the prospect of duplicative recoveries owing to the "windfall" gains sought by plaintiffs, themselves spurred on by an active class action bar.

In response to these criticisms, there have been a number of legislative proposals over the years to alter the current scheme. These proposals fall into three categories: (1) de-treble damages, (2) make treble damages discretionary with the court instead of mandatory; and (3) limit the availability of treble damages to the most severe antitrust violations. *See* ABA TREBLE DAMAGES MONOGRAPH, at 50–65. By and large, these proposals for reform have been unsuccessful, although some statutory exceptions have even been created that limit recovery to actual damages for conduct that has been reviewed and approved by government agencies. *See, e.g.*, 15 U.S.C. § 4016(a)(a) (Export Trading Company Act of 1982, § 306); 15 U.S.C. § 4303 (National Cooperative Research and Production Act of 1993, § 4). Also, as noted in Sidebar 3–1, under ACPERA, a criminal defendant who enters into a leniency agreement may be relieved of the possibility of exposure to treble damages.

On the other hand, defenders of the treble damage remedy point out that today it is more difficult than ever to prove an antitrust violation. Owing to changes in antitrust rules that have elevated burdens of proof, as well as judicially imposed restrictions on the scope of the private remedy, such as those reflected in *Brunswick*, *Illinois Brick* and *Associated General*, the threat of overdeterrence has been minimized. In part due to these changes, the cost of pursuing antitrust litigation similarly has exploded and the number of new private civil antitrust actions is quite small, ranging between 600 and 800 per year in the federal courts. Hence, they argue, the greater danger today is underdeterrence: antitrust violations will go undetected, unprosecuted and/or unpunished. Treble damages, in their view, remain critical precisely because they provide an incentive for plaintiffs to sue and because they serve to deter serious antitrust violations. Indeed, they point to cases such as *ADM* (Lysine) and *Vitamins*, which we studied in Chapter 1, and more recent and far-reaching international cartels, as evidence that even treble damages and the threat of fines and prison remain insufficient in some cases to deter the most profitable and egregious of antitrust violations.

Our next Sidebar evaluates the economic foundations of this long-running debate.

Sidebar 8–8:
The Economics of Penalties

How large should antitrust law set the penalty for a violation? Are penalties systematically too low—no more than "slaps on the wrist"—leading firms to ignore the antitrust laws? Can penalties be too high? Economists have studied questions like this under the twin assumptions that the primary purpose of antitrust sanctions is deterrence[a] and that the goal of antitrust is economic efficiency (aggregate wealth maximization). This Sidebar sketches how economists think about antitrust penalties and the incentive effects of the private treble damages system.

Net Harm to Others: An Example

An example will help clarify the economic issues. Suppose that the antitrust violation involves horizontal market division, and the only available remedy involves a fine payable by the violators to the government treasury. How large should that fine be?

To make the problem concrete, refer to Figure 8–3 (which is modeled on Figure 5–1). In the particular example set forth in Figure 8–3, the violation leads to an industry-wide price increase (from P1 to P2) and a reduction in industry output (from Q1 to Q2). The transfer from buyers to sellers resulting from the violation is 1000. The allocative efficiency loss is 400 and has two parts because had the firms not exercised market power, the buyers and sellers would have shared the foregone gains from trade that the market would have achieved. In particular, sellers lost the lower rectangle (300 in the example) and buyers lost the upper triangle (100 in the example). The violation leads to production cost savings of 50 (perhaps arising because the firms adopted a territorial market allocation

---

[a] This assumption rules out other goals of antitrust penalties that may be important in practice, including punishment to wrongdoers, compensation to victims, and the creation of incentives for private parties to bring suit to vindicate the antitrust laws. Some effects of private damages on those other goals are discussed in passing in this Sidebar, however.

scheme that kept the transportation costs of serving customers low).

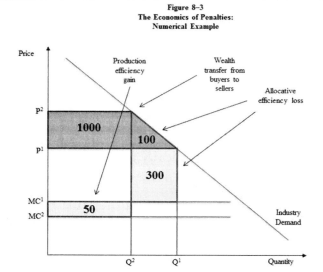

Figure 8–3
The Economics of Penalties:
Numerical Example

If detection and conviction were certain, the remedial rule that leads to economically efficient outcomes would require that the sellers, as a group, pay 1100: the sum of the transfer from buyers (here 1000) and that portion of the allocative efficiency loss that would have benefitted buyers in the absence of the violation (100). If sellers must give up as a remedy for an antitrust violation an amount equal to the harm they cause others—the transfer plus the portion of the allocative efficiency loss that would have gone to buyers—then the sellers will only go ahead with conduct if that conduct is efficient. Here's why. Absent antitrust enforcement, sellers would be expected to go ahead with their conduct (here the market division arrangement) because it would be profitable to them as a group.[b] They would benefit from the transfer from buyers (1000) plus the production cost savings (50), less the portion of the allocative efficiency loss that would have gone to sellers (300), for a net profit of 750. Take away the transfer and the portion of the allocative efficiency loss that would have gone to buyers, and sellers would profit if and only if the production cost savings exceeds the collective allocative efficiency loss—that is, if and only if there are efficiency gains to society as a whole from the conduct.

---

[b]   This discussion assumes that so long as the arrangement is profitable for the sellers as a group, they can devise a mechanism for sharing the profits among themselves so that each member of the arrangement benefits individually.

The generalization that can be taken from this example is that the efficient fine for an antitrust violation equals the net harm that the violation causes others (here the transfer plus the allocative efficiency loss to buyers), as that rule will lead prospective violators to consider the welfare of others as well as their own welfare, and take only those actions that are beneficial to society as a whole. The "net harm to others" formulation comes from William Landes, *Optimal Sanctions for Antitrust Violations,* 50 U. CHI. L. REV. 652 (1983), and the approach is implicit in the pioneering economic analysis of legal sanctions in Gary Becker, *Crime and Punishment: An Economic Approach,* 76 J. POL. ECON. 169 (1968).

Why wouldn't the efficient sanction instead set the fine at the profit to sellers (here 750)? A sanction based on disgorgement of seller profits (rather than the net harm to others) would have the virtue of making all violations unprofitable, and thus deterring them. But from an economic efficiency point of view, such a rule goes too far in principle: it deters alike inefficient conduct and efficient conduct (that nevertheless happens to violate an imperfectly-specified legal rule) because it treats the production cost savings (which add to seller profits) as bad, not good.[c] *See* A. Mitchell Polinsky & Steven Shavell, *Should Liability Be Based on the Harm to the Victim or the Gain to the Insurer?,* 10 J. L. ECON. & ORG. 427 (1994) (providing general analysis, not focused specifically on antitrust).

Overdeterrence and Underdeterrence

If the rule for determining sanctions for lawbreaking generally leads violators to pay less than the net harm to others, the legal system is said to "underdeter" violations: the harm to society from the violations of law exceeds the cost of preventing them. With underdeterrence, firms will not invest sufficient resources to ensure antitrust compliance, for example. On the other hand, if the rule for determining sanctions imposes a penalty in excess of the efficient remedial rule, more lawbreaking will be prevented, but "overdeterrence" will result. Firms will be led to spend more to stamp out the last violations

---

[c] In the example, suppose that production cost savings were 500 rather than 50. Then the profit from the market division scheme would be 1200 (1000 transfer + 500 cost savings – 300 sellers' share of allocative efficiency loss). A sanction based on seller profits would fine sellers 1200, deterring the practice. But the sanction based on net harm to others (still 1100) would be less than the profit to sellers, so the practice would not be deterred under the efficient sanctions rules—as is appropriate, given a focus on efficiency, since the production cost savings (500) exceeds the total allocative efficiency loss (400). As this example makes clear, the choice of a rule for determining sanctions for violations is tied up with views as to the purposes of antitrust law (economic efficiency or something else?) and the purposes of remedies (deterrence or something else?).

than those violations cost society (in terms of efficiency). Compliance programs may become so onerous, or executives may become so cautious, that firms will stay away from socially beneficial conduct close to the line of illegality, for fear that they will be found to violate the law and forced to pay a large penalty even though their conduct generates only a small reduction in aggregate social wealth.

For practices that would be challenged as civil violations, and particularly those that would be analyzed under the rule of reason, overdeterrence is likely as serious a concern as underdeterrence. For criminal violations—naked price-fixing, bid-rigging or market division among rivals—some take the view that the threat of overdeterrence is less troublesome, at least as the antitrust laws are enforced today in the United States. There is no evidence, for example, that firms are limiting joint venture formation or legitimate trade association activity for fear of being charged with price-fixing. But it is possible that high criminal fines could induce excessive expenditures on compliance, potentially leading to higher output prices, if the firm cannot pass those fines on to the employees responsible for the criminal conduct. *See* Bruce H. Kobayashi, *Antitrust, Agency and Amnesty: An Economic Analysis of the Criminal Enforcement of the Antitrust Laws Against Corporations*, 69 GEO. WASH. L. REV. 715 (2001).

Individual Versus Corporate Sanctions

The response to hard-core cartel activities, such as price-fixing, in the United States has largely been increased corporate fines and jail time for individual offenders. Cartels are routinely uncovered notwithstanding growing corporate fines, leading the United States to place greater effort on augmenting corporate sanctions by imposing criminal penalties on the individuals responsible for cartel behavior. The Department of Justice reasonably believes that "individual accountability through the imposition of jail sentences is the single greatest deterrent" to criminal antitrust violations such as price-fixing cartels. Scott D. Hammond, *Ten Strategies for Winning the Fight Against Hardcore Cartels*, Oct. 18, 2005 (Paris Working Party No. 3 Prosecutors Program). *See also* Brent Snyder, Deputy Assistant Attorney General, Antitrust Division, U.S. Dep't of Justice, *Individual Accountability for Antitrust Crimes* (Feb. 19, 2016), https://www.justice.gov/opa/speech/deputy-assistant-attorney-general-brent-snyder-delivers-remarks-yale-global-antitrust.

For an argument that increasing the frequency, magnitude, and variety of individual sanctions would provide greater deterrence than further increases in corporate sanctions, and so should be preferred, see Douglas H. Ginsburg & Joshua D. Wright, *Antitrust Sanctions*, 6 COMP. POL'Y INT'L 3 (2010).

Concealment and the Damage Multiple

Many antitrust violators seek to hide their actions from their victims and the government, finders of fact do not always see all the evidence, and courts do not always reach the correct conclusions from the evidence in the record. For reasons like these, it is by no means certain that all antitrust violations will be detected and successfully prosecuted. If a seller thinks that its unlawful actions have only a one in three chance of detection and conviction, it will treat the remedy of 1100 as if it were only one third that size (about 367).[d] In order to make sellers act as though the sanction for violation would be 1100 under such circumstances, the penalty must be multiplied by the inverse of what sellers, thinking about whether to violate the law, would consider the likelihood of eventual detection and judicial enforcement. In this example, with the probability of enforcement 1/3, the penalty would need to be multiplied by 3 (the inverse of 1/3), leading to an efficient sanction of 3300. More generally, *under the efficient sanction, the "net harm to others" would be the penalty base, and the full penalty would multiply that base by a multiple set at the inverse of the violator's subjective probability of detection and conviction, as the violator would have evaluated its chances at the time it engaged in the unlawful practices.*

Private Damages: Ideal vs. Reality

The structure of the efficient sanction bears a family resemblance to the private damages remedy in force today. The current remedy begins with a penalty base related to the injury to victims (the overcharge if the victims are buyers, or lost profits if the victims are excluded rivals). A successful private plaintiff recovers triple the penalty base—this is the familiar "treble damages" remedy in private antitrust litigation. *See generally* Steven C. Salop & Lawrence J. White, *Economic Analysis of Private Antitrust Litigation*, 74 GEO. L.J. 1001 (1986) (reporting an empirical study of private antitrust litigation). How does this remedy compare with the efficient sanction suggested by economic theory?

---

[d] This statement assumes that the seller is "risk-neutral:" it would not pay an insurance premium to reduce risks on the one hand, and would not pay to take gambles on the other hand.

There are many points of difference between the two, some suggesting that the private treble damages remedy is too high, others suggesting it is too low, and still others suggesting it is not set at the efficient level in any case but not clearly too high or too low on average. *See generally* William Breit & Kenneth G. Elzinga, *Private Antitrust Enforcement: The New Learning*, 28 J. L. ECON. 405 (1985).

Too low. The penalty base (and thus the private penalty as a whole) is too low in principle because it only counts the direct injury to the victim (the overcharge if the victim is a buyer) and ignores the portion of the allocative efficiency loss that would have gone to buyers absent the violation. It is also too low because antitrust law systematically understates the penalty base relative to the underlying economic concept by not awarding plaintiffs prejudgment interest and by cutting off recovery of damages for older violations through application of the statute of limitations. John M. Connor & Robert H. Lande, *Not Treble Damages: Cartel Recoveries Are Mostly Less Than Single Damages*, 100 IOWA L. REV. 1997 (2015); Robert H. Lande, *Are Antitrust "Treble" Damages Really Single Damages?*, 54 OHIO ST. L.J. 115 (1983).

Moreover, damages may be too low to the extent that some victims, injured by the violation, do not recover—for example, because their lawsuit is deterred (or they are induced to accept a weak settlement) by the transactions costs of going to court, by risk aversion, by restrictions on the ability of indirect purchasers to recover damages, or by limitations on the extraterritorial jurisdiction of the U.S. antitrust laws. In addition, the deterrent effects of private damages actions will be reduced to the extent the victims were aware that they may have been dealing with a cartel or other antitrust violator when they were charged a high price by it, and thus knew they might someday blow the whistle on the violator by filing a private lawsuit for damages. When both victim and violator are aware that the victim may sue for damages in the future, the market price will rise to counteract the later damages in an expected sense. If the violator and victim contract around the private treble damages system in this way, the private remedy does not deter violations, no matter how high the multiple. Jonathan B. Baker, *Private Information and the Deterrent Effect of Antitrust Damages Remedies*, 4 J. L. ECON. & ORG. 385 (1988); Stephen Salant, *Treble Damage Awards in Private Litigation for Price Fixing*, 95 J. POL. ECON. 1326 (1987); DANIEL F. SPULBER, REGULATION AND MARKETS § 19.4 (1989).

Too high. Private damages may be too high to the extent that the antitrust violator is subject to other penalties that also provide deterrence. Here the relevant question is not whether any individual sanction is efficient, but whether the collection of penalties, as a group, provides deterrence. Those other penalties can include fines or jail time for executives in a related Justice Department criminal prosecution, disgorgement in a related FTC case, damages in a related case under state law, and injunctive relief in civil cases brought by the DOJ, the FTC or states that raises the costs of doing business. For cases pursued by multiple enforcement authorities worldwide, the other penalties may also include sanctions in jurisdictions outside the U.S. If penalties in any one proceeding are set without consideration of the deterrent consequences of relief in earlier or simultaneous proceedings, they may, in aggregate, end up too high. Moreover, penalties may be too high if, absent proper application of the antitrust injury doctrine, plaintiffs are permitted to recover for harms that are not causally related to the efficiency loss from the violation. *See, e.g.,* William H. Page, *Antitrust Damages and Economic Efficiency: An Approach to Antitrust Injury,* 47 U. CHI. L. REV. 467 (1980); Phillip Areeda, *Antitrust Violations Without Damage Recoveries,* 89 HARV. L. REV. 1127 (1976).

Also, some suggest that the private treble damages award leads to excessive litigation, because plaintiffs, attracted by the prospect of a recovery substantially in excess of their injury, do not consider the costs to the judicial system in deciding whether to bring their case. Proposals for "decoupling" the violator's payment from the victim's recovery—splitting the payment between the victim and the government—make clear that the penalty level that best deters violations does not necessarily provide the most appropriate incentive for private antitrust enforcement or the most appropriate level of compensation for victims. *See* A. Mitchell Polinsky, *Detrebling Versus Decoupling Antitrust Damages: Lessons from the Theory of Enforcement,* 74 GEO. L. J. 1231 (1986) (asserting that the same level of deterrence could be achieved at lower social cost by raising the amount paid by the defendant while lowering the amount received by the plaintiff, with the government receiving the difference).

Not correct in individual cases. The economic approach to penalties suggests that the damage multiple in every case should equal the inverse of the violator's subjective probability of detection and conviction, measured as of the time the violator chose to engage in the unlawful practices. Assuming the penalty base were not too high or too low, this means that a multiple of three (treble damages) is correct in every case only if every violator expects that it has one chance in three of eventually being forced to pay damages. Detection and conviction are indeed uncertain, but there is no reason to think that the probability is one in three in every case. In particular, some antitrust violators, like the participants in the lysine and vitamins cartels, take steps to conceal their unlawful conduct from detection, while other violations, including many forms of exclusionary conduct, are not hidden from view. It is possible, therefore, that antitrust law deters (even overdeters) those violations that are the easiest to detect and prosecute, without adequately deterring highly concealed violations. One could imagine a system in which a rough triage is employed to address this possibility: assign a private damages multiple of three in most cases but double the multiple to six if the violators aggressively concealed their conduct and halve it to 1.5 if the violation was particularly open and easy to detect.

Conclusion

The economic approach to penalties provides a way to think about the general level of sanctions for antitrust violations, not a mathematical formula for determining damages in any particular case. Note, too, that the economic approach suggests that the effects of the system of penalties cannot be understood in a vacuum. If government enforcers devote fewer resources to investigating antitrust violations or changes in substantive law reduce the ability of certain classes of plaintiffs to challenge violations, those acts will reduce the likelihood that any particular violator will be detected and convicted. Unless the damages multiple is increased under such circumstances, the level of deterrence will be reduced. In this regard it is interesting to note that over the past thirty years, the courts have restricted the access of certain plaintiffs to the courts (for example through the antitrust injury and indirect purchaser doctrines) while Congress has simultaneously increased the penalties for criminal antitrust violations.

Finally, the relationship between penalties and deterrence also can be affected by legal rules respecting the scope of liability. *See generally* William H. Page, *The Scope of Liability for Antitrust Violations*, 37 STAN. L. REV. 1445 (1985) (scope of liability must be integrated with measurement of damages to achieve the efficient sanction). For example, in *Texas Indus., Inc. v. Radcliff Materials, Inc.*, 451 U.S. 630 (1981), the Supreme Court held that co-conspirators are jointly and severally liable for the entire amount of damages attributable to a conspiracy. In the case of a price-fixing cartel, therefore, each co-conspirator is in theory liable for three times the entire amount of the overcharges attributable to the conspiracy. No right of contribution exists, therefore, whereby one defendant found liable can implead its alleged co-conspirators to collect their share of the damages done. How might this rule affect deterrence under the economic models discussed in this Sidebar?

NOTE ON DISGORGEMENT

Note that one of the penalties discussed in Sidebar 8–8 is the option of "disgorgement"—requiring as a penalty that the antitrust violator pay over to the government or private parties the ill-gotten gains attributable to its violation, sometimes referred to as the "fruits" of its violation. In a price fixing or monopolization case, those gains might be measured by the additional profits the firm was able to obtain through its anticompetitive conduct.

As noted in the Sidebar, the economic rationale for disgorgement, sometimes also referred to as "restitution," is straight-forward—by extracting the fruits of the unlawful conduct, the economic incentive to engage in the conduct in the first place is neutralized, and hence may function as a useful deterrent. That assumes, however, that detection efforts are successful. If a firm discounts the likelihood of disgorgement due to its belief that its illegal conduct will not be detected, the mere possibility that it might lose its ill-gotten gains alone will not deter the conduct. Indeed, if disgorgement were the only remedy, unlawful conduct might be encouraged on the theory that the "worst case" means only giving back the gains.

The legal basis for seeking disgorgement, however, is less clear than the economic. In authorizing suits for damages, Section 4 of the Clayton Act focuses on the harm of the illegal conduct to its victims, typically yielding claims of overcharges from consumers in cases of collusion or monopolization, and claims of lost profits from the prey in exclusionary effects cases. It does not focus on the benefits of the violation to the violator. But what about public enforcement authorities?

In late 1998, the FTC sought to extend its injunctive powers to cover disgorgement in a highly visible case involving the generic prescription drug manufacturer Mylan Laboratories. As a generic drug manufacturer, Mylan typically licensed the information necessary to produce a drug from a specialty chemical manufacturer. In this instance, Mylan had entered into a 10-year exclusive licensing arrangement with the chemical manufacturers of the active pharmaceutical ingredients for two popular prescription drugs, lorazepam and clorazepate. According to the complaints in the case, Mylan thereafter raised its prices on one of the drugs by between 1,900 and 3,200%. On the other, it raised prices 1,900 to 19,000%.

In a typical FTC proceeding, the FTC would seek to secure an order to "cease and desist" pursuant to its authority to secure "temporary restraining orders" and "preliminary injunctions" under Section 13(b) of the FTC Act, 15 U.S.C. § 53(b). The FTC argued in *Mylan* that its authority permitted it to seek permanent injunctions rescinding the licensing agreements and preventing them from being reinstated, and, as an additional equitable remedy, disgorgement of $120 million in alleged ill-gotten profits. Although the ultimate deterrent value of disgorgement can be debated, compared to a mere order to cease and desist it was clearly a more formidable tool of enforcement.

Three significant issues related to disgorgement arose in the course of the litigation: (1) whether the FTC had the authority under § 13(b) to seek disgorgement of profits attributable to an antitrust violation; (2) whether the states that had joined in the case pursuing claims under Sections 1 and 2 of the Sherman Act also could seek disgorgement via Section 16 of the Clayton Act; and (3) whether private plaintiffs could pursue treble damages even after the FTC had secured a settlement that included disgorgement. In a series of opinions, the court answered all three of these questions in the affirmative.

Noting that five other circuit courts of appeals had read the FTC Act's grant of equitable authority as sufficient to permit the FTC to pursue monetary relief, the district court denied Mylan's motion to dismiss the disgorgement claims. *See FTC v. Mylan Labs., Inc.*, 62 F. Supp. 2d 25 (D.D.C. 1999). The court concluded that the power to seek monetary relief was consistent with the broad remedial purposes of Section 5 of the FTC Act, pursuant to which the FTC should be permitted to seek "complete relief" against violations. *Id.* at 36–37. The second question proved more challenging. Although the court initially concluded that the states could not seek disgorgement under Section 16 of the Clayton Act, *id.* at 40–42, it later modified that judgment to recognize the states' right to do so under state laws that referenced or were modeled after the FTC Act. *See FTC v. Mylan Labs., Inc.*, 99 F. Supp. 2d 1 (D.D.C. 1999).

The case brought by the FTC and the states was quickly followed by a number of private treble damage class actions initiated by, among others, health care providers and hospitals who were direct purchasers of lorazepam and clorazepate. The cases were transferred and consolidated by the Judicial Panel on Multi-district Litigation pursuant to the procedures of 28 U.S.C. § 1407. Mylan then moved to dismiss the actions on the ground that the plaintiffs "lacked standing" to pursue their damage claims given the FTC's recovery of disgorged profits through its settlement with Mylan (which followed the district court's ruling that the Commission had the authority to seek disgorgement). *See In re Lorazepam & Clorazepate Antitrust Litigation*, 202 F.R.D. 12 (D.D.C. 2001); *see also In re Lorazepam & Clorazepate Antitrust Litigation*, 289 F.3d 98 (D.C. Cir. 2002) (declining interlocutory review of district court's decision to certify class action).

Mylan argued that the rationale of *Illinois Brick* should control, even though the plaintiffs were direct, not indirect purchasers. It urged the court to embrace an "Ultimate Purchase Rule," which, consistent with *Illinois Brick*, would only recognize the right to recover damages of a single class of persons—here represented by the FTC. Any further recovery, it urged, would be duplicative. While noting that the defendants' arguments were "creative," the court nevertheless rejected them. Distinguishing *Illinois Brick*, it declined to endorse any general rule of "exclusive standing" based on the policies that animated *Illinois Brick*. Whereas *Illinois Brick* raised the question of how damages could be apportioned among two competing sets of plaintiffs seeking recovery under the same statute—Section 4 of the Clayton Act—in *Mylan* the FTC proceeded under a "wholly separate cause of action," namely Section 13(b) of the FTC Act. In further support of its position, the court cited *ARC America*, where, in rejecting the argument that state indirect purchaser statutes were preempted by *Illinois Brick*, the Supreme Court implicitly endorsed the view that complementary remedial schemes directed at the same or similar conduct can coexist without damaging the overall remedial goals of the antitrust laws (*see supra* Sidebar 8–6).

The FTC's victory in *Mylan* was deemed significant, solidifying its power to seek monetary relief and introducing the threat of disgorgement into its arsenal of remedial tools. But do you agree with all of the district court's rulings? Might they result in over-deterrence, authorizing as they do disgorgement by the FTC and the states, as well as treble damages by private direct purchasers? Or is it arguable that multiple threats are necessary to achieve adequate deterrence given the challenges of detection and the possibility that potential wrong doers will discount the likelihood of being discovered?

To clarify its enforcement intentions in light of its victory in *Mylan*, the FTC in 2003 issued a policy statement on the use of monetary equitable remedies in antitrust cases. The Policy Statement explained that the agency would consider three factors in deciding whether to seek disgorgement or restitution: (1) whether the underlying violation is clear, (2) whether there is a reasonable basis for calculating the amount of the remedial payment, and (3) the value that the Commission would contribute to effective enforcement by pursuing monetary equitable relief in light of other likely remedies, including remedies in private actions and criminal proceedings. How, if at all, do these conditions reflect the economic theory of penalties discussed in Sidebar 8–8? Responding to concerns raised during the public comment period that preceded the issuance of the policy statement, the Commission said it remains sensitive to potential duplicative recoveries by injured persons or the possibility that defendants might be required to make excessive multiple payments for the same injury.

In 2012, the FTC withdrew the 2003 Statement, citing concerns about its "overly restrictive view of the Commission's options for equitable remedies." *See* https://www.ftc.gov/system/files/documents/public_statements/296171/120731commstmt-monetaryremedies.pdf. The FTC maintained that disgorgement is an appropriate remedy in certain cases and specifically addressed the first and third factors concerning whether the underlying violation is clear and the value that the FTC would contribute by pursuing monetary equitable relief as opposed to a different remedy. As to the first factor, the FTC explained that it was an unjustified "heightened standard" that was not used by courts or relevant for evaluating anticompetitive conduct. The new statement also explained that the third factor was overly burdensome because it could be misinterpreted to require the FTC to show an inability to obtain an appropriate remedy through other means. Commissioner Maureen K. Ohlhausen dissented, asserting that withdrawing the 2003 statement created uncertainty about when the FTC would find disgorgement appropriate. *See* https://www.ftc.gov/sites/default/files/documents/public_statements/ statement-commissioner-maureen-k.ohlhausen/120731ohlhausenstatement. pdf.

The issue of disgorgement was raised again in 2015 after a settlement between the FTC and Cephalon, a drug manufacturer, and its parent company in a pay-for-delay case. The FTC alleged that Cephalon engaged in unlawful monopolization after entering into several reverse payment settlements with generic drug manufacturers over a disputed patent. In its consent order, the FTC sought $1.2 billion in equitable monetary relief. A statement on the matter explained that disgorgement was appropriate for several reasons. First, there were incentives for brand drug makers to collude with generic drug makers in the market due to the regulatory regime. Second, Cephalon was able to benefit from its settlements with generic drug makers for several years. Lastly, the patent that Cephalon settled over was fraudulently obtained. *See* https://www.ftc.gov/system/files/documents/cases/150528cephalonstatement. pdf.

Commissioners Joshua D. Wright and Maureen K. Ohlhausen approved the consent order but released a concurring statement that suggested limits on the FTC's disgorgement policy. *See* https://www.ftc.gov/system/files/documents /cases/150528cephalonohlhausenwright.pdf. Using the three-factor test in the 2003 Policy Statement as a basis for evaluating whether disgorgement was appropriate, the concurring Commissioners found that Cephalon's conduct warranted a monetary equitable remedy. Despite the appropriateness of disgorgement in the matter, they warned that lack of guidance from the Commission on its disgorgement policy created uncertainty for firms. Commissioner Ohlhausen expressed concern that the overuse of monetary equitable remedies would cause the FTC "to neglect its special mission to develop the antitrust laws through Part III litigation and other unique tools." Commissioner Wright urged the FTC to use economic analysis of penalties and optimal deterrence in evaluating whether monetary relief is an appropriate remedy. In his view, use of economic analysis would help guide the FTC to seek such relief only when "there is both a significant probability that a violation escapes detection and punishment and where other remedies are insufficient to make the unlawful activity unprofitable."

b. Calculating Antitrust Damages

To justify an award of antitrust damages, a party must overcome several distinct hurdles. First, and most obvious, it must establish an antitrust violation. Second, it must establish the "fact of injury," *i.e.*, that the conduct of the defendant that violated the antitrust laws was the proximate cause of an actual injury to its "business or property." " '[W]here the plaintiff proves a loss, and a violation by defendant of the antitrust laws of such nature as to be likely to cause that type of loss * * * the jury, as the trier of facts, must be permitted to draw from this circumstantial evidence the inference that the necessary causal relation exists.' " *Continental Ore Co. v. Union Carbide and Carbon Corp.*, 370 U.S. 690, 697 (1962). *See also Bigelow v. RKO Radio Pictures*, 327 U.S. 251, 264 (1946). Third, it must establish the amount of its antitrust damages—*i.e.*, the fact of injury alone is distinct from the amount of damages. Accommodating the current complexity of these issues is an important factor in successfully managing treble damage litigation.

All three requirements are evident in the following case excerpt from the Supreme Court's opinion in *J. Truett Payne*.

J. TRUETT PAYNE CO. v. CHRYSLER MOTORS CORP.

United States Supreme Court, 1981.
451 U.S. 557, 101 S.Ct. 1923, 68 L.Ed.2d 442.

[The Court began by noting that the mere fact that a violation of the antitrust laws has occurred does not mean that a private party seeking redress under Section 4 of the Clayton Act has suffered compensable "injury." Quoting *Brunswick Corp. v. Pueblo Bowl-O-Mat, Inc.*, 429 U.S. 477 (1977), the Court reiterated that " 'to recover damages [under § 4] respondents must prove more than that the petitioner violated [a provision of the federal antitrust laws] * * *, since such proof establishes only that injury may result.' " In the excerpt that follows, we will see how the Court integrated the traditional framework for proving fact of injury with the antitrust injury concept from *Brunswick*. Eds.]

II

* * *

Petitioner nevertheless asks us to consider the sufficiency of its evidence in light of our traditional rule excusing antitrust plaintiffs from an unduly rigorous standard of proving antitrust injury. In *Zenith Radio Corp. v. Hazeltine Research, Inc.*, 395 U.S. 100, 123–124, 89 S.Ct. 1562, 1576, 23 L.Ed.2d 129 (1969), for example, the Court discussed at some length the fixing of damages in a case involving market exclusion. We accepted the proposition that damages could be awarded on the basis of plaintiff's estimate of sales it could have made absent the violation:

"[D]amage issues in these cases are rarely susceptible of the kind of concrete, detailed proof of injury which is available in other contexts. The Court has repeatedly held that in the absence of more precise proof, the factfinder may 'conclude as a matter of just and reasonable inference from the proof of defendants' wrongful acts and their tendency to injure plaintiffs' business, and from the evidence of the decline in prices, profits and values, not shown to be attributable to other causes, that defendants' wrongful acts had caused damage to the plaintiffs.' *Bigelow v. RKO Pictures, Inc., supra* [327 U.S.], at 264 [66 S.Ct., at 579]. *See also Eastman Kodak Co. v. S. Photo Materials Co.,* 273 U.S. 359, 377–379 [47 S.Ct. 400, 404, 405, 71 L.Ed. 684] (1927); *Story Parchment Co. v. Paterson Parchment Paper Co.,* 282 U.S. 555, 561–566, 51 S.Ct. 248, 250, 75 L.Ed. 544 (1931)." Ibid.

In *Bigelow v. RKO Radio Pictures, Inc.,* 327 U.S. 251, 66 S.Ct. 574, 90 L.Ed. 652 (1946), relied on in *Zenith,* film distributors had conspired to deny the plaintiff theater access to first-run films. The jury awarded damages based on a comparison of plaintiff's actual profits with the contemporaneous profits of a competing theater with access to first-run films. Plaintiff had also adduced evidence comparing his actual profits during the conspiracy with his profits when he had been able to obtain first-runs. The lower court thought the evidence too imprecise to support the award, but we reversed because the evidence was sufficient to support a "just and reasonable inference" of damage. We explained:

"Any other rule would enable the wrongdoer to profit by his wrongdoing at the expense of his victim. It would be an inducement to make wrongdoing so effective and complete in every case as to preclude any recovery, by rendering the measure of damages uncertain. Failure to apply it would mean that the more grievous the wrong done, the less likelihood there would be of a recovery." 327 U.S., at 264–265, 66 S.Ct., at 580.

Our willingness to accept a degree of uncertainty in these cases rests in part on the difficulty of ascertaining business damages as compared, for example, to damages resulting from a personal injury or from condemnation of a parcel of land. The vagaries of the marketplace usually deny us sure knowledge of what plaintiff's situation would have been in the absence of the defendant's antitrust violation. But our willingness also rests on the principle articulated in cases such a *Bigelow,* that it does not " 'come with very good grace' " for the wrongdoer to insist upon specific and certain proof of the injury which it has itself inflicted.

* * *

————————

If all issues of directness and proximity have been resolved in the plaintiff's favor, there remains the question of how to measure damages. To provide a basis for quantifying harm, the plaintiff must attempt to demonstrate how it would have fared, and if it is a business, what profits it might have gained, were it not for the defendant's misconduct.

Although the traditional case law, reflected in *J. Truett Payne*, established the general principle that once liability is found the standards of proof on damages should not be rigorous, that traditional leniency may be on the wane. More recently, plaintiffs have faced increasingly skeptical courts in presenting their cases for damages. Today plaintiffs almost always turn to expert economic testimony to improve the odds of recovery, which in turn can trigger *Daubert* challenges to the admissibility of their testimony. *Contrast Concord Boat Corp. v. Brunswick Corp.*, 207 F.3d 1039 (8th Cir. 2000) (excluding damages expert's testimony) *with New York v. Julius Nasso Concrete Corp.*, 202 F.3d 82, 88 (2d Cir. 2000) (citing *Zenith* in support of its decision reversing district court's exclusion of plaintiff's proposed expert testimony on antitrust damages). *See also In re Scrap Metal Antitrust Litigation*, 527 F.3d 517 (6th Cir. 2008) (citing *Conwood* and affirming both admissibility of expert's damage calculation and jury's award of damages).

Here, too, the traditional legal framework is important to consider. In the past, courts generally accepted two principal models of antitrust damages: "before and after" and "yardstick." Note how these approaches are reflected in the quotation from *Zenith* in the Court's opinion in *J. Truett Payne*. "Before and after" models could be used in price fixing and other kinds of consumer damage cases, and by injured, although not destroyed, prey in cases of exclusionary conduct. In price fixing cases, "before and after models" seek to compare prices in the non-conspiracy period to prices in the conspiracy period and use the difference as a baseline approximation of overcharges. In cases of exclusionary conduct, in which the prey continued in business, the method could be used to focus on the prey's profitability before and after the alleged predatory conduct. Assuming that the diminution in profits in the period of unlawful conduct could be causally linked to the anti-competitive conduct, it too could produce an approximation of damages.

"Yardstick" models are based on a comparison of the firm or firms most directly involved in or affected by anticompetitive conduct with firms that are not, and can be used in cases of collusive or exclusionary conduct. In cases alleging collusive effects, the "yardstick" method compares the market subject to restraint with another market that is not—the "yardstick" market. A yardstick can also be used in an exclusionary effects case to compare the success of the target of predation against a comparable firm not faced with predation, or with some portion of the same firm in a distinct geographic or product market. In each circumstance, the goal of a yardstick is to seek to evaluate the damages attributable to the anticompetitive conduct by comparing the performance of the firm affected by the conduct with firms that are not. The yardstick method also can be used to establish a "going concern" value for a business that has been totally excluded.

Figure 8–4:

Typical Measures of Damages in Private Antitrust Cases

Collusive Anticompetitive Effects	Exclusionary Anticompetitive Effects	Methodologies for Proving
• Overcharges	• Lost profits • Going concern value	• Before-and-after • Yardstick • Regression • Other statistical or econometric means

While these basic models in large part continue to influence damages evidence in antitrust cases, newer, more sophisticated, and more case-specific econometric models and regression analyses are also being employed. Often, however, even those new models are influenced by the traditional methods, as we shall see in our next case.

Conwood Co. v. United States Tobacco Co., 290 F.3d 768 (6th Cir. 2002), illustrates what is at stake when a court seeks to quantify the damage done to a firm as a consequence of an antitrust violation. The plaintiff (Conwood) and the defendant (United States Tobacco Co. or USTC) manufactured moist snuff, a smokeless tobacco product. USTC accounted for 77 percent of sales in a relevant market defined as "smokeless moist snuff tobacco in the United States," and Conwood had 13–14 percent. At trial, USTC conceded that it was a monopolist. Conwood alleged that USTC engaged in illegal monopolization by: (1) removing and discarding Conwood's product display racks from stores without the store manager's permission; (2) training its sales agents to deceive store clerks into giving them permission to reorganize the store's moist snuff section, after which the sales agents hid or destroyed Conwood's racks; (3) misusing its position as a "category manager" by providing misleading information to retailers to make them believe that USTC products enjoyed better sales so that retailers would carry USTC products and drop Conwood products; and (4) entering into exclusive agreements with retailers to exclude Conwood's products.

The case was tried before a jury, which found USTC guilty of monopolization and returned a verdict of $350 million. The trebled award was $1.05 billion—one of the largest treble damage verdicts in the history of the U.S. antitrust laws. USTC appealed, challenging the trial court's denial of several of its motions, pre and post-verdict, as well as its refusal to exclude the damages study and testimony of Conwood's damage expert. The court of appeals affirmed. Concluding that USTC had engaged in improper exclusion, the Sixth Circuit endorsed the district court's rulings on evidence and other matters concerning damages. Passages of the court's opinion concerning damages appear below.

CONWOOD CO. V. UNITED STATES TOBACCO CO.

United States Court of Appeals for the Sixth Circuit, 2002.
290 F.3d 768.

CLAY, CIRCUIT JUDGE.

* * *

Damages

[William Rosson, Conwood's Chairman,] testified that had Conwood not been subjected to USTC tactics, it would have had a national market share of approximately 22 to 23 percent. Rosson testified that he had carefully tracked Conwood's market share over the past 20 years. Conwood's actual market share in its first 10 years in the moist snuff industry was 11 percent. In the next decade, starting from 1990, that figure increased by roughly 2.5 percent. Rosson testified that the lack of growth that occurred during the second decade largely resulted from USTC's tactics. He testified that his numbers are based on his studying markets where the company had a foothold and those in which it did not. In places where the company had a "foothold," *i.e.*, a relatively high market share in a given area, it saw its market share increase during the 1990s to a market share above 20 percent. Rosson testified that each additional point (one percent) of market share translates into approximately $10 million in annual profits.

[Terry Williams, Conwood's national sales manager,] testified concerning Conwood's market share with respect to the ten retail locations for which USTC offered evidence at trial. In those locations where USTC did not have rack exclusivity, Conwood's moist brands market share was well above its national average. For those locations where USTC had rack exclusivity, Conwood's market share was below its national average. Conwood argues that from these figures, a jury could have concluded that in unimpeded competition, Conwood's market share would have been approximately 25 percent instead of 13.5 percent nationally.

Finally, to prove damages, Conwood relied on the expert testimony of Professor Richard Leftwich of the University of Chicago Graduate School of Business, who is recognized as an expert on business valuation and lost profits. Leftwich apparently tested Rosson's hypothesis that Conwood's market share increased in areas in which it did not face USTC exclusivity.

Using a regression analysis, Leftwich found a statistically significant difference between states in which Conwood had a foothold and those in which it did not. Under Leftwich's model, in states where Conwood had a market share in 1990 of 20 percent or more, the market share grew on average an additional 8.1 percent from 1990 to 1997. In states where Conwood's market share in 1990 was at least 15 percent, it grew an additional 6.5 percent. In states below these thresholds, Conwood's growth was considerably lower. As the district court noted:

> Leftwich applied a regression analysis to test Conwood's hypotheses. He determined that Conwood's share in a state in 1990 is statistically related to the change in Conwood's market share between 1990 and 1997. The regression model predicts that where Conwood had a higher market share (*e.g.*, 15–20%) in 1990, Conwood's market share grew during the period 1990 to 1997. In contrast, in states where Conwood had a lower market share, the regression predicts that its share would grow very little.

Leftwich then determined that Conwood's low market growth was due to USTC's behavior. Leftwich's model also found that increases in USTC's exclusionary behavior in a state reduced Conwood's share of sales by a statistically significant amount. He found that Conwood's damages as a result of USTC's actions amounted to a figure between $313 million and $488 million, depending on whether Conwood's market share would have grown by 6.5 percent or 8.1 percent. The jury awarded damages of $350 million.

* * *

V.

USTC challenges the district court's decision to allow Leftwich to testify as to the damages sustained by USTC's conduct. USTC argues that the district court made no findings regarding the admissibility of Leftwich's report under *Daubert v. Merrell Dow Pharm., Inc.*, 509 U.S. 579, 113 S.Ct. 2786 (1993). USTC argues that Leftwich's methodology fails because it was constructed solely for this case. USTC also argues that Leftwich's study did not attempt to segregate the effects of other factors that could have contributed to Conwood's low sales in some states, and it made no attempt to test whether the slow growth in certain states was causally linked to any of USTC's conduct. Thus, USTC argues the study did not and could not fit the case at hand.

* * *

USTC does not challenge Leftwich's qualifications as an expert, but only his testimony and damages study. Pursuant to Rule 702 of the Federal Rules of Evidence, "[i]f scientific, technical, or other specialized knowledge will assist the trier of fact to understand the evidence or to determine a fact in issue, a witness qualified as an expert by knowledge, skill, experience, training, or education, may testify thereto in the form of an opinion or otherwise.* * * "In *Daubert,* the Supreme Court "established a general gatekeeping [or screening] obligation for trial courts" to exclude from trial expert testimony that is unreliable and irrelevant. The district court must determine whether the evidence "both rests on a reliable foundation and is relevant to the task at hand." In assessing relevance and reliability, the district court must examine "whether the expert is proposing to testify to (1) scientific knowledge that (2) will assist the trier of fact to understand or determine a fact in issue." This involves a preliminary inquiry as to whether the reasoning or methodology underlying the testimony is scientifically valid and whether that reasoning or methodology properly can be applied to the facts in issue. Some of the factors that may be used in such an inquiry include: (1) whether the theory or technique has been tested and subjected to peer review and publication, (2) whether the potential rate of error is known, and (3) its general acceptance. "This inquiry is a flexible one, with an overarching goal of assessing the 'scientific validity and thus the evidentiary relevance and reliability' of the principles and methodology underlying the proposed expert testimony." "[A] trial judge must have considerable leeway in deciding in a particular case how to go about determining whether particular expert testimony is reliable." *Kumho Tire Co., Ltd. v. Carmichael,* 526 U.S. 137, 152, 119 S.Ct. 1167 (1999).

USTC presents no reasoned basis for us to find that the district court abused its discretion in determining that Leftwich's methodology was sufficiently reliable or relevant to survive a *Daubert* challenge. USTC asserts two principal challenges to Leftwich's study and testimony. USTC claims that Leftwich did not relate any of Conwood's loss to specific bad acts by USTC and failed to account for other factors that could have had a negative effect on Conwood's sales. Leftwich used a regression analysis to test Rosson's hypothesis that Conwood's growth was suppressed most in states where it had only a small market share when USTC began its exclusionary practices. He also tested whether the intensity of USTC's misconduct increased in or around 1990. Rosson testified that once his company reached a 15 percent market share, USTC's exclusive vending practices were not as effective.

Leftwich employed three methods to test Conwood's claims: regression analyses, a yardstick test and a before-and-after test. All three are generally accepted methods for proving antitrust damages. *See e.g., Petruzzi's IGA Supermarkets, Inc. v. Darling-Delaware Co.,* 998 F.2d 1224, 1238 (3d Cir. 1993) (explaining that if performed properly multiple regression analysis is a reliable means by which economists may prove antitrust damages); *Eleven Line, Inc. v. North Texas State Soccer Ass'n,* 213 F.3d 198, 207 (5th Cir. 2000) (noting that the two most common methods of quantifying antitrust damages are the "before and after" and "yardstick" measures of lost profits).[8]

Leftwich found a statistically significant difference in Conwood's market share between those states in which Conwood had a foothold and those in which it did not. In those states in which Conwood enjoyed a market share of 15 and 20 percent or more, Conwood grew in share, between 1990 and 1997, on an average of 6.5 percent and 8.1 percent, respectively. He concluded that but for USTC's exclusionary acts, Plaintiff's market share would have grown by these same amounts in non-foothold states. Contrary to USTC's arguments, the record indicates that Leftwich ruled out the possibility that the statistical relationship was caused by factors other than USTC's conduct. We find particularly relevant the undisputed evidence that Leftwich examined the possible explanations that USTC's own expert suggested as possible explanations for Conwood's low market share. Leftwich testified that he tested all "plausible explanations" for his results for which he had data. Employing a regression analysis, Leftwich analyzed whether these other factors could explain Conwood's laggard growth in non-foothold states and concluded that they could not.

Leftwich also employed a before-and-after test to investigate Conwood's claims. Specifically, he tested whether the relationship between Conwood's share of moist snuff sales in a state and the rate of growth in Conwood's share of sales in that same state was the same or different for the seven year period before 1990 as it was for the seven year period after 1990. He found that Conwood's moist snuff market share did not grow significantly more in foothold states in the seven year period before 1990. Thus, there was no correlation in the pre-1990 period between Conwood's foothold status and market share growth rate.

Further, Leftwich employed a yardstick test to examine whether in the related loose leaf tobacco market, in which USTC does not participate, Conwood would always grow more in states where they started out with a high market share. He did not find a statistically significant relationship in Conwood's increase in market share in the loose leaf market between 1990 and 1997 and its share in 1990. In other words, where Conwood enjoyed a high market share or foothold in 1990 in the loose leaf market, it did not necessarily grow more in the period between 1990 and 1997.

USTC complains that Leftwich failed to take into account any USTC "bad act." However, this is not completely accurate. Using USTC's expert's own regression model, Leftwich used sworn affidavits compiled from 241

---

8 "The before and after theory compares the plaintiff's profit record prior to the violation with that subsequent to it [and] the yardstick test . . . consists of a study of the profits of business operations that are closely comparable to the plaintiff's." A regression analysis looks at the relationship between two variables. The point of a regression analysis is to determine whether the relationship between the two variables is statistically meaningful.

Conwood sales representatives detailing USTC's unethical activity in their areas. He used this information to construct three alternate measures of USTC's bad acts by state. * * * Thus, his damages study was relevant to the issues of this case.

USTC also complains that Leftwich's regression analysis ignored other market variables that could have caused Conwood's harm. However, as explained above, Leftwich ruled out all plausible alternatives for which he had data. Moreover, he accounted for all variables raised by USTC's own expert. In any event, "[i]n order to be *admissible* on the issue of causation, an expert's testimony need not eliminate all other possible causes of the injury." In sum, after reviewing the record and giving due deference to the district court's decision, we believe that the district court did not abuse its discretion in concluding that Leftwich's study satisfied *Daubert* and allowing him to testify, subject to vigorous cross examination and an opportunity for Defendant to introduce countervailing evidence of its own.

Finally, USTC contends that Rosson's testimony regarding damages and Leftwich's study were speculative and failed to support the damages awarded. We disagree. USTC essentially argues that a more rigorous standard of proof of damages was warranted. However, it is undisputed that USTC did not object to the jury instructions regarding damages. The jury was instructed that it could not award damages for injuries caused by other factors. As juries are presumed to follow the instructions given, we reject USTC's argument that Conwood failed to disaggregate the injury caused by USTC as opposed to that caused by other factors.

In addition, an award of damages may be awarded on a plaintiff's estimate of sales it could have made absent the antitrust violation. *J. Truett Payne Co. v. Chrysler Motors Corp.*, 451 U.S. 557, 565, 101 S.Ct. 1923 (1981). While USTC demands a more exacting standard, "[t]he vagaries of the marketplace usually deny us sure knowledge of what plaintiff's situation would have been in the absence of the defendant's antitrust violation." *Id.* at 566. "The antitrust cases are legion which reiterate the proposition that, if the fact of damages is proven, the actual computation of damages may suffer from minor imperfections."

We believe that there was sufficient evidence to support the jury's award of damages in this case. There was testimony that absent USTC's unlawful conduct, Conwood would have achieved market share in the mid-20s. For instance, Rosson testified that had Conwood not been subjected to USTC tactics, it would have had a national market share of approximately 22 to 23 percent. Rosson testified that he had carefully tracked the growth of Conwood's market share over the past 20 years, and its sharp decline in the 1990s was largely due to USTC's tactics. Williams, Conwood's national sales manager, also testified that in those stores where USTC practiced rack exclusivity, Conwood's market share was well below its national average. Such evidence supported Leftwich's damages analysis, and he estimated that Conwood's damages ranged between $313 million and $488 million. The jury awarded damages well within that range. Although USTC argues that there was evidence that undermined Rosson's testimony regarding whether USTC's conduct caused Conwood's injury, the jury heard all of the evidence presented to it, and apparently found other testimony supporting the award of damages more credible. In sum, we believe that there was sufficient evidence to sustain the award in this case.

* * *

Conwood highlights two important elements of calculating damages in private antitrust litigation. The first is the need to select an analytical model that best captures the results that plaintiff would have achieved had it not been for the defendant's misconduct. The second is the centrality of expert testimony—typically, by accountants and economists—in supplying a model for computing damages and in applying the model to the facts at hand

As noted above, in accordance with Section 4 of the Clayton Act, the $350 million in "actual" damages proved by Conwood was trebled to $1.05 billion. In addition, as a prevailing plaintiff, Conwood received an award of attorney's fees and costs pursuant to § 4 of the Clayton Act. What might justify this seeming windfall to Conwood?

For another illustration of the interplay of damages, economic models, and the role of expert testimony, see *LePage's Inc. v. 3M Company*, 324 F.3d 141 (3d Cir. 2003). In *LePage's*, the court rejected arguments by 3M that the plaintiff's damage expert's testimony should have been excluded. 3M asserted that the testimony was flawed in two general respects: (1) the "lost market share" model that the plaintiff's expert constructed as a yardstick to evaluate the "but for" world, *i.e.*, LePage's' likely success but for 3M's conduct, rested upon improper assumptions, and (2) that it failed to disaggregate damages based on lawful and unlawful conduct by 3M. The court rejected both arguments, sustaining the district court's treble damage award of nearly $70 million.

Sidebar 8–9:
Legal Procedure and Settlement

Notwithstanding all the attention casebook authors give to judicial decisions, most antitrust cases are resolved through settlement. This Sidebar asks why all cases are not settled. It also discusses the concern raised by some critics of private enforcement that private plaintiffs can coerce inappropriate settlements in frivolous cases. For further discussion of these issues, see Bruce L. Hay & Kathryn E. Spier, *Settlement of Litigation, in* The New Palgrave Dictionary of Economics and the Law 442 (Peter Newman ed., 1998).

Why Don't All Cases Settle?

Most court complaints between private parties, antitrust included, are settled rather than tried. A mid-1980s study found that between 70% and 88% of private antitrust damages cases that reached a final disposition (judgment or settlement) were settled. Steven C. Salop & Lawrence J. White, *Economic Analysis of Private Antitrust Litigation*, 74 Geo. L. J. 1001, 1010 (1986) (table 9). The range arises because dismissals may have been settlements or judgments for defendants. Both figures may understate the settlement rate, if many disputes are settled before trial or if private injunctive cases are more likely to settle than private damages cases. Few antitrust cases ever go to trial.

In most private cases, settlement has substantial advantages for both sides. It saves on litigation costs, which can be substantial, avoids business harms that may be associated with delay in resolving the dispute or the public airing of trial testimony, and allows risk averse parties to avoid the uncertainty of trial. Even if the parties disagree to some extent about the likely judicial resolution or the likely remedy in the event plaintiff prevails, there will typically be a range of possible settlements that make both sides better off than they would be in going to trial. In a damages case, the minimum plaintiff will take to settle is the expected damage award (its assessment of the prospects of success, times the damage payment it expects to receive if it prevails) less the future costs of continued litigation (including court costs, attorney and expert fees, the diversion of executive time, and the costs of uncertainty and delay). The maximum the defendant will pay in a settlement is its expected damage payment plus the future costs of litigation. If the maximum a defendant will pay exceeds the minimum plaintiff will accept, there is room for a deal, and the parties can usually be counted on to reach a settlement in that range. Under such circumstances, why don't all private cases settle?

The economics literature suggests two main reasons. First, the two sides may have such different beliefs or expectations about the likelihood of prevailing or the nature of the remedy as to leave no room for settlement. If one or both of the parties is overly-optimistic about its prospects for success at trial, or if defendant thinks it would not have to pay much in damages should it lose while plaintiff expects a very large award if it prevails, the maximum defendant will pay may be less than the minimum plaintiff will accept, leaving no possibility for settlement.

Second, when two sides bargain rationally with private or incomplete information, they might miss a mutually beneficial deal simply because it may rationally take a tough bargaining stance. If one side reasonably but wrongly thinks it can get a better deal by holding out for more, for example, the parties may reach an impasse even if there is room for a deal that would benefit both. Or if a plaintiff expects to bring a series of similar actions, and can't tell which defendants have particularly strong cases, it may do best by making an offer that defendants with weak cases will take and going to trial with the rest, even if it could have reached a deal with the latter defendants if it could have sorted them in advance. In this story, the plaintiff cannot make such a deal later; otherwise the defendants with weak cases will pretend to have strong ones to get the same settlement. Nor can a defendant with a strong case convincingly prove that fact in any other way than by going to trial, even through discovery.

These explanations for the failure of litigating parties to reach a negotiated deal suggest that the prospects for settlement go up if expected trial costs rise (increasing the settlement range), if the parties engage in additional discovery (reducing information differences between the sides and bringing their beliefs and expectations closer together), or through the use of alternative dispute resolution techniques like mock trials and mediation (again bringing the beliefs and expectations of the parties closer together).

Terms of Settlement

Some critics of private antitrust enforcement have expressed concern about the influence of extensive discovery and the threat of treble damages on the terms of settlement in antitrust cases. They raise the possibility that plaintiffs with weak cases could nevertheless extract substantial settlements from defendants because of these procedural aspects of antitrust litigation, encouraging the filing of frivolous claims. To understand this argument it is necessary to explore what influences the terms of settlement.

A settlement of a case would be expected to fall between the minimum plaintiff would accept and the maximum defendant would pay. But the difference will not be split 50–50 if one party has greater bargaining power than the other. In the economic literature, bargaining power depends importantly on what happens if firms do not reach a deal.[a] In the most basic analysis, if litigation is very costly for defendant, and not so costly for plaintiff, then the plaintiff has the stronger bargaining position—it can threaten to impose large costs by litigating—so a settlement will likely favor plaintiff. This simple bargaining power story may be complicated, though, by differences between the parties in their desire to avoid risk, by a party's concern that it will be adversely affected in other cases if it accedes to a weak settlement in this one, or by the possibility that lawyers with somewhat different interests than the parties they represent may control settlement talks on their side of the table.

In the picture of private antitrust litigation offered by the critics, the prospect of a treble damage award and the likelihood that discovery will be much more expensive for the defendant than the plaintiff lead systematically to settlements that favor plaintiffs, even when cases are weak. The prospect of pro-plaintiff settlements, in turn, may encourage plaintiffs to bring more cases. This theory is difficult to evaluate, however, because there is little evidence from which to gauge the social value of weak cases. If most are frivolous, then there is reason for concern. But cases may be difficult for plaintiffs to win even if they are meritorious—for example, if the substantive legal rules make it difficult for plaintiffs to succeed even when competition is harmed, if plaintiffs who would end up victorious were all the facts known frequently cannot surmount the burden they must meet to justify more complete discovery, or if standing rules exclude from the courthouse plaintiffs with knowledge of violations and the resources to litigate. Put differently, rules that encourage plaintiffs to bring antitrust lawsuits can benefit the economy by increasing the deterrent effect of the antitrust laws, or harm the economy by imposing litigation costs on wrongly accused defendants and discouraging procompetitive conduct likely to prompt a complaint. The value of private treble damage actions and easy access to discovery must be evaluated with both possibilities in mind.

---

[a]   The economic theory of bargaining suggests that in a negotiation, the lion's share of the joint benefits will go to the party that has the least to lose if no deal is reached. *See, e.g.*, Avinash Dixit & Susan Skeath, GAMES OF STRATEGY 521–47 (1999).

G. CONCLUSION

This Chapter examined the structural antitrust enforcement considerations associated with the substantive antitrust rules discussed in earlier chapters. These structural considerations begin with a determination of jurisdiction: does an applicable antitrust statute cover the potentially anticompetitive conduct? If there are no jurisdictional impediments, the next concern is who is likely to challenge the behavior in question? Is there a risk of criminal enforcement by the Justice Department, or might the FTC use Section 5 of the FTC Act to reach behavior not condemned by the Sherman or Clayton Acts? Will a state intervene? Can a private party sue? In certain circumstances, Congress or certain states actively immunize specific anticompetitive conduct against antitrust liability. Is the conduct in question exempted from or immunized against antitrust liability by federal or state regulations? If a competitor or customer sues, can she satisfy the threshold requirements of standing? Can the plaintiff bear evidentiary burdens essential to establishing liability, or are there evidentiary ambiguities or analytical weaknesses (*e.g.*, economic implausibility) that may warrant summary judgment? Finally, in case of an adverse judgment against the defendant, what remedies are available to the plaintiff?

H. PROBLEMS AND EXERCISES

Problem 8–1:
Sweet Co.

Sweet Co. is one of four principal manufacturers of artificial sweeteners in the world. Like other artificial sweeteners, Sweet Co.'s main product, SweetStuff, is used as an additive in a variety of foods, such as cereals, soda pop, juices, cookies, and cakes. Sweet Co.'s principal customers, therefore, are food manufacturers, who account for more than 75% of its sales. SweetStuff is also sold through supermarkets to consumers, who use it in place of sugar for cooking purposes and as a drink sweetener for hot drinks (coffee and tea), as well as cold drinks (lemonade and iced tea). Worldwide sales of artificial sweeteners have been growing steadily for the last decade, and are now roughly $10 billion/year. Sweet Co.'s annual sales are roughly $3 billion.

Following a two year grand jury investigation, the Antitrust Division of the Department of Justice sought and secured criminal indictments against Sweet Co. and its two largest rivals for engaging in a worldwide conspiracy to fix the prices of artificial sweeteners. Sweet Co. denied that it had conspired with its rivals and vowed to vigorously contest the government's charges. After the close of the government's case in chief at trial, a consent agreement was reached, pursuant to which Sweet Co. agreed to pay fines of $250 million.

Shortly after the indictments were announced, a number of private parties filed suit against Sweet Co., both as individuals and, in many cases, as purported class representatives. By the time the settlement agreement was reached with the government, over three dozen such suits had been filed. Four of these are summarized below.

> Suit No. 1: *Drink Manufacturers vs. Sweet Co. (Federal Court)*. In this action, filed in the United States District Court, several of the major manufacturers of soda pop and juices have joined to sue Sweet Co. for its alleged violations of Section 1 of the Sherman Act. Pursuant to Section 4 of the Clayton Act, the plaintiffs seek to recover three times the alleged overcharges they incurred as purchasers of SweetStuff during the period of the alleged conspiracy.

> Suit No. 2: *Consumers of SweetStuff v. Sweet Co. (Federal Court)*. This is a consumer class action also filed in a United States District Court, but in a different district than Suit No. 1. It too alleges violations of Section 1 of the Sherman Act and seeks three times the alleged overcharges paid by the class for SweetStuff. The complaint purports to be brought on behalf of a class of consumers who purchased SweetStuff at supermarkets and groceries for their own use as a sweetener.

> Suit No. 3: *Consumers of SweetStuff Products v. Sweet Co. (State Court)*. This too is a consumer class action, but it was filed in state court under state antitrust laws. The complaint alleges violations of state antitrust provisions that parallel those of Section 1 of the Sherman Act, and seeks to recover three times the actual damages sustained by consumers who purchased cereals, soda pop, juices, and cookies that contained SweetStuff at their local supermarkets.

> Suit No. 4: *Foreign Supermarkets vs. SweetCo. (Federal Court)*. This is a federal antitrust action filed in U.S. District Court by two of the largest supermarket chains in Europe, who allegedly purchased packaged SweetStuff from Sweet Co. during the period of the alleged conspiracy. The SweetStuff purchased was for resale to consumers in their stores in Europe, as well as in the United States. The two supermarket chains seek treble damages for the overcharges they paid for all of their purchases of SweetStuff.

Consider the following issues with respect to each suit:

(1) What motion or motions might you file challenging any of the actions on grounds of lack of jurisdiction, standing or antitrust injury?

(2) What procedural steps might you recommend to combine any of these actions, as through removal, transfer and/or consolidation?

(3) Which, if any, of the class actions strikes you as vulnerable with respect to class certification? Why?

Problem 8–2:
Maverick Motors

In response to shortages of gasoline and consequently higher gasoline prices in the early 1970s, federal government regulators imposed minimum fuel economy standards on all of the major automobile manufacturers. These standards, known as Corporate Average Fuel Economy ("CAFÉ") standards, applied to cars and light trucks, although different standards were established for each. Around the same time, federal regulators also responded to increased levels of automotive air pollution by developing standards to control and reduce vehicle emissions. Moreover, California adopted uniquely strict emissions standards that required the producers to make significant changes to engine design. Other states followed suit and adopted similarly strict standards.

Since that time, CAFÉ and low emission standards have been controversial features of government regulation of the automobile industry. Environmentalists and others urge increases in the CAFÉ standards and stricter regulation of vehicle emissions, while most automobile manufacturers oppose government-mandated increases in fuel economy and decreases in emissions, particularly at a time when consumers have made clear their preference for performance cars and larger vehicles, especially minivans and sport utility vehicles. These larger vehicles tend to be far more profitable for the automobile producers than are passenger cars, but they are also less fuel efficient and more polluting. Indeed, although the major manufacturers publicly maintain that they are interested in and diligently working to produce more fuel efficient and lower polluting vehicles, the pace of innovation to accomplish those goals has remained slow in much of the industry.

In response to renewed calls for increased CAFÉ standards for both passenger vehicles and light trucks, as well as even stricter emissions standards, five of the six largest automobile manufacturers (measured by their shares of U.S. domestic passenger vehicle sales) formed the Coalition of Car Producers ("CCP"). CCP funds studies of automotive safety, pollution and fuel economy, and lobbies at the state and federal level to oppose regulation of both fuel economy and automotive emissions. CCP has successfully lobbied to stall legislative efforts in several states to impose stricter emissions standards and has persuaded federal regulators to delay higher CAFÉ standards, which although adopted in 2007, will not take full effect until 2020.

Maverick Motors is the only major automobile producer that has refused to join the Coalition. Indeed, it has frequently opposed CCP at both state and federal hearings, attempting to refute its charges that technology is either unavailable or too costly to meet more stringent fuel economy and emissions standards. Maverick has been an industry leader for almost three decades with respect to "green" technology that lowers fuel consumption *and* engine emissions, without reducing engine horsepower or acceleration. It also is an industry leader in passenger car production techniques, and traditionally enjoys a significant cost advantage over its rivals, producing high quality cars at lower cost. Maverick's ability to offer more fuel efficient and "ultra low emission" vehicles at prices that remain competitive with its rivals is a function of these production cost advantages, as well as its persistent investment in engine technology research and development.

Maverick has filed suit against CCP and its members claiming that their collective actions constitute violations of Section 1 of the Sherman Act. In particular, the complaint alleges that its legitimate competitive advantage—a function of its efforts to develop new technologies and cut production costs—is being neutralized by the successful efforts of CCP and its members to preclude more stringent fuel economy and emissions standards. Indeed, Maverick alleges, it would be uniquely situated to meet more stringent fuel economy and emissions standards if the federal government and the states were to impose them, and could quickly gain market share from its rivals. Maverick further alleges that the coordination among members of CCP goes beyond simple lobbying and includes joint efforts to slow the pace of innovation in the industry in order to maintain current levels of profitability and deny Maverick a larger share of sales. As a consequence, consumers have been deprived of the benefits of cleaner air, reduced CO_2 emissions associated with global warming, and more fuel efficient automobiles at competitive prices.

In its complaint, brought under Sections 4 and 16 of the Clayton Act, Maverick prays for an order enjoining the defendants from continuing to engage in violations of Section 1 of the Sherman Act. It also asserts claims for treble damages, attorney's fees, and costs, alleging that but for the defendants' conduct its market share and consequent profitability would have substantially grown.

In response to the action, CCP has filed a motion to dismiss, arguing that Maverick: (1) lacks standing to bring its suit; (2) has not suffered any antitrust injury; and (3) that in any event, CCP's activities constitute petitioning conduct that is outside the scope of possible Sherman Act scrutiny. How should the motion be resolved?

APPENDIX A

SELECTED ANTITRUST STATUTES

■ ■ ■

Excerpts from the Principal U.S. Antitrust Statutes[1]

A. The Sherman Act

§ 1 Sherman Act, 15 U.S.C. § 1—Trusts, etc., in restraint of trade illegal; penalty

Every contract, combination in the form of trust or otherwise, or conspiracy, in restraint of trade or commerce among the several States, or with foreign nations, is declared to be illegal. Every person who shall make any contract or engage in any combination or conspiracy hereby declared to be illegal shall be deemed guilty of a felony, and, on conviction thereof, shall be punished by fine not exceeding $100,000,000 if a corporation, or, if any other person, $1,000,000, or by imprisonment not exceeding 10 years, or by both said punishments, in the discretion of the court.

§ 2 Sherman Act, 15 U.S.C. § 2—Monopolizing trade a felony; penalty

Every person who shall monopolize, or attempt to monopolize, or combine or conspire with any other person or persons, to monopolize any part of the trade or commerce among the several States, or with foreign nations, shall be deemed guilty of a felony, and, on conviction thereof, shall be punished by fine not exceeding $100,000,000 if a corporation, or, if any other person, $1,000,000 or by imprisonment not exceeding 10 years, or by both said punishments, in the discretion of the court.

§ 3 Sherman Act, 15 U.S.C. § 3—Trusts in Territories or District of Columbia illegal; combination a felony

(a) Every contract, combination in form of trust or otherwise, or conspiracy, in restraint of trade or commerce in any Territory of the United States or of the District of Columbia, or in restraint of trade or commerce between any such Territory and another, or between any such Territory or Territories and any State or States or the District of Columbia, or with foreign nations, or between the District of Columbia and any State or States or foreign nations, is declared illegal. Every person who shall make any such contract or engage in any such combination or conspiracy, shall

---

[1] For a comprehensive collection of the antitrust statutes enforced by the Department of Justice, *see* https://www.justice.gov/atr/file/761131/download; for a compilation of the statutes enforced by the Federal Trade Commission, *see* http://www.ftc.gov/ogc/stats.shtm.

be deemed guilty of a felony, and, on conviction thereof, shall be punished by fine not exceeding $100,000,000 if a corporation, or, if any other person, $1,000,000, or by imprisonment not exceeding 10 years, or by both said punishments, in the discretion of the court.

(b) Every person who shall monopolize, or attempt to monopolize, or combine or conspire with any other person or persons, to monopolize any part of the trade or commerce in any Territory of the United States or of the District of Columbia, or between any such Territory and another, or between any such Territory or Territories and any State or States or the District of Columbia, or with foreign nations, or between the District of Columbia, and any State or States or foreign nations, shall be deemed guilty of a felony, and, on conviction thereof, shall be punished by fine not exceeding $100,000,000 if a corporation, or, if any other person, $1,000,000, or by imprisonment not exceeding 10 years, or by both said punishments, in the discretion of the court.

§ 4 Sherman Act, 15 U.S.C. § 4—Jurisdiction of courts; duty of United States attorneys; procedure

The several district courts of the United States are invested with jurisdiction to prevent and restrain violations of sections 1 to 7 of this title; and it shall be the duty of the several United States attorneys, in their respective districts, under the direction of the Attorney General, to institute proceedings in equity to prevent and restrain such violations. Such proceedings may be by way of petition setting forth the case and praying that such violation shall be enjoined or otherwise prohibited. * * *

§ 7 Sherman Act, 15 U.S.C. § 6a (Foreign Trade Antitrust Improvements Act of 1982)—Conduct involving trade or commerce with foreign nations

Sections 1 to 7 of this title shall not apply to conduct involving trade or commerce (other than import trade or import commerce) with foreign nations unless—

(1) such conduct has a direct, substantial, and reasonably foreseeable effect—

(A) on trade or commerce which is not trade or commerce with foreign nations, or on import trade or import commerce with foreign nations; or

(B) on export trade or export commerce with foreign nations, of a person engaged in such trade or commerce in the United States; and

(2) such effect gives rise to a claim under the provisions of sections 1 to 7 of this title, other than this section.

If sections 1 to 7 of this title apply to such conduct only because of the operation of paragraph (1)(B), then sections 1 to 7 of this title shall apply to such conduct only for injury to export business in the United States.

B. The Clayton Act

§ 2 Clayton Act, 15 U.S.C. § 13—Discrimination in price, services, or facilities

(a) *Price; selection of customers*

It shall be unlawful for any person engaged in commerce, in the course of such commerce, either directly or indirectly, to discriminate in price between different purchasers of commodities of like grade and quality, where either or any of the purchases involved in such discrimination are in commerce, where such commodities are sold for use, consumption, or resale within the United States or any Territory thereof or the District of Columbia or any insular possession or other place under the jurisdiction of the United States, and where the effect of such discrimination may be substantially to lessen competition or tend to create a monopoly in any line of commerce, or to injure, destroy, or prevent competition with any person who either grants or knowingly receives the benefit of such discrimination, or with customers of either of them: *Provided,* That nothing herein contained shall prevent differentials which make only due allowance for differences in the cost of manufacture, sale, or delivery resulting from the differing methods or quantities in which such commodities are to such purchasers sold or delivered * * *.

(b) *Burden of rebutting prima-facie case of discrimination*

Upon proof being made, at any hearing on a complaint under this section, that there has been discrimination in price or services or facilities furnished, the burden of rebutting the prima-facie case thus made by showing justification shall be upon the person charged with a violation of this section, and unless justification shall be affirmatively shown, the Commission is authorized to issue an order terminating the discrimination: *Provided, however,* That nothing herein contained shall prevent a seller rebutting the prima-facie case thus made by showing that his lower price or the furnishing of services or facilities to any purchaser or purchasers was made in good faith to meet an equally low price of a competitor, or the services or facilities furnished by a competitor.

(c) *Payment or acceptance of commission, brokerage, or other compensation*

It shall be unlawful for any person engaged in commerce, in the course of such commerce, to pay or grant, or to receive or accept, anything of value as a commission, brokerage, or other compensation, or any allowance or discount in lieu thereof, except for services rendered in connection with the sale or purchase of goods, wares, or merchandise, either to the other party to such transaction or to an agent, representative, or other intermediary therein where such intermediary is acting in fact for or in behalf, or is subject to the direct or indirect control, of any party to such transaction other than the person by whom such compensation is so granted or paid.

(d) *Payment for services or facilities for processing or sale*

It shall be unlawful for any person engaged in commerce to pay or contract for the payment of anything of value to or for the benefit of a customer of such person in the course of such commerce as compensation or in consideration for any services or facilities furnished by or through such customer in connection with the processing, handling, sale, or offering for sale of any products or commodities manufactured, sold, or offered for sale by such person, unless such payment or consideration is available on proportionally equal terms to all other customers competing in the distribution of such products or commodities.

(e) *Furnishing services or facilities for processing, handling, etc.*

It shall be unlawful for any person to discriminate in favor of one purchaser against another purchaser or purchasers of a commodity bought for resale, with or without processing, by contracting to furnish or furnishing, or by contributing to the furnishing of, any services or facilities connected with the processing, handling, sale, or offering for sale of such commodity so purchased upon terms not accorded to all purchasers on proportionally equal terms.

(f) *Knowingly inducing or receiving discriminatory price*

It shall be unlawful for any person engaged in commerce, in the course of such commerce, knowingly to induce or receive a discrimination in price which is prohibited by this section.

§ 2c Clayton Act, 15 U.S.C. § 13c—Exemption of non-profit institutions from price discrimination provisions

Nothing in the Act approved June 19, 1936, known as the Robinson-Patman Antidiscrimination Act, shall apply to purchases of their supplies for their own use by schools, colleges, universities, public libraries, churches, hospitals, and charitable institutions not operated for profit.

§ 3 Clayton Act, 15 U.S.C. § 14—Sale, etc., on agreement not to use goods of competitor

It shall be unlawful for any person engaged in commerce, in the course of such commerce, to lease or make a sale or contract for sale of goods, wares, merchandise, machinery, supplies, or other commodities, whether patented or unpatented, for use, consumption, or resale within the United States or any Territory thereof or the District of Columbia or any insular possession or other place under the jurisdiction of the United States, or fix a price charged therefor, or discount from, or rebate upon, such price, on the condition, agreement, or understanding that the lessee or purchaser thereof shall not use or deal in the goods, wares, merchandise, machinery, supplies, or other commodities of a competitor or competitors of the lessor or seller, where the effect of such lease, sale, or contract for sale or such condition, agreement, or understanding may be to substantially lessen competition or tend to create a monopoly in any line of commerce.

§ 4 Clayton Act, 15 U.S.C. § 15—Suits by persons injured

(a) *Amount of recovery; prejudgment interest*

Except as provided in subsection (b) of this section, any person who shall be injured in his business or property by reason of anything forbidden in the antitrust laws may sue therefor in any district court of the United States in the district in which the defendant resides or is found or has an agent, without respect to the amount in controversy, and shall recover threefold the damages by him sustained, and the cost of suit, including a reasonable attorney's fee. * * *

§ 4A   Clayton Act, 15 U.S.C. § 15a—Suits by United States; amount of recovery; prejudgment interest

Whenever the United States is hereafter injured in its business or property by reason of anything forbidden in the antitrust laws it may sue therefor in the United States district court for the district in which the defendant resides or is found or has an agent, without respect to the amount in controversy, and shall recover threefold the damages by it sustained and the cost of suit. * * *

§ 4B   Clayton Act, 15 U.S.C. § 15b—Limitation of actions

Any action to enforce any cause of action under sections 15, 15a, or 15c of this title shall be forever barred unless commenced within four years after the cause of action accrued. * * *

§ 4C Clayton Act, 15 U.S.C. § 15c—Actions by State attorneys general

(a) *Parens patriae; monetary relief; damages; prejudgment interest*

(1) Any attorney general of a State may bring a civil action in the name of such State, as parens patriae on behalf of natural persons residing in such State, in any district court of the United States having jurisdiction of the defendant, to secure monetary relief as provided in this section for injury sustained by such natural persons to their property by reason of any violation of sections 1 to 7 of this title. The court shall exclude from the amount of monetary relief awarded in such action any amount of monetary relief (A) which duplicates amounts which have been awarded for the same injury, or (B) which is properly allocable to (i) natural persons who have excluded their claims pursuant to subsection (b)(2) of this section, and (ii) any business entity.

(2) The court shall award the State as monetary relief threefold the total damage sustained as described in paragraph (1) of this subsection, and the cost of suit, including a reasonable attorney's fee. * * *

§ 4D   Clayton Act, 15 U.S.C. § 15d—Measurement of damages

In any action under section 15c(a)(1) of this title, in which there has been a determination that a defendant agreed to fix prices in violation of sections 1 to 7 of this title, damages may be proved and assessed in the aggregate by statistical or sampling methods, by the computation of illegal overcharges, or by such other reasonable system of estimating aggregate damages as the court in its discretion may permit without the necessity of separately proving the individual claim of, or amount of damage to, persons on whose behalf the suit was brought.

§ 5   Clayton Act, 15 U.S.C. § 16 (Tunney Act)—Judgments

(a) *Prima facie evidence; collateral estoppel*

A final judgment or decree heretofore or hereafter rendered in any civil or criminal proceeding brought by or on behalf of the United States under the antitrust laws to the effect that a defendant has violated said laws shall be prima facie evidence against such defendant in any action or proceeding brought by any other party against such defendant under said laws as to all matters respecting which said judgment or decree would be an estoppel as between the parties thereto: *Provided,* That this section shall not apply to consent judgments or decrees entered before any testimony has been taken. Nothing contained in this section shall be construed to impose any limitation on the application of collateral estoppel, except that, in any action or proceeding brought under the antitrust laws, collateral estoppel effect shall not be given to any finding made by the Federal Trade Commission under the antitrust laws or under section 45 of this title which could give rise to a claim for relief under the antitrust laws.

(b) *Consent judgments and competitive impact statements; publication in Federal Register; availability of copies to the public*

Any proposal for a consent judgment submitted by the United States for entry in any civil proceeding brought by or on behalf of the United States under the antitrust laws shall be filed with the district court before which such proceeding is pending and published by the United States in the Federal Register at least 60 days prior to the effective date of such judgment. Any written comments relating to such proposal and any responses by the United States thereto, shall also be filed with such district court and published by the United States in the Federal Register within such sixty-day period. Copies of such proposal and any other materials and documents which the United States considered determinative in formulating such proposal, shall also be made available to the public at the district court and in such other districts as the court may subsequently direct. Simultaneously with the filing of such proposal, unless otherwise instructed by the court, the United States shall file with the district court, publish in the Federal Register, and thereafter furnish to any person upon request, a competitive impact statement which shall recite—

(1)   the nature and purpose of the proceeding;

(2)   a description of the practices or events giving rise to the alleged violation of the antitrust laws;

(3)   an explanation of the proposal for a consent judgment, including an explanation of any unusual circumstances giving rise to such proposal or any provision contained therein, relief to be obtained thereby, and the anticipated effects on competition of such relief;

(4)   the remedies available to potential private plaintiffs damaged by the alleged violation in the event that such proposal for the consent judgment is entered in such proceeding;

(5)   a description of the procedures available for modification of such proposal; and

(6)   a description and evaluation of alternatives to such proposal actually considered by the United States.

* * *

§ 6   Clayton Act, 15 U.S.C. § 17—Antitrust laws not applicable to labor organizations

The labor of a human being is not a commodity or article of commerce. Nothing contained in the antitrust laws shall be construed to forbid the existence and operation of labor, agricultural, or horticultural organizations, instituted for the purposes of mutual help, and not having capital stock or conducted for profit, or to forbid or restrain individual members of such organizations from lawfully carrying out the legitimate objects thereof; nor shall such organizations, or the members thereof, be held or construed to be illegal combinations or conspiracies in restraint of trade, under the antitrust laws.

§ 7   Clayton Act, 15 U.S.C. § 18—Acquisition by one corporation of stock of another

No person engaged in commerce or in any activity affecting commerce shall acquire, directly or indirectly, the whole or any part of the stock or other share capital and no person subject to the jurisdiction of the Federal Trade Commission shall acquire the whole or any part of the assets of another person engaged also in commerce or in any activity affecting commerce, where in any line of commerce or in any activity affecting commerce in any section of the country, the effect of such acquisition may be substantially to lessen competition, or to tend to create a monopoly.

No person shall acquire, directly or indirectly, the whole or any part of the stock or other share capital and no person subject to the jurisdiction of the Federal Trade Commission shall acquire the whole or any part of the assets of one or more persons engaged in commerce or in any activity affecting commerce, where in any line of commerce or in any activity affecting commerce in any section of the country, the effect of such acquisition, of such stocks or assets, or of the use of such stock by the voting or granting of proxies or otherwise, may be substantially to lessen competition, or to tend to create a monopoly.

This section shall not apply to persons purchasing such stock solely for investment and not using the same by voting or otherwise to bring about, or in attempting to bring about, the substantial lessening of competition. * * *

§ 8 Clayton Act, 15 U.S.C. § 19—Interlocking directorates and officers

(a)(1)   No person shall, at the same time, serve as a director or officer in any two corporations (other than banks, banking associations, and trust companies) that are—

(A) engaged in whole or in part in commerce; and

(B) by virtue of their business and location of operation, competitors, so that the elimination of competition by agreement between them would constitute a violation of any of the antitrust laws;

if each of the corporations has capital, surplus, and undivided profits aggregating more than $10,000,000 as adjusted pursuant to paragraph (5) of this subsection.

(2) Notwithstanding the provisions of paragraph (1), simultaneous service as a director or officer in any two corporations shall not be prohibited by this section if—

(A) the competitive sales of either corporation are less than $1,000,000, as adjusted pursuant to paragraph (5) of this subsection;

(B) the competitive sales of either corporation are less than 2 per centum of that corporation's total sales; or

(C) the competitive sales of each corporation are less than 4 per centum of that corporation's total sales.

For purposes of this paragraph, "competitive sales" means the gross revenues for all products and services sold by one corporation in competition with the other, determined on the basis of annual gross revenues for such products and services in that corporation's last completed fiscal year. For the purposes of this paragraph, "total sales" means the gross revenues for all products and services sold by one corporation over that corporation's last completed fiscal year.

(3) The eligibility of a director or officer under the provisions of paragraph (1) shall be determined by the capital, surplus and undivided profits, exclusive of dividends declared but not paid to stockholders, of each corporation at the end of that corporation's last completed fiscal year.

(4) For purposes of this section, the term "officer" means an officer elected or chosen by the Board of Directors.

(5) For each fiscal year commencing after September 30, 1990, the $10,000,000 and $1,000,000 thresholds in this subsection shall be increased (or decreased) as of October 1 each year by an amount equal to the percentage increase (or decrease) in the gross national product, as determined by the Department of Commerce or its successor, for the year then ended over the level so established for the year ending September 30, 1989. As soon as practicable, but not later than January 31 of each year, the Federal Trade Commission shall publish the adjusted amounts required by this paragraph.

(b) When any person elected or chosen as a director or officer of any corporation subject to the provisions hereof is eligible at the time of his election or selection to act for such corporation in such capacity, his eligibility to act in such capacity shall not be affected by any of the provisions hereof by reason of any change in the capital, surplus and undivided profits, or affairs of such corporation from whatever cause, until the expiration of one year from the date on which the event causing ineligibility occurred.

* * *

§ 11 Clayton Act, 15 U.S.C. § 21—Enforcement provisions

* * *

(c) Review of orders; jurisdiction; filing of petition and record of proceeding; conclusiveness of findings; additional evidence; modification of findings; finality of judgment and decree

Any person required by such order of the commission * * * to cease and desist from any such violation may obtain a review of such order in the court of appeals of the United States for any circuit within which such violation occurred or within which such person resides or carries on business * * *. The findings of the commission * * * as to the facts, if supported by substantial evidence, shall be conclusive. * * * The judgment and decree of the court shall be final, except that the same shall be subject to review by the Supreme Court upon certiorari, as provided in section 1254 of Title 28.

* * *

(l) Penalties

Any person who violates any order issued by the commission * * * under subsection (b) of this section after such order has become final, and while such order is in effect, shall forfeit and pay to the United States a civil penalty of not more than $5,000 for each violation, which shall accrue to the United States and may be recovered in a civil action brought by the United States. Each separate violation of any such order shall be a separate offense, except that in the case of a violation through continuing failure or neglect to obey a final order of the commission * * * each day of continuance of such failure or neglect shall be deemed a separate offense.

§ 12 Clayton Act, 15 U.S.C. § 22—District in which to sue corporation

Any suit, action, or proceeding under the antitrust laws against a corporation may be brought not only in the judicial district whereof it is an inhabitant, but also in any district wherein it may be found or transacts business; and all process in such cases may be served in the district of which it is an inhabitant, or wherever it may be found.

§ 15 Clayton Act, 15 U.S.C. § 25—Restraining violations; procedure

The several district courts of the United States are invested with jurisdiction to prevent and restrain violations of this Act, and it shall be the duty of the several United States attorneys, in their respective districts, under the direction of the Attorney General, to institute proceedings in equity to prevent and restrain such violations. Such proceedings may be by way of petition setting forth the case and praying that such violation shall be enjoined or otherwise prohibited. When the parties complained of shall have been duly notified of such petition, the court shall proceed, as soon as may be, to the hearing and determination of the case; and pending such petition, and before final decree, the court may at any time make such temporary restraining order or prohibition as shall be deemed just in the premises. Whenever it shall appear to the court before which any such proceeding may be pending that the ends of justice require that other parties should be brought before the court, the court may cause them to be summoned whether they reside in the district in which the court is held or not, and subpoenas to that end may be served in any district by the marshal thereof.

§ 16 Clayton Act, 15 U.S.C. § 26—Injunctive relief for private parties; exception; costs

Any person, firm, corporation, or association shall be entitled to sue for and have injunctive relief, in any court of the United States having jurisdiction over the parties, against threatened loss or damage by a violation of the antitrust laws, including sections 13, 14, 18, and 19 of this title, when and under the same conditions and principles as injunctive relief against threatened conduct that will cause loss or damage is granted by courts of equity, under the rules governing such proceedings, and upon the execution of proper bond against damages for an injunction improvidently granted and a showing that the danger of irreparable loss or damage is immediate, a preliminary injunction may issue: *Provided,* That nothing herein contained shall be construed to entitle any person, firm, corporation, or association, except the United States, to bring suit for injunctive relief against any common carrier subject to the jurisdiction of the Surface Transportation Board under subtitle IV of Title 49. In any action under this section in which the plaintiff substantially prevails, the court shall award the cost of suit, including a reasonable attorney's fee, to such plaintiff.

C. Federal Trade Commission Act (15 U.S.C. §§ 41–58, as amended)

§ 1 FTC Act, 15 U.S.C. § 41—Federal Trade Commission established; membership; vacancies; seal

A commission is created and established, to be known as the Federal Trade Commission (hereinafter referred to as the Commission), which shall be composed of five Commissioners, who shall be appointed by the President, by and with the advice and consent of the Senate. Not more than three of the Commissioners shall be members of the same political party. * * * The President shall choose a chairman from the Commission's membership. * * *

§ 5 FTC Act, 15 U.S.C. § 45—Unfair methods of competition unlawful; prevention by Commission

(a) Declaration of unlawfulness; power to prohibit unfair practices; inapplicability to foreign trade

(1) Unfair methods of competition in or affecting commerce, and unfair or deceptive acts or practices in or affecting commerce, are hereby declared unlawful.

* * *

(2) The Commission is hereby empowered and directed to prevent persons, partnerships, or corporations * * * [with some specified exceptions] from using unfair methods of competition in or affecting commerce and unfair or deceptive acts or practices in or affecting commerce.

(b) Proceeding by Commission; modifying and setting aside orders

Whenever the Commission shall have reason to believe that any such person, partnership, or corporation has been or is using any unfair method of competition or unfair or deceptive act or practice in or affecting commerce, and if it shall appear to the Commission that a proceeding by it in respect thereof would be to the interest of the public, it shall issue and serve upon such person, partnership, or corporation a complaint stating its charges in that respect and containing a notice of a hearing upon a day and at a place therein fixed at least thirty days after the service of said complaint. The person, partnership, or corporation so complained of shall have the right to appear at the place and time so fixed and show cause why an order should not be entered by the Commission requiring such person, partnership, or corporation to cease and desist from the violation of the law so charged in said complaint. * * *

(c)   Review of order; rehearing

Any person, partnership, or corporation required by an order of the Commission to cease and desist from using any method of competition or act or practice may obtain a review of such order in the court of appeals of the United States, within any circuit where the method of competition or the act or practice in question was used or where such person, partnership, or corporation resides or carries on business, by filing in the court, within sixty days from the date of the service of such order, a written petition praying that the order of the Commission be set aside. * * *

(d)   Jurisdiction of court

Upon the filing of the record with it the jurisdiction of the court of appeals of the United States to affirm, enforce, modify, or set aside orders of the Commission shall be exclusive.

* * *

(l)   Penalty for violation of order; injunctions and other appropriate equitable relief

Any person, partnership, or corporation who violates an order of the Commission after it has become final, and while such order is in effect, shall forfeit and pay to the United States a civil penalty of not more than $10,000 for each violation, which shall accrue to the United States and may be recovered in a civil action brought by the Attorney General of the United States. Each separate violation of such an order shall be a separate offense, except that in a case of a violation through continuing failure to obey or neglect to obey a final order of the Commission, each day of continuance of such failure or neglect shall be deemed a separate offense. In such actions, the United States district courts are empowered to grant mandatory injunctions and such other and further equitable relief as they deem appropriate in the enforcement of such final orders of the Commission.

* * *

(n)   Standard of proof; public policy consideration

The Commission shall have no authority under this section * * * to declare unlawful an act or practice on the grounds that such act or practice is unfair unless the act or practice causes or is likely to cause substantial injury to consumers which is not reasonably avoidable by consumers themselves and not outweighed by countervailing benefits to consumers or to competition. In determining whether an act or practice is unfair, the Commission may consider established public policies as evidence to be considered with all other evidence. Such public policy considerations may not serve as a primary basis for such determination.

§ 6 FTC Act, 15 U.S.C. § 46—Additional powers of Commission

The Commission shall also have power—

(a) Investigation of persons, partnerships, or corporations

To gather and compile information concerning, and to investigate from time to time the organization, business, conduct, practices, and management of any person, partnership, or corporation engaged in or whose business affects commerce, excepting banks, savings and loan institutions described in section 57a(f)(3) of this title, Federal credit unions described in section 57a(f)(4) of this title, and common carriers subject to the Act to regulate commerce, and its relation to other persons, partnerships, and corporations.

(b) Reports of persons, partnerships, and corporations

To require, by general or special orders, persons, partnerships, and corporations, engaged in or whose business affects commerce, excepting banks, savings and loan institutions described in section 57a(f)(3) of this title, Federal credit unions described in section 57a(f)(4) of this title, and common carriers subject to the Act to regulate commerce, or any class of them, or any of them, respectively, to file with the Commission in such form as the Commission may prescribe annual or special, or both annual and special, reports or answers in writing to specific questions, furnishing to the Commission such information as it may require as to the organization, business, conduct, practices, management, and relation to other corporations, partnerships, and individuals of the respective persons, partnerships, and corporations filing such reports or answers in writing. Such reports and answers shall be made under oath, or otherwise, as the Commission may prescribe, and shall be filed with the Commission within such reasonable period as the Commission may prescribe, unless additional time be granted in any case by the Commission.

(c) Investigation of compliance with antitrust decrees

Whenever a final decree has been entered against any defendant corporation in any suit brought by the United States to prevent and restrain any violation of the antitrust Acts, to make investigation, upon its own initiative, of the manner in which the decree has been or is being carried out, and upon the application of the Attorney General it shall be its duty to make such investigation. It shall transmit to the Attorney General a report embodying its findings and recommendations as a result of any such investigation, and the report shall be made public in the discretion of the Commission.

(d) Investigations of violations of antitrust statutes

Upon the direction of the President or either House of Congress to investigate and report the facts relating to any alleged violations of the antitrust Acts by any corporation.

(e) Readjustment of business of corporations violating antitrust statutes

Upon the application of the Attorney General to investigate and make recommendations for the readjustment of the business of any corporation alleged to be violating the antitrust Acts in order that the corporation may thereafter maintain its organization, management, and conduct of business in accordance with law.

(f) Publication of information; reports

To make public from time to time such portions of the information obtained by it hereunder as are in the public interest; and to make annual and special reports to the Congress and to submit therewith recommendations for additional legislation; and to provide for the publication of its reports and decisions in such form and manner as may be best adapted for public information and use: *Provided*, That the Commission shall not have any authority to make public any trade secret or any commercial or financial information which is obtained from any person and which is privileged or confidential, except that the Commission may disclose such information (1) to officers and employees of appropriate Federal law enforcement agencies or to any officer or employee of any State law enforcement agency upon the prior certification of an officer of any such Federal or State law enforcement agency that such information will be maintained in confidence and will be used only for official law enforcement purposes, and (2) to any officer or employee of any foreign law enforcement agency under the same circumstances that making material available to foreign law enforcement agencies is permitted under section 57b–2(b) of this title.

* * *

§ 13 FTC Act, 15 U.S.C. § 53—False advertisements; injunctions and restraining orders

* * *

(b) Temporary restraining orders; preliminary injunctions

Whenever the Commission has reason to believe—

(1) that any person, partnership, or corporation is violating, or is about to violate, any provision of law enforced by the Federal Trade Commission, and

(2) that the enjoining thereof pending the issuance of a complaint by the Commission and until such complaint is dismissed by the Commission or set aside by the court on review, or until the order of the Commission made thereon has become final, would be in the interest of the public—

the Commission by any of its attorneys designated by it for such purpose may bring suit in a district court of the United States to enjoin any such act or practice. Upon a proper showing that, weighing the equities and considering the Commission's likelihood of ultimate success, such action would be in the public interest, and after notice to the defendant, a temporary restraining order or a preliminary injunction may be granted without bond * * *. Provided further, That in proper cases the Commission may seek, and after proper proof, the court may issue, a permanent injunction. Any suit may be brought where such person, partnership, or corporation resides or transacts business, or wherever venue is proper under section 1391 of Title 28. In addition, the court may, if the court determines that the interests of justice require that any other person, partnership, or corporation should be a party in such suit, cause such other person, partnership, or corporation to be added as a party without regard to whether venue is otherwise proper in the district in which the suit is brought. In any suit under this section, process may be served on any person, partnership, or corporation wherever it may be found.

Sample State Antitrust Statute—New York's Donnelly Act (1899)

Art. 22, § 340, N.Y. Gen. Bus. § 340. Contracts or agreements for monopoly or in restraint of trade illegal and void

1. Every contract, agreement, arrangement or combination whereby

A monopoly in the conduct of any business, trade or commerce or in the furnishing of any service in this state, is or may be established or maintained, or whereby

Competition or the free exercise of any activity in the conduct of any business, trade or commerce or in the furnishing of any service in this state is or may be restrained or whereby

For the purpose of establishing or maintaining any such monopoly or unlawfully interfering with the free exercise of any activity in the conduct of any business, trade or commerce or in the furnishing of any service in this state any business, trade or commerce or the furnishing of any service is or may be restrained, is hereby declared to be against public policy, illegal and void.

* * *

Art. 22, § 340, N.Y. Gen. Bus. § 341. Penalty

Every person or corporation, or any officer or agent thereof, who shall make or attempt to make or enter into any such contract, agreement, arrangement or combination or who within this state shall do any act pursuant thereto, or in, toward or for the consummation thereof, wherever the same may have been made, is guilty of a class E felony, and on conviction thereof shall, if a natural person, be punished by a fine not exceeding one hundred thousand dollars, or by imprisonment for not longer than four years, or by both such fine and imprisonment; and if a corporation, by a fine of not exceeding one million dollars. An indictment or information based on a violation of any of the provisions of this section must be found within three years after its commission. No criminal proceeding barred by prior limitation shall be revived by this act.

Principal E.U. Treaty Provisions[2]

Article 101 (formerly Treaty Establishing the European Community (TEC) Article 81)

1.   The following shall be prohibited as incompatible with the internal market: all agreements between undertakings, decisions by associations of undertakings and concerted practices which may affect trade between Member States and which have as their object or effect the prevention, restriction or distortion of competition within the internal market, and in particular those which:

(a)   directly or indirectly fix purchase or selling prices or any other trading conditions;

(b)   limit or control production, markets, technical development, or investment;

(c)   share markets or sources of supply;

(d)   apply dissimilar conditions to equivalent transactions with other trading parties, thereby placing them at a competitive disadvantage;

(e)   make the conclusion of contracts subject to acceptance by the other parties of supplementary obligations which, by their nature or according to commercial usage, have no connection with the subject of such contracts.

2.   Any agreements or decisions prohibited pursuant to this Article shall be automatically void.

3.   The provisions of paragraph 1 may, however, be declared inapplicable in the case of:

—any agreement or category of agreements between undertakings,

---

[2]   For a comprehensive collection of the relevant provisions of the Treaty on the Functioning of the European Union ("TFEU"), as well as the various regulations, exemptions and guidelines, *see* http://ec.europa.eu/competition/antitrust/legislation/legislation.html.

—any decision or category of decisions by associations of undertakings,

—any concerted practice or category of concerted practices,

which contributes to improving the production or distribution of goods or to promoting technical or economic progress, while allowing consumers a fair share of the resulting benefit, and which does not:

(a) impose on the undertakings concerned restrictions which are not indispensable to the attainment of these objectives;

(b) afford such undertakings the possibility of eliminating competition in respect of a substantial part of the products in question.

Article 102 (formerly TEC Article 82)

Any abuse by one or more undertakings of a dominant position within the internal market or in a substantial part of it shall be prohibited as incompatible with the internal market insofar as it may affect trade between Member States.

Such abuse may, in particular, consist in:

(a) directly or indirectly imposing unfair purchase or selling prices or other unfair trading conditions;

(b) limiting production, markets or technical development to the prejudice of consumers;

(c) applying dissimilar conditions to equivalent transactions with other trading parties, thereby placing them at a competitive disadvantage;

(d) making the conclusion of contracts subject to acceptance by the other parties of supplementary obligations which, by their nature or according to commercial usage, have no connection with the subject of such contracts.

APPENDIX B

SELECTED ANTITRUST RESOURCES
ON THE INTERNET

■ ■ ■

Principal Guidelines and Policy Statements Issued by the Federal Trade Commission and the United States Department of Justice

A. Cartels and Criminal Antitrust Offenses

U.S. Department of Justice, Antitrust Division, Criminal Enforcement Resources

http://www.usdoj.gov/atr/public/criminal.htm

U.S. Department of Justice, Leniency Policy for Individuals (1993)

http://www.usdoj.gov/atr/public/guidelines/lenind.htm

U.S. Department of Justice, Corporate Leniency Policy (1993)

http://www.usdoj.gov/atr/public/guidelines/0091.htm

U.S. Department of Justice, Antitrust Resource Manual

https://www.justice.gov/usam/antitrust-resource-manual

U.S. Sentencing Commission, 2015 Guidelines Manual (Nov. 1, 2015) Section 2R1.1 addresses criminal antitrust offenses.

http://www.ussc.gov/guidelines/2015–guidelines-manual

B. Mergers

Horizontal Merger Guidelines (Aug. 19, 2010)

https://www.ftc.gov/sites/default/files/attachments/merger-review/100819hmg.pdf

Commentary on the Horizontal Merger Guidelines (2006)

http://www.usdoj.gov/atr/public/guidelines/215247.htm

Pre-Merger Notification Under the Hart-Scott-Rodino Act—Resources

https://www.ftc.gov/enforcement/premerger-notification-program

U.S. Department of Justice, Antitrust Division, Policy Guide to Merger Remedies (2004)

http://www.usdoj.gov/atr/public/guidelines/205108.htm

Non-Horizontal Merger Guidelines (1984)

http://www.usdoj.gov/atr/public/guidelines/2614.htm

Protocol for Coordination in Merger Investigations Between the Federal Enforcement Agencies and State Attorneys General (1998)

http://www.usdoj.gov/atr/public/guidelines/1773.htm

National Association of Attorneys General, Horizontal Merger Guidelines (1993)

http://www.naag.org/assets/files/pdf/at-hmerger_guidelines.pdf

C.   Other Enforcement Policy Guidelines and Related Material

Antitrust Guidelines for the Licensing of Intellectual Property (1995)

http://www.usdoj.gov/atr/public/guidelines/0558.htm

Antitrust Enforcement Guidelines for International Operations (rev. 1995)

http://www.usdoj.gov/atr/public/guidelines/internat.htm

Statements of Antitrust Enforcement Policy in Health Care (1996)

http://www.usdoj.gov/atr/public/guidelines/0000.htm

Antitrust Guidelines for Collaborations among Competitors (2000)

http://www.ftc.gov/os/2000/04/ftcdojguidelines.pdf

Statement of Enforcement Principles Regarding "Unfair Methods of Competition" Under Section 5 of the FTC Act (2015)

https://www.ftc.gov/system/files/documents/public_statements/735201/150813section5enforcement.pdf

Guides for Advertising Allowances and Other Merchandising Payments and Services ("*Fred Meyer* Guides")

https://www.ftc.gov/node/116933

U.S. Department of Justice, Antitrust Division Manual

https://www.justice.gov/atr/division-manual

D.   Selected Other Antitrust Internet Resources of Interest

U.S. Department of Justice, Antitrust Division

http://www.usdoj.gov/atr/

U.S. Federal Trade Commission

http://www.ftc.gov/

The Federal Trade Commission at 100: Into Our 2nd Century, William E. Kovacic (2009)

https://www.ftc.gov/system/files/documents/reports/federal-trade-commission-100-our-second-century/ftc100rpt.pdf

National Association of Attorneys General, Antitrust Committee

http://www.naag.org/naag/committees/naag_standing_committees/antitrust-committee.php

Links to Antitrust Enforcement Agency Web Sites Worldwide

https://www.justice.gov/atr/antitrust-sites-worldwide

American Bar Association, Section on Antitrust Law

http://www.abanet.org/antitrust/

American Antitrust Institute

http://www.antitrustinstitute.org/

Antitrust Modernization Commission

http://govinfo.library.unt.edu/amc/

European Commission, Directorate General for Competition
http://ec.europa.eu/dgs/competition/index_en.htm

The Organisation for Economic Co-operation and Development (OECD)
http://www.oecd.org/

International Competition Network (ICN)
http://www.internationalcompetitionnetwork.org/

E.   Antitrust Blogs of Interest
Antitrust & Competition Policy Blog
http://lawprofessors.typepad.com/antitrustprof_blog/

Antitrust Connect
http://antitrustconnect.com/

Antitrust Law Blog
http://www.antitrustlawblog.com/

Antitrust Lawyer Blog
http://www.antitrustlawyerblog.com/

Antitrust Today
http://constantinecannon.com/antitrusttoday/

Antitrust Unpacked
http://shearmanantitrust.com/

AntitrustWatch Blog
http://blogs.orrick.com/antitrust/

Applied Antitrust Law
http://appliedantitrust.com/

Chillin' Competition

https://chillingcompetition.com/

Kluwer Competition Law Blog

http://kluwercompetitionlawblog.com/

Truth on the Market

https://truthonthemarket.com/

INDEX

References are to Pages
